# American Government and Politics in the Information Age

## Version 5.0

David L. Paletz, Diana Owen, and Timothy E. Cook

FlatWorld

978-1-4533-3786-8

# American Government and Politics in the Information Age
## Version 5.0

David L. Paletz, Diana Owen, and Timothy E. Cook

Published by:

FlatWorld
292 Newbury Street
Suite #282
Boston, MA 02115-2832



Gen: 202110281537

# Brief Contents

# Contents

# About the Authors

## David L. Paletz

David L. Paletz is an emeritus professor of political science at Duke University. He has been director of Duke's Film/Video/Digital Program and for six years has been editor of the journal *Political Communication*. His degrees are all from the University of California, Los Angeles. Paletz specializes in American government and politics (defined broadly to include the foundations, public institutions, processes, and policies) and political communication (defined broadly to include news, opinion, and entertainment). Among the courses he has taught are American Government, Politics and the Media in the U.S., Film and Politics, Documentary Film, and Politics and the Libido. He is the author of *The Media in American Politics: Contents and Consequences*, 2nd ed. (Longman, 2002), and co-author of *Media Power Politics* (Free Press, 1983) and *Politics in Public Service Advertising on Television* (Praeger, 1977). He is the editor of and a contributor to *Political Communication in Action* (Hampton Press, 1996) and *Political Communication Research*, vols. I and II (Ablex, 1987 and 1996); a coeditor and contributor to *Taken by Storm: Media, Public Opinion, and U.S. Foreign Policy in the Gulf War* (University of Chicago Press, 1994) and *Terrorism and the Media* (Sage, 1992); coeditor of *Business as Usual* (Hampton Press, 2003) and *Glasnost and After: Media and Change in Eastern/Central Europe* (Hampton Press, 1995); and the author or co-author of some sixty other publications. He created and chaired for many years the Political Communication Research Section of the International Association for Media and Communication Research and chaired the Political Communication Section of the American Political Science Association. Among his research and teaching awards are a Congressional Fellowship from the American Political Science Association, a Humanities Fellowship from the Rockefeller Foundation, two Fulbright Scholarships, and the Alumni Distinguished Undergraduate Teaching Award from Duke University. In 2012 he received the David Swanson Award for Service to Political Communication Scholarship from the Political Communication Sections of the American Political Science Association and the International Communication Association.

## Diana Owen

Diana Owen is a professor of political science and director of the Civic Education Research Lab (https://cerl.georgetown.edu/) at Georgetown University and teaches in the Communication, Culture, and Technology graduate program. She is a graduate of George Washington University and received her doctorate in political science from the University of Wisconsin–Madison. Owen has been an American Political Science Association Congressional Media Fellow and is the recipient of the Daniel Roselle Award from the Middle States Association for the Social Studies. She is the author, with Richard Davis, of *New Media and American Politics* (Oxford, 1998) and *Media Messages in American Presidential Elections* (Greenwood, 1991). She is a coeditor of *The Internet and Politics: Citizens, Voters, and Activists* (Routledge, 2006) with Sarah Oates and Rachel Gibson; she is a coeditor of *Making a Difference: The Internet and Elections in Comparative Perspective* (Lexington, 2009) with Richard Davis, Stephen Ward, and David Taras; and a coeditor of *Internet Election Campaigns in the United States, Japan, Korea, and Taiwan* (Palgrave Macmillan, 2017). She has published numerous scholarly journal articles and book chapters in the areas of American government, mass political behavior, political communication, media and politics, political socialization, civic education, and elections and voting behavior. Her most recent work focuses on digital media in American elections and the intersection of civic education and political engagement. She is the recipient of several grants from the U.S. Department of Education supporting programs and research on high-needs primary and secondary school students. She is grateful for the support of her husband of over forty years, Jeffrey, and her cats, Bella and Gio.

## Timothy E. Cook

Timothy E. Cook (1954–2006) was a political scientist who held the Kevin P. Reilly, Sr., Chair of Political Communication at Louisiana State University from 2001 to 2006 after twenty years as a professor at Williams College. He was the first occupant of the Laurence Lombard Chair at the Joan Shorenstein Center on the Press, Politics and Public Policy at Harvard University's Kennedy School of Government and was a visiting professor of public policy at the Kennedy School. Cook was an American Political Science Association Congressional Fellow, which afforded him the opportunity to study the internal workings of Congress as a participant observer. He made lasting contributions in the fields of American government and media and politics. He is the author of the landmark works *Making News and Making Laws: Media Strategies in the House of Representatives* (Brookings Institution Press, 1987) and *Governing with the News: The News Media as a Political Institution* (University of Chicago, 1999 and 2005). Cook was a co-author of *Crosstalk: Citizens, Candidates, and the Media in a Presidential Campaign* (University of Chicago Press, 1996). Both *Governing with the News* and *Crosstalk* were honored with the Doris Graber Award of the Political Communication Section of the American Political Science Association for the best book published in ten years. Cook also was the editor of *Freeing the Presses: The First Amendment in Action* (Louisiana State University Press, 2006). Additionally, Cook published journal articles and book chapters in the fields of legislative studies; presidential politics; elections and voting behavior; political communication; political socialization; and lesbian, gay, and bisexual politics. Cook was inducted into the Louisiana State University Manship School Hall of Fame in 2011. Cook passed away from brain cancer at the age of fifty-one. He is survived by his spouse, Jack Yeager, a professor of French at Louisiana State University.

# Acknowledgments

The authors would like to thank the following colleagues who have reviewed the text and provided comprehensive feedback and suggestions for improving the material:

- Tally S. Payne, Casper College
- Heather James, Borough of Manhattan Community College CUNY
- William Jesse Barnett, Jr., Kentucky Christian University
- James Druckman, Northwestern University
- Stephen Farnsworth, George Mason University
- Brian Fogarty, University of Missouri–St. Louis
- Jeff Gulati, Bentley University
- Scott Heffner, De Anza Community College
- Diane Heith, St. John's University
- Christopher S. Kelley, Miami University of Ohio
- Jodie Drapal Kluver, Bridgewater State University
- Regina Lawrence, University of Oregon
- Jason Lindsey, St. Cloud State University
- Domenic Maffei, Caldwell College
- Danielle Vinson, Furman University
- Michael W. Wagner, University of Nebraska–Lincoln

We appreciate the contribution of John Maltese of the University of Georgia, who was with us at the start and produced the initial draft of Chapter 15 in Version 1.0.

We are also thankful for the contribution of Christopher Borick of Muhlenberg College, who produced the initial draft of Chapter 16, and Glenn Hastedt of James Madison University, who produced the initial draft of Chapter 17 both in Version 1.0.

Over the years, the following Duke University graduate and undergraduate students worked with David Paletz on the text. We give thanks to and for them all:

- Bradford Bishop
- Lisa Caldemeyer
- Haohan Chen
- Dana Edelstein
- Priya Gupta
- Ian McDonald
- Taneisha Means
- Evan Oxman
- Jill Rickershauser
- Amisha Shrimanker
- Lauren Silk
- Malina Swiatek (who also revised the PowerPoints and Instructor Manual)
- John White

*Paletz acknowledges the Camargo and Bogliasco Foundations for awarding fellowships to his wife, Toril Moi. As her companion, he was privileged to work on the manuscript in sublime surroundings overlooking the Mediterranean.*

Lastly, the authors gratefully acknowledge the talented individuals at FlatWorld, notably Sean Wakely, Lindsey Kaetzel, and Kerribeth Mello, who worked with such dedication and tolerance to produce our book.

# Dedication

For Toril (DLP)

For Jeffrey (DO)

For Jack (TEC)

For Tim (DLP and DO)

# Preface

Our text is a comprehensive introduction to the vital subjects of American government and politics.

**Governments** consist of institutions, offices, and individuals who make policies and laws involving taxation and spending, costs and benefits, even life and death. Governments possess **power**—the ability to gain compliance, to get people under their jurisdiction to obey them. They may exercise their power by using the police and military to enforce their decisions. However, power need not involve the exercise of force or compulsion; people often obey because they think it is in their interest to do so, they have no reason to disobey, or they fear punishment. Above all, people obey their government because it has **authority**; its power is seen by people as rightfully held, as legitimate. People can grant their government **legitimacy** because they have been socialized to do so; because there are processes, notably elections, that enable them to choose and change their rulers; and because they believe that their governing institutions operate justly.

**Politics** is the process by which leaders are selected and policy decisions are made and executed. It involves people and organizations, both inside and outside government, engaged in deliberation and debate, disagreement and conflict, cooperation and consensus, and power struggles.

**governments**

The institutions, offices, and individuals whose decisions are legitimate and thus enforceable on society.

**power**

The ability to gain compliance from others.

**authority**

Power seen as rightfully held, as legitimate.

**legitimacy**

People's acceptance of a political system and belief that the government's decisions should (usually) be obeyed.

**politics**

The process by which leaders are selected and policies made. It involves people and groups inside and outside of government in struggles for power.

In covering American government and politics, our text

- introduces the provisions of the Constitution and the complexities of federalism;
- describes communication in the information age;
- develops the meanings of civil liberties and the conflicts over civil rights;
- shows how people are socialized to politics, acquire and express public opinions, and participate in political life;
- describes interest groups, political parties, and elections—the intermediaries that link people to government and politics;
- details the branches of government and how they operate; and
- explains how policies are made and affect people's lives.

# A Media Approach

Learning and understanding these subjects can be a challenge. Inspired by students' familiarity with the mass media and their fluent use of communication technologies, we have chosen an approach that connects government and politics with these media and technologies.

We start with the awareness that students acquire much of their political information from four main sources of media. First, from the news media's twenty-four-hours-a-day, seven-days-a-week coverage of events, including online.

Second, many students connect with government and politics through media entertainment. They watch television reality programs and contests, dramas, situation comedies, and late-night talk and humor shows, most of which have political aspects. They see and stream movies and sometimes documentaries about social and political issues. They may listen to music containing political messages.

Third, beyond news and entertainment, students may be familiar with some of the ubiquitous and pervasive commentary emanating from opinion-mongers and partisans. Arguably, some commentary is also entertaining.

Fourth are social media. Through their forms, information can be transmitted, distributed, replicated, and searched much more quickly and be subjected to far more individual control, initiative, and choice than ever before. Their content variously repeats, amplifies, challenges, and contradicts the information purveyed by the mass media; it can also lie, outrage, shame, harass, and destroy privacy.

Despite the media's significance, students are often unfamiliar with the causes of the media's contents, especially the importance of ownership, profits, and professionalism. They may not fully grasp the influence on the media of outside forces, such as interest groups, political parties and candidates, and policymakers. Most of these forces are media savvy and use technologies to try to maximize their positive and minimize their negative coverage.

We have therefore organized our text to connect students' media- and technology-saturated lives to the world of politics and government. We want students to learn how the media interact with and depict the American political system; to recognize the similarities and differences between these media depictions and the reality of government and politics; and to understand the consequences these interactions and depictions have for the public, politics, government, and public policies. We want students to learn how to use the media in all their variety, to intervene productively in politics, and get things done.

## Incorporating the Media

If there was any question about the appropriateness of our incorporating the media, witness the January 6, 2021, insurrection at the U.S. Capitol. Supporters of President Trump stormed and invaded the building, overwhelmed law enforcement, and occupied the House and Senate chambers, putting the lives of some of the members and their staffs in danger. They smashed doors and glass and vandalized congressional offices. A rioter lounged in the House Speaker's chair. Another scrawled "Murder the Media" on a door. The media were there. Television cameras from the networks, cable channels, and especially C-SPAN vividly exposed the clashes and violence as for several hours the authorities struggled to restore order. Journalists reported from the scene. News anchors commented over what they saw. During the subsequent days, observers framed the events using the media to put them in context.

This video summarizes the events of the Capitol insurrection that took place on January 6, 2021, as Congress met to certify the 2020 presidential election results.

View in the online reader

Chapter 3 details the system of communication, the organization of media, and the transmission of information in the United States. We integrate this relevant media material throughout every chapter, including the first two, which cover the Constitution and Federalism. Thus, every chapter opens with an anecdote that ties media to the chapter's process, institution, or policy area under study.

Each chapter presents the most common media depictions of its subject. In some chapters, a few depictions dominate: in Chapter 15 the entertainment media portray the judicial system unrealistically. In other chapters, depictions are split. For example, in Chapter 4, we see that journalists' diligent defense of the civil liberties (e.g., freedom of speech) that are central to their job does not carry through to their stories about crime or war.

## Boxes

Each chapter contains two boxes designed to reveal how the media are involved in and influence politics.

The "Enduring Image" box captures a chapter's subject visually. Instantly recognizable, these images are part of our media-induced collective memory of government and politics. Each box explains the original meaning of the image, why it was so important, and its contemporary relevance. For example, the enduring image in Chapter 8 is of Dr. Martin Luther King, Jr., making his "I Have a Dream" speech from the steps of the Lincoln Memorial to the vast crowd participating in the March on Washington for Jobs and Freedom in August 1963, at the height of the civil rights movement.

The media do not simply hold a mirror up to political reality. A "Comparing Content" box presents differences among media depictions of a subject. The box may compare a political event to reports about it in the news, compare depictions of the same political event in various media outlets, or compare changes in media depictions over time. For example, the content-comparison box in Chapter 11 shows how and explains why portrayals of candidates in fiction and documentary films are dramatically different.

## Interactions and Effects

Within each chapter, we cover the interactions between people in the media and those involved in politics and government—specifically in the institutions, processes, or policy areas described in that chapter. These interactions help explain why some depictions are more common in the media than others. Thus, in Chapter 13 we describe how the media, particularly the White House press corps, are organized to report on the presidency. Then we discuss how presidents and their staff devise and deploy communication strategies and tactics to try to manage the media to obtain positive coverage.

We then identify the probable results of these interactions and depictions. For example, in Chapter 11, we discuss their effects on the election prospects of the presidential candidates.

# Pedagogical Aids

Each section of every chapter includes learning objectives, key takeaways, exercises, and key terms. These specify what material in that chapter is critical, both when read the first time and when reviewed.

For those students who want to explore a particular topic further, each chapter includes an annotated set of readings, an annotated list of noteworthy fiction and nonfiction films, and other visuals that depict the chapter's subject.

Each chapter also contains photographs, tables, and figures that we use to further our discussion. Captions explain each one's political meaning. We include links to video and audio clips, political and media websites, and research databases further to enrich the teaching and learning experience.

# Supplements

*American Government and Politics in the Information Age* v5.0 is accompanied by a robust supplements program that augments and enriches both the teaching and student learning experiences.

Faculty should contact their FlatWorld sales representative or FlatWorld support at support@flatworld.com for more information or to obtain access to the supplements upon adoption.

## Sample Syllabi

Sample syllabi based on either 16-week or 10-week terms provide useful templates that help new adopters transition from their current course textbook to *American Government and Politics in the Information Age* v5.0. Faculty can download the syllabi from the FlatWorld website, or they can be obtained by contacting your local FlatWorld representative or FlatWorld support (support@flatworld.com).

## Instructor's Manual

The instructor's manual (IM) includes Learning Objectives and an outline for each chapter. The IM also features possible responses to Exercise questions, which encourage students to more deeply engage with course material.

## PowerPoint Slides

PowerPoint slides organized by chapter include a concise and thorough outline, a list of Learning Objectives, and Key Terms contained in the text. These slides work well for both face-to-face and online learning environments, enliven lectures, and stimulate class discussions. Adopters can use the slides as composed to support lectures or customize and build upon them to suit their particular teaching goals.

## Test Item File

The Test Item File (TIF) includes more than fifty questions per chapter in multiple-choice, fill-in-the-blank, and essay-question formats. All answers are provided, including possible responses to the essay questions. The items have been written specifically to reinforce the major topics covered in each chapter and to align with FlatWorld Homework and in-text quiz items. The Test Item File questions are also available pre-formatted for easy export into popular learning management systems such as Canvas or Blackboard.

## Test Generator—Powered by Cognero

FlatWorld is pleased to provide a computer-generated test program powered by the leading assessment provider Cognero to assist instructors with selecting, randomizing, formatting, loading online, or printing exams. Please contact your local FlatWorld representative or FlatWorld support (support@flatworld.com) for more information or to request the program.

## FlatWorld Homework

FlatWorld Homework is provided in an easy-to-use interface. Multiple choice, fill-in-the-blank, matching, and other question types are available for use and are all auto-gradable. Students who utilize the homework questions should see their performance improve on examinations that are given using the Test Item File questions that accompany this book.

## Online Quizzes and Flashcards

Autograded Quiz questions and Flashcards for student self-evaluation are organized by chapter and section and embedded in the online version of the book. Students can use the Quizzes and Flashcards to test their comprehension by section as they read and learn, once they have completed a chapter, or for test review.

# What Our Text Does and Does Not Do

Our text is a comprehensive introduction to American politics and government; it covers all the basics. Then it goes beyond the basics to explain how and why, in this information age, government and politics are most commonly depicted in the media.

In each chapter, we compare the reality of American government and politics with the media's most common depictions (acknowledging that there are differences between and among the media and in their political contents). We show that the depictions range from accurate and revealing to inaccurate and misleading. We distinguish the telling accounts and insights from partial truths, false impressions, and distortions.

We do not inflate the importance of the media. We recognize that much of politics and government occurs under the media's radar screen and that the consequences of the media's coverage vary widely.

We avoid the temptation of gee-whiz utopian celebrations of new technologies. Rather, we discuss their possibilities, their limitations, and their dangers: they can and do lower the costs of political activity and organization but do not necessarily turn people into thoughtful, full-fledged activists—indeed, sometimes the reverse.

Finally, we recognize that people variously embrace, accept, ignore, reject, or rework the media's contents. Above all, in today's information age, they are able to hash and rehash the meaning and impact of what is covered, not covered, and depicted accurately or misleadingly in the media.

# Our Concern for Civic Education

One of our goals in writing this book is to encourage students to participate in civic life. In appropriate chapters, we add a "Civic Education" box showing how young people have become involved in politics, government, and the making of public policies, as well as how the media, in all their forms, can help and hinder civic work.

We hope that students will come to understand, appreciate, question, and criticize the realities of American politics and government and the media depictions of these realities. We also hope that they will learn how to use the media to intervene effectively in the American political system on their own terms.

# The Plan of the Book

We begin our text with two chapters designed to introduce and establish the background and fundamentals of American government and politics.

Chapter 1 covers the foundations and structures of authority established by the U.S. Constitution in 1789. We explain the origin, contents, development, and contemporary importance of the Constitution, noting that while American society has changed greatly since then, the political system established by the Constitution still underlies and determines much of American government and politics.

Chapter 2 describes American federalism and its complex interweaving of national, state, and local governments.

Chapter 3 describes the communication system of the United States and accounts for its contents of entertainment, news, opinion-commentary, and social media. Then it discusses how people in politics and government interact with and respond to the media.

Chapter 4 and Chapter 5 cover the conflicts and disputes, debates, and decisions made over the constitutional provisions establishing Americans' liberties and the right to be free of discrimination. Throughout this first part of the book, we show that the U.S. communication system is intimately linked to, and has sometimes buttressed or undermined, these foundations of American government and politics.

The following part of the book focuses on the public. Chapter 6 describes American political culture and how Americans acquire their politically relevant values, beliefs, attitudes, and opinions. Chapter 7 covers public opinion. Chapter 8 describes the many ways that Americans participate in politics. These chapters explain how and when the media are and are not a resource for the public in making sense of and influencing politics and government.

The next part of the book describes the three intermediaries—interest groups (Chapter 9), political parties (Chapter 10), and campaigns and elections (Chapter 11)—that connect the people to government and also link officials within government. Participants in these intermediaries often rely heavily on the media for much of their information, while also seeking to avoid media coverage of their less-appealing activities.

The penultimate part of the book examines the central institutions of the federal government—Congress (Chapter 12), the presidency (Chapter 13), the federal bureaucracy (Chapter 14), and the federal judicial system (Chapter 15)—taking them in order of their appearance in the Constitution. People in these institutions spend considerable time, energy, and resources in dealing with the media, although the ways in which they do so vary depending on their responsibilities and powers, media manipulation skills, and on the media's highly uneven interest in their activities and actions.

The book's final part brings all of these strands together to analyze policymaking and the contents of public policies. Chapter 16 describes the policymaking process and looks at social and economic policies. Chapter 17 is concerned with foreign and defense policies. We show where the media have, and have not, been influential in shaping, supporting, and undermining United States policies and their outcomes at home and abroad.

Our ultimate goals are for students to increase their knowledge of the people, processes, institutions, and policies that make up the American political system; to become more aware of the influence and political effects of the media; and to understand how they, as members of the public, can participate in politics.

## What's New in Version 5.0

Version 5.0 is updated to include information about the 2020 elections, including results of the presidential election; legal challenges to the presidential election results; the outcome of the January 5, 2021, Georgia runoff election and its impact on control of the Senate; the final days of the Trump administration and the transition process to the new Biden administration; and how democratic institutions responded to challenges to the system. Interim updates on the Black Lives Matter movement, summer 2020 protests, the coronavirus pandemic and COVID-19 relief, the death of Justice Ruth Bader Ginsburg, and the appointment of the newest Supreme Court Justice, Amy Coney Barrett, are included. Specific changes made to each chapter are listed below.

New, updated, or substantially revised coverage of the following has been included in this version:

Chapter 2: the Confederate battle flag; the intergovernmental lobby; and police reform.

Chapter 3: selective exposure; selective perception; selective retention; and polarization.

Chapter 5: recent civil rights developments and the increasing importance of Civil War Amendments.

Chapter 6: political norms and rituals and repercussions of violating them; the relationship between "Stop the Steal" and the January 6th insurrection; and political efficacy.

Chapter 7: public opinion; polling in the digital age; and the impact of the pandemic upon presidential election polling.

Chapter 8: The 2020 U.S. presidential election voter turnout; voter participation based on socioeconomic status, age, gender, and race; changes in the racial and ethnic makeup of the U.S. electorate; unsubstantiated claims of voter fraud in the 2020 U.S. presidential election; disenfranchised felons; voter suppression; and citizen activity with focus on Black Lives Matter protests.

Chapter 9: the evolution and demise of interest groups; lobbying and the President; and lobbying government agencies.

Chapter 10: Liz Cheney's ouster from House Republican Party Chair; differences between Democrats and Republicans and increased polarization; new key term "party discipline"; divided government and challenges faced by the Biden Administration due to slim party control of Congress; recent trends in Congress; data on party identification and party realignment; and parties' use of digital media to organize the electorate.

Chapter 11: the 2020 presidential and congressional elections; campaign finance data; escalating costs of political campaigns; state government efforts to curb "dark money"; big data and microtargeting; new key terms "AI" and "voter files"; new digital campaigns such as gaming; the media's treatment of Biden and Trump during the 2020 election cycle; candidate advertising; the 2020 presidential debates; and California's 2021 gubernatorial recall election.

Chapter 12: Trump's first and second impeachments; redistricting based on the 2020 census; notable congressional actions; the CARES Act; The American Rescue Plan; congressional leaders; Constitutional provisions for disciplining congressional members; demographics of congressional members; Alexandria Ocasio-Cortez and her media presence; and use of social media by congressional members.

Chapter 13: the presidency under Trump and particularly in light of the Mueller Report; the U.S. Justice Department under Attorney General Barr; the final days of the Trump presidency; and the advent of the Biden presidency.

Chapter 14: the role of Inspector General; regulatory committees and airline crashes; and J. Edgar Hoover.

Chapter 15: the nomination and confirmation of Justice Amy Coney Barrett.

Chapter 16: the government's reaction to the coronavirus pandemic with specific focus on the Biden Administration's response and new information about how former Governor Andrew Cuomo handled the crisis.

Chapter 17: the U.S. withdrawal from Afghanistan.

CHAPTER 1

# The Constitution and the Structure of Government Power

## 1.1 Preamble

On the day after the presidential election of 2000, *ABC World News Tonight* was anything but routine: candidates George W. Bush and Al Gore disputed the election results. Victory addresses and concession speeches were postponed, as the arduous process of challenging the vote in the pivotal state of Florida commenced.

As the anchor noted at the outset of the evening broadcast, "Uncertainty, intrigue and partisan politics made for a volatile mix." But he ended the broadcast with a reassuring note, much as anchors had done following previous elections: "Finally, this evening, a very brief personal note. A colleague and I who have covered the transfer of power in many unfortunate parts of the world, very often at the point of a gun, agree today on the marvel of this democracy. For all the turmoil last night and today and perhaps tomorrow, Americans, unlike so many others, take the peaceful and orderly transition of power, ultimately, for granted. A gift from the founding fathers."[1]

He thus reiterated conventional wisdom and reinforced public opinion about the wondrous design of American government contained in the Constitution. Yet his praise of the founders was misleading: in fact, the Constitution helped produce the "turmoil" of the 2000 presidential election. Presidents are selected by an Electoral College, a process whereby the winner of the popular vote in a state usually takes all of its electoral votes. Bush won a scant majority in the Electoral College, even as more people voted for Albert Gore nationwide.

Sixteen years later, Donald J. Trump won the Electoral College and thus the presidency, although his opponent, Hillary Clinton, received almost three million more votes. There were some complaints (mainly from the losing side) about the Electoral College denying the popular will and overrepresenting rural states. Proposals to try to abolish the Electoral College were bruited about but went nowhere. Reasons: It benefits Republicans, and the difficulty of amending the Constitution.

In 2020, former Vice President Joseph Biden defeated incumbent President Trump in the Electoral College and by a much larger majority of over six million in the popular vote, thus raising more qualms about the disparity with the College. President Trump and his lawyers then were able to take advantage of the federal system to challenge the results in several states, alleging fraud.

The media have long been enthusiastic about the Constitution, if not always the Electoral College. They provided crucial assistance in the processes leading up to its adoption in the 1780s. They continue to venerate it today, but less so as its defects and inadequacies become more visible.

# 1.2 The First American Political System

## Learning Objectives

After reading this section, you should be able to answer the following questions:

1. What was the Stamp Act Congress?
2. What was the Continental Congress?
3. What are the principles contained in the Declaration of Independence?
4. What were the Articles of Confederation?

We can understand what the Constitution was designed to accomplish by looking at the political system it replaced: the Articles of Confederation, the United States' first written constitution, which embodied political ideals expressed by the Declaration of Independence.

## From Thirteen Colonies to United States

By the mid-eighteenth century, Britain's thirteen colonies on North America's east coast stretched from Georgia to New Hampshire. Each colony had a governor appointed by the king and a legislature elected by landholding voters. These colonial assemblies, standing for the colonists' right of self-government, clashed with the royal governors over issues of power and policies. Each colony, and the newspapers published therein, dealt with the colonial power in London and largely ignored other colonies.

### The Stamp Act Congress

British policy eventually pushed politics and news across colonial boundaries. In 1763, the British antagonized the colonists in two important ways. A royal proclamation closed off the frontier to colonial expansion. The British also sought to recoup expenses borne defending the colonies. They instituted the first ever direct internal taxes in North America. The most famous, the Stamp Act, required the use of paper embossed with the royal seal to prove that taxes had been paid.

Such taxes on commerce alienated powerful interests, including well-off traders in the North and prosperous planters in the South, who complained that the tax was enacted in England without the colonists' input. Their slogan, "No taxation without representation," shows a dual concern with political ideals and material self-interest that persisted through the adoption of the Constitution.

Among the opponents of the Stamp Act were printers who produced newspapers and pamphlets.

The arduous technology of typesetting and hand-printing individual pages did not permit sizable production.[2] Newspapers reached large audiences by being passed around—"circulated"—or by being read aloud at taverns.[3] Printers' precarious financial condition made them dependent on commissions from wealthy people and official subsidies from government, and thus they were eager to please people in power. Crusading journalism against government authorities was rare.[4] The Stamp Act, however, was opposed by powerful interests and placed financial burdens on printers, so it was easy for newspaper printers to oppose it vigorously with hostile stories.

During the Stamp Act crisis, news began to focus on events throughout the thirteen colonies. Benjamin Franklin, postmaster of the British government for the colonies, developed a system of post roads linking the colonies. Printers now could send newspapers to each other free of charge in the mail, providing content for each other to copy. Colonial legislatures proposed a meeting of delegates from across the colonies to address their grievances. This gathering, the Stamp Act Congress, met for two weeks in 1765. Delegates sent a petition to the king that convinced British authorities to annul the taxes.

**FIGURE 1.1**
**Newspaper Printing**
Printing newspapers was a small, labor-intensive business. Printers were often identifiable around town, not only for being ink stained, but also because the physical strain of pulling their presses shut made one shoulder rise considerably higher than the other.

Source: © Thinkstock.

### Link

**Declaration of Rights**

Click here to see the text of the Stamp Act Congress's Declaration of Rights.

## The Continental Congress

In 1773, the British government awarded the East India Company a monopoly on importing and selling tea to the American colonies. This policy, too, hurt powerful interests: colonial traders and merchants. Rebellious Bostonians ransacked the East India Company's ships and pushed cartons of tea overboard. The British reacted harshly to this "Boston Tea Party": they closed the port of Boston, deported rebels to England for trial, and restricted settlement in and trade to the west of the country.

Once again, delegates from the various colonies met, this time in a gathering known as the Continental Congress, to address the difficulties with Britain. But this congress's petitions, unlike those of the Stamp Act Congress, were rebuffed. Repressive policies were kept in place. The Continental Congress launched a boycott of British products, initiated the Revolutionary War, and passed the Declaration of Independence.[5]

# The Declaration of Independence

The **Declaration of Independence**, issued on July 4, 1776, announced that the thirteen colonies were independent of Britain. It was designed to be read aloud in public and to be sent to international audiences. Its point-by-point charges against British rule give equal weight to how the king damaged America's economic interests and how he ignored principles of self-government.

**Declaration of Independence**

The document drafted by Thomas Jefferson and adopted by the Continental Congress in revised form in 1776, which declared the independence of the thirteen colonies from Britain.

The Declaration is a deeply democratic document.[6] It is democratic in what it *did*—asserting the right of the people in the American colonies to separate from Britain. And it is democratic in what it *said*: "We hold these truths to be self-evident, that all men are created equal" and have inviolable rights to "life, liberty, and the pursuit of happiness." The Declaration concludes that the people are free to "alter or abolish" repressive forms of government. Indeed, it assumes that the people are the best judges of the quality of government and can act wisely on their own behalf.

**Link**

**The Declaration of Independence**

For more information on the Declaration of Independence, visit the National Archives here.

# The Articles of Confederation

**Articles of Confederation**

The first American written constitution, adopted by the Continental Congress in 1777, ratified in 1781, and superseded when the Constitution was ratified by nine of the thirteen states in 1788.

**confederation**

A political system in which a government acts as a unit superior to the states but is dependent on their consent.

Drafted in 1777, the **Articles of Confederation** were the first political constitution for the government of the United States. They codified the Continental Congress's practices and powers. The United States of America was a **confederation** of states. Although the confederation was superior to the individual states, it had no powers without their consent.

**Link**

**The Articles of Confederation**

Click here for the text of the Articles of Confederation.

Under the Articles, the Continental Congress took over the king's powers to make war and peace, send and receive ambassadors, enter into treaties and alliances, coin money, regulate Indian affairs, and run a post office. But the confederation could not raise taxes and relied on revenues from each of the states. There was no president to enforce the laws and no judiciary to hear disputes between and among the states.

Each state delegation cast a single vote in the Continental Congress. Nine states were needed to enact legislation, so few laws were passed. States usually refused to fund policies that hampered their own interests.[7] Changes in the Articles required an all-but-impossible unanimous vote of all thirteen delegations. The weakness of the Articles was no accident. The fights with Britain created widespread distrust of central authority. By restricting the national government, Americans could rule themselves in towns and states. Like many political thinkers dating back to ancient Greece, Americans assumed that self-government worked best in small, face-to-face communities.

## Key Takeaways

The first American political system, as expressed in the Articles of Confederation, reflected a distrust of a national government. Its powers were deliberately limited in order to allow Americans to govern themselves in their cities and states.

## Exercises

1. What was it about the Stamp Act and the decision to award a monopoly on the sale of tea to the East India Company that helped bring the American colonies together? What were the motivations for forming the first Congresses?

2. In what way is the Declaration of Independence's idea that "all men are created equal" a democratic principle? In what sense are people equal if, in practice, they are all different from one another?
3. What were the weaknesses of the Articles of Confederation? Do you think the American government would be able to function if it were still a confederation? Why or why not?

# 1.3 Creating and Ratifying the Constitution

## Learning Objectives

After reading this section, you should be able to answer the following questions:

1. What was Shays's Rebellion?
2. What was the Constitutional Convention?
3. What were the three cross-cutting divides at the Constitutional Convention?
4. What were the main compromises at the Constitutional Convention?
5. Who were the Federalists and the Anti-Federalists?
6. What factors explain ratification of the Constitution?

The Constitution was a reaction against the limitations of the Articles of Confederation and the democratic experiments begun by the Revolution and the Declaration of Independence.

## The Case against the Articles of Confederation

The Articles could not address serious foreign threats. In the late 1780s, Britain denied American ships access to British ports in a trade war. Spain threatened to close the Mississippi River to American vessels. Pirates in the Mediterranean captured American ships and sailors and demanded ransom. The national government had few tools to carry out its assigned task of foreign policy.[8]

There was domestic ferment as well. Millions of dollars in paper money issued by state governments to fund the Revolutionary War lost their value after the war.[9] Financial interests were unable to collect on debts they were owed. They appealed to state governments, where they faced resistance and even brief armed rebellions.

Newspapers played up Shays's Rebellion, an armed insurrection by debt-ridden farmers to prevent county courts from foreclosing mortgages on their farms.[10] Led by Captain Daniel Shays, it began in 1786, culminated with a march on the federal arsenal in Springfield, Massachusetts, and wound down in 1787.

The Continental Congress voted unanimously to raise an army to put down Shays's Rebellion but could not coax the states to provide the necessary funds. The army was never assembled.[11]

## Link

**Shays's Rebellion**

Click here to learn more about Shays's Rebellion.

Leaders who supported national government portrayed Shays's Rebellion as a vivid symbol of state governments running wild and proof of the inability of the Articles of Confederation to protect financial interests. Ordinary Americans, who were experiencing a relatively prosperous time, were less concerned and did not see a need to eliminate the Articles.

# Calling a Constitutional Convention

**Constitutional Convention**

The gathering of delegates from twelve of the thirteen states who met in Philadelphia from June to September of 1787; originally authorized by the Continental Congress to consider amendments to the Articles of Confederation, they ultimately drafted the Constitution that replaced it.

The **Constitutional Convention** was convened in 1787 to propose limited reforms to the Articles of Confederation. Instead, the Articles would be replaced by a new, far more powerful national government.

Twelve state legislatures sent delegates to Philadelphia (Rhode Island did not attend). Each delegation would cast a single vote.

## Who Were the Delegates?

The delegates were not representative of the American people. They were well-educated property owners, many of them wealthy, who came mainly from prosperous seaboard cities, including Boston and New York. Most had served in the Continental Congress and were sensitive to the problems faced by the United States. Few delegates had political careers in the states, and so they were free to break with existing presumptions about how government should be organized in America.

**FIGURE 1.2**
**History and the Information Age**
This creative photographer brings a bust of George Washington into the information age.

Source: Photo courtesy of W. T. Chapin.

## Link

**Constitutional Convention**

Click here to learn more about the delegates to the Constitutional Convention.

The Constitutional Convention was a mix of great and minor characters. Exalted figures and brilliant intellects sat among nonentities, drunkards, and nincompoops. The convention's driving force and chief strategist was a young, bookish politician from Virginia named James Madison. He successfully pressured revered figures to attend the convention, such as George Washington, the commanding officer of the victorious American revolutionaries, and Benjamin Franklin, a man at the twilight of a remarkable career as printer, scientist, inventor, postmaster, philosopher, and diplomat.

Madison drafted the first working proposal for a Constitution and took copious notes at the convention. Published after his death in 1836, they are the best historical source of the debates; they reveal the extraordinary political complexity of the deliberations and provide remarkable insight into what the founders had in mind.[12]

Once the Constitution was drafted, Madison helped write and publish a series of articles in a New York newspaper. These Federalist papers defend the political system the Constitutional Convention had crafted.

**FIGURE 1.3**
**James Madison**
The unassuming and slight James Madison made an unusual teammate for the dashing, ex-soldier Alexander Hamilton and the august diplomat John Jay. But despite these contrasts and some political divides, they merged their voices in the Federalist papers (most of them by Hamilton), published in New York newspapers under the pseudonym "Publius." Soon after the ratification of the Constitution, *The Federalist* was widely republished in book format. Scholars now regard it as the fullest explication of the logic underlying the Constitution.

Source: Everett Collection/ Shutterstock.com

## Interests and the Constitution

In the early twentieth century, historian Charles Beard asserted that the Constitution was "an economic document for economic ends," pushed by investors and industrialists who would profit more from a national economic and political system than from one favoring small-scale agricultural interests.[13] Research has not upheld Beard's stark division of reaction to the Constitution into well-off supporters and poor, democratic adversaries. Many local, well-to-do patriarchs opposed the Constitution; many small merchants wanted a national government.

But Beard's focus on economic and social interests is revealing. Paper money, debt relief, and Shays's Rebellion concerned those committed to existing economic and social orders. Consider Federalist No. 10, the most famous of Madison's Federalist papers. In it, he decried the dangers of democracy; he started with "a rage for paper money" and "an abolition of debts," then the specter of "an equal division of property," all of which he found an "improper or wicked project." Madison paid attention to the right to acquire and maintain property, which the Declaration brushed aside. He claimed that political systems were created to maintain liberty—including the liberty to accumulate wealth. Political equality meant only that each person had a right to express himself or herself.

Nonetheless, economic inequality was deemed by Jefferson and most of the Founders to be of concern and to be a threat to popular government and political freedom.[14]

## Ideas and the Constitution

The Constitutional Convention responded to ideas, not just interests. Delegates doubted that the people could wisely rule. They sought to replace *democracy* with a *republic*, in which officials would be chosen to act on the people's behalf. Federalist No. 10 makes the case.

Madison was concerned with threats to order and stability from what he called **factions**, groups pursuing their self-interest above the public good. For Madison, factions were inevitable. His worst nightmare was of a faction becoming a political majority, trampling on the rights of its helpless opponents, and quickly enacting its program. He favored a large republic, which, he believed, would discourage a faction's rise to power. Madison expected that in a republic, the number of locally oriented interests would increase and diversify, which would make it harder for any one of them to dominate. Minority factions could pass legislation by forming temporary majorities, Madison reasoned, but these diverse majorities would not be able to agree on a single project long enough to be oppressive.

**factions**

James Madison's term for groups that pursue their self-interest or individual preferences above the public good.

# Drafting the Constitution

**constitution**

A system of fundamental laws and principles that prescribe the structure and functions of the government.

Delegates to the Constitutional Convention first gathered on May 25, 1787, in what is now called Independence Hall in Philadelphia. Their goal was to devise a **constitution**, a system of fundamental laws and principles outlining the nature and functions of the government. George Washington presided. Delegates worked in an intimate setting without committees.

The structure of power created by the Constitution resulted from a deeply political process. Political scientists have revealed the degree to which the Constitutional Convention and the ratification conventions can be understood to be the result of the manipulation of parliamentary rules, strategic voting, shifting coalitions, and the "agenda-setting" and "framing" use of mass communication.[15]

## The Secrecy of the Constitutional Convention

Deliberations took place in secret, as delegates did not want the press and the public to know the details of what they were considering (see the following "Comparing Content" for more information). Newspapers hardly mentioned the convention at all, and when they did, it was in vague references praising the high caliber of the delegates.[16]

### Comparing Content

#### The Convention's Gag Rule

Press coverage of the Constitutional Convention cannot be compared because one of the first decisions made in the Constitutional Convention was that "nothing spoken in the House be printed, or otherwise published or communicated."[17] The delegates feared that exposure through newspapers would complicate their work. The delegate who is today regarded as the great defender of civil liberties, George Mason, wrote to his son approvingly: "This I think myself a proper precaution to prevent mistakes and misrepresentation until the business shall have been completed, when the whole may have a very different complexion from that in the several crude and indigested parts might in their first shape appear if submitted to the public eye."[18]

This gag rule was rigorously enforced. One day the presiding officer, George Washington, noticed that an inattentive delegate had dropped his notes on the floor when leaving the hall. Washington broke his usual silence and rebuked the unknown infractor: "I am sorry to find that some one Member of this Body, has been so neglectful of the secrets of the convention as to drop in the State House a copy of their proceedings, which by accident was picked up and delivered to me this morning. I must entreat Gentlemen to be more careful, least [sic] our transactions get into the News Papers, and disturb the public repose by premature speculations."

Throwing the notes on the table, Washington exclaimed, "I know not whose Paper it is, but there it is, let him who owns it take it." Delegate William Pierce, who recorded this tale, noted that Washington "bowed, picked up his Hat, and quitted the room with a dignity so severe that every Person seemed alarmed."[19]

The founders were not unanimous about the threat posed by the press. Thomas Jefferson was in Paris as an ambassador. In August 1787, he wrote to his counterpart in London, John Adams, that there was no news from the convention: "I am sorry they began their deliberations by so abominable a precedent as that of tying up the tongues of their members. Nothing can justify this example but the innocence of their intentions, & ignorance of the value of public discussions. I have no doubt that all their other measures will be good & wise."[20]

In 1787, the powers of the press were identified in ways we recognize in the twenty-first century. Washington was concerned that news about the political process might produce rumors, confusion, worry, and public opposition to worthwhile policies. But as Jefferson recognized, the news can also lead to productive public debate, dialogue, and deliberation.

**FIGURE 1.4 Independence Hall Assembly Room in Philadelphia, Pennsylvania**
The membership of the Constitutional Convention was so small—never more than fifty on a given day—that they could proceed largely in "a committee of the whole." This size enabled them to continue their discussions in private at their preferred boardinghouses and taverns—and to keep a tight lid on public discussion.

Source: Photo taken by Dan Smith, http://commons.wikimedia.org/wiki/File:Independence_Hall_Assembly_Room.jpg. Reproduced via CC BY-SA 2.5: https://creativecommons.org/licenses/by-sa/2.5/deed.en

## The Cross-Cutting Divides

The delegates immediately discarded the Continental Congress's mandate that they recommend amendments to the Articles of Confederation. They agreed to draft a new Constitution from scratch in order to create a national government superior to and independent of the states.

This crucial decision was followed by disagreement about exactly how to create a national government. The states varied widely in economic bases, population sizes, and numbers of slaves.

Three cross-cutting divides existed among the states:

1. Large states versus small states[21]
2. Cosmopolitan, centrally located states (Connecticut to Virginia) versus parochial states on the northern and southern borders
3. Southern states, reliant on slavery in their economies, versus Northern states, which were not

The powers and structures of the Constitution resulted from a series of compromises designed to bridge these three divides.

## Large and Small States

The most threatening split in the convention emerged initially between large and small states.

**Virginia Plan**

James Madison's initial working draft at the Constitutional Convention, containing strong national powers, a bicameral legislature with the popularly elected lower chamber choosing the upper chamber, and a weak executive elected by the legislature.

Large states fired the first salvo. The **Virginia Plan**, drafted by Madison, foresaw a strong national government that could veto any state laws it deemed contrary to the national interest. The central institution was a bicameral (two-chamber) legislature. The people would elect the lower house, which would in turn select the members of the upper house; the two chambers together would then elect the executive and judiciary. Breaking with the Articles of Confederation's equal representation of states, the Virginia Plan allotted seats to both chambers of the legislature by population size alone.[22]

Cosmopolitan, centrally located states, provided strong initial support for the Virginia Plan against scattered opposition from border states. But Madison could not hold this coalition behind *both* a strong national government *and* a legislature allocated by population. Delegates from the small states of New Jersey, Delaware, and Maryland liked a strong national government, but they feared being overpowered. Delegates from populous Massachusetts and three fast-growing Southern states joined the two largest states, Virginia and Pennsylvania, to support legislative districts based on population, but they disliked the Virginia Plan's sweeping powers for the national government.

**New Jersey Plan**

The alternative to the Virginia Plan, offered by William Paterson of New Jersey, with reduced national powers and a single legislative body representing the states.

On June 15, the small states proposed an alternative. The **New Jersey Plan** enhanced the national government's powers to levy taxes and regulate commerce but left remaining powers to the states. The plan had a federal executive, elected by the legislature, to enforce states' compliance with national law, and a federal judiciary to settle disputes among the states and between the states and the national government. Any national law would become "the supreme law of the respective States." The New Jersey Plan preserved the core of the Articles of Confederation—equal representation of states in a unicameral (single-chamber) legislature.

Only three states voted for the New Jersey Plan, but the Virginia Plan's vulnerability was exposed. Facing an impasse, delegates from Connecticut suggested a compromise. Borrowing the Virginia Plan's idea of a bicameral legislature, they proposed that one chamber, the House of Representatives, be made up of representatives from districts of equal population, while in the Senate each state would be equally represented with two senators.

**Connecticut Compromise (also known as the Great Compromise)**

The solution worked out by delegates from Connecticut to create a bicameral legislature, with one chamber (the Senate) representing states, and the other (the House of Representatives) representing the people in districts of equal population size.

This **Connecticut Compromise (also known as the Great Compromise)** was adopted by the convention with only Virginia and Pennsylvania in opposition. Thus, the configuration of today's Congress emerged not so much from principled deliberations between the Constitution's founders as from the necessity for compromise between competing state interests. In essence, the founders decided to split the difference.[23]

## North and South

After this vote, North versus South displaced the divide between large and small states. The convention became preoccupied by how the new government would be empowered to deal with slavery. Northerners feared the South's growth and room for expansion. Southerners worried that the North would threaten the practice of slavery, which, although legal in all states, was a central part only of Southern economies.

**three-fifths clause**

Constitutional provision that, for purposes of representation, only 60 percent of the enslaved population would be counted.

Northern interests in a strong national government acceded to Southern demands on slavery. Southerners argued that slaves should be counted when allocating legislative seats. Eventually, the convention settled on a **three-fifths clause**: 60 percent of the enslaved population would be counted for purposes of representation. Northern delegates, convinced that the largest slave-holding states would never have a majority in the Senate, gave in.

### Link

**The Three-Fifths Clause**

Aaron McGruder's comic strip *The Boondocks* ran this installment during the 2004 presidential campaign. Showing a depressed black man talking about the three-fifths clause, it powerfully illustrates the Constitution's long-lasting affront to African Americans, almost all of whom were enslaved and thus, for the purpose of the census (and for that of representation in Congress and the Electoral College), would be counted as three-fifths of a person. Click here to read the comic.

As the convention considered the national government's powers, an alliance of delegates from New England and the Deep South emerged to defend local control and their states' economic self-interest. Southerners sought to maintain slavery, while New Englanders wanted national tariffs to protect their commerce. They struck a deal that resulted in New England delegates voting to require the return of fugitive slaves and to prevent Congress from regulating the slave trade until 1808.

The delegates did not confront slavery head on (indeed, the word "slavery" is not directly mentioned in the Constitution). As a result, the issue of slavery would overshadow much of federal politics until its bloody resolution in the Civil War of the 1860s.

## The Executive

By now, the Constitutional Convention could not break down, because the document had something for everybody. Small states liked the security of a national government and their equal representation in the Senate. The Deep South and New England valued the protection of their economic bases. Pennsylvania and Virginia—the two most populous, centrally located states—foresaw a national government that would extend the reach of their commerce and influence.

The convention's final sticking point was the nature of the executive. The debate focused on how many people would be president, the power of the office, the term of the office, how presidents would be elected, and whether they could serve multiple terms.

To break the logjam on the presidency, the convention created the **Electoral College** as the method of electing the president, a political solution that gave something to each of the state-based interests. The president would not be elected directly by the popular vote of citizens. Instead, electors chosen by state legislatures would vote for president. Small states got more electoral votes than warranted by population, as the number of electors is equal to the total of representatives *and* senators. If the Electoral College did not produce a majority result, the president would be chosen by the popularly elected House, but with one vote per state delegation.[24] With all sides mollified, the convention agreed that the office of president would be held by one person who could run for multiple terms.

**Electoral College**

The body of electors chosen by states to select the president and vice president of the United States.

## Bargaining, Compromise, and Deal Making

The Constitutional Convention began with a principled consensus on establishing a stronger national government; it ended with bargaining, compromise, and deal making. State delegations voted for their political and economic self-interests, and often worked out deals enabling everyone to have something to take home to constituents. Some complex matters, such as the structures of the executive and judicial branches, were left up to the new Congress. As one scholar writes, the Constitution is "a patch-work sewn together under the pressure of both time and events by a group of extremely talented . . . politicians."[25]

**Link**

**The Constitution**

To learn more about the Constitution, visit the National Constitution Center here.

# Ratifying the Constitution

The signing of the Constitution by the delegates on September 17, 1787, was just the beginning. The Constitution would go into effect only after being approved by specially elected ratifying conventions in nine states.

Ratification was not easy to win. In most states, property qualifications for voting had broadened from landholding to taxpaying, thereby including most white men, many of whom benefited from the public policies of the states. Popular opinion for and against ratification was evenly split. In key states like Massachusetts and Virginia, observers thought the opposition was ahead.[26]

## The Opposition to Ratification

The elections to the ratifying conventions revealed that opponents of the Constitution tended to come from rural inland areas (not from cities and especially not from ports, where merchants held sway). The opponents held to the ideals of the Declaration of Independence, which favored a deliberately weak national government to enhance local and state self-government.[27] They thought that the national government's powers, the complex system of government, lengthy terms of office, and often indirect elections in the new Constitution unacceptably distanced government from the people.

Opponents also feared that the strength of the proposed national government posed a threat to individual freedoms. They criticized the Constitution's lack of a **Bill of Rights**—clauses to guarantee specific liberties from infringement by the new government. A few delegates to the Constitutional Convention, notably George Mason of Virginia and Elbridge Gerry of Massachusetts, had refused to sign the document in the absence of a Bill of Rights.

**Bill of Rights**

Constitutional sections guaranteeing specific liberties from infringement by the new government; more precisely, the first ten amendments to the Constitution, passed by Congress in 1789 and ratified by 1791 to fulfill the Federalists' campaign promise during the state conventions ratifying the Constitution.

## The Campaign for Ratification

Despite such objections and obstacles, the campaign for ratification was successful in all thirteen states.[28] The advocates of the national political system, benefiting from the secrecy of the Constitutional Convention, were well prepared to take the initiative. They called themselves not nationalists but **Federalists**. Opponents to the Constitution were saddled with the name of **Anti-Federalists**, though they were actually the champions of a federation of independent states.

**Federalists**

The name adopted by those favoring the ratification of the Constitution.

**Anti-Federalists**

The name applied to those who opposed ratification of the Constitution.

By asking conventions to ratify the Constitution, the Federalists evaded resistance from state legislatures. Federalists campaigned to elect sympathetic ratifiers and hoped that successive victories, publicized in the press, would build momentum toward winning ratification by all thirteen states.

Anti-Federalists did not decry the process by which the Constitution was drafted and ratified. Instead, they participated in the ratification process, hoping to organize a new convention to remedy the Constitution's flaws.

## Newspapers and Ratification

The U.S. newspaper system boosted the Federalist cause. Of the approximately one hundred newspapers being published during the ratification campaign of 1787–88, "not more than a dozen . . . could be classed as avowedly antifederal."[29] Anti-Federalist arguments were rarely printed and even less often copied by other newspapers.[30] Printers followed the money trail to support the Federalists. Most newspapers, especially those whose stories were reprinted by others, were based in port cities, if only because arriving ships provided good sources of news. Such locales were dominated by merchants, who favored a national system to facilitate trade and commerce. Newspapers were less common in rural interior locations, where Anti-Federalist support was greatest.

Federalists also pressured the few Anti-Federalist newspapers that existed. They wrote subscribers and advertisers and urged them to cancel. Anti-Federalist printers often moved to other cities, went out of business, or began reprinting Federalist articles. Federalists hailed such results as the voice of the people. When an Anti-Federalist paper in Philadelphia halted publication, Federalists exulted, "There cannot be a greater proof that the body of the people are federal, that the antifederal editors and printers fail of support."[31]

Today the most famous part of this newspaper campaign is the series of essays (referred to earlier) written by Alexander Hamilton, John Jay, and James Madison, and published in New York newspapers under the collective pseudonym "Publius." The authors used their skills at legal argumentation to make the strongest case they could for the document that emerged from the Constitutional Convention. These **Federalist papers**, steeped in discussion of political theory and history, offer the fullest logic for the workings of the Constitution. However, they were rarely reprinted outside New York and were a minor part of the ratification campaign.

### Link

***The Federalist Papers***

Click here to read *The Federalist Papers* at the Library of Congress.

Newspapers instead played on public sentiment, notably the adulation of George Washington, presiding officer of the convention, and his support of the Constitution.[32] The most widely disseminated story concerned his return trip from Philadelphia to Virginia. A bridge collapsed, but Washington escaped unharmed. The tale implied that divine intervention had ensured Washington's leadership by "the providential preservation of the valuable life of this great and good man, on his way home from the Convention."[33]

Not all states were eager to ratify the Constitution, especially since it did not specify what the federal government could not do and did not include a Bill of Rights. Massachusetts narrowly voted in favor of ratification, with the provision that the first Congress take up recommendations for amending the Constitution. New Hampshire, Virginia, and New York followed this same strategy. Once nine states had ratified it, the Constitution was approved. Madison was elected to the first Congress and proposed a Bill of Rights, the first ten amendments to the Constitution. Only after

**FIGURE 1.5**
**Federalist Political Cartoon**

The Federalists' media strategies included images, too. A famous woodcut at the start of the Revolution was of a serpent cut into thirteen sections with the admonition "Join or Die." Federalists provided a new twist on this theme. They kept track of the ratification by an edifice of columns, elevated one by one as each state ratified. The next state convention on the list would be represented by a hand lifting the column, often accompanied by the confident motto "Rise It Will."

Source: Library of Congress (https://www.loc.gov/pictures/item/2002695523/) via Wikimedia: https://commons.wikimedia.org/wiki/File:Franklin_join_or_die.jpg.

**Federalist papers**

A series of essays written by Alexander Hamilton, John Jay, and James Madison, published in New York newspapers during the debate over the ratification of the Constitution; they are generally understood to offer the fullest logic behind the creation of the Constitution.

Congress had approved the Bill of Rights did North Carolina and Rhode Island ratify the Constitution.

## Key Takeaways

We have shown that the Constitution was a political document, drafted for political purposes, by skillful politicians who deployed shrewd media strategies. At the Constitutional Convention, they reconciled different ideas and base self-interests. Through savvy compromises, they resolved cross-cutting divisions and achieved agreement on such difficult issues as slavery and electing the executive. In obtaining ratification of the Constitution, they adroitly outmaneuvered or placated their opponents. The eighteenth-century press was crucial to the Constitution's success by keeping its proceedings secret and supporting ratification.

## Exercises

1. From what James Madison says in Federalist No. 10, what economic interests was the Constitution designed to protect? Do you agree that the liberty to accumulate wealth is an essential part of liberty?
2. What did James Madison mean by "factions," and what danger did they pose? How did he hope to avoid the problems factions could cause?
3. Why were the Constitutional Convention's deliberations kept secret? Do you think it was a good idea to keep them secret? Why or why not?
4. What were the main divisions that cut across the Constitutional Convention? What compromises bridged each of these divisions?

# 1.4 Constitutional Principles and Provisions

## Learning Objectives

After reading this section, you should be able to answer the following questions:

1. What is the separation of powers?
2. What are checks and balances?
3. What is bicameralism?
4. What are the Articles of the Constitution?
5. What is the Bill of Rights?

## The Principles Underlying the Constitution

The Constitution established a national government that did not rely on the support of the states. At the same time, it limited the federal government's powers by listing ("enumerating") them. This practice of *federalism* (as we explain in detail in Chapter 2) means that some policy areas are exclusive to the federal government, some are exclusive to the states, and others are shared between the two levels.

Federalism aside, three key principles are the crux of the Constitution: separation of powers, checks and balances, and bicameralism.

## Separation of Powers

**Separation of powers** is the allocation of three domains of governmental action—law making, law execution, and law adjudication—into three distinct branches of government: the legislative, the executive, and the judicial. Each branch is assigned specific powers that only it can wield (see Table 1.1).

**separation of powers**

The doctrine whereby legislative, executive, and judicial powers are placed in distinct, at least partially autonomous, institutions.

**TABLE 1.1 The Separation of Powers and Bicameralism as Originally Established in the Constitution**

| Branch of Government | Term | How Selected | Distinct Powers |
|---|---|---|---|
| **Legislative** | | | |
| House of Representatives | 2 years | Popular vote | Initiate revenue legislation; bring articles of impeachment |
| Senate | 6 years; 3 classes staggered | Election by state legislatures | Confirm executive appointments; confirm treaties; try impeachments |
| **Executive** | | | |
| President | 4 years | Electoral College | Commander-in-chief; nominate executive officers and Supreme Court justices; veto; convene both houses of Congress; issue reprieves and pardons |
| **Judicial** | | | |
| Supreme Court | Life (during good behavior) | Presidential appointment and Senate confirmation (stated more or less directly in Federalist No. 78) | Judicial review (implicitly in Constitution but stated more or less directly in Federalist No. 78) |

This separation is in the Constitution itself, which divides powers and responsibilities of each branch in three distinct articles: Article I for the legislature, Article II for the executive, and Article III for the judiciary.

**FIGURE 1.6** Plan of the City of Washington, 1792

In perhaps the most abiding indicator of the separation of powers, Pierre L'Enfant's plan of Washington, DC, placed the president's house and the Capitol at opposite ends of Pennsylvania Avenue. The plan notes the importance of the two branches being both geographically and politically distinct.

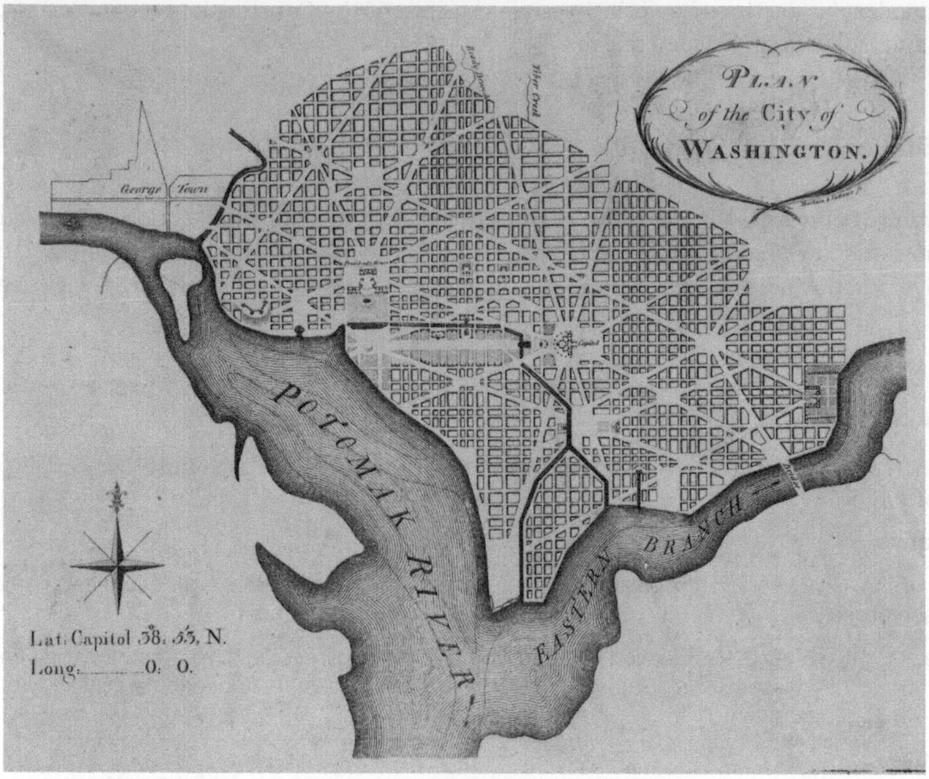


Source: Library of Congress: (https://www.loc.gov/resource/g3850.ct000509/?r=0.261,0.223,1.161,0.46,0) via Wikimedia Commons: http://commons.wikimedia.org/wiki/File:L'Enfant_plan_original.jpg.

## Checks and Balances

At the same time, each branch lacks full control over all the powers allotted to it. Political scientist Richard Neustadt put it memorably: "The Constitutional Convention of 1787 is supposed to have created a government of 'separated powers.' It did nothing of the sort. Rather, it created a government of separated institutions *sharing* powers."[34] No branch can act effectively without the cooperation—or passive consent—of the other two.

**checks and balances**

The Constitution's approach whereby every branch is equipped with powers at least partially countervailing those of the other two branches.

**judicial review**

The power of the Supreme Court to render acts of Congress or decisions of the executive null and void on the basis that they violate the Constitution.

Most governmental powers are shared among the various branches in a system of **checks and balances**, whereby each branch has ways to respond to, and if necessary, block the actions of the others. For example, only Congress can pass a law. But the president can veto it. Supreme Court justices can declare an act of Congress unconstitutional through **judicial review**. Figure 1.7 shows the various checks and balances between the three branches.

The logic of checks and balances echoes Madison's skeptical view of human nature. In Federalist No. 10 he contends that all individuals, even officials, follow their own selfish interests. Expanding on this point in Federalist No. 51, he claimed that officeholders in the three branches would seek influence and defend the powers of their respective branches. Therefore, he wrote, the Constitution provides "to those who administer each department the necessary constitutional means and personal motives to resist encroachments of the others."[35]

**FIGURE 1.7 Checks and Balances**

The following chart explains the checks and balances of the three branches of government.

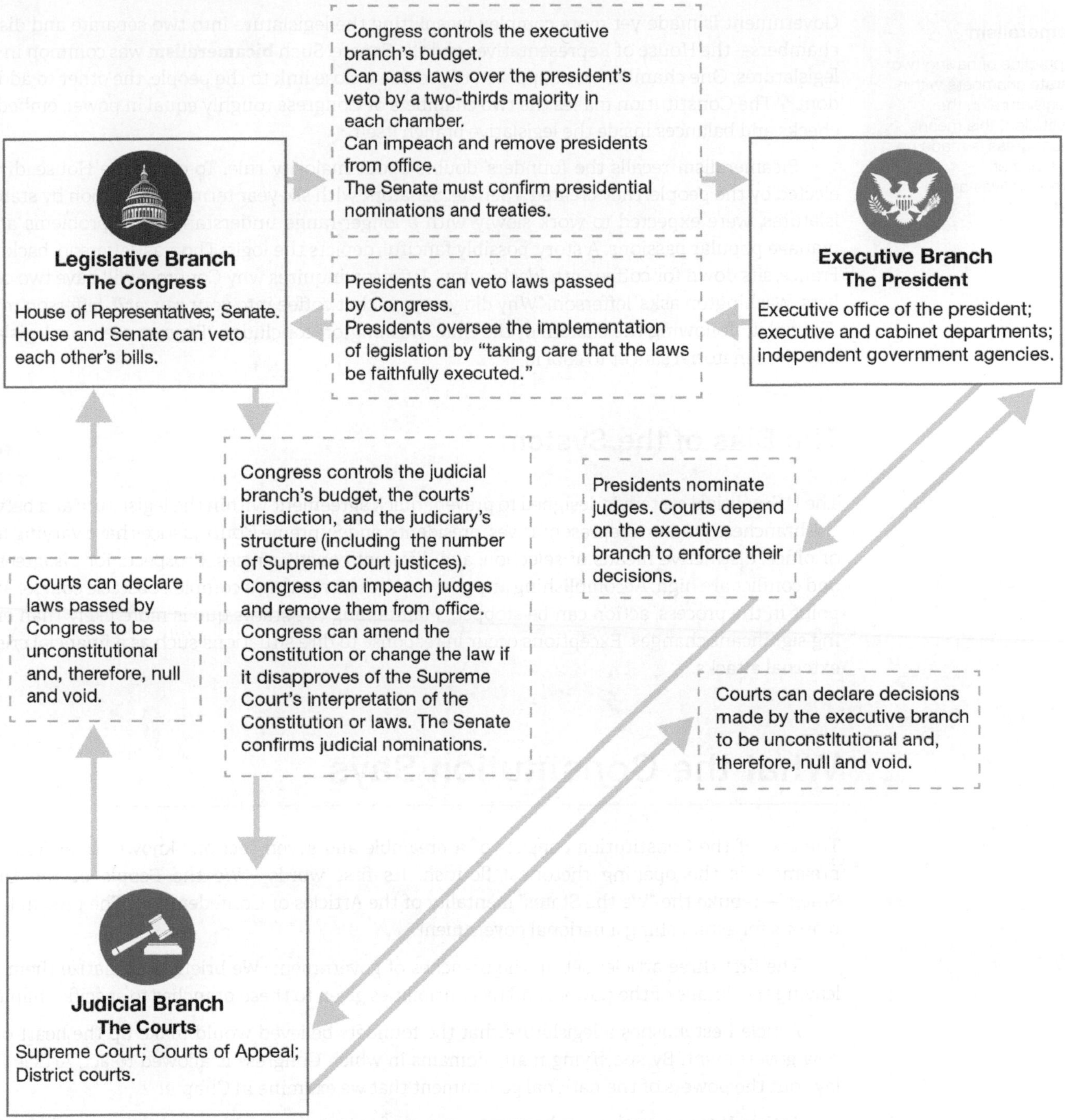

Congress controls the executive branch's budget.
Can pass laws over the president's veto by a two-thirds majority in each chamber.
Can impeach and remove presidents from office.
The Senate must confirm presidential nominations and treaties.
Legislative Branch
The Congress
House of Representatives; Senate. House and Senate can veto each other's bills.
Executive Branch
The President
Executive office of the president; executive and cabinet departments; independent government agencies.
Presidents can veto laws passed by Congress.
Presidents oversee the implementation of legislation by "taking care that the laws be faithfully executed."
Congress controls the judicial branch's budget, the courts' jurisdiction, and the judiciary's structure (including the number of Supreme Court justices). Congress can impeach judges and remove them from office. Congress can amend the Constitution or change the law if it disapproves of the Supreme Court's interpretation of the Constitution or laws. The Senate confirms judicial nominations.
Presidents nominate judges. Courts depend on the executive branch to enforce their decisions.
Courts can declare laws passed by Congress to be unconstitutional and, therefore, null and void.
Courts can declare decisions made by the executive branch to be unconstitutional and, therefore, null and void.
Judicial Branch
The Courts
Supreme Court; Courts of Appeal; District courts.


Source: Adapted from George C. Edwards, Martin P. Wattenberg, and Robert L. Lineberry, *Government in America: People, Politics, and Policy* (White Plains, NY: Pearson Longman, 2011), 46.

## Bicameralism

**bicameralism**

The practice of having two separate chambers within the legislature; in the Constitution, this means that Congress is made up of a House of Representatives and a Senate.

Government is made yet more complex by splitting the legislature into two separate and distinct chambers—the House of Representatives and the Senate. Such **bicameralism** was common in state legislatures. One chamber was supposed to provide a close link to the people, the other to add wisdom.[36] The Constitution makes the two chambers of Congress roughly equal in power, embedding checks and balances inside the legislative branch itself.

Bicameralism recalls the founders' doubts about majority rule. To check the House, directly elected by the people, they created a Senate. Senators, with six-year terms and election by state legislatures, were expected to work slowly with a longer-range understanding of problems and to manage popular passions. A story, possibly fanciful, depicts the logic: Thomas Jefferson, back from France, sits down for coffee with Washington. Jefferson inquires why Congress will have two chambers. Washington asks Jefferson, "Why did you pour that coffee into your saucer?" Jefferson replies, "To cool it," following the custom of the time. Washington concludes, "Even so, we pour legislation into the senatorial saucer to cool it."[37]

## The Bias of the System

The U.S. political system is designed to prevent quick agreement within the legislature and between the branches. Senators, representatives, presidents, and Supreme Court justices have varying terms of office, distinctive means of selection, and different constituencies. Prospects for disagreement and conflict are high. Accomplishing any goal requires navigating a complex obstacle course. At any point in the process, action can be stopped. Maintaining the status quo is more likely than enacting significant changes. Exceptions occur in response to dire situations such as a financial crisis or external attacks.

# What the Constitution Says

The text of the Constitution consists of a preamble and seven sections known as "articles." The preamble is the opening rhetorical flourish. Its first words—"We the People of the United States"—rebuke the "We the States" mentality of the Articles of Confederation. The preamble lists reasons for establishing a national government.

The first three articles set up the branches of government. We briefly summarize them here, leaving the details of the powers and responsibilities given to these branches to specific chapters.

Article I establishes a legislature that the founders believed would make up the heart of the new government. By specifying many domains in which Congress is allowed to act, Article I also lays out the powers of the national government that we examine in Chapter 2.

Article II takes up the cumbersome process of assembling an Electoral College and electing a president and a vice president—a process that was later modified by the Twelfth Amendment. The presidential duties listed here focus on war and management of the executive branch. The president's powers are far fewer than those enumerated for Congress.

The Constitutional Convention punted decisions on the structure of the judiciary below the Supreme Court to the first Congress to decide. Article III states that judges of all federal courts hold office for life "during good Behaviour." It authorizes the Supreme Court to decide all cases arising under federal law and in disputes involving states. Judicial review, the central power of the Supreme Court, is not mentioned. Asserted in the 1803 case of *Marbury v. Madison* (discussed in Chapter 15 Section 3), it is the ability of the Court to invalidate a law passed by Congress or a decision made by the executive on the basis that it violates the Constitution.

Article IV lists rights and obligations among the states and between the states and the national government (discussed in Chapter 2).

Article V specifies how to amend the Constitution. This shows that the framers intended to have a Constitution that could be adapted to changing conditions. There are two ways to propose amendments. States may call for a convention. (This has never been used due to fears it would reopen the entire Constitution for revision.) The other way to propose amendments is for Congress to pass them by a two-thirds majority in both the House and Senate.

There are two ways to approve an amendment. One is through ratification by three-fourths of state legislatures. Alternatively, an amendment can be ratified by three-fourths of specially convoked state conventions. This process has been used once. "Wets," favoring the end of Prohibition, feared that the Twenty-First Amendment—which would have repealed the Eighteenth Amendment prohibiting the sale and consumption of alcohol—would be blocked by conservative ("dry") state legislatures. The wets asked for specially called state conventions and rapidly ratified repeal—on December 5, 1933.

Thus a constitutional amendment can be stopped by one-third of either chamber of Congress or one-fourth of state legislatures—which explains why there have been only twenty-seven amendments in over two centuries.

Article VI includes a crucial provision that endorses the move away from a loose confederation to a national government superior to the states. Lifted from the New Jersey Plan, the **supremacy clause** states that the Constitution and all federal laws are "the supreme Law of the Land."

**supremacy clause**

Clause in Article VI of the Constitution stating that the Constitution and all federal laws are "the supreme Law of the Land."

Article VII outlines how to ratify the new Constitution.

# Constitutional Evolution

The Constitution has remained essentially intact over time. The basic structure of governmental power is much the same in the twenty-first century as in the late eighteenth century. At the same time, the Constitution has been transformed in the centuries since 1787. Amendments have greatly expanded civil liberties and rights. Interpretations of its language by all three branches of government have taken the Constitution into realms not imagined by the founders. New practices have been grafted onto the Constitution's ancient procedures. Intermediary institutions not mentioned in the Constitution have developed important governmental roles.[38]

## Amendments

Many crucial clauses of the Constitution today are in the amendments. The Bill of Rights, the first ten amendments ratified by the states in 1791, defines civil liberties to which individuals are entitled. After the slavery issue was resolved by a devastating civil war, equality entered the Constitution with the Fourteenth Amendment, which specified: "No State shall . . . deny to any person within its jurisdiction the equal protection of the laws." This amendment provides the basis for civil rights, and further democratization of the electorate was guaranteed in subsequent ones. The right to vote became anchored in the Constitution with the addition of the Fifteenth, Nineteenth, Twenty-Fourth, and Twenty-Sixth Amendments, which stated that such a right, granted to all citizens aged eighteen years or more, could not be denied on the basis of race or sex, nor could it be dependent on the payment of a poll tax.[39]

## Link

**The Full Text of the Constitution**

See Chapter 18 (Appendix A) for the full text of the Constitution, or click here to read this content at the National Archives.

## Constitutional Interpretation

The Constitution is sometimes silent or vague, making it flexible and adaptable to new circumstances. Interpretations of constitutional provisions by the three branches of government have resulted in changes in political organization and practice.[40]

For example, the Constitution is silent about the role, number, and jurisdictions of executive officers, such as cabinet secretaries; the judicial system below the Supreme Court; and the number of House members or Supreme Court justices. The first Congress had to fill in the blanks, often by altering the law.[41]

The Supreme Court is today at center stage in interpreting the Constitution. Before becoming chief justice in 1910, Charles Evans Hughes proclaimed, "We are under a Constitution, but the Constitution is what the Court says it is."[42] By examining the Constitution's clauses and applying them to specific cases, the justices expand or limit the reach of constitutional rights and requirements. However, the Supreme Court does not always have the last word, since state officials and members of the national government's legislative and executive branches have their own understanding of the Constitution that they apply on a daily basis, responding to, challenging, and sometimes modifying what the Court has held.[43]

## New Practices

Specific sections of the Constitution have evolved greatly through new practices. Article II gives the presidency few formal powers and responsibilities. During the first hundred years of the republic, presidents acted in limited ways, except during war or massive social change, and they rarely campaigned for a legislative agenda.[44] Article II's brevity would be turned to the office's advantage by President Theodore Roosevelt at the dawn of the twentieth century. He argued that the president is "a steward of the people . . . bound actively and affirmatively to do all he could for the people." So the president is obliged to do whatever is best for the nation as long as it is not specifically forbidden by the Constitution.[45]

## Intermediary Institutions

**intermediary institutions**

Institutions that have, largely informally, arisen to bridge the gap between the government and the people or the gaps among the three branches.

The Constitution is silent about various **intermediary institutions**—political parties, interest groups, and the media—that link government with the people and bridge gaps caused by a separation-of-powers system. The political process might stall in their absence. For example, presidential elections and the internal organization of Congress rely on the party system. Interest groups represent different people and are actively involved in the policy process. The media are fundamental for conveying information to the public about government policies as well as for letting government officials know what the public is thinking, a process that is essential in a democratic system.

## Key Takeaways

The Constitution established a national government distinguished by federalism, separation of powers, checks and balances, and bicameralism. It divided power and created conflicting institutions—between three branches of government, across two chambers of the legislature, and between national and state levels. While the structure it created remains the same, the Constitution has been changed by amendments, interpretation, new practices, and intermediary institutions. Thus the Constitution operates in a system that is democratic far beyond the founders' expectations.

## Exercises

1. Why was conflict between the different branches of government built into the Constitution? What are the advantages and disadvantages of a system of checks and balances?
2. How is the Constitution different from the Articles of Confederation? How did the authors of the Constitution address the concerns of those who worried that the new federal government would be too strong?
3. What do you think is missing from the Constitution? Are there any constitutional amendments you would propose?

# 1.5 The Constitution in the Information Age

## Learning Objectives

After reading this section, you should be able to answer the following questions:

1. How do the media portray the Constitution?
2. How do the media depict the politicians charged with fulfilling the Constitution's vision of public life?
3. What are the effects of the media's depiction of the Constitution?

We have seen that the Constitution is a political document adopted for political reasons in a highly political process. Yet the text of the Constitution, and the structure of power it created, are almost entirely above political controversy. It is an object of pride for almost all Americans.

## The Constitution as a Sacred Document

The official presentation of the Constitution in public buildings shows it as a **sacred document**, demonstrating its exalted status. The original document is ensconced in what is called a "Shrine" at the National Archives.

**sacred document**

A revered manuscript given exalted status; applied to the Constitution.

**FIGURE 1.8 Declaration of Independence, the Bill of Rights, and the U.S. Constitution Displayed in the Rotunda of the National Archives in Washington, DC**

Not far from the "Shrine" in the National Archives, the twentieth-century re-creation by Howard Chandler Christy hangs in the U.S. Capitol. The eye is carried toward the beatific glow around the document itself, George Washington standing proudly as its guardian. The atmosphere is of nobility, grandeur, and calm, not base self-interest and conflict—though the latter characterized the convention at least as much.

Source: Photo taken by Kelvin Kay, http://commons.wikimedia.org/wiki/File:ArchivesRotunda.jpg.

Aside from after recent elections, the media rarely portray the Constitution or the structure of the political system as a cause of political problems. However, media depictions of the politicians charged with fulfilling the Constitution's vision in public life are far less positive.

Let us return to our discussion at the beginning of this chapter. The news declared a "constitutional crisis" during the aftermath of the 2000 presidential election. The covers of *Time*, *Newsweek*, and *U.S. News & World Report* all displayed the manuscript of the Constitution and its boldly emblazoned preamble, "We the People." The stories reported the 4–3 vote by the Florida Supreme Court, which ordered a statewide recount of that state's vote (the vote that would decide the national outcome), and the U.S. Supreme Court's 5–4 order to halt the recount and hear the Bush campaign's appeal. Both *Newsweek* and *U.S. News & World Report* superimposed the word "CHAOS" on the Constitution; *Newsweek* showed the word looming menacingly beneath the torn, seemingly fragile document.

All three news magazines lamented that the Constitution was threatened by unscrupulous, self-interested politicians intruding into the realm of dispassionate principle. To quote *Newsweek*, "The endless election has not been a grand contest of famous legal gladiators contesting broad constitutional principles . . . [but] a local fight, a highly personal shoving match driven by old grudges and vendettas."[46] Yet it was the complex electoral and federal system devised in the Constitution itself that caused much of the crisis.

Entertainment media occasionally present stories about the Constitution and the structure of power it created. Consider the familiar tale of a lone individual bravely fighting to restore a wayward political system to its virtuous roots. In the 1930s, director Frank Capra perfected the genre in a series of Hollywood movies that reached its height in the classic 1939 film *Mr. Smith Goes to Washington* (see the following "Enduring Image" on this topic).

## Enduring Image

### *Mr. Smith Goes to Washington*

James Madison's portrayal in the Federalist papers of sacrosanct institutions and fallible politicians finds its movie version in director Frank Capra's *Mr. Smith Goes to Washington*.[47] Upon its 1939 release, it was hugely popular and a critical success, second only to *Gone with the Wind* in box office receipts and Oscar nominations. The title alone has recurred repeatedly in political talk across the decades ever since.

*Mr. Smith* begins when a senator dies. The governor, pushed to appoint either a party hack or a reformer, picks instead his sons' "Boy Ranger" leader, resonantly named Jefferson Smith (James Stewart). The naive Smith heads to the Capitol under the wing of the state's senior senator, Joseph Paine (Claude Rains), who entrusts Smith to the dead senator's cynical secretary, Clarissa Saunders (Jean Arthur). Paine is a onetime associate of Smith's father, a crusading editor, but has sold out to the state's political boss. At Paine's urging, Smith submits a bill proposing a national boys' camp but later learns that the site has been bought by the boss to sell at a huge profit to the government for a dam Paine is proposing. Smith refuses to back down, and a fake corruption charge is launched against him with devastating results. About to resign in disgrace, Smith visits the Lincoln Memorial. Sustained by the love and political know-how of Saunders, Smith fights back by a filibuster on the Senate floor. The Washington reporters who had earlier scorned his innocence are transformed into his supporters by his idealism. But his home state hears little of this: the boss controls all radio stations and newspapers and brutally quashes any support. Smith faints in exhaustion when confronted with baskets full of trumped-up hate mail, but is saved when the guilt-ridden Paine tries to shoot himself and confesses to the corrupt scheme. The movie ends in a blaze of jubilation as the Senate president, apparently satisfied with Smith's vindication, gives up gaveling for order.

Many observers see the message of *Mr. Smith* as reassuring: the system works, preserved by the idealist individual American hero. The founders and their handiwork are viewed as above criticism. During the climactic filibuster, Smith reads the Declaration of Independence and the Constitution, lecturing the senators, "Great principles don't get lost once they come to light—they're right here."

The film endures because it is richly challenging: *Mr. Smith* is both a celebration in theory and an indictment in practice of the American political system.

*Mr. Smith* has been a template for media depictions of the American political system. The Reese Witherspoon vehicle *Legally Blonde 2: Red, White and Blonde* (2003) follows the same formula of an idealistic individual going to Capitol Hill and redeeming the promise of the political system against crooked politicians.

In this photo Mr. Smith, played by James Stewart, is filibustering on the Senate floor.

Source: Allstar Picture Library / Alamy Stock Photo

# Media Interactions: Why the Media Still Affirm the Constitution

Why do the media today present a rosy picture of the Constitution and the political system it created? One historic reason is that opposition to the Constitution collapsed after the Bill of Rights was added to it in 1791. Within a few years, the Constitution was no longer an object of political controversy. Even during the Civil War, the ultimate "constitutional crisis," both sides were faithful to the cherished principles of the Constitution—at least as each side read them.

The Constitution is the essential framework for the work of reporters as well as politicians. Reporters rely on order and regularity to perform their job day in, day out. The procedures established by the Constitution—such as how presidents are elected; how a bill becomes a law; how the president, Congress, and the Supreme Court vie for power—are the basis for continuing sagas that reporters narrate across days, months, even years.[48]

The Constitution also gives the media an easy symbol with which they can display their idealism and belief in a perhaps unattainable (and un-Madisonian) political system in which officials work efficiently, cooperatively, and selflessly in the public interest. This explains the criticism heaped on President Trump for failing to acknowledge defeat in the 2020 election and delaying the transition to President-elect Biden.

## Media Consequences

This positive media portrayal of the Constitution encourages reverence for the political system even when there is much criticism of the officials in that system.[49] Typical are the results of a public opinion poll conducted during 1992, a year marked by high public unhappiness with government. Not surprisingly, the survey showed that the public was highly critical of how the president and members of Congress were handling their jobs. But the public did not criticize the *institutions* of Congress and the presidency themselves. Ninety-one percent said they approved of "the constitutional structure of government."[50] Political scientists John Hibbing and Elizabeth Theiss-Morse, who conducted the research, concluded, "People actually see two quite different political systems. . . . Anything associated with the constitutional system elicits a positive response. . . . To the extent there are problems with the political system it is because we have deviated from what was outlined in the Constitution, not because that outline was flawed."[51]

Yet many of the media's indictments against politicians are for behaviors encouraged by the Constitution. Reporters and the mass media often criticize American politicians for "squabbling" and "bickering." But the separation of powers, as the founders designed it, is supposed to *encourage* conflict within the legislature and between the three branches.

The Constitution is a remarkably terse document. Generations have worked to evolve its meanings in over two centuries of politics and policies. Americans may rarely question the Constitution itself, but they surely disagree and debate over how its principles should be applied. In the chapters to follow, we will see many contemporary examples of politics around the Constitution in the information age—from constitutional amendments, to disputes between the branches over the powers of each, to the meanings of the Constitution's clauses when applied in public policy.

### Key Takeaways

The media usually portray the Constitution favorably and above politics. Yet, the Constitution was—and remains—a political document created and developed in political ways for political purposes. In part because of the media's presentation, the public finds little to criticize in the Constitution, even as it is quick to disparage public officials. Nonetheless, the Constitution continues to be the object of political engagement in the twenty-first century.

### Exercises

1. Think about the movies you've seen. Do any of them present the Constitution in a negative light? What do they see as the source of problems with the American political system, if not the Constitution?
2. Why do you think Americans tend to idealize the Constitution? Do you think there are disadvantages to having an idealized view of the Constitution?

## Civic Education

### Gregory Watson and the Twenty-Seventh Amendment

The message of civic education is the relevance and importance of politics. If the workings of the American political system are not what we like, there are ways to change structures, policies, and political practices.

An unusual example is provided by Gregory Watson.[52] In 1982, as a sophomore at the University of Texas at Austin, Watson found a stimulating topic for a government class essay: The Bill of Rights, as drafted by Madison and passed by Congress, originally included *twelve* amendments. Only ten were ratified by the states and included in the Constitution.

In 1982, congressional pay raises were controversial, and Watson concluded that this issue made one of the two unratified amendments pertinent: "No law, varying the compensation for the services of the Senators and Representatives, shall take effect, until an election of Representatives shall have intervened." Only six of the thirteen states had ratified this amendment by 1791. But Watson noticed that the amendment had no time limit. In his essay, he laid out the history of the amendment and urged that it be ratified by thirty-two more states. His instructor, dubious that a constitutional amendment could be revived after almost two hundred years, gave Watson's paper a C.

Undeterred, Watson launched a campaign to get state legislatures to pass this congressional compensation amendment. His first successes were with Maine in 1983 and Colorado in 1984. The news media began paying attention. The story of legislators voting themselves pay raises and news of scandals over congressional perks of office resonated with the public; the momentum shifted in Watson's favor. In 1992, Michigan became the thirty-eighth state to ratify the amendment. Congress recognized Watson's efforts in what became the Twenty-Seventh Amendment to the Constitution—203 years after their congressional forebears had passed it.

# 1.6 Recommended Reading

Belkin, Carol. *A Brilliant Solution: Inventing the American Constitution*. New York: Harcourt, 2002. An astute, readable account of the creation of the Constitution.

Condon, Sean. *Shays's Rebellion: Authority and Distress in Post-Revolutionary America*. Baltimore: Johns Hopkins University Press, 2015. A compelling and concise account.

Davis, Sue, and J. W. Peltason. *Corwin and Peltason's Understanding the Constitution*, 17th ed. Belmont, CA: Wadsworth, 2003–2017. An indispensable clause-by-clause guide to the Constitution.

Devins, Neal, and Louis Fisher. *The Democratic Constitution*, 2nd ed. New York: Oxford University Press, 2015. A sweeping, persuasive account of how everyone in American politics helps define the meaning of the Constitution.

Hamilton, Alexander, James Madison, and John Jay (collective pseudonym "Publius"), *The Federalist Papers*, 1788.

Levinson, Sanford. *Our Undemocratic Constitution: Where our Constitution Goes Wrong (And How We The People Can Correct It)*, New York: Oxford University Press, 2008. Levinson's critique of the constitution for being insufficiently democratic and for producing dysfunctional government.

Riker, William H. *The Strategy of Rhetoric: Campaigning for the American Constitution*. New Haven, CT: Yale University Press, 1996. A distinguished political scientist's posthumously published work recounting the many tactics of the ratification campaign.

Storing, Herbert. *What the Anti-Federalists Were For*. Chicago: University of Chicago Press, 1988. A valuable appreciation of the Anti-Federalist approach to governance.

# 1.7 Recommended Viewing

*Founding Brothers* (2002). This History Channel documentary based on Joseph Ellis's best-selling account explores the policies and personalities of post-Revolutionary America.

*The Great McGinty* (1940). Preston Sturges's first effort as director is a comedy about a hobo rising through the ranks of a party machine to become governor and spoiling it all by going honest.

*Hamilton* (2015). The critically acclaimed and box-office triumph musical about the life of the founding father.

*Mr. Smith Goes to Washington* (1939). Frank Capra's classic drama of a lone, idealistic individual single-handedly (but with a woman's love and help) fighting corrupt individuals within a sacrosanct political system.

*The Patriot* (2000). A South Carolina farmer and veteran of the wars with France (Mel Gibson) reluctantly takes up arms as a guerrilla fighter in the Revolution and struggles with his political identity and the meaning of self-government.

*Rebels and Redcoats* (2003). A lively four-hour documentary featuring a British military historian's perspective of the Revolution as a bloody civil war.

*1776* (1972). The movie adaptation of the Broadway musical comedy hit vividly portrays the high-minded and self-interested political struggles leading to the Declaration of Independence.

# Endnotes

1. *World News Tonight* transcript, November 8, 2000, quotations on pp. 1 and 9.
2. See Stephen Botein, "'Meer Mechanics' and an Open Press: The Business and Political Strategies of Colonial American Printers," *Perspectives in American History* 9 (1975): 127–225; and "Printers and the American Revolution," in *The Press and the American Revolution*, ed. Bernard Bailyn and John B. Hench (Worcester, MA: American Antiquarian Society, 1980), 11–57. Also, Charles E. Clark, *The Public Prints: The Newspaper in Anglo-American Culture* (New York: Oxford University Press, 1994), chap. 9; and "The Press the Founders Knew," in *Freeing the Presses: The First Amendment in Action*, ed. Timothy E. Cook (Baton Rouge: Louisiana State University Press, 2005).
3. Thomas C. Leonard, *News for All: America's Coming-of-Age with the Press* (New York: Oxford University Press, 1995), chap. 1.
4. For amplification of this argument, Timothy E. Cook, *Governing with the News: The News Media as a Political Institution* (Chicago: University of Chicago Press, 1998), chap. 2.
5. See Jack N. Rakove, *The Beginnings of National Politics: An Interpretive History of the Continental Congress* (New York: Knopf, 1979).
6. Staughton Lynd, *The Intellectual Origins of American Radicalism* (New York: Vintage, 1969); Garry Wills, *Inventing America: Jefferson's Declaration of Independence* (New York: Vintage, 1979); and Pauline Maier, *American Scripture: Making the Declaration of Independence* (New York: Knopf, 1997).
7. Keith L. Dougherty, *Collective Action under the Articles of Confederation* (New York: Cambridge University Press, 2001), chaps. 4-5.
8. A synopsis is Jack N. Rakove, *Original Meanings: Politics and Ideas in the Making of the Constitution* (New York: Knopf, 1996), 25–28. More generally, see Max M. Edling, *A Revolution in Favor of Government: Origins of the U.S. Constitution and the Making of the American State* (New York: Oxford University Press, 2004).
9. Gordon S. Wood, "Interests and Disinterestedness in the Making of a Constitution," in *Beyond Confederation: Origins of the Constitution and American National Identity*, ed. Richard Beeman, Stephen Botein, and Edward C. Carter II (Chapel Hill: University of North Carolina Press, 1987), 69–109.
10. See Leonard A. Richards, *Shays's Rebellion: The American Revolution's Final Battle* (Philadelphia: University of Pennsylvania Press, 2002).
11. See Keith L. Dougherty, *Collective Action under the Articles of Confederation* (New York: Cambridge University Press, 2001), chap. 6.
12. The standard edition of Madison's notes is in *The Records of the Federal Convention of 1787*, ed. Max Farrand, 3 vols. (New Haven, CT: Yale University Press, 1937).
13. Charles A. Beard, *An Economic Interpretation of the Constitution of the United States* (New York: Macmillan, 1913).
14. See Clement Fatovic, *America's Founding and the Struggle over Economic Inequality* (Lawrence: University Press of Kansas, 2015).
15. Our analysis draws on these authors, especially John P. Roche, "The Founding Fathers: A Reform Caucus in Action," *American Political Science Review* 55 (December 1961): 799–816; Calvin C. Jillson, *Constitution Making: Conflict and Consensus in the Federal Convention of 1787* (New York: Agathon Press, 1988); and William H. Riker, *The Strategy of Rhetoric: Campaigning for the American Constitution* (New Haven, CT: Yale University Press, 1996).
16. See John K. Alexander, *The Selling of the Constitutional Convention: A History of News Coverage* (Madison, WI: Madison House, 1990).
17. Max Farrand, ed., *The Records of the Federal Convention of 1787* (New Haven, CT: Yale University Press, 1937), vol. 1, 17.
18. Max Farrand, ed., *The Records of the Federal Convention of 1787* (New Haven, CT: Yale University Press, 1937), vol. 3, 28.
19. Max Farrand, ed., *The Records of the Federal Convention of 1787* (New Haven, CT: Yale University Press, 1937), vol. 3, 86–87.
20. Max Farrand, ed., *The Records of the Federal Convention of 1787* (New Haven, CT: Yale University Press, 1937), vol. 3, 76.
21. The terms "large state" and "small state" are misleading. Some small states had larger populations than large states. The small states all shared economic vulnerability and an inability to grow, usually because they were boxed in by other states on their western edge, which made it impossible to hope for westward expansion.
22. The text of the Virginia Plan (and its main rival, the New Jersey Plan) can be found in Clinton Rossiter, *1787: The Grand Convention* (New York: Macmillan, 1966), 361–63 and 369–71.
23. David Brian Robertson, "Madison's Opponents and Constitutional Design," *American Political Science Review* 99 (2005): 225–44.
24. The quoted phrase comes from John P. Roche, "The Founding Fathers: A Reform Caucus in Action," *American Political Science Review* 55 (December 1961): 810.
25. John P. Roche, "The Founding Fathers: A Reform Caucus in Action," *American Political Science Review* 55 (December 1961): 815; see also David Brian Robertson, "Madison's Opponents and Constitutional Design," *American Political Science Review* 99 (2005): 225–44
26. Jackson Turner Main, *The Antifederalists: Critics of the Constitution, 1781–1788* (Chapel Hill: University of North Carolina Press, 1961), 249; Evelyn C. Fink and William H. Riker, "The Strategy of Ratification" in *The Federalist Papers and the New Institutionalism*, ed. Bernard Grofman and Donald Wittman (New York: Agathon Press, 1989), 220–55.
27. See Herbert Storing, *What the Anti-Federalists Were For* (Chicago: University of Chicago Press, 1988).

28. Pauline Maier, *Ratification: The People Debate the Constitution, 1787–1788* (New York: Simon & Schuster, 2010).
29. Robert Allen Rutland, *The Ordeal of the Constitution: The Antifederalists and the Ratification Struggle of 1787–1788* (Norman: University of Oklahoma Press, 1966), 38.
30. William H. Riker, *The Strategy of Rhetoric: Campaigning for the American Constitution* (New Haven, CT: Yale University Press, 1996), 26–28.
31. More specifically, see Robert A. Rutland, "The First Great Newspaper Debate: The Constitutional Crisis of 1787–88," *Proceedings of the American Antiquarian Society* (1987): 43–58. These examples come from Robert Allen Rutland, *The Ordeal of the Constitution: The Antifederalists and the Ratification Struggle of 1787–1788* (Norman: University of Oklahoma Press, 1966), 73–74, 135–38, 265–66; and John P. Kaminski and Gaspare J. Saladino, eds., *Commentaries on the Constitution, Public and Private* (Madison, WI: State Historical Society of Wisconsin, 1981), vol. 1, xxxii–xxxix.
32. On the most commonly reprinted articles, see William H. Riker, *The Strategy of Rhetoric: Campaigning for the American Constitution* (New Haven, CT: Yale University Press, 1996), chap. 6, esp. table 6.1.
33. John P. Kaminski and Gaspare J. Saladino, eds., *Commentaries on the Constitution, Public and Private* (Madison, WI: State Historical Society of Wisconsin, 1981), vol. 1, 243.
34. Richard E. Neustadt, *Presidential Power* (New York: Wiley, 1960), 33. Of course, whether the founders intended this outcome is still open to dispute.
35. James Madison. *The Federalist Number 51*, [6 February] 1788. National Archives. Retrieved from: https://founders.archives.gov/documents/Madison/01-10-02-0279.
36. Gordon S. Wood, *The Creation of the American Republic* (Chapel Hill: University of North Carolina Press, 1969), chap. 6.
37. This version comes from Richard F. Fenno Jr., *The United States Senate: A Bicameral Perspective* (Washington, DC: American Enterprise Institute, 1982), 5.
38. Bruce Ackerman, *The Failure of the Founding Fathers: Jefferson, Marshall and the Rise of Presidential Democracy* (Cambridge, MA.: Belknap Press of Harvard, 2005).
39. See Alexander Keyssar, *The Right to Vote: The Contested History of Democracy in the United States* (New York: Basic Books, 2000).
40. The power of all three branches to develop the vague language of the Constitution is well documented in Neal Devins and Louis Fisher, *The Democratic Constitution* (New York: Oxford University Press, 2004).
41. David P. Currie, *The Constitution in Congress: The Federalist Period, 1789–1801* (Chicago: University of Chicago Press, 1997).
42. Hughes was then Governor of New York. Quoted in Edward S. Corwin, *The Constitution and What It Means Today* (Princeton, NJ: Princeton University Press, 1954), xiii.
43. See Neal Devins and Louis Fisher, *The Democratic Constitution* (New York: Oxford University Press, 2004).
44. See Jeffrey Tulis, *The Rhetorical Presidency* (Princeton, NJ: Princeton University Press, 1987).
45. Jeffrey K. Tulis, "The Two Constitutional Presidencies," in *The Presidency and the Political System*, 6th ed., ed. Michael Nelson (Washington, DC: CQ Press, 2000), 93–124.
46. Evan Thomas and Michael Isikoff, "Settling Old Scores in the Swamp," *Newsweek* (December 18, 2000), 36–44, quotations on 38.
47. Insightful analyses of the film include Brian Rose, *An Examination of Narrative Structure in the Films of Frank Capra* (New York: Arno Press, 1980), chap. 3; and Charles J. Maland, *Frank Capra* (Boston: Twayne, 1980), chap. 4.
48. See Mark Fishman, *Manufacturing the News* (Austin: University of Texas Press, 1980).
49. See Samuel P. Huntington, *American Politics: The Promise of Disharmony* (Cambridge, MA: Harvard University Press, 1981).
50. John R. Hibbing and Elizabeth Theiss-Morse, *Congress as Public Enemy: Public Attitudes toward American Political Institutions* (New York: Cambridge University Press, 1995), 59.
51. John R. Hibbing and Elizabeth Theiss-Morse, *Congress as Public Enemy: Public Attitudes toward American Political Institutions* (New York: Cambridge University Press, 1995), 87, 104.
52. This example is taken from Richard B. Bernstein and Jerome Abel, *Amending America: If We Love the Constitution So Much, Why Do We Keep Trying to Change It?* (New York: Times Books, 1993), chap. 13.

CHAPTER 2

# Federalism

## 2.1 Preamble

The war in Iraq was dragging on long past President George W. Bush's declaration in May 2003 of the end of formal hostilities. In 2004, the Defense Department, wary of the political pain of reviving the military draft, called up most of the National Guard. The Guard consists of volunteers for state military units headed by the state's governor but answerable to the commander in chief, the president. Most Guard volunteers expect to serve and keep the peace at home in their states, not fight in a war overseas.

State and local governments made it known that they were being adversely affected by the war. At the 2004 annual meeting of the National Governors Association, governors from both political parties fretted that the call-up had slashed the numbers of the National Guard available for states' needs by as much as 60 percent. Their concerns made the front page of the *New York Times*. The story began, "Many of the nation's governors complained . . . that they were facing severe manpower shortages in guarding prisoners, fighting wildfires, preparing for hurricanes and floods and policing the streets."[1]

**FIGURE 2.1 Governors Mingling and Speaking at the National Governors Association**
The annual meeting of the National Governors Association provides an opportunity for state officials to meet with each other, with national officials, and with reporters.

Source: Ted Eyton via Flickr: https://www.flickr.com/photos/taedc/4374097036/. Reproduced via CC BY-SA 2.0: https://creativecommons.org/licenses/by-sa/2.0/

This involvement of state governors in foreign policy illustrates the complexity of American federalism. The national government has an impact on state and local governments, which in turn influence each other and the national government.

The story also shows how the news media's depictions can connect and affect different levels of government within the United States. The governors meet each year to exchange ideas and express common concerns. These meetings give them an opportunity to try to use the news media to bring public attention to their concerns, lobby the national government, reap policy benefits for their states, and increase their national visibility.

But the coverage the governors received in the Iraq case was exceptional. The news media seldom communicate the dynamic complexity of government across national, state, and local levels. Online media are better at enabling people to negotiate the bewildering thicket of the federal system and communicate between levels of government.

**federalism**

The allocation of powers and responsibilities among national, state, and local governments and the intergovernmental relations between them.

**Federalism** is the allocation of powers and responsibilities among national, state, and local governments and the intergovernmental relations between them. The essence of federalism is that "all levels of government in the United States significantly participate in all activities of government."[2] At the same time, each level of government is partially autonomous from the rest.[3]

# 2.2 Federalism as a Structure of Power

## Learning Objectives

After reading this section, you should be able to answer the following questions:

1. What is federalism?
2. What powers does the Constitution grant to the national government?
3. What powers does the Constitution grant to state governments?

The Constitution and its amendments outline distinct powers and tasks for the national and state governments. Some of these constitutional provisions enhance the power of the national government; others boost the power of the states. Checks and balances are designed to protect each level of government against encroachment by the others.

## National Powers

The Constitution gives the national government three types of power. In particular, Article I authorizes Congress to act in certain enumerated domains.

## Exclusive Powers

The Constitution gives **exclusive powers** to the national government that states may not exercise. These are foreign relations, the military, war and peace, trade across national and state borders, and the monetary system. States may not make treaties with other countries or with other states, issue money, levy duties on imports or exports, maintain a standing army or navy, or make war.

**exclusive powers**

Powers that the Constitution grants to the national or state governments and prevents the other level from exercising.

## Concurrent Powers

The Constitution accords some powers to the national government without barring them from the states. These **concurrent powers** include regulating elections, taxing and borrowing money, and establishing courts.

National and state governments both regulate commercial activity. In its **commerce clause**, the Constitution gives the national government broad power to "regulate Commerce with foreign Nations, and among the several States and with the Indian tribes." This clause allowed the federal government to establish a national highway system that traverses the states. A state may regulate any and all commerce that is entirely within its borders.

National and state governments alike make and enforce laws and choose their own leaders. They have their own constitutions and court systems. A state's Supreme Court decision may be appealed to the U.S. Supreme Court provided that it raises a "federal question," such as an interpretation of the U.S. Constitution or of national law.

**concurrent powers**

Powers that the Constitution specifies that either national or state governments may exercise.

**commerce clause**

The section in the Constitution that gives Congress the power to "regulate Commerce with foreign Nations, and among the several States and with the Indian tribes."

## Implied Powers

The Constitution authorizes Congress to enact all laws "necessary and proper" to execute its enumerated powers. This **necessary and proper clause** allows the national government to claim **implied powers**, logical extensions of the powers explicitly granted to it. For example, national laws can and do outlaw discrimination in employment under Congress's power to regulate interstate commerce.

**necessary and proper clause**

Constitutional provision that gives Congress vast power to enact all laws it considers "necessary and proper" to carry out its enumerated powers.

**implied powers**

Unlisted powers to the national government that are logical extensions from powers expressly enumerated in the Constitution.

# States' Powers

The states existed before the Constitution, so the founders said little about their powers until the Tenth Amendment was added in 1791. It holds that "powers not delegated to the United States . . . nor prohibited by it [the Constitution] to the States, are reserved to the States . . . or to the people." States maintain inherent powers that do not conflict with the Constitution. Notably, in the mid-nineteenth century, the Supreme Court recognized that states could exercise **police powers** to protect the public's health, safety, order, and morals.[4]

**police powers**

Inherent powers that states hold to protect the public's health, safety, order, and morals.

## Reserved Powers

Some powers are reserved to the states, such as ratifying proposed amendments to the Constitution and deciding how to elect Congress and the president. National officials are chosen by state elections.

Congressional districts are drawn within states. Their boundaries are reset by state officials after the decennial census. So the party that controls a state's legislature and governorship is able to manipulate districts in its favor. Republicans, having taken over many state governments in the 2010 elections, benefited from this opportunity.

The Constitution requires that the census count all residents of the country. Traditionally, the census count has been non-partisan and data-driven. In 2020, however, the Trump administration asked the Supreme Court for permission to stop the count ahead of schedule. The president had insisted that the numbers exclude undocumented immigrants. Yet many such immigrants were difficult to track down. Failure to include them would likely give more representation to Republicans in the House of Representatives and state and local governments. The court granted the administration's request.[5]

# National Government's Responsibilities to the States

The Constitution lists responsibilities the national government has to the states. The Constitution cannot be amended to deny the equal representation of each state in the Senate. A state's borders cannot be altered without its consent. The national government must guarantee each state "a republican form of government" and defend any state, upon its request, from invasion or domestic upheaval.

# States' Responsibilities to Each Other

Article IV lists responsibilities states have to each other: each state must give "full faith and credit" to acts of other states. For instance, a driver's license issued by one state must be recognized as legal and binding by another.

No state may deny "privileges and immunities" to citizens of other states by refusing their fundamental rights. States can, however, deny benefits to out-of-staters if they do not involve fundamental rights. Courts have held that a state may require newly arrived residents to live in the state for a year before being eligible for in-state (thus lower) tuition for public universities, but may not force them to wait as long before being able to vote or receive medical care.

Officials of one state must extradite persons upon request to another state where they are suspected of a crime.

States dispute whether and how to meet these responsibilities. Conflicts sometimes are resolved by national authority. In 2003, several states wanted to try John Muhammad, accused of being the sniper who killed people in and around Washington, DC. The U.S. attorney general, John Ashcroft, had to decide which jurisdiction would be first to put him on trial. Ashcroft, a proponent of capital punishment, chose the state with the toughest death penalty law, Virginia.

Sometimes, the courts intervene. As we discuss in Chapter 5, federal judges and eventually the U.S. Supreme Court declared state bans on same-sex marriage unconstitutional.

# "The Supreme Law of the Land" and Its Limits

Article VI's supremacy clause holds that the Constitution and all national laws are "the supreme law of the land." State judges and officials pledge to abide by the U.S. Constitution. In any clash between national laws and state laws, the latter must give way. However, as we shall see, boundaries are fuzzy between the powers national and state governments may and may not wield. Implied powers of the national government, and those reserved to the states by the Tenth Amendment, are unclear and contested. The Constitution leaves much about the relative powers of national and state governments to be shaped by day-to-day politics, in which both levels have a strong voice.

# A Land of Many Governments

"Disliking government, Americans nonetheless seem to like governments, for they have so many of them."[6] Table 2.1 catalogs the 87,576 distinct governments in the fifty states. They employ over eighteen million full-time workers. These numbers would be higher if we included territories, Indigenous American reservations, and private substitutes for local governments such as gated developments' community associations.

**TABLE 2.1** Governments in the United States

| | |
|---|---|
| National government | 1 |
| States | 50 |
| Counties | 3,034 |
| Townships | 16,504 |
| Municipalities | 19,429 |
| Special districts | 35,052 |
| Independent school districts | 13,506 |
| Total governmental units in the United States | 87,576 |

Source: Data from U.S. Bureau of the Census, categorizing those entities that are organized, usually chosen by election, with a governmental character and substantial autonomy.

## States

In one sense, all fifty states are equal: each has two votes in the U.S. Senate. The states also have similar governmental structures to the national government: three branches—executive, legislative, and judicial (only Nebraska has a one-chamber—unicameral—legislature). Otherwise, the states differ from each other in numerous ways. These include size, diversity of inhabitants, economic development, and levels of education. Differences in population are politically important as they are the basis of each state's number of seats in the House of Representatives, over and above the minimum of one seat per state.

On occasion, a state will make the news as Texas did in February 2021 when a rare winter storm caused widespread power failures. The Republican-controlled state government was blamed for lax regulation of the state's utilities. It was revealed that in contrast to much of the rest of the country that has interconnected electrical systems, the public entity, the Electricity Reform Council of Texas (ERCOT), responsible for operating the state's grid has gone it alone and insulated (avoided having) its utilities from federal regulation.[7]

States usually get less attention in the news than do national and local governments. Many state events interest national news organizations only if they reflect national trends, such as a story about states passing laws regulating or restricting abortions.[8]

A study of Philadelphia local television news in the early 1990s found that only 10 percent of the news time concerned state occurrences, well behind the 18 percent accorded to suburbs, 21 percent to the region, and 37 percent to the central city.[9] Since then, the commitment of local news outlets to covering state news has waned further. A survey of state capital news coverage in 2002 revealed that thirty-one state capitals had fewer newspaper reporters than in 2000.[10] The number has further decreased since then.

## Indigenous American Reservations

In principle, Indigenous American tribes enjoy more independence than states but less than foreign countries. Yet the Supreme Court, in 1831, rejected the Cherokee tribe's claim that it had the right as a foreign country to sue the state of Georgia. The justices said that the tribe was a "domestic dependent nation."[11] As wards of the national government, the Cherokee were forcibly removed from land east of the Mississippi in ensuing years.

Indigenous Americans have slowly gained self-government. Starting in the 1850s, presidents' executive orders set aside public lands for reservations directly administered by the national Bureau of Indian Affairs (BIA). During World War II, Indigenous Americans working for the BIA organized to gain legal autonomy for tribes. Buttressed by Supreme Court decisions recognizing tribal rights, national policy now encourages Indigenous American nations on reservations to draft constitutions and elect governments.[12]

**FIGURE 2.2 Foxwoods Advertisement**

The image of glamour and prosperity at casinos operated at Indigenous American reservations, such as Foxwoods (the largest such casino) in Connecticut, is a stark contrast with the hard life and poverty of most reservations.

Source: © Thinkstock.

In July 2020, by a vote of 5–4, the Supreme Court ruled that a three-million-acre swath of eastern Oklahoma is a reservation of the Muscogee (Creek) nation, having been granted by Congress in exchange for 100,000 of them being forced from their ancestral lands in Georgia and Alabama during the 1830s. The decision means, among other things, that indigenous people who commit crimes in that area of Oklahoma, which includes much of Tulsa, must be tried in federal or tribal courts.[13]

Since the Constitution gives Congress and the national government exclusive "power to regulate commerce . . . with the Indian tribes," states have no automatic authority over tribe members on reservations within state borders.[14] As a result, many Indigenous American tribes have built profitable casinos on reservations within states that otherwise restrict most gambling.[15]

## Local Governments

All but two states are divided into administrative units known as counties.[16] States also contain municipalities, whether huge cities or tiny hamlets. They differ from counties by being established by local residents, but their powers are determined by the state. Cutting across these borders are thousands of school districts as well as special districts for drainage and flood control, soil and water conservation, libraries, parks and recreation, housing and community development, sewerage, water supply, cemeteries, and fire protection.[17]

### Key Takeaways

Federalism is the American political system's arrangement of powers and responsibilities among—and ensuing relations between—national, state, and local governments. The U.S. Constitution specifies exclusive and concurrent powers for the national and state governments. Other powers are implied and determined by day-to-day politics.

### Exercises

1. Consider the different powers that the Constitution grants exclusively to the national government. Explain why it might make sense to reserve each of those powers for the national government.
2. Consider the different powers that the Constitution grants exclusively to the states. Explain why it might make sense to reserve each of those powers to the states.
3. In your opinion, what is the value of the "necessary and proper" clause? Why might it be difficult to enumerate all the powers of the national government in advance?

# 2.3 The Meanings of Federalism

### Learning Objectives

After reading this section, you should be able to answer the following questions:

1. How has the meaning of federalism changed over time?
2. Why has the meaning of federalism changed over time?
3. What are states' rights and dual, cooperative, and competitive federalism?

**states' rights**

An approach to federalism that holds that each state entered into a compact in ratifying the Constitution and can therefore decide whether or not to obey a law it considers unconstitutional.

**dual federalism**

An approach to federalism that divides power between national and state governments into distinct, clearly demarcated domains of authority.

**cooperative federalism**

An approach to federalism that sees national, state, and local governments working together to address problems and implement public policies in numerous domains.

**competitive federalism**

An approach to federalism that stresses the conflict and compromise between national, state, and local governments.

The meaning of federalism has changed over time. During the first decades of the republic, many politicians held that **states' rights** allowed states to disobey any national government that in their view exceeded its powers. Such a doctrine was largely discredited after the Civil War. Then **dual federalism**, a clear division of labor between national and state governments, became the dominant doctrine. During the New Deal of the 1930s, **cooperative federalism**, whereby federal and state governments work together to solve problems, emerged and held sway until the 1960s. Since then, the situation is summarized by the term **competitive federalism**, whereby responsibilities are asserted based on whether the national or state or local government claims to be best able to handle the task.

# States' Rights

The ink had barely dried on the Constitution when disputes arose over federalism. Treasury Secretary Alexander Hamilton hoped to build a strong national economic system; Secretary of State Thomas Jefferson favored a limited national government. Hamiltonian and Jeffersonian factions in President George Washington's cabinet led to the first political parties: respectively, the Federalists, who favored national supremacy, and the Republicans, who supported states' rights.

## Compact Theory

In 1798, Federalists passed the Alien and Sedition Acts, outlawing malicious criticism of the government and authorizing the president to deport enemy aliens. In response, the Republican Jefferson drafted a resolution passed by Kentucky's legislature, the first states' rights manifesto. It set forth a compact theory, claiming that states had voluntarily entered into a "compact" to ratify the Constitution. Consequently, each state could engage in "nullification" and "judge for itself" if an act was constitutional and refuse to enforce it.[18] However, Jefferson shelved states' rights when, as president, he directed the national government to purchase the enormous Louisiana Territory from France in 1803.

### Links

**Alien and Sedition Acts**

Click here to read more about the Alien and Sedition Acts.

**Jefferson's Role**

Click here to read more about Jefferson's role.

## Slavery and the Crisis of Federalism

After the Revolutionary War, slavery waned in the North, where slaves were domestic servants or lone farmhands. In the South, labor-intensive crops on plantations were the basis of Southern prosperity, which relied heavily on slaves.[19]

In 1850, Congress faced the prospect of new states carved from land captured in the Mexican War and debated whether they would be slave or free states. In a compromise, Congress admitted California as a free state but directed the national government to capture and return escaped slaves, even in free states. Officials in Northern states decried such an exertion of national power favoring the South. They passed state laws outlining rights for accused fugitive slaves and forbidding state officials from capturing fugitives.[20] The Underground Railroad transporting escaped slaves northward grew. The saga of hunted fugitives was at the heart of Harriet Beecher Stowe's 1852 novel *Uncle Tom's Cabin*, which sold more copies proportional to the American population than any book before or since.

In 1857, the Supreme Court stepped into the fray. Dred Scott, the slave of a deceased Missouri army surgeon, sued for freedom, noting he had accompanied his master for extended stays in a free state and a free territory.[21] The justices dismissed Scott's claim. They stated that Negroes, excluded from the Constitution, could never be U.S. citizens and could not sue in federal court. They added that any national restriction on slavery in territories violated the Fifth Amendment, which bars the government from taking property without due process of law. To many Northerners, the Dred Scott decision raised doubts about whether *any* state could effectively ban slavery. In December 1860, a convention in South Carolina repealed the state's ratification of the Constitution and dissolved its union with the other states. Ten other states followed suit. The eleven formed the Confederate States of America (see "Enduring Image"). The civil war drew nigh.

**FIGURE 2.3**
**Lithograph from *Uncle Tom's Cabin***
The plight of fugitive slaves, vividly portrayed in the mega best seller of the 1850s, *Uncle Tom's Cabin*, created a crisis in federalism that led directly to the Civil War.

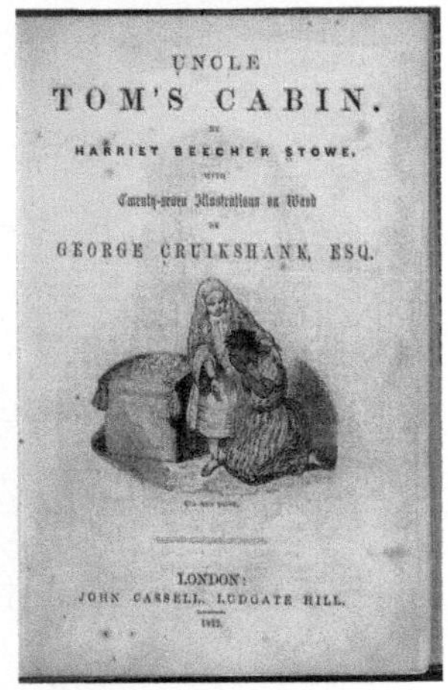


Source: moosevlt. "Uncle Tom's Cabin." Via Flickr: https://www.flickr.com/photos/48734803@N00/252322873/. Reproduced via CC BY 2.0: https://creativecommons.org/licenses/by/2.0/.

## Links

### The Underground Railroad

Learn more about the Underground Railroad here.

### The Dred Scott Case

Click here to learn more about the Dred Scott case from the Library of Congress.

## Enduring Image

### The Confederate Battle Flag

This photo shows the Confederate battle flag.

Source: Dee Browning/Shutterstock.com

The American flag is an enduring image of the United States' national unity. The Civil War battle flag of the Confederate States of America is also an enduring image, but of states' rights, of opposition to a national government, and of support for slavery. The blue cross studded with eleven stars for the states of the Confederacy was not its official flag. Soldiers hastily pressed it into battle to avoid confusion between the Union's Stars and Stripes and the Confederacy's Stars and Bars. After the South's defeat, the battle flag, often lowered for mourning, was mainly a memento of gallant human loss.[22]

The flag's meaning was transformed in the 1940s as the civil rights movement made gains against segregation in the South. One after another, Southern states flew the flag above their capitols or defiantly redesigned their state flags to incorporate it. Over the last seventy years, myriad meanings arousing deep emotions have become attached to the flag: states' rights; Southern regional pride; a general defiance of big government; nostalgia for a bygone era; racist support of segregation; or "equal rights for whites."[23]

This photo shows the new Mississippi state flag.

Source: grebeshkovmaxim/Shutterstock.com

On June 17, 2015, nine African Americans, the oldest eighty-seven, the youngest twenty-six, were shot and killed in the famed Emanuel African Methodist Episcopal Church in downtown Charleston, South Carolina. Photographs of the alleged shooter, a young white man, showing him with the flag and a racist manifesto, drew many people, particularly African Americans, to focus on the flag's racist meaning. A movement calling for the removal of the flag from government properties swiftly ensued. In relatively short order, it was taken down (by some combination of decisions of the governor and state legislature) from the state capitol grounds in South Carolina, Alabama, and elsewhere. In July 2020, the governor of Mississippi signed legislation to remove the Confederate emblem from the state flag.

The South's defeat in the Civil War discredited compact theory and nullification. Since then, state officials' efforts to defy national orders have been futile. In 1963, Governor George Wallace stood in the doorway of the University of Alabama to resist a court order to desegregate the all-white school. Eventually, he had no choice but to accede to federal marshals. In 1994, Pennsylvania Governor Robert Casey, a pro-life Democrat, decreed he would not allow state officials to enforce a national order that state-run Medicaid programs pay for abortions in cases of rape and incest. He lost in court.[24]

# Dual Federalism

After the Civil War, the justices of the Supreme Court wrote, "The Constitution, in all its provisions, looks to an indestructible Union, composed of indestructible States."[25] They endorsed dual federalism, a doctrine whereby national and state governments have clearly demarcated domains of power. The national government is supreme, but only in the areas where the Constitution authorizes it to act.

The basis for dual federalism was a series of Supreme Court decisions early in the nineteenth century. The key decision was *McCulloch v. Maryland* (1819). The Court struck down a Maryland state tax on the Bank of the United States chartered by Congress. Chief Justice Marshall conceded that the Constitution gave Congress no explicit power to charter a national bank,[26] but concluded that the Constitution's necessary-and-proper clause enabled Congress and the national government to do whatever it deemed "convenient or useful" to exercise its powers. As for Maryland's tax, he wrote, "the power to tax involves the power to destroy." Therefore, when a state's laws interfere with the national government's operation, the latter takes precedence. Nonetheless, from the 1780s to the Great Depression of the 1930s, the size and reach of the national government were relatively limited. As late as 1932, local government raised and spent more than the national government or the states.

## Link

***McCulloch v. Maryland***

Click here to read more about *McCulloch v. Maryland* (1819).

On two subjects, however, the national government increased its power in relationship to the states and local governments: sin and economic regulation.

## The Politics of Sin

National powers were expanded when Congress targeted obscenity, prostitution, and alcohol.[27] In 1872, reformers led by Anthony Comstock persuaded Congress to pass laws blocking obscene material from being carried in the U.S. mail. Comstock had a broad notion of sinful media: all writings about sex, birth control, abortion, and childbearing, plus tabloid newspapers that allegedly corrupted innocent youth.

**FIGURE 2.4 The Suppression of Vice**

The first book by Anthony Comstock, who headed the New York Society for the Suppression of Vice, aimed at the supposedly corrupting influence of the tabloid media of the day on children and proposed increasing the power of the national government to combat them.

Source: Anthony Comstock. "The Modern Newsstand and its Results." *Traps for the Young*, Fourth Edition (New York: Funk & Wagnall's Company, 1883).

As a result of these laws, the national government gained the power to exclude material from the mail even if it was legal in individual states.

The power of the national government also increased when prostitution became a focus of national policy. A 1910 exposé in *McClure's* magazine roused President William Howard Taft to warn Congress about prostitution rings operating across state lines. The ensuing media frenzy depicted young white girls torn from rural homes and degraded by an urban "white slave trade." Using the commerce clause, Congress passed the Mann Act to prohibit the transportation "in interstate commerce . . . of any woman or girl for the purpose of prostitution or debauchery, or for any other immoral purpose."[28] The bill turned enforcement over to a tiny agency concerned with antitrust and postal violations, the Bureau of Investigations. The bureau aggressively investigated thousands of allegations of "immoral purpose," including unmarried couples crossing state lines to wed and interracial married couples.

The crusade to outlaw alcohol provided the most lasting expansion of national power. Reformers persuaded Congress in 1917 to bar importation of alcohol into dry states, and, in 1919, to amend the Constitution to allow for the nationwide prohibition of alcohol. Pervasive attempts to evade the law boosted organized crime, a rationale for the Bureau of Investigations in the 1920s to bloom into the Federal Bureau of Investigation (FBI), the equivalent of a national police force.

Prohibition was repealed in 1933. But the FBI under J. Edgar Hoover, its director from 1924 to his death in 1972 at the age of seventy-seven, continued to call attention through news and entertainment media to the scourge of organized crime that justified the bureau's growth and political independence, and Hoover's power. (For more on Hoover, see Chapter 14). The FBI supervised film depictions of the lives of criminals like John Dillinger and long-running radio and television shows like *The F.B.I.* The heroic image of federal law enforcement would not be challenged until the 1960s, when the classic film *Bonnie and Clyde* romanticized the tale of two small-time criminals into a saga of rebellious outsiders crushed by the ominous rise of authority across state lines. Withal, *The FBI* is still favorably portrayed on network television today.

## Economic Regulation

Other national reforms in the late nineteenth century that increased the power of the national government were generated by reactions to industrialization, immigration, and urban growth. Crusading journalists decried the power of big business. Upton Sinclair's 1906 novel *The Jungle* exposed miserable, unsafe working conditions in America's factories. These reformers feared that states lacked the power or were reluctant to regulate railroads, inspect meat, or guarantee food and drug safety. They prompted Congress to use its powers under the commerce clause for economic regulation, starting with the Interstate Commerce Act in 1887 to regulate railroads and the Sherman Antitrust Act in 1890 to outlaw monopolies.

The Supreme Court, defending dual federalism, limited such regulation. It held in 1895 that the national government could only regulate matters *directly* affecting interstate commerce.[29] In 1918, it ruled that Congress could not use the commerce clause to deal with local matters like conditions of work. The national government could regulate interstate commerce of harmful products such as lottery tickets or impure food.[30]

# Cooperative Federalism

The massive economic crises of the Great Depression tolled the death knell for dual federalism. In its place, cooperative federalism emerged. Instead of a relatively clear separation of policy domains, national, state, and local governments would work together to try to respond to a wide range of problems.

## The New Deal and the End of Dual Federalism

Elected president in 1932, Democrat Franklin Delano Roosevelt (FDR) sought to implement a "New Deal" for Americans amid staggering unemployment. He argued that the national government could restore the economy more effectively than states or localities. He persuaded Congress to enact sweeping legislation. New Deal programs included boards enforcing wage and price guarantees; programs to construct buildings and bridges, develop national parks, and create artworks; and payments to farmers to reduce acreage of crops and stabilize prices.

**FIGURE 2.5 Dorothea Lange Photograph**

The 1930s New Deal programs included commissioning photographers to document social conditions during the Great Depression. The resultant photographs are both invaluable historical documents and lasting works of art.

Source: U.S. Farm Security Administration via Library of Congress (https://www.loc.gov/pictures/item/2017772305/) and Wikimedia: http://commons.wikimedia.org/wiki/File:Dorothea_Lange,_Country_ store_on_dirt _road,_Gordonton,_North_Carolina,_1939.jpg.

By 1939, national government expenditures equaled state and local expenditures combined.[31] FDR explained his programs to nationwide audiences in "fireside chats" on the relatively young medium of radio. His policies were highly popular, and he was reelected by a landslide in 1936. As we describe in Chapter 15, the Supreme Court, after rejecting several New Deal measures, eventually upheld national authority over such once-forbidden terrain as labor-management relations, minimum wages, and subsidies to farmers.[32] The Court thereby sealed the fate of dual federalism.

## Links

**The New Deal**

Click here to learn more about the New Deal.

**Fireside Chats**

Read the Fireside Chats online here.

## Grants-in-Aid

**grants-in-aid**

The national government's provision of funds to states or localities to administer particular programs.

**categorical grants**

Grants through which states and localities spend national funds on programs to meet the precise purposes Congress specified.

Cooperative federalism's central mechanisms were **grants-in-aid**: the national government passes funds to the states to administer programs. Starting in the 1940s and 1950s, national grants were awarded for infrastructure (airport construction, interstate highways), health (mental health, cancer control, hospital construction), and economic enhancement (agricultural marketing services, fish restoration).[33]

Grants-in-aid were cooperative in three ways. First, they funded policies that states already oversaw. Second, **categorical grants** required states to spend the funds for purposes specified by Congress but gave them leeway on how to do so. Third, states' and localities' core functions of education and law enforcement had little national government supervision.[34]

# Competitive Federalism

During the 1960s, the national government moved increasingly into areas once reserved to the states. As a result, the essence of federalism today is competition rather than cooperation.[35]

## Judicial Nationalizing

Cooperative federalism was weakened when a series of Supreme Court decisions, starting in the 1950s, caused states to face much closer supervision by national authorities. As we discuss in Chapter 4 and Chapter 5, the Court extended requirements of the Bill of Rights and of "equal protection of the law" to the states.

## The Great Society

In 1963, President Lyndon Johnson proposed extending the New Deal policies of his hero, FDR. Seeking a "Great Society" and declaring a "War on Poverty," Johnson inspired Congress to enact massive new programs funded by the national government. Over two hundred new grants programs were enacted during Johnson's five years in office. They included a Jobs Corps and Head Start, which provided preschool education for poor children.

The Great Society undermined cooperative federalism. The new national policies to help the needy dealt with problems that states and localities had been unable or reluctant or unwilling to address. Many of them bypassed states to go straight to local governments and nonprofit organizations.[36]

### Link

**The Great Society**

Click here to read more about the Great Society.

## Friction

In competitive federalism, national, state, and local levels clash, even battle with each other.[37] Overlapping powers and responsibilities create friction, which is compounded by politicians' desires to pursue their ideologies and priorities, get in the news, and claim credit for programs responding to public problems.

Consequently, in recent decades, partisan control of different state governments has led to differences in and polarization between states in their policies (such as on health care, state taxation, and abortion).[38]

The advent of the Trump presidency found competitive federalism in full bloom. Policies proposed, decisions made, and actions taken by the executive branch of the federal government have been objected to, contested, and opposed by states and sometimes city governments. Some of these challenges, such as California's against the Trump administration's policies on climate control, have received widespread news coverage.[39]

Differences between and within states and local governments over how to respond to COVID-19 have been conspicuous. For example, some local officials (school superintendents) in New Jersey declined to follow the governor's instructions to open schools for face-to-face instruction.[40]

## Mandates

Under competitive federalism, funds go from national to state and local governments with many conditions—most notably, directives known as **mandates**.[41] State and local governments want national funds but resent conditions. They especially dislike "unfunded mandates," according to which the national government directs them what to do but gives them no funds to do it.

**mandates**

Directives from the national government to state and local governments, either as orders or as conditions on the use of national funds.

After the Republicans gained control of Congress in the 1994 elections, they passed a rule to bar unfunded mandates. If a member objects to an unfunded mandate, a majority must vote to waive the rule in order to pass it. This reform has had little impact: negative news attention to unfunded mandates is easily displaced by dramatic, personalized issues that cry out for action. For example, in 1996, the story of Megan Kanka, a young New Jersey girl killed by a released sex offender living in her neighborhood, gained huge news attention. The same Congress that outlawed unfunded mandates passed "Megan's Law"—including an unfunded mandate ordering state and local law enforcement officers to compile lists of sex offenders and send them to a registry run by the national government.

### Key Takeaways

Federalism in the United States has changed over time from clear divisions of powers between national, state, and local governments in the early years of the republic to greater intermingling and cooperation, as well as conflict and competition today. Causes of these changes include political actions, court decisions, responses to economic problems (e.g., depression), and social concerns (e.g., sin).

### Exercises

1. What view of federalism allowed the Confederate states to justify seceding from the United States? How might this view make it difficult for the federal government to function in the long run?
2. What are the differences between dual, cooperative, and competitive federalism? What social forces led to the federal and state governments working together in a new way?
3. How is federalism portrayed in the movies and television shows you've seen? Why do you think it is portrayed that way?

# 2.4 Why Federalism Works (More or Less)

## Learning Objectives

After reading this section, you should be able to answer the following questions:

1. How do national, state, and local governments interact to make federalism work, more or less?
2. How are interest groups involved in federalism?
3. What are the ideological and political attitudes toward federalism of the Democratic and Republican parties?

When Hurricane Katrina hit New Orleans and the surrounding areas on August 29, 2005, it exposed federalism's frailties. The state and local governments were overwhelmed, yet there was uncertainty over which level of government should be in charge of rescue attempts. Louisiana Governor Kathleen Blanco refused to sign an order turning over the disaster response to federal authorities. She did not want to cede control of the National Guard and did not believe signing the order would hasten the arrival of the troops she had requested. President George W. Bush failed to realize the magnitude of the disaster and subsequently believed that the federal response was effective. In fact, as was obvious to anyone watching television, it was slow and ineffective. New Orleans Mayor C. Ray Nagin and state officials accused the Federal Emergency Management Agency (FEMA) of failing to deliver urgently needed help and of thwarting other efforts through red tape.

Hurricane Katrina was an exceptional challenge to federalism. Normally, competition between levels of government does not careen so much out of control, and federalism works, more or less. We have already discussed one reason: a legal hierarchy—in which national law is superior to state law, which in turn dominates local law—dictates who wins in clashes in domains where each may constitutionally act.

There are three other reasons.[42] First, state and local governments provide crucial assistance to the national government in implementing its policies; assistance that, as we shall see, is not always accepted. Second, national, state, and local levels have complementary capacities, providing distinct services and resources. Third, the fragmentation of the system is sometimes bridged by interest groups, notably the intergovernmental lobby that provides voices for state and local governments. We discuss each reason.

## Applying Policies Close to Home

State and local governments are essential parts of federalism because the federal government routinely needs them to execute national policy. State and local governments adjust the policies as best they can to meet their political preferences and their residents' needs. Policies and the funds expended on them can thus vary dramatically from one state to the next, even in national programs such as unemployment benefits.[43]

This division of labor, through which the national government sets goals and states and localities administer policies, makes for incomplete coverage in the news. National news watches the national government, covering more the political games and high-minded intentions of policies than the nitty-gritty of implementation. Local news stresses the local angle of national news, the impact of decisions in distant Washington (see the following "Comparing Content" for more information).

## Comparing Content

### Passage of No Child Left Behind Act

The No Child Left Behind (NCLB) Act vastly expanded the national government's supervision of public education with requirements for testing and accountability. Amid the final push toward enacting the law, Washington reporters for national newspapers were caught up in a remarkable story: the bipartisan coalition uniting staunch opponents President George W. Bush and liberal senator Edward M. Kennedy (D-MA) civilly working together on a bold, historic piece of legislation. Dana Milbank's *Washington Post* story was typical. Milbank termed the bill "the broadest rewriting of federal education policy in decades," and he admired "Washington's top bipartisan achievement of 2001."[44] The looming problems of funding and implementing the act were obscured in the national media's celebration of the lovefest.

By contrast, local newspapers across the country calculated the benefits and costs of the new legislation on education in their states and localities—in particular, how much money the state would receive under NCLB and whether or not the law's requirements and deadlines were reasonable. On January 9, 2002, the *Boston Globe*'s headline was "Mass. Welcomes Fed $$; Will Reap $117M for Schools, Testing," and the *Denver Post* noted, "Colorado to Get $500 million for Schools."[45]

Local newspapers sought out comments of state and local education officials and leaders of local teachers' unions, who were less smitten by the new law. The *Sacramento Bee* published a lengthy front-page story by reporter Erika Chavez on January 3, shortly before Bush signed the law. Chavez contrasted the bill's supporters who saw it as "the most meaningful education reform in decades" with opponents who found that "one crucial aspect of the legislation is nothing more than a pipe dream." Discussing the bill's provision that all teachers must be fully credentialed in four years, a staffer at the State Department of Education was quoted as saying, "The numbers don't add up, no matter how you look at them." The California Teachers' Association's president called it "fantasy legislation," adding, "It's irresponsible to pass this kind of law and not provide the assistance needed to make the goals attainable. I can't understand the reason or logic that went into this legislation. It's almost a joke."[46] In time, the critics would come closer to vindication than the law's proponents.

# Complementary Capacities

The second reason federalism often works (or not) is because national, state, and local governments specialize in different policy domains.[47] The main focus of local and state government policy is economic development, broadly defined to include all policies that attract or keep businesses and enhance property values. States have traditionally taken the lead in highways, welfare, health, natural resources, and prisons.[48] Local governments dominate in education, police and fire protection, sewerage, sanitation, airports, and parking.

The national government is central in policies to serve low-income and other needy persons. In these **redistributive policies**, those paying for a service in taxes are not usually those receiving the service.[49] These programs rarely get positive coverage in the local news, which often shows them as "something-for-nothing" benefits that undeserving individuals receive, not as ways to address national problems.[50]

**redistributive policies**

Policies whereby those who pay the taxes usually do not receive the service paid by the taxes.

States cannot effectively provide redistributive benefits. It is impossible to stop people from moving away because they think they are paying too much in taxes for services. Nor can states with generous benefits stop outsiders from moving there—a key reason why very few states enacted broad health-care coverage.[51]

The three levels of government also rely on different sources of taxation to fund their activities and policies. The national government depends most heavily on the national income tax, based in part on people's ability to pay. This enables it to shift funds away from the wealthier states (e.g., Connecticut, New Jersey, New Hampshire) to poorer states (e.g., New Mexico, North Dakota, West Virginia).

Taxes of local and state governments are more closely connected to services provided. Local governments depend mainly on property taxes—the more valuable the property, the more people pay. State governments collect state income taxes but rely most on sales taxes gathered during presumably necessary or pleasurable consumer activity.

### Links

**Tax and Budget Information for Federal, State, and Local Governments**

Find more information about government budgets and taxes at the federal level here and at the state and local levels here.

The language of "no new taxes" or "cutting taxes" is an easy slogan for politicians to feature in campaign ads and the news. As a result, governments often increase revenues on the sly, by lotteries, cigarette and alcohol taxes, toll roads, and sales taxes falling mostly on nonresidents (like hotel taxes or surcharges on car rentals).[52]

# The Intergovernmental Lobby

A third reason federalism often works (or not) is because interest groups and professional associations focus simultaneously on a variety of governments at the national, state, and local levels. With multiple points of entry, policy changes can occur in many ways (or not).[53]

These processes are reinforced by the intergovernmental lobby. State and local governments lobby the president and Congress. Their officials band together in organizations, such as the National Governors Association, National Association of Counties, the U.S. Conference of Mayors, and the National Conference of State Legislatures. These associations trade information and pass resolutions to express common concerns to the national government. Such meetings are one-stop-shopping occasions for the news media to gauge nationwide trends in state and local government.

Policy diffusion, a horizontal form of change, may occur. State and local officials watch what other state and local governments are doing or not doing. States can be "laboratories of democracy," experimenting with innovative programs that sometimes spread to other states. They can also make problems worse with ineffective or misdirected policies. Colorado's 2013 legalization of the recreational use of marijuana (the first stores opened January 1, 2014) provides benefits by reaping a harvest of tax receipts and boosting tourism but also raises concerns about safety (driving under the influence) and under-age use.

State policies can respond to long-simmering issues, as California did in 2019 by enacting a law allowing college athletes to be paid (The Fair Pay to Play Act).

State policies can be exploited by adroit businesses: in its pursuit of increasing profit from the sale of its opioid (addictive) painkiller OxyContin, Purdue Pharma focused its marketing in states with lower regulation of prescription drugs.

# Police Reform

The permeability of federalism—its openness or resistance to change—is exposed by the subject of police reform. Breaking-news events arouse calls for policy responses at various levels of the polity. Massive publicity around the police killings of Black citizens and subsequent protest demonstrations propel police brutality onto the policy agenda nationwide and inspire proposals for state and local reforms.[54]

In addition to the use of violence, police practices raise numerous issues that can be subject to challenge and change. These include violating civil rights and civil liberties; accountability for false confessions and wrongful convictions; racial profiling; whether they should be armed with surplus military equipment (off-loaded by the Pentagon); whether police budgets should be defunded or reallocated; limits on the powers of police unions (especially to protect their members from dismissal); and discouraging officers from lying in court (testi-lying).

The police's situation is complicated. Law-enforcement officers are endowed with authority, including the use of deadly force, to try to ensure order and security in society, undertakings made challenging in the face of a widely armed civilian population. Its members are often held responsible for, but are ill-equipped and untrained to handle, psychological, social, and family ills. In a profession filled with hours of boredom, the police can suddenly find themselves in harm's way and enduring moments of utter terror.

So the police are vulnerable to local and state governments looking to enact and implement some of these policies. At the same time, the police can turn to the national level for protection. Police lobbyists (Federal Law Enforcement Officers Association, National Sheriffs' Association) worked with President Trump's top advisers, Republicans and a few Democrats in Congress, to preserve the legal doctrine that protects police officers from lawsuits. They sought to retain no-knock warrants, prevent a national database of complaints against the police, and thwart legislation to ban chokeholds and to make it easier to pursue and prosecute police misconduct.[55]

# Democrats, Republicans, and Federalism

The parties stand for different principles with regard to federalism. Democrats prefer policies to be set by the national government. They opt for national standards for consistency across states and localities, often through attaching stringent conditions to the use of national funds. Republicans decry such centralization and endorse devolution, giving (or, they say, "returning") powers to the states—and seeking to shrink funds for the national government.

In an example that combines principles with politics, President Obama's Justice Department threatened to take over and administer police departments, such as in Baltimore, it deemed to be racist and to use excessive force. But its successor, the Trump Justice Department, declined to do so.

Principled distinctions can evaporate in practice. Both parties have been known to give priority to other principles over federalism and to pursue policy goals regardless of the impact on boundaries between national, state, and local governments.[56]

So, Republicans sometimes champion a national policy while Democrats look to the states and localities. In 2017, President Trump signed an executive order banning people from seven majority-Muslim countries from entry to the United States The Democratic Attorneys General of several states challenged the ban, which some federal judges then suspended as unconstitutional.

Marijuana is another example. After Colorado, in 2014, voters approved ballot measures legalizing marijuana for recreational purposes in Alaska and Oregon, and more states followed. This led to a conflict between these states and President Trump's attorney general's commitment to upholding the federal law prohibiting recreational use of the substance.

As a result of the 2010 and subsequent elections, Republicans added to their control of the executives and legislatures of state governments. This enabled them to enact policies (some proposed by the American Legislative Exchange Council—an interest group we discuss in Chapter 9). These included cutting taxes on the wealthy, reducing unemployment benefits and funds for education and public services, and limiting voting rights, immigration, and environmental protection.[57] They imposed restrictions on abortions and abortion providers, and loosened them on the ownership and possession of guns.[58] In contrast, when Democrats gained control of Illinois, they raised the minimum wage, introduced a graduated income tax, and deemed abortion a fundamental right for women.

Whether desirable or not, these actions showed competitive federalism in action, working more or less: states as places for policies and laws opposed by the Obama administration and unlikely to be enacted at the national government level.

Competitive federalism degenerated into outright conflict over the Affordable Care Act (initially derisively called "Obamacare" by its detractors). Some Republican-dominated states defied or thwarted parts of the Act by declining millions of dollars in federal funds (100 percent of the cost for the first three years and 90 percent thereafter) to expand their Medicaid programs, thus denying health care to millions of the poorest people. (The Supreme Court had ruled that the expansion of Medicaid was voluntary and thus up to each state to decide.) Some of these states also refused to operate state health exchanges, thereby forcing Washington to set them up in the state.

Then, in July 2020, conflict between U.S. governments became palpable when President Trump sent federal forces from the Department of Homeland Security (DHS), the U.S. Marshal Service, the U.S. Customs and Border Patrol (CBP), and the Federal Protection Service, into such cities as Portland, Oregon, and threatened to deploy them in Chicago and elsewhere. His justification was to stop riots, stop looting and the destruction of property, and maintain the peace. Some governors and mayors challenged the president's actions and promises on the grounds the forces were unnecessary and unneeded, wore camouflage, and drove unmarked cars. Worse, they fired pepper spray and tear gas at protesters, inciting and perpetuating violence. The local politicians charged the president with promoting a law-and-order message (bolstered by his political advertising) showing he was protecting the (mainly white) public against the national danger of (Black) unrest.[59]

## Key Takeaways

The federal system functions, more or less, because of the authority of national over state laws, which trump local laws; crucial assistance provided by the states and local governments to execute national policy; the complementary capacities of the three levels of government; and the intergovernmental lobby. The Democratic and Republican parties differ ideologically about federalism, although these differences can be changed to achieve political objectives. Competitive federalism can become quite common.

## Exercises

1. How do the perspectives of national, state, and local governments complement one another? What are the strengths of each perspective?

2. Why do you think Democrats are more likely to prefer to make policy at the national level? Why are Republicans more likely to prefer to leave policymaking to state and local governments?
3. How did conflicts between the national government and state and local governments contribute to damage caused by Hurricane Katrina? Why do you think federalism broke down in that case?

# 2.5 Federalism in the Information Age

## Learning Objectives

After reading this section, you should be able to answer the following questions:

1. What are the strengths and weaknesses of the media in covering federalism?
2. How are some public officials in the federal system able to use the media to advance their political agendas?
3. What effects could the new media have on people's knowledge of and commitment to federalism?

Federalism gives the American political system additional complexity and dynamism. The number of governments involved in a wide sweep of issues creates many ways for people in politics to act and to be heard. These processes are facilitated by a media system that resembles federalism by its own merging and mingling of national, state, and local content and audiences.

## Media Interactions

National, state, and local news and entertainment outlets all depict federalism. Now they are joined by new technologies that communicate across geographical boundaries.

### National News Outlets

News on network television, cable news channels, and public broadcasting is aimed at a national audience. A few newspapers are also national. Reporters for these national outlets are largely based in New York and Washington, DC, and in a smattering of bureaus here and there across the country.

### Local News Outlets

Local television stations transmit the news programs of the national networks to which they are affiliated. They broadcast local news on their own news shows. These shows are not devoid of substance, although it is easy to make fun of them as vapid and delivered by airheads, like Will Ferrell's character Ron Burgundy in the 2004 comic film *Anchorman*, and its 2013 sequel. But they have only scattered national and international coverage, and attention to local and state government policies and politics is overshadowed by stories about isolated incidents such as crimes, car chases, and fires.

Almost all newspapers are local. Stories from the wire services enable them to include national and international highlights and some state items in their news, but most of their news is local. As their staffs shrink, they increasingly defer to powerful official sources in city hall or the police station for the substance of news. The news media serving smaller communities are even more vulnerable to pressure from local officials for favorable coverage and from advertisers who want a "feel-good" context for their paid messages.

## From National to Local

Local newspapers and television stations sometimes have their own correspondents in Washington, DC. They can add a local angle by soliciting information and quotes from home-state members of Congress. Or, pooling of resources lets local television broadcasts make it look as though they have sent a reporter to Washington; a single reporter can send a feed to many stations by ending with an anonymous, "Now back to you."

## From Local to National

Some local stories become prominent and gain saturation coverage nationally. They are often horrific or disasters or threaten and disrupt people's lives and persist longer than a few days. Two dreadful cases occurred in early 2014. In the first, chemicals leaked from a Freedom Industries storage tank in West Virginia into a river, thereby contaminating Charleston's water. The city's 300,000 residents were warned not to drink or use the water. In the second, the giant utility Duke Power discharged toxic waste (coal ash) into a North Carolina river. It was the third largest "spill" on record.

**parachute in**

When national reporters come from the networks to cover a local event.

The often cozy relationships of local officials, company owners, and some local media are dislodged, at least temporarily, when national reporters from the networks **parachute in** to cover the event. Additional derelictions and abuses by the companies may be revealed, ineffective and antiregulation state policies exposed, knowledgeable local reporters consulted, environmentalists given their say, and investigations (some of them by federal agencies) spurred. Important issues are raised and brought to the attention of the public, such as the safety of chemicals—few of which have been tested—and their effects on health, as well as the lack of effective regulation by federal and particularly state agencies.

In 2011, federalism itself took center stage with the efforts of Republican governor Scott Walker of Wisconsin, and related steps by the Republican governors of Indiana and Ohio, to save funds by stripping most of the collective bargaining power of the state's public employee unions. Stories reported on the proposed policies, Democratic legislators' efforts to thwart them, and the workers' and supporters' sit-ins and demonstrations.

Such stories expand amid attention from local and national news outlets and discussion about their meaning and import. National, state, and local officials alike find they have to respond to the problems evoked by the dramatic event.[60]

## State News and State Politics

Except for covering certain governors and attorneys general, the local media give little space in their news to state governments and their policies. One reason is that there are only a few truly statewide news outlets like New Hampshire's *Manchester Union Leader* or Iowa's *Des Moines Register*. Another reason is that most state capitals are far from the state's main metropolitan area. Examples such as Boston and Atlanta, where the state capital is the largest city, are unusual. The four largest states are more typical: their capitals (Sacramento, Austin, Tallahassee, and Albany) are far (and in separate media markets) from Los Angeles, Houston, Miami, and New York City.

Capital cities' local news outlets do give emphasis to state government. But those cities are relatively small, so that news about state government usually goes to people involved with state government more than to the public in the state as a whole.

State officials do not always mind the lack of scrutiny of state government. It allows some of them to get their views into the media. Governors, for example, have full-time press officers as key advisors and routinely give interviews and hold news conferences. According to governors' press secretaries, their press releases are often printed word-for-word across the state, and the governors also gain positive coverage when they travel to other cities for press events such as signing legislation.[61]

# Media Consequences

The variety and range of national and local media offer opportunities for people in politics to gain leverage and influence. National policymakers, notably the president, use national news and entertainment media to reach a national public. But because local news media serve as a more unfiltered and thus less critical conduit to the public, policymakers also seek and obtain positive publicity from them.

State governors and big-city mayors, especially when they have few formal powers or when they face a state legislature or city council filled with opponents, can parlay favorable media attention into political power.[62] At best, a governor (as one wrote in the 1960s) "sets the agenda for public debate; frames the issues; decides the timing; and can blanket the state with good ideas by using access to the mass media."[63]

Some state attorneys general are particularly adept and adroit at attracting positive media coverage through the causes they pursue, the (sometimes) outrageous accusations they announce, and the people they prosecute. One result is to put intolerable pressure on their targets to settle before trial. Another is reams of favorable publicity that they can parlay into a successful campaign for higher office, as Eliot Spitzer did in becoming governor of New York in 2006, and Andrew Cuomo in 2010.

But to live by the media sword is sometimes to die by it, as Governor Spitzer discovered when the media indulged in a blizzard of stories about his engaging the services of prostitutes. He resigned from office in disgrace in March 2008. (See the documentary *Client 9*, listed in our "Recommended Viewing.") Indeed, news attention can be unwanted and destructive. After he was arrested in December 2008 for corruption, the widespread negative coverage Illinois Governor Rod Blagojevich received in the national, state, and local media contributed to his speedy impeachment and removal from office by the state legislature the next month. Convicted, he went to prison in 2012.

The media are also important because officials are news consumers in their own right. State legislators value news exposure to communicate to other legislators, the governor, and interest groups and to set the policy agenda.[64] Thus, legislative staffers in Illinois conclude that news coverage is a better indicator of public opinion than polls.[65] The news may more heavily and quickly influence officials' views of problems and policy issues than the public.

# New Media and Federalism

New technologies that enable far-flung individuals to quickly obtain news from many locales can help people understand the many dimensions of federalism. People in politics in one state can, with a few keystrokes, find out how an issue is being handled in all fifty states, thus providing a boost for ideas and issues to travel more quickly than ever across state lines. The National Conference of State Legislatures, as part of its mission to "offer a variety of services to help lawmakers tailor policies that will work for their state and their constituents," maintains a website with a motto, "Where Policy Clicks!," allowing web surfers to search the latest information from a whole range of states about "state and federal issues A to Z."

But new media create a challenge for federalism. They erode the once-close connection of media to geographically defined communities. Consumers can tune in to distant satellite and cable outlets as easily as local television stations. Cell phones make it as convenient (and cheap) to call across the country as across the street. The internet and the web, with their listservs, websites, blogs, chat rooms, and podcasts permit ready and ongoing connections to groups and communities that can displace individuals' commitment to and involvement in their physical surroundings.

In one sense, new technologies simply speed up a development launched in the 1960s, when, as one scholar writes, "one type of group—the place-based group that federalism had honored—yielded to groups otherwise defined, as by race, age, disability, or orientation to an issue or cause."[66]

Yet the vitality of state and local governments, presenting so many opportunities for people in politics to intervene, reminds us that federalism is not about to wither and die. In the end, the new technologies may enable individuals and groups more efficiently to manage the potentially overwhelming amount of information about what is going on in policymaking—and to navigate quickly and adroitly the dazzling and bemusing complexity of American federalism.

## Key Takeaways

The U.S. media system blends national, state, and local outlets. Issues and stories move from one level to another. This enables people in politics to gain influence but can undermine them. New media technologies, fostering quick communication across vast expanses, allow people to learn and understand more about federalism but challenge federalism's geographical foundation. Federalism seems like a daunting obstacle course, but it also opens up many opportunities for political action.

## Exercises

1. How do the perspectives of the national and local media differ? Why is there relatively little coverage of state politics in the national and local media?
2. Do you get any of your news about or relevant to federalism from new media? How does such news differ from the news you get from the traditional media?

### Civic Education

***Michael Barker vs. the School Board***

As Hamilton predicted in Federalist No. 28, if the people are frustrated at one level of government, they can make their voice heard and win policy battles at another. Federalism looks like a daunting obstacle course, yet it opens up a vast array of opportunities for political action.

Michael Barker did not set out to push the Louisiana state legislature for a new law. In 2003, Barker, a seventeen-year-old high school junior from the town of Jena, had wondered if his school district might save money on computer equipment by making smarter purchases. He sent four letters to the LaSalle Parish School Board requesting information about computer expenditures. He was rebuffed by the superintendent of schools, who notified him that a state law allowed public officials to deny requests for public records from anyone under the age of eighteen.

Barker did not understand why minors—including student journalists—had no right to access public information. Stymied locally, he aimed at the state government. He conducted an internet search and discovered a statewide nonprofit organization, the Public Affairs Research Council (PAR), that promotes public access. Barker contacted PAR, which helped him develop a strategy to research the issue thoroughly and contact Jena's state representative, Democrat Thomas Wright. Wright agreed to introduce House Bill 492 to strike the "age of majority" provision from the books. Barker testified in the state capital of Baton Rouge at legislative hearings on behalf of the bill, saying, "Our education system strives daily to improve upon people's involvement in the democratic process. This bill would allow young people all over the state of Louisiana to be involved with the day-to-day operations of our state government."

But Barker's crusade had just begun. A state senator who had a personal beef with Representative Wright tried to block passage of the bill. Barker contacted a newspaper reporter, who wrote a story about the controversy. The ensuing media spotlight caused the opposition to back down. After the bill was passed and signed into law by Governor Kathleen Blanco, Barker set up a website to share his experiences and to provide advice to young people who want to influence government.[67]

# 2.6 Recommended Reading


Berman, David R. *Local Government and the States: Autonomy, Politics, and Policy*. Armonk, NY: M. E. Sharpe, 2003. An overview of the relationship between state and local governments.

Derthick, Martha. *Keeping the Compound Republic: Essays on American Federalism*. Washington, DC: Brookings, 2001. A set of discerning essays on intergovernmental relations.

Kaniss, Phyllis. *Making Local News*. Chicago: University of Chicago Press, 1991. A pathbreaking account of how politicians and journalists interact to produce local news.

Lawrence, Regina G. *The Politics of Force: Media and the Construction of Police Brutality*. Berkeley: University of California Press, 2000. An eye-opening example of how local issues do and do not spread to national news and politics.

Peterson, Paul E. *The Price of Federalism*. Washington, DC: Brookings, 1995. An astute assessment of the contributions that national, state, and local levels can and do make to government..

Posner, Paul L. *The Politics of Unfunded Mandates: Whither Federalism?* Washington, DC: Georgetown University Press, 1998. A concise account of the ups and downs of unfunded mandates.

Shapiro, David L. *Federalism: A Dialogue*. Evanston, IL: Northwestern University Press, 1995. A distinguished legal scholar debates with himself on the pros and cons of federalism.


# 2.7 Recommended Viewing

*Amistad* (1997). This Steven Spielberg dramatization of the legal aftermath of a revolt on a slave ship examines interactions between local, state, national, and international law.

*Anchorman* (2004). This vehicle for comedian Will Ferrell, set in the 1970s, spoofs the vapidity of local television news.

*Bonnie and Clyde* (1967). Small-time criminals become romanticized rebels in this famous revisionist take on the expansion of national authority against crime in the 1930s.

*Cadillac Desert* (1997). A four-part documentary about the politics of water across state lines in the American West.

*City Hall* (2020). Frederick Wiseman's epic documentary showing the workings of Boston's government and conspicuously the city's ubiquitous mayor.

*Client 9: The Rise and Fall of Eliot Spitzer* (2010). Alex Gibney's interviews-based documentary about the interweaving of hubris, politics, enemies, prostitution, the FBI, and the media.

*The FBI Story* (1959). James Stewart stars in a dramatized version of the bureau's authorized history, closely overseen by FBI director J. Edgar Hoover.

*First Blood* (1982). When Vietnam vet John Rambo clashes with a monomaniacal local sheriff in this first "Rambo" movie, it takes everyone from the state troopers, the National Guard, and his old special forces colonel to rein him in.

*George Wallace: Settin' the Woods on Fire* (2000). A compelling documentary on the political transformations of the Alabama governor who championed states' rights in the 1960s.

*Monrovia, Ind.* (2019). Frederick Wiseman's documentary examines daily life in a farming community.

*Mystic River* (2003). A state police officer investigating the murder of the daughter of a childhood friend faces "the law of the street" in a working-class Boston neighborhood.

*Public Housing* (1997). Frederick Wiseman documents life in this Chicago institution.

*State Legislature* (2007). Frederick Wiseman's documentary explores the Idaho legislature at work.

# Endnotes


1. Sarah Kershaw, "Governors Tell of War's Impact on Local Needs," *The New York Times*, July 20, 2004, A1.
2. See Morton Grodzins's classic book *The American System: A New View of Government in the United States* (Chicago: Rand McNally, 1966), 13.
3. We follow the founders who reserved "national government" for the legislative, presidential, and judicial branches at the national level, saving "federal government" for the entity consisting of national, state, and local levels. See Paul E. Peterson, *The Price of Federalism* (Washington, DC: Brookings, 1995), 13–14.
4. License Cases, 5 How. 504 (1847).
5. Adam Liptak and Michael Wines, "Supreme Court Permits Freeze of Census, in Victory for Trump," *The New York Times*, October 14, 2020, A1 (21).
6. Martha Derthick, *Keeping the Compound Republic: Essays on American Federalism* (Washington, DC: Brookings, 2001), 83.
7. David Montgomery, Simon Romero and James Robbins, "Cities v. State: Grid Failure Adds to Fight Over G.O.P Governance," *The New York Times*, February 19, 2021, A 23.a
8. For example, John Leland, "Abortion Foes Advance Cause at State Level," *The New York Times*, June 3, 2010, A1, 16.
9. Phyllis Kaniss, *Making Local News* (Chicago: University of Chicago Press, 1991), table 4.4.
10. Charles Layton and Jennifer Dorroh, "Sad State," *American Journalism Review*, June 2002, http://www.ajr.org/article_printable.asp?id=2562.
11. *Cherokee Nation v. Georgia*, 30 US 1 (1831).
12. See Charles F. Wilkinson, *American Indians, Time, and the Law: Native Societies in a Modern Constitutional Democracy* (New Haven, CT: Yale University Press, 1987); George Pierre Castile, *To Show Heart: Native American Self-Determination and Federal Indian Policy, 1960–1975* (Tucson: University of Arizona Press, 1998); and Kenneth R. Philp, *Termination Revisited: American Indians on the Trail to Self-Determination, 1933–1953* (Lincoln: University of Nebraska Press, 1999).
13. Jimcy McGirt v. Oklahoma, 591U.S. 140 S. Ct. 2452 (2020).
14. *Worcester v. Georgia*, 31 US 515 (1832).
15. *Montana v. Blackfeet Tribe of Indians*, 471 US 759 (1985); *California v. Cabazon Band of Indians*, 480 US 202 (1987); *Seminole Tribe of Florida v. Florida*, 517 US 44 (1996).
16. The two exceptions are Alaska, which has boroughs that do not cover the entire area of the state, and Louisiana, where the equivalents of counties are parishes.
17. The U.S. Bureau of the Census categorizes those entities that are organized (usually chosen by election) with a governmental character and substantial autonomy. U.S. Census Bureau, *Government Organization: 2002 Census of Governments* 1, no. 1: 6, http://www.census.gov/prod/2003pubs/gc021x1.pdf.
18. Forrest McDonald, *States' Rights and the Union: Imperium in Imperio, 1776–1876* (Lawrence: University Press of Kansas, 2000), 38–43.
19. This section draws on James M. McPherson, *Battle Cry of Freedom: The Civil War Era* (New York: Oxford University Press, 1988).
20. Thomas D. Morris, *Free Men All: The Personal Liberty Laws of the North, 1780–1861* (Baltimore, MD: Johns Hopkins University Press, 1974).
21. An encyclopedic account of this case is Don E. Fehrenbacher, *The Dred Scott Case: Its Significance in American Law and Politics* (New York: Oxford University Press, 1978).
22. See especially Robert E. Bonner, *Colors and Blood: Flag Passions of the Confederate South* (Princeton, NJ: Princeton University Press, 2002).
23. For overviews of these meanings see Tony Horwitz, *Confederates in the Attic: Dispatches from the Unfinished Civil War* (New York: Random House, 1998) and J. Michael Martinez, William D. Richardson, and Ron McNinch-Su, eds., *Confederate Symbols in the Contemporary South* (Gainesville: University of Florida Press, 2000).
24. David L. Shapiro, *Federalism: A Dialogue* (Evanston, IL: Northwestern University Press, 1995), 98 n. 139.
25. *Texas v. White*, 7 Wall. 700 (1869).
26. *McCulloch v. Maryland*, 4 Wheat. 316 (1819).
27. This section draws on James A. Morone, *Hellfire Nation: The Politics of Sin in American History* (New Haven, CT: Yale University Press, 2003), chaps. 8–11.
28. Quoted in James A. Morone, *Hellfire Nation: The Politics of Sin in American History* (New Haven, CT: Yale University Press, 2003), 266.
29. *United States v. E. C. Knight*, 156 US 1 (1895).
30. *Hammer v. Dagenhart*, 247 US 251 (1918). A similar logic prevented the U.S. government from using taxation powers to the same end. *Bailey v. Drexel Furniture Company*, 259 U.S. 20 (1922).
31. Thomas Anton, *American Federalism & Public Policy: How the System Works* (Philadelphia, PA: Temple University Press, 1988), 41.
32. Respectively, *National Labor Relations Board v. Jones & Laughlin Steel*, 301 US 1 (1937); *United States v. Darby*, 312 US 100 (1941); *Wickard v. Filburn*, 317 US 111 (1942).
33. David B. Walker, *The Rebirth of Federalism: Slouching toward Washington* (Washington, DC: CQ Press, 1999), 99.
34. Martha Derthick, *Keeping the Compound Republic: Essays on American Federalism* (Washington, DC: Brookings, 2001), 17.
35. Paul E. Peterson, Barry George Rabe, and Kenneth K. Wong, *When Federalism Works* (Washington, DC: Brookings, 1986), especially chap. 5; Martha Derthick, *Keeping the Compound Republic: Essays on American Federalism* (Washington, DC: Brookings, 2001), chap. 10.
36. David B. Walker, *The Rebirth of Federalism: Slouching toward Washington* (Washington, DC: CQ Press, 1999), 123–25.
37. The term "competitive federalism" is developed in Thomas R. Dye, *American Federalism: Competition among Governments* (Lexington, MA: Lexington Books, 1990).
38. Jacob M. Grumbach, "From Backwaters to Major Policymakers: Policy Polarization in the States, 1970-2016," *Perspectives on Politics 16* (June 2018), 416–35); also Devin Caughey and Christopher Warshaw, "Policy Preferences and Policy Change: Dynamic Responsiveness in the American States, 1936-2014," *American Political Science Review*, 112 (2018): 2249–66.
39. Hiroko Tabuchi, "U.S. Climate Change Policy: Made in California," *The New York Times*, September 27, 2017, A1 (18).
40. Tracey Tully, "Murphy Wants Schools Open, but Local Officials Have Other Ideas,"
41. This definition is drawn from Michael Fix and Daphne Kenyon, eds., *Coping with Mandates: What Are the Alternatives?* (Washington, DC: Urban Institute Press, 1988), 3–4.
42. See also John D. Nugent, *Safeguarding Federalism: How States Protect Their Interests in National Policymaking* (Norman: University of Oklahoma Press, 2009).
43. Thomas R. Dye, *American Federalism: Competition among Governments* (Lexington, MA: Lexington Books, 1990), chap. 2; Paul E. Peterson, *The Price of Federalism* (Washington, DC: Brookings, 1995), chap. 4.
44. Dana Milbank, "With Fanfare, Bush Signs Education Bill," *Washington Post*, January 9, 2002, A3.
45. Ed Hayward, "Mass. Welcomes Fed $$; Will Reap $117M for Schools, Testing," *Boston Globe*, January 9, 2002, 7; Monte Whaley, "Colorado to Get $500 Million for Schools," *Denver Post*, January 9, 2002, A6.
46. Erika Chavez, "Federal Teacher Goal is Blasted; Congress' Mandate that Instructors Get Credentials in 4 Years is Called Unrealistic," *Sacramento Bee*, January 3, 2002, A1.
47. This section draws on Paul E. Peterson, *The Price of Federalism* (Washington, DC: Brookings, 1995).
48. Thomas Anton, *American Federalism & Public Policy: How the System Works* (Philadelphia, PA: Temple University Press, 1988), table 3.3.
49. This definition comes from Paul E. Peterson, Barry George Rabe, and Kenneth K. Wong, *When Federalism Works* (Washington, DC: Brookings, 1986), 15.
50. Paul E. Peterson, Barry George Rabe, and Kenneth K. Wong, *When Federalism Works* (Washington, DC: Brookings, 1986), 19.
51. Mark C. Rom and Paul E. Peterson, *Welfare Magnets: A New Case for a New National Standard* (Washington, DC: Brookings, 1990).
52. Glenn R. Beamer, *Creative Politics: Taxes and Public Goods in a Federal System* (Ann Arbor: University of Michigan Press, 1999), chap. 4.
53. Thomas Anton, *American Federalism & Public Policy: How the System Works* (Philadelphia, PA: Temple University Press, 1988), chap. 5.
54. Regina G. Lawrence, *The Politics of Force: Media and the Construction of Police Brutality* (Berkeley: University of California Press, 2000).
55. Luke Broadwater and Catie Edmondson, "Police Lobby Steers Congress Away From Major Reforms," *The New York Times*, June 26, 2020, A23.
56. Paul L. Posner, *The Politics of Unfunded Mandates: Whither Federalism?* (Washington, DC: Georgetown University Press, 1998), 223.
57. Ben Merriman, *Conservative Innovators: How States Are Challenging Federal Power* (Chicago: University of Chicago Press, 2019).
58. Joshua C. Wilson, *The New States of Abortion Politics* (Palo Alto, CA: Stanford University Press, 2016).
59. Mike Baker, Thomas Fuller,, and Shane Goldmacher, "Cities Are In Bind As Unrest Flares Over U.S. Actions," *The New York Times*, July 27, 2020, A1 (17).
60. Benjamin I. Page, *Who Deliberates?* (Chicago: University of Chicago Press, 1996).
61. Charles Layton and Jennifer Dorroh, "Sad State," *American Journalism Review*, June 2002, http://www.ajr.org/article_printable.asp?id=2562.
62. This section draws from Thad L. Beyle and Lynn R. Muchmore, eds., "The Governor and the Public," in *Being Governor: The View from the Office* (Durham, NC: Duke University Press, 1983), 52–66; Alan Rosenthal, *Governors and Legislatures: Contending Powers* (Washington, DC: CQ Press, 1990), 24–27; and Phyllis Kaniss, *Making Local News* (Chicago: University of Chicago Press, 1991), chap. 6.
63. Former governor of North Carolina, Terry Sanford, *Storm over the States* (New York: McGraw-Hill, 1967), 184–85, quoted in Thad L. Beyle and Lynn R. Muchmore, eds., "The Governor and the Public," in *Being Governor: The View from the Office* (Durham, NC: Duke University Press, 1983), 52.

64. Christopher A. Cooper, "Media Tactics in the State Legislature," *State Politics and Policy Quarterly* 2 (2002): 353–71.
65. Susan Herbst, *Reading Public Opinion: How Political Actors View the Democratic Process* (Chicago: University of Chicago Press, 1998), chap. 2.
66. Martha Derthick, *Keeping the Compound Republic: Essays on American Federalism* (Washington, DC: Brookings, 2001), 152.
67. This information comes from Jan Moller, "Teen's Curiosity Spurs Open-Records Bill," New Orleans *Times-Picayune*, April 14, 2004; and Wendy Scahetzel Lesko, "Teen Changes Open-Records Law," *Youth Activism Project, E-News*, July 2004, http://www.youthactivism.com/newsletter-archives/YA-July04.html.

CHAPTER 3

# Communication in the Information Age

## 3.1 Preamble

On the evening of April 2, 2003, the television networks' nightly news aired a brief night-vision video, supplied by the Defense Department, of U.S. forces carrying Private Jessica Lynch to safety after rescuing her from behind enemy lines in Iraq. The next day, in an exclusive on its front page that read like a Hollywood screenplay outline, the *Washington Post* reported her heroic story. Written from Washington, DC, and based on information supplied by unnamed officials, it told how the young maintenance clerk shot several enemy soldiers while "fighting to the death" before she was seriously wounded, captured, and taken to an enemy hospital. A few days later she was daringly rescued by U.S. commandos.[1] The story echoed through the broadcasting and print news media in the United States, throughout the world, and on the web. The television networks' morning news shows sent reporters to West Virginia to interview Lynch's family and friends. A website was established to receive and share tributes to her gallantry and feats.[2]

Although the *Post*'s report mentioned that the story had yet to be confirmed, the Pentagon reaped favorable publicity for the war with this tale of a Rambo-type exploit by an ordinary American woman in the battle against tyranny. This frame, or point of view, was widely used in many accounts of the event. (We explain frames and framing in detail in Section 6.)

Media companies bargained for the rights to Private Lynch's story. Viacom offered her a package: a prime-time news interview on its CBS television network; a book deal with its publishing house, Simon & Schuster; a music-video host spot on its cable channel MTV2; and a movie contract.[3] Eventually she signed with NBC, which had indicated that it was going to make a TV movie about her whether it had the rights to her story or not. NBC aired its made-for-TV movie *Saving Jessica Lynch* soon after the Veterans Day publication of a book about her ordeal written by a former *New York Times* reporter with whom she split a $1 million advance.[4] Promoting the book, Ms. Lynch appeared on ABC's *Primetime Live* for an interview with Diane Sawyer, NBC's *Today Show*, the CBS *Late Show* with David Letterman, and on CNN's *Larry King Live*. She was the subject of a cover story in *Time* magazine and was featured in *Glamour* magazine as one of its women of the year.

Accounts in both mass and social media, statements by Private Lynch herself, and a commentary by the *Post*'s ombudsman (the individual at the newspaper charged with evaluating its stories) almost three months after the original story indicated that the facts, to the extent they could be verified, were far less heroic.[5] Lynch's gun had jammed and not been fired. She did not fight or shoot at any enemy soldiers. The rescue may not have been necessary, because the Iraqi army had fled from the hospital the previous day, although it probably still controlled the town. Hospital staff had escorted the commandos to her ward. Blogs dissecting and arguing about the media's rethinking mushroomed. Over two years after the initial event, a former deputy commander at the United States Central Command wrote an op-ed column in the *New York Times* reminding people that Private Lynch had never claimed to be a hero and denying that the military had played up her rescue for publicity purposes.[6]

The Jessica Lynch story graphically reveals the interconnection of communication, information, and the media, as well as their significance for government and politics. These are the subjects of this chapter.

# 3.2 Communication, Information, and the Media

## Learning Objectives

After reading this section, you should be able to answer the following questions:

1. What are communication, information, and the media, and how are they central to American government and politics?
2. How have economics, government and politics, and technology shaped the media and their contents?
3. What are the main criticisms directed at the media business?
4. What are the main types of mass media?

**communication**

The process of transmitting or exchanging information. It can involve asserting, arguing, debating, deliberating, contacting, pressuring, appealing to, cajoling, and addressing.

**information**

Facts, knowledge, and views that people communicate about subjects and events. It encompasses news, opinion and commentary, and the contents of entertainment.

**media**

Well-established communication formats, such as newspapers and magazines, network television and radio stations, designed to reach large audiences.

**Communication** is a central activity of most everyone engaged in politics and government—people asserting, arguing, deliberating, demonstrating, and contacting public officials; candidates seeking to win votes; lobbyists pressuring policymakers; presidents appealing to the public, cajoling Congress, addressing the leaders and people of other countries. All this communication sparks more communication, actions, and reactions.

Most commonly communicated is **information** about subjects and events, people and processes.[7] It can be true or false (or fake), fiction or nonfiction, believable or not.

Most of the information that Americans obtain about politics and government comes through the media, both traditional and new. Traditional (sometimes called mainstream or legacy) **media** are discussed in this section. They consist of forms such as newspapers and magazines, television and radio, movies, books, and popular music usually designed and intended to attract audiences. Although much political information still originates in the mainstream media, it increasingly emanates from newer forms of media, such as YouTube, Facebook, Twitter, and Instagram.

Communication, information, and the media are central to this book in three ways. First, they depict the people, institutions, processes, policies, and issues of politics and government. Second, the ways in which they interact with participants in government and politics influence how these people are shown. Third, these depictions can have political and policy effects.

## Economics, Government and Politics, and Technology

Three interrelated factors are central to the development of the U.S. media business and its contents. They are economics, government and politics, and technology.

With regard to economics, journalist A. J. Liebling wrote, "The function of the press . . . is to inform, but its role is to make money."[8] Even when profit is not the motive, the media need financing to survive. The commercial media rely on advertising, sales, and subscriptions, and so the contents of their diverse products are aimed at attracting audiences sought by advertisers. Unlike many other countries, the United States has no media primarily financed by the government.

Government is involved with the media as a regulator, censor, and enabler. Regulation often involves decisions on technology: the Federal Communications Commission (FCC) has given away approximately $70 billion worth of digital spectrum, the wireless airwaves that carry television and radio broadcasts, to major media companies. Government censors by restricting content it deems obscene or by punishing media for producing such content. Government enables when, for example, it waives antitrust laws for media companies or subsidizes and thus lowers the postage costs for mailing newspapers and magazines.

Technological innovation can change media economics, relations with politicians and government, and the media's political contents. Exemplified by how Donald J. Trump's canny exploitation of television entertainment and cable news, and his use of Twitter, contributed to his public visibility and ascension to the American presidency.

Economics, government, and technology interact. The degree to which a technology influences politics depends on the way in which the technology is used. This, in turn, is shaped by the economic realities of the marketplace and by government policies concerning who can use a medium and for what purpose. Although the technology of television, even before cable, could have allowed for multiple and diverse channels, the economic search for a big audience to attract advertising revenue, combined with government regulation that favored private for-profit ownership, created the "three-networks system" that endured until the 1980s. This system provided airtime for presidents to present themselves and their programs to a huge national audience. When cable television offered more alternatives for viewers, it became harder for presidents to be heard above the clamor of competing programs—a difficulty exacerbated by the emergence of new media.

# The Media Business

Big businesses dominate much of the media. Between them, they own the main television networks and production companies, most of the popular cable channels, the major movie studios, newspapers, magazines, book publishers, and the top record companies.[9] In January 2011 the FCC approved the merger of Comcast, the nation's largest cable and home internet provider, with NBC Universal, one of the major producers of television shows and movies and the owner of several local stations, as well as such lucrative cable channels as MSNBC, CNBC, USA, Bravo, and SYFY. In 2018, AT&T acquired the majority of 21st Century Fox. In 2019, CBS and Viacom merged, reuniting the Paramount Film Studio, MTV, Nickelodeon, Comedy Central, and the (soon to be put up for sale) book publisher Simon & Schuster.

Some scholars criticize the media industry for pursuing profits and focusing on the bottom line. They accuse it of failing to cover government and public affairs in depth and of not presenting a wide range of views on policy issues.[10]

The reliance of most of the mass media on advertising as their main source of revenue and profit can discourage them from giving prominence or even attention to challenging social and political issues and critical views. Advertisers in particular want cheery contexts for their messages.

Nonetheless, the mass media can contain abundant information about politics, government, and public policies. We next specify the main types of these mass media and allude to their contents.

## Newspapers

The core of the mass media of the departed twentieth century was the newspaper. Even now, newspapers originate the overwhelming majority of domestic and foreign news, much of it about or related to government, politics, and public policies.

During recent years, sales have plummeted as many people have given up or never acquired the habit of reading print newspapers. Newer generations in particular are relying on social outlets. Although revenue from digital advertising is increasing, print advertising (automotive, employment, and real estate) has drastically declined, with classified ads moving to Craigslist and specialist job-search sites. Consequently, newspapers have slashed staff, reduced reporting, closed foreign and domestic bureaus (including in Washington, DC), and shrunk in size. With the inevitable and disastrous damage to democracy from the disappearance of reporters from courthouses, state houses, and city halls.

Nonetheless, although the number is declining, there are still around 1,200 daily newspapers in the United States with an estimated combined daily circulation of roughly forty million; many more millions read newspapers online. Chains of newspapers owned by corporations account for over half of circulation. Dramatically furthering consolidation, in August 2019 New Media Investment Group, controller of GateHouse Media, purchased Gannett, owner of *USA Today* and more than one hundred other publications.[11]

A few newspapers are available nationwide and report high average daily circulations combining print, online, and mobile apps requiring a monthly subscription. Most comprehensive of them all is the *New York Times*. Others are the *Washington Post*, *Wall Street Journal*, and *USA Today*.[12]

## Magazines

There are roughly seven thousand magazines published in the United States on every conceivable subject. Five publishers account for around one-third of the total revenue generated.

Most magazines focusing on politics, government, and public policies are ideological and available on the internet. We mention them under "Opinion and Commentary" later in this chapter. Here, however, we should mention the supermarket tabloid the *National Enquirer*, which thrives on a diet of celebrity scandals and gossip, but which also has a conservative political perspective: it has been known to acquire and then suppress stories unfavorable to President (then candidate) Trump. (A practice known as "catch and kill.")

## Television

There are approximately seventeen hundred commercial, for-profit television stations in the United States broadcast over the airwaves. They are also carried, as required by federal law, by local cable providers. Most commercial stations are affiliated with or, in a few cases, owned and operated by one of the networks (ABC, CBS, NBC, and Fox), which provides the bulk of their sports, news, and public affairs programs.

The networks commission and finance from production companies, some of which they own, the bulk of the entertainment programming shown on their stations and affiliates. The most desired viewers are between the ages of eighteen and forty-nine, the objects of advertisements. So the shows often follow standard formats with recurring characters: situation comedies, dramas about police officers and investigators, and doctors and lawyers, as well as romance, dance, singing, and other competitions. Sometimes they are spin-offs from programs that have done well in the audience ratings or are copies of successful shows from other countries. "Reality" shows, heavily edited, replete with reaction shots, and sometimes scripted, of real people put into staged situations or caught unaware, have become common because they draw an audience and usually cost less to make than other shows.

The NFL is the ratings stalwart. The highest-rated telecasts are usually special events such as the Super Bowl (which costs sponsors over $5.25 million for a thirty-second advertisement) and awards shows.

Unusual and risky programs are put on the air by networks and channels that may be doing poorly in the ratings and are willing to try something out of the ordinary to attract viewers. Executives at the then relatively new Fox network commissioned *The Simpsons*. For Matt Groening, the show's creator, it has a political message: "Figures of authority might not always have your best interests at heart.... Entertain and subvert, that's my motto."[13] Satirizing American family life, government, politics, and the media, it is one of television's longest-running and most popular series worldwide.

Network shows on explicitly political subjects have mixed fates. NBC's *West Wing*, about a liberal president and his staff ran from 1999–2005; but ABC's *Commander-in-Chief*, about a woman president, lasted for only the season 2005–2006. ABC returned to politics in 2012 with *Scandal*. The combination of the show's protagonist, a beautiful and tough Black woman, a former White House communications director embroiled in crisis management and its conspiracy, credibility-defying plots, attracted a sizable audience.

With the exception of its network and network-affiliated channels, cable (and satellite-transmitted stations) is mainly a niche medium. Its channels thrive (or at least survive) financially because they receive per subscriber fees from cable company operators for the right to include channels in the lineup. The channels also receive funds for selling advertisements. However, of the roughly 189 ad-supported cable channels, people watch an average of only seventeen. Indeed, ten (USA, Disney, ESPN, History, TNT, TBS, Fox News, A&E, FX, and AMC) have almost a third of all the viewers.

Cable channels occasionally attract audiences through programs that are surprising and challenging (*Breaking Bad* and *Mad Men* on AMC) or notorious (the *Real Housewives* franchise on Bravo). The non-commercial pay channel HBO rose to prominence with two remarkable shows, *The Sopranos* and *The Wire*, dealing with social and political subjects, and featuring psychologically complex protagonists. For several seasons it featured politics in the drama *Game of Thrones*, about battles for power and control, and the situation comedy *VEEP*, about a woman who goes from vice president to president to ex-president. It has continued in the topical comedy vein with John Oliver's *Last Week Tonight*.

Politics and government appear not only in news and public affairs, or explicitly in fiction shows on television, but also in other types of programs, particularly courtroom dramas and police shows. In the long-running and top-rated (with an audience sometimes reaching around 22 million) *NCIS* (Naval Criminal Investigative Service), a team of attractive special agents conducts criminal investigations. The show features technology, sex, villains, and suspense. The investigators and their institutions are usually portrayed favorably.

## Public Broadcasting

The Corporation for Public Broadcasting (CPB) was created by the federal government in 1967 as a private, nonprofit corporation to oversee the development of public (non-commercial) television and radio.[14] The CPB receives an annual allocation from Congress. Most of the funds are funneled to some three hundred and fifty public television stations of the Public Broadcasting Service (PBS) and to around one thousand public radio stations, most affiliated with National Public Radio (NPR), to cover operating costs and the production and purchase of programs.

The CPB's board members are appointed by the president, making public television and radio vulnerable or at least sensitive to the expectations of the incumbent administration. Congress sometimes charges the CPB to review programs for objectivity, balance, or fairness and to fund additional programs to correct alleged imbalances in views expressed. Conservatives charge public broadcasting with a liberal bias. Republicans in the House of Representatives have sought to withdraw its federal government funding.

About half of public broadcasting stations' budgets come from viewers and listeners, usually responding to unremitting on-air appeals. Other funding comes from state and local governments, state colleges and universities housing many of the stations, and from foundations.

Corporations and local businesses underwrite programs in return for on-air acknowledgments akin to advertisements for their image and products. Their decisions on whether or not to underwrite a show tend to favor politically innocuous over provocative programs. Public television and radio thus face similar pressure from advertisers as their for-profit counterparts.

Public broadcasting delves into politics, particularly with its evening news programs and documentaries in its *Frontline* series. National Public Radio, with an audience of around 27 million listeners weekly, broadcasts lengthy news programs during the morning and evening with reports from domestic and a few foreign bureaus. NPR has current-events and call-in programs. Guests from a spectrum of cultural life are interviewed by Terry Gross on her program *Fresh Air*. *On the Media* analyzes the news business in all its aspects; and Ira Glass's *This American Life* features distinctive individuals delving into important issues and quirky subjects. Most of these programs are available via podcast from iTunes. Public Radio Exchange, PRX.org, has an abundance of programs from independent producers and local NPR stations.

## Commercial Radio

Around eleven thousand commercial FM and AM radio stations in the United States broadcast over the airwaves. During the 1990s, Congress and the FCC dropped many restrictions on ownership and essentially abandoned the requirement that stations must serve the "public interest." This led to the demise of much public affairs programming and to a frenzy of mergers and acquisitions. Clear Channel Communications, then the nation's largest owner, bought the second-largest company, increasing its ownership to roughly 1,150 stations. The company was sold in 2008 to two private equity firms. In 2018, the satellite radio provider SiriusXM (controlled by Liberty Media) acquired the music streaming service Pandora Media for $3.5 billion, thus giving it access to listeners "who prefer streaming music through mobile phones."[15]

Most radio programming is aimed at an audience based on musical preference, racial or ethnic background and language, and interests (e.g., sports). Much of the news programming is supplied by a single company, Westwood One, a subsidiary of media conglomerate Viacom. Even on all-news stations, the reports are usually limited to headlines and brief details. Talk radio, dominated by conservative hosts, reaches large audiences. We discuss it in more detail in this chapter's Section 5.

## Music

Four major companies produce, package, publicize, advertise, promote, and merchandise music in the form of albums (CDs), singles (songs), and through streaming. The companies and performers also make music that is cheaply available online through services such as the Apple's iTunes Store. Some people, especially students, download music from the internet or burn CDs for themselves and others.

Music often contains political content. Contrast Green Day's scathing hit song "American Idiot" and its lyric "One nation controlled by the media" with Lee Greenwood's patriotic "God Bless the U.S.A." Some rap lyrics celebrate capitalism and consumerism, promote violence against women, and endorse—or even advocate—attacks on the police and other authority figures.

The music industry has also provided a forum for many to air grievances, giving voice to marginalized groups with historically limited access to the government. For example, politically conscious artists have emerged from the rap genre to focus on topics such as social conflict, Afro-centricism, and economic inequality. Public Enemy, Mos Def, Common, and Eminem have used songs to inform their listeners on pertinent social issues. Take Macklemore and Ryan Lewis's 2012 hit "Same Love," in which they advocate for LGBTQ rights, specifically access to marriage equality.

## Movies

Hollywood filmmakers (producers, screenwriters, directors, actors) of various political persuasions have periodically been involved in, even embroiled with, politics and government. On one hand, they and their films have been subjected to congressional investigations followed by industry-wide blacklisting (see Chapter 12 Section 7). On the other hand, Hollywood actor Ronald Reagan served two terms as president.[16]

Nowadays, the movie business is dominated by a few major studios, which finance and distribute around 130 of the 560 or so feature films made each year. Mass-market logic usually pushes them to seek stories that "are sufficiently original that the audience will not feel it has already seen the movie, yet similar enough to past hits not to be too far out."[17] Superheroes, science fiction and fantasy, sophomoric comedies, and animation dominate. Sequels are frequent. Special effects are common. In Robert Altman's satire *The Player*, the protagonist says that the "certain elements" he needs to market a film successfully are violence, suspense, laughter, hope, heart, nudity, sex, and a happy ending.

Released by Disney and Marvel in 2018, *Black Panther* contained most of these elements but differed from conventional Hollywood fare by being made by and about Black people. It became one of the ten top-grossing films ever.

It can cost well over $100 million to produce, advertise, and distribute a film to theaters. These costs are more or less recouped by U.S. and overseas box office sales, DVD sales (declining) and rentals, revenue from selling broadcast rights to television, subscription cable, video on demand, and funds received from promoting products in the films (product placement).

Many independent films are made, but few of them are distributed to theaters, and even fewer are seen by audiences. This situation is being changed by cable channels, which specialize in digital distribution and video on demand, and by streaming platforms.

It is said in Hollywood that "politics is box office poison." The financial failure of films concerned with U.S. involvement in Iraq, such as *In the Valley of Elah*, appears to confirm this axiom. Nonetheless, the major studios and independents, such as Participant Media, have sometimes made movies that are politically relevant or promote social change. Some such movies have been box office survivors, even successes. We refer to many of them in this book and provide a list at the end of each chapter. The five nominees for the 2005 Oscar for best picture all contained political content—*Brokeback Mountain* (LGBTQ+ depiction), *Capote* (a fiction writer's complex relationship to two murderers he befriends and writes about), *Crash* (racial tension in Los Angeles), *Good Night and Good Luck* (CBS's response to the Red Scare of the early 1950s), and *Munich* (Israeli–Palestinian relations). Every year several Oscar nominees are politically relevant even if only in the Documentary, Documentary Short, or Live Action Short categories.

## Books

Some 300,000 books are published annually. About "seventy percent of them will not earn back the money that their authors have been advanced."[18] There are literally hundreds of publishers, but five produce 60 percent of all books sold in the United States. Publishers' income comes mainly from sales. A few famous authors command multi-million-dollar advances: President Bill Clinton received more than $10 million and President George W. Bush around $7 million to write their memoirs. These sums are small change compared to the $65 million received by the Obamas for their memoirs. Several of the books about President Trump and his presidency, almost all of them negative, have been best-sellers.

E-books are booming. The advantage for readers is obtaining the book more cheaply and quickly than by mail or from a bookstore. For publishers, there are no more costs for printing, shipping, warehousing, and returns. But digital books could destroy bookstores if, for example, publishers sold them directly to the iPad. Indeed, publishers themselves could be eliminated if authors sold their rights directly to, say, Amazon.

Books about government, politics, and public policies, particularly if they feature revelations, can receive widespread coverage in the rest of the media. They are excerpted in magazines and newspapers. Their authors are interviewed on cable and network television, radio, and elsewhere. This can increase their visibility and effects but can also change their emphases.

### Key Takeaways

The subjects of this section are communication, information, and the media. We have explained how economics, government and politics, and technology shape the media and their contents. Market domination by a few conglomerates limits competition and, arguably, the wide availability and range of media contents. The main types of mass media are newspapers, magazines, television, public broadcasting, commercial radio, music, films, and books. Their contents relevant to politics and government are entertainment, news, opinion and commentary. They are largely aimed at a vast, undifferentiated audience but also niche audiences.

### Exercises

1. Where do you get most of your information? How do you think the type of media you consume affects the kind of information you get?
2. How does the need to attract a large audience for advertisements influence media content?

## 3.3 New and Social Media

### Learning Objectives

After reading this section, you should be able to answer the following questions:

1. In what ways are the new and social media changing the relationships between communication and government and politics?
2. What is WikiLeaks.org, and who is Edward Snowden?
3. What detracts from the ability of the new and social media to improve citizen education and enhance public life?
4. For what reasons do politicians criticize Twitter and Facebook?

The early 1980s saw the development of the mass media, with modern technologies being used in new combinations. They are muddying if not eliminating the traditional differences between media. The big five technology companies are Alphabet Inc. (the parent company of Google), Amazon, Apple, Facebook, and Microsoft. They mostly dominate their spheres; for example, Facebook also owns Instagram, WhatsApp, and Messenger, and has more than three billion monthly users.

Technology and entertainment companies increasingly compete to be involved at all levels of the media business: they seek to be able to *generate, produce, purchase, own, control, sell,* and *distribute* media content. Netflix in particular is showing politically and socially oriented documentaries and docu-dramas. Amazon is rivaling Netflix by developing its own shows and buying up exclusive rights to movies and television episodes for its streaming service. Streaming has burgeoned as movie houses have closed during the COVID-19 pandemic.

In early 2019 this competition saw three significant developments. First, the wireless provider AT&T acquired the Time Warner networks and Turner Broadcasting—the Warner Brothers movie studio and vast library of film and television programming; also CNN, TNT, and TBS—creating a streaming video business named Warner Media, to be anchored by HBO.

Second, the conglomerate Walt Disney Company purchased the 20th Century Fox movie and television studios, the National Geographic and FX cable services, and most of Hulu. Disney already ran the Disney movie studio, Marvel, Pixar, and Lucasfilm, and owned ESPN. Fox retained ownership of Fox News, a chain of local television stations, and the FSI sports channel. Then, in April 2019, Disney announced the creation of the Disney+ subscription video-streaming service of movies and shows to compete with Netflix et al.

Third, the tech giant Apple created Apple News Plus, offering content from more than three hundred titles of newspapers and magazines as well as music apps and a video service with some original television programming, including a morning show.

Meanwhile, social media, consisting of internet-based platforms, user-generated content, and social networking sites, have thrived. Facebook is by far the dominant force in social media. It owns Instagram, Snapchat, and WhatsApp and 80 percent of mobile social traffic. Also part of social media are content-sharing sites such as the Google-owned YouTube and Reddit. Platforms such as Twitter connect, communicate, express, interchange with, and respond to the views of others. A majority of people use social media for their news. They obtain information from websites, blogs, discussion boards, and podcasts.

# Changing Relationships

The new and social media have changed the relationship between communication and government and politics and public policies in four significant ways: making more information available and accessible, narrowcasting, creating content, and blogging.

## Making More Information Available and Accessible

Following the lead of the Open Government Initiative of the Obama White House, some federal agencies use new technologies to disclose—make available and accessible—their information and data.

Government is not alone in pursuing visibility. Other institutions and organizations have used the media to bring materials to light, often information the government wants to keep secret. Two key figures were Julian Paul Assange and Edward Snowden.

Assange founded **WikiLeaks.org** in 2007 to expose the secrets of governments, corporations, and other institutions. In 2010 he released a classified video showing a U.S. helicopter killing civilians, including two journalists, in Baghdad—an edited version was viewed several million times on YouTube.[19] He subsequently released thousands of intelligence and military field reports from the war in Afghanistan and from the front lines of the conflict in Iraq.

**WikiLeaks.org**

An organization that exposes the secrets of governments, corporations, and other institutions.

Assange followed up in November 2010 with a dump of classified cables sent by U.S. diplomats from their embassies during the previous three years. The cables detailed the diplomats' dealings with and honest assessments of both the foreign countries where they were stationed and the countries' leaders, revealing the reality beneath the rhetoric: that Saudi Arabia has urged that Iran be bombed, that Shell dominates the government of Nigeria, that China launched a cyber attack on Google, and that the U.S. State Department urged its employees to collect biometrical information on foreign diplomats serving at the United Nations.

WikiLeaks released this material, much of it provided by Chelsea Manning (formerly Bradley Manning), a low-level army intelligence analyst, to selected leading newspapers in the United States (*New York Times*), the United Kingdom (*Guardian*), and elsewhere, leaving it up to the journalists to decide which was news, which could be made public, and whether to redact (remove) names from it. Their release could damage the careers of some U.S. diplomats and disclose the names of informants, thereby endangering both. The cables could be subject to foreign governments' and private companies' data-mining and pattern-analysis programs.[20]

**FIGURE 3.1 Anything to Say?**

This itinerant art installation, titled *Anything to Say?,* by Davide Dormino depicts whistleblowers Edward Snowden, Julian Assange, and Chelsea Manning standing on three chairs and a fourth, empty chair that symbolizes a platform for public speaking.

Source: Davide Dormino / CC BY-SA (https://creativecommons.org/licenses/by-sa/4.0), https://commons.wikimedia.org/wiki/File:Davide_Dormino_-_Anything_to_say.jpg.

In 2016, WikiLeaks released emails, obtained by Russian hackers, that undermined Hillary Clinton's election campaign and supported that of her opponent Donald Trump. We discuss this in our Chapter 11.

In 2013, Edward Snowden, computer expert, former employee of the Central Intelligence Agency (CIA), and contractor for the National Security Agency (NSA), began releasing to selected media outlets thousands of classified documents. These revealed a vast range of U.S. global surveillance programs, some of them arguably unconstitutional, involving spying on millions of people, including American citizens. We will return to Snowden, his revelations, and their impact, in Chapter 4 and Chapter 17.

The U.S. Justice and Defense Departments and other organizations tried to stop these revelations, to avoid further leaks, and to punish the leakers. Assange was holed up for several years in the Ecuadorian embassy in London but is now in prison in London as the United States tries to have him extradited. Snowden has been charged with violations of the Espionage Act and is in Russia. Chelsea Manning was convicted in 2013 of violating the Espionage Act and sentenced to thirty-five years in prison. She was incarcerated from 2010–2017, then released when her sentence was commuted by President Obama. She has been returned to prison for refusing to testify against Assange before a grand jury.

## Narrowcasting

The new media narrowcast. Often controlled by individual communicators, their content is usually aimed at smaller and more socially, economically, and often politically distinct audiences than those sought or reached by the mass media. This fragmentation of the mass audience means that the older media's pursuit of lowest-common-denominator content may no longer be financially necessary or viable.

There are cable channels devoted to women, Black people, and Latinx people, as well as for buffs of news, weather, history, and sports. A wide range of material is produced, reported, and made available. Young people increasingly watch on a computer, tablet, video game console, or mobile phone.

Satellite radio is the fastest-growing radio market. It uses technology that broadcasts a clear signal to receivers anywhere in the world. Listeners have hundreds of program options. Broadcast radio stations are no longer limited by the range of a signal across terrain, but rather through the web can reach listeners who make up an audience that is less bounded by geography than by shared cultural, social, and political interests.

## Creating Content

As major news organizations have gone online, they have hired technologically skilled young people. At first, these technicians would primarily reprocess content. Now they sometimes create it. Thanks to cell phone cameras, webcams, and social networks, ordinary people can create, store, sort, share, and show digital videos. Home videos, remixes, and television excerpts are posted by users (also by the television networks).

Video clips can be used to hold politicians accountable by revealing their gaffes and showing the contradictions in their statements and behavior, thereby exposing their dissembling, exaggerations, and falsehoods.

People can become citizen journalists generating content by reporting on subjects usually ignored and on events unavailable to news media: for example, citizen journalists reported on the massacre of students at Virginia Tech University in 2006. They showed some of what happened and documented the effectiveness or ineffectiveness of the authorities' responses. Mainstream media have incorporated such citizen journalism into their news products.

## Blogging

**Blogs** are online diaries whose authors post information, ideas, commentary, and opinions. Blogs may permit feedback from readers and provide hyperlinks to other online content that may enrich the discussion. Many people blog, but few are widely read. Exceptions are the *Daily Kos* and the *Huff Post*.

**blogs**

Online diaries whose authors post information, including ideas and opinions.

Blogging can be seen as a new form of journalism without deadlines or broadcast schedules. But it does not replace reporting. Most bloggers lack the resources of the news media and the knowledge and expertise of journalists to investigate government, politics, and public policies. They rely on material issued elsewhere for their information: domestic and foreign newspapers, government documents, academic papers, and other media.

The "blogosphere" can hold public officials accountable by amplifying and spreading information, especially when many bloggers cover the same subject, a phenomenon known as "blogswarm."

Bloggers can hold the news media accountable. One important way is by challenging the media's framing of a story. For example, conservative bloggers criticize reporters for framing stories about abortion, gay rights, and religion from a liberal perspective.

Bloggers also challenge the media's stories. On a *60 Minutes* segment on September 8, 2004, anchor Dan Rather presented documents purportedly showing that President George W. Bush had received preferential treatment when joining the Texas Air National Guard in the early 1970s and thus avoided military service in Vietnam. The report was a scoop that had been rushed onto the air. Conservative internet forums and bloggers immediately pointed out that, because of their format and typography, the documents were forged. The accusation quickly gained national attention by the news media and was soon corroborated. Rather's long career at CBS was ended sooner than he and the network had planned.

## Limitations

The capacity of new and social media to realize their potential and promise for improving citizen education and enhancing public life is limited. They are rife with muddle, nonsense, rumor, and error: as a comic example, when the journalist Hunter S. Thompson died, a site reported President Richard Nixon's opinion that Thompson "represented the dark, venal and incurably violent side of the American character." In fact, Thompson had said that about Nixon.

Social media endanger privacy. Two examples from so many: a researcher obtained from Facebook and sold the personal information of eighty-seven million people. Google logs all the searches made on it, stores the information indefinitely, and can make it available to others.

Social media provide a platform for anger, hatred, rage, threats, and justifications for and examples of violence. They are a haven for lies and conspiracy theories. People use them to invent and spread harmful, dangerous misinformation, for example, misrepresenting; distorting, and doctoring images to support false claims about the alleged bad behavior of migrants from Central America.

Deception facilitated by the new media never ends. The *New York Times* has reported the existence of a network of roughly 1,300 websites, such as *Maine Business Daily*, *Des Moines Sun*, and *Ann Arbor Times*, in all fifty states. Supposedly filling the local news void left by departed local newspapers, they hire freelance and other reporters to write news stories. But in fact the network promotes propaganda commissioned by "conservative think tanks, political operatives, corporate executives and public relations professionals. . . . The assignments typically come with precise instructions about whom to interview and what to write. . . ."[21]

Elections are a fount of widely circulated false news stories. The 2016 presidential election featured a bevy of them, including the Pope endorsing Donald Trump and Hillary Clinton's use of a pizzeria as a child-trafficking site. Messages from Russian hackers reached roughly one hundred and fifty million users and arguably influenced the election result.

The 2020 presidential election saw a deluge of disinformation on Facebook, Twitter, and many Spanish-language platforms. They claimed that President Trump was victorious but that social media were censoring his win; that in Arizona's Maricopa County election workers had given Trump voters pens undetectable by ballot scanners; and that armed protesters funded by liberal billionaire George Soros were taking over the U.S. Capitol.[22]

Politicians are increasingly critical of Facebook and Twitter. Republicans attack them for committing censorship by deleting and attaching warning labels. Democrats complain about the hate and misinformation online.

## Key Takeaways

In this section we have seen how the new and social media are changing the relationship between communication and government and politics. They make more information than ever available and accessible. They facilitate narrowcasting, the creation of content, and blogging. However, there are serious limitations on their contents and their capacity to enhance public life and political understanding.

## Exercises

1. How do new media make it difficult for governments to keep secrets? What effect do you think that will have on politics?
2. How does blogging differ from traditional journalism? What are the advantages of blogging as a form of journalism? What are the disadvantages?
3. In what sense do new media make everyone potentially a journalist? Do you agree that this also makes everyone potentially a public figure?

### Civic Education

The communications system in the United States, with its heady mix of traditional mass media and new media, offers a startling array of options for citizens to intervene and get something done in politics and government. The opportunities are especially rich for young people who are well versed in new technologies, and they are charting new paths in political journalism.

Young journalists are bringing news that is relevant and timely to the millennial generation—the eighty million people aged eighteen to thirty-four. Positions for young journalists and technology specialists are opening at millennial news sites. These sites are taking advantage of the fact that, contrary to popular opinion, young people read more than older people.[23] There is a demand for content by and for young news consumers.

Millennial news sites tap into the diversity of the young generation. They target particular audiences based on factors like their gender or racial and ethnic background. Stories focus on issues like feminism, racial and ethnic discrimination, social justice, technology, and the environment. These topics are covered in the mainstream media, but millennial sites present them in a way that is directly relevant to young audience members. A headline on Vox.com, "A New Study Shows Even 5-year-olds Can't Escape Racism," promoted a story on racial discrimination that was invisible in the mainstream media.

The design and content of millennial news sites aim to grab the attention of a young generation. Information is presented as visual stories, videos, and graphic features. Serious political stories appear alongside lighter lifestyle and entertainment features. Right below the lead story about President Trump's travel ban appeared the BuzzFeed headline: "A 23-year-old Blogger is Fighting Back After Zillow Threatened Her With a Cease and Desist Letter."

# 3.4 News

## Learning Objectives

After reading this section, you should be able to answer the following questions:

1. What is news?
2. What is objectivity?
3. How do journalists acquire the news?
4. How do journalists assemble the news?
5. What is bias?
6. How is the news presented?
7. How do people in public life try to influence their depictions by and in the media?
8. What are three common ways journalists cover people in public life?

**news**

Reports by journalists of selected events commonly involving violence, conflict, disasters, and scandals.

**News** is an account, often dramatic, of some events happening or having usually recently happened in the world. Common subjects are conflict or violence (e.g., wars, terrorism), crime (e.g., murder, theft, scams, and corruption), natural disasters (e.g., earthquakes, hurricanes), and scandals (e.g., sexual, financial). Information about or relevant to politics, government, and public policies commonly appears in the media as news. The statements and actions of powerful or prominent people, especially the American president (e.g., former President Trump's tweets) are news. So are human-interest stories, such as the rescue of Private Jessica Lynch discussed in the preamble to this chapter. Only a few stories or issues receive extensive news coverage at any one time.

News is timely, a breaking event like an assassination attempt on a president, or newly revealed information, such as a video made years ago of presidential candidate Donald Trump expressing disdainful views about how to interact with women. Slow-moving processes that may be of vital importance (e.g., global warming) take time to become news, often requiring a "peg"—the release of an alarmist study, a congressional hearing, or presidential speech—on which to hang the story.

News can be local: for example, a student journalist reporting an outbreak of COVID-19 on her campus that administrators had hitherto down-played, denied, and kept concealed.[24]

News is usually incomplete. As the one-time reporter and Hollywood screenwriter Ben Hecht observed, "Trying to understand the day's events by reading a newspaper was like trying to tell time with a watch that had only a second hand."[25]

News can be divided into three spheres. The sphere of consensus, consisting of unquestionable values and unchallengeable truths, lacks controversy. The sphere of deviance consists of people and opinions outside convention. They are usually deemed unworthy of being reported. The sphere of legitimate controversy is where much of the news, especially about government, politics, and policies, takes place and is reported.[26]

## Journalists

News is mainly reported by journalists. They work under time pressure, often with tight deadlines to come up with stories around the clock. Competition can be intense, as can be the pursuit of readers and ratings. The job has become more difficult in recent years as budget cuts have led news organizations to rely on fewer reporters for more stories for more outlets, and as news is reported over a twenty-four-hour cycle.

The profession can be dangerous and deadly: at least seventy journalists are killed annually worldwide. A few of these deaths receive international coverage, notably that of the intrepid war correspondent Marie Colvin. Far more attention was given to the assassination and dismemberment in 2018 in the Saudi Arabian consulate in Istanbul of the Saudi citizen and U.S. resident Jamal Khashoggi, allegedly by a hit squad from his country of origin. His murder stayed in the news for several weeks because he was an occasional columnist for the *Washington Post* and because of the ineffectual and unconvincing efforts of the Saudi government, abetted by former President Trump, to deny knowledge of and then acknowledge responsibility for his death.

A majority of journalists are white, middle class, middle-aged, and male. Women now compose about one-third of the press corps and racial minorities around one-tenth. In a survey, 36 percent identified themselves as Democrats, 33 percent as Independents, and 18 percent as Republicans.[27]

Any influence of reporters' characteristics and opinions on their stories is limited by their profession's code of ethics and the norm of **objectivity** they learn in journalism school or on the job.[28] These include reporting accurate, verified information, and different sides of an issue, and being impartial and fair. They should exclude their personal opinions, not deliberately distort, and separate reporting from opinion, commentary, and advocacy.[29]

**objectivity**

In news reporting, impartiality and fairness, and the reporting of facts without opinion and including different sides of an issue.

If they are found out, journalists who deliberately and blatantly violate the profession's ethics are punished. A *New York Times* reporter was dismissed in 2013 after it was discovered that he had fabricated or plagiarized around forty of the six hundred articles he had written for the paper; editors resigned in the wake of the discoveries. A star foreign correspondent for *USA Today*, who had worked for the paper for over twenty years, resigned in January 2004, accused of plagiarism and of inventing parts or all of some of his stories.

Few journalists are guilty of such egregious violations. That said, abiding by professional standards and journalistic norms, and adhering to objectivity, can be complicated, even difficult. This will become clear in our discussion of the processes of "acquiring" news, "assembling" news, "presentation" of news, and "interactions" that follow (after "Comparing Content").

## Comparing Content

### Depictions of Journalists

Many of our impressions of journalists, their behavior, and their trustworthiness come from the media.[30] Media depictions repeat two types best captured in the classic film *His Girl Friday*: reporter Hildy Johnson (Rosalind Russell) and her editor, Walter Burns (Cary Grant).

The first type, exemplified by Hildy, is the journalist as intrepid seeker after truth and crusader for justice. The most famous real-life equivalents are Bob Woodward and Carl Bernstein, *Washington Post* reporters who helped uncover the Watergate scandal and wrote a book about it, *All the President's Men*, which was turned into a popular Hollywood movie. Even some caustic satires of the news business contain versions of the journalist as noble loner. In *Network*, Peter Finch plays a television news anchor who begins to go insane on camera, shouting, "I'm mad as hell, and I'm not going to take it anymore." In the movie, his pain and anguish are exploited by amoral network executives. In real life, his battle cry became the theme of citizens' tax revolts in the late seventies and could be heard at Tea Party rallies thirty years later.

The second type of journalist, typified by Walter Burns, is more common in the entertainment media. At their worst, as in Billy Wilder's classic *Ace in the Hole*, such reporters cynically and callously exploit the disasters of the human condition. But even less bitter films show reporters as led astray from their devotion to the truth to the point that they destroy lives and reputations in their reckless search for an exclusive story ahead of other reporters (a scoop) that is dramatic and shocking. In *Absence of Malice*, Sally Field plays a reporter who ends up besmirching a good man's (Paul Newman) reputation. In *Broadcast News*, William Hurt and Albert Brooks compete to become a news anchor. Hurt—good-looking, smooth, unscrupulous, and none too bright—wins out over the dumpier, knowledgeable, and dedicated Brooks.

A contemporary example of the second type is Rita Skeeter. Introduced by J. K. Rowling in her enormously popular Harry Potter series, Skeeter writes for the *Daily Prophet*, *Witch Weekly*, and other publications. She is untrustworthy, unscrupulous, vindictive, and vile. She justifies her behavior with the motto, "Our readers have a right to the truth." But her news stories are error-strewn and full of lies. They destroy friendships, inflict pain and suffering, and deprive decent people of their jobs. Rita Skeeter gets scoops by turning herself into a bug. The moral is that such journalists are nasty bugs.[31]

## Acquiring the News

Journalists follow standard procedures to obtain the news. They hunt it together in "packs." They go to the scene, especially of wars and disasters. They talk to people who have participated in, witnessed, or claim to know what happened. They dig into records. They invoke the Freedom of Information Act (FOIA)—see Chapter 4 Section 3. Easing their job, many events, such as press conferences, trials, and elections, are scheduled in advance.

In hunting the news, journalists, akin to the unscrupulous one in *Ace in the Hole* (discussed above), can be obnoxiously intrusive to the point of wreaking harm. Flooding with their numbers and equipment into communities stricken by violence, they violate people's privacy, demand interviews, and besiege vulnerable victims and witnesses.

### Beats

**beats**

Institutions, organizations, and subjects that a reporter is assigned to cover regularly.

News organizations guarantee stories by assigning reporters to cover certain **beats** such as the White House or specific subjects such as environmental policy. Institutions and subjects not on reporters' beats (off the beaten track, so to speak) generate few stories unless something newsworthy thrusts them into prominence, as when the banking crisis of 2008 provoked questions about the regulatory ineffectiveness of the Securities and Exchange Commission and other government agencies.

### Sources

**sources**

People, often in government, who, for one reason or another, provide reporters with information.

**scoops**

News obtained ahead of other reporters.

Journalists frequently interact with and rely on **sources**—especially people in government and politics—to provide them with information, facts, quotes, and **scoops**.

The desire and competition for scoops can lead reporters (and their editors) into egregious errors. In January 2019, BuzzFeed reported the sensational news, citing as sources "two federal law enforcement officials," that the special counsel, Robert S. Mueller III, investigating the possibility of collusion between the Trump presidential campaign and Russian authorities, had evidence that President Trump had instructed his former lawyer to lie to Congress. The story spread like wildfire through cable news and social media, becoming the object of widespread discussion, until other news outlets failed to confirm it and the Office of Special Counsel quickly denied the story's validity. Justifiably, President Trump attacked BuzzFeed for promoting fake news.[32]

Often, sources supply material openly and unreservedly. Other sources, commonly dubbed "whistle blowers," reveal dubious activities, outrages, and scandals.[33] They may "*leak*" material of their own volition or as authorized by superiors that is confidential or secret or classified. Leakers usually require anonymity.[34]

Sources can be unreliable—their memories fallible, their revelations one-sided; they may omit information, even lie. Among sources' possible motives for communicating with reporters are the national interest, dissent from or disagreement with government policies or actions, self-interest, ambition, anger, frustration, revenge, undermining rivals or opponents, and defeating secrecy.

The reporter-source relationship is symbiotic: they need each other. Reporters need sources for news that is otherwise hard to obtain. Sources need reporters to get their views and information as favorably into the news as possible.

Sometimes the relationship is adversarial, with reporters pressing a reluctant source for information. Sources must often respond to reporters' ideas of what is news. Information from one beat may produce a news story that another beat wants to keep quiet. Refusal to reveal information may result in negative coverage and in sources becoming targets in reporters' and columnists' stories.

## Government Reports

Legislative committees, regulatory agencies, and governmental departments and commissions conduct investigations, hold hearings, and issue reports and press releases. Journalists sometimes draw on these for their stories. Typical is a *New York Times* front-page story headlined "Terror Suspects Buying Firearms, Report Finds" (in the United States), based on an investigation by the Government Accountability Office.[35]

## Investigative Reporting

Some journalists specialize in **investigative reporting**, pursuing information that may involve legal or ethical wrongdoing and that is likely to be concealed.[36] Sometimes known as "muckraking," this reporting requires detailed and thorough digging into a story. It is often time-consuming and expensive. The *New York Times*, the *Washington Post*, and the *New Yorker* engage in it, as do the nonprofit Center for Public Integrity, ProPublica, and the Center for Investigative Reporting. Examples of award-winning investigative stories include exposure of secret Central Intelligence Agency prisons in Eastern Europe, the torture of Iraqi prisoners by U.S. forces, appalling care in veterans' hospitals, and job-related deaths of Mexican workers in the United States.

**investigative reporting**

Intensive research by journalists, usually into subjects that those involved don't want exposed.

## Wire Services

The media rely on the **wire services** for much of their international and national news. Wire services cover and transmit stories worldwide from their own staff and from reporters who work for the many newspapers and other organizations that belong to the services. Prominent wire services are the Associated Press (AP) and Reuters. The AP sends news to approximately 1,700 newspapers, 5,000 radio and television stations, and 8,500 other media outlets in over one hundred countries.

Video feeds supplied by the AP and Reuters are the source of much of the televised international news. Subscribers are sent video accompanied by natural sound without narration and brief printed informational scripts. Some foreign correspondents are based in London doing voice-overs for these feeds for broadcast on their networks' news programs.

**wire services**

Agencies, particularly the Associated Press (AP), that cover and transmit news stories from throughout the world to their subscribers, resulting in similar coverage in many of the news media.

# Assembling the News

**gatekeepers**

Controllers of access to information, news, etc.

In assembling the news, journalists make choices, starting with what stories, subjects, and issues to report. By making these decisions they become **gatekeepers**. They are influenced by their assumptions and values. Some of these subjects, such as individuals heroically trying to achieve democracy and freedom, usually produce positive stories. Others, such as terrorists and racism, are inherently negative. Journalists also decide how to *frame* the story, what *facts* to include (and exclude), what *words* to use, and the *tone*. As follows:

## Framing

In framing (as detailed later in this chapter) a story is given a focus, a central subject or issue around which its narrative is built and judgments rendered. Often, the frame is established by the headline, as in "White House blame game intensifies as Trump agenda stalls."[37]

## Facts

Reporters imbue their stories with facts. Facts help give them validity and credibility, but may be hard to find or establish. People can benefit from concealing them. Facts may be challenged, contradicted, or denied. Moreover, to make sense or be given meaning, many facts require context and/or interpretation.

Facts are not necessarily self-evident. Then-Secretary of Defense Donald Rumsfeld famously responded at a press conference (on February 12, 2002) to a question asking "if there was any evidence to indicate that Iraq has attempted to supply terrorists with weapons of mass destruction?"[38] with the following:

"The absence of evidence is not evidence of absence. . . . There are known knowns. These are things we know that we know. There are known unknowns. That is to say, there are things that we now know we don't know. But there are also unknown unknowns. These are things we do not know we don't know."[39]

Responding to questions on NBC's *Meet the Press* (January 22, 2017) about former President Trump's contention that the size of his inauguration crowd was larger than reported by the news media, his counselor Kellyanne Conway said the White House had put forth "alternative facts."[40] But to those who believe that a fact is a fact is a fact, the phrase "alternative fact" is problematic, a denial of reality: it is not a fact; indeed, it is more likely to be false.

Fact-checking is an integral part of reporting. Internal checking scrutinizes facts for accuracy and validity before publishing them. External fact-checking, prominent during the 2016 election and subsequently, undertaken by PolitiFact, FactCheck.Org, and the like, consists of making judgments about the veracity, the truth, of questionable factual assertions made by people in the news, especially public officials, above all by President Trump.[41] External fact-checking sometimes deters lying, but it may not stop people from believing the lie, particularly if they distrust the press.

## Words

The words used in a story can influence its meaning. Conflict in Congress is inherently negative when called "gridlock" but less so, even positive, when described as "debate" or "deliberation."

Consider the dilemma of journalists faced with untrue statements made by former President Trump but reluctant or unwilling to call them lies (that is, statements made with intent to deceive).

Among the possible synonyms, most of them less blatant than *lies*, were *erroneous assertions*, *disputable* or *bogus claims*, *post-factual*, and *truth-averse*.

## Tone

A final element in assembling a story is its tone: that is, a distinctive way of expressing its contents. There are myriad possibilities. Tone can be ironic, skeptical, snide, cynical, sarcastic, insulting, aggressive, hostile, harsh, but also sympathetic, supportive, and congratulatory.

## Bias (Slant)

It should be clear by now that the processes of acquiring and assembling the news can make it difficult for journalists, no matter how dedicated, to achieve objectivity. This has contributed to persistent accusations against the mainstream news media of and widespread discussions about bias.

We will not reiterate this extensive literature here.[42] But much depends on how one defines bias. We define it as intentional (a central term) favoring of one side (individual, ideology, perspective, viewpoint) over other possibilities, expressed through selection of subject, frame, facts (liable to omission and distortion), and skewed words (as in Fox News's "Obama fled Washington" to describe the president's departure for Camp David).

Bias assumes motivation; that is, the intent is deliberate. But intent can be hard to identify or unravel, let alone prove, unless evidence of it is persistent and consistent. Motivation is often ascribed when a story or report favors or disfavors its subject. But this may be a function of the subject itself, not the deliberate intent of the journalist: an account in the U.S. news media of a terrorist attack in the country is inherently unfavorable to the terrorists.

Omission can be a clear indication of bias. A positive story about President Trump would be shown on Fox News but be nowhere on MSNBC; a negative Trump story would be on MSNBC but not on Fox. Or, if not absent, the stories could be given much more or less prominence.

# Presentation

As a result of widely agreed-upon criteria of newsworthiness, the process of gathering the news, especially in packs, and the use of news services, the news media often report many of the same stories. Only a few stories are featured prominently at any one time due to limitations of resources and of broadcast prime time and front-page print space.

Nonetheless, there are some differences among the media in the range and type of news on which they focus. For example, the *New York Times*, with its stable of reporters in Washington, DC, and its foreign correspondents, emphasizes government and politics in the United States and abroad. Cable news channels focus mainly on U.S. politics, often repeating stories from the *New York Times* and *Washington Post*. They give short shrift to foreign stories. In fact, the Fox News Channel has a segment titled "Around the World in 80 Seconds." In contrast, the BBC World News covers the world.

The media also differ stylistically in how they present the news. The *Times* does it with relative sobriety. Cable channels dramatize their reports by announcing "breaking news," using graphic captions, accompanying stories with pulsating music, engaging in fast-paced editing, and repeatedly admonishing viewers to "stay with us."

Television news is picture driven: stories with appealing, dramatic, or even available camera footage are more likely to be played prominently than those without. Viewers are unaware of what is not shown, what happened before or after the picture was taken, and whether or not the shot was staged. Camera angles, distance from the subject, especially close-ups, length of shot, camera movement, and editing, all influence viewers' impressions. A picture may be worth a thousand words, but it can also mislead.

## Enduring Image

### The Overthrow of Saddam Hussein

The toppling of a dictator's statue is an enduring image, symbolizing the literal collapse of a regime's authority and the massive uprising and joy of a population freed at last from tyranny. On April 9, 2003, a U.S. mechanized vehicle using a cable pulled down Saddam Hussein's mammoth statue in Baghdad's Firdos Square. The square was sealed off by U.S. marines. The few people in it were U.S. soldiers, Iraqis from the United States, promoted "Free Iraqi Forces Militia" (comprising exiles who had recently been returned to the country by the Pentagon), and journalists.

On television the statue falls, the crowd cheers. On the front pages of newspapers in the United States and around the world, the Reuters news agency photograph shows the toppling of Saddam Hussein's statue under the watchful eye of an American soldier. The images symbolize the U.S. defeat of the dictator and his regime and the Iraqi people celebrating their newfound freedom. Wider shots of the square, revealing only a handful of people were in the plaza, were far less common.[43]

This clips explains how the destruction of the Saddam statue in Baghdad was used as propaganda.

View in the online reader

The first photograph of the statue being pulled down reflects news values of vividness, drama, and conflict. It spectacularly harkens back to the removal of statues of Lenin and Stalin after the collapse of communism in the Soviet Union. The alternative photos, showing much more of the relatively empty square, lacked dramatic news values and thus their symbolic effects.

Because the news media found the dramatic image to be irresistible, they reinforced a frame, pushed by the Bush administration, of a jubilant Iraqi population welcoming its liberators. But the meaning of an image can change. Now, for many people, the falling statue represents the illusion of a U.S. military success that turned into a quagmire of frustration.

# Interactions and Types of Coverage

As we document throughout this book, many of the people involved in public life understand that their election and reelection, their selection, their effectiveness in office, and their ability to achieve their objectives often depend on how the media portray them, their deliberations and debates, disagreements and conflicts, cooperation and consensus, action and inaction, struggles for power, and their decisions. They know that media depictions can influence people's opinions and understandings of policy problems and possible solutions, and can encourage or discourage participation in politics. So, they bestow favors, such as giving access to sympathetic journalists. (President Trump's press secretaries gave White House press credentials to media organizations previously denied them, but known to favor the president.)

They also know that information is power. The more they have of it, especially in advance of their opponents, the better. They have aides who gather, synthesize, and summarize the news from newspapers and television, from talk shows, political publications, polls, websites, and blogs.[44]

People in public life and their staffs look to interact with news media personnel. Of course, many of them are of little interest to the media, who ignore them. Others are of intermittent interest. A few, notably the president and his associates, party leaders in and significant members of Congress, are of consuming interest, particularly if involved in controversy or scandals.

Nonetheless, many of these individuals, abetted by aides sometimes dubbed "spin doctors," try, more or less, to manage and manipulate the news: to influence journalists' selection of stories and their contents. They deploy a plethora of techniques.

They make public appearances, give speeches, hold press conferences, and stage newsworthy events. They "stay on message": repeating it and refusing to be diverted from their position or perspective. They speak in brief, pithy phrases known as sound bites. They adhere to their "talking points." They stick to rehearsed rhetoric with which they feel comfortable. They opportunely release bad news when it is least likely to be noticed (known as taking out the trash). They deplore, decry, rail against, but may themselves engage in, leaks. They devise "scripts" or "narratives" to depict their behavior, activities, actions, policies, and the consequences of these policies as positively as possible. They try to identify themselves and their parties with positive policies, known as "branding." They conceal, minimize, or put the best gloss on their mistakes and blunders.

Former President Trump pursued a new type of attack against several news organizations, accusing them of promulgating and perpetuating "fake news," that is, stories with no basis in reality and probably intended to mislead and deceive people. His primary example was the charge that members of his campaign staff, if not the president himself, were possibly aware of, perhaps involved with, and may even have colluded with Russian agents in the hacking and release of emails from the Hillary Clinton campaign—a charge of which he would be absolved after an investigation of almost two years. (More on this in Chapter 11, Chapter 12, and Chapter 13).

People in government and politics are aware of the *news cycle*; that is, of how long an event is likely to remain newsworthy, usually twenty-four hours, before it is replaced. They come to understand "optics"; that is, how their actions, as communicated and interpreted by the media, will look to the public.

Favors! Persuasion! Manipulation! Pressure! Intimidation! Despite and because of all these techniques, the news (and often opinion) media's coverage varies. Three common types are "lap dog," "watchdog," and "attack dog." Learn more about each type in Table 3.1.

**indexing**

When journalists index the news to the debate about an issue and policy among officials and politicians.

**lap dogs**

Journalists, when the government's perspective (overwhelmingly) dominates their news stories.

**watchdogs**

Journalists, when their news stories hold people in power accountable by scrutinizing and reporting their statements, activities, claimed accomplishments, and failures.

**attack dogs**

Journalists whose stories about government and politics are highly negative and focus on blunders and disasters, scandals and corruption.

**TABLE 3.1** Types of Media Coverage

| Types of Media Coverage | Description |
|---|---|
| Lap Dogs | Journalists usually rely on policymakers as knowledgeable and convenient sources of information. Much news, therefore, consists of the issues and policies among officials and politicians. Political scientist Lance Bennett and his colleagues call this **indexing**. The news media serve as **lap dogs** when the government's perspective dominates. This particularly takes place when leaders and prominent figures of the opposition party refrain from or are reluctant to criticize and challenge the government's policies or do not articulate an alternative viewpoint for reporters to include in their stories. [45]<br><br>A notable example of the news media as lap dogs was their coverage of the George W. Bush administration's claims in 2002–2003 that the U.S. must attack Iraq because that state possessed weapons of mass destruction. Leaders of the Democratic Party did not forcefully challenge the White House's official story, plans, and rationale. Most of the news media then transmitted the administration's arguments without subjecting them to sustained analysis, criticism, and rebuttal. |
| Watchdogs | The news media are sometimes **watchdogs**, holding people in government and other powerful institutions accountable by scrutinizing and reporting their statements, activities, claimed accomplishments, and failures. This type of coverage can be provoked by dramatic events, such as Hurricane Katrina, to which the George W. Bush administration responded unconvincingly. Journalists went to the scene, saw the devastation and havoc for themselves, and showed it directly to viewers. Outraged reporters asked so many impassioned questions of administration officials about their inadequate response to Katrina that the Salon website compiled a "Reporters Gone Wild" video clip.[46]<br><br>Conversely, the media may not bark at all. As Dean Starkman documents: "The U.S. business press failed to investigate and hold accountable Wall Street banks and major mortgage lenders in the years leading up to the financial crisis of 2008."[47] |
| Attack Dogs | The news media can be **attack dogs**. President Richard M. Nixon observed, based on his many years in public life, that "for the press, progress is not news—trouble is news."[48] The news about government and politics is often negative, about blunders and disasters, scandals and corruption. This "gotcha" journalism can provoke a "feeding frenzy" in which reporters, like a pack of dogs, search for, uncover, and chew over every morsel of the story.[49] News coverage of President Clinton's relationship with White House intern Monica Lewinsky exemplified such a feeding frenzy. |

## Key Takeaways

In this section, we have explained how journalists decide what is news; how they acquire it (through beats, sources, investigative reporting, and other ways); how they assemble the news (by making decisions about stories, values, frames, facts, words, and tone); and how they present news. We briefly discussed bias. Then we described the techniques that people in public life use to manage and manipulate the news media to try to obtain positive and avoid negative depictions. And we specified three ways that the news media can behave toward people in authority, especially government and politics: as lap dogs, watchdogs, or attack dogs.

## Exercises

1. What makes something news? How do journalists decide what to report as news?

2. Why was the close-up photograph of the statue of Saddam Hussein being pulled down so much more widely used in the media than the wide-angle shot? How does the need to tell an interesting story affect how the news gets reported?
3. What factors determine how journalists cover politics? When is their coverage of politicians more likely to be favorable, and when is it more likely to be critical?

# 3.5 Opinion and Commentary

## Learning Objectives

After reading this section, you should be able to answer the following questions:

1. What are the leading liberal websites?
2. What are the right-wing media?
3. What are the leading comedy programs?

The media do far more than report the news. They are full of talking heads, journalists, pundits, outright partisans, and of course bots from fake accounts, busy expressing opinions and commenting on the news and current events. These reactions and responses can contribute to a marketplace of ideas, informed public discussion, and greater understanding of politics, government, and public policies. However, cacophony often abounds, shouting and squabbling drown out thought, **gaslighting** is frequent, and assertions dominate analysis. Important subjects are broached too briefly in too little time, while less significant, often trivial topics are inflated. Misinformation is pervasive. Lies are common. Videos are doctored to create misleading impressions. Opinion and commentary are sometimes mistaken for, confused with, or equated by the public and politicians with news, leading to (further) disdain for the news media.

**gaslighting**

Covertly creating doubts about an individual or group.

## Location

In this section, we tell you where to find some of the conspicuous opinion and commentary in the media about politics, government, and public policies. One can distinguish the ideologies of opinion and commentary media by the material they include and exclude, and what they focus on or emphasize.

### Print and Websites

Most newspapers contain editorials expressing opinions about the events of the day. The *New York Times* and *Washington Post* are liberal; the *Wall Street Journal* is conservative. They supplement their editorials with columns from regular contributors. Some newspapers add op-eds. These are opinions from people unaffiliated with the paper. Some newspapers carry a range of opinions, others are ideologically monolithic. Cartoons, when featured, often comment critically on public officials, policies, and current events. Comic strips are sometimes politically provocative, thus Garry Trudeau's sardonic *Doonesbury* and Aaron McGruder's scathing *The Boondocks*. These strip writers first published their work in their campus newspapers at Yale and the University of Maryland, respectively.

Publications provide a spectrum of analysis and opinion, and in some cases of news. A few appear in print and online; most are only on their websites. Prominent among the liberals and progressives are the *Daily Beast*, *HuffPost*, *Mother Jones*, the *Nation*, *Salon*, *Slate*, *Talking Points Memo*, and *Think Progress*. *Media Matters* monitors and corrects what it calls conservative misinformation.

Foremost among the conservatives are *Breitbart News*, the *Daily Caller*, the *Daily Wire*, *Drudge Report* (becoming less so), the *Federalist*, the *Gateway Pundit*, *Real Clear Politics*, and the *Washington Times*. By vehemently promoting Donald Trump they contributed to his election as president in 2016. The president appointed *Breitbart's* head, Stephen Bannon, as White House chief strategist, but later fired him. Conservative sites are sometimes disparagingly dubbed the "alt-right" or "right-wing ecosystem," terms they disavow. False stories are launched, particularly by the reactionary Alex Jones on radio and the internet, and his incendiary website *InfoWars*, as well as by *Parler*, *Newsmax*, and *One America News Network*, then picked up by more respectable (less outrageous) conservative outlets.[50]

The nonpartisan *Axios*, *BuzzFeed*, *CQ Roll Call*, *Center for Investigative Reporting*, and *ProPublica* cover government and politics focusing on Washington, DC. *The New Republic* inclines to be politically moderate.

## Television

After much debate among members of Congress, televised coverage of floor proceedings via the Cable Satellite Public Affairs Network (C-SPAN) was established in the U.S. House of Representatives in 1979 and in the Senate in 1986 (C-SPAN2) to transmit gavel-to-gavel coverage of floor action. These channels plus C-SPAN3 also air an array of political events, including election debates, political advertisements, press conferences, discussion forums, interviews with news makers, journalists, and authors, and book reviews.

The television networks' Sunday morning interview programs, notably *Meet the Press* and *This Week*, usually feature prominent government officials and other well-known politicians. In the face of sometimes aggressive questioning by the host and interview panelists, guests strive to set the news agenda and get their messages across to viewers. The programs, which have small audiences, are influential because they are widely watched in Washington, DC, otherwise known as "inside the Beltway," and by people interested in government and politics.

Twenty-four-hour cable television channel CNN reports some news. But it has a lot of time to fill and has cut back on reporters and news-gathering resources, particularly on foreign affairs. It focused on President Trump, increasingly relying on and reacting to news stories from the *New York Times* and organizations such as Politico. It has cut costs and raised profits by surrounding its news anchors with commentary and opinion, speculation and prediction, from panels consisting of some combination of reporters, correspondents, politicians, former government officials, pundits, political consultants, party strategists, and people from ideological think tanks. These guests, many of whom appear regularly, often express forceful points of view, deploy sound bites, and are adept at memorizing and delivering "spontaneous" observations and quips.

Arguably, CNN is liberal: President Trump called it the Clinton News Network. (See the discussion in Chapter 13 of his adverse relationship with the channel.) Certainly, however, the two other leading cable news channels are ideological.

For an adamantly pro-Trump, mainly conservative, Republican, anti-Democrat perspective (with minor exceptions), there is the Fox News Channel. Prior to President Trump's departure from office it had the highest prime-time viewership, not just of the cable news channels, but of all television. Despite its claims to separate news from opinion, the two often blend together on behalf of the latter. The channel features partisan, opinionated talk-show hosts, conspicuously the energetic—or vociferous, if you prefer—Sean Hannity, the disputatious Laura Ingraham, and Tucker Carlson, with his quizzical, indignant paying-attention expression. These commentators use multiple media platforms in addition to the Fox News Channel—radio talk shows, books, and websites—to spread their messages.

MSNBC is cable's liberal alternative to the conservative Fox News. Its leading hosts, each with their own program, are the combative Chris Hayes, academic Rachel Maddow, and the reflectively partisan Lawrence O'Donnell.

Sinclair Broadcasting Group has roughly a hundred and ninety-two local television stations in eighty-nine markets, reaching 39 percent of American viewers. The stations are affiliated with various networks. However, their owner uses them to promote his conservative ideology, to air biased political segments produced by the corporate news division, and to have anchors read from scripts prepared by Sinclair. These messages likely reach many of the approximately twenty million households that rely on local television.[51]

## Radio

Over two thousand radio stations employ a news-talk format. Hosts have ample time to vent their opinions, to cultivate, reaffirm, and cajole their callers and listeners. The bulk of the talk-radio audience listens to broadcasters who, like themselves, express conservative opinions, are pro-Republican, and are hostile to liberals, Democrats, and feminists. The most conspicuous until his death in 2021 was Rush Limbaugh. This caustic conservative was widely heard on more than six hundred stations with an estimated weekly audience of around 15 million.[52]

Other conservative radio commentators are Glen Beck, Dan Bongino, and Mark Levin.

From a countervailing radical perspective, there is the Pacifica Network, particularly its evening news program Democracy Now!, hosted by Amy Goodman and Juan Gonzalez and hear on approximately nine hundred stations. It reports stories and interviews people rarely heard on mainstream, let alone conservative, media.

There are approximately 1,500 Christian programming stations. In addition to their inspirational religious content and music, they broadcast programs on marriage and family issues and advice for the troubled. Some of their content is relevant to politics and public policy, especially their espousal of and support for traditional views and values.

## Comedy

Comedy is a genre that sometimes ventures politically where other modes of entertainment are reluctant to tread. Comedy has a point of view, offers an argument. Its treatment of authority figures and institutions ranges from supportive to benign to undermining, and rarely, as in the performances of Lenny Bruce, to subversive. It often lacerates, normally from a liberal, perhaps radical, perspective. President Trump and sometimes his associates have been the target and more or less victims, of the television shows of Samantha Bee (*Full Frontal*), John Oliver (*Last Week Tonight*), Bill Maher (*Real Time*), and Trevor Noah (*The Daily Show*), as well as of late-night hosts Stephen Colbert and Seth Meyers, perhaps the most caustic of them all in his post-monologue "A Closer Look"; also segments of *Saturday Night Live*.

The most irreverent and cogent critique of newspapers appears in *The Onion*.[53] January 2011 saw the debut on the IFC cable channel of the television version, titled *Onion News Network*.

## Link

### *The Onion*

As headlines from *The Onion* show, this fake newspaper can produce an audacious commentary on the news media and American government and politics.

Learn more about *The Onion* and the *Onion News Network* from their website and their Wikipedia page.

An exception to the liberal dominance of comedy is the satirical conservative-religious website *Babylon Bee*.[54]

Incivility is common in opinion and commentary. Jeffrey M. Berry and Sarah Sobieraj find, however, that the partisan media of talk radio, the Fox and MSNBC cable television channels, and political blogs go way beyond incivility to engage in outrage: that is, rhetoric characterized by venom, vilification of opponents, and hyperbolic reinterpretations of current events.[55] There are sensationalism, out-of-context quotes, and ad hominem attacks. Common are mockery, insulting language, and name calling. The intent is to provoke an emotional response of anger, fear, or moral righteousness. The partisan liberal and conservative media both spew outrageous speech, but conservatives are nastier.

A notorious example of outrageous disinformation was the right-wing campaign, despite all the evidence implicating Trump acolytes, that Antifa and Black Lives Matter were responsible for the January 6 invasion of the Capitol. Reporters for the *New York Times* traced the initial report by a commenter on Twitter to another pundit guest-hosting Rush Limbaugh's show. The message was then picked up and perpetuated by a host of their fellows on radio and cable television.[56]

## Key Takeaways

In this section, we have identified the incidence of opinion and commentary in the media. They are prevalent in newspapers and magazines, on television and radio, and in comedy. In addition, numerous organizations and individuals use new technology to spread their ideological gospels, including misinformation.

## Exercises

1. What is the value of having opinion and commentary in the media? Do you think they make it easier or harder for people to learn the truth and develop their own views about politics, government, and public policies?
2. How do the media influence politics and government? What do you think the media treat as the most important political issues?
3. How can humor be used to influence public opinion? Why might satire be more effective than conventional opinion in political persuasion?

# 3.6 Media Influences on People, Politics, Government, and Public Policies

## Learning Objectives

After reading this section, you should be able to answer the following questions:

1. What are four leading influences of the media on people, politics, government, and public policies?
2. Which influences do you think are the most important?
3. What are selective exposure, selective perception, selective retention, and polarization?

Our discussion of "Communication in the Information Age" leads to important ways in which media contents influence people, politics, government, and public policies. Here are four of them that will recur throughout the text.

## Agenda Setting

When the media place attention and emphasis on certain issues, people tend to see them as important problems requiring government action. The public then judges politicians according to how well or poorly they seem to respond to the issues.

Consider the television show 24. It gave its viewers the impression that terrorists were a constant threat to the United States and likely to strike with horrible destructiveness anywhere at any time. At its peak, the show had a weekly audience of approximately fifteen million viewers and reached millions more through the internet.

This "**agenda setting**" power of the media, in effect, tells people what they should be thinking about. The flip side of agenda setting is that when the media ignore issues or policy areas, often so too does the public. Thus, for people involved in government or politics, getting an issue in the media or keeping it out is important; the agenda influences the public's awareness and understanding of what should be done or safely ignored by policymakers.[57]

**agenda setting**

The power of the media to tell the public what subjects and issues to think about.

## Framing

The media are not simply important in getting people to think about an issue; they influence *how* people think about it. Scholars refer to this media power as "**framing**."[58]

As discussed in this chapter, journalists bring a perspective to bear on events, highlighting certain aspects at the expense of others, to create a more or less coherent narrative.[59] This names protagonists and antagonists, identifies some of the causes of the event described, offers moral judgments, and may suggest solutions. Framing is inherent in the process of selecting, editing, organizing, and presenting news stories and reports. It is often expressed in the television anchorperson's introduction and in newspaper headlines and opening paragraphs.

**framing**

The central idea or theme with which media personnel organize a story and thus give it a point of view.

The meaning of an event can depend dramatically on how it is framed by and in the media. For example, the public understands a demonstration quite differently depending on whether the news frames it as an exercise of freedom of speech or as a threat to or violation or breakdown of law and order.

Of course, some frames are more convincing than others. A frame's impact may depend on who is promoting it, what other frames it is competing against, and how frequently it is repeated.

Often, though, news frames are predictable.[60] They express widely shared assumptions and values. The news media framed the events of 9/11 as terrorist attacks on the United States, with a response from Americans of national heroism, horror, and mourning.

Out of habit and to simplify complex subjects, journalists tend to cover government and politics with a relatively small repertoire of familiar frames. Relations within and between the branches of government are typically framed as conflicts. Stories often frame politicians as motivated by partisanship and the desire for reelection. Stories about government agencies are frequently framed around bureaucratic incompetence, waste, and corruption.

Framing influences politics by reinforcing or changing what people think of an issue. Different frames call for different policy solutions. Thus, *24* told its viewers that in the grim choice between security and liberty, coercion must prevail, that torture is essential to extract information from terrorists to forestall (usually just in time) their lethal schemes.

# Priming

**priming**

When media (news stories) ascribe responsibility for a problem to a person or institution.

Media frames can provide criteria that audience members use to make judgments about government institutions, public officials, and issues. This is called "**priming**." It can occur when news stories identify the person or institution to blame for an event. The president is often held responsible for the nation's problems. Priming effects are strongest "when the news frames a problem as if it were the president's business, when viewers are prepared to regard the problem as important, and when they see it as entangled in the duties and obligation of the presidency."[61]

Because of its intrinsic importance, reemphasized by the news and entertainment media, fighting terrorism continues as a prominent issue. The president is seen as primarily responsible. Presidential candidates' competence to combat terrorism thus becomes an important criterion by which the electorate judges them. Note, in this respect, that some of *24*'s presidents could not be trusted to execute that duty and obligation effectively.

# Mobilizing

The media affect what people think about politics, government, and public policies and how they think about them. They also influence what, if anything, people do about them.

**mobilize**

To encourage, even inspire, individuals to engage in political behavior and action.

Media contents can **mobilize** individuals to engage in political behavior, from contacting public officials to voting, to protesting, to committing violence. In the 1960s, television coverage increased participation in the nonviolent protests of the civil rights movement against segregation in the South.[62] Continuous coverage of the 2020 Black Lives Matter demonstrations contributed to generating a wide range of participation, some of it violent.

The media can influence people in politics without the public's being much involved. Politicians are far more voracious consumers of the news than most Americans. When issues are heavily covered in the media, officials take such prominence as a sign that they may well be called to account for their actions, even if the public has not yet spoken out. And they speak and behave differently than they did when the issues were obscure. Media attention tends to encourage action and speed up the policy process, if only so politicians can get the issue off the table.

## Selective Exposure, Selective Perception, Selective Retention, and Polarization

We now turn to the relations between the media and the important concepts of *selective exposure* and its brethren. **Selective exposure** is people's decisions to expose themselves deliberately to media contents that they expect to agree with or find congenial to their views. This explains why many conservatives, Republicans, Evangelicals, and the like watch Fox News, and listened to Rush Limbaugh and similar proponents. Their ideological opposites reach for cable channel MSNBC and other outlets in the same vein.

Then, in the unlikely case that this exposure by people requires a modicum of opinion adjustment on their part, **selective perception**, leads them to perceive these media contents according to their existing beliefs. Then, through **selective retention**, they subsequently remember the contents (whether adjusted or not) in consonance with their established views.

Social media reinforce selective exposure by encouraging, even leading, people to expose and limit themselves to contents (people, perspectives, and policies) they already share or would agree with. People follow and stay with the ideological apps they favor. Social media contribute to these responses and reactions through the application of algorithms that identify, cater to, and reinforce their views. This all contributes to **polarization**: the divergence of political attitudes based on ideological extremes.

*Polarization* establishes and increases the division between people (for example, between Republicans and Democrats) on the bases of their opinions, beliefs, ideologies, partisanship, and policy preferences.

**selective exposure**

People deliberately expose themselves to media content they agree or expect to agree with.

**selective perception**

Perceiving media contents according to one's existing beliefs.

**selective retention**

Remembering media contents in accordance with one's established views.

**polarization**

The divergence of political attitudes based on ideological extremes.

### Key Takeaways

In this section we described four leading influences of the media on people, politics, government, and public policies: they are agenda setting, framing, priming, and mobilizing. We also introduced the phenomena of selective exposure, selective perception, selective retention, and polarization.

### Exercises

1. Based on your opinion, rank in order of importance the four leading influences that are discussed in this section.
2. Justify your ranking.
3. Argue for and against the benefits for government and politics of polarization.

# 3.7 Recommended Reading

Bennett, W. Lance. *News: The Politics of Illusion*, 10th ed. Chicago: University of Chicago Press, 2016. A lively, wide-ranging critique and explanation of the failure of the news media to serve democracy.

Bimber, Bruce. *Information and American Democracy: Technology in the Evolution of Political Power*. New York: Cambridge University Press, 2003. A sweeping overview of American politics in different "information ages."

Caro, Robert A. *Working: Researching, interviewing, writing*. New York: Knopf, 2019. The journalist and remarkable biographer of Lyndon B. Johnson on his skills, methods, and investigative techniques.

Chadwick, Andrew. *Internet Politics: States, Citizens, and New Communication Technologies*. New York: Oxford University Press, 2006. A thoughtful overview of the political implications, issues, and influence of the internet.

Compaine, Benjamin M., and Douglas Gomery. *Who Owns The Media?* 3rd ed. Mahwah, NJ: Lawrence Erlbaum, 2000. A detailed account of the organization and financing of the media.

Edelman, Murray. *From Art to Politics: How Artistic Creations Shape Political Conceptions*. Chicago: University of Chicago Press, 1995. A surprisingly upbeat account of political communication through art and fiction.

Hamilton, James T. *All the News That's Fit to Sell: How the Market Transforms Information into News*. Princeton, NJ: Princeton University Press, 2003. A compelling and detailed application of economic theory to explain the contents of news.

Hersh, Seymour M. *Reporter: A Memoir*. New York: Knopf, 2018. A revealing but sanitized account by the investigative journalist of his activities and experiences.

Hilsum, Lindsey. *In Extremis: The Life of War Correspondent Marie Colvin*. New York: Macmillan, 2018. A sympathetic biography based on Colvin's diaries.

Schudson, Michael. *Advertising, the Uneasy Persuasion: Its Dubious Impact on American Society*. New York: Basic Books, 1984. A distinctive discussion of the role of advertising in American society and economy.

West, Darrell M. *The Rise and Fall of the Media Establishment*. New York: Palgrave MacMillan, 2001. A brief history of professional journalism from its inception to what the author claims is its current loss of power.

Zelizer, Barbie. *About To Die: How News Images Move the Public*. New York: Oxford University Press, 2010. A thoughtful discussion of the use of visual images in the news.

# 3.8 Recommended Viewing

*Ace in the Hole* (1951 aka *The Big Carnival*). Mesmerizing portrayal of an unscrupulous reporter manipulating the victim of a mine accident to obtain a big story.

*All the President's Men* (1976). Through investigative journalism, two *Washington Post* reporters uncover the Watergate affair and bring down President Nixon's men. Based on their book.

*Battleship Potemkin* (1925). Soviet director Sergei Eisenstein's stirring tale of an incident in the abortive 1905 Russian revolution, a brilliant illustration of how to make a film with collective protagonists (notably, the people of Odessa).

*Citizen Kane* (1941). Orson Welles's investigation of the life of a media mogul is matchless moviemaking.

*Duck Soup* (1933). The Marx Brothers' anarchic send-up of the incompetence and hypocrisy of governments and of the folly of war. Groucho becomes leader of the country of Freedonia and leads it into a comedic war.

*Good Night and Good Luck* (2005). Based on the real-life conflict in the 1950s in which television newsman Edward R. Murrow defied corporate pressure and brought down demagogic Senator Joseph McCarthy.

*His Girl Friday* (1939). In this wise-cracking comedy, cynical editor (Cary Grant) uses his wiles to keep his star reporter and ex-wife (Rosalind Russell) from leaving the newspaper.

*Kill the Messenger* (2014). Fact-based saga of the life and death of journalist Gary Webb, who had writen a series of articles alleging CIA involvement in the transfer of money from cocaine sales in the U.S. to the Nicaraguan Contras.

*The Lenny Bruce Performance Film* (1965). The great comedian takes on the Supreme Court, the legal system, and the police in this devastating on-stage monologue.

*The Man Who Shot Liberty Valance* (1962). Director John Ford's meditative Western in which the news makes the myth that establishes the wrong man as the hero and successful politician.

*Network* (1976). Television company executives exploit an anchorman's madness on the air to boost ratings.

*The Player* (1992). Robert Altman's delightful satire of Hollywood, its filmmakers, and its films.

*Rashomon* (1950). Four versions of an ambush, rape, and murder are shown in Japanese director Akira Kurosawa's famous exploration of the elusive nature of truth.

*Red Hollywood* (1996). Documentary, replete with excerpts from their movies, about the writers, directors, and actors investigated postwar by the government and blacklisted by the industry.

*Shattered Glass* (2003). Fictionalized version of the true story of a journalist who is fired from *The New Republic* magazine when it is discovered that he has fabricated many of his stories.

*Sherlock Jr.* (1924). Buster Keaton's amazing comedy in which he enters into and becomes part of a film being screened.

*The Social Network* (2010). A fascinating account, partly factual and partly fictional, of the founding of Facebook.

*Spotlight* (2015). Another fictionalized true story: this time a small group of *Globe* reporters, led by an editor, expose the Boston archdiocese's cover-up of its priests' sexual abuse of children.

*Star Wars* (1977). The first of the multipart saga applies themes from the American Revolution to planetary political systems.

*Sullivan's Travels* (1941). Director Preston Sturges's tale of a director of mindless Hollywood studio films who wants to make films of social commentary but discovers the value of comedy.

*Sweet Smell of Success* (1957). Portrayal of the manipulations of a powerful New York newspaper gossip columnist.

*Triumph of the Will* (1935). Hitler's favorite filmmaker, Leni Riefenstahl, made this propaganda documentary of the 1934 Nazi party rally in Nuremberg, a celebration of the fascist state.

*Truth* (2015). Dramatized version of events ending the network career of CBS anchorman Dan Rather.

*Under the Wire* (2018). Documentary about the indomitable war correspondent Marie Colvin.

# Endnotes


1. Susan Schmidt and Vernon Loeb, "'She Was Fighting to the Death'; Details Emerging of W.V. Soldier's Capture and Rescue," *Washington Post*, April 3, 2003, A1.
2. Scott Drake, webmaster of Jessica-Lynch.com, e-mail to Tim Cook, March 6, 2005.
3. Jim Rutenberg, "To Interview Former P.O.W., CBS Offers Stardom," *The New York Times*, June 16, 2003, A1.
4. Rick Bragg, *I Am a Soldier, Too: The Jessica Lynch Story* (New York: Alfred A. Knopf, 2003).
5. Dana Priest, William Booth, and Susan Schmidt, "A Broken Body, a Broken Story, Pieced Together…," *Washington Post*, June 17, 2003, A1 and Michael Getler, "A Long, and Incomplete, Correction," *Washington Post*, June 29, 2003, B6.
6. Michael DeLong, "Politics During Wartime," *The New York Times*, April 27, 2007, A7.
7. This section draws on Bruce Bimber, *Information and American Democracy: Technology in the Evolution of Political Power* (New York: Cambridge University Press, 2003), especially 9–12.
8. A. J. Liebling, *The Press* (New York: Ballantine, 1964), 7.
9. C. Edwin Baker argues for the importance of media diversity in *Media Concentration and Democracy: Why Ownership Matters* (New York: Cambridge University Press, 2007).
10. Ben H. Bagdikian, *The New Media Monopoly* (Boston: Beacon Press, 2004).
11. Marc Tracy, "Acquisition of Gannett Creates Print Goliath In a $1.4 Billion Deal," *New York Times,* August 6, 2019, B6.
12. See Nikki Usher, *Making News at The New York Times* (Ann Arbor, MI: The University of Michigan Press, 2014), for how the newspaper is adapting to the new media environment.
13. Quoted in Sanjiv Bhattacharya, "Homer's Odyssey," *Observer Magazine*, August 6, 2000, 19.
14. William Hoynes, *Public Television for Sale* (Boulder, CO: Westview Press, 1994); and Marilyn Lashley, *Public Television* (New York: Greenwood, 1992).
15. Amie Tsang and Edmund Lee, "SiriusXM to Buy Pandora for $3.5 Billion in an Effort to Expand Its Reach," *The New York Times*, September 25, 2018, B3.
16. See Donald T. Critchlow, *When Hollywood Was Right: How Movie Stars, Studio Moguls, and Big Business Remade American Politics* (New York: Cambridge University Press, 2013) ; Alan Casty, *Communism in Hollywood: The Moral Paradoxes of Testimony, Silence and Betrayal* Lanham, Md: Scarecrow Press, 2009); and Steven J. Ross, *Hollywood Left and Right: How Movie Stars Shaped American Politics* (New York: Oxford University Press, 2011).
17. Mark Litwak, *Reel Power* (New York: Morrow, 1986), 74.
18. Ken Auletta, "Publish or Perish," *The New Yorker*, April 26, 2010, 24–31, is the source for much of this discussion; the quote is from p. 30.
19. See Raffi Khatchadourian, "No Secrets," *The New Yorker*, June 7, 2010, 40–51.
20. WikiLeaks released emails from the Hillary Clinton campaign as we discuss in Chapter 11 "Campaigns and Elections."
21. Davey Alba and Jack Nicas, "How Agendas Fill Local News Void," *The New York Times*, October 19, 2020, A1, 18.
22. Patricia Mazzei and Nicole Perlroth, "Experts Call Disinformation Targeting Spanish Speakers an 'Emergency,'" *The New York Times*, November 5, 2020, P7.
23. Neil Howe, "Millennials: A Generation of Page-Turners," *Forbes*, January 16, 2017.
24. Amelia Nierenberg, "Student Reporters Expose Clusters at Colleges," *The New York Times*, November 5, 2020, A4.
25. Adina Hoffman, *Ben Hecht: Fighting Words, Moving Pictures* (New Haven, Ct., Yale University Press, 2019).
26. Daniel C. Hallin, *The Uncensored War: The Media and Vietnam* (New York: Oxford University Press, 1989).
27. For journalists' backgrounds, see David H. Weaver, Randal A. Beam, Bonnie J. Brownlee, Paul S. Voakes, and G. Cleveland Wilhoit, *The American Journalist in the 21st Century* (Mahwah, NJ: Lawrence Erlbaum, 2007), 20.
28. Society of Professional Journalists, Code of Ethics, revised September 6, 2014.
29. David T. Z. Mindich, *Just the Facts: How "Objectivity" Came to Define American Journalism* (New York: New York University Press, 1998).
30. For a study of movie depictions of American journalism, see Matthew C. Ehrlich, *Journalism in the Movies* (Champaign: University of Illinois Press, 2004).
31. J. K. Rowling, *Harry Potter and the Goblet of Fire* (New York: Scholastic Press, 2000), especially 433–53, 511–15, 611–15, and 726–28; the quotation is on p. 450.
32. Jim Rutenberg, "'Bombshell' Relegated To Limbo," *The New York Times*, January 21, 2019, B1(5).
33. Allison Stanger, *Whistleblowers: Honesty in America from Washington to Trump*" (New Haven, CT.: Yale University Press, 2019).
34. Stephen Hess, *The Government/Press Connection: Press Officers and Their Offices* (Washington, DC: Brookings Institution, 1984), chap. 7.
35. Eric Lichtblau, "Terror Suspects Buying Firearms, Report Finds," *The New York Times*, March 8, 2005, A1.
36. James S. Ettema and Theodore L. Glasser, *Custodians of Conscience: Investigative Journalism and Public Virtue* (New York: Columbia University Press, 1998).
37. Alex Isenstadt, *Politico*, March 26, 2017.
38. U.S. Dept of Defense, 2/12/2002. https://archive.defense.gov/Transcripts/Transcript.aspx?TranscriptID=2636.
39. U.S. Dept of Defense, 2/12/2002. https://archive.defense.gov/Transcripts/Transcript.aspx?TranscriptID=2636.
40. January 21, 2017.
41. Lucas Graves, *Deciding What's True: The Rise of Political Fact-Checking in American Journalism* (New York: Columbia University Press, 2016).
42. Relevant are Robert M. Entman, "Framing Bias: Media in the Distribution of Power," *Journal of Communication* (57: February 28, 2007), 163–73; Edward S. Herman and Noam Chomsky, *Manufacturing Consent: The Political Economy of the Mass Media* (New York: Pantheon, 2002); Timothy Groseclose, *Left Turn: How Liberal Media Bias Distorts the American Mind* (New York: St. Martin's Press, 2011): and the paper "Political Bias in the News Media" (April 1, 2013), written by Duke undergraduate Susan Wang under Paletz's guidance.
43. The differences between the photographs was brought to our attention in the May/June 2003 issue of *Extra!*, p. 8.
44. Ashley Parker, "Where News Is Power, a Fight to Be Well-Armed," *The New York Times*, January 18, 2011, A14, 17.
45. W. Lance Bennettt, "An Introduction to Journalism Norms and Representations of Politics," *Political Communication* 13 no 4 (October-December 1996), 373-84.
46. See W. Lance Bennett, Regina G. Lawrence, and Steven Livingston, *When the Press Fails: Political Power and the News Media from Iraq to Katrina* (Chicago: University of Chicago Press, 2007) for a thoughtful analysis of when and why the news media are lap dogs and watchdogs (the "Gone Wild" example is on p. 167).
47. Dean Starkman, *The Watchdog That Didn't Bark: The Financial Crisis and the Disappearance of Investigative Reporting* (New York: Columbia University Press, 2014), 1.
48. Quoted in William Safire, "The Press is the Enemy: Nixon and the Media," *New York*, January 27, 1975, 44.
49. Larry J. Sabato, *Feeding Frenzy: How Attack Journalism Has Transformed American Politics* (New York: Free Press, 1991).
50. Yochai Benkler, Robert Faris, and Hal Roberts, *Network Propaganda: Manipulation, Disinformation, and Radicalization* (New York: Oxford University Press, 2018).
51. Sheelah Kolhatkar, "Breaking The News," *New Yorker*, October 22, 2018, 30-42; also, Gregory J. Martin and Joshua McCrain, "Local News and National Politics," *American Political Science Review* 113, 2 (2019): 372-84.
52. For a study of the similarities and relationships of Limbaugh, Fox News, and the *Wall Street Journal*, see Kathleen Hall Jamieson and Joseph N. Cappella, *Echo Chamber: Rush Limbaugh and the Conservative Media Establishment* (New York: Oxford University Press, 2008).
53. Susannah B. F. Paletz, "The Irreverent *Onion*," *Political Communication* 21, no. 1 (January–March 2004): 131–34; and for a collection of headlines, see Scott Dickens, ed., *The Onion Presents Our Dumb Century* (New York: Three Rivers Press, 1999).
54. Emma Goldberg, "By Lampooning Liberals, 'Babylon Bee' Aims to Be 'The Onion' of the Right," *The New York Times*, October 12, 2020, A15.
55. Jeffrey M. Berry and Sarah Sobieraj, *The Outrage Industry: Political Opinion and the New Incivility* (New York: Oxford University Press, 2014).
56. Michael M. Grynbaum, Davey Alba and Reid J. Epstein, "How a Lie Took Wings as the Capitol Riot Raged," *The New York Times*, March 1, 2021, A1 (16, 17).
57. Amber E. Boydstun, *Making the News: Politics, the Media, and Agenda Setting*, Chicago: University of Chicago Press, 2013.
58. Brian F. Schaffner and Patrick J. Sellers, *Winning with Words: The Origins and Impact of Political Framing* (New York: Routledge, 2010).
59. Stephen D. Reese, Oscar H. Gandy Jr., and August E. Grant, eds., *Framing Public Life: Perspectives on Media and Our Understanding of the Social World* (Mahwah, NJ: Lawrence Erlbaum, 2001).
60. Daniel C. Hallin, *The Uncensored War: The Media and Vietnam* (New York: Oxford University Press, 1986), 116–17.
61. Shanto Iyengar and Donald R. Kinder, *News That Matters: Television and American Opinion* (Chicago: University of Chicago Press, 1987), 97 and 110.
62. Taeku Lee, *Mobilizing Public Opinion: Black Insurgency and Racial Attitudes in the Civil Rights Era* (Chicago: University of Chicago Press, 2002).

# CHAPTER 4
# Civil Liberties

## 4.1 Preamble

The mass media are obsessed with law and order. Police shows and news about the police abound. The opening voice-over of the Fox television network series *Cops* intones that the show "is filmed on location with the men and women of law enforcement." Camera crews accompany police officers through the streets of America's cities, shooting many hours of real-life video to edit down to half-hour programs showing cops catching culprits. The police officers are the only narrators. Series producers say, "The goal is to put you in the passenger seat with them so you can experience what it is like to be a cop."[1] (After twenty-five years on Fox, *Cops* moved to the cable channel Spike in 2013.)

Spike, now Paramount, cancelled the show in May 2020 after nationwide protests at the brutal death of George Floyd, a Black man, at the hands of police.

*Cops*' approach to criminal justice is summarized in its theme music. The outcome is always the same: the "bad boys" (and bad girls) are shown to be criminals deserving to be hauled in. The end of each episode reassures us that the police are working hard to stop crime. Other central concerns of American politics—and specifically the civil liberties of individuals—are submerged. Suspects are seldom informed of their rights, rarely request a lawyer, and are not "presumed innocent until proven guilty."

In contrast to *Cops*, the media are often stalwart defenders of civil liberties, particularly freedom of the press, which is so crucial to their own activities. For **civil liberties** are the rights and freedoms of individuals that the Constitution says government should not infringe on. What these freedoms entail is much disputed in American politics and affects a wide range of policies.

Listen to the theme song for the show *Cops*.

View in the online reader

**civil liberties**

The rights and freedoms of individuals that government may not infringe on, mostly listed in the Bill of Rights.

## 4.2 The Bill of Rights

### Learning Objectives

After reading this section, you should be able to answer the following questions:

1. What is the Bill of Rights?
2. What historical periods were central to the evolution of civil liberties protections?
3. What is the relationship of the Fourteenth Amendment to civil liberties?

**Bill of Rights**

The first ten amendments to the Constitution, adopted in 1789 and ratified in 1791.

The foundation of civil liberties is the **Bill of Rights**, the ten amendments added to the Constitution in 1791 to restrict what the national government may do.

The state conventions that ratified the Constitution obtained promises that the new Congress would consider adding a Bill of Rights. James Madison—the key figure in the Constitutional Convention and an exponent of the Constitution's logic in the Federalist papers—was elected to the first House of Representatives. Keeping a campaign promise, he surveyed suggestions from state-ratifying conventions and zeroed in on those most often recommended. He wrote the amendments not just as goals to pursue but as commands telling the national government what it must do and what it cannot do. Congress passed twelve amendments, but the Bill of Rights shrank to ten when the first two (concerning congressional apportionment and pay) were not ratified by the necessary nine states.

### Link

**The Bill of Rights**

Click here to view the Bill of Rights.

The first eight amendments that were adopted address particular rights. The Ninth Amendment addresses the concern that listing some rights might undercut unspoken natural rights that preceded government. It states that the Bill of Rights does not "deny or disparage others retained by the people." This allows for unnamed rights, such as the right to travel between states, to be recognized. We discussed the Tenth Amendment in Chapter 2 as it has more to do with states' rights than individual rights.

# The Rights

**habeas corpus**

A writ issued by a judge asking the government for the reasons for a person's arrest; the Constitution protects an individual's right to ask for such a writ.

**bills of attainder**

Laws prohibited by the Constitution that punish a named individual without judicial proceedings.

**ex post facto laws**

Laws prohibited by the Constitution that retroactively make a legal act a crime.

Even before the addition of the Bill of Rights, the Constitution did not ignore civil liberties entirely. It states that Congress cannot restrict one's right to request a writ of **habeas corpus** giving the reasons for one's arrest. It bars Congress and the states from enacting **bills of attainder** (laws punishing a named person without trial) or **ex post facto laws** (laws retrospectively making actions illegal). It specifies that persons accused by the national government of a crime have a right to trial by jury in the state where the offense is alleged to have occurred and that national and state officials cannot be subjected to a "religious test," such as swearing allegiance to a particular denomination.

The Bill of Rights contains the bulk of civil liberties. Unlike the Constitution, with its emphasis on powers and structures, the Bill of Rights speaks of "the people," and it outlines the rights that are central to individual freedom.[2]

The main amendments fall into several broad categories of protection:

1. Freedom of expression (I)
2. The right to "keep and bear arms" (II)
3. The protection of person and property (III, IV, V)
4. The right not to be "deprived of life, liberty, or property, without due process of law" (V)
5. The rights of the accused (V, VI, VII)
6. Assurances that the punishment fits the crime (VIII)
7. The right to privacy implicit in the Bill of Rights

# The Bill of Rights and the National Government

Congress and the executive have relied on the Bill of Rights to craft public policies, often after public debate in newspapers.[3] Civil liberties expanded as federal activities grew.

## The First Century of Civil Liberties

The first big dispute over civil liberties erupted when Congress passed the Sedition Act in 1798, amid tension with revolutionary France. The act made false and malicious criticisms of the government—including Federalist President John Adams and Congress—a crime. While printers could not be stopped from publishing, because of freedom of the press, they could be punished after publication. The Adams administration and Federalist judges used the act to threaten with arrest and imprisonment many Republican editors who opposed them. Republicans argued that freedom of the press, before or after publication, was crucial to giving the people the information they required in a republic. The Sedition Act was a key issue in the 1800 presidential election, which was won by the Republican Thomas Jefferson over Adams; the act expired at the end of Adams's term.[4]

Debates over slavery also expanded civil liberties. By the mid-1830s, Northerners were publishing newspapers favoring slavery's abolition. President Andrew Jackson proposed stopping the U.S. Post Office from mailing such "incendiary publications" to the South. Congress, saying it had no power to restrain the press, rejected his idea. Southerners asked Northern state officials to suppress abolitionist newspapers, but they did not comply.[5]

**FIGURE 4.1 Frederick Douglass and the *North Star***

The ex-slave Frederick Douglass, like many prominent abolitionists, published a newspaper. Much of the early debate over civil liberties in the United States revolved around the ability to suppress such radical statements.

Source: Library of Congress. (https://www.loc.gov/exhibits/odyssey/archive/02/0210001r.jpg). Via Wikimedia: https://en.wikipedia.org/wiki/File:NorthStarfrontpage.jpg; Frank W. Legg. Frederick Douglass, ca. 1879. National Archives Frank W. Legg Photographic Collection of Portraits of Nineteenth-Century Notables, 1862-1884. NARA ID: 558770. https://catalog.archives.gov/id/558770. Via Wikimedia: http://commons.wikimedia.org/ wiki/File:Frederick_Douglass_portrait.jpg.

## World War I

As the federal government's power grew, so too did concerns about civil liberties. When the United States entered the First World War in 1917, the government jailed many radicals and opponents of the war. Persecution of dissent caused Progressive reformers to found the American Civil Liberties Union (ACLU) in 1920. Today, the ACLU pursues civil liberties for both powerless and powerful litigants across the political spectrum. While it is often deemed a liberal group, it has defended reactionary organizations, such as the American Nazi Party and the Ku Klux Klan, and has joined powerful lobbies in opposing campaign finance reform as a restriction of speech.

# The Bill of Rights and the States

**due process clause**

Section of the Fifth Amendment that prohibits the federal government from depriving individuals of "life, liberty, or property without due process of law."

**selective incorporation**

The Supreme Court's application of the protections of the Bill of Rights one by one to the states after it has decided that each is "incorporated" into (inherent in) the Fourteenth Amendment's protection of liberty against state actions.

In Chapter 5, we discuss the Fourteenth Amendment, added to the Constitution in 1868, and how its **due process clause**, which bars *states* from depriving persons of "life, liberty, or property, without due process of law," is the basis of civil rights. The Fourteenth Amendment is crucial to civil liberties, too. The Bill of Rights restricts only the *national* government; the Fourteenth Amendment allows the Supreme Court to extend the Bill of Rights to the states. Note, however, that in some cases, protections provided by state constitutions are greater than the U.S. Constitution and the Bill of Rights.

The Supreme Court exercised its new power gradually. The Court followed **selective incorporation**: for the Bill of Rights to extend to the states, the justices had to find that the state law violated a principle of liberty and justice that is fundamental to the inalienable rights of a citizen. Table 4.1 shows the years when many protections of the Bill of Rights were applied by the Supreme Court to the states; some have never been extended at all.

**TABLE 4.1 The Supreme Court's Extension of the Bill of Rights to the States**

| Date | Amendment | Right | Case |
|---|---|---|---|
| 1897 | Fifth | Just compensation for eminent domain | *Chicago, Burlington & Quincy Railroad v. City of Chicago* |
| 1925 | First | Freedom of speech | *Gitlow v. New York* |
| 1931 | First | Freedom of the press | *Near v. Minnesota* |
| 1932 | Fifth | Right to counsel | *Powell v. Alabama (capital cases)* |
| 1937 | First | Freedom of assembly | *De Jonge v. Oregon* |
| 1940 | First | Free exercise of religion | *Cantwell v. Connecticut* |
| 1947 | First | Nonestablishment of religion | *Everson v. Board of Education* |
| 1948 | Sixth | Right to public trial | *In Re Oliver* |
| 1949 | Fourth | No unreasonable searches and seizures | *Wolf v. Colorado* |
| 1958 | First | Freedom of association | *NAACP v. Alabama* |
| 1961 | Fourth | Exclusionary rule excluding evidence obtained in violation of the amendment | *Mapp v. Ohio* |
| 1962 | Eighth | No cruel and unusual punishment | *Robinson v. California* |
| 1963 | First | Right to petition government | *NAACP v. Button* |
| 1963 | Fifth | Right to counsel (felony cases) | *Gideon v. Wainwright* |
| 1964 | Fifth | Immunity from self-incrimination | *Mallory v. Hogan* |
| 1965 | Sixth | Right to confront witnesses | *Pointer v. Texas* |
| 1965 | Fifth, Ninth, and others | Right to privacy | *Griswold v. Connecticut* |
| 1966 | Sixth | Right to an impartial jury | *Parker v. Gladden* |
| 1967 | Sixth | Right to a speedy trial | *Klopfer v. N. Carolina* |
| 1969 | Fifth | Immunity from double jeopardy | *Benton v. Maryland* |
| 1972 | Sixth | Right to counsel (all crimes involving jail terms) | *Argersinger v. Hamlin* |
| 2010 | Second | Right to keep and bear arms | *McDonald v. Chicago* |

| Rights Not Extended to the States | |
|---|---|
| Third | No quartering of soldiers in private dwellings |
| Fifth | Right to grand jury indictment |
| Seventh | Right to jury trial in civil cases under common law |
| Eighth | No excessive bail |
| Eighth | No excessive fines |

# Interests, Institutions, and Civil Liberties

Many landmark Supreme Court civil liberties cases were brought by unpopular litigants: members of radical organizations, publishers of anti-Semitic periodicals or of erotica, religious adherents to small sects, atheists and agnostics, or indigent criminal defendants. This pattern promotes a media frame suggesting that civil liberties grow through the Supreme Court's staunch protection of the lowliest citizen's rights.

The finest example is the saga of Clarence Gideon in the book *Gideon's Trumpet* by Anthony Lewis, then the Supreme Court reporter for the *New York Times*. The indigent Gideon, sentenced to prison, protested the state's failure to provide him with a lawyer. Gideon made a series of handwritten appeals. The Court heard his case under a special procedure designed for paupers. Championed by altruistic civil liberties experts, Gideon's case established a constitutional right to have a lawyer provided, at the state's expense, to all defendants accused of a felony.[6] Similar story lines often appear in news accounts of Supreme Court cases. Reporters personalize these stories by interviewing the person who brought the suit and telling the touching individual tale behind the case.[7]

This mass-media frame of the lone individual appealing to the Supreme Court is only part of the story. Powerful interests also benefit from civil liberties protections. Consider, for example, freedom of expression: Fat-cat campaign contributors rely on freedom of speech to protect their right to spend as much money as they want to in elections. Advertisers say that commercial speech should be granted the same protection as political speech. Huge media conglomerates rely on freedom of the press to become unregulated and more profitable.[8]

Many officials have to interpret the guarantees of civil liberties when making decisions and formulating policy. They sometimes have a broader awareness of civil liberties than do the courts. For example, the Supreme Court found in 1969 that two Arizona newspapers violated antitrust laws by sharing a physical plant while maintaining separate editorial operations. Congress and the president responded by enacting the Newspaper Preservation Act, saying that freedom of the press justified exempting such newspapers from antitrust laws.

## Key Takeaways

In this section we defined civil liberties as individual rights and freedoms that government may not infringe on. They are listed primarily in the Bill of Rights, the ten amendments added in 1791 by the founders to address fears about the new federal government's potential to abuse power. Initially limited to the federal government, they now apply, though unevenly, to the states. What those liberties are and how far they extend are the focus of political conflict. They are shaped by the full range of people, processes, and institutions in American politics. Both unpopular minorities and powerful interests claim civil liberties protections to gain favorable outcomes.

## Exercises

1. How does the original text of the Constitution protect civil liberties? What kinds of rights does the Bill of Rights protect that the original body of the Constitution does not?
2. Why might landmark civil liberties cases tend to be brought by unpopular or disadvantaged groups? What are some of the ways in which powerful interests benefit from civil liberties protections?
3. Do you think the Bill of Rights does enough to protect civil liberties? In your opinion, are there any ways in which the Bill of Rights goes too far?

# 4.3 Religion, Speech, the Press, Assembly, and Petition

## Learning Objectives

After reading this section, you should be able to answer the following questions:

1. What two clauses protect freedom of religion?
2. What exceptions apply to freedom of speech?
3. What protections do the media enjoy under freedom of the press?
4. What are the benefits of and limitations on the right to assemble and petition?

Civil liberties touch upon many issues. In the next two sections, we describe the current interpretation of each right and outline the policies it affects.

## Freedom of Religion

The First Amendment addresses freedom of religion in two distinct clauses: the establishment clause and the free expression clause.

### Establishment Clause

**establishment clause**

Section of the First Amendment that prohibits the government from recognizing an official religion.

Rejecting the British legacy of "established" churches, the **establishment clause** bars Congress from giving any religion an official status. In Jefferson's much-quoted line, the establishment clause erects a "wall of separation between church and state." A public policy may advance religious objectives only if its aim and main effect have nothing to do with religion. Thus, a law forcing stores to close on Sundays can be justified to require employers to give staff a day off but not to enforce a Sabbath.[9]

The separation of church and state has generated high-profile controversies. The drama surrounding such confrontations is often captured by the press. In the 1920s, John Thomas Scopes was found guilty of teaching evolution in violation of a Tennessee law requiring that the Bible's version of creation be taught in public schools. Scopes's trial, portrayed in the stage play and film *Inherit the Wind*, was a precursor of later battles.

## Link

**The Scopes Trial**

Click here to learn more about the Scopes trial.

Starting in the 1960s, the Supreme Court, in a series of rulings, prohibited nondenominational state-issued prayers in school, Bible readings, moments of silence intended for prayer, and student-led prayers at graduation ceremonies and football games. (The Court did refrain from invalidating the Pledge of Allegiance for containing the words "under God.")[10] Court attempts to stop prayers are hard to enforce across the country—especially since they often receive saturation media coverage that gives most of the attention to those decrying what they see as judicial activism.

In 1983, the Supreme Court voted 6–3 that the practice of the Nebraska legislature of starting its sessions with a prayer offered by a chaplain paid by the state was constitutional.[11] The dissenters observed that the majority, rather than reshaping the Establishment clause, had carved out an exception to it. In May 2014, however, the Court voted by 5–4 that town boards can start their sessions with Christian sectarian prayers, even though the participants would not just be lawmakers but would include spectators and people doing business with the board.[12] Writing for the majority, Justice Anthony M. Kennedy did offer the caveat that prayers would be unacceptable if they were consistently used to "denigrate nonbelievers or religious minorities or threaten damnation or preach conversion."

In 2020, the Supreme Court, siding with religious organizations, further weakened the division between church and state. In June, it voted 5–4 to allow public funding of religious schools. Specifically, the schools could participate in programs providing scholarships to students attending private schools.[13] In July, it voted 7–2 to allow employers with religious or moral objections not to provide their employees with cost-free coverage for contraception. And by the same vote, employment discrimination laws did not apply to teachers in religious schools.[14]

## Free Exercise Clause

The First Amendment also says that Congress shall not prohibit the "free exercise" of religion. Individuals have the right to believe and practice their religions as they see fit. Government policies cannot target individuals' religious practices or force actions that violate their religions.

This **free exercise clause** gained potency in 1943 when the Supreme Court ruled that Jehovah's Witnesses could not be expelled from public schools for refusing to salute the American flag, an act contrary to their religion. More recently, the Supreme Court limited the clause's reach when it ruled, in 1990, that American Indians had no right to disobey an Oregon law barring controlled substances in order to ingest peyote as part of a religious service. The Court held that laws hindering religious practices do not violate the First Amendment if they apply to all persons and do not openly refer to religion.

**free exercise clause**

Section of the First Amendment that prohibits the government from barring individuals from freely practicing religion.

The establishment clause tries to keep religion out of government; the free exercise clause tries to keep government out of religion. The two objectives are not always compatible. For example, President George W. Bush proposed to allow government to contract with "faith-based" organizations to administer social programs. Opponents argued that this would violate the establishment clause by endorsing religion; Bush responded that existing policy violated the free exercise clause by discriminating against religious organizations.

In July 2014, the relationship between religious beliefs and the marketplace became even more legally complicated. In its "Hobby Lobby" decision, the Supreme Court voted 5–4 that the Affordable

Care Act requirement that employer-provided health insurance include coverage for contraception could not apply to for-profit companies if they had religious objections to some types of contraception.[15] This case was not decided on First Amendment grounds but rather was an interpretation of the 1993 "Religious Freedom Restoration Act," which states that the government "shall not substantially burden the exercise of religion without satisfying a demanding legal test."[16]

Link

***Burwell v. Hobby Lobby Stores Inc.***

Learn more about *Burwell v. Hobby Lobby Stores Inc.* here.

# Freedom of Speech

The Supreme Court has held that "debate on public issues should be uninhibited, robust, and wide-open."[17] Offensive speech is less detrimental than the "chilling effect" of individuals being silenced for fear of retribution. Nevertheless, freedom of speech is not absolute. Governments can regulate or restrict it under certain conditions.

## Thoughts, Words, and Actions

Thoughts are deemed beyond the scope of government regulation; actions are heavily regulated by government; words are somewhere in between. The distinctions between thoughts, words, and actions are not always clear. Two cases of protest against the Vietnam War show how lines are drawn.[18] In one, a protester burned his draft card and was charged with violating a federal law that makes it a crime to knowingly destroy draft cards. The Court upheld the law, saying that the law aimed to maintain draft records, not to stifle free expression. When two students wore black armbands to their high school to protest the war and were suspended for violating the dress code, the Court found the policy sought to suppress free expression and sided with the students.

## When Speech Can Be Regulated

The First Amendment does not protect speech that fails to contribute to the exchange of ideas that is crucial in a democracy—for instance, libel, obscenity, and "fighting words"—but such forms of speech are narrowly defined.

**libel**

Defamatory publication unprotected by the First Amendment; to win a libel suit, public figures must demonstrate "actual malice" revealed by a "reckless disregard for the truth."

The publication of defamatory information, or **libel**, can be challenged in court. But officials and other public figures must demonstrate "actual malice" displayed by a "reckless disregard for the truth."[19] Thus libel cases are hard to win. Nonetheless, some litigants sue to shame a media organization publicly or to force it to spend money defending itself in court.

There is now a right to possess most obscene material in one's home, but not to produce, sell, or ship it. Early in the twentieth century, obscenity laws had halted the circulation of works of art such as James Joyce's now classic novel *Ulysses*. In 1957, the Supreme Court shrank the definition of obscenity from anything to do with sex to "material that deals with sex in a manner appealing to prurient interest" and "utterly without redeeming social importance." This decision forced the justices to hear dozens of cases in order to distinguish obscenity from protected speech. The results were almost comical. The often elderly justices viewed numerous pornographic films, the earthy Thurgood Marshall recounting the goings-on to his patrician, sight-impaired colleague John Harlan. At one point, Justice Potter Stewart exasperatedly wrote in one opinion, "I know it when I see it." Finally, in 1973, the Court established three rules that must be met for material to be obscene: it appeals to a prurient interest by the standards of the local community; it depicts specified sexual conduct in a patently offensive way; and it lacks serious literary, artistic, political, or scientific value.[20]

In the 1920s, the Supreme Court allowed government to bar **fighting words** as long as there was a "clear and present danger" of provoking an immediate attack or acts of violence. In Justice Oliver Wendell Holmes's terms, freedom of speech does not extend to the right to falsely yell "Fire!" in a crowded theater. Such a rule allowed for suppression of radical voices. As late as 1951, the Court upheld a federal law banning advocacy of the violent overthrow of the government. But the Court, in 1969, held that speech favoring illegal action is protected unless violence is both intended and likely.[21]

**fighting words**

Speech, not protected by the First Amendment, that provokes people to immediate attack or acts of violence.

Even when the government cannot bar speech, it can direct its time, place, and manner. But policies may not target particular content and must provide alternative ways to express oneself. If public universities and colleges cannot ban political speeches, they may restrict them to certain parts of campus such as "Free Speech Alleys."

## Speech Codes

Like fighting words, intimidation and harassment are not protected forms of free speech. By this logic, colleges and universities in the 1980s proposed campus speech codes to forbid the demeaning or stigmatizing of persons on the basis of race, ethnicity, gender, or sexual orientation. Proponents argued that speech codes would actually boost free speech, since "hate speech" deterred individuals who felt under attack from speaking out. But courts struck down the codes as too broad.[22]

# Freedom of the Press

The media claim special privileges under the First Amendment's guarantee of "freedom of the press."

## Prior Restraint

The government is rarely able to stop material from being published. Even the Sedition Act of 1798, discussed previously in this chapter (Section 2), did not include **prior restraint**. The Supreme Court extended the ban to the states in 1931 when it struck down a Minnesota law allowing the state to suppress a "malicious, scandalous and defamatory" publication as a "public nuisance"—in this case, an abusively anti-Semitic periodical. Prior restraint is rarely justified: in 1971, the Court refused to issue an injunction sought by the executive branch against the *New York Times* and *Washington Post* on grounds of violations of national security. In the absence of the government's *proof* that the national interest would be harmed, the Court allowed the publication of the Pentagon Papers, a leaked classified set of documents revealing decisions leading to the Vietnam War.[23]

**prior restraint**

A practice, forbidden by the First Amendment, whereby government can prevent publication.

### Links

**Prior Restraint**

Click here to learn more about prior restraint.

***Near v. Minnesota* and *New York Times v. U.S.***

For more information on *Near v. Minnesota* and *New York Times v. U.S.*, visit here and here.

## News Media Privileges

Reporters have privileges that the public lacks: greater access to the workings of government, the ability to question officeholders, and access to government public-information offices that feed them quotations and stories. But such privileges, particularly protection from revealing confidential sources, stem from policy and practice, not from constitutional rights.

Laws aimed at public disclosure, such as sunshine laws preventing government from working behind closed doors, benefit reporters. The Freedom of Information Act (FOIA), enacted in 1966, allows for access to executive agencies and commissions' records and files closed to public inspection.[24] Information obtained under the FOIA provides documentation for stories like *USA Today*'s discovery of a huge increase in the use and dealing of crack cocaine by individuals under age fifteen. Such information can also reveal scandals. In 1990, *Washington Post* reporter Ann Devroy was frustrated with White House Chief of Staff John Sununu's refusal to answer her dogged questions about his rumored use of perquisites of office for private gain. Devroy filed for documents under the FOIA and found Sununu had used government planes to get to a dentist's appointment and to attend postage-stamp auctions. Sununu resigned in disgrace.

In contrast are government efforts to curb the release of information it deems damaging to national security. The Obama administration cracked down on government officials who, without permission, told reporters about their national security concerns, especially policies they considered problematic, unethical, or botched. Its Justice Department brought more cases under the Espionage Act (seven) against people accused of leaking information than all previous administrations combined (four). In its brief in one case, it told the Supreme Court that reporters "have no privilege to refuse to provide direct evidence of criminal wrongdoing by confidential sources."[25] This argument was consistent with the Supreme Court's 1972 ruling by 5–4 in *Branzburg v. Hayes* that the First Amendment provided no protection against grand jury subpoenas.[26]

### Link

***Branzburg v. Hayes***

More information on *Branzburg v. Hayes* can be found here.

A conspicuous subject of the Justice Department's pursuit was *New York Times* reporter James Risen. He was subpoenaed (first by the George W. Bush administration and then by the Obama administration) to reveal the sources for what became his book *State of War*.[27] His refusal embroiled him in a legal battle lasting seven years. It took him to the Supreme Court, which, in a one-line order, rejected his appeal, thereby requiring him to comply with the subpoena. Even when eventually called to testify in court, he refused to answer questions that might help the Justice Department identify his sources.

Attorney General Eric H. Holder Jr. changed direction before leaving office in 2015. (Perhaps his imminent departure allowed him to move in the direction he had always preferred.) He revised the Justice Department guidelines to make it harder "to demand phone records, notes or e-mails from news organizations" and eliminated the limitation that the protections apply "only to journalists engaged in 'ordinary news gathering.'"[28]

Nonetheless, following the Risen case, there is now legal precedent that could be used to compel journalists to testify and reveal their sources. There is as yet no federal shield law to protect them.

## Broadcast Regulation

Public policy treats different media differently. Broadcast and cable slots, being inherently limited, can be regulated by government in ways that are not allowed for print media or the internet.[29]

The Federal Communications Commission (FCC), established in 1934, has the power to issue licenses for a given frequency on the basis of "the public interest, convenience, or necessity." From the start, the FCC favored big commercial broadcasters aiming at large audiences. Such limits on competition enabled the establishment of hugely profitable radio (and later television) stations and networks, whose licenses—sometimes jokingly termed licenses to print money—the FCC almost automatically renewed.

The FCC has regulatory authority to penalize the broadcast media, but not cable television, for indecent content. During the halftime show at the 2004 Super Bowl, televised by CBS, singer Justin Timberlake tore the costume and for a split second exposed the right breast of singer Janet Jackson. The FCC fined CBS $550,000 for the Super Bowl "wardrobe malfunction." The fine was overturned by a federal court of appeals in July 2008. In May 2009, the Supreme Court returned the case to the court for reconsideration. The appeals court again ruled in favor of CBS. Again the FCC appealed. In 2012 the Supreme Court again refused to hear the case.

# Rights to Assemble and Petition

Rights to assemble and petition government allow individuals to come together as groups and voice concerns. These rights permitted groups that were denied the vote—such as women before 1920—to state views and pressure government.[30] Social movements claim that the rights protect protesting; interest groups argue that the right to petition government includes all lobbying.

Like speech, freedom of assembly can be regulated in its time, place, and manner. Thus, demonstrations outside political party conventions may be limited to given areas, sometimes far from the event. Moreover, the right is "to *peaceably* assemble." Governments have the power and responsibility to ensure that protests do not turn violent. But the failure to distinguish between an assembly and a mob has resulted in tragic consequences when unarmed protesters have lost their lives (see the following "Enduring Images" for more information).

### Enduring Images

**Kent State**

On May 4, 1970, at Ohio's Kent State University, National Guardsmen fired on unarmed student protesters who had planned a noontime antiwar rally. Four students, including two passersby, died. A photographer snapped fifteen-year-old runaway Mary Ann Vecchio kneeling and screaming over Jeffrey Miller's dead body. Another showed National Guardsmen, impersonal under gas masks, aiming rifles at defenseless students. Such images conjure up brutal, deliberate repression of rights of protest. They reappear on anniversaries of the Kent State killings, with captions like, "Americans were stunned to see photographs showing the government shooting on its own citizens, here in the world's oldest democracy where the right of political dissent is supposedly fundamental."[31]

National Guardsmen marching at Kent State.

Source: Associated Press

Here Mary Ann Vecchio kneels over the body of Jeffrey Miller.

Source: John Filo / Contributor / Getty Images

The history of these enduring images is more complex.[32] Protests began on college campuses on April 30, 1970, when President Richard Nixon announced an invasion of Cambodia, expanding the Vietnam War. Protests were not always peaceful. In Kent, students smashed store windows on May 1, and Kent State's ROTC building was burned down on May 2. Ohio's governor mobilized the National Guard to defend the campus. On May 4, the Guard, badly outnumbered, sought to stop the rally. Other photos from May 4 show students taunting the Guard, fogs of tear gas, and volleys of empty tear-gas canisters and rocks thrown at soldiers. The picture of soldiers aiming their rifles may have been an early attempt to subdue the protest without shooting. The immediate response to the shootings did not blame the Guard. Nixon's reaction was widely reprinted: "This should remind us all once again that when dissent turns to violence it invites tragedy."[33] Polls showed most of the public blamed students for the deaths and backed the Guard's actions.[34]

The enduring image, however, is of Mary Ann Vecchio. One reason is its emotional resonance: it resembles a pietà sculpture of Mary grieving over the body of Jesus. Also, American politics after the invasion of Cambodia turned from engaging in to ending the Vietnam War—in part as a response to unrest that racked the country. And President Nixon's law-and-order rhetoric lost support as revelations of illegal misdeeds surfaced in the Watergate scandal. By the fall of 1973, a majority in a Harris Poll saw the shootings as "unjustified and repressive."[35] As images of Kent State were winnowed down to the one picture of Mary Ann Vecchio over the body of Jeffrey Miller, the meaning of what happened at Kent State shifted from a tragic consequence of disorder to a vivid symbol of civil liberties denied.

### Key Takeaways

In this section we discussed the constitutional protections guaranteeing freedoms of religion, speech, the press, assembly, and petition. These important protections are far-reaching but nonetheless subject to important exceptions. The First Amendment, for example, guarantees freedom of speech, but this is not absolute: governments can regulate or restrict it under certain conditions. The media can also claim special privileges under the First Amendment's guarantee of "freedom of the press," such as the prohibition of prior restraint.

### Exercises

1. What is the difference between the establishment and the free exercise clauses of the First Amendment? How do these clauses complement one another? How might they come into conflict?
2. What kinds of speech are protected by the First Amendment? What factors determine whether speech is protected?
3. Why might it be important for citizens of a democracy to have the right to assemble and to petition their government? In your opinion, what should the limits of these rights be?

# 4.4 Arms, Searches and Seizures, Accusation, Punishment, Property, and Privacy

### Learning Objectives

After reading this section, you should be able to answer the following questions:

1. What is the Second Amendment?
2. What constitutes illegal searches and seizures?
3. What amendments protect the rights of the accused?
4. What is eminent domain?
5. What is the current state of abortion as a civil liberty?

# The Right to Keep and Bear Arms

The Second Amendment reads, "A well-regulated militia being necessary to the security of a free state, the right to keep and bear arms shall not be infringed." Is this a right of self-defense that is akin to the protection of one's dwelling guaranteed by other amendments?[36] Or is it simply a basis for states to build militias, balancing off the standing army of the national government—in which case the gradual replacement of volunteer state militias by the National Guard rendered the Second Amendment obsolete?[37]

Most crime rates in the United States are similar to those of countries such as Canada or Australia. But the United States has a far higher rate of violent crime, in part because of the greater availability of firearms. Guns are also involved in suicides and accidents.

A large majority of the public supports some restrictions on the sale of firearms, but few policies have been enacted to do so.[38] Although opponents of gun control are outnumbered, they are more likely than supporters to vote on this issue. They also enjoy the very vocal, visible, and organizational support of the National Rifle Association (NRA).

Policy debate on gun control usually occurs after a dramatic, heavily covered news event like an assassination or a massacre at a school. One political scientist described the result as "furious politics, marginal policy."[39] For example, after the killings of Martin Luther King Jr. and Robert Kennedy in 1968, Congress debated President Lyndon Johnson's proposal for a federal system of firearm registration and licensing of gun owners but passed only limited, ineffective legislation. In 1994, dramatic fights over banning assault weapons and mandating a waiting period for gun purchases produced a law with huge loopholes when it failed to cover private sales at gun shows and via the internet. The ban on assault weapons expired in 2004 and was not renewed.

Indeed, in 2005 Congress passed and President George W. Bush signed the Protection of Lawful Commerce in Arms Act. The law protected gun manufacturers, distributors, and dealers from civil liabilty law suits for damage caused by their products.

The "right to keep and bear arms" has been debated by the public and politicians more than by courts. But in June 2008, the Supreme Court, by a vote of 5–4, ruled that individuals have the right to bear arms. This decision, an interpretation of the Second Amendment, struck down the District of Columbia's thirty-two-year-old law banning the possession of handguns.[40] In June 2010, the Court, again by a vote of 5–4, applied the ruling to cities and states by overturning Chicago's ban on handguns.[41] The Court has not prohibited all legislation and limitation of guns, but some governmental actions would likely conflict with the Court's interpretation of the Second Amendment.

That is, if new gun control laws could be enacted at the federal level. After the massacre of twenty children and six adult staff by a lone gunman at Sandy Hook Elementary School in December 2012, President Obama proposed legislation to ban assault weapons, to ban magazines with more than ten rounds of ammunition, and to require background checks at gun shows and internet sales (but not between family and friends). The first two provisions were removed from the bill to help ensure Senate passage. Even so, in April 2013, it fell six votes short of the sixty required to overcome a filibuster.

Otherwise, policies dealing with the sale, possession, and use of firearms and ammunition vary by state. They cover licenses and permits, who can regulate firearms in the state (preemption by the state or allowed to localities, who can have more or less stringent policies than the state), stand your ground laws, bans on certain types of guns, and the number of rounds a magazine can hold. Also, the carrying in public of open (open carry) and concealed (closed carry) weapon. A few states (California, Colorado, Maryland, and New York) have enacted strict laws. Connecticut banned semi-automatic rifles, which the Supreme Court upheld in June 2016 when it refused to hear a challenge to the ban.

Mostly, state laws are less restrictive than those at the federal level. A conspicuous example is North Carolina, where in 2013 the Republican-controlled government decided to allow concealed guns in state parks and playgrounds, in places where a fee is charged for admission, inside bars and restaurants where alcoholic beverages are sold and consumed, and at parades and funerals. Establishment owners can post a notice that carrying a concealed handgun is prohibited on the premises, and the gun possessors are forbidden from consuming liquor while carrying. Concealed weapons can also be carried on college and school campuses, provided they are locked in vehicles.

## Searches and Seizures

The Fourth Amendment prevents the government from conducting "unreasonable searches and seizures." A reasonable search is conducted with a warrant issued by a judge and based on probable cause. What is "unreasonable" varies with how much privacy people can expect when they are being searched. Cars are less private than houses, so rules for searches of cars are less stringent. And government agencies can state reasons to compel persons not suspected of a crime to submit to searches and seizures. The goal of preventing airplanes from being hijacked authorizes mandatory searches of persons and their property before boarding aircraft and allows the confiscation of objects deemed dangerous.[42]

### Electronic Searches

New technologies complicate searches and seizures. In 1967, the Supreme Court ruled that the Fourth Amendment did not simply restrict physical entry: it "protects people, not places."[43] The pivotal test is whether a person has "a legitimate expectation of privacy" regardless of the technological means used to search. Thus, the Court has held that the use of heat-sensing devices able to find intensive marijuana farms inside closets requires a search warrant as much as would physical entry to one's house.[44]

In June 2014, the Supreme Court, in *Riley v. California*, ventured further into new technology by voting unanimously that police require a warrant before they can search the cell phones of people they arrest.[45] This decision may well apply to tablets, laptops, and such.[46] Then in 2018, the Supreme Court voted 5–4, with Chief Justice Roberts joining the liberal justices, to require the government (with limited exceptions) to obtain a warrant to collect cell phone (location) data (see *Carpenter v. United States*).

#### Links

***Riley v. California***

Click here to learn more about *Riley v. California*.

***Carpenter v. United States, No. 16-402***

Click here to learn more about *Carpenter v. United States*.

New technologies also intrude into formerly private domains hitherto more or less free from the potentially prying eye of government. Add to that the government's concern with combating terrorism and protecting Americans at home and abroad. Then add in the existence and expansion of the National Security Agency (NSA) and its congeries. All of which lead to the fear that the United States could become—might even be becoming—a surveillance state.

In May 2004, the Government Accountability Office (GAO) released a report on data mining. It documented fifty-two federal agencies conducting 122 projects to collect, analyze, and use identifiable information on U.S. persons for national security and law enforcement purposes. These numbers, which omit classified projects, are probably low-ball estimates.

## Electronic Eavesdropping

In December 2005, the *New York Times* revealed a secret executive order signed by President George W. Bush authorizing electronic eavesdropping on computerized and cell phone conversations without a warrant. The revelation, which the *Times* "under heavy administration pressure . . ." held for a year before publishing, had been leaked to the newspaper's reporters, the redoubtable James Risen and his colleague Eric Lichtblau, by a lawyer in the Justice Department.[47] President Bush claimed that the inherent powers of the president and Congress's authorization of force to respond to the 9/11 attacks allowed him to initiate this policy. (For fictional examples of warrantless wiretapping, see the Showtime drama *Homeland*).

In June 2013, Edward Snowden, a former contractor with the NSA, started to release to selected newspapers (notably, the *Washington Post* and the *Guardian* in England) a vast trove documenting the agency's collecting and searching the of telephone data (billions of phone calls) of Americans and non-Americans, data mining of online activity, of emails—virtually everything it wanted from the internet companies that people rely on to communicate.[48] The programs took place in the United States and worldwide. The Foreign Intelligence Surveillance Court (FISC), which had been created to require the NSA to obtain judicial permission to eavesdrop on Americans, had authorized the programs in 2006 and rejected hardly any (roughly ten) of the more than twenty thousand requests.

In January 2014, President Obama announced some limits on the government's surveillance programs.[49] He sought to put the records in private hands, not the government's. Meanwhile, analysts would be able to examine only records of people no more than two links removed from any telephone number which they had a reasonable and articulable suspicion of terrorism. And the NSA would have to obtain a court order ahead of time from a judge who agreed that the standard of suspicion had been met—with an exception for after-the-fact court review in a fast-moving exigency.

The president said he would ask the attorney general and the director of national intelligence to propose additional restrictions on the government's ability to retain, search, and use the communications of Americans incidentally collected without a warrant.

Gag orders restricting businesses from telling that they had received so-called national security letters (a kind of subpoena) to turn over customers' records would expire after a fixed period in most cases.

The president announced his intention of establishing a panel of advocates to represent privacy concerns before the Foreign Intelligence Surveillance Court (FISC). But it would only operate in novel and important cases. Nor, apparently, would the panel have the authority to monitor the court's caseload and independently decide when a case warranted its presence.[50]

Because the president did not announce that the government would cease taking data from Google, or stockpiling flaws from the Windows operating system, or not weaken encryption systems, observers assumed that the government would therefore continue to be able to use these and other techniques to conduct surveillance and cyber attacks.

Comparing these proposed reforms critically to the recommendations and reports of the Review Group on Intelligence and Communication appointed by the president after the Snowden revelations, and to a report of the Privacy and Civil Liberties Oversight Board, an independent watchdog created by Congress and appointed by the president, one observer called them "radically insufficient."[51]

Simply put, the president's decisions were unlikely to satisfy everybody (or even anybody). Tensions between people's privacy and fears of the intrusive power of the state on the one hand, and national security as defined and aimed for by the government on the other, would continue unabated.

Inevitably, the issue continues. In January 2015, the National Academy of Sciences (NAS) released a detailed study concluding "that there was no effective alternative to the government's 'bulk collection' of basic information about every telephone call made in the United States."[52] This does not mean that such collections must continue. And the study did conclude that ways of controlling and protecting the data could be improved.

### Link

**NAS Bulk Collection of Signals Intelligence: Technical Options Report**

Learn more about the National Academy of Sciences' Bulk Collection Report here.

Scholars have concluded that on balance over past decades the Supreme Court has favored law enforcement by, for example, allowing greater latitude for searches and seizures. Fears that have contributed to the Supreme Court's 5–4 decision, with Chief Justice Robert joining the liberal justices, to require the government (with limited exceptions such as bomb threats and child abductions) to obtain a warrant to collect cell phone (location) data.

## The Exclusionary Rule

The Fourth Amendment's **exclusionary rule** prevents evidence from an illegal search or seizure being introduced against a defendant in court. The Supreme Court adopted this rule for federal cases in 1914 and extended it to states in 1961.

**exclusionary rule**

Judicial rule applied to federal and state courts that prohibits the use of evidence in a trial when it is not legally obtained.

Law enforcement officers have long bridled at the exclusionary rule and claim that "technicalities" allow guilty suspects to be set free. The Supreme Court has permitted the use in trials of seized evidence that would have been "inevitably discovered" even without an unconstitutional search—such as that "in plain view"—or which police officers acquired under a search warrant that they did not know was improperly issued.[53]

# The Rights of the Accused

Collectively, the Fifth, Sixth and Seventh Amendments set forth procedural guarantees known as "rights of the accused," which exist through the criminal process from accusation to trial to conviction.

## Innocent until Proven Guilty

The central right of the accused is the presumption that anyone charged with a crime is innocent until proven guilty in court. This rule can be hard to preserve when an accused individual has been subjected to massive unfavorable media attention prior to or during a trial. For example, the police have perfected a technique known as the "perp walk" (for "perpetrator"), allowing television cameras to film the accused—often handcuffed and in prison garb—escorted by police. Such images, repeated over and over again in news broadcasts, can lead viewers to presume guilt rather than innocence.

## "Taking the Fifth"

**FIGURE 4.2**
**Oliver North's Swearing In at Congressional Hearing**
Congressional investigations that provide grants of immunity can complicate judicial proceedings. The conviction of Oliver North, a central figure in the arms-for-money Iran-Contra scandal of the 1980s, was overturned for that reason.

Source: J. Scott Applewhite / Associated Press

The Constitution's Fifth Amendment gives people the right to refuse to answer questions from any entity of government if they claim such responses might lead to criminal prosecution. Claiming this right not to incriminate oneself is popularly called "taking the fifth." Witnesses may be compelled to testify only if given immunity from prosecution.[54]

Such restrictions frustrate law enforcement officers, who find confessions among the best means to obtain a guilty verdict.

The right against self-incrimination originally meant only that individuals could not be forced to testify against themselves during their trials. In the 1920s, the Supreme Court threw out convictions for which evidence had been gained by torture or coercion and slowly expanded the right to cover all discussions with all law enforcement officials.

By 1966, the Court was weary of issuing case-by-case decisions about whether the police had gone too far in questioning suspects. In *Miranda v. Arizona* (384 US 436), the justices, having reviewed numerous police manuals, concluded that police often tried to create an atmosphere designed to intimidate or manipulate the accused into confessing. The justices ruled that law enforcement officials must "demonstrate the use of procedural safeguards" by ensuring that the accused is "adequately and effectively apprised of his rights." The Miranda decision required a warning to be read to suspects prior to interrogation—this warning is known as **Miranda rights**—without which their statements could not be admitted as evidence in court. Suspects must be notified of the following: that they have the right to remain silent, that whatever they say can be used against them in court, that they have the right to be represented by a lawyer before and during questioning, that they have the right to have a lawyer provided by the court if they cannot afford one, and that they have the right to terminate questioning at any time.

**Miranda rights**

List of rights that the police must tell suspects if their confessions are to be admitted as evidence in court.

These rights are familiar to anyone who has seen criminal detective movies or television shows.

But are they effective? Police officers view the reading of these rights as a mere technicality. They can get information by appealing to a suspect's desire to tell his or her story and by acting as if they are on the suspect's side. Even after suspects invoke Miranda rights, officers can try to change their minds or elicit what they term off-the-record information. Eighty percent of suspects voluntarily waive their rights; many confess.[55]

## Trial Procedures

Over time, Supreme Court decisions have outlined processes for a suspect to be tried in court. The most important are the following:

**double jeopardy**

The practice of putting someone on trial a second time for a crime after their acquittal; prohibited by the Fifth Amendment.

- Individuals cannot be subject to **double jeopardy**; in other words, they cannot be tried again for a crime after being acquitted of it in an earlier trial. This restriction does not prevent someone acquitted in a criminal case from being sued in a civil case: actor-athlete O. J. Simpson, found not guilty of the murder of his ex-wife and her friend, was found in civil court to be responsible and financially liable for their deaths.[56]
- Suspects must know and understand the charges and evidence against them; therefore, cases against those "incompetent to stand trial" for reasons of illness or insanity must be dismissed, and juvenile suspects cannot be tried as adults.

- The trial must be speedy, so that someone not yet proven guilty is not punished by lengthy incarceration before trial.
- Defendants for serious crimes (punishable by more than six months in prison or a $500 fine) and those in federal civil cases have a right to a trial by an "impartial jury" of their peers.
- Defendants have a right to face and confront witnesses against them.
- The accused has a right to a defense attorney. At first, this meant only that accused persons could pay for lawyers to represent them. But the 1932 case of seven young African American men sentenced in Scottsboro, Alabama, to die on a charge of raping two white women (a charge later found to be trumped up) persuaded the Supreme Court otherwise. The justices ruled that these defendants—poor, illiterate, and charged with a capital offense—had to be represented by a public defender, a defense attorney employed and paid by the state.[57]

This ruling gradually extended to all defendants in federal courts, then to felony defendants in state courts, and eventually to anyone facing any jail time.[58] But public defenders are underpaid and overworked. And their convicted clients can win on appeal only if they can show that public defenders made serious errors, depriving them of a fair trial.[59]

Moreover, most charges are resolved prior to trial when a defendant agrees to plead guilty to a lesser charge. They thereby avoid being charged with—and found guilty of—a more serious crime and receiving a more severe sentence, but they lose out on the many protections of trial procedures.

## The War on Terror

Civil liberties are often impaired during international crises. The "war on terrorism" is no exception. While the revelations in April 2004 of abuse and torture of Iraqi prisoners in the Abu Ghraib prison may be a matter more for international law than civil liberties, other rights of the accused were also in question after the terrorist attacks of 9/11.

In October 2001, Congress enacted the USA Patriot Act. Among other things, it authorized the attorney general to detain indefinitely a noncitizen when there are "reasonable grounds to believe" that the person is a threat to national security. Attorney General John Ashcroft praised these policies, observing, "It is difficult for a person in jail or under detention to murder innocent people or to aid or abet in terrorism."[60]

The Bush administration used these powers vigorously. Hundreds of resident aliens were detained without explanation in the fall of 2001, many in solitary confinement. When the Taliban government was overthrown in Afghanistan in late 2001, American forces captured some ten thousand soldiers and other Afghanis. Many of them were named "enemy combatants" (not "prisoners of war," who would have greater protection under international law). Shackled and hooded, they were shipped to a military prison at the base at Guantánamo Bay. Some were subjected to abusive interrogation. The base was located on land the United States had leased from Cuba in perpetuity, and thus, according to the Bush administration, it was outside the jurisdiction of the federal judiciary.[61]

Many rights of the accused were directly challenged by these policies: the right to know charges against oneself, the right to counsel, the right to a speedy and public trial, the right to a jury of one's peers, the right to confront adverse witnesses, and the ability to appeal decisions to a higher court.

In 2004, the Supreme Court upheld the president's power as commander in chief to name persons as enemy combatants, to hold them indefinitely under Congress's authorization of military force, and to fashion trial proceedings with less stringent standards of evidence. But due process required that a citizen held in the United States as an enemy combatant be given a meaningful opportunity to contest the detention's basis before a neutral decision maker. The Court also ruled that because the United States controlled Guantánamo, all detainees there had the habeas corpus right to go to federal court to challenge their detention.[62]

In response, the Bush administration began keeping detainees in a camp in Bagram, Afghanistan, in the theater of war, where judges could not go. And Congress passed the Military Commissions Act of 2006, removing the federal courts' jurisdiction to hear habeas corpus applications from detainees designated as enemy combatants. Then, in 2008, the Supreme Court, by 5–4, declared the Military Commissions Act unconstitutional, thereby giving back to enemy combatants their habeas corpus rights.[63] From 2008 to July 2010 federal judges found sufficient evidence to justify detention in nineteen of thirty-four cases. Then the federal appeals court required the judges to give a pro-government presumption in favor of U.S. intelligence reports. Afterward, only one of twelve appeals was successful.

# Punishment of Convicted Criminals

The Eighth Amendment also gives rights to people convicted of a crime. It aims to make the punishment fit the crime and to prohibit "cruel and unusual punishment." Policies affected by the Eighth Amendment include the length of prison sentences, prison conditions, and the death penalty.

## Prisons

Through the 1970s, prisoners were rarely expected to serve out their full sentences. Parole or "time off for good behavior" gave incentives to cooperate and acquire skills needed to reenter society. But media stories about crimes committed by paroled ex-cons impelled "truth-in-sentencing" laws—mandatory minimums or fixed sentences for given crimes.

States began adopting "three-strikes-and-you're-out" laws. These typically increase the sentence for a second felony conviction and require life in prison without parole for a third. These lengthy sentences often bear little connection to the gravity of the crimes committed.

Lengthy sentences, and the fact that over three-fourths of those put in state or federal prison each year commit nonviolent crimes, raise an Eighth Amendment question: does the punishment fit the crime?[64] In 2003 the Supreme Court decided that "three strikes" was not so "grossly disproportionate" as to violate restrictions on "cruel and unusual punishment."[65]

It is unclear to what extent the "cruel and unusual punishment" constitutional protection applies to the U.S. military and to time in detention before trial. Chelsea Manning (formerly Bradley Manning), the U.S. army intelligence analyst who conveyed over 700,000 classified documents to WikiLeaks, was held for nine months in solitary confinement in a military prison while awaiting trial on espionage and other charges.

The United States is the world leader in the proportion of the population that is incarcerated. When you include those on probation or parole, about 3.2 percent of adults live under the criminal justice system's direct supervision.[66]

When prison policies are reexamined, it is less for civil liberties than for their costs. States badly needed to cut expenses when the economic depression that started in 2007 slashed their tax receipts. They instituted sentencing alternatives to prison for first-time offenders, those seeking early parole, and prisoner-release programs.

Prisoners may organize to pursue common interests, such as seeking decent conditions in prison.[67] Inspired by 1960s civil rights movements, they claimed a denial of basic rights. Their perspectives were bolstered by Hollywood films of the 1960s and 1970s, such as *Birdman of Alcatraz*, *Cool Hand Luke*, and *One Flew Over the Cuckoo's Nest*, that vividly depicted inhumane conditions of involuntary confinement. Some inmates taught themselves to become lawyers and sued the prisons. Starting in the 1960s, the Supreme Court recognized prisoners' rights to bring suit and said the ban on "cruel and unusual punishment" included prison conditions. While harsh conditions may be part of a convict's penalty, prisoners cannot be subjected to "unnecessary and wanton" pain by the "deliberate indifference" of authorities.[68]

Reform arrived in December 2018 when President Trump signed the bipartisan criminal justice legislation, the federal First Step Act. Among its many provisions (intentions), it curbed inhuman practices in prison, reduced recidivism and reformed corrections, sentencing, and confinement. In particular, it shortened mandatory minimum sentences for nonviolent drug offenses and eased the federal three strikes rule. (See Chapter 16 Section 1 and the link to the First Step Act.)

## The Death Penalty

The death penalty is now reserved for the most serious of crimes: murder and treason. In 1972, the Supreme Court threw out all state laws imposing the death penalty as a violation of due process being arbitrarily applied from one case to the next. In 1976, the Court allowed states to impose capital punishment as long as it is decided on by a jury following a strict process, weighing mitigating and aggravating circumstances to decide if death is the most appropriate punishment.[69] After 1976, thirty-eight states reinstated the death penalty, which by then was endorsed by a strong majority of the public.

The main objection to the death penalty today is that it cannot be applied dependably enough to meet the Bill of Rights's standards for due process. Death sentences vary greatly based on the race of the convicted murderer and that of the murder victim; Black people convicted of murdering a white person are far more likely to receive a death sentence than are Black people convicted of murdering a Black person (see the following "Comparing Content" for more information). Arguably, executing the death penalty itself is a cruel and unusual punishment.

### Comparing Content

#### Victims and Capital Punishment

Victims are everywhere in the media. But who gets to play the part? For some investigative journalists, the answer is innocent death row inmates. Building on evidence dug up by journalism professor David Protess and his students at Northwestern University, reporters for the *Chicago Tribune* compiled two devastating series about prisoners sentenced to die on faulty evidence—"Trial and Error" and "The Failure of the Death Penalty in Illinois." The first story in the series began by listing accusations against prosecutors: "They have prosecuted Black men, hiding evidence the real killers were white. They have prosecuted a wife, hiding evidence her husband committed suicide. . . . They do it to win. They do it because they won't get punished."[70]

Evidence of mistaken convictions led Illinois Governor George Ryan to declare a moratorium on capital punishment and, just before leaving office in 2003, to commute all death penalties to life in prison without parole. Days later, Ryan went on *Oprah*. The show's host, Oprah Winfrey, aired two episodes she termed "our show with the governor who emptied death row." Before the broadcast, Winfrey videotaped interviews with surviving relatives of those whose murderers had been spared the death penalty. She confronted Ryan with this video testimony of survivors describing the gruesome crimes and their sense of betrayal.

For investigative journalism, the victims are wrongfully convicted death row inmates, whose wrongful convictions justify a halt to the death penalty so that the state does not put innocent people to death. This focus on the exoneration of the wrongfully convicted, sometimes by dramatic revelations of exculpatory DNA evidence, shifts the media's frame away from the victims of crime to the victims of prosecution, and may thereby shift public opinion. But for the daytime talk show, the victims are survivors of violent crime who rely on the justice system to give them what Winfrey called "closure." The future of capital punishment may depend on which frame wins.

# Property Rights and Eminent Domain

**takings clause**

Section of the Fifth Amendment that bars government from taking private property for public use without "just compensation."

**eminent domain**

Government's power to take private land for public use.

The Fifth Amendment includes a **takings clause**: government must provide "just compensation" (usually market value) when it uses its power of **eminent domain** to take property for public use, or if government action removes "all the purposes for which it was acquired."[71]

Some civil liberty advocates propose expanding this right to limit government regulation. They echo Chief Justice Rehnquist, who wrote, "We see no reason why the Takings Clause of the Fifth Amendment, as much a part of the Bill of Rights as the First Amendment or Fourth Amendment, should be relegated to the status of a poor relation."[72] Corporations and business associations have funded probusiness legal centers that argue that *any* regulation restricting a property's value or use is a "taking" requiring compensation. This approach would throw out such land-use policies as zoning, rent control, wetland conservation laws, and regulations like the Endangered Species Act.[73]

The Supreme Court has resisted putting property rights front and center. The justices ruled in 2005 against a homeowner who contested the city's plan to replace her economically depressed neighborhood with an office park, hotel, and conference center. They said that governments have broad discretion to take property for "public use" as long as it is put to a "public purpose," including economic development, even when the land is transferred to other private owners.[74] In reaction, several states began to limit the uses of eminent domain.

# Right to Privacy

A right to privacy is nowhere explicitly named in the Bill of Rights. However, some members of the Supreme Court recognized the right in a 1965 case. They overturned the conviction of executives of Connecticut's Planned Parenthood for violating a state law that banned advising married couples about the use of birth control and prescribing contraceptives. One justice found privacy implicit in the First, Third, Fourth, and Fifth Amendments. Other justices found it in the Ninth Amendment's reminder that the Bill of Rights does not exhaust the sum total of liberties.[75] The right could be applied to the states through the due process clause of the Fourteenth Amendment.

## *Roe v. Wade* and Abortion Rights

In this 1973 decision, the Supreme Court, invoking privacy, recognized a woman's constitutional right to an abortion in the first three months of a pregnancy.[76] Whether to have an abortion was seen as a private decision between a woman and her doctor. Before and since then, a debate has raged between two sides calling themselves "pro-choice" and "pro-life"—a debate and a divide exaggerated by the news media's preference for vivid conflicts.

**Link**

**Oral Arguments in *Roe v. Wade***

Click here to listen to oral arguments in *Roe v. Wade*.

The *Roe* decision mobilized a pro-life movement. Members of Congress sought but failed to obtain the two-thirds majorities necessary for a constitutional amendment declaring that life begins with conception, thereby recognizing the fetus as a "person" able to receive the protection of the Bill of Rights. President Reagan, elected in 1980, also pushed to reverse *Roe*. States tried to test

*Roe*'s boundaries. The Court initially rejected such efforts as requiring the written consent of the woman's spouse or her parents, demanding that abortions be performed in a hospital, or enforcing twenty-four-hour waiting periods.

By the end of the 1980s—President Reagan having named new justices to the Supreme Court—the original majority for *Roe* had eroded. In 1989, the Court limited abortion rights by ruling that the state's interest in the fetus begins at conception, not viability; states could now regulate abortions in the first trimester.[77]

## *Roe* Reaffirmed

When pro-life president George H. W. Bush named David Souter and Clarence Thomas to replace retiring pro-choice justices William Brennan and Thurgood Marshall, *Roe* seemed doomed. In 1992, the justices considered a Pennsylvania law that required a married woman's husband to be notified before she could have an abortion and a twenty-four-hour waiting period for a woman to be provided with information about risks and consequences of abortion. But Justice Anthony Kennedy, allying with Souter and Sandra Day O'Connor (a Reagan appointee), jointly wrote an opinion. They declined to overturn *Roe*'s central tenet that a woman had a right to an abortion prior to the ability of the fetus to live outside the womb. But they scrapped the trimester scheme of *Roe* and put in a new (if less clear) test of whether a law imposes an "undue burden" on a woman's right to an abortion. The decision supported most of the restrictions Pennsylvania had placed on abortion. It fit public opinion that was against reversing *Roe v. Wade* but in support of conditions and exceptions.[78]

**FIGURE 4.3 *Roe v. Wade* Anniversary**

The justices of the Supreme Court presumably did not realize when they issued the *Roe v. Wade* decision on January 22, 1973, that its anniversary would be marked by demonstrations by opponents and counterdemonstrations of proponents in front of their building.

Source: Rena Schild / Shutterstock.com

## D&X or Partial-Birth Abortion?

With the Court's reaffirmation of *Roe*, the pro-life movement was on the defensive—until it began focusing on an unusual abortion procedure known technically as "dilate and extract" (D&X). Giving it the unsettling term "partial-birth abortion" and recounting dramatic examples of its use late in a pregnancy, the pro-life side refocused the attention of the media on the fetus and away from the pro-choice emphasis on a woman's right to decide (with her physician) on abortion without government interference.

In 2003, Congress passed—and President George W. Bush signed—a law banning partial-birth abortion. The law allowed an exception to save the lives of women but no exception for their health. It was the first time since *Roe* that federal law criminalized an abortion procedure. With President George W. Bush's two appointees voting in the majority, the Supreme Court upheld the law by a vote of 5–4 in April 2007.[79]

In recent years, pro-life politicians and interest groups have turned increasingly to the states to pass and implement various policies making it more difficult for women to have abortions. These policies include prohibiting abortion after fetal viability except to preserve the woman's life or health, confining abortions to hospitals, imposing restrictions on abortion clinics, requiring a waiting period and requiring women to undergo counseling (e.g., about the alleged link between abortion and breast cancer), and disallowing the use of state funds to pay for an abortion, making it virtually impossible for a woman to obtain an abortion in much of the country.

In June 2016, the Supreme Court voted 5–3 to overturn a Texas law (and thus similar laws in other states) requiring abortion providers to have staff privileges at a hospital within thirty miles of the clinic and for the clinics to meet expensive hospital building and equipment standards. The majority ruled that Texas had failed to justify its argument that these measures would result in better treatment but rather created an undue burden for women seeking an abortion.[80] The law would have drastically reduced the number of abortion clinics in the state. Then, in June 2020, the Court by a vote of 5–4 struck down a Louisiana law similar to the Texas one. Concurring, the Chief Justice made up the crucial fifth vote majority, but only to acknowledge the precedent of the Texas case—a case that he wrote had been "wrongly decided."[81]

Now, several states have taken the draconian step of banning abortion at the first sign of a fetal heartbeat. Others are expected to follow. That is, if the Supreme Court does not first overturn or nullify *Roe v. Wade*.

In movies and television series, in contrast to restrictions in the states, discussions of abortions and actual abortions without regrets are increasing everyday.[82]

## Personal Privacy

Finally, there is the issue of what we call "personal privacy." That is privacy as a protection against the domination of business and commerce. This is the "powers of Google, Facebook, website owners, and internet service providers to collect, analyze, and sell data about (y)our most private, thoughts, desires, associates, and communications."[83] We volunteer some of this information (i.e., from posts), but much of it comes from data brokers who collect information from warranties, pharmacy records, and pay stubs, as well as from public data sets. On top of that there's the bedeviling issue of the failure of cybersecurity against fraud and theft.

We should not rely on government to protect us against these threats to our privacy—quite the reverse. On March 27, 2017, the Republican-controlled House of Representatives joined the Senate in voting to "undo rules that keep internet service providers—the companies like Comcast, Verizon and Charter that you pay for online access—from selling your personal information."[84]

But federalism can come to the rescue. As of 2020, the California Consumer Privacy Act grants residents of the state various rights over their personal information, such as the right

- to access personal data many companies have compiled on them;
- to know about employee data;
- to delete personal data; and
- of parents regarding their children's data.

## Key Takeaways

This section covered rights dealing with arms, searches and seizures, the accused, punishment, property, and privacy. The Supreme Court has interpreted the Second Amendment as allowing people to bear arms. Freedom from unreasonable searches and seizures is being infringed by the development of new technologies and the government's concern to preserve national security. Rights of the accused include the right to be considered innocent until proven guilty, protection against self-incrimination, the Miranda rights, and trial processes. Some policies initiated by the government's war on terror have challenged these rights. The rights of convicted criminals apply to punishment, prison terms, and the death penalty. Property rights can conflict with the government's power of eminent domain. Abortion is subject to Supreme Court decisions, political conflict, and policies at the national and state levels. A burgeoning issue is personal privacy.

## Exercises

1. What rationale does the Second Amendment give for protecting the right to bear arms? What are some different ways this rationale could be interpreted?
2. How have new technologies made it difficult to determine what constitutes an unreasonable search and seizure? What information about you do you think the government should have access to?
3. What are the arguments for and against the death penalty? On what grounds do some people argue that the death penalty infringes on the rights of the accused?
4. Do you think people should have a basic right to privacy? In your opinion, does any part of the Bill of Rights seem to guarantee a right to privacy?

# 4.5 Civil Liberties in the Information Age

## Learning Objectives

After reading this section, you should be able to answer the following questions:

1. Which civil liberty is vital to media operations, and why?
2. Why are civil liberties vulnerable to media frames?
3. Why is the media's depiction of civil liberties ambivalent?

"Liberty" is a word with special resonance in the United States. It is hailed in the Pledge of Allegiance. It is featured in the lyrics of patriotic songs. It is emblazoned on coins. The Liberty Bell and the Statue of Liberty are among the most central symbols of the promise of the United States.

News and entertainment often pay homage to the value of civil liberties. Indeed, the media, like the American people as a whole, are strongly committed in principle to civil liberties, especially when presented as elements of the hallowed Bill of Rights. Yet, the media often slight, even undermine, specific civil liberties.

# Media Interactions

Media personnel find civil liberties to be a vital topic because they hold fast to freedom of expression as a crucial protection to perform their jobs. Also, the frame of the virtuous individual standing up for beloved principles against the government and depredatory corporations is easily presentable as a defense of civil liberties.

The rights of the accused are the kernel of many a media story. For instance, dramas from the vantage point of a person wrongly accused by officials of a crime are perennial favorites in films and television. The television drama *Perry Mason* compiled 271 episodes from 1957 to 1966, and they are endlessly rerun. Each episode is similar: the brilliant lawyer Perry Mason defends his client in court against a rush to judgment by the district attorney and police and, in a climactic cross-examination, unveils the true guilty party. For a more contemporary example of a portrayal of the wrongly accused there is the book and film *Gone Girl*. Its subjects include media coverage of disappearance, missing persons community outreach, and televised interviews with the accused.

Nowadays, the media feature crime control. Witness the television show *Law and Order* and its various spin-offs: these shows are presented from the perspectives of police and prosecutors, not civil liberties. Or consider crime in the news: its good-guys-versus-bad-guys dynamic makes it easy to crank out accounts of crime on a day-in-day-out (or hour-in-hour-out) basis. These stories are reported almost entirely from sources in police stations and courts. Crime beat reporters call up police spokespersons every day and ask, "What have you got?" Police officers are happy to direct reporters to newsworthy events and quick, reliable information. By one estimate, newspapers report nine crime stories a day; local television news brings viewers four a day. Because reporters rely so heavily on police for information, police misconduct, including violations of civil liberties, usually get less attention, although there are exceptions such as police corruption, abuses, and violence.[85]

**sphere of consensus**

General agreement about the causes of and how to respond to a crisis.

Similarly, war or other national security crises rarely invite critical media coverage, particularly in the early phases when the media act within a **sphere of consensus**: a general agreement about the causes of and how to respond to a crisis. The media, already suspected by many of left-leaning bias, are sensitive to accusations of being unpatriotic and are attracted to the saga of the United States unified against its demonized enemies. As a result, the government's voice is usually enhanced, and dissenters' voices are muffled, making it easier for the government to advance restrictions on civil liberties in the name of national security.

In the first months after 9/11 officials and reporters began to ask if the failure to predict the terrorist attacks was occasioned by legal restrictions on cooperation between the Federal Bureau of Investigation (FBI) and the Central Intelligence Agency (CIA). These laws had been set in place to protect civil liberties and discourage the government from spying on its own citizens. Such concerns were eclipsed when the news media referred positively to legislation to lift those restrictions as "laws to make it easier for the FBI to gather information."

The media may be distracted away from civil liberties—and downplay their importance—for one other reason. Asserting civil liberties is often the way unpopular minorities struggle against being repressed or silenced in a majority-rule political system. But such outsiders have trouble getting their concerns into the news on their own terms, particularly if they are opposed to the government. They often have no choice except to make theatrical efforts to attract the news media's appetite for dramatic conflict, such as demonstrating against or disrupting official events. This behavior makes it hard for them to use the media to claim the civil liberty protections that are vital to their survival.

# Media Consequences

The mass media's choice of frames between law and order and civil liberties has powerful consequences. In one study, people were presented with different frames for a Ku Klux Klan march. When the news story framed the event as a threat to law and order, people gave high priority to the importance of order and low support for the application of civil liberties, the reverse of those who viewed a news story framing the march as an instance of freedom of expression.[86] And recent research contends that news coverage of the threat of terrorism "seems to have contributed to public acceptance of the erosion of civil liberties."[87]

Such ambivalence is not unique to the mass media. All the institutions, processes, and participants in American politics display a strong commitment to civil liberties alongside a willingness to submerge that commitment when other commitments (especially the maintenance of law and order) become more prominent—unless the issue is reframed, notably through media presentations, as one of civil liberties.

That said, the primary advocates and the main beneficiaries of civil liberties are not always—in fact, not often—the downtrodden and the underdog. Powerful political forces use the leverage of civil liberties to win battles and gain yet more power. The freedoms of the Bill of Rights are not simply dusty statements of long-held principle. Nor are they simply obligations for government to protect the vulnerable. Instead, the words of the Bill of Rights are *tools* used in politics by all—and all kinds of—political players.[88]

## Key Takeaways

In this section, we saw that the media are ambivalent about civil liberties, much like the American public and the participants in American government, as their focus on civil liberties is in tension with at least equally strong concerns about crime and the need for law and order. American politics, powerfully buttressed by the media, is thus equivocal toward civil liberties, valued in principle but often submerged by other, seemingly more pressing, concerns.

## Exercises

1. How do the television programs and movies you have seen about the legal system treat the issue of civil liberties? Who are the heroes of these shows, and what are they fighting for?
2. To what extent do you think there is a trade-off between civil liberties and law and order? To what extent is it possible to protect individual rights and maintain civil order at the same time?

# 4.6 Recommended Reading

Amar, Akhil Reed. *The Bill of Rights*. New Haven, CT: Yale University Press, 1998. An ambitious, innovative vision of the Bill of Rights as a unified entity.

Cook, Timothy E., ed. *Freeing the Presses: The First Amendment in Action*. Baton Rouge: Louisiana State University Press, 2005. A collection of essays by scholars looking at freedom of the press in theory and practice.

Donziger, Steven R. *The Real War on Crime: The Report of the National Criminal Justice Commission*. New York: Harper Collins, 1996. A national commission's eye-opening report on the looming disconnect between crime rates and punitive public policies.

Luker, Kristin. *Abortion and the Politics of Motherhood*. Berkeley: University of California Press, 1984. A discussion and analysis of pro-life and pro-choice politics.

Rapping, Elayne. *Law and Justice as Seen on TV*. New York: New York University Press, 2003. A thought-provoking analysis of the spate of "law and order" programming.

Waldron, Jeremy. *The Harm in Hate Speech*. Cambridge, Mass.: Harvard University Press, 2012.

White, Welsh S. *Miranda's Waning Protections: Police Interrogation Practices after Dickerson*. Ann Arbor: University of Michigan Press, 2001. A discerning account of the legacy of the *Miranda* case in theory and in practice.

Ziegler, Mary. *Beyond Abortion: Roe v. Wade and the Battle for Privacy*. Cambridge, Mass: Harvard University Press, 2018. Thoughtful discussion of abortion in the context of privacy.

# 4.7 Recommended Viewing

*Bowling for Columbine* (2002). Michael Moore's quirky documentary on the United States' "gun culture."

*Citizenfour* (2014). In Laura Poitras's documentary, Edward Snowden explains why he released to selected newspapers hordes of information about the NSA's spying on the communications of Americans and non-Americans.

*Cool Hand Luke* (1967). A convict (Paul Newman) becomes a hero to fellow inmates by resisting cruel prison authorities.

*Dead Man Walking* (1995). Film of Sister Helen Prejean's memoir of her ethical, emotional, and spiritual conflicts in counseling a racist (Sean Penn) on death row.

*The Farm* (1998). Absorbing documentary of six inmates in the maximum-security Louisiana State Penitentiary at Angola.

*German Concentration Camps Factual Survey*, Special Archival Edition, British Film Institute and Imperial War Museums. Initial documentary record of the horrific slaughter of the Holocaust when civil liberties were destroyed.

*Gideon's Trumpet* (1980). TV version of Anthony Lewis's book about Clarence Gideon (Henry Fonda), the indigent who went to the Supreme Court to force the state to provide him with a lawyer.

*Inherit the Wind* (1960). A dramatization of the Scopes trial over teaching evolution in public schools.

*Minority Report* (2002). In a future world, where technology allows police to arrest people before they commit crimes, wrongly accused cop (Tom Cruise) fights to save his name.

*The Post* (2017). Steven Spielberg's lightly fictionalized version, featuring publisher Kay Graham (played by Meryl Streep), of the U.S. Supreme Court's "Pentagon Papers" (free speech) decision. Note that while the *New York Times* published portions of the Papers, the more cautious *Washington Post* published articles about the Papers.

*School Prayer* (1999). Riveting documentary about a Mississippi mother who sues her local school district to remove prayer and Bible classes—and about the outrage that ensues.

*The Thin Blue Line* (1988). Errol Morris's film, combining documentary and fictional techniques, investigates the murder of a Dallas police officer and results in freeing an innocent man who had been convicted of the crime.

*United States of Secrets* (2014). Two revealing PBS Frontline documentaries about NSA spying. Part 1 "The Program" and Part 2 "Privacy Lost."

# Endnotes


1. Quoted in Aaron Doyle, "'Cops': Television Policing as Policing Reality," in *Entertaining Crime: Television Reality Programs*, ed. Mark Fishman and Gray Cavender (New York: Aldine de Gruyter, 1998), 95–116, quote at 101.
2. This section draws on Robert A. Goldwin, *From Parchment to Power* (Washington, DC: American Enterprise Institute, 1997).
3. This theme is developed in Michael Kent Curtis, *Free Speech, "The People's Darling Privilege": Struggles for Freedom of Expression in American History* (Durham, NC: Duke University Press, 2000).
4. See James Morton Smith, *Freedom's Fetters: The Alien and Sedition Laws and American Civil Liberties* (Ithaca, NY: Cornell University Press, 1956). For how the reaction to the Sedition Act produced a broader understanding of freedom of the press than the Bill of Rights intended, see Leonard W. Levy, *Emergence of a Free Press* (New York: Oxford University Press, 1985).
5. Michael Kent Curtis, *Free Speech, "The People's Darling Privilege": Struggles for Freedom of Expression in American History* (Durham, NC: Duke University Press, 2000), especially chaps. 6–8, quote at 189.
6. Anthony Lewis, *Gideon's Trumpet* (New York: Vintage Books, 1964); the case is *Gideon v. Wainwright* 372 U.S. 335 (1963).
7. Richard Davis, *Decisions and Images: The Supreme Court and the News Media* (Englewood Cliffs, NJ: Prentice-Hall, 1994).
8. Frederick Schauer, "The Political Incidence of the Free Speech Principle," *University of Colorado Law Review* 64 (1993): 935–57.
9. *Lemon v. Kurtzman*, 403 US 602 (1971).
10. Respectively, *Engel v. Vitale*, 370 US 421 (1962); *Abington School District v. Schempp*, 374 US 203 (1963); *Wallace v. Jaffree*, 472 US 38 (1985); *Lee v. Weisman*, 507 US 577 (1992); and *Santa Fe Independent School District v. Doe*, 530 US 290 (2000).
11. *March v. Chambers*, 463 U.S. 783 (1983).
12. *Town of Greece v. Galloway*, No. 12-696.
13. *Espinoza v. Montana Department of Revenue*, 591 U.S.______(2020).
14. Adam Liptak, "Court, 7-2, Allows Religious Opt-Out On Birth Control," *The New York Times*, July 9, 2020, A1 (17).
15. *Burwell v. Hobby Lobby Stores*, 573 US __ (2014) Docket No.13-354.
16. This paragraph is based on Paul Horowitz, "Hobby Lobby Is Only the Beginning," *The New York Times*, July 2, 2014, A23.
17. *New York Times v. Sullivan*, 376 US 254 (1964).
18. *United States v. O'Brien*, 391 US 367 (1968); and *Tinker v. Des Moines Independent Community School District*, 393 US 503 (1969).
19. *New York Times v. Sullivan*, 376 US 254 (1964).
20. The key cases here are *Roth v. United States*, 354 US 476 (1957); *Stanley v. Georgia*, 394 US 557 (1969); and *Miller v. California*, 413 US 15 (1973).
21. Respectively, *Schenck v. United States*, 249 US 47 (1919); *Dennis v. United States*, 341 US 494 (1951); and *Brandenburg v. Ohio*, 395 US 444 (1969).
22. James B. Jacobs and Kimberly Potter, *Hate Crimes: Criminal Law and Identity Politics* (New York: Oxford University Press, 1998), 112–21.
23. *Near v. Minnesota*, 283 US 697 (1931); and *New York Times v. United States*, 403 US 713 (1971).
24. Herbert N. Foerstel, *Freedom of Information and the Right to Know: The Origins and Applications of the Freedom of Information Act* (Westport, CT: Greenwood Press, 1999).
25. Cited in Adam Liptak, "Supreme Court Rejects Appeal From Times Reporter Over Refusal to Identify Source," *The New York Times*, June 2, 2014, A1.
26. *Branzburg v. Hayes*, 408 U.S. 665 (1972),
27. *State of War: Secret History of the CIA and the Bush Administration* (New York: Simon & Schuster, 2006).
28. Matt Apuzzo, "Holder Fortifies Protection of News Media's Phone Records, Notes or Emails," *The New York Times*, January 15, 2015, A16.
29. *Red Lion Broadcasting Company v. Federal Communication Commission*, 395 US 367 (1969) and *Turner Broadcasting System, Inc. et al. v. Federal Communication Commission*, 520 US 180 (1997).
30. See Susan Zaeske, *Signatures of Citizenship: Petitioning, Antislavery, and Women's Political Identity* (Chapel Hill: University of North Carolina Press, 2003), and Linda J. Lumsden, *Rampant Women: Suffragists and the Right of Assembly* (Knoxville: University of Tennessee Press, 1997).
31. Sue Schuurman, "Kent State Killings Shock Nation: 28 Years Ago This Week," *Weekly Alibi*, May 11, 1998, http://weeklywire.com/ww/05-11-98/alibi_skeleton.html.
32. Writings on Kent State, particularly in the immediate aftermath of the shooting, are highly politicized, with government commissions' reports being dismissed as cover-ups of conspiracies. A balanced assessment of the literature is Thomas R. Hensley and Jerry M. Lewis, eds., *Kent State and May 4th: A Social Science Perspective* (Dubuque, IA: Kendall/Hunt, 1978).
33. Quoted in Sue Schuurman, "Kent State Killings Shock Nation: 28 Years Ago This Week," *Weekly Alibi*, May 11, 1998, http://weeklywire.com/ww/05-11-98/alibi_skeleton.html.
34. See the Gallup Poll from *Newsweek*, May 25, 1970, 30, cited in James J. Best, "Kent State: Answers and Questions," in *Kent State and May 4th: A Social Science Perspective*, ed. Thomas R. Hensley and Jerry M. Lewis (Dubuque, IA: Kendall/Hunt, 1978), 25.
35. *New York Post*, October 3, 1973, as reported in J. Gregory Payne, "Aftermath," May4Archive.org, http://www.may4archive.org/aftermath.shtml.
36. Joyce Lee Malcolm, *To Keep and Bear Arms: The Origins of an Anglo-American Right* (Cambridge, MA: Harvard University Press, 1994).
37. H. Richard Uviller and William G. Merkel, *The Militia and the Right to Arms, Or, How the Second Amendment Fell Silent* (Durham, NC: Duke University Press, 2002).
38. For these data, my summary of the fate of the control legislation proposed by President Obama, and an illuminating discussion of gun control in America, see David Cole, "Facing the Real Gun Problem," *New York Review*, June 20, 2013, 12–16.
39. Robert J. Spitzer, *The Politics of Gun Control* (Chatham, NJ: Chatham House, 1995), 168.
40. *District of Columbia v. Heller*, 554 US 570 (2008).
41. *McDonald v. Chicago*, 561 US ___, 130 S.Ct. 3020 (2010).
42. Michael Gizzi and Craig Curtis, *The Fourth Amendment in Flux: The Roberts Court, Crime Control, and Digijtal Privacy* (Lawrence: University Press of Kansas, 2017).
43. *Olmstead v. United States*, 277 US 438 (1928) and *Katz v. United States*, 389 US 347 (1967).
44. *Kyllo v. US*, 533 US 27 (2001).
45. *Riley v. California*, 573 U.S. __ (2014) Docket No. 13-132.
46. Adam Liptak, "Justices, 9-0, Rule Cellphone Search Needs a Warrant," *The New York Times*, June 26, 2014, A1,17.
47. Mark Danner, "He Remade Our World," *New York Review of Books*, April 3, 2014, 80; see also James Risen, *Pay Any Price: Greed, Power, and Endless War* (New York: Houghton Mifflin Harcourt, 2014).
48. See Laura Poitras's documentary *Citizenfour* about Edward Snowden; also Glenn Greenwald, *No Place to Hide: Edward Snowden, the NSA, and the US Surveillance State* (New York: Metropolitan Books, 2014).
49. Remarks by the President on Review of Signals Intelligence, January 17th, 2014, available at www.whitehouse.gov; also Mark Landler and Charlie Savage, "Keeping Wide Net, Obama Sets Limits on Phone Spying," *The New York Times*, January 18th, 2014, A1, A6; the summary of the president's statement is quoted from A6.
50. David Cole, "Can Privacy Be Saved?" *New York Review of Books*, March 6, 2014, 23; also, "Liberty and Security in a Changing World" *Report and Recommendations of the President's Review Group on Intelligence and Communications Technologies*, December 12, 2013, www.whitehouse.gov; and "Report on the Telephone Records Program Conducted under Section 215 of the USA PATRIOT Act and on the Operations of the Foreign Intelligence Surveillance Court," *Privacy and Civil Liberties Oversight Board*, January 23, 2014.
51. David Cole, "Can Privacy Be Saved?" *New York Review of Books,* March 6, 2014, 23; also, "Liberty and Security in a Changing World" Report and Recommendations of the President's Review Group on Intelligence and Communications Technologies, December 12, 2013, www.whitehouse.gov; and "Report on the Telephone Records Program Conducted under Section 215 of the USA PATRIOT Act and on the Operations of the Foreign Intelligence Surveillance Court," Privacy and Civil Liberties Oversight Board, January 23, 2014.
52. David E. Sanger, "Report Finds No Substitute For Mass Data Collection," *The New York Times*, January 16, 2015, A23.
53. The cases that established the exclusionary rule are *Weeks v. United States*, 232 US 383 (1914) and *Mapp v. Ohio*, 367 US 643 (1961). See, more recently, *Nix v. Williams*, 467 US 431 (1984); *United States v. Leon*, 468 US 897 (1984); and *Massachusetts v. Sheppard*, 468 US 981 (1984).
54. *Quinn v. United States*, 349 US 155 (1955); *Emspak v. United States*, 349 US 190 (1955) and *Ullman v. United States*, 350 US 422 (1956).
55. Welsh S. White, *Miranda's Waning Protections: Police Interrogation Practices after Dickerson* (Ann Arbor: University of Michigan Press, 2001), especially chap. 7.

56. *Powell v. Alabama* 287 U.S. (1932).
57. *Powell v. Alabama* 287 U.S. 45 (1932).
58. *Johnson v. Zerbst*, 304 US 458 (1938); *Gideon v. Wainwright*, 372 US 335 (1963) and *Argersinger v. Hamlin*, 407 US 25 (1972).
59. *United States v. Cronic*, 466 US 648 (1984) and *Strickland v. Washington*, 466 US 668 (1984).
60. Quoted in Matthew Purdy, "Bush's New Rules to Fight Terror Transform the Legal Landscape," *The New York Times*, November 25, 2001, B4.
61. For a detailed history of abuses in the war on terror, see Jane Mayer, *The Dark Side: The Inside Story of How the War on Terror Turned into a War on American Ideals* (New York: Doubleday, 2008); and for a critique of the trade-off between liberty and security see David Cole and Jules Lobel, *Less Safe, Less Free: Why America Is Losing the War on Terror* (New York: New Press, 2007).
62. *Hamdi v. Rumsfeld*, 542 US 507 (2004) and *Rasul et al. v. Bush, President of the United States, et al.*, 542 US 466 (2004).
63. *Boumediene et al. v. Bush, President of the United States, et al.* (Nos. 06-1195 and 06-1196), 476 F. 3d 1981 (2008).
64. Steven R. Donziger, ed., *The Real War on Crime: The Report of the National Criminal Justice Commission* (New York: Harper Collins, 1996), chap. 1.
65. *Ewing v. California*, 538 US 11 (2003) and *Lockyer v. Andrade*, 538 US 63 (2003). The basis for "proportionality" as an Eighth Amendment test is *Solem v. Helm*, 462 US 277 (1983).
66. Steven R. Donziger, ed., *The Real War on Crime: The Report of the National Criminal Justice Commission* (New York: Harper Collins, 1996), 34; Fox Butterfield, "U.S. 'Correctional Population' Hits New High," *The New York Times*, July 26, 2004, A10.
67. Ronald Berkman, *Opening the Gates: The Rise of the Prisoners' Movement* (Lexington, MA: D. C. Heath, 1979).
68. *Cooper v. Pate*, 378 US 546 (1964); *Estelle v. Gamble*, 429 US 97 (1976); *Wilson v. Seiter*, 501 US 299 (1991) and *Lewis v. Casey*, 516 US 804 (1996).
69. *Furman v. Georgia*, 408 US 238 (1972); *Gregg v. Georgia*, 428 US 153 (1976); *Woodson v. North Carolina*, 428 US 280 (1976).
70. Ken Armstrong and Maurice Possley, "Trial and Error, Part 1: Verdict: Dishonor," *Chicago Tribune*, January 10, 1999.
71. This statement comes from *Duquesne Light Company v. Barasch*, 488 US 299 (1989).
72. *Dolan v. City of Tigard*, 512 US 374 at 392 (1994).
73. For an effective statement of this position, see Richard Epstein, *Takings: Private Property and the Power of Eminent Domain* (Cambridge, MA: Harvard University Press, 1985).
74. *Kelo v. New London*, 545 US 469 (2005).
75. *Griswold v. Connecticut*, 381 US 479 (1965).
76. *Roe v. Wade*, 410 US 113 (1973).
77. *Webster v. Reproductive Health Services*, 492 US 490 (1989).
78. *Planned Parenthood of Southeastern Pennsylvania v. Casey*, 505 US 833 (1992).
79. *Gonzales v. Carhart* and *Gonzales v. Planned Parent Federation of America*, 550 US 124 (2007).
80. *Whole Women's Health v. Hellerstedt*, 579 U.S.___2016.
81. *June Medical Services, LLC v.Russo*, 591 U.S.____(2020).
82. Cara Buckley, "The New Normal Onscreen: Matter-of-Fact Abortions," *The New York Times*, July 22, 2019, C1 (8).
83. David Cole, "The New America: Little Privacy, Big Terror," *The New York Review*, August 18, 2015, 18.
84. Tom Wheeler, "The G.O.P. Just Sold Your Privacy," *The New York Times*, March 29, 2017, A27; Wheeler, a Democratic appointee, had been the Chairman of the Federal Communications Commission (FCC) that instituted the rule.
85. See the ethnographic research of Steven M. Chermak in his book *Victims in the News: Crime and the American News Media* (Boulder, CO: Westview Press, 1995), especially chap. 2.
86. Thomas E. Nelson, Rosalee A. Clawson, and Zoe M. Oxley, "Media Framing of a Civil Liberties Conflict and Its Effect on Tolerance," *American Political Science Review* 91 (1997): 567–83; also George E. Marcus, John L. Sullivan, Elizabeth Theiss-Morse, and Sandra L. Wood, *With Malice toward Some: How People Make Civil Liberties Judgments* (New York: Cambridge University Press, 1995).
87. Douglas M. McLeod and Dhavan V. Shah, *News Frames and National Security: Covering Big Brother* (New York: Cambridge University Press, 2015), 3.
88. See Wayne Batchis, *The Right's First Amendment: The Politics of Free Speech & the Return of Conservative Libertarianism* (Stanford: Stanford University Press, 2016), for the argument that conservatives have adopted and co-opted constitutional free speech rights.

CHAPTER 5

# Civil Rights

## 5.1 Preamble

The campaign for the Democratic Party's nominee for president in 2008 culminated in a contest between a mixed-race man and a white woman. Both candidates addressed their identities directly and with pride. Barack Obama gave a notable speech about race, saying that Black anger and white resentments were grounded in legitimate concerns and that Americans must work together to move beyond their racial wounds. Conceding defeat in June, Hillary Clinton told her supporters, "Although we weren't able to shatter that highest, hardest glass ceiling this time, it's got about eighteen million cracks in it."[1]

**FIGURE 5.1 Obama–Clinton Rally Held in Orlando on October 20, 2008**

In 2008, a mixed-race man and a white woman made history as the leading contenders for the Democratic nomination for president.

Source: Photo courtesy of Nathan Forget via Wikimedia: https://commons.wikimedia.org/wiki/File:Obama_Stump_Speech_-_cropped.jpg. Reproduced via CC BY 2.0: https://creativecommons.org/licenses/by/2.0/deed.en.

Reporters and commentators in the media identified how race and gender played out in the campaign and in the statements of the candidates and their associates, including the polarizing statements of figures such as Obama's minister, Jeremiah Wright. At the same time, the media reported that the Democratic contest and Obama's nomination symbolized how far civil rights have come in America from the dark days of segregation. This frame became dominant when Obama was elected president in November 2008 and reelected in 2012.

**Civil rights** protect people against discrimination. They focus on equal access to society and to political activities such as voting. They are pursued by **disadvantaged groups** who, because of a single characteristic, have historically been discriminated against. In this chapter, we consider race and ethnicity, gender, sexual orientation, and disability.

The history of civil rights was created, first and most influentially, by Black people's struggle for racial equality. Their strategies and policy victories became the model for all other disadvantaged groups.[2]

**civil rights**

Equal access to society and to the political process without arbitrary discrimination.

**disadvantaged group**

Those who historically have had little or no economic, social, and political power and who have been singled out for discriminatory treatment in politics and society.

## 5.2 Civil War Amendments and African Americans

### Learning Objectives

After reading this section, you should be able to answer the following questions:

1. What are the Civil War Amendments?
2. What civil rights challenges faced African Americans?
3. What are de jure and de facto segregation?

4. What did the U.S. Supreme Court decide in *Plessy v. Ferguson* and *Brown v. Board of Education*?
5. What are the Civil Rights and the Voting Rights Acts?
6. What is affirmative action?
7. What civil rights issues persist?

## The Civil War Amendments

The Emancipation Proclamation issued on January 1, 1863, by President Abraham Lincoln during the third year of the Civil War freed all enslaved people resident in jurisdictions engaged in the rebellion against the federal government: more than three million. It did not, however, change the legal status of 800,000.

**Civil War Amendments**

The three amendments added to the Constitution (Thirteenth, Fourteenth, and Fifteenth) after the Civil War to establish the legal status and rights of the newly freed slaves.

Equality did not enter the Constitution until the **Civil War Amendments** (the Thirteenth, Fourteenth, and Fifteenth) set forth the status and rights of former slaves.

In early 1865, with the Union's triumph in the Civil War assured, Congress passed the Thirteenth Amendment. Quickly ratified by victorious Union states, it outlawed slavery and "involuntary servitude." It authorized Congress to pass laws enforcing the amendment—giving it the power to eradicate not simply slavery but all "badges of servitude."[3]

Abraham Lincoln, assassinated in 1865, was succeeded as president by Andrew Johnson, who pushed for a quick reunion of North and South. Republicans in Congress feared that the rights of newly freed enslaved people would be denied by a return to the old order. Distrusting Johnson, they decided protections had to be put into the Constitution. Congress enacted the Fourteenth Amendment in 1868 and made its ratification a condition for the Southern states' reentry into the Union.

The Fourteenth Amendment contains three key clauses. First, anyone born in the United States is a U.S. citizen, and anyone residing in a state is a citizen of that state. So it affirmed Black people as U.S. and state citizens.

Second, the amendment bars states from depriving anyone, whether a citizen or not, of "life, liberty, or property, without due process of law." It thereby extended the Bill of Rights' due process requirement on the federal government to the states.

**equal protection clause**

The section of the Fourteenth Amendment to the Constitution that requires states to ensure "equal protection of the laws" to all individuals.

Third, the amendment holds that a state may not "deny to any person within its jurisdiction the equal protection of the laws." This **equal protection clause** is the Supreme Court's major instrument for scrutinizing state regulations. It is at the heart of all civil rights. Though the clause was designed to restrict states, the Supreme Court has ruled that it applies to the federal government, too.[4]

The Fifteenth Amendment, ratified in 1870, bars federal and state governments from infringing on a citizen's right to vote "on account of race, color, or previous condition of servitude."

The Bill of Rights *limited* the powers of the federal government; the Civil War Amendments *expanded* them. These amendments created new powers for Congress and the states to support equality. They recognized for the first time a right to vote.

Political debate and conflict surround how, where, and when civil rights protections are applied. The complex U.S. political system provides opportunities for disadvantaged groups to claim and obtain their civil rights. At the same time, the many divisions built into the Constitution by the separation of powers and federalism can be used to frustrate the achievement of civil rights.

# Black People

The status of Black people continued to be a central issue of American politics after the Civil War.

## Disenfranchisement and Segregation

The federal government retreated from the Civil War Amendments that protected the civil rights of Black people. Most Black people resided in the South, where almost all were disenfranchised and segregated by the end of the nineteenth century by Jim Crow laws that enforced segregation of public schools, accommodation, transportation, and other public places.

### Link

**Jim Crow Laws**

"Jim Crow" was a derogatory term for Black people, named after "Jump Jim Crow," a parody of their singing and dancing as performed by a white actor in blackface. Click here to learn more about Jim Crow laws.

Click here to read *The Red Record* by Ida B. Wells-Barnett.

Enforcing the Fifteenth Amendment's right to vote proved difficult and costly. Black people voted in large numbers but faced violence from white people. Vigilante executions of Black people by mobs for alleged or imagined crimes reached new highs. In 1892 alone, 161 lynchings were documented, and many more surely occurred. White mob violence against Black people and their businesses and homes was pervasive. White police and National Guardsmen often looked on or joined in. Photos of lynched and mutilated Black bodies circulated in newspapers and postcards.

However, these depictions had reverse effects. Between 1880 and the 1930s, "while locals justified nearby lynchings, publicity exposed lynchings to distant un-supportive audiences and allowed African Americans to safely articulate counternarratives and condemnations."[5]

In 1894, Democrats took charge of the White House and both houses of Congress for the first time since the Civil War. They repealed all federal oversight of elections and delegated enforcement to the states.[6] Southern states quickly restricted Black voting. They required potential voters to take a literacy test or to interpret a section of the Constitution. Whites who failed an often easier test might still qualify to vote by virtue of a "grandfather clause," which allowed those whose grandfathers had voted before the Civil War to register.

The Supreme Court also reduced the scope of the Civil War Amendments by nullifying federal laws banning discrimination. The Court ruled that the Fourteenth Amendment did not empower the federal government to act against private persons.

**de jure segregation**

Separation of the races by law and public policies.

**separate but equal**

The doctrine, endorsed by the Supreme Court in *Plessy v. Ferguson* (1896) and repudiated by *Brown v. Board of Education* (1954), that racial segregation was constitutional as long as all races were treated equally.

**De jure segregation**—the separation of races by the law—received the Supreme Court's blessing in the 1896 case of *Plessy v. Ferguson*. A Louisiana law barred white and Black people from sitting together on trains. A Louisiana equal rights group, seeking to challenge the law, recruited a light-skinned Black man, Homer Plessy, to board a train car reserved for whites. Plessy was arrested. His lawyers claimed the law denied him equal protection. By a vote of 8–1, the justices ruled against Plessy, stating that these accommodations were acceptable because they were "**separate but equal**." Racial segregation did not violate equal protection, provided both races were treated equally.[7]

*Plessy v. Ferguson* gave states the green light to segregate on the basis of race. "Separate but equal" was far from equal in practice. White people rarely sought access to areas reserved for Black people, which were of inferior quality. Such segregation extended to all areas of social life, including entertainment media. Films with all-Black or all-white casts were shot for separate movie houses for Black people and white people.

## Mobilizing against Segregation

At the dawn of the twentieth century, Black people, segregated by race and disenfranchised by law and violence, debated how to improve their lot. One approach accepted segregation and pursued self-help, vocational education, and individual economic advancement. Its spokesman, Booker T. Washington, head of Alabama's Tuskegee Institute, wrote the best-selling memoir *Up from Slavery* (1901) and worked to build institutions for Black people, such as colleges for Black people only. Sociologist W. E. B. Du Bois replied to Washington with his book *The Soul of Black Folk* (1903), which argued that Black people should protest and agitate for the vote and for civil rights.

Du Bois's writings gained the attention of white and Black Northern reformers, who founded the National Association for the Advancement of Colored People (NAACP) in 1909. Du Bois served as director of publicity and research, investigating inequities, generating news, and going on speaking tours.[8]

The NAACP brought test cases to court that challenged segregationist practices. Its greatest successes came starting in the 1930s, in a legal strategy led by Thurgood Marshall, who, many years later, in 1967, would be appointed to the Supreme Court by President Lyndon Johnson. Marshall urged the courts to nullify programs that provided substandard facilities for Black people on the grounds that they were a violation of "separate but equal." In a key 1937 victory, the Supreme Court ruled that, by providing a state law school for white people without doing the same for Black people, Missouri was denying equal protection.[9] Such triumphs did not threaten segregation but made Southern states take "separate but equal" more seriously, sometimes forcing them to give funds for Black colleges, which became centers for political action.[10]

During World War I, Northern factories recruited rural Southern Black men for work, starting a "Great Migration" northward that peaked in the 1960s. In Northern cities, Black men voted freely, had fewer restrictions on their civil rights, organized themselves effectively, and participated in politics. They began to elect Black members of Congress and built prosperous Black newspapers.

When the United States entered World War II, many African Americans were brought into the defense industries but confronted discrimination in hiring and wages. Roughly one million joined the armed forces but were confined to segregated units.

Black people's war involvement in the name of freedom, equality, and democracy made their lack thereof in America more blatant and outrageous. Inevitably, many of these soldiers who returned from fighting for their country engaged in more militant politics. Membership in the NAACP swelled tenfold to 500,000.

President Harry S. Truman saw Black citizens as a sizable voting bloc. In 1946, he named an advisory commission to recommend civil rights policies. Amid his 1948 election campaign, Truman issued executive orders that adopted two of its suggestions: desegregating the armed forces and creating review boards in each cabinet department to monitor discrimination. With the crucial help of Northern Black votes, Truman won in an upset.

## The End of De Jure Segregation

In the 1940s, Supreme Court decisions on lawsuits brought by the NAACP and argued by Thurgood Marshall chipped away at "separate but equal." In 1941, Arthur Mitchell, a Black member of Congress from Chicago, was kicked out of a first-class sleeping car when his train entered Arkansas. The Court ruled that the Arkansas law enforcing segregation was unconstitutional. In 1944, the Court ruled that the Fifteenth Amendment barred Texas from running an all-white primary election. In 1948, it stopped enforcement of covenants that home buyers signed that said they would not resell their houses to Black people or Jews.[11]

Marshall decided to force the justices to address the issue of segregation directly. He brought suit against school facilities for Black people that were physically equal to those for white people. With the 1954 decision *Brown v. Board of Education*, the Supreme Court overturned *Plessy v. Ferguson* and ruled unanimously that racial segregation in public education violated the Constitution.[12] (See the Chapter 15 "Comparing Content" on *Brown v. Board of Education of Topeka, Kansas*.)

### Link

***Brown v. Board of Education***

Click here for more information on *Brown v. Board of Education*.

Only six percent of Southern schools had begun to desegregate by the end of the 1950s. In 1957, Arkansas Governor Orval Faubus, backed by white mobs, mobilized the National Guard to fight a federal court order to desegregate Little Rock's public schools. President Dwight Eisenhower reluctantly took charge of the Arkansas National Guard and called up U.S. troops to enforce the order.[13] Television images of the nine Little Rock students attempting to enter Central High School surrounded by troops and an angry mob brought the struggle for civil rights into American living rooms.

### Link

**Central High Conflicts**

Learn more about the conflicts at Central High here.

## The Black Civil Rights Movement

Even before the *Brown v. Board of Education* decision, a mass movement of Black people had emerged from Black churches and Black colleges. Such organizations provided networks for communicating with and organizing recruits. The Black press in both the North and the South publicized the movement.

Daily newspapers in the South, which covered a white power structure and were aimed at white readers, all but ignored the Black civil rights movement. Southern reporters who covered the movement were threatened, and even harmed physically, by the Ku Klux Klan, a white supremacist group.[14] Northern newspapers were slow to discover the movement, although the attention they eventually accorded civil rights protests would help the movement grow and expand.

The Montgomery Bus Boycott in 1955 was sparked when Rosa Parks refused to give up her seat to a white man and move to the back of the bus. The first mass action for civil rights took place in Baton Rouge, Louisiana, in 1953. Black people led by a Baptist minister boycotted the city's segregated public buses. Although Black people provided about three-quarters of the ridership, they had to stand behind an often near-empty white section. A deal was struck: the city council saved the first two rows for white people, but Black people could sit anywhere else as long as they were not in front of whites.

## Enduring Image

### Rosa Parks

Two enduring images of the Black civil rights movement are of Rosa Parks. In one, she is being arrested. In a later photograph taken for *Look* magazine, she is sitting on a city bus *in front of* a white passenger. Her refusal to give up her bus seat to a white person and move to the back of the bus touched off the massive Montgomery bus boycott that ended with a Supreme Court decision ordering the city to desegregate public transportation. The images endure because of the simple, moving tale of a lone individual affirming her dignity and equality by a simple act—sitting down.

Another bus boycott took place in Montgomery, Alabama. Rosa Parks, a seamstress and an activist in the local NAACP, was arrested in December 1955 after refusing to give up her bus seat to a white man. Here she is being fingerprinted by Deputy Sheriff D.H. Lackey in Montgomery, Alabama, on Feb. 22, 1956.

Source: Pictorial Press Ltd / Alamy Stock Photo

What the images do not show is that Parks was a long standing activist in local civil rights politics and was secretary of the Montgomery chapter of the NAACP. The photo of her arrest was not for her action on the bus, but for later activity in the boycott.

Parks was not the first Black woman to refuse to give up her seat on a bus. Claudette Colvin, a fifteen-year-old young woman active in the NAACP Youth Council, had refused to give up her bus seat a few months before. Colvin cried out as she was arrested, "This is my constitutional right." NAACP leaders had hoped to draw attention to Colvin's case until they realized that she was foul-mouthed and unruly—the pregnant, unmarried Colvin was not the symbol of Black resistance the NAACP wished to portray. Parks, a diminutive, devout, soft-spoken married woman, was ideal for favorable publicity.[15]

Civil rights activists receive most positive coverage when they are able to present themselves as noble, oppressed victims. The images of Parks, arrested and sitting at the front of the bus, have lasted and been widely reproduced. Other images of Parks as political activist and organizer, roles that are equally central to her life, have not.

Rosa Parks, 43, seen here sitting on a seat at the front of a bus as the bus boycott came to an end.

Source: Science History Images / Alamy Stock Photo

NAACP leaders sued the city and started a boycott led by a twenty-six-year-old Baptist preacher fresh out of divinity school—Martin Luther King Jr. The boycott lasted 381 days and ended only after the U.S. Supreme Court declared Montgomery's segregated public transportation unconstitutional.

King founded the Southern Christian Leadership Conference (SCLC) to lead Black resistance, confirmed himself as the leading orator of the movement, and honed a strategy by which Black victims of discrimination confronted repressive white power nonviolently. Rosa Parks's example revealed how this "David-and-Goliath" story was well suited to getting the issue of civil rights into the news.

Students created the next wave of activism. In 1960, four freshmen at North Carolina A&T State University sat down at a dime store, whites-only lunch counter in Greensboro and would not leave until they were served.

The students tipped off a local white photographer, who took a picture of them that gained national attention. The "Greensboro four" were arrested and jailed. Twenty-nine students sat at the lunch counter the next day, and hundreds more followed. After months of dwindling sales, Greensboro's merchants agreed to desegregate. The sit-in was rapidly imitated across the South.[16] It inspired a new, younger, more confrontational organization—the Student Nonviolent Coordinating Committee (SNCC).

In 1961, white and Black activists launched a Freedom Ride to travel together on buses from Washington, DC, to New Orleans in defiance of state laws. They did not make it. In Alabama, one bus was stopped, and its occupants were badly beaten. Another bus was set on fire, and the freedom riders barely escaped alive.

Dramatic, widely distributed photographs of these events forced President John F. Kennedy to order federal agencies to halt segregation and discrimination in interstate transportation.[17] Civil rights activists used depictions of white repression to win dramatic news coverage and generate public sympathy for their cause.

For example, in 1962, Air Force veteran James Meredith, after repeated appeals and a Supreme Court order, was rejected for admission as the first Black student to the University of Mississippi. To exclude him, the state legislature passed a law declaring that those charged with moral turpitude could not be admitted to a state university. The day it became law, Meredith was convicted of voter fraud—a crime he had not committed. To enforce the Court's ruling, the Kennedy administration federalized and called out the National Guard to escort Meredith onto campus. Riots ensued from a mob of 2,000 students and others blocking his entrance. More than a hundred and fifty federal marshals were wounded, two people died, and many were arrested. The events would become known as the Battle of Oxford.

In 1963, King and the SCLC conducted an all-out campaign, including mass meetings, sit-ins, and boycotts of downtown stores in Birmingham, Alabama. Their attempts to march to city hall were violently suppressed by police. Marchers, including young children, were chased and attacked by police dogs and pummeled with water from fire hoses so powerful it tore off their clothes and removed bark from trees. Thousands were arrested.

These protests, and the official response, received saturation coverage in the news. After five weeks, Birmingham's business leaders signed an agreement to desegregate stores and enhance Black employment.[18] In a nationally televised address in June, President Kennedy proposed a far-reaching Civil Rights Act. Riding a surge of attention, King planned a national march on Washington. A quarter of a million people jammed around the Lincoln Memorial in August to hear speeches and songs, capped off by King's "I Have a Dream" vision of racial reconciliation.

### Link

**Dr. Martin Luther King's "I Have a Dream" Speech**

Listen to King's "I Have a Dream" speech here.

## The 1964 Civil Rights Act and 1965 Voting Rights Act

After the assassination of President Kennedy in November 1963, the new president, Lyndon B. Johnson, asked Congress to pass the Civil Rights Act, which Kennedy had initiated. It became law after weeks of lobbying, concessions, deals, and filibusters by Southern senators.

The Civil Rights Act forbids discrimination on the basis of "race, color, religion, or national origin" in public accommodations and employment. It set up the Equal Employment Opportunity Commission (EEOC) to implement the law.

With the passage of the Civil Rights Act, the movement turned from discrimination to the vote. Southern Black people trying to register to vote were required to answer impossible questions, such as "how many bubbles in a bar of soap?" Those who managed to register and then tried to vote might be beaten or fired from their jobs. King and the SCLC marched on Selma, Alabama, peacefully to push the goal of registering Black citizens to vote. Such a simple message was ideal for transmission through the national news.

The SNCC organized the Freedom Summer of 1964, a campaign to register voters in Mississippi, the state with the largest percentage of Black people and the lowest rate of Black voter registration. Massive resistance from whites resulted in violence, culminating in the murder of three civil rights workers—one Black person and two white people. Murders of white civil rights activists generated more public outrage and received more news coverage than murders of Black participants.

**FIGURE 5.2 President Lyndon B. Johnson Signing the 1964 Civil Rights Act**

Landmark civil rights legislation was signed into law by a son of the Old South, Texan Lyndon B. Johnson, who pointedly invited the civil rights leader Martin Luther King Jr. to the White House for the ceremony.

Source: LBJ Library photo by O.J. Rapp. "Signing of the Civil Rights Act of 1964." Image Serial No. C522-2-WH64. Via Wikimedia: http://commons.wikimedia.org/wiki/File:LBJ_ Civil_Rights_Act_crowd.jpg.

In March of 1965, King organized a march from Selma to the state capital, Montgomery. A column of six hundred marchers was confronted by fifty Alabama state troopers, some on horseback, and ordered to disperse. When they did not move, the troopers charged them and shot tear gas, brutally injuring one hundred of the demonstrators. Television footage of this "Bloody Sunday" was widely broadcast.

The upsurge in news coverage prompted membership and funding for civil rights organizations to soar. Public opinion polls revealed that civil rights was the nation's most important problem.[19] Officials felt pressure to act. President Johnson gave a televised speech before Congress to propose the Voting Rights Act, stating, "It is all of us who must overcome the crippling legacy of bigotry and injustice." He paused, then evoked the civil rights battle cry: "We shall overcome."[20] With Johnson's leadership, the legislation sailed through Congress. (See Johnson speak here.)

The Voting Rights Act of 1965 gave new powers to the federal government. The act outlawed literacy tests and required the states to prove to the Justice Department that any changes in voting practices would not abridge the right to vote. It authorized the federal government to use poll watchers and registration examiners to supervise state and local elections. It instantly removed barriers to Black registration and voting. In Mississippi, the percentage of Black people registered to vote swelled from under 7 percent in 1964 to 60 percent in 1967.

The year 1967 saw another major decision from the Supreme Court. Richard and Mildred Loving had been sentenced to a year in prison in Virginia for violating the state's anti-miscegenation law. They fled to Washington, DC, and eventually appealed their conviction. The Supreme Court unanimously invalidated laws prohibiting interracial marriage on the grounds that they violated the due process and equal protection clauses of the Fourteenth Amendment to the Constitution.[21]

## From South to North

Victorious in the South, the Black civil rights movement turned north. Black and white people were separated by locality and attended different schools in both North and South. Separation of the races in the North was by practice more than by law; such **de facto segregation** proved tougher to address by legal efforts alone.

**de facto segregation**

Separation of the races that occurs by social practice.

Black people began rioting in Northern cities, and the rioting reached a peak in 1967. Many rioters saw their actions as protest or rebellion. Some of their violence targeted white-owned stores, which they looted, and police stations, which they set on fire. Scores of Black people died after police and soldiers were brought in to restore order.

In part due to their perennial interest in vivid, dramatic conflict, the media shifted their focus from nobly suffering victims to fiery, demanding militants. The unity, discipline, and influence of the Black civil rights movement ebbed. King's doctrine of nonviolent resistance was challenged by the rhetoric of the Black Muslim leader Malcolm X, who advocated "any means necessary" to advance equality and promoted SNCC's new motto, "Black Power." Malcolm X was assassinated in 1965 by rival Black Muslims. In 1968, King was assassinated in Memphis, where he had gone to support the sanitation workers' campaign for improved pay and working conditions.

Black militancy, amplified in the news, spawned a white backlash. Republican Richard Nixon was elected president in 1968 on a "law and order" platform that called for slowing down desegregation. The news prominently displayed the dramatic, sometimes violent, reaction by white people against the busing of Black students to white schools in supposedly liberal Northern cities such as Boston. It did not miss the irony of massive demonstrations against the busing to desegregate the public schools of Boston, the city at the center of the opposition to slavery prior to the Civil War.

In 1974, the Supreme Court rejected a Detroit plan that required busing across school district lines. The judicial push for integration slowed.[22]

## Affirmative Action

**affirmative action**

Efforts made or enforced by government to increase percentages of racial and ethnic minorities, and women, in higher education and the workplace.

In recent years, in addition to the coverage of police brutality and discrimination the main mass media focus on Black civil rights has been **affirmative action**: efforts made or enforced by government to achieve equality of opportunity by increasing the percentages of racial and ethnic minorities and women in higher education and the workplace.

Most members of racial and ethnic minorities support affirmative action; majorities of white people are opposed. Supporters tend to focus on remedying the effects of past discrimination; opponents respond that government should never discriminate on the basis of race. The media largely frame the issue as a question of one side winning and the other side losing.[23]

The Supreme Court first weighed in on affirmative action in 1978. Allan Bakke, a white applicant, was denied entrance to the medical school of the University of California, Davis. Bakke noted that his test scores were higher than other applicants admitted on a separate track for minorities. He sued, charging "reverse discrimination." The Court concluded that UC Davis's approach of separating white and minority applicants into two separate groups violated the principle of equal protection. School programs like Harvard's, which considered race as one of many criteria, were permissible.[24]

A 2003 Supreme Court decision affirmed this position by voiding the undergraduate admission program at the University of Michigan that added points to a candidate's application on the basis of race but upholding the graduate admission approach that considered race in a less quantitative way.

In 2007, the Supreme Court rejected the actions of the Seattle and Louisville school systems to promote racial integration by assigning students to particular schools in order to make the population of each school reflect the cities' racial composition. This 5–4 decision by Chief Justice John Roberts, leading the Court's conservative majority, seemed to prohibit school systems from using race to classify and thus assign students. It did, however, allow the use of other (unspecified) race-conscious measures to combat racial segregation.[25]

In 2014, the Supreme Court voted 6–2 to uphold Michigan's ban making it illegal for state entities to consider race in college admissions and in hiring and in targeting financial aid to specific races. The ban had been proposed as a ballot initiative to amend the state constitution and was approved in 2006 by 58 percent of those voting. There are similar bans in Arizona, California, Nebraska, Oklahoma, and Washington. Writing for the majority, Justice Anthony Kennedy took pains to insist that the decision was not a repudiation of affirmative action but was based on allowing the state's voters to decide whether to prohibit racial preferences in government decisions.[26] Other sorts of preferences, such as for athletes and the offspring of alumni or donors, are apparently unaffected and allowed.

Then in June 2016 the Court by 4–3 rejected a challenge to a race-conscious admissions policy at Texas University at Austin. Essentially, the Court ruled that officials could include race as a factor in admissions but that not all affirmative action programs are constitutionally acceptable.[27]

Conflicts over affirmative action continued but with a twist when, in the fall of 2018, the Trump Justice Department joined a lawsuit by some Asian American students (recruited by an organization called Students for Fair Admissions) who had been rejected by Harvard and contended that the university's admission policies are discriminatory, that in effect they favor Black Americans at the expense of Asian Americans.[28] The final decision is likely to be made by the Supreme Court and may undermine, even eviscerate, the common understanding.

## Civil Rights Issues Persist

In 2013 by a vote of 5–4 the Supreme Court essentially eviscerated key parts of the Voting Rights Act on the grounds that, according to Chief Justice Roberts, who wrote the majority opinion, "times have changed." The decision overturned the law's provision that most of nine states, primarily in the South, with histories of discriminatory voting practices, had to obtain "preclearance" from the federal government—prove to the Justice Department or a three-judge panel of the U.S. District Court for the District of Columbia, that any changes they wanted to make would protect (not harm) the rights of minority voters.[29] After the decision, preclearance was ended.

Before the Court's decision and after it, Republican-dominated state governments have made it harder to vote, particularly for Black people, those living in poverty, and students; that is, those who are inclined to vote Democratic.[30] They variously imposed strict voter identification requirements (disallowing student IDs, public employee IDs, and photo IDs issued by public assistance agencies). They reduced the number of polling places and their opening times and hours, cut the period allowed for early voting, and eliminated same-day registration.

The federal government's recourse is to pursue violations through the courts. The Justice Department has asked the federal courts to block enforcement of some of the provisions of these new laws and to return some states to federal "preclearance" oversight. But, in contrast to its powers under the Civil Rights Act, going to the courts is lengthy, expensive, and puts the burden of proof on the plaintiffs.

The legacy of slavery and segregation is evident not only in the income gap and higher rates of poverty, unemployment, and incarceration, but also the drug addiction, lower life expectancy, lack of education, easy availability of guns, and lower college completion rates of Black people compared to white people.

Visitors to the website of the NAACP will find many subjects connected to race, such as police practices of racial profiling and alleged abuse, sometimes killing, of Black suspects. But the NAACP also deals with issues that disproportionately affect Black people and that some might think have "nothing to do with race." These include what the NAACP labels "environmental racism," whereby polluting factories are placed next to poor, largely Black neighborhoods.

The mass media tend to focus on incidents of overt discrimination, such as police brutality and the killing of Black men, that arouse protests, demonstrations, and organized movements such as Black Lives Matter (and also whether police should wear body cameras), rather than on the damage caused by the poverty, poor education, and environmental hazards that disadvantaged groups often face. This media frame explains why television reporters, facing the devastation of New Orleans by Hurricane Katrina, were so thunderstruck by the overwhelming number of Black faces among the victims. The topic of Black poverty is simply not something the press routinely reports. Increasingly, though, they have turned their attention to police brutality, the possibility of reducing police budgets (defunding the police), and structural racism.

### Key Takeaways

Civil rights protect people against discrimination and focus on equal access to society and political life. In this section we have described the evolution and contents of the civil rights of Black people. We started with the Civil War Amendments added to the Constitution to guarantee newly freed slaves' legal status. We covered Black people's disenfranchisement and segregation, their mobilizing against segregation, the end of de jure segregation, and the civil rights movement. We described the 1964 Civil Rights Act, the 1965 Voting Rights Act, and the issue of affirmative action. Until recent decisions by the Supreme Court, Black people have had more success in combating segregation by law than in fighting discrimination by practice. They have variously been helped and hindered by media coverage and depictions of their situation and struggles. Civil rights issues persist today.

### Exercises

1. What basic protections did the Civil War Amendments introduce? How would life in America be different if these amendments had never been passed?
2. How were Black people denied the right to vote and equal protection even after the Civil War Amendments passed? When did that begin to change, and why?
3. How did civil rights protesters seek to bring discrimination to the public's attention? Why do you think their strategy worked?
4. To what extent do you think that the legacy of slavery and segregation is responsible for the inequalities that persist in America? How do you think the law should deal with those inequalities?

# 5.3 Latinxs, Asian Americans, Indigenous Americans

### Learning Objectives

After reading this section, you should be able to answer the following questions:

1. What civil rights challenges have Latinxs faced?
2. What civil rights challenges have Asian Americans faced?
3. What civil rights challenges have Indigenous Americans faced?

Policies protecting Black people's civil rights may extend to other racial and ethnic minorities. Most prominent of these groups are Latinxs, Asian Americans, and Indigenous Americans. They all have civil rights concerns of their own.

## Latinxs

Latinxs have displaced Black people as the largest minority group in the United States. They are disproportionately foreign born, young, and poor. They can keep in touch with issues and their community through a burgeoning Spanish-language media. Daily newspapers and national television networks such as Univision provide a mix of news and advocacy.

Politicians court Latinxs as a growing bloc of voters.[31] As a result, Latinxs have had some success in pursuing civil rights, such as the use of Spanish in voting and teaching. After Latinx groups claimed that voting rights were at risk for citizens not literate in English, the Voting Rights Act was amended to require ballots to be available in a language other than English in election districts where that language was spoken by 5 percent or more of the electorate. And the Supreme Court has ruled that school districts violate the Civil Rights Act of 1964 when students are taught in a language that they do not understand.[32]

Latinx success has not carried over to immigration.[33] Undocumented immigrants pose vexing questions in terms of civil rights. If caught, should they be jailed and expelled? Should they be eligible to become citizens?

In 2006, Congressman Jim Sensenbrenner (R-WI) introduced legislation to change undocumented immigration from a violation of civil law to a felony and to punish anyone who provided assistance to undocumented immigrants, even church ministers. Hundreds of thousands rallied in cities across the country to voice their opposition. President George W. Bush pushed for a less punitive approach that would recognize undocumented immigrants as "guest workers" but would still not allow them to become citizens.

Other politicians have proposed legislation. Mired in controversy, none of these proposals have become law. President Obama revisited one aspect of the subject in his 2011 State of the Union message:

> *Today, there are hundreds of thousands of students excelling in our schools who are not American citizens. Some are the children of undocumented workers, who had nothing to do with the actions of their parents. They grew up as Americans and pledge allegiance to our flag, and yet they live every day with the threat of deportation. . . . It makes no sense.*
>
> *Now, I strongly believe that we should take on, once and for all, the issue of illegal immigration. I am prepared to work with Republicans and Democrats to protect our borders, enforce our laws, and address the millions of undocumented workers who are now living in the shadows. I know that debate will be difficult and take time.*[34]

### Link

**UnidosUS**

Click here to learn more about Latinx civil rights at UnidosUS online.

# Asian Americans

Asian Americans claim heritage from any of some twenty-plus nations. They have been the victims of riots, lynchings, and murder. The Naturalization Act of 1790 until the middle of the twentieth century restricted many Chinese, Indian, and other Asian immigrants from obtaining citizenship or owning property because they were not considered free white people. The Chinese Exclusion Act of 1882 prohibited immigration of Chinese laborers. It was expected to last ten years but was made permanent in 1902 and not repealed until 1943.

Many landmark cases on racial discrimination going back to the nineteenth century stemmed from suits by Asian Americans. In one case, a federal court in California ruled that residents of Asian descent were not white and were ineligible for naturalization. Referencing then-current "scientific" and popular ideas about race, the court deemed "Orientals" unfit for participation in Republican government.[35] Discrimination was enforced by such cases as *The People v. Hall*—an appealed murder case in the 1850s in which the California Supreme Court established that Chinese Americans and Chinese immigrants had no rights to testify against white citizens.

World War II brought more discrimination out of an unjustified, if not irrational, fear that some Japanese Americans might be loyal to Japan and thus commit acts of sabotage against the United States: the federal government imposed curfews on them. After President Franklin D. Roosevelt signed Executive Order 9066 on February 19, 1942, roughly 120,000 Japanese Americans (62 percent of them U.S. citizens) were forcibly moved from their homes and had their businesses confiscated. They were sent to distant, desolate relocation camps. Ruling toward the end of the war, the Supreme Court did not strike down the internment policy, which violated their constitutional rights, but it did hold that classifying people by race is unconstitutional.[36]

Meanwhile, many of the Asian Americans would fight for the United States as their families were interned.

Japanese Americans who had been interned in camps later pressed for redress. Congress eventually responded with the Civil Liberties Act of 1988, whereby the U.S. government apologized to and compensated camp survivors.[37]

## Link

**Japanese Internment**

Click here to learn more about Japanese internment.

**FIGURE 5.3 Japanese Interment Camps**

Like the Mochida family pictured here, many Japanese Americans were shipped to internment camps during World War II.

Source: Dorothea Lange [Public domain]; https://commons.wikimedia.org/wiki/File:Photograph_of_Members_of_the_Mochida_Family_Awaiting_Evacuation_-_NARA_-_537505_-_Restoration.jpg.

Asian Americans have united against discrimination. During the Vietnam era, Asian American students opposing the war highlighted its impact on Asian populations. Instead of slogans such as "Bring the GIs home," they chanted, "Stop killing our Asian brothers and sisters."

These Asian American student groups—and the periodicals they spawned—provided the foundation for a unified Asian American identity and politics.[38]

A dazzling array of Asian American nationalities, religions, and cultures has emerged since 1965, after restrictions on immigration from Asia were removed. Yet vestiges of discrimination remain. For example, Asian Americans are paid less than their high level of education would warrant.[39] In the 1992 riot mostly made up of Black people reacting to the acquittal of white police for the beating of Rodney King, stores in South Los Angeles (Koreatown) were looted and vandalized.

Media stereotyping of Asian Americans is no longer so prevalent and contributing to discrimination: the detectives Charlie Chan and Mr. Moto (played by white actors), the house boy on the television western *Bonanza*, women as delicate and submissive in such films as *Sayonara* (1957). Asian Americans, like other American minorities, increasingly appear in television series and commercials. Studies programs are offered at universities and colleges.

# Indigenous Americans

Indigenous Americans represent many tribes with distinct languages, cultures, and traditions. Despite mass destruction, illegal land grabs, and broken treaties, it is unfair and misleading to diminish their legal identities into ethnicities or think of them merely as victims. They have survived, even thrived.[40] Through the American Indian Movement and Red Power, they have asserted their rights and demanded protection against discrimination just as members of racial and ethnic groups do.

For much of their history, Indigenous Americans residing outside of reservations were in a legal limbo, being neither members of self-governing tribal nations nor U.S. citizens. For example, in 1881, John Elk, an Indigenous American living in Omaha, claimed that he was denied equal protection of the laws when he was prevented from voting. The Supreme Court ruled that since he was "born to an Indian nation," Elk was not a citizen and could not claim a right to vote. Nowadays, Indigenous Americans living on or outside reservations vote as any other citizens.

HCR-108 (August 1, 1953) made it a policy to abolish federal supervision over American tribes as soon as possible and to subject Indigenous Americans to the same laws, privileges, and responsibilities as other U.S. citizens. However, it also ended government responsibility to tribe members and legal protection to territory, culture, and religion (i.e., ended U.S. recognition of sovereignty of the tribes, trusteeship over Indigenous reservations, and exclusion of state law applicability to Indigenous persons). The intent was to assimilate Indigenous people into American society.

The Indian Civil Rights Act (ICRA) of 1968 guarantees Indigenous people many civil rights, including equal protection under the law and due process; freedom of speech, press, and assembly; and protection from unreasonable search and seizure, self-incrimination, and double jeopardy.

Indigenous Americans' civil rights issues today center on tribal autonomy and self-government on reservations. Thus, some of the provisions of the Bill of Rights, such as the separation of church and state, do not apply to tribes.[41] Reservations may also legally discriminate in favor of hiring Indigenous Americans.

Indigenous Americans still face challenges and resort to protests to protect and attract media attention to their ancestral rights. Starting in 2016, they and some supporters picketed, blocked, and halted construction of the Dakota Access Pipeline that was intended to carry a half-million barrels of crude oil daily across federal land under the Missouri River a mile north of the border of the reservation of the Standing Rock Sioux Tribe. They contended that it would likely pollute the water and desecrate their ancestral burial grounds. President Obama delayed the construction. But soon after taking office, President Trump authorized the process to proceed.

For much of their history, Indigenous Americans have looked to enforce treaties granting them sovereignty, tribal boundaries, and treaty obligations; for example, a treaty promising the Cherokee

Nation a non-voting delegate in Congress. In 2020, the Supreme Court ruled that much of Tulsa and Eastern Oklahoma was a Creek reservation. (See Chapter 2.)

### Link

**The Indigenous American Civil Rights Movement**

Click here for more on the Indigenous American Civil Rights movement.

### Key Takeaways

In this section, we addressed the civil rights challenges facing Latinxs, Asian Americans, and Indigenous Americans. Latinxs have gained language but not citizenship rights for undocumented immigrants. After the horror of relocation inflicted on Japanese Americans, Asian Americans have obtained their rights, although vestiges of discrimination remain. Rights issues for Indigenous Americans concern tribal autonomy and self-government.

### Exercise

1. Are there differences between discriminating on the basis of race and of ethnicity? Are there legitimate reasons for treating people differently?

# 5.4 Women

### Learning Objectives

After reading this section, you should be able to answer the following questions:

1. What is the Nineteenth Amendment?
2. What is the Equal Rights Amendment?
3. What is sexual harassment?

## Women

Women constitute a majority of the population and of the electorate, but they have never spoken with a unified voice for civil rights, nor have they received the same degree of protection as racial and ethnic minorities.

## The First Wave of Women's Rights

In the American republic's first years, the right to vote was reserved for property owners, most of whom were male. Married women could not own property, because they were deemed the property of their husbands. The expansion of the franchise to "universal white manhood suffrage" served only to lock in women's disenfranchisement.

Women's activism arose in the campaign to abolish slavery. Women abolitionists argued that the case against slavery could not be made as long as women did not have political rights as well. In 1848, women and men active in the antislavery movement, meeting in Seneca Falls, New York, adopted a Declaration of Sentiments. Emulating the Declaration of Independence, it argued that "all men and women are created equal" and catalogued "repeated injuries and usurpations on the part of man toward woman."[42]

### Link

**The Seneca Falls Convention**

Click here to learn more about the Seneca Falls Convention.

Opponents argued that women were emotionally unstable, intellectually inferior, the vote would distract them from their domestic duties, and that the moral order would be threatened if they involved themselves in politics.

After the Civil War, women abolitionists hoped to be rewarded with the vote, but women were not included in the Fifteenth Amendment. In disgust, Susan B. Anthony and Elizabeth Cady Stanton, two prominent and ardent abolitionists, launched an independent women's movement.[43] Anthony drafted a constitutional amendment to guarantee women's right to vote: "The right of citizens of the United States to vote shall not be denied or abridged by the United States or by any state on account of sex."[44] Modeled on the Fifteenth Amendment, it was introduced in the Senate in 1878.

At first, the suffragists demurely petitioned and testified. By 1910, their patience was at an end. They campaigned against members of Congress and picketed the White House. They engaged in hunger strikes and boycotts and were heckled, spat on, knocked down, and imprisoned. Ostracized and ridiculed by the media, they formed their own press.

Their actions, widely publicized, eventually paid off in 1920, when the Nineteenth Amendment to the Constitution, which grants and protects women's right to vote, was added to the Constitution.

But the amendment failed to give Black, Indigenous American, Hispanic, and Chinese women the vote. Like their male compatriots, Black women were blocked by poll taxes, literacy tests, and the like. As documented by Martha S. Jones in her magisterial book (see Section 8) in their battle for voting participation, they had to try to overcome racism and sexism. (For example, the investigative journalist and suffragist Ida B. Wells refused demands that Black women march at the back of the 1913 suffragette parade). Novelist Alice Walker would coin the term "womanism" (womanist prose) to represent feminists of color and others concerned about race and class-based oppression. This approach is now described as "intersectionality."

**FIGURE 5.4** Women's Suffrage

Women picketing in front of the White House embarrassed President Woodrow Wilson during World War I. They pointed out that his promise "to make the world safe for democracy" did not include extending the vote to women. Wilson changed his position to one of support for the Nineteenth Amendment.

Source: The first picket line—College day in the picket line. Washington D.C, Feb 1917. Photograph. Library of Congress: https://www.loc.gov/item/97500299/.

## The Second Wave of Women's Rights

With the vote won, the women's movement lost its central focus. Women's interests in social change through suffrage and to leave the household to join the workforce were mostly concerns of white (middle-class) women.

**Equal Rights Amendment (ERA)**

Failed attempt to amend the Constitution to mandate equal treatment of women and men.

Women were also split by a proposed **Equal Rights Amendment (ERA)** to the Constitution, mandating equal treatment of men and women under the law. It had been proposed in 1923 by well-to-do Republican working professional women but was opposed by women Democrats in labor unions, who had won "specific bills for specific ills"—minimum wage and maximum hours laws for working women. Meanwhile, women constituted an increasing proportion of voters and made inroads in party activism and holding office.[45]

### Link

**The Equal Rights Amendment**

Learn more about the Equal Rights Amendment here.

Then came an unexpected breakthrough: Conservative Southern House members, hoping to slow down passage of the 1964 Civil Rights Bill, offered what they deemed frivolous amendments—one of which expanded the act to protect women. Northern and Southern male legislators joined in derision and laughter. The small contingent of congresswomen berated their colleagues and allied with Southern conservatives and Republicans to pass the amendment 168–133.

Thus, the Civil Rights Act ended up also barring discrimination in employment on the basis of sex. However, the Equal Employment Opportunity Commission (EEOC), created to implement the act, decided that its resources were too limited to focus on anything but race.

In 1966, women activists reacted by forming the National Organization for Women (NOW), which became the basis for a revived women's movement. NOW's first president was Betty Friedan, a freelance writer for women's magazines. Her 1963 best seller, *The Feminine Mystique*, showed that confining women to the domestic roles of wife and mother squelched opportunities for middle-class, educated women.[46] Women's organizations adopted the slogan "the personal is political." They pointed out that even when men and women in a couple worked outside the home equally, housework and child care fell more heavily on wives, creating a "second shift" limiting women's opportunity for political activism.

## Equality without the ERA

By 1970, Democrats and Republicans alike backed the ERA and women's rights. One House member, Bella Abzug (D-NY), later exulted, "We put sex discrimination provisions into everything. There was no opposition. Who'd be against equal rights for women?"[47]

Such laws could be far-reaching. Title IX of the Education Act Amendments of 1972, outlawing sex discrimination in federally funded educational programs, prompted little debate when it was enacted. Today it is controversial. Some charge that it pushes funds to women's sports, endangering men's sports. Defenders respond that all of women's sports put together get less funding at universities than men's sports such as basketball or football.[48]

NOW and other organizations focused on the ERA. It passed by huge bipartisan margins in the House in 1970 and the Senate in 1972; thirty of the thirty-eight states necessary to ratify approved it almost immediately. However, opposition to the ERA, led and generated by conservative women, notably Phyllis Schlafly, arose among the general public, including women. While women working outside the home generally favored the ERA to fight job discrimination, housewives feared that the ERA would remove protection for them, such as the legal presumptions that women were more eligible than men for alimony after a divorce. The public's support of the ERA declined because of fears that it might allow military conscription of women and gay marriage. The political consensus crumbled, and in 1980 the Republican platform opposed the ERA for the first time. The ERA died in 1982 when the ratification process expired.[49]

In January 2020 Virginia became the thirty-eighth state to approve the ERA. Too late? Arguably, the process must be restarted for it to be legally binding. The decision is up to the courts.

Although women have made strides toward equality, many of them continue to experience issues in their daily lives. These include not receiving equal pay for equal work, the unavailability of medical leave, the exclusion of contraception coverage in health insurance (see the Supreme Court's "Hobby Lobby" decision, discussed in Chapter 4), and difficulty in obtaining abortions (also covered in that chapter).

Moreover, women still fall behind on important measures. Even after their 2018 election influx, they make up only 25.0 percent of the United States Senate, 23.4 percent of the U.S. House of Representatives, and 28.7 percent of state legislatures. The top twenty occupations of women are the same as they were fifty years ago: they work as secretaries, nurses, and grade school teachers and in other low-paid white-collar jobs. This imbalance of power and positions between men and women brings us to sexual harassment.

## Sexual Harassment

Start with Congress: with its bevy of appealing but subordinate women and abundance of powerful men; sexual harassment is not uncommon. Lurid news accounts recount stories from some of the women abused over the years, and report that "between 1997 and 2014 the United States Treasury paid $15.2 million in 235 awards and settlements for workplace violations."[50]

**sexual harassment**

Form of discrimination on the basis of sex and gender that consists of unwelcome sexual advances or sexual conduct, verbal or physical, that interfere with a person's performance or create a hostile working environment.

But what is *sexual harassment*? In 1980, the EEOC defined **sexual harassment** as unwelcome sexual advances or sexual conduct, verbal or physical, that interfere with a person's performance or create a hostile working environment. In 1986 the Supreme Court ruled that discrimination on the basis of sex is barred in the workplace by the Civil Rights Act of 1964. They later ruled that it is also barred in colleges and universities that receive federal funds by Title IX of the Education Amendments of 1972. In a series of decisions, the Supreme Court has also ruled that employers are responsible for maintaining a harassment-free workplace. Schools may be held legally liable if they have tolerated sexual harassment. Therefore, they have established codes and definitions of what is and is not permissible. The College of William and Mary, for example, sees a power difference between students and teachers and prohibits any and all sexual contact between them. Others, like Williams College, seek to ensure that teachers opt out of any supervisory relationship with a student with whom they are sexually involved.

In theory, women who are sexually harassed have recourse to remedies. But, first, there are obstacles of definition and description. What is "inappropriate conduct"? Does a sexually hostile environment entail lewd remarks, unwelcome advances, uninvited and offensive touching? Genital exposure by the man? Must the behavior be maleficent? Require abuse? Assault? Rape?

A second problem is that of judicial determination. "Courts routinely dismiss cases brought by workers who claim their supervisors propositioned them, kissed them or grabbed their breasts. The judges declare that the conduct does not constitute harassment in a legal sense, and refuse to let the cases go to trial."[51]

Third, is the inclusion of arbitration clauses in employee contracts, requiring disputes to be settled by arbitration instead of in court. Contracts may also include employee confidentiality and nondisclosure agreements.[52]

Fourth, the women are vulnerable to accusations of making unfounded allegations and denunciations, of making unproven career- or life-destroying accusations, of money grubbing, and of lying.

Nonetheless, women who bring sexual harassment suits often find a receptive climate and generally sympathetic news media coverage. They may be emboldened by other women who join and support them with the #MeToo hashtag. Their male perpetrators have included prominent producers, executives, and entertainers in Hollywood, on-air figures and commentators at the major networks—Fox, CBS, and elsewhere. Some of the women have received substantial compensation as a result of their suits. But several of the men, especially those who worked for Fox, have also received substantial payouts for being dismissed. The men have responded to the accusations against them with some combination of silence, apologies, promises to reform, contrition, and denial.

## Key Takeaways

Women have gained less civil rights protection, in part because of policy disagreements among women and because of fear of undermining men's and women's traditional roles.

## Exercises

1. Would you favor the passage of an Equal Rights Amendment today?
2. Are there situations in which you think men and women should be treated differently?
3. Could you redefine sexual harassment?

# 5.5 LGBTQ+ People

## Learning Objectives

After reading this section, you should be able to answer the following questions:

1. In what areas have lesbians and gay men won rights?
2. In what areas have lesbians and gay men not won rights?
3. What rights issues do transgender people face?

## Lesbians and Gay Men

Gay people, lesbians and gay men, are at the forefront of controversial civil rights battles today. They have won civil rights in several areas but not in others.[53]

Lesbians and gay men face unique obstacles in attaining civil rights. Unlike race or gender, sexual orientation may or may not be seen as an "accident of birth" that merits constitutional protection. The gay rights movement is opposed by religious conservatives, who see homosexuality as a flawed behavior, not an innate characteristic. Moreover, gay people are not "born into" a visible community and identity into which they are socialized. A history of ostracism prompts some to conceal their identities. According to many surveys of gay people, they experience discrimination and violence, actual or threatened.

Election exit polls estimate that lesbians, gay men, and bisexuals make up 4 percent of the voting public. When candidates disagree on gay rights, gay people vote by a three-to-one margin for the more pro-gay of the two.[54] Some pro-gay policies are politically powerful. For instance, the public overwhelmingly condemns discrimination against gay people in the workplace.

## Gay Movements Emerge

The anticommunist scare in the early 1950s spilled into worries about "sexual perverts" in government. Gay people faced harassment from city mayors and police departments pressured to "clean up" their cities of "vice."

The first gay rights movement, the small, often secretive Mattachine Society, emerged to respond to these threats. Mattachine's leaders argued that gay people, rather than adjust to society, should fight discrimination against them with collective identity and pride. Emulating the African American civil rights movement, they protested and confronted authorities.[55]

In June 1969, during a police raid at a gay bar in New York City's Greenwich Village, the Stonewall Inn, customers fought back. Street protests and violent outbursts followed over several days and catalyzed a mass movement. The Stonewall riots were overlooked by network television and at best got only derisive coverage in the back pages of most newspapers. But discussion of the riot and the grievances of gay people blossomed in alternative newspapers such as *The Village Voice* and emerging weeklies serving gay urban enclaves. By the mid-1970s, a national newsmagazine, *The Advocate*, had been founded.

By the early 1980s, the gay movement boasted national organizations to gather information, lobby government officials, fund electoral campaigns, and bring test cases to courts.[56] The anniversary of the Stonewall riots is marked by "gay pride" marches and celebrations in cities across the country.

This video explains how the Stonewall Riots sparked a movement.

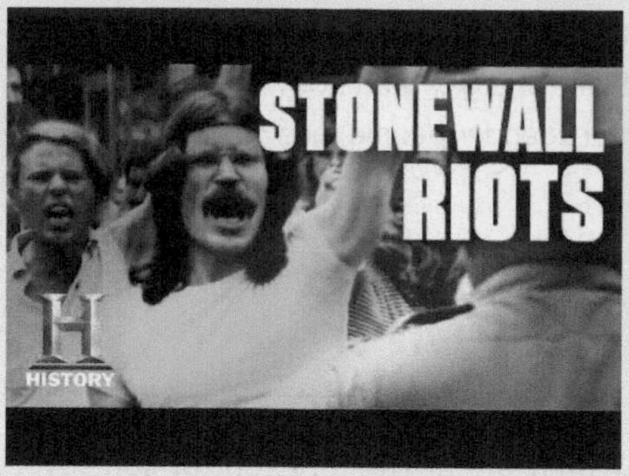


View in the online reader

## Political and Legal Efforts

The gay rights movement's first political efforts were for laws to bar discrimination by sexual orientation in employment, the first of which were enacted in 1971.[57] President Bill Clinton issued an executive order in 1998 banning discrimination on the basis of sexual orientation in federal government employment outside the military. By 2003, nondiscrimination laws had been enacted in 40 percent of American cities and towns. In 2014 President Obama signed an executive order banning job discrimination against gay people and lesbians working for federal contractors. There is not, however, a federal law preventing employees from being fired because of their sexual orientation.[58]

The first legal victory for lesbian and gay rights occurred in 1965: a federal district court held that the federal government could not disqualify a job candidate simply for being gay.[59] In 1996, the Supreme Court voided a 1992 Colorado ballot initiative that prevented the state from passing a law to ban discrimination on the basis of sexual orientation. The justices said the amendment was so sweeping that it could be explained only by "animus toward the class" of gay people—a denial of equal protection.[60]

In 2003, the Court by 6–3 rejected a Texas (sodomy) law banning same-sex sexual contact. The grounds were that it denied equal protection of the law and the right to privacy. The decision overturned a 1986 ruling that had upheld a similar law in Georgia.[61]

## The Military Ban

In 1992, presidential candidate Bill Clinton endorsed lifting the ban on gay people serving openly in the military. In a postelection press conference, Clinton said he would sign an executive order to do so. The news media, seeing a dramatic and clear-cut story, kept after this issue, which became the top concern of Clinton's first days in office. The military and key members of Congress launched a public relations campaign against Clinton's stand, highlighted by a media event at which legislators toured cramped submarines and asked sailors on board how they felt about serving with gay people. Clinton ultimately supported a compromise that was closer to a surrender—a "don't ask, don't tell" policy that had the effect of substantially increasing the number of discharges from the military for homosexuality.[62]

Over years of discussion and debate, argument, and acrimony, opposition to the policy increased and support declined. President Obama urged repeal, as did his secretary of defense and leaders of the military. In December 2010, Congress passed and the president signed legislation repealing "don't ask, don't tell." As the president put it in his 2011 State of the Union message, "Our troops come from every corner of this country—they are Black, white, Latinx, Asian, and Indigenous American people. They are Christian and Hindu, Jewish and Muslim. And yes, we know that some of them are gay. Starting this year, no American will be forbidden from serving the country they love because of who they love."[63]

## Same-Sex Marriage

Same-sex couples brought suits in state courts on the grounds that preventing them from marrying was sex discrimination barred by their state constitutions. In 1996, Hawaii's supreme court agreed. Many members of Congress, concerned that officials might be forced by the Constitution's "full faith and credit" clause to recognize same-sex marriages from Hawaii, quickly passed a Defense of Marriage Act (DOMA), which President Clinton signed. It defined marriage as the union of a man and a woman and denied same-sex couples all the federal benefits given to married people. Many states followed suit, and Hawaii's court decision was nullified when the state's voters amended the state constitution before it could take effect.

In 2000, the highest state court in Vermont ruled that the state may not discriminate against same-sex couples and allowed the legislature to create **civil unions**. These give same-sex couples "marriage lite" benefits such as inheritance rights. Going further, in 2003, Massachusetts's highest state court allowed same-sex couples legally to wed. So did the California and Connecticut Supreme Courts in 2008.

**civil unions**

Alternative to same-sex marriage, whereby a state does not allow same-sex couples to legally marry but allows them to apply for legal recognition of their relationship; this gives them the rights and privileges of marriage in that state.

Voters in thirty states, including California in 2008 (by 52 percent of the vote), passed amendments to their state constitutions banning same-sex marriage. President George W. Bush endorsed an amendment to the U.S. Constitution restricting marriage and its benefits to opposite-sex couples. It received a majority of votes in the House of Representatives, but not the two-thirds required.

In 2010, a federal judge in San Francisco struck down California's voter-approved ban on same-sex marriage on the grounds that it discriminates against gay men and women. A federal appeals court then likewise ruled the ban unconstitutional. In 2011, New York allowed same-sex marriage. The legal battle would be settled, more or less, by the Supreme Court.

In 2013, the Supreme Court ruled unconstitutional the provision of DOMA denying federal benefits to same-sex couples whose marriages were recognized by state law. The grounds were that Congress lacked the authority to restrict marriage to opposite-sex couples. The 5–4 decision did not answer the question of whether restrictions (bans) on same-sex marriages imposed by states themselves were or could be constitutional or not.[64] In a related decision the same day, the court also avoided the issue of state bans. After federal courts in California had found the ban on same-sex marriage unconstitutional, proponents of the ban had appealed the decision to the Supreme Court. By a different 5–4 the Court voted to dismiss their appeal on the narrow grounds that they lacked "standing."[65] In his dissent in the DOMA case, Justice Antonin Scalia warned presciently that sooner or later the Court would decide that denying same-sex couples the right to marry violated the Constitution.

By April 2014, seventeen states had legalized same-sex marriage: eight by their legislatures, six by courts, and three by popular vote. Thirty-three states banned it. But federal judges in some of these states were declaring the bans unconstitutional on the grounds that they violated the Constitution's equal protection clause or resulted in state-imposed inequality or because they violated the full faith and credit clause by refusing to recognize a decision made in another state.

On June 26, 2015, the Supreme Court in a 5–4 majority decision written by Justice Anthony Kennedy ruled that the Due Process and Equal Protection Clauses of the Fourteenth Amendment to the U.S. Constitution guarantee the right to same-sex marriage. The Court thereby invalidated the bans still in force in thirteen states.[66]

Nonetheless, given the absence of federal legislation banning discrimination on the basis of sexual orientation, it was still legal in many states to discriminate against LGBTQ+ people in employment, housing, and public accommodation.

# Transgender People

Transgender people identify with or express a gender different from their assigned sex. They could be uncomfortable with their external appearance and desire to transition from one sex to another. They could have gender dysphoria treatable with hormone replacement therapy, gender affirming surgery, or psychotherapy.

Transgender people have been attacked, murdered, and experienced discrimination obtaining or when at work, seeking or using public accommodations, in health care, and in other aspects of their lives.[67] But it was in 2016 that North Carolina's House Bill 2 (HB2) brought national attention, particularly through widespread media coverage, to their situation.

Enacted by the Republican-dominated state legislature and signed by the Republican governor, the legislation allowed people to only use a multi-occupancy single public restroom according to their gender as stated on their birth certificate. The law was a response to the addition by the Charlotte City Council of sexual orientation and gender identity to the city's nondiscrimination ordinance. One effect of the Charlotte action was to allow transgender people to use facilities that conformed to their gender identity. A claimed justification for the state law was to prevent straight men from putting on dresses so they could view women in women's restrooms. (Only the first part of the law dealt with bathrooms; other parts, pretty much ignored by the media, restricted minimum wage increases and child labor protections.)

The National Basketball Association (NBA), the National Collegiate Athletic Association (NCAA), and other national organizations and businesses reacted to the law by withdrawing events from and stopping expansions in North Carolina, thus costing the state, particularly its major cities, millions of dollars. Those same organizations refused to reinstate the events or return unless, or until, the state repealed the legislation.

On June 30, 2017, the still Republican-controlled state legislature passed and the newly elected governor, a Democrat, signed legislation more or less repealing HB2. More, because it permitted people to use the bathroom of the gender with which they identified. Less, because until 2020, it prevented cities from enacting nondiscrimination ordinances protecting lesbian, gay, bisexual, and transgender people.

However, transgender people have obtained some legal support and political protection. Public opinion about them and their rights is slowly improving, although with uncertainty and a lack of knowledge.[68]

## Key Takeaways

LGBTQ+ people have won protections against discrimination in states and localities and in the military and, through the courts, equality in marriage. Transgender people experience discrimination from government, as in North Carolina.

## Exercise

1. Do you feel you have faced discrimination? How do you think the type of discrimination you have faced should be addressed in the law?

# 5.6 People with Disabilities

## Learning Objective

After reading this section, you should be able to answer the following question:

1. What is the Americans with Disabilities Act?

## People with Disabilities

People with disabilities have sought and gained civil rights protections. When society does not accommodate their differences, they view this as discrimination. They have clout in part because, by U.S. Census estimates, over 19 percent of the population has some kind of disability.

### From Rehabilitation to Rights

Early in the twentieth century, federal policy began seeking the integration of people with disabilities into society, starting with returning veterans of World War I. According to these policies, disabilities were viewed as medical problems; rehabilitation was stressed.

By the 1960s, Congress began shifting toward civil rights by enacting a law requiring new federal construction to be designed to allow entrance for people with disabilities. In 1972, Congress voted, without debate, that work and school programs receiving federal funds could not deny benefits to or discriminate against someone "solely by reason of his handicap."[69] Civil servants in the Department of Health, Education, and Welfare built on this language to create a principle of **reasonable accommodation.** In the workplace, this means that facilities must be made accessible (e.g., by means of wheelchair ramps), responsibilities restructured, or policies altered so that someone with disabilities can do a job. At schools, it entails extra time for tests and assignments for those with learning disabilities.

**reasonable accommodation**

Federal policy mandating employers and schools to find ways to make it possible for people with disabilities to have equal access to employment and education.

The Americans with Disabilities Act (ADA) passed Congress by a large margin and was signed into law in 1990 by President George H. W. Bush. The act moved away from the "medical model" by defining disability as including a physical or mental impairment that limits a "major life activity." It gives people with disabilities a right of access to public buildings. It prohibits discrimination in employment against those who, given reasonable opportunity, could perform the essential functions of a job.

However, the Supreme and other courts interpreted the law and its definition of disability narrowly; for example, to exclude people with conditions that could be mitigated (e.g., by a hearing aid or artificial limb), controlled by medication, or were in remission.

In response, on September 29, 2008, President George W. Bush signed legislation overturning these decisions. It expanded the definition of disability to cover more physical and mental impairments and made it easier for workers to prove discrimination.

Then, in March 2017, the Supreme Court unanimously interpreted the Individuals With Disabilities Education Act (IDEA) to mean that schools may not settle for minimal educational progress by students with disabilities. The Court did not, however, set forth a clearer standard. The vagueness put the burden on the family to show that the child needed a particular program.[70]

## Depictions of Disabilities

Disability activists fight to be respected and accepted as they are. They advocate for what they can do when society does not discriminate against them and adapts to their needs. This effort is frustrated by the typical media frame presenting disabilities as terrible medical burdens to conquer. The mass media tend to present people with disabilities either as pitiable, helpless victims requiring a cure or as what activists call "supercrips": those courageously trying to "overcome" their handicaps[71] (see the following "Comparing Content" for more information).

### Comparing Content

#### Christopher Reeve

In 1995, the actor Christopher Reeve suffered a devastating fall in a horseback-riding accident, which paralyzed him from the neck down and forced him to use a ventilator to breathe. Reeve—best known for playing the role of Superman in a series of movies—would not be deterred. He became a film director and found award-winning acting roles, such as a television remake of director Alfred Hitchcock's classic *Rear Window* (1954), in which the principal character has a broken leg.

Above all, Reeve resolved he would walk again. He began to campaign for a cure for spinal injuries, sponsoring television specials and raising money through a newly formed foundation. He gave countless speeches, including one to the Democratic National Convention in 2000. Reeve's efforts won praise in the media, which monitored his landmarks, such as breathing without a ventilator. A *Time* magazine headline in September 2002 was typical: "Against All the Odds: Christopher Reeve, in a visit with *TIME*, tells how he is regaining control of his body, one finger at a time."

The media attention lavished on Reeve until his death in 2004 irked many people with disabilities. They saw the massive publicity he received as undermining their struggle for civil rights and equal treatment. In magazines aimed at serving people with disabilities, such as *Ability Magazine* and *Ragged Edge*, writers blasted Reeve for presenting himself as, in their words, "incomplete" or "decayed." Chet Cooper, editor of *Ability Magazine*, confronted Reeve in a 1998 interview. Cooper began, "Promoting civil rights for people with disabilities would involve encouraging people to accept and respect people with disabilities just as they are. . . . Their concept is 'I don't need to walk to be a whole human being. I am able to lead a fully functional life, independent of walking.'" Reeve answered, "We were not born to be living in wheelchairs. We were meant to be walking upright with all of our body systems fully functional and I'd like to have that back."[72]

Actor Christopher Reeve was adored by the news media—and politicians—for his committed fight to regain the use of his body after a horseback-riding accident.

Source: Featureflash Photo Agency / Shutterstock.com

## Key Takeaways

People with disabilities have won civil rights protections through national legislative and executive action.

## Exercise

1. How do you explain the success of people with disabilities to obtain rights?

# 5.7 Civil Rights in the Information Age

## Learning Objectives

After reading this section, you should be able to answer the following questions:

1. How do media portrayals of civil rights activities vary?
2. How and why do civil rights organizers exert pressure on media outlets?
3. How are new media being used to serve the interests of civil rights groups and raise awareness of civil rights issues?

The media are a potential resource for disadvantaged groups subject to discrimination to try to energize their members, attract support (sway opinion, raise funds) from the public, and achieve their policy objectives.

# Media Interactions

Generating positive media depictions can be a struggle for disadvantaged groups, but it has proved essential in their progress toward achieving their civil rights.

## Stages of Interaction

Civil rights movements' interactions with the media tend to move in stages. At first, fearing biased depictions, these groups try to stay out of the media or work defensively to limit negative coverage. Over time, activists become more sophisticated in dealing with the news media and more determined to use news attention as leverage. Their challenge is to find ways to "package" the discrimination they face every day into a compelling breaking story.

Demonstrations, marches, and protests are one way to respond, although they can quickly become "old news." Some activists end up conducting larger and more militant protests in order to get covered, but this can be detrimental. After 1965, for example, the African American civil rights movement divided, as some participants embraced the confrontational, even inflammatory rhetoric of the "Black Power" movement. Coverage of militancy easily turns negative, so activists have learned to anticipate the needs of the news media and become more disciplined when they plan their activities. As a result, they may downplay controversial issues and stress less sweeping policy changes.

Members of disadvantaged groups are quick to see the media acting as *agents of* discrimination, reinforcing derogatory stereotypes.[73] They therefore monitor media content and apply pressure on both news and entertainment media to influence how their members are portrayed.[74] They threaten boycotts of media companies and advertisers. One of the first endeavors of the National Association for the Advancement of Colored People (NAACP) was to protest against D. W. Griffith's feature film *Birth of a Nation* (1915), which, despite achieving classic status, portrayed African Americans after the Civil War as stupid and venal and celebrated the Ku Klux Klan. Even if the controversy does not end in a withdrawal of the offensive material, it sensitizes media executives to the risks of potentially inflammatory programming.

Targets of public criticism may respond by reforming their depictions. Griffith himself was stung by the accusations of insensitivity. His next film, *Intolerance* (1916), is an eloquent epic combining multiple stories across the ages to plead for understanding between groups. More recently, director Jonathan Demme faced protests from lesbian and gay groups over his film *Silence of the Lambs* (1991), whose villain was a seductive, murderous cross dresser. In response, Demme's next film, *Philadelphia* (1993), featured Tom Hanks as a sympathetic gay man with AIDS who sues the law firm that fired him.

## Supportive Media

Through old and new media, disadvantaged groups can reach out and mobilize among themselves in favor of civil rights.

Supportive media have long prospered in one old technology: newsprint. Newspapers aimed at Black readers date back to *Freedom's Journal*, a newspaper founded in 1827 in New York to rebut the racist claims of other newspapers. Today the Black press, ranging from small local weeklies to glossy high-circulation national magazines like *Ebony*, continues the tradition. It provides news items that might otherwise go unnoticed in the mainstream media and also adds information and interpretation about ongoing stories, explicitly taking the interests and viewpoints of Black people into account. The Black press is prominent online as well.[75]

The burgeoning number of foreign-language daily and weekly newspapers (many of them also online), which serve other racial and ethnic minorities, are among the few gaining readership today. Many are small, independent operations; others are offshoots of established newspapers such as *El Nuevo Herald* in Doral, Florida, or *Viet Mercury* in San Jose, California. They often provide information and perspectives that challenge narrow or stereotypical coverage. Magazines such as *Ms.* enable women to address each other about political concerns.

News and entertainment cable channels serving disadvantaged groups include Oxygen for women, Black Entertainment Television for Black people, and Logo for gay people. The small "indie" subsidiaries of Hollywood studios in 2005 produced two Oscar finalists with challenging content: *Crash* on race and *Brokeback Mountain* on sexual orientation.

## Going Online

There are numerous resources online that can inform disadvantaged individuals and groups about their civil rights. Websites such as Civilrights.org, sponsored by the Leadership Conference on Civil Rights, provide up-to-date information about a wide range of issues, such as how homeowners with disabilities can protect their homes during an economic downturn. Rich resources recounting the struggles for civil rights throughout history are available online, including the Library of Congress's Voices of Civil Rights, an online exhibition of thousands of documents, oral histories, photos, and news reports on the African American civil rights movement.

Disadvantaged groups use digital media to mobilize an often far-flung constituency and spark action for civil rights. They organize online communities on Facebook to share information and concerns. They use email alerts and text messages to keep their supporters abreast of the latest developments and to call them to action when needed. They orchestrate blast email messages and online petitions urging members of Congress to support their cause.

## Media Consequences

The media sometimes sympathetically depict and amplify disadvantaged groups' demands for civil rights, especially when they are voiced by individuals who ask only for equality of opportunity and to be judged on their own merits. Coverage is unfavorable when it frames the demands as undeserved or requiring special privileges or the issue as a conflict in which one side will win and the other lose. The media's frame of interracial conflict increases racial divides on affirmative action. If affirmative action is presented in terms that are less stark than win-lose or either-or, whites' views become more favorable.[76]

**FIGURE 5.5**
**Ellen DeGeneres and the Media**
Ellen DeGeneres's character on her situation comedy *Ellen* came out of the closet, and so did DeGeneres herself, to huge media attention.

Source: Featureflash Photo Agency / Shutterstock.com

**hate crime**

An attack on a minority because of his or her race, religion, or sexual orientation, which sometimes results in death.

**"came out of the closet"**

Gay or lesbian individuals who, having previously denied or concealed their sexual orientation, now publicly announce it.

Civil rights issues often make the news in the form of dramatic, unexpected events. Two widely publicized **hate crime** murders from 1998 drew attention to these issues. James Byrd Jr., a Black man, was chained to the back of a truck and dragged to his death in Jasper, Texas. Matthew Shepard, a gay University of Wyoming student, was beaten, tied to a remote fence in Laramie, and left to die. These murders provoked massive attention to the threat of violence against Black people and gay men.

Televised docudramas were made about both cases. The media's constant images of the dusty back roads of Jasper and the buck-and-rail fence outside Laramie evoked images of the old South and the Wild West. These media depictions sparked debates about the persistence of discrimination. But they presented it as an isolated problem, and not one that concerns mainstream America.

The media can depict members of disadvantaged groups positively to the public. Given that most Americans are surrounded by and interact with people like themselves, such visibility can push people toward understanding and tolerance. Perhaps the most notable example of this effect is the shift in the portrayal of gay people in the mass media.[77] Positive images appeared on television series such as *Modern Family* and *Will and Grace*. Familiar, openly gayLGBTQ+ showbiz personalities appear on talk shows, including Ellen DeGeneres, who **"came out of the closet"** in real life and in playing her character in her situation comedy *Ellen*. She has subsequently hosted a talk show of her own and the Oscars. Such depictions create a climate of tolerance in which gay people are more comfortable being open. As a result, more Americans report knowing someone who is gay, which in turn increases their support for equal treatment.[78]

### Key Takeaways

In this section we showed that the media are a potential resource for disadvantaged groups to energize their members, sway public opinion, and achieve their policy objectives. Such groups may engage in behavior that attracts media attention; they may monitor and try to influence media coverage. Disadvantaged groups also benefit from their own media and from their use of digital media. Depictions in mass media can be unfavorable—for example, when a group's demands are framed as undeserved or requiring special privileges—or favorable, as in portrayals of LGBTQ+ people on television entertainment shows.

Finally, we would observe the almost always negative depictions of Arabs and Muslims, especially of men, in American media. They are commonly depicted as terrorists engaged in irrational and violent behavior.

### Exercises

1. What do you think makes people sympathetic to discrimination claims? What makes them more likely to dismiss them?

2. How are people of the same race, gender, sexual orientation, or disability as you portrayed in the media? Do you think they are portrayed realistically?
3. Do you support any civil rights groups? How do these groups use the media to bring attention to their cause?

### Civic Education

**Los Angeles High School Students Walkout**

High school students in and around Los Angeles walked out of class on Friday, March 24, and Monday, March 27, 2006. They were protesting legislation passed by the House of Representatives to criminalize undocumented immigration and any sort of aid to undocumented immigrants. Through mass media coverage of the walkout they were able to raise their concerns in their own terms.[79]

As the example of the high school students shows, schools can be a fertile ground for civil rights activism. Civil rights are especially pertinent to institutions of higher learning. Public universities and colleges must be operated according to the Fourteenth Amendment's demand that governments provide "equal protection of the law." Private universities and colleges are subject to civil rights laws, since the vast majority of them receive federal funds.

# 5.8 Recommended Reading

Frank, Walter. *Law and the Gay Rights Story: The Long Search for Equal Justice in a Divided Democracy.* New Jersey: Rutgers University Press, 2014. A comprehensive history covering the issues.

García, John A. *Latino Politics in America: Community, Culture, and Interests.* Lanham, MD: Rowman & Littlefield, 3rd ed. 2016. A well-informed, inclusive account of Latinx politics.

Jones, Martha S. *Vanguard: How Black Women Broke Barriers, Won the Vote, and Insisted on Equality for All.* New York: Basic Books, 2020. The Black women who battled for their rights against racism and sexism.

Larson, Stephanie Greco. *Media and Minorities: The Politics of Race in News and Entertainment.* Lanham, MD: Rowman & Littlefield, 3rd ed. 2016. An exhaustive catalog of the many ways in which the media stereotype racial and ethnic minorities.

Lee, Harper. *To Kill a Mockingbird.* New York: J. B. Lippincott, 1960. Best-selling novel (and Hollywood film) in which liberal Southern lawyer defends falsely accused African American man; an eloquent plea for racial understanding and tolerance.

Mucciaroni, Gary. *Same Sex, Different Politics: Success and Failure in the Struggle over Gay Rights.* Chicago: University of Chicago Press, 2008. Argues that obtaining gay rights depends on interactions between advocates, public opinion, and political institutions.

Roberts, Gene, and Hank Klibanoff. *The Race Beat: The Press, the Civil Rights Struggle, and the Awakening of a Nation.* New York: Random House, 2008. Media coverage of the civil rights movement.

Scotch, Richard K. *From Good Will to Civil Rights: Transforming Federal Disability Policy*, 2nd ed. Philadelphia: Temple University Press, 2009. A revealing case study of Congress's pioneering steps on the issue of disability.

Wolbrecht, Christina. *The Politics of Women's Rights: Parties, Positions, and Change.* Princeton, NJ: Princeton University Press, 2010. A comprehensive survey and analysis.

Woodward, C. Vann. *The Strange Career of Jim Crow.* New York: Oxford University Press, 1950. The classic study of segregation in the United States.

# 5.9 Recommended Viewing

*And Then They Came For Us* (2017). Account of Executive Order 9066 signed by President Roosevelt leading to the forced incarceration of 120,000 Japanese Americans during World War II.

*Bamboozled* (2000). Spike Lee's satire of portrayals of Black people in popular culture.

*The Birth of a Nation* (1915). Director D. W. Griffith's groundbreaking epic of the Civil War and its aftermath rewrites history in its glorification of the Ku Klux Klan.

*BlacKkKlansman* (2018). Comedy in which a Black policeman infiltrates the Ku Klux Klan.

*Brokeback Mountain* (2005). A pathbreaking Hollywood movie about the doomed romance of two male Wyoming ranch hands.

*The Bronze Screen* (2002). Documentary of 100 years of the (stereotyped) images of Latinxs on film and television.

*Do the Right Thing* (1989). Director Spike Lee's troubling take on racial and ethnic tensions in the city.

*El Norte* (1983). Director Gregory Nava's pioneering drama of Guatemalans fleeing political repression to enter the United States as undocumented immigrants.

*Eyes on the Prize* (1987). A compelling multipart documentary of the American civil rights movement.

*Freedom Riders* (2010). Documentary about the Black and white men and women who flouted Jim Crow laws and faced enraged mobs by sitting together on interstate buses and trains traveling across the South.

*Fruitvale Station* (2013). Drama on the last day of Oscar Grant's life before he is killed by a BART police officer in Oakland, CA.

*Get Out (2017).* Black man visits his white girlfriend's parents with dire consequences.

*Guess Who's Coming to Dinner* (1967). Successful struggle of the parents (stars Katharine Hepburn and Spencer Tracy) of a white woman to come to terms with her engagement to a Black doctor (star Sidney Poitier).

*I Am Not Your Negro* (2016). Race relations documented through the life and eloquent words of Black author James Baldwin.

*Iron Jawed Angels* (2004). Recounts the struggle of the suffragists who fought for the passage of the Nineteenth Amendment.

*The Laramie Project* (2002). Director Moises Kaufman's video adaptation of his play based on interviews with Wyomingites in the wake of the anti-gay murder of Matthew Shepard.

*Loving* (2016). Feature film based on the documentary (below).

*The Loving Story* (2011). Nancy Buirski's moving documentary about Richard and Mildred Loving, their lawyers, and the 1967 Supreme Court decision that overturned and invalidated laws prohibiting interracial marriage (anti-miscegenation laws).

*Mississippi Burning* (1988). Loosely based on the FBI investigation, obstructed by bigotry and a conspiracy of violence, into the murder of three civil rights workers.

*North Country* (2005). The true story of the battle of a woman against sexual haarassment in a Minnesota mining company.

*Of Civil Wrongs and Rights: The Fred Korematsu Story* (2000). Absorbing documentary on the battle for vindication of a Japanese American interned by the U.S. government during World War II.

*Outrage* (2009). Kirby Dick's documentary outs closeted politicians whose anti-gay records, it contends, contradict their homosexuality.

*Scottsboro: An American Tragedy* (2001). Documentary about Black teenagers falsely accused, convicted, imprisoned, and eventually exonerated of rape in 1931.

*Selma* (2014). A moving account of the famous march in 1965 for civil rights and accompanying events, although the depiction of the Rev. Martin Luther King Jr. is pietistic and that of the motives and behavior of President Lyndon B. Johnson misleading.

*She's Beautiful When She's Angry* (2014). Documentary about the changes wrought by the women's movement between 1966 and 1971.

*The Slanted Screen* (2006). Documentary on stereotypical portrayals of Asian people in films and television.

*Smoke Signals* (1998). Trip of two young men out of a reservation shows their life and stereotypes about Indigenous Americans.

*Stonewall Uprising* (2010). Documentary recounting the 1969 "rebellion" by gay people in New York City against police raids, which catalyzed the gay liberation movement.

*The Times of Harvey Milk* (1984). A moving documentary about one of the first openly gay elected officials in the United States, gunned down by a fellow city supervisor in 1978. Made into the Hollywood film *Milk* (2008), starring Sean Penn.

*Two Towns of Jasper* (2001). A documentary about the murder of James Byrd, in which Black people interview Black people and white people interview white people in the two racially separate communities within the town.

# Endnotes


1. Meghan Keneally, "Hillary Clinton's Progress Trying to 'Shatter That Highest, Hardest Glass Ceiling,'" *ABC News*, November 9, 2016, https://abcnews.go.com/Politics/hillary-clintons-progress-shatter-highest-hardest-glass-ceiling/story?id=43420815.
2. John D. Skrentny, *The Minority Rights Revolution* (Cambridge, MA: Harvard University Press, 2002).
3. Herman Belz, *A New Birth of Freedom: The Republican Party and Freedmen's Rights, 1861–1866*, 2nd ed. (New York: Fordham University Press, 2000), chap. 7.
4. *Bolling v. Sharpe*, 347 US 497 (1954). See also *Adarand Constructors v. Peña*, 515 US 200 (1995).
5. Michael Weaver, "'Judge Lynch' in the Court of Public Opinion: Publicity and the De-legitimation of Lynching," *American Political Science Review*, 113:2 (2019): 293.DOI: https://doi.org/10.1017/S0003055418000886.
6. William Gillette, *Retreat from Reconstruction, 1869–1879* (Baton Rouge: Louisiana State University Press, 1979), chap. 2. Data on lynching are in Robert L. Zangrando, *The NAACP's Crusade Against Lynching, 1909–1950* (Philadelphia: Temple University Press, 1980), table 2.
7. *Plessy v. Ferguson*, 163 US 537 (1896).
8. Charles Flint Kellogg, *NAACP: A History of the National Association for the Advancement of Colored People*, vol. 1 (Baltimore: Johns Hopkins University Press, 1967).
9. *Missouri ex rel. Gaines v. Canada*, 305 US 676 (1937). See Mark V. Tushnet, *The NAACP's Legal Strategy Against Segregated Education, 1925–1950* (Chapel Hill: University of North Carolina Press, 1987), chaps. 2–5.
10. Doug McAdam, *Political Process and the Development of Black Insurgency, 1930–1970*, 2nd ed. (Chicago: University of Chicago Press, 1999), 100–103.
11. *Mitchell v. United States*, 313 US 80 (1941); *Smith v. Allwright*, 321 US 649 (1944); *Shelley v. Kraemer*, 334 US 1 (1948).
12. *Brown v. Board of Education*, 347 US 483 (1954).
13. Harvard Sitkoff, *The Struggle for Black Equality, 1954–1992*, rev. ed. (New York: Hill and Wang, 1993), chap. 2.
14. Gene Roberts and Hank Klibanoff, *The Race Beat*. (New York: Random House, 2006).
15. Douglas Brinkley, *Rosa Parks* (New York: Viking Penguin, 2000), chap. 5.
16. William H. Chafe, *Civilities and Civil Rights: Greensboro, North Carolina, and the Black Struggle for Freedom* (New York: Oxford University Press, 1980), chap. 3.
17. David Niven, *The Politics of Injustice: The Kennedys, the Freedom Rides, and the Electoral Consequences of a Moral Compromise* (Knoxville: University of Tennessee Press, 2003).
18. Glenn T. Eskew, *But For Birmingham: The Local and National Movements in the Civil Rights Struggle* (Chapel Hill: University of North Carolina Press, 1997).
19. Tom W. Smith, "America's Most Important Problem—A Trend Analysis," *Public Opinion Quarterly* 44, no. 2 (Summer 1980): 164–80.
20. Lyndon B. Johnson. 15 March 1965. "Special Message to the Congress: The American Promise." Public Papers of the Presidents of the United States: Lyndon B. Johnson, 1965. Volume I, entry 107, pp. 281-287. Washington, D. C.: Government Printing Office, 1966. Retrieved from: http://www.lbjlibrary.net/collections/selected-speeches/1965/03-15-1965.html.
21. *Loving v. Virginia*, 388 U.S. 1 (1967).
22. J. Harvie Wilkinson III, *From Brown to Bakke: The Supreme Court and School Desegregation* (New York: Oxford University Press, 1979), chaps. 8–9.
23. Robert M. Entman and Andrew Rojecki, *The Black Image in the White Mind: Media and Race in America* (Chicago: University of Chicago Press, 2000).
24. *Regents of the University of California v. Bakke*, 438 US 265 (1978).
25. *Parents Involved in Community Schools v. Seattle School District No. 1*, 551 US 701 (2007).
26. *Shuette v. Coalition to Defend Affirmative Action* (2014).
27. *Fisher v. University of Texas*, 579 U.S. ___ 2016; also Adam Liptak, "4 Justices Uphold Race-Aware Admissions," *The New York Times*, June 24, 2016, A1.
28. Katie Benner, "Trump's Justice Department Redefines Whose Civil Rights to Protect," *The New York Times*, September 4, 2018, A13.
29. *Shelby County v. Holder*, 570 U.S. 2013.
30. In a study of proposed and adopted voting restriction legislation from 2006–2011, Keith G. Bentele and Erin E. O'Brien concluded that they "are highly partisan, strategic, and racialized affairs" *Perspectives on Politics*, 11:4 (December 2013): 1088–1116.
31. Benjamin Márquez, *LULAC: The Evolution of a Mexican American Political Organization* (Austin: University of Texas Press, 1993); David Rodríguez, *Latino National Political Coalitions: Struggles and Challenges* (New York: Routledge, 2002).

32. *Lau v. Nichols*, 414 US 56 (1974).
33. Rodolfo O. de la Garza et al., *Latino Voices: Mexican, Puerto Rican, and Cuban Perspectives on American Politics* (Boulder, CO: Westview Press, 1992).
34. Barack Obama. 11 January 2011. "Remarks by the President in State of Union Address." Retrieved from: https://obamawhitehouse.archives.gov/the-press-office/2011/01/25/remarks-president-state-union-address.
35. *In re Ah Yup* (1878).
36. *Korematsu v. United States*, 323 US 214 (1944).
37. Leslie T. Hatamiya, *Righting a Wrong: Japanese Americans and the Passage of the Civil Liberties Act of 1988* (Stanford, CA: Stanford University Press, 1993); Mitchell T. Maki, Harry H. L. Kitano, and S. Megan Berthold, *Achieving the Impossible Dream: How Japanese Americans Obtained Redress* (Urbana: University of Illinois Press, 1999).
38. Yen Le Espiritu, *Asian American Panethnicity: Bridging Institutions and Identities* (Philadelphia: Temple University Press, 1992), chap. 2; Pei-Te Lien, *The Making of Asian America Through Political Participation* (Philadelphia: Temple University Press, 2001), chap. 5.
39. Mia Tuan, *Forever Foreigners or Honorary Whites?: The Asian Experience Today* (New Brunswick, NJ: Rutgers University Press, 1998).
40. David Treuer, *The Heartbeat of Wounded Knee* (New York: Riverhead-Penguin Books, 2019).
41. *Talton v. Mayes*, 163 US 376 (1896).
42. Nancy Isenberg, *Sex and Citizenship in Antebellum America* (Chapel Hill: University of North Carolina Press, 1998); Susan Zaeske, *Signatures of Citizenship: Petitioning, Antislavery, and Women's Political Identity* (Chapel Hill: University of North Carolina Press, 2003).
43. Louise Michele Neuman, *White Women's Rights: The Racial Origins of Feminism in the United States* (New York: Oxford University Press, 1999).
44. Jean H. Baker, ed., *Votes for Women: The Struggle for Suffrage Revisited* (New York: Oxford University Press, 2002).
45. Cynthia Ellen Harrison, *On Account of Sex: The Politics of Women's Issues, 1945–1968* (Berkeley: University of California Press, 1988).
46. On EEOC's initial implementation, see Hugh Davis Graham, *The Civil Rights Era: Origins and Development of National Policy* (New York: Oxford University Press, 1990), chap. 8; on the founding of NOW, see Jo Freeman, *The Politics of Women's Liberation* (New York: Longman, 1975).
47. Quoted in Christina Wolbrecht, *The Politics of Women's Rights: Parties, Positions, and Change* (Princeton, NJ: Princeton University Press, 2000), 35.
48. Joyce Gelb and Marian Lief Palley, *Women and Public Policies: Reassessing Gender Politics*, rev. ed. (Charlottesville: University Press of Virginia, 1998), chap.5.
49. Jane S. Mansbridge, *How We Lost the ERA* (Chicago: University of Chicago Press, 1986).
50. Yamiche Alcindor and Katie Rogers, "Congress Struggles to Confront Harassment as Stories Pile Up," *New York Times*, November 14, 2017, A19.
51. Sandra F. Sperino and Suja F. Thomas, "When Harassment Isn't Harassment," *The New York Times*, November 30, 2017, A31.
52. Sheelah Kolhatkar, "The Disrupters," *New Yorker*, November 20, 2017, 58.
53. Susan Gluck Mezy, *Beyond Marriage: Continuing Battles for LGBT Rights*, Lanham, MD: Rowman & Littlefield, 2017; and Daniel R. Pinello, *America's War on Same-Sex Couples and Their Families: And How the Courts Rescued Them*, New York: Cambridge University Press, 2017; and *Failure in the Struggle over Gay Rights* (Chicago: University of Chicago Press, 2008); and Paul Brewer, *Value War: Public Opinion and the Politics of Gay Rights* (Lanham, MD: Rowman & Littlefield, 2008).
54. Mark Hertzog, *The Lavender Vote: Lesbians, Gay Men, and Bisexuals in American Electoral Politics* (New York: New York University Press, 1996).
55. John D'Emilio, *Sexual Politics, Sexual Communities: The Making of a Homosexual Minority*, 1940–1970 (Chicago: University of Chicago Press, 1983). On news coverage of the early movement, see Edward Alwood, *Straight News: Gays, Lesbians, and the Media* (New York: Columbia University Press, 1996).
56. Craig A. Rimmerman, *From Identity to Politics: The Lesbian and Gay Movements in the United States* (Philadelphia: Temple University Press, 2002), chaps. 2 and 3.
57. James W. Button, Barbara A. Rienzo, and Kenneth D. Wald, *Private Lives, Public Conflicts: Battles Over Gay Rights in American Communities* (Washington, DC: CQ Press, 1997).
58. Peter Baker, "Obama Calls For a Ban On Job Bias Against Gays," *The New York Times*, July 22, 2014, A14.
59. *Scott v. Macy*, 349 F. 2d 182 (1965).
60. *Romer v. Evans*, 517 US 620 (1996) at 632.
61. *Lawrence v. Texas*, 539 US 558 (2003) overturning *Bowers v. Hardwick* 478 US 186 (1986).
62. Craig A. Rimmerman, ed., *Gay Rights, Military Wrongs: Political Perspectives on Lesbians and Gays in the Military* (New York: Garland Publishing, 1996).
63. "State of the Union 2011: President Obama's Full Speech," ABC News, accessed February 3, 2011, http://abcnews.go.com/Politics/State_of_the_Union/state-of-the-union-2011-full-transcript/story?id=12759395&page=4.
64. *United States v. Windsor*, 570 U.S. 12 (2013).
65. *Hollingsworth v. Perry*, 570 U.S. 12 (2013).
66. Obergefell v. Hodges, 576 US__ (2015); see Stephen Macedo, *Just Married: Same-Sex Couples, Monogamy and the Future of Marriage* (Princeton: Princeton University Press, 2015) for a thoughtful defense of marriage equality.
67. For a striking example, see *Karen Francis Ulana v. Easterm Airlines*, U.S. Court of Appeals for the Seventh Circuit, 742 F 2nd 1081, August 29, 1984.
68. Jami K. Taylor, Daniel C. Lewis, and Donald C. Haider-Markel, *The Remarkable Rise of Transgender Rights* (Ann Arbor: University of Michigan Press, 2018).
69. Richard K. Scotch, *From Good Will to Civil Rights: Transforming Federal Disability Policy*, 2nd ed. (Philadelphia: Temple University Press, 2001), chap. 3.
70. *Endrew F. v. Douglas County School District*, reported by Richard Perez-Pena, *The New York Times*, March 23, 2017, A19.
71. Charles A. Riley II, *Disability and the Media: Prescriptions for Change* (Hanover, NH: University Press of New England, 2005).
72. Christopher Reeve and Fred Fay, "The Road I Have Taken: Christopher Reeve and the Cure," interview by Chet Cooper, *Ability Magazine*, 1998, http://abilitymagazine.com/reeve_interview.
73. For an exhaustive catalog of stereotypes, see Stephanie Greco Larson, *Media and Minorities* (Lanham, MD: Rowman & Littlefield, 2005).
74. Kathryn C. Montgomery, *Target Prime Time: Advocacy Groups and the Struggle over Entertainment Television* (New York: Oxford University Press, 1989).
75. Susan Herbst, *Politics at the Margin: Historical Studies of Public Expression Outside the Mainstream* (New York: Cambridge University Press, 1994), chap. 3.
76. Paul M. Sniderman and Thomas Piazza, *The Scar of Race* (Cambridge, MA: Belknap Press of Harvard University Press, 1993).
77. Larry Gross, *Up from Invisibility: Lesbians, Gay Men, and the Media in America* (New York: Columbia University Press, 2001); Suzanna Danuta Walters, *All the Rage: The Story of Gay Visibility in America* (Chicago: University of Chicago Press, 2001).
78. On the dynamics of public opinion, see Alan S. Yang, "The Polls—Trends: Attitudes Toward Homosexuality," *Public Opinion Quarterly* 61, no. 3 (1997), 477–507; and *From Wrongs to Rights, 1973–1999: Public Opinion on Gay and Lesbian Americans Moves Toward Equality* (New York: Policy Institute, The National Gay and Lesbian Task Force, 2001).
79. See Cynthia H. Cho and Anna Gorman, "Massive Student Walkout Spreads Across Southland," *Los Angeles Times*, March 28, 2006, A1; Teresa Watanabe and Hector Becerra, "How DJs Put 500,000 Marchers in Motion," *Los Angeles Times*, March 28, 2006, A10.

CHAPTER 6

# Political Culture and Socialization

## 6.1 Preamble

Americans have strong positive feelings about the country's flag. Government leaders and candidates giving speeches often are flanked by the Stars and Stripes; flags appear in ceremonies honoring police officers, firefighters, and military personnel; and American embassies, military bases, and ships abroad are depicted with flags flying. The flag is displayed prominently in television, print, and online advertisements for many different products; car showrooms are draped with flags; clothing manufacturers present models wearing the latest fashions against American flag backdrops; and flags appear in ads for food, furniture, toys, and electronic gadgets. Flags the size of the entire field are rolled out during NFL and college football games to cheering crowds.

Immediately following the 9/11 terrorist attacks, there was a huge increase in the sale and display of the American flag. Nowhere was the trend more apparent than on television news broadcasts: news anchors wore American flag lapel pins, and background visuals featured themes such as "America Fights Back," wrapped in the flag's color scheme of red, white, and blue.

**FIGURE 6.1 Commemorated the Victims of the September 11, 2001 Terrorist Attacks**
Prior to a football game in September 2010, cadets from the U.S. Air Force Academy unfurl a large American flag in Falcon Stadium to commemorate the people who lost their lives in the 9/11 terrorist attacks.

Source: Mike Kaplan, ASAF via Wikimedia: https://commons.wikimedia.org/wiki/File:BYU_at_Air_Force_2010-09-11.jpg.

The United States flag is the core icon of American political culture. Media representations associate the flag with the two dominant values of the American creed: democracy and capitalism. News media connect the flag with aspects of democratic political culture, including elections, government institutions, and national pride. People have more positive reactions to politicians when they appear with the American flag. Advertisements send the message that to "buy American," and thereby support the free market economic system, is to be patriotic.

People gain an understanding and acceptance of the political culture of their nation through political socialization. The term "political socialization" refers to the process by which people learn their roles as citizens and develop an understanding of government and politics. This chapter explores the ways in which knowledge about politics; attitudes about government, political processes, and leaders; and citizens' political behavior—all of which are elements of American political culture—are passed on from generation to generation.

# 6.2 Political Culture

## Learning Objectives

After reading this section, you should be able to answer the following questions:

1. What is a nation's political culture, and why is it important?
2. What are the characteristics of American political culture?
3. What are the values and beliefs that are most ingrained in American citizens?
4. What constitutes a political subculture, and why are subcultures important?

This section defines political culture and identifies the core qualities that distinguish American political culture, including the country's traditions, folklore, and heroes. The values that Americans embrace, such as individualism and egalitarianism, will be examined as they relate to cultural ideals.

## What Is Political Culture?

**political culture**

Collective ideologies, values, beliefs, norms, assumptions, and patterns of behavior that characterize a particular country.

**Political culture** can be thought of as a nation's political personality. It encompasses the deep-rooted, well-established political traits that are characteristic of a society. Political culture takes into account the attitudes, values, and beliefs that people in a society have about the political system, including standard assumptions about the way that government works. As political scientist W. Lance Bennett notes, the components of political culture can be difficult to analyze. "They are rather like the lenses in a pair of glasses: they are not the things we see when we look at the world; they are the things we see with."[1] Political culture helps build community and facilitate communication because people share an understanding of how and why political events, actions, and experiences occur in their country.

Political culture includes formal rules as well as customs and traditions, sometimes referred to as "habits of the heart," that are passed on generationally. People agree to abide by certain formal rules, such as the country's constitution and codified laws. They also live by norms, which are unstated rules that allow people in a society to coexist respectfully. Examples of norms in the United States are civil discourse, respectful treatment of political opponents, and the willingness to accept the outcomes of elections without resorting to violence. Political culture sets the boundaries of acceptable political behavior in a society.[2]

**Civic culture** is an aspect of political culture that pertains to citizens' acceptance of government authority and their belief in the importance of civic duty, such as the duty to vote and serve on a jury, and the participation in political and community life.[3] While the civic culture in the United States has remained relatively stable over time, shifts have occurred as a result of transformative experiences, such as war, economic crises, and other societal upheavals that have reshaped attitudes and beliefs.[4] Key events, such as the Civil War, World War I, the Great Depression, World War II, the Vietnam War, the civil rights movement, and the terrorist attacks of 9/11 have influenced the political world views of American citizens, especially young people, whose political values and attitudes are less well established. COVID-19, and the accompanying disruption of people's lives, greatly impacted civic culture. Views about whether or not to wear masks, maintain social distance, and eat inside restaurants differed widely across states, and even within states, at times resulting in verbal and physical conflicts.

**civic culture**

Citizens' acceptance of government authority and desire to fulfill their civic duty and participate in politics.

# American Political Culture

Political culture consists of a variety of elements. Some aspects of culture are abstract, such as political beliefs and values. Other elements are visible and readily identifiable, such as rituals, traditions, symbols, folklore, and heroes. These aspects of political culture can generate feelings of national pride that form a bond between people and their country. Political culture is not monolithic. It consists of diverse subcultures based on group characteristics such as race, ethnicity, sexual preference, and social circumstances, including living in a particular place or in a certain part of the country. We will now examine these aspects of political culture in the American context.

## Beliefs

**Beliefs** are ideas that are considered to be true by a society. Founders of the American republic endorsed both equality, most notably in the Declaration of Independence, and liberty, most prominently in the Constitution. These political theories have become incorporated into the political culture of the United States in the central beliefs of egalitarianism and individualism.

**beliefs**

Ideas that are considered to be true by a society.

**Egalitarianism** is the doctrine emphasizing the natural equality of humans, or at least the absence of a preexisting superiority of one set of humans above another. This core American belief is found in the preamble to the Declaration of Independence, which states that "all men are created equal" and that people are endowed with the unalienable rights to "life, liberty, and the pursuit of happiness." Americans endorse the intrinsic equal worth of all people. Survey data consistently indicate that between 80 percent and 90 percent of Americans believe that it is essential to treat all people equally, regardless of race or ethnic background.[5]

**egalitarianism**

Doctrine emphasizing the natural equality of people in society.

The principle of **individualism** stresses the centrality and dignity of individual people. It privileges free action and people's ability to take the initiative in making their own lives as well as those of others more prosperous and satisfying. In keeping with the Constitution's preoccupation with liberty, Americans feel that children should be taught to believe that individuals can better themselves through self-reliance, hard work, and perseverance.[6]

**individualism**

Principle emphasizing the centrality and dignity of the individual and her or his capacity for free action.

The beliefs of egalitarianism and individualism are in tension with one another. For Americans today, this contradiction tends to be resolved by an expectation of **equality of opportunity**, the belief that each individual has the same chance to get ahead in society. Americans tend to feel that most people who want to get ahead can make it if they're willing to work hard.[7] This viewpoint has become somewhat less prevalent as the gap in the standard of living between rich and impoverished has grown in the past decade.[8] Americans are more likely to promote equal political rights, such as the Voting Rights Act's stipulation of equal participation for all qualified voters, than economic equality, which would redistribute income from the wealthy to those living in poverty.[9] The

**equality of opportunity**

The right of each individual to the same chance to get ahead in society.

divisive debates in the U.S. Congress over repeal of the Affordable Care Act, nicknamed Obamacare, have focused on the distribution of benefits to those unable to afford health-care coverage.

## Values

**values**

A society's shared convictions about what is just and good.

Beliefs form the foundation for **values**, which represent a society's shared convictions about what is just and good. Americans claim to be committed to the core values of individualism and egalitarianism. Yet there is sometimes a significant disconnect between what Americans are willing to uphold in principle and how they behave in practice. People may say that they support the Constitutional right to free speech but then balk when they are confronted with a political extremist or a racist speaking in public.

**American creed**

Belief in the United States "as a Government of the people, by the people, for the people, whose powers are derived from the consent of the governed."

**American exceptionalism**

Conviction that America's vast frontier offered boundless opportunities for individuals to achieve their goals.

**patriotism**

Love of one's country and respect for its symbols and principles.

Core American political values are vested in what is often called the **American creed**. The creed, which was composed by New York State Commissioner of Education Henry Sterling Chapin in 1918, refers to the belief that the United States is a government "by the people, for the people, whose just powers are derived from the consent of the governed." The nation consists of sovereign states united as "a perfect Union" based on "the principles of freedom, equality, justice, and humanity." **American exceptionalism** is the view that America's exceptional development as a nation has contributed to its special place in the world. It is the conviction that the country's vast frontier offered boundless and equal opportunities for individuals to achieve their goals. Americans feel strongly that their nation is destined to serve as an example to other countries.[10] They support the export of American culture around the world, including television programs and films. They believe that the political and economic systems that have evolved in this country are perfectly suited in principle to permit both individualism and egalitarianism.

Consequently, the American creed also includes **patriotism**: the love of one's country and respect for its symbols and principles. The events of 9/11 ignited Americans' patriotic values, resulting in many public displays of support for the country, its democratic form of government, and authority figures in public service jobs, such as police and firefighters. The press has scrutinized politicians for actions that are perceived to indicate a lack of patriotism, and the perception that a political leader is not patriotic can generate controversy. In the 2008 presidential election, a minor media frenzy developed over Democratic presidential candidate Barack Obama's "patriotism problem." The news media debated the significance of Obama's not wearing a flag lapel pin on the campaign trail and his failure to place his hand over his heart during the playing of the national anthem. Hillary Clinton also was criticized for failing to wear a flag pin when she accepted the 2016 Democratic presidential nomination.

**political tolerance**

Willingness to allow groups with whom one disagrees fundamentally to exercise their constitutionally guaranteed freedoms.

Another core American value is **political tolerance**, the willingness to allow groups with whom one disagrees to exercise their constitutionally guaranteed freedoms, such as free speech. While many people strongly support the ideal of tolerance, they often are unwilling to extend political freedoms to groups they dislike. People acknowledge the constitutional right of racist groups, such as skinheads, to demonstrate in public, but will go to great lengths to prevent them from doing so.[11]

University students on both the political right and left have protested hosting speakers on campus with whom they disagree. This situation raises the issue of whether the students are at odds with the value of political tolerance. Hundreds of students at Middlebury College in March 2017 disrupted a lecture by Charles Murray, an academic who wrote the controversial book *The Bell Curve*, that argued that intelligence is more important than social factors in predicting a range of outcomes, such as the tendency to commit crimes and job performance. In April 2017, a speech by conservative author Ann Coulter was canceled by the University of California, Berkeley, due to student protests that the administration believed raised safety concerns.

A steak fry in Iowa during the 2008 Democratic presidential primary sparked a debate over candidate Barack Obama's patriotism. Obama, standing with opponents Bill Richardson and Hillary Clinton, failed to place his hand over his heart during the playing of the national anthem. In the background is Ruth Harkin, wife of Senator Tom Harkin, who hosted the event.

View in the online reader

## Enduring Image

### Patriotism

Civil rights leaders Dr. Martin Luther King, Jr. and Rev. Ralph Abernathy kneel and lead demonstrators in prayer to protest the arrest of demonstrators in Dallas County, Alabama, in 1965.

Source: BH/Associated Press

Former NFL quarterback Colin Kaepernick ignited a public controversy when he refused to stand and took a knee as the national anthem was played before games in 2016. Kaepernick defended his action, stating, "I am not going to stand up to show pride for a flag for a country that oppresses Black people and people of color."[12] The protest gesture was taken up by football players and athletes from other sports as well as demonstrators opposing systemic racism. It sparked a controversy about the patriotism of those who supported the right to kneel during the anthem.

The act of kneeling during the national anthem divided the nation. Kneeling was viewed by some as an act of defiance and resistance to racial injustice. Demonstrators knelt on the spot where George Floyd, a Black man, was pinned to the ground by a white police officer. When visiting a Black church in Delaware while campaigning for the presidency in 2020, Joe Biden knelt in solidarity. Others considered kneeling to be an affront to American patriotism. Football fans boycotted NFL stadiums where players knelt during the anthem to show their opposition. President Donald Trump stated that Kaepernick "should find a country that works better for him."[13] On Twitter, Trump argued that the NFL should ban kneeling and "fire" NFL owners who allowed players to "disrespect our flag."

Former NFL quarterback Colin Kaepernick protested racial injustice by kneeling as the national anthem was played before games. Nate Boyer, a Green Beret and former NFL player, gave Kaepernick the idea for kneeling as a gesture.

Source: Abaca Press / Alamy Stock Photo

Kaepernick was inspired to use kneeling as a gesture of protest by a photograph of Dr. Martin Luther King, Jr., kneeling in protest against civil rights abuses in Selma, Alabama, in 1965. The image shows Dr. King leading a prayer following the arrest of 250 people who participated in a march to get Black Americans registered to vote.[14]

**rule of law**

The premise that government is based on a body of law, agreed on by the governed, that is applied equally and justly.

Democratic political values are among the cornerstones of the American creed. Americans believe in the **rule of law**: the idea that government is based on a body of law, agreed on by the governed, that is applied equally and justly. The Constitution is the foundation for the rule of law. The creed also encompasses the public's high degree of respect for the American system of government and the structure of its political institutions.

**capitalist economic values**

Values that emphasize the need for a free enterprise system, open business competition, private ownership of property, and limited government intervention in business affairs.

**Capitalist economic values** are embraced by the American creed. Capitalist economic systems emphasize the need for a free enterprise system that allows for open business competition, private ownership of property, and limited government intervention in business affairs. Underlying these capitalist values is the belief that, through hard work and perseverance, anyone can be financially successful.[15]

The primacy of individualism may undercut the status quo in politics and economics. The emphasis on the lone, powerful person implies a distrust of collective action and of power structures such as big government, big business, or big labor. The public is leery of having too much power concentrated in the hands of a few large companies. The emergence of the Tea Party, a visible grassroots conservative movement that gained momentum during the 2010 midterm elections, illustrates how some Americans become mobilized in opposition to the "tax and spend" policies of big government.[16] While the Tea Party shunned the mainstream media because of their view that the press had a liberal bias, they received tremendous coverage of their rallies and conventions, as well as their candidates. Tea Party candidates relied heavily on social media, such as Facebook and Twitter, to get their anti–big government message out to the public. Candidates continue to run under the Tea Party label and embrace the message of limited federal government and fiscal restraint. In 2016, Republican presidential candidate Donald Trump appealed to some of the same sentiments that animated the Tea Party. He relentlessly attacked the press. His call to "drain the swamp" of Washington insiders and Wall Street mega-bankers became a rallying cry for his supporters. Once in office, he proceeded to pack his cabinet with wealthy businessmen and Wall Street types. He continued to emphasize these themes during his unsuccessful reelection bid in 2020.

**FIGURE 6.2 Tea Party Protests at the Capitol Building on September 12, 2009**

Tea Party supporters from across the country staged a "March on Washington" to demonstrate their opposition to government spending and to show their patriotism.

Source: CantWinThisGame via Wikimedia: https://commons.wikimedia.org/wiki/ File:Sept_12,_2009_-_Tea_Party_Tax_Payer_Protest,_Washington_DC.jpg. Reproduced via CC BY-SA 3.0: https://creativecommons.org/licenses/by-sa/3.0/deed.en].

## Rituals, Traditions, and Symbols

**rituals**

Ceremonial acts performed by the people of a nation.

Rituals, traditions, and symbols are highly visible aspects of political culture, and they are important characteristics of a nation's identity. **Rituals**, such as singing the national anthem at sporting events and saluting the flag before the start of a school day, are ceremonial acts that are performed by the people of a nation. Some rituals have important symbolic and substantive purposes: Election Night follows a standard script that ends with the vanquished candidate congratulating the opponent on a well-fought battle and urging support and unity behind the victor.[17] The formalities surrounding the swearing in of the new president on Inauguration Day is a public ritual demonstrating the peaceful transition of power. These long-standing rituals were upended following the 2020 election, when Donald Trump refused to acknowledge that Joe Biden had won the presidential contest and refused to attend Biden's inauguration ceremony. Failure to conform to these rituals contributed to the unrest that incited an insurrection at the U.S. Capitol by Trump supporters on January 6, 2021. The State of the Union Address that the president makes to Congress every January is a ritual that, in the modern era, has become an opportunity for the president to set his policy agenda, to report on his administration's accomplishments, and to establish public trust. A more recent addition to the State of the Union ritual is the practice of having representatives from the president's party and the opposition give formal, televised reactions to the address.

**FIGURE 6.3 Inauguration Day 2021**

Inauguration Day rituals represent the peaceful transition to a new presidential administration.

Source: The White House. V20210120LJ-0376. President-elect Joe Biden, Dr. Jill Biden, Vice President-elect Kamala Harris and Mr. Doug Emhoff, Jan. 20, 2021, prior to the 59th Presidential Inauguration. (Official White House Photo by Lawrence Jackson). Via Flickr: https://www.flickr.com/photos/whitehouse/50911774223/.

Political **traditions** are customs and festivities that are passed on from generation to generation, such as celebrating America's founding on the Fourth of July with parades, picnics, and fireworks. **Symbols** are objects or emblems that stand for a nation. The flag is perhaps the most significant national symbol, especially as it can take on enhanced meaning when a country experiences difficult times. The bald eagle was officially adopted as the country's emblem in 1787, as it is considered a symbol of America's "supreme power and authority." Individual states have their own symbols, including flags, birds, and flowers, that speak to their individuality. The Calico Cat is the state cat of Maryland; the Buckeye Tree is the state tree of Ohio; and the Whiptail Lizard is the state reptile of New Mexico.

**FIGURE 6.4**
**The Statue of Liberty**
The Statue of Liberty stands in New York Harbor, an 1844 gift from France that is a symbol welcoming people from foreign lands to America's shores.

Source: Elcobbola via Wikimedia Commons: https://commons.wikimedia.org/wiki/File:Statue_of_Liberty_7.jpg. (CC BY-SA 3.0) https://creativecommons.org/licenses/by-sa/3.0/deed.en.

**traditions**

Customs and festivities passed on from generation to generation.

**symbols**

Objects or emblems that represent a nation.

**folklore**

Legends and stories shared by a nation.

## Folklore

Political **folklore**, the legends and stories that are shared by a nation, constitutes another element of culture. Individualism and egalitarianism are central themes in American folklore that are used to reinforce the country's values. The "rags-to-riches" narratives of novelists—the late-nineteenth-century writer Horatio Alger being the quintessential example—celebrate the possibilities of advancement through hard work.

Much American folklore has grown up around the early presidents and figures from the American Revolution. This folklore creates an image of men, and occasionally women, of character and strength. Most folklore contains elements of truth, but these stories are usually greatly exaggerated.

The first American president, George Washington, is the subject of folklore that has been passed on to schoolchildren for more than two hundred years. Young children learn about Washington's impeccable honesty and, thereby, the importance of telling the truth, from the legend of the cherry tree. When asked by his father if he had chopped down a cherry tree with his new hatchet, Washington confessed to committing the deed by replying, "Father, I cannot tell a lie." This event never happened and was fabricated by biographer Parson Mason Weems in the late 1700s.[18] Legend also has it that, as a boy, Washington threw a silver dollar across the Potomac River, a story meant to illustrate his tremendous physical strength. In fact, Washington was not a gifted athlete, and silver dollars did not exist when he was a youth. The origin of this folklore is an episode related by his step-grandson, who wrote that Washington had once thrown a piece of slate across a very narrow portion of the Rappahannock River in Virginia.[19]

Folklore surrounds Betsy Ross, who is purported to have designed and stitched the first American flag at the behest of George Washington. While Betsy Ross was a seamstress who made flags at the time, it is unlikely that she was responsible for the national flag. In the early days of the Republic, people were anxious for stories about the Revolutionary War. The Betsy Ross story was a patriotic tale devised to instill patriotism in girls by providing a female heroine.[20] The legend of Molly Pitcher is another example of Revolutionary War folklore. Mary Hayes, nicknamed "Molly," brought water to the Revolutionary soldiers during the Battle of Monmouth during heavy action against the British in over 100 degree temperatures. When her husband was felled in battle, she took over his post at a cannon for the remainder of the day. A musket ball flew between her legs tearing her skirt, yet she carried on unfazed. In reality, while there were women who participated in battle, the tale of Molly Pitcher grew taller over time. Numerous books and films have recounted the stories of Betsy Ross and Molly Pitcher to generations of young people.[21]

**FIGURE 6.5 Folktales about George Washington**
There are many folktales about young George Washington, including that he chopped down a cherry tree and threw a silver dollar across the Potomac River. These stories were popularized by engravings like this one by John C. McCabe depicting Washington working as a land surveyor.

Source: Photo courtesy of the National Park Service Historical Handbook Series No. 26, frontispiece, http://commons.wikimedia.org/wiki/File:Young_George_Washington.jpg.

## Heroes

**heroes**

People who, in theory, embody the best of what a country has to offer and thereby define a nation's political culture.

**Heroes** embody the human characteristics most prized by a country. A nation's political culture is in part defined by its heroes who, in theory, embody the best of what that country has to offer. Traditionally, heroes are people who are admired for their strength of character, beneficence, courage, and leadership. People also can achieve hero status because of other factors, such as celebrity status, athletic excellence, and wealth.

Shifts in the people whom a nation identifies as heroes reflect changes in cultural values. Prior to the twentieth century, political figures and war heroes were preeminent among American heroes. These included patriotic leaders, such as Clara Barton, who tended to injured soldiers during the Civil War and founded the American Red Cross; prominent presidents, such as Abraham Lincoln; and military leaders, such as Civil War General Stonewall Jackson, a leader of the Confederate army. People learned about these leaders from biographies, which provided information about the valiant actions and patriotic attitudes that contributed to their success.

Today American heroes are more likely to come from the ranks of prominent entertainment, sports, technology, and business figures than from the world of politics. Popular culture became a powerful mechanism for elevating people to hero status beginning around the 1920s. As mass media, especially motion pictures, radio, and television, became an important part of American life, entertainment and sports personalities who received a great deal of publicity became heroes to many people who were awed by their celebrity. Baseball greats Babe Ruth and Lou Gehrig became role models.[22]

In the 1990s, business leaders, such as Microsoft's Bill Gates and General Electric's Jack Welch, were considered to be heroes by some Americans who sought to achieve material success. The tenure of business leaders as American heroes was short-lived, however, as media reports of the lavish lifestyles and widespread criminal misconduct of some corporation heads led people to become disillusioned. The incarceration of Wall Street investment advisor Bernard Madoff made international headlines as he was alleged to have defrauded investors of billions of dollars.[23]

Sports figures feature prominently among American heroes, especially during their prime. Cyclist Lance Armstrong was a hero to many Americans because of his unmatched accomplishment of winning seven consecutive Tour de France titles after beating cancer. However, heroes can be quickly dethroned when their accomplishments are discredited and their character is questioned. Armstrong quickly moved from being one of the most popular American athletes of all time to being a pariah.

**FIGURE 6.6 Lance Armstrong**

Cyclist Lance Armstrong was considered by many to be an American hero because of his athletic accomplishments and his fight against cancer. He became a fallen hero after admitting to using performance-enhancing drugs and lying about it.

Source: stock_photo_world / Shutterstock.com

NBA basketball player Michael Jordan epitomizes the modern-day American hero. Jordan's hero status is vested in his ability to bridge the world of sports and business with unmatched success. The media promoted Jordan's hero image intensively, and he was marketed commercially by Nike, which produced his "Air Jordan" shoes.[24] His unauthorized 1999 film biography is titled *Michael Jordan: An American Hero*, and it focuses on how Jordan triumphed over obstacles, such as racial prejudice and personal insecurities, to become a role model on and off the basketball court. Young filmgoers watched Michael Jordan help Bugs Bunny defeat evil aliens 1996's in *Space Jam*. In the 2002 film *Like Mike*, pint-sized rapper Lil' Bow Wow plays an orphan who finds a pair of Michael Jordan's basketball shoes and is magically transformed into an NBA star. Lil' Bow Wow's story has a happy ending because he works hard and plays by the rules. In 2014, Jordan became a billionaire, further solidifying his status as an icon who has achieved the American Dream. With the 2020 release of the highly popular miniseries *The Last Dance*, which focused on his basketball career, Jordan was introduced to a new generation of fans.

The 9/11 terrorist attacks prompted Americans to make heroes of ordinary people who performed in extraordinary ways in the face of adversity. Firefighters and police officers who gave their lives, recovered victims, and protected people from further threats were honored in numerous ceremonies. Also treated as heroes were the passengers of Flight 93 who attempted to overtake the terrorists who had hijacked their plane, which was believed to be headed for a target in Washington, DC. The plane crashed in a Pennsylvania field.

As Americans have become increasingly dependent on technology, figures from the tech world are treated as heroes. Tech leaders are perceived as achieving the American Dream, starting from humble beginnings and achieving tremendous professional success. Facebook founder Mark Zuckerberg has been hailed as a hero for his ability to take an idea he developed in his college dormitory room and make it into a multi-billion-dollar platform used by millions of people worldwide. Similarly, Jeff Bezos, owner of Amazon.com, *The Washington Post*, and Whole Foods, is admired for creating the world's largest online shopping retailer.

**FIGURE 6.7 Mark Zuckerberg**

Facebook founder Mark Zuckerberg's success in building a social media empire has made him a hero to young Americans seeking a future in technology industries.

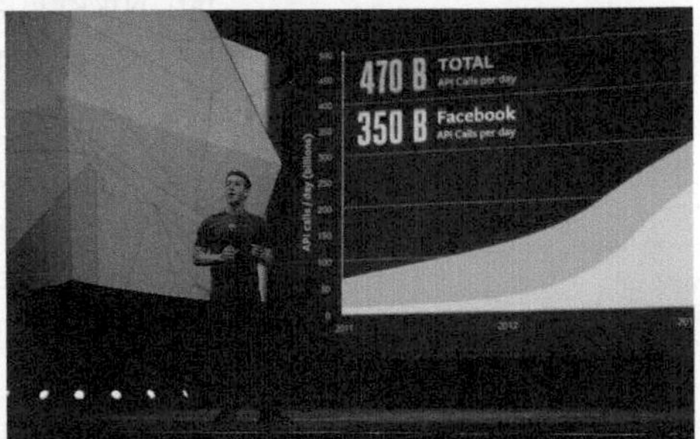


Source: Source: By Maurizio Pesce from Milan, Italia via Wikimedia: https://commons.wikimedia.org/wiki/File:Mark_Zuckerberg_on_stage_at_Facebook's_F8_Conference_(15048918191).jpg (CC BY 2.0) (http://creativecommons.org/licenses/by/2.0)], via Wikimedia Commons.

# Subcultures

**subcultures**

Distinct groups associated with particular beliefs, values, and behavior patterns and existing within the overall framework of the larger political culture.

Political **subcultures** are distinct groups, associated with particular beliefs, values, and behavior patterns, that exist within the overall framework of the larger culture. They can develop around groups with distinct interests, such as those based on age, sex, race, ethnicity, social class, religion, and sexual preference. Many Americans identify with their ethnic and racial roots, such as African Americans, Asian Americans, and Latinx Americans. Subcultures also can be geographically based. Political scientist Daniel Elazar identified regional political subcultures, rooted in American immigrant settlement patterns, that influenced the way that government was constituted and practiced in different locations across the nation. The moral political subculture, which is present in New England and the Midwest, promotes the common good over individual values. The individual political subculture, which is evident in the middle Atlantic states and the West, is more concerned with private enterprise than societal interests. The traditional political subculture, which is found in the South, reflects a hierarchical societal structure in which social and familial ties are central to holding political power.[25] Political subcultures can also form around social and artistic groups and their associated lifestyles, such as the heavy metal and hip-hop music subcultures.

Although the definition of political culture emphasizes unifying, collective understandings, in reality, cultures are multidimensional and often in conflict. When subcultural groups compete for societal resources, such as access to government funding for programs that will benefit them, cultural cleavages and clashes can result. As we will see in the section on multiculturalism, conflict between competing subcultures is an ever-present fact of American life.

## Media Frames: The Hip-Hop Subculture

A cohort of Black Americans has been labeled the hip-hop generation by scholars and social observers. The hip-hop generation is a subculture of generation X (people born between 1965 and 1984) that identifies strongly with hip-hop music as a unifying force. Its heroes come from the ranks of prominent music artists, including Grandmaster Flash, Chuck D, Run DMC, Ice Cube, Sister Souljah, Nikki D, and Queen Latifah. While a small number of people who identify with this subculture advocate extreme politics, including violence against political leaders, the vast majority are peaceful, law-abiding citizens.[26]

The hip-hop subculture emerged in the early 1970s in New York City. Hip-hop music began with party-oriented themes, but by 1982 it was focusing heavily on political issues. Unlike the preceding civil rights generation—a Black subculture of baby boomers (people born immediately after World War II) that concentrated on achieving equal rights—the hip-hop subculture does not have an overarching political agenda. The messages passed on to the subculture by the music are highly varied and often contradictory. Some lyrics express frustration about the poverty, lack of educational and employment opportunities, and high crime rates that plague segments of the Black community. Other songs provide public service messages, such as those included on the *Stop the Violence* album featuring Public Enemy and MC Lyte, and Salt-N-Pepa's "Let's Talk about AIDS." Music associated with the gangsta rap genre, which was the product of gang culture and street wars in South Central Los Angeles, promotes violence, especially against women and authority figures such as the police. It is from these lyrics that the mass media derive their most prominent frames when they cover the hip-hop subculture.[27]

Media coverage of the hip-hop subculture focuses heavily on negative events and issues, while ignoring the socially constructive messages of many musicians. The subculture receives most of its media attention in response to the murder of prominent artists, such as Tupac Shakur and Notorious B.I.G., or the arrest of musicians for violating the law, usually for a weapons- or drug-related charge. A prominent news frame is how violence in the music's lyrics translates into real-life violence. As hip-hop music became more popular with suburban white youth in the 1990s, the news media stepped up its warnings about the dangers of this subculture.

**FIGURE 6.8 Media Coverage of Hip-Hop**

Media coverage of hip-hop tends to downplay the positive aspects of the subculture.

Source: Sterling Munksgard / Shutterstock.com

Media reports of the hip-hop subculture also coincide with the release of successful albums. Since 1998, hip-hop and rap have been the top-selling record formats. The dominant news frame is that the hip-hop subculture promotes selfish, materialist values. This is illustrated by news reports about the cars, homes, jewelry, and other commodities purchased by successful musicians and their promoters.[28] Rapper and hip-hop artist Kanye West's lavish wedding to reality television star Kim Kardashian in 2014 was estimated to have cost several million dollars, and was a prominent news item for several weeks.

A new generation of hip-hop artists, such as Drake and Chance, maintain the core elements of the subculture. They are more tech-savvy than their predecessors and able to produce music more prolifically. Their message tends to be more positive, playful, and humorous than the lyrics of the past.[29]

# Multiculturalism

One of the hallmarks of American culture is its racial and ethnic diversity. In the early twentieth century, the playwright Israel Zangwill coined the phrase "**melting pot**" to describe how immigrants from many different backgrounds came together in the United States. The melting pot metaphor assumed that over time the distinct habits, customs, and traditions associated with particular groups would disappear as people assimilated into the larger culture. A uniquely American culture would emerge that accommodated some elements of diverse immigrant cultures in a new context.[30] For example, American holiday celebrations incorporate traditions from other nations. Many common American words originate from other languages. Still, the melting pot concept fails to recognize that immigrant groups do not entirely abandon their distinct identities. Racial and ethnic groups maintain many of their basic characteristics, but at the same time, their cultural orientations change through marriage and interactions with others in society.

Over the past decade, there has been a trend toward greater acceptance of America's cultural diversity. **Multiculturalism** celebrates the unique cultural heritage of racial and ethnic groups, some of whom seek to preserve their native languages and lifestyles. The United States is home to many people who were born in foreign countries and still maintain the cultural practices of their homelands.

**melting pot**

Metaphor used to describe how immigrants from many different backgrounds come together in the United States and that assumes that the distinct habits, customs, and traditions of particular groups disappear as their members assimilate into the larger culture.

**multiculturalism**

An appreciation of the unique cultural heritage of racial and ethnic groups in the United States, some of whom seek to preserve their native languages and lifestyles.

**FIGURE 6.9 Celebrating Indigenous American Heritage**
Americans celebrate their multicultural heritage by maintaining traditions associated with their homelands.

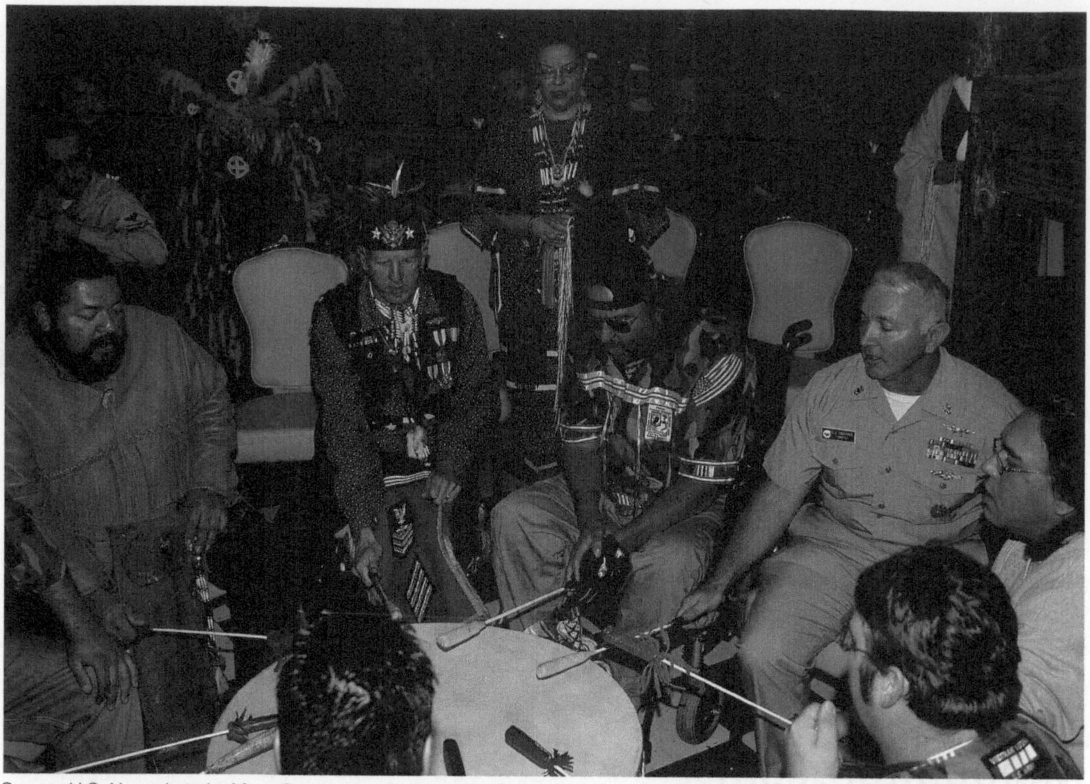

Source: U.S. Navy photo by Mass Communication Specialist Seaman Nathan L. Anderson [Public domain]; https://commons.wikimedia.org/wiki/File:US_Navy_061121-N-6159N-001_USS_John_F._Kennedy_(CV_67)_Command_Master_Chief,_Carl_L._Dassance_pounds_on_a_ceremonial_drum_during_the_Native_American_and_Alaskan_Heritage_celebration.jpg.

Multiculturalism has been embraced by many Americans, and it has been promoted formally by institutions. Elementary and secondary schools have adopted curricula to foster understanding of cultural diversity by exposing students to the customs and traditions of racial and ethnic groups. As a result, young people today are more tolerant of diversity in society than any prior generation has been. Government agencies advocate tolerance for diversity by sponsoring Hispanic and Asian American/Pacific Islander heritage weeks. The U.S. Postal Service has introduced stamps depicting prominent Americans from diverse backgrounds.

Tensions over multiculturalism and diversity were prominent during the 2016 presidential election, when Republican candidate Donald Trump raised the issue of immigration and called for the building of a wall to keep Latin American people from crossing the U.S. border. Once in office, President Trump signed an executive order blocking people from six Muslim-majority countries from entering the United States. The controversial travel ban sparked protests throughout the country.[31] In contrast, America's multicultural heritage was celebrated with the election of Kamala Harris, who is of Jamaican and South Asian descent, as vice president in the 2020 presidential election.

**FIGURE 6.10 Airport Protests**

Protesters gathered at airports throughout the United States to demonstrate their opposition to President Trump's executive order blocking people from six Muslim-majority nations from entering the country.

Source: By Dennis Bratland (Own work) via Wikimedia: https://commons.wikimedia.org/wiki/File:SeaTac_Airport_protest_against_immigration_ban_01.jpg. (CC BY-SA 4.0) (http://creativecommons.org/licenses/by-sa/4.0)], via Wikimedia Commons.

## Enduring Image

### The 9/11 Firefighters' Statue

On 9/11 Thomas E. Franklin, a photographer for Bergen County, New Jersey's *Record*, photographed three firefighters—Billy Eisengrein, George Johnson, and Dan McWilliams—raising a flag amid the smoldering rubble of the World Trade Center. Labeled by the press "the photo seen 'round the world," his image came to symbolize the strength, resilience, and heroism of Americans in the face of a direct attack on their homeland.

Developer Bruce Ratner commissioned a nineteen-foot-tall, $180,000 bronze statue based on the photograph to stand in front of the New York City Fire Department (FDNY) headquarters in Brooklyn. When the statue prototype was unveiled, it revealed that the faces of two of the three white firefighters who had originally raised the flag had been replaced with those of Black and Hispanic firefighters. Ratner and the artist who designed the statue claimed that the modification of the original image represented an effort to promote America's multicultural heritage and tolerance for diversity. The change had been authorized by the FDNY leadership.[32]

The modification of the famous photo raised the issue of whether it is valid to alter historical fact in order to promote a cultural value. A heated controversy broke out over the statue. Supporters of the change believed that the statue was designed to honor all firefighters, and that representing their diverse racial and ethnic backgrounds was warranted. Black and Hispanic firefighters were among the 343 who had lost their lives at the World Trade Center. Kevin James of the Vulcan Society, which represents Black firefighters, defended the decision by stating, "The symbolism is far more important than representing the actual people. I think the artistic expression of diversity would supersede any concern over factual correctness."[33]

The iconic photograph of 9/11 firefighters raising a flag near the rubble of the World Trade Center plaza is immortalized in a U.S. postage stamp. Thomas E. Franklin, the veteran reporter who took the photo, said that the image reminded him of the famous Associated Press image of Marines raising the American flag on Iwo Jima during World War II.

Source: Tony Baggett / Shutterstock.com

Opponents claimed that since the statue was not meant to be a tribute to firefighters, but rather a depiction of an actual event, the representation needed to be historically accurate. They drew a parallel to the famous 1945 Associated Press photograph of six Marines raising the flag on Iwo Jima during World War II and the historically precise memorial that was erected in Arlington, Virginia. Opponents also felt that it was wrong to politicize the statue by making it part of a dialogue on race. The proposed statue promoted an image of diversity within the FDNY that did not mirror reality. Of the FDNY's 11,495 firefighters, 2.7 percent are Black and 3.2 percent are Latinx, percentages well below the percentage these groups represent in the overall population.

Some people suggested a compromise—two statues. They proposed that the statue based on the Franklin photo should reflect historical reality; a second statue, celebrating multiculturalism, should be erected in front of another FDNY station and include depictions of rescue workers of diverse backgrounds at the World Trade Center site. Plans for any type of statue were abandoned as a result of the controversy.

## Key Takeaways

Political culture is defined by the ideologies, values, beliefs, norms, customs, traditions, and heroes characteristic of a nation. People living in a particular political culture share views about the nature and operation of government. Political culture changes over time in response to dramatic events, such as war, economic collapse, or radical technological developments. The core American values of democracy and capitalism are vested in the American creed. American exceptionalism is the idea that the country has a special place in the world because of the circumstances surrounding its founding and the settling of a vast frontier.

Rituals, traditions, and symbols bond people to their culture and can stimulate national pride. Folklore consists of stories about a nation's leaders and heroes; often embellished, these stories highlight the character traits that are desirable in a nation's citizens. Heroes are important for defining a nation's political culture.

America has numerous subcultures based on geographic region; demographic, personal, and social characteristics; religious affiliation; and artistic inclinations. America's unique multicultural heritage is vested in the various racial and ethnic groups who have settled in the country, but conflicts can arise when subgroups compete for societal resources.

## Exercises

1. What do you think the American flag represents? Would it bother you to see someone burn an American flag? Why or why not?
2. What distinction does the text make between beliefs and values? Are there things that you believe in principle should be done that you might be uncomfortable with in practice? What are they?
3. Do you agree that America is uniquely suited to foster freedom and equality? Why or why not?
4. What characteristics make you think of someone as particularly American? Does race or cultural background play a role in whether you think of a person as American?

# 6.3 Political Socialization

## Learning Objectives

After reading this section, you should be able to answer the following questions:

1. How do people develop an understanding of their political culture?
2. What is political socialization, and why is it important?
3. What constitutes a political generation?

This section will define what is meant by political socialization and detail how the process of political socialization occurs in the United States. It will outline the stages of political learning across an individual's life course. The agents that are responsible for political socialization, such as the family and the media, and the types of information and orientations they convey will be discussed. Group differences in political socialization will be examined. Finally, the section will address the ways that political generations develop through the political socialization process.

## What Is Political Socialization?

People are inducted into the political culture of their nation through the political socialization process.[34] Most often, older members of society teach younger members the rules and norms of political life. However, young people can and do actively promote their own political learning, and they can influence adults' political behavior as well.[35]

**political learning**

Active and passive, formal and informal ways in which people mature politically.

**political self**

Sense of personal identification with the political world, which includes belonging to a community and knowledge of the shared beliefs and values of the members of that community.

**political socialization**

Process through which people develop the attitudes, values, beliefs, and opinions conducive to becoming good citizens in their country.

**agents of socialization**

Individuals and institutions, including family, school, peer group, and mass media, responsible for imparting political orientations through the socialization process.

**political legitimacy**

Having faith in the integrity of the political system and processes.

**political efficacy**

Individuals' feeling that they can or cannot personally influence government and politics.

Political scientists Gabriel Almond and James Coleman once observed that we "do not inherit our political behavior, attitudes, values, and knowledge through our genes."[36] Instead, we come to understand our role and to "fit in" to our political culture through the political learning process.[37] **Political learning** is a broad concept that encompasses both the active and passive and the formal and informal ways in which people mature politically.[38] Individuals develop a **political self**, a sense of personal identification with the political world. Developing a political self begins when children start to feel that they are part of a political community. They acquire the knowledge, beliefs, and values that help them comprehend government and politics.[39] The sense of being an American, which includes feeling that one belongs to a unique nation in which people share a belief in democratic ideals, is conveyed through the political learning process.

**Political socialization** is a particular type of political learning whereby people develop the attitudes, values, beliefs, opinions, and behaviors that are conducive to becoming good citizens in their country. Socialization is largely a one-way process through which young people gain an understanding of the political world through their interaction with adults and the media. The process is represented by the following model:[40]

who (subjects) → learns what (political values, beliefs, attitudes, behaviors) → from whom (agents) → under what circumstances → with what effects.

**Agents of socialization**, which include parents, teachers, and the mass media, convey orientations to subjects, who are mostly passive. For example, parents who take an active role in politics and vote in every election often influence their children to do the same. Young people who see television coverage of their peers volunteering in the community may take cues from these depictions and engage in community service themselves. The circumstances under which political socialization can take place are almost limitless. Young people can be socialized to politics through dinner conversations with family members, watching television and movies, participating in a Facebook group, or texting with friends. The effects of these experiences are highly variable, as people can accept, reject, or ignore political messages.

People develop attitudes toward the political system through the socialization process. **Political legitimacy** is a belief in the integrity of the political system and processes, such as elections. People who believe strongly in the legitimacy of the political system have confidence that political institutions will be responsive to the wants and needs of citizens and that abuses of governmental power will be held in check. If political leaders engage in questionable behavior, there are mechanisms to hold them accountable. The presidential impeachment process and congressional ethics hearings are two such mechanisms.

**Political efficacy** refers to individuals' perceptions about whether or not they can influence the political process. People who have a strong sense of political efficacy feel that they have the skills and resources to participate effectively in politics and that the government will be responsive to their efforts. Those who believe in the legitimacy of the political system and are highly efficacious are more likely to participate in politics and to take strong stands on public policy issues.[41] Citizens who take part in protests voicing their frustration about the government's not meeting their needs or dealing with societal problems often have high levels of political efficacy.

The system was put to the test following the 2020 election when Donald Trump refused to acknowledge that Joe Biden had won the presidency and challenged the results in several states. He held a rally to "stop the steal" in Washington, DC, after which a mob stormed the U.S. Capitol building, where Congress was certifying the election results. After three hours, the building was secured and Congress resumed the process of certifying Biden's electoral victory.[42]

Much political socialization in the United States passes on norms, customs, beliefs, and values supportive of democracy from one generation to the next. Americans are taught to respect the democratic and capitalist values imbedded in the American creed. Young people are socialized to respect authorities, such as parents, teachers, police officers, and firefighters, and to obey laws.

The goal of this type of socialization is to ensure that the democratic political system survives even in times of political stress, such as economic crisis, war, or a pandemic.[43] One indicator of a stable political system is that elections take place regularly following established procedures and that people recognize the outcomes as legitimate.[44] Most Americans quickly accepted George W. Bush as president when the 2000 election deadlock ended with the Supreme Court decision that stopped the recounting of disputed votes in Florida. The country did not experience violent protests after the decision was announced, but instead moved on with politics as usual.[45]

This citizen-produced video shows peaceful protesters outside of the Supreme Court as the case of *Bush v. Gore* was being considered to decide the outcome of the 2000 presidential election. The close election between Republican George W. Bush and Democrat Al Gore hinged on a recount of votes in Florida to determine who would receive the state's electoral votes, which were eventually awarded to Bush.

View in the online reader

Some scholars argue that political socialization is akin to **indoctrination**, as it forces people to conform to the status quo and inhibits freedom and creativity.[46] However, socialization is not always aimed at supporting democratic political orientations or institutions. Some groups socialize their members to values and attitudes that are wildly at odds with the status quo. The Latin Kings, one of the largest and oldest street gangs in the United States, has its own constitution and formal governing structure. Leaders socialize members to follow gang rules that emphasize an "all for one" mentality; this includes strict internal discipline that calls for physical assault against or death to members who violate the rules. It also calls for violent retribution against rival gang members for actions such as trafficking drugs in the Kings' territory. The Kings have their own sign language, symbols (a five-point crown and tear drop), colors (black and gold), and holidays (January 6, "Kings Holy Day") that bond members to the gang.[47]

**indoctrination**

Process of instructing people to conform to particular doctrines, principles, and ideologies.

# Political Socialization over the Life Course

Political learning begins early in childhood and continues over a person's lifetime. The development of a political self begins when children realize that they belong to a particular town and eventually that they are Americans. Awareness of politics as a distinct realm of experience begins to develop in the preschool years.[48]

Younger children tend to personalize government. The first political objects recognized by children are the president of the United States and the police officer. Children tend to idealize political figures, although young people today have a less positive view of political actors than in the past. This trend is partially a result of the media's preoccupations with personal scandals surrounding politicians.

**FIGURE 6.11 Volunteering and Political Participation**

Young people who participate in community service projects can develop a long-term commitment to volunteering and political participation.

Source: Monkey Business Images/Shutterstock.com.

Young people often have warm feelings toward the political system. Children can develop patriotic values through school rituals, such as singing the "Star Spangled Banner" at the start of each day. As children mature, they become increasingly sophisticated in their perceptions about their place in the political world and their potential for involvement: they learn to relate abstract concepts that they read about in textbooks like this one to real-world actions, and they start to associate the requirements of democracy and majority rule with the need to vote when they reach the age of twenty-one.

**FIGURE 6.12 Student Activism**
Student activists in the 1960s protested against U.S. involvement in the Vietnam War. Some activists developed more favorable attitudes toward government as they matured, had families, and became homeowners.

Source: Courtesy of the Daily Cardinal and the University of Wisconsin-Madison Archives (ID S04779).

People are the most politically impressionable during the period from their midteens through their midtwenties, when their views are not set and they are open to new experiences. College allows students to encounter people with diverse views and provides opportunities for political engagement.[49] Young people may join a cause because it hits close to home. After the media publicized the case of a student who committed suicide after his roommate allegedly posted highly personal videos of him on the internet, students around the country became involved in antibullying initiatives.[50] Joining the workforce, getting married, and taking on new responsibilities can also influence the political orientation of an adult.

Significant events in adults' lives can radically alter their political perspectives, especially as they take on new roles, such as worker, spouse, parent, homeowner, and retiree.[51] This type of transition is illustrated by 1960s student protesters against the Vietnam War. Protestors held views different from their peers; they were less trusting of government officials but more efficacious in that they believed they could change the political system. However, the political views of some of the most strident activists changed after they entered the job market and started families. Some became government officials, lawyers, and business executives—the very types of people they had opposed when they were younger.[52]

Even people who have been politically inactive their entire lives can become motivated to participate as senior citizens. They may find themselves in need of health care and other benefits, and they have more time for involvement. Organizations such as the Gray Panthers provide a pathway for senior citizens to get involved in politics.[53]

## Agents of Political Socialization

People develop their political values, beliefs, and orientations through interactions with agents of socialization. Agents include parents, teachers, friends, coworkers, military colleagues, church associates, club members, sports-team competitors, and media.[54] The political socialization process in the United States is mostly haphazard, informal, and random. There is no standard set of practices for parents or teachers to follow when passing on the rites of politics to future generations. Instead, vague ideals—such as the textbook concept of the "model citizen," who keeps politically informed, votes, and obeys the law—serve as unofficial guides for socializing agencies.[55]

Agents can convey knowledge and understanding of the political world and explain how it works. They can influence people's attitudes about political actors and institutions. They also can show people how to get involved in politics and community work. No single agent is responsible for an individual's entire political learning experience. That experience is the culmination of interactions with a variety of agents. Parents and teachers may work together to encourage students to take part in service learning projects. Agents also may come into conflict and provide vastly different messages. The school is often a source of supportive messages about government, while the media provide a constant barrage of negative messages about government ineffectiveness and corruption.

We focus here on four agents that are important to the socialization process—the family, the school, the peer group, and the media. There are reasons why each of these agents is considered influential for political socialization; there are also factors that limit their effectiveness.

## Family

Over forty years ago, pioneering political-socialization researcher Herbert Hyman proclaimed that "foremost among agencies of socialization into politics is the family."[56] Hyman had good reason for making this assumption. The family has the primary responsibility for nurturing individuals and meeting basic needs, such as food and shelter, during their formative years. A hierarchical power structure exists within many families that emphasizes parental authority and obedience to the rules that parents establish. The strong emotional relationships that exist between family members may compel children to adopt behaviors and attitudes that will please their parents or, conversely, to rebel against them.

Parents can teach their children about government institutions, political leaders, and current issues, but this rarely happens. Government and politics is not a priority for most families, who are concerned with other matters, such as family relationships, education, and sports. Families can influence the development of political values and ideas, such as respect for political symbols or belief in a particular cause. The family as an agent of political socialization is most successful in passing on basic political identities, especially an affiliation with the Republican or Democratic Parties and liberal or conservative ideological leanings.[57]

**FIGURE 6.13 Passing on Political Interests**

Members of the Kennedy family have been prominently involved in politics for over a century, illustrating how the desire to participate in politics is passed on generationally.

Source: National Archives via Wikimedia: https://commons.wikimedia.org/wiki/File:President_Kennedy_and_his_brothers._Attorney_General_Robert_F._Kennedy,_Senator_Edward_Moore_Kennedy,_President_John..._-_NARA_-_194238.jpg.

Children can learn by example when parents act as role models. Young people who observe their parents reading the newspaper and following political news on television may adopt the habit of keeping informed. Adolescents who accompany parents when they attend public meetings, circulate petitions, or engage in other political activities stand a better chance of becoming politically engaged adults.[58] Children can sometimes socialize their parents to become active in politics; participants in the Kids Voting USA program have encouraged their parents to discuss campaign issues and take them to the polls on Election Day.

The home environment can either support or discourage young people's involvement in political affairs. Children whose parents discuss politics frequently and encourage the expression of strong opinions, even if it means challenging others, are likely to become politically active adults. Young people raised in this type of family will often initiate political discussion and encourage parents to become involved. Alternatively, young people from homes where political conversations are rare, and airing controversial viewpoints is discouraged, tend to abstain from politics as adults.[59] Politics was a central focus of family life for the Kennedys, a family that has produced generations of activists, including President John F. Kennedy and Senator Ted Kennedy.

There are limitations on the effectiveness of the family as an agent of political learning and socialization. Most families are not like the Kennedys. For many families, politics is not a priority, as they are more concerned with issues related to day-to-day life. Few parents serve as political role models for their children. Many activities, such as voting or attending town meetings, take place outside of the home.[60]

## School

Some scholars consider the school, rather than the family, to be the most influential agent of political socialization.[61] Schools can stimulate political learning through formal classroom instruction via civics and history classes, the enactment of ceremonies and rituals such as the flag salute, and extracurricular activities such as student government. Respect for authorities is emphasized, as teachers have the ability to reward and punish students through grades. Civics classes in schools also can instruct students in the responsible and effective use of social media to engage in politics.

An important task of schools as agents of political socialization is the passing on of knowledge about the fundamentals of American government, such as constitutional principles and their implications for citizens' engagement in politics. Students who master these fundamentals feel competent to participate politically. They are likely to develop the habit of following politics in the media and to become active in community affairs.[62] Schools can also help students to learn the skills necessary to take part in politics, such as contacting public officials, working in the community, and voting.

**Bennington College study**

Longitudinal study of women who attended Bennington College during the Great Depression of the 1930s and were politically socialized by their teachers and student colleagues.

The college classroom can be an environment for socializing young people to politics. Faculty and student exchanges can form, reinforce, or change evaluations of politics and government. A famous study of women students who attended **Bennington College** during the Great Depression of the 1930s illustrates how the college experience can create long-lasting political attitudes. The Bennington women came predominantly from wealthy families with conservative values. The faculty consisted of political progressives who supported the New Deal and other social programs. About one-third of the Bennington women adopted the progressive ideals of their teachers. Many of these women remained active in politics their entire lives. A number became leaders of the women's rights movement.[63]

**FIGURE 6.14 Political Socialization**

Women at Bennington College in the 1930s became active in community affairs as a result of their political socialization in college.

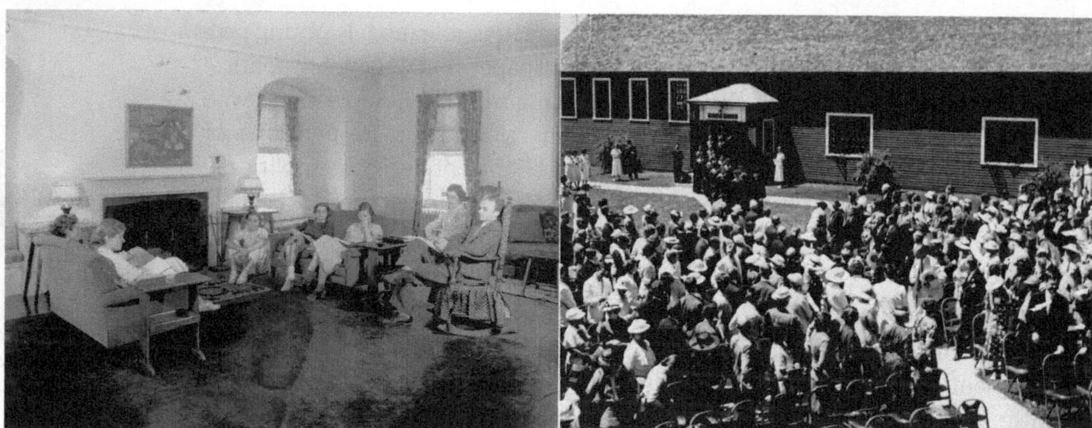

Source: Courtesy of Bennington College. Left photo by C.G. Scofield. Right photo by Rotzel.

While schools have great potential as agents of political socialization, they are not always successful in teaching even basic facts about government to students. Schools devote far less time to civics and history than to other subjects that are considered to be basic skills, such as reading and math. The average amount of classroom time spent on civics-related topics is less than forty-five minutes per week nationwide, although this figure varies widely based on the school. Students whose exposure to civics is exclusively through lectures and readings generally memorize facts about government for tests but do not remember them or make connections to real-world politics. The most effective civic education programs engage students in activities that prepare them for the real world of politics, such as mock elections and legislative hearings.[64]

Some schools have taken on the responsibility of teaching students to be good digital citizens who can use information technology to effectively access information about government and take part in politics. Students learn how to use social media to express their opinions responsibly and to contact public officials. However, there are substantial disparities in students' access to digital civics instruction. Well-resourced schools are more likely to teach digital citizenship skills than schools serving high-need populations. This inequity in access contributes to the civic empowerment gap where some people feel they do not have the capacity to contact the government to work on their behalf.[65]

**FIGURE 6.15 Learning about Politics through Civic Education**
Congressman John Lewis and We the People Students at the U.S. Capitol in Washington, DC

Source: © Copyright Cheryl Cook-Kallio. Courtesy Cheryl Cook-Kallio and the Center for Civic Education. Via https://www.civiced.org/news/congressman-john-lewis.

## Peer Group

Peers (a group of people who are linked by common interests, equal social position, and similar age) can be influential in the political socialization process. Young people desire approval and are likely to adopt the attitudes, viewpoints, and behavior patterns of groups to which they belong. Unlike the family and school, which are structured hierarchically with adults exercising authority, the peer group provides a forum for youth to interact with people who are at similar levels of maturity. Peers provide role models for people who are trying to fit in or become popular in a social setting.[66]

Peer group influence begins when children reach school age and spend less time at home. Middle-childhood (elementary school) friendships are largely segregated by sex and age, as groups of boys and girls will engage in social activities such as eating together in the lunchroom or going to the mall. Such interactions reinforce sex-role distinctions, including those with political relevance, such as the perception that males are more suited to hold positions of authority. Peer relationships change later in childhood, adolescence, and young adulthood, when groups are more often based on athletic, social, academic, and job-related interests and abilities.[67]

The pressure to conform to group norms can have a powerful impact on young people's political development if group members are engaged in activities directly related to politics, such as student government or working on a candidate's campaign. Young people even will change their political viewpoints to conform to those held by the most vocal members of their peer group rather than face being ostracized. Still, individuals often gravitate toward groups that hold beliefs and values similar to their own in order to minimize conflict and reinforce their personal views.[68] Peer activities that are not specifically political can influence political socialization. Participation on a sports team can teach tolerance of others, acceptance of rules, and respect for authority. As in the case of families, the influence of peer groups is mitigated by the fact that politics is not a high priority for most of them.

## Media

As early as the 1930s, political scientist Charles Merriam observed that radio and film had tremendous power to educate: "Millions of persons are reached daily through these agencies, and are profoundly influenced by the material and interpretations presented in impressive form, incessantly, and in moments when they are open to suggestion."[69] The capacity of mass media to socialize people to politics has grown massively as the number of media outlets has increased and as new technologies allow for more interactive media experiences. Most people's political experiences occur vicariously through the media because they do not have personal access to government or politicians.

Since the advent of television, mass media have become prominent socialization agents. Young people's exposure to mass media has increased markedly since the 1960s. Studies indicate that the typical American aged two to eighteen spends almost forty hours a week consuming mass media, which is roughly the equivalent of holding a full-time job. In one-third of homes, the television is on all day. Young people's mass media experiences often occur in isolation. They spend much of their time watching television, using a computer or cell phone, playing video games, or listening to music alone. Personal contact with family members, teachers, and friends has declined. More than 60 percent of people under the age of twenty have televisions in their bedrooms, which are multimedia sanctuaries.[70]

The use of more personalized forms of media, such as text messaging and social networking sites, has expanded exponentially in recent years. These forms of media use are more active than television and can potentially have a stronger influence on political socialization. Young people using these forms of media have greater control over their own political socialization: they can choose to follow politics through Instagram or in a Facebook group that consists largely of close friends and associates with similar viewpoints, or they may decide to avoid political material altogether. Young people, even those who have not reached voting age, can become involved in election campaigns by using social media to contribute their own commentary and videos online.

Media are rich sources of information about government, politics, and current affairs. People learn about politics through news presented on television, in newspapers and magazines, on radio programs, on internet websites, and through social media. The press provides insights into the workings of government by showcasing political leaders in action, such as gavel-to-gavel coverage of Congress on C-SPAN. People can witness politicians in action, including on the campaign trail, through videos posted on YouTube and on online news sites such as CNN and MSNBC. Entertainment media, including television comedies and dramas, music, film, and video games, also contain much political content. Television programs like *The West Wing* offer viewers accounts of how government functions that, although fictionalized, can appear realistic. Comedies depicting government, such as *Veep* and *The Politician*, also can influence people's perceptions.

Some factors work against the media as agents of political socialization. Media are first and foremost profit-driven entities that are not mandated to be civic educators; they balance their public service imperative against the desire to make money. Moreover, unlike teachers, journalists do not have formal training in how to educate citizens about government and politics; as a result, the news often can be more sensational than informative. The increased use of social media by politicians and the public has contributed to greater political polarization, as people express extreme positions and are less willing to work together toward common goals.

# Group Differences

Political learning and socialization experiences can differ vastly for people depending on the groups with which they associate, such as those based on gender and racial and ethnic background. Certain groups are socialized to a more active role in politics, while others are marginalized. Wealthier people may have more resources for participating in politics, such as money and connections, than poorer people.

There are significant differences in the ways that males and females are socialized to politics. Historically, men have occupied a more central position in American political culture than women. This tradition was institutionalized at the time of the founding, when women did not receive the right to vote in the Constitution. While strides have been made over the past century to achieve political equality between the sexes, differences in sex-role socialization still exist. Traits associated with political leadership, such as being powerful and showing authority, are more often associated with males than females. Girls have fewer opportunities to observe women taking political action, especially as few females hold the highly visible positions, such as member of Congress and cabinet secretary, that are covered by mass media. This trend has been changing as women such as Madeleine Albright, Condoleezza Rice, and 2016 presidential candidate Hillary Clinton attracted media attention in their roles as secretary of state. Speaker of the House of Representatives Nancy Pelosi has been a strong leader of the Democratic Party. Sarah Palin gained national attention as Republican John McCain's vice presidential running mate in 2008. Vice President Kamala Harris became the first woman to hold the position in 2021. President Joe Biden's cabinet includes women in top positions, including Treasury Secretary Janet Yellen, Housing and Urban Development Secretary Marcia Fudge, and Interior Secretary Deb Haaland.[71]

**FIGURE 6.16 Female Political Leaders**
Vice President Kamala Harris is one of an increasing number of women who have achieved a highly visible political leadership role.

Source: Isaac Hoops / Shutterstock.com

Despite these developments, women are not consistently represented in high-level government positions. President Donald Trump's cabinet contained fewer women than the seven who held cabinet positions under President Barack Obama.[72] Women are still socialized to supporting political roles, such as volunteering in political campaigns, rather than leading roles, such as holding higher-level elected office, but they have gained some headway. The result is that fewer women than men seek careers in public office beyond the local level. However, the number of women elected to Congress increased notably as a result of the 2018 midterm elections.[73]

# Political Generations

A **political generation** is a group of individuals, similar in age, who share a general set of political socialization experiences leading to the development of shared political orientations that distinguish them from other age groups in society. People of a similar age tend to be exposed to shared historical, social, and political stimuli. A shared generational outlook develops when an age group experiences a decisive political event in its **impressionable years**—the period from late adolescence to early adulthood when people approach or attain voting age—and begins to think more seriously about politics. At the same time, younger people have less clearly defined political beliefs, which makes them more likely to be influenced by key societal events.[74]

**political generation**

Group of individuals similar in age who share a general set of socialization experiences that leads to the development of shared political orientations that distinguish them from other age cohorts.

**impressionable years**

Period from late adolescence to early adulthood when people begin to think more seriously about politics and can take part in meaningful ways, such as by voting.

The idea of American political generations dates back to the Founding Fathers. Thomas Jefferson believed that new generations would emerge in response to changing social and political conditions and that this would, in turn, influence public policy. Today, people can be described as being part of the Depression Era/GI generation, the silent generation, the baby boom generation, generation X, and the millennial generation/generation Y. Depression Era/GIs, born between 1900 and 1924, were heavily influenced by World War I and the Great Depression. They tend to trust government to solve problems because they perceived that Franklin Delano Roosevelt's New Deal programs helped the country recover from the Depression. The silent generation, born between 1922 and 1945, experienced World War II and the 1950s during their impressionable years. Like their predecessors, they believe that government can get things done, but they are less trusting of leaders. The Vietnam War and the civil rights and women's rights movements left lasting impressions on the baby boomers, who were born between 1943 and 1960. The largest of the generations, this cohort protested against the government establishment in its youth and still distrusts government. Generation Xers, born between 1965 and 1980, came of age during a period without a major war or economic hardship. The seminal events they relate to are the explosion of the Challenger spacecraft and the Iran-Contra hearings. This generation developed a reputation for lacking both knowledge of and interest in politics.[75] The political development of the millennials, those born between 1981 and 1996, is influenced by the terrorist attacks of 9/11 and its aftermath, as well as by the rise of digital technologies. This generation is more multicultural and has more tolerance for racial and ethnic difference than older cohorts. Sociologists William Strauss and Neil Howe have identified Generation Z, consisting of people born in 1997 and beyond, which is a new political cohort. This generation is influenced by the war on terror, parents who seek to protect them from societal ills, and the COVID-19 pandemic.[76] Gen Z has been raised in a digital culture and is the most diverse generation in history, with 48% identifying as nonwhite.[77]

Some scholars have noted the emergence of Gen C, the emerging generation of very young children who have been dramatically impacted by the COVID-19 pandemic. While it is difficult to pinpoint exactly who is in Gen C because the long-term effects of the pandemic on this group are unknown, sociologists include children born in 2016 and later, as the aftereffects of COVID-19 are likely to influence people yet to be born. Gen C has had important aspects of their lives disrupted, including how they interact with others and celebrate major milestones. The overall political character of this generation will only be revealed over time.[78]

**FIGURE 6.17**
**Millennials and Technology**
The millennial generation is known for being tech savvy and for using social networks to communicate.

Source: © Shutterstock, Inc.

Conflicts between generations have existed for centuries. Thomas Jefferson observed significant differences in the political worldviews of younger and older people in the early days of the republic. Younger government leaders were more willing to adapt to changing conditions and to experiment with new ideas than older officials.[79] Today generation Xers and the millennials have been portrayed as self-interested and lacking social responsibility by their elders from the baby boom generation. Generational conflicts of different periods have been depicted in landmark films, including the 1950s-era *Rebel without a Cause* and the 1960s-era *Easy Rider*. Generation X has been portrayed in films such as *Slacker*, *The Breakfast Club*, and *Reality Bites*. Movies about the millennial generation include *Easy A* and *The Social Network*.

## Key Takeaways

- Political socialization is the process by which people learn about their government and acquire the beliefs, attitudes, values, and behaviors associated with good citizenship. The political socialization process in the United States stresses the teaching of democratic and capitalist values. Agents, including parents, teachers, friends, coworkers, church associates, club members, sports teams, mass media, and popular culture, pass on political orientations.
- Political socialization differs over the life course. Young children develop a basic sense of identification with a country. College students can form opinions based on their experiences working for a cause. Older people can become active because they see a need to influence public policy that will affect their lives. There are subgroup differences in political socialization. Certain groups, such as citizens with higher levels of education and income, are socialized to take an active part in politics, while others are marginalized.
- Political generations consist of individuals similar in age who develop a unique worldview as a result of living through particular political experiences. These key events include war and economic depression. The worldviews of the millennial generation and Gen Z are highly influenced by their use of technology.

## Exercises

1. Do you believe you have the power to make an impact on the political process?

2. What is the first political event you were aware of? What did you think about what was going on? Who influenced how you thought about it?
3. How do members of your political generation feel about the government? How do your attitudes differ from those of your parents?

# 6.4 Political Culture and Socialization in the Information Age

## Learning Objectives

After reading this section, you should be able to answer the following questions:

1. How do people's interactions with media contribute to their political socialization?
2. How do media depict political socialization in the news and on entertainment channels?

New media are becoming important agents of political socialization because they host a great deal of political content and require the active engagement of users. Both news media and entertainment media provide depictions that influence political socialization, such as models of government leaders and citizen action.

## Media Interactions

People's interactions with media are increasingly important to the process of political socialization. The explosion in communication technologies has resulted in people communicating less via face-to-face interactions with family members and peers and more through technological intermediaries, such as the internet, cell phones, and personal digital devices. Even teachers find it increasingly difficult to compete with the communications technologies that command their students' attention.

The internet is a potentially powerful agent of political socialization because of the vast amount of political information available online and the fact that people actively engage with online platforms. Not only do people get information about government from news sites and blogs, but they can also post responses to stories and debate others through discussion forums. They also can use online media to actively take part in political processes, such as election campaigns. They can post tweets expressing their opinions, share video commentaries, and organize political events using social media. They can create their own blogs and videos and publish them online.

Young people have been on the forefront of using social media to learn about and participate in politics. Over 90 percent of adults are online, and they are using social media for politics at an increasing rate.[80] Evidence suggests that young people are developing their political identities online as they learn about the differences between candidates and political parties and acquire information about issues and political events. They use social media to create collaborative online communities that organize for political causes, lobby government, and campaign for candidates. All of these activities contribute to the socialization of engaged citizens. In addition, people frequently encounter political content in their social media feeds, which has the potential to increase their levels of political information and engagement.

# Media Depictions

**FIGURE 6.18** Young Voters with Political Passion

Despite the dominant media depiction of apathy, many young voters are passionate about exercising their right to vote.

Source: Karl_Sonnenberg/Shutterstock.com.

Depictions of socialization and learning experiences abound in media. News and entertainment media are especially powerful as they provide depictions that embody the beliefs and values that make up American political culture. Core American values are crucial elements of a "good story," as they resonate with the public. Both egalitarianism and individualism are celebrated in stories in which lone, ordinary people are able to defeat powerful economic and political forces aligned against them.

A frequent media frame depicts young people as disengaged from politics. This frame is especially prevalent during election campaigns, when news stories focus on young people's lack of participation in campaign activities, such as working on behalf of a candidate, and low turnout. This frame is misleading, as many young voters take an active role in elections, and can make a difference in the outcome.[81]

## News Media

News media provide frequent depictions of political role models, including government leaders and citizens who are actively involved in community affairs. Politicians are often portrayed negatively, which can cause people to distrust leaders and lose faith in government. A prominent media frame portrays political leaders as constantly at odds and unable to reach civil agreement or compromise. This media frame is reinforced during elections when candidates attack their opponents unrelentingly in their stump speeches and ads.

## Entertainment Media

Entertainment media provide depictions of core American values central to the political socialization process. Individualism is portrayed frequently in television dramas and comedies that tell stories of average citizens taking on the political and economic systems. Politicians can use entertainment media to convey an image of themselves embodying American values. Former Alaska Governor Sarah Palin has cultivated an image of rugged individualism and self-reliance. She reinforced this image through the short-lived reality television program *Sarah Palin's Alaska*.

Depictions can take the form of fictional dramas, such as *Friday Night Lights*'s portrayal of family life and the politics of sports in rural Texas, and sitcoms, or the offbeat view of parent–child relationships shown in *Modern Family* and *The Goldbergs*. Comedy programs, like *The Connors*, depict working-class American life. The sitcom *black-ish* has tackled controversial topics like gun control and the use of the n-word. Reality television programs such as *Teen Mom* offer insights into family socialization that can invite commentary and criticism from viewers.

Children's literature and movies feature many stoic, individualist characters. The classic film *The Wizard of Oz* (1939) has been called a tale of self-reliance. Dorothy, dropped from Kansas into Oz by a tornado, is advised that, to be able to return home, she should go to the Emerald City and appeal to the superior power, the Wizard of Oz. On the way there, she meets up with a Scarecrow desiring a brain, a Tin Man in search of a heart, and a Cowardly Lion in need of courage. The four meet a fearsome Wizard who orders them to bring back the broom of the Wicked Witch of the West. After a series of adventures, they return victorious to the Emerald City, only to find that the Wizard is nothing but a small man behind a curtain who has created an illusion of the "great and powerful Oz." It turns out, he explains, that he was merely a lost itinerant balloonist who, upon descending from the clouds, was declared a Wizard by the credulous people. Dorothy and her friends learn that they each had the power they sought all along.

Teachers seeking to instill democratic and character values in their students have capitalized on the popularity of Harry Potter, the protagonist wizard in J. K. Rowling's popular books. Harry has become a hero to children (and adults) who have read about his exploits. He embodies values of individualism and bravery tempered with humility. Young people can relate to Harry because in the world of the Muggles (those without magical powers), he is average and imperfect. Even among the wizards, he is not the smartest or the most talented. Yet he is able to handle extraordinary situations with bravery and skill. Harry's heroism provides a civics lesson for readers because it illustrates the balance between the democratic values of individualism and egalitarianism. While Harry realizes that his magic powers give him the ability to distinguish himself, he chooses to include others—Hermione Granger, Ron and Ginny Weasley, and Neville Longbottom—as he fights against evil. Further, Harry does not seek public recognition for his acts of heroism.[82]

MTV's series *The Real World*, which has aired continuously for over thirty seasons since 1991, provides an intriguing look at the socialization experiences of groups of twentysomething strangers who live together for a year. The program provides insights into the effects of peers on the development of the housemates' attitudes and behaviors. In the course of learning to adapt to new surroundings, live as a group, and find jobs, cast members deal with political issues. The San Francisco season attracted national media attention because it featured the house members grappling with the issue of HIV/AIDS when roommate Pedro, who worked as an AIDS educator and counselor, tested positive for the disease. Depictions related to subgroup relations and multiculturalism abound on *The Real World*. Cast members come from a variety of racial and ethnic backgrounds, which is a source of tension in the house. Almost every season involves a Black male who stereotypically is alienated and confrontational. Most of the time, this character is shown talking about the societal injustices he suffers and picking fights with other house members. These confrontations force cast members to take sides and voice their opinions about race.

# Media Consequences

Parents and educators express concerns that socialization of young people via mass media contributes to a citizenry that is alienated from politics and distrusts government. Many of the media messages young people receive about politics are negative. They spend little time discussing these messages with other people or discovering the ways in which they can actively engage the political world. Alternatively, young people today are exposed to much more political media content than any prior generation. This exposure can contribute to greater awareness of government and opportunities for civic action. Digital communication technologies offer people increased opportunities for taking part in politics via media, such as posting to a blog or participating in a "**tweetup**," using the microblogging platform Twitter to inform people about a political event taking place online or offline.

**tweetup**

An online or offline meeting organized via the microblogging platform Twitter.

## Scandal Coverage

The influence of mass media on children's attitudes toward leaders and government has become more negative over time, as media messages focus more on personal scandals and institutional dysfunction. For the most part, young children's initial views of politics tend to be positive. Studies conducted in the 1960s showed that children idealized the president. They considered him a **benevolent leader**, someone who did good things for the country and would help a child personally. Even during the Watergate scandal of the 1970s, which involved a break-in at the Democratic National Committee headquarters and a cover-up by President Richard Nixon, children held strong, positive feelings about the office of the president. Children learned about President Nixon's

**benevolent leader**

A concept in which young children consider the president to be a personal friend who will do good things for the nation.

impeachment primarily from their parents and teachers, and not from the mass media. Media accounts focused on the political aspects of the Nixon impeachment, which went over the heads of most children. Many parents felt it was important to instill positive views of government in their children during this period of political upheaval.

The situation was much different in the 1990s when children learned about President Bill Clinton's involvement with White House intern Monica Lewinsky, predominantly from nonstop, graphic television coverage that focused on Clinton's personal life. Young children became disillusioned with President Clinton because they felt he had not told the truth. For the first time, children's views of the sitting president, as well as their opinions about the institution of the presidency, were significantly more negative than those of their parents. Fewer children aspired to become president when they grew up.[83]

Political scandal coverage can be relentless, and can be more pervasive than coverage of government actions and policies. In 2014, New Jersey Governor Chris Christie was battered by the press for weeks because of his role in "Bridgegate," where lanes on the busy George Washington Bridge allegedly were closed in retaliation against a political opponent, causing massive traffic jams. "Bridgegate Coverage" overshadowed stories about the economy, reforms of the nation's surveillance program, and same-sex marriages, which were being prominently debated at the time. Governor Christie experienced another scandal—"Beachgate"—in the summer of 2017 when New Jersey public beaches were closed due to the state's inability to pass a budget. Christie and his family vacationed at Island Beach State Park, which was closed to the public. A journalist took an aerial photo of Christie relaxing in a beach chair that became the source of many internet memes (see here).

**FIGURE 6.19 Governor Christie's "Beachgate" Scandal**

A journalist's photo of New Jersey Governor Chris Christie on a closed beach was fodder for a major scandal story over the July 4th weekend as the public was barred from the beach.

Source: Andrew Mills/Associated Press.

During the 2016 presidential election, coverage of Hillary Clinton's use of a private email server instead of the official government server when she was secretary of state saturated the media. The coverage was bolstered by Donald Trump's constantly raising the issue. With eleven days to go in the election, FBI Director James Comey announced that the Clinton email probe was being reopened. Some observers, especially members of her campaign staff, felt that the nonstop coverage of the Clinton email situation contributed to her loss to Donald Trump.

## Hollywood and Washington

The **Payne Fund studies** of motion pictures and youth, conducted between 1929 and 1933, provide early evidence that film can be a powerful agent of socialization. The studies found that people developed attitudes toward racial and ethnic groups, war, and crime based on their exposure to popular films. Audience members who saw the controversial film *Birth of a Nation* believed that Blacks in the post–Civil War era were uncivilized and dangerous. Children who watched their favorite movie stars, such as James Cagney and Humphrey Bogart, playing criminals on screen imitated their behavior patterns by acting up in school.[84]

**Payne Fund studies**

Research conducted between 1929 and 1933 that demonstrated the influence of movies on young people's attitudes about racial groups, war, and crime.

Recognizing that film has the power to impart political messages to the public, officials in Washington have forged connections with the filmmaking community in Hollywood. The Hollywood-Washington connection dates back to the 1930s when President Herbert Hoover befriended MGM mogul Louis B. Mayer, whose studio produced many of the most popular films of the era. President Franklin D. Roosevelt realized that films could influence public perceptions of the Great Depression and the United States' involvement in World War II. Roosevelt encouraged filmmakers to make movies with optimistic messages that would generate support for government action. The defeatist ending of director John Ford's Oscar-winning film *The Grapes of Wrath* (1940), based on the John Steinbeck novel, was changed to depict the Joad family persevering despite terrible hardship, due to their inner strength. In addition to prowar documentaries such as Frank Capra's *Why We Fight* series, Roosevelt requested that studio heads make popular films in support of the war effort. Films such as *Confessions of a Nazi Spy* depicted Germany as a nation out to destroy the American Constitution and the Bill of Rights. Anti-German messages were delivered in popular series films such as *Tarzan Triumphs* (1943), in which Tarzan and Cheetah fight Nazis who parachute into their jungle paradise.[85]

**FIGURE 6.20 Influence of *Birth of a Nation***

Early research indicated that film could be an influential agent of political socialization. Negative attitudes toward African Americans were transmitted to audiences through the film *Birth of a Nation*.

Source: Gado Images / Alamy Stock Photo

Immediately following the 9/11 terrorist attacks, representatives of Hollywood's major studios, television networks, trade organizations, and the creative community met with senior White House officials to discuss how the entertainment community could help in the war against terror by emphasizing that the 9/11 attacks were an affront to civilization.[86] Hollywood sought to define its political role while at the same time protecting its future at the box office. The first inclination was to feature comedy and fantasy fare that would be uplifting and noncontroversial. Films featuring terrorist themes—such as the Jennifer Lopez vehicle *Tick Tock*, which is about terrorists planting bombs in Los Angeles shopping malls, and *Nosebleed*, a Jackie Chan movie about a window washer who discovers a plan to blow up the World Trade Center—were shelved. Images of the Twin Towers were removed from films set for release, such as *Spiderman*. However, video rentals of films featuring dramatic action and terrorist plots increased by 30 percent in the months directly following the attacks, which gave Hollywood an indication that the public would be receptive to more violent offerings.[87] War films with a patriotic theme, such as *Behind Enemy Lines* and *The Last Castle*, proved to be highly popular, and coincidentally, reinforced the messages suggested by the White House delegation.

## Key Takeaways

Mass media have become compelling agencies of political learning, as young people spend a tremendous amount of time being exposed to television, the internet, video games, and other media rather than interacting with other people. Media messages about politics are often negative, which may lead young people to become alienated from the political process. Young people, in particular, may learn a good deal about politics from entertainment and popular media.

## Exercises

1. Are there any fictional characters who seem heroic to you? What qualities make him or her seem heroic?
2. Where do you get most of your news about politics? Do you think that where you get your news might affect your views about politics? In what ways?

### Civic Education

#### Kids Voting USA

Young people often have difficulty seeing the relevance of civic education to their immediate lives. Programs tend to emphasize future participation, such as voting in presidential elections, which is an activity that students cannot engage in until they reach the age of eighteen. However, innovative curriculum projects can stimulate students' interest in elections through meaningful campaign-related activities.

Kids Voting USA is a program initiated in 1988 that allows grade school teachers to use a curriculum designed around an election campaign. Students become involved by researching issues and preparing position papers, constructing informational websites, writing articles for newspapers, and serving as reporters on local television stations. On Election Day, children accompany parents to the polls and cast ballots in a special election. Children who participate are often motivated to turn out at elections when they reach voting age. In addition, children's participation in Kids Voting USA stimulates parents' interest in the campaign and thus increases voter turnout. Young people initiate discussions at home that are associated with their school projects. This enthusiasm for elections continues for some families after the program's completion, especially among families of lower socioeconomic status who previously had little incentive for participating in politics.[88]

# 6.5 Recommended Reading


Calavita, Marco. *Apprehending Politics*. Albany: State University of New York Press, 2005. Looks at how the news media influence the political beliefs and behavior of generation X.

Callahan, Rebecca M., and Chandra Miller, *Coming of Political Age*. New York: Russell Sage Foundation, 2013. Examines American schools and the civic education of American youth.

Campbell, David E. *Why We Vote*. Princeton, NJ: Princeton University Press, 2006. Examines the ways in which schools and communities socialize young people to politics.

Craig, Steven C., and Stephen Earl Bennett, eds. *After the Boom*. Lanham, MD: Rowman & Littlefield, 1997. Explores the socializing experiences and political orientations of generation X, people born between 1960 and 1980.

Delli Carpini, Michael X. *Stability and Change in American Politics*. New York: New York University Press, 1986. A study of the baby boom generation using a political socialization framework.

Elazar, Daniel J. *The American Mosaic*. Boulder, CO: Westview Press, 1994. Examines the geographical underpinnings of American political culture across generations.

Hunter, James Davison. *Culture Wars*. New York: Basic Books, 1991. Discusses how subgroups based on religious differences disagree on fundamental issues of American national identity.

Johnson, Thomas J., Carol E. Hays, and Scott P. Hays. *Trickle Up Political Socialization: The Impact of Kids Voting USA on Voter Turnout in Kansas*. Lanham, MD: Rowman & Littlefield, 1998. A collection of articles discussing how the mass media can contribute to the political socialization process and foster the development of democratic values and participation.

Kitwana, Bakari. *The Hip-Hop Generation*. New York: Basic Civitas Books, 2002. Discusses the socialization experiences of young Black Americans who find their political voice in hip-hop music.

McClosky, Herbert, and John Zaller. *The American Ethos*. Cambridge, MA: Harvard University Press, 1984. Examines the nature of Americans' commitment to democratic and capitalist values.

Niemi, Richard G., and Jane Junn. *Civic Education*. New Haven, CT: Yale University Press, 1998. Explores how schools succeed and fail in teaching civics.

Schmermund, Kathleen. *Charles Gibson vs. Jon Stewart*. New York: Lambert Academic Publishing, 2010. Compares political socialization of young people via traditional and fake news media.

Strauss, William, and Neil Howe. *Generations*. New York: William Morrow and Company, 1992. Provides an overview of American generations since the founding of America.

White, John Kenneth. *The Values Divide*. New York: Chatham House Publishers, 2003. An account of how changes in the demographic, racial, and ethnic makeup of the United States that have occurred since the 1950s have resulted in a fundamental shift in cultural values.

Youniss, James, and Miranda Yates. *Community Service and Social Responsibility in Youth*. Chicago: University of Chicago Press, 1997. A study of high school community service programs and how they work to promote future civic participation.

## 6.6 Recommended Viewing

*63: Sixty-Three Up* (2019). The eighth installment of Michael Apted's unprecedented documentary film chronicling the lives of fourteen British men and women in seven-year intervals. The subjects represent a cross section of British society, and their life stories depict a variety of socialization experiences and political orientations. This series of documentaries, beginning with *Seven Up*, is the only film depiction of socialization over the life course.

*American Family* (2002). A PBS dramatic series that examines the everyday lives of members of an extended Latinx family.

*American History X* (1998). An examination of two brothers who are drawn into a neo-Nazi skinhead gang. The film examines family socialization as the initial source of one brother's racism, which is reinforced in prison and in a gang.

*An American Family* (1973), *American Family Revisited* (1983), *Lance Loud!: A Death in an American Family* (2003). A television documentary series capturing the life and times of the Loud family; the series was one of the first forays into "reality TV" and became controversial as the family dealt publicly with many difficult life situations, including issues of sexual orientation and divorce.

*The Breakfast Club* (1985). This film explores diverse socialization experiences in the home, school, and peer group of several high school students forced to do detention together in the school library.

*Dead End* (1937). An examination of the problems, including cultural conflicts, faced by New York City residents as they live through their impressionable years during the Great Depression.

*Easy Rider* (1969). This portrayal of two young societal dropouts who ride motorcycles across the American southwest depicts various scenes of the late 1960s counterculture.

*Rebel without a Cause* (1955). James Dean portrays a troubled and misunderstood middle-class 1950s-era youth in this classic depiction of generational conflict.

*River's Edge* (1987). A dark portrayal of 1980s youth culture based on a true story of friends who do not report the murder of a woman in their group by her boyfriend. The film deals with issues such as family socialization in homes with absentee parents and peer-group influence. It was selected as the "Film That Mattered" for the 1980s by the LA International Film Festival.

*Slacker* (1991). This documentary-style film of twentysomethings living on the edge of society in Austin, Texas, contributed to the image of 1990s youth culture as aimless and bored.

*The Last Dance* (2020). The career of basketball hero Michael Jordan is documented in this Netflix miniseries that focuses on his time playing for the Chicago Bulls.

# Endnotes


1. W. Lance Bennett, *Public Opinion in American Politics* (New York: Harcourt Brace Jovanovich, 1980), 368.
2. Daniel J. Elazar, *The American Mosaic* (Boulder, CO: Westview Press, 1994).
3. Gabriel A. Almond and Sidney Verba, *The Civic Culture* (Newbury Park, CA: Sage Publications, 1986).
4. Ronald Inglehart, *Culture Shift in Advanced Industrial Society* (Princeton, NJ: Princeton University Press, 1990).
5. James Davison Hunter and Carl Bowman, *The State of Disunion* (Charlottesville, VA: In Media Res Educational Foundation, 1996); Pew Research Center for the People and the Press, *Values Survey* (Washington, DC: Pew Research Center, March 2009).
6. James Davison Hunter and Carl Bowman, *The State of Disunion* (Charlottesville, VA: In Media Res Educational Foundation, 1996).
7. Pew Research Center for the People and the Press, *Retro-Politics: The Political Typology* (Washington, DC: Pew Research Center, November 11, 1999).
8. Pew Research Center for the People and the Press, "The Growing Gap Between Rich and Poor." Report (Washington, DC: Pew Research Center, 2013).
9. Richard W. Wilson, "American Political Culture in Comparative Perspective," *Political Psychology*, 18, no. 2 (1997): 483–502.
10. James Davison Hunter and Carl Bowman, *The State of Disunion* (Charlottesville, VA: In Media Res Educational Foundation, 1996).
11. John L. Sullivan, James Piereson, and George E. Marcus, *Political Tolerance and American Democracy* (Chicago: University of Chicago Press, 1982).
12. Steve Wyche, "Colin Kaepernick explains why he sat during national anthem." NFL.com, Aug 27, 2016. Retrieved from: https://www.nfl.com/news/colin-kaepernick-explains-why-he-sat-during-national-anthem-0ap3000000691077.
13. Dan Cancian, "Everything Trump Has Said About NFL Kneeling So Far," Newsweek, June 8, 2020. Everything Trump Has Said About NFL Kneeling So Far (newsweek.com).
14. Maya Rhodan, "This Photo of MLK Kneeling Has New Power Amid the NFL Protests. Here's the Story Behind It," Time, September 25, 2017. History Behind Photo of Martin Luther King, Kr. Kneeling | Time.
15. Herbert McClosky and John Zaller, *The American Ethos* (Cambridge, MA: Harvard University Press, 1987).
16. Pew Research Center for the People and the Press, *Views of Business and Regulation Remain Unchanged* (Washington, DC: Pew Research Center, February 21, 2001).
17. Benjamin Ginsberg and Herbert Weissberg, "Elections and the Mobilization of Popular Support," *American Journal of Political Science* 22, no.1 (1978): 31–55.
18. George Washington's Mount Vernon, "Is it true that George Washington chopped down a cherry tree when he was a boy?," accessed February 3, 2011, http://www.mountvernon.org/knowledge/index.cfm/fuseaction/view/KnowledgeID/21.
19. George Washington's Mount Vernon, "Did George Washington really throw a silver dollar across the Potomac River?," accessed February 3, 2011, http://www.mountvernon.org/knowledge/index.cfm/fuseaction/view/KnowledgeID/20.
20. Lonn Taylor, Jeffrey Brodie, and Kathleen Kendrick, *The Star-Spangled Banner: An American Icon* (Washington, DC: Smithsonian, 2008).
21. Agusta Stevenson, *Molly Pitcher: Young Patriot* (New York: Aladdin Paperbacks, Simon and Schuster, 1983).
22. Fred I. Greenstein, *Children and Politics* (New Haven, CT: Yale University Press, 1969).
23. Sandra Yin, "Shifting Careers," *American Demographics*, 23, no. 12 (December 2001): 39–40.
24. Pat Walters, *Michael Jordan: The New American Hero* (Charlottesville VA: The Crossroads Project, 1997).
25. Daniel J. Elazar, *American Federalism: A View From the States*, 2nd ed. (New York: Thomas Y. Crowell, 1972).
26. Bakari Kitwana, *The Hip-Hop Generation* (New York: Basic Civitas Books, 2002).
27. Manning Marable, "The Politics of Hip-Hop," *The Urban Think Tank*, 2 (2002); http://www.hartford-hwp.com/archives/45a/594.html.
28. Autumn Lewis, "Vilification of Black Youth Culture by the Media" (master's thesis, Georgetown University, 2003).
29. James Guida, "Hip-Hop's New Wave of Lyricism," *The New Yorker*, April 12, 2017.
30. Lawrence H. Fuchs, *The American Kaleidoscope*. (Middletown, CT: Wesleyan University Press, 1990).
31. Brady Dennis and Jerry Markon, "Amid Protests and Confusion, Trump Defends Executive Order: 'This Is Not a Muslim Ban'," *The Washington Post*, January 29, 2017.
32. Rod Dreher, "The Bravest Speak," *National Review Online*, January 16, 2002.
33. "Ground Zero Statue Criticized for 'Political Correctness,'" *CNN*, January 12, 2002, http//www.cnn.com.
34. Fred I. Greenstein, *Children and Politics* (New Haven, CT: Yale University Press, 1969).
35. Michael McDevitt and Steven Chaffee, "From Top-Down to Trickle-Up Influence: Revisiting the Assumptions about the Family in Political Socialization," *Political Communication*, November 2002, 281–301.
36. Gabriel A. Almond and James S. Coleman, eds., *The Politics of the Developing Areas* (Princeton, NJ: Princeton University Press, 1960), 27.
37. Pamela Johnston Conover, "Political Socialization: Where's the Politics?" in *Political Science: Looking to the Future, Volume III, Political Behavior*, ed. William Crotty (Evanston, IL: Northwestern University Press, 1991), 125–152.
38. Carole L. Hahn, *Becoming Political* (Albany: State University of New York Press, 1998).
39. Richard E. Dawson and Kenneth Prewitt, *Political Socialization* (Boston: Little Brown and Company, 1969).
40. Fred I. Greenstein, *Children and Politics* (New Haven, CT: Yale University Press, 1969).
41. Stephen C. Craig, *Malevolent Leaders* (Boulder, CO: Westview, 1993).
42. Lauren Leatherby, Arielle Ray, Anjali Singhvi, Christiaan Triebert, Derek Watkins, and Haley Wills, "How a Presidential Rally Turned Into a Capitol Rampage," *The New York Times*, January 12, 2021. https://www.nytimes.com/interactive/2021/01/12/us/capitol-mob-timeline.html.
43. Jack Dennis, David Easton, and Sylvia Easton, *Children in the Political System* (New York: McGraw-Hill, 1969).
44. Jack Dennis, David Easton, and Sylvia Easton, *Children in the Political System* (New York: McGraw-Hill, 1969).
45. Pamela Johnston Conover, "Political Socialization: Where's the Politics?" in *Political Science: Looking to the Future, Volume III, Political Behavior*, ed. William Crotty (Evanston, IL: Northwestern University Press, 1991), 125–152.
46. Charles E. Lindblom, "Another Sate of Mind," in *Discipline and History*, ed. James Farr and Raymond Seidelman (Ann Arbor: University of Michigan Press, 1993), 327–43.
47. Felix Padilla, *The Gang as American Enterprise* (New Brunswick, NJ: Rutgers University Press, 1992).
48. Jack Dennis, David Easton, and Sylvia Easton, *Children in the Political System* (New York: McGraw-Hill, 1969).
49. Richard G. Niemi and Mary A. Hepburn, "The Robirth of Political Socialization," *Perspectives on Political Science*, 24 (1995): 7–16.
50. Virginia Sapiro, *The Political Integration of Women* (Urbana: University of Illinois Press, 1983).
51. Janie S. Steckenrider and Neal E. Cutler, "Aging and Adult Political Socialization," in *Political Learning in Adulthood*, ed. Roberta S. Sigel (Chicago: University of Chicago Press, 1988), 56–88.
52. Paul Lyons, *Class of '66* (Philadelphia: Temple University Press, 1994).
53. Anne Daugherty Miles, "A Multidimensional Approach to Distinguishing between the Most and Least Politically Engaged Senior Citizens, Using Socialization and Participation Variables" (PhD diss., Georgetown University, 1997).
54. Richard E. Dawson and Kenneth Prewitt, *Political Socialization* (Boston: Little, Brown, 1969).
55. Kenneth P. Langton, *Political Socialization* (New York: Oxford, 1969); Michael P. Riccards, *The Making of American Citizenry* (New York: Chandler Press, 1973).
56. Herbert Hyman, *Political Socialization* (Glencoe, IL: Free Press, 1959), 69.
57. Jack Dennis and Diana Owen, "The Partisanship Puzzle: Identification and Attitudes of Generation X," in *After the Boom*, ed. Stephen C. Craig and Stephen Earl Bennet (Lanham, MD: Rowman & Littlefield, 1997), 43–62.
58. Richard M. Merelman, *Making Something of Ourselves* (Berkeley: University of California Press, 1986).
59. M. N. Saphir and Steven H. Chaffee, "Adolescents' Contribution to Family Communication Patterns," *Human Communication Research* 28, no. 1 (2002): 86–108.
60. Richard M. Merelman, "The Family and Political Socialization: Toward a Theory of Exchange," *Journal of Politics*, 42: 461–86.
61. Robert Hess and Judith Torney, *The Development of Political Attitudes in Children* (Chicago: Aldine, 1967).
62. Norman H. Nie, Jane Junn, and Kenneth Stehlik-Barry, *Education and Democratic Citizenship in America* (Chicago: University of Chicago Press, 1996).
63. Duane F. Alwin, Ronald L. Cohen, and Theodore M. Newcomb, *Political Attitudes Over the Life Span* (Madison: University of Wisconsin Press, 1991).
64. Richard G. Niemi and Jane Junn, *Civic Education* (New Haven, CT: Yale University Press, 1998).
65. Meira Levinson, *No Citizen Left Behind* (Cambridge, MA: Harvard University Press, 2012).
66. Lawrence J. Walker, Karl H. Hennig, and Tobias Krettenauer, "Parent and Peer Contexts for Children's Moral Reasoning Development," *Child Development* 71, no. 4 (August 2000): 1033–48.

67. Judith Rich Harris, "Where Is the Child's Environment? A Group Socialization Theory of Development," *Psychological Review* 102, no. 3 (1995): 458–89.

68. Eric L. Dey, "Undergraduate Political Attitudes," *Journal of Higher Education*, 68 (1997): 398–413.

69. Charles Edward Merriam, *The Making of Citizens* (Chicago: University of Chicago Press, 1931), 160–61.

70. Kaiser Family Foundation, *The Media Family* (Menlo Park, CA: Kaiser Family Foundation, 2006).

71. Beatrice Jin, Allan James Vestal, Emily Cadei, and Andrew McGill, "Joe Biden's Cabinet: Who's In, and Who Voted Against Them," Politico, March 11, 2021. https://www.politico.com/interactives/2021/joe-biden-cabinet-members-confirmations-list/.

72. Jasmine C. Lee, "Trump's Cabinet So Far Is More White and Male Than Any First Cabinet Since Reagan's," *The New York Times*, March 10, 2017.

73. Virginia Sapiro, *Women in American Society* (New York: Mayfair Publishing, 2002).

74. Michael X. Delli Carpini, *Stability and Change in American Politics* (New York: New York University Press, 1986).

75. William Strauss and Neil Howe, *Generations* (New York: William Morrow, 1992).

76. William Strauss and Neil Howe, *Millennials Rising* (New York: Random House, 2000).

77. Michael Dimmock, "Defining Generations: Where Millennials End and Generation Z Begins," Fact Tank, Pew Research Center, January 17, 2019. https://www.pewresearch.org/fact-tank/2019/01/17/where-millennials-end-and-generation-z-begins/.

78. Catherine E. Shoichet, "Meet Gen C, the COVID Generation," CNN, March 11, 2021. https://www.cnn.com/2021/03/11/us/covid-generation-gen-c/index.html.

79. Daniel J. Elazar, *The Generational Rhythm of American Politics* (Philadelphia: Temple University, Center for the Study of Federalism, 1976).

80. Pew Research Center for the People and the Press, "Internet/Broadband Fact Sheet," (Accessed March, 2021). http://www.pewinternet.org/fact-sheet/internet-broadband/.

81. Diana Owen, *Youth Voting and the Media* (Washington, DC: The George Washington University, Graduate School of Political Management, 2008).

82. Jeffrey A. Becker, "Heroism and the Political Morality of Democracy in Harry Potter," paper delivered at the Annual Meeting of the American Political Science Association, Boston, MA, August 29–September 1, 2002.

83. Diana Owen and Jack Dennis, "Kids and the Presidency: Assessing Clinton's Legacy," *The Public Perspective* 10, no. 3 (April–May 1999): 41–44.

84. Garth Jowett, Ian C. Jarvic, and Kathy H. Fuller, *Children and the Movies* (New York: Cambridge, 1996).

85. Clayton R. Koppes and Gregory D. Black, *Hollywood Goes to War* (New York: Free Press, 1987).

86. "Hollywood Considers Role in War Effort," *CNN*, November 12, 2001, http://www.cnn.com.

87. "Commercial Response to September 11," *NewsHour Online*, October 24, 2001, http://www.pbs.org/newshour.

88. Michael McDevitt and Steven H. Chaffee, "Second-Chance Political Socialization: 'Trickle-Up' Effects of Children on Parents," in *Engaging the Public*, ed. Thomas J. Johnson, Carol E. Hays, and Scott P. Hays (Lanham, MD: Rowman & Littlefield, 1998), 57–66.

CHAPTER 7

# Public Opinion

## 7.1 Preamble

It has become a ritual for Americans to spend the evening of presidential elections in front of their televisions or their computer screens and tablets following the voting returns as they are announced state by state. Election Night coverage is driven by anchors making projections about which candidate will win each state's electoral votes. Typically, news organizations have a good sense by late afternoon of who will be the next president of the United States based on exit polls of voters taken as they leave the polling place, although they hold off on making a prediction until later in the evening.[1]

**FIGURE 7.1 Exit Polls Misguide 2000 Election Night Coverage**

Misguided by exit poll data, news organizations prematurely called the 2000 presidential election contest in favor of Al Gore first and then George W. Bush. The election was too close to call on election night and eventually was decided in favor of Bush.

Source: Peter Cosgrove / Associated Press

Election Night 2000 began like any other since the 1960s, when television networks began using exit polls. The election was the closest in many decades, and there was much uncertainty about whether Republican George W. Bush or Democrat Al Gore would emerge victorious. As the night unfolded, it became clear that the outcome would be decided by Florida's twenty-five electoral votes. Network and cable news anchors discussed the closeness of the election and told the public to anticipate a long and interesting evening—a statement that proved prescient. By 8 p.m., with exit polls showing Gore was leading in Florida, television news organizations speculated that Gore would be headed to the White House. Three hours later, the networks began to rescind the call of Florida for Gore when it became evident that data from exit polls conflicted with actual returns from voting precincts.[2]

Much confusion ensued. With the media's proclamation of Bush as the winner, Gore phoned Bush and conceded the election and departed from his hotel to make his concession speech. While Gore was en route, the press once again changed their position, stating that the election was too close to call. Gore returned to his hotel, as the media's Election Night prediction of a Bush victory lasted all of ninety minutes.[3] The 2000 election was not decided on Election Night—November 7. Instead, a recount of the votes in Florida was undertaken in an attempt to determine the winner. The recount was halted by the U.S. Supreme Court on December 12, 2000, and George W. Bush was sworn in as president on January 20, 2001.

The Election Night 2000 media debacle illustrates a number of points relevant to this chapter. Polling is an integral element of American politics. Polls shape the way that news organizations frame their stories and convey information to the public. In fact, many news organizations have in-house polling operations or collaborate with polling firms to have public opinion data constantly available. Poll results allow the media to convey information to the public in a concise and authoritative manner. Polls can provide guidance to decision makers about election outcomes and policy debates. However, poll results are not always accurate, as was the case with the exit polls in the 2000 presidential election, and they can misrepresent public sentiment. Therefore, it is important for people to be savvy consumers of opinion polls.

# 7.2 What Is Public Opinion?

## Learning Objectives

After reading this section, you should be able to answer the following questions:

1. What is public opinion?
2. What are the different interpretations of public opinion?
3. How does an attitude differ from an opinion?

**public opinion**

People's collective preferences on matters related to government and politics.

Public opinion is one of the most frequently evoked terms in American politics. At the most basic level, **public opinion** represents people's collective preferences on matters related to government and politics. However, public opinion is a complex phenomenon, and scholars have developed a variety of interpretations of what public opinion means. One perspective holds that individual opinions matter; therefore, the opinions of the majority should be weighed more heavily than opinions of the minority when leaders make decisions. A contrasting view maintains that public opinion is controlled by organized groups, government leaders, and media elites. The opinions of those in positions of power or who have access to those in power carry the most weight.

Public opinion is often made concrete through questions asked on polls. Pollsters ask core questions, such as "Do you feel that the country is better off now than it was four years ago?" to gauge people's feelings about the government. Politicians routinely cite public opinion polls to justify their support of or opposition to public policies. Candidates use public opinion strategically to establish themselves as front-runners or underdogs in campaigns. Interest groups and political parties use public opinion polls to promote their causes. The mass media incorporate reports of public opinion into news stories about government and politics.

## Defining Public Opinion

What exactly is public opinion? Scholars do not agree on a single definition of public opinion. The concept means different things depending on how one defines "the public" and assumptions about whose opinion should or does count the most—individuals, groups, or elites.

**attentive public**

People who pay close attention to government and politics in general.

**issue publics**

People who focus on particular public policy debates and ignore other issues.

Most simply, the public can be thought of as people who share something in common, such as a connection to a government and a society that is confronted by particular issues that form the basis of public policies. Not all people have the same connection to issues. Some people are part of the **attentive public** who pay close attention to government and politics in general. Members of the attentive public can be seen as "political junkies" who are interested and engaged in politics. Other individuals are members of **issue publics** who focus on particular public policy debates, such as abortion or defense spending, and ignore others.[4] They may focus on a policy that has personal relevance; a health-care activist, for example, may have a close relative or friend who suffers from a prolonged medical problem. Some members of the public have little interest in politics or issues, and their concerns may not be represented.

An **opinion** is the position—favorable, unfavorable, neutral, or undecided—people take on a particular issue, policy, action, or leader. Opinions are not facts; they are expressions of people's feelings about a specific political object. Pollsters seeking people's opinions often say to respondents as they administer a survey, "there are no right or wrong answers; it's your thoughts that count." Opinions are related to but not the same as **attitudes**, or persistent, general orientations toward people, groups, or institutions. Attitudes often shape opinions. For example, people who hold attitudes strongly in favor of racial equality support public policies designed to limit discrimination in housing and employment.

**opinion**

The position that a person takes on a particular issue policy, action, or leader.

**attitudes**

Persistent, general orientations toward people, groups, or institutions.

Public opinion can be defined most generically as the sum of many individual opinions. More specific notions of public opinion place greater weight on individual, majority, group, or elite opinion when considering policy decisions.

## Equality of Individual Opinions

Public opinion can be viewed as the collection of individual opinions, where all opinions deserve equal treatment regardless of whether the individuals expressing them are knowledgeable about an issue or not. Thus, public opinion is the aggregation of preferences of people from all segments of society. The use of public opinion polls to gauge what people are thinking underlies this view.[5] By asking questions of a sample of people who are representative of the U.S. population, pollsters contend they can assess the American public's mood.[6] People who favor this perspective on public opinion believe that government officials should take into account both majority and minority views when making policy.

## Majority Opinion

Another perspective maintains that public opinion is the opinion held by the most people on an issue. In a democracy, the opinions of the majority are the ones that should count the most and should guide government leaders' decision making. The opinions of the minority are less important than those of the majority. This view of public opinion is consistent with the idea of popular election in that every citizen is entitled to an opinion—in essence, a vote—on a particular issue, policy, or leader. In the end, the position that is taken by the most people—in other words, the position that receives the most votes—is the one that should be adopted by policymakers.

Rarely, if ever, does the public hold a single unified opinion. There is often significant disagreement in the public's preferences, and clear majority opinions do not emerge. Immigration is an issue that consistently has divided the American public. In 2021, the public was somewhat less concerned about undocumented immigration than it had been in the recent past, with about half indicating that increased security at the border should be a priority of the Biden administration. Instead, 65% of the public was mostly concerned about the government reuniting children and their parents who were separated at the border.[7] Gun policy is one of the most divisive issues in American politics. Also in 2021, just over half of the population supported stricter gun laws. However, there were major partisan differences of opinion, as 81% of Democrats supported stricter laws and only 20% of Republicans took this position. Where people lived also was reflected in their opinions about gun legislation. Sixty-six percent of people living in urban areas and 54% living in suburban areas favored stricter gun laws, compared to 38% of those living in rural areas.[8] This situation, where there are large disagreements about issues, poses a challenge for leaders looking to translate these preferences into policies.

## Public Debate among Groups

Some scholars contend that public opinion emerges from public debate among groups rather than from individual opinions.[9] Political parties, interest groups, trade associations, nonprofit organizations, trade unions, and corporations will articulate positions and front public discussion of issues in which they have a stake. Groups representing opposing viewpoints often find themselves in a position to define social problems. While individuals frequently find it difficult to make their views known and have them taken seriously, organized groups have the resources, such as lobbyists and funding to administer polls and pay for advertising, as well as the ability to attract the attention of policymakers and the mass media. Social media have made it easier for groups without significant resources to publicize their opinions by using Facebook groups, Twitter, Pinterest, and other platforms.

**FIGURE 7.2 Group Opinions on Social Media**
Social media facilitate people's ability to express their opinions through groups, such as those related to environmental activism.

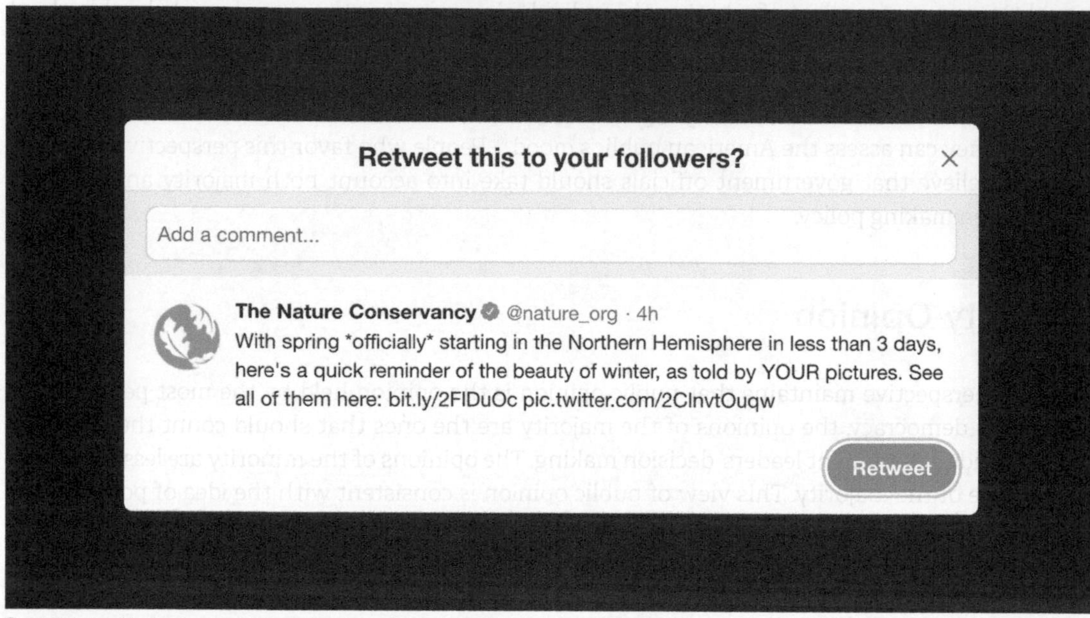


Source: https://twitter.com/nature_org?ref_src=twsrc^google|twcamp^serp|twgr^author.

Groups work hard to frame issue debates to their advantage. They often will gauge public preferences and use this information when devising media tactics to gain support for their positions.[10] Opposing groups will present competing public opinion poll data in an effort to influence decision makers and the press. Opinions can shift notably over time. In 1997, the United States' participation in a summit in Kyoto, Japan, where nations signed a climate-control treaty, sparked a barrage of media stories on the issue of global warming and the potential for deadly gases to induce climate change. Most Americans believed then that global warming existed and that steps should be taken to combat the problem.[11] Groups such as the Environmental Defense Fund, Greenpeace, and the Sierra Club, which favor government-imposed regulations on fossil fuel companies and automobile manufacturers to curb pollution, cited opinion poll data showing that over 70 percent of the public agreed with these actions. Organizations representing industry interests, such as the Legislative Exchange Council, used opinion polls indicating that the public was reluctant to sacrifice jobs or to curb their personal energy use to stop global warming.[12] Scientists with competing views weighed in on the issue. The debate in the media among competing groups and scientists' claims influenced public opinion over the following decade. There have been significant shifts in opinion about climate change over the past twenty years. Half of the public believed that global warming was a problem in 2010.[13] By 2012, 67 percent of the public believed there was solid evidence that global warming was getting worse over time.[14] In 2021, 64 percent felt global warming was a serious threat and 80 percent believed that climate change was a very serious problem for the United States and the world.[15]

## Elite Opinion

Politicians, pollsters, policy specialists, activists, and journalists have assumed the position of **opinion leaders** who shape, create, and interpret public opinion. These political elites are devoted to following public affairs—it's their job.[16] Noted journalist and social commentator Walter Lippmann observed that average people have neither the time nor the inclination to handle the impossible task of keeping up with the myriad issues that confront the nation. They do not have the opportunity to directly experience most political events and must rely on secondhand accounts conveyed by elites, primarily through mass media. In Lippmann's view, public opinion is best managed by specialists who have the knowledge and capabilities to promote policies.[17] Thus, elite opinion, and not the views of average citizens, should count the most.

**FIGURE 7.3 Pundits Offer Opinions**
"Talking heads," who provide elite opinions about issues, events, and leaders, populate cable news.

Source: U.S. Navy photo by Mass Communication Specialist 1st Class Chad J. McNeeley via Wikimedia: http://commons.wikimedia.org/wiki/ File:Admiral_Mike_Mullen_interview_on_Fox_News_ Sunday.jpg.

The mass media rely heavily on the opinions of government elites, especially when covering foreign policy and domestic issues such as the economy and employment. The breadth of news coverage about foreign affairs is constrained to reflect the range of viewpoints expressed by officials such as members of Congress who are debating the issues. The voices of average Americans are much less prominent in news coverage.[18] As political scientist V. O. Key stated, "The voice of the people is but an echo."[19]

**opinion leaders**

People who are interested in and attentive to public affairs and express their opinions to others, who follow their lead.

Elite opinion is frequently articulated by **pundits** who offer their opinion or commentary on political issues. College professors, business and labor leaders, lobbyists, public relations representatives, and pollsters are typical pundits who provide expert opinion. Some pundits represent distinctly partisan or ideological viewpoints and use public opinion data selectively to support these positions. Pundits can establish their credentials as experts on governmental affairs and politics through their frequent media appearances as "talking heads" on cable television programs such as CNN, MSNBC, and Fox News.

**pundits**

People who offer their opinion or commentary on political issues through the media.

## Key Takeaways

Public opinion can be defined broadly as the collective views of people in a society. It is a complicated concept that takes into account the opinions of individual citizens, groups, and elites. Public opinion is publicized through the media, often by pundits who promulgate elite views.

## Exercises

1. Have you ever participated in an opinion poll? Did you feel that you were able to adequately convey your feelings about the issues you were asked about?
2. What are the different ideas about what public opinion really is? What might the advantages of looking at public opinion in each of those different ways be?

# 7.3 Democracy and Public Opinion

## Learning Objectives

After reading this section, you should be able to answer the following questions:

1. Why is public opinion important in a democracy?
2. How does public opinion differ from public judgment?
3. What is deliberative polling?

Political scientist Harold Lasswell once noted, "The open interplay of opinion and policy is the distinguishing mark of popular rule."[20] Public opinion plays a number of important roles in a representative democracy. Leaders can take public opinion into account when making laws and formulating policy. Public opinion can act as a check on leadership, as the members of the public can express their dissatisfaction with politicians who refuse to take their opinions into account, and vote them out of office.

## Public Opinion and Public Policy

One purpose of public opinion in a democracy is to inform public policymaking. Opinion polls provide a mechanism for succinctly presenting the views of the mass public to government leaders who are making decisions that will affect society. Leaders often monitor the public pulse when making policy decisions, such as whether to raise taxes or to support college tuition benefits, especially when they face an election campaign.

Perspectives about the relationship of public opinion to policymaking differ vastly. On the one hand, scholars and political practitioners believe that public policy should be guided by public opinion so that the will of the people is respected. Public opinion polls are essential to ensuring democratic governance. Political scientist Sidney Verba supported this view: "Surveys produce just what democracy is supposed to produce—equal representation of all citizens. The sample survey is rigorously egalitarian; it is designed so that each citizen has an equal chance to participate and an equal voice when participating."[21] From this perspective, members of Congress, state legislators, and local officials should pay close attention to the public's views when making laws.

Others disagree with the notion that leaders should pay close attention to public opinion when making decisions. They point out that many members of the public are uninformed about issues, and the opinions they record on polls are not carefully reasoned. Journalist and scholar Walter Lippmann noted that governing by popularity is not always best. Instead, public policy should be grounded in sound principles supported by experts; decision making should not simply be the result of popular will. This view is consistent with the belief that the country is being run by pollsters and their followers and not by leaders with integrity and principle. As an editorial in the *Wall Street Journal* lamented, "Spend too much time following polls and you simply forget how to lead, especially when it matters."[22]

Some scholars take issue with Verba's assessment of the egalitarian nature of polls in democracy and argue that minority opinion is not given sufficient weight. Certain people, such as individuals with few economic resources or those without access to technology and polling apps, have a difficult time getting their views recognized. Pollsters may not reach these people because they do not have regular telephone or internet service, or they do not have the time or inclination to answer questionnaires.

# Public Judgment

Public opinion, especially as measured by polls, is a quick take on the public pulse. It often does not require that members of the public have much knowledge about politicians, government, or policies; they merely must be willing to state whatever views pop into their heads. Public opinion polls often deal with issues and abstract ideas that people have not thought much about. Many people are reluctant to say that they don't know about an issue when asked by a pollster, and so they record a response that they have not really thought much about.

**Public judgment**, in contrast, is a special type of public opinion where people carefully consider the important issues of the day, contemplate the range of viewpoints, and weigh the consequences of policy prescriptions. Rather than stating positions off the top of their heads, public judgment requires people to be knowledgeable about an issue and debate the merits of policies before arriving at an informed opinion. For example, public opinion polls conducted by the Pew Research Center indicate that the public favors tougher immigration laws and better enforcement of border security. However, when people exercise public judgment and consider the consequences of immigration policy, such as the moral issues related to the welfare of children of undocumented immigrants, they support more generous policies.[23] Public judgment is not easily achieved, but it offers an important counterbalance to the domination of elite opinion in the policy sphere.

**public judgment**

A type of public opinion where people carefully consider the range of viewpoints and policy consequences of issues.

# Deliberative Polling

**Deliberative polling** is a technique that provides members of the public with the opportunity to think carefully about issues and their relationship to public policy. It attempts to deal with the fact that many people know little about issues because they lack the time to acquire information. Deliberative polling was pioneered in 1988 and has been used around the world to gauge opinion. The Center for Deliberative Democracy at Stanford University applies and studies the use of deliberative polling. It finds that people have thoughtful discussions and reach reasoned conclusions about policies if they are given the time, opportunity, and information to engage in deliberations. Political scientist James Fishkin, who pioneered deliberative polling, observes, "The Public is very smart if you give it a chance. If people think their voice actually matters, they'll do the hard work, really study their briefing books, ask the experts smart questions and then make tough decisions."[24]

**deliberative polling**

A technique that brings people together to discuss issues with experts and other citizens in order to arrive at more informed opinions.

### Link

**Deliberative Polling**

Click here to learn more about deliberative polling.

A random, representative sample of people is first polled about their positions on targeted issues. They are then brought together for a few days to discuss a particular issue in detail. The participants are provided with briefing materials, engage in a dialogue with experts on specific topics, and discuss their views in small groups led by trained moderators. The deliberations are shared with the general public through television broadcasts. The participants are polled again after they have deliberated, to determine if their opinions have changed. Scholars believe that deliberative polls represent the opinions the public would hold on issues if they had the opportunity to exercise public judgment and carefully consider their options. After deliberating on an issue, members of the public frequently shift positions.[25] For example, people participating in a deliberative polling experiment in Texas shifted their views on the use of wind power from 54 percent to 84 percent in favor. As a result, political leaders heeded the views of Texas's population, and the state went from last to first in the use of wind power.[26]

**FIGURE 7.4 Deliberative Polling**

Deliberative polling brings people together to discuss issues in detail with policy experts so that they can develop informed opinions.

Source: AFL-CIO America's Unions via Flickr: https://www.flickr.com/photos/labor2008/2587616688/. Reproduced via CC BY 2.0: https://creativecommons.org/licenses/by/2.0/.

## Key Takeaways

Public opinion is important in a democracy, as it can guide policy decisions. There is disagreement about the extent to which political leaders should take the public's views into account compared with the advice of experts. Many people do not have a good understanding about issues and related policies. Deliberative polling is an attempt to give people the opportunity to become more informed about issues and to contemplate policy options.

## Exercises

1. How much do you think politicians should take public opinion polls into account when making policy? When do you think they should disregard public opinion?
2. What does deliberative polling attempt to measure? What are the advantages of deliberative polling?

# 7.4 Polling the Public

## Learning Objectives

After reading this section, you should be able to answer the following questions:

1. How have public opinion polls developed historically?
2. What are the different types of public opinion polls?

Public opinion polling has a long history in the United States. Polls are ubiquitous in American political life. In 2007, there were nearly 5,500 polling organizations in the United States, an increase of over 1,500 organizations in ten years.[27] Today, it is impossible to estimate the number of organizations that conduct polls, as it has become very easy for just about anyone to conduct a poll online. Polling has proliferated in the digital age as tools for assessing public opinion have become ubiquitous. Every day the public is polled about topics ranging from their views about taxes and the federal budget, to their opinions about the environment and global warming, to whether or not a principal has the right to dictate how students dress and style their hair.

Polls vary greatly in terms of their quality, content, and purpose. Reliable public opinion data are gathered by reputable commercial polling organizations, nonpartisan think tanks, academic institutions, government agencies, and news organizations. Misleading information about public opinion can result from quick polls taken online that do not employ appropriate data-gathering techniques.

## History of Opinion Polling

Public opinion polls date back to the early days of the American republic. From the outset, polls were linked closely with newspapers. The *Harrisburg Pennsylvanian* conducted the first informal "**straw poll**" in 1824 that incorrectly predicted Andrew Jackson as the winner over John Quincy Adams in the presidential election.[28] Early straw polls were administered haphazardly and without concern for drawing a proper sample, often right after people had cast their ballots in elections or even when they were checking into a hotel. They were notoriously inaccurate, yet they became a popular feature of newspapers and magazines, which treated poll data as a source of news much like today.

**straw poll**

An informal poll, often used to gauge opinions about candidates, that is administered haphazardly and without attention to proper sampling methods.

Straw polls were sponsored by publishers as a gimmick to attract readers, who would fill out mail-in ballots that included subscription offers. Over eighty straw polls were conducted during the 1924 presidential election, six of which were national polls. Newspapers also conducted polls on pressing issues of the day, such as whether or not people favored Prohibition, the constitutional ban on alcohol. Coverage of these polls in print publications generated thousands of column inches.[29]

By the 1920s, market researchers had begun to use scientific polls that employed samples representative of the population to ascertain consumer product preferences. They used polls to discover everything from what kinds of magazine stories readers enjoyed most to what automobiles people preferred.[30] Commercial pollsters applied market research techniques to determine what candidates voters favored, how satisfied the public was with the way the president was doing his job, and how people felt about the pressing issues of the day.

Despite these advances, magazines and newspapers continued to use unscientific straw polls, which were less expensive to administer and contributed to the profitability of the publication.

The problems associated with straw polls came to a head in the 1936 presidential election when the *Literary Digest*, a popular magazine with a large circulation, incorrectly predicted the presidential election outcome, prompting the public to lose faith in polls. For a time after the *Literary Digest* debacle, newspapers shied away from highlighting polls in their coverage.

## Enduring Image

### The *Literary Digest* Poll

In polling, more subjects does not necessarily yield better results. This lesson was learned all too well by the *Literary Digest* in 1936. Founded in 1890, the *Literary Digest* was a venerable general interest magazine that catered to an educated, well-off clientele. In 1916, the magazine initiated a presidential election poll that became a popular feature. Subscribers mailed in sample ballots indicating their preference in the election. The poll correctly predicted that Woodrow Wilson would be the winner, and the magazine's poll went on to successfully call the next four elections. Newspapers gave substantial coverage to the poll, which drove up the magazine's readership. In 1932, James A. Farley, chairman of the Democratic National Committee, was widely quoted as saying, "Any sane person cannot escape the implication of such a gigantic sampling of popular opinion as is embraced in the *Literary Digest* straw vote. . . . It is a Poll fairly and correctly conducted."

The 1936 *Literary Digest* election issue straw poll that incorrectly predicted that Alf Landon would defeat Franklin Roosevelt by almost 20 percentage points in the presidential election marked the end of the era of straw polls and the beginning of the use of scientific polls in reporting.

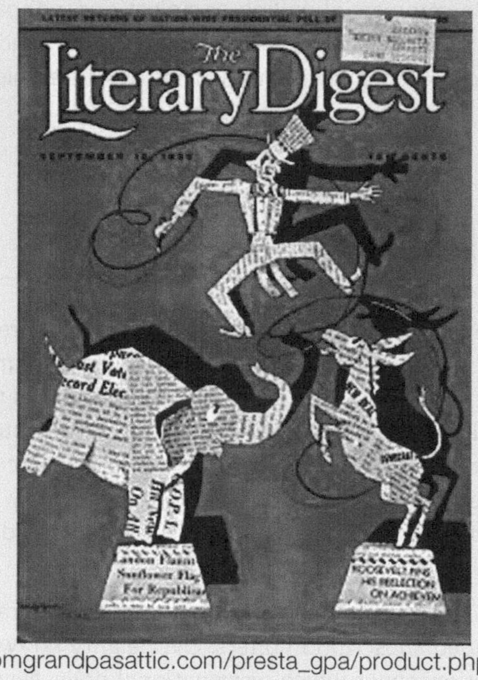


Source: http://www.fromgrandpasattic.com/presta_gpa/product.php?id_product=130.

The magazine set out to launch its most ambitious poll ever in 1936. Over 10 million postcards were mailed to *Literary Digest* subscribers, people on automobile registration lists, and names in telephone directories, of which 2.4 million were returned. The *Literary Digest* issued its predictions in an article boasting that the figures represented the opinions of "more than one in every five voters polled in our country" scattered throughout the forty-eight states. The results indicated that Republican candidate Alfred Landon would defeat Franklin Roosevelt, receive 57 percent of the popular vote, and carry thirty-two states in the Electoral College. Roosevelt won by a landslide, commanding 61 percent of the popular vote and winning in all but two states.

While the magazine made no claims of infallibility, its methodology was heavily flawed. The sample was biased toward Republican-leaning voters, who could afford telephone service, cars, and magazine subscriptions. The volunteers who tabulated the results were not carefully trained, which introduced additional error into the calculations. The backlash from the errant results was monumental. The *Literary Digest* went bankrupt, and the public's faith in polls was shattered.

Commercial pollsters using scientific techniques correctly predicted that Roosevelt would defeat Landon in the 1936 election. These pollsters conduct polls for clients for a profit. The Gallup Poll administered personal interviews with a **quota sample** of people who fit into particular demographic categories, such as sex and age groups. Gallup correctly predicted the winners of the 1940 and 1944 presidential contests. However, during the 1948 election, three major pollsters—Gallup, Roper, and Crossley all incorrectly predicted that Republican presidential candidate Thomas Dewey would defeat Democratic candidate Harry Truman. The quota sampling method used by these pollsters was problematic and was replaced by **probability sampling**, in which subjects are randomly selected to take part in a poll.[31]

**quota sample**

A method of selecting survey participants that involves choosing subjects on the basis of their fitting into particular demographic categories, such as sex and age groups.

**probability sampling**

A method of selecting survey participants at random.

## Enduring Image

### Dewey Defeats Truman

The 1948 presidential election did not start off well for Democratic candidate Harry S. Truman. As vice president, Truman was sworn in as president when Franklin Roosevelt died less than three months into his fourth term. Truman was forced to deal with a variety of controversial issues, including the decision to drop atomic bombs on Hiroshima and Nagasaki, which he believed would end World War II in the Pacific. Newspapers labeled Truman a "little man," a tag that resonated with the public who contrasted him unfavorably to the larger-than-life Roosevelt.

The Democrats were highly factionalized when they met in Philadelphia for their national nominating convention. They attempted unsuccessfully to recruit popular war hero Dwight D. Eisenhower to be their candidate. When the convention adopted a strong civil rights platform, Southern delegations bolted and nominated their own candidate, Strom Thurmond of South Carolina. Liberals who disapproved of Truman's policies formed the Progressive Party and nominated Henry Wallace of Iowa as their candidate. In the end, Truman became the nominee with Senator Alben Barkeley of Kentucky as his running mate. The pair was faced with an unenthusiastic constituency.

In contrast, the Republican Party united behind Thomas E. Dewey, the popular governor of New York. Dewey had been the Republicans' candidate in the 1944 presidential campaign, and had come close to Roosevelt in the popular vote. California Governor Earl Warren, future chief justice of the Supreme Court, was the vice presidential candidate.

Pollsters and the press anticipated that Dewey would win by a landslide. On September 9, 1948, nearly two months prior to the election, noted pollster Elmo Roper declared that there would be no more Roper Polls predicting the outcome: "My whole inclination is to predict the election of Thomas E. Dewey by a heavy margin and devote my time and efforts to other things."[32]

Normally, incumbents such as President Truman run low-key campaigns, and challengers such as Governor Dewey work hard to win. Dewey campaigned like a front-runner, remaining aloof and dignified while avoiding discussions of controversial issues. Roles were reversed in the 1948 presidential campaign. Truman, realizing he had nothing to lose, launched an aggressive "Whistle Stop" campaign. Traveling in a special Pullman railroad car nicknamed the Ferdinand Magellan, after the explorer who circumnavigated the world, Truman covered 32,000 miles and gave 355 rousing speeches. At each stop, Truman would introduce his family to the crowd, answer questions, and shake hands. As he fought his way through the campaign, he acquired the slogan "Give 'em hell, Harry!"

Even as Truman's campaign picked up steam and polls showed the gap between the candidates was closing, the press refused to concede that he could win. *Newsweek* polled fifty political journalists a month before the campaign, and all of them stated that Dewey would win. Truman had the support of only 15 percent of the nation's newspapers.[33] By Election Day, polls indicated that Truman might pull an upset, but journalists stuck to their story that Dewey would win by a landslide. Reports filtered in throughout Election Night that Truman was leading in the popular vote, but the press continued to report that he could not emerge victorious. The *Chicago Tribune* was so certain that Truman would lose, the headline of the early edition proclaimed "DEWEY DEFEATS TRUMAN." The paper had already been delivered, and the *Tribune* dispatched employees to retrieve the papers from newsstands and homes, but many remained in the hands of readers. Traveling by train from his home state of Missouri to Washington, DC, Truman made a brief stop in St. Louis, where he was presented with one of the papers bearing the infamous headline. Truman held up the paper and quipped, "This is for the books."[34]

Truman's victory, as immortalized in this enduring image of him holding up a paper with the headline "DEWEY DEFEATS TRUMAN," is one of the biggest comebacks in American election history.

Source: Everett Collection Historical / Alamy Stock Photo

Survey research organizations associated with academic institutions emerged in the 1940s with the establishment of the National Opinion Research Center (NORC) at the University of Chicago and the Survey Research Center (SRC) at the University of Michigan. These organizations and others like them, such as the Roper Center at the University of Connecticut, field and archive detailed surveys that provide researchers with a wealth of data to use in studies to gain a deeper understanding of the public's political attitudes and behavior. Nonpartisan survey research organizations, such as the Pew Research Center, provide data to news organizations and academics. Commercial pollsters, including Gallup, provide polling services to clients and also share their data with the press, scholars, and the public through their websites.[35]

# Types of Polls

The amount of polling data available today from commercial polling firms, academic survey research organizations, campaign organizations, trade associations, interest groups, media outlets, and online sources is almost overwhelming. There are great variations in the type and quality of polling data. A public opinion survey fielded by a reputable organization using proper social scientific techniques differs greatly from a **quick poll** consisting of one or two questions administered online to whoever is willing to take it.

**quick poll**

An online poll, usually consisting of one or two questions, that is asked of a nonrepresentative, self-selected sample of respondents.

Questionnaires used to measure public opinion include a variety of question types. **Closed-ended questions** provide respondents with a fixed number of options about a topic from which they can choose the one that best fits their position. A closed-ended question frequently asked to gauge people's feelings about the direction in which the country is headed is, "Generally speaking, would you say things in this country are heading in the right direction, or are they off on the wrong track?" Respondents must select one of the options: the right direction or the wrong track. Closed-ended questions are easier and less time-consuming to analyze, although they limit the respondent's ability to express their opinions to the choices offered by the researcher. **Open-ended questions** do not provide fixed options but instead allow respondents to reply to a question in their own words. This type of question elicits more information from respondents and can be useful in gaining insight into sensitive topics. The drawbacks of open-ended questions are that people may not want to take the time to answer them and they are more time-consuming for pollsters to analyze. An open-ended question about the direction in which the country is headed would ask people to express their own views in response to the question "How do you think things are going in this country?"

**closed-ended questions**

Items on a questionnaire that provide respondents with a fixed number of options about a topic from which they can choose the one that best fits their position.

**open-ended questions**

Items on a questionnaire that allow respondents to reply to a question in their own words.

Most polls provide snapshots of people's opinions at a particular point in time. Other polls track opinions over time in order to determine if people's views remain stable or change. In rare cases, studies have tracked the opinions of the same groups of people over years, even decades. A **panel study** tracks the same group of respondents at different points in time. The views of the women who attended Bennington College in the 1930s were tracked through the 1980s. The study revealed that the college experience changed some of the women's attitudes and that the views acquired in college remained stable over time.[36]

**panel study**

Panel study that tracks the same people over time.

## Polls and Surveys

The terms "poll" and "survey" often are used interchangeably, yet there are distinctions between them. A **public opinion poll** is typically conducted by a commercial organization working for a profit. A poll generally consists of a short questionnaire administered over a brief period of time to a sample of between six hundred and fifteen hundred people. A **survey** most often is conducted by academic or government researchers. Surveys consist of longer questionnaires designed to examine the foundations and consequences of opinions in some detail. Researchers may administer the survey to thousands of subjects interviewed over an extended period of time.[37]

**public opinion poll**

A short questionnaire administered to a sample of people to ascertain the views of a larger population, usually conducted by a commercial organization.

**survey**

A questionnaire typically administered by academic or government researchers to a representative sample of people drawn from a larger population.

Scientific polls and surveys are considered to be the gold standard for measuring public opinion. They adhere to established procedures that help ensure the accuracy of their results, which include using proper techniques for drawing a sample and designing questions. Scientific polls and surveys are administered to a sample of people who are representative of a larger population. The sample is drawn using probability sampling, meaning that each person in the population has a chance of being included in the sample. It is possible to get an accurate accounting of public opinion with a relatively small sample. A representative sample of twelve hundred people can accurately reflect the public opinion of the entire population of the United States. On the other hand, large samples that are not representative may not reflect public opinion accurately at all. Question wording is another important consideration when measuring public opinion. Questions need to be clearly stated, and they should not lead the respondent to choose one answer over another. A poorly worded question can be misunderstood by the respondent and ultimately can misrepresent the public's viewpoints. Answer options that do not provide the public with clear alternatives also are problematic.

**FIGURE 7.5 Survey Question Wording**

This Fox News poll taken after the 2011 State of the Union address does not provide clear options for respondents. The answers are double-barreled because people can agree with one part of the answer but not the other. For option A, you may believe that President Obama gave a wonderful speech but not reconsider at least one item on his agenda. Similarly, for option B, you may agree that President Obama gave a good speech, but you may have changed your mind about his agenda.

**If you could give Obama a grade on the State of the Union Address:**

A. He gave a wonderful speech, and I've reconsidered at least one item on his agenda.
B. A good speech, but I feel relatively the same about his agenda.
C. I was indifferent to the address, and my views remained unchanged.
D. The president could have given a much better speech, and he did not deliver in addressing the issues I care about.
E. The president failed the test.

Source: Adapted from "Fox News Poll: Give Obama a Grade on the State of the Union," Fox News, January 26, 2011, accessed April 5, 2011, http://foxnewsinsider.com/2011/01/26/poll-give-obama-a-grade-on-the-state-of-the-union/.

There are many ways in which polls and surveys can be administered, including through face-to-face interviews, telephone interviews, mail questionnaires, and online questionnaires. Each of these methods has pros and cons. Face-to-face interviews are advantageous for administering long, complicated surveys, yet they are costly, and subjects may be reluctant to talk to a stranger about their opinions. Telephone interviews are relatively easy to administer, but getting a representative sample has become more difficult as many polling organizations rely on landline telephone directories to recruit respondents, and people increasingly are dependent on cell phones. Young people are not well represented in landline polls.[38] Mail questionnaires are a low-cost method that allows subjects privacy when answering questions, which can yield more accurate results. However, mail surveys often suffer from low response rates, as people simply opt out because the questionnaire is self-administered.[39]

Online polls and polls administered through digital apps have become more popular options in recent years as the majority of the public has access to the internet, and cell phone and tablet use is prevalent. According to the Pew Research Center, more than 90 percent of American adults were online in May 2021, and 30 percent of adults say they are almost constantly online.[40] Studies indicate that online polls are no less reliable than other forms of polling. They have the advantage of being cost-effective, and allowing respondents privacy when answering questions. Online polls also provide opportunities for innovation, such as getting reactions to video clips of campaign ads. The limitation of online polls is that it is more difficult to get a representative sample using the internet than with some traditional methods, because not all of the public is online. Also, online surveys are self-administered, and people can drop out before they are completed, especially if the questionnaire is lengthy.[41]

## Exit Polls

**Exit polls** are face-to-face interviews with voters taken as they leave the voting booth to determine their candidate preference in the election and their positions on issues. These polls are fielded in a small number of voting precincts per state with the goal of acquiring representative data. They are used to predict the outcomes of elections and to determine the characteristics of voters who supported particular candidates. Exit poll data can reveal, for example, who female, Latinx, Republican voters favored in an election campaign.

**exit polls**

Face-to-face interviews with voters taken as they leave the voting booth to determine their candidate preference in the election and their positions on issues.

Exit polls are a major component of the media's Election Night coverage. Until 1992, each news network had its own in-house exit polling operation. To cut costs, an exit poll consortium, Voter News Service (VNS), was formed to provide data to all the major networks. VNS released the exit poll data that prompted the networks to prematurely declare the results of the 2000 presidential election, and the organization subsequently was disbanded. Exit poll data in the 2008, 2012, 2016, and 2020 presidential elections, and 2010, 2014, and 2018 midterm elections were provided to major television news organizations and the Associated Press by the National Election Exit Poll conducted by Edison Research.

Conducting exit polls during the 2020 presidential election was challenging due to the COVID-19 pandemic. Typically, exit polls consist of in-person interviews with a randomly selected sample of voters as they leave their polling places. Over 90 million American voters cast their votes prior to the 2020 election. Pollsters collected in-person interview data at early voting locations in eight key states using pandemic safety protocols. They also conducted telephone interviews with people who had mailed in their ballots.[42] The combination of polling techniques contributed to exit poll findings that were not very accurate, especially when the findings for racial and ethnic group voting were analyzed.[43]

### Link

**Exit Polling**

Read more about exit polling from the American Association for Public Opinion Research here.

News organizations use exit polls to declare a winner, sometimes when few of the actual returns from the voting precincts have been recorded. This practice has raised concerns, especially since the major television networks all rely on exit poll data from the same source—the National Election Exit Poll. While exit polls are often accurate, if the sample of voters is unrepresentative of the population, the survey questions are poorly written, or interviewers are not trained to properly administer the poll, the results can be wrong, as was the case in the 2000 presidential election.

Some scholars allege that media reports of exit polls can depress election turnout. When the media declare the winner in a presidential election on the basis of exit polls before the voting booths have closed across the country, people who have not yet voted may decide not to turn out. Network television newscasts declared Ronald Reagan the winner of the 1980 presidential election on the basis of exit polls hours before the voting booths had closed on the West Coast. A controversy ensued around the allegation that West Coast voters were discouraged from casting a ballot because they felt their vote was irrelevant. The networks agreed voluntarily to refrain from declaring a winner in elections until after all the polls have closed nationwide—an agreement that has not always been followed.

## Quick Polls

**robo-polling**

Administering automated polls by phone that use a recorded voice to ask the question and that require respondents to answer by pressing the touch pad on their telephone.

A quick poll usually consists of one or two questions that are posted to a website, blog, discussion board, social media platform, or podcast. Quick polls have become standard features of websites of news organizations, political leaders, issue advocacy groups, political parties, candidates, bloggers, and even average citizens. They can be distributed through website sidebars, email links, Facebook postings, and Twitter feeds. There are many platforms available that make it easy for just about anyone to field a quick poll. Quick polls also can be administered through **robo-polling**—administering automated polls by phone that use a recorded voice to ask the question and that require respondents to answer by pressing the touch pad on their telephone.[44]

Quick polls do not conform to the established protocols for conducting scientific polls, and they generally are not reliable indicators of public opinion. They often use an unscientific **convenience sample** of people who may see the poll posted online or have the link sent to them through email. Most respondents to quick polls are self-selected, and they may have a strong interest in the topic. Often it is possible for people to register their views more than once, which can bias the outcome of the poll. Quick polls may generate many responses, but the results can be wildly inaccurate. In addition, quick poll questions can be designed in a way that elicits a particular response that is then used to promote a particular position. For example, a quick poll might seek to find support for bike lanes in cities by stating, "Seven out of ten Americans favor designating bike lanes in major cities. Do you favor or oppose designating bike lanes in your city?"

Quick polls can be a fun way to generate interest in political affairs. People can express their views easily, and they often get immediate feedback about where they stand compared to others. The results of quick polls often are revealed in visually appealing infographics. Reporters and bloggers use the results of quick polls to generate story lines and supplement the text of their pieces. However, quick polls can be misused when the results are interpreted as if they truly reflect public opinion rather than just the views of the people who chose to take them.

**FIGURE 7.6 Quick Polls**
Quick polls provide snapshots of political opinion that are used by the media, interest groups, parties, and candidates. Millions of people responded to this quick poll on climate change, but the sample is self-selected, and the results may not be accurate.

Source: iSideWith.com; https://www.isidewith.com/poll/734977926.

**convenience sample**

Respondents to unscientific polls who are self-selected.

**push poll**

Not a legitimate poll but a marketing technique disguised as a poll that is designed to influence respondents' opinions about candidates and issues through leading questions.

## Push Polls

A **push poll** is a marketing technique used by political campaigns and issue advocacy groups to influence the opinions of respondents. Despite their name, push polls are not legitimate public opinion polls. They are a form of advertising masquerading in the form of an opinion survey. No one collects or analyzes the data from a push poll; instead, the questions include information—often false—about a candidate or issue. Push polls can influence vote choice in campaigns by incorporating negative attacks on a candidate into the questions asked or associating a candidate with a particular issue position that may or may not be accurate.

Push polls were used against Republican candidate John McCain during the 2000 presidential primary. Voters in South Carolina were asked questions like, "Would you be more or less likely to vote for John McCain for president if you knew he had fathered an illegitimate Black child?" Push polls were used to target Democratic candidate Barack Obama in the 2008 presidential campaign. Voters in Ohio received phone calls from Opinion Access Corporation asking if they would be more or less likely to vote for Barack Obama if they knew that he had voted to let convicted child sex offenders out early.[45] While these allegations were untrue or taken out of context, the information was spread to voters. Push polls have been outlawed in certain states, and they have been condemned by the American Association of Public Opinion Researchers (AAPOR), the organization that upholds standards for polling and survey research.[46]

## Other Ways of Measuring Public Opinion

There are a variety of ways of measuring public opinion aside from polls. The different sides of an argument expressed in public debates or at a community meeting reflect public opinion. The positions taken in letters to the editor, blog and social media posts, and the comments in response to news stories and editorials are all indicators of public sentiment. The commentary that people post in response to news stories can provide a rich source of information about public opinion, especially when people take the issue seriously and are respectful when expressing their views. This commentary also can be careless and vitriolic, as people resort to personal attacks or post quick reactions to complex issues.

**Focus groups** have been used for over eighty years to ascertain people's attitudes, beliefs, and opinions about politics within a group setting. A facilitator asks questions of a group of between eight and twelve people who can engage in a conversation about the topic. Focus groups not only are useful for gaining in-depth insights into what individuals think, but also aid in understanding the group dynamics behind public opinion. Focus groups can reveal when people feel comfortable expressing their beliefs, when they will confront others about their views, when they will withdraw from a discussion, and when they are influenced by the opinions of others.[47] Focus groups have been used to allow college students to reveal their views about government and their role in a democratic polity. Talking with students in a group setting, researchers discovered that young people are more interested and engaged in politics than survey-based studies indicate, and that they are thinking creatively about ways to become involved, especially using social media.[48] Focus groups are used extensively in election campaigns to determine what issues voters are thinking about and which candidates they prefer.

**FIGURE 7.7**
**Online Comments as Public Opinion**
Online news stories provide comment sections where people can discuss issues and events. These comments are an expression of public opinion.

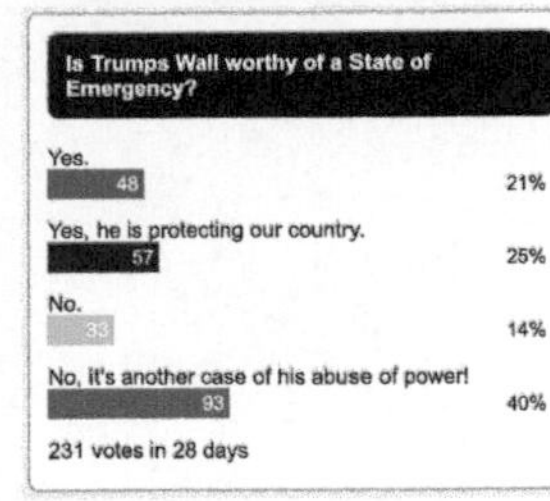


Source: PolitoPoll; https://bit.ly/33Yv6hR.

**focus groups**
Small groups that take part in guided discussions where participants express their opinions.

### Key Takeaways

Public opinion polling dates back to the early days of the republic. The abundance of poll data measuring Americans' opinions about government and politics available today is astounding. In this environment, it is important to differentiate between quality polling data generated through established scientific methods and unreliable information produced by quick polls.

### Exercises

1. Why did newspapers begin running straw polls? What incentive did newspapers have to ensure their polls were representative?
2. How was the 1936 *Literary Digest* presidential poll flawed? Why did most journalists fail to predict Truman's reelection in 1948?
3. What is the purpose of push polling? Why is it generally considered to be dishonest or manipulative?

# 7.5 Public Opinion in the Information Age

## Learning Objectives

After reading this section, you should be able to answer the following questions:

1. How are public opinion polls depicted in the media?
2. What are opinion leaders, and how do they influence the views of opinion followers?
3. What is an echo chamber? What is the effect of echo chambers on democracy?

The media's use of public opinion data has a long history. The press depends on polls as a source of information for its stories, and polling organizations need the media to publicize their results. For almost two centuries, the press has commissioned polls from professional organizations or sponsored their own in-house polling operations. Today, major news organizations join with well-established polling firms to measure public opinion. *USA Today* and CNN work with the Gallup organization to field opinion polls.

**digital polls**

Polls administered through internet platforms and smartphones that run the gamut from sophisticated surveys to quick polls.

In the information age, the press's use of opinion polls has flourished as it is easy and more cost-effective to collect opinion information. **Digital polls** are a quick way to get people to express their views and to exchange opinions with others. These polls can be taken online, on an electronic tablet, or on a cell phone. The potential for polls to not only measure public opinion but also influence opinion has increased.

## Media Depictions

The results of public opinion polls are prominently depicted in all forms of media. News organizations regularly include poll results in their stories about political issues, events, and leaders. Poll results released by the press, candidate organizations, and political parties feature prominently during elections in news stories, commentary, and campaign media. Political websites and blogs offer quick polls where people can record their views on myriad topics instantaneously. These poll results are depicted as colorful sidebars that attract audiences' attention. Poll results frequently run on the ticker on cable television news broadcasts and on media organization websites.

Poll results make headlines. They can be presented in the form of eye-catching visuals to highlight their prominence. One hundred days into Joe Biden's presidency, poll stories about his job approval dominated the press. Fox News led with the headline, "Biden approaches 100 days in office—what do Americans think?" and then discussed Biden's popularity relative to former presidents.[49] The *Washington Post* proclaimed, "Americans give Biden mostly positive marks for first 100 days,"[50] a sentiment that was echoed by CNN, "Majority of Americans approve of Biden and his priorities in first 100 days."[51] The stories generated thousands of comments expressing views, both pro and con, about President Biden's job performance. These comments represent another expression of public opinion.

Pundits and experts who appear in the media make extensive use of poll results when making their case. They appear with charts and graphs depicting poll results to emphasize that the public shares their views. They use opinion polls to speak on behalf of the public, whether or not they are truly representing the views of the people.

Polls also present depictions of the media. A Harvard-Harris poll conducted in May 2017 indicated that two-thirds of the American public felt that the mainstream press contained fake news. The findings also suggested that 84 percent of the public believed that it is hard to know what news to believe online and in social media. The same study found that 60 percent of the public believed that President Trump was treating the media unfairly, while less than half felt that the media was unfair to the president.[52] Despite the unfavorable depiction of the media, the results of the survey were reported widely in the press and can be found here.

# Media Interactions

Elites and the mass public use public opinion polls in a variety of ways. Opinion leaders use poll results to convey information to others who rely on their guidance when making political decisions. Digital media have not only created more opportunities for the public to share their opinions but have also made it possible for average citizens to field their own polls and collect opinion data.

## Opinion Leaders

An **opinion leader** is a broker who imparts information about politics and government to other people. Opinion leaders are attentive to media messages and pass on information in a simplified format to people who pay less attention to politics. The **two-step flow model** of communication posits that the media disseminate information that is received by opinion leaders, who interpret the information and pass it on to opinion followers, who are less interested in and informed about political affairs. Opinion leaders have the respect of opinion followers because of their status in a social group, their role as a political expert, or their celebrity.[53]

**FIGURE 7.8 Celebrity Opinion Leaders**

Celebrities like George Clooney can use their prominence in the media to promote causes and influence public opinion.

Source: Photo courtesy of Nando65, http://commons.wikimedia.org/wiki/File:George_Clooney_and_Fatma_Samoura.JPG.

Opinion leaders may be members of the public who are especially attentive to political matters. They follow the news religiously, pay attention to political leaders' speeches, and even may participate in governmental affairs by attending meetings or holding office. People who are in the same social group will seek cues from opinion leaders who share their interests and who can simplify their voting decisions or provide them with shortcuts for taking positions on complicated issues. Pundits, political experts, and public officials can be opinion leaders when they are held in esteem by citizens. Media personalities, including television news anchors, talk show hosts, and prominent political bloggers, increasingly have taken on the role of opinion leaders, especially when they have ideological views similar to people who follow them.[54] Celebrities from the entertainment industry can become opinion leaders. Media mogul Oprah Winfrey has expressed her views on issues and political leaders to her vast audience. Actor George Clooney has used his celebrity to bring attention to violence in the Sudan.

**opinion leader**

A broker who imparts information about politics and government to other people.

**two-step flow model**

A communication model where the media disseminate information that is processed by opinion leaders, who simplify messages and pass them on to opinion followers.

FIGURE 7.9 Two-Step Flow Model of Communication

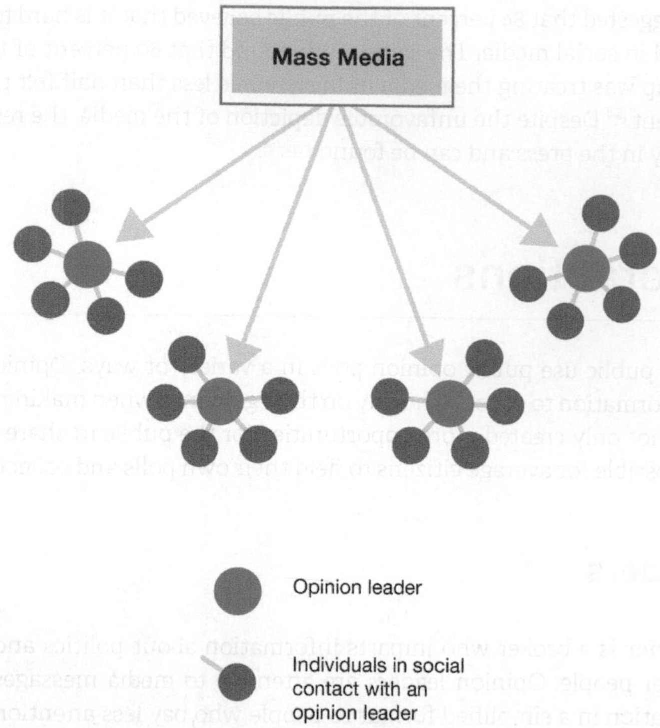


Source: Adapted from E. Katz and P. Lazarsfeld, *Personal Influence*, (New York, NY: The Free Press, 1955).

## Digital Polls and Forums

The opportunities for the public to express their opinions through the media have skyrocketed in the information age. The interactive features of digital media make it easy for people to express their views and share their opinions with others. Quick polls can be incorporated into just about any news or political site, and they can be shared virally through social media and email. Online forums allow people to post their views and react to the opinions of others.

Digital polls, which use internet platforms and smartphones to administer questions to members of the public, have proliferated in the information age. These polls run the gamut from sophisticated survey instruments to one-question quick polls. Online polls are a standard feature of news websites, political party and candidate sites, interest group and trade association sites, blogs, social media sites, and Twitter feeds. The quality of online polls varies greatly as well. Online polls administered by reputable organizations to a representative sample of the public yield reliable results. Quick polls taken by a convenience sample of people who come across the poll and decide to take it are generally inaccurate.

Digital media have made it possible for members of the public to conduct their own informal polls to solicit opinions about government and politics. There are online platforms, such as YouPolls.com and SurveyMonkey.com, where average citizens, political activists, and bloggers can post a question and solicit answers from interested members of the public. People can post a video clip of a news item and gauge the public's reaction. These informal poll results can be used to stimulate online discussions about issues, leaders, government institutions, and political events. Some of these citizen-initiated polls deal with serious debates facing the nation, such as taxes and immigration policy. Some opinion forums are designed more to entertain than to elicit serious opinions.

## Live Polls

**Live polls** record people's reactions to a speech, debate, or event in real time. The results of live polls are displayed below images of the event as it takes place, which allows viewers to see fluctuations in opinion over time. In January 2011, live polling was used to gauge the public's opinion of President Obama's State of the Union address as it was unfolding. The public was invited to participate in a nationwide poll gathering reactions to the address using their smartphones and iPads. Reactions from Democrats, Republicans, and independents were tracked and displayed on the bottom portion of the television screen on cable news channels. While the sample was not representative, hundreds of thousands of people took part.[55]

The satirical news source *The Onion* produced a parody of pundits adjusting their views in an attempt to please the public as they watch a live poll tracking the audience's opinion about their discussion.

**live polls**

Polls that record people's opinions about an event as it is unfolding; the results are depicted simultaneously with video of the event.

Watch this parody of pundits adjusting their views in an attempt to please the public.

View in the online reader

# Media Consequences

A major issue confronting opinion researchers is whether or not polls released in the media actually influence opinion. It may be the case that polls not only reflect opinion but also can change people's views about candidates and issues. It is difficult to isolate poll effects, but there is some evidence to suggest that the media's dissemination of poll results can influence personal opinions.

## The Echo Chamber

Public judgment, informed opinions about issues, requires that people be open to diverse viewpoints and consider the outcomes when supporting policy positions. Some scholars believe that a democracy requires media that provide a place where citizens can gain a broad perspective on political issues and events. However, in the current high-choice media environment that offers literally hundreds of options for getting information, people increasingly are exposed solely to viewpoints consistent with their own beliefs.

The media landscape is populated by cable news programs, talk radio shows, online news sites, and blogs that represent extreme liberal and extreme conservative positions on issues. Many people who tune into these opinionated sources of information shield themselves from other perspectives, thus cutting off the potential to meaningfully debate policy options. Communication scholars Kathleen Hall Jamieson and Joseph Cappella label this phenomenon the **echo chamber**. They observe that some people attend to media that are essentially "self protected enclaves hospitable to their own beliefs."[56] With more than three hundred cable channels alone to choose from, people gravitate toward niche media that often feature like-minded hosts. Fox News's conservative talk show host Sean Hannity and MSNBC's liberal host Rachel Maddow reach their followers on television, radio, and online. Blog readers visit sites that are in line with their views and avoid those that challenge their opinions.

**echo chamber**

The idea that people pay attention to media that conform to their ideological views to the exclusion of media that offer alternative perspectives.

Scholars have identified negative and positive consequences of the echo chamber effect. On one hand, selective exposure to ideological media may have deleterious effects on democratic discourse as people take extreme positions on issues and refuse to make compromises that are often necessary to achieve workable public policies. At the same time, people who come to feel strongly about their political beliefs are more likely to participate in politics.[57]

## Key Takeaways

The relationship between the media and public opinion has grown increasingly complicated. Poll results and opinion forums have proliferated in all forms of media. The vast number of political media sources has made it possible for people to expose themselves only to news and information that conform to their personal ideological and partisan perspectives. The implications for democratic politics are both negative and positive.

## Exercises

1. In what sense is the relationship between the media and polling organizations mutually beneficial?
2. What makes someone an opinion leader? What makes you personally pay attention to a public figure's opinion?
3. Why do some scholars argue that the current media environment has become like an echo chamber? Do you think you regularly consume any media that challenge your political views?

### Civic Education

**Increasing Issue Understanding**

In the information age, a wealth of material about issues, as well as the stands Americans take on these issues, is available from the media, government agencies, and nonprofit organizations. Accessing and sorting through the often complicated and conflicting material on issues can be a daunting task, especially when not all available information is reliable or of high quality. Only a small segment of the population has the motivation or the opportunity to become informed about most issues, especially when the costs in terms of time and effort are high. As a result, there is a knowledge gap among the public about issues. Highly educated people from upper-income brackets have a greater command of issues and thus more influence on policies that effect society than people from lower socioeconomic backgrounds.

Creative civic education initiatives can help alleviate the knowledge gap on issues and assist people in developing informed opinions. Deliberative forums can help young people develop informed views on issues and even take action. Knowledgeable opinion leaders and subject-area experts can meet with people in classes, clubs and organizations, private homes, or online to share information about issues. Due to a proliferation of online tools such as SurveyMonkey, young people can field their own polls to gain a sense of how public opinion is produced and measured.

Forums have been held across the country on the topic of climate change, which is a highly contested issue with much conflicting evidence. Experts provide information followed by discussions that are facilitated by citizen participants. Effective forums have a clear focus, such as the effect of climate change on the local area. Specific examples can be provided in order to make the issue resonate with the participants. Communities of people who are interested in climate change can form offline and continue to interact online through discussion boards and social media.[58]

# 7.6 Recommended Reading

Althaus, Scott L. 2003. *Collective Preferences in Democratic Politics.* New York: Cambridge University Press, 2003. A study examining the ways in which public opinion surveys influence democratic deliberation in ways that favor particular groups in society.

Asher, Herbert B. *Polling and the Public: What Every Citizen Should Know*, 7th ed. Washington, DC: CQ Press, 2007. A valuable guidebook providing insight into how polls are designed and reported.

Bennett, W. Lance, and David L. Paletz, eds. *Taken By Storm: The Media, Public Opinion, and U.S. Foreign Policy in the Gulf War*. Chicago: University of Chicago Press, 1994. A comprehensive study of public opinion, media, and foreign policy focusing on the Gulf War period.

Burstein, Paul. *American Public Opinion: Advocacy and Policy in Congress*, New York: Cambridge University Press, 2014. An example of the influence of public opinion on democracy, which argues that majority opinion is represented in Congress, but for only a few high-profile issues.

Donsbach, Wolfgang, and Michael W. Traugott. *The Sage Handbook of Public Opinion Research*. Thousand Oaks, CA: Sage Publications, 2008. A handbook covering topics in public opinion ranging from the development of public opinion research, methods for ascertaining opinion, and uses of public opinion data.

Erikson, Robert S., and Kent L. Tedin. *American Public Opinion*, 9th ed. New York: Longman, 2019. A text covering key topics in public opinion, including the history of polling, methodological issues, and the role of public opinion in a democracy.

Glynn, Carroll J., Susan Herbst, Garrett J. O'Keefe, and Robert Y. Shapiro. *Public Opinion*. Boulder, CO: Westview Press, 1999. A comprehensive overview of public opinion in scholarship and practice.

Goidel, Kirby, ed. *Political Polling in the Digital Age*. Baton Rouge: Louisiana State University Press, 2011. A collection of essays about the challenges of public opinion polling in the new media era.

Herbst, Susan. *Numbered Voices*. Chicago: University of Chicago Press, 1993. An insightful study of the development of consequences of public opinion polling that questions the extent to which polls truly represent the voices of the mass public.

Lippmann, Walter. *Public Opinion*. New York: Free Press, 1922. A classic work that explores the relationship between the press and public opinion, arguing that the media make events known to the public that they cannot directly experience, thereby influencing opinion.

Maxwell McCombs and Sebastian Valenzuela, *Setting the Agenda*, 3rd ed. Cambridge, UK: Polity Press, 2021. Discusses the ways in which the news media influence the issue agenda and public opinion.

Rosalee A. Clawson and Zoe M. Oxley, *Public Opinion: Democratic Ideals, Democratic Practice*, 4th ed. Washington, DC: CQ Press, 2021. A text that examines the relationship between citizens and their government in a democracy through the lens of public opinion.

Stroud, Natalie Jomini. *Niche News*. New York: Oxford University Press, 2011. A detailed exploration of Americans' growing preference for highly partisan news sources, and its implications.

Warren, Kenneth F. *In Defense of Public Opinion Polling*. Boulder, CO: Westview Press, 2003. An account of Americans' love-hate relationship with polls, which includes a brief history of polling and a discussion of the use of polling in a democracy.

Zaller, John. *The Nature and Origins of Mass Opinion*. New York: Cambridge, 1992. A study examining the ways in which the public acquires information from elites and the mass media and translates it into opinions.

# 7.7 Recommended Viewing

*Ask a Silly Question* (1998). A respected Canadian journalist employs humor to raise important issues about the power of public opinion polls to shape policy.

*Atomic Café* (1982). A lively documentary consisting entirely of government materials that were used to influence public opinion about the atomic bomb during the Cold War.

*Constructing Public Opinion* (2001). A scholarly and engaging examination of the ways in which politicians and the media use polling data to construct public opinion.

*Gentleman's Agreement* (1947). Originally titled *Public Opinion*, this Academy Award winner stars Gregory Peck as a reporter who pretends to be Jewish to uncover opinions about racial and religious prejudice.

*Irresistible* (2020). Steve Carell stars as a Democratic strategist who helps a retired veteran run for mayor in a small town. Directed by Jon Stewart, the satire examines aspects of modern-day campaigning and opinion polling.

*Magic Town* (1947). When the small Midwestern town of Grandview is found to replicate Gallup poll results for the entire nation, a pollster (Jimmy Stewart) uses the town to gauge public opinion, causing its citizens to change their behavior while shouldering this great responsibility.

*North Carolina Voices* (2005). A series of documentaries—"The State of Aging," "Looking for Work," and "Touched by War"—that examines trends in public opinion about issues. The series incorporates historical footage, interviews, and public opinion polls.

*Recount* (2008). A chronicle of the recount of Florida votes as the results of the 2000 presidential election hang in the balance.

*What America Needs: From Sea to Shining Sea* (2003). Documentary filmmaker Mark Wojahn traveled the country by train, asked more than five hundred people from all walks of life the question "What do you think America needs?" and recorded a plethora of opinions.

# Endnotes


1. Robert S. Erikson and Kent L. Tedin, *American Public Opinion*, 8th ed. (New York: Longman, 2011).
2. James W. Ceaser and Andrew E. Busch, The Perfect Tie (Lanham, MD: Rowman & Littlefield, 2001).
3. Dan Rather, CBS Evening News, Election Night Coverage, November 7, 2000, 8:15 p.m.
4. James A. Stimson, *Public Opinion in America*, 2nd ed. (Boulder, CO: Westview, 1999).
5. Carroll J. Glynn, Susan Herbst, Garrett J. O'Keefe, and Robert Y. Shapiro, *Public Opinion* (Boulder, CO: Westview, 1999).
6. Susan Herbst, *Numbered Voices* (Chicago: University of Chicago Press, 1993).
7. AP-NORC Center for Public Affairs Research, "Public Is Concerned about Biden's Handling of Immigration and Border Security," NORC at the University of Chicago, April 5, 2021. https://apnorc.org/projects/public-is-concerned-about-bidens-handling-of-immigration-and-border-security/.
8. Pew Research Center, "Amid a Series of Mass Shootings in the U.S., Gun Policy Remains Deeply Divisive," April 20, 2021. https://www.pewresearch.org/politics/2021/04/20/amid-a-series-of-mass-shootings-in-the-u-s-gun-policy-remains-deeply-divisive/.
9. Carroll J. Glynn, Susan Herbst, Garrett J. O'Keefe, and Robert Y. Shapiro, *Public Opinion* (Boulder, CO: Westview, 1999).
10. Ken Kollman, *Outside Lobbying* (Princeton, NJ: Princeton University Press, 1999).
11. Jon A. Krosnick, Penny S. Visser, and Allyson L. Holbrook, "American Opinion on Global Warming," *Resources* no. 133 (Fall 1998): 5–9.
12. Glynn R. Wilson, "Global Warming: Competing Ideas and Interest Groups," *Public Opinion Project*, May 2, 1998, accessed June 19, 2005, http://www.southerner.net/fast/pocompet.html.
13. Christopher R. Borick, Erick Lachapelle, and Barry G. Rabe, "Climate Compared: Public Opinion on Climate Change in the United States and Canada," *Issues in Governance Studies*, no. 39, April 2011, accessed April 11, 2011, http://www.brookings.edu/~/media/Files/rc/papers/2011/04_climate_change_opinion/04_climate_change_opinion.pdf.
14. Pew Research Center for the People & the Press, "More Say There Is Solid Evidence of Global Warming," (Washington, DC: Pew Research Center, October 15, 2012).
15. Lydia Saad, "Global Warming Attitudes Frozen Since 2016," Gallup News, April 5, 2021. https://news.gallup.com/poll/343025/global-warming-attitudes-frozen-2016.aspx; Jon A. Krosnick, Bo MacInnis, and Jared McDonald, Climate Insights 2020: Synthesis Report. Resources for the Future, Stanford University, February 22, 2021. https://www.rff.org/publications/reports/climateinsights2020-synthesis/.
16. John Zaller, *The Nature and Origins of Mass Opinion* (New York: Cambridge, 1992).
17. Walter Lippmann, *Public Opinion*, New York: Harcourt, Brace & Company, 1922.
18. W. Lance Bennett, Regina C. Lawrence, and Steven Livingston, *When the Press Fails* (Chicago, IL: University of Chicago Press, 2007).
19. V. O. Key Jr., *Public Opinion and American Democracy* (New York: Alfred A. Knopf, 1961).
20. Harold D. Lasswell, *Democracy through Public Opinion* (Menasha, WI: George Banta Publishing Company, 1941), 15.
21. As cited in Scott Keeter, "Public Opinion Polling and Its Problems," in *Political Polling in the Digital Age*, ed. Kirby Goidel (Baton Rouge: Louisiana State University Press, 2011), 28.
22. General Morris. *The Wall Street Journal*, April 7, 1999. Editorial. https://www.wsj.com/articles/SB923445545387550451.
23. Daniel Yankelovich, *Coming to Public Judgment* (Syracuse, NY: Syracuse University Press, 1991).
24. Joe Klein, Joe. "How Can a Democracy Solve Tough Problems?" *Time Magazine*, 9/2/2010. http://content.time.com/time/magazine/article/0,9171,2015790,00.html.
25. James S. Fishkin, *When the People Speak* (New York: Oxford University Press, 2009).
26. Joe Klein, "How Can a Democracy Solve Tough Problems?," *Time*, September 2, 2010, accessed June 6, 2011, http://www.time.com/time/politics/article/0,8599,2015481,00.html.
27. Kirby Goidel, "Public Opinion Polling in a Digital Age: Meaning and Measurement," in *Political Polling in the Digital Age*, ed. Kirby Goidel (Baton Rouge: Louisiana State University, 2011), 11–27.
28. Robert S. Erikson and Kent L. Tedin, *American Public Opinion*, 8th ed. (New York: Longman, 2011).
29. Robert S. Erikson and Ken L. Tedin, *American Public Opinion*, 8th ed. (New York: Longman, 2011).
30. Kathleen Morgan Drowne, *The 1920s* (Westport, CT: Greenwood Press, 2004).
31. Barbara A. Bardes and Robert W. Oldendick, *Public Opinion: Measuring the American Mind* (Belmont, CA: Wadsworth/Thompson Learning, 2006).
32. Elmo Roper as quoted in David McCullough, *Truman* (New York: Simon & Schuster, 1992), 657.
33. American Treasures of the Library of Congress, "Dewey Defeats Truman" (Washington, DC: Library of Congress, American Memory Collection, 2003).
34. David McCullough, *Truman* (New York: Simon & Schuster, 1992).
35. The results of polls from a range of sources are aggregated by RealClearPolitics http://www.realclearpolitics.com/epoll/latestpoll and The Cornell Institute for Social and Economic Research http://www.ciser.cornell.edu/info/polls.shtml.
36. Duane F. Alwin, Ronald L. Cohen, and Theodore M. Newcomb, *Political Attitudes over the Life Span: The Bennington Women after Fifty Years* (Madison: University of Wisconsin Press, 1991).
37. Michael W. Traugott and Paul J. Lavrakas, *The Voter's Guide to Election Polls*, 2nd ed. (New York: Chatham House, 2000).

38. Scott Keeter, "Public Opinion Polling and Its Problems," in *Political Polling in the Digital Age*, ed. Kirby Goidel (Baton Rouge: Louisiana State University Press, 2011), 28–53.
39. Michael W. Traugott and Paul J. Lavrakas, *The Voter's Guide to Election Polls*, 2nd ed. (New York: Chatham House, 2000).
40. Andrew Perrin and Sara Atske, "About three-in-ten U.S. Adults Say They Are 'Almost Constantly' Online," FactTank, Pew Research Center, March 26, 2021. https://www.pewresearch.org/fact-tank/2021/03/26/about-three-in-ten-u-s-adults-say-they-are-almost-constantly-online/.
41. Scott Keeter, "Public Opinion Polling and Its Problems," in *Political Polling in the Digital Age*, ed. Kirby Goidel (Baton Rouge: Louisiana State University Press, 2011), 28–53.
42. Jennifer Agiesta, "How the Exit Polls Will Work in a Pandemic," *CNN Politics*, November 3, 2020. https://www.cnn.com/2020/11/02/politics/exit-polls-2020-pandemic/index.html.
43. Robert Griffin, "Don't Trust the Exit Polls. This Explains Why." The Monkey Cage, The Washington Post, November 10, 2020. https://www.washingtonpost.com/politics/2020/11/10/dont-trust-exit-polls-this-explains-why/.
44. Mark Blumenthal, "The Case for Robo-Pollsters," *National Journal*, September 14, 2009, accessed April 10, 2011, http://www.nationaljournal.com/njonline/the-case-for-robo-pollsters-20090914.
45. Sam Stein, "Nasty Anti-Obama Push Poll Launched in Ohio," *Huffington Post*, September 11, 2008, accessed June 6, 2011, http://www.huffingtonpost.com/2008/09/11/nasty-anti-obama-push-pol_n_125607.html.
46. "What Is a "Push" Poll?" American Association for Public Opinion Research. Accessed May 2021. https://www.aapor.org/Education-Resources/Resources/What-is-a-Push-Poll.aspx.
47. David W. Stewart, Prem N. Shamdasani, and Dennis W. Rook, *Focus Groups: Theory and Practice*, 2nd ed. (Thousand Oaks, CA: Sage Publications, 2007).
48. Nicholas V. Longo and Ross P. Meyer, *College Students and Politics: A Literature Review*, Circle Working Paper 46 (College Park, MD: Center for Information and Research on Civic Learning and Engagement, May, 2006).
49. Jack Durschlag, "Biden Approaches 100 Days in Office—What Do Americans Think?" *Fox News*, April 26, 2021. https://www.foxnews.com/us/fox-news-poll-biden-approaches-100-days-in-office-what-do-americans-think.
50. Dan Balz, Scott, Clement, and Emily Guskin, "Americans Give Biden Mostly Positive Marks for First 100 Days, Post-ABC Poll Finds," *The Washington Post*, April 25, 2021. https://www.washingtonpost.com/politics/2021/04/25/biden-100-days-poll/.
51. Jennifer Agiesta, "CNN Poll: Majority of Americans Approve of Biden and His Priorities in the First 100 Days," *CNN Politics,* April 28, 2021. https://www.cnn.com/2021/04/28/politics/cnn-poll-biden-approval-100-days/index.html.
52. Jonathan Easley, "Poll: Majority Says Mainstream Media Publishes Fake News," *The Hill*, May 24, 2017.
53. Paul F. Lazarsfeld, Bernard R. Berelson, and Hazel Gaudet, *The People's Choice* (New York: Duell, Sloan, and Pierce, 1944).
54. Ronald S. Burt, "The Social Capital of Opinion Leaders," *Annals of the American Academy of Political and Social Science*, November 1999, 1–22.
55. David Baker, "Live-Polling the State of the Union," *Huffington Post*, January 25, 2011, accessed May 20, 2011, http://www.fightsforjobs.com/2011/01/live-polling-the-state-of-the-union.
56. Kathleen Hall Jamieson and Joseph N. Cappella, *Echo Chamber* (New York: Oxford University Press, 2008), 87.
57. Natalie Jomini Stroud, *Niche News* (New York: Oxford University Press, 2011).
58. Matthew C. Nisbet, "Civic Education about Climate Change: Opinion-Leaders, Communication Infrastructure, and Participatory Culture," White Paper (Washington, DC: Climate Change Education Roundtable, National Academies, December 6, 2010).

CHAPTER 8

# Participation, Voting, and Social Movements

## 8.1 Preamble

A prominent news story line following the 2020 presidential election focused on the surge in turnout among young voters. Headlines proclaimed, "Young Voters in the U.S. Turned Out in Record Numbers,"[1] "Youth Voting Turnout Surges in the 2020 U.S. Election,"[2] and "The 2020 Election Shows Gen Z's Voting Power for Years to Come."[3] Fifty-three percent of voters under age thirty cast a ballot in the 2020 presidential election, marking the highest level of young voter turnout in history.[4]

Media coverage of the youth vote in 2020 was a far cry from the typical story line of the "apathetic young voter" that has prevailed for decades. The night of the 2004 presidential election, the Associated Press (AP) released a story under the headline, "2004 Not the Breakout Year for Youth Vote After All." According to the story, "Fewer than one in 10 voters Tuesday were 18 to 24, about the same proportion of the electorate as in 2000. . . ."[5] The AP story implied that young voters had not turned out in the large numbers that many observers had predicted. It cited early exit polls, which are notoriously unreliable, as the basis for its conclusion. The article was reprinted in many newspapers, and it formed the basis of numerous television, radio, and online reports. The article, however, was incorrect. In fact, turnout among eighteen- to twenty-four-year-olds had risen significantly from 36 percent in the 2000 presidential election to 47 percent in 2004.[6] Youth-vote activists and scholars acted quickly to correct the inaccuracies through the media, but it was too late. This single article had a tremendous influence on candidates, campaign consultants, and political party leaders who cited the AP article as evidence that young voters were not a constituency worth targeting in elections.[7]

The assumptions underlying the "apathetic young voter" media frame were challenged time and time again, yet the headlines remained the same. Media images of the general public's political involvement are unflattering, but depictions of young people are worse. Mainstream media portray young people as irresponsible, self-centered, and lacking the motivation to become involved in government and politics. Young people were a visible and active force in the 2008 election, and turnout increased. Still, post-election stories in 2008 perpetuated the myth of the "apathetic youth voter." The frame dominated news accounts in the 2012 presidential contest as well, despite the fact that young voters represented a higher percentage of the electorate than they did in 2008. The same thing happened in 2016, despite the fact that young Republicans turned out in record numbers in the Iowa caucuses and young Democrats participated actively in the nominating campaign.[8]

**FIGURE 8.1** Young Voter Engagement in Politics

Young people participate in different ways. Media often depict young people as being disinterested in voting, but this portrayal does not reflect the fact that many young voters engage actively in elections.

Source: Allison C Bailey/Shutterstock.com

**New England town meeting**

A form of direct democratic participation as characterized by meetings of entire communities in New England during the colonial period.

Media representations of the public's political disengagement contain elements of truth. Americans do not meet the ideal of involved and fully informed citizens that derives from the concept of the **New England town meeting** of the colonial period, where the entire community took part in civic affairs. Media coverage focuses on the particular aspects of political participation that typically have low rates of civic engagement—especially political party work and campaign activity—or on the aspects that are expected to have higher rates of engagement, such as voting.

The public is more politically active and aware than much press coverage would suggest. Over 60 percent of adults have participated in politics in some way, and more than 70 percent of young people have done community service.[9] Still, the "engaged public" remains a largely untold news story.

**social movements**

Large groups of people with common concerns who have mobilized to actively pursue political objectives.

Americans participate in politics in many different ways, such as voting, contacting leaders, holding public office, and protesting. **Social movements** that mobilize large numbers of people on behalf of a cause are an important dimension of American political involvement. This chapter examines the origins, development, and influence of social movements. The media's depiction of citizens' political participation is complex and even contradictory.

# 8.2 What Is Political Participation?

## Learning Objectives

After reading this section, you should be able to answer the following questions:

1. What are the ways in which Americans participate in politics?
2. What factors influence voter turnout in elections?
3. How do Americans participate in groups?

Americans have many options for taking part in politics, including voting, contacting public officials, campaigning, running for and holding office, protesting, and volunteering. Voting is the most prominent form of political participation. Voter registration and turnout is influenced by legal and structural factors, voter qualifications, the type of election, and voters' enthusiasm about a particular campaign.

# Types of Political Participation

**Political participation** is action that influences the distribution of social goods and values.[10] People can vote for representatives, who make policies that will determine how much they have to pay in taxes and who will benefit from social programs. They can take part in organizations that work to directly influence policies made by government officials. They can communicate their interests, preferences, and needs to government officials by engaging in public debate and expressing their opinions on social media.[11] Such political activities can support government officials, institutions, and policies, or aim to change them.

**political participation**

Actions directed explicitly toward influencing the distribution of social goods and values.

Far more people participate in politics by voting than by any other means. Yet there are many other ways to take part in politics that involve varying amounts of skill, time, and resources. People can work on an election campaign, contact public officials, circulate a petition, join a political organization, and donate money to a candidate or a cause. Serving on a local governing or school board, volunteering in the community, and running for office are forms of participation that require significant time and energy. Organizing a demonstration, protesting, and even rioting are other forms of participation.[12]

**FIGURE 8.2 Supporting Causes Can Lead to Advocacy**

People take part in support activities on behalf of a cause, which can lead to more active involvement, such as advocating for an issue or fundraising.

Source: BABAROGA/Shutterstock.com.

Digital media enable people to engage in politics. They provide new opportunities for people to take part in conventional forms of politics. Contacting public officials is facilitated by new media, allowing people to express their concerns about and support for policy issues. People can sign an online petition. They can use social media, like Facebook, Twitter, and Instagram, to raise awareness of issues or to support a candidate for office. They can organize political events and rallies online, and stimulate offline participation. They can work collaboratively to solve community problems.[13]

People can take part in **support activities**, which are more passive forms of political involvement. They may attend concerts or participate in sporting events associated with causes, such as the "Race for the Cure" for breast cancer. These events are designed to raise money and awareness of societal problems such as poverty and health care. However, most participants are not activists for these causes. Support activities can lead to active participation, as people learn about issues through these events and decide to become involved.

**support activities**

Passive forms of political involvement, such as attending a concert on behalf of a cause.

People also can engage in **symbolic participation**, routine or habitual acts that show support for the political system. People salute the flag and recite the Pledge of Allegiance at the beginning of a school day, and they sing the national anthem at sporting events. Symbolic acts are not always supportive of the political system. Some people may refuse to say the Pledge of Allegiance to express their dissatisfaction with government. Citizens can show their unhappiness with leadership choices by the symbolic act of not voting.

**symbolic participation**

Routine or habitual acts that show support for or dissatisfaction with the political system.

# Voting

For many people, voting is the primary means of taking part in politics. A unique and special political act, voting allows for the views of more people to be represented than any other activity. Every citizen gets one vote that counts equally. Over 90 percent of Americans agree with the principle that citizens have a duty to vote.[14] Still, many people do not vote regularly.

## Voter Qualifications

Registered voters meet eligibility requirements and have filed the necessary paperwork that permits them to vote in a given locality. In addition to the requirement that voters must be eighteen years of age, states can enforce residency requirements that mandate the number of years a person must live in a place before being eligible to vote. According to the U.S. Census Bureau, 69 percent of eligible Americans were registered to vote in 2016.[15] A large majority of those people who have registered to vote participate in presidential elections—59.2 percent of registered voters turned out in the 2016 general election. The number of eligible voters who took part in the 2020 presidential election increased markedly to 66.2%, with 158.4 million ballots cast.[16]

The composition of the electorate has changed radically throughout American history. The pool of eligible voters has expanded from primarily white, male property owners at the founding to include Black men after the Civil War, women after 1920, and eighteen- to twenty-year-olds after 1971. The eligible electorate in the 1800s, when voter turnout consistently exceeded 70 percent, was far different than the diverse pool of eligible voters we see today.

The American electorate has become more racially and ethnically diverse over time. White voters made up almost 70% of the electorate in 2020, a percentage that has declined from 85% in 1996. Hispanic and Black voters each accounted for 11% of voters.[17] Over 4 million Asian American and Pacific Islanders, representing about 3% of the electorate, voted in 2020 compared to 1.25 million in 2016.[18]

## Barriers to Voting

**FIGURE 8.3** Voter Registration

Organizations conducting voter registration drives register as many voters as government voter registration sites.

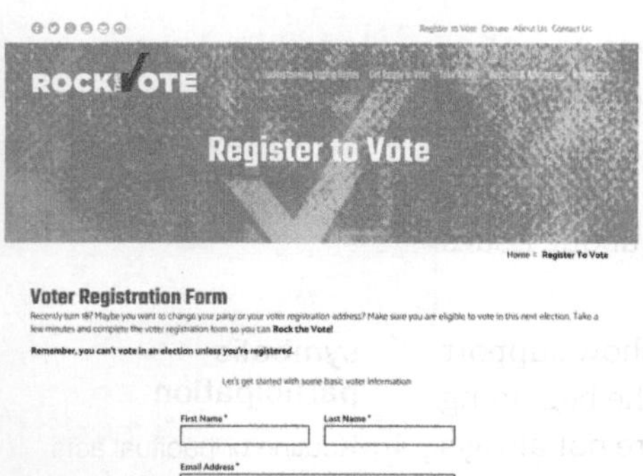


Source: https://www.rockthevote.org/register-to-vote/.

Social, cultural, political, and economic factors can keep people from voting. Some barriers to voting are informal. The United States holds a large number of elections, and each is governed by specific rules and schedules. With so many elections, people can become overwhelmed, confused, or just plain tired of voting.

Other barriers are structural. Voter registration laws were implemented in the 1860s by states and big cities to ensure that only citizens who met legal requirements could vote. Residency requirements limited access to registration offices. Closing voting rosters weeks or months in advance of elections effectively disenfranchised voters. Over time, residency requirements were relaxed. Beginning in the 1980s, some states, including Maine, Minnesota, and Wisconsin, made it possible for people to register on Election Day. Turnout in states that have Election Day registration averages ten points higher than in the rest of the country.[19]

The United States is one of the few democracies that require citizens to register themselves rather than having the government take responsibility for automatically registering them. Significant steps have been taken to make registration easier. In 1993, Congress passed the **National Voter Registration Act**, also known as the "motor voter" law, allowing citizens to register at motor vehicle and social services offices. "Motor voter's" success in increasing the ranks of registered voters differs by state, depending on how well the program is publicized and executed.

**National Voter Registration Act**

A law that allows citizens to register to vote at motor vehicle and social services offices; also known as the "motor voter" law.

Voter registration also has been assisted by online registration. In most cases, individuals must download the form, sign it, and mail it in. Rock the Vote (RTV), a nonpartisan youth mobilization organization, established the first online voter registration initiative in 1992 with official backing from the Congressional Internet Caucus. RTV registered over 2 million new voters in 1992, 80 percent of whom cast a ballot, and signed up over 2.5 million voters in 2008.[20] Following the 2008 election, RTV lobbied the Obama administration to institute fully automated online voter registration nationally. As of 2018, it is possible to register online in thirty-seven states plus the District of Columbia.[21]

## Voter Suppression

**Voter suppression** attempts to prevent eligible voters from registering to vote or voting. Voting rights can be suppressed by laws that make it difficult for citizens to exercise their right to vote. Often voter-suppression laws make it harder for disadvantaged people, members of diverse racial and ethnic groups, and people with disabilities to cast a ballot. Prior to the Voting Rights Act of 1965, which made them illegal, these laws included poll taxes and literacy tests. Today, voter-suppression laws include limiting early voting, voter ID laws, purges of voter rolls without notifying voters, and making polling places difficult to find or physically inaccessible to people with mobility issues. Voter ID laws require a person to present an official form of identification, often including a photo, at the polls, which deprives voters who cannot afford or are not able to obtain these documents from exercising their right to vote.[22]

**voter suppression**

Deliberate attempts, both legal and informal, to discourage people from registering and voting; voter suppression most often affects disadvantaged people, members of diverse racial and ethnic groups, and people with disabilities.

During the COVID-19 pandemic in 2020, twenty-nine states and the District of Columbia enacted seventy-nine laws to increase voting rights by expanding access to voter registration, mail-in voting, and early voting, and increasing services for voters with disabilities and non–English language speakers. At the same time, six states enacted laws restricting voting access.[23] Following the 2020 election, over 250 new laws were proposed in forty-three states that would create barriers to voting for millions of citizens.[24]

In the new media era, voter suppression has expanded to include deliberate efforts by campaigns and political organizations to discourage people from voting. Digital ads in the 2016 election run by the Russia-backed Internet Research Agency urged Black voters to "boycott the election" because neither candidate would represent their interests. Research conducted at the University of Wisconsin–Madison indicated that incorrect information about polling places and the date that balloting would take place was posted on Twitter. Social media posts also emphasized that voting is pointless and even attempted to intimidate voters by attempting to organize violence at polling places.[25]

Successful efforts to combat voter suppression have been launched. Stacey Abrams ran as the Democratic candidate for governor of Georgia in 2018, losing narrowly to Republican Brian Kemp. Kemp was also the secretary of state overseeing the election, which posed a potential conflict of interest.[26] Abrams became an outspoken advocate for voter protection. She formed the groups Fair Fight and the New Georgia Project, which worked with other voting rights organizations to register hundreds of thousands of voters who had been purged from voting rolls.[27] Her network's efforts expanded the number of first-time voters, young voters, and voters of color who registered and cast a ballot in the 2020 presidential election and the runoff election determining the senators for Georgia.[28] A **runoff election** is held in certain states, including Georgia, that require that candidates meet a threshold percentage of votes in a primary or general election in order to be declared the winner. However, in 2021, the Georgia state legislature passed a 98-page voting law that restricts

**runoff election**

A voting system where if a candidate does not win a minimum percentage of votes, such as 50%, in a general election, a second election is held among the top vote getters.

access to absentee ballots, imposes strict ID requirements, limits polling centers and ballot drop boxes, and makes it a misdemeanor charge to offer food or water to voters waiting in line.[29]

## Disenfranchisement of Felons

In all states except Maine and Vermont, inmates serving time for committing felonies lose their right to vote. At least ten states prohibit former felons from voting even after they have served their time. States argue that their legal authority to deny convicted felons voting rights derives from the Fourteenth Amendment, which stipulates that voting rights of individuals guilty of "participation in rebellion, or other crime" can be denied. This practice excluded 5.2 million people from the voting rolls in the 2020 election.[30]

Opinions are divided on this issue. Some people believe that individuals who have committed a serious crime should be deprived of the privileges enjoyed by law-abiding people. Others contend that the integrity of the democratic process is at stake and that individuals should not be denied a fundamental right once they have served their time. They contend that denying convicted felons the right to vote is unfair, as it discriminates against Black Americans. One out of thirteen Black people is denied the right to vote due to felony conviction, compared to one out of fifty-six people from other racial groups.[31]

## Turnout

**midterm elections**

Elections held in the midpoint of a president's term where members of Congress, governors, state legislators, and local leaders are elected.

Voter turnout depends on the type of election. A large number of elections are held in the United States every year, including local elections, elections for county and statewide offices, primaries, and general elections. Only a small number of people, generally under one-quarter of those eligible, participate in local, county, and state elections. **Midterm elections**, in which members of Congress run for office in nonpresidential-election years, normally draw about one-third of eligible voters.[32] Voter turnout in presidential elections is generally higher than for lower-level contests; usually more than half the eligible voters cast a ballot.

Much is made about low levels of voter turnout for presidential elections in the current era. However, there have not been great fluctuations in turnout since the institution of universal suffrage in 1920. Forty-nine percent of the voting-age public cast a ballot in the 1924 presidential contest, the same percentage as in 1996. Turnout in presidential elections in the 1960s was over 60 percent. More voters were mobilized during this period of political upheaval in which people focused on issues of race relations, social welfare, and the Vietnam War.[33] Turnout was lower in the 1980s and 1990s, when the political climate was less tumultuous. There has been a steady increase in turnout since the 2000 presidential election, in which 51 percent of the voting-age public cast a ballot. Turnout was 55 percent of the voting-eligible population in 2004, 57 percent in 2008, 58 percent in 2012, 61.4 percent in 2016, and 66.7 percent in 2020.[34]

Almost 160 million voters cast a ballot in the 2020 presidential election—the most in U.S. history. Only two elections have had higher turnout—the election of 1900 with 73.7% and the election of 1876 with 82.6%. Like these historic elections, the 2020 presidential contest was high in controversy, sparking a high level of interest among voters.[35]

Young voters are less likely to turn out in presidential elections than are older citizens. Turnout among eighteen- to twenty-nine-year-olds declined steadily from 1972, when the voting age was lowered to eighteen, until 1988. Young voters turned out in large numbers in 1992 to support Democratic candidate Bill Clinton, who campaigned on issues that appealed to young people, like education and jobs. The increase in young voter participation declined to all-time lows in 1996 and 2000. However, there was a surge in young voter turnout in 2004 and 2008. Thirty-eight percent of eligible eighteen- to twenty-nine-year-olds cast a ballot in 2012. Young voters turned out at about the same rate in 2016 as they had in 2012, which was close to 50 percent of eligible voters.[36] More than half of young voters—53 percent—cast a ballot in 2020, signaling that young people have emerged as a substantial voting bloc that candidates should take seriously.[37]

In 2016, the youth vote was even higher—55 percent—in **battleground states** where the race between the presidential candidates was close. Hillary Clinton gained 55 percent of the youth vote compared to 37 percent for Donald Trump and 8 percent for independent candidates Jill Stein and Evan McMullin. Clinton fared well among young women and diverse groups, while Trump gained votes from young white evangelicals living in rural areas. In the 2020 election, the youth vote reached at least 53 percent, with young voters preferring Biden to Trump by at least a 25 percentage point margin. Young voters of color preferred Biden to Trump at much higher rates than did young white voters.[38]

**battleground states**

States where the presidential election is hotly contested and the Democratic and Republican candidates each have a chance of winning.

**FIGURE 8.4 Voter Turnout 1980–2020**

Compare rates of voter turnout across different age groups from 1980 to 2020. At this time, there is not conclusive data on the 2020 voter turnout for thirty- to forty-five-year-olds; forty-five to sixty-four-year-olds; and those sixty-five and older, although it is estimated to be similar to the 2016 data.

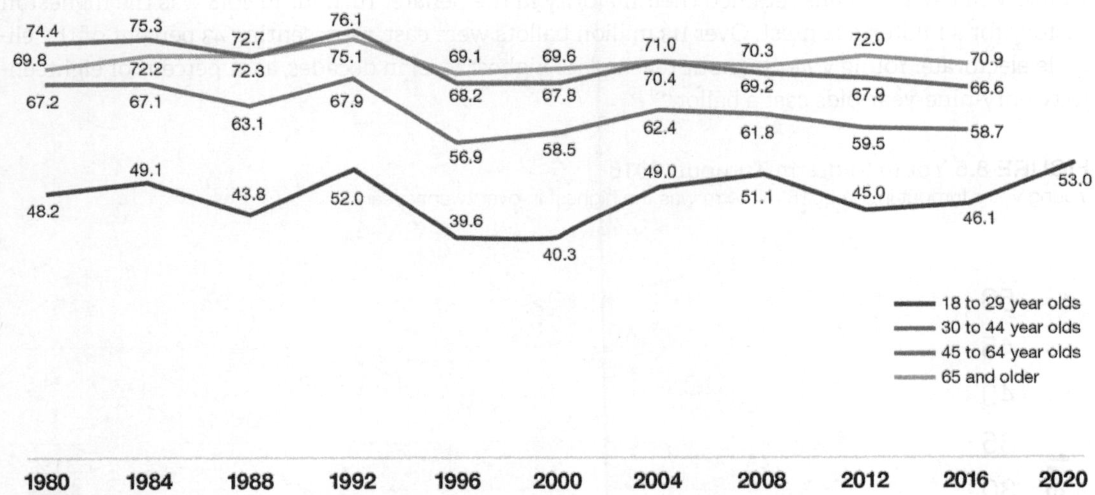


Sources: Data from https://census.gov/newsroom/blogs/random-samplings/2017/05/voting_in_america.html; CIRCLE. 2020. "Young People Increase Turnout, Lead Biden to Victory," November 25. Medford, MA: Tufts University. https://circle.tufts.edu/latest-research/election-week-2020; "Voter Turnout," MIT Election Data Science Lab, April 28, 2021. https://electionlab.mit.edu/research/voter-turnout.

Turnout varies significantly across localities. Some regions have an established culture of political participation. Local elections in small towns in New England draw up to 80 percent of qualified voters. In 2020, 80 percent of voters in Minnesota and 76 percent of those in Maine and Wisconsin turned out in the 2020 presidential election, compared to around 55 percent in Arkansas and Oklahoma.[39]

Turnout figures can be skewed by undercounting the vote. This problem gained attention during the 2000 election. The contested vote in the Florida presidential race resulted in a recount in several counties. Ballots can be invalidated if they are not properly marked by voters or are not read by antiquated voting machines. Political scientists have determined that presidential election turnout is underestimated on average by 4 percent, which translates into hundreds of thousands of votes.[40]

Unsubstantiated claims of voter fraud were purported by former President Donald Trump and echoed by his supporters following the 2020 presidential election. The charges focused on states where Trump was unsuccessful, and alleged problems with counting ballots, ballot-box stuffing, and unmatched signatures on mail-in ballots.[41] A handful of Republican members of Congress objected to certifying the election, but Joe Biden was formally confirmed as president-elect by Congress on January 7, 2021.[42]

Voters in midterm elections choose all the members of the U.S. House of Representatives and one-third of the Senate, along with officeholders at the state and local levels. Voter turnout levels have hovered around 40 percent in recent midterm elections. Turnout for the 2010 midterm election was 41.6 percent, compared with 41.4 percent in 2006 and 40.5 percent in 2002.[43] However, voter turnout in the 2014 midterm contest was the lowest since World War II, as only 36.4 percent of eligible voters cast a ballot. Young voters are less likely to turn out in midterm elections than are older citizens. In 2010, only about 23 percent of eligible eighteen- to twenty-nine-year-olds cast a ballot.[44] Young voter turnout dropped markedly in 2014. Fourteen million fewer eighteen- to twenty-nine-year-olds went to the polls.

Interest in the 2018 midterm elections was exceptionally high. The campaign was viewed by many voters as a referendum on the presidency of Donald Trump. Voters were engaged by a variety of issues about which they felt strongly, especially health care for Democrats and immigration for Republicans. Democrats sought to gain control of Congress, as Republicans had the majority in both the House and the Senate. President Donald Trump was active on the campaign trail, holding rallies to support candidates in states where he was popular. The Democrats took control of the House, while Republicans retained their majority in the Senate. Turnout in 2018 was the highest in history for a midterm contest. Over 113 million ballots were cast, representing 43 percent of the eligible electorate. Young voter turnout reached its highest level in decades, as 31 percent of eighteen- to twenty-nine-year-olds cast a ballot.[45]

**FIGURE 8.5 Youth Midterm Turnout, 2018**
Young voter turnout in the 2018 midterm was the highest in over twenty years.

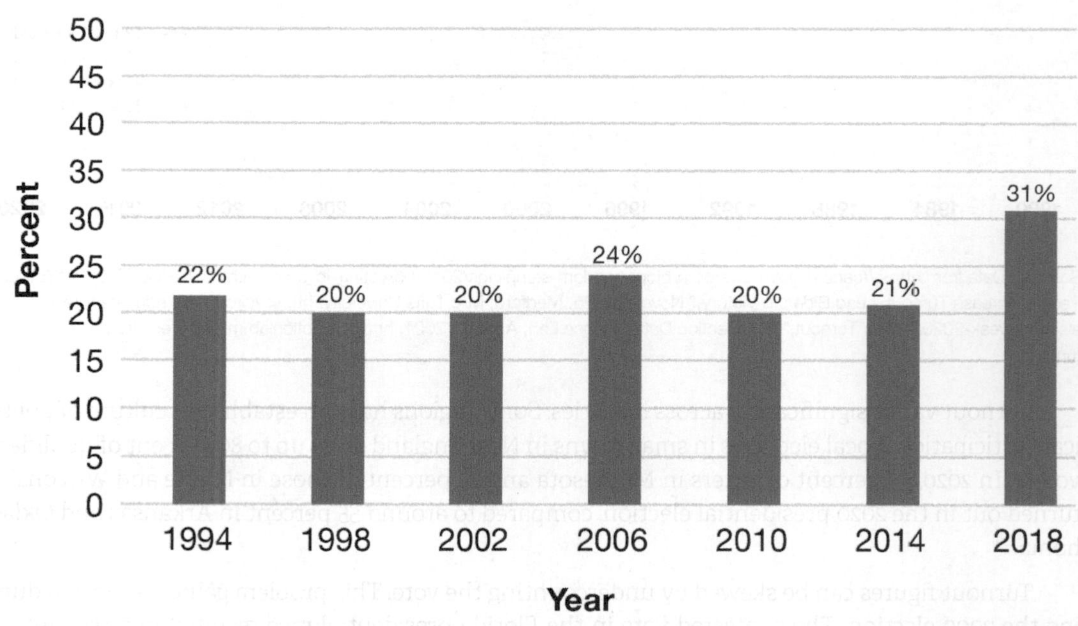


Source: Data from Young People Dramatically Increase their Turnout to 31%, Shape 2018 Midterm Elections, CIRCLE, https://civicyouth.org/young-people-dramatically-increase-their-turnout-31-percent-shape-2018-midterm-elections/.

The United States Election Project provides information about voter turnout in presidential and midterm election campaigns.

# Democratic Participation

People have many options for engaging in politics. People can act alone by writing letters to members of Congress or staging acts of **civil disobedience**. Some political activities, such as boycotts and protest movements, involve many people working together to attract the attention of public officials. Increasingly, people are participating in politics via the media, especially the internet.

**civil disobedience**

Deliberate, nonviolent violation of laws that people consider to be unjust, committed in order to draw attention to a cause.

## Contacting Public Officials

Expressing opinions about leaders, issues, and policies has become one of the most prominent forms of political participation. The number of people contacting public officials at all levels of government has risen markedly over the past three decades. Seventeen percent of Americans contacted a public official in 1976. By 2008, 44 percent of the public had contacted their member of Congress about an issue or concern.[46] Email has made contacting public officials cheaper and easier than the traditional method of mailing a letter.

**FIGURE 8.6** Contacting Congress

The directive to "write your member of Congress" is taken seriously by increasing numbers of citizens: legislators' email boxes are filled daily, and millions of letters are processed by the Capitol Hill post offices.

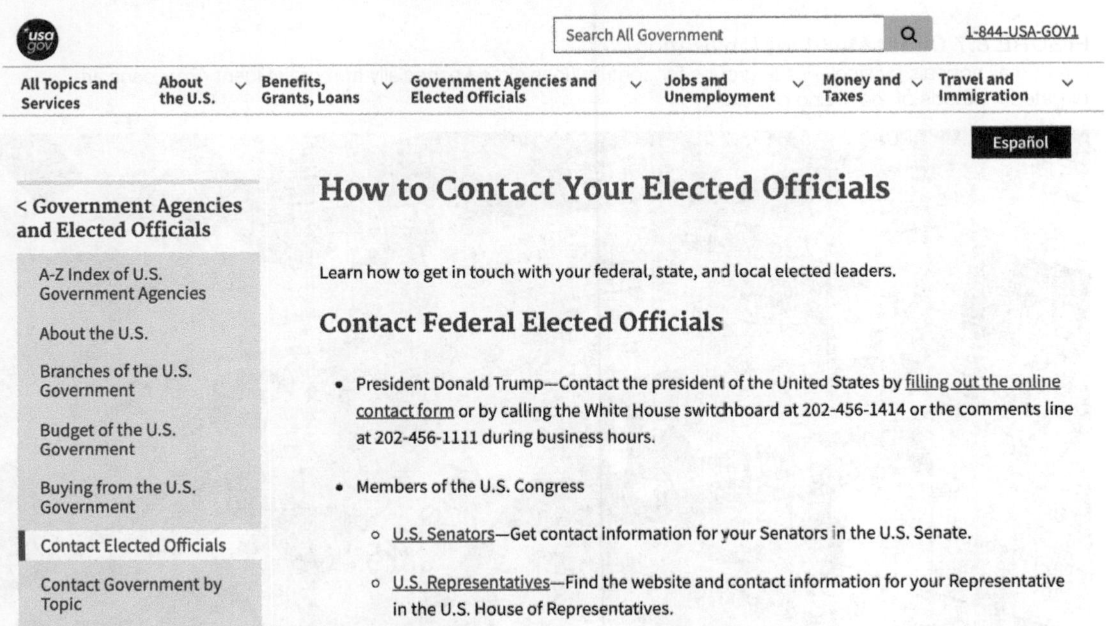


Source: USA.gov; https://www.usa.gov/elected-officials.

Students interning for public officials soon learn that answering constituent mail is one of the most time-consuming staff jobs. Every day, millions of people voice their opinions to members of Congress. Over 7 million constituents per year contact their senators using "snail mail." A member of Congress can receive as many as 5,000 letters and phone calls from the public in a single month.[47] The Senate alone receives an average of over four million email messages per week and more than two hundred million email messages per year.[48] Still, email may not be the most effective way of getting a message across, because officeholders believe that an email message takes less time, effort, and thought than a traditional letter. Leaders frequently are "spammed" with mass emails that are not from their constituents. Letters and phone calls almost always receive some kind of a response from members of Congress. The U.S. government hosts a site to help people contact government officials (see here).

## Contributing Money

**super PACs**

Super PACs are political committees that are allowed to raise and spend unlimited amounts of money from corporations, unions, individuals, and associations to influence the outcome of state and federal elections.

The number of people who give money to a candidate, party, or political organization has increased substantially since the 1960s. Small donors are people who make contributions of $200 or less to campaigns. Bernie Sanders raised funds from over 3.25 million small donors in his bid for the 2016 Democratic presidential nomination, which he lost to Hillary Clinton. However, only 33 percent of funds in the 2016 election came from small donors. The 2020 presidential election was the most expensive in history, with the candidates hauling in nearly $4 billion in campaign funds. Joe Biden raised over $400 million and Donald Trump raised $378 million from small donors.[49] The bulk of campaign funding in the 2020 presidential race—representing about 70 percent of all contributions—came from big donors, some of whom contributed over $10 million of their own funds to the presidential election through **super PACs**.[50] Men are more likely to make a campaign donation than women, as are people with higher levels of education and socioeconomic status.

**direct mail**

Fundraising targeting voters by mailing solicitations to them.

**Direct mail** and email solicitations make fundraising easier, especially when donors can contribute through candidate and political party websites. A positive side effect of fundraising campaigns is that people are made aware of candidates and issues through appeals for money.[51]

Americans are more likely to make a financial contribution to a cause or a candidate than to donate their time. As one would expect, those with higher levels of education and income are the most likely to contribute time and money. Those who give money are more likely to gain access to candidates when they are in office.

**FIGURE 8.7** Direct Mail for Mobilization

Direct mail appeals by single-issue groups for contributions aimed especially at more affluent Americans are targeted methods of mobilizing people.

Source: Matt Gush/Shutterstock.com

## Campaign Activity

In addition to voting, people engage in a range of activities during campaigns. They work for political parties or candidates, organize campaign events, and discuss issues with family and friends. Generally, about 15 percent of Americans participate in these types of campaign activities in an election year.[52]

New media offer additional opportunities for people to engage in campaigns. People can blog or participate in discussion groups, or tweet about candidates, issues, and events. They can create and post videos on behalf of or opposed to candidates. They can use social networking sites, like Facebook, to recruit supporters, enlist volunteers for campaign events, or encourage friends to donate money to a candidate.

The 2008 presidential election sparked high levels of public interest and engagement, especially as social media emerged as new platforms for election activity. The race was open, as there was no incumbent candidate, and voters felt they had an opportunity to make a difference. Democrat Barack Obama, the first African American to be nominated by a major party, generated enthusiasm, especially among young people. In addition to traditional forms of campaign activity, like attending campaign rallies and displaying yard signs, the internet provided a gateway to involvement for 55 percent of Americans.[53] Young people in particular used social media, like Facebook, to organize online on behalf of candidates. Students advertised campus election events on social media sites, such as candidate rallies and voter registration drives, which drew large crowds.[54]

**FIGURE 8.8** Increased Voter Participation in 2008

Participation in the 2008 presidential election was greater than usual, as people were motivated by the open race and the candidate choices.

Source: Action Sports Photography / Shutterstock.com

During the 2016 election, young voters were mobilized by Vermont Senator Bernie Sanders's candidacy for the Democratic presidential nomination. "Feeling the Bern," they enthusiastically attended his campaign rallies and canvassed door-to-door to build support for his candidacy. They actively promoted Sanders on social media, where Sanders had 5.7 million Facebook followers. Sanders engaged regularly in conversations with his followers on social media, who were more engaged than followers of Donald Trump or Hillary Clinton. Young voters' support for Sanders was surprising given that he was seventy-four years old, but young people found him to be smart, open to new ideas, and trustworthy. They admired Sanders's background as a civil rights activist in the 1960s and former mayor of Burlington, Vermont, who fought against corporations. Sanders's candidacy contrasted with that of Hillary Clinton, who was perceived as an establishment candidate with ties to Wall Street banks and big corporations. During the election, Sanders spoke of a political "revolution" that would transform the country, a message that appealed to young voters.[55] He railed against entrenched corporate interests as well as big donor control over campaign financing. He favored taking strong measures to protect the environment. He advocated free college education for all. Early on, Sanders's edge over Hillary Clinton was strong. He gained 70 percent of voters aged eighteen to twenty-nine in the Iowa caucuses.[56] While Sanders remained competitive until late in the Democratic primary campaign, he ultimately was not able to win enough delegates to the national nominating convention to gain the party's presidential nomination.

**FIGURE 8.9** Young People for Bernie Sanders

Young voters rallied around Democratic presidential hopeful Bernie Sanders during the 2016 nominating campaign. After losing the nomination, Sanders continued to promote his progressive agenda in person and online.

Source: BestStockFoto / Shutterstock.com

Young voters in the 2020 presidential election used social media in new ways to engage in the campaign. They employed platform alternatives to Facebook and Twitter, such as TikTok and Twitch, to get people to the polls. They formed groups, such as Future Coalition and Gen-Z for Change, to organize youth phone banking and **text banking** efforts. They met online via Zoom to train volunteers in how to create and post content that would reach and appeal to young voters. They disseminated video and audio clips of candidates showing their personal sides, such as the inside of Georgia Democratic Senate candidate Jon Ossoff's home, showcasing his "snack closet."[57]

**text banking**

The digital equivalent of phone banking, where volunteers reach out to voters via text with targeted personalized messages.

They also employed online gaming as a tool for voter mobilization. Rep. Alexandria Ocasio-Cortez (D-NY) used Twitch to stream herself playing the game *Among Us*. She directed viewers to go to IWillVote.com, where they could pledge to turn out in the election. Over 5.4 million people, whose average age was twenty-one, viewed the video, with many visiting the voting site.[58]

## Running for and Holding Public Office

Being a public official requires a great deal of dedication, time, energy, and money. About 3 percent of the adult population holds an elected or appointed public office.[59] Although the percentage of people running for and holding public office appears small, there are many opportunities to serve in government. Young people have successfully run for local and state-level offices. In 2016, Jewell Jones, at age twenty-one, became the youngest person elected to the Michigan state legislature after having served on his local town council.[60]

Potential candidates for public office must gather signatures on a petition before their names can appear on the ballot. Some people may be discouraged from running because the signature requirement seems daunting. For example, running for mayor of New York City requires 7,500 signatures and addresses on a petition. Once a candidate gets on the ballot, she must organize a campaign, solicit volunteers, raise funds, develop a social media presence, and garner press coverage.

## Protest Activity

**civil rights movement**

A social movement begun in the 1950s to combat discrimination against African Americans.

Protests involve unconventional, and sometimes unlawful, political actions that are undertaken in order to gain rewards from the political and economic system. Protest behavior can take many forms. People can engage in nonviolent acts of civil disobedience, where they deliberately break a law that they consider to be unjust.[61] This tactic was used effectively during the 1960s **civil rights movement**, when African Americans sat in whites-only sections of public buses. Other forms of protest behavior include marking public spaces with graffiti, demonstrating, and boycotting. Extreme forms of protest behavior include acts that cause harm, such as when environmental activists place spikes in trees that can seriously injure loggers, terrorist acts like bombing a building, and civil war.

Extreme discontent with a particular societal condition can lead to rioting. Riots are frequently spontaneous and are sparked by an incident that brings to a head deep-seated frustrations and emotions. Members of social movements may resort to rioting when they perceive that there are no conventional alternatives for getting their message across. Riots can result in destruction of property, looting, physical harm, and even death. Racial tensions sparked by a video of police beating Rodney King in 1991 and the subsequent acquittal of the officers at trial resulted in the worst riots ever experienced in Los Angeles.

**FIGURE 8.10 Watts Riots, 1965**

The Watts riots in 1965 were the first of a number of civil disturbances in American cities. Although their participants thought of them as political protests, the news media presentation rarely gave that point of view.

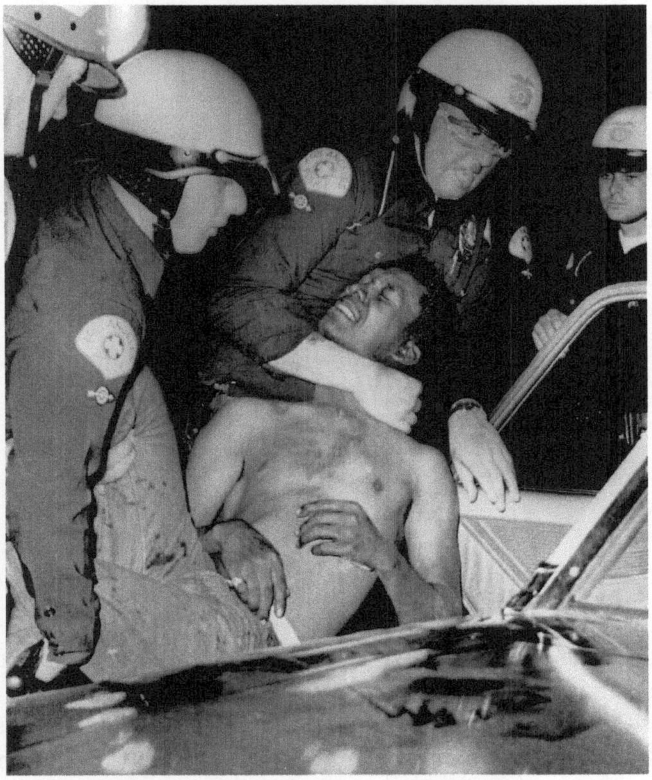

Source: Everett Collection Inc / Alamy Stock Photo

## Comparing Content

### The Rodney King Video

In March 1991, KTLA News at Ten in Los Angeles interrupted programming to broadcast an eighty-one-second amateur videotape of several police officers savagely beating Black motorist Rodney King as he stood next to his vehicle. A nineteen-second edit of the tape depicted the most brutal police actions and became one of the most heavily broadcasted images in television news history. The original and the edited tape tell two different stories of the same event.

Viewing the entire tape, one would have seen a belligerent and violent Rodney King, who was difficult for police to constrain. Not filmed at all was an intoxicated King driving erratically, leading police on an eight-mile, high-speed chase through crowded streets.

The edited video showing the beating of King told a different story of police brutality and was the basis of much controversy. Race relations in Los Angeles in 1991 were strained. The tape enraged Blacks in Los Angeles who saw the police's actions as being indicative of widespread problems within the Los Angeles Police Department and not an isolated incident.

Four white officers were tried in criminal court for the use of excessive force, and they were acquitted of all but one charge. Jurors were shown the entire tape, not just the famous nineteen-second clip. Soon after the verdict was announced, riots broke out. Demonstrators burned buildings and assaulted bystanders. Fifty-four people were killed and two thousand were wounded. Property damage was in the millions of dollars.

This video discusses both the Rodney King beating and the 1992 riots in Los Angeles.

View in the online reader

The *CBS News* report on the Rodney King incident included the following controversial video.

View in the online reader

College students in the 1960s used demonstrations to voice their opposition to the Vietnam War. Today, students demonstrate to draw attention to causes. For more than two decades, young people have made use of digital communications strategies to organize protests by forming groups online and on social media. In 1999, online strategies were used to organize demonstrations against the globalization policies of the World Trade Organization and the World Bank. Over two hundred websites were established to rally support for protests in Seattle, Washington; Washington, DC; Quebec City, Canada; and other locations. Protest participants received online instructions at the protest website about travel and housing, where to assemble, and how to behave if arrested. Extensive email listservs keep protesters and sympathizers in contact between demonstrations. The social messaging platform Twitter has been used to convey eyewitness reports of protests worldwide.

The Occupy movement, which began in the United States as Occupy Wall Street in 2011, was an international protest against social and economic inequality. Protests were organized locally, as people camped out in public places for long periods of time to publicize their concerns. Tfhe movement used the slogan, "We are the 99%," to support their contention that wealth is concentrated among 1 percent of income earners, who have inordinate political power. Media coverage focused on the movement's lack of clearly defined goals and demands. It also highlighted skirmishes with authorities and lack of sanitary conditions in the camps. By 2012, the Occupy encampments had disbanded, while protest activities continue both online and offline.[62]

Black Lives Matter (BLM) is a movement that began in 2013 with protests after a Florida jury issued a not-guilty verdict in the shooting death of unarmed teenager Trayvon Martin by George Zimmerman, a man who lived in his neighborhood. The movement gained traction as protesters took to the street after Michael Brown was killed by a white police officer in Ferguson, Missouri in 2014. A grand jury refused to indict the police officer in the case. Further protests followed the deaths of other Black men who were confronted by police.[63]

**systemic racism**

A system where public policies, institutional practices, cultural norms, and historic representations perpetuate racial group inequity.

Protests over **systemic racism** coincided with the 2020 presidential election. Galvanized by the killing by police officers of George Floyd, Breonna Taylor, and other Black Americans, activists and average citizens took to the street in protest across the nation and the world. It is estimated that between 15 million and 26 million people in the United States had participated in Black Lives Matter protests as of June 6, 2020.[64]

## Participation in Groups

About half the population takes part in national and community political affairs by joining an interest group, issue-based organization, civic organization, or political party. Organizations with the goal of promoting civic action on behalf of particular causes, or **single-issue groups**, have proliferated. These groups are as diverse as People for the Ethical Treatment of Animals (PETA), which supports animal rights, the Concord Coalition, which seeks to protect Social Security benefits, and the Aryan Nation, which promotes white supremacy.

**single-issue groups**

Organizations with the goal of promoting action on behalf of particular causes.

There are many ways to advocate for a cause. Members may engage in lobbying efforts and take part in demonstrations to publicize their concerns. They can post their views on blogs and energize their supporters using Facebook groups that provide information about how to get involved. Up to 70 percent of members of single-issue groups show their support solely by making monetary contributions.[65]

## Volunteering

Even activities that on the surface do not seem to have much to do with politics can be a form of political participation. Many people take part in neighborhood, school, and religious associations. They act to benefit their communities without monetary compensation.

Maybe you coach a Little League team, visit seniors at a nursing home, or work at a homeless shelter. If so, you are taking part in **civil society**, the community of individuals who volunteer and work cooperatively outside of formal governmental institutions.[66] Civil society depends on **social networks**, based on trust and goodwill, that form between friends and associates and allow them to work together to achieve common goals. Community activism is thriving among young people who realize the importance of service that directly assists others. Almost 70 percent of high school students and young adults aged eighteen to thirty report that they have been involved in community activities at some point in their lives.[67] About 20 percent of people aged fifteen to twenty-five volunteer on a regular basis.[68]

**civil society**

The community of individuals who volunteer and work cooperatively outside of formal governmental institutions.

**social networks**

Associations of friends and acquaintances, based on trust and goodwill, that are able to work together to achieve common goals.

### Key Takeaways

There are many different ways that Americans can participate in politics, including voting, joining political parties, volunteering, contacting public officials, contributing money, working in campaigns, holding public office, protesting, and rioting. Voting is the most prevalent form of political participation, although many eligible voters do not turn out in elections. People can take part in social movements in which large groups of individuals with shared goals work together to influence government policies. New media provide novel opportunities for political participation, such as using Facebook to campaign for a candidate and Twitter to keep people abreast of a protest movement.

### Exercises

1. What are some of the ways you have participated in politics? What motivated you to get involved?
2. What political causes do you care the most about? What do you think is the best way for you to advance those causes?
3. Do you think people who have committed serious crimes should be allowed to vote? How do you think not letting them vote might affect what kind of policy is made?

# 8.3 Why People Participate

## Learning Objectives

After reading this section, you should be able to answer the following questions:

1. How do people become politically mobilized?
2. How interested are Americans in taking part in politics?

People get involved in politics for a variety of reasons. They may be personally motivated because of an event that changed their lives. They may perceive a problem or injustice in society and want to take action. They may receive invitations to participate from friends, organizations, political parties, or a candidate's campaign. A person's socialization, life experience, and attitude toward politics can influence their participation. Some people have a strong sense of civic duty and efficacy, a belief that they can influence government, which compels them to act. Barriers such as legal obstacles may preclude some people from engaging politically.

## Mobilization Efforts

**FIGURE 8.11 Religion in Politics**
Religious convictions can influence people to participate in politics.

Source: Photo courtesy of dbking https://commons.wikimedia.org/wiki/File:Christian_protester_-_Tea_Party_march.jpg. Reproduced via CC BY 2.0: https://creativecommons.org/licenses/by/2.0/deed.en.

**executive order**

An executive order is a directive by the president or a state governor that enacts a policy and has the force of law.

Most people do not wake up one morning and decide that they are going to engage in politics. They must be motivated to participate, often by people or organizations reaching out to them and asking them to get involved. Increasingly, people receive digital invitations to participate through groups formed by friends on Facebook, calls to action posted on Twitter and Instagram, email solicitations from campaigns and interest groups, and podcasts from political organizations. People also can be mobilized in response to events, such as a violent act in their community or their opposition to a government policy. The **executive order** by President Donald Trump banning people from many Muslim nations from entering the country sparked protests at airports across the country.

Traditionally, political parties helped mobilize people by recruiting volunteers for campaigns and other political events. Parties provided a training ground for candidates and leaders and rallied people around issues. Today parties' role in directly mobilizing people to participate in politics has diminished. Fewer people identify with a political party than in the past. People are more inclined to act on behalf of a candidate who represents their interests than a political party.[69]

Interest groups and candidates' campaigns can encourage people to take part in politics. They use marketing strategies to target potential activists based on demographic characteristics and political orientations. Organizations acquire lists of prospects from political parties and market research firms, and they use these lists to contact people by mail, telephone, and email.[70] They can **microtarget** supporters based on specific characteristics, such as voters who are in their twenties, drink Starbucks coffee, enjoy Judd Apatow films, and work in the legal field.

**microtarget**

To use a marketing strategy in which potential political activists are identified and solicited on the basis of their demographic characteristics and consumer behavior.

Trade unions mobilize blue-collar workers, especially on behalf of the Democratic Party. Black churches are instrumental in organizing political action in the Black community, fundamentalist congregations provide a base for the Christian Right, and the Catholic Church helps mobilize the pro-life movement against abortion and anti–death-penalty activists.

# Socialization and Life Experience

People can establish the habit of participating in politics through **political socialization**, the process by which people acquire their political beliefs, attitudes, and actions. Political experiences with families, schools, friendship groups, churches, community organizations, and mass media can motivate people to become lifelong political participants. If your parents are community activists, there is a good chance that you also will be active at some point in your life.[71] People can be socialized to participation through civic education when they learn in school how democracy works and how they can take part. Students can gain experience by participating in extracurricular activities, student government, or community volunteer programs. These activities place young people in social and political networks with others who have a strong sense of **civic duty**, the belief that one has a responsibility to take part in community life.

**political socialization**

The process by which people acquire their political beliefs, attitudes, and behaviors.

**civic duty**

The responsibility of a citizen to take part in community life.

People's integration into their communities is strongly related to their level of political activity. Those who are mobile and have not established community roots find it more difficult to participate in politics because they are not part of a social network. It takes about three to five years to develop friendship networks, learn about the problems facing a community, and identify which people are the key players.[72] As a result, young people, who tend to be more mobile, may be less likely to engage politically.

Difficult life experiences can cause people to act who never thought they would become involved. President Bill Clinton pardoned Dorothy Gaines, Kemba Smith, and her father who had received long mandatory prison sentences on drug charges with no hope of parole. They were not involved with drugs but had boyfriends who were dealers. It is a crime under federal law to associate with known drug dealers. Ms. Gaines lobbied for her freedom from her jail cell, working with civil rights organizations, and she drew media attention to her problem, including a widely read article in *People* magazine. Kemba Smith's father, Gus, an accountant who had never been politically active, worked to secure his daughter's release. A cover story in *Ebony* magazine rallied support for her case, and a film was made about her life. Since the pardons, Dorothy Gaines, her father, and Kemba Smith have continued to lobby for changes in the sentencing laws. Kemba Smith has established a foundation to educate young people about making proper decisions.

## Link

**Kemba Smith Foundation**

Learn more about Kemba Smith's foundation here.

# Attitudinal Factors

**political efficacy**

An individual's perception that she can make a difference in politics and governmental affairs.

People's attitudes about government and politics can influence their decision to participate. People who have a strong sense of **political efficacy**, are interested in politics, and have a sense of civic duty are more likely to participate. Political efficacy is the belief that you personally can make a difference in governmental affairs.[73] During elections, people who believe that their vote can make a difference are more likely to cast a ballot than those who feel that their vote doesn't matter.[74]

Americans' interest in politics declined for about two decades beginning in the 1980s. Only about one-quarter of the public in 2000 expressed much interest in the presidential campaign, and there was even less interest in other aspects of politics. Only about 40 percent of citizens felt strongly that voting was an important civic duty. The 2008 presidential campaign bucked this trend: around 80 percent of the public expressed interest in the election and over 60 percent considered voting to be their civic duty. Interest in the 2012 presidential contest dipped somewhat from 2008, with about 70 percent of the public expressing interest.[75] Despite the fact that voters were less satisfied with the presidential candidates in 2016 than they had been in two decades, interest in the election was high. According to the Pew Research Center, 80 percent of voters had thought about the election and felt that the outcome really mattered.[76] The high level of interest in the presidential election continued in 2020, with 83 percent of voters saying that it "really matters who wins."[77] Americans are typically less interested in nonpresidential elections.[78]

Political interest is bolstered by the ability of people to take part in politics and express their opinions more easily through digital media. People feel like they have a greater say in government and can reach out to leaders through email and online discussion forums. Political leaders have established social media accounts on Facebook and Twitter in order to share information and to enable greater interaction with their constituents.

# Personal Gratification

The expectation that political participation will be rewarding can spark people to become active. Some people are motivated by the belief that they will be connected to powerful leaders and receive material benefits, such as a chance to further their careers or get help with a personal problem. Others embrace the opportunities to meet people and socialize while working together, or they are happy to do something good for the community. High schools and colleges throughout the nation have instituted community service programs to stimulate lifelong participation based on the personal gratification students experience when they realize that their efforts make a difference.

**FIGURE 8.12** Young People in Community Service

A majority of U.S. high school students and many other young people participate in community service activities ranging from tutoring after school to cleaning up public spaces.

Source: Photo courtesy of U.S. Navy Mass Communication Specialist 3rd Class Daniel Viramontes, http://commons.wikimedia.org/wiki/File:US_Navy_090804-N-7280V-398 _Sailors_paint_a_classroom_during_a _community_service_project.jpg.

## Key Takeaways

People often are motivated to participate in politics because they are targets of mobilization efforts by political parties and interest groups. They also can acquire the habit of participating politically through the process of political socialization or have a life experience that prompts them to act. Political attitudes such as civic duty and a sense of political efficacy can influence a person's decision to participate. People may seek personal gratification through political action, as they enjoy working with others and helping their community. Legal factors such as voter registration requirements can impede participation.

## Exercises

1. Are you aware of interest groups' and political campaigns' efforts to mobilize you? What techniques do they use to try to reach people like you?
2. Why do you think Americans have become less engaged in politics? Why do you think they were more engaged during the 2008 election? Why were they less interested in the 2012 presidential campaign?

# 8.4 Who Participates and Who Does Not

## Learning Objectives

After reading this section, you should be able to answer the following questions:

1. What types of people are the most and the least likely to participate in American government and politics?
2. What barriers to political participation do some groups face?

Meaningful and regular opportunities for all people to participate must be guaranteed by a democratic political system, whether or not everyone chooses to take part. But not all Americans engage in politics, nor are the opportunities for participation equal. Voters and political activists generally are older, more educated, and better off financially than the general population. These people have the best chance of having their views represented in government. Meanwhile, those who rely the most on government programs and policies, such as recipients of public assistance, often have fewer opportunities to participate and are less engaged.

## Socioeconomic Status

**socioeconomic status**

People's levels of education, income, and occupation, which are strongly linked to patterns of political participation.

**Socioeconomic status** (SES) is determined by people's levels of education, income, and occupation. Wealthier and better educated people tend to vote more often, participate more in political activities, and donate more money to causes than poorer or less educated people. They also have greater access to the resources that facilitate political activity, including contacts with people in powerful positions. People's occupations also are related to their participation, as people in managerial and professional positions are the most politically active, followed by craftspersons, service workers, and laborers. Many managers and professionals follow politics as part of their jobs. The unemployed are the least inclined to take part.

Education has the strongest impact on participation, as it provides people with background knowledge of how the political system works. Educated people develop the skills that allow them to follow and understand events through the mass media. They are likely to form opinions about political issues and engage in discussions. The political blogs with the most readers, such as Daily Kos and Huffington Post, are written and read by well-educated people.[79] Education prepares people to deal with the bureaucratic aspects of participation, such as registering to vote or organizing a petition drive.

Political scientists Martin Gilens[80] and Larry Bartels[81] have found that the public policy preferences of well-off people in the 90th income percentile are supported over 90 percent of the time. The government rarely responds to the preferences of people in low-income groups, who often lack the resources and skills to advocate on their own behalf.

## Age

Political participation differs notably by age. People between the ages of thirty-five and sixty-five are the most politically active. At this stage in life, people are more likely than younger people to have established homes, hold steady jobs, and be settled into communities. Those with stable community roots often have strong incentives and greater resources for becoming involved in politics.

**FIGURE 8.13** Young People Pushing for Change

Young people have brought issues to the attention of public officials and worked effectively for positive change.

Source: Photo courtesy of the U.S. Department of State, http://www.flickr.com/photos/statephotos/5085000843/.

While younger people turn out in elections less often than do older people, youth voting has been on the rise in presidential elections since 2004. Turnout among eighteen- to twenty-four-year-olds dropped from 50 percent in 1972, the first presidential election year after the voting age was lowered to eighteen, to 36 percent in 2000. Turnout among senior citizens, people sixty-five and older, increased to nearly 70 percent in that same time period.[82] Young voter turnout rose to 47 percent in 2004 and 51 percent in 2008, partly as a result of voter registration and mobilization efforts by groups like Rock the Vote. The youth vote contributed to the success of Democratic presidential candidate Barack Obama in 2008, as young volunteers provided countless hours of campaign support.[83] Young voters were instrumental to Democratic candidate Joe Biden's win in the 2020 election, especially in battleground states. Sixty-one percent of eighteen- to twenty-nine-year-olds voted for Biden, with 87 percent of young Black voters, 83 percent of young Asian voters, and 73 percent of young Latinx voters supporting him. Information about young voters can be obtained from the Center for Information & Research on Civic Learning and Engagement.[84]

People under the age of thirty are among the least involved in mainstream forms of participation, such as contacting officials and running for public office. Young people often lack the money and time to participate. They also are more mobile. Still, many young people realize that participation matters. Reacting to problems they see in their hometowns, youth have formed groups to work for change. They have successfully lobbied government officials, spoken out at public meetings, and provided formal testimony at hearings. Young people have established safety policies in schools, protested against increases in college tuition rates, and prompted the creation of recreational facilities for biking, skateboarding, and ice hockey. Despite the COVID-19 pandemic, teens and twenty-somethings were a strong presence at protests against racial injustice and encouraged their peers to speak out and take action.[85]

## Gender

Political scientists and journalists often talk about the **gender gap** in participation, which assumes women lag behind men in their rates of political engagement. The gender gap is closing for some forms of participation, such as voting, but still exists for activities such as running for office. Over 10 million more women than men are registered to vote.[86] Women turn out to vote at significantly higher rates than men. Around 63 percent of women turn out in presidential elections compared to 59 percent of men.[87]

**gender gap**

The difference that exists between men's and women's political participation.

### Link

**Gender Differences in Politics**

Click here to learn about women voters and officeholders from the Center for American Women and Politics (CAWP).

Since the 1990s, women have been as likely as men to contact members of Congress, sign and circulate petitions, attend local political meetings, and donate their time to political causes. They take part in local and state political activities more than they do in the national realm, where most media attention is focused. While initially women were less likely than men to access digital media and engage politically on social media, by 2020 the gender gap had closed.[88]

A significant gender gap in participation exists for running for and holding political office, although the gap has been closing in recent years. While women make up more than half the population, they constitute far less than half of elected officeholders, especially at the national level. A total of 366 women have served in Congress since 1917, when Jeannette Rankin (R-MT) was the first woman elected to Congress. A total of 131 women were sworn in to the 116th Congress—101 members of the House of Representatives and 25 senators. Women make up 24 percent of the members of Congress.[89]

**FIGURE 8.14 Increasing Numbers of Women in Politics**

An increasing number of women are running for and winning national office. Representative Nancy Pelosi (D-CA) was the first woman speaker of the House of Representatives. Representative Elise Stefanik (R-NY) is the House Republican conference chair.

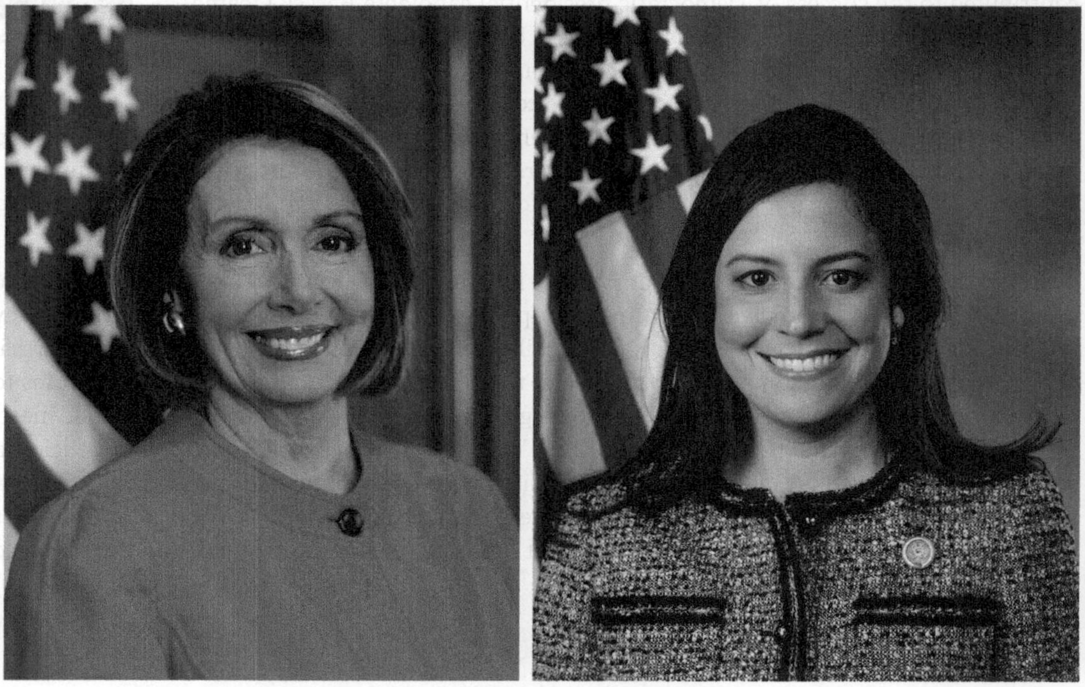

Sources: Lauren Victoria Burke [Public domain]; http://commons.wikimedia.org/wiki/File:Speaker_Nancy_Pelosi.jpg. United States House of Representatives, Public domain, via Wikimedia Commons; https://commons.wikimedia.org/wiki/File:Elise_Stefanik,_115th_official_photo.jpg.

## Link

**Women in Congress**

Visit the Women in Congress website of the Office of the Clerk of the U.S. Capitol to see historical information and data on women members of Congress.

# Race and Ethnicity

Participation differs among members of racial and ethnic groups. Specific patterns of participation are associated with Black people, Latinxs, and Asian Americans and Pacific Islanders.

## Black People

Discriminatory practices kept Black voter turnout low until after the passage of the Voting Rights Act of 1965. **Poll taxes**, fees that had to be paid before a citizen could register to vote, disenfranchised people living in poverty, many of whom were Black. **Literacy tests**, which required people to demonstrate their ability to read, write, and interpret documents prior to voting, were applied unfairly to Black people. The "**white primary**" restricted voting in Democratic primaries to white people in certain Southern states. The Southern Democratic party was so dominant that winning the primary was tantamount to election to office. Intimidation and violence by groups such as the Ku Klux Klan kept Black voters from the polls. Eventually, civil rights protests and litigation resulted in the elimination of formal barriers to voting.[90]

**poll taxes**

Fees that had to be paid before a citizen could register to vote; this requirement disenfranchised people living in poverty, including Black citizens.

**literacy tests**

Tests requiring people to demonstrate their ability to read, write, and interpret documents before being allowed to register to vote and that were used to deny Blacks voting rights.

**white primary**

Democratic Party primary elections in certain Southern states that permitted only whites to vote.

Today, Black citizens vote at least as often as white citizens do who share the same socioeconomic status. Sixty-five percent of Black voters turned out in the 2008 presidential election compared with 66 percent of white voters. Over 90 percent of Black voters supported African American candidate Barack Obama.[91] In 2012, Obama received the votes of 96 percent of Black voters, constituting 13 percent of the electorate.[92] Black voter turnout declined for the first time in twenty years in the 2016 election, dropping to 59.6 percent after reaching an all-time high of 66.6 percent in 2012, which was a seven-point difference. Black voters were less enthusiastic about Donald Trump and Hillary Clinton than they had been about Barack Obama in 2008 and 2012.[93] Black voter turnout in 2020 was 63%, an increase over 2016, but not quite as high as in 2008.[94]

Black and white Americans are about equal in how much time and effort they devote to activities other than voting. However, they differ in the types of activities in which they engage. White people are more likely to contact public officials and join political organizations. Black citizens are active in election campaigns and social movements.

## Latinxs

The Latinx population in the United States is well established and, according to the U.S. Census Bureau, has grown to over 53 million people from diverse countries of origin. They form a substantial political bloc, although their turnout rate is lower than the national average. Only 49 percent of eligible Latinx voters turned out in the 2008 presidential election, and 48 percent cast a ballot in 2012. Fifty-four percent of Latino voters cast a ballot in 2020 compared to 48 percent in 2016.

FIGURE 8.15
**Reaching Out to Hispanic Voters**
Candidates routinely aim campaign ads at the fast-growing Latinx and Asian American populations. Political websites frequently contain Spanish language content to appeal to Latinx voters.

Source: Photo courtesy of Brian via Flickr: https://www.flickr.com/photos/16176291@N08/2306292301/. (CC BY-SA 2.0); https://creativecommons.org/licenses/by-sa/2.0/.

Latinxs tend to participate in other forms of political activity with less frequency than either white or Black citizens. Latinxs are underrepresented among elected officeholders. While there are an estimated 59 million Latinxs in the U.S. population, only 6,700—or one percent—hold elected office at the local, state, or federal levels.[95] In 2010, three Latinx candidates were elected to top offices, including two governors and one senator, for the first time in history. The 116th Congress sat forty-seven Latinx members—forty House members, four senators, and three territorial delegates. The Pew Hispanic Center provides information and data on Latinx American politics.

Language is one barrier to Latinx participation. However, candidates increasingly recognize that Latinxs constitute a large and growing voting bloc and have begun campaigning in Spanish. During the 2000 presidential election campaign, candidate George W. Bush ran nearly as many ads in Spanish as in English.[96] Since 2008, presidential candidates' websites routinely feature extensive Spanis-language content, as do the websites of a good number of congressional candidates.[97]

## Asian Americans and Pacific Islanders

According to the U.S. Census, Asian Americans and Pacific Islanders are the fastest growing and most diverse ethnic group. Yet their rates of participation are lower than those for other groups. In 2008, 48 percent of Asian Americans turned out to vote.[98] Turnout among this group was down slightly to 47 percent in 2012, and remained low in 2016.[99] Asian American voter turnout was 59% in 2020, marking a ten percentage point increase over 2016.[100] Cultural factors contribute to the lower levels of Asian American and Pacific Islander voting. Almost 75 percent of Asian adults in the United States are immigrants. Some are recent immigrants who still maintain strong ties to their ethnic culture. Asian Americans who have been victims of hate crimes or consider themselves to be part of a deprived group find their way to the polls in greater numbers.[101]

Cultural factors contribute to the lower levels of Asian American and Pacific Islander voting. Almost 75 percent of Asian adults in the United States are immigrants. Some are recent immigrants who still maintain strong ties to their ethnic culture. Asian Americans who have been victims of hate crimes or consider themselves to be part of a deprived group find their way to the polls in greater numbers.[102] As a result of a severe rise in attacks against Asian Americans during the COVID-19 pandemic, the community responded by organizing protests and urging government officials to take action. In 2021, the U.S. Senate passed legislation to strengthen the federal government's ability to address hate crimes.[103]

## Key Takeaways

Who participates in politics depends on a variety of factors, including socioeconomic status, age, gender, and race and ethnicity. Those with the most money, time, and skills are more likely to participate. Older people with higher education and income are the most likely to vote and take part in politics. People who have the least in society, and who are most in need of government assistance, are often the most poorly equipped to take action to improve their lot.

## Exercises

1. Which groups are the least likely to participate in politics? What are the obstacles to participation that these groups face?
2. What effect do you think it has on politics and government that some groups participate more than others? What effect do you think it has on politics and government that there are relatively few women in Congress?

# 8.5 Social Movements

## Learning Objectives

After reading this section, you should be able to answer the following questions:

1. What is a social movement?
2. Why did the civil rights movement form, and how did it work toward its objectives?
3. What were the goals of the women's movement, and how were they achieved?

Thus far our discussion has focused primarily on how and why individuals decide to participate in politics by engaging in activities such as voting, contacting officials, or running for office. There are times when groups of people who are concerned about a particular issue or idea join forces to demand government action. A social movement is formed when large numbers of people organize and mobilize to actively pursue common political objectives.[104]

A social movement has a formal and enduring organizational structure as well as recognized leaders. Movements begin with people who share concerns about long-standing societal problems and believe that their rights and interests are not being adequately represented. They can evolve from grassroots groups into national organizations and even become interest groups that lobby government officials. Social movements can last for months, years, or even decades. The farmworkers' movement was founded in the 1960s by César E. Chávez and still exists today. Its national organization, the United Farm Workers, seeks congressional legislation to guarantee fair wages and treatment of undocumented workers.[105]

Movement participants assume that **collective action**, cooperative activities by groups in pursuit of a common goal, will be more effective in gaining the attention of media and government officials to instigate change than individuals acting on their own. Establishing a communications network to energize participants and mobilize them for action is a key component of a social movement. The digital media have become important organizing tools for social movements. They can use websites, Twitter feeds, social media, text messages, and other platforms to publicize their cause, recruit members, fundraise, and organize events.

**collective action**

Cooperative activities by groups in pursuit of a common goal.

# A Brief History of Social Movements

**abolitionist movement**

A social movement in the mid-1800s that sought to end slavery.

**temperance movement**

A movement that prompted Congress to pass the Eighteenth Amendment in 1919, instituting Prohibition, which forbade the sale or transportation of alcohol. Prohibition was repealed in 1935.

The United States has a long tradition of social movements that have sparked major changes in political processes and government policies. The **abolitionist movement** of the mid-1800s sought to end slavery, an issue that contributed to the outbreak of the Civil War. The **temperance movement**, led by the Anti-Saloon League and the Women's Christian Temperance Union, prompted Congress to pass the Eighteenth Amendment in 1919 prohibiting the sale or transportation of alcohol. Prohibition was repealed in 1935.

Guaranteeing the right to vote to all citizens has been the focus of some of the most important social movements. The Constitution at the time of the founding guaranteed suffrage only to white, male landowners. States placed restrictions on voting based on race, age, gender, religion, and even personal character. All states had dropped the requirement for land ownership by 1344, but constitutional restrictions based on race remained until 1870 and gender until 1920 with the passage of the Nineteenth Amendment to the U.S. Constitution.

**FIGURE 8.16 The Abolitionist Movement**

People, including many women, were involved in the abolitionist movement against slavery in the mid-1800s.

ANTI-SLAVERY MEETING ON THE COMMON.

Source: North Wind Picture Archives / Alamy Stock Photo

## The Civil Rights Movement

**Civil Rights Act of 1964**

Legislation passed by the U.S. Congress with the goal of guaranteeing African Americans equal rights under the law.

The Fifteenth Amendment to the Constitution formally ended race-based limitations on voting in 1870. However, minority citizens were not truly enfranchised until the passage of the **Civil Rights Act of 1964** and the Voting Rights Act of 1965. This legislation was the result of pressure on the government by the civil rights movement.

The civil rights movement emerged in the 1950s in reaction to discrimination against African Americans in Southern states. Segregationist policies placed restrictions on Black citizens' right to vote and violated their basic civil rights in other ways. African Americans were forced to use facilities separate from whites, such as restrooms and water fountains, and to sit at the back of public buses. Black students attended schools that were usually inferior to schools for whites.

United under the Southern Christian Leadership Conference, Black churches formed one foundation of the civil rights movement. Dr. Martin Luther King Jr., one of the movement's leaders, emphasized that nonviolent direct action would be used to expose racial injustices. Civil rights activists boycotted businesses that employed discriminatory practices. They engaged in acts of civil disobedience that disrupted established patterns of daily life. Black people ate at white lunch counters, were arrested, and were jailed. Southern Black people mounted large-scale voter registration drives. In the summer of 1963 alone, over fourteen hundred demonstrations and marches were staged to protest disenfranchisement and other forms of discrimination.

These tactics were designed to attract media attention that would help to galvanize the movement and force political leaders to take notice, and they worked. Politicians perceived that Black voters were becoming powerful and listened to their demands. President John F. Kennedy agreed to sponsor legislation that would ensure Black civil and voting rights, which Congress passed and President Lyndon Johnson signed into law after Kennedy's assassination.

The Black Lives Matter movement has revitalized the quest for civil rights. It began as a series of protests against the shooting of unarmed Black men, often by members of law enforcement. Three women began posting their reactions to the deaths and subsequent legal trials of the shooters using the Twitter hashtag #BlackLivesMatter. The hashtag was first used after George Zimmerman, a member of a neighborhood watch group, was acquitted of killing Trayvon Martin in 2013. The hashtag became widespread after Michael Brown was shot by a police officer in Ferguson, Missouri in 2014. The use of social media helped to focus attention on the issue of police violence against Black citizens. It helped to transform Black Lives Matter from a series of protests into a movement that urges police reform. Activists were able to get their narrative across using social media, which was picked up by the mainstream press.[106] The women who originated the hashtag created the Black Lives Matter network, which has chapters in cities around the country. The network mobilizes large grassroots protests advocating for racial justice. Movement leaders have become involved in mainstream politics, running for local office and writing for established newspapers.[107]

**FIGURE 8.17 Black Lives Matter**
Social media popularized the Black Lives Matter movement, and helped supporters to publicize their message of racial justice.

Source: Joseph Sohm / Shutterstock.com

Widespread protests against systemic racism were sparked by the murder of George Floyd on May 25, 2020. Floyd, a Black man, was murdered by Derek Chauvin, a white police officer who knelt on his neck for nine minutes and twenty-nine seconds until he stopped breathing. Chauvin was later arrested and found guilty of murder by a jury. Outrage over the deaths of Floyd, Breonna Taylor, Daunte Wright, and others by police set in motion the largest social movement in American history. Black Lives Matter protests were held in over 2,000 communities in the United States and sixty countries.[108]

## Enduring Images

### "I Have a Dream"

One of the most enduring, indeed revered, images of the civil rights movement is of Dr. Martin Luther King Jr. addressing a crowd of more than 250,000 people on the Washington Mall from the steps of the Lincoln Memorial. King was joined by thousands of protesters from across the nation participating in the March on Washington for Jobs and Freedom in August 1963.

King delivered the stirring keynote speech extemporaneously. The backdrop of the Lincoln Memorial dramatized the fact that a century after the Emancipation Proclamation had been signed, freeing the slaves, Black people were still crippled by segregation and discrimination. King uttered the famous words, "I have a dream that one day this nation will rise up and live out the true meaning of its creed: 'We hold these truths to be self-evident, that all men are created equal.'"[109]

Dr. Martin Luther King Jr. giving the "I Have a Dream" speech. The image of Dr. Martin Luther King Jr. addressing the crowd on the National Mall endures as a symbol of the civil rights movement.

Source: Associated Press

The speech was covered on television in its entirety and received widespread attention in newspapers and magazines. The image of King, arm extended and head held high, addressing the crowd marks a memorable moment in our nation's history and has come to symbolize the civil rights movement and its leaders. It has been replicated in history books and popular films, like *Forrest Gump*.

Video of the "I Have a Dream Speech" delivered by Dr. Martin Luther King Jr. in August 1963.

View in the online reader

## The Women's Movement

Throughout much of American history, a woman was considered to be an extension of her husband and, as such, did not need her own vote. Women were not granted the constitutional right to vote until 1920, but they were politically involved. Women formed charitable institutions to fight poverty and were active in reform movements, such as protecting children working in factories and textile mills. They participated in abolitionist groups that formed in the 1830s to achieve freedom for slaves. Lucretia Mott and Elizabeth Cady Stanton were denied voting rights as delegates to a world-wide antislavery convention in London. This event compelled them to organize the **women's movement** in the United States, with the primary goal of gaining the fundamental right to vote.[110]

**women's movement**

A social movement that began with the goal of seeking women's suffrage and extended to other aspects of women's equality.

Women acquired organizing skills that were central to their movement from their involvement with other causes. They lobbied Congress and state legislatures, spoke passionately in public forums, held rallies, circulated petitions, and even went to jail for their beliefs. The Nineteenth Amendment, ratified in 1920, granted women suffrage.

**FIGURE 8.18 Suffragettes Fighting for the Right to Vote**

Women who had been active in the movement to abolish slavery had thought that demands for women's equality would be next on the agenda. As it turned out, they had to pressure for another fifty years before the Nineteenth Amendment guaranteed the right of women to vote.

Source: American Press Association, *Youngest parader in New York City suffragist parade*. New York, ca. 1912. Via Library of Congress: https://www.loc.gov/item/97500068/.

**Women's Educational Equity Act**

Legislation passed by the U.S. Congress to guarantee women the same educational opportunities as men, including Title IX, which requires schools to remove barriers to females' full participation in sports.

Even as women won the legal right to vote, barriers to their participation remained. States made registration difficult. Some women were discouraged from voting by their husbands and friends.[111] From the 1960s to the 1980s, the women's movement was revitalized around the basic goals of achieving equal rights for women in politics, business, organized religion, and sports. Women fought for equal pay for equal work, for women to be ordained as clergy, and for girls to have the same opportunities to compete in school sports as boys. They were successful in achieving many of their goals. Congress passed the **Women's Educational Equity Act** in 1974, which included Title IX, requiring schools to remove barriers to females' full participation in sports.

Today, there is no longer a single mass women's movement. Instead, there are many organizations working on a wide range of issues related to women, such as health care, social justice, and domestic violence.[112] They make use of digital communication to reach out to the public and to support one another. The National Organization for Women (NOW), which takes action on issues of women's equality, provides information and opportunities for participation online. Through its website "Take Back The Night" it promotes action against domestic violence, sexual assault, and all forms of sexual abuse by providing an online guide to organizing events, making T-shirts and posters available, and offering access to legal assistance.[113]

## A Society of Many Movements

**Americans with Disabilities Act**

Legislation passed by the U.S. Congress guaranteeing that no individual will be excluded from the benefits of any program or activity that receives public funding because of a handicap.

**Christian Right**

A loose coalition of evangelical Protestants who share common ideological beliefs, such as support for traditional marriage and a pro-life position on abortion.

Following in the footsteps of the civil rights movement and the women's movement, other movements have formed in reaction to policies that disadvantage particular segments of society. The LGBTQ+ rights movement has succeeded in having policies enacted to fight discrimination in the workplace, increase access to medical benefits, and stop bullying in schools. The movement also has been able to mobilize support for same-sex marriage, which led to the Supreme Court's declaring same-sex marriage legal in all fifty states and the District of Columbia in the 2015 case of *Obergefell v. Hodges*. Americans with disabilities formed a movement that resulted in the passage of the **Americans with Disabilities Act** of 1990, guaranteeing that no individual will be excluded from the benefits of any program or activity receiving public funding because of a handicap.

Some social movements have become a force in the political mainstream. The **Christian Right** emerged in the 1980s as groups of evangelical Protestants found common ground in shared ideological beliefs, including support for marriage and traditional two-parent families, a pro-life position on abortion, local control of education and home schooling, and the protection of young people from pornography. It has become aligned with the conservative wing of the Republican Party.[114]

Social movements can employ tactics to reverse the law or to challenge outcomes using extralegal, illegal, and even violent means. Antiabortion activists who seek legislation making abortions illegal have bombed clinics and attacked and even killed doctors who perform abortions. Self-described "ecoterrorists" have set fire to housing developments that they see as contributing to suburban sprawl.

Some movements invoke the Constitution as a justification for violent action against the government. The militia movement believes it must preserve the Constitution's Second Amendment right to keep and bear arms. Members conduct regular drills in military dress during which they fire high-powered weapons. The movement uses an elaborate system of websites and independent radio stations to present their position and communicate with one another.

# Insurrection

On January 6, 2021, a mob stormed the U.S. Capitol as members of Congress met to certify Joe Biden as the winner of the 2020 presidential election. The action constituted an **insurrection**, a violent uprising against the government, as opposed to a legitimate social movement advocating for societal change. A crowd of about 2,000 people had gathered for a "Rally to Save America," prompted by Donald Trump's false allegations that the election had been stolen. They were mobilized by a call on Twitter to #StopTheSteal that had gone viral and was posted by Trump supporters.[115] The participants in the attack on the Capitol included a range of groups, including pro-Trump activists and media outlets, members of the Proud Boys and Boogaloo Bois, anti-government groups that promote violence, unsanctioned militias from across the country, and believers in the **QAnon** conspiracy theory.[116]

**insurrection**

A violent uprising against a government or authority.

**QAnon**

An entirely unfounded theory that Donald Trump is waging a secret war against Satan-worshipping pedophiles in government, business, and the media who will be arrested and executed.

Stoked by a speech by Trump, members of the crowd marched to the Capitol and forcibly gained entrance to the building, smashing windows and doors while overpowering police. Some were armed with weapons and bear spray. They disrupted the congressional proceedings as members of the House and Senate took cover, fearing for their lives. The insurrectionists broke into the offices of prominent leaders, such as Speaker of the House Nancy Pelosi, and destroyed public property. After several hours, law enforcement secured the Capitol and Congress returned to the business of certifying the election. In the end, five people were killed, and several police officers were seriously wounded in the riot. More than four hundred people who took part in the insurrection were arrested. The U.S. Justice Department launched an investigation into the riot.[117]

Images of the Capitol insurrection taken by a reporter who was on the scene.

View in the online reader

# Social Movements and the Media

Social movements rely on media attention to gain public support, recruit members, and present their agendas to political leaders. The media can shape the public's views about particular movements and the causes they represent. Movement leaders attempt to gain control over their message through interviews and staged events.

The press can influence a movement's success or failure. The 1960s student movement provides an illustration. At first the student movement was virtually ignored by the media. As the Vietnam War escalated, students expressed their opposition through demonstrations and sit-ins on college campuses. Media coverage was abundant and favorable. News stories about student activists along with graphic televised images of the war helped attract new members to the antiwar effort. Press coverage became more negative as government officials who opposed the antiwar movement emerged and were featured in media reports. Negative coverage galvanized the movement, as supporters rallied to defend the cause. It also radicalized the movement, as members pursued more militant tactics to ensure coverage. The bombing of a building at the University of Wisconsin, which killed a graduate student, caused people to lose sympathy with the activists. Journalists grew tired of the story and portrayed the movement as factionalized into different groups with rival leaders. The student movement eventually fell apart.[118]

Social media have become important tools for social movements. People can harness the power of their social networks to mobilize their friends and associates. Today, social media contributes as much to igniting and sustaining social movements as television news did in earlier times.[119] Research by the Annenberg School for Communication showed that a core group of activists uses social media to energize people to take action, organize movements, and communicate during protests. Messages and images posted on social media can provide strong impetus for political action. Video of police officer Derek Chauvin kneeling on the neck of George Floyd circulated widely through social media and became a catalyst for Black Lives Matter protests. People on the periphery of social movements can show their support by liking and sharing messages posted by activists even if they don't take to the streets.[120]

## Key Takeaways

America has a long tradition of social movements wherein people work collectively for a cause. Movements have sought equal rights for women, members of racial and ethnic groups, and LGBTQ+ citizens. They have worked to create better opportunities for people with disabilities and senior citizens. Social movements rely on collective action that brings individua's together to work toward a joint goal. Insurrections aimed at overthrowing the government are not legitimate social movements. The media are important for attracting attention to these efforts, which can increase participation in the movement and force political leaders to take notice. Social movements use websites and social media to keep their supporters informed and mobilized.

## Exercises

1. What were the goals of the civil rights movement? How did civil rights activists work to achieve them?
2. What were the original goals of the women's movement? How has the women's movement evolved since then?
3. What are the most important social movements today? How are these different movements portrayed in the media?
4. How do social movements use social media?

# 8.6 Participation, Voting, and Social Movements in the Information Age

## Learning Objectives

After reading this section, you should be able to answer the following questions:

1. In what ways can people participate in government through the media?
2. What influence do the media have on political participation?

The media are central to political participation and mobilization. The public uses all forms of media to express opinions, contact leaders, and engage in politics. Journalists, pollsters, and political consultants create media depictions of peoples' participation and inactivity. These depictions shape the public's perceptions about political participation. Individuals may be prompted to engage in public affairs when they view media accounts of people like themselves taking part. The public can participate in politics through media, especially online, on digital platforms, and through social media.

## Media Interactions

The interaction between media and political participation is complicated. Media can encourage or discourage participation by drawing attention to political leaders, events, and issues. New media, in particular, not only allow people to monitor politics but also provide them with options for active engagement.

## Participation through Media

Americans rely on newspapers, television, radio, and digital media to stay informed about politics. Media connect people to political events, such as election campaigns and rallies on the National Mall in Washington, DC, to which they may have limited direct, personal contact. People also can actively take part in politics through media. Television and radio call-in talk shows and internet chat rooms accommodate political discussion between the public, political activists, government leaders, and the press.

Televised town meetings allow the public to ask questions directly of politicians and journalists. CNN regularly holds televised town meetings with political leaders, such as President Joe Biden and Vice President Kamala Harris, that they make available as podcasts. During election campaigns, televised presidential debates that allow voters, rather than journalists, to ask questions draw the largest audiences. People see others like themselves taking part in political life through media depictions, which can make them more likely to become engaged. Social media can make it easier for people to participate by spreading awareness of issues and informing people about political events. The Black Lives Matter movement was able to get supporters to participate in its protest activities through its social media networks.

## Media Events and Civic Action

Devastating events extensively reported in the media can spark people to organize and lobby for policy change. National media attention can prompt leaders to take activists seriously. Coverage of the 1999 shootings at Colorado's Columbine High School, which left fifteen people dead, rallied support for tougher gun-control legislation. In the wake of the Columbine shootings, students from across the state formed SAFE—Sane Alternatives to the Firearms Epidemic. A ninety-person SAFE delegation traveled in August 1999 to Washington, DC, where they met with President Bill Clinton, Vice President Al Gore, and House Minority Leader Richard Gephardt (D-MO), who pledged support for the group's position advocating tougher gun-control laws. In a made-for-media moment on the steps of Capitol Hill, the students grilled members of Congress who opposed tough gun-control legislation.[121] Students continued to take action against gun violence following the mass shooting at Marjory Stoneman Douglas High School in Parkland, Florida, in 2018. The students gained nationwide media attention, even making the cover of *Time* magazine, for their anti–gun violence movement, March for Our Lives. The Parkland students used their media fame to organize for racial justice and equality.[122]

### Link

**March for Our Lives**

March for Our Lives began as an anti–gun violence movement and has branched out to promote other causes, including racial justice. You can learn more here.

Digital media have made it easier for people to bring public attention to issues and causes. Sites that host online petitions have become prevalent. Change.org allows people to start petitions and appeal for signatures using email and social media. Petitions have been circulated for issues as diverse as calling for improvements in health-care coverage, requesting that police investigate criminal behavior, and advocating that the United States take action in international matters. Some online petitions have been effective in getting legislation passed. As of 2021, the site had attracted over 440,116,060 million people.

## e-Activism

New information technologies provide additional options for people who wish to take part in acts of civil disobedience and protest. Digital tools, such as websites, blogs, email lists, and social network sites, can be used to organize people online. These tools can be used to spread information, recruit participants, and provide logistical information about events. People who are geographically dispersed can share stories and strategies that provide incentives for engagement.

**smart mobs**

Acts of civil disobedience or protest organized through digital communication technology.

**Smart mobs** are groups of people who are organized through networks facilitated by computers and smartphones. Smart mobs are more spontaneous, have less structure, and exist for a shorter time period than social movements. Antiglobalization and environmental activists protesting the World Trade Organization Ministerial Conference in Seattle in 1999 used smart-mob tactics to coordinate their efforts. Over time, the use of social media for political activism has become more sophisticated. It is now commonplace for demonstrations to be organized as smart mobs. Protest guides providing strategies to activists, such as how to post images and videos online so that they go viral, are shared over Twitter and Instagram.[123]

# Activism or Slacktivism?

**slacktivism**

Slacktivism refers to actions people take on social media in support of a cause that require little time or effort, such as "liking" a political blog post.

Some people express concern that social media actually depresses political participation by promoting slacktivism instead of activism. **Slacktivism** refers to actions people take on social media in support of a cause that require little time or effort. "Feel-good" measures, such as sharing a political post, have been referred to as "armchair activism," as a person's time commitment may be no more than the few seconds it takes to click a "like" button. However, social media can drum up support for a cause in a way that makes a difference.

The Ice Bucket Challenge that was popularized on social media in 2014 was designed to bring attention to ALS, better known as Lou Gehrig's Disease. The idea originated with Pete Frates, the former captain of Boston College's baseball team who was diagnosed with the disease at a young age. Frates doused himself with a bucket of freezing cold water, and challenged others to post pictures of themselves taking the challenge. Those who chickened out were expected to donate money for ALS research. The challenge went viral on Facebook, and received attention from sports, entertainment, and political celebrities who took the challenge. Many people who completed the challenge also contributed to the fund, which raised $115 million in its first year and had generated $250 million in three years. The funds went to good use, as a global team of researchers made a breakthrough in identifying a gene related to ALS, which is a step in the direction of finding a cure.[124]

Celebrities take the Ice Bucket Challenge to raise awareness of and funds to fight ALS, a degenerative disease with no known cure.

View in the online reader

# Media Depictions

This chapter opened with an anecdote that illustrates a dominant theme of media coverage—that the public does not participate very much in politics, especially voting. While such depictions are not entirely inaccurate, the media's emphasis on the disengaged public is misleading. Voter turnout in presidential elections has been on the rise. Americans are contacting public officials in record numbers, joining issue organizations, and participating in community service activities. Reporting that emphasizes the public's disengagement can discourage people from taking part in politics. On the other hand, reports that highlight the ways that people participate can spark political interest and engagement.

## Media Stereotypes and Political Participation

The media employ a number of stock frames in their stories about political participation. These frames generate stereotypes of the public's participation that are at best partially accurate. Stereotypes assume that all members of the group share the same political orientations, but often this is not the case.

The media use stereotypes in their campaign reporting to characterize groups of voters. Media attention focused on the "angry voter" for almost two decades beginning in the 1980s. At first, it was "angry white males," who emerged in response to political correctness. By the 1990s, the focus had shifted to "soccer moms," who were portrayed as being disgusted with politics. Yet studies showed that most white males and soccer moms were not upset about politics and that they did not vote as a bloc. During the 2008 campaign, the press highlighted McCain and Obama's outreach to "NASCAR dads," who were portrayed as a rowdy, beer-guzzling crowd with lower levels of education and income than other voters. In fact, NASCAR fans' socioeconomic status mirrors that of the general population, and they hail from all walks of life.[125] "Dot.com moms" emerged as a stereotypical group that was courted by candidates in the 2012 presidential campaign. These moms not only took their kids to soccer practice, but also were sophisticated users of digital media who were influential in their extensive social networks. The "angry voter" resurfaced as a characterization of the American electorate that was fueled by "political rage" in the 2020 presidential contest.[126]

**FIGURE 8.19 Searching for Swing Voters**

The news media often try to identify a swing voter group that will be key to an election campaign. Sometimes, their choices say more about the demographics of their audiences (or even of their reporters) than about the group's impact on the election.

Sources: Rido/Shutterstock.com; SeventyFour/Shutterstock.com; Aaron of L.A. Photography/Shutterstock.com

Stereotyping has implications for political participation and policymaking. Stereotypes can form the basis of campaign and policy agendas. The media give the impression that the votes and opinions of "angry white males" who saw taxes and defense as priority issues, and "soccer moms" who were concerned about child care and education, count more than those of other people. As a result, candidates and political leaders may direct more of their attention toward this issue. Media stereotypes legitimate the ideas and causes of particular groups, while discounting those of others.[127]

## Civic Education

### Parkland Students Take Action After Shooting

On February 14, 2018—Valentine's Day—a former student armed with an AR-15 assault rifle entered Marjory Stoneman Douglas High School in Parkland, Florida, and opened fire. Terrified students and faculty sheltered in classrooms while the young gunman made his way down the corridors, firing his weapon again and again. Students used their cell phones to document the shooting, creating a compelling and lasting record of the carnage. In the end, fourteen students and three teachers were killed in the rampage.

Immediately after the shooting, Parkland students began organizing to advocate against gun violence and school safety. The students made it clear they were tired of the "thoughts and prayers" typically offered by politicians following a school shooting. Emma Gonzalez, a Parkland senior who became one of the key faces of the Parkland movement, held up her AP government notes at a rally in Florida shortly after the shooting. She spoke about the need to put the lessons learned in class into action.

March for Our Lives held a rally on March 24, 2018, to protest gun violence.

Source: Rob Crandall/Shutterstock.com.

> *Instead of worrying about our AP Gov chapter 16 test, we have to be studying our notes to make sure that our arguments based on politics and political history are watertight. The students at this school have been having debates on guns for what feels like our entire lives. AP Gov had about three debates this year. Some discussions on the subject even occurred during the shooting while students were hiding in the closets. The people involved right now, those who were there, those posting, those tweeting, those doing interviews and talking to people, are being listened to for what feels like the very first time on this topic that has come up over 1,000 times in the past four years alone (CNN Staff, 2018).*[128]

Unlike survivors of previous school shootings, the Parkland students were able to command extensive media coverage. They appeared on cable TV programs, including CNN, MSNBC, and Fox News. These media-savvy students understood how to leverage social media to support their goals. Consequently, they kept the story and their proposals to keep schools safe through more effective gun ownership regulations in the media spotlight for weeks. Parkland students tweeted about their fallen classmates, shared memes, jokes, video clips, and news stories to their over 2 million followers. Moreover, they publicly challenged political leaders, such as Secretary of Education Betsy DeVos, Senator Marco Rubio (R-FL), and National Rifle Association spokesperson Dana Loesch, to address their concerns in meaningful ways (Bromwich, 2018).[129]

Six weeks after the shooting, the Parkland students organized the March for Our Lives. Hundreds of thousands of people packed the streets in Washington, DC, and cities across the country to protest gun violence and demand action. The students shared the stage not only with celebrities, but also ordinary people whose lives had been changed by gun violence. They successfully emphasized the fact that shootings affect people from all walks of life. Nine-year-old Yolanda Renee King, the granddaughter of Martin Luther King Jr. and Coretta Scott King, led the crowd in a chant about the power of younger generations to make change. The march concluded with Emma Gonzalez standing silent for six minutes and twenty-four seconds—the time it took for the gunman to wage his deadly attack at Parkland (Garber, 2018).[130]

Parkland students were successful in raising awareness of gun violence in schools and even succeeded in persuading some leaders to take up their cause. For example, Florida Governor Rick Scott, a long-time supporter of the pro-gun National Rifle Association, signed a $400 million school safety bill that tightened gun regulations in the state. Governor Scott's actions were made over the objection of the NRA (Scherer, 2018).[131]

The students also learned firsthand about difficult aspects of political activism. For example, critics lashed out at David Hogg and Emma Gonzalez, prominent Parkland student activists. Hogg was publicly ridiculed for not being accepted at his top choices for college (Scott, 2018),[132] and a faked photo of Gonzalez tearing up the Constitution was widely circulated on the internet (see here). These students' irreverent statements have included attacks on older generations of Americans for their lack of action regarding gun safety. However, it is that same generation whose support and votes the movement needs to be successful, at least in the short run.

# Media Consequences

**virtuous circle**

Political interest and engagement stimulated by the media.

**spiral of cynicism**

A cycle of distrust of government and politics created by the media's scandal-ridden coverage of government and politics.

Scholars disagree about the effects of mass media on political participation. Some argue that the media serve the public by providing information that stimulates political interest, furthers information gathering, and encourages participation. The result is a "**virtuous circle**" that promotes political engagement.[133] During presidential elections, the media stimulates public interest with its campaign coverage that incorporates voters' voices through its reports and social media channels. Others contend that the media's scandal-ridden and negative coverage of government and politics creates a "**spiral of cynicism**" by generating public distrust, discouraging interest, eroding attention to the news, and ultimately hindering participation.[134] Public opinion about government fell in the wake of the nonstop coverage of President Bill Clinton's affair with white House intern Monica Lewinsky. Constant coverage of the bickering and polarized politics in Congress has contributed to very low public assessments of the institution. Neither of these perspectives alone tells the full story, as both positive and negative media effects can result, depending on coverage.

The media, in some instances, may have no effect on participation. People may not pay attention to political media or take media messages seriously. They assess politics on the basis of their own personal experiences or those of their families and friends. The decision to participate is related to their membership in groups and social networks, being contacted by a political party or interest group, or a sense of civic duty and efficacy. Thus, some individuals' participation or inaction is influenced by their personal realities rather than mediated realities.

**bowl alone**

The idea, put forward by political scientist Robert Putnam, that television is making Americans a nation of watchers rather than doers.

Some scholars contend that the media create a situation wherein passive monitoring of politics substitutes for real action.[135] People spend time watching television instead of participating in community activities, such as holding local office or volunteering at a homeless shelter. Political scientist Robert Putnam argues that television may be making the United States a nation of watchers rather than doers who are more likely to "**bowl alone**" than to work with others.[136]

## Key Takeaways

The media offer opportunities for political participation. People can engage using the internet to express their opinions, share information, organize political events, support candidates, and encourage others to get involved. Digital media offer constantly expanding possibilities for taking political action.

The media's relationship to political participation is complex. The press can stimulate or depress political activity, or it may have no effect on it. Media stereotypes of groups and their political participation can influence the amount of attention these groups get from political leaders. While some of the traditional institutions that mobilize people, such as political parties, have become less of a force, the mass media's potential to have an impact on political action has grown.

## Exercises

1. How do people use the media to get involved in politics and make their opinions heard? What opportunities do new media create for people to become involved?
2. In your opinion, is the way the media covers politics more likely to encourage people to become involved in politics or more likely to turn them off from politics? Why do you think that is?

## Civic Education

### A New Generation of Civil Rights Activists

The historic election of an African American president, Barack Obama, energized a new generation of civil rights activists. Young people have become active in organizations whose membership was aging and ranks dwindling. They have sought to keep the momentum of the election alive by organizing around issues, taking part in community affairs, and seeking positions in government and public affairs.

The NAACP convention offers young people the opportunity to learn about issues related to civil rights.

Source: Associated Press

The National Association for the Advancement of Colored People (NAACP) was founded in 1909 and is the nation's largest grassroots civil rights organization. The average age of NAACP members is fifty-five years old. The NAACP sought to revitalize its mission and membership on the coattails of the Obama election by ramping up its youth movement. The organization has seen a rise in the number of chapters on college campuses throughout the country. Young people also have activated more than six hundred "youth units" to carry out a campaign to increase college access and affordability.

Young civil rights leaders are working to change injustices faced by the LGBTQ+ community, women, immigrants, and the Muslim community. They are seeking quality public education for students of color, energizing the Black youth vote, and working to improve immigration policy.[137] Demar Lamont Roberts, a graduate of South Carolina State University in his twenties, became active in the NAACP to experience "the camaraderie, seeing civil rights persons that have come before me and paved the way for me."[138] He joined the leadership of the NAACP National Youth Work Committee, which is mobilizing around voting rights and other issues. Roberts used the social messaging platform Twitter to keep friends and associates informed about the convention. The NAACP website provides information about the organization's history, current news, and ways to become involved.

# 8.7 Recommended Reading

Abrams, Stacey. *Our Time Is Now: Power, Purpose, and the Fight for a Fair America*. New York: Henry Holt and Company, 2020. Abrams details the disenfranchisement and suppression of voters, especially voters of color, and provides a roadmap for countering these trends.

Conway, M. Margaret. *Political Participation in the United States*, 3rd ed. Washington, DC: CQ Press, 2000. An overview of trends in political participation.

Foot, Kirsten A, and Steven M. Schneider. *Web Campaigning*. Cambridge, MA: MIT Press, 2006. An examination of the evolution of the use of the internet in election campaigns.

Frantzich, Stephen E. *Citizen Democracy*. Lanham, MD: Rowman & Littlefield, 1999. A series of compelling stories of how average people have made a difference through political participation.

Freeman, Jo, and Victoria Johnson, eds. *Waves of Protest*. Lanham, MD: Rowman & Littlefield, 1999. A collection of articles on a variety of protest movements, including AIDS activism, the fight for the rights of people with disabilities, and the women's movement of the 1990s.

Hindman, Matthew. *The Myth of Digital Democracy*. Princeton, NJ: Princeton University Press, 2008. Hindman discusses the common contention that the internet has made political participation more accessible to the general public and finds instead that online politics are dominated by a new, technologically savvy elite.

Jacobs, Lawrence R., Fay Lomax Cook, and Michael X. Delli Carpini. *Talking Together: Public Deliberation and Political Participation in America*. Chicago: University of Chicago Press, 2009. The authors examine how and why citizens engage in political conversations that can contribute to political participation.

Jaffe, Sarah. *Necessary Trouble: Americans in Revolt*. New York: Nation Books, 2016. This book discusses twenty-first century social movements, such as the Tea Party, Occupy Wall Street, and Black Lives Matter.

Johnson, Thomas J., Carol E. Hays, and Scott P. Hays, eds. *Engaging the Public*. Lanham, MD: Rowman & Littlefield, 1998. Scholars and journalists discuss ways in which government and the mass media can stimulate political activity.

Martyn Barrett and Dimitra Pachi. *Youth Civic and Political Engagement*. New York: Routledge, 2019. An overview of the ways that young people participate in politics and civic life in the digital age.

Perrin, Andrew J. *American Democracy: From Tocqueville to Town Halls to Twitter*. Malden, MA: Polity Press, 2014. Provides a theoretical and historical discussion of American democracy and participation, updated for the information age.

Piven, Frances Fox, and Richard A. Cloward. *Why Americans Still Don't Vote*. Boston: Beacon Press, 2000. Discusses historical trends in voter turnout and provides explanations for nonvoting.

Schier, Stephen E. *By Invitation Only: The Rise of Exclusive Politics in the United States*. Pittsburgh, PA: University of Pittsburgh Press, 2000. Contends that American political participation falls short of democratic ideals because political parties, interest groups, and campaigns target small, exclusive segments of the population with their activation strategies. The importance of money for successful mobilization efforts is emphasized.

Schudson, Michael. *The Good Citizen*. New York: Free Press, 1998. Schudson provides a historical overview of civic participation in the United States, including a discussion of the part played by mass media at each stage of development.

Skocpol, Theda, and Morris P. Fiorina, eds. *Civic Engagement in American Democracy*. Washington, DC: Brookings, 1999. A collection of essays that attempts to sort out the reasons for and implications of Americans' disappointing levels of political participation.

Taylor, D'Angelo S. and Robert J. Flinn, *A Political Life: Black Culture, Civic Engagement, Education, and Hope*. D'Angelo S. Taylor Publisher, 2016. A perspective on Black political participation from both an academic and a personal perspective.

# 8.8 Recommended Viewing

*All In: The Fight for Democracy* (2020). A documentary where Stacey Abrams explores the history and present-day mechanism of voter suppression, its effect on voters, and ways of combatting these trends.

*Election* (1999). A dark comedy, starring Reese Witherspoon and Matthew Broderick, about a high school election that goes awry.

*Eyes on the Prize* (1988). An award-winning documentary about the civil rights movement.

*Forrest Gump* (1994). Tom Hanks stars in this film about a simple man who witnesses historical events between the 1950s and the 1980s, including social movements and protests.

*John Lewis: Good Trouble* (2020). A documentary chronicling the life of the late John Lewis from his years in the civil rights movement to his career as a member of the House of Representatives.

*Seeing Red* (1984). A documentary film about the political dedication, activities, lives, and fates of American communists.

*This Is What Democracy Looks Like* (1999). A documentary covering the World Trade Organization (WTO) protests in 1999.

*Unfinished Symphony* (2001). A documentary film that focuses on a three-day protest march in 1971 tracing the path of Paul Revere's 1775 ride by newly returned veterans of the Vietnam War, including a young John Kerry, who became a U.S. senator.

*The War at Home* (1980). This documentary film chronicles the evolution of the Vietnam protest movement focusing on the college town of Madison, Wisconsin, in 1969.

*The World's Civil Rights Movement* (2016). An examination of civil rights movements around the world from the 1950 through Occupy Wall Street and Black Lives Matter.

# Endnotes


1. Dorman, John L. Dorman, "Young Voters in the US Turned Out in Record Numbers in 2020, Powering Bident's Presidential Victory," Business Insider, November 22, 2020. https://www.businessinsider.com/young-voters-record-voting-turnout-biden-trump-presidential-election-2020-11.
2. Poppy Noor, "Youth Voting Turnout Surges in the 2020 U.S. Election," The Guardian, November 9, 2020. https://www.theguardian.com/us-news/2020/nov/09/youth-turnout-us-election-biden-victory-young-voters.
3. Abigail Johnson Hess, "The 2020 Election Shows Gen Z's Voting Power for Years to Come," CNBC.com, November 18, 2020. https://www.cnbc.com/2020/11/18/the-2020-election-shows-gen-zs-voting-power-for-years-to-come.html.
4. Noah Pransky, "How Record-Setting Youth Turnout in the 2020 Election Surpassed 2016 Levels," LX News, NBC Universal, November 10, 2020. https://www.lx.com/politics/how-record-setting-youth-turnout-in-the-2020-election-blew-away-expectations/24200/.
5. Siobahn McDonough, "2004 Not the Breakout Year for Youth Vote After All," *Associated Press*, November 2, 2004.
6. Center for Information & Research on Civic Learning and Engagement (CIRCLE), "Youth Voting," http://www.civicyouth.org/?page_id=241#1.
7. Diana Owen, *Youth Voting and the Media* (Washington, DC: George Washington University Graduate School of Political Management, 2006).
8. Renee Montagne, "How Engaged Are Young Voters In The 2016 Presidential Election?" NPR, February 3, 2016.
9. Allstate/National Journal, *Heartland Monitor Survey*, April 2014. Accessed June 17th, 2014: http://www.nationaljournal.com/next-economy/big-questions/only-one-percent-of-americans-are-really-politically-active-20140509; Michael Schudson, *The Good Citizen* (New York: Free Press, 1998).
10. Steven J. Rosenstone and John Mark Hansen, *Mobilization, Participation, and Democracy in America* (New York: Macmillan, 1993), 4.
11. Sidney Verba, Kay Lehman Schlozman, and Henry E. Brady, *Voice and Equality: Civic Voluntarism in American Politics* (Cambridge, MA: Harvard University Press, 1995).
12. Lester W. Milbrath and M. L. Goel, *Political Participation*, 2nd ed. (Chicago: Rand McNally, 1977).
13. Pew Research Center, *Civic Engagement in the Digital Age*. Report. (Washington, DC: Pew Research Center, 2013).media/Files/Reports/2013/PIP CivicEngagementintheDigitalAge.pdf.
14. Working Group on Universal Voting, Lift Every Voice: The Urgency of Universal Civic Duty Voting." *The Brookings Institution* and The Ash Center for Governance and Innovation, Harvard Kennedy School, July 20, 2020. https://www.brookings.edu/research/lift-every-voice-the-urgency-of-universal-civic-duty-voting.
15. United States Census Bureau, *Voting and Registration in the Election of November 2016* (Washington, DC: U.S. Department of Commerce, 2017). https://census.gov/data/tables/time-series/demo/voting-and-registration/p20-580.html.
16. Drew DeSilver, "Turnout Soared in 2020 as Nearly Two-thirds of Eligible U.S. Voters Cast Ballots for President," Facttank: News in the Numbers. Pew Research Center, January 28, 2021.
17. John Gramlich, "What the 2020 Electorate Looks Like by Party, Race and Ethnicity, Age, Education, and Religion," Facttank: News in the Numbers. Pew Research Center, October 26, 2020.
18. Jennifer Baik, "APIA Vote Celebrates Record-Breaking Asian American and Pacific Islander Voter Turnout Amidst Presidential Election," Asian and Pacific Islander American Vote, November 13, 2020. https://www.apiavote.org/press/apiavote-celebrates-record-breaking-asian-american-and-pacific-islander-voter-turnout-amidst.
19. Raymond E. Wolfinger and Steven J. Rosenstone, *Who Votes?* (New Haven, CT: Yale University Press, 1980).
20. "The Campaign: Rockers and Rappers," *The Economist*, June 20, 1993, 25.
21. National Conference of State Legislatures, "Online Voter Registration," January 31, 2017. http://www.ncsl.org/research/elections-and-campaigns/electronic-or-online-voter-registration.aspx.
22. Van R. Newkirk II, "Voter Suppression Is Warping Democracy," *The Atlantic*, July 17, 2018. https://www.theatlantic.com/politics/archive/2018/07/poll-prri-voter-suppression/565355/ Joshua Clark, "Widening the Lens on Voter Suppression." Research Brief. Berkeley, CA: Haas Institute for a Fair and Inclusive Society at UC Berkeley, July 2018. https://haasinstitute.berkeley.edu/sites/default/files/haas_institute_wideningthelensonvotersuppression_july2018_publish.pdf.
23. Brennan Center for Justice, "Voting Laws Roundup 2020," December 8, 2020. https://www.brennancenter.org/our-work/research-reports/voting-laws-roundup-2020-0.
24. Amy Gardner, Kate Rabinowitz, and Harry Stevens, "How GOP-backed Voting Measures Could Create Hurdles for Tens of Millions of Voters," The Washington Post, March 11, 2021. https://www.washingtonpost.com/politics/interactive/2021/voting-restrictions-republicans-states/.
25. Young Mie Kim, "Voter Suppression Has Gone Digital," Brennan Center for Justice, November 20, 2018. https://www.brennancenter.org/blog/voter-suppression-has-gone-digital.
26. Astead W. Herndon and Trip Gabriel. "Showdown in Georgia Governor's Race Reflects a Larger Fight Over Voting Rights," *The New York Times*, October 15, 2018. https://www.nytimes.com/2018/10/15/us/politics/georgia-abrams-kemp-voting.html.
27. Sarah Polus. "Stacey Abrams: Fighting Voter Suppression 'Changed the Trajectory of the Nation," *The Hill*, November 10, 2020. https://thehill.com/homenews/state-watch/525345-stacey-abrams-fighting-voter-suppression-changed-the-trajectory-of-the.
28. Maya King, "How Stacey Abrams and Her Band of Believers Turned Georgia Blue," *Politico*, November 8, 2020. https://www.politico.com/news/2020/11/08/stacey-abrams-believers-georgia-blue-434985.
29. Nick Corasaniti and Reid J. Epstein, "What Georgia's Voting Law Really Does," The New York Times, April 2, 2021. https://www.nytimes.com/2021/04/02/us/politics/georgia-voting-law-annotated.html.
30. Chris Uggen, Ryan Larson, Sarah Shannon, and Arleth Pulido-Nava, "Locked Out 2020: Estimates of People Denied Voting Rights Due to a Felony Conviction," The Sentencing Project, October 30, 2020. https://www.sentencingproject.org/publications/locked-out-2020-estimates-of-people-denied-voting-rights-due-to-a-felony-conviction/.
31. Human Rights Watch, *Felony Disenfranchisement* (Washington, DC: The Sentencing Project, 2017). http://www.sentencingproject.org/issues/felony-disenfranchisement/.
32. Steven J. Rosenstone and John Mark Hansen, *Mobilization, Participation, and Democracy in America* (New York: Macmillan Publishing Company, 1993), 1.
33. Frances Fox Piven and Richard A. Cloward, *Why Americans Still Don't Vote* (Boston: Beacon Press, 2000).
34. Michael McDonald, "Voter Turnout," *United States Election Project*, http://elections.gmu.edu/voter_turnout.htm; James M. Lindsay, "The 2020 Election by the Numbers," Council on Foreign Relations, December 15, 2020. https://www.cfr.org/blog/2020-election-numbers.
35. James M. Lindsay, "The 2020 Election by the Numbers," *Council on Foreign Relations*, December 15, 2020. https://www.cfr.org/blog/2020-election-numbers.
36. Circle Staff, Young Voters in the 2016 General Election (Boston, MA: Johnathan M. Tisch College of Civic Life at Tufts University, 2017).
37. "Youth Voting in 2020," CIRCLE, Tufts University, April 30, 2021. https://circle.tufts.edu/.
38. Lili Pike, "Why So Many Young People Showed Up on Election Day," Vox, November 7, 2020.
39. U.S. Census Bureau, "Reported Voter Registration and Voting by States, 2016" (Washington, DC: U.S. Department of Commerce, 2017). https://census.gov/data/tables/time-series/demo/voting-and-registration/p20-580.html.
40. William H. Flanigan and Nancy H. Zingale, *Political Behavior of the American Electorate*, 9th ed. (Washington, DC: CQ Press, 1999).
41. Saranac Hale Spencer, "Nine Election Fraud Claims, None Credible," FactCheck.org, Annenberg Public Policy Center, December 11, 2020. https://www.factcheck.org/2020/12/nine-election-fraud-claims-none-credible/.
42. Jeremy Herb, Clare Foran, Manu Raju, and Phil Mattingly, "Congress Completes Electoral Count, Finalizing Biden's Win After Violent Delay from Pro-Trump Mob," CNN Politics, January 7, 2021.
43. Michael McDonald, "Voter Turnout," *United States Election Project*, http://elections.gmu.edu/voter_turnout.htm.
44. Center for Information & Research on Civic Learning and Engagement (CIRCLE), "Young Voters in the 2010 Elections," http://www.civicyouth.org/wp-content/uploads/2010/11/2010-Exit-Poll-FS-Nov-17-Update.pdf.
45. Center for Information & Research on Civic Learning and Engagement, "The Youth Vote in the 2018 Elections." https://mail.google.com/mail/u/1/#search/Center+for/FMfcgxvzLhdxlnkPLPBprWFNxxwCvZMW.
46. Congressional Management Foundation, *Communicating with Congress: How the Internet Has Changed Citizen Engagement* (Washington, DC: Congressional Management Foundation, 2008).
47. Issie Lapowsky, "What It Takes to Make Congress Actually Listen," Wired, February 1, 2018. https://www.wired.com/story/opengov-report-congress-constituent-communication/.
48. Congressional Management Foundation, *Communicating With Congress: How the Internet Has Changed Citizen Engagement* (Washington, DC: Congressional Management Foundation, 2008).
49. Center for Responsive Politics, "2020 Presidential Race: Small Donors," OpenSecrets.org, April 30, 2021. https://www.opensecrets.org/2020-presidential-race.
50. Matea Gold, Anu Narayanswamy, and Tom Hamburger, "Donations, Big and Small, Continue to Pour Into 2016 Race," *The Washington Post*, February 1, 2016.
51. Gary C. Jacobson, *The Politics of Congressional Elections* (New York: HarperCollins, 1997).
52. Sidney Verba, Kay Lehman Schlozman, and Henry E. Brady, *Voice and Equality: Civic Voluntarism in American Politics* (Cambridge, MA: Harvard University Press, 1995), 70.

53. Diana Owen, "The Campaign and the Media," in *The American Elections of 2008*, ed. Janet M. Box-Steffensmeier and Steven E. Schier (Lanham, MD: Rowman & Littlefield, 2009), 9–32.
54. Diana Owen, "The Campaign and the Media," in *the American Elections of 2012,* ed. Janet M. Box-Steffensmeier and Steven E. Schier (New York: Routledge, 2013).
55. Nathan Heller, "Feeling the Bern With the Youth Vote," *The New Yorker*, August 25, 2015.
56. Kathleen Chaykowski, "Why Bernie Sanders's Social Media Followers Are More Engaged Than Donald Trump's," *Forbes*, March 25, 2016.
57. Rebecca Klar. "Teens Expand TikTok Playbook to Help Democrats in Georgia Runoffs," *The Hill*, December 27, 2020. https://thehill.com/homenews/campaign/531490-teens-expand-tiktok-playbook-to-help-democrats-in-georgia-runoffs.
58. Imad Khan, "AOC's Twitch Get-Out-the-Vote Efforts Will Help Democrats in 2020—and Beyond," *NBC News*, October 29, 2020. https://www.nbcnews.com/think/opinion/aoc-s-twitch-get-out-vote-efforts-will-help-democrats-ncna1245318.
59. Sidney Verba, Kay Lehman Schlozman, and Henry E. Brady, *Voice and Equality: Civic Voluntarism in American Politics* (Cambridge, MA: Harvard University Press, 1995), 51–52.
60. Stephanie Steinberg, "Jewell Jones Makes History as Youngest State Rep," *The Detroit News*, December 6, 2016.
61. Michael Lipsky, "Protest as a Political Resource," *American Political Science Review*, December 1968, 1145.
62. Todd Gitlin. *Occupy Nation*. (New York: Harper Collins, 2012).
63. Elizabeth Day, "#BlackLivesMatter: The Birth of a New Civil Rights Movement," The Guardian, July 15, 2015.
64. Larry Buchanan, Quoctrung Bui, and Jugal K. Patel, "Black Lives Matter May Be the Largest Movement in U.S. History, The New York Times, July 3, 2020. https://www.nytimes.com/interactive/2020/07/03/us/george-floyd-protests-crowd-size.html.
65. Robert D. Putnam, *Bowling Alone: America's Declining Social Capital* (New York: Simon & Schuster, 2000).
66. Don E. Eberly, *America's Promise: Civil Society and the Renewal of American Culture* (Lanham, MD: Rowman & Littlefield, 1998).
67. Peter D. Hart Research Associates, *New Leadership for a New Century* (Washington, DC: Public Allies, August 28, 1998).
68. Center for Information and Research on Civic Learning and Engagement, *Volunteering/Community Service Fact Sheet. Report*. (Medford, MA: Tufts University, 2014). Accessed June 18, 2014; http://www.civicyouth.org/quick-facts/volunteeringcommunity-service/#2.
69. Jack Dennis and Diana Owen, "The Partisanship Puzzle," in *After the Boom: The Politics of Generation X*, ed. Stephen C. Craig, and Stephen Earl Bennett (Lanham, MD: Rowman & Littlefield, 1997), 43–61.
70. Steven E. Schier, *By Invitation Only: The Rise of Exclusive Politics in the United States* (Pittsburgh, PA: University of Pittsburgh Press, 2000).
71. Richard M. Merelman, *Making Something of Ourselves* (Berkeley: University of California Press, 1984).
72. M. Margaret Conway, *Political Participation in the United States*, 3rd ed. (Washington, DC: CQ Press, 2000).
73. Sidney Verba and Norman H. Nie, *Participation in America: Political Democracy and Social Equality* (New York: Harper & Row, 1972).
74. "Views of the 2020 Campaign and Voting in November," Election 2020, Pew Research Center, August 13, 2020. https://www.pewresearch.org/politics/2020/08/13/views-of-the-2020-campaign-and-voting-in-november/.
75. Pew Research Center for the People & the Press, "GOP Holds Early Turnout Edge, But Little Enthusiasm for Romney: Section 1: Campaign Interest and Engagement." Report. Washington, DC: Pew Research Center, 2012. Accessed June 19th, 2014: http://www.people-press.org/2012/06/21/section-1-campaign-interest-and-engagement-2/.
76. Pew Research Center, *2016 Campaign:* http://www.people-press.org/files/2016/07/07-07-16-Voter-attitudes-release.pdf.
77. "Views of the 2020 Campaign and Voting in November," Election 2020, Pew Research Center, August 13, 2020. https://www.pewresearch.org/politics/2020/08/13/views-of-the-2020-campaign-and-voting-in-november/.
78. Pew Research Center for the People & the Press, "Pew Weekly News Interest Index Poll, Oct, 2010," *Poll Database*, http://people-press.org/questions/?qid=1772828&pid=51&ccid=51#top: "Thinking about this year's (2010) Congressional elections, would you say that you are interested in what's happening in elections around the country?"
79. Matthew Hindman, *The Myth of Digital Democracy* (Princeton, NJ: Princeton University Press, 2008).
80. Martin Gilens, "Inequality and Democratic Responsiveness," Public Opinion Quarterly, vol. 69, no. 5, Special Issue, 2005: 778-796.
81. Larry Bartels. Unequal Democracy: The Political Economy of the New Gilded Age, 2nd ed. Princeton, NJ: Princeton University Press, 2016.
82. Project Vote-Smart, Democracy Inclusion Project, http://www.vote-smart.org/yip.
83. Center for Information & Research on Civic Learning and Engagement (CIRCLE), "Youth Voting," http://www.civicyouth.org/?page_id=241#1.
84. Angela Nelson, "Young Voters Were Crucial to Biden's Win," TuftsNow, April 30, 2021. https://now.tufts.edu/articles/young-voters-were-crucial-biden-s-win.
85. "Youth Are Standing Up Against Racism," United National Human Rights, Office of the High Commissioner, March 21, 2021. https://www.ohchr.org/EN/NewsEvents/Pages/anti-racism-day-2021.aspx.
86. Claire Gothreau, "Everything You Need to Know About the Gender Gap," Center for American Women and Politics, Rutgers University, February 26, 2021. https://cawp.rutgers.edu/election-analysis/everything-you-need-know-about-gender-gap.
87. Jens Manuel Krogstad and Mark Hugo Lopez, "Black Voter Turnout Fell in 2016, Even as a Record Number of Americans Cast Ballots," *Fact Tank* (Washington, DC: Pew Research Center, May 12, 2017).
88. Monica Anderson and Dennis Quinn, "46% of U.S. Social Media Users Say They Are 'Worn Out' by Political Posts and Discussions," FactTank, Pew Research Center, August 8, 2019. https://www.pewresearch.org/fact-tank/2019/08/08/46-of-u-s-social-media-users-say-they-are-worn-out-by-political-posts-and-discussions/.
89. Congressional Research Service, Women in Congress: Statistics and Brief Overview. Research Report. Updated December 4, 2020. https://fas.org/sgp/crs/misc/R43244.pdf.
90. Jens Manuel Krogstad and Mark Hugo Lopez, "Black Voter Turnout Fell in 2016, Even as a Record Number of Americans Cast Ballots," *Fact Tank* (Washington, DC: Pew Research Center, May 12, 2017).
91. Michael McDonald, "Current Population Survey Voting and Registration Supplement," *United States Election Project*, http://elections.gmu.edu/CPS_2008.html.
92. David Paul Kuhn, "Exit Polls: How Obama Won," *Politico*, November 5, 2012.
93. Jens Manuel Krogstad and Mark Hugo Lopez, "Black Voter Turnout Fell in 2016, Even as a Record Number of Americans Cast Ballots," *Fact Tank* (Washington, DC: Pew Research Center, May 12, 2017).
94. Jacob Fabina, "Despite Pandemic Challenges, 2020 Election Had Largest Increase in Voting Between Presidential Elections on Record," The United States Census Bureau, April 29, 2021. https://www.census.gov/library/stories/2021/04/record-high-turnout-in-2020-general-election.html.
95. Dianna M. Nanez, "Latinos Make Up Only 1% of All Local and Federal Elected Officials," USA Today, January 6, 2020.
96. Rush Schriefer, Bush campaign media consultant, interview by Owen, May 22, 2001.
97. Jens Manuel Krogstad, "Key Facts About the Latino Vote in 2016," *Fact Tank* (Washington, DC: Pew Research Center, October 4, 2016).
98. Douglas R. Hess, "Analysis of the 2008 Current Population Survey (CPS) Voter and Registration Supplement," http://www.projectvote.org/images/publications/Reports on the Electorate/Analysis of the 2008 CPS Voting Supplement.pdf.
99. Lian Bunny, Sami Edge, and Hillary Davis, "Asian-American Population Surges, but Voter Turnout Still Lacks," NBC News and News21, August 22, 2016. http://www.nbcnews.com/news/asian-america/asian-american-population-surges-voter-turnout-still-lacks-n633146.
100. Jacob Fabina, "Despite Pandemic Challenges, 2020 Election Had Largest Increase in Voting Between Presidential Elections on Record," The United States Census Bureau, April 29, 2021. https://www.census.gov/library/stories/2021/04/record-high-turnout-in-2020-general-election.html.
101. The White House Commission on Asian Americans and Pacific Islanders, *A People Looking Forward* (Washington, DC: U.S. Government, 2001); Pew Research Center, "Fact Tank: Asian American Voter Turnout Lags Behind Other Groups," Report. (Washington, DC: Pew Research Center, 2014). Accessed June 19, 2014: http://www.pewresearch.org/fact-tank/2014/04/09/asian-american-voter-turnout-lags-behind-other-groups-some-non-voters-say-theyre-too-busy/.
102. The White House Commission on Asian Americans and Pacific Islanders, A People Looking Forward (Washington, DC: U.S. Government, 2001); Pew Research Center, "Fact Tank: Asian American Voter Turnout Lags Behind Other Groups," Report. (Washington, DC: Pew Research Center, 2014). Accessed June 19, 2014: http://www.pewresearch.org/fact-tank/2014/04/09/asian-american-voter-turnout-lags-behind-other-groups-some-non-voters-say-theyre-too-busy/.
103. Catie Edmondson, "Senate Resoundingly Passes Bill to Target Anti-Asian Hate Crimes," *The New York Times*, April 22, 2021. https://www.nytimes.com/2021/04/22/us/politics/senate-anti-asian-hate-crimes.html.
104. Jo Freeman and Victoria Johnson, eds., *Waves of Protest* (Lanham, MD: Rowman & Littlefield, 1999).
105. United Farm Workers of America, "Action Alert! Urge Congress to Support UFW-Sponsored Bills Allowing an Undocumented Farm Worker to Earn Legalization," 2001, http://www.ufw.org/gallowact.htm.
106. Deen Freelon, Charlton D. McIlwain, and Meredith D. Clark, "Beyond the Hashtags: Center for Media & Social Impact," February 29, 2016.
107. McLaughlin, Michael, "The Dynamic History of #BlackLivesMatter Explained," *Black Voices*, December 26, 2016.
108. Larry Buchanan, Quoctrung Bui, and Jugal K. Patel, "Black Lives Matter May Be the Largest Movement in U.S. History," *The New York Times*, July 3, 2020. https://www.nytimes.com/interactive/2020/07/03/us/george-floyd-protests-crowd-size.html.
109. Martin Luther King, Jr., "I Have A Dream." March on Washington, 1963.
110. Rebecca DeWolf, *Gendered Citizenship: The Original Conflict over the Equal Rights Amendment, 1920–1963*. Lincoln, NE: University of Nebraska Press, 2021.

111. M. Margaret Conway, *Political Participation in the United States* (Washington, DC: CQ Press, 1991), 98–107.
112. Barbara Epstein, "What Happened to the Women's Movement," *Monthly Review*, April 2000, 1–13.
113. "Take Back The Night" website http://www.takebackthenight.org.
114. Christian Coalition of America, "Our Mission," http://www.cc.org.
115. DFRLab, "#StopTheSteal: Timeline of Social Media and Extremist Activities Leading to 1/6 Insurrection," Atlantic Council, February 10, 2021. https://www.justsecurity.org/74622/stopthesteal-timeline-of-social-media-and-extremist-activities-leading-to-1-6-insurrection/.
116. Dan Barry, Mike McIntire, and Matthew Rosenberg, "'Our President Wants Us Here': The Mob That Stormed the Capitol," *The New York Times*, January 9, 2021. https://www.nytimes.com/2021/01/09/us/capitol-rioters.html.
117. Hannah Rabinowitz, Marshall Cohen, and Caroline Kelly, "Justice Department Has Charged at Least 400 People in Capitol Riot So Far," CNN Politics, April 27, 2021.
118. Todd Gitlin, *The Whole World Is Watching* (Berkeley: University of California Press, 1980).
119. Baris Coban, ed. Social Media and Social Movements. New York: Lexington Books, 2016.
120. Gabriel Granillo, "The Role of Social Media in Social Movements," Portland Monthly, June 10, 2020. https://www.pdxmonthly.com/news-and-city-life/2020/06/the-role-of-social-media-in-social-movements.
121. Michael Grunwald, "At Capitol, Young Friends and Foe of Gun Control Test Each Other," *Washington Post*, July 19, 1999, A10.
122. Kelli Kennedy, "Students Against Gun Violence Rallying for Racial Justice," AP News, June 24, 2020.
123. Jane Hu, "The Second Act of Social-Media Activism," The New Yorker, August 3, 2020. https://www.newyorker.com/culture/cultural-comment/the-second-act-of-social-media-activism.
124. ALS Association, "Ice Bucket Challenge Donations Lead to Discovery of New ALS Gene" ALS Association Website.http://www.alsa.org/fight-als/ice-bucket-challenge.html.
125. Liz Clarke, *One Helluva Ride* (New York: Villard, 2008).
126. Steven Webster, "Angry Americans: How Political Rage Helps Campaigns But Hurts Democracy," The Conversation, September 10, 2020. https://theconversation.com/angry-americans-how-political-rage-helps-campaigns-but-hurts-democracy-145819.
127. Barbara L. Poole and Melinda A. Mueller, "Alienation and the 'Soccer Mom': A Media Creation or a New Trend in Voting Behavior," in *Engaging the Public*, ed. Thomas J. Johnson, Carol E. Hays, and Scott P. Hays (Boulder, CO: Rowman & Littlefield, 1998), 29–40; Susan J. Carroll, "The Disempowerment of the Gender Gap: Soccer Moms and the 1996 Elections," *PS Online*, March, 1999, http://www.apsanet.org.
128. Emma Gonzalez. (2018) "March for Our Lives speech, March 24, 2018." Via CNN Staff, "Florida Student Emma Gonzalez to Lawmakers and Gun Advocates: 'We Call BS,'" CNN, February 17. https://www.cnn.com/2018/02/17/us/florida-student-emma-gonzalez-speech/index.html.
129. Bromwich, Jonah Engel. 2018. "How the Parkland Students Got So Good at Social Media," *The New York Times*, March 7. https://www.nytimes.com/2018/03/07/us/parkland-students-social-media.html.
130. Garber, Megan. 2018. "The Powerful Silence of the March for Our Lives," *The Atlantic*, March 24. https://www.theatlantic.com/entertainment/archive/2018/03/the-powerful-silence-of-the-march-for-our-lives/556469/.
131. Scherer, Michael. 2018. "Florida Gov. Rick Scott Breaks with NRA to Sign New Gun Regulations," *The Washington Post*, March 9.
132. Scott, Eugene. 2018. "Parkland's David Hogg Challenges Students to Remain Activists, Even If They Don't Go To College," *The Washington Post*, March 30. https://www.washingtonpost.com/news/the-fix/wp/2018/03/30/parklands-david-hogg-challenges-students-to-remain-activists-even-if-they-dont-go-to-college/?utm_term=.ce1c4034937b.
133. Pippa Norris, *A Virtuous Circle: Political Communications in Postindustrial Societies* (New York: Cambridge University Press, 2003).
134. Joseph Cappella and Kathleen Hall Jamieson, *Spiral of Cynicism: The Press and the Public Good* (New York: Oxford University Press, 1997).
135. Roderick P. Hart, *Seducing America: How Television Charms the Modern Voter* (New York: Oxford University Press, 1994).
136. Robert Putnam, *Bowling Alone: America's Declining Social Capital* (New York: Simon & Schuster, 2000).
137. Matt Pearce and Kurtis Lee, "The New Civil Rights Leaders: Emerging Voices in the 21st Century," Los Angeles Times, March 5, 2015. https://www.latimes.com/nation/la-na-civil-rights-leaders-br-20150304-htmlstory.html.
138. Associated Press. "NAACP reports resurgence of youth activism." *Associated Press* via *The Augusta Chronicle*, July 12, 2009. Retrieved from: https://www.augustachronicle.com/article/20090712/LIFESTYLE/307129989.

CHAPTER 9

# Interest Groups

## 9.1 Preamble

The media often depict interest group lobbyists negatively in the news and in entertainment. One particular episode of *The Simpsons* provides an extreme example. Lisa Simpson writes an essay titled "The Roots of Democracy" that wins her a trip to Washington, DC, to compete for the best essay on patriotism award. She writes, "When America was born on that hot July day in 1776, the trees in Springfield Forest were tiny saplings . . . and as they were nourished by Mother Earth, so too did our fledgling nation find strength in the simple ideals of equality and justice."[1]

In Senator Bob Arnold's office a lobbyist proposes razing the Springfield National Forest. Arnold responds, "Well, Jerry, you're a whale of a lobbyist, and I'd like to give you a logging permit, I would. But this isn't like burying toxic waste. People are going to notice those trees are gone." The lobbyist offers a bribe, which Arnold accepts.

Lisa sees it happen and tears up her essay. She sits on the steps of the Capitol and envisions politicians as fat cats scratching each other's backs and lobbyists as pigs feeding from a trough. Called to the microphone at the "Patriots of Tomorrow" awards banquet, Lisa reads her revised essay, now titled "Cesspool on the Potomac." A whirlwind of reform-minded zeal follows. Senator Arnold is caught accepting a bribe to allow oil drilling on Mount Rushmore and is arrested and removed from office. Lisa does not win the essay contest.[2]

Senator Arnold is corrupt, but the cartoon's unpunished instrument of corruption is the lobbyist.

## 9.2 The Interest Group System

### Learning Objectives

After reading this section, you should be able to answer the following questions:

1. What are interest groups?
2. What are the main types of interest groups?
3. What are the most important elements of interest groups?
4. What incentives encourage interest group membership?
5. How do interest groups recruit members?
6. How do the media portray unions and union activity?
7. How do interest groups influence elections?

**FIGURE 9.1**
**University of Texas Logo**

The words *Disciplina*, *Praesidium*, and *Civitatis* translate as "The cultivated mind is the guardian genius of democracy." Devoted to education (and sports), universities try to influence government policies that affect their interests.

Source: Courtesy of the University of Texas at Austin.

**interest groups**

Organizations that, on behalf of an interest or ideal, try to influence politics and public policies.

**public interest groups**

Organizations that work for the common good as they define it, such as for consumers, the environment, the family, or reform of government.

**Interest groups** are intermediaries linking organizations and people to government, often through lobbyists. They make demands on government and try to influence public policies in their favor. Their most important difference from political parties is that they do not seek elective office. Interest groups can be single entities, join associations, and have individual members.

The University of Texas at Austin is an educational institution. Its main purposes are teaching and research. Like other educational institutions, it is an interest group when it tries to influence public policies. These policies include government funding for facilities and student grants, loans, and work study. It may also try to influence laws and court decisions applying to research, admissions, gender equality in intercollegiate athletics, and student records. It may ask members of Congress to earmark funds for some of its projects, thereby bypassing the normal competition with other universities for funds based on merit.[3]

Single entities often join forces in associations. Associations represent their interests and make demands on government on their behalf. The University of Texas belongs to the Association of American Universities. General Electric (GE) belongs to over eighty trade associations, each representing a different industry, such as mining, aerospace, and home appliances.[4]

Many interest groups have individuals as members. People join labor unions and professional organizations (e.g., associations for lawyers or political scientists) that claim to represent their interests.

**TABLE 9.1 Types of Interest Groups**

Interest groups can be divided into five types: economic, societal, ideological, public interest, and governmental.

| | |
|---|---|
| Economic Interest Groups | The major economic interest groups represent businesses, labor unions, and professions. Business interest groups consist of industries, corporations, and trade associations. Unions usually represent individual trades, such as the International Brotherhood of Teamsters. Most unions belong to an association, such as the American Federation of Labor and Congress of Industrial Organizations (AFL-CIO).<br>Economic interest groups represent every aspect of our economy, including agriculture, the arts, automobiles, banking, beverages, construction, defense, education, energy, finance, food, health, housing, insurance, law, media, medicine, pharmaceuticals, science, sports, technology, telecommunications, transportation, travel, and utilities. These groups cover from head (i.e., the Headwear Institute of America) to toe (i.e., the American Podiatric Medical Association) and from soup (i.e., the Campbell Soup Company) to nuts (i.e., the Peanut Butter and Nut Processors Association). |
| Societal Interest Groups | Societal interest groups focus on interests based on people's characteristics, such as age, gender, race, and ethnicity, as well as sexual preference. The National Association for the Advancement of Colored People (NAACP) is one of the oldest societal interest groups in the United States. Immigrant rights organizations are among the newest.<br>Religious institutions sometimes behave as societal interest groups when, for example, they make demands on government to maintain their tax-exempt status. Or when they lobby individually against abortion or as part of such organizations as the National Association of Evangelicals. |
| Ideological Interest Groups | Ideological and partisan interest groups (sometimes overlapping with religious entities), promote a reactionary, conservative, liberal, progressive, or a radical political philosophy. They may be funded by very wealthy individuals, foundations, or other organizations. On the left, are the Center for American Progress and the Democracy Alliance, which channels millions of dollars annually to liberal advocacy groups. On the right are FreedomWorks and the Ethics and Public Policy Center; also, the brothers Charles and David Koch have created and fund a network of groups (notably, Americans for Prosperity) to promote their policy priorities.[5]<br>We categorize interest groups that take stands on such controversial issues as abortion and gun control as ideological, although some might argue that they are actually public interest groups. |

| | |
|---|---|
| Public Interest Groups | **Public interest groups** work for widely accepted concepts of the common good, such as the family, human rights, and consumers. Although their goals are usually popular, some of their specific positions (e.g., environmental groups opposing offshore drilling for oil) may be controversial and challenged. |
| Government Interest Groups | Government interest groups consist of local, state, and foreign governments. They seek to influence the relevant policies and expenditures of the federal government. |

# Life Stages of Interest Groups

Interest groups commonly experience a life cycle of creation (or birth), growth and change (or evolution), and sometimes death.[6]

## Creation

As the United States has become more complex, with new technologies, products, services, businesses, and professions, the government has become more involved in the economy and society. People with common interests organize to solicit support and solutions from government to their problems. Policies enacted in response to the efforts of these groups affect other people, who then form groups to seek government intervention for themselves. These groups may give rise to additional groups.[7]

No surprise, then, that Amazon, Apple, Facebook, and Google have hired numerous lobbyists (some in-house, others on contract from lobbying and law firms) and are spending millions of dollars to protect themselves against possible investigation, regulation, anti-trust actions, legislation, censorship, and other hostile activities by governments and competitors.[8]

Some interest groups are created in reaction to an event or a perceived grievance. The National Right to Life Committee (NRLC) was founded in 1973 in response to the U.S. Supreme Court's *Roe v. Wade* decision earlier that year legalizing abortion. However, groups may form long after the reasons for establishing them are obvious. The NAACP was not founded until 1909 even though segregation of and discrimination against African Americans had existed for many years.

### Link

**Oral Arguments in *Roe v. Wade***

Listen to oral arguments in *Roe v. Wade* here.

**Interest group entrepreneurs** usually are important in the creation of groups. Often they are responding to events in their lives. After a drunk driver killed one of her daughters, Candy Lightner founded Mothers Against Drunk Driving (MADD) in 1980. She thereby identified **latent interests**: people who could be grouped together and organized to pursue what she made them realize was a shared goal: punishing and getting drunk drivers off the road. She was helped by widespread media coverage that brought public attention to her loss and cause.

**interest group entrepreneurs**

People who see the need for and create an interest group.

**latent interests**

Shared goals that an interest group can organize people to pursue.

Some interest groups, such as those supporting immigrants, are sustained by wealthy individuals, foundations, and other sources that provide them with funds, thereby enabling them to recruit members, engage in political activities (demonstrations, marches, rallies), conduct research, and bring pressure on government to enact their policy objectives.[9]

## Evolution and Demise

Interest groups can change over time. The National Rifle Association (NRA) started out in the late nineteenth century as a sports organization dedicated to improving its members' marksmanship. It became an advocate for law and order in the 1960s, until its official support for the 1968 Gun Control Act brought dissension in its ranks. Since the election of new leaders in 1977, the NRA has focused on the Second Amendment right to bear arms, opposing legislation restricting the sale or distribution of guns and ammunition.[10]

An interest group may be beset by internal conflict, subject to revelations. In 2020, after he was fired, the NRA's former second in command published a book describing the organization as focused on money and rife with fraud and intrigue; and its chief executive was described as a woefully inept manager (although skillful lobbyist). More dramatically, the author contradicted the organization's policy preferences by calling for gun control.[11]

Interest groups can die. They may run out of funds or be undermined by scandals. Their issues may lose popularity or become irrelevant. Slavery no longer exists in the United States and thus neither does the American Anti-Slavery Society.

# How Interest Groups Are Organized

Interest groups have leaders and staff. They control the group, decide its policy objectives, and recruit and represent its members.

## Leaders and Staff

Leaders and top staff usually run the interest group. They do so because they command its resources and information flow and have the experience and expertise to deal with public policies that are often complex and technical. Over a century ago, Robert Michels identified this control by an organization's leaders and staff and called it "the iron law of oligarchy."[12]

This oligarchy, or rule by the few, applies to single-entity interest groups and to most associations. Their leaders are appointed or elected and select the staff. Even in many membership organizations, the people who belong do not elect the leaders and have little input when the leaders decide policy objectives.[13] Their participation is limited to sending in dues, expressing opinions, and if membership is voluntary, leaving when dissatisfied.

By increasing individuals' autonomy, new technologies and networks challenge group leaders' control or dominance, even the viability, of their organizations. But as Bruce Bimber and his colleagues show (among other findings) in a study of AARP, the American Legion, and MoveOn, group leaders have responded by effectively deploying these instruments for interaction and mobilization to their and their organizations' advantage. They have developed ways (e.g., rapid response and feedback) of bringing potential members into the group, increasing existing members' attachment to it, and encouraging supporters to participate in, and engage with the organization.[14]

## Voluntary Membership

People join membership interest groups voluntarily or because they have no choice.

When membership is voluntary, interest groups must recruit and try to retain members. Members help fund the group's activities, legitimize its objectives, and add credibility with the media.

Some people may not realize or accept that they have shared interests with others on a particular issue. For example, many young adults download music from the internet, but few of them have joined the Future of Music Coalition, which is developing ways to do this legally. Others may be unwilling to court conflict by joining a group representing oppressed minorities or espousing controversial or unpopular views even when they agree with the group.[15]

People do not need to join an interest group voluntarily when they can benefit from its activities without becoming a member. This is the problem of collective goods. Laws successfully lobbied for by environmental organizations that lead to cleaner air and water benefit members and nonmembers alike. However, the latter get a free ride.[16]

There are three types of incentives that, alone or in combination, may overcome this **free-rider problem**. A **purposive incentive** leads people to voluntarily join and contribute money to a group because they want to help the group achieve its goals. Membership in the American Civil Liberties Union (ACLU) increased by one hundred thousand in the eighteen months following the 9/11 attacks as the group raised concerns that the government's antiterrorism campaign was harming civil liberties.[17] In addition, people may join groups such as the Union of Concerned Scientists because of a **solidary incentive**. The motivation to join the group stems from the pleasure of interacting with like-minded individuals and the gratification of publicly expressing one's beliefs.

**free-rider problem**

A situation in which people can benefit from an interest group's accomplishments without joining it.

**purposive incentive**

When people join a group to accomplish its goals.

**solidary incentive**

When people join a group for friendship and belonging.

**material incentives**

When people join a group for the goods and services it provides.

People may also join groups to obtain **material incentives** available only to members. AARP, formerly the American Association of Retired Persons, has around thirty-five million members. It obtains this huge number by charging a nominal annual membership fee and offering such material incentives as health insurance and reduced prices for prescription drugs. The group's magazine is sent to members and includes tax advice, travel and vacation information, and discounts.

## Recruitment

One way interest groups recruit members is through media coverage. The appealingly named Center for Science in the Public Interest (CSPI) is a consumer organization that focuses on food and nutrition issues, produces quality research, and has media savvy. It is a valuable source of expertise and information for journalists. The frequent and favorable news coverage it receives brings the group and its activities to the public's attention and encourages people to support and join it.

News coverage of an interest group does not always have to be favorable to attract members. Oftentimes, stories about the NRA in major newspapers are negative. Presenting this negative coverage as bias and hostility against and attacks on gun owners, the group's leaders transform it into purposive and solidarity incentives. They use email "to power membership mobilization, fundraising, single-issue voting and the other actions-in-solidarity that contribute to [their] success."[18] And add to the group's roughly five million members.

Groups also make personalized appeals to recruit members and solicit financial contributions. Names of people who might be sympathetic to a group are obtained by purchasing mailing lists from magazines, other groups, and political parties. Recruitment letters and emails often feature scare statements, such as a claim that Social Security is in jeopardy.

Interest groups recruit members, publicize their activities, and pursue their policy objectives through the new media. The Save Our Environment Action Center consists of national environmental groups pooling their databases of supporters and establishing a website. Through this network, people can receive informational newsletters via email, sign petitions, and contact their representatives.

## Required Membership

Employment in most automobile plants requires that workers be members of the International Union, United Automobile, Aerospace and Agricultural Implement Workers of America (UAW).

Workers long fought to establish unions to improve their wages, working conditions, and job opportunities. One way of achieving these objectives was to require all workers at a plant to be union members. But union membership has plummeted as the United States has moved from a manufacturing to a service economy, and employers have effectively discouraged unionization. Many jobs do not have unions for workers to join whether they want to or not. Today only about 10.5 percent of wage and salary workers belong to a union, compared to a high of 35.5 percent in 1945. In June 2018, the Supreme Court voted by 5–4 that government workers who refrain from joining a union do not have to pay for collective bargaining, or union negotiations on their behalf.

### Media Depictions of Unions

One reason for the decline of unions is their mainly negative portrayal in the media.[19] There are hardly any labor-beat reporters in the news media, so union officials are infrequently used as sources and are consequently unable to frame union news to their advantage.

Strikes are the union action most often shown in the news. These are usually framed not as legitimate collective tactics to improve wages and working conditions, but as hurting or inconveniencing consumers by disrupting services (e.g., suspending classes in elementary and high schools) and causing the cancellation of events (e.g., professional sporting games).[20]

Unions are rare in movies. *Norma Rae* (1979), *Matewan* (1987), and the documentary *Harlan County, USA* (1976), favorably portray workers' struggles to organize and strike for better working conditions, wages, and security, against exploiting employers. But in the classic union film, the Academy Award–winning *On the Waterfront* (1954), the union is corrupt, violent, and linked to organized crime; the union leaders exploit members to enrich themselves.

### Representation

Groups claim to represent the interests of their members or constituents, but these interests may conflict. In an extensive study, Dara Z. Strolovitch found that civil rights organizations prioritized the interests of their middle-class members over the interests of people living in poverty and the working class. For example, they pushed for affirmative action rather than welfare and antipoverty policies.[21]

A problem for AARP is that its members may have little in common. In 1988, AARP supported legislation setting up a catastrophic health insurance plan in Medicare to provide insurance for older people faced with huge medical bills for major illnesses. After the plan went into effect, many seniors objected to the increase in their Medicare premiums and an annual surtax of as high as $800. Their complaints were widely covered in the media. Congress repealed the program the next year.

Even when members share a group's general goals, they may reject some of its policy proposals or tactics. In 2009, Apple quit the U.S. Chamber of Commerce because the chamber opposed global-warming legislation.

## Interest Groups and Elections

Interest groups become involved in elections to influence policymakers. They may contribute funds, make independent expenditures, advocate issues, and mobilize voters. Wealthy groups help pay for the presidential nominating conventions and the presidential inauguration. They give funds to political parties because "by helping party leaders retain or regain control of the House or Senate, policymaking rewards . . . follow."[22]

## Endorsing Candidates

Interest groups may endorse candidates for office and, if they have the resources, mobilize members and sympathizers to work and vote for them. President Bill Clinton blamed the NRA for Al Gore's losing the 2000 presidential election because it influenced voters in several states, including Arkansas, West Virginia, and Gore's home state of Tennessee. Had any of these states gone for Gore, he would have won the election.

Interest groups can promote candidates through television and radio advertisements. During the 2004 presidential election, the NRA ran a thirty-minute infomercial in battleground states favoring President George W. Bush and calling his opponent "the most anti-gun presidential nominee in United States history." In subsequent years, the NRA again issued ads endorsing the Republican presidential candidates.

Endorsements do carry risks. If the endorsed candidate loses, the unendorsed winner is likely to be unsympathetic to the group. Thus, relatively few interest groups endorse presidential candidates, and most endorsements are based on ideological congruence.

The NRA grades candidates for federal and state government on how committed they are to gun rights. It supports those with the higher grades, then tracks those in office to ensure they remain faithful to the group, campaigning for those who do and against those who do not.

## Funding Candidates

Made possible by the 1971 Federal Election Campaign Act (FECA), **political action committees (PACs)** are a means for organizations, including interest groups, to raise funds and contribute to candidates in federal elections. Approximately one-third of the funds received by candidates for the House of Representatives and one-fifth of funds for Senate candidates come from PACs.

**political action committees (PACs)**

Political committees that raise and spend money to elect or defeat candidates that are associated with businesses, trade associations, labor organizations, and ideological groups.

However, in January 2010 the Supreme Court ruled by 5–4 in the *Citizens United* case, discussed in more detail in Chapter 11, that the government cannot ban political spending by corporations in candidate elections. The court majority justified the decision on the grounds of the First Amendment's free speech clause. The dissenters argued that allowing unlimited spending by corporations on political advertising would corrupt democracy.[23]

Many interest groups value candidates' power above their ideology or voting record. Most PAC funds, especially from corporations, go to incumbents. Chairs and members of congressional committees and subcommittees who make policies relevant to the group are particularly favored. The case of Enron, although extreme, graphically reveals such funding. Of the 248 members of Congress on committees that investigated the 2002 accounting scandals and collapse of the giant corporation, 212 had received campaign contributions from Enron or its accounting firm, Arthur Andersen.[24]

Some interest groups do fund candidates on the basis of ideology and policy preference. Ideological and public interest groups base support on candidates' views even if their defeat is likely. Pro-life organizations mainly support Republicans; pro-choice organizations mainly support Democrats.

The interest group–candidate relationship is a two-way street. Many candidates actively solicit support from interest groups on the basis of an existing relationship or the promise of a future one. Candidates obtain some of the funds necessary for their campaigns from interest groups; the groups who give them money get the opportunity to make their case to sympathetic legislators. A businessman defending his company's PAC is quoted as saying, "Talking to politicians is fine, but with a little money they hear you better."[25]

Much better. The Center for Responsive Politics shows correlations between campaign contributions and congressional voting. After the House of Representatives voted 220–215 in 2003 to pass the Medicare drug bill, the organization reported that "lawmakers who voted to approve the legislation have raised an average of roughly twice as much since 1999 from individuals and PACs associated with health insurers, HMOs [health maintenance organizations] and pharmaceutical manufacturers as those who voted against the bill."[26]

## Key Takeaways

Interest groups are diverse in membership and purpose. They are created, may evolve in composition and goals, and sometimes die out. Interest group entrepreneurs can be integral to the creation of interest groups. Different types of incentives encourage interest group membership. Organizations use various methods to recruit new members. The media are particularly critical of labor unions. Interest groups try to influence elections in order to advance their policy objectives.

## Exercises

1. Why do you think some interest groups have a bad reputation? What social purpose do interest groups serve?
2. Do you support any interest groups? What made you decide to support them?
3. What are the different ways interest groups can influence policies? Do you think interest groups should be allowed to contribute as much as they want to political campaigns?

# 9.3 Lobbying: The Art of Influence

## Learning Objectives

After reading this section, you should be able to answer the following questions:

1. What is lobbying?
2. How do lobbyists gain access to public officials?
3. What is grassroots lobbying?
4. How do lobbyists attempt to influence Congress, the president, the bureaucracy, and the courts?
5. How is lobbying regulated?

**lobbyists**

Representatives of interest groups who try to influence public officials.

**lobbying**

Activities that lobbyists perform, such as informing, persuading, and pressuring in order to influence policymakers to support a group's interests.

Interest groups employ **lobbyists** to protect and advance their interests. Lobbyists do this through **lobbying**: informing, persuading, and pressuring policymakers to support the group's objectives.

The more policies the government proposes, the more lobbyists become involved. In response to the greatest financial crisis since the Great Depression of the 1930s, the Obama administration proposed to overhaul the regulation and increase oversight of the financial system. This generated a bonanza of business for lobbyists. Lobbyists represented banks, mutual funds, hedge funds, credit card companies, as well as companies in manufacturing, retail, and service industries who could be affected by changes in the laws.

# The Lobbyists

The number of people in Washington, DC, who lobby ranges up to 80,000. Some work for organizations, others for law firms organizations hire.[27] Some of them go through a revolving door (sometimes called "cashing in" between government service and lobbying. Former presidential aides are prominent and powerful among them. More than two hundred lobbyists are former members of Congress. Others have worked for congressional committees or the agencies they now lobby. These former public servants have expertise, access, and contacts with policymakers.

This move from public service to private enrichment, cashing in on connections, is grist for the news media. The *New York Times* reported that Wall Street's financial firms had more than 125 former members of Congress and congressional aides working to limit the policies proposed by the Obama administration and the Democratic majority in Congress to overhaul and intensify regulation of the industry. They included Richard H. Baker, a former chairman of a subcommittee of the House Financial Services Committee. As president of hedge funds' Managed Funds Association, Baker led the fight to prevent government oversight of hedge funds. The association spent $3.7 million in 2009 lobbying federal officials.[28]

The *Times* later reported that government agencies (such as the Securities and Exchange Commission, the Commodity Futures Trading Commission, the Office of Thrift Supervision, and the Federal Reserve) that were deciding on at least 243 regulations to implement the new 2,300-page banking law were being lobbied by 148 of their former employees, who had recently been hired away from the agencies. Asked by the *Times* reporter if his previous employment gave him an edge in lobbying, one of them replied, "The answer is yes, it does. If it didn't, I wouldn't be able to justify getting out of bed in the morning and charging the outrageous fees that we charge our clients, which they willingly pay."[29]

Lobbyists also take positions in the federal government. They bring expertise from their jobs and usually take a pay cut. They are familiar with and may be sympathetic to their industry's policy agenda. Before he became President George W. Bush's chief of staff, Andrew Card was General Motors's chief lobbyist in Washington, DC.

# What Lobbyists Do

Lobbying is done by members of the group's or association's staff, a law or lobbying firm that specializes in representing clients before government, or both. In addition to lobbying, firms may offer such services as public relations, research, polling, direct mail, and grassroots campaigns.[30]

Arguably, nonprofit research organizations (think tanks such as the Brookings Institution and the Center for Strategic and International Studies) also engage in lobbying when they receive "tens of millions of dollars from foreign governments . . . while pushing United States government officials to adopt policies that often reflect the donors' priorities."[31] We write "arguably" because the think tanks claim they are engaged in research, not lobbying.[32]

## Gaining Access

Lobbyists need **access** to policymakers in order to make their cases. But public officials are not obliged to meet with lobbyists, take their telephone calls, or look at their text and email messages. Access is granted when the policymaker has received campaign contributions from the group or is sympathetic to its interests, or the group's policy objectives are important to constituents back home.

**access**

The opportunity to meet with and communicate with policymakers.

Ensuring access often involves building relationships. Lobbyists attend elected officials' fundraisers and receptions and hand over campaign checks from their groups. They meet policymakers informally at dinners, golf games, sporting events, parties, and weddings. They enable lawmakers to fly on corporate jets at discounted rates and then join them for the ride. However, legislation has limited some of these benefits.

### Providing Information

After being granted access, lobbyists try to convince public officials to support or accept or, at least, not oppose the interest group's policy positions. They supply three types of information. First, they offer information about current or proposed laws and regulations that are relevant to the group's interests. Second, they supply political information about whether the policymakers' constituents would be affected by a new policy and whether public opinion would support or oppose a policy change. Third, they offer technical information about the implications and possible effects of policy proposals.

The sections below focus on lobbying of the branches of the federal government. We would note, however, that some lobbyists operate at the state level. In particular, they actively deal with the states' attorneys general (SAGs). They participate in fundraisers, give campaign contributions, sponsor conferences, and offer other inducements. The purposes are to push the SAGs to "drop investigations, change policies, negotiate favorable settlements or pressure federal regulators. . . ." Facilitating this success, there is usually less transparency and fewer disclosure requirements at the state level.[33]

## Lobbying Congress

**grassroots lobbying**

A strategy pursued by interest groups to influence elected officials by having their constituents contact them.

Some interest groups encourage their members and others to contact their legislators on behalf of a policy position the group advocates. This is called **grassroots lobbying**. Hired firms use data banks, telephone banks, and direct mail to contact people likely to be responsive to the group. Messages are crafted through focus groups and surveys. All this costs money, so grassroots lobbying is mainly done by amply funded interest groups on major public policy issues like the minimum wage.

Lobbyists may have extensive involvement with members of Congress and their staff in personal, committee, and leadership offices. Some lobbyists intervene from the start of the congressional policymaking process, encourage or discourage the introduction of proposed legislation, and try to influence its contents. They may draft a bill and work with congressional staff to sign up cosponsors. They may help organize congressional hearings, decide on the timing of the hearings, identify people to testify, write testimony for some of them, and provide questions for legislators to ask witnesses.[34]

Lobbyists may be involved with the subcommittee or committee markup of a bill. They may attempt to modify its language, add amendments, and work to have the bill approved or defeated by subcommittee or committee vote. They try to persuade members to vote for or against the bill on the floor.

These activities take place in both the House of Representatives and the Senate, as well as the House-Senate conference committee held to reconcile and resolve differences between bills passed by each chamber, and in the final House and Senate votes.

Lobbyists can also try to influence the amount of money Congress appropriates for agencies and programs. After the U.S. Department of Justice brought an antitrust lawsuit against Microsoft in October 1997, the company called upon lawmakers to approve the lowest possible budget for the department. Its objectives were to punish the Justice Department and reduce its enforcement funds.

## Lobbying the President

Depending on personal preferences, ideological inclinations, and political needs, the president may be in contact with business, industry, labor, and other interest group leaders. Normally, however, communications with interest groups are made on the president's behalf by individual members of the White House staff and by the White House Office of Public Engagement, and, on occasion, the Office of Management and Budget (OMB). Indeed, the OMB process of reviewing regulations issued by government agencies provides an opportunity for interest groups, especially business groups, to change them.[35]

Presidents can cater to interest groups they favor or that have supported them or whose support they seek by pushing policies the interest groups desire. Usually, these are policies the president favors anyway. For example, President George W. Bush imposed restrictions on stem cell research, while President Barack Obama removed these restrictions shortly after taking office.

Interest groups supporting a presidential proposal can try to convince members of Congress with whom they have influence to vote in their favor. The White House may solicit such support as the George W. Bush administration did to gain the endorsement of AARP, using an expensive advertising campaign in support of the bill adding drug coverage to Medicare. But interest groups may not be permanent or even reliable allies. For example, in 2005, AARP opposed President Bush's proposal to "reform" Social Security.

During his 2016 campaign, Donald Trump promised that as president he would "drain the swamp." Meaning, one assumes, diminish, if not eliminate, the influence of lobbyists. Given that few lobbyists had supported him or expected him to win, he was in a position to move toward that goal. But, as documented by The *New York Times*, businesses quickly hired and lavishly remunerated influential lobbyists who had backed and had connections to the new president and prominent cabinet members. In a mutually beneficial arrangement, they would enjoy and exploit concomitant access and influence, and in turn contribute to and raise funds for the president's reelection campaign.[36]

Readers of this chapter will anticipate the *New York Times'* headline that would soon greet newly elected president Joe Biden in 2020: "Companies and Countries Rush to Lobby Biden."[37]

## Lobbying Governmental Agencies

Bureaucrats are important to interest groups because they usually have leeway to decide what laws mean and how to administer and implement them. For example, the guidelines bureaucrats issued to carry out the Medicare drug benefit determined which drugs and medical devices would be covered. Lobbyists for doctors, hospitals, insurers, drug companies, pharmacies, and medical equipment manufacturers contacted bureaucrats directly about these decisions.[38]

In a dramatic example of the importance of regulators' discretion and the influence of groups, Toyota saved roughly $100 million by negotiating with regulators at the National Highway Traffic Safety Administration (NHTSA) to limit the recall of 2007 Toyota Camry and Lexus ES models for sudden acceleration. Toyota was allowed to recall the floor mats it claimed could become lodged under the accelerator pedal.[39]

Even more striking, lobbyists were able to negotiate with senior officials in the Trump administration's Treasury Department to transform the federal tax law of December 2017 to slash taxes even more for the biggest American and foreign corporations and their shareholders. The lobbyists were benefited by the sloppy way the original bill was written and rushed through Congress, giving the Treasury Department extra leeway to interpret the law.[40]

# Lobbying the Courts

Interest groups are affected by court decisions. It matters to them who the judges are, in terms of their legal philosophy, policy preferences, and partisan affiliation. Interest groups who have the attention of the White House seek to influence the president's selection of federal judges by suggesting candidates and screening those on the short list.

Groups for or against nominees lobby senators to approve, delay, or reject confirmation. Media-oriented tactics include testifying at hearings of the Senate Judiciary Committee, feeding negative or positive information about nominees to senators and reporters, sponsoring radio and television advertisements, and organizing grassroots campaigns.[41]

Interest groups pursue their goals in court.[42] They may challenge a policy, appeal adverse decisions by other branches of government, and file suits against public officials to require them to take or refrain from taking some action. The U.S. Chamber of Commerce's National Chamber Litigation Center represents the interests of business before the courts.

Certain interest groups use the courts as the main way to try to achieve their objectives. Thus, the ACLU often brings cases before the courts to assert and protect constitutional rights. During the 1970s, the ACLU's Women's Rights Project, headed by Ruth Bader Ginsburg (later to be appointed to the Court by President Clinton), filed the majority of cases that challenged discrimination against women and were heard by the Supreme Court.

Formed in 1994, Judicial Watch used much of its annual budget of $35 million to use the courts to attack Hillary Clinton. In 2016 it was the plaintiff in more than twenty Freedom of Information Act lawsuits against her. Most of its suits have been dismissed, but the organization hit pay dirt over her use of a private email server when she was secretary of state. The suits required Ms. Clinton and her staff to answer detailed questions, and the media coverage perpetuated the impression that she was untrustworthy.[43]

Interest groups may also go to court when they lack influence in the legislative and executive branches. The NAACP mounted a litigation campaign against segregation laws, culminating in its notable victory in the Supreme Court's 1954 unanimous school desegregation decision of *Brown v. Board of Education*.

### Link

***Brown v. Board of Education***

Click here for more information on *Brown v. Board of Education.*

# Regulation of Lobbying

As the opening anecdote from *The Simpsons* illustrates, interest groups in general and lobbyists in particular receive a bad press. The media send out a drumbeat of criticism featuring stories of conflict of interest, corruption, and scandals in the relations of policymakers and lobbyists.

The media's negative depictions of lobbying, and the concern of members of Congress to refute accusations of being beholden to "special interest groups" (a derogatory term), have produced proposals to regulate lobbyists and lobbying. These are designed to correct abuses, placate the media, and reassure the public. They increase the amount of information about and the visibility of lobbying, eliminate the appearance of corruption, and may reduce lobbyists' influence over the policymaking process.

## Comparing Content

### Jack Abramoff

Jack Abramoff's meteoric rise began in 1995, soon after the Republicans took over Congress and interest groups and lobbying firms hired lobbyists connected to Republican legislators and conservative organizations. His lobbying successes started with keeping the government of the Northern Mariana Islands, an American territory in the Pacific, exempt from American labor laws; the islands' factories could pay their workers a pittance yet still label their products "Made in America." Then he saved an Indigenous American tribe, the Mississippi Band of Choctaws, hundreds of millions in possible taxes by helping defeat a proposal to tax casino revenues. Other Indigenous American tribes hired him, as he worked to defeat legislation to subject them to state taxes.

Initial media coverage of Abramoff was favorable. On July 3, 2000, the *Wall Street Journal* published a front-page story describing his "money, methods and results" as "exceptional."[44] In April 2002, the *New York Times* published a similar front-page story, with quotes such as "'I call Jack Abramoff, and I get results'" and, from the lobbyist himself, "'All of my political work . . . is driven by philosophical interests, not by a desire to gain wealth.'"[45] Both stories included criticisms of the lobbyist but depicted the man and his power and accomplishments positively overall.

On February 22, 2004, a front-page story in the *Washington Post* exposed Abramoff in the first of a series of investigative reports that would continue over three years.[46] According to an article in *Vanity Fair*, "Abramoff believes the media's negative coverage, leading to his downfall, began with competing Republican lobbyists who coveted his clientele and fed damaging information about him to the newspaper."[47]

The stories revealed that Abramoff had exploited the Indigenous American tribes. Casino-rich tribes had paid him and a public relations firm more than $45 million over three years. Abramoff had used some of the money to bribe members of Congress, make campaign contributions, hold fundraising events, and provide lavish trips, seats in sports boxes, and dinners for members of Congress as well as jobs for their relatives.

Adding to Abramoff's woes, Republican Senator John McCain held several days of media-covered hearings in 2004 and 2005 exposing his activities. According to Abramoff, McCain's aides heightened the negative media coverage by doling out embarrassing emails to the press in which the lobbyist ridiculed his Indigenous American clients as "morons" and "monkeys" and threatened to crush rival lobbyists like bugs.[48]

On January 3, 2006, Abramoff pled guilty to fraud, tax evasion, and conspiracy to bribe public officials.

The first comprehensive lobbying regulation was enacted in 1946. The Legislative Reorganization Act required lobbyists to register their affiliation and record their finances.[49] Later, the 1995 Lobbying Disclosure Act required lobbying firms and lobbyists to register with Congress and file reports twice per year listing their compensation, clients, lobbying expenses, and issues they are following for each of their clients.[50] Only trivial gifts from lobbyists to legislators are allowed.[51]

In 2006, a series of corruption scandals contributed to the Republicans, losing control of Congress. During the election, Democrats pledged to reform the culture of Washington, DC. In 2007, the Democratic-controlled Congress passed and President George W. Bush signed a law establishing new ethics and lobbying rules for Congress. Its main provisions bar members from accepting gifts, meals, or trips from lobbyists or the organizations that employ them, requires the filing of lobbying reports on the internet, and increases the civil and criminal penalties for failing to comply with lobbying laws.

However, the manipulation of legal loopholes and a lack of stringent enforcement can undermine the effectiveness of any lobbying regulations, as with "destination fundraisers," exposed by *New York Times* reporter Eric Lipton, in which lawmakers get together, discuss policy issues with, and raise funds from lobbyists, corporate executives, and other donors at lavish resorts. Because the expenses for the events are paid for by political campaigns and leadership PACs controlled by the lawmakers, they are not considered gifts, even though the money is in fact "collected from the corporate executives and lobbyists . . ."[52]

When Barack Obama became president in 2009, he issued an executive order forbidding appointees in every executive agency from accepting gifts, participating for two years on any matter they had worked on in prior employment, lobbying Congress for two years after leaving the administration, and ever lobbying the Obama administration.[53]

President Trump increased the ban to five years after they leave office, preventing executive branch employees, including those in the White House, from lobbying the federal agency where they had worked. He also permanently banned them from serving as foreign lobbyists. But rules banning lobbyists from taking a job with any agency they had tried to influence during the past two years were removed, and former executive branch employees could informally lobby the administration as long as they were not registered as a lobbyist.[54] President Trump allowed for waivers to the rules without written explanation or public disclosure for any White House employees.

## Key Takeaways

Interests groups use lobbyists to influence public officials. Lobbyists seek access to public officials in all government branches. Lobbyists try to influence government officials by providing information regarding their group's interests and through grassroots lobbying. Many lobbyists are former public officials. The media are often critical of lobbying, and various attempts have been made to regulate lobbyists and lobbying. The manipulation of legal loopholes and the lack of stringent enforcement sometimes undermine lobbying regulations. What should they be allowed to do?

## Exercises

1. Do you think it matters that so many government servants become lobbyists and vice versa? What are the advantages and disadvantages of having a "revolving door" between lobbying and government service?
2. What makes lobbyists valuable to their clients? What can lobbyists do for groups seeking to influence politics?
3. How are lobbyists regulated? What can lobbyists still legally do under lobbying regulations?

# 9.4 Interest Groups and the Political System

## Learning Objectives

After reading this section, you should be able to answer the following questions:

1. What factors determine an interest group's success?
2. What are the levels of influence that interest groups can possess in their relations with policymakers?
3. What is pluralism?
4. What are the strengths and weaknesses of business interest groups?

In their book, *The Israel Lobby and U.S. Foreign Policy*, John J. Mearsheimer and Stephen M. Walt argue that the activities of interest groups, particularly the American Israel Public Affairs Committee, are one reason why, since World War II, the United States has provided more direct economic and military support to Israel than any other ally has and pursues a policy of preserving and enhancing Israel's security.[55] This raises the questions of why interest groups succeed or fail to achieve their policy objectives.[56]

## Why Interest Groups Are (or Are Not) Successful

The main factors determining an interest group's effectiveness are its assets, objectives, alliances, the visibility of its involvement in policy decisions, its responses to political change and crises, plus, of course, the media's depiction of it.

### Assets

Successful interest groups have prestige, respected leadership, political skills, and ample finances. The Business Roundtable, composed of the chief executives of the two hundred leading corporations, has them all and thus has access to and influence on policymakers. Monetary assets allow groups to contribute to political campaigns through their political action committees (PACs).

The status and distribution of an interest group's members also contribute to its success. Automobile dealers are influential and live, as do their employees, in congressional districts across the country. After President Barack Obama proposed putting automobile loans under the oversight of a new federal consumer authority aimed at protecting borrowers from abusive lenders, the dealers' lobbying arm, the National Automobile Dealers Association, organized opposition, including trips to Washington for some of the eighteen thousand dealers to meet and plead their case with their legislators.[57] Congress exempted auto dealers from the regulation.

## Objectives

The ease or difficulty of achieving a group's goals can determine its success. Preventing legislation from being enacted is usually easier than passing it. In a comprehensive study of interest group activities during the last two years of the Clinton administration and the first two years of the George W. Bush administration, researchers found that although some advocates succeed eventually in changing policy, "[t]he vast bulk of lobbying in Washington has to do not with the creation of new programs, but rather with the adjustment of existing programs or with the maintenance of programs just as they are."[58]

Moreover, legislation enacted over the opposition of powerful interest groups tends to be watered down, or the political costs of its passage are so heavy that its proponents in the presidential administration and Congress are discouraged from challenging the groups again.

## Alliances

Interest groups sometimes cooperate with other groups to help achieve a policy objective they could not accomplish alone. A coalition expands resources, broadens expertise, and adds to the credibility of the policy objective. Alliances are often of natural allies such as the National Restaurant Association, the American Nursery and Landscape Association, and the National Council of Agricultural Employers, which united to oppose restrictions on immigration and penalties on businesses that employ undocumented immigrants. But alliances can be made up of strange bedfellows, as when the ACLU and the NRA allied to oppose the U.S. Department of Justice's putting raw, unsubstantiated data into a national computer network. For the ACLU, it was a violation of people's right to privacy; for the NRA, it was a move toward denying people the right to bear arms.[59]

## Visibility of Policy Involvement

Interest groups are often most successful when their activities are unreported by the media, unscrutinized by most policymakers, and hidden from the public. Opposition to a group's activities is difficult when they are not visible. As one lobbyist observed, "A lobby is like a night flower, it thrives in the dark and dies in the sun."[60]

**iron triangles**

Congressional committees or subcommittees, bureaucratic agencies, and interest groups that together dominate policymaking in a policy area, oftentimes with little visibility.

In what are called **iron triangles**, or subgovernments, policy on a subject is often made by a relatively few people from Congress, the bureaucracy, and interest groups. A classic iron triangle was veterans' affairs policy. Members of Congress chairing the relevant committees and subcommittees and their aides, key agency administrators from the U.S. Department of Veterans Affairs, and representatives from interest groups such as the American Legion and the Veterans of Foreign Wars (VFW) have interacted and dominated policymaking.[61] This policymaking has taken place with low visibility and very little opposition to the benefits provided for veterans. In general, the news media pay little attention to iron triangles in the absence of conflict and controversy, and interest groups are likely to achieve many of their objectives.

## Political Change and Crises

Whether interest groups defend what they have or go on the offense to gain new benefits often depends on who is in control of the government. Some interest groups' goals are supported or opposed far more by one political party than another. A new president or a change in party control of Congress usually benefits some groups while putting others at a disadvantage. The Republican takeover of the presidency and control of Congress in the 2016 election put a brake on new regulation of business, reduced funds for regulators to hire staff and enforce regulations, and limited investigations of industry practices.

Crises, especially ones extensively depicted by the media, often involve politicians and interest groups trying to achieve or prevent policy changes. Looking to exploit the horrific BP (British Petroleum) oil spill of 2010 in the Gulf of Mexico (which was widely covered in the media, replete with images of oil-infested waters and oil-coated beaches and wildlife), environmentalists and their congressional allies worked for "measures to extend bans on new offshore drilling, strengthen safety and environmental safeguards, and raise to $10 billion or more the cap on civil liability for an oil producer in a spill."[62] Opposing them were the oil and gas industry, which, according to the Center for Responsive Politics, spent $174.8 million on lobbying in 2009, and its allies in Congress from such oil states as Texas and Louisiana.

# Relations between Interest Groups and Policymakers

When viewed overall, there is a hierarchy in the influence of relations between interest groups and policymakers.[63]

- At the top, the interest group makes policy. This is uncommon.
- More common, the group maintains close political relations with policymakers.
- The group has an unchallengeable veto status over some governmental decisions, for example, over a presidential appointment.
- The group receives some attention from policymakers but mainly has a pressure relationship with them.
- The group has only a potential reprisal relationship with policymakers; it can threaten to oppose a member of Congress at the next election.
- At the bottom of the ladder, rejected by policymakers, the group is left to agitate and resist; its public demonstrations usually signify its inability to achieve its objectives by less visible means.

The relationships between interest groups and policymakers vary depending on the administration in power. Energy companies had a close political support and referral relationship with the George W. Bush and Trump administrations but primarily a pressure relationship with the Obama administration. Relationships also vary by subject. For example, a Democratic president's choice to head the U.S. Department of Labor may have to be acceptable to the AFL-CIO, but the union organization has little influence over other cabinet appointments.

Our categorization of the relationships between interest groups and policymakers brings us to the anomalous American Legislative Exchange Council (ALEC). Information about this organization became widespread in the media after a batch of its internal documents was leaked to and published in *The Guardian* newspaper.[64]

Although not legally classified as an interest group, ALEC can be very effective in achieving its policy preferences, particularly in Republican-controlled state governments. The organization's modus operandi is to bring together representatives of corporations with state legislators (overwhelmingly Republican) from across the United States to develop "model" bills. At the sessions, the companies make presentations, there is a discussion, then a vote. At least 50 percent of the companies and of the legislators at a meeting must approve a piece of legislation if it is to go forward as a "model" bill. Thus both sides have a veto. Lawmakers can customize the bills, introduce, and try to pass them in their state legislatures.

Bills already enacted in various states deal with such issues as cutting taxes and regulation of business, reducing the compensation of public employees, privatizing public education (e.g., with school vouchers), tightening voter identification requirements, preventing regulations designed to reduce global warming, and opposing "Obamacare." Around two hundred become law annually.

Among the laws was "Stand Your Ground." First passed in 2005 in Florida, it was subsequently adopted by ALEC as a "model" and enacted in around twenty-six states. The law attracted considerable attention, much of it negative, when in 2012, neighborhood watch coordinator George Zimmerman killed Black high school student Trayvon Martin. This event, and Zimmerman's acquittal, gave ALEC unwanted publicity, disrupting its hitherto cozy and secretive relationship with corporations and state legislators. Civil rights groups attacked major corporations, threatening them with boycotts for their involvement with ALEC and therefore support of "Stand Your Ground." Some forty-one major companies, including Amazon, Coca-Cola, General Electric, McDonald's, and Walmart, left ALEC.

According to ALEC, it is a private members club that does not lobby. Its nonprofit status means it does not have to identify the participants in its sessions and its members can use their dues as a tax deduction. Yet critics pointed out that it gains access for corporations to legislators, presents and promotes industry-backed legislation, collaborates with legislators in designing the legislation, and encourages legislators to introduce and vote for bills in their state legislatures. In 2013, ALEC, perhaps in response to this criticism, created an organization allowing it to lobby more overtly without damaging its charitable status.[65]

# Who Benefits from Interest Groups?

In Federalist No. 10, James Madison warns of the dangers of factions: "[A] number of citizens, whether amounting to a majority or minority of the whole, who are united and actuated by some common impulse of passion, or of interest, adverse to the rights of other citizens, or to the permanent and aggregate interests of the community."[66] Madison believed that factions were inevitable, because their causes were "sown in the nature of man."[67]

Madison's factions are not exactly today's interest groups. Indeed, interest groups, by representing diverse segments of society, offset one of Madison's concerns—the domination of the majority. Nonetheless, his warning raises important questions about the effects of interest groups.

## Pluralism: Competition among Groups

**pluralism**

The theory that interest groups' competition leads to policy balance through compromise and negotiation.

**overlapping membership**

The theory that when people belong to several interest groups, they encourage negotiation and compromise and thereby limit any one group from dominating areas in which its interests are paramount.

Briefly stated, **pluralism** is the theory that competition among interest groups produces compromise and balance among competing policy preferences. For pluralists, the abundance of interest groups, the competition between them, and their representation of interests in society are inherent in American democracy. Bargaining between groups and ever-changing group alliances achieve a desirable dispersion of power or at least an acceptable balancing of the various interests in society.[68]

Pluralists acknowledge that some groups might dominate areas where their interests are paramount. But they believe two factors rectify this situation. In **overlapping membership**, people belonging to several interest groups encourage negotiation and compromise. Underrepresented people will in time establish groups to assert their interests.

## The Advantage of Business

An argument against pluralism is that business has an advantage over other segments of society, particularly people living in poverty and the working class.[69] These Americans lack the disposable income and political skills to organize. The issues that concern them are often absent from the policy agenda.[70] Business sponsors political advertisements, gives campaign contributions, donates to political parties, hires law and public relations firms, and funds research advocacy groups promoting free-market economics. A corporation can deploy multiple lobbyists and obtain access to various policymakers by joining several trade groups, belonging to business associations such as the U.S. Chamber of Commerce, and using its CEO and other personnel from headquarters to lobby.[71]

Business and trade associations make up approximately 70 percent of the organizations with representation in Washington, DC.[72] Add interest groups representing professionals, and they account for approximately 85 percent of total spending on lobbying.[73]

Quite often a policy appears only to affect specific corporations or industries and therefore does not receive much media or public attention.[74] The Walt Disney Company's copyright on Mickey Mouse was due to expire in 2003, and those on Pluto, Goofy, and Donald Duck would expire soon after. In 2000, after lobbying and well-placed campaign contributions by Disney, Congress extended all copyrights for twenty more years.[75]

Business is not monolithic. Interests conflict between and among industries, individual corporations, and organizations representing professionals. Large businesses can have different objectives than small businesses. The interests of manufacturers, distributors, and retailers can clash. Moreover, even when business is united, its demands are not necessarily gratified immediately and absolutely, especially when the issue is visible and the demands provoke opposition.

## Negative Depictions of Business

The media often depict business interest groups negatively, which can limit the groups' influence. For example, stories about the dubious dealings and bankruptcy of corporations such as Enron, the trials of corporate leaders who have pillaged their companies, and the huge salaries and bonuses paid in financial and related business sectors.

Corporations and their executives are commonly the villains in popular films, including *RoboCop* (1987), *Wall Street* (1987), *The Naked Gun 2½: The Smell of Fear* (1991), and the documentaries of Michael Moore, particularly *Roger and Me* (1989). Television news stories oftentimes portray the big business sector as buying access and favors with lavish campaign contributions and other indulgences, wielding undue influence on the policy process, and pursuing its interests at the expense of the national interest.[76] Newspapers similarly frame business interest groups and their lobbyists as involved in dubious activities and exercising power for private greed. Typical is the *New York Times* headline: "Vague Law and Hard Lobbying Add Up to Billions for Big Oil."[77]

These stories could frame business interest groups more positively. They could point out that business lobbyists favor essential and deserving objectives, present information and valid arguments to policymakers, and make their proposals in a political arena (i.e., Congress) in competition with other groups. However, the negative view of business is incarnated in the enduring image of the chairmen of the seven leading tobacco companies testifying before Congress (see the following "Enduring Image" for more info).

### Enduring Image

#### Big Tobacco Testifies Before Congress

On April 14, 1994, the chief executives of the leading tobacco companies stood up, raised their right hands, and swore before members of the subcommittee on Health and the Environment of the House of Representatives' Committee on Energy and Commerce that nicotine was not addictive. The photograph of this moment, prominently featured in the U.S. and foreign media, has become an enduring image of business executives who place the interests and profits of their corporations above the public interest even if it requires them to engage in self-deception, defy common sense about the dangers of their products, and give deceptive testimony under oath.

Had one sat through the several hours of hearings, watched them on television, or read the transcript, the executives would have come across as less defiant and more reasonable. They agreed to give Congress unpublished research documents, acknowledged that cigarettes may cause various health problems, including cancer and heart disease, and admitted that they would prefer that their children not smoke.[78] But the photo and its brief explanatory caption, not the complicated hearings, is the enduring image.

Why does this image of venal, almost criminal, tobacco executives endure? Simply put, television news's continuing coverage of the litigation by state attorneys general against the tobacco companies required vivid video to illustrate and dramatize an otherwise bland story. What better choice than the footage of the seven tobacco executives? Thus, the image circulated over and over again on the nightly news and is widely available on the internet years later.

The chairmen of the seven leading tobacco companies swear that nicotine is not addictive.

Source: John Duricka / Associated Press

## Key Takeaways

Numerous factors determine the success or failure of interest groups in achieving their policy objectives. These include their assets, objectives, alliances, visibility of their involvement in policy decisions, responses to political change and crises, and depictions in the media. Relatedly, there is a hierarchy of interest groups' (like ALEC's) relations with policymakers. Pluralists regard interest groups as essential to American democracy; critics, however, believe that business interest groups are too dominant. Business interest groups have several advantages enabling them to achieve their policy objectives but also several disadvantages, including negative media depictions.

## Exercises

1. What makes an interest group effective? What do you think are the most effective interest groups in the United States?
2. Why might interest groups be more effective when their activities are not widely known? Why might publicity make lobbying less effective?
3. What advantages do business interest groups have in influencing public policies? What factors limit the effectiveness of business interest lobbying?

# 9.5 Interest Groups in the Information Age

## Learning Objectives

After reading this section, you should be able to answer the following questions:

1. How do interest groups interact with the media?
2. How do the media depict interest groups?
3. What are the consequences of these depictions?

## Media Interactions

The National Rifle Association covets attention. It operates NRATV, a pugilistic online video channel. The NRA has assumed that most of its coverage, even when unfavorable, benefits it by showing it under attack, thereby rallying more members to its ranks, donations to its coffers, and proponents to its views. But in 2019, depictions in the news of an organizational crisis, the departure of its president, the removal of its second-in-command, its severed relationship with advertising agency, the shutdown of online production of NRATV, the investigations of its finances by congressional committees, and the scrutiny by the New York state attorney general, may have undermined the faith of some of its existing and potential adherents.[79]

Many business interest groups remain restrained and try not to interact with the news media at all. They avoid media attention, particularly when it is likely to be negative. They prefer to pursue their policy objectives out of the media's and the public's sight and scrutiny.

### Public Relations

Other interest groups have the need or the resources to strive for a favorable image and promote themselves and their policy preferences. One way is through advertising. They place advertisements on the television networks' evening news shows in policymakers' constituencies, such as Washington, DC, and New York, where opinion leaders will see them, and in prominent newspapers, such as the *New York Times*, the *Washington Post*, and the *Wall Street Journal*. Even media outlets with tiny audiences may be suitable for advertisements. The Lockheed Martin Corporation has advertised in the policy-oriented *National Journal* in order to reach Washington insiders and policymakers.

**public relations**

Techniques designed to promote an interest group's activities, image, and policy preferences positively.

Some interest groups engage in **public relations** campaigns. Walmart paid $10 million annually to counter lobbying groups that were funded by two unions. These unions were critical of the retail giant's low wages, inadequate health care, and discrimination against women. The public relations campaign promoted the company's positive activities and responded to criticisms.[80]

Public relations is not confined to American interest groups. Numerous foreign governments have U.S. public relations consultants or lobbyists representing them in communicating with the U.S. media, policymakers, and public. The firms instruct their clients on how to deal with the media, arrange meetings for them with journalists, set up editorial briefings, pitch stories to reporters and editors, and try to create newsworthy events. These tactics usually succeed in increasing and improving the countries' news coverage and images.[81]

Occasionally, the media expose this public relations activity. The *New York Times* revealed that, in part because fifteen of the nineteen terrorists involved with the attacks on 9/11 were Saudi Arabian, the Saudi "government spent millions of dollars on well-connected lobbyists and national television advertisements after 9/11 in a drive to improve its image among Americans."[82]

## Advocacy Campaigns

A few interest groups engage in advocacy campaigns through the media. A notable example took place during the 1994 attempt by the Clinton administration to change the U.S. health-care system. Some $60 million was spent on advertising, with opponents outspending supporters two to one.

The Health Insurance Association of America (now named America's Health Insurance Plans), representing small to medium-sized insurance companies, waged the most effective public campaign. Under the appealing name of the Coalition for Health Insurance Choices, it spent around $14 million creating and showing television ads in which a woman (Louise) and her spouse (Harry) critically comment on alleged defects in the president's health-care proposal. "Having choices we don't like is no choice at all," says Louise in one ad. No direct reference was made to the health insurance industry behind the ad.[83]

The ads were aimed at members of Congress and thus aired mostly in Washington, DC, and on CNN. They attracted news coverage, which amplified awareness about, attributed influence to, and enhanced their effects. By framing the administration's proposal in terms of high cost and big government, the ads contributed to its defeat in Congress. It would not be until 2010 that reform of health care would be achieved, as discussed in Chapter 16.

Advocacy campaigns may not be above board. FTI Consulting was hired by some of the world's largest oil and gas companies to influence public opinion, to appear to be speaking for ordinary people. Among the consultant's fancy-named creations: Texans for Natural Gas (to support fracking), the Arctic Energy Center (for drilling in Alaskan waters and the Arctic wildlife refuge); and the Main Street Investors Coalition (warning about the threat of climate activism to small-time investors in the stock market).[84]

## Attracting Media Attention

Most interest groups lack sufficient funds to advertise at all. Yet coverage in the news media can be essential, especially for many public interest groups, if they are to recruit members, raise funds, improve their access to policymakers, and obtain public support for their objectives.[85] So they hold news conferences, issue press releases, release research studies, give interviews to journalists, and try to have their spokespeople appear on talk radio and television public affairs shows. Their problem is that there are far more groups seeking news coverage than the media can accommodate.

Interest groups deploy several techniques to attract media coverage. Among them are the catchy phrase, the telling statistic, the scorecard, and the poll. Charlton Heston embodied the catchy phrase. While he was president and spokesperson of the NRA, he held up a musket during its annual meeting and stated to members that the only way he would give up his gun is when they pry it "from my cold dead hands."

This media-attention-getting phrase became his trademark, which he repeated with other guns at subsequent conventions. They were the last words he uttered before he officially stepped down from the NRA's presidency in 2003.

Another technique is the telling statistic. A report titled *City Slickers: How Farm Subsidy Checks End Up in Big Cities* from the Environmental Working Group achieved widespread and prominent publicity when it revealed that $1.2 million per year in agricultural subsidies was going to people living in the 90210 zip code, which is, as most Americans know from the television show of the same name, urban and affluent Beverly Hills.[86] Because farm subsidies are traditionally justified as preserving and protecting family farms, the report persuasively reframed the issue as government subsidies to wealthy corporate farm interests.[87]

Some interest groups issue scorecards that enable journalists to report easily how policymakers have voted on issues of concern to the group's members and the public. The League of Conservation Voters has released a list to the press during election years of the "Dirty Dozen" members of Congress with the supposedly worst records on the environment. The legislators targeted are usually in close races, and some 60 percent of them have been defeated.

**FIGURE 9.2** Charlton Heston and the NRA

As its president, this hero of some of Hollywood's greatest epics brought the NRA even more prominence, especially when he uttered his defiant phrase.

Source: Getty Images/Staff

Interest groups also pay for or conduct public opinion polls, sometimes with questions that frame the issue to push the public toward their point of view. During the California water shortage of 2001, the California Farm Bureau released a poll showing that 71 percent of those polled believed "that the federal government has a financial responsibility to help keep California's farmers in agriculture production." The actual question asked about "California family farmers" (the word "family" encouraged a positive response), the phrase "financial responsibility" is quite vague, and the 71 percent figure was achieved by adding the 44 percent "definite yes" response to the 27 percent "probably yes" response.[88]

## Disproportionate Coverage

Most news coverage of societal and public interest groups goes only to a few. According to Lucig H. Danielian and Benjamin Page, "The media seize upon a few prominent individuals or groups to speak for broad sets of interests."[89]

Witness a study of 244 interest groups in fourteen major newspapers, two news magazines, and the top three television networks.[90] The single most-covered group in each of four policy areas received around 40 percent of all the coverage in that area. These were the Sierra Club on the environment, the Council on Foreign Relations on national security and foreign policy, the ACLU for civil rights, and the Christian Coalition of America on broad matters of public policy. The figure reaches approximately 68 percent of total coverage when the number of groups is lowered to twelve (5 percent of the total number) to include the NAACP, Greenpeace, and a few others. In contrast, 34 percent of the 244 interest groups did not appear in a single story.

The larger a group's budget, the more likely it is to be covered. These groups have staff to communicate with the media, hold regular press conferences, provide the press with dependable information, stage events with dramatic visuals and symbolism, and make news by suing the government. They also are covered because reporters return repeatedly to sources familiar to them and their audiences.

Most news organizations are not inclined to incur the expense of investigating interest groups' organization and claims of accomplishments. Nor are they able to obtain easy access to the groups' records. For ten years, the Christian Coalition was the most prominent interest group of the religious right. Journalists took the claims of its leaders at face value. Only later did a former national leader who had left the group reveal to the press that the number of members had been inflated.[91]

## Media Consequences

Media depictions matter. Favorable coverage of public interest groups seeking to protect the environment and consumers has helped get their issues on the policy agenda and some of their proposals enacted.[92] The breast cancer lobby is far more successful at shaping media coverage and thus influencing public opinion and determining public policy (including government funding) than the prostate cancer lobby, even though the diseases have almost identical morbidity and mortality rates.[93]

Disproportionate coverage of a few societal and public interest groups enhances their importance and the impression that each one represents a policy area. Instead, there is often a spectrum of interest groups across areas. Sparse or nonexistent coverage of these interest groups means that the media do not bring their demands, activities, and policy perspectives to the attention of policymakers and the public.

Unfavorable media depictions of labor unions reinforce their negative stereotypes. This coverage reduces public support for unions' organizing efforts and discourages people from voluntarily joining unions. It discredits striking as a desirable or even appropriate way for unions to achieve their objectives.

Media coverage of business interest groups conveys their power. It limits this power by framing it as excessive and adverse to the public interest and by exposing some of it as greed and exploitation. This coverage affects public opinion. Of the people polled about "the power of different groups in influencing government policy, politicians, and policymakers in Washington" and which groups had "too much" influence, 86 percent selected "big companies," 83 percent chose "political action committees which give money to political candidates," and 71 percent picked "political lobbyists."[94] Overwhelmingly, people have the impression that government is run by a few big interests.[95] In November 2005, 90 percent of respondents to a Harris poll (up from 83 percent the previous year) said big companies had too much influence on government.

No wonder interest groups become issues in elections. Each party accuses the other of being beholden to "special interests" and of unsavory relationships with lobbyists. The media pursue stories about interest group contributions and of lobbyists holding prominent staff positions in candidates' campaigns. Democratic presidential candidate Barack Obama refused in the 2008 presidential election to accept contributions from registered lobbyists and political action committees (PACs). Republican nominee John McCain established a conflict-of-interest policy that resulted in the resignation or dismissal of several members of his campaign staff who were registered as lobbyists.

### Key Takeaways

Interest groups use a variety of techniques to interact with the news media and obtain favorable coverage. These include advertising, public relations, and advocacy. Despite the vast number of interest groups in existence, the news media tend to cover the activities of only a few leading organizations. Media depictions of interest groups can have a significant impact on public opinion about them and support for or opposition to their policy preferences. The media often depict big business groups negatively, while they usually portray other groups, such as environmental organizations, more positively. The overall effect of the media's depictions of interest groups is to give people the impression that government is run by a few big interests.

## Exercises

1. Why do you think some interest groups avoid media exposure? Why do others try to use the media to achieve their objectives?
2. Which interest groups do you view negatively? Which do you view positively? What do you think made you view those groups that way?

### Civic Education

**SAVE**

Forming an interest group and keeping it going takes a strong commitment, but many young people have done just that. They recognize that there is power in numbers and that having a group of people unite behind a cause can be more effective than acting alone. Enterprising young people have established interest groups representing a wide range of causes and issues.

An example of a youth-focused interest group is the Student Association for Voter Empowerment (SAVE), a national organization of college students whose mission is to promote civic education in order to increase voter participation and help young people navigate the public policy process and interact with government. In addition to voter advocacy, SAVE lobbies government officials to pass legislation promoting jobs, health insurance, and college financial aid for young people. SAVE was founded by Kenyon College graduates Matthew Segal and Anna Salzberg and has over ten thousand members on campuses in fifteen states. The organization makes use of online media to facilitate its operations. Students wishing to start a chapter of SAVE on their campus can access an online tool kit with directions for creating a constitution, building an organization, and becoming active. The organization provides information about key issues, advertises its activities, including conferences and outreach projects, fundraises, and facilitates communication among its members. Group leaders also publish a blog on the Huffington Post. SAVE was instrumental in getting the House of Representatives to introduce the bipartisan Student Voter Opportunity to Encourage Registration (VOTER) Act of 2008, which requires colleges to take measures to register students to vote.

In 2011, SAVE combined with "Declare Yourself" to become "Our Time" promoting greater representation of Americans under thirty.

# 9.6 Recommended Reading

Ainsworth, Scott H. *Analyzing Interest Groups: Group Influence on People and Policies*. New York: W. W. Norton, 2002. An analysis of interest groups and their activities using a theoretical approach.

Baumgartner, Frank R., Jeffrey M. Berry, Marie Hojnacki, David C. Kimball, and Beth L. Leech. *Lobbying and Policy Change: Who Wins, Who Loses, and Why*. Chicago: University of Chicago Press, 2009. An account showing that because the entrenched Washington system favors the status quo, 60 percent of lobbying campaigns fail to change policy.

Berry, Jeffrey M., and Clyde Wilcox. *The Interest Group Society*, 6th ed. New York: Routledge, 2018. A leading text providing basic information about most aspects of interest groups.

Cigler, Allan J., Burdett A. Loomis, and Anthony Nowness, eds. *Interest Group Politics*, 9th ed. Washington, DC: Sage, 2021. An informative and wide-ranging collection of research on interest groups in American politics.

Dahl, Robert A. *A Preface to Democratic Theory*. Chicago: University of Chicago Press, 1956. The leading statement of the pluralist position and the democratic role of interest groups.

Hertel-Fernandez, Alexander. *State Capture: How Conservative Activists, Big Businesses and Wealthy Donors Reshaped the American States—and the Nation*. New York: Oxford University Press, 2019. The American Legislative Exchange Council, State Policy Network, and Americans for Prosperity revealed.

Olson, Mancur, Jr. *The Logic of Collective Action: Public Goods and the Theory of Groups*. Cambridge, MA: Harvard University Press, 1965. An influential study using an economic approach to understand groups' organization, membership, and effectiveness.

Schattschneider, Elmer E. *The Semi-Sovereign People*. New York: Holt, Rinehart, and Winston, 1960. A powerful critique of pluralism and American democracy.

Schlozman, Kay Lehman, and John T. Tierney. *Organized Interests and American Democracy*. New York: Harper & Row, 1986. A comprehensive account of Washington-based interest groups in the early 1980s.

Truman, David B. *The Governmental Process: Political Interests and Public Opinion*, 2nd ed. New York: Alfred A. Knopf, 1971 (originally published 1951). This book revived the study of interest groups as central to U.S. politics and raised many subjects, concepts, and questions that are still important.

## 9.7 Recommended Viewing

*Casino Jack and the United States of Money* (2010). Droll documentary about Jack Abramoff, his confederates, and his victims.

*Citizen Ruth* (1996). A satire in which a delinquent, pregnant girl (Laura Dern) is exploited and then exploits the pro-life and pro-choice movements battling over her.

*Harlan County, U.S.A.* (1976). Powerful documentary about the strike of Kentucky mine workers against a mining company.

*Matewan* (1987). John Sayles' film, based on actual events in West Virginia in 1920, of the bitter and violent conflict when coal miners struggled to organize a union over the repression of the mine owners.

*The Naked Gun 2½: The Smell of Fear* (1991). In one of the plots, oil, coal, and nuclear interests kidnap and replace the president's pro-environment energy policy appointee.

*Norma Rae* (1979). Southern mill worker becomes an independent woman as she protests working conditions and strives to organize a union.

*On the Waterfront* (1954). Marlon Brando is memorable as a man who accepts then fights against union corruption.

*The People and the Power Game: The Lobbies* (1996). A television program that analyzes the relationship between members of Congress and the lobbyists who seek to influence them.

*Roger & Me* (1989). A docucomedy in which Michael Moore pursues General Motors' president to show him how the closing of automobile plants and firing of workers affected Flint, Michigan.

*Thank You for Smoking* (2005). Comedy about the tribulations and triumphs of a public relations operative for big tobacco.

# Endnotes


1. "Mr. Lisa Goes to Washington." *The Simpsons*. Season 3 Episode 2, 20th Century Fox, September 26, 1991.
2. Matt Groening, James L. Brooks, Sam Simon, and George Meyer, "Mr. Lisa Goes to Washington," *The Simpsons*, Season 3, Episode 2, originally aired September 26, 1991. This episode is loosely based on the movie *Mr. Smith Goes to Washington*.
3. James D. Savage, *Funding Science in America: Congress, Universities, and the Politics of the Academic Pork Barrel* (New York: Cambridge University Press, 1999); and Jeffrey Brainard and J. J. Hermes, "Colleges' Earmarks Grow, Amid Criticism," *Chronicle of Higher Education*, March 28, 2008.
4. Kay Lehman Schlozman and John T. Tierney, *Organized Interests and American Democracy* (New York: Harper & Row, 1986), 72–73.
5. Theda Skocpol and Alexander Hertel-Fernandez, "The Koch Network and Republican Party Extremism," *Perspectives on Politics* (14:1), September 2016, 681–99.
6. See McGee Young, *Developing Interests: Organizational Change and the Politics of Advocacy* (Lawrence: University Press of Kansas, 2010), for a discussion of groups' founding and evolution through time.
7. This is known as disturbance theory. It was developed by David B. Truman in *The Governmental Process: Political Interests and Public Opinion*, 2nd ed. (New York: Alfred A. Knopf, 1971), chap. 4; and it was amplified by Robert H. Salisbury in "An Exchange Theory of Interest Groups," *Midwest Journal of Political Science* 13 (1969): 1–32.
8. Ceilia Kang and Kenneth P. Vogel, "Tech Titans Build Lobbyist Army, Trying to Repel Threats to Power," *The New York Times*, June 6, 2019, A1 (16).
9. Julia Preston, "Cash Amplifies Call to Reshape Immigration," *The New York Times*, November 15, 2014, A1.
10. Scott H. Ainsworth, *Analyzing Interest Groups: Group Influence on People and Policies* (New York: W. W. Norton, 2002), 87–88.
11. Joshua L. Powell, *Inside the N.R.A.: A Tell-All Account of Corruption, Greed, and Paranoia Within the Most Powerful Political Group in America* (New York: Grand Central Publishing, 2020).
12. Robert Michels, *Political Parties: A Sociological Study of the Oligarchical Tendencies of Modern Democracy* (New York: Dover Publications, 1959; first published 1915 by Free Press).
13. Scott H. Ainsworth, *Analyzing Interest Groups: Group Influence on People and Policies* (New York: W. W. Norton, 2002), 114–15.
14. Bruce Bimber, Andrew J. Flanagin, and Cynthia Stohl, *Collective Action in Organizations: Interaction and Engagement in an Era of Technological Change* (New York: Cambridge University Press, 2012); also David Karpf, *The MoveOn Effect: The Unexpected Transformation of American Political Advocacy* (New York: Oxford University Press, 2012).
15. Scott Sigmund Gartner and Gary M. Segura, "Appearances Can Be Deceiving: Self Selection, Social Group Identification, and Political Mobilization," *Rationality and Society* 9 (1977): 132–33.
16. See Mancur Olson Jr., *The Logic of Collective Action: Public Goods and the Theory of Groups* (Cambridge, MA: Harvard University Press, 1965).
17. Eric Lichtblau, "F.B.I. Leader Wins a Few at Meeting of A.C.L.U.," *The New York Times*, June 14, 2003, accessed March 23, 2011, http://www.nytimes.com/2003/06/14/us/fbi-leader-wins-a-few-at-meeting-of-aclu.html?ref=ericlichtblau.
18. Brian Anse Patrick, *The National Rifle Association and the Media: The Motivating Force of Negative Coverage* (New York: Peter Lang, 2002), 9.
19. William J. Puette, *Through Jaundiced Eyes: How the Media View Organized Labor* (Ithaca, NY: ILR Press, 1992).
20. For an exception, see Deepa Kumar, *Outside The Box: Corporate Media, Globalization, and the UPS Strike* (Urbana: University of Illinois Press, 2007).
21. *Affirmative Advocacy: Race, Class, and Gender in Interest Group Politics* (Chicago: University of Chicago Press, 2007).
22. Michael M. Franz, *Choices and Changes: Interest Groups in the Electoral Process* (Philadelphia, PA: Temple University Press, 2008), 7.
23. The case is *Citizens United v. Federal Election Commission*, No. 08–205. See also Adam Liptak, "Justices, 5-4, Reject Corporate Spending Limit," *The New York Times*, January 21, 2010, accessed March 23, 2011, http://www.nytimes.com/2010/01/22/us/politics/22scotus.html.
24. Don Van Natta Jr., "Enron's Collapse: Campaign Finance; Enron or Andersen Made Donations to Almost All Their Congressional Investigators," *The New York Times*, January 25, 2002, accessed March 23, 2011, http://www.nytimes.com/2002/01/25/business/enron-s-collapse-campaign-finance-enron-andersen-made-donations-almost-all- their.html.
25. Mark Green, "Political PAC-Man," *New Republic* (December 13, 1982): 18.
26. Center for Responsive Politics, "Money and Medicare: Campaign Contributions Correlate with Vote," *OpenSecrets Blog*, November 24, 2003, http://www.opensecrets.org/capital_eye/inside.php?ID=113.
27. John R. Wright, *Interest Groups and Congress* (Boston: Allyn and Bacon, 1996), 9–10.
28. Eric Lichtblau, "Lawmakers Regulate Banks, Then Flock to Them," *The New York Times*, April 13, 2010, accessed March 23, 2011, http://www.nytimes.com/2010/04/14/business/14lobby.html.
29. Eric Lichtblau, "Ex-Regulators Get Set to Lobby on New Financial Rules," *The New York Times*, July 27, 2010, accessed on March 23, 2011, http://www.nytimes.com/2010/07/28/business/28lobby.html.
30. The Center for Responsive Politics has compiled a comprehensive database of lobbyist activities. "Lobbying Database," Center for Responsive Politics, accessed March 23, 2011, http://www.opensecrets.org/lobbyists/index.php.
31. Eric Lipton, Brooke Williams and Nicholas Confessore, "Foreign Powers Buy Influence at Think Tanks," *The New York Times*, September 6, 2014, A1.
32. On think tanks generally, see Thomas Medvetz, *Think Tanks in America* (Chicago: University of Chicago Press, 2012).
33. For detailed revelations about and examples of the relationships, see Eric Lipton, "Lobbyists, Bearing Gifts, Pursue Attorneys General," *The New York Times*, October 29, 2014, A1, 16–18.
34. Rogan Kersh, "Corporate Lobbyists as Political Actors: A View from the Field," in *Interest Group Politics*, 6th ed., ed. Allan J. Cigler and Burdett A. Loomis (Washington, DC: CQ Press, 2002), 227.
35. Simon F. Haeder and Susan Webb Yackee, "Influence and the Administrative Process: Lobbying the U.S. President's Office of Management and Budget," *American Political Science Review* 109:3 (2015): 507–22.
36. Michael LaForgia, et al., "D.C.'s Swamp Has New Aim: Another Term," *The New York Times*, July 6, 2020, A1 (17).
37. Kenneth P. Vogel and Eric Lipton, "Companies and Countries Rush to Lobby Biden," *The New York Times*, November 18, 2020, A1 (20).
38. Robert Pear, "Medicare Law Prompts a Rush for Lobbyists," *The New York Times*, August 23, 2005, accessed March 23, 2011, http://www.nytimes.com/2005/08/23/politics/23health.html.
39. Micheline Maynard, "House Panel Says Toyota Misled Public on Safety," *The New York Times*, February 23, 2010, accessed March 23, 2011, http://www.nytimes.com/2010/02/23/business/global/23toyota.html?ref=michelinemaynard.
40. Jesse Drucker and Jim Tankersley, "Business Got Big TaxCut; Lobbyists Made It Bigger," *The New York Times*,December 31, 2019, A1 (12).
41. Lauren Cohen Bell, *Warring Factions: Interest Groups, Money, and the New Politics of Senate Confirmation* (Columbus: Ohio State University Press, 2002).
42. For the advantages and disadvantages of going to the courts, see Julianna S. Gonen, *Litigation as Lobbying* (Columbus: Ohio State University Press, 2003).
43. Jonathan Mahler, "Group's Path on Clinton: Sue Early and Often," *The New York Times*, October 13, 2016, A17.
44. Jim VandeHei, "Rain Dance: Mississippi Choctaw Find an Unlikely Ally In a GOP Stalwart…," *Wall Street Journal*, July 3, 2000.
45. David E. Rosenbaum, "At $500 an Hour, Lobbyist's Influence Rises with G.O.P.," *The New York Times*, April 3, 2002, accessed March 23, 2011, http://query.nytimes.com/gst/full-page.html?res=9A01E6DC103AF930A35757C0A9649C8B63.
46. Susan Schmidt, "A Jackpot from Indian Gaming Tribes," *Washington Post*, February 22, 2004, accessed March 23, 2011, http://www.washingtonpost.com/ac2/wp-dyn/A60906-2004Feb21?language=printer.
47. David Margolick,"Washington's Invisible Man," *Vanity Fair*, April 2006, 247.
48. David Margolick,"Washington's Invisible Man," *Vanity Fair*, April 2006, 200.
49. U.S. Government Printing Office, "Legislative Reorganization Acts: Provisions of the Legislative Reorganization Acts of 1946 and 1970 Applicable to Both Houses," accessed April 4, 2011, http://www.gpo.gov/congress/house/hd106-320/pdf/hrm85.pdf.
50. U.S. House of Representatives, Office of the Law Revision Counsel, "2 USC Chapter 26: Disclosure of Lobbying Activities," accessed April 4, 2011, http://uscode.house.gov/download/pls/02C26.txt.
51. Lobbying Disclosure Act of 1995, Pub. L. No. 104-65, 109 Stat. 691–706 (December 19, 1995).
52. Eric Lipton, "A Loophole Allows Lawmakers To Reel In Trips and Donations," *The New York Times*, January 20, 2014,10.
53. Executive Order, "Ethics Commitments by Executive Branch Personnel," January 21, 2009, http://www.whitehouse.gov/the_press_office/Executive Order-Ethics Commitments.
54. Michael S. Schmidt and Eric Lipton, "Executive Order Toughens Some Facets of Lobbying Ban and Weakens Others," *The New York Times*, January 29, 1917, A16.
55. John J. Mearsheimer and Stephen M. Walt, *The Israel Lobby and U.S. Foreign Policy* (New York: Farrar, Straus & Giroux, 2007); see also the critique by Robert C. Lieberman, "The 'Israel Lobby' and American Politics," *Perspectives on Politics* 7, no. 2 (June 2009): 235–57; the rebuttal by John J. Mearsheimer and Stephen M. Walt, "The Blind and the Elephant in the Room: Robert Lieberman and the Israel Lobby," *Perspectives on Politics* 7, no. 2 (June 2009): 259–73; and the rejoinder by Robert Lieberman, "Rejoinder to Mearsheimer and Walt," *Perspectives on Politics* 7, no. 2 (June 2009): 275–81; also Connie Bruck, "Friends of Israel," *New Yorker* (September 1, 2014): 50–63.
56. Also see Matt Grossmann, *The Not-So-Special Interests: Interest Groups, Public Representation, and American Governance* (Stanford: Stanford University Press, 2012).

57. Eric Lichtblau, "Auto Dealers Campaign to Fend Off Regulation," *The New York Times*, May 16, 2010, accessed March 23, 2011, http://www.nytimes.com/2010/05/17/business/17dealers.html.
58. Frank R. Baumgartner, Jeffrey M. Berry, Marje Hojnacki, David C. Kimball, and Beth L. Leech, *Lobbying and Policy Change: Who Wins, Who Loses, and Why* (Chicago: University of Chicago Press, 2009), 240. See also R. Kenneth Godwin and Barry J. Seldon, "What Corporations Really Want from Government: The Public Provision of Private Goods," in *Interest Group Politics*, 6th ed., ed. Allan J. Cigler and Burdett A. Loomis (Washington, DC: CQ Press, 2002), 205–224.
59. Jeffrey M. Berry, and Clyde Wilcox, *The Interest Group Society*, 3rd. ed. (New York: Longman, 2008), 188–190.
60. Jeffrey Goldberg, "Real Insiders," *New Yorker*, July 4, 2005, accessed March 23, 2011, http://www.newyorker.com/archive/2005/07/04/050704fa_fact.
61. J. Leiper Freeman, *The Political Process: Bureau-Legislative Committee Relations*, rev. ed. (New York: Random House, 1965).
62. Eric Lichtblau and Jad Mouaward, "Oil Companies Weigh Strategies to Fend Off Tougher Regulations," *The New York Times*, June 2, 2010, accessed March 23, 2011, http://www.nytimes.com/2010/06/03/us/03lobby.html.
63. These categories come from Samuel J. Eldersveld, "American Interest Groups," in *Interest Groups on Four Continents*, ed. Henry W. Ehrmann (Pittsburgh, PA: University of Pittsburgh Press, 1958), 187.
64. See "How ALEC Serves As A 'Dating Service' For Politicians And Corporations" broadcast on National Public Radio's Fresh Air, December 10, 2013; the story is based on ALEC internal documents leaked to the *Guardian* newspaper; see also, Alexander Hertel-Fernandez, "Who Passes Business's 'Model Bills'? Policy Capacity and Corporate Influence in U.S. State Politics,' *Perspectives on Politics,* 12:3 (September 2014): 582–602.
65. For a definitive discussion, see the book by Alexander Hertel-Fernandez in 9.6 Recommended Reading.
66. James Madison, "Federalist #10," in Clinton Rossiter, ed., *The Federalist Papers* (New York: New American Library, 1961), 78; see also Library of Congress, THOMAS, "Federalist No. 10," accessed April 4, 2011, http://thomas.loc.gov/home/histdox/fed_10.html.
67. James Madison, "Federalist #10," in *The Federalist Papers*, ed. Clinton Rossiter (New York: New American Library, 1961), 79.
68. See Robert A. Dahl, *A Preface to Democratic Theory* (Chicago: University of Chicago Press, 1956); also Arthur F. Bentley, *The Process of Government: A Study of Social Pressures* (Chicago: University of Chicago Press, 1908); and William P. Browne, *Groups, Interests, and U.S. Public Policy* (Washington, DC: Georgetown University Press, 1998).
69. Kay Lehman Schlozman, Sidney Verba, and Henry E. Brady, *The Unheavenly Chorus: Unequal Political Voice and the Broken Promise of American Democracy* (Princeton: Princeton University Press, 2012).
70. Frank R. Baumgartner, Jeffrey M. Berry, Marje Hojnacki, David C. Kimball, and Beth L. Leech, *Lobbying and Policy Change: Who Wins, Who Loses, and Why* (Chicago: University of Chicago Press, 2009), 254–55.
71. Jeffrey M. Berry and Clyde Wilcox, *The Interest Group Society*, 3rd. ed. (New York: Longman, 2008), 221.
72. Kay Lehman Schlozman and John T. Tierney, *Organized Interests and American Democracy* (New York: Harper & Row, 1986), 67.
73. Frank R. Baumgartner and Beth L. Leech, "Interest Niches and Policy Bandwagons: Patterns of Interest Group Involvement in National Politics," *Journal of Politics* 63, no. 4 (November 2001): 1197. The figure is for 1996.
74. Mark A. Smith, *American Business and Political Power: Public Opinion, Elections, and Democracy* (Chicago: University of Chicago Press, 2000).
75. James Surowiecki, "Righting Copywrongs," *New Yorker*, January 21, 2002, accessed March 23, 2011, http://www.newyorker.com/archive/2002/01/21/020121ta_talk_surowiecki.
76. Lucig H. Danielian and Benjamin Page, "The Heavenly Chorus: Interest Group Voices on TV News," *American Journal of Political Science* 38, no. 4 (November 1994): 1056.
77. Edmund L. Andrews, "Vague Law and Hard Lobbying Add Up to Billions for Big Oil," *The New York Times*, March 27, 2006, accessed March 23, 2011, http://www.nytimes.com/2006/03/27/business/27royalties.html.
78. For an account of the hearing, see Philip J. Hilts, "Tobacco Chiefs Say Cigarettes Aren't Addictive," *The New York Times*, April 15, 1994, accessed on March 23, 2011, http://www.nytimes.com/1994/04/15/us/tobacco-chiefs-say-cigarettes- aren-t-addictive.html.
79. Danny Hakim, "N.R.A. Shuts Down Production of NRATV as Its No.2 Official Resigns," *The New York Times*, June 27, 2019, A20.
80. Jeffrey Goldberg, "Selling Wal-Mart," *New Yorker*, April 2, 2007, accessed March 23, 2011, http://www.newyorker.com/reporting/2007/04/02/070402fa_fact_goldberg.
81. Jarol B. Manheim, *Strategic Public Diplomacy and American Foreign Policy* (New York: Oxford University Press, 1994); also Jarol B. Manheim and Robert B. Albritton, "Changing National Images: International Public Relations and Media Agenda Setting," *American Political Science Review* 78, no. 3 (September 1984): 641–57; and Pat Choate, *Agents of Influence: How Japan's Lobbyists in the United States Manipulate America's Political and Economic System* (New York: Knopf, 1990).
82. Christopher Marquis, "Worried Saudis Pay Millions to Improve Image in the U.S.," *The New York Times*, August 29, 2002, accessed March 23, 2011, http://www.nytimes.com/2002/08/29/world/worried-saudis-pay-millions-to-improve-image-in-the-us.html.
83. Quoted from "Harry and Louise Health Care Ad Compilation." William J. Clinton Presidential Library. https://www.youtube.com/watch?v=Cd_xPNT1Fh8.
84. Hiroko Tabuchi, "Global Firm Cast Big Oil's Messages as Grass-Roots Campaigns," *The New York Times*, November 12, 2020, A1 (24).
85. Kay Lehman Schlozman and John T. Tierney, *Organized Interests and American Democracy* (New York: Harper & Row, 1986), chap. 10; also Ken Kollman, *Outside Lobbying: Public Opinion & Interest Group Strategies* (Princeton, NJ: Princeton University Press, 1998).
86. Ken Cook, Clark Williams, Andrew Art, and Chris Campbell, *City Slickers: How Farm Subsidy Checks End Up in Big Cities*, March 1995, accessed April 4, 2011, http://www.ewg.org/reports/slickers.
87. Jeffrey M. Berry and Clyde Wilcox, *The Interest Group Society*, 3rd. ed. (New York: Longman, 2008), 235–36.
88. California Farm Bureau Federation, "Farm leader calls for Federal action on farm crisis," May 8, 2001.
89. Lucig H. Danielian and Benjamin Page, "The Heavenly Chorus: Interest Group Voices on TV News," *American Journal of Political Science* 38, no. 4 (November 1994): 1069.
90. A. Trevor Thrall, "The Myth of the Outside Strategy: Mass Media News Coverage of Interest Groups," *Political Communication* 23, no. 4 (2006): 407–20.
91. Laurie Goodstein, "Debt and Leadership Turmoil Sap Christian Coalition's Political Strengths," *International Herald Tribune*, August 3, 1999, 3.
92. Jeffrey M. Berry, *The New Liberalism: The Rising Power of Citizen Groups* (Washington, DC: Brookings Institution Press, 2000).
93. Karen M. Kedrowski and Marilyn Stine Sarow, *Cancer Activism: Gender, Media, and Public Policy* (Urbana: University of Illinois Press, 2007).
94. The Harris Poll, April 26–May 5, 2001.
95. 1995 poll cited in Jeffrey M. Berry and Clyde Wilcox, *The Interest Group Society*, 3rd. ed. (New York: Longman, 2008), 19.

CHAPTER 10

# Political Parties

## 10.1 Preamble

A favorite pastime of political journalists is periodically assessing the state of political parties, usually in conjunction with national elections. Journalists are rarely optimistic or complimentary when describing parties' present status or forecasting their future, often predicting the decline of the two major political parties. However, history has shown that the two major American political parties, the Democrats and Republicans, are amazingly enduring institutions, even when the mass media have sold them short. The strength and popularity of parties in the political process shift regularly. Political parties are adaptive institutions whose organization and functions change in response to different political and historical circumstances.[1] The Republican and the Democratic parties each have gone through periods of popularity, decline, and resurgence.

**FIGURE 10.1**
**Rep. Liz Chaney Lost Leadership Position**
Rep. Liz Cheney (R-WY) lost her leadership position in the Republican Party following a highly publicized intraparty fight.

Source: U.S. House of Photography via Wikimedia: https://en.wikipedia.org/wiki/Liz_Cheney#/media/File:Liz_Cheney_official_116th_Congress_portrait.jpg.

Reporters routinely take stock of the parties, and their prognosis is typically bleak and filled with foreboding. Stories about intraparty conflict within the Republican Party in 2021 eclipsed news about the COVID-19 pandemic, employment concerns, and health care. Republican Party leaders were divided about whether or not to remain loyal to Donald Trump amidst his false claims that he had won the 2020 presidential election and his subsequent impeachment over the insurrection at the U.S. Capitol on January 6, 2021.[2] The battle came to a head when Rep. Liz Cheney (R-WY) was ousted as House Republican Conference chair, the third highest ranking position within the party. Headlines from major news outlets trumpeted "Party Purge" and "The Battle for the Soul of the Republican Party," as party leaders duked it out. Some leaders sided with Cheney, who voted to impeach Trump, while others pledged their loyalty to the former president.[3]

The Democratic and Republican parties have dominated for over 150 years because of their ability to adapt to changing political and cultural circumstances. In the early decades of the republic, when voting rights were limited to male landowners, parties formed around charismatic leaders such as Thomas Jefferson and John Adams. When voting rights were extended, parties changed to accommodate the mass public more fully. As immigrants came to the United States and settled in urban areas, party machines emerged and socialized the immigrants to politics.

Parties also have adapted to changes in the media environment. When radio and television were new technologies, parties incorporated them into their strategies for reaching voters, including through advertising. More recently, the Republican and Democratic parties have advanced their use of online platforms and social media for campaigning, fundraising, and issue advocacy. Parties maintain contact with voters during non-election periods through their sophisticated websites and social media.

**FIGURE 10.2** Michelle Obama Addresses Delegates

Political parties are important mechanisms for citizen involvement at the grassroots level.

Source: Photo courtesy of QQQQQQ via Wikimedia: https://commons.wikimedia.org/wiki/File:Michelle_Obama_DNC_2008.jpg. Reproduced via CC BY-SA 3.0: https://creativecommons.org/licenses/by-sa/3.0/deed.en.

# 10.2 History of American Political Parties

## Learning Objectives

After reading this section, you should be able to answer the following questions:

1. What is a political party?
2. What were James Madison's fears about political factions?
3. How did American political parties develop?
4. How did political machines function?

**political parties**

An enduring organization under whose label candidates seek and hold office.

**Political parties** are enduring organizations under whose labels candidates seek and hold elective office.[4] Parties develop and implement rules governing elections. They help organize government leadership.[5] Political parties have been likened to public utilities, such as water and power companies, because they provide vital services for a democracy. American voters align themselves with political parties, which help them to make decisions about candidates and public policies.

The endurance and adaptability of American political parties is best understood by examining their colorful historical development. Parties evolved from factions in the eighteenth century to political machines in the nineteenth century. In the twentieth century, parties underwent waves of reform that some argue initiated a period of decline. The renewed parties of today are service-oriented organizations dispensing assistance and resources to candidates and politicians.[6] Political parties maintain a connection with voters through their websites and social media between election campaigns.

**Link**

**The Development of Political Parties**

A timeline of the development of political parties can be accessed here.

# Fear of Faction

The founders of the Constitution were fearful of the rise of **factions**, groups in society that organize to advance a political agenda. They designed a government of checks and balances that would prevent any one group from becoming too influential. James Madison famously warned in **Federalist No. 10** of the "mischiefs of faction," particularly a large majority that could seize control of government.[7] The suspicion of parties persisted among political leaders for more than a half-century after the founding. President James Monroe opined in 1822, "Surely our government may go on and prosper without the existence of parties. I have always considered their existence as the curse of the country."[8]

Despite the ambiguous feelings expressed by the founders, the first modern political party, the Federalists, appeared in the United States in 1789, more than three decades before parties developed in Great Britain and other western nations.[9] Since 1798, the United States has only experienced one brief period without national parties, from 1816 to 1827, when infighting following the War of 1812 tore apart the Federalists and the Republicans.[10]

**FIGURE 10.3 Conflicts between Federalists and Republicans**
Newspaper cartoons depicted conflicts that arose between the Federalists and Republicans, who sought to control government.

Source: Congressional Pugilists, 1798. [Philadelphia] Photograph. Library of Congress: https://www.loc.gov/item/2008661719/.

# Parties as Factions

The first American party system had its origins in the period following the Revolutionary War. Despite Madison's warning in Federalist No. 10, the first parties began as political factions. Upon taking office in 1789, President George Washington sought to create an "enlightened administration" devoid of political parties.[11] He appointed two political adversaries to his cabinet, Alexander Hamilton as treasury secretary and Thomas Jefferson as secretary of state, hoping that the two great minds could work together in the national interest. Washington's vision of a government without parties, however, was short-lived.

Hamilton and Jefferson differed radically in their approaches to rectifying the economic crisis that threatened the new nation.[12] Hamilton proposed a series of measures, including a controversial tax on whiskey and the establishment of a national bank. He aimed to have the federal government assume the entire burden of the debts incurred by the states during the Revolutionary War. Jefferson, a Virginian who sided with local farmers, fought this proposition. He believed that moneyed business interests in the New England states stood to benefit from Hamilton's plan. Hamilton assembled a group of powerful supporters to promote his plan, a group that eventually became the Federalist Party.[13]

**factions**

Organized groups that often represent interests that differ from those of the larger community.

**Federalist No. 10**

James Madison's essay in the *Federalist Papers* that deals with the need to guard against the danger of factions whose interests might be at odds with those of the wider community.

## The Federalists and the Republicans

**Federalists**

Supporters of the U.S. Constitution who believed in a strong national government.

The Federalist Party originated at the national level but soon extended to the states, counties, and towns. Hamilton used business and military connections to build the party at the grassroots level, primarily in the Northeast. Because voting rights had been expanded during the Revolutionary War, the **Federalists** sought to attract voters to their party. They used their newfound organization for propagandizing and campaigning for candidates. They established several big-city newspapers to promote their cause, including the *Gazette of the United States*, the *Columbian Centinel*, and the *American Minerva*, which were supplemented by broadsheets in smaller locales. This partisan press initiated one of the key functions of political parties—articulating positions on issues and influencing public opinion.[14]

**Anti-Federalists**

People who opposed the ratification of the U.S. Constitution and favored small, localized government.

**Whiskey Rebellion**

In 1794, farmers on the western frontier protested against a tax on whiskey that was part of Treasury Secretary Alexander Hamilton's plan to eliminate the national debt; the rebellion was suppressed by an army dispatched by the newly formed national government.

Disillusioned with Washington's administration, especially its foreign policy, Jefferson left the cabinet in 1794. Jefferson urged his friend James Madison to take on Hamilton in the press, stating, "For God's sake, my Dear Sir, take up your pen, select your most striking heresies, and cut him to pieces in the face of the public."[15] Madison did just that under the pen name of Helvidius. His writings helped fuel an **Anti-Federalist** opposition movement, which provided the foundation for the Republican Party. This early Republican Party differs from the present-day party of the same name. Opposition newspapers, the *National Gazette* and the *Aurora*, communicated the Republicans' views and actions, and inspired local groups and leaders to align themselves with the emerging party.[16] The **Whiskey Rebellion** in 1794, staged by farmers angered by Hamilton's tax on whiskey, reignited the founders' fears that violent factions could overthrow the government.[17]

**FIGURE 10.4 The Whiskey Rebellion**

Farmers protested against a tax on whiskey imposed by the federal government. President George Washington established the power of the federal government to suppress rebellions by sending the militia to stop the uprising in western Pennsylvania. Washington himself led the troops to establish his presidential authority.

Source: Metropolitan Museum of Art https://www.metmuseum.org/art/collection/search/11302); Accession Number: 63.201.2. Gift of Edgar William and Bernice Chrysler Garbisch, 1963. Public Domain.

## First Parties in a Presidential Election

Political parties were first evident in presidential elections in 1796, when Federalist John Adams was barely victorious over Republican Thomas Jefferson. During the election of 1800, Republican and Federalist members of Congress met formally to nominate presidential candidates, a practice that was a precursor to the nominating conventions used today. As the head of state and leader of the Republicans, Jefferson established the American tradition of political parties as grassroots organizations that band together smaller groups representing various interests, run slates of candidates for office, and present issue platforms.[18]

The early Federalist and Republican parties consisted largely of political officeholders. The Federalists not only lacked a mass membership base but also were unable to expand their reach beyond the moneyed classes. As a result, the Federalists ceased to be a force after the 1816 presidential election, when they received few votes. The Republican Party, bolstered by successful presidential candidates Thomas Jefferson, James Madison, and James Monroe, was the sole surviving national party by 1820. Infighting soon caused the Republicans to cleave into warring factions: the National Republicans and the Democratic-Republicans.[19]

# Establishment of a Party System

A true political party system with two durable institutions associated with specific ideological positions and plans for running the government did not begin to develop until 1828. The Democratic-Republicans, which became the Democratic Party, elected their presidential candidate, Andrew Jackson. The Whig Party, an offshoot of the National Republicans, formed in opposition to the Democrats in 1834.[20]

The era of **Jacksonian Democracy**, which lasted until the outbreak of the Civil War, featured the rise of mass-based party politics. Both parties initiated the practice of grassroots campaigning, including door-to-door canvassing of voters and party-sponsored picnics and rallies. Citizens voted in record numbers, with turnouts as high as 96 percent in some states.[21] Campaign buttons publicly displaying partisan affiliation came into vogue. The **spoils system**, also known as patronage, where voters' party loyalty was rewarded with jobs and favors dispensed by party elites, originated during this era.

The two-party system consisting of the Democrats and Republicans was in place by 1860. The Whig Party had disintegrated as a result of internal conflicts over patronage and disputes over the issue of slavery. The Democratic Party, while divided over slavery, remained basically intact.[22] The Republican Party was formed in 1854 during a gathering of former Whigs, disillusioned Democrats, and members of the Free-Soil Party, a minor antislavery party. The Republicans came to prominence with the election of Abraham Lincoln.

**Jacksonian Democracy**

A period lasting from the election of President Andrew Jackson in 1828 until the outbreak of the Civil War, which featured the rise of mass-based party politics.

**spoils system**

Also known as patronage, a system in which voters were rewarded for their party loyalty and votes with jobs and favors dispensed by party leaders.

**FIGURE 10.5** Thomas Nast Cartoon of the Republican Elephant

The donkey and the elephant have been symbols of the two major parties since cartoonist Thomas Nast popularized these images in the 1860s.

Source: Everett Historical/Shutterstock.com

# Parties as Machines

**party machines**

Partisan command structures headed by bosses who exacted loyalty and services from underlings in return for jobs and favors; machines were found primarily in cities.

Parties were especially powerful in the post–Civil War period through the Great Depression, when more than 15 million people immigrated to the United States from Europe, many of whom resided in urban areas. **Party machines**, cohesive, authoritarian command structures headed by bosses who exacted loyalty and services from underlings in return for jobs and favors, dominated political life in cities. Machines helped immigrants obtain jobs, learn the laws of the land, gain citizenship, and take part in politics.

Machine politics was not based on ideology, but on loyalty and group identity. The Curley machine in Boston was made up largely of Irish constituents who sought to elect their own.[23] Machines also brought different groups together. The tradition of parties as ideologically ambiguous umbrella organizations stems from Chicago-style machines that were run by the Daley family. The Chicago machine was described as a "hydra-headed monster" that "encompasses elements of every major political, economic, racial, ethnic, governmental, and paramilitary power group in the city."[24] The idea of a "balanced ticket" consisting of representatives of different groups developed during the machine-politics era.[25]

Because party machines controlled the government, they were able to sponsor public works programs, such as roads, sewers, and construction projects, as well as social welfare initiatives, which endeared them to their followers. The ability of party bosses to organize voters made them a force to be reckoned with, even as their tactics were questionable and corruption was rampant.[26] Bosses such as William Tweed in New York were larger-than-life figures who used their powerful positions for personal gain. Tammany Hall boss George Washington Plunkitt describes what he called "honest graft":

*My party's in power in the city, and its goin' to undertake a lot of public improvements. Well, I'm tipped off, say, that they're going to lay out a new park at a certain place. I see my opportunity and I take it. I go to that place and I buy up all the land I can in the neighborhood. Then the board of this or that makes the plan public, and there is a rush to get my land, which nobody cared particular for before. Ain't it perfectly honest to charge a good price and make a profit on my investment and foresight? Of course, it is. Well, that's honest graft.*[27]

## Enduring Image

### Boss Tweed Meets His Match

The lasting image of the political party boss as a corrupt and greedy fat cat was the product of a relentless campaign by American political cartoonist Thomas Nast in *Harper's Weekly* from 1868 to 1871. Nast's target was William "Boss" Tweed, leader of the New York Tammany Hall party machine, who controlled the local Democratic Party for nearly a decade.

Nast established the political cartoon as a powerful force in shaping public opinion and the press as a mechanism for "throwing the rascals" out of government. His cartoons ingrained themselves in American memories because they were among the rare printed images available to a wide audience in a period when photographs had not yet appeared in newspapers or magazines, and when literacy rates were much lower than today. Nast's skill at capturing political messages in pictures presented a legacy not just for today's cartoonists but for photographers and television journalists. His skill also led to the undoing of Boss Tweed.

Tweed and his gang of New York City politicians gained control of the local Democratic Party by utilizing the Society of Tammany (Tammany Hall), a fraternal organization, as a base. Through an extensive system of patronage whereby the city's growing Irish immigrant population was assured employment in return for votes, the Tweed Ring was able to influence the outcome of elections and profit personally from contracts with the city. Tweed controlled all New York state and city Democratic Party nominations from 1860 to 1870. He used illegal means to force the election of a governor, a mayor, and the speaker of the assembly.

The *New York Times*, *Harper's Weekly*, reform groups, and disgruntled Democrats campaigned vigorously against Tweed and his cronies in editorials and opinion pieces, but none was as successful as Nast's cartoons in conveying the corrupt and greedy nature of the regime. Tweed reacted to Nast's cartoon, "Who Stole the People's Money," by demanding of his supporters, ". . . stop them damned pictures. I don't care what the papers write about me—my constituents can't read; but damn it, they can see pictures!"[28]

The Tweed Ring was voted out in 1871, and Tweed was ultimately jailed for corruption. He escaped and was arrested in Spain by a customs official who didn't read English, but who recognized him from the *Harper's Weekly* political cartoons. He died in jail in New York.

Thomas Nast's cartoon, "Who Stole the People's Money," implicating the Tweed Ring appeared in *Harper's Weekly* on August 19, 1871.

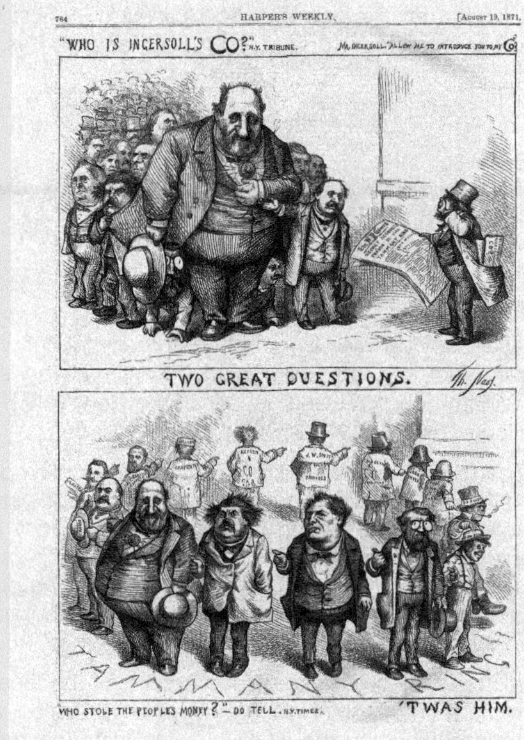


Source: *Harper's Weekly*: https://www.harpweek.com/09Cartoon/BrowseByDateCartoon.asp?Month=August&Date=19.

## Parties Reformed

Not everyone benefited from political machines. There were some problems that machines either could not or would not deal with. Industrialization and the rise of corporate giants created great disparities in wealth. Dangerous working conditions existed in urban factories and rural coal mines. Farmers faced falling prices for their products. Reformers blamed these conditions on party corruption and inefficiency. They alleged that party bosses were diverting funds that should be used to improve social conditions into their own pockets and keeping their incompetent friends in positions of power.

## The Progressive Era

The mugwumps, reformers who declared their independence from political parties, banded together in the 1880s and provided the foundation for the **Progressive Movement**. The Progressives initiated reforms that lessened the parties' hold over the electoral system. Voters had been required to cast color-coded ballots provided by the parties, which meant that their vote choice was not confidential. The Progressives succeeded by 1896 in having most states implement the secret ballot. The secret ballot is issued by the state and lists all parties and candidates. This system allows people to split their ticket when voting rather than requiring them to vote the party line. **Ticket-splitting** is the practice of voting for candidates of different parties on the same ballot during an election. The Progressives also hoped to lessen machines' control over the candidate selection process. They advocated a system of direct **primary elections** in which the public could participate rather than **caucuses**, or meetings of party elites. The direct primary had been instituted in only a small number of states, such as Wisconsin, by the early years of the twentieth century. The widespread use of direct primaries to select presidential candidates did not occur until the 1970s. Today, a majority of states employ direct primaries for presidential candidate selection.

The Progressives sought to end party machine dominance by eliminating the patronage system. Instead, employment would be awarded on the basis of qualifications rather than party loyalty. The merit system, now called the **civil service**, was instituted in 1883 with the passage of the Pendleton Act. The merit system wounded political machines, although it did not eliminate them.[29]

Progressive reformers ran for president under party labels. Former president Theodore Roosevelt split from the Republicans and ran as the Bull Moose Party candidate in 1912, and Robert LaFollette ran as the Progressive Party candidate in 1924. Republican William Howard Taft defeated Roosevelt, and LaFollette lost to Republican Calvin Coolidge.

**FIGURE 10.6 Progressive Reformers Political Cartoon**
The Progressive Reformers' goal of more open and representative parties resonates today.

Source: Edward Windsor Kemble, "The Latest Arrival at the Political Zoo." Harper's Weekly, 7/20/1912. Via Wikimedia: https://commons.wikimedia.org/wiki/File:Theodore_Roosevelt_Progressive_Party_Cartoon,_1912_copy.jpg

**Progressive Movement**

Reformers who came together in the 1880s to fight party corruption and inefficiency that they felt was the legacy of party machines.

**ticket-splitting**

The practice of voting for candidates of different parties on the same ballot during an election.

**primary election**

An election that decides who will be a political party's nominee for an office in the general election.

**caucuses**

Meetings held by party members to select candidates who will run for office.

**civil service**

Government employment that would be awarded on the basis of qualifications rather than party loyalty.

## New Deal and Cold War Eras

**New Deal**

The program instituted by President Franklin Roosevelt to lead the country out of the Great Depression; it included the creation of jobs and executive agencies to oversee the economic recovery.

Democratic President Franklin Delano Roosevelt's **New Deal** program for leading the United States out of the Great Depression in the 1930s had dramatic effects on political parties. The New Deal placed the federal government in the pivotal role of ensuring the economic welfare of citizens. Both major political parties recognized the importance of being close to the power center of government and established national headquarters in Washington, DC.

An era of executive-centered government also began in the 1930s, as the power of the president was expanded. Roosevelt became the symbolic leader of the Democratic Party.[30] Locating parties' control centers in the national capital eventually weakened them organizationally, as the basis of their support was at the local grassroots level. National party leaders began to lose touch with their local affiliates and constituents. Executive-centered government weakened parties' ability to control the policy agenda.[31]

**Cold War**

A period of hostility between the Soviet bloc countries and Western powers led by the U.S. that lasted from 1945 to 1990.

The **Cold War** period that began in the late 1940s was marked by concerns over the United States' relations with Communist countries, especially the Soviet Union. Following in the footsteps of the extremely popular president Franklin Roosevelt, presidential candidates began to advertise their independence from parties and emphasized their own issue agendas even as they ran for office under the Democratic and Republican labels. Presidents such as Dwight D. Eisenhower, Ronald Reagan, and George H. W. Bush won elections based on personal, rather than partisan, appeals.[32]

## Candidate-Centered Politics

**national party nominating convention**

A convention held by political parties to select their presidential candidate and develop the party's platform.

Political parties instituted a series of reforms beginning in the late 1960s amid concerns that party elites were not responsive to the public and operated secretively in so-called smoke-filled rooms. The Democrats were the first to act, forming the McGovern-Fraser Commission to revamp the presidential nominating system. The commission's reforms, adopted in 1972, allowed more average voters to serve as delegates to the **national party nominating convention**, where the presidential candidate is chosen. The result was that many state Democratic parties switched from caucuses, where convention delegates are selected primarily by party leaders, to primary elections, which make it easier for the public to take part. The Republican Party soon followed with its own reforms that resulted in states adopting primaries.[33]

**candidate-centered politics**

Rather than relying heavily on party support, candidates form their own campaign organizations when running for office.

The unintended consequence of reform was to diminish the influence of political parties in the electoral process and to promote the **candidate-centered politics** that exists today. Candidates build personal campaign organizations rather than rely on party support. The media have contributed to the rise of candidate-centered politics. Candidates can appeal directly to the public through television rather than working their way through the party apparatus when running for election.[34] Candidates use social media, such as Facebook and Twitter, to connect with voters. Campaign professionals and media consultants assume many of the responsibilities previously held by parties, such as developing election strategies, managing media tactics like producing and running campaign ads, and getting voters to the polls.

**FIGURE 10.7 Jimmy Carter Campaigning in the 1976 Presidential Campaign**

Democrat Jimmy Carter, a little-known Georgia governor and party outsider, was one of the first presidential candidates to run a successful campaign by appealing to voters directly through the media. After Carter's victory, candidate-centered presidential campaigns became the norm.

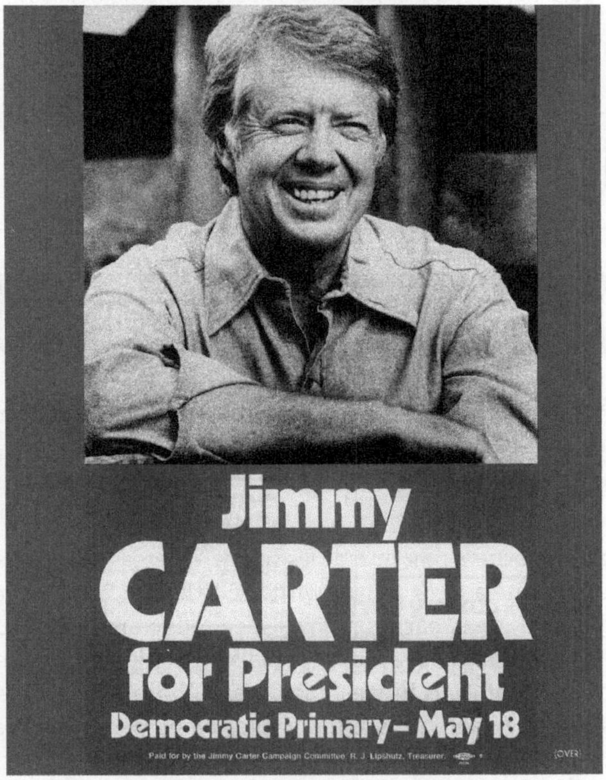


Source: Flyer from Jimmy Carter's presidential campaign. Via Wikimedia: https://commons.wikimedia.org/wiki/File:1976_Presidential_campaign_flyer.jpg.

## Key Takeaways

Political parties are enduring organizations that run candidates for office under a given label. American parties developed quickly in the early years of the republic despite concerns about factions expressed by the founders. A true, enduring party system developed in 1828. The two-party system of Democrats and Republicans was in place before the election of President Abraham Lincoln in 1860.

Party machines became powerful in the period following the Civil War when an influx of immigrants brought new constituents to the country. The Progressive Movement initiated reforms that fundamentally changed party operations. Party organizations were weakened during the period of executive-centered government that began during the New Deal.

Reforms of the party nominating system resulted in the rise of candidate-centered politics beginning in the 1970s. The media contribute to candidate-centered politics by allowing candidates to take their message to the public directly without the intervention of parties.

## Exercises

1. What did James Madison mean by "the mischiefs of faction?" What is a faction? What are the dangers of factions in politics?
2. What role do political parties play in the U.S. political system? What are the advantages and disadvantages of the party system?

3. How do contemporary political parties differ from parties during the era of machine politics? Why did they begin to change?
4. How have the media influenced the rise of candidate-centered politics?

# 10.3 Political Parties Today

## Learning Objectives

After reading this section, you should be able to answer the following questions:

1. What are the characteristics of modern-day American political parties?
2. What are political party platforms?

Political parties play an important role in politics today. Whereas observers like the *Washington Post*'s David Broder could write a book in 1972 with the title *The Party's Over*, such eulogies were premature. Compared to the 1970s, party organizations today are larger, further reaching, more highly organized, and better financed. Parties provide support to candidates who are running for office. Relations among party officials in Washington and those in the states have improved dramatically. Voters are still more likely to cast their votes along partisan lines than independently, even as a greater number of people consider themselves independent of parties.

American political parties have a number of distinctive characteristics. The two major political parties have been dominant for a long period of time. The parties are permeable, meaning that people are able to join or leave the party ranks freely. The two major parties are ideologically ambiguous in that they are umbrella organizations that can accommodate people representing a broad spectrum of interests. At the same time, the Democratic and Republican parties have become more polarized—representing more extreme ideological positions—in recent years.

## Two-Party Domination

**two-party system**

A party system like that in the United States, where nearly all elected offices are held by candidates associated with the two parties that are able to garner the vast majority of votes.

A **two-party system** is one in which nearly all elected offices are held by candidates associated with the two parties that are able to garner the vast majority of votes. The Republican Party and the Democratic Party are the major parties that have monopolized American politics since the early 1850s.[35] A major party runs candidates for local, state, and federal offices in a majority of states and holds one of the two largest blocs of seats in the U.S. Congress.[36]

Many people consider the two-party system to be a uniquely American phenomenon. Some scholars argue that this acceptance of the two-party norm is a result of Americans' aversion to radical politics and their desire to maintain a stable democratic political system.[37] Having too many parties can destabilize the system by confusing voters and allowing parties that take extreme ideological positions to become prominent in government, much like Madison feared factions at the founding.

# Ideological Ambiguity

Traditionally, rather than assuming strong ideological alignments, the two major parties have represented the core values of American culture that favor the centrist positions inherent in the liberal tradition of liberty, democracy, and equal opportunity.[38] Former Democratic Speaker of the House Thomas P. "Tip" O'Neill was fond of saying, "In any other country, the Democratic Party would be five parties."[39] O'Neill was referring to the fact that the Democratic Party has no clear ideological identity and instead accommodates interests from across the liberal–conservative spectrum. Groups that both favor and oppose gun control can find a home in the Democratic Party. The Democratic Party is loosely associated with a liberal attitude toward politics, which proposes that government should take a more active role in regulating the economy, provide a social safety net, and ensure equality in society through programs like affirmative action. Similar things have been said about the Republican Party,[40] although the Republicans have had a more unified message than the Democrats. The Republican agenda favors capitalism and limited government intervention in people's lives. The Republican Party's base includes fewer disparate groups than the Democratic base. The Republican Party is associated with a conservative outlook and support for a free-market economy.

In recent years, the differences between Democrats and Republicans have become more starkly divided along ideological lines. Overt hostility to members of the opposing party and their viewpoints has been on the rise since the 2016 election. Republicans have become strongly wedded to conservative positions, while Democrats have moved further to the liberal end of the ideological spectrum. One consequence of this increased partisan polarization is an inability for government leaders to compromise, which can result in stalemates on passing legislation.[41]

## Party Platforms

Political parties develop **policy platforms** that outline their positions on issues and the actions leaders will take to implement them if elected.[42] Parties frequently assume middle-of-the-road positions or waffle on issues to avoid alienating potential supporters.[43] For example, party platforms may oppose abortion—except in cases of rape or incest.[44] Both Republicans and Democrats agreed that the COVID-19 pandemic was a major threat to the U.S. economy and that government action was needed.[45]

**policy platforms**

Plans outlining political party positions on issues and the actions that leaders will take to implement them if elected to office.

Some scholars contend that American parties have become more ideologically distinct over the last three decades. Party leaders are expressing polarized opinions—opinions that are at opposite ends of the ideological spectrum—on issues, especially at the national level. These differences can be seen in the highly partisan debate over the health-care system. Democrats in Congress support government involvement in the health-care system and worked to pass the Patient Protection and Affordable Care Act (ACA), commonly known as "Obamacare," endorsed by President Obama in 2010. Republicans have sought to repeal the act since 2011, arguing that it can cost people their jobs. The top health-care concern for Democratic members of Congress in 2021 was protecting health-care coverage for patients with preexisting conditions, while almost half of Republican members sought to repeal the ACA.[46]

## Permeability

**mass membership organizations**

Political parties that require people to pay dues to belong, which is not the case for American parties.

**umbrella organizations**

Party organizations that accommodate a wide range of groups and interests.

Political parties in the United States are porous, decentralized institutions that can be joined readily by people who choose to adopt the party label, usually Democrat or Republican.[47] American parties are not **mass membership organizations** that require people to pay dues if they want to belong, which is the case in many European democracies. Instead, party membership is very loosely defined often by state laws that are highly variable. In some states, citizens declare a party affiliation when registering to vote. People also can join a state or local party organization, or work for a candidate associated with a particular party.

Parties are **umbrella organizations** that accommodate labor and business federations, interest groups, racial and ethnic constituencies, and religious organizations. Traditionally, the Democratic Party has been home to labor unions, and the Republican Party has accommodated business interests, although these relationships are not set in stone.

The fact that groups seeking to achieve similar political goals are found in both parties is evidence of their permeability. Pro-choice and antiabortion forces exist within the two major parties, although the Democratic Party is far more accommodating to the pro-choice position, while the Republican Party is overwhelmingly pro-life. One Democratic organization that supports pro-choice women candidates is Emily's List. Democrats for Life of America and Republican National Coalition for Life represent antiabortion constituencies.

Parties compete for the allegiances of the same groups in an effort to increase their bases of support. As the Latinx population has swelled to almost 60 million people, according to the U.S. Census Bureau, the Democratic and Republican parties have stepped up their efforts to attract Latinx voters and organizations. Both parties have produced Spanish-language television ads and websites, tailored their messages about health care and education to appeal to this group, and recruited Latinx candidates.[48] The parties also have increased their appeals to Asian American voters, who at almost 19 million people are a growing political constituency.

### Key Takeaways

Political parties today are experiencing a period of renewal. They have strengthened their organizations, improved their fundraising techniques, and enhanced the services they offer to candidates and officeholders.

American parties have three major characteristics. 1) Two parties, the Republicans and the Democrats, have dominated for over 150 years. 2) These major parties typically have been ideologically ambiguous in that they take middle-of-the-road rather than extreme positions on issues, although in recent years they have become more politically polarized. 3) Parties are permeable institutions that allow people and groups to move easily in and out of their ranks. Rather than having strong ideological predispositions, American parties devise broad platforms to outline their stances on issues.

### Exercises

1. How does the two-party system differ from other party systems? What are the advantages of a two-party system? What are its disadvantages?
2. What do you think explains the enduring appeal of the two major parties? How are they able to adapt to the changing ideas of the electorate?
3. What are the implications of the Democratic and Republicans parties becoming more ideologically polarized?

# 10.4 Party Organization

## Learning Objectives

After reading this section, you should be able to answer the following questions:

1. What is the organizational structure of American political parties?
2. How do national party organizations differ from state and local party organizations?
3. What functions do political parties perform?

The organizational structure of political parties consists of the machinery, procedures, and rituals party leaders and professionals employ so that parties operate effectively in the electoral and governing processes.[49] Party organizations establish connections between leaders and followers so that they can build and maintain a base of supportive voters they can count on during elections. Parties maintain permanent offices to assist their constituencies. They engage in party-building activities, including voter registration and get-out-the-vote drives. They provide candidate support, such as collecting polling data and running ads.[50]

Party organizations take many forms. National and state parties are large and complex organizations. They have permanent headquarters, chairpersons, boards of directors, and full-time employees with specialized responsibilities. They maintain lists of officers and members, operate under established bylaws and rules, and hold scheduled meetings and conventions. Local parties range from highly active, well-organized, professional structures to haphazard, amateur operations.[51]

# National Parties

**National party committees** today are the power centers of the Republican and Democratic parties. They are the ultimate authority in the parties' organizational hierarchy. The Democratic National Committee (DNC) and the Republican National Committee (RNC) are located in Washington, DC. The DNC and RNC chairs are the leaders of their party organization and are visible representatives of the parties in the press.

**national party committees**

The central authority in the organizational hierarchy of American political parties.

National organizations are responsible for putting on the **nominating conventions** where each party's presidential candidates are selected every four years. Nominating conventions provide an opportunity to rally the troops and reward the party faithful by having them participate as delegates. They also provide an opportunity for parties to showcase their leaders and policies in front of a national television audience. The nominating conventions kick off the general election for president every four years.

**nominating conventions**

Conventions held by the national Republican and Democratic parties where the candidates who will run for president are formally selected every four years.

National parties have adapted to the era of candidate-centered politics, in which candidates form their own campaign organization that orchestrates their bids for office. They have become service-oriented organizations, providing resources for candidates and officeholders. They stepped up their fundraising activities, expanded their staffs, and established stronger linkages with state, local, and candidate campaign organizations. The DNC and the RNC have established multimedia strategies that include traditional mass media appeals through press releases and staged events. They also get their message out using sophisticated websites, Facebook pages, Twitter feeds, and YouTube channels. They maintain lists of supporters whom they target directly through social media with specialized messages. Party websites are a one-stop shop for information about candidates and officeholders, issue positions, and voting logistics. They also provide a gateway for people to become involved in politics by providing information about volunteer activities and offering opportunities to contribute to the party.

## Legislative Campaign Committees

**legislative campaign committees**

Party committees that finance and manage congressional elections.

**Legislative campaign committees** finance and manage legislative elections. Members of Congress officially oversee the committee staffs. The National Republican Congressional Committee, National Republican Senatorial Committee, Democratic Congressional Campaign Committee, and the Democratic Senatorial Campaign Committee help candidates for the House and Senate meet the demands of modern campaigning. They provide survey research to determine voters' candidate preferences and stands on issues. They recruit volunteers and raise funds for campaigns. These committees organize media appeals to promote the party's leaders and agenda through television advertising, press briefings, direct mail, email solicitations, and social media.[52]

# State Parties

State party organizations operate in vastly different environments because of the varied political culture of individual states. There is fierce competition between parties in some states, while other states lean more favorably toward one party. Party competition, however, exists in every state. The press often discusses states as being "blue" for Democratic leaning, and "red" for Republican leaning. "Purple" states consist of nearly equal numbers of Democrats and Republicans. According to Gallup, the two parties were competitive in a majority of states in 2011. Only fourteen states were solidly Democratic and five states were solidly Republican.[53] This dynamic changed in just two years, as seventeen states leaned Democratic and fourteen states favored the Republicans in 2013. These changes in state party loyalty came about as voters were preparing for the 2014 midterm elections.[54]

Party and election laws vary greatly among states. In Maryland, voters must register and declare their party identification twenty-nine days before a primary election in order to participate. In Massachusetts, Independents can register with a party to vote in that party's primary on Election Day. In Wisconsin, party preference is part of the secret ballot. On Election Day, voters check a box on the ballot indicating their party choice, find that party's section of the ballot, and mark their preferences.

Like their national counterparts, state parties provide candidates with services, such as volunteer recruitment and polling. They offer citizens access to government leaders and information about issues. State parties have become multimillion-dollar organizations, most of which own their headquarters, employ full-time staff, and have operating budgets of over a half-million dollars. State legislative campaign committees assist in campaigns by dispensing funds to candidates.[55]

# Local Parties

Local party organizations exist at the legislative district, county, city, ward, and precinct levels. Some local parties are extremely vital, providing the link between average people and parties. In addition to fulfilling the basic election functions, they sponsor public affairs programs, provide services to senior citizens and young people, and organize community events. Some local parties are less active because many community-level positions, like town council seats, are nonpartisan.

## Key Takeaways

Party organization refers to the officials, activists, and members who set up the administration, make the rules, and carry out the collective goals and activities of the party. The Democratic and Republican national party committees are the central authorities for the two major American parties. Party organizations at the state and local levels are influenced by the political environment in which they are situated.

## Exercises

1. What kinds of services do contemporary parties provide? Why does it make sense for them to provide these kinds of services?
2. How do national, state, and local party organizations differ from one another? What are the main functions of each level of party organization?

# 10.5 Party in Government

## Learning Objectives

After reading this section, you should be able to answer the following questions:

1. What constitutes the party in government?
2. How do presidents use their position as symbolic leader of their political party?
3. What are legislative parties?
4. What is divided government, and what challenges does it pose for presidential leadership?

The **party in government** constitutes the organized partisans who serve in office, such as members of the Democratic and Republican parties in Congress. Parties provide an organizational structure for leaders in office, develop policy agendas, and ensure that majority and minority party opinions are voiced. The party in government seeks to represent its supporters, achieve policy objectives, and enhance the prospects for reelection. It is the center of democratic action. Party coalitions of many officeholders can be more powerful mechanisms for voicing opinions than individual leaders acting on their own. Coalitions from opposing parties spar openly by taking different positions on issues.[56]

**party in government**

The organized party members who serve in office, such as members of the Democratic and Republican parties in Congress.

## Presidential Leadership

Since the 1990s, presidents have assumed a major responsibility for party fundraising. President Bill Clinton made fundraising a priority for the Democratic Party. He was the headliner at major events that drew big crowds and raised millions of dollars. President George W. Bush became the top fundraiser for the Republican Party, raising a record $84 million in six months en route to achieving a $170 million goal by the 2004 presidential election.[57] During his 2008 campaign for the presidency, Barack Obama raised over $600 million, mostly through online appeals. Once in office, President Obama continued to raise funds for Democratic Party candidates through appearances at dinners and events as well as through his campaign organization's website, Organizing for America.[58] Obama's fundraising reached $1.23 billion for his 2012 presidential bid.[59] While in office, Donald Trump focused more on fundraising than did any prior president. He held over sixty political rallies and raised over $1 billion for his reelection campaign. Following his loss in the 2020 presidential contest, Trump raised over a half-billion dollars from his supporters who believed his false claim that the election had been stolen.[60]

# Legislative Parties

**legislative parties**

The internal party organizations within each house of Congress.

**party discipline**

Democratic and Republican leaders seek to get all of their members to vote with the majority of their colleagues in the party on policy legislation.

**party unity**

A vote in Congress where a majority of Democrats opposes a majority of Republicans.

**Legislative parties** are the internal party organizations within each house of Congress. The Speaker of the House and the Senate majority leader, the highest ranking leaders in Congress, are members of the majority party. They work closely with the majority leader, whip, chair of the policy committee, and chair of campaign committee in each body. The House and Senate minority leaders head a similar cast on the opposite side of the partisan fence. The Democratic Caucus and the Republican Conference, consisting of all members elected from a party, are the internal party organizations within each house of Congress. They oversee committee assignments and encourage **party discipline** by asking members to vote along party lines.

Party discipline can be difficult to enforce given the diversity of constituency interests and personalities in Congress. The extent to which party members are willing to vote in a bloc varies over time. **Party unity** voting represents the number of congressional votes where a majority of Democrats has opposed a majority of Republicans. Party unity in congressional voting rose from 40 percent in the early 1970s to 90 percent or more since 2000. According to *Congressional Quarterly*, party unity was higher in 2013 than it had been since World War II, and remained high through 2017. Party unity for Democrats reached record levels in 2020, with Democratic members of Congress voting with their caucus 98 percent of the time. The percentage was somewhat lower for Republicans, who exhibited party unity on 88 percent of congressional votes.[61]

Members of the same party in Congress are more similar ideologically in recent years than in the past. The Democratic Party in Congress contains few conservatives compared to the period before 1980, when conservative southern Democrats often disagreed with the liberal and moderate members of their party. Republicans in Congress today are more united in taking conservative positions than in the past.[62] Legislative parties like those in Congress are found in forty-nine of the fifty state legislatures. Nebraska, which has a nonpartisan, unicameral legislature, is the exception.

# Divided Government

**divided government**

Divided government is when a majority of members of the House and/or Senate are of a different party than the president.

The American system of separation of powers and checks and balances devised by the framers presents some obstacles to elected officials, using their party connections to wield power. **Divided government**, which occurs when the chief executive is of a different party from the majority in the legislature, is a common occurrence in American government. Divided government can get in the way of cooperative policymaking. Presidential vetoes of legislation passed by Congress can be more frequent during periods of divided government.[63]

Just because members of Congress belong to the same political party does not guarantee that they will agree on policy or legislation. Despite the fact that Republicans controlled the House and the Senate during the first two years of his presidency, President Donald Trump had difficulty getting Congress to enact legislation that backed up his campaign promises, such as building a wall between the United States and Mexico to keep out undocumented immigrants.[64] However, President Trump was able to get his cabinet nominees confirmed by the Senate despite vocal opposition by the Democrats to some of his appointees.[65] President Joe Biden began his presidency with his party having control of the House and Senate by very small margins. The Democratic Party held a slim majority in the House of Representatives and had a slight edge in the Senate as the two Independent members caucused with the Democrats.

## Key Takeaways

The party in government constitutes the organized partisans who serve in office, such as members of the Democratic and Republican parties in Congress. The president is the symbolic leader of his political party and can use this position to urge party members to achieve policy goals. Legislative parties seek to impose discipline on party members in Congress, which is not always easily accomplished because members represent vastly different constituencies with particular needs. Divided government—periods when the president is of a different party from the majority in Congress—can create challenges for presidents seeking to enact their policy agendas.

## Exercises

1. What role does the president play in party politics? What role do legislative parties play?
2. What might the advantages and disadvantages of divided government be? Would you prefer the executive and legislative branches be controlled by the same party or by different parties?

# 10.6 Party Identification

## Learning Objectives

After reading this section, you should be able to answer the following questions:

1. How do Americans affiliate with a political party?
2. What are partisan coalitions?
3. What happens during a partisan realignment or dealignment?

People who identify with a political party either declare their allegiance by joining the party or show their support through regular party-line voting at the polls. People can easily switch their party affiliation or distance themselves from parties entirely. However, people who do not declare a partisan affiliation when they register to vote lose the opportunity to participate in primary election campaigns in many states.

## Partisan Identification

A person's **partisan identification** is defined as a long-term attachment to a particular party.[66] Americans are not required to formally join party organizations or to pay dues to a party, as is the case in other democracies. Instead, people self-identify as Republicans, Democrats, or members of minor parties. They also can declare themselves Independent and not aligned with any political party.[67]

**partisan identification**

A person's long-term attachment to a particular political party.

Since the 1960s there has been a gradual decline in identification with political parties and a rise in the number of Independents. In 2000, more people identified as Independents (40 percent of the voting population) than were affiliated with either the Democratic (34 percent) or Republican (24 percent) parties for the first time in history.[68] The proportion of people registering as Independents increased 57 percent between 1990 and 1998, while those registering as Democrats declined by 14 percent and as Republicans by 5 percent. According to Gallup, in 2021, 30 percent of the population identified as Democrats and 19 percent as Independent-leaning Democrats, while 25 percent identified as Republicans and 15 percent as Independent-leaning Republicans. The nine-percentage-point difference between Democrats and Republicans was one of the largest in history. Eleven percent of Americans were pure Independents or did not affiliate with either political party.[69]

### Link

**Trends in Party Identification**

Trends in party identification have been compiled by the Pew Research Center in the interactive graph found here.

Gallup tracks Americans' party identification here.

As strong voter identification with political parties has declined, so has dedication to the two-party system. According to a national survey, citizens have more trust in product brands, such as Nike, Levi's, Honda, and Clorox, than in the Democrats and Republicans.[70] Since the 1980s, Americans have become skeptical about the two major parties' ability to represent the public interest and to handle major issues facing the country, such as crime, the environment, and saving Social Security.[71] Still, the two-party system continues to dominate the political process, as a viable multiparty alternative has not emerged.

## Party Coalitions

**party coalitions**

Groups that have long-term allegiances to a particular political party and whose members vote for that party consistently in elections.

**realignment**

A major, enduring shift in party coalition loyalties that results in a change in the balance of power between the two major parties.

**critical elections**

An election where a minority party becomes the majority party following electoral victory and remains dominant for an extended period of time.

**Party coalitions** consist of groups that have long-term allegiances to a particular political party. Regions of the country establish loyalties to a specific party as a result of the party's handling of a war, a major social problem, or an economic crisis. Social, economic, ethnic, and racial groups also become aligned with particular parties. Catholics and labor union members in the Northeast form a part of the Democratic coalition. White fundamentalist Protestants are a component of the Republican coalition.[72] Parties count on coalition members to vote for them consistently in elections.

A major, enduring shift in coalition loyalties that results in a change in the balance of power between the two major parties is called a **realignment**.[73] Realignments can be sparked by **critical elections**, where a minority party wins and becomes the majority party in government following an election, and remains dominant for an extended period of time. American parties realign about once every thirty or forty years. A critical election in 1932 brought the Democrats and President Franklin Roosevelt to power after a period of Republican domination dating from the 1890s. This New Deal coalition was based on an alliance of white Southerners and liberal Northerners who benefited from the social welfare policies of the Democratic administration during the Great Depression. The election of Ronald Reagan in 1980 marked the beginning of a realignment favoring the Republicans. In this coalition, white Southerners moved away from the Democratic Party as they favored the more conservative values espoused by the Republicans.[74]

Some political observers believe that the 2016 presidential election marked the beginning of a partisan realignment. The Republican Party has become a home for Midwestern, white, working-class people. The Democratic Party has become a coalition of educated whites with racial and ethnic minorities located in cities. Republican and Democratic party supporters differ less on social issues, and are more alike on their views on LGBTQ+ rights and abortion than are the officeholders in their respective parties.[75] They are more divided on policies related to immigration and trade.[76] However, partisan realignments can only be identified retrospectively when the trends are observed over the long haul. The election of Democrat Joe Biden in 2020 was an indication that the predictions that a partisan realignment had begun in 2016 may be premature.[77]

Partisan **dealignment** occurs when party loyalty declines and voters base their decisions on short-term, election-specific factors, such as the leadership qualities of a candidate.[78] The inclination of people to identify as Independents rather than as partisans is evidence that a dealignment is occurring.[79] A partisan dealignment may be occurring today, as more people are identifying as Independents or not affiliating with parties, and more voters select their candidates on the basis of personal traits, such as honesty. Mass media can contribute to partisan realignment by focusing attention on candidates' personalities and scandals, which are short-term factors that can influence vote choice.

**dealignment**

A decline in party strength that occurs when party loyalty decreases and voters base their decisions on short-term, election-specific factors.

## Key Takeaways

People indicate their identification with a political party either by declaring their allegiance to a particular party or by regularly supporting that party at the polls. Societal groups that gravitate toward particular political parties can form partisan coalitions. These coalitions can shift during critical elections, which result in a minority party becoming the majority party in government.

## Exercises

1. Do you consider yourself either a Republican, a Democrat, or an Independent? What makes you identify with one party rather than the other or to not identify with one of the two major political parties?
2. Why do parties go through realignment? How does realignment allow parties to adapt to a changing electorate? Is there evidence that American political parties are in the process of realigning today?

# 10.7 Minor Parties

## Learning Objectives

After reading this section, you should be able to answer the following questions:

1. What is a minor party, also known as a third party?
2. What are the types of minor parties in American politics?
3. What difficulties do minor parties face in winning elections?

**minor party**

Also known as a third party, it is an organization that is not affiliated with the Democrats or Republicans, contests in a limited number of elections, and does not receive large pluralities of votes.

A **minor party**, or third party, is an organization that is not affiliated with the two major American parties—the Democrats or Republicans. Minor parties run candidates in a limited number of elections, and they do not receive large pluralities of votes. They arise when the two major parties fail to represent citizens' demands or provide the opportunity to express opposition to existing policies. Citizens often form a minor party by uniting behind a leader who represents their interests.

# Functions of Minor Parties

Minor parties raise issues that the Democrats and Republicans ignore because of their tendency to take middle-of-the road positions. As a result, minor parties can be catalysts for change.[80] The Progressive Party backed the women's suffrage movement in the early twentieth century, which led to the passage of the Nineteenth Amendment. Child labor laws, the direct election of U.S. senators, federal farm aid, and unemployment insurance are policies enacted as a result of third-party initiatives.[81]

**Tea Party**

A grassroots movement with conservative leanings that emerged in 2009 to protest government taxing and spending policies.

The **Tea Party** raised issues related to the national debt, government bailouts to failing industries, and the health-care-system overhaul. The Tea Party is a conservative-leaning grassroots political movement that emerged in 2009 when the Young Americans for Liberty in the state of New York organized a protest against state government "tax and spend" policies. The Tea Party–themed protest recalled events in 1773, when colonists dumped tea into Boston Harbor to demonstrate their opposition to paying a mandatory tax on tea to the British government. Subsequent Tea Party protests took place in states across the country. Tea Party supporters participated in national protests in Washington, DC, which drew thousands of supporters. Tea Party–backed candidates ran for office for the first time in 2010, and gained seats in the House and Senate as well as in state and local offices. As has been the case with minor parties historically, the Tea Party was less prominent in the 2016 and 2020 elections. However, the movement maintains 750 local organizations, raises funds for candidates, and holds weekly webinars for supporters and campaign organizers.[82]

CNBC editor Rick Santelli called for a "Chicago Tea Party" protest, which ignited the movement. The Tea Party's efforts were publicized through new media, including websites such as Tea Party Patriots, Facebook pages, blogs, and Twitter feeds.

The national protests were prompted by a video of a rant by CNBC editor Rick Santelli opposing government subsidies of mortgages that went viral after being posted on the Drudge Report.

View in the online reader

Minor parties can invigorate voter interest by promoting a unique or flamboyant candidate and by focusing attention on a contentious issue.[83] Voter turnout increased in the 1992 presidential contest for the first time in over two decades in part because of minor-party candidate Ross Perot.[84] Perot, a wealthy businessman, was a candidate for president in 1992 for the minor party United We Stand America, receiving nearly twenty million votes. He ran again in 1996 as a member of the Reform Party and earned nearly eight million votes.[85] Perot supporters were united in their distrust of professional politicians and opposition to government funding of social welfare programs. The presence of the Tea Party in the 2010 midterm elections stimulated interest in the campaign and helped to elevate turnout.

**FIGURE 10.8 Ralph Nader and Ross Perot Campaigning**
Minor-party candidates Ross Perot and Ralph Nader did not come close to winning the presidency, but they did bring media attention to issues during the elections in which they ran.

Sources: (left) Joseph Sohm / Shutterstock.com; (right) Courtesy of Sage Ross via Wikimedia: http://commons.wikimedia.org/wiki/File:Ralph_Nader_and_crowd,_October_4,_2008.jpg. Reproduced via CC BY-SA 3.0: https://creativecommons.org/licenses/by-sa/3.0/deed.en.

Minor-party candidates can be **spoilers** in elections by taking away enough votes from a major party candidate to influence the outcome without winning. Minor parties collectively have captured over 5 percent of the popular vote in every presidential election since 1840, although individual minor parties may win only a small percentage of votes.[86] Green Party candidate Ralph Nader was considered by some analysts to be a spoiler in the 2000 presidential campaign by taking votes away from Democratic contender Al Gore in Florida. George W. Bush received 2,912,790 votes in Florida compared to Al Gore's 2,912,253 votes.[87] If 540 of Nader's 96,837 votes had gone to Gore, Gore might have ended up in the White House.[88]

**spoiler**
A minor-party candidate who takes away enough votes from a major-party candidate to influence the outcome of the election while not winning the election himself.

Third-party candidates had a greater influence in the 2016 presidential contest than they have had in recent campaigns. Independent candidates Gary Johnson, Jill Stein, and Evan McMullen (Better for America) collectively earned 6 percent of the vote. The Independent candidates were especially popular among young voters who were dissatisfied with the two major party candidates. Their impact was felt in battleground states, such as Michigan and Wisconsin, where analysts found that they took votes away from Democratic candidate Hillary Clinton.[89]

Although seventeen third-party candidates were on ballots during the 2020 presidential election, they had little impact on the outcome. Rapper Kanye West, running under the Birthday Party label, gained some publicity as a celebrity but earned few votes.[90]

# Types of Minor Parties

Minor parties can be classified as enduring, single-issue, candidate-centered, and fusion parties. Learn more about each type in Table 10.1.

**enduring minor party**

A minor party that has existed for a long time and regularly runs candidates for office.

**single-issue minor party**

A minor party that exists to promote a particular policy agenda.

**candidate-centered minor party**

A minor party formed around a candidate who is able to rally support based on her own message.

**fusion minor party**

Also known as alliance party, this is an enduring or single-issue minor party that engages in the practice of cross endorsement, backing candidates who appear on a ballot under more than one party label.

**cross endorsement**

The minor-party practice of backing candidates who appear on a ballot under more than one party label.

**TABLE 10.1** Types of Minor Parties

| | |
|---|---|
| **Enduring Minor Parties** | Some minor parties have existed for a long time and resemble major parties in that they run candidates for local, state, and national offices. They differ from major parties because they are less successful in getting their candidates elected.[91] The Libertarian Party, founded in 1971, is an **enduring minor party**, which is a type of minor party that has existed for a long time and regularly fields candidates for president and state legislatures. The Libertarians are unable to compete with the two major parties because they lack a strong organizational foundation and the financial resources to run effective campaigns. The party also holds an extreme ideological position, which can alienate voters. Libertarians take personal freedoms to the extreme and oppose government intervention in the lives of individuals, support the right to own and bear arms without restriction, and endorse a free and competitive economic market.[92] |
| **Single-Issue Minor Parties** | Sometimes called ideological parties, **single-issue minor parties** exist to promote a particular policy agenda. The Green Party is a product of the environmental movement of the 1980s. It advocates environmental issues, such as mandatory recycling and strong regulations on toxic waste.[93] The Green Party holds annual meetings and has run presidential candidates in six elections since 1996, when consumer advocate Ralph Nader was its first presidential nominee. |
| **Candidate-Centered Minor Parties** | **Candidate-centered minor parties** form around candidates who are able to rally support based on their own charisma or message. Former World Wrestling Federation star Jesse "The Body" Ventura was elected governor of Minnesota in 1998 under the Independence Party label, an offshoot of the Reform Party. The plainspoken, media-savvy Ventura made the need for an alternative to two-party domination a core theme of his campaign: "It's high time for a third party. Let's look at Washington. I'm embarrassed. We've got a lot of problems that the government should be dealing with, but instead, for the next nine months, the focus of this nation will be on despicable behavior by career politicians. If this isn't the right time for a third-party, then when?"[94] Ventura was a third party presidential candidate in the 2020 election. |
| **Fusion Minor Parties** | **Fusion minor parties**, also known as alliance parties, are enduring or single-issue minor parties that engage in the practice of **cross endorsement**, backing candidates who appear on a ballot under more than one party label. Fusion parties routinely endorse candidates who have been nominated by the two major parties and support their causes. Cross endorsement allows minor parties to contribute to the election of a major-party candidate and thus gain access to officeholders. In addition to giving a major-party candidate an additional ballot position, fusion parties provide funding and volunteers. Fusion parties are explicitly banned in eighteen states. Only eight states permit the practice of cross endorsement. The most active fusion parties are in New York. The Liberal Party and the Democratic Party cross endorsed Mario Cuomo in the 1990 New York governor's race, leading him to defeat his Republican Party and Conservative Party opponents handily. The Conservative Party and the Republican Party cross endorsed George Pataki in the 2000 governor's race, leading him to victory.[95] During the 2010 midterm elections, the Tea Party cross endorsed several successful candidates running in the primary under the Republican Party label, upsetting mainstream Republican candidates. Some of the Tea Party–endorsed candidates, such as U.S. Senate candidate Rand Paul in Kentucky, went on to win the general election. The Green Liberty Party was a fusion party that ran Mark Paul Miller as a write-in candidate for president in 2016. The party's platform called for making medical marijuana available to veterans.[96] In 2020, the Working Families Party, a progressive minor party in Arizona, sought to establish fusion voting in Arizona.[97] |

## Comparing Content

### The Tea Party

There has been almost as much discussion about media coverage of the Tea Party as there has been about the organization's issue positions, candidate endorsements, and protest activities. Tea Party activists, such as former Alaska governor and Republican vice presidential candidate Sarah Palin, have lambasted the traditional news media for being tied to special interests and irrelevant for average Americans. Instead, Tea Party leaders have embraced social media, preferring to communicate with their supporters through Facebook and Twitter. In recent years, as the Tea Party has become more established, media coverage of the party has waned.

Media coverage of Tea Party rallies focused on racially charged signs, prompting the movement's leaders to decry the mainstream press.

Source: Photo courtesy of Bonzo McGrue via Wikimedia: https://commons.wikimedia.org/wiki/File:BirthCertificate.jpg. Reproduced via CC BY 2.0: https://creativecommons.org/licenses/by/2.0/deed.en.

Early Tea Party protests against government economic policies received little mainstream press attention. Media coverage increased as the Tea Party staged rowdy protests against government health-care reform, and public interest in the movement grew. Stories by major news organizations focused on the evolution of the Tea Party, its positions on issues, its membership, and its most vocal spokespersons. Tea Party rallies garnered extensive attention from mainstream media as well as political bloggers. The Tea Party received the lion's share of media coverage on election night in 2010, as the mainstream press framed the election results in terms of public dissatisfaction with the political status quo as evidenced by victories by Tea Party–backed candidates.[98] The Tea Party continues to attract press coverage even as its novelty and support ebb and flow. However, it was not as dominant a story in the 2012 or 2014 elections. Tea Party–affiliated activists made headlines following the 2020 presidential election as they amplified Donald Trump's allegations of a stolen election by protesting at locations where ballots were being counted.[99]

Coverage of the Tea Party differs widely by media outlet. CNN reports of a Tea Party protest in Chicago featured on-site reporters aggressively interviewing average citizens who were participating in the event, challenging them to defend the Tea Party's positions on issues. CNN and network news outlets reported that members of Congress had accused Tea Party protesters of anti-Obama racism based on racially charged statements and signs held by some protesters. Fox News, on the other hand, assumed the role of Tea Party cheerleader. Fox analyst Tobin Smith took the stage at a Tea Party rally in Washington, DC, and encouraged the protesters. Reporting live from a Boston Tea Party protest, Fox Business anchor Cody Willard encouraged people to join the movement, stating, "Guys, when are we going to wake up and start fighting the fascism that seems to be permeating this country?"[100]

Rally signs depict issue positions.

Source: Photo courtesy of Sage Ross. https://commons.wikimedia.org/wiki/File:Tea_Party_Protest,_Hartford,_Connecticut,_15_April_2009_-_009.jpg. ((CC BY-SA 3.0); https://creativecommons.org/licenses/by-sa/3.0/deed.en.

Studies of mainstream press coverage of the Tea Party also vary markedly depending on the source. A 2010 report by the conservative Media Research Center found that the press first ignored and then disparaged the Tea Party. The report alleged that ABC, CBS, NBC, and CNN framed the Tea Party as a fringe or extreme racist movement.[101] Conversely, a 2010 survey conducted by the mainstream newspaper the *Washington Post* found that 67 percent of local Tea Party organizers felt that traditional news media coverage of their groups was fair, compared to 23 percent who considered it to be unfair. Local organizers also believed that news coverage improved over time as reporters interviewed Tea Party activists and supporters and gained first-hand knowledge of the group and its goals.[102] Both reports were debated widely in the press. Over time, Tea Party coverage has become increasingly mainstream.

# Challenges Facing Minor Parties

A minor-party candidate has never been elected president. In the past five decades, minor parties have held few seats in Congress or high-level state offices. Few minor party candidates have won against major-party candidates for governor, state representative, or county commissioner in the past two decades. Minor-party candidates have better luck in the approximately 65,000 nonpartisan contests for city and town offices and school boards in which no party labels appear on the ballot. Hundreds of these positions have been filled by minor-party representatives.[103]

A majority of the public favors having viable minor-party alternatives in elections.[104] Why, then, are minor parties unable to be a more formidable presence in American politics?

## Winner-Take-All Elections

One major reason for two-party dominance in the United States is the prominence of the **single-member district plurality system** of elections,[105] also known as winner-take-all elections. Only the highest vote getter in a district in federal and most state legislative elections gains a seat in office. Candidates who have a realistic chance of winning under such a system are almost always associated with the Democratic and Republican parties, which have a strong following among voters and necessary resources, such as funding and volunteers to work in campaigns.

**single-member district plurality system**

Also known as first-past-the-post or winner-take-all, the system in which the highest vote getter in a district in federal and most state legislative elections gains a seat in office.

In contrast, **proportional representation (PR) systems**, such as those used in most European democracies, allow multiple parties to flourish. PR systems employ larger, multimember districts where five or more members of a legislature may be selected in a single election district. Seats are distributed according to the proportion of the vote won by particular political parties. For example, in a district comprising ten seats, if the Democratic Party got 50 percent of the vote, it would be awarded five seats; if the Republican Party earned 30 percent of the vote, it would gain three seats; and if the Green Party earned 20 percent of the vote, it would be granted two seats.[106] PR was used for a short time in New York City Council elections in the 1940s but was abandoned after several communists and other minor-party candidates threatened the Democratic Party's stronghold.[107]

**proportional representation (PR) systems**

Elections are held for multiple seats in a district, allowing seats to be distributed according to the proportion of the vote won by particular political parties.

## Legal Obstacles

Minor parties are hindered by laws that limit their ability to compete with major parties. Democrats and Republicans in office have created procedures and requirements that make it difficult for minor parties to be listed on ballots in many states. In Montana, Oklahoma, and several other states, a candidate must obtain the signatures of least 5 percent of registered voters to appear on the ballot. A presidential candidate must collect over one million signatures to be listed on the ballot in every state. This is an insurmountable barrier for most minor parties that lack established organizations in many states.[108]

Campaign finance laws work against minor parties. The 1974 Federal Election Campaign Act and its amendments provide for public financing of presidential campaigns. Rarely has a minor-party candidate been able to qualify for federal campaign funds, as the party's candidates must receive 5 percent or more of the popular vote in the general election. Similar barriers hinder state-level minor-party candidates from receiving public funding for taxpayer-financed campaigns, although some states, such as Connecticut, are debating plans to rectify this situation.

## Lack of Resources

The financial disadvantage of minor parties impedes their ability to amass resources that are vital to mounting a serious challenge to the two major parties. They lack funds to establish and equip permanent headquarters. They cannot hire staff and experienced consultants to conduct polls, gather political intelligence, court the press, generate new media outreach, or manage campaigns.[109]

## Lack of Media Coverage

Minor parties rarely receive significant media coverage except when they field a dynamic or outlandish candidate, such as Kanye West or Jesse Ventura, or when they are associated with a movement that taps into public concerns, such as the Tea Party. The dominant horserace frame employed by the media focuses on who is ahead and behind in an election and usually tags minor-party candidates as losers early in the process. Media treat minor parties as distractions and their candidates as novelty acts that divert attention from the main two-party attractions.

Minor parties often are unable to air televised campaign ads because they lack funds. Even in the digital era, television advertising is an essential part of campaigns because it allows candidates to control their own message and reach large numbers of voters. Minor-party candidates have difficulty gaining publicity and gaining recognition among voters when they cannot advertise. Some minor-party candidates have established sophisticated websites to compensate for their lack of television and newspaper coverage. However, websites alone cannot generate the kind of attention that television can muster for a candidate.

**FIGURE 10.9 Ross Perot Participating in the 1992 Presidential Debate**

Minor-party candidates rarely have the opportunity to participate in televised presidential debates. An exception was Reform Party candidate Ross Perot, whose campaign was bolstered by his inclusion in the 1992 presidential debate with Republican George H. W. Bush and Democrat Bill Clinton.

Source: Dennis Brack / Alamy Stock Photo

Minor-party candidates routinely are excluded from televised debates in which major-party candidates participate.[110] By being allowed to participate in the 1992 presidential debates, Independent candidate Ross Perot achieved national visibility and symbolic equality with incumbent president George H. W. Bush and Democratic candidate Bill Clinton.

These benefits were denied Ralph Nader when he was excluded from the presidential debates in 2000 because the Commission on Presidential Debates ruled that Nader did not have enough voter support to warrant inclusion. No third-party candidate participated in the presidential debates with major candidates in 2016 or 2020.

## Absorption by Major Parties

When a minor-party movement gains momentum, the Republican and Democratic parties move quickly to absorb the minor party by offering enticements to their members, such as support for policies that are favored by the minor party. Major-party candidates appeal to minor-party supporters by arguing that votes for minor-party candidates are wasted.[111] Major parties are often successful in attracting minor-party voters because major parties are permeable and ambiguous ideologically.[112]

After the Democrats in Congress were instrumental in passing the Voting Rights Act in 1964, the Republican Party absorbed the southern Dixiecrats, a Democratic Party faction opposed to the legislation. The two major parties tried to attract Ross Perot's Reform Party supporters after his 1996 presidential bid, with the Republican Party succeeding in attracting the lion's share of votes. The Republican Party's position against big government appealed to Perot supporters.[113] Even though the Tea Party gravitates toward the Republican Party, and most Tea Party–backed candidates are Republicans, Republican elites and voters have not universally accepted it.

## Online Political Party Alternatives

The information age has made possible digital alternatives to political parties that perform some of the key functions of parties. Political organizers have built online alternatives to the two long-dominant parties through a variety of new organizations, including Americans Elect, No Labels, Unity08, and the 1787 Party. In 2012, Americans Elect sought to nominate a bipartisan presidential slate through a website that they promoted widely through a nationwide bus tour and numerous campus visits that gained presidential attention. While unsuccessful in fulfilling their goal, the organization gained ballot access in over thirty states. Americans Elect fulfilled at least part of Leon Epstein's definition of political parties as public utilities that recruit candidates who contest elections. So far, however, the capacity of these online organizations to redefine the role of parties in the American electoral process has fallen short, as they either disband, as was the case with Americans Elect, or go on hiatus in non-election years. Some of these organizations, like No Labels, have gone on to become prominent bipartisan organizations that provide opportunities for citizens to learn about issues and leaders to work together across party lines.

### Link

**No Labels**

No Labels is a national online movement of Democrats, Republicans, and Independents that mobilizes people to get elected officials to work together on policy issues. The organization has been active for more than a decade.

## Key Takeaways

Minor parties offer an alternative to the dominant Republican and Democratic parties, but they have difficulty surviving. They arise to challenge the two major parties when people feel that their interests are not being met. There are four major types of minor parties: enduring, single-issue, candidate-centered, and fusion parties. Minor parties have difficulty winning high-level office but are able to fill seats at the county and local levels. There are numerous challenges faced by minor parties in American politics, including winner-take-all elections, legal obstacles, lack of resources, and limited media coverage.

## Exercises

1. When do minor parties tend to arise? How can minor parties have an impact on national politics if they cannot usually compete in national elections?

2. What minor parties are you familiar with? How are minor parties generally portrayed in the media?
3. What makes it difficult for minor parties to win state and local elections?

# 10.8 Political Parties in the Information Age

## Learning Objectives

After reading this section, you should be able to answer the following questions:

1. How do political parties publicize their leaders, candidates, and causes?
2. How do the media depict political parties?
3. In what ways has the relationship of the media and political parties changed over time?

Political parties thrive when they are able to manage the media and effectively promote their candidates, leaders, and causes. Their goal is to use the media to publicize policy positions, activities, and leaders. Party organizations launch media blitzes and provide technical communications assistance to campaigns and government officials so that they can attract media attention. They also use media to inform and mobilize their loyalists. Media depictions tend to be dramatic, emphasizing infighting among party members as well as conflicts between different parties. Social media have become important tools for political parties to publicize their activities, recruit members, fundraise, and advocate for public policies.

## Media Interactions

Political parties are obsessed with keeping their names and representatives in the public eye. Publicity gives the impression that the party is active and influential. A party with a strong media presence can attract volunteers and financial contributors. Parties use a variety of tactics in their efforts to control the media agenda and get their message out to the public and to journalists. They employ many of the same tactics as interest groups, such as holding news conferences, issuing press releases, giving interviews to journalists, and appearing on television and radio talk shows. Democratic and Republican officials provide competing commentary about issues. Party leaders participate in "spin sessions" to get their views heard. Parties engage in aggressive advertising campaigns. Finally, they maintain significant web and digital media presences to reach their supporters and to court the press.

## Partisan Spin

Political parties seek to influence political debate on a daily basis by confronting the opposition in the media. They engage in **spin**, the practice of providing an interpretation of events or issues that favors their side. High-profile partisans make the rounds of political talk programs such as *Meet the Press*, and visit news shows and give interviews to print journalists to spin their views. Partisan spin doctors routinely appear on television immediately following candidate debates or major speeches to interpret what has been said and to recast any misstatements.[114] Spin doctors can be elected leaders, party officials, or interest group leaders.

**spin**

The practice of providing an interpretation of events or issues that favors a particular side, such as the Democratic or Republican parties.

Specific media outlets are associated with spin doctors who favor a specific party. Conservative Fox News host Tucker Carlson favors the Republican Party and draws a large audience. Liberal talk show hosts such as MSNBC's Rachel Maddow tend to support Democrats.

## Advertising

Political advertising is a way for parties to disseminate messages without having them filtered by journalists. Parties engage extensively in **issue advocacy**, advertising campaigns that focus on legislative policies. They also develop ads supportive of their candidates and leaders and critical of the opposition. Online video is a cost-effective alternative to television advertising. Millions of people are reached by online political ads each day in their social media feeds. Political party organizations spent over $100 million on digital advertising between April 2018 and January 2021.[115]

**issue advocacy**

Advertising campaigns that focus on legislative policies.

### Links

**Democratic and Republican Party YouTube Channels**

The Democratic and Republican parties feature online ads on their YouTube channels, which makes them readily available to supporters as well as journalists.

Democratic Party YouTube Channel

Republican Party YouTube Channel

## Websites

Party websites offer a vast amount of information to average citizens, political activists, and journalists who take the initiative to visit them. Websites provide an effective mechanism for communicating information to citizens and can lessen the administrative burden on party organizations. They reach a large number of people instantaneously and have become more effective mechanisms for raising funds than the earlier method of direct mail. The sites include general political information, such as facts about American democracy and party history. Press releases, platforms, and position papers give the lowdown on issues and candidates. Party sites also host discussion boards and blogs where party elites, including candidates, interact with rank-and-file members.[116] Websites hype symbols that create a sense of identity as well as a party brand. The technical delivery of this content is an important aspect of outreach, so developing email lists of party members, especially visitors to the website, is a priority.

**FIGURE 10.10**
**Democratic Party's Logo**
The Democratic Party uses its website to promote its logo. After Hillary Clinton's defeat in 2016, the party dropped its Obama-era slogan, "Democrats: Change that Matters."

Source: Photo courtesy of Cliff, http://www.flickr.com/photos/nostri-imago/4994523865/.

**FIGURE 10.11**
**Republican Party's Logo**
The Republican Party logo has been simplified to the party's acronym, GOP, which stands for "Grand Old Party." It includes a small elephant, a symbol of the Republican Party. The donkey is a symbol of the Democratic Party.

Source: https://www.gop.com/.

The Democratic and Republican parties have logos that they use to promote their brands. The Democratic Party logo is a "D" surrounded by a circle, and the Republican Party logo is the acronym "GOP" on a red background. Blue is the color associated with the Democratic Party, and red is the color of the Republican Party. The logos' designs are simple and meet the requirement of being easy to integrate in advertising materials and to use on social media.

The Democratic Party's and Republican Party's websites are sophisticated. In addition to the sites' content, visitors are offered the opportunity to connect with the party through email, Facebook, Twitter, YouTube, Flickr, and other social media. Some of the material on Democratic and Republican websites consists of negative, at times vicious, attacks on the opposing party. Democratic Party websites focus heavily on the accomplishments of the Biden administration. Republican Party websites feature content critical of Biden and his policies.

# Media Depictions of Political Parties

In depicting political parties, the media highlight conflicts between the two major parties and divisions within each party. The press also focuses on the strategies parties employ in their pursuit of political power.

## Partisan Conflict

Parties as adversaries is an accurate characterization of one of their primary functions, representing opposing viewpoints and providing platforms for debate. The modern party has been called "a fighting organization."[117] Indeed, parties actively promote this image. Reporters consulting party websites and reading partisan blogs get their fill of negative hyperbole about the opposition.

The press coverage can exaggerate the conflicts between parties by employing sports and war metaphors. Parties often are described as attacking, battling, fighting, jousting, beating, and pummeling one another. This type of media coverage becomes a problem when parties genuinely try to work together while the press continues to frame their relations in conflict terms. When the Republican congressional leadership held a meeting at the White House in 1995 and agreed to work with Democratic President Bill Clinton on public policy, Republican House Speaker Newt Gingrich told reporters that the meeting was "great." When the press immediately speculated about when the cordial relations would break down, Gingrich reacted by dressing down reporters: "[Y]ou just heard the leaders of the Republican Party say that the Democratic President today had a wonderful meeting on behalf of America; we're trying to work together. Couldn't you try for twenty-four hours to have a positive, optimistic message as though it might work?"[118]

A study by the Pew Research Center in 2017 revealed that hostile partisan disagreements in Congress generate the highest amount of engagement on social media. When members of opposing parties "go negative," they spark the public to post on Twitter and Facebook. The findings suggest that while the public says that it would prefer the political parties to be less polarized, people react more to partisan disagreements. Studies find that engagement on social media solidifies communities of political party loyalists online and heats up partisan conflicts.[119] The press exacerbates these polarizing trends as the majority of media coverage focuses on disagreements and partisan polarization rather than on harmony and compromise.[120]

## Party Strategies

Media depictions often focus on the strategies parties use to win elections and control government. The press is obsessed with how the Republicans and Democrats manage their messages to attract or lose supporters.

One strategy typically portrayed by mass media is that parties routinely compromise the public good to achieve self-interested goals. The Democratic Party is continually criticized for catering to organized labor, Hollywood liberals such as Barbara Streisand and Alec Baldwin, and feminists. The Republican Party is chided for favoring conservatives and corporate interests. The press argues that both parties support these privileged groups because they make large financial donations to party organizations and campaigns.

Media depictions suggest that parties fail to live up to campaign promises about policies they will enact if their candidates are elected. A recurring media theme during President Obama's presidency was that Obama did not represent his party's interests, such as on the issue of tax cuts. President Donald Trump has been depicted as undercutting the Republican Party's efforts to pass legislation by making controversial statements that diverted attention from their policy agenda.[121] President Joe Biden's efforts in his first hundred days to deal with the COVID-19 pandemic through a mask mandate, universal vaccinations, and financial stimulus were portrayed as forwarding liberal Democratic Party ideals.[122] However, press coverage is not consistent with research demonstrating that party leaders keep campaign promises at least two-thirds of the time.[123]

**FIGURE 10.12 Biden Addresses the Nation about COVID-19**

President Biden addresses the nation about his plans to handle the COVID-19 pandemic, which were supported by the Democratic Party.

Source: Official White House Photo by Adam Schultz. The White House via Wikimedia Commons: https://commons.wikimedia.org/wiki/File:P20210311AS-0800_(51102889360).jpg.

# Media Consequences

**"Checkers" speech**

A speech delivered by vice presidential candidate Richard Nixon during the 1952 presidential campaign. The speech was a defense against media reports that he had misused funds given to him by supporters.

Political parties have had to adapt to a dynamic mass media environment that at times has weakened their position in the political process. The introduction of television in the 1950s allowed candidates and government officials to circumvent parties and take their appeals directly to the public. An example is Nixon's **"Checkers" speech**. Richard Nixon, who was running on a ticket headed by Republican presidential candidate General Dwight D. Eisenhower, had been accused of taking money from campaign supporters. The Republican Party was unhappy with Nixon and considered dropping him from the ticket. To save his political career, Nixon went on television to make his case to the American people by detailing his personal finances and denying any wrongdoing. With his wife, Pat, by his side, Nixon declared that there was one gift from supporters he would not return, a dog named Checkers that had become a beloved family pet. The tactic worked, as the public bought into Nixon's impassioned television appeal. Eisenhower and Nixon went on to win the election.

A defining moment was the "Checkers" speech delivered by vice presidential candidate Richard Nixon on September 23, 1952. Part 1 is shown here.

View in the online reader

By the 1980s, party elites had less influence on public opinion than media elites, especially journalists.[124] The press had assumed parties' responsibility for recruiting candidates, organizing the issue agenda, and informing and mobilizing voters.[125] Journalists controlled the amount of publicity parties and candidates received, which contributed to their recognition among voters.

Consultants work directly with candidates to develop media strategies, often leaving parties out of the loop. In his bid for the 2004 Democratic presidential nomination, former governor of Vermont Howard Dean worked with consultants to develop an innovative campaign strategy centered on using the internet to build a base of online supporters through sites including Meetup.com and MoveOn.org, and to raise funds. The Democratic Party expressed concerns about Dean's tactics because he ignored the traditional bases of the party's support, such as environmental activists and other liberal interest groups.[126] Dean was successful in raising funds on the internet but was unable to secure the presidential nomination.

A defining moment was the "Checkers" speech delivered by vice presidential candidate Richard Nixon on September 23, 1952. Part 2 is shown here.

View in the online reader

Parties responded in the 1990s by developing media strategies to enhance their proficiency as service providers to candidates, officeholders, and voters. They engaged in aggressive fundraising schemes so that they could afford to hire the services of consultants and purchase expensive advertising time on television and space in print publications. Parties have facilities where politicians do on-air television and radio interviews and tape messages for local media markets. They invest heavily in advertising during and between election cycles.

Today, major parties are at the forefront of innovation with communications technology as they seek ways of making the internet and digital media more effective and exciting for party members. Parties use websites and social media to engage the public during non-election periods. These media efforts have been paying off. Seventy-seven percent of the public believes that political parties are important to them for providing political information.[127] Party advertisements can influence the opinions of up to 4 percent of voters, enough to sway an election, although this does not happen in every contest.[128]

## Key Takeaways

Political parties have a double-edged relationship with the media. On the one hand, the press is important for political parties because it publicizes the activities and positions of party organizations, leaders, and candidates, which can build a base of support. On the other hand, media coverage of parties emphasizes conflict and the failure of parties to make good on promises they make about policies. Thus, parties are continually revising their strategies as they attempt to garner as much positive coverage and publicity as possible.

Parties need to manage the media and attract sufficient attention to remain viable in the public eye and inform and mobilize their constituents. They interact with journalists by engaging in spin, producing and airing advertisements, hosting websites, and populating social media. Media depictions highlight the conflicts between parties and the strategies they employ to attract voters. Parties have adapted to a changing media environment by developing in-house media facilities to allow candidates and officeholders to communicate with constituents.

## Exercises

1. Why is publicity important to political parties? What are the different strategies parties employ to stay in the public eye and get their messages across?
2. Why does media coverage of political parties tend to exaggerate the conflicts between them? What incentive do the media have to portray politics as conflictual?

## Civic Education

### Youth Engagement in Political Parties

Political parties provide a gateway to involvement in public affairs. Parties offer opportunities for taking part in political campaigns, advocating on behalf of a policy issue, and even running for office. The experience of involvement with a political party can help people hone their organizational skills, develop as public speakers, and learn how to use media for outreach.

Young people traditionally have been somewhat resistant to participation in political parties. They often feel that political parties are targeted more toward older citizens. Yet active party organizations aimed at young people exist at the national, state, and local levels. The College Democrats and College Republicans have national organizations with local affiliates on campuses. These organizations are integral to the parties' voter registration and campaign efforts. They host conferences to give young people a voice in the party. They provide training in campaign techniques, including the use of social media, that instruct young people in reaching out to their peers so that they can make a difference in elections.

College party organizations offer a wide range of opportunities for young party activists to get involved in government and politics.

Source: Photo courtesy of John Edwards 2008 via Flickr: https://www.flickr.com/photos/forallofus/1254455614/. Reproduced via CC BY-SA 2.0: https://creativecommons.org/licenses/by-sa/2.0/.

# 10.9 Recommended Reading

Bibby, John, and Sandy Maisel. *Two Parties or More? The American Party System.* Boulder, CO: Westview Press, 2002. An exploration of the strengths, weaknesses, and functions of minor parties in a two-party dominant system.

Brewer, Mark, and Jeffrey Stonecash. *Dynamics of American Political Parties.* New York: Cambridge University Press, 2009. A historical account of the evolution of American political parties.

Chambers, William Nisbet, and Walter Dean Burnham. *The American Party Systems,* 2nd ed. New York: Oxford University Press, 1975. An excellent collection of essays discussing the historical stages of development of the political party system.

Epstein, Leon D. *Political Parties in the American Mold.* Madison: University of Wisconsin Press, 1986. An impressive investigation into political parties' ability to adapt to changing political, social, economic, and technological conditions.

Galaway, Terry. *Machine Made: Tammany Hall and the Creation of Modern American Politics.* New York: Liveright Publishing, 2014. Exploration of the influence of New York City's Tammany Hall machine on political parties today that takes into account not only well-documented corruption but also the more positive aspects, such as socializing immigrant populations to politics.

Gibson, Rachel, Paul Nixon, and Stephen Ward, eds. *Political Parties and the Internet: Net Gain?* London: Routledge, 2003. A timely collection of articles assessing the positive and negative implications of political parties and the internet.

Green, Donald, Bradley Palmquist, Eric Schickler, and Giordano Bruno. *Partisan Hearts and Minds.* New Haven, CT: Yale University Press, 2002. A comprehensive study of the party in the electorate that argues for the enduring centrality of partisanship as a political cue for many Americans.

Johnson, Dennis W. *No Place for Amateurs.* New York: Routledge, 2001. Argues that political consultants, pollsters, media experts, political action committees, fundraisers, and debate coaches have take on the functions of political parties, diminishing parties' significance in the political process.

Key, V. O. Jr. *Politics, Parties, & Pressure Groups,* 5th ed. New York: Thomas Y. Crowell, 1964. The classic treatise on political parties, covering their history and development, structure, and function.

Lepore, Jill. *The Whites of Their Eyes.* Princeton, NJ: Princeton University Press, 2010. An examination of the Tea Party in historical context.

Maisel, L. Sandy. *American Political Parties and Elections: A Very Short Introduction.* New York: Oxford University Press, 2016. A short, focused introduction to political parties and their role in American politics.

Maisel, L. Sandy, and Jeffrey M. Berry. *The Oxford Handbook of American Political Parties and Interest Groups.* New York: Oxford University Press, 2010. A comprehensive handbook defining terms related to political parties and interest groups.

Riechley, A. James. *The Life of the Parties.* New York: Free Press, 1992. A lively, detailed account of the history of American parties from the founding to the present day.

Riordon, William L. *Plunkitt of Tammany Hall.* St. James, NY: Brandywine Press, 1994. Political wisdom dispatched by a New York party boss in the 1800s.

Sifry, Micah L. *Spoiling for a Fight.* New York: Routledge, 2003. A survey of contemporary third parties, including case studies of Ross Perot and Jesse Ventura of the Reform Party and Ralph Nader of the Green Party.

White, John Kenneth, and Daniel M. Shea. *New Party Politics.* Boston: Bedford/St. Martin's, 2000. An account of the influence of new communications technologies, including the internet, on American political parties.

# 10.10 Recommended Viewing

*Advise and Consent* (1962). This political thriller depicts hardcore partisan politics when a president seeks Senate confirmation of a candidate for secretary of state in the Cold War era.

*All the Way* (2016). Bryan Cranston plays President Lyndon Johnson as he attempts to navigate rifts in the Democratic Party during the civil rights movement in 1963–64.

*America's Political Parties: The Democratic Party, 1960–1992* (1992). Documentary beginning with the swearing in of President John F. Kennedy and following developments in the Democratic Party through the years of reform to the election of President Bill Clinton.

*America's Political Parties: The Republican Party, 1960–1992* (1992). Documentary tracing the evolution of the Republican Party and its various constituent groups from the candidacy of conservative Barry Goldwater through the Nixon, Reagan, and first Bush presidencies.

*Daley: The Last Boss* (1995). Award-winning documentary of mayor of Chicago Richard J. Daley, who reigned from 1955 to 1976 and was considered to be the last of the big-city bosses affiliated with the Democratic machine.

*Gangs of New York* (2002). Director Martin Scorsese's depiction of the Five Points section of New York during the reign of Boss Tweed.

*Head of State* (2003). Chris Rock stars as a Washington, DC, alderman who is recruited to run for president by party leaders who want to gain support from minority groups.

*The Last Hurrah* (1958). The last stand of a venerable political boss in a northeastern city is explored in this classic film based loosely on the last race run by famous Boston mayor James Michael Curley.

*The People and the Power Game—the Elected: The Presidency and Congress* (1996). Author Hedrick Smith's production focuses on the difficulties faced by President Bill Clinton and the Democrats in enacting their policy agenda after the Republican takeover of the House of Representatives in 1995.

*Perot: The Rise and Fall of a Presidential Contender* (1992). A CNN-produced film that explores the third-party presidential bid of millionaire businessman Ross Perot in 1992; the film includes compelling interviews and news footage.

*Power, Politics and Latinos* (1992). A documentary focusing on efforts by Latinxs to promote political awareness and participation in the United States; the film includes an examination of the development of the La Raza Unida party.

*Tea Party: The Documentary Film* (2010). A pro–Tea Party film investigating the grassroots bases of Tea Party support.

*A Third Choice* (1996). A documentary exploring minor parties over the course of over two hundred years.

*The Time of the Lincolns* (2001). A documentary based on biographies of Abraham and Mary Todd Lincoln that spends significant time exploring the evolution of the political party system from 1836 to 1864.

# Endnotes

1. Leon D. Epstein, Political Parties in the American Mold (Madison: University of Wisconsin Press, 1986).
2. Paul LeBlanc, "House Republicans Are Preparing to Oust Liz Cheney from Leadership This Week," CNN Politics, May 10, 2021. https://www.cnn.com/2021/05/10/politics/liz-cheney-vote-what-to-watch/index.html
3. James Downie, "The Big Myth of Cheney, Trump, and the GOP," The Washington Post, May11, 2021. https://www.washingtonpost.com/opinions/2021/05/09/big-myth-about-cheney-trump-gop/
4. Leon D. Epstein, *Political Parties in the American Mold* (Madison: University of Wisconsin Press, 1986), 3.
5. V. O. Key Jr., *Politics, Parties, & Pressure Groups*, 5th ed. (New York: Thomas Y. Crowell Company, 1964).

6. John H. Aldrich, *Why Parties? The Origin and Transformation of Party Politics in America* (Chicago: University of Chicago Press, 1995); Samuel J. Eldersveld and Hanes Walton Jr., *Political Parties in American Society*, 2nd ed. (Boston: Bedford/St. Martin's, 2000).
7. Publius (James Madison), "The Federalist No. 10," in *The Federalist*, ed. Robert Scigliano (New York: The Modern Library Classics, 2001), 53–61.
8. Richard Hofstadter, *The Idea of a Party System* (Berkeley: University of California Press, 1969), 200.
9. William Nisbet Chambers and Walter Dean Burnham, *The American Party Systems* (New York, Oxford University Press, 1975).
10. William Nisbet Chambers, *Political Parties in a New Nation* (New York: Oxford University Press, 1963).
11. John Kenneth White and Daniel M. Shea, *New Party Politics* (Boston: Bedford/St. Martin's, 2000).
12. Joseph Charles, *The Origins of the American Party System* (New York: Harper & Row, 1956).
13. Richard Hofstadter, *The Idea of a Party System* (Berkeley: University of California Press, 1969).
14. See William Nisbet Chambers, *Political Parties in a New Nation* (New York: Oxford University Press, 1963).
15. William Nisbet Chambers, *Political Parties in a New Nation* (New York: Oxford University Press, 1963), 58.
16. See William Nisbet Chambers, *Political Parties in a New Nation* (New York: Oxford University Press, 1963).
17. Michael Schudson, *The Good Citizen* (New York: Free Press, 1998).
18. John Kenneth White and Daniel M. Shea, *New Party Politics* (Boston: Bedford/St. Martin's, 2000).
19. Ronald P. Formisano, "Federalists and Republicans: Parties, Yes—System, No," in *The Evolution of the American Electoral Systems*, ed. Paul Kleppner, Walter Dean Burnham, Ronald P. Formisano, Samuel P. Hays, Richard Jensen, and William G. Shade (Westport, CT: Greenwood Press, 1981), 37–76.
20. Michael F. Holt, *The Rise and Fall of the American Whig Party* (New York: Oxford University Press, 2003).
21. Michael F. Holt, *The Rise and Fall of the American Whig Party* (New York: Oxford University Press, 2003).
22. Michael F. Holt, *The Rise and Fall of the American Whig Party* (New York: Oxford University Press, 2003).
23. John Kenneth White and Daniel M. Shea, *New Party Politics* (Boston: Bedford/St. Martin's, 2000).
24. Milton Rakove, *Don't Make No Waves, Don't Back No Losers: An Insider's Analysis of the Daley Machine* (Bloomington: Indiana University Press, 1975), 3.
25. Gerald M. Pomper, *Passions and Interests* (Lawrence: University Press of Kansas, 1992).
26. A. James Riechley, *The Life of the Parties* (New York: Free Press, 1992).
27. William L. Riordon, *Plunkitt of Tammany Hall* (St. James, NY: Brandywine Press, 1994), 3.
28. Chris Lamb, "DRAWING POWER: The limits of editorial cartoons in America," *Journalism Studies*, September 11, 2007, accessed July 17, 2918, https://www.tandfonline.com/doi/abs/10.1080/14616700701504666.
29. Charles Merriam and Harold F. Gosnell, *The American Party System* (New York: MacMillan, 1922).
30. A. James Riechley, *The Life of the Parties* (New York: Free Press, 1992).
31. John Kenneth White and Daniel M. Shea, *New Party Politics* (Boston: Bedford/St. Martin's, 2000).
32. James W. Caeser, *Presidential Selection* (Princeton, NJ: Princeton University Press, 1979).
33. William Crotty, *American Parties in Decline* (Boston: Little, Brown, 1984).
34. Diana Owen, *Media Messages in American Presidential Elections* (Westport, CT: Greenwood Press, 1991).
35. William Nisbet Chambers and Walter Dean Burnham, eds., *The American Party Systems* (New York: Oxford University Press, 1975).
36. Steven J. Rosenstone, Roy L. Behr, and Edward H. Lazarus, *Third Parties in America*, 2nd ed. (Princeton, NJ: Princeton University Press, 2000), 9.
37. Clinton Rossiter, *Parties and Politics in America* (Ithaca, NY: Cornell University Press, 1960).
38. John Gerring, *Party Ideologies in America, 1828–1996* (New York: Cambridge, 1998).
39. Adam Clymer, "Buoyed by Resurgence, G.O.P. Strives for an Era of Dominance," *The New York Times*, May 25, 2003, accessed March 23, 2011, http://query.nytimes.com/gst/fullpage.html?res=950CE1D91531F936A15756C0A9659C8B63&pagewanted=all.
40. Gerald M. Pomper, *Passions and Interests* (Lawrence: University Press of Kansas, 1992).
41. Frank Newport, "The Impact of Increased Political Polarization," Gallup, Polling Matters, December 5, 2019. https://news.gallup.com/opinion/polling-matters/268982/impact-increased-political-polarization.aspx.
42. Leon D. Epstein, *Political Parties in the American Mold* (Madison: University of Wisconsin Press, 1986); Gerald M. Pomper, *Passions and Interests* (Lawrence: University Press of Kansas, 1992).
43. Anthony Downs, *An Economic Theory of Democracy* (New York: Harper, 1957).
44. John C. Green and Paul S. Herrnson, eds., *Responsible Partisanship?* (Lawrence: University Press of Kansas, 2002).
45. Katherine Schaeffer, "Despite Wide Partisan Gaps in Views of Many Aspects of the Pandemic, Some Common Ground Exists," Fact Tank, Pew Research Center, March 24, 2021. https://www.pewresearch.org/fact-tank/2021/03/24/despite-wide-partisan-gaps-in-views-of-many-aspects-of-the-pandemic-some-common-ground-exists/.
46. John Connolly, Praynay Nadella, David Grande, "Health Care in the Next Congress—Policy Positions of the Incoming 2021 House of Representatives, Health Affairs Blog, December 24, 2020. https://www.healthaffairs.org/do/10.1377/hblog20201221.179370/full/.
47. Leon D. Epstein, *Political Parties in the American Mold* (Madison: University of Wisconsin Press, 1986).
48. Susan Milligan, "Midterms May Hinge on Votes of Latinos: Both Major Parties Tailoring Messages to Growing Minority," *Boston Globe*, October 31, 2002.
49. V. O. Key Jr., *Politics, Parties, & Pressure Groups*, 5th ed. (New York: Thomas Y. Crowell Company, 1964).
50. Samuel J. Eldersveld, and Hanes Walton Jr., *Political Parties in American Society*, 2nd ed. (Boston: Bedford/St. Martin's, 2000).
51. Stephen E. Frantzich, *Political Parties in the Technological Age* (New York: Longman, 1989).
52. John Kenneth White and Daniel M. Shea, *New Party Politics* (Boston: Bedford/St. Martin's, 2000).
53. Jeffrey M. Jones, "Number of Solidly Democratic States Cut in Half from '08 to '10," *Gallup*, February 21, 2011, accessed March 26, 2011, http://www.gallup.com/poll/146234/Number-Solidly-Democratic-States-Cut-Half.aspx?utm_source= tagrss&utm_medium=rss&utm_campaign=syndication&utm_term= State Politics.
54. Lydia Saad, "Not as Many U.S. States Lean Democratic in 2013," *Gallup*, January 29, 2014, accessed July 8, 2014, http://www.gallup.com/poll/167030/not-states-lean-democratic-2013.asp.
55. Sarah M. Morehouse and Malcolm E. Jewell, "State Parties: Independent Partners in the Money Relationship," in *The State of the Parties*, ed. John C. Green and Rick Farmer (Lanham, MD: Rowman & Littlefield, 2013), 151–68.
56. Samuel J. Eldersveld and Hanes Walton Jr., *Political Parties in American Society*, 2nd ed. (Boston: Bedford/St. Martin's, 2000).
57. "Bush Campaign Has Raised Nearly $84 Million Since Last Spring," *Washington Post*, October 14, 2003.
58. Jose Antonio Vargas, "Obama Raised Half a Billion Online," *Washington Post*, November 20, 2008, accessed March 26, 2011, http://voices.washingtonpost.com/44/2008/11/obama-raised-half-a-billion-on.html.
59. Kenneth P. Vogel, et al., "Barack Obama, Mitt Romney Both Topped $1Billion in 2012," *Politico*, December 7, 2012. Accessed July 8, 2014. http://www.politico.com/story/2012/12/barack-obama-mitt-romney-both-topped-1-billion-in-2012-84737.html.
60. Louis Jacobson, "What We Know About Trump's Fundraising Off the False Claim of Election Fraud," *PolitiFact*, January 8, 2021. https://www.politifact.com/article/2021/jan/08/what-we-know-about-trumps-fundraising-false-claim-/.
61. Shawn Zeller, "No Quarter for Centrists in the House: 2020 Vote Studies," *Roll Call*, March 3, 2021.
62. Larry Schwab, "The Unprecedented Senate: Political Parties in the Senate after the 2000 Election," in *The State of the Parties*, ed. John C. Green and Rick Farmer (Lanham, MD: Rowman & Littlefield, 2013), 241–53; Lee Drutman, "Why There Are So Few Moderate Republicans Left," FiveThirtyEight, August 24, 2020. https://fivethirtyeight.com/features/why-there-are-so-few-moderate-republicans-left/.
63. Gary W. Cox and Samuel Kernell, *The Politics of Divided Government* (Boulder, CO: Westview Press, 1991).
64. Christopher Ingraham, "Trump Has Signed Twice As Many Bills As Obama Had at This Point," *The Washington Post*, April 6, 2017.
65. Russell Berman, "The Donald Trump Cabinet Tracker," *The Atlantic*, April 27, 2017.
66. Angus Campbell, Philip E. Converse, Warren E. Miller, and Donald E. Stokes, *The American Voter* (New York: John Wiley and Sons, 1960).
67. Donald Green, Bradley Palmquist, and Eric Schickler, *Partisan Hearts and Minds* (New Haven, CT: Yale University Press, 2002).
68. Data computed using the American National Election Studies, http://www.electionstudies.org. Two percent of the sample consider themselves "apolitical."
69. Jeffrey M. Jones, "Quarterly Gap in Party Affiliation Largest Since 2012," Gallup, April 7, 2021. https://news.gallup.com/poll/343976/quarterly-gap-party-affiliation-largest-2012.aspx.
70. Patricia Winters Lauro, "According to a Survey, the Democratic and Republican Parties Have Brand-Name Problems," *The New York Times*, November 17, 2000.
71. Diana Owen and Jack Dennis, "Antipartyism in the USA and Support for Ross Perot," *European Journal of Political Research* 29: 383–400.
72. Paul Allen Beck, "A Tale of Two Electorates: The Changing American Party Coalitions, 1952–2000," in *The State of the Parties*, 4th ed., ed. John C. Green and Rick Farmer (Lanham, MD: Rowman & Littlefield, 2003), 38–53.
73. V. O. Key Jr., "A Theory of Critical Elections," *Journal of Politics* 21: 198–210.

74. Walter Dean Burnham, "Realignment Lives: The 1994 Earthquake and Its Implications," in *The Clinton Presidency: First Appraisals*, ed. Colin Campbell and Bert A. Rockman (Chatham, NJ: Chatham House, 1996), 363–95.
75. Jeff Diamant, "Three-in-Ten or More Democrats and Republicans Don't Agree with Their Party on Abortion," *Pew Research Center*, June 18, 2020. https://www.pewresearch.org/fact-tank/2020/06/18/three-in-ten-or-more-democrats-and-republicans-dont-agree-with-their-party-on-abortion/.
76. Michael Lind, "This is What the Future of American Parties Looks Like," *Politico*, May 22, 2016.
77. George Packer, "Is America Undergoing a Political Realignment?" *The Atlantic*, April 8, 2019. https://www.theatlantic.com/ideas/archive/2019/04/will-2020-bring-realignment-left/586624/.
78. Walter Dean Burnham, *Critical Elections and the Mainsprings of American Politics* (New York: Norton, 1970).
79. Paul Allen Beck, "A Tale of Two Electorates: The Changing American Party Coalitions, 1952–2000," in *The State of the Parties*, 4th ed., ed. John C. Green and Rick Farmer (Lanham, MD: Rowman & Littlefield, 2003), 38–53.
80. Daniel A. Mazmanian, *Third Parties in Presidential Elections* (Washington, DC: Brookings Institution, 1974).
81. Micah L. Sifry, *Spoiling for a Fight* (New York: Routledge, 2003).
82. Jenny Beth Martin, "The Tea Party Movement Is Alive and Well—And We Saw Trump Coming," *Politico*, November 19, 2016.
83. Daniel A. Mazmanian, *Third Parties in Presidential Elections* (Washington, DC: Brookings Institution, 1974).
84. Diana Owen and Jack Dennis, "Antipartyism in the USA and Support for Ross Perot," *European Journal of Political Research* 29 (1996): 383–400.
85. John C. Green and William Binning, "Surviving Perot: The Origins and Future of the Reform Party," in *Multiparty Politics in America*, ed. Paul S. Herrnson and John C. Green (Lanham, MD: Rowman & Littlefield, 1997), 87–102.
86. Steven J. Rosenstone, Roy L. Behr, and Edward H. Lazarus, *Third Parties in America*, 2nd ed. (Princeton, NJ: Princeton University Press, 2000).
87. Committee for the Study of the American Electorate, "Votes Cast for Presidential Candidates," accessed March 26, 2011, http://www.fairvote.org/turnout/prrevote2000.htm.
88. Micah L. Sifry, *Spoiling for a Fight* (New York: Routledge, 2003).
89. Alexandra Jaffe, "By the Numbers: Third-Party Candidates Had an Outsize Impact on Election," NBC News, November 9, 2016.
90. Adam Forgie, "3rd Party Candidates: An In-Depth Look at Who Else Is Running for President," CBS KUTV News, October 13, 2020. https://kutv.com/news/beyond-the-podium/know-your-candidate/2020-3rd-party-candidates-an-in-depth-look-at-who-else-is-running-for-president.
91. Steven J. Rosenstone, Roy L. Behr, and Edward H. Lazarus, *Third Parties in America*, 2nd ed. (Princeton, NJ: Princeton University Press, 2000).
92. Terry Savage, "The Libertarian Party: A Pragmatic Approach to Party Building," in *Multiparty Politics in America*, ed. Paul S. Herrnson and John C. Green (Lanham, MD: Rowman & Littlefield, 1997), 141–45.
93. Greg Jan, "The Green Party: Global Politics at the Grassroots," in *Multiparty Politics in America*, ed. Paul S. Herrnson and John C. Green (Lanham, MD: Rowman & Littlefield, 1997), 153–57.
94. Micah L. Sifry, *Spoiling for a Fight* (New York: Routledge, 2003).
95. J. David Gillespie, *Politics at the Periphery* (Columbia: University of South Carolina Press, 1993).
96. Green Liberty Party. Website: http://greenliberty.weebly.com/.
97. Morgan Lee, "New Minor Party Pushes for 'Fusion Voting' in New Mexico," *Associated Press*, July 3, 2020. https://www.usnews.com/news/best-states/new-mexico/articles/2020-07-03/new-minor-party-pushes-for-fusion-voting-in-new-mexico.
98. Brian Stelter, "In News Coverage, Tea Party and Its 'New Personalities' Hold the Spotlight," *New York Times*, November 3, 2010.
99. Lois Beckett, "Tea Party-linked Activists Protest Against 'Election Fraud' in U.S. Cities," *The Guardian*, November 6, 2020. https://www.theguardian.com/us-news/2020/nov/06/tea-party-linked-activists-protestagainst-election-fraud-us-cities.
100. Tony Rogers, "Both Fox News and CNN Made Mistakes in Tea Party Protest Coverage," About.com Journalism, accessed March 26, 2011, http://journalism.about.com/od/ethicsprofessionalism/a/teaparty.htm.
101. Rich Noyes, "TV's Tea Party Travesty," Media Research Center, April 15, 2010, accessed March 26, 2011, http://www.mrc.org/specialreports/uploads/teapartytravesty.pdf.
102. Amy Gardner, "Tea Party Groups Say Media Have Been Fair, Survey Finds," *Washington Post*, October 26, 2010, accessed March 26, 2011, http://www.washingtonpost.com/wp-dyn/content/article/2010/10/26/AR2010102602796.html.
103. Micah L. Sifry, *Spoiling for a Fight* (New York: Routledge, 2003), 45.
104. Micah L. Sifry, *Spoiling for a Fight* (New York: Routledge, 2003), 45.
105. Maurice Duverger, *Party Politics and Pressure Groups* (New York: Thomas Y. Crowell, 1972).
106. Douglas J. Amy, *Real Choices/New Voices* (New York: Columbia University Press, 1993).
107. Clinton Rossiter, *Parties and Politics in America* (Ithaca, NY: Cornell University Press, 1960).
108. Steven J. Rosenstone, Roy L. Behr, and Edward H. Lazarus, *Third Parties in America*, 2nd ed. (Princeton, NJ: Princeton University Press, 2000).
109. Steven J. Rosenstone, Roy L. Behr, and Edward H. Lazarus, *Third Parties in America*, 2nd ed. (Princeton, NJ: Princeton University Press, 2000).
110. Steven J. Rosenstone, Roy L. Behr, and Edward H. Lazarus, *Third Parties in America*, 2nd ed. (Princeton, NJ: Princeton University Press, 2000).
111. Clinton Rossiter, *Parties and Politics in America* (Ithaca, NY: Cornell University Press, 1960).
112. J. David Gillespie, *Politics at the Periphery* (Columbia: University of South Carolina Press, 1993).
113. Ronald B. Rapoport and Walter J. Stone, "Ross Perot Is Alive and Well and Living in the Republican Party: Major Party Co-optation of the Perot Movement and the Reform Party," in *The State of the Parties*, 2nd ed., ed. John C. Green and Rick Farmer (Lanham, MD: Rowman & Littlefield, 2003), 337–53.
114. Stephen Bates, *The Future of Presidential Debates* (Boston: Joan Shorenstein Barone Center on the Press, Politics and Public Policy, 1993).
115. "Online Political Ad Spending," Open Secrets, January, 2021. https://www.opensecrets.org/online-ads.
116. Rachael Gibson and Stephen Ward, "A Proposed Methodology for Studying the Function and Effectiveness of Party and Candidate Web Sites," *Social Science Computer Review* 18: 301–19.
117. Robert Michels, *Political Parties*, ed. Seymour Martin Lipset (1915; New York: Collier Books, 1962), 78.
118. Joseph N. Cappella and Kathleen Hall Jamieson, *Spiral of Cynicism* (New York: Oxford University Press, 1997).
119. Lee De-Wit, Sander Van Der Linden, and Cameron Brick, "Are Social Media Driving Political Polarization," Greater Good Magazine, January 16, 2019. https://greatergood.berkeley.edu/article/item/is_social_media_driving_political_polarization.
120. Pew Research Center, "Partisan Conflict and Congressional Outreach" (Washington, DC: Pew Research Center, February 23, 2017). http://www.people-press.org/2017/02/23/partisan-conflict-and-congressional-outreach/.
121. Jeff Zeleny and Kevin Liptak, "Another Trump Crisis Craters GOP Agenda," *CNN Politics*, May 16, 2017. http://www.cnn.com/2017/05/15/politics/trump-gop-agenda-stalled/index.html.
122. Lisa Lerer and Annie Karni, "At 100 Days, Biden Is Transforming What It Means to Be a Democrat," *The New York Times*, April 29, 2021. https://www.nytimes.com/2021/04/29/us/politics/biden-democrats.html.
123. Joseph N. Cappella and Kathleen Hall Jamieson, *Spiral of Cynicism* (New York: Oxford University Press, 1997).
124. Nelson Polsby, *The Consequences of Party Reform* (New York: Oxford University Press, 1983).
125. Thomas E. Patterson, *Out of Order* (New York: Knopf, 1994).
126. Thomas B. Edsall, "Dean Sparks Debate on His Potential to Remold Party," *Washington Post*, October 20, 2003.
127. James A. Thurber, Erin O'Brien, and David A. Dulio, "Where Do Voters Get Their Political Information," *Campaigns and Elections*, April, 2001, 9.
128. Will Lester, "About $1B Spent on Televised Midterm Ads," *Associated Press*, December 5, 2002.

# CHAPTER 11
# Campaigns and Elections

## 11.1 Preamble

It has become commonplace for reality programs to hold elections. The *American Idol* winner is chosen in an elimination contest by receiving the most votes from viewers who, just like voters in regular elections, make decisions based on any number of reasons: voice, song selections, looks, gender, race, even hometown. Unlike in government elections, on *American Idol* people vote as often as they want by telephone and text message.

The connection between reality television and American elections was reinforced with the election of Donald Trump as president. President Trump had achieved celebrity status due to his position as the host of *The Apprentice* and *The Celebrity Apprentice* for fifteen seasons. Researchers at the University at Buffalo found that frequent viewers of *The Apprentice* were more likely to form a positive impression of Trump as a decision maker and to vote for him in the 2016 presidential election.[1]

Elections are ingrained in American culture, so it is no surprise that the winner of an entertainment contest would be chosen through a voting process. Elections are the heart and voting is the voice of American democracy. Elections legitimize the winners and the political system. They enable Americans to influence the decisions of their elected leaders.

## 11.2 Election Campaigns

### Learning Objectives

After reading this section, you should be able to answer the following questions:

1. How are American election campaigns organized?
2. How are campaigns funded? What are the regulations that guide campaign fundraising and spending?
3. What strategies do candidates use when pursuing elected office?

This section covers campaign organization, funding, and strategy. Getting elected often requires defeating opponents from the same political party in a **primary election** in order to become that party's nominee. The nominees from each party run to gain office in the **general election**. Election campaigns require organization, funding, and strategy. Legal guidelines, especially for campaign finance, influence the environment within which elections take place. The media are central to the electoral process.

**primary election**

An election that decides who will be a political party's nominee for an office in the general election.

**general election**

An election, typically held after the political parties have chosen their nominees through caucuses or primaries, that decides who will hold an office, such as a congressional representative or president.

## Campaign Organization

Candidates form organizations to manage their electoral bids. It takes the coordinated effort of a staff to run a successful campaign for office. The staff is headed by the campaign manager, who oversees personnel, allocates expenditures, and develops strategy. The political director deals with other politicians, interest groups, and organizations supporting the candidate. The finance director helps the candidate raise funds directly and through a finance committee. The research director is responsible for information supporting the candidate's position on issues and for research on the opponents' statements, voting record, and behavior, including any vulnerabilities that can be attacked.

FIGURE 11.1
Exit Polls
Outside the polls, some voters answer questions on exit polls that are used in media reports.

Source: Sergieiev / Shutterstock.com

The communications team promotes the candidate to the news media and at the same time works to deflect negative publicity. This entails briefing journalists, issuing press releases, responding to reporters' questions and requests, and meeting informally with journalists. The communications team's job has become more complicated in the digital age. Getting the candidate's message out to voters on **social media**, such as Facebook and Twitter, has become a priority. The communications team members craft messages that they hope will be picked up and amplified by voters in their social media networks, bloggers, and the established press. Campaigns now routinely hire social media directors to coordinate their digital outreach to voters and journalists. Both Hillary Clinton and Donald Trump had staffs of over one hundred people to run their digital operations in the 2016 presidential election.[2] The size of the digital operations staffs of Joe Biden and Donald Trump in the 2020 presidential contest were even larger.[3] Campaigns also have consultants responsible for media strategy, specialists on political advertising, and speechwriters.

**social media**

Digital media platforms that allow users to create and share content easily and that have been used in elections to share candidate information and videos, organize events, and collect campaign donations.

Pollsters are essential because campaigning without polls is like "flying without the benefit of radar."[4] Polls conducted by campaigns, not to be confused with the media's polls, can identify the types of people who support or oppose the candidate and those who are undecided. They can reveal what people know and feel about the candidates, the issues that concern them, and the most effective appeals to win their votes. Tracking polls measure shifts in public opinion, sometimes daily, in response to news stories and events. They test the effectiveness of the campaign's messages, including candidates' advertisements. Polls are released by the press almost every day during presidential elections, and are part of the horserace coverage of campaigns.

Relatedly, **focus groups** bring together a few people representative of the general public or of particular groups, such as undecided voters, to find out their reactions to such things as the candidate's stump speech delivered at campaign rallies, debate performance, and campaign ads. Television news programs will air campaign focus groups as an entertaining way of examining the public's views about candidates at particular junctures in a campaign, such as following debates.

**focus groups**

Small groups that take part in guided discussions where participants express their opinions.

FIGURE 11.2 Campaign Focus Groups
Campaigns convene focus groups consisting of voters who share their views about candidates and the election in order to guide strategic decisions.

Source: fizkes/Shutterstock.com

# Funding Campaigns

"Money is the mother's milk of politics," observed the longtime and powerful California politician Jesse Unruh. The cost of organizing and running campaigns has risen precipitously. The 2008 presidential and congressional elections cost $5.3 billion dollars, a 25 percent increase over 2004.[5] The 2012 election continued the cycle of increased spending, topping $6 billion. Candidates spent a total of $2.6 billion in the presidential election and $3.6 billion in congressional races.[6] According to the Center for Responsive Politics, candidates spent $3.77 billion in the 2014 race, which was a historic high point for midterm elections. The cost of midterm elections rose even higher in 2018, when over $5 billion was spent.[7] Presidential candidates' campaigns in 2016 raised $1.46 billion.[8] The escalating costs of election campaigns continues unabated. The 2020 presidential election was the most expensive in history, topping $14 billion. The election cost more than twice the amount of the 2016 campaign.[9] Around 60 percent of this money goes to media costs, especially television advertising. The Campaign Finance Institute and the Federal Election Commission have a wealth of information about the funding of American election campaigns.

## Limiting Contributions and Expenditures

In an episode of *The Simpsons*, Homer's boss tells him, "Do you realize how much it costs to run for office? More than any honest man could afford."[10] Spurred by media criticisms and embarrassed by news stories of fundraising scandals, Congress periodically passes, and the president signs, laws to regulate money in federal elections.

**Federal Election Campaign Act (FECA)**

A federal law originally passed in 1971 that limited the amount of money that individuals, political parties, and political groups could contribute to campaigns.

**Federal Election Commission (FEC)**

The institution that oversees campaign finance, including campaign contributions and candidate expenditures.

The **Federal Election Campaign Act (FECA)** of 1971, amended in 1974, limited the amount of money that individuals, political parties, and political groups could contribute to campaigns and provided guidelines for how campaign funds could be spent. The FECA also provided a system of public financing for presidential campaigns. It required that campaigns report their financial information to a newly established enforcement institution, the **Federal Election Commission (FEC)**, which would make it public.

Opponents challenged the constitutionality of these laws in the federal courts, arguing that they restrict political expression.[11] In the 1976 case of *Buckley v. Valeo*, the Supreme Court upheld the limits on contributions and the reporting requirement but overturned all limits on campaign spending except for candidates who accept public funding for presidential election campaigns.[12] The Supreme Court argued that campaign spending was the equivalent of free speech, so it should not be constrained. In the 2014 case of *McCutcheon, et al. v. Federal Election Commission*, the Supreme Court, in a divided 5–4 decision, extended this logic by striking down limits on individual contributions to federal candidates during a two-year election cycle because it violated First Amendment free speech provisions.[13]

**FIGURE 11.3 Republican National Committee Ad Featuring Presidential Candidate Bob Dole**
In 1996, the Republican National Committee used "soft money" to produce an ad that devoted fifty-six seconds to presidential candidate Bob Dole's biography and only four seconds to issues. Similarly, the Democratic National Committee used "soft money" on ads that promoted candidate Bill Clinton. These ads pushed the limits of campaign finance laws, prompting a call for reform.

Source: Photo courtesy of the U.S. Department of Defense by Samantha Quigley, http://commons.wikimedia.org/wiki/File:Bob_Dole_VE_Day_60th_Anniversery.jpg.

For around twenty years, **"hard money"** that was contributed directly to campaigns was regulated through the FECA. However, campaign advisors were able to exploit the fact that **"soft money"** given to the political parties for get-out-the-vote drives, party-building activities, and issue advertising was not subject to contribution limits. Soft money could be spent for political advertising as long as the ads did not ask viewers to vote for or against specific candidates. Nonparty organizations, such as interest groups, also could run issue ads as long as they were independent of candidate campaigns. The Democratic and Republican parties raised more than $262 million in soft money in 1996, much of which was spent on advertising that came close to violating the law.[14] Parties have been prohibited from raising and spending "soft money" since 2002. However, the Supreme Court decision in *McCutcheon, et al. v. Federal Election Commission* in 2014 made it possible to funnel large amounts of soft money into political party coffers.[15]

**"hard money"**

Funds, contributed directly to candidate campaigns, that are subject to government regulation.

**"soft money"**

Funds contributed to political parties for get-out-the-vote drives, party-building activities, and issue advertising that was not subject to contribution or expenditure limitations as long as it was not used directly for candidate advertising.

Congress responded with the **Bipartisan Campaign Reform Act (BCRA)** of 2002, better known by the names of its sponsoring senators, as McCain–Feingold. It banned soft-money contributions by political committees and prohibited corporations and labor unions from advocating for or against a candidate via broadcast, cable, or satellite prior to presidential primaries and the general election. A constitutional challenge to the law was mounted by Senate Majority Whip Mitch McConnell, who believed that the ban on advertising violated First Amendment free-speech rights. The law was upheld by a vote of 5–4 by the Supreme Court.[16] This decision was overruled in 2010 when the Supreme Court decided that restricting independent spending by corporations in elections violated free speech.[17] The case concerned the rights of Citizens United, a conservative political group, to run a caustic ninety-minute film, *Hillary: The Movie*, on cable television to challenge Democratic candidate Hillary Rodham Clinton as she ran in the 2008 primary election campaign. The 5–4 decision divided the Supreme Court, as justices weighed the interests of large corporations against the Constitutional guarantee of free speech.[18] The ruling in *Citizens United* combined with the elimination of limitations on individual donations in the case of *McCutcheon, et al. v. Federal Election Commission* have paved the way for money to play an even more prominent role in election campaigns than it has in the past.

**Bipartisan Campaign Reform Act (BCRA)**

Also known as McCain–Feingold, this federal law placed limitations on soft-money contributions by political committees and prohibited corporations and labor unions from advocating for or against a candidate via broadcast, cable, or satellite prior to presidential primaries and the general election.

YouTube trailer for *Hillary: The Movie*.

View in the online reader

In April 2011, comedic news anchor Stephen Colbert announced his intention to form a "super PAC" to expose loopholes in the campaign finance laws that allow corporations to form political action committees, which can spend unlimited amounts of money in elections on advertising. Colbert testified in front of the FEC and was granted permission to form his PAC, which would be funded by Viacom, the media corporation that owns Comedy Central, which hosted *The Colbert Report*. The decision sparked concern that media organizations would be free to spend unlimited amounts of money in campaigns; however, the FEC's decision imposed the strict limitation that Colbert could only show the ads on his program. Colbert announced the FEC's decision to allow him to form a PAC to raise and spend funds in the 2012 election in this video.

Colbert eventually signed his PAC over to comedian Jon Stewart when he decided to run for office in South Carolina. This video discusses how candidate Colbert was prohibited from coordinating with the PAC now overseen by Stewart.

The public supports actions to curb the influence of wealthy people and groups in elections even as the federal government's actions have been limited. Voters indicated their frustration with the Supreme Court's decision in *Citizens United* that has resulted in skyrocketing election costs by endorsing state-level measures to curb campaign contributions. In 2020, Oregon voters passed an amendment to the state constitution capping contributions to candidates. Alaska voters supported a measure aimed at controlling dark money where the donors' identities are unknown.[19]

## Sources of Funding

There are seven main sources of funding for federal elections. These sources include individuals, political action committees, super PACS, public financing, candidates' contributions to their own campaigns, political party committees, and advocacy organizations or "527 committees." Individuals contribute the most to election campaigns. The 2014 Supreme Court decision in *McCutcheon, et al.*

*v. Federal Election Commission* removed restrictions on donations in federal elections, which will allow this amount to grow. Individual donations amounted to just under $1 million in the 2012 presidential contest and climbed to $1.8 billion in 2020.[20]

**political action committees**

Political committees that raise and spend money to elect or defeat candidates that are associated with businesses, trade associations, labor organizations, and ideological groups.

**Political action committees** (PACs) sponsored by advocacy organizations are an other source of direct funding to candidates. PACs were developed by business and labor organizations to fund candidates, and were institutionalized through the Federal Election Campaign Act of 1972. Politicians also have created PACs to generate funds for candidates they support. PACs can give up to $5,000 per candidate per election. In 2012, they gave $41,643,399 to congressional candidates. Presidential candidates in 2016 received $2,945,552 from PACs. Super PACs differ from PACS in that they cannot make donations directly to candidates or political parties. They can, however, spend an unlimited amount of money independently, such as by making ads for or against a candidate without coordinating with a campaign committee or party. The 2,276 super PACs that were active in the 2020 election raised almost $3.5 billion and spent over $2 billion of those funds.[21]

Presidential candidates can opt for public funding of their election campaigns. The funds come from an income tax checkoff, where people can check a box to contribute $3 to a public funding account. To qualify for public funding, candidates must have raised $100,000 in amounts of $250 or less, with at least $5,000 from each of twenty states. The first $250 of every individual contribution is matched with public funds starting January 1 of the election year. However, candidates who take public funds must adhere to spending limits.

**FIGURE 11.4 Presidential Candidate John McCain on the Campaign Trail in 2008**

In 2008, Republican candidate John McCain criticized his Democratic opponent, Barack Obama, for failing to use public financing for his presidential bid, as he had promised. McCain felt disadvantaged by taking public funds because the law limits the amount of money he could raise and spend, while Obama was not subject to these restrictions.

Source: Photo courtesy of Matthew Reichbach, http://commons.wikimedia.org/wiki/File:Sarah_Palin_and_John_McCain_in_Albuquerque.jpg. Reproduced via CC BY 2.0: https://creativecommons.org/licenses/by/2.0/deed.en.

Party committees at the national, state, and local levels, as well as the parties' Senate and House campaign committees, can give a Senate candidate a total of $35,000 for the primary and then general election and $5,000 to each House candidate. There is no limit on how much of their own money candidates can spend on their campaigns. Neither John McCain nor Barack Obama used personal funds for his own campaign in 2008. Barack Obama and Mitt Romney also refrained from self-financing in 2012, as did Hillary Clinton and Donald Trump in 2016. Continuing the trend, Joe Biden and Donald Trump did not self-finance in 2020. Self-financed presidential candidates do not receive public funds.

Known as **"527 committees"** after the Internal Revenue Service regulation authorizing them, advocacy groups, such as the pro-Democratic ActBlue and the pro-Republican GOPAC, can receive and spend unlimited amounts of money in federal elections as long as they do not coordinate with the candidates or parties they support and do not advocate for the election or defeat of a candidate. They spent approximately $400 million in all races in the 2008 election cycle. In the wake of the Supreme Court decision supporting the rights of Citizens United to air *Hillary: The Movie*, spending by independent committees grew tremendously. The 527 committees spent $280 million in 2010, an increase of 130 percent from 2008.[22] Spending by advocacy groups decreased substantially in 2012 in the presidential race, but increased in state and local elections. In the 2014 midterm elections, liberal groups spent $354 million, conservative groups spent $412.2 million, and other groups spent $29.8 million. Advocacy groups spent large amounts in the 2016 elections, especially during the presidential primary campaign. Advocacy groups spent $220.9 million in state and local elections and $182.2 million national elections in the 2018 midterms.[23]

**"527 committees"**

Advocacy groups that can receive and spend unlimited amounts of money in elections as long as they do not coordinate with candidates' campaign organizations or political parties in support of or opposition to a candidate.

Funds spent by political groups promoting a candidate without reporting their activities to the Federal Election Commission are considered **"dark money."** Nonprofit political organizations are not legally required to reveal their donors, and can run ads or promote social media messages for or against candidates without accountability. Super PACs can also spend "dark money" under some circumstances. The amount of "dark money" is difficult to determine because there are no reporting requirements, but some estimates place the amount of "dark money" spent in the 2016 election at over $181 million. In the 2018 midterm elections, over $100 million that could not be traced to its original source was spent.[24] The amount of "dark money" in the 2020 election skyrocketed to over $1 billion, with a higher percentage supporting liberal candidates than conservative candidates.[25]

**dark money**

Funds spent by political organizations promoting a candidate that are not reported to the Federal Election Commission. Nonprofit groups can spend unlimited funds in campaigns without revealing the donors.

# Campaign Strategy

Most campaigns have a strategy to win an election by raising funds, recruiting volunteers, and courting voters. Campaign strategies take into account voters' party identification, the candidate's image, and issues. Candidates carry out their strategy through retail politics and the media.

In **retail politics**, also known as field operations, candidates engage in person-to-person campaigning. Even in the current new media era, personal appearances by candidates are important. Candidates and surrogates representing their campaign, such as their spouses, campaign and political party officials, and celebrities, speak at rallies, knock on doors in neighborhoods, visit voters in their homes, and put in appearances at schools, religious institutions, and senior-citizen centers. They greet workers outside factories and in eateries and hold town hall meetings. The campaign distributes posters, lawn signs, T-shirts, baseball caps, and buttons. In the state of New Hampshire, which holds the first presidential primary in the nation, it is not unusual for residents to meet and talk with several candidates vying for their party's nomination in their neighbors' homes, coffee shops, and walking down the street.

**retail politics**

Campaign activity, also known as field operations, in which candidates engage in person-to-person encounters with potential voters.

## Big Data and Microtargeting

**microtargeting**

The process of mining people's personal data in order to devise specific messages that appeal to particular voters.

**big data**

Extremely large data sets that can be analyzed by computers to identify patterns of voters, preferences and behaviors.

**Microtargeting** is the process of mining people's personal data to devise specific messages that appeal to particular voters. The use of **big data**, extremely large data sets that can be analyzed by computers to identify patterns of voters' preferences and behaviors, has become commonplace in campaigns. During the 2012 presidential election, the Obama campaign used information gleaned from the trail of data that people leave behind on social media to develop voter profiles that they used to target messages to voters.[26] The data included information about voters' political opinions, candidate preferences in past campaigns, and consumer behavior. A text message from a campaign can be tailored specifically to appeal to particular members of the electorate, such as a young, female voter who enjoys lattes at Starbucks. Campaigns pay Facebook, Google, YouTube, and Twitter to post ads and short videos based on their big data analysis.

Microtargeting reached new levels of sophistication during the 2016 presidential election. The national Republican and Democratic parties provided candidates with access to the voter file, a public record of citizens' voter registration and turnout history. The campaigns supplemented the voter file with information from commercial data brokers about each voter's demographic profile, occupation, political contributions, memberships, property ownership, permits and licenses, magazine subscriptions, film rentals, community volunteering, and political opinions. The campaigns could match over 5,000 different traits to each voter. They used this information to create messages targeted directly to particular voters through telephone calls, door-to-door outreach, and pop-up ads in social media.[27]

**FIGURE 11.5 Microtargeting Voters**

Campaigns use microtargeting to develop voter profiles that they use for microtargeting ads and videos. The majority of voters do not know that their personal data are being gathered and used for this purpose.

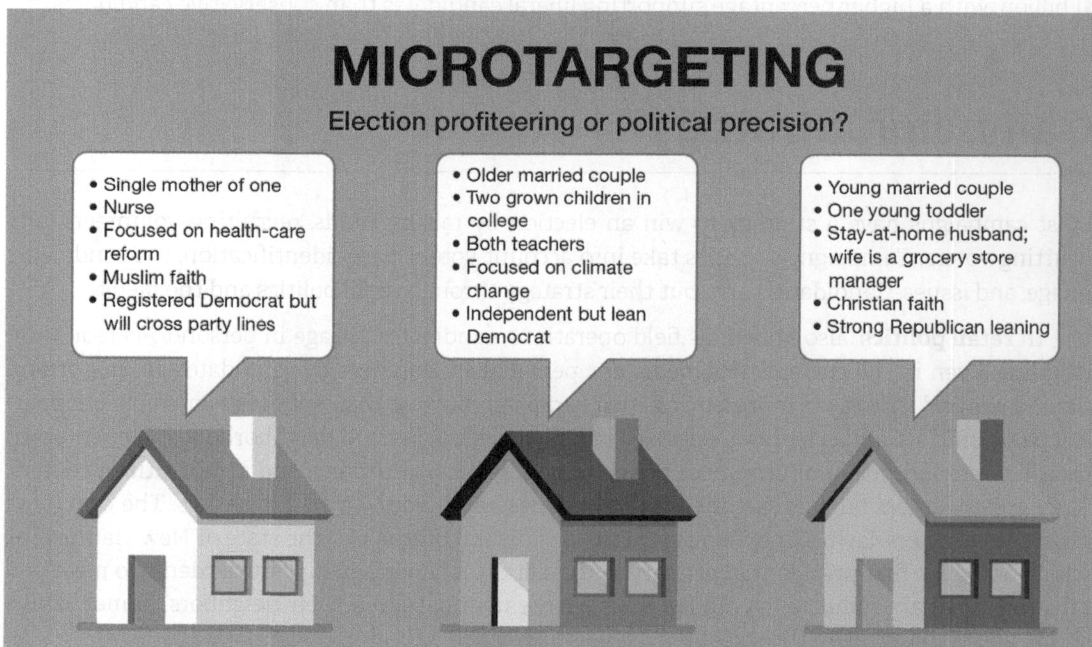


The use of personal data for campaign microtargeting was exposed during the 2016 election when it was revealed that Cambridge Analytica, a political data analysis firm, had gained access to personal information on over 50 million Facebook users without their knowledge. The firm was hired by Donald Trump's campaign to develop personality profiles of voters that could be used for microtargeting late in the campaign in battleground states where candidates from both parties had a good chance of winning. A majority of Americans had no idea that their data were being collected and used for microtargeting.[28] According to a study by the Annenberg School at the University of Pennsylvania, 86 percent of Americans oppose the use of their personal data in this way.[29]

The use of big data and microtargeting became more advanced in the 2020 election. Campaigns had access to unprecedented amounts of data on voters. The **voter files** used by campaigns contained between 500 and 2,500 bits of information on each voter. Campaign strategists use **AI**-powered predictive modeling to target voters based on their personal and political characteristics.[30]

**voter files**

Integrated data sets that add personal information about voters to their state-level voter registration record.

**AI**

An acronym for "artificial intelligence" that refers to the ability of a computer or robot to do things that are typically handled by humans.

## Party Identification

Candidates have a base of support, usually from people who are registered with and consistently vote for the candidate's party. For a candidate whose party has a majority of the people registered to vote in an electoral district, all it takes to win the election is getting enough of them out to vote. This may be easier said than done. There are still many people who identify as political independents rather than affiliate themselves with the Republican or Democratic parties.

**Party identification** seldom decides elections alone, although it is a strong predictor of a person's vote choice. A candidate's image and their position on issues are also important, particularly when independents and undecided voters hold the balance. Party identification does not apply in a primary election, when all the candidates are of the same party.

**party identification**

A person's affiliation with a political party that can be a strong predictor of his vote choice in an election.

There are deep divisions based on partisanship in the American electorate. **Partisan polarization** between Republicans and Democrats has increased in recent years. Candidates and government officials disagree strongly on issues such as immigration and health care. Voters have become more rigid in their policy preferences and in their conservative and liberal ideologies. They are unlikely to trust leaders from the opposite side of the aisle to govern effectively. Partisanship has become a social identity for many people. According to the Pew Research Center, one third of Democrats and half of Republicans would be angry if their child married someone from the opposing party.[31]

**partisan polarization**

Deep divisions in the American electorate between people who identify as Democrats and those who identify as Republicans.

## Candidate Image

**Candidate image** consists of the background, experiences, and personal qualities of people running for elected office. Campaigns strive to present an image of their candidate that fits the public's expectations of the office sought, especially in comparison with the opponent, who is portrayed as less qualified. Voters expect the president to have strong leadership skills and to be principled, decisive, and trustworthy. Other qualities, such as military service and compassion, may be deemed by the public and the media to be important as well.

**candidate image**

Those aspects of a candidate's background, experience, and personal qualities that are presented to the public in order to influence people's voting decisions.

Images are not entirely malleable. Age, gender, race, and military service cannot be changed willy-nilly. But they can be manipulated by selective accounting and shrewd presentation of the facts. Images are easiest to create early in a campaign when many people may not know much about a candidate. Which of a candidate's possible images the public accepts often depends on the media's depictions.

The media's coverage of candidates Republican Donald Trump and Democrat Hillary Clinton during the 2016 presidential election influenced public perceptions. Both candidates were depicted as being untrustworthy by news organizations. Trump was construed as being dishonest in his business dealings. Clinton was hounded for being secretive and using a private email server while she was secretary of state.

ABC news coverage of the October 19, 2016, presidential debate.

View in the online reader

The media paid much less attention to Joe Biden than to Donald Trump in the 2020 presidential contest. Biden, who had a reputation for being, as he called himself, "a gaffe machine," had fewer opportunities to misspeak because he often was out of the limelight. Adhering to COVID-19 mitigation strategies, Biden conducted much of his campaign virtually from his home in Delaware. The media portrayed Biden as empathetic and somewhat boring. Trump, on the other hand, used outrageous Twitter posts and relentless attacks on his enemies to gain the lion's share of press attention.[32]

## Issues

Issues, subjects, and public policy positions on matters of concern are central to campaigns. Candidates take positions on issues that are designed to increase their chances of election. Issues raised during campaigns are often based on voters' concerns that are identified by polls. The media can make issues a prominent part of the election agenda, which can work for or against a candidate.

Many candidates have past records indicating their stands on issues, leaving them little choice about how to manage some issues. Incumbents claim credit for their accomplishments. Challengers blame the incumbent for the country's problems. Moreover, each party is associated with certain issues. Democrats are seen as the party to protect Social Security, improve the economy by creating jobs, increase the minimum wage, and expand health-care coverage. Republicans are viewed as the party to strengthen national defense, cut taxes, and be tough on crime.

**wedge issues**

Issues that cut across party lines and that can be used by candidates to attract voters who affiliate with the opposition party.

**Wedge issues** are issues that cut across party lines. A candidate can increase her vote by splitting off some of the people who usually support the other party and its candidates.[33] Republicans have employed immigration and the threat to Americans' jobs as a way of attracting the Democrats' base of working-class white men. Democrats are using affordable health care as a way of reaching across party lines.

## Staying on Message

**FIGURE 11.6 Barack Obama's Campaign Slogan**

Presidential candidate Barack Obama reinforced his campaign slogan, "Forward," during his campaign trail appearances in 2012.

Source: Photo courtesy of Bbsrock via Wikimedia: https://commons.wikimedia.org/wiki/File:ObamaAbingtonPA.JPG. Reproduced via CC BY 3.0: https://creativecommons.org/licenses/by/3.0/deed.en.

Implementing strategy effectively requires staying on message. **Branding** is one strategy that candidates use to link themselves with a message. Candidates develop their own brand that associates them with a logo and a catchy slogan. Their brands are marketed as if they are products, like Nike or Coke. Candidates are like barkers at a fairground, each promoting his or her own show. At every opportunity they repeat their message and slogan. In 1992 the main message of Bill Clinton's presidential campaign was "It's the economy, stupid," which was aimed at blaming President George H. W. Bush for the country's economic problems. The Mitt Romney campaign slogan was similar to the 2008 Obama slogan, "Believe in America." Barack Obama's campaign slogan in 2008, "Change we can believe in," was a fresh take on a familiar call for change in American politics. The Obama campaign had multiple slogans in 2012 that were targeted at particular groups or occasions, but his overall campaign slogan was "Forward." A version of Obama's logo, the red, white, and blue rising sun, was used in both the 2008 and 2012 races.

Donald Trump's campaign brand in 2016 was built around the slogan "Make America Great Again." The slogan appeared most prominently on red ball caps, which became a trademark of the campaign. Hillary Clinton's campaign slogan was "Stronger Together," and her logo featured an H with an arrow pointing forward. After losing the election, Clinton started a political organization aimed at promoting progressive causes called Onward Together, which builds from her campaign slogan. In 2020, Trump's campaign slogan was "Keep America Great," which played off his 2016 slogan. The Biden campaign, after a few false starts, settled on the slogan, "Build Back Better."

**branding**

Candidates develop their brand by associating themselves with a logo and slogan.

Staying on message is not easy. Campaigns constantly have to react to unexpected events and to the other side's statements and actions—all in a twenty-four-hour news cycle. They usually respond rapidly to new subjects and issues, deflecting, reframing, or exploiting them.

**FIGURE 11.7**
**Candidate Slogans and Logos**
Donald Trump and Joe Biden used slogans and logos to brand their candidacies.

Sources: Biden-Harris Build Back Better. Via Wikimedia: https://commons.wikimedia.org/wiki/File:Biden-Harris_Build_Back_Better_61WnP4A6qVL._AC_SL1500.jpg; BottonsOnline, Public domain, via Wikimedia Commons; https://commons.wikimedia.org/wiki/File:Donald-trump-bs-531.png.

## Key Takeaways

Elections are crucial in a representative democracy like the United States. They enable people to choose their leaders and thereby influence public policy. They endow elected officials with legitimacy. There are two main types of elections: primary and general elections. Candidates from the same political party contest for the party's nomination in primary elections. Candidates from different parties run in the general election, which decides who will take office.

Campaign finance is an integral element of American elections. Individuals, PACs, public funds, political parties, candidates themselves, 527 committees, and super PACs fund campaigns. Campaign finance laws have shaped the way that candidates raise and spend money in elections, especially presidential candidates who accept public funding.

Candidates engage in retail politics by meeting with voters on the campaign trail. Campaigns employ strategies that take into account party identification, candidate image, issues, and message cohesion.

## Exercises

1. How do you think the fact that it takes so much money to run for political office affects what politicians do in office? Why might we want to limit the role money plays in politics?
2. Do you think it makes sense to treat money spent on campaign advertising as a form of free speech? How is campaign spending like other forms of self-expression? How is it different?
3. What do you think the most important factors in choosing leaders should be? How effective do you think political campaigning is in influencing your opinion?

# 11.3 Media and Election Campaigns

## Learning Objectives

After reading this section, you should be able to answer the following questions:

1. How has new media's role in campaigns evolved?
2. How do the news media cover campaigns?
3. How do candidates present and use political advertising in their campaigns?
4. How do candidates manage campaign debates? How do media influence debates?

Campaigns want to influence media coverage in their candidate's favor. They seek to dominate the election agenda, frame and prime issues, and have the media transmit their message of the day. The proliferation and diversity of modes of communication make this complicated. Campaigns attempt to control their political advertisements and influence debates. They use social media to publicize messages that they hope the press will cover. They try to set the news media agenda, but the relationship is uncertain at best.[34]

The current media environment is complex and poses challenges for candidates running for office, political parties, and journalists. Traditional media, such as newspapers and television news, continue to be important in elections. At the same time, the role of digital media, especially online news sources and social media, has become increasingly prominent.

## The Evolution of Modern Campaign Media

**mass media election**

Campaigns in the television era beginning in the late 1970s, when candidates took their message directly to the public rather than relying on political parties.

American election campaigns have been candidate-centered and media-centered since the late 1970s. The **mass media election,** where candidates took their messages directly to the public through television, began in 1976. Jimmy Carter, a Georgia governor who had little exposure to national politics, bypassed the Democratic Party leadership and won over voters by appealing to them on television. An outsider candidate, Carter became the Democratic nominee and went on to become president. Candidates were heavily focused on getting television coverage throughout the 1980s and 1990s, as elections became increasingly media-centric. Campaigns would time events to coincide with the broadcast schedule of television news.[35] Television remains the main source of election information for many Americans, although more voters are now turning to digital media for news about campaigns.

In 1992, Democratic candidate Bill Clinton launched the rudimentary first presidential election website that was dubbed brochureware. The site posted basic biographical information, position papers, speeches, and simple newspaper-style ads that were very similar to Clinton's paper campaign brochures. The website had very few visitors. By 1996, campaigns were experimenting with flashier websites and basic discussion boards where voters could contact the campaign. Candidates had websites with interactive features that could be used to fundraise and recruit volunteers by the 2000 election. Journalists and average citizens were establishing political blogs where they would comment on the campaign.[36]

The 2004 presidential election was important in the development of the American digital campaign. Candidates took advantage of the unique qualities of the internet, and used their websites, blogs, and email to communicate more directly and interactively with voters. Voters began to contribute to coverage of campaigns through eyewitness reports of candidates on the stump. Howard Dean, a contender for the Democratic presidential nomination, broke new ground with his online media efforts. He used the internet to fundraise and recruit volunteers through "meet-ups," a precursor to Facebook for organizing networks. Dean supporters would connect online and meet up offline.[37]

Democratic presidential candidate Barack Obama's campaign developed a new media strategy in 2008 that was game-changing. Obama's team revolutionized the use of social media in elections, which is now standard in campaigns. They used advanced features of digital media to network and collaborate with voters. The Obama campaign website was a full-service, multimedia center that introduced voters and journalists to a candidate about whom little was known outside of his home state of Illinois. People could locate information about Obama's background and issue positions, access and share videos and ads, post comments, blog, donate money, volunteer, and purchase campaign T-shirts and caps. Obama also was active on Facebook, Twitter, and YouTube, as he reached out to voters on a more personal level via social media. The digital strategies that the Obama campaign pioneered have become more sophisticated in subsequent elections. Candidates now aggressively pursue a social media campaign strategy to communicate with voters and attract mainstream media attention.[38]

Since the 2008 election, social media have become essential to campaigning. Donald Trump used Twitter prolifically to reach out to his nearly 50 million Twitter followers, many of whom had started following him while he was on *The Apprentice.* Trump's inflammatory statements and personal attacks often led news coverage of the 2016 and 2020 presidential races and were the subject of hundreds of hours of discussions by panels of commentators on cable news networks. In an interview with Fox News, Trump described how his tweets drove the mainstream media news cycle:

"Tweeting is like a typewriter—when I put it out, you put it immediately on your show. I mean, the other day, I put something out, two seconds later I am watching your show, it's up."[39]

## The Dean Scream

While new media have helped candidates reach out to voters and the press, they also can have unintended negative consequences. Democratic presidential hopeful Howard Dean's presidential campaign was derailed in 2004 by a viral video that foreshadowed the power of new media to create problems for candidates. Dean gave a pep talk to his campaign workers after a disappointing finish in the Iowa caucuses—the first contest of the presidential nominating campaign—and let out a scream that has become infamous. Shouting over the din of his supporters, he committed to continuing his campaign and then let out a loud scream. A video of "the scream" went viral and was replayed on cable news hundreds of times, but without the loud audience noise over which he was attempting to be heard. Dean was considered an eccentric and unconventional candidate, and this video reinforced that image and made him appear unhinged. Parodies of "the scream" proliferated online.[40]

Videos posted by people attending campaign events and fundraisers that have gone viral have harmed other candidates. During the 2012 election, Republican presidential candidate Mitt Romney was secretly filmed during a private fundraiser telling wealthy contributors that "47 percent" of the people voting for Barack Obama are dependent on the government.[41] Hillary Clinton was filmed at a private fundraiser in 2016 stating that half of Donald Trump's supporters fell into a "basket of deplorables."[42] Both Romney and Clinton were plagued by these comments, which were viewed as being insensitive to large groups of voters, for the remainder of their campaigns.

2004 Democratic presidential candidate Howard Dean's campaign was effectively ended by an amateur video of the "Dean Scream" that went viral following the Iowa caucuses.

View in the online reader

## News Media

Even in the new media era, television news, especially cable news, is the mainstay of election media as it attracts the largest audience of voters.[43] The speed of the twenty-four-hour news cycle and the range of media outlets make it difficult for campaigns to control what the news media report. Still, candidates try to stick to one message each day, embellishing it with **sound bites** to appeal to the reporters. They stage events and photo opportunities, or **photo ops**, with carefully selected locations, backdrops, and crowds. Staging can backfire. To show that he was strong on defense, Democratic presidential candidate Michael Dukakis appeared in a tank during the 1988 campaign. The press reported that his helmet made him look like the comic strip character Snoopy.

**sound bites**

Brief phrases uttered by candidates that are designed to be compelling and fit into news stories.

**photo ops**

Staged events designed to depict a candidate favorably in the media.

In the past, reporters would travel with candidates and were able to get stories based on personal interviews and insights gained from experiencing the campaign firsthand. As news budgets have become tighter, fewer reporters are "on the bus" with the candidates. Instead, reporting relies more heavily on video of candidates' rallies and campaign stops, voters' accounts of candidates' activities, and social media posts, including tweets from campaigns.

The media set the agenda for the campaign by directing voters' attention to particular stories and events. Through its **agenda-setting** role, the press tells the public what to think about, even if they don't always tell people what to think. In 2016, a Knight Foundation report found that journalists gave prominence to Donald Trump's campaign, as he received 63 percent of media attention compared to 37 percent for Hillary Clinton. Cable news often covered Trump rallies in real time. Trump continued to dominate election news in 2020. For every ten candidate mentions in major newspapers, eight were about Trump and two were about Biden.[44] News media coverage of presidential elections tends to be negative. Seventy-seven percent of news coverage of Donald Trump and 64 percent of stories about Hillary Clinton during the 2016 general election were negative.[45] The tone of media coverage in 2020 differed radically based on the news outlet. Almost 90 percent

**agenda-setting**

The press does not necessarily tell people what to think, but it does tell voters what to think about and to what they should pay attention.

of CBS News reporting on Biden was positive, while 95 percent of coverage of Trump was negative. On Fox News, about 60 percent of coverage of both candidates was negative.[46]

**FIGURE 11.8 Michael Dukakis in a Tank during the 1988 Presidential Election**

Democratic presidential candidate Michael Dukakis's campaign advisors felt that depicting him in a tank would prove that he was not weak on defense. Provoking mockery from the press corps, cartoonists, and late-night comedians, the photo op had the reverse effect.

Source: Michael E. Samojeden / Associated Press

### Link

**President Trump's Tweets**

The *New York Times* kept a running list of President Trump's tweets starting from the campaign trail up to mid-2019, which can be seen here.

Reporters and editors have the final say over the subjects and frames of campaign news. Bill Clinton's campaign manager, James Carville, described the power of the news media as "staggering" and said that his staff dubbed them "The Beast."[47]

**horserace coverage**

News media election coverage that emphasizes who is winning and losing the race.

**Horserace coverage** focuses on which candidate is leading and which is trailing based on their standing in the polls, and it dominates campaign news. The horserace became a prominent form of campaign news coverage in the 1960s when media polling became prevalent. This coverage of strategy gives reporters a fresh angle that plays up the suspense of an election campaign.[48] Coverage also focuses heavily on the campaign process and strategies, including the actions, decisions, and conflicts of the candidate's staff. The press highlights candidates' attacks on one another, as well as conflicts, controversies, blunders, and gaffes. Scandal, such as misconduct in office and illegal drug use, sometimes brought to reporters' attention by a candidate's opponents and spread on the internet's rumor mills, is a news staple.[49]

Coverage of policy issues in the news is slight, even in presidential elections. Candidates focus on only a few policy positions, which they repeat throughout the campaign. Journalists have little reason to report them frequently. Americans are less interested in foreign policy than domestic policy, and so international issues receive the least campaign coverage. Besides, policies lack the excitement and drama of the horserace.

# Political Advertisements

Television and radio advertisements are essential elements of election campaigns.[50] Ads capitalize on people's beliefs and values. They are often designed to arouse emotions, such as anxiety and fear, hope and enthusiasm.[51] They attract attention with dramatic visuals, sounds, and slogans. They sometimes exaggerate, even distort, information.

Candidate advertising in the information age has become more complex as campaigns seek to disseminate their ads through multiple platforms. Candidates release ads on candidate and political-party websites and on video-sharing platforms, such as YouTube and Hulu. Ads also are posted or linked on news sites and blogs. Candidate ads targeted at particular voters pop up when people access websites. Voters also share candidates' ads with their friends on social networks.

## Ad Formats

Ads come in many formats, but even now when glitzy techniques are available, the talking head, in which the candidate speaks directly to the audience, is common. Other formats are testimonials from people enthusiastically supporting the candidate and documentary ads utilizing footage of the candidate campaigning. Ads that utilize a "self-incrimination" of the opponent can be devastating. In 1992, the Clinton campaign ran an effective ad juxtaposing President George H. W. Bush's positive comments about the economy with data showing its decline.

Ads can use a panoply of visual and sound techniques. Distance (tight close-ups can be unflattering), angles (camera shots that look up make an individual seem more powerful), movement (slow motion suggests criminality), editing (people looking at a candidate with adoration or disgust)—all these techniques influence viewers' reactions. Color also influences perceptions: blue reassures, red threatens. Candidates often are shown in flattering color while the opponent is depicted in sinister black and white. Morphing, electronically changing and blending photographs and other visuals, can identify candidates with unpopular figures such as Adolf Hitler.

## Attack Ads

**Attack ads** denounce elements of the opponent's record, image, and issue positions.[52] They have been criticized as "the crack cocaine of politics" and for being demeaning and misleading. They also have been praised as "political multivitamins," providing voters with pertinent and substantial evidence-backed information about policies they would otherwise not encounter. Attack ads can allow voters to contrast candidates' qualifications and issue stance.[53] They can mark memorable moments in campaigns, such as the "**Daisy Ad**" attacking Republican presidential candidate Senator Barry Goldwater in 1964.

Attack ads employ a number of techniques to convey their points. They can point out "flip-flops," exposing apparent contradictions in the opponent's voting record and public statements. They can chastise the opponent for "not being on the job" and missing votes. Ads can convey "guilt by association," linking the opponent to unpopular individuals and organizations. Candidates can attempt to refute attack ads with denials, explanations, rebuttals, and apologies. However, many attack ads are effective in generating negative impressions of candidates. Rebuttals tend to repeat the original charge and prolong the ad's visibility.[54] The Wisconsin Advertising Project provides information and research about candidate, political-party, and interest-group advertising.

**attack ads**

Campaign ads that disparage the opposing candidate's qualifications, character, image, record, and issue positions.

**Daisy Ad**

A famous ad, produced by Democratic presidential candidate Lyndon Johnson's campaign against Republican Barry Goldwater in 1964, that appealed to voters' fear of a nuclear attack.

## Enduring Image

### The Daisy Ad

The Daisy Ad, an enduring attack ad, was designed for the 1964 election campaign of Democratic President Lyndon Johnson. It exploited the fear that Johnson's Republican opponent, Senator Barry M. Goldwater of Arizona, was willing to use nuclear weapons.

The ad shows a little girl plucking the petals from a daisy as she counts from one to ten out of order. A doomsday-sounding male voice takes over the countdown from ten to one. At zero, there is a nuclear explosion, and the girl's face turns into a mushroom cloud that fills the screen. Over the roar of the cloud, President Johnson intones, "These are the stakes. To make a world in which all of God's children can live, or to go into the dark." The word *stakes*, with its suggestion of being burnt at the stake, fits the Johnson campaign slogan, which ends the ad: "Vote for President Johnson on November 3. The stakes are too high for you to stay home."

The ad, which only ran once on television, never mentions Goldwater's name. It was not necessary. People were soon informed by the news media that it referred to him. Outraged Republican leaders unintentionally publicized the ad. The news media replayed the ad, increasing its visibility and the negative effect it had on the Goldwater candidacy.

View the ad in its entirety here.

The Daisy Ad remains a classic example of negative advertising.

View in the online reader

## Links

### Political Advertising Archives

The Living Room Candidate is a rich archive of campaign advertising dating back to the 1952 presidential election.

The Wisconsin Advertising Project provides data and research on ads in addition to copies of historic ads.

## Ads in the 2018 Midterm Elections

Ads in the 2018 midterm elections reflected the themes that candidates wanted to emphasize in their campaigns. The wedge issues of immigration, health care, taxes, jobs, guns, and education were raised in ads for both Democratic and Republican candidates. Negative ads were prevalent, as has become the norm. The midterm elections were viewed as a referendum on President Donald Trump, and this was reflected in ads. Candidates in parts of the country where President Trump was highly popular, such as Tennessee and Georgia, ran ads that featured Trump speaking at rallies and making candidate endorsements. In Florida, Republican gubernatorial candidate Rep. Ron DeSantis ran an ad where he is depicted teaching his children to support Trump. DeSantis is shown urging his toddler to "build the wall" using cardboard play bricks. He reads Trump's *The Art of the Deal* to his child with the caption "PITBULL TRUMP DEFENDER" displayed across the screen, as he states, "Then Mr. Trump said, 'You're fired!' I love that part." Finally, DeSantis teaches his daughter to talk by using a Trump "Make America Great Again" lawn sign. DeSantis won the election to become Florida's governor.

During the 2018 midterms, the Republican candidate for governor in Florida, Rep. Ron DeSantis, ran this ad where he teaches his children about Donald Trump.

View in the online reader

## Ads in the 2020 Presidential Election

Candidates spent an unprecedented $2.75 billion on advertising in the 2020 presidential election. Ads were especially important for Joe Biden, as he did not go out on the campaign trail as often as Donald Trump did as he followed COVID-19 distancing protocols. Biden campaign ads focused heavily on the candidate's ability to handle the pandemic and deal with the issues of racial justice and police reform. Some of his ads sought to provide voters with assurances of a better future and emphasized "one America" that was not divided by partisan polarization. Trump ads countered by vilifying protestors seeking racial justice as a threat to law and order and warned of a "left-wing" government takeover. Trump's message of "America First" was a theme that ran through many of his ads.

This is one of Biden's campaign ads in 2020.

View in the online reader

This is one of Trump's campaign ads in 2020.

View in the online reader

## Ad Watches

**ad watches**

Media and academic efforts to analyze campaign ads and point out their inaccuracies.

Some newspapers, a few television stations, and websites such as FactCheck.org analyze ads and point out their inaccuracies. These **ad watches** may limit the deceptiveness of ads in an election. But they may boomerang by showing the ads to people who might not otherwise have seen them. Toward the end of a campaign, ad checks have trouble standing out amid the clutter of so many ads for so many candidates. People also can ignore them, skip over them with remotes, and delete them with a keyboard stroke.

### Link

**Ensuring Accuracy**

FactCheck.org is a project of the Annenberg Public Policy Center, which checks ads and news stories for inaccuracies on a continuing basis. Learn more at FactCheck.org.

# Debates

**Debates** between candidates running for office have become a campaign ritual. They allow voters to assess how candidates respond to questions and think on their feet. Debates also provide an opportunity for voters to directly compare candidates' stands on issues. While television is the most popular medium, voters can tune into debates via a wide range of platforms, including radio and internet sites. YouTube debates have been held where candidates answer questions that are submitted on video by average citizens.

**debates**

Formal meetings between candidates running for office, typically moderated by an impartial party, that allow candidates to discuss issues and policy positions.

Candidates seek to influence their debates by negotiating with the sponsoring organization and their opponents.[55] They negotiate over who will participate, the number and timing of debates, the subjects that will be addressed, and who will be the moderators and questioners. No detail is left out, including whether questions can be followed up, the type of audience involvement, the length of answers, the height of the podium behind which the candidates will stand, whether and how much the candidates can move about the stage, and whether the camera can cut away from the speaker to an opponent.

**FIGURE 11.9 The Televised Kennedy–Nixon Debate**

Vice President Richard Nixon, confident about his debating skills, underestimated the importance of appearance. He was wan and sweating in contrast to his assured opponent, Senator John F. Kennedy, during the first televised debate of the 1960 presidential election.

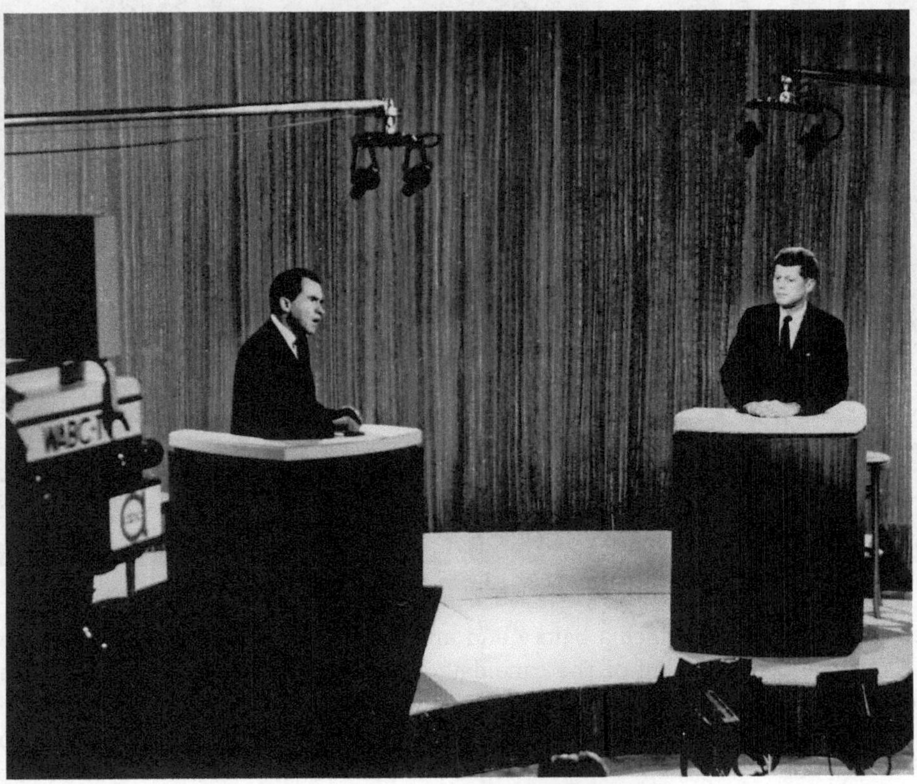


Source: Pictorial Press Ltd / Alamy Stock Photo

In the first-ever televised presidential debate, the **Kennedy–Nixon debate** in 1960, the camera cut away to show Vice President Richard Nixon, who was recovering from the flu and wearing heavy pancake makeup, sweating, while his opponent, Senator John F. Kennedy (D-MA), coolly answered questions. Viewers who saw the debate on television declared Kennedy the debate winner. However, people who listened to the debate on radio were turned off by Kennedy's heavy Boston accent and felt that Nixon had won the debate.

**Kennedy–Nixon debate**

The first-ever televised presidential debate between Vice President Richard Nixon and Senator John F. Kennedy in 1960.

## Link

**1960 Kennedy–Nixon Debate (Part I) (1960)**

Watch this video of the Kennedy–Nixon debate in 1960.

President Bush checks his watch during a presidential debate in 1992.

View in the online reader

Candidates are coached for debates. They prepare answers to anticipated questions that can be designed to catch them off guard, which might result in a gaffe. They memorize words and phrases from their campaign strategists that have been tested in focus groups and polls. They try to project leadership, appear likable and sincere, stay on message, emphasize issues that favor them, be critical of, but not nasty toward, their opponent, and avoid gaffes.

**FIGURE 11.10 Debate Formats**

The format of debates varies. Candidates may address questions formally from behind podiums or they may sit on stools and move about the stage. Hillary Clinton and Donald Trump engaged in animated exchanges during a debate featuring a more relaxed format.

Source: Julio Cortez/Associated Press

The campaigns spin the media before and after the debates. Predebate, they lower expectations about the debating skill of the candidate and raise them for the opponent. Campaign supporters try to convince journalists that their candidate won the debate. This spin is essential because journalists' judgments, more than the substance of the debate, influence public opinion.[56] Journalists and pundits, in their instant analysis and polls of viewers, frame debates in terms of who won or lost. They focus on "defining moments," identifying memorable lines and gaffes. In his debate with Jimmy Carter in 1976, President Gerald Ford, trying to make a statement about the spirit of the East Europeans, said that the Soviet Union did not dominate Eastern Europe. Although people watching the debate registered little reaction, reporters picked up on this apparent blunder and hounded Ford for days. Public opinion swung from seeing the debate as essentially a tie to seeing it as a crippling loss for Ford. The first presidential debate in 2020—described as "90 minutes of chaos"—devolved into a shouting match as Donald Trump heckled and interrupted Joe Biden over the objections of the moderator, Fox News' Chris Wallace.[57]

## Key Takeaways

News media focus heavily on the horserace and strategy elements of campaigns, especially who's ahead and who's behind in the polls. Candidates' messages are conveyed in short sound bites. Journalists pay more attention to a candidate's image, gaffes, campaign strategies, and scandals than to issues.

Candidates attempt to control their image, establish their campaign theme, and set the issue agenda through their campaign advertising. They design ads that will appeal to their supporters and reach out to undecided voters. Negative ads are prevalent in campaigns, as they can be effective in creating negative views of opponents and allowing voters to compare candidates.

Debates allow voters to assess candidates one-on-one. Candidates seek to control debates by negotiating the logistics and engaging in intense preparation. Candidates' representatives provide analyses of the debate. Media engage in post-debate assessments of the candidates' performances.

## Exercises

1. What kind of political ads are you personally most likely to see? Do you think you are more likely to be influenced by direct mailers, television and radio ads, or online ads?
2. How do you think having televised debates changes how people evaluate political candidates? Does actually seeing candidates debate help people evaluate their qualifications for office?
3. Why do you think candidates try to stick with just one message every day? What do you think the advantage of "staying on message" is?

# 11.4 Presidential Elections

## Learning Objectives

After reading this section, you should be able to answer the following questions:

1. How are political party nominees for president selected?
2. What is the purpose of presidential nominating conventions?
3. What is the Electoral College, and how does it work?

The presidential election gets the most prominent American campaign. It lasts the longest and receives far more attention from the media than any other election. The Constitution requires the president to be a natural-born U.S. citizen, at least thirty-five years old when taking office, and a resident of the United States for at least fourteen years. It imposes no limits on the number of presidential terms, but the first president, George Washington, established a precedent by leaving office after two terms. This stood until President Franklin D. Roosevelt won a third term in 1940 and a fourth in 1944. Congress then proposed, and the states ratified, the Twenty-Second Amendment to the Constitution, which limited the president's term of office to two terms.

# Caucuses and Primaries

**convention delegates**

Party regulars who attend the national nominating conventions and choose the presidential nominee.

Becoming a political party's presidential nominee requires obtaining a majority of the delegates at the party's national nominating convention. Delegates are party regulars, both average citizens who are active in party organizations and officeholders, who attend the national nominating conventions and choose the presidential nominee. The parties allocate **convention delegates** to the states, the District of Columbia, and to U.S. foreign territories based mainly on their total populations and past records of electing the party's candidates. The Republican and Democratic nominating conventions are the most important, as third-party candidates rarely are serious contenders in presidential elections.

Most candidates begin building a campaign organization, raising money, soliciting support, and courting the media months, even years, before the first vote is cast. Soon after the president is inaugurated, the press begins speculating about who might run in the next presidential election. Potential candidates test the waters to see if their campaign is viable and if they have a chance to make a serious bid for the presidency. President Donald Trump held a fundraising rally in anticipation of a reelection bid in June of 2017—less than six months after taking office.

**caucuses**

Meetings of party members at which delegates to the nominating convention are selected; these delegates then decide on the party's nominee, who will run in the general election.

**primaries**

Elections in which party members vote for delegates to the nominating convention; these delegates then choose the party's nominee, who will enter the general election.

**front-load primaries**

Primaries that states hold early in the process to increase their influence over who secures the presidential nomination.

**super delegates**

Delegates to the Democratic National Convention who are party luminaries, members of the Democratic National Committee, governors, and members of Congress. These delegates do not have to run for delegate in caucuses or primaries.

Delegates to the party nominating conventions are selected through **caucuses** and **primaries**. Some states hold caucuses, often lengthy meetings of the party faithful who choose delegates to the party's nominating convention. The first delegates are selected in the Iowa caucuses in January. Most convention delegates are chosen in primary elections in states. Delegates are allocated proportionally to the candidates who receive the most votes in the state. New Hampshire holds the first primary in January, ten months before the general election. More and more states **front-load primaries**—hold them early in the process—to increase their influence on the presidential nomination. Candidates and the media focus on the early primaries because winning them gives a campaign momentum.

The Democrats also have **super delegates** who attend their nominating convention. Super delegates are party luminaries, members of the National Committee, governors, and members of Congress. Most super delegates are allocated one vote, although some have only a partial vote, which explains why the delegate count is higher than the vote count at the Democratic convention. The number of super delegates has changed slightly in every presidential year since 2008. In 2020, superdelegates made up 16% of the Democratic convention delegates.

# The National Party Conventions

The Democratic and Republican parties hold their **national nominating conventions** toward the end of the summer of every presidential election year to formally select the presidential and vice presidential candidates. The party of the incumbent president holds its convention last. Conventions are designed to inspire, unify, and mobilize the party faithful as well as to encourage people who are undecided, Independent, or supporting the other party to vote for its candidates.[58] Conventions also approve the party's **platform** containing its policy positions, proposals, and promises. Platforms are guideposts for candidates, and do not bind them to support specific policy prescriptions once in office.

**national nominating conventions**

Meetings held by political parties to formalize the selection of their candidates for president and vice president and to establish a party platform.

**platform**

A document developed by political party elites that contains policy positions and proposals that candidates promise to enact once in office.

Selecting the party's nominees for president and vice president is potentially the most important and exciting function of national conventions. But today conventions are coronations, as the results are already determined by the caucuses and primaries. The last presidential candidate not victorious on the first ballot was Democrat Adlai Stevenson in 1952. The last nominee who almost lacked enough delegates to win on the first ballot was President Gerald Ford at the 1976 Republican National Convention.

**FIGURE 11.11** Senator Kamala Harris at the Democratic National Convention

Senator Kamala Harris was the first Black and Asian American woman vice presidential candidate.

Source: Nuno21/Shutterstock.com

Presidential candidates choose the vice presidential candidate, who is approved by the convention. The vice presidential candidate is selected based on a number of criteria. They might have experience that complements that of the presidential nominee, such as being an expert on foreign affairs while the presidential nominee concentrates on domestic issues. The vice presidential nominee might balance the ticket ideologically or come from a battleground state with many electoral votes. Three women have been prominent vice presidential candidates. New York Congresswoman Geraldine Ferraro was on the 1984 Democratic ticket with former Minnesota Senator Walter Mondale. Arizona Republican Senator John McCain selected Alaska Governor Sarah Palin as his running mate in 2008. Democratic presidential candidate Joe Biden chose Senator Kamala

Harris, the first Black and Asian American woman vice presidential candidate. The choice for a vice presidential candidate can sometimes be met with dissent from party members.

Hillary Clinton made history in 2016 when she accepted the Democratic nomination at the party convention in Philadelphia as the first female major party presidential candidate. Donald Trump, whose background in the real estate business and reality television made him an unconventional choice, officially became the Republican nominee at the party convention in Cleveland.

**FIGURE 11.12 2016 Democratic and Republican National Conventions**
On the left is Hillary Clinton at the 2016 Democratic National Convention. On the right is Donald Trump at the 2016 Republican National Convention.

Source: mark reinstein/Shutterstock.com.

**postconvention "bounce"**

A temporary increase in opinion-poll standings experienced by presidential nominees immediately following the national nominating convention.

Modern-day conventions are carefully orchestrated by the parties to display the candidates at their best and to demonstrate enthusiasm for the nominee. The media provide gavel-to-gavel coverage of conventions and replay highlights. As a result, candidates receive a **postconvention "bounce"** as their standing in the polls goes up temporarily just as the general election campaign begins.

## The Electoral College

**Electoral College**

The 538 electors who choose the president and vice president by majority vote.

The president and vice president are chosen by the **Electoral College** as specified in the Constitution. Voters do not directly elect the president but choose electors—representatives from their state who meet in December to select the president and vice president. To win the presidency, a candidate must obtain a majority of the electors, at least 270 out of the 538 total. The statewide winner-take-all by state system obliges them to put much of their time and money into swing states where the contest is close. Except for Maine and Nebraska, states operate under a winner-take-all system: the candidate with the most votes cast in the state, even if fewer than a majority, receives all its electoral votes.

### Link

**Electoral College Information**

The U.S. National Archives and Records Administration has a resource for the Electoral College here.

It is possible to win the election without winning the popular vote. George W. Bush won in 2000 with about a half-million fewer votes than Democrat Al Gore. The Electoral College decision depended on who won the popular vote in Florida, where voting was contested due to problems with ballots and voting machines. The voting in Florida was so close that the almost two hundred thousand ballots thrown out far exceeded Bush's margin of victory of a few hundred votes. The election was called on December 12, more than a month after Election Day, when the U.S. Supreme Court stopped the recounting of votes in Florida and Al Gore conceded victory to George W. Bush. In 2016, Donald Trump won the Electoral College with 306 electoral votes compared to Hillary Clinton's 232 electoral votes. However, Clinton prevailed with 48.5 percent of the popular vote compared to 46.4 percent for Trump. CNN has compiled 2016 election statistics here.

## Key Takeaways

Presidential elections involve caucuses, primaries, the national party convention, the general election, and the Electoral College. Presidential hopefuls vie to be their party's nominee by collecting delegates through state caucuses and primaries. Delegates attend their party's national nominating convention to select the presidential nominee. The presidential candidate selects his or her vice presidential running mate, who is approved at the convention. Voters in the general election select electors to the Electoral College, who select the president and vice president. It is possible for a candidate to win the popular vote and lose the general election.

## Exercises

1. What is the difference between a caucus and a primary? Why might caucuses and primaries produce different results?
2. What is the purpose of national party conventions, if presidential nominees are no longer really chosen at them?
3. How does the Electoral College system differ from a system in which voters choose the president directly?

# 11.5 George W. Bush Reelected in 2004

## Learning Objectives

After reading this section, you should be able to answer the following questions:

1. What were the key issues in the 2004 presidential election?
2. How did the media depict the candidates during the campaign?

Republican President George W. Bush ran for reelection against Democratic candidate Senator John Kerry (MA) and won. The campaign hinged on the candidates' performance in battleground states, where the race was close. Terrorism and the war in Iraq were key campaign issues. Candidates made greater use of the internet for fundraising and recruiting volunteers than in the past.

# The Nominating Campaign

**FIGURE 11.13 Howard Dean Speaking at a DNC Event**

The candidacy of Governor Howard Dean, who was vying for the Democratic presidential nomination in 2004, was derailed after a video of the scream he let out when addressing his supporters at the Iowa caucuses ignited an unfavorable media blitz.

Source: Photo courtesy of Matt Wright, https://commons.wikimedia.org/wiki/File:HowardDeanDNC.jpg. (CC BY-SA 3.0); https://creativecommons.org/licenses/by-sa/3.0/deed.en.

In 2003, Governor Howard Dean (VT) was the Democratic presidential candidate most vociferously opposing the Iraq War. His stance and forceful rhetoric gave his campaign unprecedented success in obtaining funds and volunteers through the web.[59] This accomplishment surprised the news media, generated reams of favorable coverage for him, helped him to raise funds, and transformed him from a marginal candidate to the front-runner—all before a single vote was cast. But in the Iowa caucuses, Governor Dean came in third behind Senators John Kerry of Massachusetts and John Edwards of North Carolina. As previously mentioned in Section 3, that night, Dean let out a loud scream now described as "the scream heard around the political world."

After the Iowa caucuses the news media reported that Senator Kerry was likely to be nominated. Dean received less coverage than before, most of it negative. His support shrank by 50 percent in the polls, while Kerry's popularity in the polls grew. Kerry won New Hampshire and other primaries, locking up the nomination on Super Tuesday, March 2.

The theme of the Democratic convention and John Kerry's acceptance speech centered on Kerry's status as a Vietnam War hero with the strength and determination to be president and commander in chief, and to wage the war on terrorism. Missing from the convention were a vision and program for the future of the country. There were few attacks on President George W. Bush or his record. For these reasons, Kerry did not experience much of a postconvention bounce.

The media endlessly replayed Democrat Howard Dean's scream after the Iowa caucuses in 2004.

View in the online reader

The Republicans renominated the incumbents, President George W. Bush and Vice President Dick Cheney, who were unchallenged in their party's caucuses and primaries. Their convention was held in New York City around the anniversary of the 9/11 terrorist attack on the World Trade Center and within staging distance of the Ground Zero site. The convention portrayed President Bush as a strong and decisive leader. Convention speakers attacked Kerry as weak, a waffler, and unqualified to be president. In his acceptance speech, President Bush laid out programs and policies he would pursue if reelected, which included security and defense in order to ensure that America "is safer." In polls, his postconvention bounce ranged from 4 to 11 percent.

The Iraq War was an issue that posed problems for both candidates. For Bush, it was the continued insurgency against the U.S. occupation and the failure to find weapons of mass destruction. He tried to finesse this by equating the war in Iraq with the war on terrorism. Kerry offered few alternatives to existing policy. He compounded his problem by saying in a speech at Marshall University about his vote for funding the war, "I actually did vote for the $87 billion before I voted against it." This statement, at best confusing, at worst contradictory, was a major news story the next day and was pounced on by the Bush camp.

The Republicans had a wedge issue in same-sex marriage. For many months this subject had been prominent in the news. Eleven states had propositions on their ballots amending their constitutions to limit marriage to one man and one woman. An ad supporting this position used the sound of wedding bells to remind people that the amendment would protect traditional marriage. The issue primed people's vote when evaluating the presidential candidates, attracting some Democratic voters to choose the Republican candidate. Nine of the eleven states went for President Bush.

# The General Election

Campaigning focused on eighteen **battleground states** that either candidate could win, a number reduced as Election Day neared to Florida, Iowa, Ohio, and Wisconsin.[60] Candidates used their ads strategically in these states. Bush's ads were more memorable and effective than Kerry's. One "documents" Kerry's supposed flip-flops by editing scenes of the senator wind surfing, so that he goes one way then another to the accompaniment of Strauss's "Blue Danube" waltz, while the voice-over states his different (contradictory) positions. The ad ends with this voice-over: "John Kerry: Whichever way the wind blows."

**battleground states**

States where the presidential election is hotly contested and the Democratic and Republican candidates each have a chance of winning.

The most damaging ads attacking Kerry were made by Swift Boat Veterans for Truth. As a 527 organization, they relieved the Bush campaign of any responsibility for the ads and from having to justify or defend them. The first **Swift Boat ad** opens with Kerry's running mate, Senator John Edwards (NC), saying that the best way to understand Kerry is to "spend three minutes with the men who served with him." The ad spliced together short interviews with veterans who accused Kerry of lying about his Vietnam War record and betraying his comrades by later opposing the war. The ad appeared in only a few states, but its incendiary charges dominated election-news coverage, where the ad was shown repeatedly. Senator Kerry's campaign waited two weeks before showing an ad responding to the accusations. In that time, the attack stuck, casting doubts about Kerry's heroism, integrity, and fitness to lead the fight against terrorism.

**Swift Boat ad**

An ad produced by the Swift Boat Veterans for Truth, challenging Democratic presidential candidate John Kerry's Vietnam War record, that aired during the 2004 election.

Kerry revived his election prospects through his performance in televised presidential debates. Polls showed that Kerry won the first debate, as he appeared presidential and seemed to be more certain than his opponent in answering the questions. However, President Bush improved in the two subsequent debates. People do not necessarily equate winning a debate with deserving their vote.

In 2004, the news media overwhelmingly emphasized the horserace. Only 18 percent of the stories on network news discussed candidates' stands on policy issues, their qualifications, or previous records.[61] Two events given prominent media coverage benefited the president: Chechen terrorists killed teachers and children in a school-hostage massacre in Beslan, Russia, and Osama bin Laden released a videotaped statement the weekend before the election. These events made the Republicans' issue of the terrorism threat resonate with voters.

President Bush won the Electoral College 286 to 252. He gained 50.7 percent of the popular vote compared to 48.3 percent for John Kerry. Bush held all the states he had won in 2000 except for New Hampshire, and he picked up Iowa and New Mexico. The key state was Ohio with twenty electoral votes, which President Bush won with 51 percent of the vote.

## Link

**Party Voting in Presidential Elections by State**

Maps depicting presidential-election voting by party from 1960 to 2008, produced by Robert Vanderbei of Princeton University, can be found here.

## Key Takeaways

Republican President George W. Bush was reelected in the 2004 presidential election against Democratic candidate John Kerry. Media coverage focused on the horserace between the candidates, especially in battleground states where the race was tight. Kerry faced opposition from a 527 organization, Swift Boat Veterans for Truth, which ran ads that cast aspersions on Kerry's service in the Vietnam War.

## Exercises

1. How did the issue of the Iraq War pose problems for George Bush in 2004? In what ways did he manage to turn the issue to his advantage?
2. How did John Kerry try to present himself in the 2004 presidential campaign? How did he end up coming across in the media?

# 11.6 Barack Obama Elected in 2008

## Learning Objectives

After reading this section, you should be able to answer the following questions:

1. In what ways did the 2008 election campaign stand out from other American presidential elections?
2. What were the key issues in the 2008 campaign?
3. What part did media play in the election?

The year 2008 marked the first time since 1952 that no incumbent president or incumbent vice president was a candidate in the presidential election. Media speculation about the possible Democratic and Republican nominees started earlier than ever before. The field of candidates seeking the nomination for both parties was large. Senator John McCain became the Republican nominee, and Senator Barack Obama clinched the Democratic nomination. The 2008 election witnessed unprecedented use of social media, such as Facebook, and video-sharing media, like YouTube, by candidates, journalists, and voters.

## The Nominating Campaign

Eleven men competed for the Republican nomination. The leading candidates were former Massachusetts Governor Mitt Romney, former New York Mayor Rudolph Giuliani, former Arkansas Governor Mike Huckabee, and Senator John McCain of Arizona. McCain had been written off by pundits the previous summer when his campaign was in disarray and out of money. He placed fourth in the Iowa caucuses but continued to campaign, winning the New Hampshire and South Carolina primaries. Both Giuliani and Romney withdrew after disappointing primary performances, leaving Huckabee to run against McCain. The Arizona senator swept the four primaries on March 5, giving him a majority of the total number of delegates for the nomination.

Senator McCain surprised pundits and politicians by choosing little-known Alaska Governor Sarah Palin as his vice presidential candidate. During the primaries, the senator had been attacked by conservative talk-radio host Rush Limbaugh and other right-wing commentators as being too liberal. Putting Palin on the ticket aimed to placate conservatives and appeal to women.

Eight men and one woman competed for the Democratic nomination. Bias against women seeking elective office by party elites, fundraisers, the media, and voters has greatly diminished, but obstacles remain for women aspiring to be president. Women face gender stereotyping that calls into question their ability to lead the country, and they must overcome the fact that the president has always been male.[62] Hillary Clinton sought to overcome these odds. She had name recognition and fundraising prowess from her eight years as First Lady and her election as senator from New York. Her most formidable challenger was Barack Obama, a first-term senator from Illinois and an African American (more accurately, he is of mixed race, from a Kenyan father and white American mother). The Democratic primary was a landmark contest between the first female candidate and first African American candidate to make a serious bid for the presidency.

The campaign for the Democratic nomination was hotly contested. Hillary Clinton's campaign made several strategic mistakes and lacked a coherent message. Obama ran the more effective campaign and was able to make his call for "change" resonate with voters. Both campaigns had sophisticated websites that not only included the usual biographical and issue information but also featured videos, ads, and interactive features that allowed users to participate in the campaign by donating, volunteering, posting messages and videos, and recruiting supporters. The Obama campaign also made extensive use of microtargeting, designing specialized messages delivered through email and **podcasts** that appealed to particular voters, such as young professionals who frequented Starbucks and used Blackberries to communicate.

**podcasts**

Digital audio or video pieces distributed by political campaigns, parties, and interest groups about a candidate, issue, or event that can be accessed conveniently on a computer or handheld digital device.

Clinton lost to Obama in the first contest, the Iowa caucuses. She recovered by winning the New Hampshire primary. On **Super Tuesday**, a date when a large number of states hold their primaries, Clinton won nine of twenty-two primaries, including California, New York, and New Jersey. Obama won the other thirteen and subsequently went on to take twelve straight caucus and primary states. Clinton won primaries in Texas, Ohio, and Pennsylvania, while Obama gained North Carolina and Indiana and picked up most of the delegates in the remaining caucus states. Clinton stayed in the race until June 7, 2008, when she withdrew and endorsed him. With 2,118 delegates needed to win the nomination, she had 1,923, and he had 2,154. Obama also had the support of 463 of the nonelected super delegates compared to 257 who backed Clinton. As his running mate, Obama chose longtime Delaware Senator Joseph Biden, who possessed the Washington and foreign policy experience he lacked.

**Super Tuesday**

A Tuesday, usually in February or March, when a large number of states hold their presidential primary elections.

## Images and Issues

Media images of the candidates varied widely. On the one hand, Barack Obama was portrayed positively as an American success story. Abandoned by his father when he was two, he was raised by a single mother who struggled financially, he worked his way through law school, and he was elected to the United States Senate. Alternately, he was depicted as a Black man with a strange name and as an elitist with a Harvard law degree and radical ideas. Depictions of John McCain also were greatly at odds. McCain was shown to be an experienced leader, wise in the ways of national security, and as a maverick not wedded to Republican orthodoxy. On the other hand, he was portrayed as a tired, old Washington politician and as a conventional conservative averse to change.

The Democrats were able to capitalize on campaign issues that worked against the Republicans, the party of the incumbent president, George W. Bush, whose popularity was low. The fading economy took precedence over terrorism. The Iraq war was increasingly seen as a mistake to be ended. Obama denounced the Bush administration and attacked his opponent, stating, "I am not going to be Bush but McCain will." He promised to respond to the problems of energy, education, and health care. He stated that taxes would be raised, but only for the wealthy.

## The General Election

One of the hallmarks of the Obama campaign was its superior use of new media. His website was more sophisticated that McCain's, despite the fact that McCain was one of the first candidates to use the internet for fundraising when he had previously sought the Republican presidential nomination in 2000. His website included "My Neighborhood" profiles of voters in the same zip code; "Take Action Now" email alerts; and "National Voter Protection Center," a space for reporting voting irregularities.[63] The Obama campaign had its own media channel, where viewers could tune in to campaign events. The campaign used digital tools to develop an email list and collect millions of cell phone numbers of potential voters.

Obama opted out of the public financing system and raised nearly $750 million. McCain took public financing and received $84 million to spend from his party convention to Election Day. Obama outspent McCain in battleground states by more than four to one. Obama had funds to air a half-hour prime-time "infomercial" on network and cable television just before the election.

During the campaign, uncertainty about Sarah Palin's qualifications for the vice presidency were raised. Her performance in the vice presidential debate showed weaknesses in her command of foreign policy issues. In addition, the news media reported that the Republican National Committee had spent $150,000 at upscale department stores for her campaign wardrobe. Palin was further undermined by Tina Fey's imitations of her on *Saturday Night Live*, which became popular online videos that were downloaded millions of times.

About 62 percent of the public turned out to vote in the 2008 presidential election. Barack Obama obtained 53 percent of the popular vote and 365 Electoral College votes, including 112 from nine states that had gone for Bush in 2004. John McCain received 46 percent of the popular vote and 173 electoral votes.

Comedian Tina Fey's parody of Republican vice presidential candidate Sarah Palin was the subject of much media discussion. Almost 25 percent of voters attributed to Palin statements that Fey had fabricated, including, "I can see Russia from my house." Here Amy Poehler parodies Hillary Clinton alongside Fey to send a bipartisan "Address to the Nation."

View in the online reader

Governor Sarah Palin appeared on *Saturday Night Live* alongside Tina Fey, who parodied her throughout the campaign.

View in the online reader

### Link

**2008 Presidential Election and Exit Poll Results**

The results of the 2008 general election are available here.

## Key Takeaways

Senator Barack Obama was the first African American elected to the position of U.S. president. He faced a strong challenge for the Democratic nomination from Senator Hillary Rodham Clinton and won the general election against Republican Senator John McCain. Social media were used to inform and mobilize voters in the election.

## Exercises

1. In what ways do you think it might be harder for a woman or Black man to win the presidency than it would be for a white man? Are there ways in which being a woman or Black person might be an advantage?
2. What were the key issues in the 2008 campaign? Why did they present problems for a Republican candidate?
3. How did the Obama campaign use the media to mobilize voters in a way that was different than the way previous campaigns had?

# 11.7 Barack Obama Reelected in 2012

## Learning Objectives

After reading this section, you should be able to answer the following questions:

1. How did the 2012 presidential election compare to the 2008 contest?
2. What were the key issues in the 2012 campaign?
3. What part did mainstream and social media play in the election?

## The Nominating Campaign

Mitt Romney, former governor of Massachusetts and organizer of the Olympics in Salt Lake City, won the Republican nomination for president after a long and hotly contested primary battle. While a large number of candidates threw their hats into the ring early on, four serious candidates emerged—Mitt Romney, former House Speaker Newt Gingrich, U.S. Congressman Ron Paul, and U.S. Senator Rick Santorum. While Romney was considered the front-runner, he faced a formidable challenge in his quest for the nomination. Some members of the Republican Party felt that he did not represent the social conservative wing of the party, especially as he had supported a health-care mandate in Massachusetts. His Mormon faith also was raised as an issue during the campaign. Much press coverage of the nominating process surrounded the twenty debates held with a rotating cast of candidates around the country. The debates were sponsored by myriad groups, including the Tea Party, nonpartisan groups, and news organizations, including Fox and CNN.

Mitt Romney was an able fundraiser, and accumulated an ample campaign war chest. This was the first campaign where super PACs were able to spend unlimited funds to support or oppose candidates. Mitt Romney and Newt Gingrich especially benefited from super PACs, running ads on their behalf. The key issues in the campaign were the economy, unemployment, taxes, how to manage the deficit in the federal budget, health care, and immigration reform. The candidates not only campaigned against each other, but also targeted President Obama. Romney gained enough votes to clinch the nomination in May, but the hard-fought campaign left the Republican Party fractured. Romney felt that the overly long nominating campaign was "absolutely nuts," as it tires voters, causes rifts within the parties, and causes the press to focus on candidate gaffes to fill the news hole.[64]

A memorable moment at the Republican National Convention, where Mitt Romney and Paul Ryan officially became the party's presidential and vice presidential nominees, came when actor Clint Eastwood talked to an empty chair that he claimed represented "invisible Obama" for twelve minutes. The press too coined a new term, "Eastwooding," which means to talk angrily to an inanimate object. The empty chair inspired one of the campaign's most popular **memes**, as people altered photos of the speech and provided captions. Social media sites encouraged people to "go ahead, make Eastwood's day and tweet your own chair pictures." A Twitter account @InvisibleObama was set up to spread the Eastwood meme, and quickly attracted more than 40,000 followers. Obama's social media team tweeted a photo of Obama presiding over a meeting at the White House in a chair labeled "The President" with the caption, "This seat's taken." A widely circulated image depicted a photo of cartoon character Grandpa Simpson under a newspaper headline, "Old Man Yells at Chair."[65]

**memes**

Slogans, images, and videos used as shortcuts to convey a message on social media that take on different meaning as they are passed on from user to user.

Clint Eastwood's rambling speech to an empty chair representing "invisible Obama" generated media buzz and many humorous memes.

View in the online reader

As the incumbent president, Barack Obama was the presumptive Democratic nominee; he did not face a serious challenge. Sixteen candidates officially opposed Obama for the nomination. Opponents appeared on only eight state ballots. Most of the opponents were issue-advocacy candidates seeking publicity for their cause. Randall Terry was a pro-life activist who ran against Obama because of his pro-choice stance on abortion. Other candidates falsely claimed that Obama was not a natural-born citizen and could not run for president, a charge that also was brought in the 2008 campaign. Obama acquired the number of delegates necessary to win the nomination in early April.[66]

## Images and Issues

Barack Obama was in a very different position as he faced the electorate in 2012 compared to 2008. As a relative unknown in 2008, Obama was an attractive candidate who represented hope and the possibility for positive change. In 2012, the incumbent president needed to defend his record and overcome the perception that he was personally aloof from the general public. The economy was in poor shape, and controversy surrounded Obama's health-care reform efforts. Young people were disenchanted by the high rate of unemployment and the rising cost of education. Obama's perceived smugness was emphasized by the press when he failed to perform well during the first debate with Mitt Romney and claimed that he didn't have time to prepare. The media also pointed to Obama's awkward body language when Romney was answering debate questions and talking about the failure of Obama's policies. The Republican National Committee released an ad called, "Smirk," that spotlighted Obama's body language during the debate. The ad was reminiscent of George H. W. Bush checking his watch during a debate with Democratic candidate Bill Clinton in 1992. Voters reacted negatively to both debate incidents.[67]

The "Smirk," an ad produced by the Republican National Committee in support of Mitt Romney, focused on President Barack Obama's smug body language as Romney challenged his positions on issues.

View in the online reader

Mitt Romney also was considered to be standoffish, which some media reports attributed to his being financially welloff. This point was driven home when a video of his remarks at a private fundraising event was leaked by the left-leaning magazine *Mother Jones*, which depicted Romney stating that 47 percent of Americans feel they are entitled to government assistance. The video had been surreptitiously recorded in May at a private Romney fundraiser in Boca Raton, Florida. Romney stood behind the substance of his remark, which played directly into the narrative of Romney as a candidate who favors the interests of the rich.[68]

Video of Governor Mitt Romney's remarks at a fundraiser in Boca Raton, Florida, where he alleged that 47 percent of Americans feel entitled to government assistance. The 47 percent statement was evoked throughout the campaign as evidence of Romney's affiliation with the rich and lack of empathy for people living in poverty.

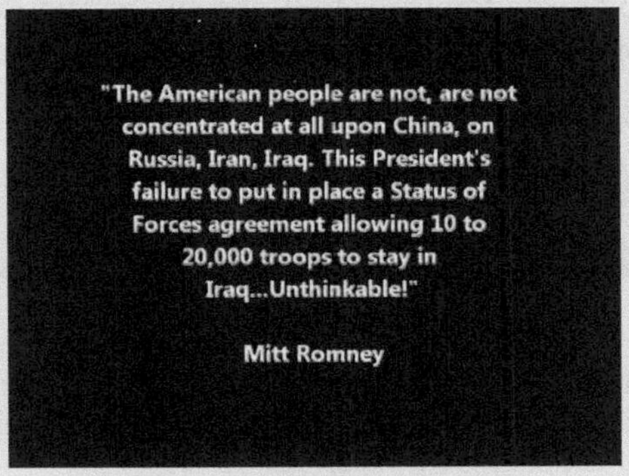

"The American people are not, are not concentrated at all upon China, on Russia, Iran, Iraq. This President's failure to put in place a Status of Forces agreement allowing 10 to 20,000 troops to stay in Iraq...Unthinkable!"
Mitt Romney


View in the online reader

# The General Election

The Obama campaign urged voters to stay the course and allow the president to continue to work on the tough issues facing the nation. Mitt Romney criticized Barack Obama's inability to deal successfully with the flagging economy, unemployment, and health care, and tried to position himself as a strong leader. The general election campaign generated a tremendous amount of media coverage and message traffic on social media. As usual, much of the media coverage focused on the horserace, which used polls to assess the relative positions of the candidates in the race. Media coverage about the race in key battleground states of Ohio, Florida, and Virginia, where the election was up for grabs, was especially intense. As the candidates headed into the final lap of the campaign, Hurricane Sandy devastated the country's east coast. Both candidates tried to demonstrate their leadership abilities and their humanity. They temporarily suspended campaigning. Obama oversaw the government response to the storm. Romney raised funds and collected supplies for victims. Journalists continued to use the horserace frame when covering the campaign and speculated about how the storm might influence the outcome of the election.[69]

The use of social media that had begun in the 2008 campaign was amplified in 2012. The Obama and Romney campaigns invested significant resources to mount extensive social media operations. The candidates' social media teams used a range of social media platforms, including Facebook, Twitter, YouTube, and Pinterest, to push out a tremendous amount of information. Obama had many more followers on social media than Romney. Obama had over 20 million more Facebook likes than Romney and 19 million more Twitter followers. While these metrics provide a rough picture of the relative size of the candidates' social media networks, they do not tell the entire story. Romney's social media users tended to interact more with the platforms, posting more and retweeting items, than Obama's users.[70] The public was less engaged in the social media campaign than they had been in 2008. Journalists used the candidates' social media as an information source. The social media war between the two campaigns was covered extensively by the press.

Advertising in the election was prolific. In addition to traditional thirty-second televised ads, spots were placed online and distributed through websites, video-sharing sites, social media, and email messages. They could be readily accessed through computers, tablets, and cell phones. The amount of money spent producing and placing ads reached an historic high at over $1 billion. The candidates' committees allocated significant resources to online ads. The Obama campaign committed over $52 million to online ads while Romney spent about half that amount, $26.2 million. The amount spent by the campaigns on online advertising represented a 251 percent increase over 2008. The vast majority of televised campaign ads were negative. Eighty-two percent of Obama's TV ads and 91 percent of Romney's spots were negative.[71]

Voter turnout in 2012 was 58 percent, which was somewhat lighter than in 2008. Barack Obama won 50.5 percent of the popular vote compared to 48 percent for Mitt Romney, but the Electoral College, and not the popular vote, determines the winner. Obama won 332 electoral votes to Romney's 206, which made Obama's win more decisive.

### Key Takeaways

President Barack Obama was able to defeat Republican challenger Mitt Romney to remain in the White House despite the public's concerns about the economy and health care. The use of social media in the campaign increased markedly from prior elections. Spending on campaign ads exceeded that in past campaigns by millions of dollars.

### Exercises

1. What challenges did President Barack Obama face as the incumbent in the White House?
2. What role do political memes play in election campaigns? Do memes have the potential to influence voters' decisions?
3. How can videos of candidates taken by citizens and posted online impact campaign media coverage?

# 11.8 Donald Trump Elected in 2016

### Learning Objectives

After reading this section, you should be able to answer the following questions:

1. What was unique about the 2016 presidential election?
2. What were the key issues in the election?
3. What role did social media play in the campaign?

## The Nominating Campaign

Without an incumbent president in the race, the 2016 election was up for grabs. As has become the norm in American politics, candidates began planning their campaigns years before they officially filed to run for the presidency. They tested the waters to see if their candidacy would be viable. They set up preliminary campaign committees and started to fundraise.

The Republican nominating campaign was hotly contested. Seventeen candidates initially were vying for the presidential nomination. The field quickly dwindled, as five candidates withdrew before the Iowa caucuses, which come early in the campaign. Three others departed after poor performances in New Hampshire, which holds the first primary. While it is typical for the top candidates to come from the ranks of seasoned politicians, two early front-runners—Ben Carson, a brain surgeon, and Donald Trump, a real estate magnate and reality TV star—had no prior political experience. Other candidates, including former Florida Governor Jeb Bush, Florida Senator Marco Rubio, and Wisconsin Governor Scott Walker, had solid political credentials. By March, only Texas Senator Ted Cruz, Ohio Governor John Kasich, and Donald Trump remained in the race. In May, Trump had passed the threshold of 1,237 delegates needed to win the nomination. He went to the Republican National Convention with 1,441 delegates in his pocket and clinched the nomination on the first ballot. Trump selected Indiana Governor Mike Pence as his running mate.

**FIGURE 11.14 2016 Republican Presidential Candidates**
The large field of Republican presidential candidates in 2016 face off in debates.

Source: Joseph Sohm/Shutterstock.com.

Presidential nominating campaigns pit candidates from their own party against each other, which can be divisive. The 2016 Republican campaign was especially contentious. Candidates participated in nine debates that at times produced testy exchanges and name-calling. During a debate in South Carolina where Ted Cruz criticized his position on abortion, Donald Trump retorted: "You are the single biggest liar. You probably are worse than Jeb Bush. This guy lied."[72] The acrimony continued in candidates' stump speeches on the campaign trail and on social media. Trump tweeted an unflattering photo of Cruz's wife, Heidi, attacking her looks and struggles with depression. During a factory tour in Wisconsin, Cruz addressed the controversy, stating, "Donald, you're a sniveling coward and leave Heidi the hell alone."[73] These personal attacks often diverted attention away from the key issues in the election. As a result of the divisive nominating campaign, some of Trump's primary opponents refused to back their own party's candidate during the general election campaign, and others only did so reluctantly.

The Democratic race for the presidential nomination had fewer contestants. Former Maryland Governor Martin O'Malley dropped out soon after the Iowa caucuses, leaving former New York Senator and U.S. Secretary of State Hillary Clinton and U.S. Senator Bernie Sanders in a two-person race. Hillary Clinton announced her candidacy on April 12, 2015, which meant that her presidential bid lasted for nineteen months. Clinton's candidacy was historic in two respects. She would be the first woman presidential candidate to be nominated by a major political party. Her candidacy would mark the only time a former First Lady had sought the presidency. In a reversal of roles, her husband, former president Bill Clinton, would accompany her on the campaign trail. Bernie Sanders announced his candidacy on May 26, 2015, not long after Clinton had entered the race. He is the longest serving Independent in Congress, having been elected to the House of Representatives in 1991 and subsequently to the Senate in 2007. Despite identifying as an Independent, Sanders has caucused with the Democratic Party in Congress, which justified his contesting to run for president under the Democratic Party banner. At age seventy-four, Sanders was the oldest candidate in the field. Information about all of the candidates who ran in the 2016 presidential election can be found here.

**FIGURE 11.15 2016 Democratic Primary Debate**
Hillary Clinton and Bernie Sanders share a lighthearted moment during Democratic primary debates.

Source: By Joseph Sohm/Shutterstock.com.

With her long history in Democratic Party politics, Hillary Clinton was considered to be the establishment candidate. She was viewed as a political insider due to her experience as secretary of state during the Obama administration and her terms in the Senate. She espoused liberal political views during the campaign, such as guaranteed equal pay for women and paid family leave.[74] Bernie Sanders described himself as a Democratic Socialist and an advocate for working-class people. He ran against Wall Street and big business, and had a strong populist appeal to voters who felt that they had not been represented by politicians in office. Sanders's platform denounced income inequality and promoted providing free college education for all students and increasing the minimum wage. Sanders's outsider status and progressive positions gained him support among young people, who appreciated his unpolished style and straightforward manner of speaking.[75]

The Democratic contenders matched up in nine primary debates as well as a series of forums where the candidates did not directly address one another. The debates were generally civil in tone, but became more contentious over time. Sanders called out Clinton for receiving large amounts of money for giving speeches to Wall Street bankers and for using the racially insensitive term "super predator" in a 1999 speech to donors.[76] Clinton attacked Sanders for being weak on gun control and unrealistic in his approach to protecting the environment. The battle between Clinton and Sanders lasted until June 7, 2016, when Clinton earned enough delegates to receive the Democratic nomination. Clinton secured 2,845 delegates to Sanders's 1,865. She received the nomination on the first ballot. Clinton selected Virginia Senator Tim Kaine as her vice presidential candidate.

## Images and Issues

Images of the candidates in the 2016 election were highly polarized. Both candidates had high profile media images before the campaign that carried over to the election. Donald Trump was known for his television program, *The Apprentice*, where his tagline was "You're fired!" Among his supporters, Trump was perceived to be an advocate for people who felt they had little hope of getting ahead. They viewed him as a successful businessman who epitomized a "take charge" style of leadership. Trump's detractors viewed him as underqualified and lacking the temperament to hold the presidency. They also felt he was a misogynist, an image that was reinforced by crude comments he made about women on the campaign trail. The image of Hillary Clinton also was mixed. She was viewed as being an experienced and competent candidate, but she was not considered to be personally likable. Even among some of her supporters, Clinton was viewed as dishonest and untrustworthy. She had been associated with a number of scandals, such as Whitewater, while her husband was president. She also was plagued by concerns about her use of a private email server while she was secretary of state.[77]

There were clear differences in the issue positions of Democratic candidate Hillary Clinton and Republican candidate Donald Trump. Immigration was one of the defining issues of the presidential campaign. Trump repeatedly emphasized that he would build a wall to stop undocumented immigration from Mexico, and that Mexico would pay for the wall. He alleged that immigrants were inordinately responsible for committing violent crimes, stating in the third presidential debate, "We have some bad *hombres* here, and we're going to get them out." Hillary Clinton agreed that border security was necessary, but advocated for a pathway to citizenship for undocumented workers. Clinton and Trump disagreed vigorously on gun control. Clinton supported more rigorous regulation of gun sales, while Trump's position would make it easier for people to carry a concealed weapon. Trade was another prominent campaign issue. Clinton supported the idea of "free trade" without tariffs, which are duties on imports from other countries to the United States Trump advocated for increasing tariffs on America's trading partners. The two nominees differed markedly on tax policy, with Trump advocating for tax cuts and Clinton supporting small tax increases on the wealthy. The environment was another area where the two candidates parted ways. Trump believed that restrictions placed on the production of coal due to environmental concerns should be lifted. Clinton supported clean energy as an alternative to coal and other fossil fuels. Information about the candidates' stands on issues can be found here.

# The General Election

The 2016 presidential election was like no other. The campaign pitted a businessman with no prior political experience against the first female major party candidate. Social media played an extraordinary role in the campaign as an integral component of the candidates' strategies that shaped media coverage. The number of people who got campaign information from social media was substantially higher than in the past. Over 16 million people followed Donald Trump's official Twitter feed, and 11 million followed Hillary Clinton's.[78] While negative campaigns are common in American politics, the level of mudslinging in the 2016 election was unprecedented.

Trump used social media aggressively to reach out to voters and gain press attention. He attacked his opponent and nicknamed her "crooked" Hillary. He labeled people who disagreed with him as "stupid," "bad," "crazy," "horrible," "dumb," and "overrated." He used Twitter to publicize his campaign slogans of "Build the Wall" and "Lock Her Up." Trump responded with a tweet storm to Clinton bringing up an incident where Trump had called a former Miss Universe "Miss Piggy" and "Miss Housekeeping." He accused Clinton of using Ms. Machado as a prop, called the former pageant winner "a con," and told people to check out her nonexistent sex tapes. This over-the-top social media strategy gained nonstop media attention that helped Trump to control the press agenda.

Clinton's social media strategy was more conventional. She used social media to solidify her voting base, and asked followers to post "I'm with her" to show their support. Her feed publicized support from celebrities, including Beyoncé, Jay-Z, Lady Gaga, Katy Perry, and Bruce Springsteen. In the past, this type of social media strategy would have been more effective, as it allows the candidate to control the message and avoid gaffes. However, in the circus-like atmosphere of the 2016 campaign, Clinton's social media messages were drowned out by the Trump campaign's antagonistic missives.

Media coverage focused heavily on scandals rather than issues. The press agenda was dominated for more than a week by the release of a video of a 2005 conversation between Donald Trump and *Access Hollywood* correspondent Billy Bush where Trump boasts about how his celebrity status allows him to do what he pleases with women. The video reinforced the image of Trump as a misogynist, and was firmly denounced by the Clinton camp. Trump and his campaign surrogates dismissed the statements as "locker room talk." Numerous women came forward alleging that Trump had sexually harassed or assaulted them, countering Trump's denials.

Throughout the campaign, Hillary Clinton was scrutinized for her use of a private email server rather than the official government server when she was secretary of state. Early in the campaign, she was cleared of wrongdoing by FBI Director James Comey. However, ten days before Election Day, Director Comey reopened the investigation when email messages were found on a computer used by former New York Congressman Anthony Weiner, the estranged husband of Clinton aide Huma Abedin. A rumor claiming that the new emails pointed to a pedophilia ring with Hillary Clinton and her campaign manager, John Podesta, at the center that was run out of a pizza restaurant in a residential neighborhood in Washington, DC, was retweeted thousands of times. The "pizzagate" rumor quickly spread across social media platforms, and inspired a man to attempt to liberate the purported child sex slaves. He fired an assault rifle inside the pizza restaurant as staff and patrons fled into the street.

A number of factors contributed to Donald Trump's victory. Trump was able to mobilize a group of people, including white, working-class voters, who felt politically disenfranchised. His supporters were enthralled by Trump's success in business, which they believed would carry over to governing the country. The email issue contributed to voters' lack of enthusiasm for Clinton, and reopening the investigation at the end of the election cycle created doubts about her trustworthiness. Key segments of the Democratic Party's electoral base, such as Black and Latinx people, did not turn out to vote for her as expected.

Voter participation in the presidential election was 59.2 percent of the eligible electorate, which was the lowest since the 1996 campaign, and down significantly from the 64 percent of the electorate who cast a ballot in 2008. A sizable number of voters were dissatisfied with both presidential candidates. Some 2.4 million people voted for down-ballot candidates, such as members of Congress, but did not pull a lever for president.

## Key Takeaway

With no incumbent in the race, the Republican and Democratic nominating campaigns were hotly contested. Hillary Clinton emerged as the first female candidate and the first former First Lady to run for the presidency from a major party. Donald Trump captured the Republican nomination after running against a large field of candidates. Clinton and Trump articulated strongly opposing views on issues. Trump's aggressive approach to using social media captured the attention of the mainstream press. He was able to mobilize voters who felt politically disenfranchised and attain the White House.

## Exercises

1. In what ways did Hillary Clinton being the first female major party presidential candidate work for and against her in the election?
2. How did the fact that Hillary Clinton and Donald Trump were both well-known public figures before the 2016 election impact their candidacies?
3. How did the candidates' use of social media in the 2016 presidential contest differ from the past?

# 11.9 Joe Biden Elected in 2020

## Learning Objectives

After reading this section, you should be able to answer the following questions:

1. How did the COVID-19 pandemic affect the 2020 presidential election?
2. What were the differences in the strategies employed by the Biden and Trump campaigns?
3. What options for casting a ballot were available to voters?
4. What were the circumstances that led to the insurrection at the U.S. Capitol?
5. What caused the House to impeach Donald Trump for a second time?

## The Nominating Campaign

The road to the White House took a drastic turn in 2020 due to the COVID-19 pandemic. The nominating campaign began in earnest in the summer of 2019, as candidates solidified their campaign organizations, raised funds, and participated in debates. The schedule of Democratic primaries and caucuses proceeded as usual until March of 2020, when the pandemic disrupted the process. On March 13, Louisiana was the first state to postpone its primary until June for safety reasons. Other states followed, delaying their nominating contests and switching to mail-in balloting, as the rate of infection increased and in-person voting became less feasible. Joe Biden won the Democratic nomination and Donald Trump was the Republican presidential nominee.

Democrats viewed the 2020 presidential election as a referendum on Trump's presidency. Twenty-nine candidates—the largest Democratic field in history—vied for their party's presidential nomination. The field consisted of familiar candidates and some fresh faces. Former Vice President Joe Biden, Senator Bernie Sanders, Senator Elizabeth Warren, Senator Kamala Harris, and New York Mayor Michael Bloomberg were candidates with the greatest initial name recognition. Mayor Pete Buttigieg of South Bend, Indiana, was the first openly gay candidate to launch a presidential campaign. Andrew Yang, an entrepreneur with limited political experience, gained attention for his focus on technology as well as his appeal to young voters and Asian Americans.[79]

A series of twelve official primary-election debates was held between the Democratic candidates starting in June of 2019 in locations across the country. Media sponsors, including ABC, CBS, NBC, and *Politico*, were selected to host the debates with the stipulation that there had to be at least one female moderator for each event. All major news organizations were eligible with the exception of Fox News. Because of the large size of the field, candidates had to meet minimum polling and fundraising requirements to qualify to participate. Only Biden and Sanders took part in all the debates, with Warren, Buttigieg, and Senator Amy Klobuchar missing just one because they did not meet the polling and fundraising requirements. Several candidates, especially those with legal backgrounds and experience in arguing cases, distinguished themselves as strong debaters. Warren, Klobuchar, Buttigieg, Senator Cory Booker, and former Housing and Urban Development Secretary Julian Castro were able to drive home points about health care, immigration, climate change and the Green New Deal, the opioid crisis, unemployment, and foreign affairs with animated exchanges. A landmark moment of the first debate came when Harris criticized Biden over his record on school busing and for working with senators who supported segregation during his long career in office.[80] The debates helped to narrow the field of contenders, as the public evaluated candidates' performances and the press declared winners and losers. Biden, at times, was portrayed as struggling in the debates, especially early on, but he managed to maintain a consistent lead in the polls and kept his position at center stage.[81]

Biden's campaign for the Democratic presidential nomination got off to a rocky start. His age was a factor as he would be the oldest president to take office at seventy-eight years old. His long career in government as a senator for thirty-six years and as vice president for eight years meant that he had an extensive record that he had to defend. Biden had also run unsuccessfully for president twice before, in 1988 and 2008.[82] The field of competitors he faced included candidates who were younger, racially and ethnically diverse, more ideologically progressive, and better able to raise funds. Biden lost the first three nominating contests in New Hampshire, where he came in fifth place; Iowa, where he came in fourth; and Nevada, where he came in second. Despite these significant defeats, Biden remained in the race, moving on to South Carolina, where he won the primary resoundingly after being endorsed by Rep. Jim Clyburn, the highest-ranking African American Democrat in Congress. With the support of Black voters, the South Carolina primary became the turning point in the race. Biden's rivals began to drop out as the campaign moved online in March due to the pandemic. By early April, only Sanders remained as a serious opponent.[83] Sanders dropped out of the race on April 8 after losing several primaries to Biden. He conceded by admitting that he could not continue to mount a campaign that he could not win when the country was dealing with a deadly pandemic. Former rivals endorsed Biden to present a united front at the national nominating convention.[84]

After securing enough convention delegates to gain the nomination, Biden sought to make a statement with his vice presidential selection. He indicated during the primaries that he was open to having a woman as his running mate. He had considered a long list of potential candidates, including Warren, Michigan Governor Gretchen Whitmer, and former national security advisor Susan Rice. Biden made the historic choice of Kamala Harris, who is of Black and South Asian descent. Biden looked past Harris' attacks on him during the debates and based his decision on the ways she would help him win the November election, such as her strength as a debater, her experience in government, and the racial diversity she brought to the ticket.[85]

As a sitting president with a sizable base of supporters, Donald Trump faced little opposition as he sought a second term. Trump also commanded the lion's share of media attention through his actions as president and by producing a steady stream of controversial tweets. Only three candidates challenged Trump for the nomination—former South Carolina Governor Mark Sanford, former Illinois Representative Joe Walsh, and former Massachusetts Governor Bill Weld; none were able to gain traction. No official Republican debates were held, although the challengers participated in debates without Trump that were sponsored by independent organizations. Some states decided not to hold Republican primaries, including Arizona, Kansas, Nevada, and South Carolina. Party officials argued that the cost was not justified given that there were no viable challengers to Trump for the nomination. This decision prompted concerns that Republican voters were being denied their say in choosing the party's ticket.[86]

The pandemic forced major changes in the nominating conventions for both parties. The Democratic National Convention took place from August 17 to 20, 2020. While the convention was hosted at the Wisconsin Center in Milwaukee, most events took place virtually. No delegates, with the accompanying hoopla on the convention floor, were physically present, but the speeches and party meetings went on unabated. The convention set the tone for Biden's campaign by emphasizing his decency, strength, and empathy in the face of personal tragedy. Biden's first wife and daughter had been killed in a car crash soon after he was first elected to the Senate in 1972, and his son, Beau, died of brain cancer in 2015. A convention highlight was the roll call nominating Biden and Harris as the Democratic presidential ticket, which was a video tour of the country. Each state's short nominating video featured iconic images, told inspirational stories, and showcased issues, like California's pitch to end environment pollution. A fan favorite featured a state lawmaker and a restauranteur on a beach holding a plate of fried appetizers and proclaiming Rhode Island as the "calamari comeback state" while calling attention to the hardship the fishing and restaurant industries faced because of the pandemic.[87] Biden's acceptance speech at the convention emphasized a theme of unifying the country, stating, "While I will be a Democratic candidate, I will be an American president."[88]

The Republican National Convention, where Trump officially became the party's nominee, was held from August 24 to 27, 2020. Controversy arose when limitations on the crowd size were imposed in Charlotte, North Carolina, the intended host city, to curb the spread of COVID-19. Consequently, Trump announced that the event would be moved to Jacksonville, Florida. The Florida convention plans were eventually cancelled, with party business meetings taking place in Charlotte and prime-time events held remotely from different locations, including Fort McHenry and the White House. Speakers and prerecorded videos sought to promote a positive narrative on Trump's handling of the pandemic that was not consistent with reality.[89] Trump delivered a seventy-minute-long acceptance speech on the White House South Lawn, a space that traditionally is off-limits to campaigning, flanked by American flags and Trump–Pence signs. The Hatch Act, a federal law passed in 1939, prevents employees in the federal government, with the exception of the president and vice president, from taking part in political activities. Since White House staff and other federal employees were involved in organizing the event, there were concerns that the Hatch Act should apply. His speech took aim at Biden, claiming without evidence that his election would result in economic disaster and unchecked violence in American cities. Trump spoke to a packed crowd, most of whom were not wearing masks.[90]

With the pandemic necessitating a shift to a virtual convention, the Democratic Party took an innovative approach to the roll call by having each state submit a short video. Rhode Island's "calamari comeback state" clip went viral.

View in the online reader

## Images and Issues

The opposing images of the presidential candidates could not have been more stark. Biden's core message was that the election was about character. He presented himself as an honest and empathetic person who lives by the social justice teachings of his Catholic faith. Biden took an aspirational and positive tone during the election, emphasizing the country's ability to overcome adversity. He framed his campaign as a mission to salvage "the soul of America" by restoring decency and saving the country from Trump's divisive and bigoted policies.[91] Biden drew a contrast between himself and Trump, whom he characterized as a wealthy snob who inherited his money and position in society. Biden drew upon his modest upbringing in Scranton, Pennsylvania, and Wilmington, Delaware, and associated himself with working people. He proudly announced that he would be the only president in over thirty years not to have an Ivy League education, with his degrees from the University of Delaware and Syracuse University. He cited Trump's references to members of the military as "suckers" and "losers" as an example of how Trump thought he was too good to serve his country like average Americans did.[92]

The Biden campaign emphasized two consistent themes—that the country was ready to be united and that the coronavirus was "a really big deal."[93] Biden initiated the call for unity during the nominating campaign and amplified it throughout the general election. His campaign website epitomized the "Unity" theme by incorporating ideas from his primary competitors in an effort to convey digital unity when the pandemic had driven much of his campaign online.[94] "Let's stop fighting and let's start fixing," became a Biden mantra that emphasized his desire to work across party lines and compromise to get the country back on track after what he perceived to be the damage done by the Trump administration.[95] The message was not only aimed at his Democratic supporters, but also at Republicans who were defecting from their party.

Trump faced the reality that he had been unable to fulfill several of his biggest campaign promises from 2016. He did not reform the health-care system by repealing and replacing "Obamacare." He had built only a small portion of a wall to halt undocumented immigration while replacing and repairing other parts, and the bill was not footed by Mexico as he had pledged, but by U.S. taxpayers.[96] The Trump campaign downplayed issues that were most problematic for his administration, such as the failed response to the coronavirus and rising unemployment rates. Instead, he claimed that the virus was a hoax and no worse than the flu.[97] He falsely proclaimed that effective treatments were widely available, including taking the drug hydroxychloroquine and drinking bleach, all of which were discredited.[98] During the final week of the campaign, Trump declared that the alarming spike in COVID-19 cases across the country was "a fake news conspiracy."[99]

Rather than looking forward and providing a vision for his second term, Trump largely employed an attack strategy and rehashed his 2016 campaign slogan: "Make America Great Again, Again."[100] Trump warned that dark days were to come if Biden were elected. Trump's attacks on Biden were relentless and included gross misrepresentations of Biden's policy positions. He stated incorrectly that Biden had "a plan to eliminate U.S. borders,"[101] supported rioters and looters, and planned to decimate police forces. He repeated unsubstantiated claims about Biden's son, Hunter, and called for his investigation and arrest. He intensified his well-worn assaults on the "liberal" media and labeled stories as "fake news" if he disagreed with them or if he was criticized. Trump peddled false narratives about the summer demonstrations against racial injustice as well. The demonstrations were precipitated by the death of George Floyd while in the custody of Minneapolis police on May 25, 2020. Trump went on to equate the Black Lives Matter movement with Antifa—a loosely affiliated group of left-wing, anti-fascists who sometimes engaged in militant tactics that Trump wanted to declare a terrorist organization.[102] He also endorsed or retweeted posts about the QAnon conspiracy theory, which claimed that Trump was waging a secret war against elite Satan-worshipping pedophiles and cannibals in government, business, and the media.[103]

## The General Election

The 2020 election took place amidst the backdrop of a deadly pandemic, demonstrations against police violence against Black Americans and people of color, systemic racism, and economic distress as businesses closed and unemployment skyrocketed. The Biden and Trump camps took very different approaches to campaigning during the pandemic. Biden and Harris combined virtual campaigning with small rallies that were socially distanced. They engaged in grassroots politics by video-chatting with groups of supporters. These video chats doubled as fundraising events and urged participants to spread the word about the Democratic ticket. Along with their surrogates, including four of Biden's granddaughters, Biden and Harris did off-the-cuff, livestreamed interviews with social media influencers to reach young voters. In a particularly creative twist, the Biden–Harris campaign held drive-in rallies where supporters watched from their cars as the candidates spoke while appearing on large screens. The candidates always made it a point to wear masks when making public appearances to encourage others to do the same.

Trump, in keeping with his denial about the severity of the pandemic, proceeded to hold large-scale rallies that were his signature during the 2016 contest. The rallies flouted medical guidelines to mitigate the spread of the virus, as his supporters often did not wear masks or practice social distancing. During the rallies, where he would talk for ninety minutes or more, Trump would inflate his accomplishments, bash the press, lie about his status in the polls, make fun of the Democratic candidates, and undermine the advice of medical professionals such as Dr. Anthony Fauci, the nation's most prominent infectious disease expert.[104] The Trump campaign's social media strategy was an extension of his regular prolific posting on Twitter. His messages were often inflammatory and narrowly targeted to appeal to his base.[105] They were designed to stir controversy that would keep him in the headlines.

Televised debates between the presidential and vice presidential candidates were scheduled and overseen by the Commission on Presidential Debates, as per the norm. However, the debates turned out to be anything but typical. The first presidential debate took place on September 29 in Cleveland, Ohio, and was co-hosted by Case Western Reserve University and the Cleveland Clinic. It was held in-person with coronavirus precautions in place. The debate was facilitated by Fox News' Chris Wallace, a veteran journalist with prior experience moderating debates. The debate was broadcast by sixteen television networks and was watched by 73.1 million people.[106] Domestic policy was the focus of the debate, and the topics included the composition of the Supreme Court,

COVID-19, the economy, race and violence in our cities, and the integrity of the election.[107] The debate was acrimonious from the start and devolved into ninety minutes of chaos. Rather than addressing the questions, Trump attacked Biden relentlessly. Biden, facing the camera, attempted to present his policy positions as Trump talked over him. At one point, Biden turned to Trump and said, "Will you shut up, man?" This became a campaign slogan emblazoned on T-shirts.[108] Wallace seemed to lose control of the event as he was interrupted ninety times by the candidates, seventy-one times by Trump and nineteen by Biden. The candidates shouted and cut one another off, with Trump disrupting Biden sixty times and Biden interrupting Trump twenty-four times.[109] Wallace's repeated attempts to get the candidates to stop interrupting and obey the debate rules were futile. A key moment from the debate came when Biden mentioned that he ran for president because he was concerned about white nationalists, and suggested that Trump condemn the Proud Boys, a far-right organization known as a hate group prone to violence. Trump declared, "Proud Boys, stand back and stand by," which was interpreted as a positive message to the group.[110] Trump would be asked to denounce white nationalists by journalists throughout the campaign, only doing so when pressed on Fox News.[111]

The vice presidential debate between Kamala Harris and Mike Pence was held on October 7 in Salt Lake City, Utah, and was moderated by Susan Page of *USA Today*. Harris made history as the first woman of color to participate in a vice presidential debate. Due to COVID-19, the candidates were seated twelve feet apart and were separated by acrylic glass barriers. The candidates sparred over the Trump administration's response to the pandemic, police reform, Trump's taxes, and trade policy.[112] However, the moment that drove headlines for over a week and lit up the Twitterverse was when a fly landed on Pence's head as he debated racial justice and police brutality.[113]

After months of downplaying the severity of the pandemic and ignoring safety precautions, Trump came down with COVID-19 on October 2, 2020. His diagnosis came after a week of in-person activities without social distancing or mask requirements, including a White House Rose Garden reception for Supreme Court nominee Amy Coney Barrett and several large campaign rallies. He was admitted to Walter Reed Medical Center and received state-of-the-art treatment that was not widely available to the public. Trump was forced to take a break from the campaign trail one month ahead of the election. He sought publicity by taking a car ride around the perimeter of the hospital, removing his mask while he grinned and waved to a small group of his supporters.[114]

While receiving treatment for COVID-19, Donald Trump took a ride in a motorcade. He was not wearing a mask and was in close quarters with others in the car, raising questions about how seriously he was taking his illness and the pandemic.

View in the online reader

The second presidential debate was initially scheduled to take place in-person on October 15, but it was cancelled when the Commission announced that it would take place virtually due to concerns raised by Trump's COVID-19 diagnosis. Trump refused to debate in a virtual format, and Biden instead scheduled a town hall with ABC News for that evening. The candidates ended up holding head-to-head televised town halls during primetime, with Trump appearing on NBC. The forums were a stark contrast in style and spectacle. Biden addressed issues facing the country in a somber tone in his town hall, moderated by George Stephanopoulos. Trump, when asked by moderator Savannah Guthrie if he would denounce QAnon and white supremacy and to clear up concerns about his health, pushed back, deflected, and evaded the questions. Biden won the ratings race, garnering 16.7 million viewers to Trump's 13.5 million viewers.[115]

Twelve days before the election, the presidential candidates met in Nashville for their final debate. The pandemonium surrounding the first debate sparked the Commission on Presidential Debates to consider taking steps to prevent a repeat performance, such as giving the moderator the ability to cut the mic, but they were not enacted. The debate was moderated by NBC's Kristen Welker, who maintained tight control over the proceedings. She asked questions about the COVID-19 pandemic, the economy, climate change, foreign interference in the presidential election, and the candidates' finances.[116] This debate was more subdued than the first one, although the candidates continued to share jabs.

Trump spent much of his energy during the presidential campaign attempting to discredit the integrity of the electoral process. Poll results reported in the press consistently showed Biden with a significant edge over Trump throughout the campaign. Biden's lead over Trump in national polls increased from January until June and remained sizable at around 8 percentage points until election day.[117] On the campaign trail and in his Twitter feed, Trump argued, even before a single vote was cast, that the only way that he could lose was if the election was rigged against him. He sought to sow doubt about mail-in ballots that were being cast in record numbers due to the pandemic, falsely claiming that millions of unsolicited ballots were sent to voters without any oversight. He appointed Louis DeJoy, a donor to his campaign, as postmaster general. DeJoy cut resources to the Post Office that caused service disruptions and delays.[118] Trump repeatedly tweeted that the election would be the "most INACCURATE & FRAUDULENT Election in history," and that it should be delayed.[119] He accused the Democrats of trying to "steal the election." His own administration's Justice Department and Department of Homeland Security issued statements assuring that the election was the most secure in American history. FBI director Christopher Wray, in testimony before the U.S. Congress, warned that this misinformation campaign would undermine American voters' confidence in the validity of their vote.[120]

Due to the pandemic, the voting process was a hybrid of in-person and mail-in balloting. All states extended the window of time in which votes could be cast ahead of Election Day, November 3, 2020.[121] A little more than half of the votes nationwide were cast in-person, with about one-quarter of voters going to the polls on Election Day. The remaining half voted by mail or absentee ballot. Over 60 percent of Trump supporters voted in-person compared to 40 percent of Biden voters.[122] The large number of mail-in ballots meant that counting the votes would take more time than usual in some states. In addition, the race was too close to call on election night in the battleground states of Georgia, Nevada, North Carolina, and Pennsylvania. The vote count and validation of the results continued for several days after the election until Biden was announced by the media as the winner on November 7. Biden won 306 electoral votes to Trump's 232 electoral votes. Voter turnout was the highest in over a century, with 66.3 percent of the voting-eligible population casting a ballot. Biden received the most popular votes ever cast for a presidential candidate with 81,281,502, compared to 74,222,593 for Trump, which was a record for a losing candidate.[123]

## Insurrection

In the aftermath of the election, Trump disputed the outcome and refused to concede that he had lost to Biden. Director Wray of the FBI stated publicly that the agency had not seen "any kind of coordinated national fraud effort . . . by mail or otherwise."[124] Trump launched a legal strategy to have the results of the election invalidated in several key states where he had lost, including Arizona, Georgia, Michigan, Nevada, Pennsylvania, and Wisconsin. In their failed effort, Trump and his allies filed sixty-two lawsuits in state and federal courts, and all but one—which involved a narrow technical issue—failed. Two of Trump's lawsuits were brought to the U.S. Supreme Court, which refused to take them up.[125] In an hour-long call, Trump implored the Georgia secretary of state, Republican Brad Raffensperger, to "find 11,780 votes" so that the results of the election would be overturned in Trump's favor. A recording of the phone call revealed Raffensperger responding to Trump's allegations of voter fraud by stating, "the data you have is wrong," and refusing to take action. Trump made a similar phone call to the Michigan secretary of state.[126]

Trump repeatedly threatened to undermine the well-established precedent of the peaceful transfer of power from the outgoing president to his successor. He held in-person rallies of his supporters where he rehashed his unsubstantiated allegations of election fraud and urged them to "take revenge." Trump's son, Eric, requested on social media that his followers report cases of voter fraud using the hashtag #StoptheSteal. Within a week, there were over 3.5 million posts referencing #StoptheSteal, which became a catalyst for rallies and protests.[127] On the day that the election of Joe Biden would be certified by a Joint Session of Congress, Trump held a "Save America" rally near the White House on the Ellipse. He tweeted to his supporters, "Big protest in D.C. on January 6th. Be there, will be wild!"[128]

Trump implored his supporters who had gathered for the rally to stop the certification of the votes. Urging them "to fight," Trump insinuated that he would be taking part, stating, "We're going to walk down to the Capitol and we're going to cheer on our brave senators and congressmen and women."[129] In fact, Trump returned to the White House, where he watched the violent insurrection unfold on flat-screen televisions in a tent on the lawn while his family members and staff celebrated.[130]

Fifty minutes into Trump's speech, rally attendees headed to Capitol Hill, where they joined other Trump supporters who were already on the grounds. Wearing Trump's signature red MAGA hats and waving Trump banners, neo-Nazi flags, and rebel flags, the protesters forced their way through police barricades and stormed the Capitol building, where the process of certifying the election was under way. They scaled the sides of the building and broke through glass windows and doors with bats and pipes. Many were armed with weapons, including guns, Molotov cocktails, explosive devices, and zip ties that could be used to secure hostages. Vice President Mike Pence, who was presiding, stopped the proceedings as members of Congress were evacuated from their chambers and escorted to secure locations.

**FIGURE 11.16 Insurrection at the Capitol**

Rioters stormed the U.S. Capitol in Washington, DC, disrupting the certification of the results of the 2020 presidential election.

Mayhem ensued at the Capitol for four hours until the building was secured. The rioters clashed with police officers who were seriously outnumbered. They attempted to breach the House and Senate chambers and were nearly successful. They threatened to shoot and kill Speaker Nancy Pelosi, ransacked her office, and stole souvenirs. Chanting "Hang Mike Pence," they erected gallows with the intention of hanging Pence as a "traitor" for carrying out his constitutional duty to oversee the certification of the presidential vote. In the end, a police officer was killed, along with four other people.[131]

Once the Capitol was secured, Congress came back into session late that evening and certified the election. Biden was thereby officially confirmed as the winner of the Electoral College vote despite opposition raised by a small group of Republican senators and 139 Republican House members who objected to at least one state's certified electoral results.[132]

# Second Impeachment

Donald Trump became the only president, in American history to be impeached twice for his role in inciting the riot at the U.S. Capitol. The Article of Impeachment drafted by the House of Representatives cited Trump for "high crimes and misdemeanors" for "incitement of insurrection." The charges against Trump included repeatedly issuing false statements asserting that the results of the presidential election were fraudulent and should not be accepted by the American people or certified, that he had willfully encouraged the crowd at his rally to engage in lawless action at the Capitol, and that he had threatened the Georgia secretary of state if he failed to find the votes to change the election outcome in Trump's favor. The Article concluded:

> *In all this, President Trump gravely endangered the security of the United States and its institutions of Government. He threatened the integrity of the democratic system, interfered with the peaceful transition of power, and imperiled a coequal branch of Government. He thereby betrayed his trust as President, to the manifest injury of the people of the United States.*[133]

As a consequence of these actions, the Article stated that Trump should be removed from office and "disqualified from holding and enjoying any office of honor, trust, or profit under the United States." On January 13, 2021—a week after the insurrection at the Capitol—the House voted to impeach Trump by a vote of 232 to 197. Ten Republicans joined all of the House Democrats in voting to impeach, which is an unprecedented number of members of a president's own party supporting impeachment.[134] Once charges are passed in the House, an impeachment trial must be held in the Senate before actions can be taken based on the Impeachment Article. However, Trump left office when Biden was inaugurated and before the Article was sent to the Senate. Therefore, for the first time in history there was the prospect of a Senate impeachment trial of a president who had left office.

# Inauguration

The inauguration of Joe Biden as the forty-sixth president of the United States and Kamala Harris as vice president took place in the wake of the breach of the U.S. Capitol and the second impeachment of Donald Trump. Threats of mob violence by right-wing extremist groups prompted Washington, DC, to be placed on an unprecedented lockdown. At least 25,000 National Guard troops were called in to provide security, and checkpoints were fortified with miles of fencing and barricades topped with razor wire. Metro stations and the four bridges leading across the Potomac River to the city were closed while armored military vehicles blocked streets to traffic.[135] Events such as the traditional inaugural parade and inaugural balls that had survived COVID-19 restrictions were further limited, cancelled, or held virtually. Fears that attacks might be imminent at state capitols led to additional lockdowns across the nation.

On January 20, 2021, Biden and Harris took their oaths of office in a scaled-down ceremony outside the Capitol. Biden was only the second Roman Catholic president, with President John F. Kennedy being the first. Harris was the first woman and the first person of Black and South Asian descent to hold the office of vice president.

The night before, Biden and Harris had honored victims of the pandemic at a ceremony where lights were placed at the Lincoln Memorial.[136] A small number of invited guests attended the inaugural ceremony, as opposed to the many thousands of Americans who typically flock to witness the historic transfer of power. A-list musicians Lady Gaga, Jennifer Lopez, and Garth Brooks made appearances. Biden was sworn in by Chief Justice John Roberts while placing his hand on a family bible. Justice Sonia Sotomayor administered the oath of office to Harris, who used two bibles, one belonging to the late Justice Thurgood Marshall, the first Black member of the Supreme Court, and one owned by a close family friend. Biden's inaugural address stressed the themes of unity and the resilience of democracy even in the face of violent challenges like the attack on the Capitol. He sent a message to other nations that he would work to rebuild trust and alliances. A highlight of the ceremony was the reading of an original poem entitled "The Hill We Climb," by Amanda Gorman, a twenty-two-year-old Black woman and the youngest person ever to be chosen as an inaugural poet.[137] Biden and Harris made their way to the White House accompanied by the marching bands of their alma maters, the University of Delaware and Howard University.

Former presidents Barack Obama, George W. Bush, and Bill Clinton attended the inauguration along with the outgoing vice president, Mike Pence. Ninety-six-year-old former president Jimmy Carter sent well wishes, although he was not able to attend due to COVID-19 health concerns. Missing was Donald Trump, who refused to attend. Only three presidents have skipped their successor's swearing in—John Adams, John Quincy Adams, and Andrew Johnson, who, like Trump, had been impeached.[138] Rather than follow established protocol, Trump chose to leave the White House without greeting the incoming president. On the morning of the inauguration, Trump made short remarks addressing small groups of family members, staffers, and supporters before flying to his golf resort at Mar-a-Lago in Florida.[139]

Twenty-two-year-old Amanda Gorman read her original poem, "The Hill We Climb," at the inauguration of Joe Biden and Kamala Harris. Gorman set out to write a poem that would inspire hope and collective purpose at a time when the country was dealing with a pandemic and recovering from the assault on the U.S. Capitol.

View in the online reader

## Key Takeaways

The COVID-19 pandemic changed how candidates campaigned and how voters cast their ballots. The 2020 election was contested during a time of great political turmoil resulting from the quickly spreading virus, racial unrest, and a declining economy. Joe Biden and Kamala Harris defeated Donald Trump, who contested the results of the election. Biden was only the second Roman Catholic to be elected president. Harris became the first woman vice president. Trump's attempts to overturn the election by claiming fraud contributed to his supporters' assault on the U.S. Capitol. Trump became the only president in U.S. history to be impeached twice.

## Exercises

1. What do you think were the most effective ways that candidates campaigned during the pandemic? If you were a presidential campaign manager in 2020, how might you innovate to get your message out to young voters?
2. If you were a member of the Commission on Presidential Debates, what steps would you take to ensure a civil and meaningful exchange between candidates?
3. Do you think Congress should hold an impeachment trial of a president after he has left office? What are the problems with and benefits of taking such action?

# 11.10 Congressional and Other Elections

## Learning Objectives

After reading this section, you should be able to answer the following questions:

1. What are the differences between House and Senate elections?
2. What is the significance of midterm elections?
3. What is gerrymandering, and how can it influence the outcomes of campaigns?
4. What are ballot measures?

Every two years the entire House of Representatives and one-third of the Senate face election. Congressional elections command far less attention from the media and voters than do presidential campaigns. However, their outcomes can determine the partisan composition of Congress, which can influence the course of public policy for decades to come. Americans can have a direct say in state policy proposals, laws, and constitutional amendments through ballot measures. They also can remove an elected official from office through a recall election.

## Congressional Elections

**midterm elections**

Elections held in nonpresidential election years that often are viewed as a referendum on the performance of the sitting president or the party controlling the House or Senate.

**divided government**

Divided government is when a majority of members of the House and/or Senate are of a different party than the president.

Congressional elections, in which all 435 House seats and one-third of Senate seats are contested, take place every two years, including years when there is a presidential election. **Midterm elections** occur in years when there is no presidential contest. Frequently, midterm elections are treated as referenda on the performance of the sitting president and can determine the balance of power in Congress. National issues, such as the economy and unemployment, can become prominent factors in midterm campaigns. Since 1926, the president's party has lost an average of thirty seats in the House and four seats in the Senate during midterm elections.

In 2016, Republicans kept their majority in the House, winning 241 seats to the Democrats' 194 seats. House Speaker Paul Ryan and Minority Leader Nancy Pelosi were both reelected. With 34 seats up for election in the Senate, the Republicans maintained a slim margin of 52 seats compared to 48 seats that went to the Democrats. The partisan balance remained stable after special elections to replace members who assumed cabinet appointments. Democratic President Barack Obama held office during a time of **divided government**, as the majority of House members were Republican. Republican President Donald Trump had the advantage of a majority of Republicans in the House and Senate for the first two years of his presidency, which made it easier for him to enact his agenda, such as instituting tax cuts and securing positions for two nominees on the U.S. Supreme Court.

The 2018 midterm elections were among the most highly contested in decades. The election resulted in a return to divided government. The Democrats took control of the House from Republicans, while the Republicans maintained their advantage in the Senate. The House election in 2018 was called a "blue wave," as Democrats gained a net of forty-one seats—the most in any election since 1974 after President Richard Nixon resigned in the wake of the Watergate scandal.[140] The Democrats' majority in the House was 233 seats compared to 197 for Republicans, taking into account vacancies. Republicans held control of the Senate in 2018, winning fifty-three seats compared to forty-five seats for the Democrats and two for Independents. The Independents caucus with the Democrats, so they are typically counted as Democratic senators.

**FIGURE 11.17** Rand Paul at His Victory Celebration in 2010

Republican Rand Paul, an ophthalmologist, won the Senate race in Kentucky against Democrat Jack Conway, the state's attorney general, with the backing of the Tea Party.

Source: Photo courtesy of Gage Skidmore via Wikimedia: http://commons.wikimedia.org/wiki/File:Will,_Rand_&_Ron_Paul.jpg. Reproduced va CC BY-SA 2.0: https://creativecommons.org/licenses/by-sa/2.0/deed.en.

Democrats took control of both houses of Congress following the 2020 election, although their margins in both the House and the Senate are razor thin. Despite President Biden's victory in the election, Democrats lost 11 House seats to Republican candidates. Democrats maintained control of the chamber with 222 seats to the Republicans' 212 seats, but they have the smallest House majority since the 1940s.[141] Democratic candidates won four seats and lost one for a net gain of three seats.[142] While both the Republicans and the Democrats occupy fifty seats, the Democrats gained control of the Senate because Vice President Kamala Harris, a Democrat, is the deciding vote in the case of a tie.

Local and regional media are in the best position to cover congressional elections, and they can set the agenda for national media. Typically, there is less media coverage of midterm elections compared with presidential campaigns, as was the case in 2008 and 2012. The 2010 midterm election received more coverage than usual, as voters expressed frustration with incumbent President Barack Obama's performance in office. The **Tea Party**—a grassroots, conservative-leaning movement that opposed the government's taxing and spending policies—staged protests that brought media attention to the election. The 2018 midterm elections received ample media coverage as they were viewed as a referendum on Donald Trump's presidency.

**Tea Party**

A grassroots movement with conservative leanings that emerged in 2009 to protest government taxing and spending policies.

## The Senate

There are one hundred senators in the U.S. Congress, two elected from each state, who serve six-year terms. One-third of Senate seats are up for election every two years. Senators are constitutionally required to be at least thirty years old and to have been a U.S. citizen for at least nine years when they take office.

**FIGURE 11.18** Beto O'Rourke on the Campaign Trail

Beto O'Rourke energized the electorate in Texas, as he ran a close race against incumbent Senator Ted Cruz that gained national media attention.

Source: 1082492116/Shutterstock.com.

Many Senate elections are competitive in both the primary and the general election. Having been in office for six or more years, incumbents have records and controversial votes, and may have upset some of their constituents. Their opponents may have name recognition and ample funding, and may have run an effective campaign using the new media and political advertising. Especially when the election is close, challengers receive almost as much visibility as incumbents. They are able to publicize their images, get some of their issues on the campaign agenda, and have attention paid to their attacks on their opponent.

In 2012, 84 percent of incumbent senators kept their seats, while 91 percent won their races in 2014. The 2014 midterm Senate elections were seen as a referendum on Democratic President Barack Obama, whose popularity had dwindled as voters perceived that he was not able to handle tough policy problems facing the nation, especially the struggling economy. President Obama's low public approval rating of 42 percent—compared to 50 percent in 2012—contributed to the loss of Democratic seats in the Senate.[143] Eighty-two percent of senators were reelected in 2014.[144]

The electoral map in 2018 favored the Republicans, as many of the thirty-five seats that were up for election were located in states where President Trump had done well in the 2016 presidential election. A number of Senate races gained national attention. In Texas, Republican incumbent Ted Cruz, who had sought his party's presidential nomination in 2016, faced Democratic challenger Beto O'Rourke, a first-term member of Congress, in a close race. O'Rourke broke records by raising over $39 million in three months. He appealed to new voters who registered and turned out in record numbers. In the end, O'Rourke was unable to top Cruz in the election.[145]

**special election**

An election held to fill a seat that has been vacated by the incumbent before a scheduled election is to take place.

One reason that the 2020 elections were so closely watched was that control of the Senate was at stake. Republicans attempted to hold onto their slim advantage while Democrats were seeking to gain enough seats to become the majority party. A total of thirty-five of the one hundred seats were up for election. Typically, thirty-three Senate seats would be at stake, but there were special elections for seats in Arizona and Georgia. A **special election** takes place when a seat has been vacated before an officeholder's term is up, often due to illness, death, or a decision to take another position. Control of the Senate passed to the Democrats after the defeat of two Republican candidates in Georgia.

**runoff election**

An election held when no candidate has received the required number of votes to win during the general election.

The partisan balance of power in the Senate hinged on the results in the state of Georgia, as no winners emerged after the November election. State election rules in Georgia require a candidate to have 50 percent or more of the votes in the general election to win a Senate seat. None of the candidates met this standard. A **runoff election**, a second election held to determine a winner when no candidate has met the required threshold of votes, took place on January 5, 2021, several weeks after the general election. The Democratic candidates won both seats. Jon Ossoff, a documentary film producer and investigative journalist who had never held public office, beat Republican Senator David Perdue, an incumbent who had just finished his first term in the Senate. Normally, only one senator at a time is up for election in a state. In this case, a special election was held in 2020 to fill a position that had been vacated when a Georgia senator retired. Republican Senator Kelly Loeffler was appointed to that seat in December 2019 and faced a challenge to fill the remainder of the term from Rev. Raphael Warnock, a Democrat. Rev. Warnock, a Baptist preacher and pastor at Ebenezer Baptist Church, where Rev. Dr. Martin Luther King, Jr. had preached, defeated Senator Loeffler. Because the results would influence President-elect Joe Biden's ability to enact his legislative agenda, the election gained national attention. The campaign was very contentious, with the Republican candidates labeling their rivals as "radical," "socialist," and worse,[146] while the Democratic candidates attacked their opponents for their handling of the COVID-19 pandemic and their support of Trump's unproven claims of voter fraud.[147] Perdue and Loeffler were both criticized for selling stocks at the start of the pandemic after they received privileged briefings.[148] Rev. Warnock, who was attacked more than any other candidate during this Senate campaign, sought to neutralize the attacks with lighthearted ads where he demonstrated his love of puppies.[149] President Donald Trump and Vice President Mike Pence, as well as President-elect Biden and Vice President–elect Kamala Harris, campaigned for their respective candidates in Georgia. The results of the Georgia runoff election made history. Jon Ossoff was the first Jewish person and Rev. Warnock was the first Black person to be elected to the Senate from Georgia.[150] Rev. Warnock was only the eleventh Black person to become a U.S. senator.[151]

To counter attacks by his opponent, Warnock ran a humorous ad that gained national attention. He brought Alvin the beagle, the puppy featured in the ad, to Washington, DC, with him when he joined the Senate.

View in the online reader

## The House of Representatives

There are 435 voting members of the House of Representatives elected in separate districts within states for two-year terms. Candidates must be at least twenty-five years old and need to have been a citizen for at least seven years.

Members of the House who are seeking reelection in districts designed to favor their party have an advantage. They usually have better organized campaigns, greater name recognition, far more funds, and more support from interest groups than do their opponents. Since 1954, 93 percent of House incumbents have been reelected. This rate dropped slightly in 2010, as 87 percent of incumbents were reelected, which is the lowest percentage since 1964.[152] Ninety percent of incumbent House members were reelected in 2012. Almost all House incumbents—95 percent—running in 2014 were returned to office.[153] The trend continued in 2018 as 93 percent of incumbents running in the midterms were reelected.[154] The incumbency rate for House members who ran for reelection remained exceptionally high at 95 percent in the 2020 elections.[155]

The media contribute to this **incumbency advantage**. Challengers often lack the funds to air political ads. News coverage of House elections favors incumbents. Local television coverage pays little attention to even the most competitive House elections.[156] Indeed, four thousand local television newscasts in eleven major markets during the four weeks before the 2004 election gave eight times as much air time to car crashes and other accidents than to House campaigns.[157] The use of social media, such as Facebook and Twitter, can benefit challengers, especially if their messages are picked up by the mainstream press. However, many voters get most of their campaign information from television. Debates can sometimes improve a challenger's chances if they are televised and widely seen. But nearly 70 percent of debates held by House candidates are not televised.[158]

**incumbency advantage**

The advantage generally enjoyed by sitting members of the House of Representatives in getting reelected to office due to better organized campaigns, greater name recognition, more funding, and support from interest groups.

## Redistricting

Each state is awarded a number of seats in the House of Representatives based on its population as determined by the national census, which is taken every ten years as required by the Constitution. If the census reveals shifts in the size of the population within districts, state legislators redraw the district lines to equalize the number of people within each congressional and state district.

President Trump tried to have a question about citizenship added to the 2020 census. The question had been dropped in 1950 to improve the response rate and accuracy.[159] The Commerce Secretary's rationale for adding the question now was to provide data to help the Justice Department enforce the Voting Rights Act. Opponents, mainly Democrats, argued that the question would make more noncitizens and minority residents unwilling to be counted, thereby weakening Democratic representation in, and reducing the allotment of millions of dollars to, states with many noncitizens.

On June 27, 2019, the Supreme Court ruled 5–4, in a decision written by Chief Justice John G. Roberts Jr., voting with the court's four liberals, to reject the action on the grounds that the "sole stated reason" by the Commerce Secretary for the addition of the citizenship question was unacceptable: it "seems to have been contrived." The decision did leave open the possibility for the administration to come up with an acceptable rationale (see here). After expressing his disagreement with the decision, the president reluctantly said he was instructing federal departments and agencies to provide their citizenship data to the Census Bureau.

**gerrymander**

To draw congressional districts in such a way as to give one political party the advantage in electing its candidates.

Redistricting is often a highly partisan and contentious activity because it can change the number of House seats each party wins in a state. The party in control of the state legislature can design districts so as to protect its incumbents and increase its House seats. The party in power can obtain more seats by having small but usually safe majorities in several districts and cramming large numbers of the other party's voters into just a few districts. This is achieved through a **gerrymander**, drawing congressional district lines to give one party the advantage in electing its candidates to the House of Representatives.[160] Incumbents in gerrymandered districts are usually reelected. For example, in the 2018 elections in North Carolina, the Republicans won 50.4 percent and ten seats, while the Democrats won 48.3 percent of the votes for the House of Representatives but only three seats.

**FIGURE 11.19** Gerrymander (Gerry-Mander)

In 1812, Massachusetts Governor Elbridge Gerry pushed through electoral redistricting that ensured his Republican Party's majority in the township of Marblehead would outweigh the Federal majority in eleven other townships. Artist Elkanah Tisdale drew a cartoon map of the salamander-shaped district for the *Boston Gazette* and coined the term "Gerry-mander" (now "gerrymander") that became a staple of political language. The visual and the term are therefore both media creations.

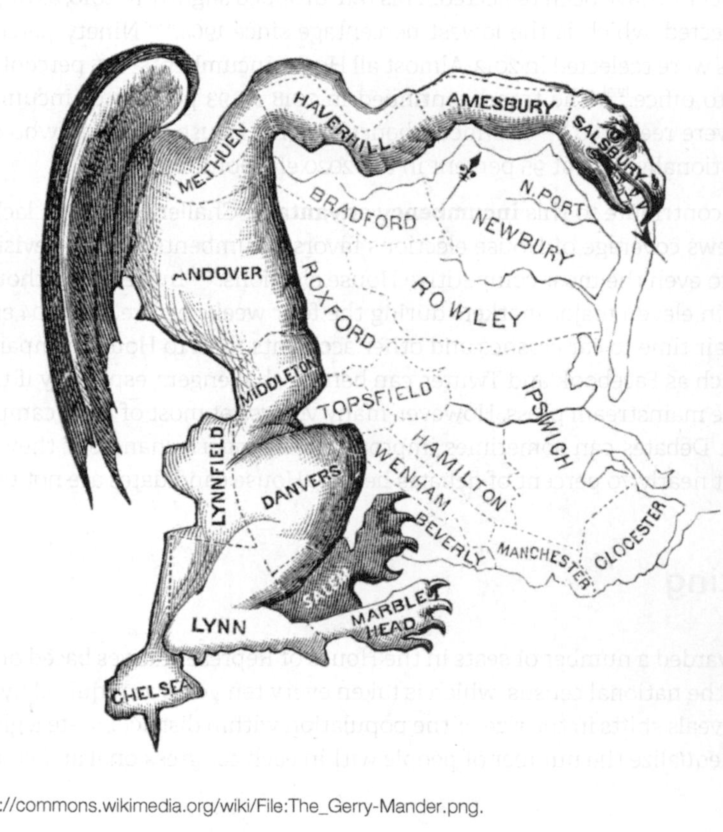


Source: Wikimedia: http://commons.wikimedia.org/wiki/File:The_Gerry-Mander.png.

Also, on June 27, 2019, the Supreme Court ruled by 5–4, in another decision by Chief Justice John G. Roberts Jr., this time joining his conservative colleagues, that the federal courts have no jurisdiction over partisan gerrymandering, no matter how blatant. He wrote that the decision recognized the limits of judicial power. Speaking from the bench to show the intensity of her dissent, Justice Elena Kagan argued that American democracy would suffer (see here).

The decision may be somewhat less draconian than it appears. Already there is litigation in state courts invoking provisions of state constitutions that might allow for preventing or limiting gerrymandering. More states could establish independent redistricting commissions to forestall gerrymandering (although independence is easier said than done). Also, the court has banned gerrymandering on the basis of race.

## Comparing Content

### Candidates in Fiction and Documentary Films

There are two types of films about candidates: Hollywood fiction seen by millions of people and documentaries seen by far fewer.[161] In Hollywood films, the candidates are glamorous and charismatic. They run for high office, usually the presidency or Senate. The focus is on their character. They are cynical and hypocritical from the start (the presidential candidate played by John Travolta in *Primary Colors*, 1998), or they become cynical and compromise their ideals and principles over the course of their campaigns (the senatorial candidate played by Robert Redford in *The Candidate*, 1972), or they are disillusioned career politicians trying but failing to change a corrupt campaign process (Warren Beatty as the senator up for reelection in *Bulworth*, 1998). Their campaign consultants use whatever tactics and techniques will win the election. The candidates have an adversarial relationship with the news media.

Documentaries offer a wider range of candidates and circumstances. *A Perfect Candidate* (1996) covers Republican Oliver North's 1994 senatorial campaign in Virginia from the perspective of the candidate, his campaign manager, and a *Washington Post* reporter. The subject of *Taking on the Kennedys* (1996) is a Republican doctor running against Senator Edward Kennedy's son Patrick for an open House of Representatives seat in Rhode Island. In *I'm a Candidate* (2001), two young men, one a Black Republican in Georgia and the other a white Democrat in Cincinnati, challenge incumbent members of the House.

The candidates in the documentaries are idealists, even a bit naive. They have principles and policy preferences. Campaigning is an all-consuming activity requiring perseverance and the sacrifice of personal life. Money is crucial for their campaigns, and they spend a lot of time trying to raise it. They engage in retail politics: shaking hands, meeting people, visiting senior-citizen centers, and marching in parades. They struggle to break through to an indifferent electorate; yet, even after they have campaigned for several months, many people remain unaware of them. They are vulnerable to the news media, which define and depict them.

Hollywood movies and documentaries convey the drama and conflict of elections, the demands on the candidates, and the strategies required to have a chance of winning. But for the lived experience of a political campaign, watch the documentaries.

# Ballot Measures

Many states offer people the opportunity to vote on ballot measures on proposed laws, ordinances, or constitutional amendments. Two types of ballot measures are the initiative and the referendum. In the 2010 midterm election, a total of 160 questions were considered on ballots in thirty-seven states. Another type of ballot measure is the recall election, whereby voters can remove an elected official from office. Learn more in Table 11.1.

**referendum**

A process whereby the state legislature refers a proposal to citizens, who vote to either approve or reject the measure.

**initiative**

A process whereby voters propose and pass laws to amend the state constitution or place a proposal on an election ballot.

**recall**

An election that allows voters to remove an elected officeholder.

**TABLE 11.1** Types of Ballot Measures

| Type of Ballot Measure | Description |
|---|---|
| Referendum | In a **referendum**, the state legislature refers a proposal to citizens, who vote to either approve or reject the measure. In every state except Delaware, amendments to the state's constitution passed by the legislature go on the ballot automatically.[162] State legislatures put other measures on the ballot to let voters make a choice or to avoid deciding a controversial issue. Referenda also can work as an end run around decisions made by a state governor. |
| Initiative | The **initiative** is similar to the referendum except that voters propose and pass laws and present them to the state legislature. Citizens also can propose an amendment to the state constitution. In some states, the legislature can adopt the proposal outright. In most cases, registered voters can place a proposal on the ballot, sometimes with a counterproposal from the state legislature. If the initiative wins a majority of the votes in an election, it goes into effect. In recent years, initiatives have been passed to cap property taxes, curtail immigration, and allow medicinal marijuana and euthanasia. States also have had ballot initiatives to recognize gay marriage.<br><br>The initiative was originally designed to combat powerful interests such as those controlling the railroads in the nineteenth century.[163] Today, initiatives are sometimes a way for wealthy individuals or interest groups to put policies into effect while bypassing the state legislature. Consulting firms specializing in initiative campaigns are paid to collect the signatures required to put a measure on the ballot.[164]<br><br>Critics attack initiatives for congesting ballots and confusing voters, and for their sometimes deceptive titles and descriptions. "Keep California Green" was the slogan for a proposition to keep taxes low on private golf courses. However, research shows that "the initiative has a significant impact on state and local government and in doing so pushes policy in the direction a majority of people say they want to go."[165] In 2016, ballot measures related to legalization of marijuana, gun control, and health care—important issues facing states and the nation—were considered. |
| Recall | Originally intended to root out corruption among elected officials, the **recall** allows voters to remove public officials from office through a direct election. A recall is initiated when a designated number of voters sign a petition requesting a special election. Fourteen state constitutions provide for recall elections for state officials, and many localities have provisions for the recall of lower-level elected officials.<br><br>Until 2003, only one governor, North Dakota's Lynn J. Frazier in 1921, had been successfully recalled. In 2003, a California Republican congressman initiated and mainly funded the recall of California's Democratic Governor Gray Davis for his alleged policy failings. Spurred by conservative talk-radio hosts, websites run by Republican operatives, disenchanted Democrats, and anti-tax organizations, and coordinated by email, more than 900,000 eligible voters signed the petition to put the recall on the ballot. The ballot asked voters two questions: if the governor should be removed from office, and who they would select from a list of candidates to replace him if the governor were recalled. The voters selected Republican Arnold Schwarzenegger to replace Governor Davis. Californians again threatened to recall their governor in 2021, alleging that Democratic Governor Gavin Newsom failed in his handling of the COVID-19 pandemic as unemployment rose and businesses failed.[166] Top leaders from the Democratic Party, including President Joe Biden and Vice President Kamala Harris, attended rallies in support of Newsom, who won the recall election handily. |

## Link

**State Ballot Measures in the 2010 Elections**

Voters in thirty-seven states considered over 160 ballot initiatives in the 2010 midterm elections. In 2012, 176 ballot issues were considered in thirty-eight states. In the presidential election year of 2016, 147 statewide ballot measures were certified in thirty-five states. Sixty-seven of these measures were put on the ballot by citizens through signature petitions, rather than by state legislatures. Ballotpedia is an active archive of ballot initiatives.

**FIGURE 11.20 Governor Arnold Schwarzenegger**

Movie action hero Arnold Schwarzenegger was elected governor of California in the recall election of 2003. This is a stellar example of how prominence in the entertainment media can be translated into visibility in the news media and victory in politics.

Source: Federal Emergency Management Agency, https://commons.wikimedia.org/wiki/File:FEMA_-_33305_-_Community_Relations_workers_in_California.jpg.

## Key Takeaways

Congressional candidates run for either the Senate or the House of Representatives. There are no limits on the number of terms a member of Congress can serve. Senators are elected in states and Representatives in congressional districts within states. Congressional districts are based on the U.S. census and are reconfigured periodically. Elections for the Senate tend to be more competitive than those for the House, where incumbent officeholders have an advantage.

Ballot measures, consisting of the initiative and the referendum, are mechanisms that allow voters to have a more direct say in state laws, government proposals, and constitutional amendments. In certain states, voters can remove elected officials from office through a recall election.

## Exercises

1. Why do you think the president's party tends to lose seats in Congress in midterm elections? Why might holding the presidency be a disadvantage in elections?

2. What advantages do incumbents have in running for office? What advantages do challengers have?
3. What are the advantages of using ballot measures to let people vote on legislative issues directly, rather than letting elected representatives decide them? What might be the disadvantages of using ballot measures?

# 11.11 Campaigns and Elections in the Information Age

## Learning Objectives

After reading this section, you should be able to answer the following questions:

1. How do campaigns use new media?
2. How has social media created new opportunities for campaign engagement?
3. How are candidates depicted in campaigns?

Candidates in the information age not only have to manage traditional news media, such as newspaper and television news coverage; they also must contend with an ever-increasing number of social media platforms. More than 200 million Americans use Facebook each month, and more than 50 percent of them get their news from the platform.[167] New media enable candidates, voters, and journalists to engage in elections in novel ways. Voters can participate in elections through social media by posting comments, organizing events, and contributing to campaigns. Entertainment media provide candidates with the opportunity to present their human side to voters. Candidates can attempt to exert control over political commentary, but they are not always successful.

## Media Interactions

Campaigns use new media, such as websites, email, text messages, social networking sites, Twitter, and blogs, in three overlapping ways.[168] New media can be used to inform voters about the candidate, including their biography, speeches and press releases, policy record, issue positions, endorsements, and attacks on the opponent. Candidates also can employ new media to get people involved in the election. New media can be used to recruit supporters and volunteers, raise funds, register voters, and get people to the polls on Election Day.[169] Finally, new media can connect voters by enabling people to exchange information on behalf of the campaign, promote the candidate to people in their social networks, and interact with others who share their views. Social media use has been pervasive since the 2008 presidential election and was a major source of information for voters in 2020. Journalists increasingly used social media as a source of news, which allowed candidates to have greater sway over the press agenda.

## Social Media

The importance of social media in elections has grown in recent election campaigns.[170] Congressional candidates have become increasingly sophisticated in their use of social media. Successful candidates used social media to promote their own brands to set themselves apart from the presidential candidates, who were not particularly popular. Younger candidates, such as Rep. Alexandria Ocasio-Cortez (D-NY), Rep. Scott Peters (D-CA), and Jared Polis (D-CO), court the "gamer vote" by streaming their video game play while urging viewers to cast their ballots.[171]

**FIGURE 11.21** O'Rourke and Cruz Post-2018 Campaign

Students pose for a photo with Texas Senate election rivals Senator Ted Cruz and Congressman Beto O'Rourke following the 2018 midterm campaign.

Source: Twitter.

People use digital media to participate in new ways, often outside the context of campaign organizations. Facebook and Twitter have emerged as the most popular platforms for political expression and networking, but other formats such as Instagram and Tumblr appeal to particular groups. Social media are versatile and allow users to post their support for or opposition to a candidate, link to outside content, such as a candidate's website, share photos and videos, express issue opinions, and share comments. Millions of people use the "I Voted" button on Facebook to let their friends know that they have taken part in an election. A study conducted during the 2012 election showed that a Facebook message showing the faces of people who clicked the "I Voted" button drove 340,000 people to the polls who may not have otherwise voted.[172]

Social media have made it possible for average people to document their interactions with candidates. Soon after the 2018 midterm elections, students from Texas A&M University encountered Republican Senator Ted Cruz, the winner of the Texas Senate race, and his opponent, Democrat Beto O'Rourke. The two rivals in the election shook hands and discussed ways that they could work together in the future. They took a photo with the students, who posted the encounter on Facebook with a caption emphasizing the importance of civil discourse and civic education.

The mainstream media have incorporated social media into their election coverage. Information gleaned from social media was a major source of election news in 2020. News organization websites feature social media applications, such as Facebook links. The *Washington Post* sponsors a promoted trend, #Election, on the Twitter.com homepage to allow users to view election coverage. The *New York Times* and CNN analyze voter tweets as part of their campaign reporting.

## Video Sharing

Campaigns make use of **video-sharing platforms** to make their ads, speeches, and appearances available to voters and journalists. Videos are posted on candidate and political party websites as well as on public video-sharing platforms such as YouTube and Hulu. Online videos have become a popular source of information for voters. In 2008, videos produced by the Obama campaign were accessed 37 million times during the primary.[173] According to the Pew Research Center, 55 percent of all voters viewed an online video during the 2012 campaign.[174] An increasing amount of candidates' advertising budgets—as much as $2.5 billion in 20202—is dedicated to online ads. These ads can be specifically targeted at voters based on their profiles; this has greater potential to influence their vote choice.[175]

**video-sharing platforms**

Digital media that allow people to post campaign-related videos and share them with others through links, email, and social media.

People post campaign videos on YouTube that are circulated virally through email messages, blog posts, and Facebook messages. While most videos posted by voters are selections from media broadcasts, such as debates, and clips of live events, such as candidate rallies, original user-generated videos can attract extensive mainstream press coverage.

**mashup**

A digital presentation that combines material from a variety of sources, such as voter-produced campaign videos, that combine existing footage of candidates with original content.

The most popular user-generated videos to date were aired during the 2008 presidential campaign. "Vote Different" was first aired in March 2007 and featured a **mashup** of Hillary Clinton speeches with an Apple commercial that depicted Clinton in the fearful role of "Big Brother." The video was the creation of a producer with tenuous ties to the Obama campaign, who had placed the ad on YouTube without authorization. This video was viewed millions of times and generated thousands of comments. It sparked a tidal wave of user-produced campaign videos.

"Vote Different" was a user-produced video attacking Hillary Clinton that aired during the 2008 presidential primary campaign.

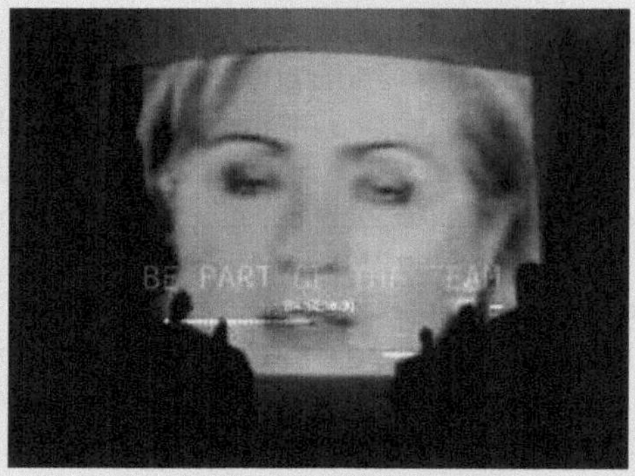

View in the online reader

Comedic videos are popular with voters and can garner mainstream media publicity. Perhaps the most popular video of the 2008 campaign was "Obama Girl . . . Cause I got a crush on Obama." The video, which first aired in November 2007, starred aspiring actress-model Amber Lee Ettinger wearing a bikini and lip-syncing a song about her love for Obama. "Obama Girl" prompted copycat videos for other candidates, including the "Incredible McCain Girl," who turns into the Incredible Hulk as she defends her candidate.

"Obama Girl" video from the 2008 presidential campaign.

View in the online reader

"Incredible McCain Girl" video from the 2008 presidential campaign.

View in the online reader

Another prominent video featured a mashup of clips from Barack Obama's concession speech after he failed to win the New Hampshire primary, along with clips of actors and musicians stating, "Yes, We Can," a line from Obama's speech. The video, produced by will.i.am of the rock group Black Eyed Peas, was posted on dipdive.com and YouTube. The video received over 16 million views during the campaign and helped to mobilize voters after Obama's New Hampshire primary defeat.

"Yes, We Can" video from the 2008 presidential election.

View in the online reader

## Media Depictions

Media depictions of candidates often focus on candidates' personalities, personal lives, flaws, and faults. For this reason, candidates seek to convey a positive personal image through entertainment media. Presidential candidates are as likely to grace the cover of the entertainment weekly *People* magazine as they are to be depicted on the front of news magazines, such as *Time* and *Newsweek*.

Depictions of candidates in American elections have become increasingly uncivil. They often violate social norms for face-to-face communication, and can be rude and offensive. Frequently, candidates fail to exhibit even a minimum of decorum when addressing their opponents. Campaign discourse has coarsened, as candidates and their surrogates do not hesitate to use vulgar terms to address their adversaries. "Talking heads" on cable television argue loudly with those holding opposing views.[176]

Depictions of the media by candidates also have become highly negative. During the 2016 and 2020 campaigns, Donald Trump waged war against the press. He sought to discredit the media in his stump speeches and through Twitter rants. He often labeled respected news organizations, such as the *Washington Post* and the *New York Times* as "fake news," despite the fact that their stories were accurate. Trump bullied journalists who he felt covered him unfairly. He made fun of a *New York Times* reporter with a disability. He banned certain media organizations from his events, including the *Washington Post*. He threatened to sue publications for stories about his finances and issues with women. At a rally in Scranton, Pennsylvania, on the final day of the campaign, Trump launched into a diatribe against the *New York Times* that was characteristic of his treatment of the press throughout the election. "They are so dishonest, folks. You can't even read articles in certain papers anymore. *New York Times* is a total lie. You can't, I mean, you can't—it is so false. Nothing to do with me. I'm just telling you, such lies. Such lies, such fabrications, such made-up stories. Now the *Times* is going out of business pretty soon. That's the good news." The *New York Times*'s circulation has actually increased since Trump entered the political arena.[177]

## Entertainment Media

Candidates and their spouses participate in popular culture and go on entertainment shows to display their human touch, identify with ordinary folk, and connect with members of an audience that is otherwise hard to reach. Their ability to influence the contents of these shows varies.

Easiest are shows with hosts such as Oprah Winfrey, because they usually ask softball questions easy to anticipate and answer. Oprah endorsed Obama for president, and his slogan "Yes, We Can" evoked her theme of helping people help themselves.

Candidates go on late-night talk shows, engaging in conversation with hosts Stephen Colbert, Jimmy Kimmel, and Jimmy Fallon. They also appear on *Saturday Night Live* and participate in its sketch comedy. They are interviewed by Trevor Noah on *The Daily Show*, which is popular with young voters.

In these appearances they try to come across as people rather than politicians, and by jesting with the hosts, they dissipate the negative effects of the jokes previously made about them. Some of these interchanges may be less spontaneous and more controlled by the candidates than it appears. According to former *Tonight Show* host Jay Leno, "Plenty of times when politicians are here, we write jokes for them. We try to make it comfortable."[178]

### *SNL* Apology Urges Country to Come Together

Often entertainment programs heighten political divides around campaigns as they court audiences with biting satire and jokes targeted at one side or the other. However, entertainment shows can also be effective in conveying political messages that seek to unite the country during times of political polarization.

The weekend before the 2018 midterm elections, *Saturday Night Live* comedian Pete Davidson made a comment about the appearance of Republican congressional candidate Dan Crenshaw, who wears an eye patch as a result of his service as a Navy Seal in Afghanistan. Davidson's poor attempt at a joke generated a great deal of criticism, especially on social media. The following week, Davidson apologized to Crenshaw, who then appeared on the set. Crenshaw accepted his apology, and then made several jokes at Davidson's expense. At one point Crenshaw's phone rang with a ringtone playing a song by Davidson's ex-fiancée, pop star Ariana Grande. Crenshaw, who won election to the House, concluded with lessons about politics and service. "We can remember what brings us together as a country and still see the good in each other." He urged people to "never forget" the dedication of veterans and public servants, and specifically paid tribute to Davidson's father, a firefighter who died responding to the attacks on the World Trade Center on 9/11. The *SNL* episode was widely viewed, and the exchange gained traction in the press and on social media.

Comedian Pete Davidson apologizes to Congressman-elect Dan Crenshaw on *SNL*.

View in the online reader

## Memes

**Memes** are images that combine symbols and slogans to convey a message or make an argument about politics. They have become a prominent form of communication in elections. Memes are popular among voters because they often are humorous in the way they transmit messages about candidates. Many memes are created by members of the public who doctor an image or supply a funny caption. They are easily spread by social media and can gain attention from the mainstream media.

**memes**

Images that combine symbols and slogans to convey a message or make an argument about politics; memes are often humorous and are easily spread via social media.

### Links

**Political Memes**

See some examples of political memes here.

This article contains several memes, including one using a famous scene from *Parks and Recreation*, celebrating Biden's 2020 victory.

## Commentary

Campaigns have some influence over the contents of the cable television shows that generate commentary through the legions of candidates' representatives and party strategists ushered in and out of the studios. However, they often are granted insufficient time to make their cases, which can result in argument and conflict rather than constructive discussion. The candidate's social media has become a source of information for commentators, which gives skillful campaigns a tool for controlling the message. However, campaign social media also can provide fodder for negative commentary.

Campaigns' influence with commentators also varies. These editorialists, columnists, and pundits are paid to have opinions and express them. Some of them are open to argument and persuasion. Others—such as staunch conservatives Tucker Carlson on Fox News and liberal Rachel Maddow on MSNBC—are impervious to the efforts of candidates and campaign media advisors they disagree with to change their minds. They are more inclined to transmit the message of the day or talking points of a candidate with whom they agree and promote.

# Fake News

**fake news**

Fabricated, sensational stories made to appear as if they are real news articles; it is also a term that is used by Donald Trump against the mainstream press.

**Fake news** describes fabricated, sensational stories made to appear as if they are real news articles. Fake news stories abounded on websites such as *Infowars, The Rightest, The Denver Guardian*, and *National Report* during the 2016 election. Fake news authors create outlandish, false stories that play into voters' preexisting beliefs about parties and candidates, making them appear credible. While some stories were outright fabrications and hyper-partisan screeds, others contained elements of truth that gave them credibility. Fake news stories in 2016 include, the claim that Pope Francis voted for Donald Trump and Hillary Clinton sold arms to ISIS. Conspiracy theories, hoaxes, and lies were spread efficiently through Facebook, Snapchat, and other social media. As the votes were being tallied during the 2020 presidential election, a photo allegedly providing evidence that 1,000 mail-in ballots had been discovered in a dumpster was posted by a conservative media personality and shared by over 25,000 Twitter users, including Donald Trump, Jr., who had 5.7 million followers. The photo, in fact, depicted envelopes from the 2018 midterm election that were being readied for recycling.[179] Fake news reaches millions of people during election campaigns, some of whom are more willing to believe an anonymous Facebook post than an attributed article in the *New York Times*.[180] Once he took office, President Trump appropriated the term "fake news" and used it against the mainstream press.

# Media Consequences

The election media environment is fast paced and saturated with information. The internet enables campaigns to send journalists a barrage of emails containing endorsements, policy pronouncements, negative information about the opponent, and instant responses to news stories. Campaigns can post ads and videos of candidates for journalists to use in their reports. The new media make available reams of election-related content—an endless swirl of poll data, commentary, speculation on sites such as RealClearPolitics.com, Politico.com, and HuffingtonPost.com. Partisan argument abounds on blogs such as Daily Kos and Instapundit, providing insights, passion, humor, and rambling screeds.

The electoral environment, with its plethora of traditional and new media sources, can overwhelm voters with information. Despite this abundance, voters are not well informed about issues, which take a back seat to the horserace in campaign reporting.

Journalists check the accuracy of candidates' statements, compare past votes and positions with current assertions, and analyze political advertisements. The media themselves are watched, checked, and corrected by sites like campaigndesk.org, mediamatters.org, and daily-howler.com. Yet, it is challenging for reporters to fact-check carefully and meet the demands of the twenty-four-hour news cycle. Bloggers and other commentators who are not schooled in journalistic practices and ethics can disseminate information without checking its veracity. As a result, voters increasingly encounter misleading information during elections. Forty-two percent of voters believed that Barack Obama was not born in the United States, a fallacy that was widely circulated in all types of media and persisted in the 2016 election when Obama was not a candidate.[181]

Candidates must be more guarded than ever. Any careless or provocative comment can be caught on camera and immediately distributed around the world. Incidents from the past, preserved on tape, can haunt candidates. A media feeding frenzy developed around Delaware Republican Senate candidate Christine O'Donnell, who was backed by the Tea Party, as a result of statements that she had made on *Politically Incorrect* with Bill Maher in 1999 that she had "dabbled in witchcraft" when she was in high school. The clip was circulated through social media and made national news. O'Donnell lost the election. Hillary Clinton in 2016 was caught off-guard making a statement to a group of campaign donors where she appeared to refer to Donald Trump's supporters as a "basket of deplorables," a statement that was reported only in part.

## Key Takeaway

The campaign media environment in the information age is complex and fast paced. Candidates, voters, and journalists must contend with a wide array of old and new media platforms. While traditional media primarily serve to inform voters, new media also involve voters in campaigns and help them to interact with others. Candidates' appearances in entertainment media as well as discussions on commentary programs can influence voters' perceptions. Today, candidates face intensive scrutiny not only from journalists but also from average people who report their actions using new media.

## Exercises

1. What social media platforms do you use? How does the way people use social media differ from the way they use newspapers and broadcast media?
2. How do candidates use the media to control their image? If you could give advice to candidates trying to improve their image, what would it be?

## Civic Education

### Young People Taking Part in Campaigns and Elections

One of the primary goals of American civic education is to prepare young people to take part in election campaigns. Traditionally, this involves studying the democratic principles underlying elections, learning how the electoral process works, registering to vote and locating a polling place, and acquiring the basic skills necessary to follow campaigns through mainstream media. All of these things are fundamental precursors to exercising the right to vote.

In the current era, civic education also needs to take into account the new ways that people are engaging in elections. The next generation of voters should be schooled in how social media and other digital tools can be used in campaigns. Young people have been effective in developing new media election applications. They have innovated with established formats, such as campaign websites and blogs, to produce content that is more appealing to younger voters. Online versions of college newspapers have featured first-person accounts of campaign events using streaming video and interviews with candidates from dorm rooms. Young people were among the first to use Facebook, YouTube, and Twitter for campaign participation. As the number of platforms continues to evolve, such as microblogging sites like Tumblr, young voters will surely be among the first to develop them for campaign use.

Young people are ahead of the curve in using new media, compelling candidates to catch up. While candidates have incorporated social media into their campaigns, they have not always made good use of these platforms. Young citizens can be essential to campaign organizations in getting candidates up to speed with new media.

### Link

**Rock the Vote**

The Rock the Vote website offers a gateway to participation in elections. It includes a feature called "Democracy Class" that provides interactive lesson plans for teaching about civics and the voting process, including new media use. Learn more about Rock the Vote's mission at their website.

# 11.12 Recommended Reading


Bartels, Larry, and Lynn Vavreck, eds. *Campaign Reform*. Ann Arbor: University of Michigan Press, 2000. Thoughtful proposals to reform all aspects of the campaign process.

Box-Steffensmeier, Janet M., and Steven E. Schier, eds. *The American Elections of 2008*. Lanham, MD: Rowman & Littlefield, 2009.

Box-Steffensmeir, Janet M., and Steven E. Schier, eds. *The American Elections of 2012*. Lanham, MD: Rowman & Littlefield, 2009.

Cornog, Evan (text), and Richard Whelan (illustrations selected and captioned). *Hats in the Ring: An Illustrated History of American Presidential Campaigns*. New York: Random House, 2000. Instructive summaries accompanied by well-chosen illustrations of presidential campaigns.

Foot, Kirsten A., and Steven M. Schneider. *Web Campaigning*. Cambridge, MA: MIT Press, 2006. A study of web practices based on numerous sites.

Hart, Roderick P. *Campaign Talk: Why Elections Are Good for Us*. Princeton, NJ: Princeton University Press, 2000. An unusual appraisal of election campaigns as a means to sustain democracy through the dialogue among candidates, the media, and the public.

Hollihan, Thomas A. *Uncivil Wars: Political Campaigns in a Media Age*, 2nd ed. Boston: Bedford/St. Martins, 2009. A text covering all aspects of the campaign process.

Jacobson, Gary C. *The Politics of Congressional Elections*, 5th ed. New York: Longman, 2001. A comprehensive and systematic text.

Just, Marion R., Ann N. Crigler, Dean E. Alger, Timothy E. Cook, Montague Kern, and Darrell M. West. *Crosstalk: Citizens, Candidates, and the Media in a Presidential Campaign*. Chicago: University of Chicago Press, 1996. Award-winning, comprehensive study of the interactions of candidates, the public, and all forms of media in the 1992 presidential election.

Schill, Dan, and John Allen Hindricks, eds. *The Presidency and Social Media: Discourse, Disruption, and Digital Democracy in the 2016 Presidential Election*. New York: Routledge, 2017.

Schroeder, Alan. *Presidential Debates: Fifty Years of High-Risk TV*, 2nd ed. New York: Columbia University Press, 2008. An exhaustive survey of and discussion of all aspects of debates.

Skelley, Jeffrey, and Larry Sabato, eds. *Trumped: The 2016 Election that Broke All the Rules*. Lanham, MD: Rowman and Littlefield, 2017. An overview of the 2016 election campaign covering campaign dynamics and the media's role.

Towner, Terri, and Jody Baumgartner, eds. *Social Media and the 2016 Presidential Election Campaign*. New York, Lexington Books, 2017. A collection of cutting-edge research studies on the role of social media in elections.

West, Darrell M. *Air Wars: Television Advertising in Election Campaigns 1952–2004*, 4th ed. Washington, DC: CQ Press, 2005. A major study of the contents and effects of political advertising.

Williams, Christine B., and Bruce I. Newman, eds. *Social Media, Political Marketing and the 2016 U.S. Election*. New York: Routledge, 2018.

# 11.13 Recommended Viewing

*The Best Man* (1964). Film version of Gore Vidal's mordant portrayal of the candidates' machinations at a convention to become their party's presidential nominee.

*Bob Roberts* (1992). A fake documentary about a folksinging conservative candidate (Tim Robbins) that shows elections reduced by the media to easy entertainment.

*Boogie Man: The Lee Atwater Story* (2008). A documentary chronicling the career of the Republican mastermind of contemporary slash-and-burn election campaigns.

*The Campaign* (2012). A comedic take on congressional elections as a naive candidate is funded by corrupt billionaires.

*The Candidate* (1972). The classic "authentic" campaign movie in which a candidate (Robert Redford) increasingly compromises his ideals as he is seduced by the prospects of victory.

*The Front Runner* (2018). Gary Hart, the leading candidate for the Democratic presidential nomination in 1988, is brought down by an extramarital relationship exposed by reporters from *The Miami Herald*.

*Game Change* (2012). A dramatized account of the 2008 presidential campaign of Republican John McCain and his running mate Sarah Palin.

*Journeys with George* (2001). A network television producer's droll video diary of herself and the press covering George W. Bush's 2000 presidential campaign.

*The Last Hurrah* (1958). In John Ford's film, a machine-politics, big-city mayor (Spencer Tracy) seeks reelection at a time when television media image-making is taking over campaigns.

*Medium Cool* (1969). Radical in content and form: the clashes between police and demonstrators at the 1968 Democratic National Convention as seen from the perspective of a news cameraman.

*Our Brand Is Crisis* (2015). American political consultants attempt to reelect a controversial politician in Bolivia using techniques prevalent in U.S. campaigns.

*Primary* (1960). The first documentary on a campaign focuses on candidates Senators John F. Kennedy and Hubert H. Humphrey in Wisconsin's 1960 presidential primary.

*Unprecedented: The 2000 Presidential Election* (2002). A corrosive documentary about the contest between Governor George W. Bush and Vice President Al Gore for Florida.

*The War Room* (1993). A riveting documentary about the people, particularly James Carville, running Bill Clinton's 1992 presidential campaign.

# Endnotes

1. Shira Gabriel, Elaine Parvati, and Melanie C. Green, "From *Apprentice* to President: The Role of Parasocial Connection in the Election of Donald Trump," *Social Psychology and Personality Science*, vol. 9, no. 3: 299-301, 2018.
2. Rebecca Ruiz, "How the Clinton Campaign Is Slaying Social Media," *Mashable*, July 15, 2016.
3. Sarah Mucha, "Biden Campaign Grows Digital Operation to Contend with Virtual Trail," *CNN Politics*, June 24, 2020. https://www.cnn.com/2020/06/24/politics/biden-campaign-digital-staff/index.html.
4. Paul S. Herrnson, *Congressional Elections: Campaigning at Home and in Washington*, 5th ed. (Washington, DC: CQ Press, 2007), 75.
5. Brody Mullins, "Cost of 2008 Election Cycle: $5.3 Billion," *Wall Street Journal*, October 23, 2008.
6. Russ Choma, "The 2012 Election: Our Price Tag (Finally) for the Whole Ball of Wax," *Center for Responsive Politics*, March 13, 2013. Accessed July 9, 2014 http://www.opensecrets.org/news/2013/03/the-2012-election-our-price-tag-fin/.
7. Open Secrets, "Cost of 2018 Election to Surpass $5 Billion, CRP Projects," October 17, 2018. Accessed November 12, 2018. https://www.opensecrets.org/news/2018/10/cost-of-2018-election/.
8. The Federal Election Commission was still compiling data on 2016 races as of July 2017.
9. "2020 Election to Cost $14 Billion, Blowing Away Spending Records," *OpenSecrets.org*, October 28, 2020. httos://www.opensecrets.org/news/2020/10/cost-of-2020-election-14billion-update/.

10. "Two Cars in Every Garage, Three Eyes on Every Fish," *The Simpsons*, November 1990.
11. See Bradley A. Smith, *Unfree Speech: The Folly of Campaign Finance Reform* (Princeton, NJ: Princeton University Press, 2001); and John Samples, *The Fallacy of Campaign Finance Reform* (Chicago: University of Chicago Press, 2006).
12. *Buckley v. Valeo*, 424 US 1 (1976).
13. Adam Liptak, "Supreme Court Strikes Down Overall Donation Cap," *The New York Times*, April 25, 2014. Accessed July 9, 2014. http://www.nytimes.com/2014/04/03/us/politics/supreme-court-ruling-on-campaign-contributions.htm?_r=0.
14. Dan Froomkin, "Special Report: Campaign Finance: Overview Part 4, Soft Money—A Look at the Loopholes," *Washington Post*, September 4, 1998.
15. John Shinkle, "Soft Money Is Back—And Both Parties Are Cashing In," *Politico*, August 4, 2017. https://www.politico.com/magazine/story/2017/08/04/soft-money-is-backand-both-parties-are-cashing-in-215456.
16. *McConnell v. Federal Election Commission*, 540 US 93 (2003).
17. *Citizens United v. Federal Election Commission*, 130 S.Ct. 876 (2010).
18. Adam Liptak, "Justices 5–4, Reject Corporate Spending Limit," *The New York Times*, January 21, 2010.
19. Ian Vandewalker, "Campaign Finance Victories in 2020 Elections," *Brennan Center for Justice*, December 1, 2020. https://www.brennancenter.org/our-work/analysis-opinion/campaign-finance-victories-2020-elections.
20. Campaign finance data for the 2012 and 2016 campaigns are available from the Federal Election Commission. "Presidential Campaign Finance: Contributions to All Candidates for the Presidential Election Cycle." http://www.fec.gov/disclosurep/pnational.do; Stacy Montemayor, Pete Quist, Karl Evers-Hillstrom, and Douglas Weber, "Joint Report Reveals Record Donations in 2020 State and Federal Races," FollowThe-Money.org., Novembe 19, 2020. https://www.followthemoney.org/research/institute-reports/joint-report-reveals-record-donations-in-2020-state-and-federal-races.
21. "2020 Outside Spending, by Super Pac," *OpenSecrets.org*, May 18, 2021. https://www.opensecrets.org/outsidespending/summ.php?chrt=V&type=S.
22. Campaign Finance Institute, "Non-Party Spending Doubled in 2010 But Did Not Dictate the Results" press release, November 5, 2010.
23. The Center for Responsive Politics tracks 527 committee spending at this site: https://www.opensecrets.org/527s/index.php.
24. Jane Mayer, *Dark Money: The Hidden History of the Billionaires Behind the Rise of the Radical Right* (New York: Doubleday, 2016). Ciara Torres-Spelliscy, "The 2018 Elections Have $100 Million in Dark Money and Counting," The Brennan Center, October 22, 2018. https://www.brennancenter.org/blog/2018-elections-dark-money.
25. Anna Massoglia and Karl Evers-Hillstrom, "'Dark Money' Topped $1 Billion in 2020, Largely Boosting Democrats," *Opensecrets.org*, March 17, 2021. https://www.opensecrets.org/news/2021/03/one-billion-dark-money-2020-electioncycle/.
26. Sasha Issenberg, "How Obama's Team Used Big Data to Rally Voters," MIT Technology Review, December 19, 2012. https://www.technologyreview.com/s/509026/how-obamas-team-used-big-data-to-rally-voters/.
27. Meta S. Brown, "Big Data Analytics and the Next President: How Microtargeting Drives Today's Campaigns," Forbes, May 29, 2016.
28. Kevin Granville, "Facebook and Cambridge Analytica: What You Need to Know as Fallout Widens," *The New York Times*, March 19, 2018. https://www.nytimes.com/2018/03/19/technology/facebook-cambridge-analytica-explained.html.
29. Joseph Turrow, Michael X. Delli Carpini, Nora A. Draper, and Rowan Howard-Williams, "Americans Roundly Reject Tailored Political Advertising," Departmental Papers, Annenberg School for Communication. Philadelphia, PA: University of Pennsylvania, July 2012. https://repository.upenn.edu/cgi/viewcontent.cgi?article=1414&context=asc_papers.
30. Tate Ryan-Mosley, "The Technology That Powers the 2020 Campaigns, Explained," MIT Technology Review, September 28, 2020. https://www.technologyreview.com/2020/09/28/1008994/the-technology-that-powers-political-campaigns-in-2020-explained/.
31. Pew Research Center, "Political Polarization in the American Public," Washington, DC, June 12, 2014. https://www.people-press.org/2014/06/12/political-polarization-in-the-american-public/?beta=true&utm_expid=53098246-2.Lly4CFSVQG2lphsg-Koplg.1&utm_referrer=https://www.google.com/.
32. Owen, Diana. "Media Coverage of the 2020 Election: Journalists and Influencers in the Misinformation Age," in Larry Sabato, Kyle Kondik, and J. Miles Coleman, eds. *A Return to Normalcy? The 2020 Election that (Almost) Broke America*. Lanham, MD: Rowman and Littlefield, 2021: 167-184.
33. D. Sunshine Hillygus and Todd G. Shields, *The Persuadable Voter: Wedge Issues in Presidential Campaigns* (Princeton, NJ: Princeton University Press, 2008).
34. For an award-winning study of media in the 1992 presidential election, see Marion R. Just, Ann N. Crigler, Dean E. Alger, Timothy E. Cook, Montague Kern, and Darrell M. West, *Crosstalk: Citizens, Candidates, and the Media in a Presidential Campaign* (Chicago: University of Chicago Press, 1996).
35. Thomas E. Patterson. *Out of Order*. New York: Alfred A. Knopf, 1994.
36. Bruce Bimber and Richard Davis. *Campaigning Online: The Internet in U.S. Elections*. New York: Oxford University Press, 2003.
37. David Plouffe. *The Audacity to Win*. New York: Viking, 2009.
38. John Heilemann and Mark Halperin. *Game Change*. New York: Harper, 2010.
39. Nolan D. McCaskill, "Trump Credits Social Media for His Election," *Politico*, October 20, 2017. https://www.politico.com/story/2017/10/20/trump-social-media-election-244009.
40. Mark Murray, "As Howard Dean's 'Scream' Turns 15, Its Impact on American Politics Lives On," NBC News, January 17, 2019. https://www.nbcnews.com/politics/meet-the-press/howard-dean-s-scream-turns-15-its-impact-american-politics-n959916.
41. David Corn, "SECRET VIDEO: Romney Tells Millionaire Donors What He REALLY Thinks of Obama Voters," *Mother Jones*, September 17, 2012. https://www.motherjones.com/politics/2012/09/secret-video-romney-private-fundraiser/.
42. Katie Reilly, "Read Hillary Clinton's 'Basket of Deplorables' Remarks About Donald Trump Supporters," *Time*, September 10, 2016. http://time.com/4486502/hillary-clinton-basket-of-deplorables-transcript/.
43. Monica Anderson, "TV Still the Top Source for Election Results, But Digital Platforms Rise." Washington, DC: Pew Research Center, November 21, 2016. https://www.pewresearch.org/fact-tank/2016/11/21/tv-still-the-top-source-for-election-results-but-digital-platforms-rise/.
44. Stuart Soroka, "News Coverage of the 2020 Presidential Election," Institute for Social Research, Center for Political Studies, University of Michigan, October 16, 2020. https://cpsblog.isr.umich.edu/?p=2871.
45. Thomas E. Patterson, "News Coverage of the 2016 General Election: How the Press Failed the Voters," Cambridge, MA: Shorenstein Center on Media, Politics and Public Policy, Harvard Kennedy School, December 7, 2016. https://shorensteincenter.org/news-coverage-2016-general-election/.
46. Thomas E. Patterson, "Tale of Two Elections: CBS and Fox News' Portrayal of the 2020 Presidential Campaign," Shorenstein Center on Media, Politics, and Public Policy, Harvard Kennedy School, December 17, 2020. https://shorensteincenter.org/patterson-2020-election-coverage/.
47. Mary Matalin and James Carville, with Peter Knobler, *All's Fair: Love, War, and Running for President* (New York: Random House, 1994), 185.
48. Thomas E. Patterson, "Tale of Two Elections: CBS and Fox News' Portrayal of the 2020 Presidential Campaign," Shorenstein Center on Media, Politics, and Public Policy, Harvard Kennedy School, December 17, 2020. https://shorensteincenter.org/patterson-2020-election-coverage/.
49. See Stephen J. Farnsworth and S. Robert Lichter, *The Nightly News Nightmare: Television's Coverage of U.S. Presidential Elections, 1988–2004*, 2nd ed. (Lanham, MD: Rowman & Littlefield, 2007) for an analysis and denunciation of the television news networks' coverage of presidential elections.
50. See Edwin Diamond and Stephen Bates, *The Spot* (Cambridge, MA: MIT Press, 1992); and Kathleen Hall Jamieson, *Packaging the Presidency*, 3rd ed. (New York: Oxford University Press, 1996).
51. Ted Brader, *Campaigning for Hearts and Minds* (Chicago: University of Chicago Press, 2006).
52. For a discussion of how candidates go negative as circumstances warrant or allow, see Emmett H. Buell Jr. and Lee Sigelman, *Attack Politics: Negativity in Presidential Campaigns since 1960* (Lawrence: University Press of Kansas, 2008).
53. See Michael M. Franz, Paul B. Freedman, Kenneth M. Goldstein, and Travis N. Ridout, *Campaign Advertising and American Democracy* (Philadelphia, PA: Temple University Press, 2008); and John G. Geer, *In Defense of Negativity: Attack Ads in Presidential Campaigns* (Chicago: University of Chicago Press, 2006). "Multivitamin" quote is from Michael M. Franz, Paul B. Freedman, Kenneth M. Goldstein, and Travis N. Ridout, *Campaign Advertising and American Democracy* (Philadelphia: Temple University Press, 2008), 143 and "crack" quote by Senator Tom Daschle is from John G. Geer, *In Defense of Negativity: Attack Ads in Presidential Campaigns* (Chicago: University of Chicago Press, 2006), 1.
54. Michael Pfau and Henry C. Kenski, *Attack Politics* (New York: Praeger, 1990), 53.
55. On debates, see Alan Schroeder, *Presidential Debates: Fifty Years of High-Risk TV*, 2nd ed. (New York: Columbia University Press, 2008); and Newton N. Minow and Craig L. LaMay, *Inside the Presidential Debates: Their Improbable Past and Promising Future* (Chicago: University of Chicago Press, 2008).
56. Diana Owen, "The Debate Challenge," in *Presidential Campaign Discourse*, ed. Kathleen E. Kendall (Albany: State University of New York Press, 1995), 135–55.
57. Shane Goldmacher, "Six Takeaways from the First Presidential Debate," *The New York Times*, September 30, 2020. https://www.nytimes.com/2020/09/30/us/politics/debate-takeaways.html.
58. Costas Panagopoulos, ed., *Rewiring Politics: Presidential Nominating Conventions in the Media Age* (Baton Rouge: Louisiana State University Press, 2007).
59. Zephyr Teachout and Thomas Streeter, eds., *Mousepads, Shoe Leather, and Hope* (Boulder, CO: Paradigm, 2008).
60. For the campaign from the consultants' perspectives, see Kathleen Hall Jamieson, ed., *Electing the President, 2004: The Insider's View* (Philadelphia: University of Pennsylvania Press, 2005).
61. Content analysis provided by Media Tenor.

62. Lori Cox Han and Caroline Heldman, eds., *Rethinking Madam President: Are We Ready for a Woman in the White House?* (Boulder, CO: Lynne Rienner Publishers, 2007); also Jennifer Lawless and Richard L. Fox, *It Takes a Candidate: Why Women Don't Run for Office* (New York: Cambridge University Press, 2005).
63. Matthew R. Kerbel, *Netroots* (Boulder, CO: Paradigm Press, 2009).
64. Janet M. Box-Steffensmeier and Steven E. Schier, eds. *The American Elections of 2012* New York: Routledge, 2013.
65. *The Caucus, The New York Times Blog*, August 31, 2012. Accessed July 11, 2014 http://thecaucus.blogs.nytimes.com/2012/08/31/doh-east-woods-convention-speech-spawns-fake-simpsons-meme/.
66. Mark Halperin and John Heilemann, *Double Down: Game Change in 2012* (New York: Penguin, 2013).
67. Diana Owen, "The Campaign and the Media," in Janet M. Box-Steffensmeier and Steven E. Schier, eds. *The American Elections of 2012* New York: Routledge, 2013.
68. Jim Rutenberg and Ashley Parker,"Romney Says Remarks on Voters Help Clarify Position," *New York Times*, September 18, 2012. Accessed July 10, 2014 http://www.nytimes.com/2012/09/19/us/politics/in-leaked-video-romney-says-middle-east-peace-process-likely-to-remain-unsolved-problem.html.
69. Jena McGregor, "In Superstorm Sandy, Gov. Chris Christie Praises Obama's Crisis Leadership," *Washington Post*, October 30, 2012. Accessed July 11, 2014 http://www.washingtonpost.com/national/on-leadership/in-superstorm-sandy-new-jersey-governor-chris-christie-praises-president-obamas-crisis-leadership/2012/10/30/89769e32-22b5-11e2-ac85-e669876c6a24_story.html.
70. Brittany Darwell, "Obama and Romney Facebook Stores and Donation Apps Tied for Users," *Inside Facebook*, November 6, 2012. Accessed July 11, 2014 http://www.insidefacebook.com/2012/11/06/obama-and-romney-facebook-stores-and-donation-apps-tied-for-users-but-obama-2012-app-beats-commit-to-mitt/.
71. Kenneth Rosen,"Who Spent More on Online Ads This Election?," *Mashable*, November 5, 2012. Accessed July 11, 2014 http://mashable.com/2012/11/05/online-ads-election.
72. Gregory Krieg, "Here are the Memorable Quotes From the Republican Debate," CNN, February 13, 2016. http://www.cnn.com/2016/02/13/politics/republican-debate-best-quotes/index.html.
73. Katie Zezima, "Cruz Defends Wife From Trump Attack," *Washington Post*, March 23, 2016. https://www.washingtonpost.com/news/post-politics/wp/2016/03/23/cruz-defends-wife-from-trump-attack/?utm_term=.f70933d41ef0.
74. Derek Willis, "Hillary Clinton and the 2016 Democrats: Mostly Liberal, Together," *New York Times*, February 15, 2015.
75. Young Democrats Flock to Bernie Sanders, Spurning Hillary Clinton's Polish and Poise," *New York Times*, February 24, 2016.
76. Anne Gearan and Abby Phillip, "Clinton Regrets 1996 Remark on 'Super Predators" After Encounter With Activist," *Washington Post*, February 26, 2016.
77. Laura Morgan Roberts and Robin J. Ely, "Why Did So Many White Women Vote for Donald Trump?"*Fortune*, November 17, 2016. http://fortune.com/2016/11/17/donald-trump-women-voters-election/.
78. Diana Owen, "Twitter Rants, Press Bashing, and Fake News: The Shameful Legacy of Media in the 2016 Election," in Larry J. Sabato, Kyle Kondik, and Geoffrey Skelley, eds., *Trumped: The 2016 Election that Broke All the Rules.*
79. Alexander Burns, Matt Flegenheimer, Jasmine C. Lee, Lisa Lerer, and Jonathan Martin, "Who's Running for President in 2020?" *The New York Times*, April 8, 2020. https://www.nytimes.com/interactive/2019/us/politics/2020-presidential-candidates.html.
80. Jacob Pramuk, "Here Are the Democrats Who Gained and Lost the Most in the First 2020 Presidential Primary Debate," *CNBC*, June 27, 2019. https://www.cnbc.com/2019/06/27/2020-democratic-presidential-primary-debate-winners-and-losers.html.
81. Lexington, "Joe Biden Struggles in the Democratic Primary Debate," *The Economist*, June 28, 2019. https://www.economist.com/democracy-in-america/2019/06/28/joe-biden-struggles-in-the-democratic-primary-debate.
82. Tanner Curtis, Antonio de Luca, Thomas Kaplan, and Umi Syam, "Joe Biden's Long Road to the Presidency," *The New York Times*, January 20, 2021. https://www.nytimes.com/interactive/2021/01/20/us/politics/joe-biden-photos.html.
83. John Wagner and Felicia Sonmez, "Election Highlights: Buttigieg, Klobuchar, Beto O'Rourke and Harry Reid Endorse Biden," *The Washington Post*, March 2, 2020. https://www.washingtonpost.com/politics/2020/03/02/campaign-live-updates/.
84. Sydney Ember, "Sanders Suspends Campaign: 'I Do Not Make This Decision Lightly,'" *The New York Times*, April 8, 2020. https://www.nytimes.com/2020/04/08/us/politics/bernie-sanders-drops-out.html.
85. Alexander Burns, Jonathan Martin, and Katie Glueck, "How Biden Chose Harris: A Search That Forged New Stars, Friends and Rivalries," *The New York Times*, August 13, 2020. https://www.nytimes.com/2020/08/13/us/politics/biden-harris.html.
86. Alex Seitz-Wald, "More GOP Challengers Line Up Against Trump, More States Cancel Their Primaries," *NBC News*, September 9, 2019. https://www.nbcnews.com/politics/2020-election/more-gop-challengers-line-against-trump-more-states-cancel-their-n1051511.
87. William J. Kole, "'Calamari Comeback': Tiniest State's DNC Video Gets Big Buzz," *Associated Press*, August 19, 2020. https://apnews.com/article/9d8f36096c3b28f0e7f2052f0b190837.
88. Elaine Kamarck, "Joe Biden's Convention Was About the Content of Our Character," *FixGov, The Brookings Institution*, August 21, 2020. https://www.brookings.edu/blog/fixgov/2020/08/21/joe-bidens-convention-was-about-the-content-of-our-character/.
89. Jonathan Martin, Alexander Burns, and Annie Karni, "Nominating Trump, Republicans Rewrite His Record," *The New York Times*, August 24, 2020. https://www.nytimes.com/2020/08/24/us/politics/republican-convention-recap.html.
90. Ed Mazza, "Trump's Mask-Free White House Speech A Potential 'Super-Spreader Event,'' *HuffPost*, August 28, 2020.
91. Jonathan Chait, "Biden's Campaign Has a New, Populist Theme. Will It Work?" *New York Magazine*, September 18, 2020. https://nymag.com/intelligencer/2020/09/bidens-campaign-scranton-park-avenue-theme-economic-populism-trump.html.
92. Jeffrey Goldberg, "Trump: Americans Who Died in War Are 'Losers' and 'Suckers,'" *The Atlantic*, September 3, 2020. https://www.theatlantic.com/politics/archive/2020/09/trump-americans-who-died-at-war-are-losers-and-suckers/615997/.
93. Gerald F. Seib, "Biden's Election Formula: It's About Two Big Themes, Man," *The Wall Street Journal*, October 12, 2020. https://www.wsj.com/articles/bidens-election-formula-its-about-two-big-themes-man-11602512600.
94. Annie Linskey, "Biden's New Campaign Website Drives Unity Theme by Incorporating Ideas from Former Rivals," *The Washington Post*, August 5, 2020. https://www.washingtonpost.com/politics/bidens-new-campaign-website-drives-unity-theme-by-incorporating-ideas-from-former-rivals/2020/08/04/dd1337b4-d6bf-11ea-9c3b-dfc394c03988_story.html.
95. Philip Elliott, "'Let's Stop Fighting and Let's Start Fixing.' Joe Biden Settles on Election Theme," *Time*, May 20, 2020. https://time.com/5591469/joe-biden-campaign-launch-philadelphia-2/.
96. Michael Albertus, 'Why Trump's Border Wall Failed," The Monkey Cage, *The Washington Post*, February 17, 2021. https://www.washingtonpost.com/politics/2021/02/17/why-trumps-border-wall-failed/.
97. Philip Bump, "210 000 Deaths Later, Trump Reverts to Comparing the Coronavirus to the Flu," *The Washington Post*, October 6, 2020. https://www.washingtonpost.com/politics/2020/10/06/210000-deaths-later-trump-reverts-comparing-coronavirus-flu/.
98. Nicholas Reimann, "Some Americans Are Tragically Still Drinking Bleach As a Coronavirus 'Cure,'" *Forbes*, August 24, 2020. https://www.forbes.com/sites/nicholasreimann/2020/08/24/some-americans-are-tragically-still-drinking-bleach-as-a-coronavirus-cure/?sh=788154e86748.
99. Susan Glasser, "Donald Trump's 2020 Superspreader Campaign: A Diary," *The New Yorker*, October 26, 2020. https://www.newyorker.com/news/letter-from-trumps-washington/donald-trumps-2020-super-spreader-campaign-a-diary.
100. Kathryn Krawczyk, "Trump's New Campaign Slogan Is Apparently 'Make America Great Again—Again,'" *The Week*, July 17, 2020. https://theweek.com/speedreads/926237/trumps-new-campaign-slogan-apparently-make-america-great-again--again.
101. Daniel Dale, "Fact Check: At Florida Rally, Trump Continues His Attacks Against Imaginary Version of Joe Biden," *CNN Politics*, October 13, 2020. https://www.cnn.com/2020/10/13/politics/fact-check-trump-biden-sanford-florida-rally/index.html.
102. Nicholas Bogel-Burroughs and Sandra E. Garcia, "What Is Antifa, the Movement Trump Wants to Declare a Terror Group?" *The New York Times*, September 28, 2020. https://www.nytimes.com/article/what-antifa-trump.html.
103. Barbara Guitierrez, "Conspiracy Theories Abound This Election Season," News@TheU, University of Miami, October 7, 2020. https://news.miami.edu/stories/2020/10/conspiracy-theories-abound-this-election-season.html; Mike Wendling, "QAnon: What Is It and Where Did It Come From?" *BBC News*. January 7, 2021. https://www.bbc.com/news/53498434.
104. Susan Glasser, "Donald Trump's 2020 Superspreader Campaign: A Diary," *The New Yorker*, October 26, 2020. https://www.newyorker.com/news/letter-from-trumps-washington/donald-trumps-2020-super-spreader-campaign-a-diary.
105. Jacob Jarvis, "Donald Trump, 'King of Twitter,' Is Being Outperformed by Joe Biden," *Newsweek*, September 29, 2020. https://www.newsweek.com/donald-trump-joe-biden-twitter-facebook-comparison-1534671.
106. David Bauder, "Debate Commission Says It Will Make Changes to Format," *ABC News*, September 30, 2020. https://abcnews.go.com/Entertainment/wireStory/moderator-chris-wallace-debate-runaway-train-73331763.
107. The Commission on Presidential Debates, "Moderator Announces Topics for First Presidential Debate," *Debates.org*, September 22, 2020. https://www.debates.org/2020/09/22/moderator-announces-topics-for-first-presidential-debate-2/.

108. Neil Vigdor, "'Will You Shut Up, Man' Quickly Becomes a Biden Campaign T-shirt," *The New York Times*, September 30, 2020. https://www.nytimes.com/2020/09/30/us/elections/will-you-shut-up-man-quickly-becomes-a-biden-campaign-t-shirt.html.
109. Jeremy Stahl, "We Counted Every Single Time Trump Interrupted During the First Presidential Debate," *Slate*, September 30, 2020. https://slate.com/news-and-politics/2020/09/trump-interruptions-first-presidential-debate-biden.html.
110. Shane Goldmacher, "Six Takeaways From the First Presidential Debate," *The New York Times*, September 30, 2020. https://www.nytimes.com/2020/09/30/us/politics/debate-takeaways.html.
111. Scott Neuman, "Trump Now Says He Condemns 'All White Supremacists,' After Declining to at Debate," *NPR.org*, October 1, 2020. https://www.npr.org/sections/live-updates-protests-for-racial-justice/2020/10/01/919375470/trump-now-says-he-condemns-all-white-supremacists-after-declining-to-at-debate.
112. Melissa Macaya, Fernando Alfonso III, Veronica Rocha, Jessica Estepa, and Kyle Blaine, "2020 Vice Presidential Debate," *CNN*, November 23, 2020. https://www.cnn.com/politics/live-news/vp-debate-coverage-fact-check-10-07-20/index.html.
113. Quint Forgey, "'I Didn't Know He Was There': Pence Says He Wasn't Bugged by Debate Fly," *Politico*, October 12, 2020. https://www.cnn.com/politics/live-news/vp-debate-coverage-fact-check-10-07-20/index.html.
114. Peter Baker and Maggie Haberman, "Trump Tests Positive for the Coronavirus," *The New York Times*, October 2, 2020. https://www.nytimes.com/2020/10/02/us/politics/trump-covid.html.
115. Michael M. Grynbaum and John Koblin, "Biden Beats Trump in Ratings Battle of the Network Town Halls," *The New York Times*, October 26, 2020. https://www.nytimes.com/2020/10/16/business/media/biden-trump-town-hall-ratings.html.
116. Kevin Breuniger, "Here Are the Key Moments from the Final Trump-Biden Presidential Debate," *CNBC*, October 22, 2020. https://www.cnbc.com/2020/10/22/final-presidential-debate-highlights-trump-vs-biden.html.
117. Visual and Data Journalism Team, "U.S. Election 2020 Polls: Who Is Ahead—Trump or Biden," *BBC News*, November 3, 2020. https://www.bbc.com/news/election-us-2020-53657174.
118. Grace Panetta, "What You Need to Know Abou US Postal Service's Funding Crisis, and How It Could Impact Your Vote in the November Election," *Business Insider*, August 14, 2020. https://www.businessinsider.com/us-postal-service-delay-funding-crisis-mail-election-trump-explainer-2020-8.
119. Eugene Kiely and Rem Rieder, "Trump's Repeated False Attacks on Mail-In Ballots," *FactCheck.org*, September 25, 2020. https://www.factcheck.org/2020/09/trumps-repeated-false-attacks-on-mail-in-ballots/.
120. Devlin Barrett, "FBI Director Affirms Russia's Aim to 'Denigrate' Biden Ahead of Election," *The Washington Post*, September 17, 2020. https://www.washingtonpost.com/national-security/wray-fbi-election-security-threats-hearing/2020/09/16/4461526e-f869-11ea-a275-1a2c2d36e1f1_story.html.
121. National Conference of State Legislatures, "Absentee and Mail Voting Policies in Effect for the 2020 Election," https://www.ncsl.org/research/elections-and-campaigns/absentee-and-mail-voting-policies-in-effect-for-the-2020-election.aspx; Miles Parks, "Rule Changes in Swing States Mean More Votes Will Count, Results May Take Longer," *NPR.org*, September 23, 2020. https://www.npr.org/2020/09/23/916012284/rule-changes-in-swing-states-mean-more-votes-will-count-results-may-take-longer.
122. Pew Research Center, "The Voting Experience in 2020," *U.S. Politics & Policy*, November 20, 2020. https://www.pewresearch.org/politics/2020/11/20/the-voting-experience-in-2020/.
123. David Wasserman, Sophie Andrews, Leo Saenger, Lev Cohen, Ally Flinn, and Griff Tatarsky, "2020 National Vote Tracker," *The Cook Political Report*, January 21, 2021. https://cookpolitical.com/2020-national-popular-vote-tracker.
124. Cooper Gatewood and Ciaran O'Connor, Disinformation Briefing: Narratives around Black Lives Matter and Voter Fraud. *Research Report*. London: ISD, 2020. file:///C:/Users/owend/Dropbox/2020 Election Book Chapters/Disinfo-Briefing-BLM-and-Voter-Fraud.pdf.
125. William Cummings, Joey Garrison, and Jim Sergent, "By the Numbers: President Donald Trump's Failed Efforts to Overturn the Election," *USA Today*, January 6, 2021. https://www.usatoday.com/in-depth/news/politics/elections/2021/01/06/trumps-failed-efforts-overturn-election-numbers/4130307001/.
126. Amy Gardner, "'I Just Want to Find 11,780 Votes': In Extraordinary Hour-Long Call, Trump Pressures Georgia Secretary of State to Recalculate the Vote in His Favor," *The Washington Post*, January 3, 2021. https://www.washingtonpost.com/politics/trump-raffensperger-call-georgia-vote/2021/01/03/d45acb92-4dc4-11eb-bda4-615aaefd0555_story.html.
127. Sheera Frenkel, "How Misinformation 'Superspreaders' Seed False Election Theories," *The New York Times*, November 23, 2020. https://www.nytimes.com/2020/11/23/technology/election-misinformation-facebook-twitter.html.
128. Dan Barry and Sheera Frenkel, "'Be There. Will Be Wild!': Trump All but Circled the Date," *The New York Times*, January 6, 2021. https://www.nytimes.com/2021/01/06/us/politics/capitol-mob-trump-supporters.html.
129. Read Trump's Jan. 6 Speech, A Key Part Of Impeachment Trial. *NPR*, February 10, 2021. Retrieved from: https://www.npr.org/2021/02/10/966396848/read-trumps-jan-6-speech-a-key-part-of-impeachment-trial.
130. Steve Holland, Jeff Mason, and Jonathan Landay, "Trump Summoned Supporters to 'Wild' Protest, and Told Them to Fight. They Did," *Reuters*, January 6, 2020. https://www.reuters.com/article/us-usa-election-protests/trump-summoned-supporters-to-wild-protest-and-told-them-to-fight-they-did-idUSKBN29B24S.
131. Shelly Tan, Youjin Shin, and Danielle Rindler, "How One of America's Ugliest Days Unraveled Inside and Outside the Capitol," *The Washington Post*, January 9, 2021. https://www.washingtonpost.com/nation/interactive/2021/capitol-insurrection-visual-timeline/.
132. John Wagner, Felicia Sonmez, Mike DeBonis, Karoun Demirjian, Amy B. Wang, Colby Itkowitz, and Paulina Firozi, "Pence Declares Biden Winner of the Presidential Election After Congress Finally Counts Electoral Votes," *The Washington Post*, January 7, 2021. https://www.washingtonpost.com/politics/2021/01/06/congress-electoral-college-vote-live-updates/.
133. 117th Congress (2021-2022). "H.Res.24 - Impeaching Donald John Trump, President of the United States, for high crimes and misdemeanors." Retrieved from: https://www.congress.gov/bill/117th-congress/house-resolution/24/text.
134. Nicholas Fandos, "Trump Impeached for Inciting Insurrection," *The New York Times*, January 13, 2021. https://www.nytimes.com/2021/01/13/us/politics/trump-impeached.html.
135. Dionne Searcey and Matthew Rosenberg, "An Inaugural Lockdown Comes at a Price for Washingtonians," *The New York Times*, January 18, 2021. https://www.nytimes.com/2021/01/18/us/washington-inauguration-security.html.
136. Alana Wise, "'We Must Remember': Biden, Harris Memorialize COVID-19 Victims," *NPR*, January 19, 2021. https://www.npr.org/sections/biden-transition-updates/2021/01/19/958548751/we-must-remember-biden-harris-memorialize-covid-19-victims.
137. Alexandra Alter, "Amanda Gorman Captures the Moment, in Verse," *The New York Times*, January 20, 2021. https://www.nytimes.com/2021/01/19/books/amanda-gorman-inauguration-hill-we-climb.html.
138. Jacey Fortin, "Trump Is Not the First President to Snub an Inauguration," *The New York Times*, January 19, 2021. https://www.nytimes.com/2021/01/19/us/politics/presidents-who-skipped-inaugurations.html.
139. Jill Colvin, "Trump Bids Farewell to Washington, Hints of Comeback," *Associated Press*, January 20, 2021. https://apnews.com/article/donald-trump-leaves-white-house-ad718c0048c341d0044c4709fb23c8dd.
140. Domenico Montanaro, "It Was a Big, Blue Wave: Democrats Pick Up Most House Seats in a Generation," *NPR*, November 14, 2018. https://www.npr.org/2018/11/14/667818539/it-was-a-big-blue-wave-democrats-pick-up-most-house-seats-in-a-generation.
141. Sarah D. Wire, "Slim Majorities in the New Congress Will Make Big Legislation Difficult," *Los Angeles Times*, January 3, 2021. https://www.latimes.com/politics/story/2021-01-03/house-democrats-small-majority-nancy-pelosi-challenges.
142. "U.S. Senate Election Results: Democrats Win," *The New York Times*, January 18, 2021. https://www.nytimes.com/interactive/2020/11/03/us/elections/results-senate.html.
143. Sean Trende, "Midterm Demographics Didn't Sink the Democrats," *Real Clear Politics*, November 19, 2014. http://www.realclearpolitics.com/articles/2014/11/19/midterm_demographics_didnt_sink_the_democrats_124701.html.
144. Center for Responsive Politics, "Reelection Rates Over the Years." http://www.opensecrets.org/bigpicture/reelect.php.
145. Amy B. Wang and Robert Moore, "Beto O'Rourke Concedes to Ted Cruz in El Paso Speech," *The Washington Post*, November 7, 2018. Accessed November 15, 2018. https://www.washingtonpost.com/politics/2018/live-updates/midterms/midterm-election-updates/beto-orourke-concedes-to-ted-cruz-in-el-paso-speech/?utm_term=.287b653e32ea.
146. Amber Phillips, "Are Georgia's Senate Democratic Candidates as 'Radical' as Republicans Are Making Them Out to Be?" *The Washington Post*, December 30, 2020. https://www.washingtonpost.com/politics/2020/12/31/are-georgias-senate-democratic-candidates-radical-republicans-are-making-them-out-be/.
147. Briana Steward, "Amid Georgia Senate Race, Democrat Rephael Warnock Slams Kelly Loeffler for Not Acknowledging Biden's Win," *ABC News*, December 17, 2020. https://abcnews.go.com/Politics/difficult-overstate-stake-warnock/story?id=74725230.
148. Tia Mitchell, "A Timeline of Investigations Into Purdue, Loeffler Stock Trading," *Atlanta Journal Constitution*, December 16, 2020. https://www.ajc.com/politics/a-timeline-of-investigations-into-perdue-loeffler-stock-trading/L6TU65WK5JBFXKDC4YWBKGGNPU/.
149. Marc Caputo and Maya King, "Why Warnock Talks Puppies Instead of Race," *Politico*, January 3, 2021. https://www.politico.com/news/2021/01/03/raphael-warnock-georgia-race-453222.
150. Lisa Lerer and Richard Fausset, "For Democrats in Georgia, 'There's No Going Back,'" *The New York Times*, January 6, 2021. https://www.nytimes.com/2021/01/06/us/politics/georgia-democrats-senate.html.
151. United States Senate, "African American Senators," *Senate.gov, Art & History*. January 18, 2021. https://www.senate.gov/pagelayout/history/h_multi_sections_and_teasers/Photo_Exhibit_African_American_Senators.htm.

152. Benjamin Knoll, "Incumbent Losses in the 2010 Midterms," *Information Knoll*, November 4, 2010, http://informationknoll.wordpress.com/2010/11/04/incumbent-losses-in-the-2010-midterms.
153. The Center for Responsive Politics, "Reelection Rates Over the Years." http://www.opensecrets.org/bigpicture/reelect.php.
154. Open Secrets, "Reelection Rates Over the Years." Accessed November 15, 2018. https://www.opensecrets.org/overview/reelect.php.
155. Tom Murse, "Do Members of Congress Ever Lose Re-Election," *ThoughtCo.*, December 10, 2020. https://www.thoughtco.com/do-congressmen-ever-lose-re-election-3367511.
156. Darrell M. West and L. Sandy Maisel, "Conclusion: Discourse and Beyond," in *Running on Empty? Political Discourse in Congressional Elections* (Lanham, MD: Rowman & Littlefield, 2004), 237.
157. "Local TV News Largely Ignores Local Political Races, New Lear Study Finds," *Lear Center Local News Archive*, USC Annenberg School for Communication, February 15, 2005, http://www.localnewsarchive.org/pdf/LCLNARelease2005.pdf.
158. Committee for the Study of the American Electorate, press release, May 16, 2001.
159. Margo J. Anderson, *The American Census: A Social History*, 2nd ed. (New Haven: Yale University Press, 2015).
160. Mark S. Monmonier, *Bushmanders and Bullwinkles: How Politicians Manipulate Electronic Maps and Census Data to Win Elections* (Chicago: University of Chicago Press, 2001).
161. Relevant is Bradley Hunt, "On the Campaign Trail: Depictions of Political Campaigns in Films," paper submitted to Paletz's "Politics and Media" seminar, April 16, 2001.
162. Matthew Mendelsohn and Andrew Parkin, eds., *Referendum Democracy: Citizens, Elites and Deliberation in Referendum Campaigns* (New York: Palgrave, 2001).
163. For its history and an evaluation of the arguments for and against the initiative, see Joseph F. Zimmerman, *The Initiative: Citizen Law-Making* (Westport, CT: Praeger, 1999).
164. For criticisms of the initiative see Richard J. Ellis, *Democratic Delusions: The Initiative Process in America* (Lawrence: University Press of Kansas, 2002).
165. John G. Matsusaka, *For the Many or the Few* (Chicago: University of Chicago Press, 2004), xi.
166. Ron Brownstein, "The Trouble With the Gavin Newsom Recall," *The Atlantic*, May 13, 2021. https://www.theatlantic.com/politics/archive/2021/05/newsom-recall-california/618872/.
167. Elisa Shearer and Amy Mitchell, "News Use Across Social Media Platforms in 2020," Pew Research Center, January 12, 2021. https://www.journalism.org/2021/01/12/news-use-across-social-media-platforms-in-2020/.
168. Adapted from Kirsten A. Foot and Steven M. Schneider, *Web Campaigning* (Cambridge, MA: The MIT Press, 2006).
169. Bruce Bimber and Richard Davis, *Campaigning Online: The Internet in U.S. Elections* (New York: Oxford University Press, 2003).
170. Matthew McWilliams, Edward Erikson, and Nicole Berns, "Can Facebook Predict Who Wins the Senate in 2014?," *Politico Magazine*, January 20, 2014. Accessed July 14, 2014 http://www.politico.com/magazine/story/2014/01/facebook-predict-who-wins-senate-2014-102401.html#.U8RX6fldWCV.
171. Rebecca Nelson, "Meet the Members of Congress Who Play Video Games," *Politico Magazine*, May 15, 2018. https://www.politico.com/magazine/story/2018/05/15/congress-video-games-scott-peters-darrell-issa-jared-polis-218367.
172. David Talbot, "How Facebook Drove Voters to the Polls," *MIT Technology Review*, September 12, 2012. Accessed July 14, 2014 http://www.technologyreview.com/news/429169/how-facebook-drove-voters-to-the-polls/.
173. Ron Brownstein, "The First 21st Century Campaign," *National Journal*, April 26, 2008, 26–32.
174. Aaron Smith and Maeve Duggan, "Online Political Videos and Campaign 2012," Pew Research Internet Project, November 2, 2012. Accessed July 14, 2014 http://www.pewinternet.org/2012/11/02/online-political-videos-and-campaign-2012/.
175. Danielle Kurtzleben, "2016 Campaigns Will Spend $4.4 Billion On TV Ads, But Why?" NPR, August 19, 2015.
176. Ashley A. Anderson, Danielle Brossard, Dietram A. Scheufele, Michael A. Xenos, and Peter Ladwig. *Journal of Computer-Mediated Communication*, vol. 19: 373–387.
177. Matthew Belvedere, "*New York Times* Subscription Growth Soars Tenfold, Adding 132,000, After Trump's Win," CNBC, November 29, 2016.
178. Marshall Sella, "The Stiff Guy vs. the Dumb Guy," *The New York Times Magazine*, September 24, 2000, 75.
179. Greg Miller, "As U.S. Election Nears, Researchers Are Following the Trail of Fake News," *Science*, October 26, 2020. https://www.sciencemag.org/news/2020/10/us-election-nears-researchers-are-following-trail-fake-news.
180. Will Oremus, "Stop Calling Everything 'Fake News'," *Slate*, December 6, 2016. http://www.slate.com/articles/technology/technology/2016/12/stop_calling_everything_fake_news.html.
181. Clay Ramsay, Steven Kull, and Evan Lewis, "Misinformation and the 2010 Election: A Study of the U.S. Electorate," *WorldPublicOpinion.org*, Program on International Policy Attitudes, University of Maryland, College Park, MD, December 10, 2010. http://www.worldpublicopinion.org/pipa/pdf/dec10/Misinformation_Dec10_rpt.pdf.

CHAPTER 12

# Congress

## 12.1 Preamble

Democratic members of the U.S. House of Representatives staged a sit-in on the House floor to advocate for gun-control measures. The sit-in took place on June 22, 2016, and lasted for twenty-five hours. House Democrats wanted to force a vote on gun-control legislation that was being blocked in the wake of a shooting at an Orlando nightclub where forty-nine people were killed and fifty-eight were wounded. The bill, known colloquially as "no fly, no buy," would prevent people on the terrorist watch list from purchasing guns. Leaders of the Republicans, who controlled the House, would not allow the bill to come to a vote. Members settled in for the long night by ordering in pizza and donuts; some brought pillows and blankets. The sit-in technically violated House rules. Republicans decried the sit-in as a "publicity stunt." Rep. John Lewis (D-GA), a civil rights leader, minority leader Nancy Pelosi (D-CA), and other members refused to leave the House floor. In response, Speaker of the House Paul Ryan (R-WI) pulled the plug on the C-SPAN cameras covering the sit-in. Democratic members pulled out their cell phones and began livestreaming the protest using Twitter Periscope. The feed was picked up by CNN, which broadcast the Periscope streams. Members tweeted messages under the hashtags #NoBillNoBreak and #holdthefloor to recruit supporters. Although members are not permitted to use cell phones in the House chamber, the sit-in participants broke the rules to make a point.[1]

While the sit-in did not prompt a vote on the gun- control measures under consideration in the House, it garnered significant attention in newspapers and on television news as well as on social media. The press drew parallels to lunch counter sit-ins during the civil rights movement in the 1960s, which Rep. Lewis had helped to organize when he was a college student. Despite the media attention to the sit-in and a rise in mass shootings, as of 2021, Congress has failed to pass gun-control legislation.[2]

Comedy Central host Trevor Noah talks about the sit-in by House members over gun control.

View in the online reader

Congress receives significantly less media attention than does the president. Yet members rely on the media to publicize their actions, rally support for their positions, and run for reelection. It takes extraordinary efforts and publicity-seeking strategies for even prominent members to get press attention. In the current era, these strategies include making use of digital media, such as Twitter feeds and YouTube videos, to drive media coverage.

The media's relationship with Congress maintains the distinction between the national institution of Congress and its locally elected members. Congress as an institution commands national media attention, while members of Congress are covered extensively in their local press.[3] Congress is a national institution composed of locally elected politicians who represent distinct constituencies. Members rely on the support of voters in their home districts to keep their job in Congress. Members of Congress must work together to consider policy issues and make laws. Yet getting one hundred senators and 435 members of the House of Representatives to work collectively is a gargantuan task. The cumbersome legislative procedure outlined by the Constitution favors inaction. Members seeking to represent the interests of people back home can come into conflict with prevailing sentiments in Washington, creating obstacles to lawmaking.

Representative John Lewis, an organizer of the sit-in on the floor of the House of Representatives over gun control, had been a civil rights activist when he was in college.

View in the online reader

The institution of Congress is slow to change. A large body with an intricate organizational structure, Congress operates under a complex system of rules and traditions (e.g., the filibuster in the Senate), some of which are Byzantine. Congress adapts to innovations, including developments in communications media (e.g., television and the internet), at a snail's pace.

This chapter begins with discussions of the powers of Congress and the institution's bicameral structure. It examines the party and leadership organizations as well as committees and their work. This chapter details the legislative process—how a bill becomes law—as well as the process of establishing the nation's budget. It also covers the characteristics of members of Congress, their job description, and their staffs. Finally, Congress's interactions with the media in the information age are investigated. The Center on Congress at Indiana University is a good source of information about Congress, including its relationship with the media.

# 12.2 The Powers of Congress Including Impeachment

## Learning Objectives

After reading this section, you should be able to answer the following questions:

1. What are the powers of Congress as enumerated in the U.S. Constitution?
2. What powers are reserved specifically for the House of Representatives, and what powers are held by the Senate alone?
3. What is the Constitution's elastic clause, and how is it used to expand the powers of Congress?
4. What is the Constitutional basis for impeachment?
5. How does the impeachment process differ in the House and the Senate?

**Article I of the Constitution**

The article that enumerates the powers of Congress.

The institution of Congress is responsible for carrying out the legislative duties of the federal government. The powers of Congress are enumerated in **Article I of the Constitution**. The founders established Congress in Article I, Section 1, which states, "All legislative Powers herein granted shall be vested in a Congress of the United States, which shall consist of a Senate and House of Representatives." By instituting Congress in the first article of the Constitution the founders asserted their belief that the legislative branch should be the chief policymaking body. They preferred a government with power vested in the legislature, which they considered most representative of the people, rather than one where the executive was preeminent. They associated the executive branch with the British monarchy, which they had fought against in the Revolutionary War, so they relegated the presidency to the second article of the Constitution. As James Madison wrote in Federalist No. 51, "In a republican government, the legislative authority necessarily predominates."[4]

## Constitutional Powers

Congress was granted tremendous political power by the founders. These powers are listed primarily in Article I, Section 8, of the Constitution, which states that Congress has broad discretion to "provide for the common defense and general welfare of the United States." To achieve this end, Congress has the authority to make and implement laws.

The Constitution lists a number of specific powers entrusted to Congress. These include responsibility for the nation's budget and commerce, such as the power to lay and collect taxes, to pay the debts, to regulate commerce with foreign nations and among the states, to coin money, and to establish post offices. Congress is assigned the power to declare war and to raise an army and navy. Congress has the right to propose amendments to the Constitution and to create new states. Congress also has the power to impeach public officials, including the president of the United States.

Certain powers are granted specifically to the House, such as the power to initiate all tax and spending bills. While the Senate cannot propose such bills, it can accept, reject, or amend them. The Senate has certain authority not vested in the House. High-level presidential nominees, such as cabinet officers, Supreme Court justices, and ambassadors, must gain Senate approval. The Senate also must concur in treaties with foreign countries. Another example of differentiating Congressional powers can be see in the impeachment process.

**FIGURE 12.1** Constitutional Powers of Congress

**Constitutional Powers of Congress**

**Article I, Section 8**

The Congress shall have power to lay and collect taxes, duties, imposts and excises, to pay the debts and provide for the common defense and general welfare of the United States; but all cuties, imposts and excises shall be uniform throughout the United States;
To borrow money on the credit of the United States;
To regulate commerce with foreign nations, and among the several states, and with the Indian tribes;
To establish a uniform rule of naturalization, and uniform laws on the subject of bankruptcies throughout the United States;
To coin money, regulate the value thereof, and of foreign coin, and fix the standard of weights and measures;
To provide for the punishment of counterfeiting the securities and current coin of the United States;
To establish post offices and post roads;
To promote the progress of science and useful arts, by securing for limited times to authors and inventors the exclusive right to their respective writings and discoveries;
To constitute tribunals inferior to the Supreme Court;
To define and punish piracies and felonies committed on the high seas, and offenses against the law of nations;
To declare war, grant letters of marque and reprisal, and make rules concerning captures on land and water;
To raise and support armies, but no appropriation of money to that use shall be for a longer term than two years;
To provide and maintain a navy;
To make rules for the government and regulation of the land and naval forces;
To provide for calling forth the militia to execute the laws of the union, suppress insurrections and repel invasions;
To provide for organizing, arming, and disciplining, the militia, and for governing such part of them as may be employed in the service of the United States, reserving to the states respectively, the appointment of the officers, and the authority of training the militia according to the discipline prescribed by Congress;
To exercise exclusive legislation in all cases whatsoever, over such District (not exceeding ten miles square) as may, by cession of particular states, and the acceptance of Congress, become the seat of the government of the United States, and to exercise like authority over all places purchased by the consent of the legislature of the state in which the same shall be, for the erection of forts, magazines, arsenals, dockyards, and other needful buildings;—And
To make all laws which shall be necessary and proper for carrying into execution the foregoing powers, and all other powers vested by this Constitution in the government of the United States, or in any department or officer thereof.

**Article IV, Section 3**

New states may be admitted by the Congress into this union; but no new states shall be formed or erected within the jurisdiction of any other state; nor any state be formed by the junction of two or more states, or parts of states, without the consent of the legislatures of the states concerned as well as of the Congress.
The Congress shall have power to dispose of and make all needful rules and regulations respecting the territory or other property belonging to the United States; and nothing in this Constitution shall be so construed as to prejudice any claims of the United States, or of any particular state.

**Amendment XVI**
**(Ratified February 3, 1913)**

The Congress shall have power to lay and collect taxes on incomes, from whatever source derived, without apportionment among the several States, and without regard to any census or enumeration.

The final paragraph of Article I, Section 8, grants to Congress the power "to make all laws which shall be necessary and proper for carrying into execution the foregoing powers." This provision is known as the **elastic clause** because it is used to expand the powers of Congress, especially when national laws come into conflict with state laws. Legislation making it a federal crime to transport a kidnapped person across state lines was justified on the basis that the elastic clause allowed Congress to apply its power to regulate commerce in this situation.

**elastic clause**

The constitutional provision that Congress shall make all laws that are "necessary and proper" for executing their powers, which has been used to expand its authority; also known as the "necessary and proper" clause.

# Constitutional Basis for Impeachment

**impeachment**

A formal charge alleging misconduct against a public official, such as the president, that is a first step in their removal from office.

The framers of the Constitution intentionally made it difficult to remove a president or other public official from office by specifying a process that involved both the House and the Senate. Article II of the U.S. Constitution (see Appendix A Section 2) provides that members of the executive branch, specifically "the President, Vice President, and all civil Officers in the United States," shall be removed from office for "Treason, Bribery, or other high Crimes and Misdemeanors" if convicted in an impeachment trial. **Impeachment** is a formal charge alleging misconduct against a public official and is the first step in removing them from office. Article 1, Section 2, Clause 5 provides that the House "shall have the sole power of impeachment," the ability to bring charges against the president. The Senate's role in impeachment is articulated in Article 1, Section 3, Clause 6, which states, "The Senate shall have the sole Power to try all Impeachments" (see Appendix A Section 1). The chief justice of the Supreme Court presides over the impeachment in the Senate. Two-thirds of the senators present are required to convict the president and thus remove him from office.

The Constitution provides a broad framework for the impeachment process. Within the rubric of these constitutional provisions, the House and Senate can determine the specific rules that will govern the impeachment proceedings in the chamber.[5]

The House initiates the impeachment process by conducting an investigation into whether actions by the president constitute impeachable offenses. Witnesses are called to testify and relevant documents are solicited and examined. After the inquiry, the House decides whether there is enough evidence of presidential wrongdoing to draft articles of impeachment. The House Judiciary Committee drafts articles of impeachment, which are then debated on the House floor. A vote is taken on each article and requires a simple majority to pass. The president is impeached—or charged—if one or more articles of impeachment is passed by the House.

**impeachment managers**

A committee of House members acting as prosecutors who have prepared the case the case for impeachment and present it in the Senate.

The Constitution does not specifically state how the Senate should act on articles of impeachment referred from the House, and does not require a trial. Once the House votes to impeach, the Speaker of the House sends the articles of impeachment to the Senate. The Senate serves as a High Court of Impeachment. **Impeachment managers** from the House prosecute the case. Senators are presented with evidence and witness testimony prior to voting to acquit or convict. The Constitution requires a two-thirds vote to convict an official, who will be removed from office. In some instances, the Senate can disqualify an official from ever holding public office again. Convicted officials cannot appeal the Senate's decision. No presidents have been convicted by the Senate. However, about half of the public officials impeached since 1789 have been removed from office.[6]

## The First Impeachment of President Donald Trump

President Donald Trump became only the third president of the United States to be formally impeached by the House of Representatives and the only president to be impeached twice. Trump also was the only president to be impeached in the House just prior to leaving office and before the Senate voted to acquit or convict. Prior to President Trump, only Andrew Johnson and Bill Clinton had been formally impeached; neither was removed from office. Richard Nixon, when faced with an impeachment inquiry, resigned from office.

On September 24, 2019, House Speaker Nancy Pelosi (D-CA) announced that the House would open an investigation into allegations that President Trump had pressured Ukrainian President Volodymyr Zelensky to investigate former vice president and Democratic presidential candidate Joe Biden, who became his rival in the 2020 election. Biden's son, Hunter Biden, had been on the board of Burisma Holdings, a Ukrainian natural gas producer. There was no evidence of any wrongdoing on the part of the Bidens. Trump withheld U.S. military aide to Ukraine, an ally facing aggression from Russia, on the condition that it would be restored when Ukraine announced it was investigating the Bidens.[7] On December 18, 2019, the House charged Trump with abusing the power of his office by asking Ukraine, a foreign government, to investigate a political opponent and with obstructing Congress as it was conducting its investigation. The congressional inquiry was sparked by a complaint filed by an anonymous **whistleblower**.

**whistleblower**

A person, often someone working inside an organization or agency, who discloses information to an authority about wrongdoing. The identity of whistleblowers often remains anonymous, and three are laws to protect them from losing their jobs.

The formal impeachment inquiry was conducted by the House Intelligence Committee chaired by Rep. Adam Schiff (D-CA) and assisted by the Judiciary Committee chaired by Rep. Jerrold Nadler (D-NY). Witnesses, including career diplomats, military officers, and Trump appointees, gave extensive testimony making the case that Trump expected Ukraine to investigate Biden, his rival, in return for military funding. Controversy arose when more than a dozen key witnesses, including Trump's personal attorney, Rudy Giuliani, Secretary of State Mike Pompeo, former National Security Advisor John Bolton, Vice President Mike Pence, and Energy Secretary Rick Perry, defied subpoenas to testify at the direction of the White House. The Trump administration also refused to turn over documents, such as emails, instant messages, and diplomats' notes, related to the case. The House passed two articles of impeachment, the first on abuse of presidential power and the second on obstruction of Congress related to blocking witnesses and withholding documents (see Appendix B).[8] Speaker Pelosi delayed transmitting the articles to the Senate for a month as she sought to pressure Senate Republicans to allow witnesses during the trial. The House delivered the articles of impeachment to the Senate on January 15, 2020.

Senate Majority Leader Mitch McConnell (R-KY) decided to hold a trial in the Trump impeachment case. The details of the process were contentious, as Republicans refused the Democrats' request for witnesses and documents. Seven impeachment managers from the House—all Democrats with strong legal backgrounds—were appointed by Speaker Pelosi to argue the case for removing the president from office. President Trump's defense team was led by White House counsel Pat Cipollone and included outside attorneys and a number of Republican House members. Members of Trump's team, such as Harvard law professor emeritus Alan Dershowitz and former Florida Attorney General Pam Bondi, were regulars on cable TV programs, including Fox News. Supreme Court Chief Justice John Roberts presided. Senators served as jurors during the trial, with strict rules governing their actions in the chamber. They were required to be present and attentive for the deliberations, which meant staying seated for long periods with only water or milk as refreshments. They also could not speak from the floor, but could submit written questions to Justice Roberts that were answered by the prosecution and defense teams. Opening arguments in the trial began on January 22, 2020, with each side allowed up to twenty-four hours over three days to make their case. Next, senators had sixteen hours to ask questions followed by two hours of arguments by the impeachment managers and the Trump team's lawyers. A hotly contested motion to allow new witnesses and documents at the trial was voted down by a slim majority of Republicans, as Senator Susan Collins (R-ME) and Senator Mitt Romney (R-UT) sided with the Democrats. On February 5, 2020, the final vote was taken on whether to convict or acquit President Trump on each article of impeachment. A two-thirds majority vote—sixty-seven senators—was required to convict, while a simple majority—fifty-one senators—was needed to acquit. The vote on Article I, abuse of power, was fifty-two to forty-eight to acquit; the vote on Article II, obstruction of Congress was fifty-three to forty-seven to acquit. The votes to impeach in the House, which held a Democratic majority, and to acquit in the Senate, which was controlled by Republicans, were almost all along party lines.

## The Second Impeachment of President Donald Trump

The second impeachment of Donald Trump took place in the wake of the insurrection at the U.S. Capitol on January 6, 2021. The House introduced a single article of impeachment (see Appendix B Section 2) alleging that Trump had instigated a mob that stormed the Capitol as the results of the 2020 presidential election confirming Joe Biden as the winner were being certified by Congress.[9] On January 13, the House voted to impeach Trump by a vote of 232 in favor and 197 opposed. Ten House Republicans voted with the Democratic majority to impeach, which was unprecedented. Among these was Rep. Liz Cheney (R-WY), the third highest ranking member of the Republican House leadership. Cheney was voted out of her leadership position on May 12, 2021, largely due to her vote in support of impeaching Trump.

Donald Trump's term as president ended on January 20, as Joe Biden took office. The House sent the article of impeachment to the Senate on January 25. Senate Republicans immediately raised a motion to dismiss the trial on the basis that it was unconstitutional because Trump had left office, but it was narrowly defeated. Even though he was no longer in office, Trump could have been banned from holding public office in the future if convicted. Each side presented its case, although no witnesses were called. The ten House impeachment managers, led by Rep. Jamie Raskin (D-MD), argued that Trump was "singularly responsible" for the insurrection at the Capitol because of his false claims of election fraud. At a rally prior to the attack, Trump urged his supporters to walk to the Capitol and "fight much harder."[10] Trump's attorneys argued that he had not incited the insurrection and that the impeachment case was partisan "political theater." The Senate vote was fifty-seven in favor of conviction and forty-three opposed, which fell short of the two-thirds majority required to convict. Seven Republicans joined all fifty Democrats in voting for conviction.[11]

### Enduring Images

#### Senator Mitt Romney (R-UT): The Lone Republican Vote to Convict President Trump

Mitt Romney, the junior senator from Utah, became the first senator in history to vote to convict and remove a president of his own party during impeachment. Members of a president's party have always closed ranks to protect their hold on the office and to negate the impression that impeachment was a bipartisan effort.[12] In his closing arguments at the Senate trial, House impeachment manager Representative Adam Schiff (D-CA), anticipating that Republican senators would vote to acquit Trump based on party loyalty, implored: "Is there one among you who will say, 'Enough'?" Senator Romney bucked his party and voted "yes" on the first article of impeachment on abuse of power—a vote for removing President Trump from office.

Romney had faced intense pressure from his Republican colleagues to vote for acquittal, but in the end voted his conscience. In a statement from the Senate floor, Romney explained his decision to his colleagues and the nation. He drew upon his strong faith in making his decision, stating, "I am a profoundly religious person. I take an oath before God as enormously consequential. I knew from the outset that being tasked with judging the President, the leader of my own party, would be the most difficult decision I have ever faced. I was not wrong." He offered an interpretation of what the Founders meant by "high crimes and misdemeanors," and indicated that President Trump had committed an egregious act against the public trust by asking a foreign government to investigate his political rival and withholding vital military funds from that foreign government to exert pressure. Romney noted that he had received numerous calls and texts demanding that he "stand with the team," and indicated that he was "sure to hear abuse from the President and his supporters." However, he maintained that: "Were I to ignore the evidence that has been presented, and disregard what I believe my oath and the Constitution demands of me for the sake of a partisan end, it would, I fear, expose my character to history's rebuke and the censure of my own conscience."[13]

Romney's bold act of defying his party radically influenced the impeachment news agenda. His vote and impassioned speech caused journalists to rework the impeachment narrative that Trump's acquittal was achieved with the unanimous support of his party. While Romney's vote did not change the outcome of the impeachment, it garnered headlines, gained extensive coverage, dominated talk on cable news programs, and ignited commentary on social media.

Watch the following video of Senator Mitt Romney's speech about his vote to convict President Trump during the impeachment trial.

View in the online reader

## Key Takeaways

Article I of the Constitution establishes Congress as the legislative branch of government with broad powers to provide for the "common defense and general welfare of the United States," along with specific powers in important areas of domestic and foreign affairs. Certain powers, such as the ability to initiate taxing and spending bills, rest exclusively with the House of Representatives. Other powers, including the approval of presidential appointments, lie solely with the Senate. The powers of Congress have been extended through the elastic clause of the Constitution, which states that Congress can make all laws that are "necessary and proper" for carrying out its duties. Congress also has the power to impeach the president and remove him from office. The House initiates impeachment inquiries and can charge a president of wrongdoing. The Senate can hold a trial and remove a president from office. President Donald Trump was only the third president of the United States to be formally impeached by the House and the only president to be impeached twice. The Senate voted against removing him from office on both occasions.

## Exercises

1. What are the advantages of making Congress the chief policymaking body? What might the disadvantages be?
2. What are the limits of congressional power? How do the powers of the House and Senate differ?
3. Is the impeachment process an effective way to deal with extreme forms of presidential misconduct? How does political partisanship impact the impeachment process?
4. What are the pros and cons of impeaching officials after they have left office?

# 12.3 A Bicameral Legislative Branch

## Learning Objectives

After reading this section, you should be able to answer the following questions:

1. What is a bicameral legislative structure, and why was it established in Congress?
2. What are the different characteristics of the House and Senate?

The bicameral structure of the U.S. Congress was established by the founders to minimize the possibility of any one governmental body becoming too powerful. The House was meant to be the most democratic of the national institutions, as its members are subject to reelection every two years. The Senate was designed by the framers as an elite body that would act as a check on the House. The two bodies differ in terms of characteristics and norms as well as in the way they operate.

## Bicameral Legislative Structure

**bicameral legislature**

Congress consists of two bodies: (1) the House of Representatives, whose membership is based on proportional representation and (2) the Senate, whose membership is based on equal representation.

The founders established Congress as a **bicameral legislature** as a check against tyranny. They feared having any one governmental body become too strong. This bicameral system distributes power within two houses that check and balance one another rather than concentrating authority in a single body. The House of Representatives is the larger body, with membership based on each state's population. The Senate is the smaller body, with each state having two delegates. With one hundred members, the Senate is a more intimate, less formal legislative body than the House, which has 435 members elected from districts that are roughly the same size in population.

Members of Congress must reside in the district or state that elects them, although the Constitution does not specify for how long. Residency can become a campaign issue. In 2017, Democrat Jon Ossoff was charged with being an "outsider" and a "carpetbagger" when he ran in and lost a hotly contested special election to represent Georgia in the House of Representatives. His Republican opponent ran an ad saying, "He's just not one of us." Ossoff was born and raised in the district, but had attended Georgetown University in Washington, DC. At the time of the election, he lived just a mile and a half outside of the district lines, where his girlfriend was attending medical school. Ossoff ran for Senate and won a tight runoff election in 2021.[14] The term "carpetbagger" refers to a politician who runs for office from an area where he or she has lived for only a short time and has few community ties. It derives from a derogatory term coined after the Civil War referring to Northerners who went south to profit from Reconstruction, carrying "carpet bags" for luggage.

Members of Congress are elected locally to serve nationally. All aspects of members' jobs, whether it be making laws or providing service to people in their home districts, are influenced by this dual concern with representing local constituencies while dealing with national policy.

# The Electoral Connection

The Constitution anticipated that the House would be more attentive to the people than the Senate. The House is designed to be the most democratic institutional body in the U.S. government because each member represents a particular district within a state rather than the entire state, which is the case for the Senate. House members stand for election every two years to ensure that they keep in close touch with the opinions and interests of the people they represent or face defeat at the polls. There are no limits on the number of terms a member can serve. Consequently, many members are constantly campaigning to keep their seats in office.

**FIGURE 12.2 Continuous Campaigns for Reelection**

Members of Congress engage in a permanent campaign for reelection that begins the minute they take office.

Source: IowaPolitics.com. "DSC_0020." (Harkin Steak Fry). Via Flickr: https://www.flickr.com/photos/iowapolitics/4984484879/in/photostream/. Reproduced via CC BY-SA 2.0: https://creativecommons.org/licenses/by-sa/2.0/.

Congress establishes the number of House members by enacting legislation. In 1787, there were sixty-five members, and the founders anticipated that House members would never represent more than 30,000 people. In 1910, the current number of 435 representatives was reached. The number of people represented by a single member has increased from 210,583 in 1910 to 646,947 in 2000 and 710,767 in 2010. The U.S. Census Bureau calculates these apportionment figures, which can be viewed on an interactive map on its website. This number of people per congressional district is projected to top 900,000 in 2050.[15] Some observers question if the democratic character of the House will be compromised if constituencies grow even larger, while others oppose enlarging an institution that is already difficult to manage.

House members are elected in districts whose lines are drawn by state legislatures after the census, which takes place every ten years. States can gain or lose representatives if there are population shifts. Following the 2020 census, six states that gained in population—Texas (two seats), Colorado, Florida, Montana, North Carolina, and Oregon—added House seats. Seven states—California, Illinois, Michigan, New York, Ohio, Pennsylvania, and West Virginia, each lost a seat.[16]

**gerrymandering**

The practice of drawing the lines of a congressional district to favor one party.

Redistricting can be controversial as legislators seek to draw district lines that advantage their own political parties. **Gerrymandering** is the practice of manipulating the size and shape of a congressional district to unduly favor one party over another. Gerrymandered districts can be oddly shaped as irregular lines are drawn to ensure the concentration of voters of a particular party. In 2003, the process of redrawing congressional district lines in Texas attracted national media attention. Democratic state legislators twice fled to neighboring states to prevent a vote on a redistricting plan that they felt favored Republicans. The media depicted the fugitive Democratic legislators hanging out on the balcony of a cheap hotel in New Mexico as the infuriated Republicans threatened to call out the Texas Rangers to forcibly return them to the state. The media attention did not stop the redistricting plan.[17] Many voters are opposed to gerrymandering and have organized efforts to stop the practice. In 2017, a group called Voters Not Politicians was organized on Facebook to establish an independent citizens commission on redistricting in Michigan. The proposal appeared on the ballot during the 2018 elections, and passed with over 60 percent of the vote.[18]

Democratic members of the Texas state assembly garnered national press attention by fleeing to a neighboring state to avoid having to vote on a redistricting plan they felt would give seats to Republicans.

View in the online reader

The framers felt that the Senate should be constituted as an elite body that would act as a check on the House, the branch closest to the mass public. Senators serve six-year terms of office, and like the House, there are no limits on the number of terms they can serve. Senators, in theory, should have more time than House members to think about something besides reelection. However, as the cost of elections has grown and Senate elections have become more competitive, fundraising has become a constant concern for many senators.[19] The founders' expectations that the House would be close to the people and the Senate would be more distant have not been realized. House members often hold safe seats and do not face serious challenges to reelection, so they often hold office for years.

House members are chosen in districts whose boundaries can cut across media markets and other political jurisdictions, such as county or city lines. Some parts of Maryland and Virginia receive most of their news from the District of Columbia, and their House members are given limited coverage. As a result, it can be difficult for local television news to cover House members and their reelection challengers. Senators, having won statewide races, receive more attention. Their opponents also are likely to receive significant media coverage, which often makes for hotly contested elections.

# House and Senate Comparisons

**seniority**

Long-standing members of Congress, especially in the Senate, hold leadership positions and have more influence over decision making than their junior colleagues.

The House and Senate are institutions that have decidedly different characters. Because of its large size and more frequent turnover in membership, the House is an impersonal institution. House members may not recognize their colleagues, and some have staff members assigned as "spotters," who whisper names into their ears to avoid embarrassment. The House operates under formal rules. It is hierarchical, and **seniority** is important. Members serve for a long time before they become leaders. Senior members hold positions on the most prestigious committees and have more influence over decision making than their junior colleagues.

The Senate does not rely as heavily on hierarchy as the House. It is less rule-bound and operates more loosely and unpredictably than the House, especially as the Senate requires the unanimous consent of its members for any bill to be taken up. This means that a lone senator has the power to stop legislative action, a power that House members do not possess. For example, in 2019 the House passed the "For the People Act" that would require all states to offer automatic voter registration, make Election Day a federal holiday, and institute measures to curtail gerrymandering. Senate Majority Leader Mitch McConnell (R-KY) killed the bill by preventing it from coming to a vote in the Senate.[20] Senators serve long terms and get to know their colleagues. Seniority is less meaningful, as junior senators have considerable power to make decisions along with their senior colleagues. The smaller size of the chamber allows members to pursue a fast track to leadership and increased public visibility early in their careers.

The differences between the House and Senate are reflected in their respective chambers. The House meets in the largest parliamentary room in the world. Members do not have assigned seats and take any available place on padded benches. Few members spend time in the chamber other than when they are speaking or voting. The Senate chamber is smaller and more ornate. Senators are assigned desks and chairs, many of which have been held by distinguished members. Since the introduction of television to the Senate chamber in 1986, senior senators have taken back-row seats, which provide favorable camera angles against a flattering blue backdrop and have space for displaying charts and graphs.

The distinctions between the chambers extend to their ability to attract media coverage, although this has changed somewhat in the new media era. The Senate routinely garners greater press attention than the House because it is easier for journalists to cover the smaller chamber and establish long-term relationships with its members, who serve six-year terms. The hierarchical structure of the House makes it easy for leaders to become national media headliners, while other members must compete for attention.[21] The proliferation of digital media outlets has made it somewhat easier for media-savvy members to get their message out through websites, blogs, Twitter feeds, and online videos. Members who are able to use Facebook, Twitter, and YouTube effectively are able to gain media attention even when they do not hold high-profile positions in Congress.

### Key Takeaways

The framers provided for a bicameral legislative branch with equal representation in the Senate and proportional representation based on state population in the House. The two bodies differ in a number of important ways that influence the way that they operate. The House is a more formal institution, where hierarchy and seniority are important factors. The Senate, as a smaller, more intimate body, is less bound by formal rules than the House. Senators typically garner more media attention than House members because they serve statewide constituencies and serve longer terms of office.

### Exercises

1. How is the design of the House intended to make its members particularly responsive to their constituents?
2. What makes the House and Senate differ in character? How do the media portray the two bodies?

# 12.4 Parties in Congress

### Learning Objectives

After reading this section, you should be able to answer the following questions:

1. How are political parties in Congress organized?
2. What role do political party organizations play in Congress?
3. How do factional organizations function in Congress?

Maintaining order in an institution consisting of hundreds of individuals with often competing agendas is about as easy as herding cats. Political parties and the House and Senate leadership help members work together to perform their duties effectively. The Constitution says little about how Congress should be organized. Most of the functions of parties and congressional leaders have developed as members have sought to shape the institution over time.

## Party Organization

Political parties provide Congress with organizational structure and discipline. The Democratic and Republican parties are a robust presence in Congress. Almost all members of Congress are either Republicans or Democrats. Party organizations have permanent offices and staffs on the Hill. Parties facilitate lawmaking and are the basis for the most stable coalitions in Congress. They unite individuals who share ideological orientations and policy goals and help them work together to pass legislation. Congressional campaign committees help party members get elected to Congress.

**caucuses**

Democratic and Republican organizations in the House and Senate that include all members and provide a forum for selecting leaders, approving committee assignments, and studying and debating issues.

**majority party**

The party in Congress holding a majority of the seats in the House or Senate; the majority party also controls top leadership positions.

**minority party**

The party in Congress holding a minority of the seats in the House or Senate; the minority party forms an organized opposition to the majority party.

Formal party organizations consist of **caucuses** and committees. The **majority party** controls the top leadership positions. The **minority party** forms an organized opposition to the majority party.

## Party Caucuses

All members of the House and Senate belonging to a political party form that party's caucus or conference. Currently, members elected as Independents caucus with the Democrats. Caucuses elect leaders, approve committee assignments, and appoint task forces to study specific issues. They provide a forum for debating policies and developing strategies for passing legislation. Party staffers serve members by supplying reports on pending legislation and assisting them with media relations by producing radio and television interviews, webcasts, and podcasts in studios on Capitol Hill.

Caucuses promote party loyalty by granting rewards to members, such as prestige committee assignments. For this reason, few members switch parties, with only twenty-seven instances in the Senate and fewer than ninety in the House since the 1880s.[22] In May 2001, Senator Jim Jeffords (I-VT) left the Republican Conference and became an Independent. His defection caused the Republicans to lose their majority position in the Senate. Jeffords was appointed to a committee chair by the Democratic Party, but his prestige was short-lived. When the Republicans became the majority party after winning additional seats in the 2002 election, Jeffords lost his chair. Senator Arlen Specter of Pennsylvania, a Republican senator since 1980, became a Democrat in 2009 due to his support of an economic stimulus package that was opposed by Republicans. Specter faced a difficult reelection bid as a Democrat in 2010 and lost to Joe Sestak in the primary, ending over four decades in Congress.[23]

## Party Committees

**party committees**

Committees established by the two major parties to perform specific tasks, such as recommending members to serve on committees and conducting issue research.

The two major parties have established **party committees** that perform specific tasks. In the House, steering committees consisting of party leaders recommend members to serve on legislative committees. Each party's House and Senate policy committee conducts research and advises members about legislative proposals. The campaign committees raise funds, conduct election research, organize volunteers, and develop campaign publicity to promote the election of party members to Congress. House Democrats' Organization, Study, and Review Committee recommends changes in party organization and rules.

## Party Voting

Congressional parties promote party voting on bills. Party-line votes occur when a majority of members of one party votes against a majority of members of the opposing party on major legislation.[24] Most votes in Congress are routine and non-divisive and therefore do not precipitate a party vote. Until the 1980s, 60 percent of congressional votes on public policy issues were along party lines. From the 1990s until recently, 70 to 80 percent of votes were partisan. Since the 2016 election, congressional voting has become even more partisan, with close to 90 percent of members casting votes consistently with their party.[25]

Political parties' influence on members' decisions and actions has been on the rise since the 1970s. One explanation for this increase in partisanship is that members come from districts where constituents are strongly affiliated with the Democratic or Republican Party.[26] As polarization between the parties has risen, members have become much less likely to defect from their party on key votes. Another explanation is that reforms instituted when Republicans took control of the House in 1994 have given more power to congressional leaders to handle procedural matters. When policy preferences among majority party members are consistent, members will delegate responsibility to the Speaker of the House and committee chairs to advance the party's legislative program.[27] Some scholars argue that this results in the majority party promoting policy goals that are closer to the ideals of the leadership than to those of rank-and-file members and the general public.[28]

The tension between the institution of Congress and individual members is evident in party voting. The primary source of conflict within party ranks stems from members' disagreement with a party's policy position because it deviates from their commitment to the voters back home. Party voting usually declines in election years, as members are less willing to face criticism in their districts for supporting unpopular positions.

Media reports on Congress commonly emphasize conflicts between the Republican and Democratic parties. The partisan conflict frame is prevalent when high-profile legislative issues are being debated. Journalists find it easier to focus on partisan dynamics, which are a legitimate part of the story, than to cover the often complicated details of the legislation itself.

Media coverage of the congressional debate over health care in recent years illustrates the use of the conflict frame, which often excludes coverage of the substance of policy issues. During the original debates over the Affordable Care Act, nicknamed "Obamacare," the media focused heavily on the strategies employed by President Barack Obama and Democratic members of Congress on the one hand and Republican members on the other to advance their positions on health care. Lawmakers on each side of the debate conducted extensive research and issued reports detailing the policy issues involved, yet news organizations focused primarily on fights between members and parties. According to the Pew Research Center, over 70 percent of the public felt that news organizations provided only fair or poor coverage of the details of various health-care proposals and their effect on people despite the health-care debate's dominating the news agenda.[29] Media coverage of the Republican effort to repeal and replace "Obamacare" in 2017 continued to focus on partisan bickering over the bill and the strategies employed by Republicans and Democrats to assert their positions. The House narrowly voted in favor of a bill that weakened some of the provisions of the Affordable Care Act, and sent it on to the Senate, where it failed to pass.[30] In 2021, reforms of the Affordable Care Act to expand subsidies for purchasing insurance were included in the $1.9 trillion American Rescue Plan passed by Congress. There was little partisan discussion of these subsidies during the COVID-19 pandemic.[31]

The late Sen. John McCain (R-AZ) gives a dramatic thumbs down as he votes against the Republican overhaul of the Affordable Care Act, defeating a measure favored by his own party.

View in the online reader

Members have very different legislative experiences depending on whether or not their party is in power. Majority party members profit from **pork barrel spending** on projects that benefit their districts. Earmarks are legislative provisions that provide funding for pork barrel projects. Pork barrel projects include federally funded parks, community centers, theaters, military bases, and building projects that benefit particular areas. These projects can help members curry favor with their constituents and help their reelection prospects. However, opponents of pork barrel spending argue that these projects should be funded by state and local budgets in the places they benefit rather than by the federal treasury. A proposal calling for a moratorium on earmarks in the 112th Congress was introduced by the Republican leadership in the House.[32] The moratorium on earmarks was passed in 2010, and the Senate voted to maintain the moratorium in 2017. However, the effectiveness of the ban has been questioned, as earmarks still make their way into legislation. After a decade, the House ended the moratorium on earmarks in 2021 in order to give more power to lawmakers on the appropriations committee.[33]

**pork barrel spending**

Legislation that provides funding for projects that benefit a member of Congress's district.

# Factions and Policy Groups

**FIGURE 12.3 Congressional Causes**

Congressional causes can form around surprising issues. The Congressional Soccer Caucus (https://ussoccerfoundation.org/about/congressional-soccer-caucus) encourages legislation, activities, and events that promote soccer, including improvement of fields and use of soccer for building communities.

Source: imtmphoto/Shutterstock.com

Outside of parties, like-minded members can form factions or specialized coalitions to promote a particular agenda. Some factions are long-standing groups with pronounced ideological leanings. They form coalitions to support or oppose legislation.[34] Some factions are based on members' identification with a group. These include the Congressional Black Caucus and the Congressional Hispanic Caucus.

In addition to the major party caucuses of the Democrats and Republicans, there also are caucuses representing offshoots of the major parties. The Tea Party caucus consists of Republicans who gained office with the backing of the Tea Party grassroots movement, although its membership has been dwindling. The House Freedom Caucus consists of conservative Republicans. It seeks to shift power away from the House leadership to rank-and-file members, and to push an agenda that includes defunding Planned Parenthood, repealing "Obamacare," and opposing President Biden's ambitious legislative agenda.[35]

There are specialized party caucuses on the Democratic side of the aisle as well. The New Democrat Coalition consists of over 100 members who have moderate views on the economy. The Blue Dog Coalition represents the conservative wing of the Democratic Party in Congress. More liberal members join the Congressional Progressive caucus. The Blue Collar Caucus comprises pro-labor Democratic members. The membership of these caucuses tend to vote together, especially on controversial issues.[36]

**policy groups (factions)**

Specialized coalitions in Congress that promote a particular agenda.

**Policy groups (factions)** also unite members interested in a particular policy area and include both Republicans and Democrats. The Congressional Wine Caucus consists of 250 House and Senate members who share a concern with the wine industry's cultural and financial significance. In addition to sponsoring wine seminars and tastings, and legislative briefings, the Wine Caucus holds fundraisers for charities.

## Key Takeaways

Political parties are central to the organizational structure of Congress. Parties provide a measure of discipline that helps the House and Senate to function more efficiently. Members who switch parties often lose the benefits of seniority, such as committee chair positions, and face an uncertain future when they seek reelection.

## Exercises

1. What is a caucus? What are some of the different caucuses in Congress?
2. How do political parties help organize Congress? Why does media coverage tend to focus on party conflicts?

# 12.5 House Leadership

## Learning Objectives

After reading this section, you should be able to answer the following questions:

1. What criteria do House members use when selecting their leadership?
2. What roles do the Speaker, floor leaders, and whips play in the House?

The House leadership consists of the Speaker, **floor leaders**, and **whips**. Committee chairs also are part of the House leadership, and they will be discussed in Section 7, which is about committees. The rules of the House give extensive power to leaders to direct the legislative process.

**floor leaders**

Leaders from each party who coordinate legislative initiatives.

**whips**

Members who promote party unity in voting.

## Leadership Criteria

House members consider a number of factors when choosing leaders. A member's personal reputation, interactions with other members, legislative skills, expertise, experience, length of service, and knowledge of the institution are taken into account. Members tend to choose leaders who are in the ideological mainstream of their party and represent diverse regions of the country. The positions that a member has held in Congress, such as service on important committees, are evaluated. Fundraising ability, media prowess, and communications skills are increasingly important criteria for leadership. The ability to forge winning coalitions and the connections that a member has to leaders in the Senate or the executive branch are factored into the decision.[37]

Holding a congressional leadership position is challenging, especially as most members think of themselves as leaders rather than followers. Revolts can occur when members feel leaders are wielding too much power or promoting personal agendas at the expense of institutional goals. At times, a leader's style or personality may rub members the wrong way and contribute to their being ousted from office.[38]

## Speaker of the House

The **Speaker of the House** is at the top of the leadership hierarchy. The Speaker is second in succession to the presidency and is the only officer of the House mentioned specifically in the Constitution. The Speaker's official duties include referring bills to committees, appointing members to select and conference committees, counting and announcing all votes on legislation, and signing all bills passed by the House. He or she rarely participates in floor debates or votes on bills. The Speaker also is the leader of his or her political party in the House. In this capacity, the Speaker oversees the party's committee assignments, sets the agenda of activities in the House, and bestows rewards on faithful party members, such as committee leadership positions.[39]

**Speaker of the House**

The top-ranking member and presiding officer of the House of Representatives.

In addition to these formal responsibilities, the Speaker has significant power to control the legislative agenda in the House. The Rules Committee, through which all bills must pass, functions as an arm of the Speaker. The Speaker appoints members of the Rules Committee who can be relied on to do his or her bidding. He or she exercises control over which bills make it to the floor for consideration and the procedures that will be followed during debate. Special rules, such as setting limits on amendments or establishing complex time allocations for debate, can influence the contents of a bill and help or hinder its passage.[40]

Speakers' personal styles have influenced the evolution of the position. Speaker Joe Cannon (R-IL) became the most powerful Speaker of the House by using strong-arm tactics to control members of both parties. "Czar" Cannon's style so angered his colleagues that he was forced to step down as chairman of the Rules Committee during the St. Patrick's Day Revolt of 1910, which stripped him of his ability to control appointments and legislation. The position lost prestige and power until Speaker Sam Rayburn (D-TX) took office in 1940. Rayburn was able to use his popularity and political acumen to reestablish the Speakership as a powerful position.[41]

**FIGURE 12.4 Strong Speakers of the House**

Strong Speakers of the House, such as Joe Cannon (left) and Sam Rayburn (right), were able to exert influence over other members. Strong speakers are no longer prominent in the House.

Sources: (left) Library of Congress, Prints & Photographs Division, photograph by Hartsook Photo via LOC: http://loc.gov/pictures/resource/cph.3f06266. Via Wikimedia: https://en.wikipedia.org/wiki/File:JGCannon.jpg#/media/File:Joseph_Gurney_Cannon_by_Hartsook_Photo,_1915.jpg; (right) Library of Congress, Prints & Photographs Division, photograph by Harris & Ewing via LOC: https://www.loc.gov/pictures/item/2016858635/. Via Wikimedia: https://commons.wikimedia.org/wiki/File:Sam_Rayburn3.jpg.

A Speaker's personal style can influence the amount of media coverage the position commands. The Speaker can become the public face of the House by appearing frequently in the press. A charismatic speaker can rival the president in grabbing media attention and setting the nation's issue agenda. On April 7, 1995, Speaker Newt Gingrich (R-GA) made an unprecedented prime-time television "State of the Congress" address on CBS indicating that the House had passed the Contract with America, a plan that proposed extensive changes to the social welfare system and tax policy. Despite the fact that the Contract with America died in the Senate, Gingrich became a "multimedia Whirling Dervish of books, writings, lectures, tapes, and television, spewing out ideas."[42] He was a constant presence on the television and radio talk show circuit, which kept attention focused on his party's issue platform. This strategy worked at the outset, as the Republicans were able to push through some of their proposals. Gingrich's aggressive personal style and media blitz eventually backfired by alienating members of both parties. This experience illustrates that the media can have a boomerang effect—publicity can make a political leader and just as quickly can bring him down.

In contrast, Speaker Dennis Hastert (R-IL), who took office in 1999, exhibited an accommodating leadership style and was considered a "nice guy" by most members. He worked behind the scenes to build coalitions and achieve his policy initiatives. After the election of President George W. Bush, Hastert coordinated a communications strategy with the executive branch to promote a Republican policy agenda. He shared the media spotlight, which other members appreciated. His cooperative approach was effective in getting important budget legislation passed.[43]

Speaker Nancy Pelosi (D-CA) was the first woman Speaker of the House, serving from 2006 to 2010. She regained the Speaker's post following the Democrats' retaking the majority in the House after the 2018 midterm elections. Media coverage of Pelosi frequently included references to her gender, clothing, emotions, and personal style. Pelosi's choice of Armani suits was much noted in the press following her selection. Syndicated *New York Times* columnist Maureen Dowd wrote a piece on November 6, 2006, titled "Squeaker of the House." Dowd alleged that Pelosi's first act after becoming Speaker was to "throw like a girl" and that she was "making her first move based on relationships and past slights rather than strategy."[44] "Squeaker of the House" became a moniker that stuck with Pelosi throughout her tenure as Speaker and was the subject of a YouTube parody. Pelosi was replaced by Rep. John Boehner (R-OH) when the Republicans took control of the House following the 2010 midterm elections. Speaker Boehner abruptly resigned his position in 2015. He was replaced by Wisconsin Representative Paul Ryan before Pelosi regained the speakership in 2018. Rep. Pelosi was reelected as speaker following the 2020 election.

**FIGURE 12.5**
**Speaker of the House Nancy Pelosi**

Nancy Pelosi, the first female Speaker of the House, regained the Speaker's post following the 2018 midterm elections.

Source: United States Government [Public domain], via Wikimedia Commons; https://commons.wikimedia.org/wiki/File:Nancy_Pelosi,_official_photo_portrait,_111th_Congress.jpg.

## Floor Leaders

The Republicans and Democrats elect floor leaders who coordinate legislative initiatives and serve as the chief spokespersons for their parties on the House floor. These positions are held by experienced legislators who have earned the respect of their colleagues. Floor leaders actively work at attracting media coverage to promote their party's agenda. The leadership offices all have their own press secretaries.

The **House majority leader** is second to the Speaker in the majority party hierarchy. Working with the Speaker, they are responsible for setting the annual legislative agenda, scheduling legislation for consideration, and coordinating committee activity. The majority leader operates behind the scenes to ensure that the party gets the votes it needs to pass legislation. They consult with members and urge them to support the majority party and work with congressional leaders and the president, when the two are of the same party, to build coalitions. The majority leader monitors the floor carefully when bills are debated, to keep their party members abreast of any key developments.[45] Rep. Kevin McCarthy (R-CA), a self-described conservative, was elected majority leader in 2014, replacing Rep. Eric Cantor (R-VA). Rep. McCarthy was replaced by Rep. Steny Hoyer (D-MD), who was chosen as House majority leader by his Democratic colleagues following the 2018 midterm elections. Rep. Hoyer held this position when the Democrats were last in the majority from 2007 through 2010. Rep. Hoyer remained House majority leader after the 2020 election.

**House majority leader**

Second in the majority party hierarchy, the majority leader works with the Speaker of the House to set the legislative agenda, coordinate committee activity, and schedule legislation for consideration.

### Link

**House Leadership**

Click here to see the current leadership in the House of Representatives.

**FIGURE 12.6 House Majority Leader Steny Hoyer and House Minority Leader Kevin McCarthy**
On the left is Rep. Steny Hoyer (D-MD) who became House majority leader following the 2018 midterm elections. On the right is Rep. Kevin McCarthy (R-CA) who became House minority leader following the 2018 midterm elections.

Sources: United States Congress [Public domain], via Wikimedia Commons; https://commons.wikimedia.org/wiki/File:Steny_Hoyer,_official_photo_as_Whip.jpg. United States Congress [Public domain]; https://commons.wikimedia.org/wiki/File:House_Maj._Leader_Kevin_McCarthy_official_photo.jpg.

**House minority leader**

The head of the party with the fewest members in the House, who conveys the minority party's positions on issues and courts the press.

The **House minority leader** is the head of the party—Democrat or Republican—that has the fewest members in the chamber. They are the head of their party in the House and receives significant media coverage. They articulate the minority party's policies and rally members to court the media and publicly challenge the policies of the majority party. They devise tactics that will place the minority party in the best position for influencing legislation by developing alternatives to legislative proposals supported by the majority. During periods of divided government, when the president is a member of the minority party, the minority leader serves as the president's chief spokesperson in the House.[46] Rep. Kevin McCarthy (R-CA) became minority leader following the 2018 midterm elections when the Republicans lost their majority in the House. Previously, McCarthy had held the position of House majority leader, beginning in 2014. Rep. McCarthy kept his position as House minority leader after the 2020 election.

## Whips

Members of Congress from the Republican and Democratic parties elect whips, who are responsible for encouraging party loyalty and discipline in the House. Aided by extensive networks of deputies and assistants, whips make sure that the lines of communication between leaders and members remain open. In 2002, whip Steny Hoyer (D-MD) greatly expanded his organization to include forty senior whips and thirty assistant whips to enforce a "strategy of inclusion," which gives more members the opportunity to work closely with party leaders and become vested in party decisions. This strategy made more party leaders with expertise available to the press in the hopes of increasing coverage of the Democratic Party's positions. Whips keep track of members' voting intentions on key bills and try to persuade wayward members to toe the party line.[47]

## Key Takeaways

An extensive leadership structure provides an organizational framework that helps House members work effectively, if not efficiently. At the top of the leadership hierarchy is the Speaker of the House, who is the body's presiding officer. Majority and minority leaders help set their party's agenda on issues. The whips encourage party unity on House votes.

## Exercises

1. What is the House Rules Committee? What makes it important to controlling what legislation gets through the House?
2. How do the roles of Speaker of the House and majority leader differ? What do party whips do?

# 12.6 Senate Leadership

## Learning Objectives

After reading this section, you should be able to answer the following questions:

1. Who makes up the Senate leadership?
2. What roles do the presiding officer, floor leaders, and whips play in the Senate?

The Senate leadership structure is similar to that in the House. The smaller chamber lacks the extensive formal rules of the House and thus requires its leaders to use their political and personal relations skills to move legislation through the institution.

## Presiding Officer

The **presiding officer** convenes floor action in the Senate. Unlike the Speaker of the House, the Senate's presiding officer is not the most visible or powerful member. The Senate majority leader has this distinction.

The Constitution designates the vice president as president of the Senate, although they rarely preside and can vote only to break a tie. Since the founding, the vice president has cast 268 tie-breaking votes. During his term, Vice President Mike Pence cast thirteen tie-breaking votes, the most of any modern vice president.

**presiding officer**

The Constitution designates the vice president as the president of the Senate; when the vice president is absent, the majority leader of the Senate becomes the president pro tempore and presides over the Senate.

**president pro tempore**

The second-highest ranking member of the Senate after the vice president, who presides over the Senate in the absence of the vice president.

In the absence of the vice president, the Constitution provides for the **president pro tempore** to preside. The president pro tempore is the second-highest ranking member of the Senate behind the vice president. By convention, the president pro tempore is the majority party senator with the longest continuous service. The president pro tempore shares presiding officer duties with a handful of junior senators from both parties, who take half-hour shifts in the position. Following the 2020 election, Vice President Kamala Harris became the first female to hold the position of president of the Senate.

**FIGURE 12.7 Current Presiding Officer and President Pro Tempore**
Vice President Kamala Harris (on the left) serves as presiding officer of the Senate and only casts a vote in case of a tie. Senator Patrick Leahy (on the right) serves as the president pro tempore of the Senate.

Sources: Office of Senator Kamala Harris via Wikimedia: https://commons.wikimedia.org/wiki/File:Kamala_Harris_official_photo_(cropped2).jpg.; Senate Judiciary Committee, Public domain, via Wikimedia Commons; https://commons.wikimedia.org/wiki/File:Leahy2009.jpg.

# Floor Leaders

**Senate majority leader**

The most influential member of the Senate, who is responsible for managing the Senate's business and managing the floor.

**right of first recognition**

The right of the Senate majority leader to speak on the floor before all other senators.

The **Senate majority leader**, who is elected by the majority party, is the most influential member of the Senate. They are responsible for managing the business of the Senate by setting the schedule and overseeing floor activity. They are entitled to the **right of first recognition**, whereby the presiding officer allows them to speak on the floor before other senators. This right gives them a strategic advantage when trying to pass or defeat legislation, as they can seek to limit debate and amendments. Senator Mitch McConnell (R-KY) was elected majority leader by the Republican Party in the Senate in 2016 and continued in that post following the 2018 midterm elections. He was replaced by Senator Charles Schumer (D-NY) following the 2020 election, and McConnell became the Senate minority leader.

**FIGURE 12.8** Senate Majority and Minority Leaders

On the left is Senate Majority Leader Charles Schumer, a Democrat from New York. On the right is Senator Mitch McConnell, a Republican from Kentucky and the Senate minority leader.

Source: Senate Photographic Studio/Jeff McEvoy [Public domain]; https://commons.wikimedia.org/wiki/File:Chuck_Schumer_official_photo.jpg; Office of Senator Mitch McConnell via Wikimedia: https://commons.wikimedia.org/wiki/File:Mitch_McConnell_portrait_2016.jpg.

The **Senate minority leader** is the head of the opposing party. They work closely with the majority leader on scheduling. They confer regularly with members of their party to develop tactics for promoting their interests in the Senate. Senator Mitch McConnell (R-KY) became the Senate minority leader following the 2020 election.

**Senate minority leader**

The head of the opposing party in the Senate, who works closely with the majority leader on scheduling business while also developing strategies for their party to promote its policy objectives.

## Whips

**Senate whips (assistant floor leaders)** are referred to as assistant floor leaders, as they fill in when the majority and minority leaders are absent from the floor. Like their House counterparts, Senate whips are charged with devising a party strategy for passing legislation, keeping their party unified on votes, and building coalitions. The Senate whip network is not as extensive as its House counterpart. The greater intimacy of relationships in the Senate makes it easier for floor leaders to know how members will vote without relying on whip counts.

**Senate whips (assistant floor leaders)**

Senators who work to devise party strategies on policy issues and to ensure party unity on Senate votes.

### Key Takeaways

The Senate leadership consists of the presiding officer, majority leader, minority leader, and whips. Unlike in the House, where the Speaker wields considerable power, the presiding officer is not the most visible member of the Senate and can only vote in case of a tie. The majority and minority leaders work together to schedule and manage Senate business. Whips are less important in the Senate than in the House because the closer personal relationships that develop in the smaller body make it easier to know how members will vote without a formal whip count.

## Exercises

1. What formal power does the vice president wield in the Senate? Who presides over the Senate when the vice president is absent?
2. What is the right of first recognition? How does it give the Senate majority leader an advantage in legislative battles?

# 12.7 Committees

## Learning Objectives

After reading this section, you should be able to answer the following questions:

1. What criteria do members use when seeking congressional committee assignments?
2. What are the prestige committees in the House and Senate?
3. What is the function of investigative committees?

In 1885, Woodrow Wilson famously observed, "Congress in session is Congress on public exhibition, whilst Congress in its committee-rooms is Congress at work."[48] This statement is no less true today. Committees are the lifeblood of Congress. They develop legislation, oversee executive agencies and programs, and conduct investigations.

**FIGURE 12.9 Senate Armed Services Committee Hearing**

This 2007 image shows Admiral Mike Mullen and General James E. Cartwright testifying during their confirmation hearing in front of the Senate Armed Services Committee for appointment to chairman and vice chairman of the Joint Chiefs of Staff.

Source: Petty Officer 1st Class Chad J. McNeeley. United States Navy image ID 070731-N-0696M-301. Via Wikimedias: https://en.wikipedia.org/wiki/File:Deense.gov_photo_essay_070731-N-0696M-301.jpg#filelinks.

There are different types of committees that are responsible for particular aspects of congressional work. **Standing committees** are permanent legislative committees. **Select committees** are special committees that are formed to deal with a particular issue or policy. **Special committees** can investigate problems and issue reports. **Joint committees** are composed of members of the House and Senate and handle matters that require joint jurisdiction, such as the Postal Service and the Government Printing Office. **Subcommittees** handle specialized aspects of legislation and policy.

**standing committees**

Permanent legislative committees in the House and Senate.

**select committees**

Special congressional committees that are formed to deal with particular issues or policies.

**special committees**

Committees that investigate problems and issue reports.

**joint committees**

Committees composed of members of the House and Senate who handle matters that require the attention of both bodies.

**subcommittees**

Committees under the standing committees that handle specific aspects of legislation and policy.

# Committee Assignments

Members seek assignments to committees while considering the overlapping goals of getting reelected, influencing policy, and wielding power and influence. They can promote the interests of their constituencies through committee service and at the same time help their chances at reelection. Members from rural districts desire appointments to the Agriculture Committee, where they can best influence farm policy. Those most interested in foreign policy seek appointment to committees such as the House Foreign Relations and Senate International Affairs Committees, where they can become embroiled in the pressing issues of the day. Power or **prestige committee** assignments in the House include Appropriations, Budget, Commerce, Rules, and Ways and Means. The most powerful committees in the Senate are Appropriations, Armed Services, Commerce, Finance, and Foreign Relations.

**prestige committee**

The most powerful congressional committees; in the House these include Appropriations, Budget, Commerce, Rules, and Ways and Means; in the Senate these include Appropriations, Armed Services, Commerce, Finance, and Foreign Relations.

The U.S. Constitution authorizes the House and Senate to discipline or "punish" its own members for "disorderly Behaviour," criminal conduct, or civil liability in order to protect the integrity of the institution.[49] In February 2021, the House voted to strip Rep. Marjorie Taylor Greene (R-GA) of her committee assignments due to false and incendiary statements she made prior to taking office, including some about executing public officials.[50]

## Link

### House and Senate Committees

A list and description of House and Senate committees can be found here.

**TABLE 12.1 Congressional Committees**

| Committees of the U.S. Congress | |
|---|---|
| **House** | **Senate** |
| **Standing Committees** | |
| • Agriculture | • Agriculture, Nutrition, and Forestry |
| • Appropriations | • Appropriations |
| • Armed Services | • Armed Services |
| • Budget | • Banking, Housing, and Urban Affairs |
| • Education and Labor | • Budget |
| • Energy and Commerce | • Commerce, Science, and Transportation |
| • Ethics | • Energy and Natural Resources |
| • Financial Services | • Environment and Public Works |
| • Foreign Affairs | • Finance |
| • Homeland Security | • Foreign Relations |
| • House Administration | • Health, Education, Labor, and Pensions |
| • Judiciary | • Homeland Security and Governmental Affairs |
| • Natural Resources | • Judiciary |
| • Oversight and Reform | • Rules and Administration |
| • Rules | • Small Business and Entrepreneurship |
| • Science, Space, and Technology | • Veterans' Affairs |
| • Small Business | |
| • Transportation and Infrastructure | |
| • Veterans' Affairs | |
| • Ways and Means | |
| **Special, Select, and Other Committees** | |
| • House Permanent Select Committee on Intelligence | • Aging (Special) |
| • Select Committee on Economic Disparity and Fairness in Growth | • Caucus on International Narcotics Control |
| • Select Committee on the Climate Crisis | • Ethics (Select) |
| • Select Committee on the Modernization of Congress | • Indian Affairs |
| • Select Committee to Investigate the January 6th Attack on the United States Capitol | • Intelligence (Select) |
| **Joint Committees** | |
| • Joint Committee on Printing | |
| • Joint Committee on Taxation | |
| • Joint Committee on the Library | |
| • Joint Economic Committee | |
| **Commissions and Caucuses** | |

| Committees of the U.S. Congress | |
|---|---|
| • Commission on Security and Cooperation in Europe (U.S. Helsinki Commission)<br>• Congressional-Executive Commission on China<br>• Tom Lantos Human Rights Commission | • Congressional Oversight Commission<br>• Senate Commission on Art |

Source: Based on "Committees of the U.S. Congress." Congress.gov. Retrieved from: https://www.congress.gov/committees.

Most House members end up getting assigned to at least one committee that they request. In the House, committee assignments can be a ticket to visibility and influence. Committees provide House members with a platform for attracting media attention, as journalists will seek them out as policy specialists. Senate committee assignments are not as strongly linked to press visibility, as virtually every senator is appointed to at least one powerful committee. The average senator serves on eleven committees and subcommittees, while the average House member serves on five.

Service on powerful subcommittees can provide a platform for attracting media attention. In 1955, the Senate Subcommittee on Juvenile Delinquency staged three days of hearings in New York City as part of its investigation into allegations brought by Senator Estes Kefauver (D-TN), a subcommittee member, that violent comic books could turn children into criminals. The press-friendly hearings featured controversial speakers and slides of comic books depicting a machine gun–toting woman character named "Frisco Mary" blowing away law enforcement officials without remorse, that were circulated widely in the media. Kefauver anticipated that the press generated by these hearings would help him gain publicity for a bid to get on the 1956 Democratic presidential ticket. He lost the presidential nomination battle but ended up the vice presidential candidate for the losing side.[51]

**FIGURE 12.10 Attracting Media Attention**

In the 1950s, Senator Estes Kefauver used controversial comics like "Frisco Mary" to generate press attention for his hearings on juvenile delinquency. This practice of using powerful exhibits to attract media attention to issues continues today.

Source: From Crime Must Pay the Penalty #3. ©1948 by Ace Magazines.

# Committee Work

Committees are powerful gatekeepers. They decide the fate of bills by determining which ones will move forward and be considered by the full House and Senate. Committee members have tremendous influence over the drafting and rewriting of legislation. They have access to experts and information, which gives them an advantage when debating bills on the floor.[52]

Committee chairs are especially influential, as they are able to employ tactics that can make or break bills. Powerful chairs master the committee's subject matter, get to know committee members well, and form coalitions to back their positions. Chairs can reward cooperative members and punish those who oppose them by granting or withholding favors, such as supporting pork barrel legislation that will benefit a member's district.[53]

Most committee work receives limited media coverage. Investigative hearings are the exception, as they can provide opportunities for high drama.

## Committee Investigations

**muckraking journalists**

Reporters in the late 1800s to early 1900s who employed an aggressive and dramatic style to expose corruption through newspaper exposés.

Conducting investigations is one of the most public activities in which congressional committees engage. During the Progressive Era of the 1890s through 1920s, members could gain the attention of **muckraking journalists** by holding investigative hearings to expose corruption in business and government. The first of these was the 1913 "Pujo hearings," in which Rep. Arsene Pujo (D-LA) headed a probe of Wall Street financiers. High-profile investigations in the 1920s included an inquiry into the mismanagement of the Teapot Dome oil reserves. During the Great Depression of the 1930s, Congress conducted an investigation of the stock market, targeting Wall Street once again. Newspapers were willing to devote much front-page ink to these hearings, as reports on the hearings increased newspaper readership. In 1950, Senator Kefauver held hearings investigating organized crime that drew 30 million television viewers at a time when the medium was new to American homes.[54]

**FIGURE 12.11 Senate Watergate Hearings, 1973**

The Senate Watergate hearings in 1973 were a major television and radio event that brought Congress to the attention of the entire nation. Film clips of highlights from the Watergate hearings are available on the Watergate Files website of the Gerald R. Ford Library & Museum.

Source: Everett Collection Historical / Alamy Stock Photo

**Watergate hearings**

Senate investigation in 1973 into the burglaries at the Democratic National Committee headquarters that led to the resignation of President Richard Nixon.

The Senate convened a special committee in 1973 to investigate the Watergate burglaries and cover-up. The burglars had been directed by President Richard Nixon's reelection committee to break into and wiretap the Democratic National Committee headquarters at the Watergate building complex. The **Watergate hearings** became a national television event as 319 hours of the hearings were broadcast and were watched by 85 percent of American households. Gavel-to-gavel coverage of the hearings was broadcast on National Public Radio. The senators who conducted the investigation, especially Chairman Sam Ervin (D-NC) and Senator Howard Baker (R-TN), became household names. The hearings resulted in the conviction of several of President Nixon's aides for obstruction of justice and ultimately led to Nixon's resignation.[55]

In 2002, the House Financial Services Committee held thirteen hearings to uncover how Enron Corporation was able to swindle investors and drive up electricity rates in California while its executives lived the high life. Prior to the hearings, which made "Enron" a household word, there was little press coverage of Enron's questionable operating procedures.

A clip of the Enron hearings before the House illustrates how Congress exercises its investigative power.

View in the online reader

In 2014, the Senate Intelligence Committee released the results of an investigation into an attack on the U.S. diplomatic compound in Benghazi, Libya, which killed four Americans, including the American ambassador, J. Christopher Stevens. The report criticized the U.S. State Department for failing to increase security at the compound after intelligence indicated a potential for violence. The House and Senate Intelligence Committees held hearings in 2017 related to an investigation into the alleged hacking of U.S. elections by the Russians.

The House Judiciary Committee held hearings in 2019 following the release of the *Report on the Investigation into Russian Interference in the 2016 Presidential Election* prepared by special counsel Robert Mueller. The 448-page report found that Russia wanted to help the Trump campaign, although the report did not establish that the campaign had coordinated directly with Russia. The report outlined at least ten instances where the president had attempted to impede the special counsel's investigation and stated that the president could not be exonerated on the question of **obstruction of justice**: whether he specifically intended to interfere with a judicial proceeding.[56] However, the Mueller report left the interpretation of the evidence of obstruction of justice up to others in the Justice Department and Congress. The report was released with portions redacted—blacked out so that they could not be read—and the Judiciary Committee sought to gain access to the full report. The committee sought testimony from the attorney general and others about the findings in the report.[57]

**obstruction of justice**

The act of intentionally interfering with a judicial proceeding. The Mueller report examined whether President Trump sought intentionally to impede the investigation into Russian interference in the 2016 election.

Attorney General William Barr testifies before the Senate Judiciary Committee.

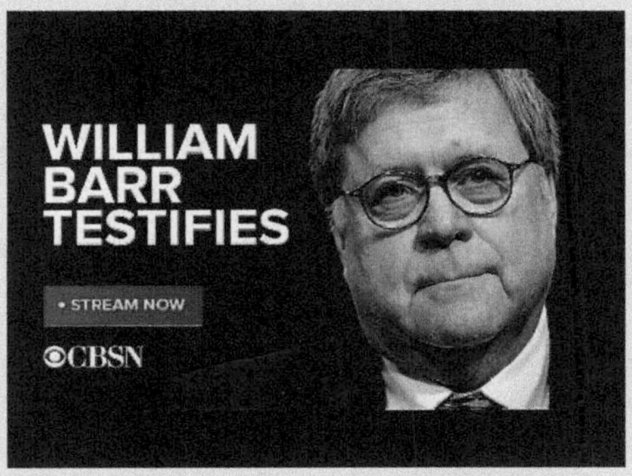


View in the online reader

Special Counsel Robert Mueller testifies before the House Judiciary Committee.

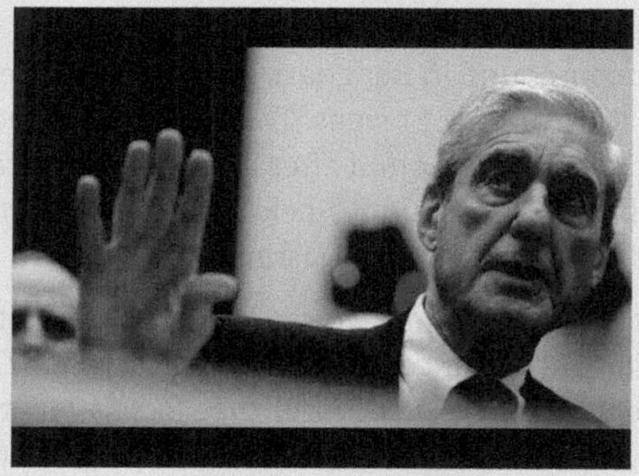

View in the online reader

## Enduring Image

### The House Un-American Activities Committee and Hollywood

Following World War II, chilly relations existed between the United States and the Communist Soviet Union, a nation that had emerged as a strong power and had exploded an atomic bomb.[58] The House Un-American Activities Committee (HUAC), which was established in 1938 to investigate subversive activities, decided to look into allegations that Communists were threatening to overthrow American democracy using force and violence. People in government, the labor movement, and the motion picture industry were accused of being communists. Especially sensational were hearings where Hollywood actors, directors, and writers were called before the HUAC. It was not uncommon for people in Hollywood to have joined the Communist Party during the Great Depression of the 1930s, although many were inactive at the time of the hearings. The HUAC alleged that film "was the principle medium through which Communists have sought to inject their propaganda."[59]

Those accused of being Communists, nicknamed "reds," were called before the HUAC. They were subject to intense questioning by members of Congress and the committee's counsel. In 1947, the HUAC held hearings to investigate the influence of Communists in Hollywood. The "Hollywood Ten," a group of nine screenwriters, including Ring Lardner Jr. and Dalton Trumbo, and director Edward Dmytryk, were paraded before the committee. Members of Congress shouted to the witnesses, "Are you now or have you ever been a member of the Communist Party?" They were commanded to provide the names of people they knew to be Communists or face incarceration. Some of the Hollywood Ten responded aggressively to the committee, not answering questions and making statements asserting their First Amendment right to free expression. Blinding flashbulbs provided a constant backdrop to the hearings, as photographers documented images of dramatic face-offs between committee members and the witnesses. Images of the hearings were disseminated widely in front-page photos in newspapers and magazines and on television.

The HUAC hearings immortalized the dramatic image of the congressional investigation featuring direct confrontations between committee members and witnesses.

Source: Library of Congress, Prints & Photographs Division, photograph by Harris & Ewing, https://www.loc.gov/pictures/item/2016876692/. Via Wikimedia: https://commons.wikimedia.org/wiki/File:Agnes_Reynolds_and_Joseph_P_Lash_1939.jpg.

The Hollywood Ten refused to cooperate with the HUAC, were cited for contempt of Congress, and were sent to prison.[60] They were blacklisted by the leaders of the film industry, along with two hundred other admitted or suspected Communists, and were unable to work in the motion picture industry. Pressured by personal and financial ruin, Edward Dmytryk eventually gave in to the HUAC's demands.

Commercial films have perpetuated the dramatic image of congressional hearings made popular by the HUAC investigations. Films released around the time of the hearings tended to justify the actions of the HUAC, including *Big Jim McClain* (1952) and *On the Waterfront* (1954). The few films made later are more critical. Woody Allen plays a small-time bookie who fronts for blacklisted writers in *The Front* (1976), a film depicting the personal toll exacted by the HUAC and blacklisting. In *Guilty by Suspicion* (1991), Robert DeNiro's character refuses to name names and jeopardizes his career as a director. *One of the Hollywood Ten* (2000) graphically depicts film director Herbert Biberman's experience in front of the HUAC before he is jailed for not cooperating.

## Key Takeaways

Much of the important work in Congress is accomplished through committees. The fate of legislation—which bills will make it to the floor of the House and Senate—is determined in committees. Members seek committee assignments based on their desire to influence policy, exert influence, and get reelected. Most committee work receives little, if any, media coverage. Investigative committees are the exception when media cover hearings on high-profile matters.

## Exercises

1. What is the role of congressional committees? What determines which committees members of Congress seek to be on?
2. What are generally considered to be the most powerful and prestigious committees in Congress? What do you think makes those committees so influential?

# 12.8 The Legislative Process

## Learning Objectives

After reading this section, you should be able to answer the following questions:

1. How does a bill become law?
2. How do members of Congress develop and draft legislation?
3. How does the congressional budget process work?

The primary responsibility of Congress is making laws. Lawmaking is no easy task. Political scientists have characterized Congress as "a procedural obstacle course that favors opponents of legislation and hinders proponents."[61] It often takes years before a bill is passed. Only a small number of bills that are introduced, or formally proposed by members of the House and Senate, become law. On average, close to eleven thousand bills are introduced in the House and Senate during a two-year legislative session, and fewer than four hundred become laws.[62]

**Jefferson's Manual**

The rule book developed by Vice President Thomas Jefferson in 1779 to help carry out his responsibilities as president of the Senate that also was adopted by the House.

The process of making laws involves complex written rules and procedures, some of which date back to 1797, when Vice President Thomas Jefferson prepared a rule book to help him carry out his responsibilities as president of the Senate. **Jefferson's Manual** was adopted by the House and remains the authoritative statement of rules except where it has been superseded by provisions passed by members. In addition, there are fifteen volumes of parliamentary procedures and supplementary manuals of notes specifying current rules that pertain to lawmaking in the House. Similar reams of codes exist in the Senate.[63]

## Making Laws

FIGURE 12.12 How a Bill Becomes a Law

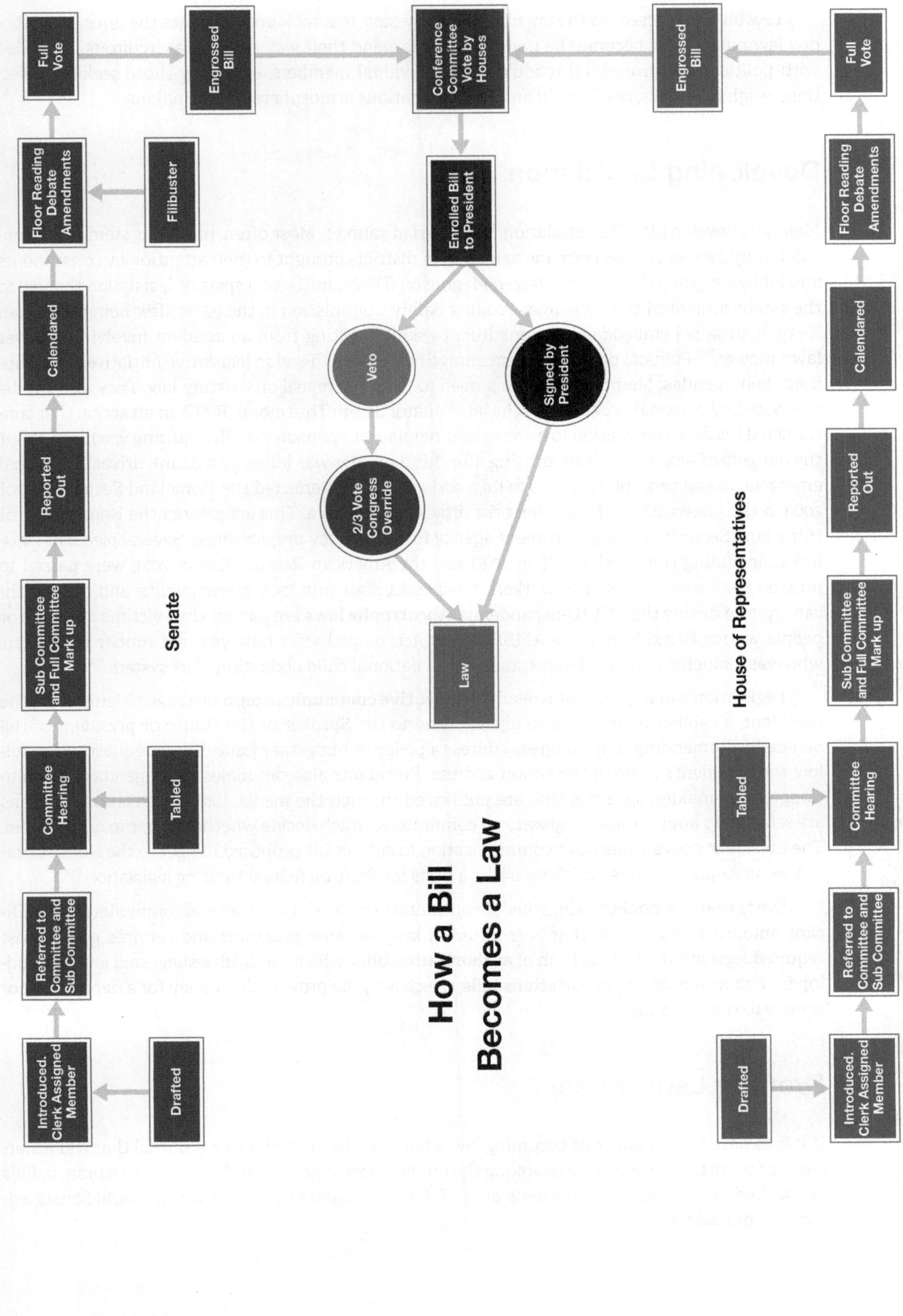


Source: Based on "How a Bill Becomes a Law," http://www.cybertelecom.org/images/howlaw.gif.

The textbook legislative process begins when a member of the House or Senate introduces a bill, which then is referred to appropriate committees within each body. Committees decide whether or not a bill is recommended for floor action, where it will be debated and voted on. The House and Senate must pass identical versions of a bill before it can be sent to the president to be signed into law.

Few bills are passed via the organized, step-by-step, textbook process. Since the 1970s, "unorthodox lawmaking" has become the norm. Most bills wend their way through a circuitous path filled with political and procedural roadblocks.[64] Individual members, especially those seeking reelection, weigh in on bills, resulting in an often contentious atmosphere for lawmaking.

## Developing Legislation

**apostrophe laws**

Laws named after people who experienced harm or were the victims of crimes.

Members develop ideas for legislation from myriad sources. Most often, proposals stem from campaign promises and issues germane to members' districts brought to their attention by constituents and lobbying groups.[65] Senator Warren Magnuson (D-WA) initiated a spate of legislation that led to the establishment of the Consumer Product Safety Commission in the 1970s after being shown an X-ray of shrapnel embedded in a constituent's skull resulting from an accident involving a power lawn mower.[66] Political parties may encourage members to develop legislative initiatives that support their agendas. Members may see a need to revise or repeal an existing law. They also can be motivated by personal experiences. The late Senator Strom Thurmond (R-SC), in an action that contradicted his fierce opposition to government regulation, sponsored a bill requiring warnings about the dangers of alcohol in all advertising after his daughter was killed by a drunk driver.[67] National emergencies can prompt members to take action. Congress enacted the Homeland Security Act of 2002 in the aftermath of the 9/11 terrorist attacks on America. This act created the Department of Homeland Security, a new government agency for emergency preparedness. Several pieces of legislation, including the CARES ACT in 2020 and the American Rescue Plan in 2021, were passed to provide resources and relief to workers, businesses, state and local governments, and the healthcare system during the COVID-19 pandemic. **Apostrophe laws** are named after victims of crimes or people who suffered harm. The AMBER Alert Act, named after nine-year-old Amber Hagerman, who was abducted and murdered, established a national child abduction alert system.[68]

**executive communication**

A message from the president, a cabinet member, or an agency head to the Speaker of the House or president of the Senate recommending that Congress address a policy or budgetary issue.

**docket**

The schedule outlining the congressional workload.

**authorization bills**

Bills that establish the level of funding for a program.

**appropriations bills**

Bills that provide the funding for a department or agency program.

Legislation can originate as a result of **executive communication**, a message or letter from the president, a cabinet member, or an agency head to the Speaker of the House or president of the Senate recommending that Congress address a policy or budgetary issue. These requests often follow the president's State of the Union address. Presidents also can make their agendas known to Congress by making speeches that are publicized through the media. Executive communications are referred to appropriate congressional committees, which decide whether or not to act on them. The president uses an executive communication to submit his proposed budget to the House Committee on Appropriations, which uses it as a basis for drafting federal funding legislation.[69]

Every year, the **docket**—the schedule outlining Congress's workload—accommodates a significant amount of legislation that is required to keep existing programs and services going. Most required legislation takes the form of **authorization bills**, which establish a suggested level of funding for a program, and **appropriations bills**, which actually provide the money for a department or agency to run the program.[70]

## Drafting Legislation

If it is to have much chance of becoming law, a bill must be drafted into a proposal that will generate support in Congress as well as among the public, interest groups, and the executive branch. Bills are drafted by members with the assistance of their staffs and experts in the House and Senate legislative counsel offices.

A bill's language can be instrumental in generating media publicity and subsequently support for or opposition to it. The title can position the bill in the public debate, as it captures the ideas and images proponents wish to convey. Megan's Law, which requires communities to publicize the whereabouts of convicted sex offenders, is named after Megan Kanka, a New Jersey girl who was murdered by a sex offender after his release from prison. Politically charged shorthand often is used to characterize bills. The health-care reform legislation passed by Congress and signed into law by President Barack Obama in 2010 has been labeled "Obamacare" by opponents seeking to repeal the legislation. The House has voted to repeal it more than sixty times without success.[71]

## Introducing Legislation

Members from either the House or Senate can introduce legislation. The member who introduces a bill is its **sponsor**. Other members can sign on as cosponsors, or supporters, of the bill. Having a large number of cosponsors or having congressional leaders sign onto a bill can boost its chances of success.

**sponsor**

The member of Congress who introduces a bill.

Bills are the most typical form of legislation. They can originate in either the House or Senate, with the exception of bills for raising revenue, which must be initiated in the House.[72] The same bill must pass through all the formal procedural hurdles in the House and Senate before it can be sent to the president to be signed into law.

**FIGURE 12.13 Introducing Bills and Debating on the Floor**

Members of the House or Senate introduce bills and open the floor to debate.

Source: Photo courtesy of Leader Nancy Pelosi via Flickr: https://www.flickr.com/photos/speakerpelosi/3721370691/. Reproduced via CC BY 2.0: https://creativecommons.org/licenses/by/2.0/.

## Committee Consideration

After a bill is introduced, it is referred to the standing committee having jurisdiction over its subject matter, such as energy or homeland security, by the presiding officers in each chamber. Having a bill referred to a friendly committee is a key to its potential for success. In the House, but not the Senate, a bill may be considered by more than one committee.[73] Committees in both chambers frequently pass a bill on to a subcommittee that deals with a specialized area of policy contained in the legislation. As more people work on a bill, the less likely it is they will reach consensus and that the bill will move beyond the committee stage.[74]

Committees sometimes request input about a bill from government departments and agencies and hold public hearings where expert witnesses testify. When members seek media coverage of committee hearings, they sometimes will bring in celebrities as witnesses.

Facebook's chief executive, Mark Zuckerberg, testified before Congress about data privacy after Facebook released 87 million users' personal data to firms that used it to target voters during the 2016 election. Members also grilled Zuckerberg about "fake news" stories and misinformation that appears on Facebook. Zuckerberg pledged that Facebook would take steps to ensure that data privacy was maintained.[75]

**FIGURE 12.14 Elmo Testifies in the House**

*Sesame Street*'s Elmo testified in front of the House Education Appropriations Subcommittee in 2002 in support of funding for school music programs.

Source: Scott J. Ferrell / Contributor / Getty Images

**Link**

Click here for a list of celebrities who have appeared before Congress.

Facebook chief executive Mark Zuckerberg testifies before Congress about internet privacy.

View in the online reader

Stephen Colbert's highly publicized testimony before Congress on behalf of immigration reform was both praised and criticized.

View in the online reader

The full committee votes to determine if the bill will be reported, meaning it will be sent to the floor for debate. If the vote is successful, the committee holds a **markup** session to revise the bill. The committee prepares a report documenting why it supports the bill. The report is sent to the whole chamber, and the bill is placed on the calendar to await floor debate.

In the House, bills must go the **Rules Committee** before reaching the floor. The Rules Committee assigns a bill a rule that sets the procedures under which the bill will be considered on the floor. The rule establishes the parameters of debate and specifies if **amendments**, proposed changes to the bill, will be permitted or not. A bill can become stalled if the Rules Committee does not assign it a rule at all or in a timely manner. Rules must be approved by a majority of the members of the House before floor action can begin. There is no Rules Committee in the Senate, where the process of bringing a bill to the floor is simpler and less formal. The Senate majority leader makes a motion to proceed with floor debate.

**markup**

Process of revising a bill.

**Rules Committee**

The committee that sets the procedure under which bills will be considered on the House floor.

**amendments**

Proposed changes to a bill.

## Floor Action

Once a bill reaches the House or Senate floor, it is debated, amended, and voted on. Many of the bills that make it to the floor are minor bills—noncontroversial measures that have symbolic value, such as naming a post office.[76] Floor consideration of most minor bills is brief, and they are approved by voice vote. Major bills focusing on divisive issues, such as budgetary proposals, health care, and national security, will prompt lengthy debate and amendment proposals before coming to a vote. A bill dies if either chamber fails to pass it.

**Committee of the Whole**

The entire House when it meets to consider a bill.

In the House, bills are considered by the full House meeting in the chamber, which is referred to as the **Committee of the Whole**. The Speaker of the House chooses a chairperson to oversee floor action. Speakers for and against the bill have an equal amount of time. A general debate of the bill is followed by debate of amendments. A quorum of 218 members is required for a vote on the bill. Yeas and nays are recorded using a computerized system.

**filibuster**

Extended debate in the Senate that blocks or delays the passage of legislation.

**unanimous consent agreements**

Negotiated agreements that set time limits on debate in the Senate.

**cloture**

A motion to limit consideration of a bill and close debate.

Senate floor action is less structured and more unpredictable than the House procedure. Senators are free to speak as long as they like. The **filibuster** can be used by skillful senators to defeat a bill by "talking it to death." To avoid lengthy and unproductive floor sessions, the Senate can employ **unanimous consent agreements**, negotiated agreements that set time limitations on debate.[77] Debate also can be restricted if three-fifths of the senators vote to invoke **cloture**, a motion to limit consideration of a bill. Getting sixty senators to agree to close debate is not easy, especially on controversial issues. Senators vote on the bill using a traditional call of the roll, with each voice vote recorded manually.

## Conference Committee

**conference committee**

A committee that works out differences between House and Senate versions of a bill.

If House and Senate versions of a bill are not the same, a **conference committee** is formed to work out the differences. Conference committees consist of members of both houses. In 1934, Senator George Norris (R-NE) characterized conference committees as the "third house of Congress" because of the power they wield in the legislative process.[78] They are the last places in which big changes in legislation can be made. Major changes in the provisions and language of bills are negotiated in conference committees. Up to 80 percent of important bills during a session of Congress end up in conference committees.[79]

During conference committee negotiations, conferees meet informally with party leaders and members who have an interest in the bill. Representatives of the executive branch work with conferees to devise a final bill that the president will be likely to sign. Once an agreement has been reached, the conference committee issues a report that must be passed by the House and Senate before the bill moves forward to be signed into law by the president.[80]

## Presidential Approval

**veto**

The president's power to reject a bill by not signing it into law.

A bill becomes law when it is signed by the president. A president can **veto**, or reject, a bill by sending it back to Congress with a memorandum indicating any objections. Congress can override a veto with a two-thirds vote in each chamber, enabling the bill to become a law over the president's objections.[81]

**FIGURE 12.15 Signing Bills into Laws**

After passing through both houses of Congress, a bill does not become a law until it is signed by the president.

Source: The White House. P20210608CW-1394. President Joe Biden, joined by Vice President Kamala Harris, lawmakers and guests, signs the Juneteenth National Independence Day Act Bill on Thursday, June 17, 2021. Via Flickr: https://www.flickr.com/photos/whitehouse/51269120779/in/album-72157719342698874/.

# The Budget Process

One of the most arduous tasks faced by Congress is passing legislation authorizing the nation's annual budget. House and Senate members, their staffs, and congressional committees in conjunction with the president and the executive branch are responsible for preparing the budget. The president submits a detailed budget proposal to Congress, which serves as a starting point. The House and Senate Budget Committees hold hearings on the budget to get advice about how funds should be spent.

The nonpartisan **Congressional Budget Office** (CBO), with a staff of over 230 economists and policy analysts, provides expert budgetary advice to Congress. It reviews the president's budget plan, projects the actual costs of budget items, and develops options for changes in taxing and spending. CBO staffers prepare detailed reports on the budget and testify before Congress.[82]

**Congressional Budget Office**

Provides expert budgetary advice to Congress.

A two-step authorization and appropriations process is required to establish and fund specific programs within the guidelines set by the annual budget. Congress must first pass laws authorizing or recommending that federal programs receive funding at a particular level. The appropriations process, where funds are actually allocated to programs for spending, is the second step. The House Appropriations Committee initiates all bills to fund programs, and its counterpart in the Senate must approve funding bills. The budget resolution that ultimately passes the House and Senate Budget Committees is usually markedly different from the president's budget proposal.

The budget process rarely goes smoothly. The process can stall, as was the case in 2011 when the inability of Congress to reach an agreement on the budget threatened to result in a government shutdown. Media coverage highlighting partisan bickering over what to fund and what to cut from the budget added to the drama surrounding the budget process. In 2014, members of Congress reached a compromise and passed a budget with less controversy than in recent years. After much negotiation, Congress passed a bill in April 2017 to keep the government open until September. The government then shut down for thirty-five days, from December 22, 2018, to January 25, 2019, as President Trump demanded more than $5 billion in the budget to fund a wall along the U.S.–Mexico border. The longest government shutdown in history was ended when the president signed a bill passed by the House to reopen the government without funding for the border wall.[83]

## C-SPAN

**C-SPAN**

The cable network that provides gavel-to-gavel coverage of congressional floor proceedings, committee hearings, and special events.

Members of the public can follow congressional action live on television. After much debate, televised coverage of floor proceedings via the Cable Satellite Public Affairs Network (C-SPAN) was established in the House in 1979 and in the Senate in 1986. **C-SPAN** transmits gavel-to-gavel coverage of floor action. It covers committee hearings and broadcasts educational panels and events.

C-SPAN affirmed Congress as a media-conscious institution.[84] A top Rules Committee staffer explained that Congress had tired of losing the battle with the president for media attention: "President Richard Nixon was dominating the airwaves with defenses of his Vietnam War policies, while congressional opponents were not being given equal access by the networks."[85]

C-SPAN's cameras show Congress at its best and worst, at its most dramatic and most mundane. They showcase members' elegant floor speeches and capture them joking and looking bored during hearings. C-SPAN is monitored continuously in most congressional offices and is a source of information and images for other mass media.

C-SPAN has expanded its operation beyond cable television and provides extensive radio and online coverage of Congress, the White House, and national politics. In addition to livestreams of television and radio feeds from Capitol Hill, the C-SPAN website includes news stories, opinion pieces, history, educational materials, and event coverage. C-SPAN has an extensive social media presence.

### Link

**C-SPAN's Channel on YouTube**

People can follow C-SPAN via Twitter, Facebook, and Foursquare. C-SPAN has its own YouTube channel that hosts an extensive political video library.

### Key Takeaways

Making laws is a complex process guided by volumes of rules and influenced by politics. While many bills are proposed each congressional session, few make it all the way through the process to be signed by the president and made law. Congress is responsible for passing legislation enacting the nation's annual budget, which is frequently a difficult task. The activities of Congress are reported by C-SPAN, which began as a cable network providing gavel-to-gavel coverage of floor proceedings and has expanded to become an extensive resource for information about government and politics.

## Exercises

1. Who can introduce legislation? What are the various stages at which bills face votes as they move through Congress?
2. What are the two steps of the budget process? Which committee has the power to initiate funding bills?

# 12.9 Members of Congress

## Learning Objectives

After reading this section, you should be able to answer the following questions:

1. What kinds of people are elected to Congress?
2. How do members make news and generate publicity for themselves?
3. What jobs are performed by congressional staff members?
4. Why do members of Congress emphasize constituent service?

Members of Congress are local politicians serving in a national institution. They spend their days moving between two worlds—their home districts and Washington. While many come from the ranks of the social and economic elite, to be successful they must be true to their local roots.

Members tailor the job to their personalities, interests, objectives, and constituent needs.[86] They engage in activities that better their chances for reelection. This strategy works, as the reelection rate for incumbents is over 90 percent.[87] They promote themselves and reach out to constituents by participating in events and public forums in their home districts. Outreach includes using social media to connect with the public. Members of Congress take positions on issues that will be received favorably. They claim success for legislative activity that helps the district—and voters believe them.[88] Successful members excel at **constituent service**, helping people in the district deal with problems and negotiate the government bureaucracy.

**constituent service**

Members of Congress help people in their home districts deal with problems and negotiate government bureaucracy.

**FIGURE 12.16 Safety of Congresspeople**

Congresswoman Gabrielle Giffords (D-AZ) was shot outside a grocery store where she was holding a "Congress on Your Corner" event to meet personally with constituents in her district in 2011. Six people were killed, including a nine-year-old girl, in the incident, which raised issues about the safety of members of Congress. Today, Giffords and her husband, former astronaut Mark Kelly, who was elected as senator from Arizona in 2020, are activists seeking to curb gun violence.

Source: Photo courtesy of Wayno Guerrini via Wikimedia: http://commons.wikimedia.org/wiki/File:Memorial_in_front_of_office_of_Gabrielle_Giffords. jpg. Reproduced via CC BY-SA 3.0: https://creativecommons.org/licenses/by-sa/3.0/deed.en.

# Profile of Members

The vast majority of members of Congress are white males from middle- to upper-income groups. A majority are baby boomers, born between 1946 and 1964. The 111th Congress—which coincided with the administration of President Barack Obama, one of the nation's youngest presidents, who took office at age forty-seven—was the oldest in history. Most members have a college education, and many have advanced degrees. While members have diverse religious affiliations, the majority of members are Christian. Roman Catholics represent the single largest religious denomination.[89]

For the first time in 2018, almost half of the members elected to the House were not white men. More women were elected than at any other time in the over two-hundred-year history of the institution. Congress became more racially and ethnically diverse. More younger members were elected than in the past. Alexandria Ocasio-Cortez, who beat a long-time incumbent to win the Democratic nomination in the Bronx, New York, was the youngest person elected, at age twenty-nine.[90] Despite these recent demographic shifts, the 117th Congress remains predominantly white, male, and older. See Table 12.2 for more information.

**TABLE 12.2** Who Makes Up the U.S. Congress?

| | |
|---|---|
| **Gender and Race** | Since the 1980s, more women and members of diverse ethnic and racial groups have been elected, but they are still massively underrepresented. Women won an unprecedented number of congressional seats in the 2018 midterm contests. Some political analysts have called this increase in female representation a "pink wave" that heavily favored the Democratic Party. One-hundred forty-six of the seats in the 117th Congress, or 27 percent, were held by women. The number of women in the House reached 122, which includes three non-voting delegates, and twenty-four in the Senate.[91]<br>The freshman congressional class that took office in 2019 was the most racially diverse of all time. The number of Latinx and Black people increased as a result of the 2018 midterm elections. The freshman congressional class also includes the first Indigenous American congresswomen and the first Muslim congresswomen. In 2021, the 117th Congress seated a record sixty Black people, fifty-four Latinx people, and eleven Asian American Pacific Islanders.[92]<br>Women and minority group representation in Congress can make a difference in the types of policy issues that are debated. Women members are more likely to focus on issues related to health care, poverty, and education. They have brought media attention to domestic violence and child custody. Members of minority groups raise issues pertinent to their constituents, such as special cancer risks experienced by Latinxs and hate crimes experienced by Asian Americans during the COVID-19 pandemic. However, the small number of women and minorities serving can hinder their ability to get legislation passed.[93] |
| **Wealth** | Members of Congress are a wealthy group. More than half of all members in are millionaires. More than fifty had a net worth of over $10 million.[94] In 2020, members' median net worth was over $1 million.[95] In comparison, less than one percent of Americans are millionaires. Members of the House and Senate earn a salary of $174,000; leaders are compensated slightly more. The Speaker of the House is the highest paid member, earning $223,500 in 2021, and the majority and minority leaders earn $193,400.[96] While this may seem like a lot of money, most members must maintain residences in Washington, DC, and their districts and must pay for trips back home.[97] |
| **Occupations** | For many members, serving in Congress is a career. Members of the House serve an average of nine years, or almost five terms. Senators average nearly eleven years, or almost two terms. Almost 75 percent of members seek reelection each cycle.[98] Members leave office because they seek more lucrative careers, such as in lobbying offices, or because they are ready to retire or are defeated.<br>Many members come from backgrounds other than politics, such as medicine, and bring experience from these fields to the lawmaking process. Business, law, and public service have been the dominant professions of members of Congress for decades.[99] Members who have come from nontraditional occupations include an astronaut, a magician, a musician, a professional baseball player, an NFL football player, and a bartender. Members also come from media backgrounds, including television reporters and an occasional sportscaster. Previous legislative experience is a useful qualification for members. Many were congressional staffers or state legislators in earlier careers.[100] |

# Members Making News

Because disseminating information and generating publicity are keys to governing, gaining reelection, and moving careers forward, many members of Congress hungrily seek media attention. They use publicity to rally public opinion behind their legislative proposals and to keep constituents abreast of their accomplishments. Media attention is especially important when constituents are deciding whether to retain or replace their member during elections or scandals.[101]

**show horse**

A member of Congress who actively seeks press attention.

**work horse**

A member of Congress who works behind the scenes to carry out the business of the institution and get legislation passed.

Members of Congress toe a thin line in their relations with the media. While garnering press attention and staying in the public eye may be a useful strategy, grabbing too much of the media spotlight can backfire, earning members a reputation for being more "**show horse**" than "**work horse**" and raising the ire of their colleagues.

Attracting national media attention is easier said than done for most members.[102] Members engage a variety of promotional tactics to court the press. They distribute press releases and hold press conferences. They use the Capitol's studio facilities to tape television and radio clips that are distributed to journalists via the internet. Rank-and-file members can increase their visibility by participating in events with prominent leaders. They can stage events or hold joint press conferences and photo ops.

## Enduring Image

Rep. Alexandria Ocasio-Cortez (D-NY), known as AOC, gained more media attention than any of the Democratic candidates who ran for president in 2020. In fact, she has gotten more national press coverage in the short time she has been in Congress than most members get in their entire careers. Much of the coverage of AOC is generated by her strong social media presence, especially her frequent use of Twitter. Even when press stories about AOC are negative, she manages to use the publicity to advocate for causes that she supports, such as the Green New Deal.[103]

Rep. Alexandria Ocasio-Cortez receives more national press coverage than most members of Congress, which she uses to publicize issues and policies that she cares about.

Source: nrkbeta. Alexandria Ocasio-Cortez @ SXSW 2019.

Just before she was sworn in as the youngest woman ever elected to the House, a video of AOC dancing barefoot on a rooftop while she was in college was posted anonymously in an effort to embarrass her. Instead, the video became a viral sensation as supporters shared it widely, edited the video to make ads, and generated memes. The video gained over 12 million views on Twitter in less than one day and was widely reported in the mainstream press. The positive response to the video far outweighed any negative reactions and helped to bring her to national attention.[104]

Video of Rep. Alexandria Ocasio-Cortez (D-NY) dancing generated press coverage for the newly elected House member.

View in the online reader

Members of Congress use new media strategies to inform the public, court the media, and gain publicity. All members have websites that publicize their activities and achievements. Some members make their views known through blog posts, including in online publications like TheHill.com and the Huffington Post. The vast majority of members of Congress use Twitter to post brief announcements ranging from alerts about pending legislation to shout-outs to constituents who are celebrating anniversaries to Bible verses. In 2014, about fifty members refused to join the Twitter revolution, claiming that it was impossible to talk about policy using the then 140-character limit. By 2017, staying off Twitter was not an option for most members of Congress, and today virtually all members have a Twitter account.

# Congressional Staff

Members have personal staffs to help them manage their workload. They also work with committee staff who specialize in particular policy areas. Most Hill staffers are young, white, male, and ambitious. Most members maintain a staff in their home districts to handle constituent service.

Congressional staff has grown substantially since the 1970s as the number of policy issues and bills considered by Congress increased. Today, House personal staffs consist of an average of fourteen people. Senate staffs range in size from thirteen to seventy-one and average about thirty-four people.[105] As a result of staff expansion, each member has become the head of an enterprise—an organization of subordinates who form their own community that reflects the personality and strengths of the member.[106]

Congressional staffers have specialized responsibilities. Some staffers have administrative responsibilities, such as running the office and handling the member's schedule. Others are responsible for assisting members with policy matters. Personal staffers work in conjunction with committee staffers to research and prepare legislation. They write speeches and position papers. Some act as brokers for members, negotiating support for bills and dealing with lobbyists. Staff influence over the legislative process can be significant, as staffers become experts on policies and take the lead on issues behind the scenes.[107]

Some staff members focus on constituent service. They spend a tremendous amount of time carefully crafting answers to the mountains of correspondence from constituents that arrive every day via snail mail, email, fax, and phone. People write to express their views on legislation, to seek information about policies, and to express their pleasure or dissatisfaction about a member's actions. They also contact members to ask for help with personal matters, such as immigration issues, or to alert members of potential public health menaces, such as faulty wiring in a large apartment building in the district.

**franking privilege**

The ability of Congress members to post mail without cost.

Members of Congress resisted using email to communicate until recent years. Members were not assigned email addresses until 1995. Despite the daunting flood of messages, email has helped congressional offices communicate with constituents efficiently. While the **franking privilege**, members' ability to post mail without cost, is still important, email has reduced the significance of this perk.

All members of Congress have press secretaries to coordinate their interactions with the media. They bring a journalistic perspective to congressional offices, acting as consultants in devising media strategies. In recent years, the press secretary's job has expanded to include using social media to publicize the member's actions and positions. A press secretary for a publicity-seeking member who faces tough reelection bids constantly courts the media, making personal contacts, writing press releases, staging photo ops and events, and helping the member prepare video and audio interviews. The press secretary constantly updates the member's Facebook and Twitter messages and YouTube videos. A press secretary for a member in a secure seat who prefers a low-key media presence concentrates on maintaining contact with constituents through newsletters and the member's website. Some offices now employ staff members whose primary responsibility is to handle digital media.

## Key Takeaways

In recent years, the membership of Congress has become increasingly diverse, as more women and minority group members have been elected. Still, the dominant profile of the typical member of Congress is an older, white male. Members of Congress are far more wealthy than average Americans. In addition to their constitutional duties, members of Congress engage in a host of other activities, many of which are related to getting reelected. Members strive to maintain close connections with their constituents while serving in Washington. They seek to publicize their activities through the mainstream press as well as social media. Congressional staffers aid members in keeping abreast of policy issues, performing constituent service, and dealing with the press.

## Exercises

1. Who represents you in Congress? How do they compare with the typical member of Congress?
2. How can members of Congress attract media attention? What are the dangers of trying too hard for media attention?

# 12.10 Congress in the Information Age

## Learning Objectives

After reading this section, you should be able to answer the following questions:

1. How has Congress's relationship to the media differed from that of the president?
2. How do members communicate with their constituents and the press?
3. How are members depicted by news media and popular media?
4. What are the effects of media coverage of Congress on public perceptions of the institution?

Congressional media relations in the information age are as complex as the 535 members of the House and Senate are unique. The size, convoluted organization, and many rules governing Congress do not make for a media-friendly institution. The media environment has become more complicated to negotiate, as members must contend with both traditional news media and social media, which provide a two-way flow of information between legislators and their constituents. Members now frequently take to social media to get their message out to the press and the public as well as to communicate with one another.

## Media Interactions

When asked by a *Time* magazine reporter to identify the most underplayed story of our times, former news anchor Walter Cronkite replied, "Congress. This is where our laws are made, where our laws are debated, and we don't cover Congress the way it ought to be."[108]

Cronkite's observation speaks to the changing relations between the national press and Congress over time. For the first century of the republic, Congress and its members were far more visible in newspapers than presidents, who felt it was beneath the dignity of the office to speak on public issues. Debates on Capitol Hill were widely reprinted in partisan papers. The profit-minded penny press of the 1830s found Washington news attractive but often focused on members' personal escapades, which raised the ire and suspicion of congressmen. Congress adopted the practice of reviewing reporters' credentials, granting them permission to sit in the drafty public gallery on a case-by-case basis. When the Capitol was rebuilt in the 1850s, the construction included press galleries, separate areas to which reporters were automatically admitted on the recommendation of their editors.

By the 1920s, the president made most of the news, Congress was relegated to a distant second place, and the Supreme Court received the least press.[109] The modern relationship between the media and Congress took shape in the 1970s, when *Washington Post* reporters Bob Woodward and Carl Bernstein broke the story about the break-in at the Democratic National Committee headquarters at the behest of the Nixon White House to uncover Democrats' campaign strategies. Hundreds of reporters were sent to Washington to cover the Watergate scandal, and many stayed after discovering that the town was ripe with stories. The Watergate scandal prompted Congress to pass **sunshine laws**, which opened most hearings to the public and the press. Many members welcomed the opportunity offered by the invigorated Washington press corps to promote themselves to their constituents.

**sunshine laws**

Laws passed by Congress to open hearings to the public and the press.

Today, members of Congress often seek media attention for their actions and policy preferences, thinking that it will sway public opinion in their favor. However, much media coverage focuses on the partisan conflict and extreme positions taken by members seeking publicity, which turns off the public. As the amount of media coverage of Congress has grown in the era of social media, policymaking has become more difficult.[110]

## Congress versus the President

There are a number of reasons why President Trump was the newsmaker-in-chief while Congress remained in his shadow. The president was a media magnet because he was a single individual at the hub of the executive branch. President Donald Trump drew a great deal of attention to himself through his impulsive and sensational tweets, which were reported widely by the press. This made it more difficult for reporters to cover Capitol Hill. Congress has many potential newsmakers and story lines that take journalists' time and energy to track down. Congress also has been resistant to new communications technologies that might elevate its profile but at the same time subject members to greater public criticism. Radio journalists were not admitted to the press gallery until 1939. Television cameras filmed the opening session of the House in 1947; they would not be allowed back for almost thirty-five years. The institution did not begin to embrace the internet until 1995, when websites for the House and Senate were established but used by only a handful of members.

## Congress Online

The tradition-bound Congress embraced the internet slowly. Political scientist Stephen Frantzich describes the situation: "One can almost hear the crunch of metal as one ancient institution and one new technology collide. For all the promises of cyberdemocracy and enhanced political linkages, in some ways the interface of Congress and the internet is a match made in Hell. Divorce is not possible, but tensions are inevitable."[111]

Members were reluctant to change the way they conducted business and were wary of receiving a barrage of email messages that would create more work for their overtaxed staffs. This attitude changed as members used the internet to get elected, staff members became tech savvy, and constituents became internet users. Today, all members communicate through online media, although some members are more sophisticated in their digital communication strategies than others.

Websites are an important resource for members' public relations efforts. They provide a platform for publicizing members' views and accomplishments that can be readily accessed by reporters. Members use websites to present their image to the public without journalistic filters. Websites can promote grassroots support for members through tools, such as printable brochures and buttons. Websites have improved constituent service. They are "virtual offices" open twenty-four hours a day, providing information and opportunities for interaction. Members can solicit opinions from constituents quickly through online polls, message boards, and social media.[112]

The websites for the House, Senate, and committees provide the public with a wealth of information about hearings and legislative action. The complete text of bills, the *Congressional Record*, which provides transcripts of floor debate, committee action, and institutional history, is available here.

The U.S. Congress has now embraced social media. Today most members use social media to communicate with their constituents, the press, and one another. Social media have made it easier for members to carry out their duties, reach out to people in their districts, and gauge public opinion. Members began using social media in 2009; by 2017, every House member and senator was using

Facebook, Twitter, and YouTube. A majority of members are on at least six social media platforms, including Instagram, Flickr, Snapchat, Medium, LinkedIn, Pinterest, Periscope, and Tumblr.[113]

Members of Congress maintain over 2,000 active social media accounts. They produce more than 100,000 tweets and Facebook posts every month, which generate tens of millions of audience reactions. Democrats are more active on social media than Republicans. Democratic members of Congress post an average of 130 times each a month on Twitter compared to 73 posts for Republicans.[114]

Social media–savvy members can reach their constituents and the press within seconds using their smartphones. Congresswoman Alexandria Ocasio-Cortez (D-NY) regularly posts messages to her almost 13 million followers on Twitter and 9 million followers on Instagram. She uses social media to publicize everything from her questions to witnesses during congressional hearings to her dance moves.

There are Facebook pages for the U.S. House and Senate as well as numerous related groups, such as U.S. Marines as Members of Congress. Many members used social media to connect with voters during their election campaigns. Once in office, members use Facebook and Twitter to share information about their policy viewpoints, committee assignments, and participation in events. They promote themselves to the press and their constituents using social media. They upload videos of their speeches and visits to their home districts. C-SPAN keeps a public list of members on Twitter, of which there were 561 in 2017. Members' feeds focus heavily on their constituent relations and positive messages about their accomplishments.

The rise in social media use has put more pressure on congressional office staffs. Members receive far more messages in the digital era than they did when constituents would contact them primarily by posted letter. Members have added social media staffers to their offices to handle the increased demands to put out and respond to social media messages.

# Media Depictions

Media depictions of Congress are a mixed bag. National news coverage focuses on the institution of Congress and tends to highlight conflict and partisan bickering. Local news covers individual members and is more positive. Depictions of Congress in television and film often exaggerate stereotypes, such as the corrupt senator or the crusading House representative.

## News Coverage

The distinction between the institution of Congress and individual members is evident in media coverage. There are distinct differences in the tone, content, and scope of news reports on Congress in the national compared to local press. National news reports focus more on the institution than individual members. Stories emphasize the investigative side of reporting in that they seek the "smoking gun," a problem, or a scandal. Reports convey the impression that Congress is populated by power brokers who are in the pocket of political insiders such as interest groups; reports often portray members of Congress as being ignorant of public concerns. When the media uncover evidence of a member of Congress misbehaving, the result is frenzied scandal coverage.

Local media coverage focuses on members more than the institution. Journalists value the access they have to members when they come home to their districts. Few local media organizations have Washington bureaus, so they rely heavily on press releases, wire feeds, canned video, members' websites, blogs, and social media. Members spend much more time courting the local press than national media. The local press serves as an intermediary between members and their constituents by focusing on the congressional stories most relevant to the district. Social media have enhanced local coverage of members of Congress as they are able to provide personalized videos and commentary from Washington quickly.

Local stories generally are more positive than national news reports. Journalists even may become unofficial cheerleaders for members. This does not mean that members never receive bad press from local news sources. During reelection bids, especially, local journalists emphasize their watchdog role, and reporting can become more critical of members.[115]

## Congress on Television and in Film

Congress has been the subject of numerous television programs and movies. Like media coverage in general, television and film treatment of Congress pales in comparison to that of the presidency.

There has been a stream of television sitcoms and dramas set in Congress, most of which have been short-lived. Programs exaggerate images of the institution that are predicated in reality. Others reinforce unflattering stereotypes of members as criminals or buffoons.[116] The television version of Congress is even more of a male bastion than the institution itself. Women primarily serve as support staff or love interests of male members. *Mister Sterling*, the congressional counterpart to *The West Wing* that survived one season, is typical. It featured an idealistic but all-too-serious young senator who uses his intelligence to outsmart his older, white, male colleagues. Women members on the show were few, and none held leadership positions. Sterling used talk radio, which is dominated by male hosts and listeners, as his primary means of communicating to the public.[117] Another quickly cancelled program was *Women of the House*, in which a scatterbrained Southern belle inherits the Senate seat of her deceased fifth husband and schemes her way through her congressional duties. The popular Netflix series *House of Cards* focuses on a fictional Democratic House member from South Carolina who ruthlessly seeks to increase his political power base.

Congress has been depicted in more than a dozen feature films since the 1930s, far fewer than the more than one hundred films that have focused on the presidency. Many of them overdramatize legislative processes and committee actions and oversimplify the workings of the institution. Floor action and committee hearings are ridden with conflict and full of surprises. In reality, floor action almost invariably proceeds by the rules with great decorum. The work of congressional committees is deliberate and complicated. On film, members of Congress are often pitted against one another. In fact, members rarely engage in direct confrontation.[118]

In *Legally Blonde 2: Red, White & Blonde* (2003), pink-clad Harvard Law School graduate Elle Woods goes to Washington with the aim of passing an animal rights bill to save the mother of her pet Chihuahua, Bruiser. To promote "Bruiser's Bill," Elle barges into a congressional hearing, interrupting the proceedings in a way that, in real life, would have guaranteed her an escort out by security. Instead, she gains enough support to get the bill passed. A clip of *Mr. Smith Goes to Washington* (1939) is cleverly inserted into the film to position it in the tradition of films in which the young, idealistic underdog takes on the corrupt lifelong politician.

Films depict members of Congress as politically and morally flawed. Blinded by ambition, they compromise their beliefs and values to achieve position and power.[119] In *The Seduction of Joe Tynan* (1979), a well-intentioned senator has an extramarital affair, even as he considers but ultimately resists caving in to powerful members to advance his career. *Charlie Wilson's War* (2007) tells the true story of a Democratic congressman from Texas who helped fund a covert war in Afghanistan against the Soviets in the 1980s. Wilson was portrayed as a flamboyant womanizer who drank too much and engaged in recreational drug use.[120]

# Media Consequences

The media can influence the behavior of members of Congress, the public's perception of the institution, and constituents' feelings about their members.

## Legislative Behavior

Perspectives on the influence of the news media on Congress's legislative activities differ. Some scholars contend that because the media do not cover much of what goes on in Congress, members are largely able to do their jobs without interference. Members with high public visibility can get into trouble, as they are subject to scrutiny and criticism. Therefore, members who pursue **insider strategies**—working behind the scenes to forge coalitions—can avoid press interference.[121]

**insider strategies**

Tactics used by members to work behind the scenes in Congress to forge coalitions while avoiding press scrutiny.

Another perspective argues that the media have dramatically changed Congress by promoting **outsider strategies** for governing. To be successful, members must court media publicity rather than forge congressional relationships that are essential for building consensus. The result is that legislative actions can be held up as members seek to influence public opinion.[122]

**outsider strategies**

Members court media publicity in order to achieve their legislative goals.

A third, more realistic perspective posits that both the insider and outsider strategies are essential for lawmaking. It is important for members to publicize their views via the media in order to rally public opinion and at the same time work to build cooperation within the institution.[123]

## Public Trust

Public confidence in Congress has declined over the past three decades. Congressional approval also is highly volatile, as the public changes its collective mind about the institution. Congress has the lowest approval ratings of the three national institutions. In 2010, Congress received its lowest approval rating in the history of the Gallup poll, with 83 percent of the public disapproving of the way the institution is handling its job. By 2014, the public's approval of Congress was even lower. Congressional approval was at approximately 20 percent in 2019, and had declined to 15% in December of 2020. In April of 2021, congressional approval had climbed to 33%, likely in response to the passage of the American Recovery Act that provided stimulus checks to most people.

### Link

**Congressional Approval over Time**

A graph and explanation of congressional approval over time is available on the Gallup website here.

Scholars offer competing views about whether or not the media contribute to this trend of declining approval of Congress. Some suggest that the image of an institution characterized by conflict and deal-making that pervades media coverage has a negative impact on public perceptions. Most Americans abhor the squabbling between members and acrimonious interactions between Congress and the presidency that they see in the media. They feel that congressional leaders have lost touch with average people and that the institution is dominated by special interests.[124] Other researchers disagree and believe that evidence of a direct connection between media coverage and declining public opinion about Congress is lacking. People's low opinion of Congress is based on the public's holding the institution accountable for negative societal conditions, such as a bad economy.[125]

## National versus Local Coverage

FIGURE 12.17 Connecting to Home Districts

The close connection that many members of Congress have with constituents in their home districts is reflected in positive media coverage.

Source: Photo courtesy of Medill DC, via Flickr: http://www.flickr. com/photos/medilldc/5389481016/. Reproduced via CC BY 2.0: https://creativecommons.org/licenses/by/2.0/.

The more critical national coverage of the institution compared to the more favorable local press accorded to members may account for differences in public opinion. People dislike the institution even as they hold favorable views of their own members of Congress. Citizens claim to be unhappy with the "pork barrel" politics of the institution but are pleased when the media report that their own member has brought home the bacon.[126]

There may be a connection between positive local coverage of members and the large number of incumbents who win reelection. The public does not think that most members of the House should be reelected but are more supportive of returning their own member to Congress.[127]

## Digital Media Effects

Digital communication, especially online news and social media, has influenced how citizens view Congress. On the one hand, Congress's online presence fosters positive attitudes toward the institution and its members. Congressional websites have been successful in facilitating the flow of information to the public. People feel that members' websites convey a sense of accountability and transparency when they report voting records, rationales for policy decisions, schedules, and issue information. Websites create trust, as people feel that members are not "hiding something."[128]

At the same time, online news sites, blogs, social media, and video-sharing sites have placed Congress and its members under a microscope. While mainstream media coverage of Congress is less prevalent than it is for the presidency, bloggers generate a continual barrage of commentary and criticism of congressional action, often taking aim at particular members. Citizens armed with smartphones can capture a member at her or his worst moment, post an embarrassing photo or video online, and have it go viral within a short period of time. Social media commentary about Congress is highly unfavorable. These negative depictions can play into the unpopular view of Congress that citizens frequently hold and contribute to declining trust in the institution.

## Key Takeaways

Congress historically has been slow to adapt to new media technologies such as radio, television, and the internet. More recently, members have integrated new media into their communications strategies. Members use websites, social media, and email to communicate efficiently with constituents.

Media reports may have a negative influence on the public's perceptions of the institution and a favorable impact on feelings about individual members. Online media, including blogs and video-sharing sites, place the institution and its members under increased scrutiny.

## Exercises

1. What makes Congress difficult for the media to cover? What do the media tend to focus on when covering Congress?

2. How do the insider and outsider strategies for having influence in Congress differ in the way they use the media?
3. Why do you think public approval of Congress has declined? To what extent are Congress's low approval ratings a result of the way media cover the institution?

## Civic Education

### Young People Testify Before Congress

Testifying before Congress is not just for celebrities and policy wonks. Average citizens can make a powerful case for a cause in front of congressional committees, an act that is frequently covered by the press. Young people have testified on behalf of research for illnesses (e.g., diabetes and cancer), educational reform, credit card company practices, and a variety of other issues.

Vicky Flamand was a young single mother in Florida working a double shift and attending college part-time. With an annual income of $13,500, she relied on government-subsidized child-care benefits to keep her tenuous lifestyle going. When the benefits expired, she reapplied, only to be turned down because the county had run out of funds. A hard worker who did not want to go on welfare, she bombarded public officials, including members of Congress, with letters and emails describing her plight and those of more than forty-six thousand families who were denied child care in Florida alone. As a result, she was asked to testify in front of the Senate Finance Committee in support of the Child Care and Development Block Grant, which funds transitional child-care benefits. She worked with the Children's Defense Fund to prepare her testimony.

Flamand felt that the senators were attentive to her testimony and sympathetic to her story. She had a powerful ally in Senator Christopher Dodd (D-CT), a cosponsor of the bill, who mentioned her testimony in his official statement at the Senate Finance Committee hearing. "I was a little person who could put a face on a problem that was hurting many, many families," Flamand said. "Testifying before Congress gave me confidence that I had the power to make a difference. You must make an effort to be heard. Someone, somewhere, will listen and hear you." Flamand's child-care benefits were restored, and she enrolled full-time in college with the goal of attending law school.

Meeting face-to-face with political leaders is one of the best ways to present your concerns about a policy and to learn about how legislative institutions work. Despite their rigorous schedules, arranging for members or former members of Congress and their staffs to speak at your school or club is not as hard as it may seem. Members of Congress and their staffs often welcome the chance to meet with young people in their districts.

Internships with members of Congress are an excellent way to get a real sense of how government works. There are many congressional internship opportunities available both in members' personal offices on Capitol Hill and in state district offices and with congressional committees. Interns have a range of duties, including answering constituent mail, researching issues, preparing press releases, and helping with constituent service. They also do their fair share of grunt work—making photocopies, answering the phones, and running errands. Committee internships tend to offer greater opportunity for research and issue-related work than those in personal offices.

# 12.11 Recommended Reading

Arnold, R. Douglas. *Congress, the Press, and Political Accountability*. Princeton, NJ: Princeton University Press, 2004. A comprehensive account of national and local media coverage of congress and its influence on citizens.

Atkinson, Mary Layton. *Combative Politics: The Media and Public Perceptions of Lawmaking*. Chicago: University of Chicago Press, 2017. An analysis of the influence of media on congressional policymaking arguing that getting legislation passed has become difficult in an era of intense media scrutiny.

Bader, John B. *Taking the Initiative*. Washington, DC: Georgetown University Press, 1999. Study of leadership agendas and the "Contract with America" during the era when Newt Gingrich was Speaker of the House.

Baker, Ross K. *House and Senate*, 3rd ed. New York: W. W. Norton, 2001. A comprehensive comparison of the two houses of Congress that relies on hundreds of interviews with members and their staffs, journalists, and lobbyists.

Casey, Chris. *The Hill on the Net*. Boston: AP Professional, 1996. An overview of Congress and the internet covering the background history, uses, and challenges faced when legislative offices go online.

Cook, Timothy E. *Making Laws & Making News*. Washington, DC: The Brookings Institution, 1989. An exploration of the interactive relationship between the press and the House of Representatives that illustrates how media strategies influence lawmaking.

Davidson, Roger H., and Walter J. Oleszek. *Congress and Its Members*, 12th ed. Washington, DC: CQ Press, 2009. A comprehensive guide covering the formal and informal aspects of the institution of Congress and its members.

Fenno, Richard F. Jr. *Home Style*. New York: Longman, 2003. A landmark ethnographic study of members of Congress and their relationship to their constituents.

Franken, Al. *Giant of the Senate*. New York: Hachette Book Group, 2017. Democratic Senator Al Franken, a former comedian and star of *Saturday Night Live*, offers humorous insights into the relationships between members of Congress.

Jacobson, Gary C. *The Politics of Congressional Elections*, 7th ed. New York: Longman, 2007. Examines the connection between legislating and running for reelection.

Kaiser, Robert. *Act of Congress: How America's Essential Institution Works, and How it Doesn't*. New York: Vintage, 2014.

Kedrowski, Karen M. *Media Entrepreneurs and the Media Enterprise in the U.S. Congress*. Cresskill, NJ: Hampton Press, 1996. Examines the growing trend of members of Congress who are proficient at courting media attention as well as legislating effectively.

Mayer, Kenneth R., and David T. Canon. *The Dysfunctional Congress?* Boulder, CO: Westview Press, 1999. A study of the dilemma faced by members of Congress who need to satisfy both the needs of the institution and their interests of their constituents.

Mayhew, David. *Congress: The Electoral Connection*. New Haven, CT: Yale University Press, 1971. Classic study arguing that members make policy decisions with the single-minded goal of getting reelected.

Rhode, David W. *Parties and Leaders in the Postreform House*. Chicago: University of Chicago Press, 1991. Argues that majority party control of the legislative agenda has increased since the 1970s.

Richie, Donald A. *The U.S. Congress: A Very Short Introduction*. New York: Oxford University Press, 2010. A good overview of the institution of Congress and how it works.

Sellers, Patrick. *Cycles of Spin*. New York: Cambridge University Press, 2009. Discusses the communication strategies of members of Congress.

Sinclair, Barbara. *Unorthodox Lawmaking*, 3rd ed. Washington, DC: CQ Press, 2007. An accounting of changes in the legislative process that deviate from the textbook notion of how a bill becomes a law.

Tate, Katherine. *Concordance: Black Lawmaking in the U.S. Congress from Carter to Obama*. Ann Arbor: University of Michigan Press, 2020. Provides a history of the Congressional Black Caucus and examines how the influence of Black lawmakers has evolved over time.

Vinson, Danielle C. *Local Media Coverage of Congress and Its Members.* Cresskill, NJ: Hampton Press, 2002. A study of patterns in local media coverage of Congress focusing on the amount and substance of coverage.

# 12.12 Recommended Viewing

*Advise and Consent* (1962). This political thriller depicts hardcore partisan politics when a president seeks Senate confirmation of a candidate for secretary of state in the Cold War era.

*Big Jim McClain* (1952). A film starring John Wayne that celebrates the House Un-American Activities Committee.

*Born Yesterday* (1950). A journalist uncovers corruption when a wealthy businessman attempts to buy influence in Congress.

*Committee on Un-American Activities* (1962). The first film made by a private citizen to question the legitimacy of a governmental agency, this documentary views the congressional investigation into alleged members of the Communist Party from the perspective of an average person seeking to understand the proceedings.

*The Congress: History and Promise of Executive Government* (1988). A Ken Burns documentary that examines the history and functions of Congress as well as some of the colorful characters who have been members.

*The Congressman* (2016). A congressman who is caught on video failing to say the "Pledge of Allegiance" is battered by the media, and spends time with people in a remote part of his Maine district and connects with a cause.

*The Distinguished Gentleman* (1992). This Eddie Murphy comedy provides some insights into the ways in which interest groups and their associated political action committees interact with Congress.

*The Front* (1976). Woody Allen stars as a small-time bookie who lends his name to blacklisted entertainment industry writers in this landmark film whose credits include six Hollywood artists blacklisted in the 1950s.

*Guilty by Suspicion* (1991). A prominent film director (Robert De Niro) is falsely accused of being a Communist and must appear before a congressional committee in the first major Hollywood film to portray the 1950s House Un-American Activities Committee hearings.

*H.R. 6161: An Act of Congress* (1979). An award-winning documentary about the conception, committee action, and passage of an amendment to the Clean Air Act featuring an unprecedented look at the behind-the-scenes workings of Congress.

*I'm Just a Bill* (1973). A popular "Schoolhouse Rock!" cartoon featuring an animated bill named Bill who goes through the steps of becoming law, which are recounted in a catchy song.

*Legally Blonde 2: Red, White & Blonde* (2003). A comedy following the escapades of a debutante-turned-lawyer who fights for animal rights on Capitol Hill, which provides a somewhat accurate view of office politics on congressional staffs.

*A Member of the Hollywood Ten* (1999). Documents the life of director Herbert Biberman during the period of the HUAC hearings.

*Mr. Smith Goes to Washington* (1939). Jimmy Stewart stars in this Frank Capra classic about an idealistic small-town youth-group leader who is appointed to the Senate, where he fights against political bosses.

*On the Waterfront* (1954). A film by director Elia Kazan, who cooperated with the HUAC, in which the protagonist testifies in front of a state investigative committee to expose corrupt union practices.

*The Seduction of Joe Tynan* (1979). A drama focusing on the political dilemma faced by a young, liberal senator who holds a deciding vote in a U.S. Supreme Court confirmation hearing.

*Taxes Behind Closed Doors* (1986). An examination of the relationship between lobbyists and members of Congress, depicting strategy sessions and meetings as real estate interests fight a major tax bill.

*That Delicate Balance 1—The President versus Congress: Executive Privilege and Delegation of Powers* (1984). This documentary examines the extent to which the executive branch is bound by limitations imposed by Congress.

*True Colors* (1991). Two law school graduates take divergent political paths, as one becomes an aide to an influential senator and is involved in political maneuvering while the other works for the Justice Department prosecuting criminals in government.

# Endnotes

1. Will Drabold, "House Democrats Stage Sit-In Over Gun Control," Time, June 22, 2016.
2. Christopher Poliquin, "Gun Control Fails Quickly in Congress After Each Mass Shooting, but States Often Act—Including to Loosen Gun Laws," *The Conversation*, March 25, 2021. https://theconversation.com/gun-control-fails-quickly-in-congress-after-each-mass-shooting-but-states-often-act-including-to-loosen-gun-laws-157746.
3. Wendy J. Schiller, *Partners and Rivals* (Princeton, NJ: Princeton University Press, 2000).
4. Clinton Rossiter, ed., "Federalist 51," in *The Federalist*, Alexander Hamilton, James Madison, and John Jay (New York: Mentor, 1961), 322.
5. United States Congress. 2020. "The Power of Impeachment: Overview." *Constitution Annotated*. https://constitution.congress.gov/browse/essay/artI_S2_C5_1_1/.
6. United States Senate, "About Impeachment," *Senate Historical Office*, 2021. https://www.senate.gov/about/powers-procedures/impeachment.htm#:~:text=After the House of Representatives,as prosecutors before the Senate.
7. Davey Alba, "Debunking 4 Viral Rumors About the Bidens and Ukraine," *The New York Times*, October 29, 2019. https://www.nytimes.com/2019/10/29/business/media/fact-check-biden-ukraine-burisma-china-hunter.html
8. Jonathan Shaub, "Executive Privilege Should Have No Power When It Comes to an Impeachment," *The Atlantic*, November 15, 2020. https://www.theatlantic.com/ideas/archive/2019/11/no-executive-privilege-in-impeachment/602044/.
9. Nicholas Fandos, "Trump Impeached for Inciting Insurrection," *The New York Times*, January 13, 2021. https://www.nytimes.com/2021/01/13/us/politics/trump-impeached.html.
10. Charlie Savage, "Incitement to Riot? What Trump Told Supporters Before Mob Stormed Capitol," *The New York Times*, January 10, 2021. https://www.nytimes.com/2021/01/10/us/trump-speech-riot.html.
11. Weiyi Cai, "A Step-by-Step Guide to the Second Impeachment of Donald J. Trump," *The New York Times*, February 13, 2021. https://www.nytimes.com/interactive/2021/02/08/us/politics/trump-second-impeachment-timeline.html.
12. Sarah Binder. "Mitt Romney Changed the Impeachment Story, All by Himself. Here Are Three Reasons That Matters," *The Monkey Cage*, The Washington Post, February 6, 2020. https://www.washingtonpost.com/politics/2020/02/06/mitt-romney-changed-impeachment-story-all-by-himself-here-are-3-reasons-that-matters/.
13. "Romney Remarks Prepared for Delivery," *NBC News*, February 3, 2020. https://www.documentcloud.org/documents/6768911-Romney-RemarksPreparedForDelivery.html#document/p1.
14. Alana Wise, "Jon Ossoff Wins Georgia Runoff, Handing Democrats Senate Control," NPR, January 6, 2021. https://www.npr.org/2021/01/06/952417689/democrat-jon-ossoff-claims-victory-over-david-perdue-in-georgia-runoff.
15. Roger H. Davidson and Walter J. Oleszek, *Congress and Its Members*, 8th ed. (Washington, DC: CQ Press, 2002), 27.
16. Congressional Research Service, "Apportionment and Redistricting Following 2020 Census," *CRS Reports*, April 27, 2021. https://crsreports.congress.gov/product/pdf/IN/IN11360#:~:text=On January 27, 2021, the,data by September 30, 2021.
17. "Texas District Fight Goes to Court," CBSNews.com, October 15, 2003, accessed February 15, 2011, cbsnews.com/stories/2003/10/09/politics/main577340.shtml.
18. Paul Egan, "Michigan's Anti-Gerrymandering Proposal Is Approved. Now What?," *Detroit Free Press*, November 7, 2018.
19. Quoted in Roger H. Davidson and Walter J. Oleszek, *Congress and Its Members*, 8th ed. (Washington, DC: CQ Press, 2002), 25.
20. Miles Park, "House Passes Extensive Election And Campaign Finance Overhaul Bill," *NPR*, March 8, 2–19.
21. Patrick J. Sellers, "Winning Media Coverage in the U.S. Congress," in *U.S. Senate Exceptionalism*, ed. Bruce I. Oppenheimer (Columbus, OH: Ohio State University Press, 2002), 132–53.
22. Steven S. Smith, Jason Roberts, and Ryan Vander Wielen, *The American Congress*, 3rd ed. (New York: Houghton Mifflin Company, 2003).
23. Paul Kane, "Arlen Specter's Party Switch Haunts Him in Primary Campaign," *Washington Post*, May 12, 2010, accessed February 12, 2011, http://www.washingtonpost.com/wp-dyn/content/article/2010/05/11/AR2010051105084.html.
24. Keith T. Poole and Howard Rosenthal, *Congress: A Political-Economic History of Roll Call Voting* (New York: Oxford, 2000).
25. Gary W. Cox and Matthew D. McCubbins, *Legislative Leviathan* (Berkeley: University of California Press, 1993).
26. Keith Krehbiel, *Pivotal Politics* (Chicago: University of Chicago Press, 1998).
27. David W. Rohde, *Parties and Leaders in the Postreform House* (Chicago: University of Chicago Press, 1991); Nicol C. Rae and Colton C. Campbell, eds., *New Majority or Old Minority?* (Lanham, MD: Rowman & Littlefield, 1999).
28. John H. Aldrich, David W. Rohde, and Michael W. Tofias, "One D Is Not Enough: Measuring Conditional Party Government, 1887–2002," Paper presented at the History of Congress Conference, Stanford University, Palo Alto, CA, April 9–10, 2004, accessed January 29, 2011, http://www.duke.edu/nmwt/papers/ART3.pdf.
29. Pew Research Center for the People & the Press, "Many Fault Media Coverage of Health Care Debate," August 6, 2009, accessed June 6, 2011, http://people-press.org/report/533/many-fault-media-coverage-of-health-care.
30. Robert Pear and Thomas Kaplan, "Senate Rejects Slimmed-Down Obamacare Repeal as McCain Votes No," *The New York Times*, July 27, 2017.
31. Benjy Sarlin, "Obamacare Would Get a Big (and Quiet) Overhaul in the Covid Relief Bill," *NBC News*, March 2, 2021. https://www.nbcnews.com/politics/congress/obamacare-would-get-big-quiet-overhaul-covid-relief-bill-n1259343.
32. "Tea Party's First Legislative Victory: McConnell Backs Earmark Ban," *Newsweek*, November 15, 2010, accessed December 16, 2010, http://www.newsweek.com/blogs/the-gaggle/2010/11/15/tea-party-s-first-legislative-victory- mcconnell-backs-earmark-ban.html.
33. Ryan Bernstein, "The Return of Earmarks to Congress," *JD Supra*, March 15, 2021. https://www.jdsupra.com/legalnews/the-return-of-earmarks-to-congress-9708521/.
34. Steven S. Smith, Jason Roberts, and Ryan Vander Wielen, *The American Congress*, 3rd ed. (New York: Houghton Mifflin Company, 2003).
35. Drew Desilver, "What Is the House Freedom Caucus, and Who's In It?" *Fact Tank* (Washington, DC: Pew Research Center, October 20, 2015).
36. Geoffrey Skelley, "The House Will Have Just as Many Moderate Democrats as Progressives Next Year," *FiveThirtyEight*, December 20, 2018.
37. Robert L. Peabody, *Leadership in Congress* (Boston: Little, Brown, 1976).
38. Joseph Cooper and David W. Brady, "Institutional Context and Leadership Style: The House from Cannon to Rayburn," *American Political Science Review* 75, no. 2 (June 1981): 411–25.

39. Thomas P. Carr, "Party Leaders in the House: Election, Duties, and Responsibilities," *CRS Report for Congress*, October 5, 2001, order code RS20881.
40. Nicol C. Rae and Colton C. Campbell, eds. *New Majority or Old Minority?* (Lanham, MD: Rowman & Littlefield, 1999).
41. Ronald M. Peters Jr., *The American Speakership* (Baltimore: Johns Hopkins University Press, 1997).
42. Dan Balz and Ronald Brownstein, *Storming the Gates* (Boston: Little Brown, 1996), 143.
43. Roger H. Davidson and Walter J. Oleszek, *Congress and Its Members*, 8th ed. (Washington, DC: CQ Press, 2002).
44. Maureen Dowd. "Squeaker of the House." *The New York Times*, November 6, 2006. Retrieved from: https://www.nytimes.com/2006/11/18/opinion/18dowd.html.
45. Richard C. Sachs, "Leadership in the U.S. House of Representatives," *CRS Report for Congress*, September 19, 1996, order code 96-784GOV.
46. Thomas P. Carr, "Party Leaders in the House: Election, Duties, and Responsibilities," *CRS Report for Congress*, October 5, 2001, order code RS20881.
47. Roger H. Davidson and Walter J. Oleszek, *Congress and Its Members*, 8th ed. (Washington, DC: CQ Press, 2002).
48. Woodrow Wilson, *Congressional Government* (New York: Houghton Mifflin, 1885), 69.
49. Congressional Research Service, "Expulsion, Censure, Reprimand, and Fine: Legislative Discipline in the House of Representatives," *EveryCRSReport.com*, June 27, 2016. https://www.everycrsreport.com/reports/RL31382.html.
50. Clare Foran, Daniella Diaz, and Annie Grayer, "House Votes to Remove Marjorie Taylor Greene from Committee Assignments," *CNN Politics*, February 4, 2021. https://www.cnn.com/2021/02/04/politics/house-vote-marjorie-taylor-greene-committee-assignments/index.html.
51. Amy Kiste Nyberg, *Seal of Approval* (Oxford: University of Mississippi Press, 1998).
52. Kenneth A. Shepsle and Barry R. Weingast, "The Institutional Foundations of Committee Power," *American Political Science Review* 81: 85–104.
53. Richard Fenno, *Congressmen in Committees* (Boston: Little, Brown, 1973).
54. David R. Mayhew, *America's Congress* (New Haven, CT: Yale University Press, 2000).
55. Ronald Gray, *Congressional Television: A Legislative History* (Westport, CT: Greenwood Press, 1984).
56. "Obstruction of Justice," *Wex Legal Dictionary*, Cornell Law School. Accessed April, 2019. https://www.law.cornell.edu/wex/obstruction_of_justice.
57. Peter Baker, "What We Know So Far From the Mueller Report," *The New York Times*, April 19, 2019.
58. Ernest Giglio, *Here's Looking at You* (New York: Peter Lang, 2000).
59. Phillip L. Gianos, *Politics and Politicians in American Film* (Westport, CT: Praeger, 1998), 65.
60. Larry Ceplair, "The Hollywood Blacklist," in *The Political Companion to American Film*, ed. Gary Crowdus (Chicago: Lakeview Press, 1994), 193–99.
61. "Structure and Powers of Congress," in *Congress A to Z*, ed. David R. Tarr and Ann O'Connor, 4th ed. (Washington, DC: CQ Press), 428.
62. John V. Sullivan, *How Our Laws Are Made*, research report (Washington, DC: Thomas Online, 2008), accessed May 21, 2011, http://thomas.loc.gov/home/lawsmade.bysec/foreword.html.
63. Charles W. Johnson, *How Our Laws Are Made* (Washington, DC: U.S. Government Printing Office, January 31, 2000).
64. Barbara Sinclair, *Unorthodox Lawmaking* (Washington, DC: Congressional Quarterly Press, 1997).
65. John V. Sullivan, *How Our Laws Are Made*, research report (Washington, DC: Thomas Online, 2008), accessed May 21, 2011, http://thomas.loc.gov/home/lawsmade.bysec/foreword.html.
66. Eric Redman, *The Dance of Legislation* (Seattle, WA: University of Washington Press, 2001).
67. Roger H. Davidson and Walter J. Oleszek, *Congress and Its Members*, 8th ed. (Washington, DC: CQ Press, 2002).
68. Irina Fanarraga, "What's In a Name? An Empirical Analysis of Apostrophe Laws," *Criminology, Criminal Justice, Law & Society*, vol 21, no. 3: 39-68.
69. Charles W. Johnson, *How Our Laws Are Made* (Washington, DC: U.S. Government Printing Office, January 31, 2000).
70. Lawrence D. Longley and Walter J. Oleszek, *Bicameral Politics* (New Haven, CT: Yale University Press, 1989).
71. Dhrumil Mehta, "Does Trying to Repeal Obamacare Actually Increase Its Appeal?" *FiveThirtyEight*, March 29, 2019. https://fivethirtyeight.com/features/does-trying-to-repeal-obamacare-actually-increase-its-appeal/.
72. John V. Sullivan, *How Our Laws Are Made*, research report (Washington, DC: Thomas Online, 2008), accessed May 21, 2011, http://thomas.loc.gov/home/lawsmade.bysec/foreword.html.
73. John V. Sullivan, *How Our Laws Are Made*, research report (Washington, DC: Thomas Online, 2008), accessed May 21, 2011, http://thomas.loc.gov/home/lawsmade.bysec/foreword.html.
74. Barbara Sinclair, *Unorthodox Lawmaking* (Washington, DC: Congressional Quarterly Press, 1997).
75. "Mark Zuckerberg Testimony: Senators Question Facebook's Commitment to Privacy," *The New York Times*, April 28, 2018. https://www.nytimes.com/2018/04/10/us/politics/mark-zuckerberg-testimony.html.
76. Brent Kendall, "Capitol Hill's Odd Bills," *The American Observer*, April 17, 2002.
77. Roger H. Davidson and Walter J. Oleszek, *Congress and Its Members*, 8th ed. (Washington, DC: CQ Press, 2002).
78. David J. Vogler, *The Third House* (Evanston, IL: Northwestern University Press, 1971).
79. Stephen D. Van Beek, *Post-Passage Politics* (Pittsburgh, PA: University of Pittsburgh Press, 1995).
80. Lawrence D. Longley and Walter J. Oleszek, *Bicameral Politics* (New Haven, CT: Yale University Press, 1989), 6.
81. Roger H. Davidson and Walter J. Oleszek, *Congress and Its Members*, 8th ed. (Washington, DC: CQ Press, 2002).
82. "CBO's Role in the Budget Office" (Washington, DC: Congressional Budget Office, 2005), accessed February 16, 2011, http://www.cbo.gov/visitorsgallery/budgetprocess.shtml.
83. Matthew Haag and Niraj Chokshi, "Government Shutdown Updates: Where Things Stand," *The New York Times*, January 21, 2019. https://www.nytimes.com/2019/01/21/us/politics/government-shutdown-update.html.
84. Timothy E. Cook, *Making Laws & Making News* (Washington, DC: Brookings, 1989).
85. Walter J. Oleszek, "The Internet and Congressional Decisionmaking," report prepared for the Chairman of the House Rules Committee, September 19, 2001.
86. Richard Fenno, *Home Style* (New York: Longman Classics, 2003).
87. Gary Jacobson, *The Politics of Congressional Elections*, 5th ed. (Boston: Allyn and Bacon, 2002).
88. Alan I. Abramowitz, "Name Familiarity, Reputation, and the Incumbency Effect in a Congressional Election," *Western Political Quarterly* 28 (September 1975): 668–84; Morris P. Fiorina, *Congress: Keystone of the Washington Establishment* (New Haven, CT: Yale, 1977); David R. Mayhew, *Congress: The Electoral Connection* (New Haven, CT: Yale University Press, 1974).
89. Jennifer E. Manning, "Membership of the 117th Congress: A Profile," *CRS Report for Congress* (Washington, DC: Congressional Research Service, May 12, 2021).
90. Jennifer E. Manning, "Membership of the 116th Congress: A Profile," CRS Report for Congress (Washington, DC: Congressional Research Service, December 17,2020).
91. Center for American Women and Politics, "Women in the U.S. Congress 2021" (Rutgers University, Eagleton Institute of Politics, 2021). https://cawp.rutgers.edu/women-us-congress-2021.
92. Jennifer E. Manning, "Membership of the 117th Congress: A Profile," CRS Report for Congress (Washington, DC: Congressional Research Service, May 12, 2021).
93. Michele L. Swers, *The Difference Women Make* (Chicago: University of Chicago Press, 2002).
94. Eric Lipton, "Half of Congress Are Millionaires," *The New York Times*, January 4, 2012. Accessed July 15, 2014 http://www.nytimes.com/2014/01/10/us/politics/more-than-half-the-members-of-congress-are-millionaires-analysis-finds.html.
95. Karl Evers-Hillstrom, "Majority of Lawmakers in 116th Congress Are Millionaires," OpenSecrets.org, April 23, 2020. https://www.opensecrets.org/news/2020/04/majority-of-lawmakers-millionaires/.
96. Ida Brudnick and Eric Peterson, *Congressional Pay and Perks* (Alexandria, VA: TheCapitolNet.com), 2010.
97. Amy Keller, "The *Roll Call* 50 Richest," *Roll Call*, September 8, 2003.
98. Gary Jacobson, *The Politics of Congressional Elections*, 5th ed. (Boston: Allyn and Bacon, 2002).
99. David T. Canon, *Actors, Athletes, and Astronauts* (Chicago: University of Chicago Press, 1990).
100. Mildred L. Amer, "Membership of the 108th Congress: A Profile," *CRS Report for Congress*, May, 2003.
101. R. Douglas Arnold, *Congress, the Press, and Political Accountability* (Princeton, NJ: Princeton University Press, 2004).
102. Timothy E. Cook, *Making Laws & Making News* (Washington, DC: Brookings, 1989).
103. Sara Fischer, Neal Rothschild, and Stef W. Knight, "Alexandria Ocasio-Cortez Is the Democrats' Trump," *Axios*, February 11, 2019. https://www.axios.com/alexandria-ocasio-cortez-social-media-donald-trump-ee71d6b7-3aef-44aa-afcb-4826f8782a51.html.
104. Margaret Sullivan, "Alexandria Ocasio-Cortez Is Freaking Out the News Media. And It's Working for Her," The Washington Post, January 14, 2019. https://www.washingtonpost.com/lifestyle/style/alexandria-ocasio-cortez-is-freaking-out-the-news-media-and-its-working-for-her/2019/01/14/53d12b04-1803-11e9-8813-cb9dec761e73_story.html.
105. Roger H. Davidson and Walter J. Oleszek, *Congress and Its Members*, 8th ed. (Washington, DC: CQ Press, 2002).
106. Robert H. Salisbury and Kenneth A. Shepsle, "U.S. Congressman as Enterprise," *Legislative Studies Quarterly* 6, no. 4 (November 1981): 559–76.

107. Susan Webb Hammond, "Recent Research on Legislative Staffs," *Legislative Studies Quarterly* 21, no. 4 (November 1996): 543–76.
108. "10 Questions for Walter Cronkite," *Time*, November 3, 2003, 8.
109. Timothy E. Cook, *Making Laws & Making News* (Washington, DC: Brookings, 1989).
110. Mary Layton Atkinson. 2017. *Combative Politics: The Media and Public Perceptions of Lawmaking*. Chicago: University of Chicago Press.
111. Stephen E. Frantzich, "RepresNETation: Congress and the Internet," in Colton C. Campbell and James A. Thurber, *Congress and the Internet*, New York: Prentice-Hall, 2003: 31-51.
112. Congress Online Project, *Nine Benefits of a Good Website*, research report (Washington, DC: George Washington University, 2003).
113. Jacob R. Straus, "Social Media Adoption by Members of Congress: Trends and Congressional Considerations." Washington, DC: Congressional Research Service, October 9, 2018. https://fas.org/sgp/crs/misc/R45337.pdf.
114. Patrick Van Kessel, Regina Widjaya, Sono Shah, Aaron Smith, and Adam Hughes, "Congress Soars to New Heights on Social Media," Washington, DC: Pew Research Center, July 16, 2020. https://www.pewresearch.org/internet/2020/07/16/congress-soars-to-new-heights-on-social-media/.
115. Danielle Vinson, *Local Media Coverage of Congress and Its Members* (Cresskill, NJ: Hampton Press, 2002).
116. Tracey L. Gladstone-Sovell, "Criminals and Buffoons: The Portrayal of Elected Officials on Entertainment Television," in *It's Show Time!*, ed. David A. Schultz (New York: Peter Lang, 2000), 119–32.
117. Garrett Epps, "Sterling Character," *The American Prospect*, January 17, 2003.
118. David L. Paletz and Daniel Lapinski, "Movies on Congress," in *The Encyclopedia of the United States Congress*, ed. Donald C. Bacon, Roger H. Davidson, and Morton Keller (New York: Simon and Schuster, 1995).
119. Gary Crowdus, "Politicians in the American Cinema," *The Political Companion to American Film* (Chicago: Lakeview Press, 1994), 322–30.
120. A.O. Scott, "Good-Time Charlie's Foreign Affairs," *The New York Times*, December 21, 2007.
121. Stephen Hess, *The Ultimate Insiders* (Washington, DC: Brookings, 1986).
122. Todd Gitlin, *Media Unlimited* (New York: Metropolitan Books, 2002).
123. Timothy E. Cook, *Governing with the News* (Chicago: University of Chicago Press, 1998).
124. John Hibbing and Elizabeth Theiss-Morse, *Congress as Public Enemy* (New York: Cambridge, 1995).
125. Pippa Norris, "The News Media and Democracy," in *Political Communication Transformed*, ed. John Bartle and Dylan Griffiths (Basingstoke: Palgrave Macmillan, 2001), 163–80.
126. John Hibbing and Elizabeth Theiss-Morse, *Congress as Public Enemy* (New York: Cambridge, 1995).
127. CNN/USA Today/Gallup Poll, October 10–12, 2003, http://pollingreport.com/cong2004.htm.
128. Congress Online Project, *Nine Benefits of a Good Website*, research report (Washington, DC: George Washington University, 2003).

CHAPTER 13

# The Presidency

## 13.1 Preamble

On May 21, 2009, President Barack Obama gave a speech explaining and justifying his decision to close the Guantánamo Bay detention center (prison). The facility had been established in 2002 by the Bush administration to hold detainees from the war in Afghanistan and later Iraq. President Obama spoke at the National Archives, in front of portraits of the founding fathers, pages of the Constitution open at his side. He thereby identified himself and his decision with the founding fathers, the treasured Constitution, and the rule of law.

Yet, years later, after the president left office in 2017 (having won reelection in 2012), the prison remained open, albeit with fewer inmates. The president had failed to offer a practical alternative or present one to Congress. Lawmakers had proved unwilling to approve funds to close it. The Republican National Committee had conducted a television advertising campaign implying that terrorists were going to be dumped onto the U.S. mainland, presenting a major terrorist threat.

**FIGURE 13.1 Connecting Policies to the Past**

Presidents can connect their policy proposals to revered American forebears and documents, but this does not guarantee success.

Source: Obama White House Archives. P052109PS-0174. President Barack Obama delivers an address on national security at the National Archives May 21, 2009. (Official White House photo by Pete Souza). Via Flickr: https://www.flickr.com/photos/obamawhitehouse/3583575606/.

Watch President Obama's *Our Security, Our Values* speech given on May 21, 2009.

View in the online reader

# 13.2 The Powers of the Presidency

## Learning Objectives

After reading this section, you should be able to answer the following questions:

1. How is the presidency personalized?
2. What powers does the Constitution grant to the president?
3. How can Congress and the judiciary limit the president's powers?
4. How is the presidency organized?
5. What is the bureaucratizing of the presidency?

The presidency is seen as the heart of the U.S. political system. This system is personalized in the president as advocate of the national interest, chief agenda-setter, and chief legislator.[1] Scholars evaluate presidents according to such abilities as "public communication," "organizational capacity," "political skill," "policy vision," and "cognitive skill."[2] The media personalize the office and push the ideal of the bold, decisive, active, public-minded president who altruistically governs the country.[3]

**FIGURE 13.2**
**Presidents Portrayed on Screen**
Whether swaggering protagonists of hit movies *Independence Day* and *Air Force One* in the 1990s or more down-to-earth heroes of the hit television series *The West Wing*, presidents are commonly portrayed in the media as bold, decisive, and principled.

Source: Photo courtesy of U.S. Navy Chief Journalist Daniel Ross, http://commons.wikimedia.org/wiki/File:Martinsheennavy.jpg.

Two big summer movie hits, *Independence Day* (1996) and *Air Force One* (1997), are typical: ex-soldier presidents use physical rather than legal powers against (respectively) aliens and Russian terrorists. The president's tie comes off and heroism comes out, aided by fighter planes and machine guns. The television hit series *The West Wing* recycled, with a lot more realism, the image of a patriarchal president boldly putting principle ahead of expedience.[4]

Presidents are even presented as redeemers.[5] There are exceptions: presidents depicted as "sleazeballs" or "simpletons."[6]

## Enduring Image

### Mount Rushmore

Carved into the granite rock of South Dakota's Mount Rushmore, seven thousand feet above sea level, are the faces of Presidents George Washington, Thomas Jefferson, Abraham Lincoln, and Theodore Roosevelt. Sculpted between 1927 and 1941, this awe-inspiring monument achieved even greater worldwide celebrity as the setting where the hero and heroine must survive the bad guys at the climax of director Alfred Hitchcock's classic and ever-popular film *North by Northwest* (1959).

This national monument did not start out devoted to American presidents. It was initially proposed to acknowledge regional heroes: General Custer, Buffalo Bill, the explorers Lewis and Clark. The sculptor, Gutzon Borglum, successfully argued that "a nation's memorial should . . . have a serenity, a nobility, a power that reflects the gods who inspired them and suggests the gods they have become."[7]

George W. Bush speaking in front of Mount Rushmore.

Source: The White House. President Discusses Homeland and Economic Security at Mt. Rushmore. Via Wikimedia: https://commons.wikimedia.org/wiki/File:Bush_at_Mount_Rushmore.jpg.

Mount Rushmore monument is an enduring image of the American presidency by celebrating the greatness of four American presidents. The successors to Washington, Jefferson, Lincoln, and Roosevelt do their part by trying to associate themselves with the office's magnificence and project an image of consensus rather than conflict, sometimes by giving speeches at the monument itself. A George W. Bush event placed the presidential podium at such an angle that the television camera could not help but put the incumbent in the same frame as his glorious predecessors.

The enduring image of Mount Rushmore highlights and exaggerates the importance of presidents as the decision makers in the American political system. It elevates the president over the presidency, the occupant over the office. All depends on the greatness of the individual president—which means that the enduring image often contrasts the divinity of past presidents against the fallibility of the current incumbent.

News depictions of the White House also focus on the person of the president. They portray a "single executive image" with visibility no other political participant can boast. Presidents usually get positive coverage during crises foreign or domestic. The news media depict them speaking for and symbolically embodying the nation: giving a State of the Union address, welcoming foreign leaders, traveling abroad, representing the United States at an international conference. Ceremonial events produce laudatory coverage even during intense political controversy.

The media are fascinated with the personality and style of individual presidents. They attempt to pin them down. Sometimes, the analyses are contradictory or may change over time. In one best-selling book, Bob Woodward depicted President George W. Bush as, in the words of reviewer Michiko Kakutani, "a judicious, resolute leader . . . firmly in control of the ship of state." In a later book, Woodward described Bush as "passive, impatient, sophomoric and intellectually incurious . . . given to an almost religious certainty that makes him disinclined to rethink or re-evaluate decisions."[8]

This media focus tells only part of the story.[9] The president's independence and ability to act are constrained in several ways, most notably by the Constitution.

# The Presidency in the Constitution

Article II of the Constitution outlines the office of president. Specific powers are few; almost all are exercised in conjunction with other branches of the federal government.

**TABLE 13.1 Bases for Presidential Powers in the Constitution**

| | |
|---|---|
| Article I, Section 7, Paragraph 2 | Veto |
| | Pocket veto |
| Article II, Section 1, Paragraph 1 | "The Executive Power shall be vested in a President . . ." |
| Article II, Section 1, Paragraph 7 | Specific presidential oath of office stated explicitly (as is not the case with other offices) |
| Article II, Section 2, Paragraph 1 | Commander in chief of armed forces and state militias |
| Article II, Section 2, Paragraph 1 | Can require opinions of departmental secretaries |
| Article II, Section 2, Paragraph 1 | Reprieves and pardons for offences against the United States |
| Article II, Section 2, Paragraph 2 | Make treaties |
| | Appoint ambassadors, executive officers, judges |
| Article II, Section 2, Paragraph 3 | Recess appointments |
| Article II, Section 3 | State of the Union message and recommendation of legislative measures to Congress |
| | Convene special sessions of Congress |
| | Receive ambassadors and other ministers |
| | "He shall take Care that the Laws be faithfully executed" |

Presidents exercise only one power that cannot be limited by other branches: the pardon. So controversial decisions like President Gerald Ford's pardon of his predecessor Richard Nixon for "crimes he committed or may have committed" or President Jimmy Carter's blanket amnesty to all who avoided the draft during the Vietnam War could not have been overturned.

Presidents also have the power to bestow, at their discretion, the Presidential Medal of Freedom. Initiated by President John F. Kennedy in 1963, this award is supposed to recognize people for an especially meritorious contribution to the security or national interests of the United States, world peace, or a cultural or other significant public or private endeavor. In practice, recipients also include financial donors and friends of the White House. President Obama gave it to his vice president, Joseph Biden. President Trump gave it to the conservative commentator Rush Limbaugh.

Presidents have more powers and responsibilities in foreign and defense policy than in domestic affairs. Although Congress has the right to declare war, the president is the commander in chief of the armed forces and, in practice, decides how (and increasingly when) to wage war. Presidents have the power to make treaties to be approved by the Senate; the president is America's chief diplomat. As head of state, the president speaks for the nation to other world leaders and receives ambassadors. We discuss the president's "war powers" later in this chapter. Otherwise, we cover the president's foreign and defense policies in Chapter 17.

The Constitution directs presidents to be part of the legislative process. In the annual State of the Union address, presidents point out problems and recommend legislation to Congress. Presidents can convene special sessions of Congress, possibly to "jump-start" discussion of their proposals. As we shall discuss in more detail, presidents can veto a bill passed by Congress, returning it with written objections. Congress can then override the veto.

The Constitution instructs presidents to be in charge of the executive branch. Along with naming federal judges, presidents appoint ambassadors and executive officers. These appointments require Senate confirmation. If Congress is not in session, presidents can make temporary appointments known as **recess appointments** without Senate confirmation, good until the end of the next session of Congress. However, in 2017, the Supreme Court ruled by 6–2 that the president could not appoint a person to fill a vacant government post on an acting basis if that person had been nominated for it but not confirmed by the Senate. This decision makes it more difficult for the president to install hundreds of his preferred choices in federal jobs.[10]

**recess appointments**

Judicial or executive appointments made by the president while Congress is out of session that do not require Senate confirmation; they last until the end of the congressional session.

The Constitution's phrase "he shall take Care that the Laws be faithfully executed" gives the president the job to oversee the implementation of laws. Thus, presidents are empowered to issue executive orders to interpret and carry out legislation. They supervise other officers of the executive branch and can require them to justify their actions.

## Congressional Limitations on Presidential Power

Almost all presidential powers rely on what Congress does (or does not do). Congress can obstruct the president, particularly when the opposing party controls both chambers, as the Republicans did against President Obama after the 2014 election; or as the Democrats did the House of Representatives after the 2018 election.

Presidential executive orders implement the law, but Congress can overrule such orders by changing the law. And many presidential powers are **delegated powers** that Congress has accorded presidents to exercise on its behalf—and that it can cut back or rescind.

**delegated powers**

Presidential prerogatives accorded by legislation, where Congress gives authority under the powers given to it by the Constitution.

Congress can challenge presidential powers single-handedly. One way is to amend the Constitution. The Twenty-Second Amendment was enacted in the wake of the only president to serve more than two terms, the powerful Franklin D. Roosevelt (FDR). Presidents now may serve no more than two terms. The last presidents to serve eight years, Ronald Reagan, Bill Clinton, George W. Bush, and Barack Obama, quickly became "lame ducks" after their reelection and lost momentum toward the ends of their second terms, when attention switched to contests over their successors.

**Impeachment** gives Congress "sole power" to remove presidents (among others) from office.[11] It works in two stages. The House decides whether or not to accuse the president of wrongdoing. If a simple majority in the House votes to impeach the president, the Senate acts as jury, House members are prosecutors, and the chief justice presides. A two-thirds vote by the Senate is necessary for conviction, the punishment for which is removal and disqualification from office.

**impeachment**

Congress's power to remove executive officers and judges from office for "treason, bribery and high crimes and misdemeanors."

Prior to the 1970s, presidential impeachment was deemed the founders' "rusted blunderbuss that will probably never be taken in hand again."[12] Only one president (Andrew Johnson in 1868) had been impeached—over policy disagreements with Congress on the Reconstruction of the South after the Civil War. Johnson avoided removal by a single senator's vote.

### Links

**Presidential Impeachment**

Read about the impeachment trial of President Johnson here.

Read about the impeachment trial of President Clinton here.

Since the 1970s, the blunderbuss has been dusted off. A bipartisan majority of the House Judiciary Committee recommended the impeachment of President Nixon in 1974. Nixon surely would have been impeached and convicted had he not resigned first. President Clinton was impeached by the House in 1998, for perjury and obstruction of justice in the Monica Lewinsky scandal. He was acquitted by the Senate in 1999.

**FIGURE 13.3 Media Attention on Impeachment**

Bill Clinton was only the second U.S. president to be impeached for "Treason, Bribery, or other High Crimes and Misdemeanors" and stand trial in the Senate. Not surprisingly, in this day of huge media attention to court proceedings, the presidential impeachment trial was covered live by television and became endless fodder for twenty-four-hour news channels. Justice William Rehnquist presided over the trial. The House "managers" (i.e., prosecutors) of the case are on the left, the president's lawyers on the right.

Source: Senate in session. C-SPAN image via Wikimedia: https://en.wikipedia.org/wiki/File:Senate_in_session.jpg.

Much of the public finds impeachment a standard part of the political system. For example, a June 2005 Zogby poll found that 42 percent of the public agreed with the statement "If President Bush did not tell the truth about his reasons for going to war with Iraq, Congress should consider holding him accountable through impeachment."[13] However, some people confuse impeachment with conviction, not understanding that impeachment is by the House of Representatives and that only a trial and conviction by the Senate can lead to removal from office.

Impeachment can be a threat to presidents who chafe at congressional opposition or restrictions. The two impeached presidents had been accused by members of Congress of abuse of power well before allegations of law-breaking. Impeachment is handy because its criteria of official misconduct—"treason, bribery, or other high crimes and misdemeanors"—are rather vague.

From Congress's perspective, impeachment can work. Nixon resigned because he knew he would be removed from office. Even presidential acquittals help Congress out. Impeachment forced Johnson to pledge good behavior and thus "succeeded in its primary goal: to safeguard Reconstruction from presidential obstruction."[14] Clinton had to go out of his way to assuage congressional Democrats, who had been far from content with a number of his initiatives; by the time the impeachment trial was concluded, the president was an all-but-lame duck.

During President Trump's first two years in office, some Democrats raised the possibility of impeaching him but were deterred by the existence of a Republican majority in the House of Representatives. However, the 2018 election gave the Democrats a majority in the House. In 2019, the president's alleged pressure on the president of Ukraine to serve his reelection interests against his potential opponent, former Vice President Joseph R. Biden, Jr., was brought to light. Emboldened by these events, the Democratic leadership in the House initiated and pursued the president's impeachment. They did so knowing they were unlikely to enjoy any Republican support; and that the Republican majority in the Senate guaranteed the president's acquittal.

Democrats and a few Republicans in the House of Representatives impeached President Trump for a second time a week before his term expired. The charge was incitement of insurrection. He was tried and acquitted by the Senate after he left office.

We describe and detail the impeachment process, participants, the concatenation of events, and the outcome in Chapter 12 Section 2.

## Judicial Limitations on Presidential Power

**inherent powers**

Presidential prerogatives claimed by presidents as implied by either the office of the president itself or the provisions of the Constitution.

Presidents claim **inherent powers** not explicitly stated but that are intrinsic to the office or implied by the language of the Constitution. They rely on three key phrases. First, in contrast to Article I's detailed powers of Congress, Article II states that "The Executive Power shall be vested in a President." Second, the presidential oath of office is spelled out, implying a special guardianship of the Constitution. Third, the job of ensuring that "the Laws be faithfully executed" can denote a duty to protect the country and political system as a whole.

Ultimately, the Supreme Court can and does rule whether and to what extent presidents have inherent powers. Its rulings have both expanded and limited presidential power. For instance, the justices concluded in 1936 that the president, the embodiment of the United States outside its borders, can act on its behalf in foreign policy.

But the court often looks to congressional action (or inaction) to define when a president can invoke inherent powers. In 1952, President Harry Truman claimed inherent emergency powers during the Korean War. Facing a steel strike that he said would interrupt defense production, Truman ordered his secretary of commerce to seize the major steel mills and keep production going. The Supreme Court rejected this move: "the President's power, if any, to issue the order must stem either from an act of Congress or from the Constitution itself."[15]

Presidents do usually win about two-thirds of their cases decided by the Supreme Court. The Obama administration was the big exception. Despite some significant victories on such issues as LGBTQ+ rights, abortion, and affirmative action, its winning percentage was 50.5 percent, lower than any president of this century. One explanation is that the conservative court was hostile to Obama's liberal agenda. This argument was somewhat bolstered by the Supreme Court's responsiveness to President Trump's assertions of executive power.[16]

## The Vice Presidency

Only two positions in the presidency are elected: the president and vice president. With ratification of the Twenty-Fifth Amendment in 1967, a vacancy in the latter office may be filled by the president, who appoints a vice president subject to majority votes in both the House and the Senate. This process was used twice in the 1970s. Vice President Spiro Agnew resigned amid allegations of corruption; President Nixon named House minority leader Gerald Ford to the post. When Nixon resigned during the Watergate scandal, Ford became president—the only person to hold the office without an election—and named former New York Governor Nelson Rockefeller vice president.

**FIGURE 13.4**
**Vice President Mike Pence**
Mike Pence as President Trump's ideal-looking vice president.

Source: Trump White House Archived. Official White House Photo by D. Myles Cullen via Wikimedia: https://commons.wikimedia.org/wiki/File:Mike_Pence_official_Vice_Presidential_portrait.jpg.

Section 4 of the Twenty-Fifth Amendment provides for the removal of a president who is unable to discharge or unwilling to admit that he can no longer discharge his duties. The vice president, plus "a majority of either the principal officers of the executive departments or of such other body as Congress may by law provide" can declare the president unfit and install the vice president as acting president. This provision has yet to be invoked.

The vice president's sole duties in the Constitution are to preside over the Senate and cast tie-breaking votes, and to be ready to assume the presidency in the event of a vacancy or disability. Eight of the forty-three presidents have been vice presidents who succeeded a dead president (four times from assassinations). Otherwise, vice presidents have few official tasks. The first vice president, John Adams, told the Senate, "I am Vice President. In this I am nothing, but I may be everything." More earthily, FDR's first vice president, John Nance Garner, called the office "not worth a bucket of warm piss."

In recent years, vice presidents are more publicly visible and have taken on more tasks and responsibilities. Ford and Rockefeller began this trend in the 1970s, demanding enhanced day-to-day responsibilities and staff as conditions for taking the job. Vice presidents now have a West Wing office, are given prominent assignments, and receive distinct funds for a staff under their control parallel to the president's staff.[17]

Arguably the most powerful occupant of the office ever was Dick Cheney. This former doctoral candidate in political science (at the University of Wisconsin–Madison) had been a White House chief of staff, member of Congress, and cabinet secretary. He possessed an unrivaled knowledge of the power relations within government and of how to accumulate and exercise power. As George W. Bush's vice president, he had access to every cabinet and subcabinet meeting he wanted to attend, chaired the board charged with reviewing the budget, took on important issues (security, energy, economy), ran task forces, was involved in nominations and appointments, and lobbied Congress.[18]

According to President Trump, when he was hesitating over choosing Mike Pence as his vice president, his aides were insistent: "They're telling me I have to pick him. It's central casting. He looks like a vice president."[19] Vice President Mike Pence's role was to be a loyal, unobtrusive, behind-the-scenes lackey to the far more flamboyant President Trump. But given the latter's age, vulnerability to investigation, propensity for controversy, and hostility from Democrats, Pence's eventual elevation to the presidency was never beyond the realm of possibility.

# Organizing the Presidency

The presidency is organized around two offices. They enhance but also constrain the president's power. Aside from their formal duties, their occupants' behavior is often characterized by intrigue, ambition, back-stabbing, conflicts, and battles.

## The Executive Office of the President

**Executive Office of the President (EOP)**

An umbrella organization started in 1939 by Franklin D. Roosevelt for various presidential staff agencies, many established by law.

The **Executive Office of the President (EOP)** is an umbrella organization encompassing all presidential staff agencies. Most offices in the EOP, such as the Office of the Vice President, the National Security Council (NSC), and the Office of Management and Budget (OMB), are established by law; some positions require Senate confirmation.

### Link

**The EOP**

Click here to learn about the EOP.

**White House Office (WHO)**

An organization within the EOP that contains the president's personal advisors and staffers.

Inside the EOP is the **White House Office (WHO)**. It contains the president's personal staff of assistants and advisors; most are exempt from Congress's purview. Though presidents have a free hand with the personnel and structure of the WHO, its organization has been the same for decades. Starting with Nixon in 1969, each president has named a chief of staff to head and supervise the White House staff. See the television documentary *The Presidents' Gatekeepers*; in his review, Jon Caramanica lists some of the terms used in the show to describe the chief of staff: "consigliere, enforcer, point guard, battlefield commander, director of traffic, reality therapist, heat shield."[20]

Other leading staffers are a press secretary to interact with the news media, and a director of communication to oversee the White House message. The national security advisor is well placed to become the most powerful architect of foreign policy, rivaling or surpassing the secretary of state. New offices, such as President Bush's creation of an office for faith-based initiatives, are rare; such positions get placed on top of or alongside old arrangements.

Even activities of a highly informal role, such as those of the first lady, the president's spouse, are standardized. It is no longer enough for them to host White House social events. They are brought out to travel and campaign. They may be the president's intimate confidante, have staffers of their own, and advocate popular policies (e.g., Lady Bird Johnson's highway beautification, Nancy Reagan's anti-drug crusade, and Barbara Bush's literacy programs). Hillary Rodham Clinton faced controversy as first lady by defying expectations of being above the policy fray; she was appointed by her husband to head the task force to draft a legislative bill for a national health-care system. Clinton's successor, Laura Bush, returned the first ladyship to a more social, less policy-minded role. Michelle Obama's cause was healthy eating. She went beyond advocacy to having Walmart lower prices on the fruits and vegetables it sells and reducing the amount of fat, sugar, and salt in foods.

## Bureaucratizing the Presidency

The media and the public expect presidents to put their marks on the office and on history. But "the institution makes presidents as much if not more than presidents make the institution."[21]

The presidency became a complex institution starting with FDR, who was elected to four terms during the Great Depression and World War II. Prior to FDR, presidents' staffs were small. As presidents took on responsibilities and jobs, often at Congress's initiative, the presidency grew and expanded.

Not only is the presidency bigger since FDR, but the division of labor within an administration is far more complex. Fiction and nonfiction media depict generalist staffers reporting to the president, who makes the real decisions. But the WHO is now a miniature bureaucracy. The WHO's first staff in 1939 consisted of eight generalists: three secretaries to the president, three administrative assistants, a personal secretary, an executive clerk. Since the 1980s, the WHO has consisted of around eighty staffers; almost all either have a substantive specialty (e.g., national security, women's initiatives, environment, health policy) or emphasize specific activities (e.g., White House legal counsel, director of press advance, public liaison, legislative liaison, chief speechwriter, director of scheduling). The White House Office adds another organization for presidents to direct—or lose track of.

The large staff in the White House, and in the Old Executive Office Building next door, is no guarantee of a president's power. These staffers "make a great many decisions themselves, acting in the name of the president. In fact, the majority of White House decisions—all but the most crucial—are made by presidential assistants."[22]

Most of these labor in anonymity unless they make impolitic remarks or otherwise attract media attention. For example, two of President George W. Bush's otherwise obscure chief economic advisors got into hot water, one for (accurately) predicting that the cost of war in Iraq might top $200 billion, another for praising the outsourcing of jobs.[23] Relatively few White House staffers—the chief of staff, the national security advisor, the press secretary—become household names in the news, and even they are quick to be quoted saying, "as the president has said" or "the president decided." But often what presidents say or do is what staffers told or wrote for them to say or do (see "Comparing Content").

## Comparing Content

### Days in the Life of the White House

On April 25, 2001, President George W. Bush was celebrating his first one hundred days in office. He sought to avoid the misstep of his father, who had ignored the media frame of the first one hundred days as the make-or-break period for a presidency and who thus seemed confused and aimless.

As part of this campaign, Bush invited Stephen Crowley, a *New York Times* photographer, to follow him and present, as Crowley wrote in his accompanying text, "an unusual behind-the-scenes view of how he conducts business."[24] Naturally, the photos implied that the White House revolves completely around the president. At 6:45 a.m., "the White House came to life"—when a light came on in the president's upstairs residence. The sole task shown for Bush's personal assistant was peering through a peephole to monitor the president's national security briefing. Crowley wrote "the workday ended 15 hours after it began," after meetings, interviews, a stadium speech, and a fund raiser.

We get a different understanding of how the White House works from following not the president but some other denizen of the West Wing around for a day or so. That is what filmmaker Theodore Bogosian did: he shadowed Clinton's then press secretary Joe Lockhart for a few days in mid-2000 with a high-definition television camera. In the revealing one-hour video, *The Press Secretary*, activities of the White House are shown to revolve around Lockhart as much as Crowley's photographic essay showed they did around Bush. Even with the hands-on Bill Clinton, the video raises questions about who works for whom. Lockhart is shown devising taglines, even policy with his associates in the press office. He instructs the president on what to say as much as the other way around. He confides to the camera he is nervous about letting Clinton speak off-the-cuff.

Of course, the White House does not revolve around the person of the press secretary. Neither does it revolve entirely around the person of the president. Both are lone individuals out of many who collectively make up the institution known as the presidency.

## Key Takeaways

The entertainment and news media personalize the presidency, depicting the president as the dynamic center of the political system. The Constitution foresaw the presidency as an energetic office with one person in charge. Yet the Constitution gave the office and its incumbent few powers, most of which can be countered by other branches of government. The presidency is bureaucratically organized and includes agencies, offices, and staff. They are often outside a president's direct control.

## Exercises

1. How do the media personalize the presidency?
2. How can the president check the power of Congress? How can Congress limit the influence of the president?
3. How is the executive branch organized? How is the way the executive branch operates different from the way it is portrayed in the media?

# 13.3 How Presidents (Try to) Get Things Done

## Learning Objectives

After reading this section, you should be able to answer the following questions:

1. How does the president try to set the agenda for the political system, especially Congress?
2. What challenges do presidents face in achieving their agendas?
3. What are the strengths and weaknesses of the presidential veto?
4. Can and do presidents lead Congress?
5. What are the president's powers as chief executive?
6. Why do presidents give so many speeches?
7. How do presidents seek public approval?

The U.S. political system was designed by the framers to be infrequently innovative, to act with neither efficiency nor dispatch. Authority is decentralized. Interests are diverse, and political parties not envisaged in the Constitution. Conflict is pervasive, as for example when Congress investigates the president.[25]

Yet, as we have explained, presidents face high expectations for action. Adding to these expectations are the soaring rhetoric and explicit commitments of their election campaigns. In 2008 candidate Obama promised to deal with the problems of the economy, unemployment, housing, health care, the situations in Iraq and Afghanistan, and much more. In 2016, candidate Trump promised to renegotiate trade agreements, fix health care, protect and bring back and increase the number of American jobs, deal with immigration, destroy ISIS, make America great again, and more.

As we have also explained, presidents do not always or even often have the power to meet these expectations. Consider the economy. Because the government and media report the growth, inflation, and unemployment rates, and the number of new jobs created (or not created), the public is consistently reminded of these measures when judging the president's handling of the economy. And certainly the president does claim credit when the economy is doing well or better. Yet the president has far less control over the economy and these economic indicators than the media convey and many people believe.

A president's opportunities to influence public policies also depend in part on the situation left by the preceding administration and the political circumstances under which the new president takes office.[26] Presidents often face intractable issues, encounter unpredictable events, have to make complex policy decisions, and are beset by outrages and scandals (policy, financial, sexual). During the first two years of his second term, President Obama had to deal with and often be blamed for, to mention just a few, the botched HealthCare.gov website and for erroneously telling people they could keep their existing health insurance plans, the inability (unwillingness) of Congress to pass gun control and immigration legislation, the sixteen-day shutdown or curtailment of federal government services, and the National Security Agency's massive spying revealed by Edward Snowden.

Once the president is in office, reality sinks in. Interviewing President Obama on *The Daily Show*, Jon Stewart wondered whether the president's campaign slogan of "Yes we can" should be changed to "Yes we can, given certain conditions." President Obama replied, "I think I would say 'yes we can, but . . . it's not going to happen overnight.'"[27]

So how do presidents get things done? Presidential powers and prerogatives do offer opportunities for leadership.

### Link

**Presidential Recordings**

Between 1940 and 1973, six American presidents from both political parties secretly recorded around five thousand hours of their meetings and telephone conversations. Learn more here.

Presidents indicate what issues should garner most attention and action; they help set the policy agenda. They lobby Congress to pass their programs, often via campaign-like swings around the country. As head of their political party they are able to try to retain or gain allies (and win reelection). Inside the executive branch, presidents make policies by well-publicized appointments and executive orders. They use their ceremonial position as head of state to get into the news and seek public approval, sometimes making it easier to persuade others to follow their lead.

## Agenda-Setter for the Political System

Presidents try to set the political agenda. They call attention to issues and solutions, using constitutional powers such as calling Congress into session, recommending bills, and informing its members about the state of the union, as well as by giving speeches and making news.[28]

**FIGURE 13.5** The State of the Union Address

The president's constitutional responsibility to inform Congress on "the state of the union" has been elevated into a performance, nationally broadcast on all major networks and cable news channels before a joint session on Capitol Hill, that summarizes the key items on his policy agenda.

Source: Obama White House Archives. P012511CK-0230. President Barack Obama waves at the conclusion of his State of the Union address in the House, Jan. 25, 2011. (Official White House Photo by Chuck Kennedy). Via Flickr: https://www.flickr.com/photos/obamawhitehouse/5391631576/.

Congress does not always defer to and sometimes spurns the president's agenda.[29] Its members serve smaller, more distinct constituencies for different terms. When presidents hail from the same party as the majority of Congress members, they have more influence to ensure that their ideas receive serious attention on Capitol Hill. So presidents often work hard to keep or increase the number of members of their party in Congress: raising funds for the party (and their own campaign), campaigning for candidates, and throwing weight (and money) in a primary election behind the strongest or their preferred candidate. Presidential coattails—where members of Congress are carried to victory by the winning presidential candidate—are increasingly short and may not exist at all. Some legislators win by larger margins in their district than does the president. In the elections midway through the president's term, the president's party generally loses seats in Congress. In 2010, despite President Obama's efforts, the Republicans gained a whopping sixty-three seats and took control of the House of Representatives.

**divided government**

Divided government is when a majority of members of the House and/or Senate are of a different party than the president.

Since presidents usually have less support in Congress from their party in the second halves of their terms, they most often expect that Congress will be more amenable to their initiatives in their first two years. But even then, **divided government**, where one party controls the presidency and the other party controls one or both chambers of Congress, has been common over the last fifty years. For presidents, the prospect of both a friendly House and Senate became the exception.

Even when the White House and Congress are controlled by the same party, as with President Obama and the Democrats in 2009 and 2010 and President Trump and the Republicans after the 2016 election, presidents do not monopolize the legislative agenda. Congressional leaders, especially of the opposing party, push other issues—if only to pressure or embarrass the president. Members of Congress have made campaign promises they want to keep despite the president's policy preferences. Interest groups with pet projects crowd in.

Withal, presidents are better placed than any other individual to influence the legislative agenda. In particular, their high prominence in the news means that they have a powerful impact on what issues will—and will not—be considered in the political system as a whole.

What about the contents of "the president's agenda"? The president is but one player among many shaping it. The transition from election to inauguration is just over two months (Bush had less time because of the disputed 2000 Florida vote). Presidents are preoccupied first with naming a cabinet and White House staff. To build an agenda, presidents "borrow, steal, co-opt, redraft, rename, and modify any proposal that fits their policy goals."[30] Ideas largely come from fellow partisans outside the White House. Bills already introduced in Congress or programs proposed by the bureaucracy are handy. They have received discussion, study, and compromise that have built support. And presidents have more success getting borrowed legislation through Congress than policy proposals devised inside the White House.[31]

Nonetheless, an activist Democrat such as President Obama was committed to taking up certain issues from the start, notably health care and bank regulation. Other issues, such as climate change, undocumented immigration, and gun control, arose or became more prominent over the course of his presidency. This attention often stemmed from crises and unexpected events and was elevated by the questions and stories of White House reporters and by media coverage. Other issues pursue the president rather than he pursuing them—for George W. Bush, a hugely destructive hurricane on the Gulf Coast propelled issues of emergency management, poverty, and reconstruction onto the policy agenda—whether a president wants them there or not.

Finally, many agenda items cannot be avoided. Presidents are charged by Congress with proposing an annual budget. Raw budget numbers represent serious policy choices.

## Chief Lobbyist in Congress

After suggesting what Congress should do, presidents try to persuade legislators to follow through. But without a formal role, presidents are outsiders to the legislative process. They cannot introduce bills in Congress and must rely on members to do so.

Presidents are often judged in the media by how effectively they interact with Congress, especially the leaders of the opposition party. President Lyndon Johnson was famous for his knowledge and understanding of the institution and its members based on his years there, particularly as majority leader of the Senate. His ability to seduce and skill at persuasion, known as "The Treatment," was legendary—as was his willingness to berate, threaten, and punish those who refused to accede to his demands or opposed him.[32]

In (dire) contrast, President Obama was seen as failing to build personal relationships; as reserved, reluctant to schmooze or glad-hand; and as aloof from Congress and its members. It was observed that "several members of Congress have said that the president's phone manner has all the charm of a robocall."[33] He was reluctant to exert his power against his enemies. His distance and disdain, commentators averred, explained in part his failure to accomplish much in or with Congress after his first two years in office, which saw passage of the Affordable Care Act, financial reform, repeal of "don't ask, don't tell" in the military, ratification of an arms-control treaty with Russia, and more.[34] But, as we shall document, there are other (important) reasons.

## Legislative Liaison

**legislative liaison**

Now called the Office of Legislative Affairs, an office consisting of presidential staffers whose job is to interact with and lobby members of Congress.

Presidents aim at legislative accomplishments by negotiating with legislators directly or through their **legislative liaison** officers: White House staffers assigned to deal with Congress who provide a conduit from president to Congress and back again. These staffers convey presidential preferences and pressure members of Congress; they also pass along members' concerns to the White House. They count votes, line up coalitions, and suggest times for presidents to rally fellow party members. And they try to cut deals.

Legislative liaison focuses less on twisting arms than on trying to maintain "an era of good feelings" with Congress. Some favors are large: supporting an appropriation that benefits members' constituencies; traveling to members' home turf to help them raise funds for reelection; and appointing members' cronies to high office. Others are small: inviting them up to the White House, where they can talk with reporters; sending them autographed photos or extra tickets for White House tours; and allowing them to announce grants. Presidents hope the cordiality will encourage legislators to return the favor when necessary.[35]

Such good feelings are tough to maintain when the president and opposition party espouse conflicting policies, especially when that party has a majority in one or both chambers of Congress or enough members in the Senate to filibuster effectively. Or when it is determined to thwart the president. All these conditions existed during the second half of President Obama's first term and the entirety of his second.

## The Veto

**veto**

The president's power to reject a bill by not signing it into law.

**overrides**

The congressional power to enact legislation over a president's veto by a two-thirds majority in each chamber.

**line-item veto**

The power, available to most state governors but not to the president, to reject parts of a bill.

When Congress passes a bill, it goes to the White House. The president can sign it, whereupon it becomes law, or return it to the originating chamber with objections, thereby vetoing it. This is a regular veto. Or he can neither sign nor return it within ten days (not counting Sundays), in which case, if Congress is no longer in session, it does not become law. This is a pocket veto. The bill does become law if Congress is still in session.[36] This **veto**—Latin for "I forbid"—heightens the stakes. Congress can get its way only if it **overrides** the regular veto with two-thirds majorities in each chamber. Presidents who use the veto can block almost any bill they dislike; only around 4 percent of all vetoes have ever been successfully overridden. The major exception is when the opposition party controls Congress—four of president George W. Bush's twelve vetoes (33 percent) were overturned. The threat of a veto can be enough to get Congress to enact legislation closer to the president's preference.

The veto does have drawbacks for presidents:

- Vetoes alienate members of Congress who worked hard crafting a bill. So vetoes are mostly used as a last resort. After the 1974 elections, the Republican president, Gerald Ford, faced an overwhelmingly Democratic Congress. A Ford legislative liaison officer recalled, "We never deliberately sat down and made the decision that we would veto sixty bills in two years. . . . It was the only alternative."[37]
- The veto is a blunt instrument. It is useless if Congress does not act on legislation in the first place. In his 1993 speech proposing health-care reform, President Clinton waved a pen and vowed to veto any bill that did not provide universal coverage. Such a threat meant nothing when Congress did not pass *any* reform. And unlike governors of most states, presidents lack a **line-item veto**, which allows a chief executive to reject parts of a bill. Congress sought to give the president this power in the late 1990s, but the Supreme Court declared the law unconstitutional.[38] Presidents must take or leave bills in their totality.
- Congress can turn the veto against presidents. For example, it can pass a popular bill—especially in an election year—and dare the president to reject it. President Clinton faced such "veto bait" from the Republican Congress when he was up for reelection in 1996. The Defense of

Marriage Act, which would have restricted federal recognition of marriage to opposite-sex couples, was deeply distasteful to the LGBTQ+ community (a key Democratic constituency) but strongly backed in public opinion polls. A Clinton veto could bring blame for killing the bill or provoke a humiliating override. Signing it ran the risk of infuriating LGBTQ+ voters. Clinton ultimately signed the legislation—in the middle of the night with no cameras present.

- Veto threats can backfire. After the Democrats took over the Senate in mid-2001, they moved the "patients' bill of rights" authorizing lawsuits against health maintenance organizations to the top of the Senate agenda. President Bush said he would veto the bill unless it incorporated strict limits on rights to sue and low caps on damages won in lawsuits. Such a visible threat encouraged a public perception that Bush was opposed to any patients' bill of rights, or even to patients' rights at all.[39] Veto threats thus can be ineffective or create political damage (or, as in this case, both).

Savvy presidents use "vetoes not only to block legislation but to shape it. . . . Vetoes are not fatal bullets but bargaining ploys."[40] Veto threats and vetoing ceremonies become key to presidential communications in the news, which welcomes the story of Capitol Hill–versus–White House disputes, particularly under divided government. In 1996, President Clinton faced a tough welfare reform bill from a Republican Congress whose leaders dared him to veto the bill so they could claim he broke his 1992 promise to "end welfare as we know it." Clinton vetoed the first bill; Republicans reduced the cuts but kept tough provisions denying benefits to children born to welfare recipients. Clinton vetoed this second version; Republicans shrank the cuts again and reduced the impact on children. Finally, Clinton signed the bill—and ran ads during his reelection campaign proclaiming how *he* had "ended welfare as we know it."

## Signing Statements

In a **signing statement**, the president claims the right to ignore or refuse to enforce laws, parts of laws, or provisions of appropriations bills even though Congress has enacted them and he has signed them into law. This practice was uncommon until developed during President Ronald Reagan's second term. It escalated under President George W. Bush, who rarely exercised the veto but instead issued almost 1,200 signing statements in eight years—about twice as many as all his predecessors combined. As one example, he rejected the requirement that he report to Congress on how he had provided safeguards against political interference in federally funded research. He justified his statements on the "inherent" power of the commander in chief and on a hitherto obscure doctrine called the unitary executive, which holds that the executive branch can overrule Congress and the courts on the basis of the president's interpretation of the Constitution.

**signing statement**

The president claims the right to ignore or refuse to enforce laws, parts of laws, or provisions of appropriations bills that Congress has enacted and he has signed into law.

President Obama ordered executive officials to consult with the attorney general before relying on any of President Bush's signing statements to bypass a law. Yet he initially issued some signing statements himself. Then, to avoid clashing with Congress, he refrained from doing so. He did claim that the executive branch could bypass what he deemed to be unconstitutional restraints on executive power. But he did not invoke the unitary executive theory.[41]

## Presidential Scorecards in Congress

How often do presidents get their way on Capitol Hill? On roll call votes, Congress usually goes along with about three-fourths of presidential recommendations; the success rate is highest earlier in the term.[42] Even on controversial, important legislation for which they expressed a preference well in advance of congressional action, presidents still do well. Congress seldom ignores presidential agenda items entirely. One study estimates that over half of presidential recommendations are substantially reflected in legislative action.[43] However, these studies preceded the deadlock between congressional Republicans and President Obama we discuss herein.

Can and do presidents lead Congress, then? Not exactly. Most presidential success is determined by Congress's partisan and ideological makeup. Divided government and party polarization on Capitol Hill have made Congress more willing to disagree with and even ignore the president. So recent presidents are less successful even while being choosier about bills to endorse. Eisenhower, Kennedy, and Johnson staked out positions on well over half of congressional roll call votes. Their successors have taken positions on fewer than one-fourth of them—especially when their party did not control Congress. "Presidents, wary of an increasingly independent-minded congressional membership and anxious to minimize defeat, have come actively to support legislation only when it is of particular importance to them."[44]

For President Obama, frustration and failure became common in the face of obdurate and recalcitrant opposition by Republicans who, after gaining control of the House of Representatives in the 2010 congressional election, refused to consider, let alone pass, most of his important legislative proposals.

# Chief Executive

As chief executive, the president can move first and quickly, daring others to respond. Presidents like both the feeling of power and favorable news stories of them acting decisively. Though Congress and courts can respond, they often react slowly; many if not most presidential actions are never effectively challenged.[45] Such direct presidential action is based in several powers: to appoint officials, to issue executive orders, to "take care that the laws be faithfully executed," and to wage war.

## Appointment Powers

Presidents hire and (with the exception of regulatory commissions) fire executive officers. They also appoint ambassadors, the members of independent agencies, and the federal judiciary.[46]

**cabinet**

The group of advisors to presidents made up of the secretaries of departments (e.g., secretary of defense) and the heads of agencies given cabinet-level status by the president.

The months between election and inauguration are consumed by the need to rapidly assemble a **cabinet**, a group that reports to and advises the president, made up of the heads of the executive departments and whatever other positions the president accords cabinet-level rank. Finding "the right person for the job" is but one criterion. Cabinet appointees overwhelmingly hail from the president's party; choosing fellow partisans rewards the winning coalition and helps achieve policy.[47] Presidents may also try to create a team that, in Clinton's phrase, "looks like America." In 1953, President Dwight Eisenhower was stung by the news media's joke that his first cabinet—all male, all white—consisted of "nine millionaires and a plumber" (the latter was a union official, a short-lived labor secretary). By contrast, George W. Bush's and Barack Obama's cabinets had a generous complement of persons of color and women (President Biden's even more so)—and at least one member of the other party. Even then, President Obama was criticized for failing to consult with his cabinet members or to use them to promote his policy agenda in Congress.[48]

These presidential appointees must be confirmed by the Senate. A nominee may be stopped in a committee. About one out of every twenty key nominations is never confirmed, usually when a committee does not schedule it for a vote.[49]

Confirmation hearings are opportunities for senators to quiz nominees about pet projects of interest to their states, to elicit pledges to testify or provide information, and to extract promises of policy actions.[50] To win confirmation, cabinet officers pledge to be responsive and accountable to Congress. Sub-cabinet officials and federal judges, lacking the prominence of cabinet and Supreme Court nominees, are even more belatedly nominated and more slowly confirmed. Even senators of the president's party routinely block nominees to protest poor treatment or win concessions.

After a committee approves (assuming it does) a nomination can be scheduled for a vote by the Senate. The Senate rarely votes down nominees on the floor, but it no longer rubber-stamps them even if they are scandal-free. An important reason is that they can be filibustered (discussed below).

As a result, presidents sometimes have to wait quite a while before their appointees take office—if they take office at all. Five months into President George W. Bush's first term, one study showed that of the 494 cabinet and sub-cabinet positions to fill, under half had received nominations; under one-fourth had been confirmed.[51] One scholar observed, "In America today, you can get a master's degree, build a house, bicycle across country, or make a baby in less time than it takes to put the average appointee on the job."[52] With presidential appointments unfilled, initiatives are delayed and day-to-day running of the departments is left by default to career civil servants. No wonder presidents install acting appointees or use their power to make recess appointments.

In 2014 the Supreme Court unanimously ruled that President Obama had overreached in 2012 by issuing recess appointments during a Senate break of only three days. (From the president's perspective, the Senate convening every three days was to prevent him from making recess appointments. In 2006 Democrats had adopted the same tactic against President George W. Bush.) But the Court by 5–4 ruled that recess appointments were permissible if made during breaks of ten or more days. The four conservative justices would have limited the appointments "to breaks between Congress's formal annual sessions, and even then to vacancies that arose during those breaks."[53]

Presidents have the authority to appoint, but the appointed are not anointed. The president may remove them for whatever reasons; or they may resign because of principle, scandal, or frustration. The Trump administration was notorious for its turnover in the positions, for example, of Homeland Security secretary, Veterans Affairs secretary, and Health and Human Services secretary; national security advisers; secretaries of defense; and press secretaries.[54]

## Executive Orders

Presidents make policies by **executive orders**.[55] This power comes from the constitutional mandate that presidents "take care that the laws be faithfully executed."

**executive order**

A directive to administrators in the executive branch on how to implement legislation already enacted; courts treat them as having the status of law, but they may be superseded by congressional legislation.

Executive orders are directives to administrators in the executive branch on how to implement legislation. Courts treat them as equivalent to laws. Dramatic events have resulted from executive orders. Some famous executive orders include Lincoln's Emancipation Proclamation, Franklin D. Roosevelt's closing the banks to avoid runs on deposits and his authorizing the internment of Japanese Americans during World War II, Truman's desegregation of the armed forces, Kennedy's establishment of the Peace Corps, and Nixon's creation of the Environmental Protection Agency. More typically, executive orders reorganize the executive branch and impose restrictions or directives on what bureaucrats may or may not do. The attraction of executive orders was captured by an aide to President Clinton: "Stroke of the pen. Law of the land. Kind of cool."[56]

In his State of the Union addresses and other statements, President Obama threatened-promised to resort to executive orders to achieve, at least in part, policies he was unable to get through Congress. Immigration served as a prominent example. At its heart, he offered temporary legal status to around eleven million undocumented immigrants. His Republican opponents sought to pass legislation rescinding his action. They took him to court, arguing that he had exceeded his authority.

President Obama also used executive orders to commit the U.S. to the Paris Agreement on climate change and institute other environmental measures, to cap many student loan payments, raise the minimum wage, and make it easier for women to discover unfair differences in their pay compared to men.

Executive orders are imperfect for presidents; unless they have gone through a formal rule-making process, they can be easily overturned. One president can do something "with the stroke of a pen"; the next can undo it. President Reagan's executive order withholding American aid to international population control agencies that promote or provide abortion services was rescinded by an executive order by President Clinton in 1993, then reinstated by another executive order by President Bush in 2001, rescinded once more by President Obama in 2009, reinstated by President Trump soon after he took office in January 2017, then rescinded by President Biden soon after he took office in 2021.

Besides, rules that can't be rescinded can be left unenforced or undermined by appointing someone who disagrees with them to head the agency. Moreover, since executive orders are supposed to be a mere execution of what Congress has already decided, they can be superseded by congressional action.

Another way for presidents to try to get things done is to have government agencies issue regulations based on existing laws. Thus, President Obama, unable to get legislation alleviating climate change through Congress, pursued it through the authority of the Environmental Protection Agency, relying on the Clean Air Act of 1970 and its re-authorization of 1990. Such rules would, for example, limit emissions of various hazardous pollutants from factory and power plant smokestacks that contribute to global warming.[57]

Other ways of getting things done are by memoranda to cabinet officers and proclamations authorized by legislation. Potentially most telling are (usually secret) national security directives—to be discussed in Chapter 17.[58]

## War Powers

Opportunities to act on behalf of the entire nation in international affairs are irresistible to presidents. Presidents almost always gravitate toward foreign policy as their terms progress. Domestic policy wonk Bill Clinton metamorphosed into a foreign policy enthusiast from 1993 to 2001. Even prior to 9/11 the notoriously untraveled George W. Bush was undergoing the same transformation. President Obama was just as if not more involved in foreign policy than his predecessors.

Congress—as long as it is consulted—is less inclined to challenge presidential initiatives in foreign policy than in domestic policy. This idea that the president has greater autonomy in foreign than domestic policy is known as the "Two Presidencies Thesis."[59]

War powers provide another key avenue for presidents to act unilaterally. After the 9/11 attacks, President Bush's Office of Legal Counsel to the U.S. Department of Justice argued that as commander in chief President Bush could do what was necessary to protect the American people.[60]

Since World War II, presidents have never asked Congress for (or received) a declaration of war. Instead, they rely on open-ended congressional authorizations to use force (such as for wars in Vietnam and "against terrorism"), United Nations resolutions (wars in Korea and the Persian Gulf), North American Treaty Organization (NATO) actions (peacekeeping operations and war in the former Yugoslavia), and orchestrated requests from tiny international organizations like the Organization of Eastern Caribbean States (invasion of Grenada). Sometimes, presidents amass all these: in his last press conference before the start of the invasion of Iraq in 2003, President Bush invoked the congressional authorization of force, UN resolutions, *and* the inherent power of the president to protect the United States derived from his oath of office.

Congress can react against undeclared wars by cutting funds for military interventions. Such efforts are time consuming and not in place until long after the initial incursion. But congressional action, or its threat, did prevent military intervention in Southeast Asia during the collapse of South Vietnam in 1975 and sped up the withdrawal of American troops from Lebanon in the mid-1980s and Somalia in 1993.[61]

Congress's most concerted effort to restrict presidential war powers, the War Powers Act, which passed over President Nixon's veto in 1973, may have backfired. It established that presidents must consult with Congress prior to a foreign commitment of troops, must report to Congress within forty-eight hours of the introduction of armed forces, and must withdraw such troops after sixty days if Congress does not approve. All presidents denounce this legislation. But it gives them the right to commit troops for sixty days with little more than requirements to consult and report—conditions presidents often feel free to ignore. And the presidential prerogative under the War Powers Act to commit troops on a short-term basis means that Congress often reacts after the fact. Since Vietnam, the act has done little to prevent presidents from unilaterally launching invasions.[62]

President Obama did not seek congressional authorization before ordering the U.S. military to join attacks on the Libyan air defenses and government forces in March 2011. After the bombing campaign started, Obama sent Congress a letter contending that as commander in chief he had constitutional authority for the attacks. The White House lawyers distinguished between this limited military operation and a war.

# Presidents and the People

Public approval helps the president assure agreement, attract support, and discourage opposition. Presidents with high popularity win more victories in Congress on high-priority bills.[63] But obtaining public approval can be complicated. Presidents face contradictory expectations, even demands, from the public: to be an ordinary person yet display heroic qualities, to be nonpolitical yet excel (unobtrusively) at the politics required to get things done, and to be a visionary leader yet respond to public opinion.[64]

## Public Approval

For over fifty years, pollsters have asked survey respondents, "Do you approve or disapprove of the way that the president is handling his job?" Over time there has been variation from one president to the next, but the general pattern is unmistakable.[65] Approval starts out fairly high (near the percentage of the popular vote), increases slightly during the honeymoon, fades over the term, and then levels off. Presidents differ largely in the *rate* at which their approval declines. President Kennedy's support eroded only slightly, as opposed to the devastating drops experienced by Ford and Carter. Presidents in their first terms are well aware that, if they fall below 50 percent, they are in danger of losing reelection or of losing allies in Congress in the midterm elections.

Events during a president's term—and how the news media frame them—drive approval ratings up or down. Depictions of economic hard times, drawn-out military engagements (e.g., Korea, Vietnam, and Iraq), unpopular decisions, and bad news drag approval ratings lower. The main upward push comes from quick international interventions, as with President Obama after the killing of Osama bin Laden in 2011, or successfully addressing national emergencies, which boost a president's approval for several months. Under such conditions, official Washington speaks more in one voice than usual, the media drop their criticism as a result, and presidents depict themselves as embodiments of a united America. The successful war against Iraq in 1991 pushed approval ratings for the elder Bush to 90 percent, exceeded only by the ratings of his son after 9/11. It may be beside the point whether the president's decision was smart or a blunder. Kennedy's press secretary, Pierre Salinger, later recalled how the president's approval ratings actually climbed after Kennedy backed a failed invasion by Cuban exiles at the Bay of Pigs: "He called me into his office and he said, 'Did you see that Gallup poll today?' I said, 'Yes.' He said, 'Do you think I have to continue doing stupid things like that to remain popular with the American people?'"[66]

But as a crisis subsides, so too do official unity, tributes in the press, and the president's lofty approval ratings. Short-term effects wane over the course of time. Bush's huge boost from 9/11 lasted well into early 2003; he got a smaller, shorter lift from the invasion of Iraq in April 2003 and another from the capture of Saddam Hussein in December before dropping to levels perilously near, then below, 50 percent. Narrowly reelected in 2008, Bush saw his approval sink to new lows (around 30 percent) over the course of his second term.

## Polls

Naturally and inevitably, presidents employ pollsters to measure public opinion. Poll data can influence presidents' behavior, the calculation and presentation of their decisions and policies, and their rhetoric.[67]

After the devastating loss of Congress to the Republicans midway through his first term, President Clinton hired public relations consultant Dick Morris to find widely popular issues on which he could take a stand. Morris used a "60 percent rule": if six out of ten Americans were in favor of something, Clinton had to be too. Thus the Clinton White House crafted and adopted some policies knowing that they had broad popular support, such as balancing the budget and "reforming" welfare.

Even when public opinion data have no effects on a presidential decision, they can still be used to ascertain the best way to justify the policy or to find out how to present (i.e., spin) unpopular policies so that they become more acceptable to the public.[68] Polls can employ the words and phrases that best sell policies to people. President George W. Bush referred to "school choice" instead of "school voucher programs," to reducing taxes for wealthy Americans as a "jobs" package, and to "wealth-generating private accounts" rather than "the privatization of Social Security." He damned a policy he opposed by calling it a "death tax" instead of an "inheritance tax."[69]

Polls can even be used to adjust a president's personal behavior. After a poll showed that some people did not believe that President Obama was a Christian, he attended services, with photographers in tow, at a prominent church in Washington, DC.

# Speechmaker-in-Chief

Presidents speak for various reasons: to represent the country, address issues, promote policies, and seek legislative accomplishments; to rally supporters, raise funds for their campaign, their party, and its candidates; and to berate the opposition. They also speak to control the executive branch by publicizing their thematic focus, ushering along appointments, and issuing executive orders.[70] They aim their speeches at those physically present and, often, at the far larger audience reached through the media.[71]

In their speeches, presidents celebrate, express national emotion, educate, advocate, persuade, and attack. Their speeches vary in importance, subject, and venue. They give major ones, such as the inauguration and State of the Union. They memorialize events such as 9/11 and speak at the site of tragedies (as President Obama did on January 12, 2011, in Tucson, Arizona, after the shootings of Rep. Gabrielle Giffords and bystanders by a crazed gunman). They give commencement addresses. They speak at party rallies. And they make numerous routine remarks and brief statements. Above all, assuming they run again, they speak almost daily during their reelection campaign; however, their stump speech is essentially the same every time and place.

Presidents are more or less engaged in composing and editing their speeches. For speeches that articulate policies, the contents will usually be considered in advance by the people in the relevant executive branch departments and agencies, who make suggestions and try to resolve or meld conflicting views, for example, on foreign policy by the State and Defense Departments, the CIA, and National Security Council. It will be up to the president, to buy in on, modify, or reject themes, arguments, and language.

Watch President Obama's full speech at the Tucson Memorial in 2011.

View in the online reader

The president's speechwriters are involved in the organization and contents of the speech.[72] They contribute memorable phrases, jokes, applause lines, transitions, repetition, rhythm, emphases, and places to pause. They write for ease of delivery, the cadence of the president's voice, mannerisms of expression, idioms, pace, and timing.

In search of friendly audiences, congenial news media, and vivid backdrops, presidents often travel outside Washington to give their speeches.[73] In his first one hundred days in office in 2001, George W. Bush visited twenty-six states to give speeches; this was a new record even though he refused to spend a night anywhere other than in his own beds at the White House, at Camp David (the presidential retreat), or on his Texas ranch.[74]

Memorable settings may be chosen as backdrops for speeches, but they can backfire. On May 1, 2003, President Bush emerged in a flight suit from a plane just landed on the aircraft carrier USS *Abraham Lincoln* and spoke in front of a huge banner that proclaimed "Mission Accomplished," announcing the end of major combat operations in Iraq. The banner was positioned for the television cameras to ensure that the open sea, not San Diego, appeared in the background. The slogan may have originated with the ship's commander or sailors, but the Bush people designed and placed it perfectly for the cameras and choreographed the scene.

**FIGURE 13.6 "Mission Accomplished"**

As violence in Iraq continued and worsened, the banner would be framed by critics of the war as a publicity stunt, a symbol of the administration's arrogance and failure.

Source: U.S. Navy photo by Photographer's Mate 3rd Class Juan E. Diaz via Wikimedia: https://en.wikipedia.org/wiki/Manning_the_rail#/media/File:USS_Abraham_Lincoln_(CVN-72)_Mission_Accomplished.jpg.

Speechmaking can entail **going public**: presidents give a major address to promote public approval of their decisions, to advance their policy objectives and solutions in Congress and the bureaucracy, or to defend themselves against accusations of illegality and immorality. Going public is "a strategic adaptation to the information age."[75]

**going public**

Presidents give a major address to promote public approval of their decisions, advance their policy objectives, or to defend themselves against accusations.

**rally phenomenon**

The president's approval rating rises during periods of international tension and likely use of American force.

According to one study of presidents' television addresses, they fail to increase public approval of the president and rarely increase public support for the policy action the president advocates.[76] There can, however, be a **rally phenomenon**. The president's approval rating rises during periods of international tension and likely use of American force. Even at a time of policy failure, the president can frame the issue and lead public opinion. Crisis news coverage likely supports the president.

Moreover, nowadays, presidents, while still going public—that is, appealing to national audiences—increasingly go local: they take a targeted approach to influencing public opinion. They go for audiences who might be persuadable, such as their party base and interest groups, and to strategically chosen locations.[77]

## Key Takeaways

The president gets things done through personal persuasion as an agenda-setter and the chief lobbyist and via his veto power and signing statements. To what extent he can lead Congress depends on its party composition and ideological makeup. As the chief executive, the president gets things done through the appointment powers, executive orders, and war powers. The president seeks power and public approval through speeches and by heeding public response to polls.

## Exercises

1. What tools does the president have to set the political agenda? What determines what's on the president's own agenda?
2. How do presidents use their veto power? What are the disadvantages of vetoing or threatening to veto legislation?
3. How does the president's position as chief executive allow him to act quickly and decisively? What powers does the president have to respond to events directly?
4. What factors affect the president's public approval ratings? What can presidents do to increase their approval ratings or stop them from declining?

# 13.4 The Presidency in the Information Age

## Learning Objectives

After reading this section, you should be able to answer the following questions:

1. What are the basic purposes of the White House communications operation?
2. How do presidents interact with the news media?
3. How does the White House press corps interact with the president?
4. What challenges did President Obama face from the media, and how did he deal with them?

5. What challenges did President Trump face from the media, and how did he and his staff try to deal with them?
6. What are the consequences of media coverage for the presidency?

Before detailing the presidency in the information age, we would remind our readers that presidents have long tried to influence the media. Abraham Lincoln was a notorious example. He engaged in infiltrating, co-opting, buying off, repressing, and cutmaneuvering.[78]

Nor was Lincoln a darling of the press. In 1864, Harper's listed the many epithets that the Northern press had hurled at him Filthy Story-Teller, Despot, Liar, Thief, Braggart, Buffoon, Monster, Ignoramus, Scoundrel, Perjurer, Robber, Swindler, Tyrant, Fiend, Butcher, Ape, Demon, Beast, Baboon, Gorilla, Imbecile.[79]

The current White House communications operation has four basic purposes.

- *Advocating*. Promoting the president and the president's policies and goals.
- *Explaining*. Providing information, details, answering questions.
- *Defending*. Responding to criticism, unanticipated events, cleaning up after mistakes, and challenging unfair or what are deemed to be unfair news stories.
- *Coordinating*. Bringing together White House units, governmental agencies (bureaucracies), allies in Congress, and outside supporters (interest groups) to publicize and promote presidential actions.[80]

How is the White House organized to go about achieving these purposes?

# Media Interactions: White House Press Operations

Presidents decide whether, when, where, at what length, and under what conditions they will talk to reporters and, usually, what they will say. Most presidential interactions with the media are highly restricted and stage-managed.

## Press Conferences

The presidential press conference evolved from Franklin D. Roosevelt's informal, off-the-record bull session in the Oval Office to a full-fledged staged event when President Kennedy invited television cameras to broadcast the conference live.

Nowadays in the best-known form of press conference, the president appears alone, usually before television cameras, to answer questions on the record from the assembled reporters who can ask anything on their minds for a given period of time (usually up to an hour). Presidents generally hold such press conferences when they need to respond to important issues or mounting criticism—or if they have been accused of avoiding direct questions from the press.

Press conferences allow presidents to dominate the news, pay obeisance to or at least acknowledge the importance of a free press, galvanize supporters, and try to placate opponents. Presidents, as much as reporters, control press conferences. They make a sometimes lengthy opening statement thereby advocating their views and cutting the number of questions. They choose who asks questions. They can recover from a tough question by finding someone to toss them a softball. Follow-up questions are not guaranteed. Presidents can run out the clock, blather on in evasive or convoluted language, and refuse to take or answer questions on a subject.[81]

**FIGURE 13.7 Press Conferences**

On the left is an informal bull session between President Franklin D. Roosevelt and the press. On the right is a televised press conference held by President John F. Kennedy.

Sources: Henry Griffin / Associated Press; Joseph Scherschel / Contributor / Getty Images

Nonetheless, press conferences have risks for presidents. As reporters' questions have become more challenging over time, so presidents shy away more and more from holding formal press conferences. They sometimes resort to joint press conferences, most often with foreign leaders. Such sessions add questioners from another country's press corps, limit the number of questions to a handful, and reduce the amount of time for the president to answer them.

Presidents favor ever more controlled interactions with reporters. They make a statement or give a speech without answering questions, or pose in a photo opportunity, where they are seen but not heard. Controversial announcements may be made in writing so that television news has no damaging footage to air.

## Press Secretary

The most visible member of a White House publicity apparatus—and the key person for reporters—is the presidential press secretary.[82] The press secretary is "responsible for creating and disseminating the official record of the president's statements, announcements, reactions, and explanations."[83] The press secretary has three constituencies with different expectations: "the president, White House staff, reporters and their news organizations."[84]

### Link

**White House Press Briefings**

Search the archives of press briefings here.

**gaggle**

The White House press secretary's 9:30 a.m. meeting with reporters, neither formal nor public; an important "dry run" for the on-the-record afternoon briefing.

In every presidency starting with Ronald Reagan's, press secretaries usually began their day with meetings with the central coordinator of policy and message, the White House chief of staff, and other senior staffers to study overnight news developments (a news summary is circulated each day to senior staff), forecast where stories are going, and review the president's schedule. Press secretaries next prepare for their first interaction with reporters, the morning's daily, less formal discussion known as the **gaggle**.[85] Cameras are not usually allowed into the gaggle. Reporters use recorders only to gather information, not for sound bites.

**FIGURE 13.8 White House Press Briefings**
The daily White House press briefing is a central event of the day for both reporters and press secretaries.

Source: Michael Candelori/Shutterstock.com

The press secretary begins the gaggle by reviewing the president's schedule before entering into a fast-moving question-and-answer session. The gaggle benefits reporters: it provides responses to overnight news, gives guidance for the workday ahead, reveals the line the White House is pushing and allows them to lobby for access to the president. The gaggle helps press secretaries too by enabling them to float ideas and slogans and, by hearing what's on reporters' minds, prepare for the afternoon briefing.

The press secretary spends the hours between the gaggle and the next briefing looking for answers to questions raised (or anticipated) and checking with other spokespersons elsewhere in the administration, such as at the Departments of State and Defense. The press secretary leads this more official 12:30 p.m. briefing, which is as close as anything to a daily enunciation of White House policy. Here, cameras are allowed; the briefing is broadcast live on cable television if news is brewing. The session is transcribed and disseminated (electronically and on paper) to reporters at the White House and beyond.

Briefings do not necessarily always benefit the White House. The presence of television cameras sometimes pushes reporters to be—or act—tough and combative for viewers. Reporters try to throw the press secretary off balance or to elicit a juicy or embarrassing admission. Briefings offer reporters a rare chance to quiz officials on matters the White House would prefer not to discuss. Press secretaries are often unresponsive to reporters' questions, stonewall, and repeat set phrases. During a single briefing when he was peppered by questions about President George W. Bush's National Guard service, press secretary Scott McClellan dutifully uttered the phrase "The president met all his responsibilities" some thirty-eight times.

## Office of Communications

The press secretary on the front line is not always the key presidential public relations strategist. Richard Nixon was the first president to craft long-range communication strategies. A bevy of public relations veterans defined a White House priority or storyline, coordinated who said what, and planned public schedules of administration officials. They brought local reporters from outside Washington to the capital. The aim was to emphasize a single White House position, woo softer local news media, and silence contrary messages in the administration.

**Office of Communications**

The part of the White House Office devoted to long-term planning of communication, headed by the director of communications.

**line of the day**

The issue or stance designated by the White House and sent to the remainder of the executive branch and to the media that day.

Such tasks were given to the newly established **Office of Communications**—retained by all subsequent presidents. Directors of communications rarely interact with reporters on a regular basis; their job is to stress the big picture. Even when Nixon's first successors, Gerald Ford and Jimmy Carter, pledged open and free interactions with reporters, they found they had to reopen the Office of Communications for central control of the all-important message.

Another lasting innovation of the Nixon presidency was the **line of the day**. Specific topics and storylines are repeated throughout the administration as the focus for all discussion on that day. Presidents use the Office of Communications to centralize a marketing strategy on issues. They are often open about this. In 2002, White House Chief of Staff Andrew Card said the Bush administration waited until after Labor Day to lobby Congress to authorize war against Iraq because, in his words, "From a marketing point of view . . . you don't introduce new products in August."[86]

## "Manipulation by Inundation"

The public must be reached *through* the news media. Reagan's election campaign took such efforts to new heights. Like Nixon, Reagan downgraded the news conference in favor of stage-managed appearances. A press officer who worked for both presidents noted a crucial distinction. The Nixon administration was restrictive, but he said, "The Reagan White House came to the totally opposite conclusion that the media will take what we feed them. They've got to write their story every day. . . . Hand them a well-packaged, premasticated story in the format they want, they'll go away. The phrase is 'manipulation by inundation.'"[87]

Reagan's lesson has been learned by subsequent presidents and media advisors. Presidents rarely have to "freeze out" given reporters (when officials do not return their calls). Staff do sometimes cajole and berate reporters, but frontal assaults against the press usually only occur in clear cases of journalistic bungling.

More typically, presidents and their staffs try to manage the news. Presidents cultivate reporters, columnists, and pundits: they host lunches, dine with them, and hold off-the-record sessions. The staff members anticipate what reporters will ask in briefings and prepare the president accordingly. They design events to meet news values of drama, color, and terseness. And they supply a wealth of daily, even hourly, information and images.

## The End Run around White House Reporters

Inundation is not sufficient. George W. Bush was typical of all presidents when he groused in 2003 to a regional reporter, "There's a sense that people in America aren't getting the truth. I'm mindful of the filter through which some news travels, and sometimes you have to go over the heads of the filter and speak directly to the people."[88]

All new presidents try novel strategies to do an end run around what they perceive to be a biased press. President Franklin D. Roosevelt relished behind-the-scenes Oval Office conferences to woo Democratic-leaning reporters (and bypass Republican-leaning editorial pages).

President Richard Nixon shunned press conferences and sought other ways to get his messages out, such as through star-struck local news. President Bill Clinton instituted cozy miniconferences with other world leaders and brought in local television weather reporters for a confab on global warming. Nowadays, the White House deals directly with the regional and local press, special interest media, and ethnic news organizations.

# Media Interactions: The White House Press Corps

Presidents head the state, government, and their political party. So almost anything they do or that happens to them is newsworthy.[89] They are the sole political person whose activities are followed around the clock. Presidents fit news values perfectly. The ongoing saga of a familiar figure engaged in myriad controversies and conflicts, international and domestic, is far simpler to explain and present than complex scenarios of coalition-building in Congress.

Which brings us to the White House Press Corps. About seventeen hundred reporters are granted White House press passes. But the key members of the White House press corps are the few dozen regulars assigned to go there day in and day out and who spend their work days there. "A White House press pass provides merely the privilege to wait—wait for a briefing; wait to see the president; wait until a press conference is called; wait to see the press secretary; wait to see senior officials; wait to have phone calls returned. There may be propinquity to power, but there is little control over when and how the news is gathered."[90]

**FIGURE 13.9 Reporters at the White House**

The White House accommodates television reporters to allow them to do their "stand-ups" with the august background of the White House portico. This area can become packed w th reporters when big stories are developing.

Source: ZUMA Press, Inc. / Alamy Stock Photo

The regulars make up an intimate society with its own culture, norms, manners, friendship networks, and modes of interaction. The White House layout reinforces this in-group mentality. The briefing room, where the press secretary and reporters meet daily, is a claustrophobic, cluttered space with forty-eight scuffed and battered seats. Beyond the dais at one end, reporters can wander down the hall to buttonhole press officers, though they cannot go much farther (the Oval Office, just fifty feet away, is inaccessible). Hallways leading to two floors of press rooms are in the back; the rooms are crammed with desks and broadcasting equipment for the use of reporters. Along the corridor are bins that contain press releases, official statements, and daily schedules (which are also available electronically). Outside, on a once graveled-over and now paved section of the lawn named "Pebble Beach," rows of television cameras await television reporters.

Rather than foster enterprise, the White House herds reporters together, gives them all the same information, and breeds anxiety by leading them to believe they may be missing the big story everyone else is chasing.

# Media Interactions: Negotiating News at the White House

Reporters submit to the conditions established by presidents and their staffers in receiving information. But they are less docile when they actually assemble that information in White House news.

## Cooperation and Conflict

The relationship between the White House and its press corps is ongoing. The "village" feel to the newsbeat includes presidents and their staffers. But while this day-to-day continuity favors cooperation, the divergent interests and notions of the White House and reporters make for a constant tension. Most reporters do not like appearing as "mouthpieces" for presidents. They embrace the notion of acting as watchdogs and seek ways to present an independent and critical account whenever possible in their White House stories.

What reporters consider news and what presidents consider news are often at odds. Presidents prefer to speak at length, be alone at center stage, favor nuance if not ambiguity, and focus on questions of policy. Reporters like terse sound bites, dramatic conflict, clear-cut comments, and a new installment on how the president is doing politically.

## Assembling the Story

Reagan's first White House spokesperson, Larry Speakes, had a plaque on his desk that read: "You don't tell us how to stage the news, and we won't tell you how to cover it."[91] Though he was being playful, Speakes revealed how the White House and the press corps each control one part of the news.

The White House controls whether, when, how, and where White House officials will meet reporters and what information to release. Pictures and video of the president are packaged along with slogans that make a visual case regardless of the angle the reporter advances. Clinton's aides affixed captions to the presidential podium during ceremonies to underscore the theme they wished to communicate. George W. Bush's assistants went one better, crafting twenty different canvasses that could be placed behind him, each emblazoned with a motto of the day, such as "Protecting the Homeland" or "Corporate Responsibility." Dan Bartlett, then Bush's director of communication, defended such branding: "The message should be seen and read and understood on TV. It's a good reinforcement."[92]

But reporters take the raw material provided by presidential news operations and craft it into a coherent and dramatic story. In a typical television news story, the president's words and images make up a tiny fraction of the allotted time. Television reporters add old video, interview critics in Congress, cite poll numbers, and give their own interpretations. Even on cable television news, which often airs presidential remarks and tweets live during the day, reporters and commentators will hash over and contest the White House "angle." Presidential statements have a different effect once placed into the news media's sometimes dramatically divergent context.

The dilemma for presidents, as Clinton's press secretary Mike McCurry noted, is that "ninety percent of what happens at the White House is pure boredom."[93] Reporters need drama. If presidents do not fit the heroic roles of "decisive problem solver" and "representative of the nation," they can be slotted into a less positive frame. Politics will displace policy; criticism and conflict overwhelm praise and unity. Even in presidents' supposed "honeymoon" periods, critical coverage is not unknown. Presidents are, then, in the unenviable position of needing the news and being routinely in its spotlight without being able consistently to control the images of themselves and their policies in that news.

# President Obama and the Media

During his first term in office, President Obama could claim several significant accomplishments. They included health-care reform, an economic stimulus program, financial regulation, educational innovations, consumer protections, the withdrawal of combat troops from Iraq, banning torture of prisoners in U.S. custody, ratification of a new strategic arms reduction treaty with Russia, and repeal of the "Don't ask, don't tell" law regarding gay and lesbian people in the military.

His accomplishments, with the exception of the killing of Osama bin Laden, were not as widely recognized as they could have been. One reason was, as the president told a reporter, "we probably spent much more time trying to get the policy right than trying to get the politics right. . . . And I think anybody who's occupied this office has to remember that success is determined by an intersection in policy and politics and that you can't be neglecting of marketing and P.R. and public opinion."[94] His media operation was accused of being reactive instead of proactive in responding to reporters and of lacking the skill to promote and the language to sell the president, his policies, and his party.

Compounding this neglect, the media environment imposed four challenges to any attempts by President Obama to communicate effectively with the American people.

First, presidents' prime-time addresses, even when carried by all networks, reach a smaller portion of the audience than they did in years past.[95] The profit-minded media discourage presidents from taking to the airwaves too often. When presidents request air time, broadcast television networks can conclude the subject is not adequately newsworthy and turn them down.

Second, the news media are more than ever obsessed with conflict. As President Obama observed to interviewer news anchor Bob Schieffer, "the twenty-four-hour news cycle and cable television and blogs and all this, they focus on the most extreme elements on both sides. They can't get enough of conflict."[96]

Third, the media are more and more partisan—intensely so. For President Obama, this meant virulent attacks and relentless denunciations by Fox News, America's most watched cable news channel; the editorial page of the *Wall Street Journal*, America's most widely circulated newspaper; and a conservative squadron led by Rush Limbaugh on talk radio. Plus, a farrago of critics, partisan commentators, and pundits subject presidential behavior, policies, speeches, press conferences, and statements to constant analysis and dissection.

Watch President Obama's Inaugural Address given on January 20, 2009.

View in the online reader

Fourth, the media audience is increasingly dispersed, fragmented, and sometimes separated into mutually exclusive segments. People are divided by whether they read newspapers (and which ones), the movies and television programs they watch, their level of involvement with and the social media, and the websites they follow. Consequently, people can be intensely partisan, adhering to one political party or another, favoring particular policies, embracing or opposing the president.

Given this media environment, President Obama faced two daunting problems: (1) to reach as many of the various audiences as possible and (2) to do so with messages in support of his personal, political, and policy objectives.[97]

One approach was to take advantage of new technologies through an Office of New Media. The president's inauguration was the first to be put on YouTube, as were his weekly radio addresses. The White House website contained the president's activities and agenda and featured videos. Text messages and Twitter alerts were sent out to the president's followers under his name. He also conducted the first internet video news conference by an American president.

Watch this clip that discusses President Obama's media blitz to push for his health-care proposal.

View in the online reader

A second approach was to appear in many media venues. On September 20, 2009, President Obama gave separate back-to-back interviews advocating his health-care proposal to each of the hosts of the Sunday morning talk shows. (The interviews had been taped the previous Friday in the Roosevelt Room in the White House).

**FIGURE 13.10 President Obama and the Media**

President Obama ventured far and wide in the media landscape to find audiences—including *The View*.

Source: Obama White House Archives. P072810PS-0640. President Barack Obama records an episode of The View at ABC Studios in New York, N.Y., July 28, 2010. (Official White House Photo by Pete Souza). Via Flickr: https://www.flickr.com/photos/obamawhitehouse/4876619097/.

In seeking and finding audiences, the president ranged far beyond Sunday morning interview programs. He appeared on late-night television talk shows, on *The Daily Show*, on *Oprah*, and the morning talk show *The View*. He gave an interview to Buzzfeed and was featured in its video "Things Everybody Does But Doesn't Talk About."

The president reached new audiences, appeared in comfortable settings, and was usually treated with deference and respect. Conversation took place in a relaxed atmosphere. He discussed his accomplishments and displayed mastery of policies yet at the same time was humanized as a family man with a sense of humor.

There were risks. Appearances on entertainment shows and casual familiarity with hosts could undermine the majesty of the office. Commercial interruptions could diminish presidential dignity. Some interviewers questioned the president's policies and competence, as Jon Stewart did. Others challenged the president's authority, as commentator Bill O'Reilly did in interviews conducted with him just before Fox televised the 2011 and 2014 Super Bowls.

# President Trump and the Media

American presidents have distinctive personalities, styles, and modes of governing. The same could be said of Donald J. Trump, but more so. A celebrity billionaire, he made his name and fortune as a real estate mogul, television "reality" show host, and entrepreneur (huckster, to his detractors). He became president by advocating populist themes, overcoming a plethora of candidates in the Republican party's primaries, and then winning the general election by defeating his Democratic opponent in the Electoral College, although losing the popular vote to her by close to three million.

Mr. Trump took over the presidency as an insurgent, an outsider challenging the established ways of doing things. He promised to "drain the swamp"—the supposed corrupt government, media, and powerful interest groups and lobbyists he claimed controlled Washington. He disparaged and dismissed some members of his staff and cabinet, criticized the FBI and CIA.

As president, Mr. Trump repudiated, rejected, and disavowed the norms and conventions of governing pursued by his predecessors and adumbrated throughout much of this chapter. Typically, at a rally speech he gave for a Republican gubernatorial candidate, he mocked and parodied the ways he said members of his staff wanted him to speak and act to be presidential.

President Trump mocking "being presidential" during a rally for a Republican gubernatorial candidate.

View in the online reader

During his election campaign, Mr. Trump proposed policies, most of which, as chief agenda-setter, he then sought in office. They were represented in his cabinet and staff appointments. Some of these policies were vague: "Make America great again" and "Win big again." More specific ones include building a "great" wall on the Mexican border (which he said Mexico would pay for), repealing the Affordable Care Act and replacing it with something much better and less expensive, bringing back jobs, and renegotiating trade agreements. He would massively upgrade the military, destroy ISIS, and keep radical Islamic terrorists out of the country. He would fix America's infrastructure and rebuild its inner cities. Many of the president's policies, such as cutting taxes, eliminating regulations, and denying climate change, were explicitly advocated by the Republican Party.

Mr. Trump brought to office little experience in government and politics and was relatively uninformed and apparently uncaring about the details and intricacies of public policies. He was reportedly disinclined to read, requiring that his briefing papers be reduced to a few key bullet points. He was an obsessive watcher of cable television, especially Fox, and coverage of himself and his actions. He possessed a powerful ego and dominating personal style, sometimes making it difficult for his intimates and staff to check, let alone reverse, his inclinations and decisions.

President Trump lacked verbal fluency and nuance, so that his remarks, although boisterous, tended to verge on incoherence and were susceptible to misunderstanding, intentional or inadvertent misinterpretation, and mockery. He indulged in hyperbole: "This administration is running like a fine-tuned machine," he told reporters at his first solo press conference in office. During the election and from the start of their time in office, the president and members of his staff were accused of misstatements, dissembling, and outright lying.

**FIGURE 13.11 President Trump Greeting Other World Leaders**
Here President Trump demonstrates his sometimes awkward initial greetings with other world leaders including Supreme Leader of North Korea Kim Jong-Un, President of Egypt Abdel Fattah Al Sisi, Prime Minister of Canada Justin Trudeau, and Prime Minister of Singapore Lee Hsien Loong.

Sources: Trump White House Archived. President Trump Meets with Chairman Kim Jong Un. (Official White House Photo by Shealah Craighead). Via Flickr: https://flickr.com/photos/whitehouse45/48164732141/; Trump White House Archived. President Donald Trump greets the President of Egypt, Abdel Fattah Al Sisi, prior to their bilateral meeting, Sunday, May 21, 2017. (Official White House Photo by Shealah Craighead). Via Flckr: https://www.flickr.com/photos/whitehouse45/33994178993/in/album-72157680930810334/; Trump White House Archived. President Donald J. Trump, Prime Minister Justin Trudeau, Prime Minister Theresa May, and Prime Minister Narendra Modi, July 7, 2017 (Official White House Photo by Shealah Craighead). Via Flckr: https://www.flickr.com/photos/whitehouse45/35781983265/; Trump White House Archived. President Donald J. Trump and Prime Minister Lee Hsien Loong, July 8, 2017 (Official White House Photo by Shealah Craighead). Via Flckr: https://www.flickr.com/photos/whitehouse45/35706153951/in/album-72157685885349776/.

Members of the president's communication staff devised tactics to try to deal with the media. Aside from tax legislation, Trump had few significant policy achievements passed by Congress during his first year in office. To create the impression of accomplishments, his communications team presented him in action (or at least motion), before the television cameras and reporters, signing and displaying executive orders handed to him in a blue leather binder by his chief of staff and other associates. This was visibility although not transparency. The president was also shown at ceremonial events, and meeting, greeting and, above all, shaking hands with foreign leaders, in sessions usually described by the White House as successful. Few substantive details about the meetings were provided, if indeed there were any.

Conservative news media outlets and conservative websites were added to the White House Press Corps, and thus to the press secretary's briefings. These reporters were relied on for softball questions and favorable coverage. But the benefits were vitiated by the press secretary's embattled interactions—variously incensed, spluttering, and contradictory—with other reporters. So conflictual did these press conferences become that his press secretary stopped holding them and left the White House at the end of June 2019 until later replaced by White House Press Secretary Kayleigh McEnany in May of 2020.

President Trump avoided formal (sit-down) interactions with the White House press corps. But he did take a few questions at joint sessions with visiting foreign leaders and spared with journalists at "photo ops." He responded sporadically, sometimes off-the-cuff, to reporters' shouted questions as he crossed the tarmac, leaving from or returning to the White House or elsewhere, or peering out from a plane. These actions could signal openness and accessibility, but he often undermined his purpose and intended effects by going off message, making misstatements, and uttering defensive denials.

The president took frequently to Twitter: he could be dubbed "the tweeter and retweeeter-in-chief." This was beneficial, allowing him to deliver thousands of message, many of them attacks on his opponents, untrammeled to 45–80 million viewers-readers (calculations and estimates vary), including the media. Unbound by self-censorship, he told them what was on his mind, who and what were making him angry, and his reactions, thereby trying to set and reset the news agenda in his favor. But he oftentimes lost the agenda; the messages often lacked clarity, were untrustworthy, and raised more questions and issues than they resolved.

**FIGURE 13.12 President Trump Signs Executive Order**

Here President Trump proudly displays one of his executive orders.

Source: Trump White House Archived. President Donald J. Trump, joined by Vice President Mike Pence, displays his signed Executive Order for the Establishment of a Presidential Advisory Commission on Election Integrity, Thursday, May 11, 2017.Vvia Flickr: https://www.flickr.com/photos/whitehouse/33803971533/.

In May 2017 the president fired the head of the FBI, James B. Comey Jr., who was in charge of investigating the president's campaign and associates for alleged contacts and conspiracy (collusion) with the Russians to influence the 2016 election results in his favor. He thereby violated President Lyndon Johnson's dictum for retaining his FBI director, the long-serving J. Edgar Hoover: "better to keep him in the tent pissing out than outside the tent pissing in." No longer in office, Comey was able to speak to the media himself or through others or testify to Congress about the investigation and his relationship with the president. He would write a best-selling book, highly critical of the president, and widely covered by the media.

**FIGURE 13.13 President Trump and the News Media**

This is an example of one of the many negative tweets toward the news media that President Trump shared on his Twitter account.

Donald J. Trump
@realDonaldTrump
Follow
The Fake News is working overtime. Just reported that, despite the tremendous success we are having with the economy & all things else, 91% of the Network News about me is negative (Fake). Why do we work so hard in working with the media when it is corrupt? Take away credentials?
4:38 AM - 9 May 2018
25,232 Retweets 112,558 Likes
53K 25K 113K


Source: Twitter.com.

The firing led to the appointment of a former head of the FBI, Robert S. Mueller III, by the Justice Department as a special counsel to undertake the investigation (including the circumstances of Comey's dismissal) and the search for incriminating evidence of the president's campaign's ties to and alleged collusion with the Kremlin's meddling.

Throughout his election campaign, President Trump attacked reporters, undermining their credibility and professionalism, a verbal assault that resonated with many of his supporters. He continued unabated when he became president, discrediting and disparaging the press. For example, during his first solo press conference on February 16, 2017, he called the press "so dishonest," accused it of engaging in "distortion," of "misrepresentation," of "inventing sources," and of being "out of control." He complained about "leaks" and reporters' use of classified information from "leakers."

According to President Trump, "it's frankly disgusting the way the press is able to write whatever they want to write." And, "it wasn't until I became a politician that I realized how nasty, how mean, how vicious the press can be, and how fake."[98] He called the press "a great danger to our country" and several news organizations the "enemy of the American people." He told those at a campaign rally that he wanted to make it easier to sue news organizations and publishers for libel and defamation.

Again and again President Trump returned to the subject of "fake news." He referred to CNN and MSNBC as "fake news" (tweet December 11, 2017). He defined "fake news" as what the news media don't or won't tell you; what is not covered; and fake polls. He called it presenting false information as news. Sometimes, it seemed as if false news was anything that depicted him negatively.

Above all, he reiterated his contention that the news media's coverage of the alleged relationship between members of his campaign staff and the Kremlin during the 2016 election was "fake news."

Fake news does exist. It could be defined as false information usually intended to deceive or mislead. One such story during the 2016 election reported the Pope endorsing candidate Trump for president. Another alleged that the chairman of Hillary Clinton's presidential campaign abused children in a Washington, DC pizza restaurant. Much fake news was perpetrated and spread by the Russians during the 2016 election.

Naturally, journalists make mistakes, get things wrong.[99] But they would resent and deny the validity of presidential press secretary Sarah Huckabee Sanders's admonition to the White House press corps: "You cannot say that it's an honest mistake when you're purposefully putting out information that you know to be false . . . or when you're taking information that hasn't been validated, that hasn't been offered any credibility, and that has been continually denied by a number of people, including people with direct knowledge of an instance."[100] And they would reject Counselor to the President Kellyanne Conway's invocation of "alternative facts" to contest objective news. (A related term is "post-truth.")[101]

This assault by President Trump and his staff was one reason for his fraught relations with the mainstream media. It was not the only reason. What, then, of President Trump and his administration, was covered by the media, how was it framed, and what went uncovered or little reported?

Although, when asked for their opinions, people often blur the different forms of media together, we will distinguish three categories: mainstream media, focusing on *The New York Times* and *Washington Post*; cable television's CNN; and humor-comedy. We skip over MSNBC and Fox, the former with its "attack dog" approach to President Trump, the latter with its "lap dog" devotion to him and its hostility to his critics and opponents. (Fox could be labelled the president's "safe space" as he called into the channel far more often than any other). Mr. Trump was also a devout watcher of Fox: after *Fox & Friends* featured a supposed "STUDY: 90% RECENT TRUMP COVERAGE IS NEGATIVE" from the (conservative) Media Research Center, President Trump retweeted it with the comment "Wow, more than 90% of Fake News Media coverage of me is negative," naming as his source "@foxandfriends." Nor do we discuss here the prevalence of commentary and opinion in support of Trump and damning his opponents and critics (including the mainstream media) by right wing radio bloviators.

The mainstream media claim to be truth-seeking, nonideological, objective, and pursuing facts. As we show throughout this book, these are more aspirations than inevitable realizations. This particularly applies in their treatment of President Trump. Dedicated, even wedded, to tradition and convention in government, the mainstream press was ill-prepared for, if not appalled by, how he shattered its image, assumptions, and understanding of the ways a president should behave in and conduct his office. He should not have left thousands of jobs unfilled (declaring some to be unnecessary), appointed people the media deem unqualified, lacked trust in expertise (scientists, diplomats), and feuded with the security services. He should have chosen his words and communicated with care. Witness the *Times*'s two-page spread headlined "All the People, Places and Things Donald Trump has Insulted on Twitter Since Being Elected President of the United States."[102]

The president should not have lied so much and should have been called to account when he did. Thus, fact-checking. Witness the *Post*'s "President Trump has made more than 2,000 false or misleading claims over 355 days," and the *Times*'s "Much That Wasn't True in a 30-Minute Interview."[103]

*The New York Times* and *Washington Post* tend to be ideologically liberal, and were therefore prone to frame unsympathetically many of Trump's policies, such as on the environment (global warming), health care, science, abortion, education, taxation, and his ban on travelers from several mainly Muslim countries. They criticized his appointees who opposed or questioned their departments' existing policies at, for example, the Environmental Protection Agency and the Departments of Justice, Education, and Housing. They denounced many of the president's budget proposals, such as defunding the National Endowments for the Arts and Humanities, and his budget as a whole.

The mainstream media expressed disdain over the president's and his administration's inability, during their early period in office, to achieve congressional passage of his policy agenda, despite having a Republican majority in both chambers. When acknowledging a policy success, as with tax reform and cuts, coverage also pointed out that its effects overwhelmingly benefitted corporations and the wealthy and would vastly increase the national debt.

The mainstream media responded critically to the barrage of statements, decisions, and actions by the president, his surrogates, and his lawyers that were or could be construed, as provocative, such as a meeting with the Russian foreign secretary and ambassador to the U.S. at which President Trump reportedly told them classified information.

Trump and his aides sometimes mishandled, gave changing, conflicting, and contradictory accounts of events, and left questions unanswered; particularly when these questions applied to scandals affecting the president, the White House, and his administration. So a story would stay in the news and play out several days longer than it would have otherwise.

No surprise, then, that the mainstream media were dismissive of the administration's communications operation, charging it with being heavy-handed and ineptly executed, lacking knowledgeable individuals and the requisite discipline and control in relations with the media that its predecessors aspired to and often developed. President Trump often gave the impression that he was his own director of communications, and pretty much his own press secretary.

We would note that on the infrequent occasions the president performed appropriately, for example, by soberly reading from the teleprompter his address to a joint session of Congress, praise from the mainstream media was positive, if not unstinting.

In sum, for the reasons we have specified, the mainstream news media viewed the Trump presidency critically. *The New York Times* and *Washington Post* produced a plethora of investigative, usually negative stories, such as the *Times*'s May 1, 2017, "President's Growing Trade Gap: A Gulf Between Talk and Action," and "In Lawsuit After Lawsuit, It's Everyday People v. the President."

Which brings us to CNN. Cable news was blessed (so to speak) with a continuous supply of grist from, by, and about Donald Trump: it was as if its content was all Trump, all the time. Certainly, significant events were covered: natural disasters, terrorism, school and other shootings. But even with these events, the focus was often on President Trump's statements, actions, and reactions.

In fact, three stories and their expansive (one might say expensive) ramifications, involving the president and various of his associates dominated coverage. First and foremost was the investigation by special counsel Robert S. Mueller III (and to some extent by congressional committees).

**FIGURE 13.14 Special Counsel Robert Mueller**

The "Mueller Investigation" as it became known began in May of 2017 and wrapped up in March of 2019.

Source: Obama White House Archives. P072012PS-0298 [cropped]. Via Wikimedia: https://commons.wikimedia.org/w/index.php?curid=61494902.

Second was Mr. Trump's alleged sexual affairs. One, with a *Playboy* playmate of the year, started in 2006 and lasted nine months. Another was at least a one-night stand, also in 2006, with an adult (pornographic) film actress and director. Both women received payments ("pay-offs?") before the 2016 presidential election for their stories. The former received $150,000 from a tabloid whose chairman and chief executive was a friend of Mr. Trump and which engaged in "catch and kill" (having obtained the story declining to publish it). The second woman received $130,000 from the president's personal lawyer. Both signed legal agreements preventing them from talking freely about their supposed relations with the president. They later struggled to extricate themselves from these restraints, although by that time they had already appeared in the media and been interviewed by journalists. The porn star hired a new lawyer who, publicity conscious, instituted lawsuits against the president, promoting the suits (and her and himself) through television appearances.

Third were tell-all books, among them, Michael Wolff's, *Fire and Fury: Inside the Trump White House* (New York: Henry Holt & Co., 2018), a demolition of President Trump's conduct in office; the fired head of the FBI. James B. Comey Jr.'s memoir/attack account of his experiences with the president, (in which he compared Trump's circle to the Mafia) *A Higher Loyalty: Truth, Lies and Leadership* (New York: Macmillan Publishers' Flatiron Books, 2018); and Bob Woodward's, *Fear: Trump in the White House* (New York: Simon & Schuster, 2018). All these authors and others undertook book tours, were widely interviewed in the mainstream media and on cable, given ample opportunity to detail their findings and views without much contradiction, and sold millions of books.

CNN went for these and related Trump stories to help attract and retain viewers. Its format was also designed to embellish its programs with an entertainment gloss. A sonorous male voice intoned: "This is CNN. The Most Trusted Name in News." (President Trump called it "The Least Trusted Name in News.") The anchorman announced "Happening Now: Breaking News" to a background of exciting (excited) dramatic music. After each segment, before going to commercial, the anchor instructed/admonished/pleaded with viewers to "stay with us." (Appropriately for the dramatic news, the seductive commercials were often for prescription drugs about which viewers were instructed to talk to their doctors, assuming they could afford to have one.)

A plethora of panelists-analysts, variously identified as correspondents, experts, party strategists, former government officials, or members of Congress, were arrayed on the screen, commenting/venting, offering occasional insights, speculating, predicting, and frequently disagreeing, under the "guidance" of an often opinionated anchor. CNN does have some of its own reporters, but the channel infrequently originates news. It relies on journalists from *The New York Times*, *Washington Post*, and, less so, on other outlets, who sometimes appear on screen, usually to repeat and discuss stories they have already reported in their own outlets.

For many years Mr. Trump had been a palpable presence in the media, spouting opinions and appearing on television entertainment. CNN was prone to use the president's past pronouncements against him: for example, juxtaposing the holding of his first state dinner with visuals of his previously (before entering office) decrying of such events as expensive wastes of money.

CNN and the other cable channels were inattentive to the Trump administration's policies and their effects. They ignored the weeds, so to speak. They gave short shrift to such actions as deregulation, benefit cuts, and judicial appointments below the Supreme Court, neglecting, for example, reductions at the Department of Agriculture in food stamps, looser rules for meat inspection, and instructions to stop using the term "climate change."[104]

Presidents have long been butts of humor but, arguably, none more so than President Trump. Actor Alec Baldwin portrayed him as a self-protective, pouting buffoon on *Saturday Night Live*. His associates and staff, such as press secretary Sarah Huckabee Sanders, were also imitated and mocked on the show.

Watch Alec Baldwin imitate President Trump during this *SNL* sketch.

View in the online reader

President Trump was the comedy gift that kept on giving. As we noted above, he was especially vulnerable given the availability of visuals from his career and 2016 campaign that could be used to show conflicts and contradictions between his past pronouncements and more recent behavior, for example, attacking Hillary Clinton for revealing confidential information while later doing the same himself.

Trump jokes abounded on the three late-night TV shows of Stephen Colbert (sometimes tough), Jimmy Kimmel (moderate), and Jimmy Fallon (mild). *The Daily Show with Trevor Noah* was hostile, but not as much as *Full Frontal*, on which the impassioned Samantha Bee excoriated the president regularly.

Scathing critiques came from Seth Meyers on his "A Closer Look" segment on his show *Late Night*. He called the president's proposed budget "cruel and delusional,"[105] referred to "chaos caused by the president's recklessness," said the president had "repeatedly shown himself to be temperamentally unfit for handling issues as serious as national security," and called him "deeply unfit for the office."[106]

Some commentators went so far as to bruit about the possibility of trying to remove President Trump from office through application of the Twenty-Fifth Amendment to the Constitution or through impeachment followed by conviction.[107] The former has been most common as a plot device on fictional television shows such as *Scandal*, *Madam Secretary*, and *Designated Survivor*.

Four shields protected or insulated the president from this assault. First, his efforts to delegitimize and undermine the mainstream news media seem to have succeeded, at least with some of his supporters. Trump voters who rejected or discredited news stories as lacking a factual base or saw them as part of a conspiracy against the president could characterize them as "fake," as Mr. Trump was wont to do.

The second bulwark consisted of the former president's supporters and allies in the media: Fox News and Fox Business News, the conservative commentators on talk radio, the *Wall Street Journal* editorial page, plus websites and blogs.

These two shields contributed to the third: the stability of President Trump's public support, remaining at around 40 percent throughout his presidency. Fourth was the Republican party's control first of Congress and then, after the 2018 election, just the Senate. The Democrats required some Republican agreement or cooperation to convict after impeachment.

Meanwhile, President Trump might have tried to better stage manage his presidency; that is, control his interactions with reporters, engage in more ceremonies, rely more on a teleprompter, restrict off-the-cuff remarks, send out talking points, minimize hyperbole and lies, and devise effective frames for his messages. He could have also improved his general communications operation. And there was always the possibility of significant policy achievements or failures (real or construed).

# Media Consequences

The president's visibility in the news is a double-edged sword. The news personalizes the presidency and presents the office through the individual incumbent. There is high pressure for dramatic action and quick results. The constant presence of the White House press corps means that reporters clamor for presidential reaction to and action about any breaking news, which can overwhelm the president's agenda.

The media encourage presidents to find policy areas that enable them to play the role of bold, public-minded leader. But because reporters seek conflict and drama at the White House newsbeat, stories are subject to what columnist Jonathan Alter has termed "the manic-depressive media."[108] In the way the media frame stories, each event is a make-or-break moment for the president, suitable for triumph or humiliation. Highs are higher; lows are lower. New issues that emerge can change the president's depiction in the news.

Success in news coverage should not be equated with policy success. Consider the news image of the elder George Bush in the fall of 1990. The news contrasted his glory in the Gulf War against his bungle on the budget. From the start, Bush laid out a straightforward line in the 1990 crisis leading up to the war—push Iraq out of Kuwait—with such clarity and intransigence that it perfectly fit the media frame of decisive action. But when Bush engaged in complex budget negotiations with key members of Congress, the news media found him looking confused and waffling. The war was a media success; the budget was a media failure. But was the war a policy success and the budget a policy failure? Not necessarily. The war solved few of the problems that provoked Iraq's invasion of Kuwait and almost led to civil war in Iraq. The budget agreement stanched the growth of the budget deficit and led to its later erasure.

It is hard for presidents to resist the temptation to appear in the news constantly, even though chasing after the readily available publicity might push them in policy directions that are far from desirable. If they want positive media attention, they must usually either opt for charged, straightforward issues and clear-cut commitments or make complex issues seem simpler than they are. They and their staffers try to package actions to balance the complexity of policies against the simplicity of news (and commentary) and the need to keep options open as long as possible against the news media's desire for drama, conflict, and closure.

## The Mueller Report

On March 24, 2019, special counsel Robert S. Mueller III submitted his Report to Attorney General William P. Barr. It concluded that "the Russian government had interfered in the 2016 election in sweeping and systematic fashion." Barr, in turn, summarized the report to exonerate Mr. Trump and his campaign from collusion with the Russians and from obstruction of justice. Three days later, Mueller wrote informing Barr that he had not exonerated Trump from obstruction of justice. This left the situation open, with the following documents and testimony possibly to become publicly available as part of partisanship and a battle for public opinion:

### Links

**Redacted Mueller Report**

Read the redacted Mueller report here.

**Barr's Summary of the Mueller Report**

Read Barr's summary of the Mueller report here.

**Mueller's Letter to Barr**

Click here to read Robert Mueller's letter to Barr regarding how Barr handled presenting the Mueller report to the public.

**Mueller's Statement, May 29, 2019**

Watch Robert Mueller give his statement on the recently concluded investigation into Russian interference in the 2016 election here.

**Mueller's Testimony Before the House Judiciary Committee**

Watch Robert Mueller's full testimony to the House Judiciary Committee on July 24, 2019 here.

### Aftermath: Trump Departs, Biden Assumes the Presidency

As we describe in Chapter 11, Joe Biden won the 2020 presidential election. President Trump persistently but baselessly claimed voter fraud, and thus his victory. Refusing to acknowledge, let alone accept, the election results, left him mainly legal and rhetorical recourses? His lawyers filed innumerable suits in state courts challenging the results; But judges rejected all save one. Twitter and other social media permanently suspended his account for violating their public interest framework. His speech to supporters at the Ellipse on January 6 (2021) contributed to that day's insurrection at and invasion of the Capitol and to his second impeachment.

According to *The New York Times*, President Trump sought to replace the acting attorney general with a loyalist who would apply the department's power to compel Georgia state legislators to overturn its presidential election results—a plan he was persuaded to abandon.[109]

The president issued numerous pardons (wiping out convictions) and commutations (shortening sentences). In the process, he ignored Justice Department guidelines. Most of the recipients had connections with the president or with people, such as his lawyer Rudolph W. Giuliani. Or they were allies, friends, or family connected to the president. During his final weeks, they included his former campaign chairman and a longtime advisor who had declined to cooperate with prosecutors in respect to the special counsel's Russia investigation; also four former Republican congressmen convicted of corruption; and his former chief strategist Stephen K. Bannon, pardoned even before his criminal trial.[110]

The Trump administration hastened to try to put various rules and regulations into effect before it left office. It defined millions of workers in industries like construction, cleaning and the gig economy as contractors and thus ineligible for unemployment and other benefits; narrowed regulatory authority over airlines; and asked the Federal Communications Commission to limit its interpretation of legal protection for social media platforms.

President Trump issued a video message on January 13 disavowing violence on the right or on the left, as well as law breaking, and vandalism. He gave a Farewell Address on January 19 celebrating his accomplishments. The next day he spoke at a Departure Ceremony invoking other achievements.

## Links

Watch this video from Twitter of Trump disavowing violence on January 13, 2021.

Watch this video of President Donald J. Trump's farewell address given on January 19, 2021.

Watch this video of President Trump Remarks given on January 20, 2021.

Biden's immediate concerns, as promised during his election campaign, were the deadly pandemic and the faltering economy (particularly jobs); interspersed with promoting his cabinet and senior advisor nominees. Then, as soon as he assumed the presidency, he set about overturning some key Trump policies. He issued memoranda, proclamations, and signed thirty executive orders during his first week in office. These included returning the U.S. to the Paris climate accord and to the World Health Organization. He rescinded rollbacks of vehicle emissions standards. He ordered the Affordable Care Act's health insurance marketplace reopened. He began dismantling some of Trump's immigration laws: reuniting migrant children with their families. He revoked the Trump administration's plan to exclude noncitizens from the census count.[111] He reopened the military to transgender troops.[112]

Other changes wrought by the Biden administration were in nomenclature: "non-citizen" replaced "illegal alien," "Tribal" people replaced Native Americans, "climate change" reappeared in government lexicons," as did LGBTQ+ references.

The president moved cautiously in foreign affairs but did cut off arms sales and support to Saudi Arabia for its war in Yemen. And he rescinded Trump's travel ban on predominantly Muslim and African countries.

Above all, with united Democratic support and against united Republican opposition, President Biden successfully achieved Congressional passage of and signed a long-delayed $1.9 trillion economic aid bill to limit the ravages of the coronavirus.

**FIGURE 13.15 President Biden Remembrance Vigil for COVID-19 Victims**
President Biden, Vice President Harris, and their spouses stand before the candlelit facade to memorialize the half-million Americans dead from the COVID-19 virus.

Source: The White House. P20210222CW-0289. President Joe Biden and First Lady Jill Biden, joined by Vice President Kamala Harris and Second Gentleman Doug Emhoff, observe a moment of silence in honor of the 500,000 Americans who have died from the COVID-19 virus Monday, Feb. 22, 2021.

## Key Takeaways

Presidents interact with the media through press conferences, the press secretary, the Office of Communications, manipulation by inundation, and end runs around White House reporters. The White House press corps, in search of dramatic stories, is engaged in ongoing conflict and cooperation with the White House. President Obama encountered several problems with the media that he tried to resolve through new technologies and appearing in many media venues. It can be difficult for presidents to balance their policy interests with the media's criteria of news and expectations of dramatic action and quick results. For several reasons, President Trump had hostile relations with the mainstream media that were never rectified.

## Exercises

1. What are the functions of the White House communications operation? What are the main ways the White House communicates with the media and the public?
2. What are some of the ways the White House can "stage" the news? Why are reporters sometimes reluctant to take the way the White House presents the news at face value?
3. How did the way President Obama interacted with the media differ from the way other presidents have interacted with the media? What new challenges did President Obama face in dealing with the media?
4. What problems did President Trump experience in his relations with the media?

# 13.5 Recommended Reading

Alter, Jonthan. *His Very Best: Jimmy Carter, a Life*. New York: Simon & Schuster, 2020. A positive re-evaluation of the man and his presidency.

Cameron, Charles M. *Veto Bargaining: Presidents and the Politics of Negative Power*. New York: Cambridge University Press, 2000. How presidents can and do use the power of the veto.

Hinckley, Barbara. *Less than Meets the Eye: Foreign Policy Making and the Myth of the Assertive Congress*. Chicago: University of Chicago Press, 1994. How Congress rarely blocks presidents' foreign policy initiatives.

Howell, William G. *Power without Persuasion: The Politics of Direct Presidential Action*. Princeton, NJ: Princeton University Press, 2003. What presidents can get done with unilateral powers.

Kernell, Samuel. *Going Public: New Strategies of Presidential Leadership*, 4th ed. Washington, DC: CQ Press, 2007. What presidents can—and cannot—get done with speechmaking.

Kessel, John H. *Presidents, the Presidency, and the Political Environment*. Washington, DC: CQ Press, 2001. An overview of the presidency beyond the president.

Kumar, Martha Joynt. *Managing the President's Message: The White House Communications Operation*. Baltimore: Johns Hopkins University Press, 2007. The definitive study of White House–media relations.

Lewis, David E. *The Politics of Presidential Appointments: Political Control and Bureaucratic Performance*. Princeton, NJ: Princeton University Press, 2010. An analysis of the evolution and increasing politicization of the appointment process.

Light, Paul C. *The President's Agenda: Domestic Policy Choice from Kennedy to Clinton*, 3rd. ed. Baltimore: Johns Hopkins University Press, 1999. A compelling study of what goes into presidents' decisions on recommendations to Congress.

Neustadt, Richard E. *Presidential Power and the Modern Presidents*. New York: Macmillan, 1990. The classic 1960 treatise on presidential power and presidential weakness, updated with postscripts and emendations on presidents from JFK to Reagan.

Peterson, Mark A. *Legislating Together: The White House and Capitol Hill from Eisenhower to Reagan*. Cambridge, MA: Harvard University Press, 1990. A painstaking account of conflict and cooperation between president and Congress.

Ragsdale, Lyn. *Vital Statistics on the Presidency*, 3rd ed. Washington, DC: CQ Press, 2008 (online January 24, 2014). A compendium of everything that can be numerically measured about the presidency, further illuminated by incisive interpretive essays.

Smith, Jeff. *The Presidents We Imagine*. Madison: University of Wisconsin Press, 2009. A detailed survey of two centuries of imaginings of U.S. presidents.

# 13.6 Recommended Viewing

*Air Force One* (1997). Air Force One is hijacked by Russian terrorists, and the president (Harrison Ford) must physically recapture the plane himself.

*All the Presidents' Movies* (2009). A documentary about which presidents watched what movies when—based on the logs of the White House theater.

*The American President* (1995). A liberal what-might-have-been fantasy of the Clinton presidency: a widowed president (Michael Douglas), amid a tough reelection fight, falls in love with an environmental lobbyist. Written by Aaron Sorkin, creator of the series *The West Wing*.

*The Clinton Affair* (2018). Description of what occurred with recollections and comments by those involved, notably Monica Lewinsky herself.

*Dave* (1993). A nice-guy body double (Kevin Kline) for a president, shows that all he needs to live up to his responsibilities are common sense and decency.

*Farenheit 9/11* (2004). Michael Moore's documentary-style assault on President George W. Bush and his administration for the Iraq war and more.

*Gabriel Over the White House* (1933). The classic White House film: a party-hack president (Walter Huston), comatose after a car accident, awakes under the guidance of the angel to end crime and unemployment and accomplish disarmament.

*Independence Day* (1996). The president (Bill Pullman) reclaims his military past to rid the world of an alien invasion.

*Kisses for My President* (1964). Curious comedy about the first woman president and her husband's gender panic as the first man to be "first lady."

*Lincoln (2012). Steven* Spielberg's historical, biographical drama.

*The Manchurian Candidate* (1962). John Frankenheimer's riveting, compellingly performed, political thriller about brainwashing.

*Nixon* (1995). Director Oliver Stone's hallucinatory attempt to make sense of the Nixon presidency, with uncanny performances by Anthony Hopkins as Nixon and Joan Allen as his wife, Pat.

*Nixon by Nixon: In His Own Words* (2014). Fascinating documentary contrasting President Nixon's private (taped) observations and comments with his public rhetoric.

*The Presidents' Gatekeepers* (2013). Interviews with all twenty living White House chiefs of staff covering fifty years and nine administrations, but is scattershot and lacks a coherent narrative.

*The Press Secretary* (2001). An insightful fly-on-the-wall documentary about several days in the professional life of Joe Lockhart, who was then President Clinton's press secretary.

*Reagan* (2011). Eugene Jarecki's documentary traces the fascinating life and career, while struggling to understand the personality, of the fortieth president.

*Vice* (2018). Adam McKay's mordant comedy-drama biography showing how Dick Cheney wielded vast power as George W. Bush's vice president and involved the United States into war against Iraq.

*W* (2008). Oliver Stone's restrained biopic of President George W. Bush.

*Wag the Dog* (1998). A political consultant (Robert De Niro) and Hollywood producer (Dustin Hoffman) try to distract attention from a presidential sex scandal by staging a fake war.

*Watergate* (2018). A four plus hours documentary of the constitutional crisis.

*The World According to Dick Cheney* (2013). Study of the most influential Vice President as he establishes and maintains his power in the executive branch

# Endnotes

1. Jeffrey K. Tulis, *The Rhetorical Presidency* (Princeton, NJ: Princeton University Press, 1988).
2. Fred I. Greenstein, *The Presidential Difference: Leadership Style from FDR to Barack Obama*, 3rd ed. (Princeton, NJ: Princeton University Press, 2009).
3. For presidential depictions in the media, see Jeff Smith, *The Presidents We Imagine* (Madison: University of Wisconsin Press, 2009).
4. Trevor Parry-Giles and Shawn J. Parry-Giles, *The Prime-Time Presidency:* The West Wing *and U.S. Nationalism* (Champaign: University of Illinois Press, 2006).
5. Mark Sachleben and Kevan M. Yenerall, *Seeing the Bigger Picture: Understanding Politics through Film and Television* (New York: Peter Lang, 2004), chap. 4; and for a detailed survey, see Jeff Smith, *The Presidents We Imagine* (Madison: University of Wisconsin Press, 2009).
6. Stephanie Greco Larson, "Political Cynicism and Its Contradictions in the Public, News, and Entertainment," in *It's Show Time! Media, Politics, and Popular Culture*, ed. David A. Schultz (New York: Peter Lang, 2000), 101–116.
7. "Primary Sources: Documents in the Hall of Records," PBS.org. Accessed on July 17 2019 at http://www.shoppbs.pbs.org/wgbh/amex/rushmore/filmmore/ps_records.html.

8. Michiko Kakutani, "A Portrait of the President as the Victim of His Own Certitude," review of *State of Denial: Bush at War, Part III*, by Bob Woodward, *The New York Times*, September 30, 2006, A15; the earlier book is *Bush at War* (New York: Simon & Schuster, 2002).
9. On the contrast of "single executive image" and the "plural executive reality," see Lyn Ragsdale, *Presidential Politics* (Boston: Houghton Mifflin Harcourt, 1993).
10. Richard Perez-Pena, "Supreme Court Limits President's Power to Fill Posts," *The New York Times*, March 22, 2017, A20.
11. The language in the Constitution comes from Article I, Section 2, Clause 5, and Article I, Section 3, Clause 7. This section draws from Michael Les Benedict, *The Impeachment and Trial of Andrew Johnson* (New York: Norton, 1973); John R. Labowitz, *Presidential Impeachment* (New Haven, CT: Yale University Press, 1978); and Michael J. Gerhardt, *The Federal Impeachment Process: A Constitutional and Historical Analysis*, 2nd ed. (Chicago: University of Chicago Press, 2000).
12. The early twentieth-century political scientist Henry Jones Ford quoted in John R. Labowitz, *Presidential Impeachment* (New Haven, CT: Yale University Press, 1978), 91.
13. Polling Report, http://www.pollingreport.com/bush.htm, accessed July 7, 2005.
14. Michael Les Benedict, *The Impeachment and Trial of Andrew Johnson* (New York: Norton, 1973), 139.
15. Respectively, *United States v. Curtiss-Wright Export Corp*, 299 US 304 (1936); *Youngstown Sheet & Tube Company v. Sawyer*, 343 US 579 (1952).
16. Adam Liptak, "Some Big Wins in Court, But Weak Record Overall," *The New York Times*, January 24, 2017, A11, based on Lee Epstein and Eric A. Posner, "The Decline of Supreme Court Deference to the President," March 6, 2017, University of Chicago, Coase-Sandor Institute for Law & Economics, Research Paper No. 800.
17. Paul C. Light, *Vice-Presidential Power: Advice and Influence in the White House* (Baltimore: Johns Hopkins University Press, 1984).
18. Barton Gellman and Jo Becker, "Angler: The Cheney Vice Presidency," *Washington Post*, June 24, 2007, A1.
19. Jane Meyer, "The President Pence Delusion," *New Yorker*, October 23, 2017, p. 54.
20. Jon Caramanica, "Television Review," *The New York Times*, September 11, 2013. [1] See Jeffrey E. Cohen, *The President's Legislative Policy Agenda*, 1789–2002 (New York: Cambridge University Press, 2012).
21. Lyn Ragsdale and John J. Theis III, "The Institutionalization of the American Presidency, 1924–92," *American Journal of Political Science* 41, no. 4 (October 1997): 1280–1318 at 1316. See also John P. Burke, *The Institutional Presidency: Organizing and Managing the White House from FDR to Clinton*, 2nd ed. (Baltimore: Johns Hopkins University Press, 2000).
22. John H. Kessel, *Presidents, the Presidency, and the Political Environment* (Washington, DC: CQ Press, 2001), 2.
23. Edmund L. Andrews, "Economics Adviser Learns the Principles of Politics," *The New York Times*, February 26, 2004, C4.
24. Stephen Crowley, "And on the 96th Day…," *The New York Times*, April 29, 2001, Week in Review, 3.
25. Douglas L. Kriner & Eric Schickler, *Investigating the President: Congressional Checks on Presidential Power* (Princeton, NJ: Princeton University Press, 2016).
26. Stephen Skowronek, *Presidential Leadership in Political Time: Reprise and Reappraisal* (Lawrence: University Press of Kansas, 2008).
27. Sheryl Gay Stolberg, "Hope and Change as Promised, Just Not Overnight," *The New York Times*, October 28, 2010, A18.
28. Donna R. Hoffman and Alison D. Howard, *Addressing the State of the Union* (Boulder, CO: Lynne Rienner Publishers, 2006).
29. See Jeffrey E. Cohen, *The President's Legislative Policy Agenda*, 1789–2002 (New York: Cambridge University Press, 2012).
30. Paul C. Light, *The President's Agenda: Domestic Policy Choice from Kennedy to Clinton*, 3rd ed. (Baltimore: Johns Hopkins University Press, 1999), 89.
31. Andrew Rudalevige, *Managing the President's Program: Presidential Leadership and Legislative Policy Formulation* (Princeton, NJ: Princeton University Press, 2002).
32. See Book 3, *Master of the Senate: The Years of Lyndon Johnson*, and Book 4, *The Passage of Power*, of Robert A. Caro's magisterial biography published by Alfred A. Knopf in 2002 and 2012 respectively; Book 5 will cover his presidency.
33. Quoted in Jason Horowitz, "G.O.P. Leader's New Role Could Take Strained White House Ties to Next Level," *The New York Times*, November 6, 2014, A2.
34. David Remnick, "Annals of the Presidency: Going the Distance," *New Yorker*, January 27, 2014, 41–67.
35. This section relies on Kenneth Collier, *Between the Branches: The White House Office of Legislative Affairs* (Pittsburgh: University of Pittsburgh Press, 1997).
36. This section relies most on Charles M. Cameron, *Veto Bargaining: Presidents and the Politics of Negative Power* (New York: Cambridge University Press, 2000); see also Robert J. Spitzer, *The Presidential Veto: Touchstone of the American Presidency* (Albany: State University of New York Press, 1988).
37. Quoted in Paul C. Light, *The President's Agenda: Domestic Policy Choice from Kennedy to Clinton*, 3rd ed. (Baltimore: Johns Hopkins University Press, 1999), 112.
38. *Clinton v. City of New York*, 524 US 427 (1998).
39. Frank Bruni, "Bush Strikes a Positive Tone on a Patients' Bill of Rights," *The New York Times*, July 10, 2001, A12.
40. Charles M. Cameron, *Veto Bargaining: Presidents and the Politics of Negative Power* (New York: Cambridge University Press, 2000), 171.
41. Charlie Savage, "Obama's Embrace of a Bush Tactic Riles Congress," *The New York Times*, August 9, 2009, A1; and Charlie Savage, "Obama Takes a New Route to Opposing Parts of Laws," *The New York Times*, January 9, 2010, A9.
42. Jon R. Bond and Richard Fleisher, *The President in the Legislative Arena* (Chicago: University of Chicago Press, 1990). For overall legislative productivity, the classic starting point is David R. Mayhew's *Divided We Govern: Party Control, Lawmaking, and Investigations, 1946–1990* (New Haven, CT: Yale University Press, 1991).
43. Andrew Rudalevige, *Managing the President's Program: Presidential Leadership and Legislative Policy Formulation* (Princeton, NJ: Princeton University Press, 2002), 136.
44. Lyn Ragsdale, *Vital Statistics on the Presidency*, 3rd ed. (Washington, DC: CQ Press, 2008), 360. See also Steven A. Shull and Thomas C. Shaw, *Explaining Congressional-Presidential Relations: A Multiple Perspective Approach* (Albany: State University of New York Press, 1999), chap. 4.
45. Terry M. Moe, "The Presidency and the Bureaucracy: The Presidential Advantage," in *The Presidency and the Political System*, 6th ed., ed. Michael Nelson (Washington, DC: CQ Press, 2000), 443–74; and William G. Howell, *Power without Persuasion: The Politics of Direct Presidential Action* (Princeton, NJ: Princeton University Press, 2003).
46. See David E. Lewis, *The Politics of Presidential Appointments: Political Control and Bureaucratic Performance* (Princeton, NJ: Princeton University Press, 2008); and G. Calvin Mackenzie, ed., *Innocent until Nominated: The Breakdown of the Presidential Appointments Process* (Washington, DC: Brookings Institution Press, 2001).
47. Jeffrey E. Cohen, *The Politics of the U.S. Cabinet: Representation in the Executive Branch, 1789–1984* (Pittsburgh, PA: University of Pittsburgh Press, 1988).
48. See the memoir by former Republican congressman and President Obama's Secretary of Transportation Raymond H. LaHood, with Frank H. Mackaman, *Seeking Bipartisanship: My Life in Politics* (Amherst, NY: Cambria Press, 2015).
49. Glen S. Kurtz, Richard Fleisher, and Jon R. Bond, "From Abe Fortas to Zoë Baird: Why Some Presidential Nominations Fail in the Senate," *American Political Science Review* 92 (December 1998): 871–81.
50. G. Calvin Mackenzie, *The Politics of Presidential Appointments* (New York: Free Press, 1981), especially chap. 7.
51. James Dao, "In Protest, Republican Senators Hold Up Defense Confirmations," *The New York Times*, May 10, 2001, A20; and Crystal Nix Hines, "Lag in Appointments Strains the Cabinet," *The New York Times*, June 14, 2001, A20.
52. G. Calvin Mackenzie, "The State of the Presidential Appointments Process," in *Innocent Until Nominated: The Breakdown of the Presidential Appointments Process*, ed. G. Calvin Mackenzie (Washington, DC: Brookings Institution Press, 2001), 1–49 at 40–41.
53. Adam Liptak, "Justices Rebuke Obama On Right Of Appointment," *The New York Times*, June 27, 2014, A1, 14, the quote is on p.14; the case is *National Labor Relations Board v. Noel Canning*, 573 US (2014).
54. Editorial, "Mr. Acosta Won't Be the Last to Go," *The New York Times*, July 13, 2019, a20.
55. Kenneth R. Mayer, *With the Stroke of a Pen: Executive Orders and Presidential Power* (Princeton, NJ: Princeton University Press, 2001).
56. Paul Begala, quoted in James Bennet, "True to Form, Clinton Shifts Energies Back to U.S. Focus," *The New York Times*, July 5, 1998, 10.
57. Coral Davenport, "Obama Builds Green Legacy With '70 Law," *The New York Times*, November 27, 2014, A1, 23.
58. Phillip J. Cooper, *By Order of the President: The Use and Abuse of Executive Direct Action* (Lawrence: University Press of Kansas, 2002).
59. See Barbara Hinckley, *Less than Meets the Eye: Foreign Policy Making and the Myth of the Assertive Congress* (Chicago: University of Chicago Press, 1994). Such deference seems largely limited to presidents' own initiatives. See Richard Fleisher, Jon R. Bond, Glen S. Krutz, and Stephen Hanna, "The Demise of the Two Presidencies," *American Politics Quarterly* 28 (2000): 3–25; and Andrew Rudalevige, *Managing the President's Program: Presidential Leadership and Legislative Policy Formulation* (Princeton, NJ: Princeton University Press, 2002),148–49.
60. John Yoo, *The Powers of War and Peace: The Constitution and Foreign Affairs after 9/11* (Chicago: University of Chicago Press, 2005).
61. William G. Howell and Jon C. Pevehouse, *While Dangers Gather: Congressional Checks on Presidential War Powers* (Princeton, NJ: Princeton University Press, 2007).
62. Louis Fisher, *Presidential War Power* (Lawrence: University of Kansas Press, 1995); Barbara Hinckley, *Less than Meets the Eye: Foreign Policy Making and the Myth of the Assertive Congress* (Chicago: University of Chicago Press, 1994), chap. 4.
63. Brandice Canes-Wrone, *Who Leads Whom? Presidents, Policy, and the Public* (Chicago: University of Chicago Press, 2006).

64. On President Obama, see George C. Edwards III, *Predicting the Presidency: the Potential of Persuasive Leadership* (Princeton, NJ: Princeton University Press, 2016).
65. James A. Stimson, "Public Support for American Presidents: A Cyclical Model," *Public Opinion Quarterly* 40 (1976): 1–21; Samuel Kernell, "Explaining Presidential Popularity," *American Political Science Review* 72 (1978): 506–22; and Richard A. Brody, *Assessing the President: The Media, Elite Opinion, and Public Support* (Stanford, CA: Stanford University Press, 1991).
66. Quoted in Daniel C. Hallin, ed., *The Presidency, the Press and the People* (La Jolla: University of California, San Diego, 1992), 21.
67. Jeffrey F. Cohen, *Presidential Leadership in Public Opinion: Causes and Consequences* (New York: Cambridge University Press, 2015); also, Lawrence Jacobs and Robert Shapiro, *Politicians Don't Pander* (Chicago: University of Chicago Press, 2000).
68. James N. Druckman and Lawrence R. Jacobs, *Who Governs? Presidents, Public Opinion, and Manipulation* (Chicago: University of Chicago, 2015).
69. Joshua Green, "The Other War Room," *Washington Monthly* 34, no. 4 (April 2002): 11–16; and Ben Fritz, Bryan Keefer, and Brendan Nyhan, *All the President's Spin: George W. Bush, the Media, and the Truth* (New York: Touchstone, 2004).
70. See Michael Baruch Grossman and Martha Joynt Kumar, *Portraying the President: The White House and the News Media* (Baltimore: Johns Hopkins University Press, 1980); and John Anthony Maltese, *Spin Control: The White House Office of Communications and the Management of Presidential News* (Chapel Hill: University of North Carolina Press, 1992).
71. Diane J. Heith, *The Presidential Road Show: Public Leadership in a Partisan Era* (New York: Routledge, 2012).
72. This discussion is based on Robert Schlesinger, *White House Ghosts: Presidents and Their Speechwriters* (New York: Simon & Schuster, 2008).
73. Roderick Hart, *The Sound of Leadership: Presidential Communication in the Modern Age* (Chicago: University of Chicago Press, 1986); Barbara Hinckley, *The Symbolic Presidency* (New York: Routledge, 1991); and Gregory L. Hager and Terry Sullivan, "President-Centered and Presidency-Centered Explanations of Presidential Public Activity," *American Journal of Political Science* 38 (November 1994): 1079–1103.
74. David E. Sanger and Marc Lacey, "In Early Battles, Bush Learns Need for Compromises," *The New York Times*, April 29, 2001, A1.
75. Samuel Kernell, *Going Public: New Strategies of Presidential Leadership*, 4th ed. (Washington, DC: CQ Press, 2007), 2; and Stephen J. Farnsworth, *Spinner in Chief: How Presidents Sell Their Policies and Themselves* (Boulder, CO: Paradigm Publishers, 2009).
76. George C. Edwards III, *On Deaf Ears: The Limits of the Bully Pulpit* (New Haven, CT: Yale University Press, 2003), 241.
77. Jeffrey E. Cohen, *Going Local: Presidential Leadership in the Post-Broadcast Age* (New York: Cambridge University Press, 2010).
78. Harold Holzer, *Lincoln and the Power of the Press: The War for Public Opinion* (New York: Simon and Schuster, 2014); we took the categories we list from Garry Wills's book review entitled "How Lincoln Played the Press," *New York Review*, November 6, 2014: 25-26.
79. Cited by David Remnick, "Comment: Real News," *New Yorker*, December 7, 2020, 15.
80. With slight modifications, these are taken from Martha Joynt Kumar, *Managing the President's Message: The White House Communications Operation* (Baltimore: Johns Hopkins University Press, 2007), xx–xxi and chap. 1.
81. Jarol B. Manheim, "The Honeymoon's Over: The News Conference and the Development of Presidential Style," *Journal of Politics* 41 (1979): 55–74.
82. Woody Klein, *All the President's Spokesmen* (Westport, CT: Praeger, 2008).
83. Martha Joynt Kumar, *Managing the President's Message: The White House Communications Operation* (Baltimore: Johns Hopkins University Press, 2007), 179.
84. Martha Joynt Kumar, *Managing the President's Message: The White House Communications Operation* (Baltimore: Johns Hopkins University Press, 2007), 180.
85. See Howard Kurtz, *Spin Cycle: Inside the Clinton Propaganda Machine* (New York: Free Press, 1998), and Kumar, "Daily White House Press Briefings: A Reflection of the Enduring Elements of a Relationship," unpublished paper, April 1999.
86. Quoted in Elisabeth Bumiller, "Bush Aides Set Strategy to Sell Policy on Iraq," *The New York Times*, September 7, 2002, A1.
87. Les Janka, quoted in Mark Hertsgaard, *On Bended Knee: The Press and the Reagan Presidency* (Boston: Houghton Mifflin Harcourt, 1988), 52.
88. Quoted in Elisabeth Bumiller, "Trying to Bypass the Good-News Filter," *The New York Times*, October 20, 2003, A12.
89. Stephen J. Farnsworth and S. Robert Lichter, *The Mediated Presidency: Television News and Presidential Governance* (Lanham, MD: Rowman & Littlefield, 2006).
90. Martha Joynt Kumar, "The President and the News Media," in *The Presidency and the Political System*, 6th ed., ed. Michael Nelson (Washington, DC: CQ Press, 2000) 835–80 at 867.
91. Timothy E. Cook, ed. *Freeing the Presses: The First Amendment in Action*. (Baton Rouge: Louisiana State University Press, 2005), p14.
92. Quoted in Anne E. Kornblut, "President Is Keeping His Messages Front and Center," *Boston Globe*, July 23, 2002, A4.
93. Quoted in Andrew Miga, "White House Drama More Colorful than the Real White House," *Boston Herald*, September 23, 1999, 3.
94. Peter Baker, "What Does He Do Now?" *The New York Times Magazine*, October 17, 2010, 42.
95. Joe S. Foote, *Television Access and Political Power: The Networks, the Presidency, and the "Loyal Opposition"* (New York: Praeger, 1990); and Matthew A. Baum and Samuel Kernell, "Has Cable Ended the Golden Age of Presidential Television?" *American Political Science Review* 93 (March 1999): 99–114.
96. CBS News. "Transcript: Obama on 'Face the Nation.'" *CBS*, September 20, 2009. Retrieved from: https://www.cbsnews.com/news/transcript-obama-on-face-the-nation-5324077/.
97. This discussion is based on Ken Auletta, "Non-Stop News," *New Yorker*, January 25, 2010, 38–47.
98. ABC News via Twitter: https://twitter.com/ABCPolitics/status/956899488672591873.
99. Michael M. Grynbaum and Sydney Ember, "CNN Corrects Trump Story Fueling 'Fake News' Claims," *The New York Times*, December 9, 2017, B3.
100. Wemple, Erik. "White House Briefing Room Descends into Chaos Over 'Fake News.'" *The Washington Post*, December 11, 2017. Retrieved from: https://www.washingtonpost.com/blogs/erik-wemple/wp/2017/12/11/white-house-briefing-room-descends-into-chaos-over-fake-news/.
101. Cited in Peter Baker and Sydney Ember, "Trump Escalates His Criticism of News Media, Fueling Partisan Debate," *The New York Times*, December 12, 2017, A21.
102. "All the People, Places and Things Donald Trump has Insulted on Twitter Since Being Elected President of the United States," *The New York Times*, January 29, 2018, 14-15.
103. Linda Qiu, "Much That Wasn't True in a 30-Minute Interview," *The New York Times*, December 30, 2017, A16.
104. See Michael Lewis, "Inside Trump's Cruel Campaign Against the USDA's Scientists," *Vanity Fair*, November 2, 2017.
105. Seth Meyers, *Late Night With Seth Meyers*, "A Closer Look," May 24, 2017.
106. Seth Meyers, *Late Night With Seth Meyers*, "A Closer Look," May 16, 2017.
107. See Elizabeth Drew, "Terrifying Trump," *New York Review*, March 9, 2017, 37-41, and Evan Osnos, "Endgames," *New Yorker*, May 8, 2017, 34–45.
108. Jonathan Alter, "The Manic-Depressive Media," *Newsweek*, February 8, 1993, 29.
109. Katie Benner, "Trump and Justice Dept. Lawyer Said to Have Plotted to Oust Acting Attorney General," *The New York Times*, January 22, 2021,1.
110. See also, Eric Lipton, "In the End, Trump Undid Years of Prosecutions," *The New York Times*, January 22, 2021, A1 (18).
111. Michael D. Shear, "With His Pen, Biden Moves to Dismantle Predecessor's Legacy," *The New York Times*, January 21, 2021, A20.
112. Helene Cooper and Michael D. Shear, "Biden Reopens Military to Transgender Troops," *The New York Times*, January 26, 2021, A1 (15).

CHAPTER 14

# The Bureaucracy

## 14.1 Preamble

On August 28, 2005, Hurricane Katrina inflicted widespread devastation on New Orleans and the Gulf Coast.

**FIGURE 14.1 Devastation Wrought by Hurricane Katrina**
This aerial shot of Gulfport, Mississippi shows how Hurricane Katrina devastated the area.

Source: Photo courtesy of the Federal Emergency Management Agency, http://commons.wikimedia.org/wiki/File:Hurricane_katrina_damage_gulfport_mississippi.jpg.

Reporters from the television networks and cable channels rushed to chronicle the catastrophe. They emotionally expressed their horror on camera and in print at the woefully tardy and inadequate response to the disaster by the government's Federal Emergency Management Agency (FEMA). The head of FEMA confessing on television that he had only learned belatedly that thousands were stranded at the New Orleans Convention Center without food or water symbolized this incompetence. Through the media and the internet, Americans and people throughout the world witnessed an inept federal agency and learned that it was led not by a disaster expert but by a political appointee whose previous employer was the International Arabian Horse Association.

**agencies**

Organizations within the federal executive branch designed to apply the law.

**federal bureaucracy**

That part of the executive branch outside the presidency that carries out laws and regulations.

FEMA is just one of over two thousand executive **agencies**—governmental organizations in the executive branch that are authorized and designed to apply the law. Collectively these agencies make up the **federal bureaucracy**. The bureaucracy consists of career civil servants and of political appointees. Most of these bureaucrats competently carry out their duties largely unnoticed by the media. Few reporters cover agencies on a regular basis. Agencies sometimes get into the news on their own terms; all of them employ public relations experts to crank out press releases and other forms of mass communication containing information on their programs and to respond to reporters' requests for facts and information. But the media often portray the bureaucracy negatively as a haven of incompetence and, as with their coverage of FEMA and Hurricane Katrina, are quick to chase after stories about bungling, blundering bureaucrats.

# 14.2 What Is Bureaucracy?

## Learning Objectives

After reading this section, you should be able to answer the following questions:

1. What is bureaucracy?
2. How do the media depict the federal bureaucracy?
3. How has the federal government bureaucracy evolved?
4. What is the Pendleton Act? How has the merit system changed the makeup of the federal bureaucracy?
5. What are the four main types of federal agencies?

**bureaucracy**

An organization marked by hierarchical division of labor, internal specialization, and adherence to fixed rules.

The influential early-twentieth-century sociologist Max Weber suggested that bureaucracy is an efficient way to govern large, complex societies. For Weber, the ideal form of **bureaucracy** has four characteristics:

1. A rational division of labor into specialized offices with fixed jurisdictions
2. Employees chosen for their skills, knowledge, or experience, not for their politics
3. A chain of command wherein officials report to higher-ups
4. Impersonal reliance on written rules to limit arbitrary variation from one case to the next[1]

## Bureaucracy in the Media

Such a depiction of bureaucratic organization and effectiveness is rarely found in the news. When the media consider bureaucracy, it is most often to excoriate it. One scholar examined a year's worth of newspaper editorials and concluded, "Mismanagement, wasteful spending, ethical lapses, and just plain incompetence stimulated editorial responses regularly. . . . By contrast, editors rarely devoted much space to agencies' success."[2] Likewise, television news zeroes in on waste, fraud, and abuse. The federal bureaucracy is a favorite target in such occasional segments as NBC's "The Fleecing of America."

This frame finds government bureaucracies rife with incompetence and bureaucrats squandering public funds. The millions of dollars misspent are drops in the bucket of a federal budget that is more than a trillion dollars, but bureaucratic inefficiency and ineptitude seem to be the rule, not the exception.

Such stories are easy for journalists to gather—from investigations by the Government Accountability Office of Congress, from congressional hearings, and from each agency's inspector general. (We would note that, post Watergate, Congress created inspector generals to investigate allegations of fraud and abuse brought by whistleblowers in federal agencies. Dismayed by their actions, President Trump would replace several Inspector Generals with his loyalists.)

The media widely covered the damning reports of the inspector general of the Securities and Exchange Commission on the reasons for the agency's failure, despite many warnings and complaints from credible sources, to investigate what was later revealed as Bernard Madoff's $65 billion ($20 billion if you only count what he stole) Ponzi scheme.[3]

Entertainment media depictions of bureaucracy are often negative. The movie *The Right Stuff* (1983), based on Tom Wolfe's best-selling history, eulogizes an era of test pilots' daring individualism. Test pilot Chuck Yeager bravely and anonymously breaks the sound barrier and then returns to the fraternity of fellow pilots in a tavern whose walls are covered with pictures of gallant men lost in the quest. But when the Soviet Union launches the Sputnik satellite in 1957, panic-stricken Washington sends buffoonish bureaucrats to recruit test pilots—excluding Yeager—into a stage-managed bureaucracy for the astronauts chosen to go into space.

The entertainment media do sometimes show bureaucracy as collectively effective and adaptable. *Apollo 13* (1995) portrays NASA and its astronauts as bureaucratic *and* heroic. After a blown-out oxygen tank aboard the space capsule threatens the lives of three astronauts, the NASA staff works to bring them back to Earth. The solution to get the astronauts home is clearly an ingenious collective one thought up by the various NASA workers together.

Bureaucracy is the problem in *The Right Stuff* and the solution in *Apollo 13*. *The Right Stuff* tanked at the box office. *Apollo 13* cleaned up, probably because of its reassuring story, tribute to the astronauts' gallantry (it is hard to view astronauts as bureaucrats), and happy ending.

We will show that the federal bureaucracy is far more complex than the media allow. Then, at the end of the chapter, we will discuss the bureaucracy in the information age.

# Evolution of the Federal Bureaucracy

The federal bureaucracy is not explicitly laid out in the Constitution. It was never instituted and planned; it evolved by the gradual accretion of agencies and tasks over time.

When Thomas Jefferson became president in 1801, the administrative civilian workers employed by the federal government—the **civil service**—numbered under three thousand. One-third of them were part-time employees. Nine-tenths worked outside Washington, DC.[4]

**civil service**

The administrative civilian workforce employed by the federal government.

## The Spoils System

**patronage**

The distribution of governmental jobs and grants to members and allies of the political party in power.

**spoils system**

The term given by its detractors to the practice started by President Andrew Jackson in 1829 of a new president replacing all civil servants with party faithful.

When political parties developed, so did the practice of rewarding friends and allies with jobs and grants. It was also a democratic reaction to an era when the bureaucracy was run by aristocrats. Andrew Jackson made political **patronage** a matter of principle when he became president in 1829. He wanted to make sure that federal workers were accountable to the executive branch—and to him as president.[5] His ally, Senator William Marcy, cried, "To the victors belong the spoils!" And Jackson's detractors coined the term the **spoils system**: when the party in power changed, there was a full-scale replacement of officials by party faithful—who donated some of their salary to party coffers.

After the Civil War, the federal government grew enormously. Presidents and legislators were overwhelmed with finding jobs for party members. Representative James Garfield griped in 1870, "[O]ne-third of the working hours of senators and representatives is hardly sufficient to meet the demands made upon them in reference to appointments of office."[6] Garfield was elected president ten years later, during which time the federal government workforce almost doubled (from 51,020 in 1870 to 100,020 in 1880). As president, Garfield was besieged with requests for patronage. He did not satisfy everyone. In 1881, Charles Guiteau, frustrated in his bid for a high-ranking appointment, shot Garfield in a Washington train station. Garfield's long agony, eventual death, and state funeral made for a dramatic continuing story for newspapers and magazines seeking a mass audience. The media frenzy pushed Congress to reform and restrict the spoils system.

### Link

**The Garfield Assassination**

Click here to learn more about the Garfield assassination.

**FIGURE 14.2** Garfield's Assassination

An illustration of the assassination of President Garfield

Source: Scene of the assassination of Gen. James A. Garfield, President of the United States. ca. 1881. Dec. 21. Photograph. Library of Congress: https://www.loc.gov/item/2003671706/.

## The Merit System

Congress passed the Pendleton Act in 1883.[7] The act sorted federal employees into two categories: merit and patronage. In a **merit system**, jobs are classified and appointments are made on the basis of performance determined by exams or advanced training. The merit system at first covered only 10 percent of the civil service, but presidents and Congress gradually extended it to insulate agencies from each other's political whims.[8] By its peak in the 1920s, 80 percent of civil servants held merit positions.

**merit system**

The practice of classifying positions in the civil service according to technical standards and of naming civil servants to lifetime appointments based on tests or advanced training.

The merit system has shrunk since the 1920s.[9] Just under half of today's civilian federal workers are merit employees. A notable reform in 1978 instituted the Senior Executive Service, a merit pool of highly trained, highly experienced, highly educated, and highly paid officers that managers can move and transfer at will.

In 2002, President George W. Bush got Congress to give him discretion over whether 170,000 employees of the new Department of Homeland Security fall under the merit system; presidents can move employees in that department in or out of the civil service as they deem conditions dictate. Bush wished to go further: he unsuccessfully sought to transfer up to 850,000 government jobs to private companies, which he claimed would cut costs and enhance efficiency.[10]

## The Line between Merit and Politics

The line between the merit system and politicized hiring and firing is not always clear. Consider U.S. attorneys, who prosecute federal crimes. They are appointed by the president, usually from his party, but it is understood that they will operate without partisanship. That is, they will not base their decisions on the interests of their party. In 2006, eight U.S. attorneys were dismissed, allegedly at the direction of the Bush White House because of their reluctance to serve Republican interests by, for example, investigating Democratic officeholders and office seekers for corruption. The story was widely and, as new revelations appeared, continually reported in the media. It led to investigative hearings in the Democratic-controlled Congress.

Then, in July 2008, the Justice Department's inspector general and internal ethics office revealed that senior aides to Attorney General Alberto R. Gonzalez had in fact broken civil service laws by using political criteria in making nonpolitical career appointments in the department; the inspector general and ethics office also revealed that White House officials were actively involved in some of the hiring decisions. Screened in interviews and through internet searches, people had been hired if they were conservative on "god, guns + gays."[11]

## Who Are the Civil Servants?

Detailed rules and procedures govern hiring, promoting, and firing civil servants. To simplify and standardize the process, each position gets a GS (General Schedule) rating, ranging from GS 1 to GS 18, which determines its salary.

Unlike other parts of government, women and racial and ethnic minorities are well represented in the civil service. Women are 46 percent of the civilian workforce and 43 percent of the federal workforce. People of color are 26 percent of the civilian workforce and 29 percent of the federal workforce. But women and people of color are clustered at lower levels of the civil service. Those at higher levels are largely white and male.[12] Lifetime job security allows many civil servants to stay in government until retirement or death, so progress into high-level positions is slow.

# The Variety of Agencies

It is hard to get an overall picture of the federal bureaucracy. First, rather than unfold from a master plan, the bureaucracy developed piecemeal, with agencies and departments added one at a time. Second, many federal responsibilities are not carried out by federal employees but by state and local government workers under federal mandates and by private companies contracted for services.

The thousands of agencies in the federal bureaucracy are divided into rough, often overlapping areas of specialization. The division of labor easily defies logic. A food writer's overview of government regulation of food found thirty-five distinct laws implemented by twelve offices within six cabinet departments. For instance, "The Department of Agriculture oversees production of hot dogs cooked in pastry dough and corn dogs, while for no discernible reason, the Food and Drug Administration regulates bagel dogs and hot dogs meant to be served in buns."[13]

Any attempt to make sense of this complex structure and to find an agency's place in the overall bureaucracy does little more than bolster an image of mind-numbing intricacy.

### Enduring Image

#### The Nightmare Organizational Chart

Organizational charts were designed to give clear and easy indications of the chain of command and who reports to whom. They are equally Byzantine for large corporations as for government. But they are often used in political debate to show the sheer incomprehensibility of bureaucracy.

This tactic was famously used in 1993 by Senate Republican leader Bob Dole (R-KS) when he opposed First Lady Hillary Rodham Clinton's ambitious health-care reform proposal. The picture of Dole and the nightmare organizational chart was widely circulated and contributed to the proposal's demise the next year. Ten years later, Republicans in the Senate proposed a reform of the Medicare system. Then-senator Hillary Rodham Clinton (D-NY) took to the floor of the Senate with nightmare organizational charts of what the Medicare system would look like if Republicans had their way.

Images endure when they can be used again and again for multiple purposes by multiple players. Hillary Clinton showed that, in politics as in life, turnabout is fair play.

Watch Bob Dole use a complex chart to explain Hillary Clinton's health-care proposal here.

Complicating the federal bureaucracy, there are several types of agencies. We look at the four main ones: (1) cabinet departments, (2) independent executive agencies, (3) government corporations, and (4) regulatory commissions.

## Cabinet Departments

**cabinet departments**

The major administrative units responsible for specified broad areas of government operations, headed by a cabinet secretary appointed by the president and confirmed by the Senate.

Fifteen agencies are designated by law as **cabinet departments**: major administrative units responsible for specified areas of government operations. Each department controls a detailed budget requested by the White House and authorized and appropriated by Congress and has a designated staff. Each is headed by a department secretary appointed by the president and confirmed by the Senate. Many departments subsume distinct offices directed by an assistant secretary. For instance, the Interior Department includes the National Park Service, the Bureau of Indian Affairs, and the U.S. Geological Survey.

Department secretaries are automatically members of the president's cabinet. For other agency heads, it is up to the president's discretion: President Clinton elevated the head of the Federal Emergency Management Agency (FEMA) to the cabinet, but the position lost cabinet status under President George W. Bush.

Cabinet departments are not equally prominent in the news. A few, such as the Departments of State, Defense, Treasury, and Justice, are covered by newsbeat reporters who regularly focus on their activities, heads, and personnel. Other departments attract consistent interest of reporters for specialized publications. No department can assume obscurity, since crises and unexpected events may thrust it into the news. For example, the Department of Energy was suddenly newsworthy after a massive power blackout in the Northeast in the summer of 2003.

## Independent Executive Agencies

The remaining government organizations in the executive branch outside the presidency are **independent executive agencies**. The best known include NASA, the Environmental Protection Agency (EPA), and the Social Security Administration (SSA). Apart from a smaller jurisdiction, such agencies resemble cabinet departments. Their heads are appointed by (and report directly to) the president and must be confirmed by the Senate. They simply lack the symbolic prestige—and literal place at the table—of a cabinet appointment. Independent executive agencies can smoothly become cabinet departments: in 1990, Congress upgraded the Veterans Administration to the cabinet-level Department of Veterans Affairs.

**independent executive agencies**

Agencies similar to cabinet departments but usually with smaller jurisdictions.

## Government Corporations

Some agencies, such as the U.S. Postal Service and the national rail passenger system Amtrak, are **government corporations**. They charge fees for services too far-reaching or too unprofitable for private corporations to handle. Ideally, they bring in enough funds to be self-sustaining. To help them make ends meet, Congress may give government corporations a legal monopoly over given services, provide subsidies, or both.[14] Government corporations are more autonomous in policymaking than most agencies. For instance, the Postal Rate Commission sets rates for postage on the basis of revenues and expenditures.

**government corporations**

Agencies that provide services for which they charge fees, usually under a government-granted monopoly, with the hope they will be fiscally self-sustaining.

Complicating the picture are the Federal National Mortgage Association (FNMA), known as Fannie Mae, and the Federal Home Loan Mortgage Corporation (FHLMC), known as Freddie Mac. These were government-sponsored enterprises and also stockholder-owned corporations. As of 2008, they owned or guaranteed about half of the country's $12 trillion mortgage market. Thus, as we discuss in Chapter 16, they were both partly responsible for and victims of the severe decline in the housing market. In September 2008, as their stock prices declined precipitously and they sank ever deeper into debt, they were taken over by the Federal Housing Finance Agency (FHFA). This was an extraordinary intervention by the federal government in the financial market.

## Regulatory Commissions

**regulation**

The use of governmental oversight, particularly of the economy, intended to protect the public interest and ensure fairness.

**regulatory commission**

An agency charged with writing rules and arbitrating disputes dealing with some specific part of the economy, with appointees having greater independence from Congress and the president.

In the late nineteenth century, the Industrial Revolution provoked economic **regulation**, the use of governmental power to protect the public interest and try to ensure the fair operation of the economy. This new domain was paired with an innovation, the **regulatory commission**, an agency charged with writing rules and arbitrating disputes in a specific part of the economy. Chairs and members of commissions are named by the president and confirmed by the Senate to terms of fixed length from which they cannot be summarily dismissed. (Probably the most prominent regulatory commission in the news is the Federal Reserve Board [known as "the Fed"]. We discuss it in Chapter 16.)

Regulatory commissions' autonomy was meant to take the politics out of regulation. But "most regulatory commissions face united, intensely interested industries, and passive, fragmented, and large consumer groups."[15] The commissions may be or become unsympathetic to the regulations they are supposed to enforce, even liable to being captured by the industries they are supposed to regulate.[16] Consider the Federal Communications Commission (FCC). It grants licenses to radio and television broadcast frequencies in exchange for vague promises to pursue "the public interest." Broadcasters are well organized, but viewers and listeners are not; the FCC's policies have favored commercial broadcasters. If the FCC does diverge from industry views, its decisions can be challenged in the courts and repealed by Congress. Broadcasters' power is weak only when the industry itself is divided.

The frailty or dereliction of regulatory commissions are often little noted unless they are so dramatic and disastrous that they eventually attract the attention of other officials, such as investigations by Congress, and arouse media coverage. As happened with the two crashes of the Boeing 737 Max airliner that killed 346 people. After the second crash in March 2019, the Federal Aviation Administration (FAA) grounded the plane.

The crashes raised questions about the rushed effort to build and approve the plane. The House Transportation Committee held several hearings during which the FAA administrator and Boeing personnel were excoriated and held to account. These hearings were assiduously covered by reporters for the *The New York Times:* examples are a scathing report by a multiagency task force critical of Boeing and the FAA; and a report from the Transportation Department's inspector general, that during the plane's certification process Boeing had failed to share essential documents with the FAA.[17]

The crashes raised questions about the rushed effort to build and approve the plane. The House Transportation Committee held several hearings during which the FAA administrator and Boeing personnel were excoriated and held to account. These hearings were assiduously covered by reporters for the *The New York Times:* examples are a scathing report by a multiagency task force critical of Boeing and the FAA; and a report from the Transportation Department's inspector general, that during the plane's certification process Boeing had failed to share essential documents with the FAA.[18]

The case cost Boeing billions of dollars, including compensation to victims, airlines, and the FAA (for two employees who withheld information from the agency), as well as the ouster of its chief executive. Withal, after being grounded for twenty months, the plane was cleared to fly again from December 29, 2020.

# The Size of the Federal Bureaucracy

Politicians pledge to shrink the size and enhance the efficiency of the federal bureaucracy. By one measure—how many civilian federal employees there are—they have succeeded: the number has not increased since the 1960s.

How, then, are politicians able to proclaim that "the era of big government is over" while providing the increase in government services that many people expect? They have accomplished this by vastly expanding the number of workers owing jobs to federal money. As a result, over sixteen million full-time workers administer federal policy.

There is the federal civilian workforce of 1.9 million, uniformed military personnel of 1.5 million, and 850,000 postal workers. Add "the federal shadow workforce," state and local government workers subject to federal mandates (discussed in Chapter 4). They devote, on the average, one-fourth of their work carrying out federal directives. There are 16.2 million state and local government workers, so the federal government does not need to hire approximately 4.05 million workers to carry out its policies.

There are billions of dollars annually in federal grants and contracts. Grants, such as those for highway construction, scholarly research, job training, and education, go through state and local government to private contractors. The government contracts with private companies to provide goods and, more recently, services in ways rarely reported in the news. The fact that the Defense Department contracted out for military interrogators and security officers in war zones did not become public knowledge until the Abu Ghraib prison abuse scandal broke in April 2004. The federal government directly supports 5.6 million jobs through contracts and 2.4 million jobs through grants.[19]

## Thickening Government

As a result of the reliance on mandates and contracts, fewer and fewer civil servants directly interact with and provide services to the public as "street-level bureaucrats."[20] Instead, federal employees are, more and more, professionals and managers. From the 1960s to the 1990s, even as the size of the civil service stayed constant, the number of senior executives and political appointees in the bureaucracy more than quintupled.[21]

This proliferation of managers creates "thickening government." The average number of layers between president and street-level bureaucrat swelled from seventeen in 1960 to thirty-two in 1992, as new administrative titles multiplied in bewildering combinations of "assistant," "associate," "deputy," and "principal" to monitor, streamline, and supervise state and local workers, contractors, and grantees—and each other. Consequently, much of the federal bureaucracy now consists of "managers managing managers."

### Key Takeaways

The federal bureaucracy is the sum total of all executive agencies and personnel. It is a complicated mix. It contains civil servants with lifetime merit appointments and political appointees. It includes distinct kinds of agencies. And its small size is misleading because some federal responsibilities are carried out through mandates to state and local governments and by the contracting out of goods and services.

### Exercises

1. What did the sociologist Max Weber think the function of a bureaucracy was? How did he think bureaucrats should differ from political leaders?

2. What was the spoils system? How did the Pendleton Act change the rules to prevent politicians from using political appointments for personal gain?
3. How have politicians managed to keep the number of federal employees the same since the 1960s? In what sense has the federal bureaucracy "thickened"?

# 14.3 Policymaking, Power, and Accountability in the Bureaucracy

## Learning Objectives

After reading this section, you should be able to answer the following questions:

1. How do government agencies exercise power through rulemaking, implementation, and adjudication?
2. What role does standard operating procedure play in agency accountability?
3. How do agencies and the president influence each other?
4. How do agencies and Congress influence each other?

The federal bureaucracy is a creature of Congress and the president. But agencies independently make policies and exert power: *legislating* by rulemaking; *executing* by implementation; and *adjudicating* by hearing complaints, prosecuting cases, and judging disputes.

## Rulemaking

Congresses and presidents often enact laws setting forth broad goals with little idea of how to get there. They get publicity in the media and take credit for addressing a problem—and pass tough questions on how to solve the problem to the bureaucracy.

**rulemaking**

The process by which agencies issue statements that implement, interpret, and prescribe policy in an area authorized by legislation passed by Congress.

Take the Occupational Safety and Health Act of 1971. It seeks "to assure so far as possible every working man and woman in the Nation safe and healthy work conditions."[22] Congress created the Occupational Safety and Health Administration (OSHA) and directed it to "establish regulations suitable and necessary for carrying this law into effect, which regulations shall be binding." OSHA began a process of **rulemaking**: issuing statements to clarify current and future policy in an area authorized by the law. It had to decide on answers for questions: What work conditions produce or endanger safety? What work conditions threaten workers' health? *How* far is "so far as possible"?[23]

### Link

**OSHA**

Click here to learn more about the history of OSHA.

When not all specified goals are equally simple to pursue, agencies gravitate toward those easier to put into effect. OSHA was championed by labor organizations that deemed health hazards on the job to be a bigger problem than safety. But OSHA's rulemaking focused more on safety than on health. It is simpler to calculate short-term costs and benefits of safety hazards than long-term costs and benefits of health hazards: for example, it's easier to install protective railings than it is to lessen exposure to potentially carcinogenic chemicals.[24]

In addition to hostility from business and industry, OSHA is handicapped by a limited budget and resources, and weak penalties to apply. It does have the weapon of exposing violations of the law using the news media.

Congress requires agencies to follow prescribed detailed procedures in issuing a rule. The explosion of New Deal agencies in the 1930s created inconsistency from one agency to the next. In 1934, the **Federal Register**, which prints all rules and decisions made by agencies, was launched to provide a common source. The ever-rising number of pages annually in the *Register* shows ever lengthier, ever more intricate rules.

**Federal Register**

The government publication that prints all rules and decisions made by agencies.

### Link

**The *Federal Register***

The *Federal Register* is available here.

In the first round, the agency interprets the statute to be applied and lists grounds for a preliminary decision. Next, it invites feedback: holding hearings or eliciting written comments from the public, Congress, and elsewhere in the executive branch. Then it issues a final rule, after which litigation can ensue; the rule may be annulled if courts conclude that the agency did not adequately justify it. Thus, in March 2009, a federal judge ordered the Food and Drug Administration to lower the minimum age at which women could obtain the Plan B birth control pill without a prescription from age eighteen to seventeen. He ruled the agency had improperly bowed to pressure from the Bush administration in setting the limit at eighteen. The pill is now available over the counter, without a prescription, with no proof of age required.

Any rule listed in the *Federal Register* has the status and force of law. The agency can modify the rule only by the same arduous process. The Bush administration worked diligently over its first three years to repeal the Clinton administration's policy forcing utility plants to spend billions of dollars on pollution upgrades during any renovations that, in the language of the Clean Air Act, exceeded "routine maintenance."[25] Environmental Protection Agency (EPA) administrator Christine Todd Whitman sought to make a "clarification" of "routine maintenance" that was more lenient to the power plants than her predecessor's strict interpretation. The new rule, first unveiled in 2002, went through lengthy review before being finally issued in late 2003. Several states in the Northeast subject to acid rain caused by Midwestern power plants promptly sued but did not win in court. Such rulemaking deep in the federal bureaucracy rarely achieves the media attention that an open debate and decision in Congress would attract—making it an unobtrusive way for officials to accomplish something politically unpopular, such as relaxing clean-air standards.[26]

# Implementing Policy

The bureaucracy makes policy through **implementation**, or applying general policies to given cases. Agencies transform abstract legal language into specific plans and organizational structures. There are rarely simple tests to assess how faithfully they do this. So even the lowliest bureaucrat wields power through implementation. Immigration agents decide which foreigners to grant asylum in the United States. Internal Revenue Service agents decide which tax returns to audit.

**implementation**

The process of applying general policies to specific cases in order to put legislation or rules into effect.

Some implementation can be easily measured. Examples are the Postal Service's balance sheet of income and expenditures or the average number of days it takes to deliver a first-class letter over a certain distance in the United States. But an agency's goals often conflict. Congress and presidents want the Postal Service to balance its budget but also to deliver mail expeditiously and at low cost to the sender and to provide many politically popular but costly services—such as Saturday delivery, keeping post offices open at rural hamlets, and adopting low postal rates for sending newspapers and magazines.[27]

Ambiguous goals also pose problems for agencies. When the SSA was formed in the 1930s, it set up an efficient way to devise standards of eligibility (such as age and length of employment) for retirement benefits. In the 1970s, Congress gave the SSA the task of determining eligibility for supplementary security income and disability insurance. Figuring out who was disabled enough to qualify was far more complex than determining criteria of eligibility for retirement. Enmeshed in controversy, the SSA lost public support.[28]

## Adjudicating Disputes

**adjudication**

Applying rules and precedents to individual cases in an adversarial setting with a defense and prosecution.

Agencies act like courts through administrative **adjudication**: applying rules and precedents to individual cases in an adversarial setting with a defense and prosecution. Some, like the National Labor Relations Board (NLRB), act as both prosecutor and judge.[29] Federal law directs workers complaining about unfair labor practices to go to regional directors of NLRB, who decide if there is probable cause that the law has been violated. If so, NLRB's general counsel brings a case on behalf of the complainant before NLRB's special administrative law judges, who hear both sides of the dispute and issue a decision. That ruling may be appealed to the full NLRB. Only then may the case go to federal court.

## Standard Operating Procedures

**standard operating procedures (SOPs)**

Recurring routines to manage particular cases.

How can civil servants prove they are doing their jobs? On a day-to-day basis, it is hard to show that vague policy goals are being met. Instead, they demonstrate that the agency is following agreed-on routines for processing cases—**standard operating procedures (SOPs)**.[30] So it is hard for agencies to "think outside the box": to step back and examine what they are doing, and why. The news media's lack of day-to-day interest in the vast majority of agencies only further dampens attention to the big picture. Sometimes, only severe crises jar agencies out of their inertia. For example, following the terrorist attacks of 9/11 the Central Intelligence Agency (CIA) moved to revive old-fashioned forms of human intelligence, such as planting spies in terrorist camps and increasing its number of Arabic-language speakers, when it became clear that its standard operating procedure of using high-tech forms of intelligence, such as satellite images and electronic eavesdropping, had been inadequate to forecast, let alone prevent, the attacks.

## Agencies' Power

Agencies are alert to and heed the power of the president and Congress over their activities. But agencies can effectively influence Congress and presidents as much as the other way around. And if Congress and presidents disagree, agencies are in the happy situation of responding to the branch that is closer to what they want to do.[31]

The signs of an agency's power include (1) the legal authority Congress and presidents accord it, (2) the size and continuity of its budget, and (3) the deference it gains from expertise. But each of these hallmarks amounts to little without political support—especially from those individuals and groups most interested in or affected by an agency's decisions. Without such support, agencies find their programs confined by others, their budgets slashed, and their claims to expertise doubted.

J. Edgar Hoover was the quintessentially powerful bureaucrat. His weapons were longevity (Director of the Federal Bureau of Investigation for forty-eight years from 1924 until his death in 1972), domination of the organization and its members, ruthlessness in his use of power (smearing and silencing critics, opponents and enemies), minimizing oversight, a host of informants, cultivation of the media, and master deployer of information. Some of that information was obtained through break-ins, bugging and wiretaps (he kept tapes on the personal lives of politicians, officials, and public figures including the philandering of President John F. Kennedy and the sex life of the Rev. Martin Luther King, Jr., prurient contents he shared with presidents). He went to great, often illegal lengths, to undermine radicals. Nonetheless, still visibly celebrating his memory is the bureau's massive headquarters, the J. Edgar Hoover FBI Building, on Pennsylvania Avenue in Washington, DC.[32]

Director Hoover may have been *sui generis* but his example shows that agencies "are not helpless, passive pawns in the game of politics as it affects their lives; they can be active, energetic, persistent participants."[33] They work to create and maintain political support from the president, Congress, and the public. Favorable media coverage is instrumental in building this political support.

Agencies also obtain political support by shifting policies when new political participants challenge their standard approach.[34] For example, in the 1970s the Army Corps of Engineers moved away from a rigid pro-development stance when environmental groups arose and lobbied for a law requiring the corps to draft environmental impact statements.

On occasion, an agency's scandals will be exposed and its head fired or allowed to resign voluntarily. His replacement, appointed by the president to clear up the mess, will work through the news and opinion media to help the agency recover, affirm his and the agency's reputation for accountability, and placate the agency's critics in Congress. This scenario took place after revelations about lengthy wait times and delays in treatment at the VA medical center in Phoenix and elsewhere, delays that staff members manipulated, deleted from the records, covered up, and that contributed to the deaths of several patients.[35]

Robert A. McDonald replaced Eric Shinseki as secretary of Veterans Affairs, a department of 300,000. He got his message of change across to the media by testifying before Congress and meeting with reporters. At his first news conference he even gave the journalists his cell phone number. He talked about changing the agency's culture, what was needed to rectify the situation, and what he had accomplished (hiring doctors and nurses, extending clinic hours, and encouraging whistleblowers).[36]

As we show throughout our book, those who try to use the media can be damaged by the media. While in Los Angeles on a program to find and house homeless vets, a homeless man identified himself as having served in the Army's elite special forces. McDonald replied that so had he. Unfortunately, this was not true; he had served in the 82nd Airborne Division. Unfortunately, his remark was captured by the CBS camera crew accompanying him and included in a news story. His lie eventually came to the media's attention and he was compelled to admit it.[37]

# How Presidents Influence the Federal Bureaucracy

Within the Executive Office of the President is the Office of Management and Budget (OMB). Its purpose is to manage the agencies of the federal government on behalf of the president. OMB oversees preparation of the budget, supervises the administration, and measures (to the extent possible) the quality and effectivenes of agencies' programs and procedures, and compliance with the president's policies. Inside OMB, the Office of Information and Regulatory Affairs (OIRA) reviews and signs off on drafts of federal rules and regulations before they are published. It is also responsible for developing and overseeing the implementation of government-wide policies on information technology, information policy, privacy, and statistical policy.

Presidents select heads of agencies and make numerous other political appointees to direct and control them. But political appointees have short careers in office; they average just over two years.[38] Civil servants' long careers in government in a single agency can easily outlast any political appointee who spars with them.[39]

**administrative presidency**

Political scientist Richard Nathan's term for the tactics presidents use with the bureaucracy to implement policy goals blocked by Congress.

Presidents are tempted to pursue implementation by agencies to accomplish policy goals that Congress has frustrated. Tools of this **administrative presidency** include establishing agencies, strategic appointments, internal reorganization, and budget cuts.[40]

## Establishing Agencies

Presidents can set up an agency by executive order—and dare Congress not to authorize and fund it. President John F. Kennedy issued an executive order to launch the Peace Corps after Congress did not act on his legislative request. Only then did Congress authorize, and allocate money for, the new venture. Agencies created by presidents are smaller than those begun by Congress; but presidents have more control of their structure and personnel.[41]

## Strategic Appointments

Presidents make strategic appointments. Agency personnel are open to change when new appointees take office. Presidents can appoint true-believer ideologues to the cabinet or an agency who become prominent in the news, stand firm against the sway of the civil service, and deflect criticism away from the president.[42] After the 9/11 attacks, President Bush let Attorney General John Ashcroft take the lead—and the flak—on aggressive law enforcement policies that many saw as threats to civil liberties.[43]

Presidents also can and do fire agency officials who question the White House line. In 2002, Mike Parker, head of the Army Corps of Engineers and former member of Congress, testified on Capitol Hill that the president's budget for the Corps was too low. His remarks were covered heavily in the news—as was his dismissal.[44]

Presidents who dislike an agency's programs can decide not to replace departing staffers. Early in his term, George W. Bush (the first president to graduate from business school) made few appointments to the Securities and Exchange Commission that regulates the stock market; he only boosted its staff after financial scandals rocked Wall Street in 2002.[45]

## Internal Reorganization

Presidents can rearrange an agency's organizational chart. President Richard Nixon faced a ballooning welfare budget after taking office in 1969. Congress failed to act on welfare reform. Nixon turned to administrative measures to slow federal outlays. Deeply conservative appointees initiated new rules; instead of worrying about denying welfare to someone who was qualified, they stressed reducing the number of ineligible persons receiving benefits. Civil servants were moved out of offices devoted to specific programs and reported to managers who graded them on their ability to cut costs. The result? Welfare rolls leveled off despite a worsening economy.[46]

## Backlash

Presidents pursue the administrative presidency most effectively with programs that are obscure or unpopular with the public. Otherwise, they risk reactions on Capitol Hill. For example, President Ronald Reagan, seeking more leeway for business, successfully restrained the EPA in his first term. He appointed loyal, lightning-rod individuals who went to Congress and asked for budget *reductions*. He left positions vacant. He shifted authority to the states. He subjected environmental laws to cost-benefit calculations that emphasized tangible costs of regulation over intangible benefits. After two years, fewer new regulations were issued, and environmental standards and enforcement were relaxed. (By "he" we do not mean that the president personally took these actions; rather, that with his agreement and acceptance, they were carried out by members of his administration.)

These victories produced a backlash. Civil servants felt excluded. Environmental interest groups made Reagan's appointees into villains they railed against in media campaigns. The resultant shift in public opinion made itself known to Congress, which eventually led Reagan to fire the agency heads. Under new, more moderate leadership, the EPA veered away from its relentlessly probusiness stance.[47]

The administrative presidency does not work unless presidents and their political appointees clearly articulate what they wish to accomplish at the outset. Bureaucrats cannot respond to conflicting or confused signals from political appointees. Communicating clearly to a far-flung executive branch is a key reason why presidents are determined to craft a "line of the day" and disseminate it through the executive branch.

George W. Bush carried coordination of presidential and agency communication one step further by ensuring that the White House, not the department secretary, appoint the press officers in each cabinet department. As Bush's first chief of staff, Andrew Card, explained, "Our communications team is not just a team for the White House. It is a communications team for the executive branch of government."[48]

In 2016, President Trump promised to dismantle the regulatory state. In office, he sought to rollback governmental regulations and change policies designed to protect workers, consumers, and the environment, particularly those of the Environmental Protection Agency, and the Interior, Labor, and Commerce Departments. Many of his cabinet and bureaucratic appointees were antagonistic to the agencies they were chosen to run and their policies.

Trump's first appointee to head the EPA was a climate change skeptic determined to slash many of the agency's plans and regulations adopted and approved by its predecessor Obama administration. One technique he adopted was to "turkey farm" some of his opponents and critics (deprive them of power by shuffling them off to unimportant posts in the agency). But people in agencies can fight back in defense of their preferred policies and against their enemies. Officials and staff members in the agency revealed his actions to pro-environmental journalists and figures in environmental interest groups. By helping expose his ethical scandals, they also precipitated his resignation from office.

Sometimes the president-agency relationship, abetted by the judiciary, can become tricky, as with enforcement of immigration policy. The Trump administration imposed a get-tough on asylum seekers and immigrants regime that many career officials at the Homeland Security Department supported. When he entered office, however, President Biden looked to modify that policy. He issued an order to pause deportations for one hundred days. A judge in Texas temporarily blocked his order. Whereupon, some Immigration and Customs (ICE) agents, who agreed with the Trump policy, moved to continue enforcing it.[49]

Posing a major problem for President Biden, he also encountered over a thousand rules and regulations, revisions to forms, buried by Trump's aides designed to make it difficult if not impossible for immigrants or asylum seekers to enter or remain in the country: "163 changes to forms and information collection; 106 official rule changes; 416 agency directives; 57 presidential orders; 301 changes in practice by agencies and their employees; 16 program terminations: 40 modifications to data and reports; 29 formal changes to the way immigration law is adjudicated; and six legislative proposals." Every one of these changes needs to be identified and eliminated to ease immigration.[50]

# How Agencies Influence Presidents

Presidential appointments, especially of cabinet secretaries, are one way to control the bureaucracy. But cabinet secretaries have multiple loyalties. The Senate's power to confirm nominees means that appointees answer to Congress as well as the president. In office, each secretary is not based at the White House but at a particular agency "amid a framework of established relations, of goals already fixed, of forces long set in motion [in] an impersonal bureaucratic structure resistant to change."[51]

## Cabinet Secretaries

Surrounded by civil servants who justify and defend department policies, cabinet secretaries are inclined to advocate the departments' programs rather than presidential initiatives. For example, while Republicans have long proposed abolishing the Department of Energy, Republican energy secretaries resist such an effort. As a senator, Spencer Abraham (R-MI) proposed the abolition of the Department of Energy. After Abraham was defeated for reelection in 2000, President Bush offered him a cabinet post as energy secretary as a consolation prize. With what a reporter termed "the enthusiasm of a convert," Secretary Abraham changed his tune: "We have a clearer mission . . . and the department is . . . a much more effective place to do business."[52] In 2017, President Trump's first appointee as secretary of energy had called for the abolition of the department when campaigning for the Republican nomination for the presidency.

Some cabinet secretaries value their independence and individuality above the president's agenda. Treasury secretaries often come to Washington directly from success as chief executive officers of corporations. In 2001, Paul O'Neill left Alcoa to become George W. Bush's first treasury secretary. O'Neill was unprepared for the scrutiny his frank, off-the-cuff public comments attracted. At odds with the public relations approach of the Bush administration and sometimes out of step with presidential statements, O'Neill was marginalized and ultimately dismissed in late 2002. O'Neill got his revenge by including inside information critical of President Bush in a "kiss and tell" memoir published in 2004.

Cabinet secretaries craft strategies of getting into the news to boost their reputations and influence both inside and outside their departments. But seeking an image of being "in charge" of their agency does not always work. Homeland Security Secretary Tom Ridge's mission included reassuring an anxious public after 9/11. But his attempts to do so, such as devising or agreeing to a color-coded system of terrorism alerts and suggesting that plastic sheeting and duct tape could effectively shield houses from the dangers of biological warfare, were mocked in the media and did more damage than good to that effort and Ridge's reputation.

## Civil Servants Shape Policies

Cabinet members are high-profile officials known to the news media and the president. With the executive branch's increasing layers, civil servants often shape outcomes as much as presidents and cabinet secretaries. The decisions they make may or may not be in line with their superiors' intentions. Or they may structure information to limit the decisions of those above them, changing ambiguous shades of gray to more stark black and white. As a political scientist wrote, "By the time the process culminates at the apex, the top-level officials are more often than not confronted with the task of deciding which set of decisions to accept. These official policy-makers, in many respects, become policy ratifiers."[53]

# How Congress Influences the Federal Bureaucracy

The Senate confirms cabinet secretaries and other nominees, thereby having a say in who controls and staffs the bureaucracy. Congress makes laws fixing the functions, jurisdictions, and goals of agencies. It sets agency budgets and conditions for how funds must be used (for example, by trying to eliminate funds for public relations).[54] It can demote, merge, or abolish any agency it finds wanting; longevity does not guarantee survival.[55] Every agency's challenge is to find ways to avoid such sanctions.

If an agency's actions become politically unpopular, Congress can cut its budget, restrict the scope of regulation or the tools used, or specify different procedures. For example, the National Endowment for the Arts (NEA) in the early 1990s made a series of controversial decisions to fund gay and lesbian performance artists. The NEA's budget was cut by Congress and its existence threatened. If such sanctions are seldom applied, their presence coaxes bureaucrats to anticipate and conform to what Congress wants.

Congress monitors agency activities by **oversight**: members gather information on agency performance and communicate to agencies about how well or, more often, how poorly they are doing.[56] Oversight ranges from a lone legislator's intervention over a constituent's late Social Security check, to mandating reports on actions and targets/achievements, to high-profile investigations and committee hearings. It is neither centralized nor systematic. Rather than rely on a "police-patrol" style of oversight—dutifully seeking information about what agencies are doing—Congress uses a "fire alarm" approach: interest groups and citizens alert members to problems in an agency, often through reports in the news.[57]

**oversight**

The process by which Congress monitors the activities of government agencies.

The Congressional Review Act gives Congress a special weapon: lawmakers have sixty legislative days to repeal major new regulations issued by federal agencies. As we discuss in Chapter 16, Policymaking and Domestic Policies, it was deployed by President Trump and the Republican-controlled Congress to overturn rules they opposed that had been enacted late in the Obama presidency.

# How Agencies Influence Congress

Agencies can work for continued congressional funding by building public support for the agency and its programs. The huge budget of the Defense Department is facilitated when public opinion polls accord high confidence to the military. To keep this confidence high is one reason the Defense Department aggressively interacts with the media to obtain favorable coverage.

Agencies can make it hard for Congress to close them down or reduce their budget even when public opinion is mixed. Agencies choose how much money to spend in implementing a program; they spread resources across many districts and states in the hope that affected legislators will be less inclined to oppose their programs.[58] For example, numerous presidents have proposed that the perennially money-losing government corporation Amtrak be "zeroed out." But Amtrak has survived time and again. Why? Although train riders are few outside the Northeast, Amtrak trains regularly serve almost all the continental forty-eight states, providing local pressure to keep a national train system going.

**FIGURE 14.3 Amtrak Map**

This Amtrak map shows routes, service type, and frequency by color and line thickness.

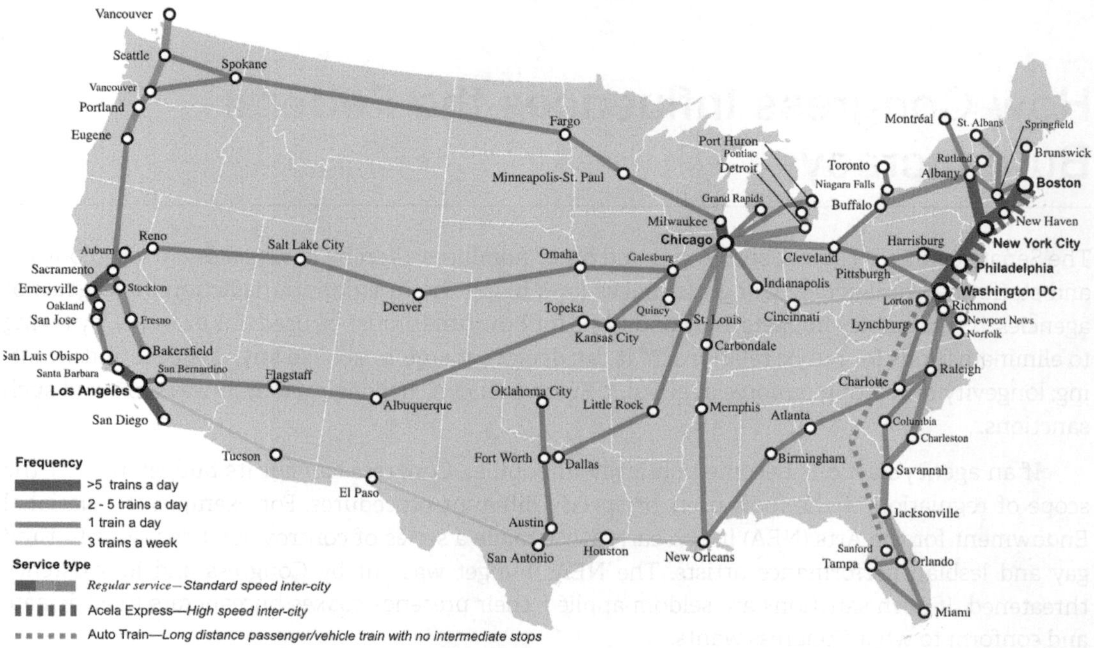


Source: PerryPlanet via Wikimedia: https://commons.wikimedia.org/wiki/File:Amtrakfreqmapcolor_svg.svg#filelinks. Reproduced via CC BY-SA 3.0: https://creativecommons.org/licenses/by-sa/3.0/deed.en.

Likewise, when faced with extinction, an agency can alter its policies to affect more congressional constituencies. For example, after the NEA was threatened with extinction, it shifted funding away from supporting artists in trendy urban centers toward building audiences for community-sponsored arts found in a multitude of districts and states—whose residents could push Congress to increase the NEA's budget. Sure enough, President Bush's tight budgets saw rises for the NEA.

## Key Takeaways

The bureaucracy often makes sweeping policy decisions. It legislates by rulemaking, executes the law by implementing it, and adjudicates by addressing individual cases in adversarial settings with defense and prosecution. Agencies constantly search for political support to ensure an adequate budget and enhance their independence. They are subject to control by but also influence the president, who proposes their budgets, creates new agencies, and appoints their leaders. Agencies are also subject to control by Congress, which funds their programs and determines their scope.

## Exercises

1. What government agencies have you had to deal with? How much authority do you think they had to decide what to do in your case?
2. What is the value of standard operating procedures? What are the limitations of having bureaucracies follow standard procedures?
3. How can agencies influence policymakers? How does the perspective of bureaucrats working in government agencies tend to differ from the perspective of the president and members of Congress?

# 14.4 The Federal Bureaucracy in the Information Age

## Learning Objectives

After reading this section, you should be able to answer the following questions:

1. How do the bureaucracy and the media interact?
2. Why and when do agencies need the media?
3. Why and when do the media need agencies?
4. What impact do media depictions of the bureaucracy have on public opinion and on agencies themselves?

We have seen the many ways the federal bureaucracy makes crucial contributions to government and public policies. Yet its depiction in the media is mixed. On the one hand, emphasizing waste, incompetence, malfeasance, and abuse, the media tend to be critical, even dismissive. On the other hand, many agencies are portrayed as competent and effective. These differences can be explained by an analysis of agency-media interactions.

# Media Interactions

There is so much variety in the agencies, commissions, and offices that make up the federal bureaucracy that we might expect their interactions with the media to differ greatly. After all, some agencies, such as the Department of Defense, have enormous budgets that might seem, at least on occasion, to require justification. Others, like the far leaner Department of State, may require justification because its mission is unclear. Some, like the National Institutes of Health, deal with technical and intricate policy areas, and their officials fear that their work will be distorted when it is translated by journalists. Others, like the Federal Trade Commission, are deemed by reporters to be dull, narrow and, most of the time, unsuitable for dramatic, exciting news.

In practice, media operations from one agency to the next resemble each other. Media scholar Stephen Hess studied those of the Food and Drug Administration and Departments of Defense, State, and Transportation. He concluded, "Regardless of how they were organized or how different their sizes, each performed the same duties in a similar manner. … The Pentagon's press operations appear much like the FDA's writ large."[59] The agencies spend millions on advertising, public relations, an internet presence, Twitter, YouTube, and the like.

As in the White House, the relationship of bureaucrats and reporters is both adversarial and cooperative. Political appointees and civil servants may be anxious about reporters' power to frame and reinterpret policy decisions. Yet they understand the importance of maintaining a friendly relationship with reporters to try to get their agency reported favorably, to boost public support for their programs and budgets. Moreover, they can never assume that the media will ignore them; they must be prepared to deal with reporters at a moment's notice. In practice, both sides usually need each other—journalists for information, bureaucrats for favorable coverage or at least to mitigate negative news.

**press officers**

People scattered through the bureaucracy who serve as official spokespersons for their agencies.

To meet the media's never-ending appetite for news, reporters turn to readily accessible **press officers**, who serve as official spokespersons for their agencies. Press officers, who are often former journalists, sympathize with the reporters who cover agencies and strive to represent their needs within the agency. They work to provide information, a quick quote, or a tidbit on a given topic that will satisfy any and all journalists who contact them.

At the same time, reporters often search for and thrive on leaks (unauthorized anonymous disclosures). These may come from high-ranking appointees in the agency seeking to float trial balloons or to place decisions in context. The source may be deep in the bureaucracy, as in the Abu Ghraib prisoner abuse scandal. Reporters also gain revelations through official reports and investigations conducted by officials in an agency.

# Why and When Agencies Need the Media

Agencies need the media for external and internal communication.

## External Communication

An agency may need favorable media depictions (1) to help it enhance its public image and build public support, (2) to ensure that the budget it receives from Congress is at least adequate for its mission, and (3) to reduce interference from presidents and their political appointees. Media stories that laud an agency's indispensable skill at solving important problems affecting a large public discourage such threats. For example, if the Centers for Disease Control and Prevention swiftly sends out warnings about a new outbreak of illness, it not only alerts the public but also provides clear evidence of its competence—and justification for an ample or increased budget.

The agencies' attention to the media goes beyond the news. Hollywood directors shooting a war movie routinely contact the Defense Department for assistance, ranging from technical advice to the use of military equipment. Nothing obliges the Pentagon to cooperate with an applicant, so it grants requests only to projects that depict it favorably. Hollywood classics raising serious questions about the military—*Fail-Safe*, *Dr. Strangelove*, and *Apocalypse Now*, for example—asked for but did not receive Pentagon help. By contrast, *Top Gun*, the top-grossing film of 1986, ended up acting as a recruiting poster for Navy pilots: it gained box-office cachet from aerial sequences filmed in several $37 million F-14 jets the navy provided free of charge.[60]

Yet, there is an issue that has come to light over the last few years that the military has been unable to control or contain from the media. It is sexual violence against women. The Defense Department estimates that in 2010 there were 19,000 cases. Of these, 3,198 were reported, but with only 244 convictions. Through news stories, an award-winning documentary film by Kirby Dick (see Section 6) and the efforts of female senators, the issue has become increasingly visible and victims emboldened to recount their experiences, with the result being that the Pentagon has begun to change and improve its procedures for offering recourse to and achieving justice for survivors.

## Internal Communication

Agencies find it hard to communicate internally as they grow bigger. Top agency officials worry that subordinates will not grasp what the agency is doing or that leaks from deep in the bureaucracy will negatively characterize policy. So they have incentives to communicate what the agency's policy is, stifle disagreement, and remind personnel of its mission. What appears on the surface to be a service to reporters actually meets these crucial internal needs of a bureaucracy. For instance, the State Department's daily noon briefing for reporters is indispensable for the State Department;

it sets a deadline to establish U.S. foreign policy and uses the news media to communicate that policy throughout government and to foreign service officers around the globe.[61]

Agency press officers communicate internally by searching for news stories bearing on the agency and reproducing them in compilations circulated through the agency called "the clips." Since the clips exaggerate the prominence—and importance—of news coverage of each agency, an agency's personnel becomes ever more sensitive to—and influenced by—media attention.

# Why and When the Media Need Agencies

At the few agencies regularly covered by news outlets—for example, the "inner cabinet" of the Departments of State, Defense, Treasury, and Justice—dynamics resemble the White House. Cabinet secretaries heading these departments become the public faces of their agencies, even celebrities worthy of mockery on comedy shows, jokes on late-night talk shows, and mimicry on *Saturday Night Live*. Like presidents, their influence is constantly monitored and measured by the observing media.

Reporters covering inner cabinet departments use their assignments to benefit both them and the department they cover. To land a front-page or lead story, they stress the importance of the agency's policy area within their news organizations. But to get the information that impresses editors and producers, reporters must rely on the input of top officials. Based at the department itself and interacting heavily with its personnel, inner cabinet reporters begin to reflect the department's procedures, approaches, and priorities.

Reporters gravitate to the Pentagon for stories about operational guns-and-ammo firepower. This approach is handy for the Defense Department, which tries to "educate" reporters—and through them, the public—on the benefits of sophisticated weapons systems (and reasons for a huge budget). The Pentagon fosters favorable coverage by giving conditional access: providing captivating video to reporters of successful military sorties, sending them to reporters' boot camp to help them appreciate the soldier's life, or "embedding" them in military units, which enables them to file compelling human interest stories of brave warriors. Even skeptical reporters find the drama and vividness of such content irresistible for the news.

## The Media Expose an Agency

What happens when a dramatic event develops into a crisis and thrusts an obscure agency into the news?

On April 20, 2010, the Deepwater Horizon oil rig in the Gulf of Mexico exploded, killing eleven workers. For the next several months, millions of gallons of oil poured into the Gulf of Mexico. A giant oil slick destroyed the ecology, polluted coastlines, killed animals and ruined their habitats, and damaged the fishing industry, tourism, and real estate businesses. It was the worst oil spill in American history.[62]

The federal government, which had leased the area to British Petroleum (BP), initially deferred to the oil company, relying on it for the technology, personnel, and financing to stem the flood of oil and initiate the cleanup. But BP's efforts were woefully ineffective, and the company drastically underestimated the amount of oil pouring into the gulf and the rate at which the oil leaked.

The media, led by *The New York Times*, looked for the government agency most responsible for the disaster. Their pursuit led them to the Minerals Management Service (MMS) of the Interior Department. MMS is required by the Outer Continental Shelf Act to inspect the approximately four thousand offshore platform facilities in the gulf for safety and operational compliance.

The *Times* reported that MMS had approved at least three huge lease sales, 103 seismic blasting projects, and 346 drilling plans, including Deepwater Horizon, without getting required permits from the National Oceanic and Atmospheric Administration (NOAA). The newspaper also reported that the MMS routinely overruled the safety and environmental concerns of its staff biologists and engineers, pressuring them to change their findings that predicted accidents. The MMS was reported to have routinely exempted BP and other companies from having to provide environmental impact statements.[63] Yet "from 2001 to 2007, there were 1,443 serious drilling accidents in offshore operations, leading to 41 deaths, 302 injuries and 356 oil spills."[64]

MMS essentially allowed the oil industry to regulate itself. With respect to the Deepwater Horizon rig, as reported in the *Times*, MMS gave BP permission to test the blowout preventer at a lower pressure than federally required and granted another exception to the company to delay mandatory testing of the preventer because it had lost well control. It did not require BP to keep a containment dome on the rig: BP took seventeen days to build one on shore and ship it to sea, where it did not work.[65]

Investigating MMS, the Interior Department's inspector general reported on its coziness with the industry, such as the MMS's allowance of oil and gas personnel to fill out inspection forms that would then be completed or signed by the MMS inspector. Many MMS inspectors had worked for the oil and gas industry. They accepted gifts from the companies and were friends with its employees.[66]

The Obama administration had not totally ignored MMS, which had a reputation for scandal and corruption. New Secretary of the Interior Ken Salazar had started to try to reform the agency with ethics standards. A new head had been appointed, but she apparently did little to fix or even change the agency.

After the revelations, she resigned. That was not enough. The conflict (contradiction) between the MMS missions of policing and supporting the oil industry was too blatant. The agency was responsible for oversight of safety and environmental protection in all offshore activities, including oil drilling, and for leasing energy resources in federal waters. But at the same time, it collected and distributed royalties of $13 billion annually from these leases. Thus, it had a vested financial interest in the industry. On May 19, 2010, Salazar announced the separation of the three responsibilities into different divisions.

The agency's name was changed to the Bureau of Ocean Energy Management, Regulation and Enforcement. Its new director issued guidelines to tighten the regulation of drilling and end or at least curtail the bribery, favoritism, and cozy relationship with the oil companies.[67]

Yet, according to Margaret Brown's remarkable documentary film *The Great Invisible* (see Section 6), four years after the spill, BP had only cleaned up around one-third of it, Congress had failed to pass any safety legislation dealing with the petroleum industry, and there are more rigs operating in the Gulf of Mexico than before the disaster.

## Comparing Content

### Torture

At any time, an agency may have to devise and implement a controversial policy embroiling it with the presidency, Congress, political parties, and public opinion. It may find itself under attack and having to battle in the media to defend, even trying to vindicate, its actions. Such was the fate of the Central Intelligence Agency (CIA) which, after 9/11, required by political leaders to prevent more attacks, established a detention and interrogation program that lasted for several years. President Obama ended it and closed the agency's secret overseas prisons after he took office.

For five years, the Democratic members and staff of the United States Senate Select Committee on Intelligence, chaired by Senator Dianne Feinstein (CA), worked to assemble a report on the program. Their investigation was confined to the actions of the operational agency, the CIA. The Republicans refused to agree to the Senate investigation unless the office of the president and the vice president and the National Security Council were excluded.[68]

The report was based on internal CIA documents, statements, and testimony. As it was being compiled, the staff and agency clashed. Suspecting that the committee staff had improperly obtained an agency review of the program, CIA officers had illegally penetrated a computer network used by the committee to write its report.

After lengthy negotiating between Senator Feinstein and the White House chief of staff over its contents, the Democrats released the 524-page executive summary of the report on December 9, 2014. Accompanying it was a 167-page rebuttal by Republican members of the committee. The date enabled the Democrats to release the summary before the Republicans took control of the committee following their takeover of the Senate in the 2014 election. (The committee classified and did not release the full report of over 6,000 pages.) The executive summary received enormous coverage in the news and opinion media and online.[69]

According to the executive summary, the CIA, poorly equipped to detain and interrogate terrorism suspects after the 9/11 attacks, had bungled the job. It had used extreme (gruesome) methods, euphemistically called enhanced interrogation techniques by the agency. Some of them, such as waterboarding, had been authorized by Justice Department lawyers during the Bush administration. Others, such as sleep deprivation, rectal feeding and rectal hydration, and worse, had not been approved. Indeed, contrary to inflated claims made by successive CIA directors in secret briefings of the president and Congress and in public statements, these interrogation methods did not result in disrupting terrorism plots, the capture of terrorist leaders, or finding bin Laden (despite the implications of the 2012 film *Zero Dark Thirty*). The executive summary documented that some agency officers had questioned whether the techniques were effective and had been offended by what they saw.

In a speech on the Senate floor just after release of the summary, Senator Feinstein called the interrogation program "a stain on our values and our history."

During the years of the program, the CIA had leaked classified information to reporters portraying it as effective. Now, upon release of the executive summary, the agency's current and past leadership and Republican allies mobilized to defend what the agency called its "aggressive counterterrorism policies and programs." The rebuttal by six Republican members of the committee denounced the report as factually inaccurate and partisan The agency released a lengthy response. Director John O. Brennan issued a statement as Senator Feinstein was preparing to speak on the Senate floor. While acknowledging mistakes, he challenged some of the findings as incomplete and selective. A website, ciasavedlives.com, was created by former officials of the agency. Three former directors and three former deputy directors jointly wrote a long op-ed essay for the *Wall Street Journal*.[70] In sum, these responses denounced the executive summary for taking a "prosecutorial" approach, inadequately considering the context of threat and danger of the time, and criticized the Democratic staff for failing to interview any agency officials who had established or run the program. More specifically, the responses claimed that the program had led to the takedown of bin Laden, the capture of senior operatives, the disruption of terrorist plots, and added enormously to knowledge about al-Qaeda. According to the responses, the agency had briefed administration officials and members of Congress, and its methods had been approved by the president and declared lawful by the Justice Department's Office of Legal Counsel.[71]

Comparing content here we have two accounts (or stories) differing in facts, interpretations, and claims of effects. They concern national security, the CIA's reputation, relations between the bureaucratic agency and Congress, contrasting perspectives of the Democratic and Republican parties, and a battle for public opinion using the news and partisan media.[72]

## Links

### The CIA's Detention and Interrogation Program

Find the executive summary online here.

Click here to read the op-ed by former CIA directors in the *Wall Street Journal.*

# Media Consequences

The media's depictions of the federal bureaucracy, ranging from highly positive to direly negative, provoke mixed feelings in the public.[73] Asked to choose in polls between "a smaller government providing fewer services" or "a bigger government providing more services," Americans opt for the former by a two-to-one margin. Like the media, the public finds waste, fraud, and abuse to be endemic to the bureaucracy. Year after year of National Election Studies surveys reveal that when asked, "Do you think that people in the government waste a lot of the money we pay in taxes, waste some of it, or don't waste very much of it?" the majority answers "a lot."[74]

Yet year after year polls also show the public strongly in favor of many specific programs and agencies. The General Social Survey, regularly conducted since 1973, has asked the public if it thinks too much money, not enough money, or about the right amount is being spent on particular policies. With few exceptions (welfare, foreign aid, and sometimes the space program), the public overwhelmingly favors keeping the level of funding the same or increasing it. Public opinion surveys asking respondents to evaluate individual agencies routinely show most people giving them favorable grades.

**FIGURE 14.4 Closed Public Building During 1995–96 Government Shutdown**
During the 1995–96 government shutdown caused by a deadlock over the federal budget between Democrats in the White House and Republicans in Congress, the news media prominently featured images of closed government facilities like the Washington Monument, the Smithsonian Institution, and many national parks. These reminders of what the federal bureaucracy provides led public opinion to pressure the Republicans to back down.

Source: Doug Mills / Associated Press

Like the portrayal in the news media, Americans scorn bureaucracy as a whole *and* admire many individual agencies. Such ambivalent public opinion provides opportunities for both shrinking and growing government responsibilities and activities. Amid a budget standoff with the Republican Congress during the government shutdown of late 1995, President Clinton was able to prevail and force the Republicans to accept fewer government cutbacks than they demanded. Clinton's victory was not simply the superior position of the president over Congress vis-à-vis the news media, it was also due to the news media's prominent coverage of the government's withdrawal of key services. (See the section on the Budget in Chapter 16 for a similar situation that occurred in October 2013.)

Federal bureaucrats are sensitive to media content because they have few gauges of public opinion apart from what is in the news. Interviewed by the Pew Research Center for the People & the Press, members of Congress, presidential appointees, and civil servants in the Senior Executive Service, all said they were heavy consumers of the news. When asked about their principal sources of information on how the public feels about issues—and allowed multiple responses—an overwhelming majority of presidential appointees and civil servants cited the media as their main source of information about public opinion.[75]

Bureaucrats not only respond to but try to craft media content that will serve their interests. When agency personnel note public distrust, they do not say that the answer is to engage in dialogue with the public so much as explaining effectively the good jobs they see themselves as already performing.[76] As a result, most agency websites avoid the huge potential of the internet for interactivity. Instead, they are designed to make it easier for the agency to communicate with the public than the other way around.[77]

When the news media do spotlight a particular agency, this attention often makes the wheels of bureaucracy turn fast and be more responsive to public opinion. Positive coverage provides an opportunity for an agency to further its public image and enhance its programs. Even more strongly negative coverage, such as the Obama administration's response to the revelations about

MMS, becomes a prod to do something to get the bad news off the front page. Either way, news coverage speeds up decision making by pushing it to higher levels of officials.[78]

## Key Takeaways

Agencies need the media for external and internal communication. They try to maintain and enhance their independence and power by fostering public approval that makes it hard for the president and Congress to challenge decisions or to cut budgets. Agencies pursue such approval by seeking positive images in the media of themselves and the programs they run. Reporters rely on official spokespersons and leaks. Media depictions encourage Americans to scorn the bureaucracy but value individual bureaucrats and programs. They motivate agencies to anticipate the needs of news in their decision making and to speed up their policymaking processes.

## Exercises

1. In what sense do government agencies and the media need each other? In what ways do their interests differ?
2. Why do you think the public tends to believe the federal bureaucracy is too large, even though it generally has a favorable opinion of most government agencies? Why might the media help create this impression in the public?

### Civic Education

**The Lesson of Room 421**

In 2003, a class of fifth-grade students at Byrd Academy, a school in Chicago's Cabrini-Green housing project, took on the city's bureaucracy in an effort to improve conditions at their dilapidated school. Byrd Academy was a magnet school for students with high academic credentials who lived in one of the most rundown and crime-ridden neighborhoods in the city. The students' ultimate goal was the building of the new school that had been promised—a sign announcing the planned construction was visible from their classroom window.

Their teacher, Brian Schultz, encouraged the class to take part in Project Citizen, a program that stresses working together to get government to act on a problem. The students identified the difficulties with their current facility, developed a series of concrete action plans, conducted research to support their position, and began a fundraising campaign. They placed their need for a new facility within the larger context of the difficulties facing their community. They wrote letters and sent emails to public officials, earned the support of high-profile figures, including Ralph Nader, and enlisted over nine hundred students from other schools to take up their cause. They circulated petitions, including an online version that was signed by thousands of people. The students appeared before the city council. They worked different bureaucratic avenues, including city officials charged with education, buildings and facilities, and finances.

The students engaged the media in a variety of ways to draw attention to their campaign for a new school. They sent press releases to local and national media, which generated television and newspaper coverage. They did interviews and wrote pieces that were published in print and online. They documented their progress on a website that served as a resource for journalists. They created a video documentary titled *Spectacular Things Happen Along the Way*, which they posted on video-sharing sites such as YouTube and linked to websites.

Not all actions end in success. Despite the best efforts of the students in Room 421, Byrd Academy was closed down, and no new school was built. Still, some good things came out of the experience. The students were relocated to schools for the gifted and talented throughout the city. They went on to relate their story to other groups and inform people about how to work the bureaucracy. Some became involved in other projects to improve their community that were successful.[79]

# 14.5 Recommended Reading

Coglianese, Cary, ed. *Regulatory Breakdown: The Crisis of Confidence in U.S. Regulation*. Philadelphia: University of Pennsylvania Press, 2012.

Fenno, Richard F. Jr. *The President's Cabinet*. Cambridge, MA: Harvard University Press, 1959. The best study of how cabinet secretaries "go native."

Golden, Marissa Martino. *What Motivates Bureaucrats?* New York: Columbia University Press, 2000. An illuminating study of four agencies amid Reagan's administrative presidency.

Goodsell, Charles T. *The New Case for Bureaucracy*. Washington, DC: CQ Press, 2014. A corrective to misconceptions about government bureaucracies.

Heclo, Hugh. *A Government of Strangers*. Washington, DC: Brookings Institution Press, 2011. The classic guide to the relationship between political appointees and civil servants.

Hess, Stephen. *The Government/Press Connection*. Washington, DC: Brookings Institution, 1984. A penetrating, readable account of press operations in the bureaucracy, comparing four disparate agencies.

Light, Paul C. *The True Size of Government*. Washington, DC: Brookings Institution, 1999. An innovative look at how bureaucratic tasks grow even as the civil service stays small.

Weiner, Tim. *Enemies: A History of the F.B.I.* New York: Random House, 2012. A critical discussion focusing on the power, paranoia, and disgraceful behavior of longtime director J. Edgar Hoover

Wilson, James Q. *Bureaucracy: What Government Agencies Do and Why They Do It*. New York: Basic Books, 2000. An examination of the bureaucracy from "the bottom up" that synthesizes experiences from examples.

# 14.6 Recommended Viewing

*Apollo 13* (1995). A jeopardized NASA moon mission saved by bureaucratic ingenuity.

*Catch-22* (1970). Joseph Heller's classic tale of army bureaucracy gone awry.

*A Certain Kind of Death* (2003). A remarkable documentary showing the bureaucrats of the Los Angeles Coroner's Office efficiently and effectively at their somewhat gruesome work.

*The Great Invisible* (2014). Margaret Brown's remarkable documentary on the 2010 explosion of the Deepwater Horizon rig and disastrous oil "spill" and their devastating effects on the lives and livelihoods of the residents and survivors.

*The Invisible War* (2012). Kirby Dick's powerful documentary exposing violence against women in the military.

*MLK/FBI* (2020). Documentary revealing how, at Director Hoover's instigation, in an attempt to destabilize the civil rights movement, the Bureau tracked and recorded thousands of hours of Rev. King.

*The Right Stuff* (1983). An elegy for the passing of the era of the lone hero of the desert test pilot and its succession by politics-bedazzled and publicity-minded astronautics.

*Top Gun* (1986). Probably the most famous hit movie as military recruiting poster. Tom Cruise plays a wild-living American who settles down and grows up to be a navy pilot.

*Welfare* (1975). The great fly-on-the-wall documentarian Frederick Wiseman's inspection of the welfare system and how it affects well-meaning civil servants and welfare recipients alike.

*Well-Founded Fear* (2000). A revealing documentary showing how Immigration and Naturalization Service (INS) officers interview people seeking political asylum to the United States and decide their fate.

# Endnotes


1. Donald P. Warwick, *A Theory of Public Bureaucracy: Politics, Personality, and Organization in the State Department* (Cambridge, MA: Harvard University Press, 1975), 4.
2. Jan P. Vermeer, *The View from the States: National Politics in Local Newspaper Editorials* (Lanham, MD: Rowman & Littlefield, 2002), 93–94.
3. Zachery Kouwe, "In Harsh Reports on S.E.C.'s Fraud Failures, a Watchdog Urges Sweeping Changes," *The New York Times*, September 30, 2009, B10.
4. Paul P. Van Riper, *History of the United States Civil Service* (Evanston, IL: Row, Peterson and Company, 1958), 19.
5. Matthew A. Crenson, *The Federal Machine: Beginnings of Bureaucracy in Jacksonian America* (Baltimore: Johns Hopkins University Press, 1975); Daniel P. Carpenter, *The Forging of Bureaucratic Autonomy: Reputations, Networks, and Policy Innovation in Executive Agencies, 1862–1928* (Princeton, NJ: Princeton University Press, 2001), chap. 2.
6. Ronald N. Johnson and Gary D. Libecap, *The Federal Civil Service System and the Problem of Bureaucracy: The Economics and Politics of Institutional Change* (Chicago: University of Chicago Press, 1994), 18.
7. Ourdocuments.gov, "Pendleton Act (1883)," accessed April 4, 2011, http://www.ourdocuments.gov/doc.php?flash=old&doc=48.
8. Ronald N. Johnson and Gary D. Libecap, *Federal Civil Service System and the Problem of Bureaucracy: The Economics and Politics of Institutional Change* (Chicago: University of Chicago Press, 1994); Stephen Skowronek, *Building a New Administrative State: The Expansion of National Administrative Capacities, 1877–1920* (New York: Cambridge University Press, 1982), chap. 3.
9. Patricia Wallace Ingraham, *The Foundation of Merit: Public Service in American Democracy* (Baltimore: Johns Hopkins University Press, 1995).
10. Richard W. Stevenson, "The Incredible Shrinking Government, Bush Style," *The New York Times*, December 8, 2002, Week in Review, 4.
11. Eric Lichtblau, "Report Faults Aides In Hiring At Justice Department," *The New York Times*, July 29, 2008, A1 and 16.
12. Katherine C. Naff, *To Look Like America: Dismantling Barriers for Women and Minorities in Government* (Boulder, CO: Westview Press, 2001).
13. Marion Burros, "Something to Read Before Your Next Meal," *The New York Times*, April 23, 2003, D3.
14. John T. Tierney, "Government Corporations and Managing the Public's Business," *Political Science Quarterly* 99 (Spring 1984): 73–92.
15. Jack H. Knott and Gary J. Miller, *Reforming Bureaucracy: The Politics of Institutional Choice* (Englewood Cliffs, NJ: Prentice Hall, 1987), 127.
16. Daniel Carpenter and David A. Moss, eds., *Preventing Regulatory Capture: Special Interest Influence and How to Limit It* (New York: Cambridge University Press, 2013).
17. David Gelles and Natalie Kitroeff, "Scathing Report Rebukes Boeing And the F.A.A., *The New York Times*, October 12, 2019, A1 (14); and Niraj Chokshi, "U.S. Faults Disclosure By Boeing On 737 Max," *The New York Times*, July 3, 2020, B4.
18. David Gelles and Natalie Kitroeff, "Scathing Report Rebukes Boeing And the F.A.A., *The New York Times*, October 12, 2019, A1 (14); and Niraj Chokshi, "U.S. Faults Disclosure By Boeing On 737 Max," *The New York Times*, July 3, 2020, B4.
19. Paul C. Light, *The True Size of Government* (Washington, DC: Brookings, 1999), 19–30; also Donald F. Kettl, *Sharing Power: Public Governance and Private Markets* (Washington, DC: Brookings, 1993).
20. Michael Lipsky, *Street-Level Bureaucracy: Dilemmas of the Individual in Public Services* (New York: Russell Sage Foundation, 1980).
21. Paul C. Light, *Thickening Government: Federal Hierarchy and the Diffusion of Accountability* (Washington, DC: Brookings, 1995), 7.
22. United States Department of Labor. OSH Act of 1970. Retrieved from: https://www.osha.gov/laws-regs/oshact/section_2.
23. Cornelius M. Kerwin, *Rulemaking: How Government Agencies Write Law and Make Policy*, 3rd ed. (Washington, DC: CQ Press, 2003), 7–8 and chap. 2.
24. James Q. Wilson, *Bureaucracy: What Government Agencies Do and Why They Do It* (New York: Basic Books, 1989), 42–43.
25. Katharine Q. Seelye, "White House Seeks Changes in Rules on Air Pollution," *The New York Times*, June 14, 2002, A1.
26. Bruce Barcott, "Changing All the Rules," *The New York Times Magazine*, April 4, 2004, 38–44ff.
27. John T. Tierney, *The U.S. Postal Service: Status and Prospects of a Public Enterprise* (Dover, MA: Auburn House, 1988), 2.
28. The distinction of "goal" and "task" is well described in James Q. Wilson, *Bureaucracy: What Government Agencies Do and Why They Do It* (New York: Basic Books, 1989), chap. 3. On the SSA, see Martha Derthick, *Agency under Stress: The Social Security Administration in American Government* (Washington, DC: Brookings, 1990).
29. See William B. Gould IV, *A Primer on American Labor Law*, 2nd ed. (Cambridge, MA: MIT Press, 1986), especially chap.4.
30. Charles E. Lindblom, "The Science of 'Muddling Through,'" *Public Administration Review* 19 (1959): 79–88.
31. Dan B. Wood and Richard W. Waterman, *Bureaucratic Dynamics: The Role of Bureaucracy in a Democracy* (Boulder, CO: Westview Press, 1994), 96.
32. Tim Weiner, *Enemies: A History of the FBI* (New York: Random House, 2012).
33. Herbert Kaufman, *Are Government Organizations Immortal?* (Washington, DC: Brookings, 1976), 9.
34. Daniel A. Mazmanian and Jeanne Nienaber, *Can Organizations Change?: Environmental Protection, Citizen Participation, and the Corps of Engineers* (Washington, DC: Brookings, 1979); and John Brehm and Scott Gates, *Working, Shirking, and Sabotage: Bureaucratic Response to a Democratic Public* (Ann Arbor: University of Michigan Press, 1997).
35. Richard A. Oppel Jr., "Watchdog Says V.A. Officials Lied," *The New York Times*, September 10, 2014, A19.
36. Jada F. Smith, "Veterans Affairs Chief Calls Culture Change Key to Improving System's Health Care," *The New York Times*, November 7, 2014, A15; also Dave Philipps, "After Hospital Scandal, V.A. Officials Jump Ship," *The New York Times*, October 17, 2014, A20; and Richard A. Oppel Jr., "New V.A. Secretary Says Hiring Spree Is Needed To Meet Patient Demand," *The New York Times*, September 9, 2014, A18.
37. David Wood, "VA Secretary Robert McDonald Falsely Claimed He Served In 'Special Forces,'" *Huntington Post*, February 23, 2015.
38. Joel D. Aberbach and Bert A. Rockman, *In the Web of Politics: Three Decades of the U.S. Federal Executive* (Washington, DC: Brookings, 2000), chap. 4.
39. Joel D. Aberbach and Bert A. Rockman, *In the Web of Politics: Three Decades of the U.S. Federal Executive* (Washington, DC: Brookings, 2000), 74.
40. The term was coined by Richard Nathan, *The Plot that Failed: Nixon and the Administrative Presidency* (New York: Wiley, 1975). Richard Nathan developed it beyond the Nixon case in *The Administrative Presidency* (New York: Wiley, 1983).
41. William G. Howell and David E. Lewis, "Agencies By Presidential Design," *Journal of Politics* 64 (2002): 1095–1114.
42. Richard J. Ellis, *Presidential Lightning Rods: The Politics of Blame Avoidance* (Lawrence: University Press of Kansas, 1994).
43. Todd S. Purdum, "Mr. Heat Shield Keeps Boss Happy," *The New York Times*, December 6, 2001, B7.
44. Joan McKinney, "Too Much Mouth—Or a New Policy?," *Baton Rouge Sunday Advocate*, March 10, 2002, 9B.

45. Stephen Labaton, "S.E.C. Suffers from Legacy of Nonbenign Neglect," *The New York Times*, September 20, 2002, B1.
46. Ronald Randall, "Presidential Power versus Bureaucratic Intransigence: The Influence of the Nixon Administration on Welfare Policy," *American Political Science Review* 73 (1979): 795–810.
47. This case study draws from Richard Waterman, *Presidential Influence and the Administrative State* (Knoxville: University of Tennessee Press, 1989), chap. 5; and Marissa Martino Golden, *What Motivates Bureaucrats?* (New York: Columbia University Press, 2000), chap. 6.
48. Quoted in Martha Joynt Kumar, "Communications Operations in the White House of President George W. Bush: Making News on His Terms," *Presidential Studies Quarterly* 33 (2003).
49. Zolan Kanno-Youngs and Michael D. Shear, "Trump Loyalists May Undercut Biden's Agenda on Immigration," *The New York Times, February 4, 2021, A1 (14).*
50. Michael D. Shear and Miriam Jordan, "Immigration Overhaul May Hinge on Finding Rules Buried by Trump," *The New York Times*, February 11, 2021, A19.
51. Richard F. Fenno Jr., *The President's Cabinet* (Cambridge, MA: Harvard University Press, 1959), 226.
52. Katharine Q. Seelye, "Steward of a Department He Once Sought to Scrap," *The New York Times*, August 31, 2003, 24.
53. Louis C. Gawthrop, *Bureaucratic Behavior in the Executive Branch: An Analysis of Organizational Change* (New York: Free Press, 1969), 18.
54. Mordecai Lee, *Congress vs. the Bureaucracy: Muzzling Agency Public Relations* (Norman: University of Oklahoma Press, 2011).
55. David E. Lewis, "The Politics of Agency Termination: Confronting the Myth of Agency Immortality," *Journal of Politics* 64 (2002): 89–107.
56. See Christopher H. Foreman Jr., *Signals from the Hill: Congressional Oversight and the Challenge of Social Regulation* (New Haven, CT: Yale University Press, 1988), 13.
57. Mathew D. McCubbins and Thomas Schwartz, "Congressional Oversight Overlooked: Police Patrols and Fire Alarms," *American Journal of Political Science* 28 (February 1984): 165–79.
58. This section is based on R. Douglas Arnold, *Congress and the Bureaucracy: A Theory of Influence* (New Haven, CT: Yale University Press, 1979).
59. Stephen Hess, *The Government/Press Connection: Press Officers and their Offices* (Washington, DC: Brookings, 1984), 17.
60. Lawrence H. Suid, *Guts and Glory: The Making of the American Military Image in Film* (Lexington: University Press of Kentucky, 2002).
61. On the State Department's noon briefings as policymaking occasions, see Stephen Hess, *The Government/Press Connection: Press Officers and their Offices* (Washington, DC: Brookings, 1984). On the role of news in an agency's internal communication, see Doris A. Graber, *The Power of Communication: Managing Information in Public Organizations* (Washington, DC: CQ Press, 2003), chap. 8.
62. See the report *Deep Water: The Gulf Oil Disaster and the Future of Offshore Drilling,* by the National Commission on the BP Deepwater Horizon Oil Spill and Off-shore Drilling, submitted to President Obama, January 2011.
63. Ian Urbina, "U.S. Said to Allow Drilling Without Needed Permits," *New York Times*, May 13, 2010, A1.
64. Erik Lipton and John M. Broder, "Regulator Deferred to Oil Industry on Rig Safety," *New York Times*, May 8, 2010. Accessed July 2, 2019 at https://www.nytimes.com/2010/05/08/us/08agency.html.
65. Ian Urbina, "In Gulf, It Was Unclear Who Was in Charge of Oil Rig," *New York Times*, June 5, 2010, A1.
66. Mary L. Kendall, "Investigative Report—Island Operating Company, et al.," U.S. Department of the Interior, Office of Inspector General, March 31, 2010, posted to web May 25, 2010, accessed November 11, 2010, http://abcnews.go.com/images/Politics/MMS_inspector_general_report_pdf.pdf.
67. John M. Broder, "Rules Tighten for Oil Regulators to Avoid Favoritism to Drillers," *New York Times*, September 1, 2010, A14.
68. Mark Danner and Hugh Eakin, "The CIA: The Devastating Indictment," *New York Review*, February 5, 2015, 31–32.
69. For example, the *New York Times*, December 10, 2014, A1, 12–14, 16. See also *The Report* (2019), the movie about the program and the CIA's conflict with the Committee.
70. "Ex-CIA Directors: Interrogations Saved Lives," *Wall Street Journal*, December 10, 2014; see also Sheryl Gay Stolberg and Eric Lichtblau, "Ex-Chief Leads Vocal Defense of Spy Agency," *New York Times*, December 13, 2014, A1,3.
71. But for a scathing critique of the agency by a former officer, see John Nixon, *Debriefing the President: The Interrogation of Saddam Hussein* (New York: Blue Rider Press, 2016).
72. A Republican exception was Senator John McCain, who had been tortured when a prisoner in North Vietnam.
73. Lloyd Fair and Hadley Cantril, *The Political Beliefs of Americans* (New York: Free Press, 1967); and Albert H. Cantril and Susan Davis Cantril, *Reading Mixed Signals: Ambivalence in American Public Opinion Toward Government* (Washington, DC: Woodrow Wilson Center Press, 1999).
74. American National Election Studies via https://electionstudies.org/.
75. Pew Research Center on the Press & the Public, "Washington Leaders Wary of Public Opinion: Public Appetite for Government Misjudged," news release, April 17, 1998, http://www.people-press.org/leadrpt.htm with questionnaire results at http://www.people-press.org/leadque.htm.
76. Pew Research Center on the Press & the Public, "Washington Leaders Wary of Public Opinion: Public Appetite for Government Misjudged," April 17, 1998, http://www.people-press.org/leadrpt.htm.
77. Darrell M. West, *Digital Government: Technology and Public Sector Performance* (Princeton, NJ: Princeton University Press, 2005), 179.
78. Martin Linsky, *Impact: How the Press Affects Federal Policy Making* (New York: Norton, 1988), 97.
79. Brian D. Schultz, *Spectacular Things Happen Along the Way* (New York: Teachers College Press, 2008).

CHAPTER 15

# The Courts

## 15.1 Preamble

A brief item in the *Washington Post* titled "A Nation of Stooges" reported that, in a nationwide poll, fewer than 50 percent of Americans could name one justice of the Supreme Court and only 17 percent could name three. In contrast, 59 percent of the people could identify the character names of the comedic trio The Three Stooges.[1]

This is the kind of cute item the media relish reporting; they have, as noted in the aforementioned article, fun with "new facts and hot stats from the social sciences." But the comparison is unfair. The Stooges appeared in close to two hundred short movies still shown on television and available online. Years after their deaths, they remain cult figures known by their nicknames, with apparel, toys, and candy merchandised in their name. In contrast, most Supreme Court justices do not have nicknames, although it is tempting to imagine what they might be. They usually crave anonymity, avoid publicity, keep cameras out of their courtroom, and rarely appear in the media.

In fact, the public's knowledge of the Supreme Court and the justices is greater than most surveys indicate.[2] Moreover, the media are much to blame that it is not higher: their coverage of the Court is sparse compared to that of the president and Congress.

## 15.2 The U.S. Legal System

### Learning Objectives

After reading this section, you should be able to answer the following questions:

1. What are the differences between civil and criminal cases, and how are these cases usually resolved?
2. How do the news and entertainment media depict trials?
3. How are the federal courts organized?
4. How does the Supreme Court work?

The American legal system handles numerous disputes and controversies. Our concern in this text is with civil and criminal cases, the main ways by which courts wield power and influence and make policies.[3]

# Civil Cases

In civil cases, plaintiffs (people or organizations) initiate lawsuits against defendants; courts resolve disputes by deciding or mediating between the two sides. Civil cases can involve money, contracts, property, personal injury, divorce, or child custody. "I'll sue you" is a threat to instigate a civil action.

The vast majority of civil cases, over sixteen million annually, are filed in state courts, compared to around four hundred thousand in federal courts. State and federal laws establish the type of civil cases their courts can hear. For example, because there is no federal divorce law, all divorce cases are heard in state courts; because Social Security is a federal program, all civil disputes involving it are heard in federal courts.

Many people are denied effective access to the courts. Among the reasons: they are unable to afford a lawyer, or the costs of pursuing a lawsuit to conclusion; they are required to submit to arbitration (which usually favors the employer, company, institution) or to a regulatory agency. As a result, particularly in a majority of family law and housing law cases, which are the most common, at least one of the litigants represents himself or herself. In a mortgage foreclosure case initiated by a bank or other lender (who may have inveigled them into taking out the loan in the first place), they are thus likely to lose the case and their home.

Because of their costs and the often lengthy delays until they are heard in court, only about 1.3 percent of civil suits filed go to trial. Most civil cases are resolved by other means, such as settlements, plea deals, mediation, or arbitration. Frequently, borrowers do not contest collection lawsuits (particularly on student loans), allowing creditors to win by default.

# Criminal Cases

Criminal cases are initiated by the government. They run the gamut from misdemeanors, such as trespassing and disorderly conduct, to felonies, such as armed robbery, rape, and murder. Unlike civil cases, criminal cases can result in the loss of liberty: a jail or (rarely) death sentence. Around seven million people in the United States are either in prison, on probation, or on parole for crimes committed; or in prison for violating the terms of their probation or parole. Note that parole has been abolished in the federal system. Many people remain in prison for weeks, months, years, awaiting trial because they cannot afford bail. Most criminal defendants are Black or Latino.[4]

Most criminal laws are passed by states, and the vast majority of criminal cases originate in state courts: roughly twenty-one million criminal cases annually, compared to about seventy-six thousand in federal courts.

Around 27 percent of the criminal cases heard in federal courts involve alleged violations of federal drug laws. Often requiring mandatory sentences without parole, these federal laws are much tougher than state laws, so it makes an enormous difference for the defendant whether a drug offense case is tried in a federal or state court.

**plea bargain**

Agreement whereby a defendant agrees to plead guilty in return for a lighter sentence, a reduced charge, or both.

Only about 3 percent of criminal cases are decided by trial. Prosecutors drop, or do not continue with charges, another 25 percent. Most of the rest are resolved by guilty pleas without going to trial. Even for murder or manslaughter, a majority of defendants plead guilty. This often entails a **plea bargain** negotiated with the prosecutor in which a defendant pleads guilty in exchange for a reduced charge. The judge must approve the plea bargain and usually does so.[5]

Except for affluent defendants with high-powered and well-paid attorneys, people involved in criminal cases have an incentive to plea bargain. Defendants who insist on going to trial face sentences that can be far longer than those received by defendants who plead guilty and cooperate with the government. Other problems defendants face include prosecutors withholding exonerating evidence, faulty identification by witnesses, unreliable forensic science, ineffective and inadequate representation by their defense attorney, and racism.[6]

For lawyers and judges, plea bargains save both time and trial costs and also lighten their workloads. In part because so many plead guilty, around forty-seven million Americans have criminal records.[7] Given the difficulty of calculating accurately, the figure could be far higher—or lower, if people's records in more than one state are excluded or included.

## Media Depictions of Trials

Dubbed "tabloid justice," news depictions of the criminal justice system, especially on cable television, focus on dramatic, sensational, and lurid cases.[8] A notorious instance was the Duke University lacrosse team rape story, which provoked a prodigious amount of often erroneous news coverage as well as outrageous opinions and judgments (notoriously from television commentator Nancy Grace) from March 2006 until April 2007, when all charges against the students were dropped and the case dismissed.

The types of cases receiving excessive and inflammatory coverage include those of a basketball star (Kobe Bryant) charged with rape; an actor (Robert Blake) accused of killing his wife; a decorating diva (Martha Stewart) charged with lying to the FBI; a pop star (Michael Jackson) accused of molesting children; and a mother (Casey Anthony) accused of killing her daughter. The media want, as the chief executive of truTV (formerly Court TV) put it, "the type of trials that have all the melodrama of a soap opera."[9]

Even trials covered live on television may be unrealistic examples of how the U.S. criminal justice system operates. The trial of O. J. Simpson, accused of the murder of his ex-wife and a friend of hers, attracted huge attention from the news media and the public during the mid-1990s. Simpson was a celebrity defendant with sufficient wealth to hire a cast of attorneys and undergo a lengthy trial. In reality, most criminal trials take little time. The Los Angeles Superior Court disposed of nearly fifty-two thousand cases between the time of Simpson's arrest and his acquittal.[10]

**FIGURE 15.1**
**Judge Judy**
Many people's understanding of and opinions about courts are based on watching judges on television.

Source: lev radin/Shutterstock.com

Trials are a staple of entertainment drama.[11] Many television series and their spin-offs involve trials. These shows differ drastically from the reality of courts and trials through the addition of drama and emotion: the highlights of cross-examination, attorneys browbeating witnesses and making speeches, and the guilty confessing. They rarely contain procedural elements, or the issues of "jurisdiction, notices to defendants, pleadings, discovery, and choice of a judge or jury trial, all of which can be argued, replied to, and motioned against."[12] As David E. Kelley, show-runner of *L.A. Law*, creator of *Ally McBeal* and *The Practice*, and a former lawyer, said, "I am writing the world of law in the way I would like it to be. It's all a conceit, because most trials are boring."[13]

Trial judges are usually portrayed on television as legitimate and judicious, and their decisions almost always as correct. Consider the pseudorealistic television courtroom show represented by *Judge Judy*.

Frequent viewers believe that judges should—as these "judges" do—ask questions, be aggressive with litigants, express views about testimony, and make known their opinions about the outcome of the cases.[14] This is, in fact, the opposite of how most real judges behave.

# Organization of the Federal Courts

The first sentence of Article III of the U.S. Constitution created the U.S. Supreme Court—a major innovation. The Articles of Confederation had made no provision for a federal judiciary, only for courts created and controlled by the states.

Article III also gave Congress the authority to create lower federal courts. After the Constitution was ratified in 1789, Congress quickly did so through the Judiciary Act of 1789.

### Link

**The Judiciary Act**

Click here to learn more about the Judiciary Act of 1789.

## The Federal District and Appeals Courts

There are 94 federal district courts staffed by 673 permanent and several temporary judges. Every state has at least one district with a district court in it responsible for hearing cases that arise within that geographic area.

Above the district courts are the federal courts of appeal. They decide whether or not district courts have made an error in conducting a trial. Judges serving on appeals courts base their rulings on written and oral legal arguments presented by lawyers for each side. There are no witnesses, no testimony, and no jury. Appellate courts answer questions of law rather than questions of fact.

There are currently thirteen courts of appeals, twelve of them based on geographic districts called "circuits." There are eleven numbered circuits, each of which has jurisdiction over several states. No state straddles more than one circuit.

There is a twelfth circuit for the District of Columbia (known as the "DC Circuit"). The thirteenth circuit is the court of appeals for the "Federal Circuit," which hears appeals from U.S. Courts of Federal Claims, International Trade, the Patent and Trademark Office, and others. There are approximately 179 judges on the courts of appeals.

A case in district court is usually presided over by one judge, whereas an appeal before a court of appeals is typically heard by a panel of three judges. A majority vote of the panel is necessary to overturn a lower-court ruling. The court of appeals issues a written ruling explaining its decision.

Every litigant in federal court has the right to appeal an unfavorable ruling from the district court. However, because it is expensive to appeal, only about 17 percent of eligible litigants do so. Moreover, higher courts hear few of the cases appealed and rarely reverse lower-court decisions.[15]

## The Supreme Court

The Supreme Court, the nation's highest tribunal, hears cases arising under the Constitution or the laws of the United States. The Constitution gives Congress the authority to set the number of Supreme Court justices, and it has changed the number several times. The Court started with five justices; it now has nine.

The Constitution does not stipulate any specific qualifications, not even a minimum age or legal training, for Supreme Court justices and other federal judges. Of the over one hundred individuals who have served on the Supreme Court, all except five women and two Black males have been white men.

# How the U.S. Supreme Court Works

Article III and the Eleventh Amendment of the Constitution require that the Supreme Court be the first court to hear certain types of cases. This original jurisdiction is limited to cases

- between the United States and one of the states,
- between two or more states,
- involving foreign ambassadors or other ministers,
- brought by one state against citizens of another state or against a foreign country.

Only about 1 percent of the Supreme Court's cases fall under its original jurisdiction. The rest reach it as appeals from civil and criminal cases that have been decided by lower federal and by state courts. As the highest appellate court in the nation, the Supreme Court is the ultimate arbiter in many areas of the law.

If the case involves a federal question, an appeal can be made from the state's appellate court of last resort to the U.S. Supreme Court. A federal question exists if a state law is alleged to violate federal law (an act of Congress), a treaty ratified by the U.S. Senate, or the U.S. Constitution; or because something that state officials do is claimed to violate the Constitution or federal law. Grounds for appeal include evidence gathered from an unreasonable search and seizure, a coerced confession, and infringement of a constitutional right to a fair trial.

With rare exceptions, the Supreme Court has absolute control over the appeals it chooses to hear. Of the roughly seven thousand cases appealed to the Court every year, the justices typically agree to review around seventy-five. They normally decide most of them with comprehensive written opinions during the Court's annual term from October through late June to early July. The Court occasionally issues **per curiam decisions**: brief, unsigned opinions, usually for cases it decides without oral argument.

The justices do not have to give any reasons for accepting or rejecting a case. Even after deciding to hear a case, they can change their minds and **"DIG" (dismiss as improvidently granted)** it: in other words, say that they won't decide the case after all, again without giving any reason.

**per curiam decisions**

Short, unsigned opinions by the Supreme Court, usually for cases it decides without oral argument.

**"DIG" (dismiss as improvidently granted)**

To refuse to hear a case after initially accepting it. Supreme Court justices may change their minds about hearing a case without giving any reason.

## Writ of Certiorari

Most cases reach the Court by way of a **writ of certiorari**. *Certiorari* is Latin for "to make more certain." Litigants who receive an adverse ruling in the federal appeals courts or, in cases involving a federal question, from a state's highest appellate court can submit a petition for a writ of certiorari to the Supreme Court, asking it to review the case.

It takes four of the nine justices to "grant cert." This is called the **Rule of Four**. If the Supreme Court does not grant cert, the lower court ruling is left standing. This does *not* mean that the Supreme Court agrees with that ruling, only that the Court has chosen not to review it.

When the Supreme Court grants cert, it is usually because four or more of the justices believe the case represents an important issue, such as an unresolved constitutional or statutory question on which they are interested in ruling. Sometimes disputes between different courts need to be resolved, or Congress and lower courts need the Court's guidance on the Constitution. However, it is not unknown for justices to avoid granting cert to important cases because they do not want to rule on them.[16]

**writ of certiorari**

Petition asking the Supreme Court to review a case.

**Rule of Four**

Rule stipulating that at least four justices of the Supreme Court must vote to accept an appealed case before it can be heard.

## The Solicitor General

**solicitor general**

Justice department official responsible for presenting the position of the presidential administration before the courts.

The case for cert is strengthened if it is backed by the **solicitor general**, the presidential appointee in the Justice Department responsible for presenting the position of the U.S. government to the courts. The solicitor general screens cases before most agencies of the federal government can appeal them to the Court. Consequently, more than half of the Supreme Court's workload comes from cases under the solicitor general. The justices pay special attention to the recommendations of the solicitor general, nicknamed "the 10th Justice" in the news.

### Link

**The Solicitor General's Office**

Visit the solicitor general's office online here.

## Briefs

**brief**

Written argument presented to a court by lawyers on behalf of clients prior to a hearing.

**amicus curiae brief**

Brief raising additional arguments, filed by a third party to a lawsuit.

When cert is granted, the lawyers for each side file a **brief** making their arguments. Others with a stake in the outcome of the case may, with the permission of the Court, each file an **amicus curiae brief** on behalf of one or the other parties to the case. (They may also persuade the Court to take a case.) Some ideological foundations fund and orchestrate organizations that file briefs. These "friend of the court" briefs expose the justices to additional arguments and enable them, should they be so inclined, to gauge interest-group attention to a case and the amount of support from the different sides.[17]

## Oral Arguments

After reviewing the briefs, the justices hear oral arguments, usually limited to an hour split equally between the sides. The justices often interrupt the attorneys with questions, probe arguments made in the briefs, and raise new issues; they may indicate their thinking about the case and possible decision. A key purpose is to persuade the other justices. The arguments can be used by the justices to reach the legal and policy decisions that they prefer[18]—unless, that is, one side's lawyer makes a more convincing argument than the other.[19] Oral arguments are the only public part of the Supreme Court's work.

### Link

**Oral Arguments Heard by the Supreme Court**

Find and listen to archived oral arguments online here.

## Law Clerks

Each justice selects a few **law clerks** (usually four). They are commonly honors graduates from the most prestigious law schools. They assist in researching cases, deciding which ones to accept, and drafting opinions. Most of the justices share their law clerks to streamline decisions about which cases to hear. They receive a pool memo analyzing each petition for cert and recommending whether or not it should be accepted. Only Justice Samuel A. Alito Jr. and recently confirmed Justice Neil M. Gorsuch do not participate in the pool; they each rely on their own law clerks to review the petitions.[20]

**law clerks**

Assistants to Supreme Court justices, selected to assist them in researching cases, deciding which ones to accept, and drafting opinions.

A clerkship betokens a promising future in the legal profession—the clerks are coveted by prestigious law firms. Because the clerks' work is confidential and rarely revealed, the extent of justices' reliance on their clerks is uncertain. One former clerk writing about the Court charged that the justices granted "great and excessive power to immature, ideologically driven clerks, who in turn use that power to manipulate their bosses."[21] Yet, most justices are so self-confident and versed in the law that it is hard to imagine them being led to make decisions against their will.

## Opinions

Some time after oral arguments, the justices meet in a conference and vote in order of seniority, starting with the chief justice, on how the case should be decided. Many opinions, dubbed "dogs" by the justices, are technical and relatively unimportant. They are "routine cases involving taxes, bankruptcy, pensions, and patents."[22]

### Link

**Supreme Court Decisions**

Click here to read archived Supreme Court decisions.

The Supreme Court decides cases by majority rule: at least five of the nine justices need to agree for a **majority opinion**. They do not, however, have to agree on the reasons for their decision. It is possible for a majority to be composed of justices who agree on their rationale for the decision plus justices who join the decision (but for other reasons) and thus write a joint or individual **concurring opinion**. Justices who disagree with the majority opinion almost always write a **dissenting opinion** or join in a colleague's dissenting opinion, explaining why they think the majority is wrong. On rare occasions, when a justice wants to make a dramatic statement arguing that the majority is profoundly wrong, she or he will read this written dissent aloud in the chamber.

**majority opinion**

Decision by a majority of the members of the Supreme Court.

**concurring opinion**

Decision by a Supreme Court justice that agrees with the majority decision, but for different reasons.

**dissenting opinion**

Decision by one or more Supreme Court justices that disagrees with the majority decision.

**FIGURE 15.2 Conference Room of the Supreme Court**

The intimacy of the Supreme Court is best captured by the conference room, where the nine justices meet to vote on which cases to hear, to discuss opinions, and to decide cases. The junior member of the Court is responsible for opening and closing the doors.

Source: Photo by Theodor Horydczak, http://www.loc.gov/pictures/item/thc1995011442/PP/.

Approximately one-third of the Court's decisions are unanimous. This figure increases to a majority if cases in which only one justice dissented are added. Scholars who have studied this phenomenon "argue that various potential influences all operate in each case and many times, in complex interactive fashion."[23]

Bargaining and compromise can ensue in an effort to create a majority coalition.[24] A study of justices' conference notes concludes that the Court's decisions come from "an intricate and shifting composite of law, politics, policy, principle, efficiency, expedience, pragmatism, dogmatism, reason, passion, detachment, individual personality, group psychology, institutional forces, and external pressures."[25] To this list, we would add the desire for approval from social groups with which they identify or associate and from the legal community of law professors and law students.[26]

The chief justice, if voting with the majority, which for current Chief Justice John G. Roberts Jr. is often the case, determines who will write its opinion. Thus, many of the Court's most important decisions are penned by the chief justice.[27] He (someday, she) may also assign the opinion to a "swing" justice (one who could decide either way), thereby ensuring that justice becomes part of the majority.[28]

If the chief justice is not in the majority, the justice in the majority who has served on the Court the longest takes on the assignment of determining who will write its opinion.

## Key Takeaways

Most criminal cases are decided by plea bargains. A few trials attract excessive coverage in news and entertainment media, which depict them unrealistically. The federal court system consists of ninety-four district courts, with at least one in each state, and thirteen appeals courts, each one with jurisdiction over several states. At the top of the judicial system is the Supreme Court. Its decisions involve briefs, oral arguments, conferences, clerks, and opinions.

## Exercises

1. Why do you think our legal system makes a distinction between civil and criminal cases? What are the key differences between the two types of cases?
2. Why do you think the media devote more coverage to the president and to Congress than to the Supreme Court? What impression of our legal system do you get from the media?
3. How many Supreme Court decisions can you name? How might your life be different if those cases had been decided differently?

# 15.3 Power of the U.S. Supreme Court

## Learning Objectives

After reading this section, you should be able to answer the following questions:

1. What is judicial review?

2. Why is *Marbury v. Madison* important?
3. What is judicial power, and how is it constrained?
4. What are the leading judicial philosophies?
5. How important are judges' ideologies and political preferences in their decisions?

In Federalist No. 78, Alexander Hamilton described the courts as "the least dangerous" branch of government because they have no direct power over "sword or purse." President Andrew Jackson (a former Indian fighter) is reputed to have said of the Supreme Court decision favoring Indigenious Americans, that Chief Justice "John Marshall has made his decision; now let him enforce it."[29] Certainly, officials charged with enforcing Supreme Court orders can sometimes evade them.[30] Yet, the Justices do possess considerable power. For example, because of the Court's 5–4 decision in 2002, the more than seven million public high school students engaged in "competitive" extracurricular activities—including cheerleading, Future Farmers of America, Spanish club, and choir—can be required to submit to random drug testing.[31]

# Judicial Review

The federal courts' most significant power is **judicial review**. Exercising it, they can refuse to apply a state or federal law because, in their judgment, it violates the U.S. Constitution.

**judicial review**

The authority of the federal courts, especially the Supreme Court, to decide whether a state or federal law violates the U.S. Constitution.

## *Marbury v. Madison*

Judicial review was asserted by the U.S. Supreme Court in 1803 in the decision of Chief Justice John Marshall in the case of *Marbury v. Madison* (5 US 137, 1803).

After losing the election of 1800, John Adams made a flurry of forty-two appointments of justices of the peace for Washington, DC, in the last days of his presidency. His purpose in doing so was to ensure that the judiciary would remain dominated by his Federalist party. The Senate approved the appointments, and Secretary of State John Marshall stamped the officials' commissions with the Great Seal of the United States. But no one in the outgoing administration delivered the signed and sealed commissions to the appointees. The new president, Thomas Jefferson, instructed his secretary of state, James Madison, not to deliver them. One appointee, William Marbury, sued, asking the Supreme Court to issue a writ of mandamus, a court order requiring Madison to hand over the commission.

**FIGURE 15.3**
**John Marshall**
Marshall was chief justice of the Supreme Court from 1801 to 1835 and the author of many decisions, including *Marbury v. Madison*.

Source: Everett Historical / Shutterstock.com

The case went directly to the Supreme Court under its original jurisdiction. John Marshall was now chief justice, having been appointed by Adams and confirmed by the Senate. He had a dilemma: a prominent Federalist, he was sympathetic to Marbury, but President Jefferson would likely refuse to obey a ruling from the Court in Marbury's favor. However, ruling in favor of Madison would permit an executive official to defy the provisions of the law without penalty.

Marshall's solution was a political masterpiece. The Court ruled that Marbury was entitled to his commission and that Madison had broken the law by not delivering it. But it also ruled that the part of the Judiciary Act of 1789 granting the Court the power to issue writs of mandamus was unconstitutional because it expanded the original jurisdiction of the Supreme Court beyond its definition in Article III; this expansion could only be done by a constitutional amendment. Therefore, Marbury's suit could not be heard by the Supreme Court. The decision simultaneously supported Marbury and the Federalists, did not challenge Jefferson and relinquished the Court's power to issue writs of mandamus. Above all, it asserted the prerogative of judicial review for the Supreme Court.[32]

## Judicial Review Assessed

For forty years after *Marbury*, the Court did not overturn a single law of Congress. And when it finally did, it was the Dred Scott decision, which dramatically damaged the Court's power. The Court ruled that people of African descent who were slaves (and their descendants, whether or not they were slaves) were not protected by the Constitution and could never be U.S. citizens. The Court also held that the U.S. Congress had no authority to prohibit slavery in federal territories.[33]

The pace of judicial review picked up in the 1960s and continues to this day. The Supreme Court has invalidated an average of eighteen federal laws per decade. The Court has displayed even less compunction about voiding state laws. For example, the famous *Brown v. Board of Education of Topeka, Kansas* desegregation case overturned statutes from Kansas, Delaware, South Carolina, and Virginia that either required or permitted segregated public schools. The average number of state and local laws invalidated per decade is 122, although it has fluctuated from a high of 195 to a low for the period 2000–2008 of 34.[34]

Judicial review can be seen as asserting the power of the Supreme Court and reinforcing the system of checks and balances. It is a way of policing the actions of Congress, the president, and state governments to ensure that they are in accord with the Constitution. But its power may be less decisive than it seems. For one scholar, although judicial review enables it to supervise the legislative branch, the Court has tended to remain subservient to the executive branch.[35] Another scholar, who studied several prominent judicial review rulings, found that "courts were unable to settle constitutional debates, and in addition were often unable to achieve their policy aims or did not actually require other political actors to do anything."[36] Moreover, whether an act violates the Constitution is often sharply debated, not least by members of the Court.

# Constraints on Judicial Power

There are three types of constraints on the power of the Supreme Court and lower court judges: precedents, internal limitations, and external checks.

## Ruling by Precedent

**precedent**

A previous court decision used to guide and justify the Court's decision in a similar case.

Judges look to **precedent**, previously decided cases, to guide and justify their decisions.[37] They are usually expected to follow the principle of *stare decisis*, which is Latin for "to stand on the decision." They identify the similarity between the case under consideration and previous ones. Then they apply the rule of law contained in the earlier case or cases to the current case. Often, one side is favored by the evidence and the precedents.

Precedents, however, have less of an influence on judicial power than would be expected. According to a study, "justices interpret precedent in order to move existing precedents closer to their preferred outcomes and to justify new policy choices."[38]

Precedents may erode over time. The 1954 Brown school desegregation decision overturned the 1896 Plessy decision that had upheld the constitutionality of separate but equal facilities and thus segregation.[39] Or they may be overturned relatively quickly. In 2003, the Supreme Court by 6–3 struck down a Texas law that made homosexual acts a crime, overruling the Court's decision seventeen years earlier upholding a similar antisodomy law in Georgia. The previous case "was not correct when it was decided, and it is not correct today," Justice Anthony M. Kennedy wrote for the majority.[40]

Judges may disagree about which precedents apply to a case. Consider students wanting to use campus facilities for prayer groups: if this is seen as violating the separation of church and state, they lose their case; if it is seen as freedom of speech, they win it. Precedents may allow a finding for either party, or a case may involve new areas of the law.

## Internal Limitations

For the courts to exercise power, there must be a case to decide: a controversy between legitimate adversaries who have suffered or are about to suffer in some way. The case must be about the protection or enforcement of legal rights or the redress of wrongs. Judges cannot solicit cases, although they can use their decisions to signal their willingness to hear (more) cases in particular policy areas.

Judges, moreover, are expected to follow the Constitution and the law despite their policy preferences. In a speech to a bar association, Supreme Court Justice John Paul Stevens regretted two of his majority opinions, saying he had no choice but to uphold the federal statutes.[41] That the Supreme Court was divided on these cases indicates, however, that some of the other justices interpreted the laws differently.

A further internal limitation is that judges are obliged to explain and justify their decisions to the courts above and below. The Supreme Court's written opinions are subject to scrutiny by other judges, law professors, lawyers, elected officials, the public, and of course, the media.

## External Checks on Power

The executive and legislative branches can check or try to check judicial power. Through their authority to nominate federal judges, presidents influence the power and direction of the courts by filling vacancies with people likely to support their policies.

Presidents may object to specific decisions in speeches, press conferences, or written statements. In his 2010 State of the Union address, with six of the justices seated in front of him, President Obama criticized the Supreme Court's expansive decision that corporations have a First Amendment right to make unlimited expenditures in candidate elections.[42]

Presidents can engage in frontal assaults. Following his overwhelming reelection victory, President Franklin D. Roosevelt proposed to Congress in February 1937 that another justice be added to the Supreme Court for each sitting justice over the age of seventy. This would have increased the number of justices on the court from nine to fifteen. His ostensible justification was the Court's workload and the ages of the justices. Actually, he was frustrated by the Court's decisions, which gutted his New Deal economic programs by declaring many of their measures unconstitutional.

The president's proposal was damned by its opponents as unwarranted meddling with the constitutionally guaranteed independence of the judiciary. It was further undermined when the justices pointed out that they were quite capable of coping with their workload, which was not at all excessive. Media coverage, editorials, and commentary were generally critical, even hostile to the proposal, framing it as "court packing" and calling it a "scheme." The proposal seemed a rare blunder on FDR's part. But while Congress was debating it, one of the justices shifted to the Roosevelt side in a series of regulatory cases, giving the president a majority on the court at least for these cases. This led to the famous aphorism "a switch in time saves nine." Within a year, two of the conservative justices retired and were replaced by staunch Roosevelt supporters.[43]

Congress can check judicial power. It overcomes a decision of the Court by writing a new law or rewriting a law to meet the Court's constitutional objections without altering the policy. It can threaten to—and sometimes succeed in—removing a subject from the Court's jurisdiction, or propose a constitutional amendment to undo a Court decision.

Indeed, the first piece of legislation signed by President Obama overturned a 5–4 Supreme Court 2007 decision that gave a woman a maximum of six months to seek redress after receiving the first check for less pay than her peers.[44] Named after the woman who at the end of her nineteen-year career complained that she had been paid less than men, the Lilly Ledbetter Fair Pay Act extends the period to six months after *any* discriminatory paycheck. It also applies to anyone seeking redress for pay discrimination based on race, religion, disability, or age.

The Constitution grants Congress the power to impeach judges. But since the Constitution was ratified, the House has impeached only eleven federal judges, and the Senate has convicted just five of them. They were convicted for such crimes as bribery, racketeering, perjury, tax evasion, incompetence, and insanity, but not for wrongly interpreting the law.

**FIGURE 15.4 Controversial Warren Court**

The controversial decisions of the Warren Court inspired a movement to impeach the chief justice.

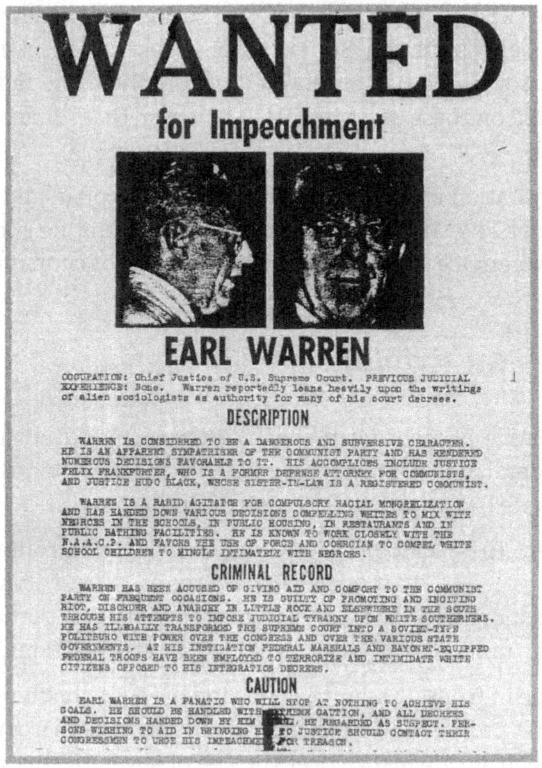


Source: Wikimedia: http://en.wikipedia.org/wiki/File:Impeach_Warren.png.

The Supreme Court may lose power if the public perceives it as going too far. Politicians and interest groups criticize, even condemn, and fail to implement particular decisions. They stir up public indignation against the Court and individual justices. This happened to Chief Justice Earl Warren and his colleagues during the 1950s for their school desegregation and other civil rights decisions.

How the decisions and reactions to them are framed in media reports can support or undermine the decisions' effectiveness and the Court's legitimacy. (See "Comparing Content" below.)

## Comparing Content

### *Brown v. Board of Education of Topeka, Kansas*

How a decision can be reported and framed differently is illustrated by news coverage of the 1954 Supreme Court school desegregation ruling.

The *New York Times* of May 18, 1954, presents the decision as monumental and historic, and school desegregation as both necessary and desirable. Southern opposition is acknowledged but downplayed, as is the difficulty of implementing the decision. The front-page headline states

"High Court Bans School Segregation; 9–0 Decision Grants Time to Comply." A second front-page article is headlined "Reactions of South." Its basic theme is captured in two prominent paragraphs: "underneath the surface . . . it was evident that many Southerners recognized that the decision had laid down the legal principle rejecting segregation in public education facilities" and "that it had left open a challenge to the region to join in working out a program of necessary changes in the present bi-racial school systems."[45]

There is an almost page-wide photograph of the nine members of the Supreme Court. They look particularly distinguished, legitimate, authoritative, decisive, and serene.

In the South, the story was different. The *Atlanta Constitution* headlined its May 18, 1954, story "Court Kills Segregation in Schools: Cheap Politics, Talmadge Retorts." By using "Kills" instead of the *Times*'s "Bans," omitting the fact headlined in the *Times* that the decision was unanimous, and including the reaction from Georgia Governor Herman E. Talmadge, the *Constitution* depicted the Court's decision far more critically than the *Times*. This negative frame was reinforced by the headlines of the other stories on its front page. "Georgia's Delegation Hits Ruling" announces one; "Segregation To Continue, School Officials Predict" is a second. Another story quotes Georgia's attorney general as saying that the "Ruling Doesn't Apply to Georgia" and pledging a long fight.

The *Times*'s coverage supported and legitimized the Supreme Court's decision. Coverage in the *Atlanta Constitution* undermined it.

External pressure is also applied when the decisions, composition, and future appointments to the Supreme Court become issues during presidential elections.[46] In a May 6, 2008, speech at Wake Forest University, Republican presidential candidate Senator John McCain said that he would nominate for the Supreme Court "men and women with . . . a proven commitment to judicial restraint." Speaking to a Planned Parenthood convention on July 17, 2007, Senator Barack Obama identified his criteria as "somebody who's got the heart, the empathy, to recognize what it's like . . . to be poor or African American or gay or disabled or old."[47]

# Judges as Policymakers

Judges have power because they decide cases: they interpret the Constitution and laws, and select precedents. These decisions often influence, even make, public policy and have important ramifications for social conflict. For example, the Supreme Court has declared term limits for members of Congress unconstitutional, and it has upheld state laws making it extremely difficult for third parties to challenge the dominance of the two major parties.[48]

## Judicial Philosophies

How willing judges are to make public policy depends in part on their judicial philosophies.[49] Some follow **judicial restraint**, deciding cases on the narrowest grounds possible. In interpreting federal laws, they defer to the views expressed in Congress by those who made the laws. They shy away from invalidating laws and the actions of government officials. They tend to define some issues as political questions that should be left to the other branches of government or the voters. When the Constitution is silent, ambiguous, or open ended on a subject (e.g., "freedom of speech," "due process of law," and "equal protection of the laws"), they look to see whether the practice being challenged is a long-standing American tradition. They are inclined to adhere to precedent.

**judicial restraint**

Judicial philosophy whereby judges decide cases on the narrowest grounds possible by, for example, deferring to the legislature's decisions.

**strict constructionism**

Judicial philosophy of applying the Constitution according to what the judges believe was its original meaning to a reasonable person when it was framed.

**judicial activism**

Judicial philosophy whereby judges are willing to substitute their policy views for the policy actions or inaction of the other branches of government.

**loose constructionism**

Judicial philosophy embodying the view that the Constitution requires interpretation to respond to changing public needs.

Judicial restraint is sometimes paired with **strict constructionism**. Judges apply the Constitution according to what they believe was its original meaning as understood by a reasonable person when the Constitution was written. In sum, their judicial philosophy is originalism and textualism.

Other judges follow a philosophy of **judicial activism** (although they may not call it that). Activist judges are willing to substitute their policy views for the policy actions or inaction of the other branches of government.

Judicial activism is often paired with **loose constructionism**, viewing the Constitution as a living document that the founders left deliberately ambiguous. In interpreting the Constitution, these judges are responsive to what they see as changes in society and its needs. A plurality of the Supreme Court found a right to privacy implicit in the Constitution and used it to overturn a Connecticut law prohibiting the use of contraceptives.[50] The justices later used that privacy right as a basis for the famous *Roe v. Wade* decision, "discovering" a woman's constitutional right to an abortion.

The distinction between judicial restraint and strict constructionism on the one hand and judicial activism and loose constructionism on the other can become quite muddy. In 1995, the Supreme Court, by a 5–4 vote, struck down the Gun-Free School Zone Act—an attempt by Congress to keep guns out of schools.[51] The ruling was that Congress had overstepped its authority and that only states had the power to pass such laws. This decision by the conservative majority, interpreting the Constitution according to what it believed was the original intentions of the framers, exemplified strict constructionism. It also exemplified judicial activism: for the first time in fifty years, the Court curtailed the power of Congress under the Constitution's commerce clause to interfere with local affairs.[52] A 5–4 conservative majority has also interpreted the Second Amendment to prohibit the regulation of guns.[53] This decision, too, could be seen as activist.

Relatedly, a decision based on judicial restraint can have liberal, even radical, policy effects. Justice Neil Gorsuch has ruled for a six to three majority (including Chief Justice John Roberts) that an employer firing an employee for being gay or transgender violated the law, specifically the literal words of the Civil Rights Act. In his dissent, the conservative Justice Samuel Alito called the ruling "preposterous."[54]

## Political Views in Action

One doesn't have to believe that judges are politicians in black robes to understand the relevance of ideology to some of their decisions. Ideology is based on their values, on their affiliations with social groups such as business, and with political groups such as political parties. Ideological perspectives can translate into, even permeate, their positions on the issues before them. Some judges' decisions are influenced, if not determined, by their ideology.[55] The Roberts' Court has consistently favored business; for example, ruling that companies can require customers to relinquish their right to sue in court so that suits have to be settled by a private arbitrator, usually favoring the company.[56]

Most decisively, based on a past half-century of research, scholar Adam Cohen argues that the Supreme Court has exacerbated economic inequality.[57]

Judges may also be influenced by their political preferences.[58] Those appointed by a Democratic president are more liberal than those appointed by a Republican president on labor and economic regulation, civil rights and liberties, and criminal justice.[59] Republican and Democratic federal court judges decide differently on contentious issues such as abortion, racial integration and racial preferences, church-state relations, environmental protection, and LGBTQ+ rights.[60]

These differences lead to "forum shopping" in which lawyers, if they have the the opportunity, file their cases in jurisdictions likely to favor them. A notorious judge has been Reed O'Connor, the only active judge in the Fort Worth Division of the Federal District Court for the Northern District of Texas. He has consistently ruled for Texas and other states in major cases against the Obama administration on its health-care law and other legislation.[61]

On occasions, the Supreme Court renders a controversial decision that graphically reveals its power and is seen as motivated by political partisanship. In December 2000, the Court voted 5–4, with the five most conservative justices in the majority, that the Florida Election Code's "intent of the voter" standard provided insufficient guidance for manually recounting disputed ballots and that there was no time left to conduct recounts under constitutionally acceptable standards.[62] This ensured that Republican George W. Bush would become president.

The decision was widely reported and discussed in the media. Defenders framed it as principled, based on legal considerations. Critics deplored it as legally frail and politically partisan. They quoted the bitter comment of dissenting Justice Stevens: "Although we may never know with complete certainty the identity of the winner of this year's presidential election, the identity of the loser is perfectly clear. It is the nation's confidence in the judge as an impartial guardian of the rule of law."[63]

### Key Takeaways

In this section, we have explained how judicial review originated, how it is exercised, and what its effects are. We described the power of the courts, especially of the Supreme Court, and how it may be constrained by precedent, internal limitations, and external pressures. Justices make policy and may be influenced by their judicial philosophies, ideologies, and political preferences.

### Exercises

1. What role does judicial review play in our legal system? Why might it be important for the Supreme Court to have the power to decide if laws are unconstitutional?
2. In *Marbury v. Madison*, how did Chief Justice Marshall strike a balance between asserting the Supreme Court's authority and respecting the president's authority? Do you think justices should take political factors into account when ruling on the law?
3. Why do you think it might be important for judges to follow precedent? What do you think would happen if judges ignored precedent?
4. Which of the four judicial philosophies described in the text makes the most sense to you? What do you think the advantages and disadvantages of that philosophy might be?
5. In what ways might judges be "politicians in black robes?"

## 15.4 Selecting Federal Judges

### Learning Objectives

After reading this section, you should be able to answer the following questions:

1. What factors influence the selection of federal judges?
2. What is the confirmation process?
3. Under what circumstances are the media important in the confirmation (or not) of Supreme Court nominees?
4. Why are some nominations unsuccessful and others successful?

The president nominates all judges to the federal courts. President George W. Bush's nominees were screened by a committee of fifteen White House and Justice Department officials headed by the White House legal counsel. They looked for ideological purity, party affiliation, and agreement with the president on policy issues, often turning to the Federalist Society for nominees.[64] President Trump relied entirely on recommendations from the Federalist Society, which has provided him with lists to choose from of ideologically pure conservatives to nominate for the Supreme and lower courts.

Other factors sometimes influencing who is nominated are the nominee's characteristics (gender, ethnicity, race), time remaining in the president's term and, when they exist, divided government and interest group support and opposition.

The candidate's home state senators may also be relevant through the "blue slip" custom whereby both of them must sign off on the nominee to allow a committee hearing. They thereby can (and do) block nominees to judgeships in their states. President Obama had to reach agreement about the acceptability of his nominees with any Republican senator in a state where he nominated a judge.

The selection of judges for the lower federal courts is important because almost all federal cases end there. Thus, through these appointments, a president "has the opportunity to influence the course of national affairs for a quarter of a century or more after he leaves office."[65]

Following selection by the president, nominees are usually considered by the Senate Judiciary Committee, which holds hearings on their (variously and broadly defined) fitness for office. Whether senators should concern themselves with anything more than the nominee's professional qualifications is often debated. Arguably, "nothing in the Constitution, historical experience, political practice, ethical norms, or statutory enactments prohibits senators from asking questions that reveal judicial nominees' views on political and ideological issues."[66] If approved by a majority of the committee, nominations are normally sent to the Senate floor for a vote of approval or disapproval.

But this process is not always followed, particularly during a time of divided government. After the 2014 election, with a majority in the Senate, Republicans were reluctant to consider President Obama's judicial nominees, and thereby left some judgeships unfilled.

Then, after the 2016 election, during President Trump's four years in office and with a majority in the Senate, Republicans obtained Senate Judiciary Committee and floor confirmation of 174 district court judges, 54 appeals court judges, and 3 Supreme Court justices, most of them conservative; almost as many as his predecessors appointed in eight years.

It used to be that Senate floor approval vote was subject to the filibuster, but in November 2013, the Senate voted to change the Senate filibuster rules. Now, debate on executive and judicial nominations could be ended by a simple majority of senators instead of the sixty previously required. Initially, the new rule did not apply to Supreme Court nominees. That would be changed with the confirmation of Neil Gorsuch in 2017.

Once in office, federal judges can be removed only by impeachment and conviction. Unless compelled to retire due to illness or incapacity, judges may time their departures so that their replacements are appointed by a president who shares their political views and policy preferences.[67] Supreme Court Justice David Souter retired in 2009 and Justice John Paul Stevens retired in 2010, enabling President Obama to nominate, and the Democratic-controlled Senate to confirm, their successors.

## Choosing Supreme Court Justices

In nominating Supreme Court justices, presidents seek to satisfy their political, policy, and personal goals.[68] They do not always succeed; justices sometimes change their views over time or may surprise the president from the start. "Biggest damfool mistake I ever made," said President Dwight D. Eisenhower about his appointment of Chief Justice Earl Warren, who led the Supreme Court's liberal decisions on civil rights and criminal procedure. Table 15.1 discusses important factors that influence presidents' choices of Supreme Court nominees.[69]

**TABLE 15.1 Factors Presidents Use When Choosing Supreme Court Nominees**

| Factor | Explanation |
|---|---|
| Senate composition | Whether the president's party has a majority or a minority in the Senate. In 1990, when the Democrats had a majority, Republican President George H. W. Bush nominated the judicially experienced and reputedly ideologically moderate David H. Souter, who was easily approved. |
| Timing | The closer to an upcoming presidential election the appointment occurs, the more necessary it is to appoint a highly qualified, noncontroversial figure acceptable to the Senate, or at least someone senators would be reluctant to reject. Otherwise, senators have an incentive to stall until after the election, when it may be too late to obtain confirmation. |
| Public approval of the president | The higher the president's approval ratings, the more nominating leeway the president possesses. But even presidents riding a wave of popularity can fail to get their nominees past the Senate, as was the case with Richard Nixon and his failed nominations of Clement Haynsworth and G. Harrold Carswell in 1970. So lacking were Carswell's qualifications that a senator defended him saying "Even if he were mediocre, there are a lot of mediocre judges and people and lawyers. They are entitled to a little representation . . . and a little chance."[70] |
| Interest groups | Nominees must usually be acceptable to interest groups that support the president and invulnerable (or at least resistant) to being depicted negatively—for example, as ideological extremists—by opposition groups, in ways that would significantly reduce their chances of Senate approval. |

# The Media and Supreme Court Nominees

Presidents have few opportunities to nominate Supreme Court justices, so the media provide intensive coverage of every stage of the nomination, from the time an incumbent justice leaves office until a replacement is confirmed by the Senate. The scrutiny is not necessarily damaging. President Clinton's nominees, Ruth Bader Ginsburg and Stephen Breyer, enjoyed Senate confirmation by votes of 97–3 and 87–9, respectively.

Sometimes the media determine a nominee's fate. President Reagan's nominee Douglas H. Ginsburg withdrew when news stories reported that he had smoked marijuana with some of his Harvard Law School students. The media were also intimately involved with the fates of other nominees, particularly Robert H. Bork, Clarence Thomas, and Brett M. Kavanaugh, through their coverage of and commentary on the Senate Judiciary Committee's hearings.

## The Nomination of Robert H. Bork

Bork was a distinguished lawyer who had taught at Yale University, served as solicitor general and acting attorney general of the United States, and was a judge on the U.S. Court of Appeals for the DC Circuit. He opposed civil rights laws and such Supreme Court decisions as *Roe v. Wade* allowing abortion. More than three hundred, mostly liberal, interest groups publicly opposed him.

The anti-Bork coalition adroitly used the media against him. It barraged two thousand journalists and seventeen hundred editorial writers with detailed packets of material criticizing him. It sponsored television and newspaper advertisements attacking him and asking Americans to urge their senators to vote against him.[71]

**"murder boards"**

Sessions in which nominees for the Supreme Court are coached by administration officials on how to respond effectively to tough questions from senators at their hearings.

The nominee, touted by his supporters as urbane, witty, and brilliant, contributed to the demise of his candidicy by the impression he made on national television during five contentious days of hearings, during which he candidly testified about his legal and political philosophy, defended his views on issues and cases, and responded to questions from members of the Senate Judiciary Committee. Having refused the practice sessions (known as **"murder boards"**) and coaching offered by the White House, the professorial, scraggly bearded Bork was outmaneuvered by his opponents on the committee, who came up with such sound bites—featured on the evening television news—as "You are not a frightening man, but you are a man with frightening views."[72]

**"to bork"**

To defeat a Supreme Court nominee by means of a lobbying and public relations campaign using and facilitated by the media.

The Senate rejected the nominee on October 23, 1987, by a vote of 58–42. The process generated a new verb in politics: "**to bork**," which means to unleash a lobbying and public relations campaign, using and facilitated by the media.

**FIGURE 15.5** Robert Bork with President Reagan

Self-confident at his public nomination by President Reagan, Bork would be defeated by the campaign waged against him by his opponents.

Source: Series: Reagan White House Photographs, 1/20/1981 - 1/20/1989 Collection: White House Photographic Collection, 1/20/1981 - 1/20/1989 [Public domain]; https://commons.wikimedia.org/wiki/File:President_Ronald_Reagan_Meeting_with_Judge_Robert_Bork_in_The_Oval_Office.jpg.

## Link

**The Bork Hearings**

Watch video of the Bork hearings online here.

## The Confirmation of Clarence Thomas

When a similar attack was waged against Clarence Thomas in the fall of 1991, the White House and the nominee's defenders were ready with a highly organized public relations campaign.

President George H. W. Bush nominated Clarence Thomas for the seat of retiring Justice Thurgood Marshall. Both were Black men. But in contrast to the liberal Democrat Marshall, Thomas was a conservative Republican. The nomination was opposed by leaders of liberal and feminist organizations, and supported by their conservative counterparts. It divided the civil rights community, which wanted a Black justice, but not one as conservative as Thomas.

Because the nomination was shrewdly announced on the Monday afternoon preceding the Fourth of July weekend, reporters only had time to transmit the favorable story, spoon-fed from the White House, of the nominee's rise from poverty to prominence. Later, they reported some of his more controversial decisions during his one-year tenure as a federal appeals court judge.

News coverage of the nomination resumed with the Senate Judiciary Committee's hearings during which Thomas, in contrast to Bork, steadfastly avoided taking clear stands on controversial issues. He had been told by his White House advisors to "(1) stress his humble roots; (2) [not] engage Senators in ideological debate; and (3) stonewall on abortion."[73] At the conclusion of the hearings, Senate confirmation seemed narrowly assured. Then law professor Anita Hill accused Thomas of having engaged in sexual improprieties when she worked for him at the Department of Education and the Equal Employment Opportunity Commission.

With the salacious accusations, media coverage skyrocketed, especially when the hearings reopened featuring Hill's testimony and Thomas's rebuttals. Entertainment media made light of the issue: on *Saturday Night Live*, Chris Rock observed that "if Clarence Thomas looked like Denzel Washington this thing would never have happened." Thomas angrily denounced his detractors for carrying out "a high-tech lynching for uppity blacks who in any way deign to think for themselves." In the end, most senators voted as they had been leaning prior to Hill's testimony. Thomas was confirmed by a vote of 52–48.

### Links

**The Thomas Hearings**

Watch the Thomas hearings online here and here.

## The Confirmation of John G. Roberts Jr.

In July 2005, President George W. Bush made the first Supreme Court nomination in eleven years. He chose John G. Roberts Jr., a federal appeals court judge on the DC Circuit, to replace the moderate Republican Sandra Day O'Connor, who was retiring. Roberts was then nominated to be chief justice after the death of incumbent William H. Rehnquist.

During three days of testifying before the Senate Judiciary Committee, the erudite and engaging Roberts compared judges to umpires and deflected questions, saying that he would be guided by the law. On September 29, 2005, the Republican-controlled Senate approved him as chief justice of the U.S. Supreme Court by a vote of 78–22.

### Link

**John G. Roberts Jr.'s Opening Statement**

Watch the opening statement of John G. Roberts Jr. online here.

**FIGURE 15.6 Supreme Court Nominees and the Media**
The media pays intense attention to Supreme Court nominees. In this photo George W. Bush holds a press conference to announce that he has nominated John G. Roberts Jr. to succeed William H. Rehnquist as chief justice.

Source: Charles Dharapak/Associated Press

## The Nomination of Harriet Miers and Confirmation of Samuel A. Alito Jr.

Bush next turned to fill Sandra Day O'Connor's vacant seat. He was under pressure, even in public statements from his wife, to appoint a woman to succeed O'Connor. He nominated his White House general counsel and close friend, Harriet Miers. She had never served as a judge, had little expertise on constitutional matters, and held few reported positions on important issues.

Conservatives, including officeholders, interest-group leaders, columnists, pundits, and bloggers, rejected the president's assurance that she was a candidate they could trust to rule as a reliable conservative. Leaders of the Senate Judiciary Committee rejected her answers to their questions as "inadequate, insufficient and insulting." Senators expressed doubts to the news media about her qualifications and knowledge of the Constitution. After twenty-four days of a ferocious barrage of criticism, all reported and amplified by the media, Ms. Miers withdrew from consideration.

President Bush then nominated a federal appeals court judge, Samuel A. Alito Jr. The judge had a consistent conservative record from his time in the Reagan administration and from fifteen years of judicial decisions of deferring to the executive branch, favoring business, and rejecting abortion rights.

In testifying before the members of the Senate Judiciary Committee, Judge Alito followed the stonewalling script. Nothing he said could be used against him by Democratic senators on the committee or by the media. A dramatic moment in his favor, shown on television, occurred when his wife, upset by the questioning directed at him, walked out of the hearings in tears. Soon after the hearings, Judge Alito was approved by 58–42 (54 Republicans plus 4 Democrats against 40 Democrats plus 1 Republican and 1 Independent).

### Links

**The Miers Nomination**

Click here to learn more about the Miers nomination.

**The Alito Confirmation**

Click here to learn more about the Alito confirmation.

## The Confirmations of Sonia Sotomayor and Elena Kagan

When Justice Souter resigned from the Court, President Obama, making his first nomination, picked Federal Appeals Court Judge Sonia Sotomayor to replace him. Her confirmation hearings in July 2009 followed the script that had worked for Roberts and Alito. She refused to opine about cases or identify a judicial philosophy other than "fidelity to the law." Sotomayor would be the first Latinx and third woman ever appointed to the Court. She would not change its ideological balance, and there were no media revelations to derail her prospects. Since the Democrats had sixty votes in the Senate, it came as no surprise that she was confirmed by a vote of 68–31.

A similar pattern followed the resignation of Justice John Paul Stevens. Obama's nominee, solicitor general and former dean of Harvard Law School Elena Kagan, was unlikely to change the ideological balance on the Court. She, too, largely stonewalled the hearings and was confirmed by the Senate on August 5, 2010, by a vote of 63–37.

### Links

**The Sotomayor Confirmation**

Click here to learn more about the Sotomayor confirmation

**The Kagan Confirmation**

Click here to learn more about the Kagan confirmation.

## The Confirmation of Neil M. Gorsuch

Justice Antonin Scalia unexpectedly died in February 2016 while on a hunting trip, whereupon Senate Majority Leader Mitch McConnell announced that the Republican-controlled chamber would not take up any replacement nominated by President Obama but would leave it up to the next president (even though Obama had nearly a year left in office).

Despite Democratic outrage and media commentary criticism, the Republicans held fast. There were no hearings on President Obama's nominee, Appeals Court Judge Merrick B. Garland. The scheme succeeded perfectly when, in the 2016 election, Donald Trump was elected president and the Republicans retained control of the Senate.

As he had promised during his campaign, President Trump nominated a conservative, in the person of Federal Appeals Court Judge Neil M. Gorsuch, to the Supreme Court. The Republican-controlled Senate took up the nomination with alacrity. During the hearings, the judge followed the now well-established formula. He denied partisanship, stating, "There's no such thing as a Republican judge or a Democratic judge, we just have judges," and thanked his friends, "liberals and conservatives and independents from every kind of background and belief" for attending the hearing. He deflected questions about the outside group that had spent $7 million lobbying against Merrick Garland and $10 million supporting his nomination.

On April 7, 2017, the Senate approved the nomination by a vote of 54–45. It came after Republicans changed the chamber's rules to allow confirmation of a Supreme Court nominee by a simple majority instead of the sixty votes required to overcome a filibuster. (Democrats had changed the rule when they controlled the Senate in 2013, barring the filibuster for lower judgeships. But they had left it in effect for Supreme Court nominees.)

## The Confirmation of Brett M. Kavanaugh

With the arrival of Justice Gorsuch, the Supreme Court continued to be essentially, ideologically divided into four conservatives, four liberals, and the moderate Justice Anthony M. Kennedy, who held the balance between the two sides. Although Kennedy more often voted with the conservatives, he occasionally joined the liberals as the decisive vote in important 5–4 decisions, notably on climate change, LGBTQ+ rights, abortion, and affirmative action.

Kennedy retired effective July 31, 2018 (reportedly partly in response to blandishments from President Trump), enabling the president to nominate his successor.[74] That man, nominated on July 9, 2018, was Brett Kavanaugh, a clear-cut conservative, who had been staff secretary in the White House for President George W. Bush and a judge for ten years on the U.S. Court of Appeals for the District of Columbia, and came recommended by the Federalist Society.

Watch the first day of the Kavanaugh confirmation hearings.

View in the online reader

Senate confirmation of Judge Kavanaugh would likely ensure a conservative majority on the Supreme Court for many years (the younger members, who would probably live longer, were conservative). Moreover, the Republicans held a majority on both the Senate Judiciary Committee and in the Senate. So Kavanaugh's confirmation seemed assured. Democratic senators on the committee, therefore, sought to delay the hearings until after the upcoming congressional elections when their party might have a majority in the chamber. They looked to discredit him by demanding documents from his time in the White House that would reveal him as a political operative. The Republicans withheld around 100,000 of them (claiming executive privilege) and submitted a last-minute document dump allowing little time for them to be read. The Republicans also argued that to understand Kavanaugh's judicial philosophy all the Democrats had to do was read his three hundred decisions as a member of the court of appeals.

Initially, the hearings followed the by now usual pattern, with the nominee stonewalling and offering banalities in response to attacks from Democratic senators and accepting the praise bestowed upon him by Republican members of the committee.

Then, heightening the drama, psychology professor Christine Blasey Ford accused the judge of having drunkenly sexually assaulted her during the 1980s when they were both high school students. Initially reluctant to come forward publicly, she eventually agreed to testify before the committee. The judge would follow her. Their testimonies would be watched by around twenty million people.

All eleven Republican members of the Senate Judiciary Committee were men. Concerned about the optics of their cross-examining Professor Blasey Ford, they delegated (ceded) the job to a woman Republican prosecutor from Arizona. The tactic failed because the prosecutor was only able to interrogate her in brief segments (thus no sustained interrogation) between positive questions asked by each of the Democratic members (six men and four women) of the committee.

FIGURE 15.7 Senate Judiciary Committee, October 2018

Source: Images from https://www.judiciary.senate.gov/about/members.

Despite some lack of recall and details, Professor Blasey Ford's calm demeanor and compelling testimony were widely acknowledged, even on Fox News, as convincing and credible, thus posing a significant rebuttal challenge to Judge Kavanaugh when he testified during the afternoon.

Watch Dr. Christine Blasey Ford's full testimony to the Senate Judiciary Committee.

View in the online reader

The judge, accompanied by his wife, had appeared on Fox News three nights earlier. Answering the questions of a friendly interviewer, he relatively mildly denied the accusations against him, saying, "I've never sexually assaulted anyone." Now, his statement and subsequent testimony to the committee were virulently, bellicosely, partisan; he claimed there was a "well-funded plot against him" and blasted the Democrats for "destroying his family and career." His words were far from judge-like: they seemed aimed at rallying President Trump and the Senate Republicans, if they required it, to his side. For their part, the Republicans dispensed with the prosecutor and supportively addressed Judge Kavanaugh themselves. In contrast to the Republicans' protective interactions toward him, the Democratic senators were challenging and hostile.

Watch as Kavanaugh responds to sexual assault allegations during his Senate hearing.

View in the online reader

The upshot of the hearings was an agreement to allow the FBI to investigate the charges against the judge and perhaps interview other accusers and potential witnesses. But the investigation had to be carried out in a few days and its parameters were set (limited) by the White House. Neither Judge Kavanaugh nor Professor Blasey Ford, nor additional accusers, nor some of the other people who asked or expected to be questioned, were interviewed. No incriminating evidence was uncovered.

Before, during, and after the hearings, Kavanaugh's proponents and opponents larded cable channels, the television networks, Facebook, Twitter and other social networks with political advertisements urging viewers to have their senators block or speed up the confirmation process, or to vote for or against confirmation.

See this advertisement sponsored by the Judicial Crisis Network defending Judge Kavanaugh.

This is one of the many ads paid for by the Judicial Crisis Network which pushed for Brett Kavanaugh's confirmation.

View in the online reader

There were mass protests, mostly by women opposed to Kavanaugh and in support of Blasey Ford. Some may have been inspired by the #MeToo movement. Demonstrators accosted senators in elevators. They filled and were sometimes forcibly removed from, the committee hearing room, the halls of Congress, the Senate's public gallery, and elsewhere. These actions were often shown by the media.

With the Senate divided 51 to 49 in favor of the Republicans and several votes uncertain, confirmation was in suspense. Two Republican women senators were concerned about whether the nominee would vote to overrule or further undermine the court's *Roe v. Wade* abortion decision. Several Democratic senators, running for reelection in states Trump had carried in 2016, were concerned about jeopardizing their chances. In the end, every Republican senator except for two voted for confirmation (one of the women voted present, pairing her vote with a colleague who was absent, giving his daughter away at her wedding). Every Democratic senator except for one from West Virginia voted against. Judge Kavanaugh was confirmed by 50–48. On October 6, 2018, he was sworn in as an Associate Justice of the Supreme Court by the man he succeeded, Anthony Kennedy, and by Chief Justice John G. Roberts Jr.

## The Confirmation of Amy Coney Barrett

Justice Ruth Bader Ginsburg died on September 18, 2020, at the age of eighty-seven, forty-six days before the November 3 election. On September 26, President Trump nominated a conservative jurist to succeed her. Forty-eight-year-old Amy Coney Barrett graduated from Notre Dame Law School in 1997 and taught there as a professor from 2000 to 2017. She was confirmed in October 2017 as a judge on the 7th Federal Appeals Court by a Senate vote of 55–43. She held conservative positions on abortion, health care (ending Obamacare), LGBTQ+ rights, and gun regulations.

When Justice Scalia died roughly nine months before the 2016 presidential election, Senate Majority Leader Mitch McConnell (R-KY) refused to bring President Obama's replacement nominee up for Senate consideration and a confirmation vote. He kept the number of seats on the court to eight for more than a year. His argument: in an election year, voters should decide who selected the next justice. In 2020, he reversed his position, arguing that the decision should be made by the incumbent president. Committee Republicans said that the decision to go ahead was "based on constitutional principle and born of a necessity to protect the will of the American people."[75] Democrats accused the Republicans of hypocrisy; of forcing confirmation through during an election, and despite a raging pandemic. It was power in action. The Republicans had the votes on the Judiciary Committee and in the Senate to confirm Judge Barrett, thereby cementing a 6–3 conservative majority on the court for the foreseeable future.

The three days of hearings began on October 12. Customarily, the chair of the Senate Judiciary Committee opens its hearings by announcing that it will be considering the nomination. However, this time, Senator Lindsey Graham convened the committee, saying confidently that "the hearing to confirm Judge Amy Barrett to the Supreme Court will now begin." The intent was to secure her confirmation before the election.

Interest groups were rampantly active. Among them were the conservative Judicial Crisis Network, the Federalist Society (which had received more than $6 million from the Koch brothers from 1997 to 2017), and anonymously funded organizations on one side; and Demand Justice, the National Women's Law Center, and Alliance for Justice on the other. They created and sponsored political advertisements, contacted sympathetic senators, and appeared on the media.

**FIGURE 15.8 President Donald Trump with Supreme Court Associate Justice Amy Coney Barrett after Attending Barrett's Swearing-in Ceremony**

See how she is dressed attractively and wearing one strand of pearls, to convey a feminine (not feminist) unchallenging capability and competence. Male candidates are not subject to such expectations.

Source: Trump White House Archived. "The Swearing-in Ceremony of the Honorable Amy Coney Barrett." Via Flickr: https://www.flickr.com/photos/whitehouse45/50547408266/.

The *New York Times* described and showed photographs of Judge Barrett, focusing on her clothing and jewelry (attention they would not have devoted to a male candidate). The effect of this image of the mother of seven, according to Vanessa Friedman of the *Times*, was to present her as the opposite of an extremist. So that "she doesn't look like someone who will take away your health care.... She looks decorous. She looks like someone who would ... respect history and authority."[76]

The Republican senators lavished praise upon her for her legal qualifications and personal virtues. They accused Democrats of attacking her Catholic faith (they had not).

She stressed her impartiality and independence and expounded on her legal philosophy of textualism and originalism popularized by her mentor, Justice Scalia. She responded to the Judiciary Committee senators' questions, as her predecessors had learned to do after Judge Robert H. Bork's debacle at his 1987 confirmation hearings, with platitudes and accounts of Supreme Court precedents, declining to say whether they were correct, and with judicious silence. She refused to say how she would rule in pending and potential cases. She tried to separate herself from the praise President Trump had heaped on her.

Democratic senators accused the Republicans of an illegitimate power grab. They pointed out that the nominee had signed a 2006 advertisement in support of overturning "the barbaric legacy" of *Roe v. Wade*; that she had criticized Chief Justice John G. Roberts Jr. for upholding a central provision of Obamacare; and they filled the hearing room with large posters of beneficiaries of the program.

The Committee Democrats' strategy was led by its senior Democrat and the chamber's oldest member, California Senator Diane Feinstein. To her party's dismay, her management of the case against Judge Barrett was faltering, her questioning meandering and repetitive. At the conclusion of the hearings, she hugged Chairman Graham, thanking him for his "fairness" and for running "one of the best set of hearings I've participated in." At the end of the hearings, public opinion favoring the nominee had increased. Feinstein would later step down from her leadership position on the committee.

The timetable was tight: the panel voted on October 22, just over a month after Justice Ginsburg's death, less than two weeks before the election. All twelve Republicans voted to confirm; all the Democrats boycotted the vote. On October 26, Judge Barrett was confirmed as an Associate Justice of the Supreme Court by a Senate vote of 52–48. All the yea votes came from Republican senators. The nays consisted of one Republican, all forty-five Democrats, and two independents. On October 27, she took the oath of office. The Republican majority on the Court was likely assured.

As allowed by the Constitution, Congress has added and reduced the number of justices on the Supreme Court. It has ranged from as few as five to as many as ten justices. But there have been no changes since 1869. (Changes in state supreme courts have been more common.) Invariably, the changes have been made for partisan advantage. In our section "External Checks on Power," we discuss President Franklin Roosevelt's efforts to change the balance of the Court and how it was negatively depicted as "court packing." Challenged by his supporters and opponents to tell them what he would do about a Supreme Court dominated by conservatives, candidate Joe Biden Jr. at first equivocated, and then promised that, if elected, he would create a bipartisan commission to study whether to expand or restructure the judiciary.

## Key Takeaways

Presidents usually look to nominate as federal judges people who share their ideological, policy, and partisan views. Nominations attract intense scrutiny from interest groups and the media and can be controversial and contentious. They are subject to confirmation by the Senate, which may delay, block, or approve them. We explain why the nominations of Robert H. Bork and Harriet Miers failed and those of Clarence Thomas, John G. Roberts Jr., Samuel A. Alito Jr., Sonia Sotomayor, and Elena Kagan were successful, as was Neil Gorsuch after controversial manipulation of the process by the Senate's Republican majority leader. We highlight the cases of Brett M. Kavanaugh and Amy Coney Barrett.

## Exercises

1. What qualities do you think are important in Supreme Court justices? Do you think the confirmation process is a good way of selecting justices?
2. How does public opinion affect who gets appointed to the Supreme Court? What role do you think public opinion should play?
3. How important are interest groups in determining successful or unsuccessful nominations to the Supreme Court?
4. Imagine you were helping prepare a nominee for the Senate Judiciary Committee hearings process. What advice would you give?
5. Should President Biden try to add justices to the Supreme Court?

# 15.5 The Courts in the Information Age

## Learning Objectives

After reading this section, you should be able to answer the following questions:

1. How do Supreme Court justices interact with the media?
2. How do reporters go about covering the Supreme Court?
3. How are the Supreme Court and its decisions depicted in the information age?
4. What are the consequences of these depictions?

## Media Interactions

Occasionally, Supreme Court justices give speeches about broad constitutional issues, talk off the record with a journalist, or rarely, engage in an on-the-record interview.[77] They may write a book setting forth their judicial philosophies and even go on television to publicize it.[78] Justice Stephen Breyer appeared on *Larry King Live* to promote his latest book. He was circumspect, carefully avoiding discussing cases in any detail or revealing the Court's deliberations.[79]

The flamboyant Justice Antonin Scalia appeared on *60 Minutes* to promote a book he coauthored on how to persuade judges. During the interview, he did discuss some of his views.[80] Nor did he shy away from voicing controversial opinions in statements and speeches, saying, for example, "You would have to be an idiot" to believe that the Constitution is a living document.[81]

On the other side, Justice Ruth Bader Ginsburg, in a speech that could be seen as a response to "strict constructionism" and that was posted on the Court's website, expressed her preference for "dynamic" over "static, frozen-in-time constitutional interpretation."[82]

(A proponent of "strict constructionism," Justice Scalia would later reject the term, preferring "reasonable interpretation.")[83]

Justice Ginsburg attracted controversy when, in an interview during the 2016 presidential election, she said, "I can't imagine what the country would be—with Donald Trump as our president." Experts said she was "unwise to speak out." Trump called her "a disgrace to the Court," and she conceded that her remarks were "ill advised."[84] She obtained even more visibility as the subject of the 2018 documentary film *RBG*, which favorably portrayed her life and career, and the 2018 feature film *On the Basis of Sex*.

Justice Ginsburg's name even percolated down to the quite young, namely Paletz's then seven-year-old granddaughter Dalia, as the following dialogue attests:

Dalia: Darth Vader Ginsburg

Susannah (her mother): She's a Supreme Court Justice who has done a lot of things for women's rights.

Dalia: So the opposite of Darth Vader.

Susannah: Yes, basically.

President Trump had no compunction about publicly disparaging judges who get in his way. As one example, he described the U.S. district judge who blocked his first immigration ban as a "so-called judge" who should be held responsible for future terrorist acts in America.

Withal, most judges shun the media. They rarely hold press conferences or discuss past, let alone current, cases.[85] Toni House, who served as the Supreme Court's public information officer for many years, described her job as "peculiar in Washington because this office doesn't spin, it doesn't flap, it doesn't interpret . . . When an opinion comes down, we put it in the hands of a reporter."[86]

The main way in which justices communicate with the media is through the legal language of their written opinions. Even when a case is controversial and the Supreme Court is divided 5–4, the justices use such language in their opinions to justify their decisions. No matter how impassioned the decision, this legal language makes it difficult for reporters to raise the subjects of partisanship or politics when writing stories about the Court's actions.

## Majesty and Secrecy

The justices have two powerful weapons that help them present to the public an image of themselves as above politics and partisanship: majesty and secrecy.

Majesty begins with the Supreme Court building, which commands awe and respect. It continues with what reporters see inside the courtroom—all that they see—which is designed to elevate the justices and the judicial process to a magisterial and impersonal status: the ornate setting, the ritual, the ceremony, the justices presiding in their robes, seated on high-backed chairs, physically and metaphorically raised up. This effect is conveyed most visibly in the official photograph of the nine justices ("Enduring Image").

The second way in which judges obtain favorable media coverage is through secrecy. Denied to reporters—and therefore absent from the news—are the justices' discussions on granting review, conference proceedings, and the process of creating a majority through opinion writing. The press is not privy to the role of law clerks, the decision-making processes, the informal contacts among the justices, the appeals and persuasion, the negotiation and bargaining, and the sometimes pragmatic compromises.[87]

**FIGURE 15.9 U.S. Supreme Court Building**

The Supreme Court building: so magisterial and redolent of justice achieved away from the hurly-burly of politics.

Source: Steven Frame/Shutterstock.com

### Enduring Image

**Photo of the Supreme Court Justices**

The traditional group photograph that the members of the Supreme Court allow to be taken shows them arrayed and authoritative in their impressive institutional setting. This enduring image enhances the justices' standing and contributes to people's acceptance of their rulings.

But what if they were shown discussing cases as bargainers? Or engaged in a nonjudicial activity? Or caught in an embarrassing moment in the way that celebrities are trapped by the tabloids? Such photographs would detract from the justices' authority and the Court's legitimacy.

Note the furor provoked by *America (The Book)*[88] by Jon Stewart and the writers of *The Daily Show with Jon Stewart*. Walmart refused to stock it. The reason: One page of this parody of a civics textbook shows the faces of the Supreme Court justices superimposed over naked elderly bodies. The facing page has cutouts of the justices' robes and a caption asking readers to "restore their dignity by matching each justice with his or her respective robe."

In the front row, left to right: Associate Justice Samuel A. Alito, Jr., Associate Justice Clarence Thomas, Chief Justice John G. Roberts, Jr., Associate Justice Stephen G. Breyer, and Associate Justice Sonia Sotomayor. In the back row, left to right: Associate Justice Brett M. Kavanaugh, Associate Justice Elena Kagan, Associate Justice Neil M. Gorsuch, and Associate Justice Amy Coney Barrett (who replaced Associate Justice Ruth Bader Ginsburg after her passing in late 2020).

Source: Fred Schilling, Collection of the Supreme Court of the United States. Retrieved from: https://www.supremecourt.gov/about/justices.aspx.

## Cameras in the Courtroom

Cameras are prohibited in the Supreme Court during public sessions. The stated reasons for the ban are that it prevents lawyers and justices from playing to the cameras and avoids any physical disruption of the chamber. There is also concern that news coverage would emphasize excerpts from the brief oral arguments, which can be misleading—since the essence of appellate advocacy before the Court is in the written briefs. The unstated reasons are that cameras might not only cause the justices to lose their cherished anonymity and privacy but also undermine the Court's mystique by allowing people to see and judge the justices' behavior.

Television cameras are excluded from most other federal courts for many of the same reasons. They are allowed in all state courts under conditions and restrictions, such as consent of the judge, agreement of the attorneys for both sides, fixed placement, and a prohibition against showing jurors.

## Reporters

Reporters covering the Supreme Court tend to be protective of the institution and the justices. In part, this is because they see law and politics as separate and different. Besides, they do not always have access to the kind of behavior and information that might lead them to think of and frame the Court in terms of policy and, particularly, politics.

Even when reporters at the Court are familiar with the facts and the oral arguments and have read the briefs of cases, they have more than enough to do just summarizing the justices' decisions. These can be complex, containing fifty to a hundred or more pages of dense text, with detailed concurring and dissenting opinions. At its busiest time of the year, the Court releases several opinions at once; over 40 percent are issued during the last three weeks of the Court's term. Reporters have little time to check over the cases and opinions, decide which ones are important, and prepare a report in layperson's language.

On controversial cases, reporters are bombarded by reactions and analyses from the parties to the case, their attorneys, legal experts, and interest groups. Some of these people are available on the plaza in front of the Supreme Court, where microphones are set up for them.

**FIGURE 15.10 Supreme Court Plaza**
After a controversial Supreme Court decision, reporters can interview the attorneys, their clients, and interest-group spokespersons.

Source: Photo courtesy of David, http://www.flickr.com/photos/bootbearwdc/22009192/. (CC BY 2.0); https://creativecommons.org/licenses/by/2.0/.

Reporters may include some of these views in their stories and show that the justices' decisions have effects on people's lives. But they usually lack the time and space to explain the decisions in explicitly political terms.

# Media Depictions of the Supreme Court

After the acrimony of *Bush v. Gore*, the justices more or less returned to collegiality. Media and public discussion of the decision as partisan politics died down. The authority and legitimacy of the Court and the justices were reaffirmed.

But no longer. Two factors keep a political perspective in sight. First, as we have shown in our accounts of the contentious and even uncontroversial presidential nominations to the Supreme Court, ideology can be a feature of the Senate's hearings, discussion, and debate, and of the media's coverage. Second, this perspective can be even more prominent when the Court is obviously ideologically divided.[89]

## Apolitical Coverage?

Because of the recent prominence of these two factors, the media now characterize the Court's blocs ideologically as conservative and liberal. What they have not yet done is to depict the Court as an explicitly political institution. To be determined is whether their coverage will remain essentially **apolitical**, showing the Court as above and beyond politics and partisanship. Will news stories and commentary on individual decisions spell out their political implications and the justices' partisan positions? Will the terms "partisan" or "partisanship" and the words "Democrat," "Republican," "political," and "politics" become more common?[90]

**apolitical**
Above and beyond politics and partisanship.

A fresh reporter at the Court can see it politically. The *New York Times*'s Adam Liptak, summarizing the 2010 term, cited studies by and data from political scientists to identify the Court as "the most conservative one in living memory."[91] He subsequently documented the justices' selection of law clerks who shared their ideological views.[92] In later articles, Liptak has drawn on research by scholars to delve more deeply into ideology on the Court: he reported, for example, that conservatives interrupt liberals (and men interrupt women) significantly more than the reverse.[93]

## Limited Coverage

Media coverage of the Supreme Court, let alone lower federal courts and state courts, is limited. Many of the Court's decisions are not reported by the news media and cable news or are recounted only briefly. The television networks give less than 4 percent of their coverage of the three branches of government to the Supreme Court. The leading news magazines focus on only 10 percent of the cases. Even a reader relying on The *New York Times* would not know about many of the Court's decisions.

A few cases, unrepresentative of the Court's docket, usually those involving the First Amendment or other rights, receive extensive coverage, as do cases arousing intense interest-group involvement. Typical is the widespread coverage given to the Court's 5–4 decision upholding a voucher system that partially pays tuition at religious schools.[94] Missing are decisions about contracts and taxes, criminal law and procedure, and federal statutes and regulations, except for cases involving big-name litigants.[95]

## Oversimplified Coverage

Coverage of the Supreme Court is often oversimplified. In news accounts, its refusal to grant certiorari is said to endorse the lower court's decision, when all it means is that the Court has refused to review the case. In a typical example, an NBC news anchor misleadingly announced that "the Court *upheld* a ban on dances in the public school of Purdy, Missouri, where many people are Southern Baptists who believe that dancing is sinful and satanic."[96]

## New Media

The new media can breach the bulwark of majesty and secrecy protecting the Supreme Court. They can provide political and critical perspectives and cover more cases in more detail. Blogs and social media are increasingly important.[97]

Reluctantly and cautiously, the Supreme Court has entered the information age. The Court's official website now contains transcripts of oral arguments on the same day they are made and audio recordings some days later. It also provides the complete opinions of each case on the docket since the 2003 term and instructions on how to obtain opinions for earlier cases. The Court now makes briefs and other filings available electronically. And, after a law review article revealing the problem was publicized and reported by the media, the Court discloses after-the-fact changes (substantial and trivial) to its opinions.[98] Still, much of the other information available, such as on Scotusblog.com, the go-to site for Supreme Court coverage—is intended for the legal community.

The internet does contain commentary on the Court's decisions. Blogs have ranged from the lighthearted and gossipy "Underneath Their Robes," which during its existence broke with judges' aloofness and inaccessibility (its creator now runs "Above the Law"), to more academic commentary.

In an example of new-media innovation in covering a politically significant trial, six bloggers joined together to create Firedoglake (http://firedoglake.com), now known as Shadow Proof. The site offered, from a liberal perspective, intensive, real-time coverage of the perjury trial of Lewis Libby Jr., former top aide to Vice President Dick Cheney. The coverage went beyond anything provided by the mainstream media.

# Media Consequences

The news media's coverage can make it hard for people to see the political orientation of judges engaged in making and changing public policies. This has reinforced the legitimacy of the courts and confidence in judges.

Indeed, 80 percent of the people in a survey conducted for the American Bar Association strongly agreed or agreed that "in spite of its problems, the American justice system is still the best in the world."[99] Fifty-four percent strongly agreed that "most judges are extremely well qualified for their jobs." Most faith was expressed in the Supreme Court, with 50 percent having strong confidence in it and only 15 percent having slight or no confidence.[100] But will this confidence persist if the advent of Justice Barrett and her decisions causes media coverage of the Court to turn political and to focus on its ideological blocs?

Reports of dramatic and sensational cases and their depictions in popular culture do make people quite critical of the way the legal system appears to operate.[101] Fifty-one percent of those surveyed agreed that it "needs a complete overhaul." Close to 80 percent agreed that "it takes too long for courts to do their job" and "it costs too much to go to court."

Tabloid trials can increase people's knowledge of some aspects of the legal system. In a survey conducted in the wake of the overwhelmingly publicized criminal and civil cases involving O. J. Simpson, almost everyone knew that anyone accused of a crime has the right to be represented in court by a lawyer and that a defendant found not guilty in a criminal trial can be sued in a civil trial. Two-thirds knew that a criminal defendant is innocent until proven guilty, although one-third mistakenly believed the reverse.

## Key Takeaways

The justices of the Supreme Court interact with reporters mainly through the legal language of their written decisions. They accentuate the Court's majesty while concealing its inner workings and excluding cameras from the courtroom. Reporters perceive the Supreme Court primarily as a legal institution. They lack the time and space to report in detail on its activities. Most coverage is therefore incomplete and oversimplified. News media coverage of the Supreme Court has been apolitical, a depiction reinforcing its legitimacy and people's confidence in it. But this public perception may be changing as the media increasingly show the court as ideologically divided. Overall, Americans believe that their legal system is the best in the world, but are critical of how it operates.

## Exercises

1. How does the way the Supreme Court presents itself enhance its authority? Are there any disadvantages to seeing the Supreme Court this way?
2. Imagine that Congress kept its deliberations as secret as the Supreme Court does. Why might it be more acceptable for the Supreme Court to keep its deliberations secret than it would be for Congress to do the same thing?
3. Do you think it would be a good thing if reporters and bloggers told us more about the inner workings of the Supreme Court? What are the advantages and disadvantages of keeping the workings of the Court secret?
4. What might be the consequences of the media's depicting the Supreme Court as apolitical or ideological (conservative-liberal) or politically partisan?
5. Do you think the advent of Justice Barrett will make this more likely?

### Civic Education

**The Medill Justice Project**

Students in Professor David Protess's "Miscarriage of Justice" class at Northwestern University (called "The Medill Justice Project" after his 2011 retirement) not only studied the criminal justice system but also got the chance to influence it. They used investigative reporting techniques to unearth information that was then used to reverse wrongful convictions in Illinois, including death-penalty sentences. They pore over case documents, reinterview witnesses, and track down tips from informants.

Their work has helped change public opinion about the death penalty, as people have become less supportive of a policy that could result in the execution of innocent people.

The media contributed to the erosion of support for the death penalty by putting these stories into a new (irresistible) innocence frame: that of an error-prone, sometimes corrupt, judicial system that executed innocent defendants. This frame became far more prevalent than the frame that was less sympathetic to the convicted, for example, of murderers and their victims.[102]

Students enrolled in the course sometimes complain about the heavy workload, but most devote their time and energy willingly. "Once you get that involved in a case, you make it your life's work. You know you could have an innocent life at stake, and if you don't save it, nobody will," stated one graduate.[103] Some of the students go on to cover the criminal court beat or become lawyers working for the rights of the accused.

The program did become involved in some controversy, leading to Professor Protess's retirement, but is continuing under new leadership.[104]

Programs in which students and faculty work together have accounted for the vast majority of the exonerations of death-row inmates since the 1970s. A few programs, such as the Innocence Project at the Benjamin Cardozo Law School of Yeshiva University, specialize in death-penalty cases. Legal clinics associated with many law schools help those who cannot afford representation with their cases. You do not have to be a law student to be involved.

(See also "Comparing Content".)

# 15.6 Recommended Reading

Bergman, Paul, and Michael Asimow. *Reel Justice: The Courtroom Goes to the Movies*, 2nd ed. Kansas City, KS: Andrews and McMeel, 2006. A droll discussion of the (mainly inaccurate) depictions in movies of various aspects of the judicial process.

Carp, Robert A., Ronald Stidham, Kenneth L. Manning, and Lisa M. Holmes. *Judicial Process in America*, 10th ed. Washington, DC: CQ Press, 2019. A comprehensive and enlightening text.

Davis, Richard. *Decisions and Images: The Supreme Court and the Press*. New York: Prentice Hall, 1994. An authoritative study of the relationship between the Supreme Court and the press.

Dickson, Del, ed. *The Supreme Court in Conference (1940–1985): The Private Discussions Behind Nearly 300 Supreme Court Decisions*. New York: Oxford University Press, 2001. Justices' conference notes organized and annotated around key decisions.

Fox, Richard L., Robert W. Van Sickel, and Thomas L. Steiger. *Tabloid Justice: Criminal Justice in an Age of Media Frenzy*, 2nd ed. Boulder, CO: Lynne Rienner Publishers, 2007. Documents how the media's obsession with high-profile trials has distorted the public's understanding of the judicial system.

Gilman, Howard. *The Votes That Counted: How the Court Decided the 2000 Presidential Election*. Chicago: University of Chicago Press, 2001. The single best book on the subject.

Goldman, Sheldon. *Picking Federal Judges: Lower Court Selection from Roosevelt Through Reagan*. New Haven, CT: Yale University Press, 1999. The definitive analysis of the process.

Gottschalk, Marie. *Caught: The Prison State and the Lockdown of American Politics*. Princeton, NJ: Princeton University Press, 2015. A magisterial study of the causes and consequences of mass incarceration in the United States.

Irons, Peter H., and Stephanie Guitton. *May It Please The Court . . . 23 Live Recordings of Landmark Cases as Argued Before The Supreme Court*. New York: New Press, 1993. Historical treasures—tapes of oral arguments before the Supreme Court.

Johnson, Timothy R., and Jerry Goldman, eds. *A Good Quarrel: America's Top Legal Reporters Share Stories From Inside the Supreme Court*. Ann Arbor: University of Michigan Press, 2009. Provides a website with audio links to excerpts of the oral arguments discussed in the book.

Maltese, John Anthony. *The Selling of Supreme Court Nominees*. Baltimore: Johns Hopkins University Press, 1998. A study of the evolution and condition of the nomination and confirmation process.

Paul, Joel R. *Without Precedent: Chief Justice John Marshall and His Times*. New York: Riverhead Books, 2018. The essential biography.

Sherwin, Richard K. *When Law Goes Pop: The Vanishing Line Between Law and Popular Culture*. Chicago: University of Chicago Press, 2000. Argues that high-profile trials and programs with judges on television threaten to turn law into spectacle.

Slotnick, Elliot E., and Jennifer A. Segal. *Television News and the Supreme Court*. New York: Cambridge University Press, 1998. Shows that Supreme Court rules and television news norms produce coverage that is infrequent, brief, and sometimes inaccurate.

# 15.7 Recommended Viewing

*Adam's Rib* (1949). A classic comedy in which a woman defense attorney (Katharine Hepburn) and her prosecutor husband (Spencer Tracy) battle in court and at home over law, justice, and her client, a woman accused of shooting her husband.

*Anatomy of a Murder* (1959). Superior courtroom drama of a murder trial.

*Created Equal: Clarence Thomas in His Own Words* (2020). A sympathetic documentary interview based on the Supreme Court justice's autobiography.

*Erin Brockovich* (2000). Based on a true story. Marginal nonlawyer employee (Julia Roberts) at small law firm battles successfully against a polluting corporation to achieve justice for decent, ordinary people.

*First Monday in October* (1981). Romance blossoms between a crusty, conservative Supreme Court justice and his new, liberal, female colleague.

*Inherit the Wind* (1960). Based on a true story. In a steamy Southern courtroom, celebrated lawyer Clarence Darrow (Spencer Tracy) defends a schoolteacher accused of violating the law by teaching evolution.

*Juvenile Court* (1973). Frederick Wiseman's fascinating documentary reveals a juvenile court in action (and inaction).

*On the Basis of Sex* (2018). How Ruth Bader Ginsburg helped bring about the end of sex discrimination.

*Philadelphia* (1993). A lawyer with AIDS (Tom Hanks) sues the sanctimonious law firm that dismissed him.

*RBG* (2018). Documentary positively portraying the life and career of Supreme Court Justice Ruth Bader Ginsburg.

*To Kill a Mockingbird* (1962). Small-town Southern lawyer (Gregory Peck) braves the hostility of his fellow citizens by defending a Black man falsely accused of raping a white woman.

*Twelve Angry Men* (1957). One man (Henry Fonda) convinces the other jury members to change their verdict to innocent.

*The Verdict* (1982). A failed lawyer with an alcohol abuse disorder (Paul Newman) struggles to regain his dignity and win a medical malpractice case against a Catholic archdiocese, despite the opposition of a powerful law firm and a corrupt judge.

# Endnotes


1. Richard Morin, "A Nation of Stooges," *Washington Post*, October 8, 1995, C5.
2. James L. Gibson and Gregory A. Caldeira, *Citizens, Courts and Confirmations: Positivity Theory and the Judgments of the American People* (Princeton, NJ: Princeton University Press, 2009).
3. Patricia Ewick and Susan S. Silbey, *The Common Place of Law* (Chicago: University of Chicago Press, 1998), 18–19.
4. For the argument and evidence that criminal courts are pervasively racist, see Nicole Gonzalez Van Cleve, *Crook County* (Stanford: Stanford University Press, 2016).
5. Jed S. Rakoff, "Why Innocent People Plead Guilty," *New York Review*, November 20, 2014, 16–18.
6. Mark Godsey, *Blind Injustice: A Former Prosecutor Exposes the Psychology and Politics of Wrongful Convictions* (Berkeley:University of California Press, 2017).
7. Amy Beach, *Ordinary Injustice: How America Holds Court* (New York: Metropolitan, 2009).
8. Richard L. Fox, Robert W. Van Sickel, and Thomas L. Steiger, *Tabloid Justice: Criminal Justice in an Age of Media Frenzy*, 2nd ed. (Boulder, CO: Lynne Rienner Publishers, 2007).
9. Quoted in Lola Ogunnaike, "As Court TV Gets Even Bolder, So Does Its Star," *The New York Times*, December 2, 2004, B1.
10. "Simpson Trial and Trivia," *US News & World Report*, October 15, 1995, 43.
11. See Timothy O. Lenz, *Changing Images of Law in Film & Television Crime Stories* (New York: Peter Lang, 2003); and Anthony Chase, *Movies on Trial: The Legal System on the Silver Screen* (New York: New Press, 2002).
12. Wende Vyborney Dumble, "And Justice for All," in *Television Studies*, ed. Gary Burns and Robert J. Thompson (Westport, CT: Praeger, 1989), 106.
13. Thane Rosenbaum, "Where Lawyers with a Conscience Get to Win Cases," *The New York Times*, May 12, 2002, AR 23.
14. Kimberlianne Podlas, "Should We Blame Judge Judy? The Messages TV Courtrooms send Viewers," *Judicature* 86, no. 1 (July–August 2002): 38–43.
15. Donald R. Songer, Reginald S. Sheehan, and Susan B. Haire, *Continuity and Change on the United States Courts of Appeals* (Ann Arbor: University of Michigan Press, 2000).
16. Lisa A. Kloppenberg, *Playing It Safe: How the Supreme Court Sidesteps Hard Cases and Stunts the Development of Law* (New York: New York University Press, 2001).
17. Paul M. Collins Jr., *Friends of the Court: Interest Groups and Judicial Decision Making* (New York: Oxford University Press, 2008).
18. Timothy R. Johnson, *Oral Arguments and Decision Making on the United States Supreme Court* (Albany: State University of New York Press, 2004).
19. Timothy R. Johnson, Paul J. Wahlbeck, and James F. Spriggs II, "The Influence of Oral Arguments on the U.S. Supreme Court," *American Political Science Review* 100 (February 2006): 99–113.
20. Adam Liptak, "A Sign of Independence From the Newest Justice," *The New York Times*, May 2, 2017, A22.
21. Edward Lazarus, *Closed Chambers: The First Eyewitness Account of the Epic Struggles Inside the Supreme Court* (New York: Times Books, 1998), 6.
22. https://www.nytimes.com/2015/08/28/us/justice-clarence-thomas-rulings-studies.html.
23. Pamela C. Corley, Amy Steigerwalt, and Artemus Ward, *The Puzzle of Unanimity: Consensus on the United States Supreme Court* (Stanford, CA:, Stanford University Press, 2013), 6.
24. The classic early study of such bargaining is Walter Murphy's *Elements of Judicial Strategy* (Chicago: University of Chicago Press, 1964); see also Forrest Maltzman, James F. Spriggs II, and Paul J. Wahlbeck, *Crafting Law on the Supreme Court* (New York: Cambridge University Press, 2000); and Saul Brenner and Joseph W. Whitmeyer, *Strategy on the United States Supreme Court* (New York: Cambridge University Press, 2009).
25. Del Dickson, ed., *The Supreme Court in Conference (1940–1985): The Private Discussions Behind Nearly 300 Supreme Court Decisions* (New York: Oxford University Press, 2001), xxvii.
26. Lawrence Baum, *Judges and Their Audiences: A Perspective on Judicial Behavior* (Princeton, NJ: Princeton University Press, 2006).
27. On the Chief Justice, see David Danelski and Artremus Ward, eds. *The Chief Justice: Appointment and Influence* (Ann Arbor: University of Michigan Press, 2016).
28. Adam Liptak, ""Doling Out Major Opinions and 'Dogs,' Roberts Pursues a Strategy," *The New York Times*, November 10, 2015, A16, referencing the research of law professor Richard J. Lazarus.
29. The case was *Worcester v. Georgia*, 31 U. S. (6 Pet) 515 (1832).
30. Martin Sweet, *Merely Judgment: Ignoring, Evading, and Trumping the Supreme Court* (Charlottesville: University of Virginia Press, 2010).
31. *Board of Education v. Earls*, 536 US 822 (2002).
32. This discussion is based in part on Jean Edward Smith, *John Marshall: Definer of a Nation* (New York: Holt, 1996), introduction and chap. 13. For an analysis of the distinction between judicial review and judicial supremacy (the obligation of officials to follow the Court's reasoning in the future), and the politics involved in the latter, see Keith E. Whittington, *Political Foundations of Judicial Supremacy: The Presidency, the Supreme Court, and Constitutional Leadership in US History* (Princeton, NJ: Princeton University Press, 2007).
33. *Dred Scott v. Sandford*, 60 US 393 (1857).
34. Lawrence Baum, *The Supreme Court*, 10th ed. (Washington, DC: CQ Press, 2010).
35. Joel R. Paul, *Without Precedent: Chief Justice John Marshall and His Times* (New York: Riverhead Books, 2018).
36. Scott E. Lemieux, "Judicial Supremacy, Judicial Power, and the Finality of Constitutional Rulings," *Perspectives on Politics* 15(4) (December 2017): 1067.
37. For a thoughtful analysis, see Randy J. Kozel, *Settled Versus Right: A Theory of Precedent* (New York: Cambridge University Press, 2017).
38. Thomas G. Hansford and James F. Spriggs II, *The Politics of Precedent on the U.S. Supreme Court* (Princeton, NJ: Princeton University Press, 2006), 130.
39. *Plessy v. Ferguson*, 153 US (1896); *Brown v. Board of Education of Topeka, Kansas*, 347 US 484 (1954).
40. The earlier case was *Bowers v. Hardwick*, 478 US 1861 (1986); it was overruled by *Lawrence v. Texas*, 02-102 (2003).
41. Linda Greenhouse, "Justice Weighs Desire v. Duty (Duty Prevails)," *The New York Times*, August 25, 2005, A1.
42. *Citizens United v. Federal Election Commission*, 558 US 50 (2010), discussed in Chapter 11 "Campaigns and Elections".
43. Jeff Shesol, *Supreme Power: Franklin Roosevelt vs. the Supreme Court* (New York: Norton, 2010).
44. *Ledbetter v. Goodyear Tire & Rubber Co.* 550 US (2007).
45. John J. Popham, "Reaction of South: 'Breathing Spell' for Adjustment Tempers Region's Feelings RULING TEMPERS REACTION OF SOUTH Southern Leaders Comment on Segregation Decision." Special to *The New York Times*. May 18, 1954, p.1/20.
46. Donald Grier Stephenson Jr., *Campaigns and the Court: The U.S. Supreme Court in Presidential Elections* (New York: Columbia University Press, 1999).
47. Quoted in Zimmerman, Eric. "Obama: We Need a Justice with 'Empathy.'" *The Hill*. May 1, 2009. Retrieved from: https://thehill.com/blogs/blog-briefing-room/news/36170-obama-we-need-a-justice-with-empathy.
48. See David K. Ryden, ed., *The U.S. Supreme Court and the Electoral Process* (Washington, DC: Georgetown University Press, 2000), especially the editor's "Overview," 1–4.
49. For the argument that the justices' behavior is largely determined by their individual policy preferences, see Jeffrey A. Segal and Harold J. Spaeth, *The Supreme Court and the Attitudinal Model Revisited* (New York: Cambridge University Press, 2002); see also Brian Z. Tamanaha, *Beyond the Formalist-Realist Divide: The Role of Politics in Judging* (Princeton, NJ: Princeton University Press, 2009).
50. *Griswold v. Connecticut*, 381 US 479 (1965).
51. *United States, Petitioner v. Alfonso Lopez, Jr.*, 514 US 549 (1995).
52. In *The Supreme Court and the American Elite, 1789–2008* (Cambridge, MA: Harvard University Press, 2009), Lucas A. Powe Jr. argues that the Court "serves ruling political coalitions" and attacks the conservative Rehnquist Court for overturning legislation that extended rights and privileges, and protected and improved society.
53. The cases are *District of Columbia et al. v. Heller*, 554 US (2008) and *McDonald et al. v. City of Chicago et al.* 561 US (2010).
54. Michael D. Shear, "A Reliably Conservative Justice Surprises, and Disappoints," *New. York Times*, June 16, 2020, A15; the case is Bostock v. Clayton Co., 590 U.S. – 2020.
55. Lawrence Baum, *Ideology in the Supreme Court* (Princeton, NJ: Princeton University Presss, 2017).
56. *AT&T Mobility v. Concepcion*, 563 U.S. 333 (2011).
57. Adam Cohen, Supreme *Inequality: The Supreme Court's Fifty-Year Battle for More Unjust America* (New York: Penguin Press, 2020).
58. For the argument that there is nothing wrong with a political court or with political motives in constitutional adjudication, see Terri Jennings Peretti, *In Defense of a Political Court* (Princeton, NJ: Princeton University Press, 1999), 73.
59. Robert A. Carp, Kenneth L. Manning, and Ronald Stidham, "President Clinton's District Judges: 'Extreme Liberals' or Just Plain Moderates?" *Judicature* 84, no. 5 (March–April 2001): 282–88; and "The Decision-Making Behavior of George W. Bush's Judicial Appointees: Far-Right, Conservative, or Moderate?" *Judicature* 88, no. 1 (July–August 2004): 20–29.
60. See also, Thomas C. Keck, *Judicial Politics in Polarized Times* (Chicago: University of Chicago Press, 2014).
61. Adam Liptak, "How Judge Shopping in Texas Led to Ruling Against Health Law," *The New York Times*, December 25, 2018, A17.
62. *Bush v. Gore*, 121 S. Ct. 525 (2000); also see David Margolick, Evgenia Peretz, and Michael Shnayerson, "The Path to Florida," *Vanity Fair*, October 2004.

63. Quoted in Linda Greenhouse's analysis "Bush v. Gore: A Special Report; Election Case a Test and a Trauma for Justices," *The New York Times*, February 20, 2001, A1.

64. Jeffrey Toobin, "Full Court Press," *New Yorker*, April 17, 2017, 24–28; also Amanda Hollis-Brusky, *Ideas with Consequences: The Federalist Society and the Conservative Counterrevolution* (New York: Oxford University Press, 2014).

65. From Tom Charles Huston to President Richard Nixon, 25 March 1969, in WHCF ExFG 50, the Judicial Branch (1969-1970), Box 1, White House Central Files FG50. Nixon Presidential Materials Project, College Park, Maryland.

66. Albert P. Melone, "The Senate's Confirmation Role in Supreme Court Nominations and the Politics of Ideology versus Impartiality," *Judicature* 75:2 (August-September 1991) 529.

67. Lee Epstein and Jeffrey A. Segal, *The Politics of Judicial Appointments* (New York: Oxford University Press, 2005).

68. Michael Comiskey, *Seeking Justices: The Judging of Supreme Court Nominees* (Lawrence: University Press of Kansas, 2004), thinks the confirmation process is acceptable and effective; but Christopher L. Eisgruber, *The Next Justice: Repairing The Supreme Court Appointments Process* (Princeton, NJ: Princeton University Press, 2007), wants the selection process to produce justices with moderate judicial philosophies; and Richard Davis, *Electing Justice: Fixing the Supreme Court Nomination Process* (New York: Oxford University Press, 2005), thinks the process is a mess and proposes various ways of electing Supreme Court justices.

69. See David Alistair Yalof, *Pursuit of Justices: Presidential Politics and the Selection of Supreme Court Nominees* (Chicago: University of Chicago Press, 1999), 4–7 and 17.

70. Quoted in Warren Weaver Jr., "Carswell Nomination Attacked and Defended as Senate Opens Debate on Nomination," *The New York Times*, March 17, 1970, A11.

71. Michael Pertschuk and Wendy Schaetzel, *The People's Rising* (New York: Thunder's Mouth Press, 1989), 155; also Ethan Bronner, *Battle for Justice: How the Bork Nomination Shook America* (New York: Norton, 1989).

72. Senator Howard Metzenbaum (D-Ohio), cited in Mark Gitenstein, *Matters of Principle* (New York: Simon & Schuster, 1992), 239.

73. Mark Gitenstein, *Matters of Principle* (New York: Simon & Schuster, 1992), 337.

74. See Adam Liptak and Maggie Haberman, "Behind Scenes, Urging Justice To Move Aside," *The New York Times,* June 29, 2018, A1 (19).

75. Congressional Record. Proceedings and Debates of the 116th Congress, Second Session. Senate. Sunday, October 25, 2020. Issue: Vol. 166, No. 184, Part II, p.S6561. Via https://www.congress.gov/116/crec/2020/10/25/CREC-2020-10-25-bk2.pdf.

76. Vanessa Friedman, "Unbuttoned," *The New York Times*, October 15, 2020, D4.

77. An exception was Justice William J. Brennan Jr., who, in 1986, engaged in sixty hours of candid interviews with reporter Stephen Wermiel and allowed him to go through his papers. The agreement was that, after Brennan retired, the reporter would write his biography. Brennan retired in 1990. The book finally appeared in 2010: Sol Stern and Stephen Wermiel, *Justice Brennan: Liberal Champion* (Boston: Houghton Mifflin Harcourt, 2010).

78. Antonin Scalia, with replies by scholars, *A Matter of Interpretation: Federal Courts and the Law* (Princeton, NJ: Princeton University Press, 1998); also Stephen G. Breyer, *Active Liberty: Interpreting Our Democratic Constitution* (New York: Knopf, 2005).

79. Stephen G. Breyer, *Making Our Democracy Work: A Judge's View* (New York: Knopf, 2010); the interview was on September 15, 2010.

80. April 27, 2008; the book is Antonin Scalia and Bryan Garner, *Making Your Case: The Art of Persuading Judges* (Eagan, MN: Thomson West, 2008).

81. Justice Scalia appeared on the American Civil Liberties Union (ACLU) panel on the state of civil liberties televised by C-SPAN (October 15, 2006), explaining and defending some of his decisions.

82. Adam Liptak, "Public Comments by Justices Veer Toward the Political," *The New York Times*, March 19, 2006, 22.

83. Antonin Scalia, with Bryan A. Garner, *Reading Law: The Interpretation of Legal Texts* (New York: Thomson/West, 2012).

84. Adam Liptak, "Ginsburg Has A Lot to Say About Trump," *The New York Times*, July 11, 2016, A1(3); Michael D. Shear, "Trump Calls Ginsburg 'A Disgrace To The Court,'" *The New York Times*, July 13, 2016, A9; and Michael D. Shear, "Ginsburg Says Her Remarks On Trump Were 'Ill Advised,'" *The New York Times,* July 15, 2016, A1(15).

85. Our discussion of interactions draws from Richard Davis, *Decisions and Images: The Supreme Court and the Press* (New York: Prentice Hall, 1994); also Robert E. Drechsel, *News Making in the Trial Courts* (New York: Longman, 1983).

86. Quoted in Elliot E. Slotnick and Jennifer A. Segal, *Television News and the Supreme Court* (New York: Cambridge University Press, 1998), 33–34.

87. When he retired in 1994, Justice Harry Blackmun gave his papers to the Library of Congress on the condition that they remained closed for five years.

88. Jon Stewart, *America (The Book)* (New York: Warner Brothers, 2004).

89. For a trenchant attack on the Roberts court as serving "Republican corporate interests" see Senator Sheldon Whitehouse, "Kavanaugh Confirmation Hearing Opening Statement," September 4, 2018.

90. Moving in this direction, see Peter Baker, "Conservatives Close In On 3-Decade Dream: Tipping Court to Right," *The New York Times*, July 10, 2018, A1 (15); and Lee Epstein and Eric Posner,"Above Politics No More," *The New York Times*, July 10, 2018, A23.

91. Adam Liptak, "Court Under Roberts Is Most Conservative in Decades," *The New York Times*, July 24, 2010, A1.

92. Adam Liptak, "Choice of Clerks Highlights Court's Polarization," *The New York Times*, September 7, 2010, A1, 14, and 15.

93. Adam Liptak, "Let Me Finish, Please: Conservative Men Dominate the Debate," *The New York Times*, April 18, 2017, A13.

94. *Zelman v. Simmons-Harris*, US Lexis 4885 (June 27, 2002).

95. Susan Michelich, "Media Coverage of the Supreme Court, 1999–2000 Term in *USA Today* and *ABC News*" (paper for "Politics and the Media," Duke University, November 2000), 7–8.

96. NBC News, April 15, 1990, cited in Elliot E. Slotnick and Jennifer A. Segal, *Television News and the Supreme Court* (New York: Cambridge University Press, 1998), 205 (their emphasis).

97. Richard Davis, ed., *Covering the United States Supreme Court in the Digital Age* (New York: Cambridge University Press, 2014).

98. Richard J. Lazarus, "The (Non)Finality of Supreme Court Opinions," 108 *Harvard Law Review* 540 (2014).

99. The American Bar Association, "Perceptions of the U.S. Justice System," http://www.abanet.org/media/perception/perception.html.

100. But see Michael A. Zilis, *The Limits of Legitimacy: Dissenting Opinions, Media Coverage, and Public Responses to Supreme Court Decisions* (Ann Arbor: University of Michigan Press, 2015).

101. These data come from Richard L. Fox and Robert W. Van Sickel, *Tabloid Justice: Criminal Justice in an Age of Media Frenzy* (Boulder, CO: Lynne Rienner Publishers, 2001), chap. 4 and the second edition, coauthored with Thomas L. Steiger (2007), chap. 4.

102. Frank R. Baumgartner, Suzanna L. De Boef, and Amber E. Boydstun, *The Politics of the Death Penalty* (New York: Cambridge University Press, 2008).

103. David Moberg, "Carrying Justice," Salon.com, March 1, 2000, http://www.salon.com/books/it/2000/0301/deathpenalty.

104. David Carr and John Schwartz, A Watchdog Professor, Now Defending Himself, *New York Tmes*, June 18, 2011, A1 (11).

# CHAPTER 16

# Policymaking and Domestic Policies

## 16.1 Preamble

During the 1990s, the U.S. crime rate declined precipitously.[1] Yet the amount of coverage of crime in the news media increased dramatically. Crime shows filled television. Hollywood films moved from a liberal to a conservative image of law.[2] The media broadened what is considered "criminal behavior."[3] This abundance of fictional depictions and factual reports framed crime as a threat, increased the public's fear, and primed crime as a problem demanding a response from policymakers.

Public officials implemented tough policies to stop this imagined outbreak of crime. These included treating juvenile offenders like adults, instituting mandatory minimum and longer sentences, the imposition of a lengthy prison term after a third conviction no matter how minor the crime (the catchy "three strikes" provision), and increasing the number of offenses subject to the death penalty.[4] These policies made little sense to experts as ways of preventing crime. They also cost a lot of money: California spent more on prisons than on all its public universities combined. Eventually, the federal government and some states, looking to save money, would change or modify the policy through alternatives to incarceration, especially of low-level drug offenders.

But as the years followed, media coverage changed. The system's abuses were exposed, its depredations revealed. Public officials changed their minds too. Eventually, Congress overwhelmingly passed and on December 21, 2018 President Trump signed "The First Step Act" in landmark prison reform.

Clearly, media depictions—amount of coverage, framing, and priming—can influence public policies for better or worse.

This chapter is devoted to policymaking and domestic policies. It starts with the U.S. economy, the economic crisis, and the government's response. Then it describes economic policymaking and the budget. Next come the influences on policies of political parties, the courts, interest groups, and public opinion. Four major policies follow: welfare, Social Security, education, and health care. The chapter concludes with policymaking, domestic policies in the information age, civic education, and with the coronavirus COVID-19 pandemic.

### Link

**First Step Act Signed on December 21, 2018**

Click here to learn more about the details of the First Step Act.

# 16.2 The U.S. Economy

## Learning Objectives

After reading this section, you should be able to answer the following questions:

1. What are some of the major economic disparities in the United States?
2. How did mortgage, credit, and regulatory policies contribute to the most recent economic crisis?
3. How did the government respond to the economic crisis?
4. Who makes economic policies, including the federal budget, in the United States?

**capitalism**

An economic system that emphasizes a free market, individual entrepreneurship, and limited government intervention in the economy and produces economic inequality.

The U.S. economic system is **capitalism**. It encourages individual enterprise, a free market, and relatively low taxation. It discourages government intervention in and regulation of the economy.

Capitalism can produce vast wealth and vast economic inequality. Ten percent of Americans possess 77 percent of the nation's wealth (distribution of assets); the bottom 80 percent have 12 percent.

The country's employment pattern is changing as some middle-class jobs are replaced by jobs paying less than the median wage. Many of these jobs are held by family breadwinners and no longer by teenagers. The biggest employers are major retailers, restaurant chains, and supermarkets, most of which have built their businesses on low pay (and low prices). Their combined profits are smaller than Apple's alone. Yet they employ 5.6 million people compared to Apple's 147,000.[5]

Economic inequality is related to social inequality. Women and men now attain similar levels of education. The earnings gap between them is shrinking slightly. On average, working women earn seventy-seven cents (to every dollar earned by working men. Professions most populated by women usually pay less than professions most populated by men: thus nurses (mostly women) are paid less than physicians (mostly men). Income gaps exist even in the same profession. Female university professors are generally paid less than male university professors, even at the same rank and with similar years of service.

Income differs dramatically by race and ethnicity. The median household income of white, Asian American, and Pacific Islander people averages above $55,000; for Black and Latinx people it is under $32,000. Black families and Latinx families are three times more likely to live in poverty than white families, although this gap, particularly between Black and white individuals, has shrunk over time due in part to government programs.

**inflation**

A rise in prices.

In 2007, the U.S. economy was humming along with the stock market soaring, employment high, and **inflation** (increases in the cost of living) low. Earlier in the decade, the media had reported the financial frauds and scandals of individual companies such as Enron and WorldCom, and the failure of the companies' accountants to catch them. Now, especially in the *Wall Street Journal* and on cable channel CNBC, they reported the booming economy, especially housing.

## Home Ownership

Public policies encourage the dream of home ownership by enabling people to deduct on their tax returns the interest they pay on their mortgage loan (a boon for the wealthy because the more interest you pay, the more you deduct) and by a Clinton-era law excluding from tax all or most of the profit they make from selling their homes. But these policies did little for people unable to obtain mortgages because of low income and poor credit records. President George W. Bush, promoting an "ownership society," pushed policies to enable the disadvantaged and those with poor credit, especially minorities, to buy homes.

This vastly increased the number of **subprime mortgages**—home loans made to people usually unqualified to receive them. Lenders peddled easy credit, asked for low or no down payments, and did not require incomes to be documented. Some borrowers were given adjustable mortgages with low initial teaser interest rates, which would later rise much higher, and were charged big fees hidden in the interest rates.

**subprime mortgages**
Loans to buy a house or apartment made to someone usually unqualified to receive them.

The Federal National Mortgage Association (Fannie Mae) and Federal Home Loan Mortgage Association (Freddie Mac) were shareholder-owned and profit-driven corporations sponsored by the government to buy mortgages from banks, thereby freeing up cash for new mortgages. They financed most of the home loans made in America. In part because of pressure from the Department of Housing and Urban Development (HUD), they plunged deeply into the market for subprime mortgages, relaxing credit requirements on the loans they bought from lenders. They also spent heavily on lobbying so that Congress did not raise their capital requirements.

## Complicated and Opaque Securities

Propelling the subprime mortgage market was the tremendous growth in complicated and opaque securities. Lenders sold the original mortgages to Wall Street and then used the cash to make still more loans. The investment and commercial banks sold packages of mortgages as mortgage-backed securities (MBS). These were then combined with other securities (e.g., commercial mortgages, credit card debt, and student loans) and sold as collateral debt obligations (CDOs).

Taking fees each time a loan was sold, packaged, securitized, and resold, the sellers made rich profits. They reaped even more by leveraging—borrowing to invest in more loans and packages. In 2004, the Securities and Exchange Commission allowed large investment banks to increase their leverage, a policy change the media barely reported. At its height, the ratio of borrowed funds compared to total assets soared to 33:1. Investors thereby vastly increased their purchases and profits—but also their potential losses.

To protect investors from losses, each package could be insured by a credit default swap (CDS). These guaranteed that if any borrowers in an MBS defaulted, the seller of the swap would pay the loss. The leading issuer was the American Insurance Group (AIG), with insurance on more than $400 billion in securities.

These arcane securities were rated "very safe" by the rating agencies. But these raters had an obvious conflict of interest: they were paid by the institutions whose securities they rated—rather like a movie producer paying a reviewer to write favorable reviews of his movies.

## Regulation

Gripped by a fervor for deregulation, the government had reduced its oversight of the financial system. In 1999, Congress enacted and President Clinton signed legislation enabling commercial banks, which collect deposits and loan money, to deal in securities—and thereby engage in speculative investments. The government also abolished many restrictions on affiliations between banks, investment companies, and insurance companies.

Regulation was the responsibility of an "alphabet soup" of federal agencies. These included the Federal Reserve Board, the Securities and Exchange Commission, the Office of the Comptroller of the Currency, the Office of Thrift Supervision, and the Federal Deposit Insurance Corporation. Their jurisdictions were splintered and confusing. Some mortgage lenders did not fall under any regulatory agency.

The government sometimes refused to seek regulatory authority even when it was desirable. The Federal Reserve Board, the Securities and Exchange Commission, the Clinton administration, and bipartisan majorities in Congress blocked proposals to regulate credit default swaps. Even when they had regulatory authority, agencies did not necessarily use it. The Federal Reserve Board did not investigate mortgage risks, and the Securities and Exchange Commission did not limit the amount of debt assumed by investment banks.

# Disaster and Collapse

As long as home prices went up, the value of homes increased, and interest rates remained low, homeowners could continue to pay their mortgages or sell at a profit. Flipping, or buying and selling property repeatedly to make money, became common.

Disaster loomed beneath this glittering surface. The American dream of home ownership turned into a nightmare. The Federal Reserve Board raised interest rates, thus increasing monthly payments for the many people with adjustable-rate mortgages. Some of them defaulted on their loans, losing their homes. House prices fell by around 25 percent in many major markets. Lenders or mortgage holders repossessed property, reselling it for less than the amount owed on the mortgage and thus taking a loss. There were so many failed mortgages that the sellers of credit default swaps did not have enough money to pay the claims.

Starting in June 2007, but only fully acknowledged in the fall of 2008, the financial system failed. Investment firms and banks declared bankruptcy or were taken over at fire-sale prices. The stock market collapsed. People's retirement accounts and the endowments of universities and colleges dropped precipitously. Fannie Mae and Freddie Mac, which had taken on debt to finance their purchases of mortgages, experienced huge losses on the defaults and were on the verge of insolvency.

There was a liquidity crisis: the credit market froze, making credit unavailable. Banks hoarded their capital and refused to lend. They assumed that other financial institutions were in financial trouble and would not be able to repay them. State and local governments, businesses, and families had difficulty borrowing and thus spending. There was a drastic fall in the demand for construction, investments, goods, and services.

Millions of Americans lost their jobs and thus their employer-provided health insurance. The crisis affected not only those with subprime mortgages but also those with regular mortgages; both groups often faced foreclosure on their homes. Nearly a quarter of all homes with mortgages became worth less than the money owed; these homeowners were thereby encouraged to default on (i.e., walk away from) their loans. Governments at all levels faced massive budget deficits as their income from taxes decreased and their expenditures to pay for the safety net of unemployment compensation and welfare increased.

# Policy Responses

**Great Depression**

The period of high unemployment, severe decreases in business activity, and falling prices in the United States that started in 1929 and ended with the onset of World War II.

The federal government's involvement in the economy, once controversial, is now tolerated if not expected. It was spurred by the **Great Depression** of the late 1920s and 1930s, in which the unemployment rate reached 25 percent. The task of policymakers faced with the new crisis was to rescue the economy and try to prevent the meltdown from happening again. This would entail far more government action to manage the economy than ever before.

Policymakers' responses initially lagged behind the crisis and were improvised and contradictory. The Bush administration requested $700 billion to buy up toxic mortgage securities but then used the funds to purchase stock in banks.

The responses became more focused. The Federal Reserve Board slashed interest rates to lower borrowing costs, bolster the real estate market, and encourage spending. Intervening in Wall Street in unprecedented ways, it committed trillions of dollars to rescue (bail out) the financial system and prevent the failure of major financial institutions. It gave them loans, guaranteed their liabilities, and brokered deals (e.g., takeovers or sales of one financial institution to another). It carried out these actions on the grounds that an economic collapse would cost millions of jobs.

President Obama's Treasury secretary, Timothy Geithner, devised a Public-Private Investment Program (PPIP) to buy up and hold as much as $1 trillion in toxic assets. The Treasury and Federal Reserve Board carried out stress tests to determine whether individual banks had the resources to survive a recession.

The government took over Fannie Mae and Freddie Mac. It extended as much as $400 billion credit to them and spurred them to refinance millions of homeowners at risk of losing homes. It left the future and fate of the corporations to be decided later. The government also funneled $185 billion into the insurance company American International Group (AIG) to keep it in business.

The Obama administration sought to create 2.5 million new jobs or at least protect existing jobs with a stimulus recovery plan of $787 billion. It invested in infrastructure—roads, bridges—and alternative sources of energy. It sent billions to the states for public schools, higher education, and child-care centers.

These programs would take time to be effective. For immediate relief, the administration provided funds for some people unable to pay their mortgages and sent the states additional monies for the safety net: unemployment insurance and other benefits.

On July 21, 2010, President Obama signed legislation imposing new regulations on the financial industry. The law was the result of detailed negotiations, compromises, and intense lobbying.

- It established a council consisting of government officials led by the Treasury secretary to track risks to the financial system.
- It set up a Bureau of Consumer Financial Protection inside the Federal Reserve Board.
- It empowered the board to liquidate failing large banks.
- It authorized the Securities and Exchange Commission to oversee private equity and hedge funds with assets of more than $150 million.
- It regulated some of the riskiest business practices and exotic investments (including credit derivatives).
- It curbed commercial banks' ability to make speculative investments for themselves (proprietary trading), although they could still make them for their clients.[6]

It was up to the regulators to work out the numerous details and implement the new law. Their actions would be subject to intensive lobbying by those affected. Meanwhile, the law was attacked by Republicans and the financial industry for creating more government bureaucracy and, they argued, undermining the economy's competitiveness. Advocates of more stringent regulation criticized it for, they claimed, doing little to reduce economic risk and not ending the likelihood of government bailouts.[7] In 2017, in control of both chambers of Congress and with President Trump in the White House, Republicans began to cut the regulations. Meanwhile, the benefits of the Obama policies carried over to the Trump presidency as the economy blossomed and unemployment dropped to an all-time low.

# Economic Policies

The government's dramatic response to the economic crisis was unusual, although it established a precedent for drastic governmental actions that could be more or less repeated, even expanded, under similar or even different circumstances. We now turn to the government's usual economic policies and the institutions, some of which we have already mentioned, responsible for deciding on and implementing them.

## Monetary Policy

**monetary policy**

Economic policy enacted by the Federal Reserve Board to manipulate the money supply and interest rates.

**Federal Reserve Board (the Fed)**

The body that supervises the U.S. banking system and executes monetary policy.

**Monetary policy** involves the amount of money available to the economy from such sources as banks, savings and loans, and credit unions. The **Federal Reserve Board (the Fed)** is responsible for monetary policy. The Fed supervises and regulates banking institutions and maintains the financial system to attain economic stability and promote growth. (This assumes that growth is desirable.) It uses three tools: the discount rate, reserve requirements, and open market operations.

### Link

**Federal Reserve Board (the Fed)**

Learn more about the Fed here.

The discount rate is what the Fed charges commercial banks for short-term loans. Lowering rates increases the banks' access to money, allowing banks to offer cheaper credit to businesses and the public, thereby stimulating the economy. The Fed does the reverse to slow down an "overheating" economy.

Reserve requirements stipulate the portions of deposits that banks must hold in reserve. By reducing reserve requirements, the Fed increases the money supply, thereby stimulating economic activity. Increasing the reserve requirements combats inflationary pressures.

Through its open market operations the Fed controls the money supply by buying and selling U.S. government securities. To stimulate the economy, the Fed increases the money supply by buying back government securities. To combat inflation, the Fed sells securities to the public and to businesses. This reduces the money supply as the Fed can take the cash paid out of circulation.

## Fiscal Policy

**fiscal policy**

Government economic policy involving taxation and spending.

**Fiscal policy** is the government taxing, spending, and borrowing. In theory, cutting taxes and increasing spending expand the economy and increase employment, while raising taxes and decreasing spending contract the economy and reduce inflation. Reality is more complex. Higher corporate and personal tax rates reduce the profit margins for companies and disposable income for the population at large. But the higher tax rates may be necessary for the government to afford its expenditure program, much of which can also increase demand and activity in the economy.

Fiscal policies are inherently political, favoring some people and groups more than and often at the expense of others. No wonder fiscal policies are debated and disputed by politicians and the political parties and lobbied by interest groups. Witness the Trump administration's tax cuts mainly favoring business and the wealthy, finally passed by the Republican-controlled Congress over Democratic objections in December 2017.

## The Administration

The main devisers of the president's economic program, in consultation with the political advisors, are the director of the White House National Economic Council (NEC), the secretary of the Treasury, the chair of the Council of Economic Advisors (CEA), and the director of the Office of Management and Budget (OMB).

The NEC coordinates domestic and international economic policymaking. Its director has an office in the West Wing and is responsible for brokering the ideas of the other economic policy advisors and controlling the president's daily economic briefings (assuming he has them).

The secretary of the Treasury usually comes from the financial or business world. The degree to which a Treasury secretary influences economic policy depends on his political skill and relations with the president. The Treasury Department is largely responsible for tax collection, payments and debt services, and enforcing federal finance and tax laws. Its interests include trade and monetary policy, international finance, and capital movements.

The CEA consists of three economists, usually academics. Ostensibly nonpartisan, they are appointed by the president and are members of the presidential staff. The chair of the CEA represents the council at the president's economic briefings. The CEA's job is to diagnose the health of the economy, analyze trends and developments, and offer recommendations. It also helps produce the president's annual economic report to Congress stating and justifying the administration's fiscal and monetary policy and priorities.

The OMB is largely responsible for preparing the president's budget and for establishing the budgets of federal agencies. It has substantial authority to control the bureaucracies and to enact the presidential policy agenda. It reviews every piece of proposed legislation submitted to Congress. Changes in agency regulations require OMB approval.

We've just described what these institutions do in theory. Reality is much messier. As insider accounts by journalists and participants can reveal, the institutions are run by individuals with sizable egos and often conflicting views of what to do about relatively simple, let alone complicated, policy issues. Some of them are adroit at political infighting. A book based on interviews with and documents from those involved tells (claims to tell) how the Obama economic "team" (including his chief of staff) struggled to decide the administration's response to the financial crisis and economic recession. It describes rivalries and disagreements; an imperious and domineering chief advisor who antagonized and alienated the others; and a Treasury secretary who was reluctant and on occasion failed to enforce decisions with which he disagreed (he denied the charge).[8] In a memoir, that (now former) Treasury secretary gives a milder account of responses to the crises. He focuses on the details of the discussions, arguments, disagreements, agreements, and the reasons for decisions.[9]

## Congress

The legislative branch influences fiscal policy through its "power of the purse" and authority over approval of the president's budget. The president needs congressional consent on all taxes and nearly all federal expenditures as well as any increase of the national debt limit. Congressional committees revise and alter the president's policies. Congress can also check the Fed by lessening its autonomy in setting monetary policy.

Members of Congress have party preferences, constituency needs, and interest group objectives in mind when considering policies. One or more of these may cause them to oppose or support the president's proposals. For example, Congress has historically been more protectionist (of domestic industries) on trade policies than presidents.

## The Budget

**budget**

A statement of the president's policy goals and priorities for the next fiscal year. It consists of receipts and expenditures.

The **budget** is a statement of the president's policy goals and priorities for the next fiscal year. It consists of two main parts. Receipts are the amounts anticipated in taxes and other revenue sources. Expenditures (outlays) are what the federal government expects to spend.[10]

The budget is submitted to Congress by February 1 of each year. It is studied by the House and Senate Budget Committees with the help of the Congressional Budget Office (CBO). The two committees prepare a budget resolution that sets ceilings for each of the items in the budget. In May, Congress adopts these budget resolutions. Over the summer, the House and Senate Appropriations Committees and their subcommittees decide on the specific appropriations. In September, Congress passes a second budget resolution that reconciles the overall and itemized budget ceilings with the overall and itemized appropriations. By the end of this process the specific budgetary allocations to various spending areas such as health, education, and defense have been approved by Congress. The modified document is then submitted to the president for signing, which he does if he accepts the congressional modifications. The president may choose to veto them, compelling the process of reconciliation to continue.

In reality, the timing of the passage of budget resolutions and the budget itself are dependent on the degree and intensity of partisan conflict, disagreement between Congress and the White House, disagreement between the House and Senate, and other clashes.

Conflict was particularly virulent during the second, two years of President Obama's first term and much of his second when Republicans controlled the House of Representatives. There were fights over stimulus packages, tax cuts, raising the ceiling on the national debt, and shutting down the government.

A showdown took place in fall 2013 when Congress failed to pass any federal spending bills for the 2014 fiscal year by the October 1 deadline. There were two main disagreements. First, members of the Republican majority in the House of Representatives offered to keep the government open but only in return for an end to financing for the Affordable Care Act. President Obama and the Democrats rejected it out of hand. The second disagreement was what to do about the sequester, the automatic spending cuts that had gone into effect on March 1, 2013. Republicans wanted to keep the entire amount of $85.4 billion for fiscal year 2013 but take less from the Pentagon and more from entitlements. Democrats sought the reverse. The deadlock partially shut down the federal government. The disruption and costs of the closings and curtailments were widely reported by the media. In addition to the usual examples of closed monuments and museums, government agencies announced the cessation of services, for example, by the Centers for Disease Control (CDC) of its seasonal flu-prevention program. These brought pressure on the antagonists, particularly the Republicans, to end the stoppage, which they did on October 16. The Affordable Care Act remained in force.

A fundamental issue persists. The federal government's expenditures significantly exceed its income from taxes and the like. There are mandatory entitlements: government programs such as Social Security, Medicare, Medicaid, veterans benefits, and interest payments on the national debt, that guarantee payments to all who are eligible. There is discretionary spending: government funds expended for defense, education, energy programs, environmental protection, law enforcement, infrastructure, and much more. The political parties disagree about the seriousness for the economy of the budget deficit and possible solutions.[11]

## Key Takeaways

The U.S. capitalist economic system produces vast wealth and vast inequality. In recent years, credit, mortgage, and regulatory policies contributed to an economic crisis. Responding to it, the government became more involved in managing the economy than ever before. Monetary policy is mainly determined by the Federal Reserve Board. Fiscal policy is mainly made by the president's economic advisors and Congress. Deciding the federal budget is a complicated process. It was particularly contentious between President Obama and the Republican-controlled House of Representatives.

## Exercises

1. What are some of the major social and economic inequalities in the United States? What do you think creates these inequalities?
2. What policies contributed to the economic crisis? What were those policies intended to achieve?
3. How did the federal government respond to the economic crisis? Who were the main actors behind formulating and implementing the government's response?
4. What are some of the differences between the formal organization of economic policymaking and the reality?
5. How is the federal budget decided?

# 16.3 Making Public Policies

## Learning Objectives

After reading this section, you should be able to answer the following questions:

1. What government actions make public policies?
2. Why and how do the political parties differ on policies?
3. How do the courts, interest groups, and public opinion influence policymaking and public policies?
4. What are the reasons for policy stability?
5. What are the reasons for policy change?

The institutions and agencies of government are involved in making public policies. They do so through enacting laws, imposing or cutting taxes, funding programs or not, issuing and enforcing regulations and rulings or not, and their use of force.

Under certain circumstances, changing all or some aspects of policies can be relatively uncomplicated. Witness President Trump's executive orders, followed in the early months of 2017 by President Trump and the Republicans in Congress taking advantage of the Congressional Review Act, which gives lawmakers sixty legislative days to overturn by majority votes major new regulations issued by federal agencies. They rescinded rules enacted late during the Obama presidency on "the environment, labor, financial protections, internet privacy, abortion, education, and gun rights."[12]

Usually, however, deciding on important public policies is much more difficult, even daunting, requiring the involvement of and decisions by more than one part of more than one branch of government. Consider the complexity of energy and immigration policies.

Energy policy involves a host of issues. They include (1) air and water pollution, (2) subsidies for oil and gas companies, (3) the risks and costs of allowing offshore drilling for oil (see discussion of the Gulf of Mexico oil "spill" in Chapter 14), (4) the dangers posed by nuclear reactors (vivid in the March 2011 catastrophe at Japan's Fukushima Daiichi power station), (5) coal mine disasters and sludge contamination, (6) the development and dangers of alternative technologies such as fracking, (7) building a pipeline to carry oil from Canada, (8) the dangers posed by industrial chemicals, and (9) what to do about global warming?

There are policy disagreements, especially between the political parties, about such proposals as raising energy efficiency standards, requiring utilities to derive more of their power from renewable sources, imposing a cap on carbon emissions from power plants, and increasing taxes on gasoline. President after president addressed energy issues and committed the United States to energy independence, all without success. (This was mocked by Jon Stewart when he showed eight presidents' rhetoric in a segment called "An Energy-Independent Future" on the June 16, 2010, episode of *The Daily Show*; view the segment here.)

Presidents and Congress and their political parties have also struggled over immigration policy:

- How to protect the nation's border? To construct a wall as demanded by President Trump?
- What to do about undocumented immigrants? Should they be deported?
- What do we do about those immigrants who stay in the country after their temporary visas expire?
- Should undocumented immigrants who have been living in America for some time be granted a path to citizenship?
- What about undocumented immigrants brought to the country as children?
- Should employers who hire undocumented immigrants be penalized—even when they claim they cannot distinguish real documents from fakes?
- Should Muslims from certain countries be banned?
- What migrants should be refused admission at the border and what should happen to them?

Proposed legislation, even with presidential support, to tackle such issues has encountered divisions between (and sometimes within) the political parties; passionate support (e.g., from some Latinx organizations) and opposition (e.g., from NumbersUSA) from interest groups; intense hostility from talk show hosts; and public attention. The Senate did pass an immigration bill in 2006, but it was defeated in the House of Representatives. The Senate then defeated a similar bill in June 2007.[13] Some states have taken action: as one example, Arizona passed a law in 2010 requiring the police, during a "lawful stop, detention or arrest," to check the immigration status of people they suspect are in the country illegally. Many of these laws have been appealed to the courts. In 2016 the Supreme Court, by a vote of 4–4, upheld an appeals court decision overturning President Obama's program to shield some five million undocumented immigrants from deportation and permitting them to work in the country.[14] President Obama's administration did expel over three million people. President Trump deported millions of undocumented immigrants, especially criminals.

As our discussions of energy and immigration policy indicate, political parties, the courts, interest groups, public opinion, and of course the media influence public policy.

## Political Parties and Policies

As we detailed in Chapter 10 and our discussion of the budget in this chapter, the political parties disagree on many policies. These differences may stem from conflicting values: for example, on abortion, the Republican Party is mostly pro-life, while Democrats are mostly pro-choice.

Politicians also espouse or oppose policies in their search for political advantage: while most leaders of the Republican Party oppose same-sex marriage from religious or ideological conviction, this position also represents the views of many of the party's adherents and a sizable (although decreasing) minority of the public.

The policy differences between the parties are clearly expressed in how they favor their constituencies. When Republicans gained control of the House of Representatives in 1994, the average Democratic district was receiving $35 million more annually in federal spending. By 2000, the average Republican district was receiving $612 million more than the average Democratic district. This change was based on policy: the Republicans increased business loans and farm subsidies and reduced public housing grants and funding for food stamps. It was also a conscious strategy of directing federal spending toward districts where the Republican incumbents were vulnerable to election defeat.[15]

## Unemployment

The economic issue with the most potent political repercussions for President Obama and both parties was unemployment. People's unhappiness about the lack of jobs helps explain the Republicans' victories and the Democrats' defeats in the 2010 elections. The official unemployment rate hovered around 9 percent in 2011. Adding some eleven million people who had given up looking for jobs or accepted part-time work increased unemployment to around 17 percent. Almost half of the unemployed had been without work for six months or more. The public sector laid off workers as state and local governments reduced their budget deficits. Although the private sector added jobs, it was barely adequate to absorb people entering the workforce. Many of these jobs paid hardly enough to live on, if that. Gradually over the years, the official unemployment rate improved, reaching an all-time low in April 2019.

The parties differed on the best policies to create jobs and reduce unemployment. For Republicans, it has been cutting taxes and reducing regulation of business. For Democrats, the federal government should stimulate the economy by "investing" (Republicans replace that positive term with the negative "spending") in infrastructure, education, child care, and other programs. Doing so would likely increase the budget deficit, which Republicans oppose. However, the advent of President Trump could have worsened the deficit situation, but he did fulfill his promise to embark on a major infrastructure program.

# The Courts and Policies

As we showed in Chapter 15, the courts make public policies. In a notable example, the Supreme Court in 2014, reversing an appeals court decision, upheld by 6–2 the authority of the Environmental Protection Agency (EPA) to regulate the pollution from coal-fired power plants in twenty-eight Midwestern and Appalachian states that wafts over East Coast states. The Court rejected the arguments of fifteen polluting states and the utilities that the rules gave the EPA too much authority and placed too heavy a burden on the utilities (about a thousand power plants) to install equipment to control the pollution.[16] In effect, the Court approved the Obama administration's efforts to use the Clean Air Act to combat global warming.

# Interest Groups and Policies

As detailed in Chapter 9, interest groups strive to influence public policy. They seek access to and provide information to policymakers, lobby the institutions of government, and try to use the media to transmit their perspectives and arguments.

Here it is appropriate to mention interest groups known as think tanks. They have an impact on policy because they advocate ideas and specialize in research. They cover the ideological spectrum—the Brookings Institution is centrist, the Center for American Progress and the Economic Policy Institute are liberal. But until the advent of the Obama administration, those promoting conservative views, such as the American Enterprise Institute, were the most influential. The Trump presidency brought the conservatives back in favor. Think tanks market their policy prescriptions through public relations and media outreach strategies. Their claimed policy expertise, access to and contacts with policymakers, and visibility in the media contribute to their influence on policy.[17] Then there are organizations such as the Employment Policies Institute and the Center for Consumer Freedom, which, despite their authoritative-sounding names, were founded by an advertising and public relations executive to challenge the studies and findings of liberal groups (e.g., in favor of raising the minimum wage).[18]

## Public Opinion and Policies

Policymakers often look to follow public opinion, especially if doing so harmonizes with their political interests. At the same time, they are skeptical about public opinion, which, as we discussed in Chapter 7, can be contradictory or unclear. Few of a representative sample of members of Congress, presidential appointees, and civil servants in the Senior Executive Service agreed with the statement that "Americans know enough about issues to form wise opinions about what should be done."[19]

So policymakers often track public opinion less as a guide to policies they should adopt than to find the frames, arguments, and phrases to try to move it and policymakers closer to their policy preferences. (See our discussion in Chapter 13.) Republicans and conservatives increased support for repeal of the estate tax by framing it as the "death tax," leading people to think that it applied to far more Americans than the 2 percent who fell under it.[20]

Yet public opinion, if probed in depth, can be revealing and compelling. A study of more than 80,000 Americans by the Program for Public Consultation at the University of Maryland found majorities of both political parties agreeing on significant policies. These included "police reform, immigration, poverty and jobs, social security, budget and taxes, health care, trade, energy and the environment, nuclear weapons and government reform."[21]

## Policy Stability

Much policymaking consists of continuing existing policies or of making incremental, that is small, changes to them. Obstacles to change include the separation of powers, the bicameral legislature, the filibuster in the Senate, and the presidential veto.

Members of Congress may resist a president's initiative because they view it as bad policy, think it will damage their reelection prospects, or believe it will hurt their party.[22] Bureaucrats, existing in a stable hierarchy, are usually comfortable administering existing policies. The federal courts exercise judicial review finding new policies constitutional or not. Powerful interest groups often benefit from prevailing policies and therefore want to maintain rather than change them.

Another reason for policy stability is the existence of policy subsystems in a policy area. (See the discussion of iron triangles in Chapter 9.) These consist of the leading members and staff of the congressional committee or subcommittee that makes the laws on the subject, the bureaucrats responsible for enforcing the laws, and the interest groups affected by the laws. The participants in these subsystems may compete over specifics, but they agree on core beliefs, control information, and have a low profile. Too complex and detailed to attract much media attention and thus public mobilization against them, the policies of these subsystems are infrequently changed significantly. For example, the government continues to subsidize agriculture to the sum of some $20 billion annually.

# Policy Change

Policy stability is sometimes punctuated. Significant policy changes and innovations do take place.[23] There are several causes that often overlap. They are (1) changes in control of the government, (2) crises and disasters, and (3) media depictions and framing. They are abetted by public awareness, the involvement of advocacy and interest groups, and policy ideas about what the changes should be.

A dramatic shift in policies often follows a sweeping election victory of a president and his party, as with the enactment of the Voting Rights Act and the antipoverty program of President Lyndon Johnson's Great Society after the 1964 election. Or it happens after a change of party control of Congress: the Republicans enacted elements of their Contract with America after they won Congress in 1994. Policy change can follow a change in party control of the presidency, as in the tax cuts and increases in defense spending after Republican Ronald Reagan was elected president in 1980. Or the drastic changes intended by President Trump (see Chapter 13 Section 4, The Presidency).

Rapid policymaking can take place after crises or situations portrayed by the president and the media as crises.[24] The Patriot Act was passed on October 29, 2001, less than two months after the 9/11 attacks on the World Trade Center and the Pentagon.

For events to change an existing policy or produce a new one, media attention is usually required. Useful is a "focusing event" that puts or elevates an issue on the policy agenda. The near-catastrophic 1979 accident at a nuclear power plant at Three Mile Island in Pennsylvania raised awareness of nuclear power as a problem for, rather than a solution to, America's energy needs. The accident was framed by the news media with alarmist coverage and by "I told you so" warnings from antinuclear groups, which increased public fear about nuclear safety. It stopped new construction of nuclear plants for many years.

Policy changes can have different fates. They may become entrenched, eroded, reversed, or reconfigured.[25] In particular, general interest reforms "to rationalize governmental undertakings or to distribute benefits to some broad constituency," such as changes in taxation, are not necessarily sustained. The politicians who achieve them leave the scene or move on to other issues.

## Key Takeaways

Policymaking involves government deciding on laws, taxing and spending, and regulations and rulings, and responding to and dealing with situations and events. It often requires negotiation and compromise and is influenced by interest groups, public opinion, and the media. Policy stability is common, but policy change can take place, particularly after a crisis or when party control of the presidency or Congress (or both) changes.

## Exercises

1. Which are the most important policymaking parts of the government?
2. Which party's policies make more sense to you?
3. How do you explain policy stability?

4. What are the obstacles to making major changes in federal government policy?
5. What can lead to dramatic changes in policy?

# 16.4 Major Domestic Policies

## Learning Objectives

After reading this section, you should be able to answer the following questions:

1. What were the main changes in welfare policy?
2. What are the main problems with Social Security and the proposals to rectify them?
3. What were the strengths, weaknesses, and fate of No Child Left Behind and "Common Core"?
4. What are the differences between Medicare and Medicaid?
5. What are the significant provisions of and problems with Obamacare?

We now describe the development and current conditions of four of the federal government's main domestic policies: welfare, Social Security, education, and health care.

But before doing so, we would note a vital distinction in expenditures for these policies, which we call *public social spending*, and of *social benefits* that are delivered by or subsidized through the tax code. The latter include tax deductions for retirement pensions, home mortgage interest, and for charitable giving. Overwhelmingly favoring the affluent, these social benefits cost the federal government billions of dollars a year but are not particularly perceived as benefits bestowed on them.[26]

## Welfare Policies

**welfare**

Government aid to those in need.

For some scholars and American policymakers, the need for welfare (public assistance) arises from the very conditions of life itself. Researchers Theodore R. Marmor, Jerry L. Mashaw, and John Pakutka identify "six threats to family income." They are: "birth into a poor family," "early death of a family breadwinner," "ill-health," "involuntary unemployment," "disability," and "outliving one's savings."[27] Some would add the failure of the economic system to provide enough jobs at a living wage, racism, and sexism. From these perspectives, people are not much to blame for needing **welfare**. Policymakers should therefore support policies to alleviate poverty (e.g., by increasing the minimum wage or lengthening the period of unemployment compensation) and try to eliminate the causes of the need for welfare.

An alternative view blames people for their fate. Public assistance violates the American values of individual enterprise and responsibility. Welfare recipients would rather collect government handouts than work. Benefits should be designed to put them to work. Welfare is to be reviled. It should be given grudgingly and with stringent conditions attached.

The services and benefits governments provide through their social policies vary widely. Scandinavian countries, such as Norway, establish a safety net from the cradle to the grave. Americans rely more on employment and private sources (insurance policies) than the government for their income and to protect them against economic misfortune.

There are several sources of income from the government for people with no or low income. They include the Earned Income Tax Credit, housing subsidies, Special Supplementary Nutrition Program for Women, Infants and Children (WIC), National School Lunch Program, and Low Income Home Energy Assistance. Whether all the people who would benefit from any of these programs know about, are eligible or qualify for, claim, and receive them, is questionable.

Food stamps are an example of an extensive welfare program. Around 46 million people receive them, with an average benefit of $500 a month for a family of four. Removing the stigma of welfare from the stamps, the government changed the name to Supplemental Nutrition Assistance Program. Making it even more acceptable, it is supported by farmers and grocery stores.[28] The Agriculture Department has tried to protect the program from its adversaries, particularly Republicans in Congress, by announcing steps to fight fraud and ensure benefits only go to the eligible. Nonetheless, in February 2014, Congress passed and the president signed a five-year farm bill that cut funds for food stamps by $800 million a year. President Trump subsequently proposed more cuts.

## Changes in Welfare Policies

In his successful 1991 campaign for the presidency, Democrat Bill Clinton preempted what had been a Republican issue by promising to "put an end to welfare as we know it." In 1996, after rejecting previous versions, he signed a Republican bill, the Personal Responsibility and Work Opportunity and Reconciliation Act (PRWORA). It helped him get reelected later that year.

This law replaced Aid for Dependent Children (AFDC) with the Temporary Assistance to Needy Families (TANF) program. The federal government gives states grants in aid and greater autonomy in structuring their welfare systems if they follow rules. Adult welfare recipients are limited to a lifetime total of five years of TANF benefits. State governments lose some of their TANF funding unless they show that significant numbers of their welfare recipients are entering the workforce. To receive benefits, children under eighteen must live with their parents or in an adult-supervised setting.

### Links

**Welfare Policies**

Read the Personal Responsibility and Work Opportunity and Reconciliation Act (PRWORA) and information on the Temporary Assistance to Needy Families (TANF) program.

Since the law was passed, some states have reported decreases of over 50 percent in their number of welfare recipients. However, it remains to be seen if the changes in welfare policy have led to less poverty or simply removed people from the welfare rolls.[29] Given the economic decline stemming from the coronavirus, the effects on people who had moved from welfare to employment and then lost their jobs have been severe.

# Social Security

Some policies are controversial at the start, then build up powerful support from their current and future beneficiaries, becoming widely accepted, even treasured, by the public. Over time, they grow in complexity and cost. **Social Security** is a notable example.

**Social Security**

Social insurance program for older adults.

## Link

**Social Security**

Click here for more information about Social Security.

Among Americans most distressed by the Great Depression were the nation's older adults, many of whom lost their savings and were unable to support themselves. President Franklin D. Roosevelt and Congress attempted to address this problem through the Social Security Act of 1935.

**FIGURE 16.1 Franklin D. Roosevelt and the Great Depression**
These figures, part of the "Breadline Sculpture" memorial to President Franklin D. Roosevelt, symbolize the desperate conditions and economic hard times for the general populace during the Great Depression, and President Roosevelt's Social Security policy in response.

Source: © Shutterstock, Inc.

**social insurance**

Government invests individuals' mandatory payroll deductions in a trust fund to be distributed according to specific criteria (e.g., age).

It established a system of **social insurance** in which taxes on payrolls were used to provide benefits to some older Americans, although not to Black agricultural and domestic workers until the fifties. Social Security was soon expanded to cover benefits for "survivors," including widows, dependent children, and orphans. In 1956, Americans living with disability were added to the list of beneficiaries, thus formally creating the Old-Age, Survivors, and Disability Insurance (OASDI) system.[30] In 1972, benefit levels were tied to the consumer price index—benefit levels go up when the consumer price index does.

Social Security now provides benefits to over sixty-one million Americans. It is the main source of economic survival for two-thirds of the older adults and the only source of income for over 30 percent of the aged.

## Social Security's Solvency

Traditionally, more money has been paid into the Social Security Trust Fund than drawn out, leading to a revenue surplus. But Americans are living longer than ever. Longer lives mean larger payouts from the fund, as there is no limit on the number of years people receive benefits. Also, recent generations entering the workforce are generally smaller in size than their predecessors. By 2040, there will not be enough money in the fund to finance recipients at the current level.[31]

Special commissions have issued reports, with alarmist stories by the press, about these problems. Proposals to "fix" Social Security have been developed by these commissions, think tanks, other interest groups, and a few politicians (most of them no longer in office). Policymakers are wary of suggesting that they may tamper with the revered system; they propose change with delicacy. Thus, in 1983 the age of eligibility for full retirement benefits was increased from sixty-five to sixty-six, but the change wasn't effective until 2009; the age increases to sixty-seven in 2027.

Additional revenue could be generated by increasing the percentage of the payroll tax or the amount to which it is applied on employees' wages and employers' contributions. However, tax increases are never popular among elected officials, so these options lack advocates in Congress.

## President Bush's Proposals

Thinking to trade on the momentum of his 2004 reelection, President George W. Bush went public with a campaign to inspire public and congressional support for his proposals to "save" Social Security.[32] Launching his campaign in his State of the Union address, he embarked on a high-profile "60 Cities in 60 Days" tour. His theme: Social Security was in perilous condition. He proposed to save it through personal (private) savings accounts. People would be allowed to invest a third of their Social Security withholdings into a variety of investment options such as the stock market.

The argument for privatization is that the stock market greatly outperforms the Social Security's trust fund over the long term.[33] Over time, therefore, privatized investment would be a boon to the overall size of the trust fund and protect the solvency of the system.

The president appeared at town hall meetings with handpicked, sympathetic audiences. Signs saying "Protecting our Seniors" flanked him. He used the positive and evocative words "choice" and "ownership" to describe his proposals.

President Bush was supported by such powerful interest groups as the U.S. Chamber of Commerce and the Business Roundtable. He also received support from potential beneficiaries of his proposed changes: Wall Street firms would receive billions of dollars to manage personal accounts.

The president faced opposition from Democrats and powerful interest groups such as organized labor and AARP (formerly the American Association of Retired Persons). They were bolstered by experts in Social Security policy who provided information challenging and undermining Bush's arguments and claims.

Critics of the president's proposals argued that there was no crisis; that the stock market goes down as well as up, so investing in it is risky and people could end up with reduced retirement income, and that private investment accounts would require the government to borrow about $2 trillion to offset the reduction in payroll taxes to avoid a shortfall in payments owed to current retirees. Most dramatically, the president's opponents contended that his proposals would destroy the program.

## Media Coverage

It was a perfect setup for the news media. On one side were the president and his nationwide campaign; on the other side was the opposition. Experts could be called on to assess the validity of both sides' arguments. This was all done on a policy issue—the future of Social Security—of public interest and concern.

From the start, media coverage undermined the president. The very first story in the *New York Times* set the pattern. It was headlined, "As White House Begins Campaign for Overhauling Social Security, Critics Claim Exaggeration."[34] It cited "outside analysts," including the nonpartisan Congressional Budget Office and academics casting doubt on the president's arguments. It contained this devastating paragraph: "White House officials privately concede that the centrepiece of Mr. Bush's approach to Social Security—letting people invest some of their payroll taxes in private accounts—would do nothing in itself to eliminate the long-term gap."

Perhaps because there was no new news in the president's appearances and statements, stories reporting them focused on the rigged audiences, the "carefully screened panelists," and meticulously staged "conversations."[35]

The more the president spoke, the less the public supported his proposals. From early January into May 2005, public opinion approval about the way Bush was handling Social Security decreased from 41 to 31 percent, while disapproval increased from 52 to 64 percent.[36]

The president ended his campaign. Personal retirement accounts disappeared from Congress's policy agenda.

# Education Policies

Traditionally, education policy has been the domain of state and local governments. Schools are funded mainly by local property taxes. Consequently, schools' resources and thus their quality of education depend on their location, with vast differences between and often within school districts.

**FIGURE 16.2 Education Funding from Property Taxes**
Because much of their funding comes from property taxes, the quality of schools differs drastically, even in the same city and district.

Sources:WhisperToMe. Via Wikimedia: https://commons.wikimedia.org/wiki/File:WestsideHSHouston.JPG; WhisperToMe. Via Wikimedia: https://commons.wikimedia.org/wiki/File:LeeHighSchoolHouston.JPG.

The federal government's limited involvement began to change in the 1960s as part of President Lyndon Johnson's War on Poverty. The 1965 Elementary and Secondary Education Act (ESEA) allotted funds for developing remedial programs, hiring teachers and aides, and purchasing supplies and equipment. The Head Start Program, also established in 1965, provided low-income children with preschool education. The Department of Education was created in 1979.

## No Child Left Behind (NCLB)

Fulfilling his campaign pledge, repeated in his inaugural address, to close the gap in achievement between minority children and those living in poverty and white children attending primarily schools in the suburbs and to improve school performance, President George W. Bush obtained overwhelming passage of significant amendments to the ESEA in the **No Child Left Behind Act** of 2001. He signed the legislation into law in an elaborate ceremony accompanied by his bipartisan congressional allies.

**No Child Left Behind Act**

President George W. Bush's policy, enacted into law, to improve education.

### Link

**The No Child Left Behind Act of 2001**

Read the complete No Child Left Behind Act here.

The law was a major policy accomplishment by the president. Placing its administration in the Education Department, he overcame the opposition of some of his party's leaders who wanted to abolish the department. Imposing federal requirements on schools, he radically changed federal-state relations in education.[37]

The law called for states to implement accountability systems covering all public schools and students and to test all students in grades 3–8 in reading and math. Schools failing to make adequate yearly progress toward goals are subject to corrective actions and restructuring. To increase parental choice for children attending an underperforming school, schools are required to let low-income parents use allotted federal funding to pay for tuition at a school in the district that has attained acceptable standards.

### Comparing Content

**No Child Left Behind**

President Bush touted No Child Left Behind as a great domestic accomplishment of his administration. He promoted it from the White House, on radio, and in speeches.[38] Education Secretary Rod Paige talked it up throughout the country. The Department of Education created a website and issued publications and press releases describing the act and how its objectives were being achieved.

The *New York Times* persistently contradicted the administration's beguiling rhetoric. Reporters detailed problems in how the program was administered and implemented. The newspaper's education writer critically evaluated the policy, and the editorial page's verdict on the program was caustic.

The newspaper pointed out that states had widely different standards for measuring students' progress—there was no agreement on how much students needed to know to be considered proficient. Many states had low proficiency standards. Students aced these state tests only to fail more rigorous federal exams.[39] States with high standards could be penalized by having many failing schools, while states with low standards and poor performance would be left alone.[40]

According to the newspaper, schools reported implausibly high graduation rates and low dropout rates even as they were pushing out low achievers in order to keep up test scores. School districts were not enforcing and failed to meet a provision in the law requiring a "highly qualified" teacher in every classroom by 2006.[41] Only 12 percent of the two million students in public schools eligible for free tutoring were receiving it. Above all, the Bush administration's funding of the program was billions of dollars short of the amount authorized by Congress.

The *Times* printed an op-ed about the Department of Education's rankings of reporters on a one hundred–point scale "depending on whether their stories were critical or favorable toward the law."[42] Repeated revelations (first reported in *USA Today*) came up that media commentators had been paid to promote the policy, including one pundit who received $240,000 and often appeared on television and radio without mentioning the payment.

The *Times* coverage focused on the program's inadequacies and failures, its duplicity and deception. Exposure is a news value, common in journalism; the *Times* reporters were doing their job. Missing, though, was an adequate acknowledgment and appreciation of the program's accomplishments and the difficulty of achieving its goals.

In time, NCLB was widely criticized for demanding unachievable targets and punishing schools for failing to meet them. In response to this criticism and a bevy of complaints, the Department of Education granted waivers to states from the requirements, including on the states' willingness to accept charter schools (a broad term describing more than five thousand private schools, some run for profit, set up mainly in urban areas, some operating over the internet, with local, state, and private funds, to compete with public schools).

Nonetheless, the emphasis on test scores was condemned: for not measuring creativity, judgment, and character, and for driving out of the curriculum subjects such as art and music, as they are difficult to test. Moreover, teacher ratings based on their students' test scores are said to reflect who the students are, not how well they are taught.

## The Obama and Trump Administrations

President Obama's secretary of education, Arne Duncan, promised to rectify the defects of NCLB. He embraced competition, accountability, parental choice, and incentives. He proposed to raise academic standards, end the misleading identification of thousands of schools as failing, turn around schools that were truly failing, recruit and retain effective teachers, track students' and teachers' performance, and tie teacher evaluation to students' test scores. He wanted to increase the number of charter schools.

Duncan promoted the development of "Common Core State Standards," national standards in English and math, specifying the skills students should have at each grade level. They were adopted by many states which therefore had to rethink teacher training, textbooks, and testing.

Secretary Duncan also created the Race to the Top competition, allocating $4.3 billion in education aid to states that complied with the Obama administration's educational goals. But this was a modest sum, won by only a few states, compared with the approximately $650 billion spent on K–12 education annually.

So even though the federal government became far more involved in education than ever before, it could only prod rather than compel the states and localities to do its bidding.

Then, in December 2015, Congress passed and President Obama signed bipartisan legislation that marked a major retreat by the federal government from its oversight role. It left education standards, ratings, sanctions, and how to fix failures up to the states and localities. It still required standardized testing in reading and math but turned the responsibility of what weight to give them in ratings over to the states and local education authorities.[43]

President Trump, his education secretary, Betsy DeVos, and their Republican allies seemed determined to reduce the federal government's involvement even more and to return power over K–12 education back to the local and state levels.[44] They also favored reducing the importance of public schools, and replacing them with charter schools, vouchers, tuition tax credits, and home and for-profit schooling.

This conflict extended to higher education. In June 2019, to take effect in July 2020, DeVos announced a repeal of the Obama administration's "gainful employment rule" that required career and certificate programs, most from for-profit colleges and universities, to prove their graduates could find gainful employment in order for them to keep access to federal financial aid. This rule also required ads for for-profit colleges and universities to compare the student debt load of their graduates with their expected career earnings. Democrats criticized the repeal for propping up low-quality for-profit colleges at the expense of students and taxpayers.[45]

# Health-Care Policies

Program by program, the federal government has contributed to the costs of medical care for some of the people who have difficulty paying their medical bills or have no health insurance. The media have encouraged the creation of such government policies by consistently reporting, with examples, about the large number of uninsured Americans without adequate doctor, prescription drug, and hospital care.

## Medicare

In 1965, the most extensive health coverage legislation in American history became law. **Medicare** helps citizens sixty-five and older meet their primary medical care needs. It covers around fifty-five million people.

**Medicare**

Federal program of medical benefits to those over age sixty-five.

Medicare has two parts. Part A pays some of the hospital charges for individuals who are eligible for Social Security benefits. It is funded by payroll deductions and matching contributions from a patient's employer. People are responsible for both a deductible charge that must be paid before Medicare payments are authorized and copayments for many hospital-related services. There are no limits on the total costs people can incur.

Part B is an optional insurance system covering health-care costs outside of hospital stays for physician services, medical tests, and outpatient visits. Participants pay a monthly fee, deductible charges, and copayments. The government contributes about three-fourths of the overall costs.

## Prescription Drugs

Medicare's lack of a prescription drug benefit was particularly hard on the older adults and those living with a disability, who commonly take several prescription drugs. Responding to this need, the Medicare Prescription Drug and Modernization Act of 2003 contains two types of assistance programs (see here). The first is a prescription drug discount card program that saves Social Security recipients roughly 15 percent to 25 percent annually.

In the program's more substantial part, individuals pay an annual premium and deductible in return for the federal government paying 75 percent of their prescription drug costs up to a certain maximum.

Because of exploding health-care costs and the new prescription drug benefit, Medicare may be in worse financial shape than Social Security. According to the program's trustees, its hospital insurance trust funds might run out of money soon.[46]

## Medicaid

**Medicaid**

Program that finances medical and long-term care for adults and children living with a disability or living in poverty.

**Medicaid** was created in 1965. It provides health-care coverage for approximately fifty million Americans who are living in poverty or living with a disability. More than a third of them are over sixty-five. The federal government pays about half the costs of their medical care, including hospital stays, physician fees, and various diagnostic services. States pay the remainder of the costs of the coverage.

### Link

**Medicaid**

Click here to learn more about Medicaid.

The federal government requires coverage of the blind, those living with a disability, and children (Children's Health Insurance Program) under the age of eighteen whose family's income is below the poverty level. Otherwise, states decide eligibility for inclusion in Medicaid. State standards vary significantly; someone eligible in California might be excluded in Texas. Nonetheless, Medicaid pays approximately two-thirds of the costs of nursing home care in this country.

Because of the high cost of health-care services covered under Medicaid, state governments have become increasingly burdened financially. Other than education, Medicaid takes up the single greatest percentage of state budgets, a cost that is increasing. This situation has caused states to cut back on a number of the program's optional medical services.

## The Uninsured

When President Obama took office, around fifty-one million Americans lacked health insurance. This figure included approximately nine million under the age of eighteen who were eligible for but not enrolled in Medicaid or the Children's Health Insurance Program. Some twenty-eight million people came from households with income above the poverty line but whose employers did not provide them with health insurance. Their work was often temporary or part-time and low-paid. About fifteen million of the uninsured had income below the poverty line yet were not receiving Medicaid.

Politicians proposed policies in response to the lack of health care. Most notably, the Clinton administration, led by First Lady Hillary Clinton, proposed health-care coverage for all United States citizens. This 1994 initiative died for lack of sufficient support in Congress, in part because of its complexity and partly because of a negative advertising campaign run by interest groups against it.[47]

## President Obama and Health Care

After he assumed office in 2009, President Obama took up health care as a major policy initiative. His administration negotiated (i.e., bargained) with every major sector of the health-care industry to support its health-care proposals. Motivating the industry was the drop in the number of employers insuring their employees or providing generous coverage and the number of employees who could afford to pay their share of the cost of insurance. This resulted in fewer Americans with insurance coverage and thus unable to pay for hospital care, doctors, and drugs.

At the heart of the bargain "was a simple quid quo pro: accept greater government regulation and involvement in return for greater guaranteed financing."[48] The government would require people to have insurance, thereby not only leaving the for-profit private insurance group industry in place, but also greatly expanding the market. This bargain did not prevent each industry group from lobbying to modify or scuttle provisions in the legislation that might reduce its members' income. The drug industry opposed studying the effectiveness of treatment; the American Medical Association lobbied to kill the proposal for a government-run insurer (i.e., the public option); hospital lobbyists objected to a Medicare oversight board that could reduce payments.[49]

In March 2010, the Democratic majority in Congress passed the Patient Protection and Affordable Care Act, arguably the most important domestic legislation in decades. It passed without a single Republican vote; Republicans believe it interferes with the free market, relies far too much on government regulation, and is a bureaucratic nightmare. It also passed despite the millions of dollars of advertising aimed at the forty Democrats in the House deemed vulnerable to defeat if they voted for the bill. In this instance, party loyalty, appeals from party leaders (especially the president), advertisements from supporters of the legislation, and the realization that this was the most propitious opportunity to enact health-care reform in many years overcame the opponents' arguments and advertising.

The 2,700-page-long law is complicated; many provisions would not go into effect until 2014 or later. Bureaucrats had to write thousands of pages of regulations to define terms such as "benefits" and clarify the details. States would have to implement many provisions. Lobbying was intense. The Republican majority in the House of Representatives voted numerous times to repeal the law (futilely, because the Senate never took up the House bills).

The law was designed eventually for around thirty-two million uninsured Americans to have health insurance through their employer, by purchasing it, or through Medicaid. Although some Democratic legislators favored a "public option" alternative, that is, insurance the government would sell, the administration deemed it politically unfeasible and it was not a part of the law.

Instead, the law expanded eligibility and subsidized lower premiums for Medicaid, transforming it from a government health-insurance program for families living in poverty into a much wider program covering millions of Americans, including able-bodied adults under age sixty-five who earn no more than 133 percent of the federal poverty level. People not covered by their employers and who earn too much to qualify for Medicaid would be able to buy coverage from state-based insurance purchasing organizations. The law also prohibited insurance companies from rejecting people for preexisting medical conditions, removed annual and lifetime limits on payments by insurance companies, and enabled children to stay on their parents' policies until they turned twenty-six.

In June 2012, the U.S. Supreme Court ruled on the Affordable Care Act.[50] By a 5–4 vote it upheld the law's individual mandate requiring almost all Americans to buy health insurance or pay a penalty. Chief Justice Roberts called the penalty a kind of tax that Congress could impose using its taxing power (but not its power under the Constitution's commerce clause).

However, the Court by 7–2 overturned the provision in the law that states failing to comply with the requirements that they expand their Medicaid program to cover low-income people lose all their Medicaid funding. Only new funds would be lost. Given the opportunity afforded by the Supreme Court, around half the states, almost all of them controlled by Republicans, refused to expand their Medicaid programs, thereby leaving millions of people without medical coverage even though the federal government would pay approximately 93 percent of the cost through the nine years from 2014.

Then in June 2015, by 6–3, the Court ruled that the Internal Revenue Service could continue to issue subsidies to people buying plans on the federal website.[51]

From the start, however, opponents and some supporters of the law, and of course the media, focused on its problems. First, the site was a disaster: cumbersome, subject to overload, and plagued by hundreds of bugs.[52] Later on, the costs of insurance increased considerably; many people remained uninsured; and choice disappeared as insurance companies canceled policies even though President Obama had repeatedly but erroneously told people, "If you like your plan, you can keep it."

Determined to end Obamacare, the Republicans had a dilemma: repeal or replace it and, if the latter, with what? The law's popular provisions and the number of people it covered made repeal politically risky, a risk increased by President Trump's unconvincing promise to replace it with a far less expensive and far better program. In control of the House, Democrats sought to protect the program, while some of their more ambitious presidential candidates proposed such ambitious policies as Medicare for All.

## Key Takeaways

This section discussed the development and current conditions of four of the main domestic policies: welfare, Social Security, education, and health care. We explained why and how the federal government, particularly the presidency, became involved, changes in involvement over time, the policies pursued, which ones were enacted into law, their effects, and concomitant issues.

## Exercises

1. What led the federal government to consider major changes to its welfare, Social Security, education, and health-care policies? What were the obstacles to change in each case?
2. Should No Child Left Behind be repealed or modified?
3. Should the Affordable Care Act be repealed or modified?
4. What major domestic policy do you think the government needs to take action on? What factors do you think prevent the government from doing something about it?

# 16.5 Policymaking and Domestic Policies in the Information Age

## Learning Objectives

After reading this section, you should be able to answer the following questions:

1. What are the five stages of the policymaking process?
2. What are some of the ways the media depict policymaking?
3. What are some of the ways the media influence policymaking?

According to a former White House staffer in the George W. Bush administration, the shifts "from discussing any actual policy pros and cons to discussing political communications, and media strategy" were "near instant."[53] The Bush administration may have gone to extremes, but as we have documented throughout this book, people in government and politics interact with the media in myriad ways to promote their interests and policy preferences. Rather than describe these interactions again, we focus here on their consequences. Far more than his predecessors combined, President Trump deployed a daily army of tweets to assert his opinions and policy preferences on the media, public opinion, and the political system.

# Media Consequences

All elements of the media can influence public policy: news, opinion and commentary, fiction and documentary films, and advertising. The internet in particular is a space for policy discussion.[54] But media attention is intense on some subjects, intermittent on others, and nonexistent on many policies. This is understandable and predictable, given the abundance of policies and the several stages and complexity of the policymaking process.

We break this policy process into five stages: (1) agenda setting, (2) formulation, (3) adoption, (4) implementation and administration, and (5) evaluation. Naturally, reality is more complex (sometimes simpler): stages overlap, do not necessarily follow in this order, and are not fulfilled for every policy. Nonetheless, the breakdown does ease understanding.

## Agenda Setting

People have many concerns. These become part of the policy agenda when they are seen as requiring government attention and action (e.g., global warming). In **agenda setting**, then, what were conditions ignored or to be endured become problems requiring government intervention.[55]

**agenda setting**

Conditions are seen as requiring government attention and action.

The media often put subjects on the policy agenda by covering the speeches and actions of policymakers, particularly the president. They also move a subject onto the policy agenda when they give it extensive coverage and frame it as a problem demanding a response by policymakers. For example, widespread reporting of how many Americans were sickened by tainted eggs and spinach eventually resulted in a law that overhauled the food safety system and gave more authority to the Food and Drug Administration.

The media can put a topic on the policy agenda by transforming it into a **news icon**. A garbage barge that for three months unsuccessfully sought a port on the East Coast to unload its cargo received extensive news coverage, was joked about in the monologues of late-night talk show hosts and mentioned in comedy shows, and became the subject of polls. With environmental interest groups weighing in, the barge grew into an icon symbolizing a wasteful society with ever-mounting garbage and nowhere to dump it. It put garbage firmly on the policy agenda.[56]

**news icon**

Through extensive media coverage, something or someone symbolizes a situation that then is put on the policy agenda.

This barge and its load became a media icon, putting the garbage problem on the policy agenda.

View in the online reader

The media can keep subjects off the policy agenda or enable policymakers to keep them off by ignoring or downplaying them. Or their coverage can give the impression, rightly or wrongly, that a subject does not require resolution through the policy process. Coverage may be insufficient when policymakers are disinterested: the scant media attention to the AIDS epidemic during its early years did not put it on the policy agenda in the face of the Reagan administration's indifference.

## Formulation

When an issue is on the agenda, policymakers often propose policies to solve it. They sometimes have several alternative policies from which to choose. Traffic safety can be sought by "building more highways (the solution of the 1950s), requiring safer cars (the solution of the 1960s), putting drunk drivers behind bars (that of the 1980s and 1990s)."[57]

**policy formulation**

Policies proposed to solve an issue on the agenda.

The media influence **policy formulation** by how they frame the subject, their coverage of policymakers' arguments and debates, and the policy alternatives they report. Thus, the production, distribution, and consumption of cannabis (marijuana) has been framed as a law-and-order problem (resulting in millions of arrests, mainly of people age twenty-four and under and mainly for possession), or increasingly as a health issue (e.g., medical marijuana) or as an everyday recreational activity that contributes to a state's revenue from taxation, as with the legal market for its sale in some states.

Media coverage of policy formulation infrequently dwells on substantive arguments and alternatives. Depiction of the legislative process is typical: the news media usually frame it as conflict and strategy. And because the news media cover only a few major issues, policymakers are often able to formulate the details of policies without much scrutiny or public awareness.

The media spotlight can speed up policy formulation on major issues. But speed tends not to work well for deliberation: deciding what to do about a problem can take sifting and winnowing. News coverage pushes for a quick response from policymakers, thereby often favoring the most available alternative, perhaps regardless of whether it effectively addresses the problem.

## Adoption

**policy adoption**

The relevant institutions of government enact a formulated policy.

For formulated policies to be put into effect, they must be adopted by the relevant institutions of government. The media can be a forum in which various sides argue their cases for **policy adoption**. But coverage is sometimes one-sided. When favorable, it enhances a policy proposal's likelihood of adoption. When unfavorable, it can undermine a proposal, as we documented in our discussion of President Bush's proposals to change Social Security. As we also noted, negative advertising helped kill the Clinton administration's health-care proposal.

Adoption of a policy legitimizes it.[58] The media usually give positive coverage to the enactment of significant laws, thereby adding to their legitimacy. But not always—see the criticism of and attacks on the Affordable Care Act.

## Enduring Images

### The Law-Signing Ceremony

An enduring image of the U.S. government is the president signing into law a piece of legislation just passed by Congress. The president is surrounded by the members of Congress responsible for and citizens benefiting from the law's passage. The ceremony requires many pens because after each stroke the president gives one to someone associated with the legislation.

The ceremony is a photo op for all the participants. It presents the president as intimately involved in policymaking as head of the government, Congress and its members as effective lawmakers, ordinary people benefiting from the law, and the law as final.

The image is compelling, but the impressions it conveys are disputable. The president may not have been intimately involved in proposing the law, deciding on its key details, and pushing for its passage. Members of Congress are more or less satisfied with the law, which may have been jerry-built out of compromises, concessions, the dropping of vital provisions, and the inclusion of unnecessary or damaging ones as favors to legislators and interest groups who would otherwise oppose passage. And with implementation and administration to come, the effects of the law are far from final.

President Eisenhower signs the Atomic Energy Act. These types of signing ceremonies give the impression of harmony and finality in the policy process.

Source: National Park Service. Dwight D. Eisenhower Presidential Library, Museum, and Boyhood Home; (https://www.eisenhowerlibrary.gov/media/2999). Image ID: 72-1031-1. Via Wikimedia: https://commons.wikimedia.org/wiki/File:EisenhowerAtomicEnergyAct.jpg.

President Johnson signs an immigration bill.

Source: LBJ Library photo (Image ID: A1421-33a) by Yoichi Okamoto via Wikimedia: http://commons.wikimedia.org/wiki/ File:Immigration _Bill_Signing_-_A1421-33a_-_10-03-1965.jpg.

President Obama signs the repealing of Don't Ask Don't Tell.

Source: Chuck Kennedy, White House photographer via Wikimedia: https://commons.wikimedia.org/wiki/File:Obama_signs_DADT_repeal.jpg.

## Implementation and Administration

Policy decisions require **policy implementation and administration**. Congress relies on the bureaucracy to develop the specific standards and procedures that fulfill the intent of the policy.

**policy implementation and administration**

Development of the specific standards and procedures that fulfill the intent of the policy.

Messy reality can make administration and implementation difficult for even the most conscientious and dedicated bureaucrat. Nor are bureaucratic defiance, incompetence, dereliction, ineptitude, and scandals unknown. Policies may be ignored or subverted at the state or local level.

The media can be a significant force at this stage of the policy process. But most policy implementation and administration take place out of the media's view and are time-consuming to find and expose, even with investigative reporting, for media coverage is sporadic and focused on a few policies.

## Evaluation

**Policy evaluation**, or assessing a policy's effectiveness, can be complicated.[59] Many public policies aim to achieve broad conceptual goals such as "healthy air quality." Or a policy may have multiple, not necessarily compatible, objectives. The 1996 Telecommunications Act was intended to unleash the power of competition, spur technological innovation, create jobs, and reduce cable rates.[60]

**policy evaluation**

Assessing a policy's effectiveness.

Nonetheless, as we showed in our box on No Child Left Behind, the media can evaluate policies through their reporting. They also report and therefore publicize some of the policy assessments of government agencies, policy oversight studies by congressional committees, and congressional hearings. They report the findings of public interest groups (e.g., that many of the recipients of tobacco subsidies do not grow tobacco) and transmit the revelations of whistle-blowers (e.g., documents showing that the tobacco companies long knew that smoking causes diseases).

Such journalism can lead to outrage from the public and from policymakers, demands for reform, and governmental action. Policies are reappraised, changed, and even junked.

Here is a list of outstanding or continuing domestic issues, most of them discussed in the media and in this chapter, that policymakers will have to face (or not) in the future:

- Budget deficit
- Drug war (its persistence)
- Education
- Employment (and income)
- Energy
- Global warming
- Health
- Homelessness
- Immigration (laws and walls)
- Inequality
- Infrastructure
- Medicare
- Natural disasters
- Opioids (pharmacy manufacturers and chains)
- Prescription drugs (distribution, costs, sales, use)
- Race relations
- Social Security
- Technology

Can you think of any others?

## Key Takeaways

The five stages of the policy process are (1) agenda setting, (2) formulation, (3) adoption, (4) implementation and administration, and (5) evaluation. The media are more or less involved and influential at every stage.

## Exercises

1. How can media coverage put an issue on the policy agenda? What issue can you think of that has been brought to public attention by media coverage?
2. How do the media depict the policymaking process in the United States? Why do you think the media portray it that way?

### Civic Education

**Student Loans**

Many students take out loans to finance their education. Their college's financial aid office guides them through the process, often steering them to certain lenders.

The government paid billions annually to subsidize lenders and guaranteed repayment of up to 97 percent of the loan. Lenders were guaranteed a rate of return by law. They therefore made large profits with minimal risk.

Raza Khan and Vishal Garg, then twenty-nine, founded MyRichUncle in 2005 on the assumption that their company would prosper in this $85 billion business by offering students lower interest rates and a better deal. But they soon discovered that students followed the recommendations of their college's financial aid officers and that MyRichUncle was excluded from many of the lists of recommended lenders. So they ran advertisements questioning and challenging the cozy relationship between financial aid officials and large lenders.

In January 2007, New York Attorney General Andrew M. Cuomo (who in 2010 would be elected governor) investigated the industry. His findings were widely reported. The media frame was the dubious and possibly illegal ways some student-loan companies used "payola" and "bribery" (e.g., giving stocks, consulting fees, gifts, trips) to financial aid officers to put them on preferred lender lists, push their loans, and exclude other lenders. They had also entered into revenue-sharing agreements (i.e., kickbacks) giving institutions a cut of all the loans their students took out with the lender.

The revelations had consequences. In May 2007, the House of Representatives voted by 414–3 to ban student loan companies from giving gifts and payments to universities. The directors of financial aid at several universities, including the University of Texas at Austin, Columbia University, Johns Hopkins University, and the University of Southern California, left their positions. New York University, the University of Pennsylvania, and other schools repaid students the money that lenders had given to the universities for steering loans to them.[61] In New York and other states, lenders promised to adhere to a code of conduct prohibiting the dubious practices.

In August 2007, the Government Accountability Office issued a report criticizing the Department of Education for failing to detect misconduct by lenders and failing to protect student borrowers. It was released by congressional Democrats and widely reported.[62]

In September 2007, President Bush signed legislation reducing the size of the federal government's subsidy to lenders and halving interest rates on student loans the government originated.[63] The new law did not, however, significantly change the relationship between the government and the student loan industry.

In March 2010, President Obama signed a law to end the loan program, eliminate the fees paid to private banks, and allocate the $80 billion saved over ten years to expand the Pell Grants program for needy students.[64] The federal government would make loans directly to students through their college's financial aid office. As a consolation, the banks, which had lobbied fiercely against the changes, would continue to earn income by servicing the loans.

This story tells us that ordinary Americans can challenge the established powers and long-standing cozy relationships of an industry that affects the lives—and debts—of students and their families. Media depictions and frames influence the policies adopted. Sadly, the challengers themselves are not always financially rewarded: MyRichUncle went bankrupt in February 2009. Worse, many Americans continue to bear the burden of crushing debt from their student loans.[65]

# 16.6 The Coronavirus, COVID-19 Pandemic

## Learning Objectives

After reading this section, you should be able to answer the following questions:

1. What were the three alternatives the U.S. government had to combat the coronavirus?
2. What are the purposes of the tests for the coronavirus?
3. What were the main measures recommended by the White House Coronavirus Task Force and President Trump to limit the coronavirus?
4. What were the most important economic effects of these measures?
5. What are the most important issues currently?

On January 20, 2020, a Seattle man who had recently traveled to Wuhan in China became the first known infection from **COVID-19**, a disease caused by a particular strain of **coronavirus**, on U.S. soil. January 30 saw the first case of person-to-person transmission in the United States. On that same date, the World Health Organization (WHO), an affiliate of the United Nations, called the coronavirus a global public health emergency. On March 11, the WHO upped the designation to a **pandemic**, a global outbreak of a disease able to infect people easily.

**COVID-19**

The disease caused by the coronavirus.

**coronavirus**

An infectious, easily transmitted, sometimes deadly, virus.

**pandemic**

A global outbreak of an infectious disease like the coronavirus.

The first American citizen reportedly died from the coronavirus in the United States on February 29, 2020. By the end of May, the virus had spread throughout the country, infecting around two million people and killing roughly 100,000.

People die all the time. Some by disease: almost a million a year worldwide from AIDS. Others bring about their own demise: roughly 190,000 people annually in the U.S. from suicide, alcohol-related causes, and drug overdoses. So why was COVID-19 deemed concerning?

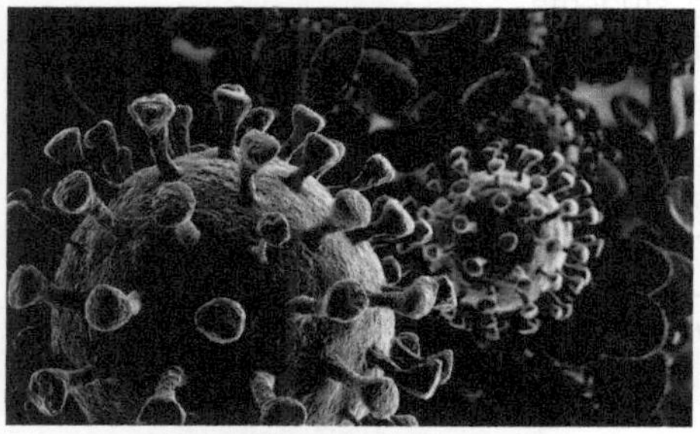

FIGURE 16.3 The Coronavirus
The coronavirus that infects and kills people worldwide with COVID-19.

Source: creativeneko/Shutterstock.com

First, the virus is highly contagious, including transmission by people who exhibit no symptoms at all (asymptomatic) or not during the fourteen days symptoms are most likely to appear. Second, it became clear that more people than initially detected were contracting COVID-19: those dying at home, care homes, and elsewhere without being tested for the virus were not necessarily included in the official count. Moreover, the nationwide lack of reliable testing during the first few months of 2020 contributed to an overall lack of information about the prevalence of the virus.

The most vulnerable were people over age sixty-five with chronic medical conditions (diabetes, obesity, hypertension, and heart disease, etc.), those living in nursing homes and long-term-care facilities, and those deprived of primary medical care.

Most at risk of exposure were first responders (police, fire fighters, etc.) and health-care, transit, and food-service workers, those whose jobs made sheltering at home difficult. Also at risk of exposure were prison inmates (including people in jail because they had been convicted and those who were simply unable to pay bail), detained immigrants, farmworkers, and the impoverished and homeless. A disproportionate number of Black and Latinx people, especially in such cities as New York, Baltimore, Chicago, the District of Columbia, Detroit, and New Orleans, contracted and died from the virus.

# The Government's Response

The initial U.S. response to the pandemic was not well coordinated. It spawned conflicts between the executive, legislative, and bureaucratic branches at the government's national, state, and local levels. The response would require government policies to be based on a combination of scientific and political judgments, taking into account medical and economic recommendations. Political participation and interest groups would be involved. Choosing between public health and the economy became a contentious policy issue. There were predictable clashes between the political parties over funding and oversight, all within the context of the looming presidential election. This turmoil was accompanied by a continuous barrage of media coverage.

In addition to the president, a range of prominent and lesser-known individuals and institutions were involved and visible in the policymaking process, more or less, at one time or another. We identify them below to give a sense of some of the public service affiliations, specializations, and skills originally called upon to deal with the coronavirus pandemic.

We start with President Trump's January 29 announcement of the administration's White House Coronavirus Task Force and his February 26 appointment of Vice President Mike Pence to chair it. The leading members and their institutional affiliations were:

- Surgeon General
- Secretary of the Department of Health and Human Services (HHS)
- Deborah L. Birx, AIDS researcher, coronavirus response coordinator for the White House
- Secretary of Housing and Urban Development (HUD)
- Dr. Anthony S. Fauci, director of the National Institute of Allergy and Infectious Diseases at the National Institutes of Health (NIH)
- Food and Drug Administration (FDA) Commissioner
- Director of the National Economic Council (NEC)
- Secretary of the Treasury
- National Security Advisor (NSA)
- Director of the Centers for Disease Control and Prevention (CDC)

Over time, supplemental task forces were established:

- The "Doctors group," an offshoot of the task force that met to discuss medical and public health issues.
- The "Opening Our Country Council" formed to strategize for reopening certain sectors of the economy.
- An unnamed group reporting directly to the president's senior adviser and son-in-law, Jared Kushner.[66]

These three groups each reported to Pence and the main task force.

The following list indicates the profusion of other federal government institutions and personnel that were or would become involved in deciding and/or executing policies related to the COVID-19 pandemic:

- Armed Services
- Army Corps of Engineers
- Federal Emergency Management Agency (FEMA)
- Federal Reserve Board
- Food and Drug Administration (FDA)
- Internal Revenue Service (IRS)
- Justice Department
- National Guard
- National Security Council (NSC)
- Occupational Safety and Health Administration (OSHA)
- Small Business Administration

Given the prevalence of scams, fraud, and con artists pursuing access to people's money, Social Security numbers, and bank and credit card accounts, federal, state, and local law enforcement authorities were called upon. As just one example, a man was arrested for "seeking investments in a nonexistent company that he claimed was just days away from marketing pills that would ward off the virus and injections that would cure COVID-19 . . . his YouTube and Instagram videos, in which he displayed a syringe of clear liquid or white pills, had been viewed more than two million times."[67]

The United States was inadequately prepared for the virus. It did not have nearly enough **personal protective equipment (PPE)** to avoid infections of first responders such as doctors, nurses, and hospital personnel. Based on initial projections, it was feared there would be an insufficient number of ventilators for critically ill patients; however, in March and April of 2020 supplies kept up with overall demands. A lack of medical supplies manufactured in China did cause shortages of key equipment and pharmaceuticals. Above all, there was a lack of effective test kits to determine who was infected with COVID-19.

**personal protective equipment (PPE)**

Medical and hospital equipment designed to protect first responders.

The medical system was also a concern. Projected hospital capacity, meaning the number of available beds and emergency and intensive care facilities, showed that if measures were not put into place, health-care providers were unlikely to be able to manage and properly treat the abundance of patients with COVID-19. In turn, this meant postponing elective surgery and routine medical care for many people. For a time in New York City, funeral homes were full and refrigerated trailers were used as portable morgues.

For three weeks starting in late February, as the virus spread, the federal government offered little guidance and coordination. Instead, federal executive authority deferred to the states, pressuring governors, mayors, and local officials to handle the crisis essentially on their own. States competed with each other but then cooperated to secure vital supplies and equipment. For example, on April 6 California announced its plan to send 500 state-owned ventilators to the Strategic National Stockpile specifically earmarked for distribution to New York state. As Governor Gavin Newsom stated, "We still have a long road ahead of us in the Golden State—and we're aggressively preparing for a surge—but we can't turn our back on Americans whose lives depend on having a ventilator now. We're meeting this moment with compassion. I know that if the tables were turned and we were experiencing a hospital surge, other states would come to our aid and provide ventilators just as we are today."[68]

In theory the U.S. government could adopt one or more of the strategies in Table 16.1 in order to meet the COVID-19 threat.

**herd immunity**

When a sufficient number of individuals in a population are resistant to an infection by virtue of a successful vaccination or possesses antibody defenses because they previously had the disease, recovered and, it is assumed, can now fight it off effectively.

**containment**

Keeping the coronavirus outside the U.S. and immediately isolating anyone who comes into contact with it.

**mitigation**

Slowing the spread of the virus within the U.S. by taking certain measures.

**social distancing**

A guideline telling people to keep at least six feet apart thus avoiding infecting or being infected by the virus.

**flattening the curve**

Avoiding a surge of cases that might overwhelm the health-care system in general, and intensive-care units in particular, with seriously ill individuals.

**TABLE 16.1 Strategies for Meeting the COVID-19 Threat**

| Strategy | Explanation |
|---|---|
| **Herd immunity** | This results when a sufficient number of individuals in a population is resistant to an infection by virtue of a successful vaccination or possesses antibody defenses because they previously had the disease, recovered, and, it is assumed, can now fight it off effectively. At least seventy percent of a population would need to be immune to infection by COVID-19 to confer herd immunity. At that level, the virus would have a difficult time finding sufficient numbers of susceptible individuals to be easily transmitted and as a result, even those who are not resistant are unlikely to become ill with the virus. |
| **Containment** | Keep the coronavirus outside the U.S. and immediately isolate anyone who came into contact with an infected person. By early March, the administration confirmed it was too late to implement this strategy effectively. On March 8, the Surgeon General of the United States, announced that the U.S. was abandoning a containment strategy and would move to a mitigation effort. |
| **Mitigation** | The mitigation effort following the failed containment strategy is intended to take measures, such as **social distancing**, to slow the spread of the virus. Social distancing guidelines direct individuals to stay at least six feet apart from other people unless they are family members, roommates, or others who share a residence. Public health experts point to research on the coronavirus that suggests one is unlikely to catch the virus from another person at distances of more than six feet. Other measures, such as wearing masks, even homemade face coverings, can amplify the effectiveness of social distancing. One of the goals of social distancing is to inhibit the coronavirus' spread from person to person, a phenomenon that popularly became known as **flattening the curve**. The purpose of flattening the curve is not to eradicate the virus, but to avoid a surge of cases that might overwhelm the healthcare system in general, and intensive-care units in particular, with seriously ill individuals. Instead of a briefer, higher peak of COVID-19 cases, a flattened curve represents a plateau of cases at a lower number rather than a sharp spike of cases at a higher number. In this way, the daily number of infections and resulting cases becomes more manageable by the health-care system. |

Models forecasting the spread and impact of the virus predicted that 100,0000 to 240,000 Americans would die. However, public health officials warned that complacency or relaxing of social-distancing behaviors without proper public health measures and testing in place could cause transmission of the virus to accelerate very quickly. In spite of heroic efforts to flatten the curve, the number turned out to be much higher than initially predicted.

On March 16, the president and the White House Coronavirus Task Force strongly recommended social distancing, including stay-at-home or shelter-in-place orders that discouraged any activities outside the home that were not essential, such as grocery shopping. To encourage people to stay at home and to protect workers, recommendations to cease commercial (e.g., shops and restaurants) and non-commercial activity and transactions, including entertainment, sports, and other gatherings of more than ten people, were put into place.

The immediate economic consequences were dire: a veritable shutting down of the country. Unemployment claims exceeded thirty-three million in a few weeks (a figure that undercounted the unemployed by excluding people barred from applying for state benefits). The stock market declined precipitously (and then partially recovered). Absent income, many employers were unable to meet payrolls, pay rents, etc. and had to eliminate jobs. Laid off or furloughed workers lacked funds for food, housing, and other essentials. Demand soared at food banks, with lines sometimes stretching for miles.

**FIGURE 16.4** Closed Due to COVID-19 Sign

Red closed due to COVID-19 sign in shop window.

Source: BreizhAtao/Shutterstock.com

With most schools moving to virtual off-campus instruction, often called **distance learning**, teachers and students scrambled to establish a way to teach and learn online. But a number of students, mainly from disadvantaged backgrounds, did not have the proper equipment or were unable to log online due to lack of web access. With college campuses emptied, courses taught remotely varied in quality, certain programs were suspended, fundraising fell dramatically, and students, both American and foreign, reconsidered their college choices and educational plans for the summer and fall of 2020.

**distance learning**

Off-campus teaching and learning using technology as a substitute for in-class education.

## Congress Takes Action

With the economy in free fall, Congress came to the rescue, at least temporarily, with a massive stimulus and stabilization package. Republicans had traditionally tried to shrink the safety net and make eligibility for support dependent on being employed or in a work program. Due to the looming economic crisis, these same Republicans supported the **Coronavirus Aid, Relief, and Economic Security Act (CARES)**.

**Coronavirus Aid, Relief, and Economic Security Act (CARES)**

The bipartisan Congressional act signed into law on March 27, 2020 that provided approximately $2 trillion in stimulus and relief to U.S. business and citizens in response to the economic crisis caused by the burgeoning pandemic.

Partisan differences had to be resolved before final passage of the legislation and its signing by the president. Among the issues in dispute: Democrats sought congressional oversight over the loans to corporations, $150 billion for hospitals, and added funding for health-care workers, the unemployed, and state and local governments.[69]

The highlights of the $2 trillion 880-page bill were as follows:[70]

- A stimulus payment based on income
- Unemployment benefits that vary by state, including self-employed and part-time workers, freelancers, and independent contractors
- Small business loans and grants, forgiven if used for payrolls (Paycheck Protection Program)
- Student loan payments suspended until September 30 for any student loan held by the federal government
- Funds for hospitals, health-care systems, and providers
- Cash grants and loans to airlines, air cargo carriers, etc.
- Funds for state and local governments
- Loans to corporate America (dubbed "a slush fund" by Democrats), disbursed by the Treasury
- Food and health-care aid to those living in poverty

Separately, the Federal Reserve provided up to $2.3 trillion in loan guarantees to banks so they could continue to make loans to local governments, businesses, and households. This action was intended to ensure credit markets remained liquid during the crises.

Bureaucratic problems in executing CARES were widespread. State unemployment offices were overwhelmed, websites crashed, leaving people unable to apply. Many people were unable to file claims because they were kept waiting for hours on the telephone. Programs quickly ran out of money. The sum of new unemployment claims filed was swelled by the number of gig workers, self-employed, and others whom the CARES Act made eligible for unemployment benefits for the first time in history.

The funds set aside for emergency relief for small businesses were quickly overwhelmed by demand. The Small Business Administration's insufficient staff and aging technology were unprepared to meet the avalanche of demands for small business loans. With decisions about disbursing program funds outsourced to banks, millions of dollars intended for small businesses to pay items like rent and payroll went to large companies. This left it to some of the companies to decide whether or not to voluntarily return the money and for the Treasury to try to recoup some of the loans.

## President Trump

President Trump was accused by his critics of not taking the coronavirus threat seriously, inadequately anticipating its effects, failing to plan or provide for sufficient testing for it, and neglecting to organize necessary health equipment and hospital care to treat it. What's the evidence?

In 2018, the administration disbanded the NSC's pandemic office that, according to its director, had been established to do everything possible to prepare for the next disease outbreak and to coordinate the government's response.[71] Arguably, though, the NSC was overstaffed, and the cut could be justified as streamlining. The Trump administration had also repeatedly tried to cut funds for the Centers for Disease Control and Prevention and the National Institutes of Health.

During the first few months of 2020, the Trump administration's response to the COVID-19 outbreak was erratic. On January 3, the administration received its first formal notification of the outbreak in China. Soon thereafter, intelligence agencies began including a warning about the coronavirus in the President's Daily Brief. But in late January and early February the president still insisted that the outbreak was "totally under control," and declared that in warm weather the virus "miraculously goes away." Nevertheless, on January 31, the administration banned any foreign nationals (with eleven categories of exceptions) who had been in China for two weeks from entering the U.S. Nonetheless, during the two months after the ban, 40,000 people came to the U.S. from that country. The President waited until March 11 to restrict travel to and from Europe. On March 13, he finally declared a national emergency. Only a few days later the President began to tout unproven treatments and praise his own performance: "I always treated the Chinese Virus very seriously, and have done a very good job from the beginning."[72]

The president's optimistic line was (faithfully) observed by his supporters on Fox News and conservative talk radio. Rush Limbaugh stated during his February 2 radio show: "The coronavirus is the common cold, folks." Relatedly, many Republicans were inclined to dismiss the virus and decline to follow the CDC guidelines to combat it.[73]

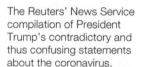

The Reuters' News Service compilation of President Trump's contradictory and thus confusing statements about the coronavirus.

View in the online reader

By early April the president shifted to blaming others for the problems in responding to the virus early on. In particular, he attributed the shortage of lifesaving equipment on states' failure to build their own stockpiles, and attacked the World Health Organization as subservient to China and complicit in offering misinformation about the virus. He then proceeded to suspend the WHO's funding from the United States, citing the need to halt it until his administration could further research the matter.

## Governors and Local Officials

Two interrelated issues pervaded (and muddied) the governmental response to the coronavirus. The first, as previously discussed, and as continued later, was a lack of presidential leadership.

The second, briefly considered here, was federalism. Our Constitution and Federalism chapters delve into the diverse and sometimes unclear relations between the national government and the states, between the states themselves, and within states. In the case of the coronavirus, these were all at play, raising myriad questions. How much authority did each level of government possess to combat the virus? How reliant should the states have been on national authority for policies and resources? How much independence did state and local governments possess to control their inhabitants' behavior? How did they respond to the burdens posed by the coronavirus?

Some of the news media played a part in considering these questions, particularly by giving airtime and visibility to more or less obscure officials such as the Republican governors of Ohio and Maryland and the Democratic governors of Michigan and New Jersey.

**FIGURE 16.5 New York Governor Andrew M. Cuomo Holds His Daily Press Conference**
New York Democratic Governor Cuomo rivaled President Trump by holding daily press conferences that attracted cable television coverage.

Source: Hans Pennink/Shutterstock.com

Notable was the attention paid to the daily press conferences of the Democratic governor of New York, Andrew Cuomo. Cuomo went into considerable detail about the effects of the virus in his state and his struggles to contain and overcome it. In the process, he complained about and complimented President Trump and his administration's responses: complained about their lack of leadership, planning, and coordination, while also finding reasons to compliment the administration when possible—all from a reluctance to incur the president's wrath and be denied or forced to compete for needed equipment and supplies. For Governor Cuomo, the national government served as a backup to the states. One of Cuomo's main complaints was over the disproportionate distribution of federal cash aid per patient between states, with New York receiving $12,000 per patient compared to Nebraska's $379,000.[74]

Eventually, the *New York Times* blasted Governor Cuomo, New York City Mayor Bill de Blasio, and their aides for projecting "an unswerving confidence that the outbreak would be readily contained,"[75] a criticism the newspaper had also leveled at the president. Still, the governor benefitted from his new-found visibility: his favorability among voters soared from 44 percent before the pandemic, to 71 percent following his daily press conferences.[76] But the governor would get his comeuppance later: he resigned from office in a sexual harassment scandal and amid revelations that his aides hid COVID-19 data for several months.

## The News Media

President Trump dominated the White House Coronavirus Task Force's daily briefings with lengthy riffs, boasts, and digressive replies to reporters' questions. He was accompanied by the Task Force's head, Vice President Pence, and other members who often invoked the president's name, attributed accomplishments to him, and celebrated his supposed decisive leadership. With infrequent exceptions, the commentators of Fox News echoed the president. The foremost exception to the chorus of approval was Dr. Anthony Fauci, director of the National Institute of Allergy and Infectious Diseases at the NIH, whose reliance on science and facts made him reluctant to kowtow to the president, bringing him many fans and threats.

**FIGURE 16.6 President Trump speaks at the White House Coronavirus Daily Briefings**
President Trump dominated the televised daily briefings of the White House Coronavirus Task Force.

Source: The White House / Public domain; https://commons.wikimedia.org/wiki/File:Coronavirus_Press_Conference_-_49659509512.jpg.

On occasion, the event lasted over two hours. It often appeared on CNN, MSNBC, Fox News, ABC, CBS, NBC, Facebook, and was streamed, which raised the question of whether it should have been shown uncut. Its average audience of several million was overwhelmingly Republican. About 79 percent of Republicans but only 16 percent of Democrats were satisfied with the information presented by the president. His approval rating initially rose to a high of 49 percent but subsequently declined.[77] This led some of his White House aides to urge him to cut back on his briefings, which eventually he did. Soon thereafter the briefings ended entirely.

Death is ubiquitous, but people dependent on the news media would have thought COVID-19 its only avatar. Coverage was continuous, to the exclusion of most else; replete with press conferences, statistics, advice, and analysis from medical experts, panels of pundits and commentators, and the repetition ad nauseam to "stay with us." Aside from portrayals of heroes, good deeds, and sad stories, much of the coverage was critical, particularly of President Trump, whose press conference utterances were assessed and fact checked. The president was not alone. The *New York Times* especially reported government ineptitude and the like. Some examples:

- "Unfilled Posts Force Scramble by Washington."[78]

- "The Needy Will Face Obstacles to Getting Stimulus Payments."[79]
- "Business Relief Program Is Facing a Messy Start."[80]
- "Strings on Bailout Money Put Off Some Executives."[81]

**FIGURE 16.7** **Dr. Anthony S. Fauci, Director of the National Institute of Allergy and Infectious Diseases of the National Institutes of Health (NIH)**
Dr. Anthony S. Fauci, whose reliance on science and facts sometimes puts him at odds with President Trump, has garnered many fans, some critics, and threats.

Source: Trump White House Archived via Flickr: https://www.flickr.com/photos/148748355@N05/49659509512/.

# How Will This End, If It Ever Does?

We conclude with a summary of key recent events and outstanding issues.

Over the waning months of the Trump administration the epidemic drastically worsened. The president shifted to the states the leadership in the fight against the virus and the decisions as to whether to reopen businesses and schools. (He himself favored a return to normal life.) He was skeptical of masks and reluctant to encourage people to use them. Many Americans, especially Republicans, emulated his bravado. During his final days in office he continued to project optimism about getting the coronavirus under control, even while new confirmed cases and deaths soared. With respect to the virus itself, the president seemed disengaged.

The Trump administration's public–private partnership Operation Warp Speed, for which the president took credit, did successfully produce effective coronavirus vaccines in record time and ahead of expectations. But in its early stages the vaccination rollout was slowed by snags and delays.

Presidential candidate Joe Biden vowed that solving the COVID-19 crisis and repairing its economic destruction would be his and his administration's top priority. He promised much greater federal funding, logistical coordination, and availability of vaccines to combat the coronavirus.

On March 11, soon after becoming president, Biden signed a nearly $1.9 trillion aid bill, that had been stalled for several months but was now passed by Congress over unanimous Republican opposition. Among its particularly significant funding provisions:

- extended and expanded unemployment benefits
- direct payments to individuals
- emergency paid leave
- increase in food stamps benefit
- expand child tax credit
- tax increases on large corporations and wealthy individuals
- grants to small businesses
- paycheck protection program (additional funding and expanded eligibility)
- state, local, and tribal governments (bridge budget shortfalls)
- K–12 schools to reopen safely
- colleges and universities
- homeless and at risk

Coronavirus cases trended downward as the vaccine rollout progressed. President Biden instructed the states to make vaccines conferring immunity available to all American adults by May 1, 2021. He predicted a return to some kind of normalcy by July 4.

Some governors were prepared to ease restrictions and embark on phased reopenings without meeting such CDC guidelines as waiting for a decline of fourteen days in fatalities. Paraphrasing President Trump, who took the phrase from a Fox News commentator, they argued that the cure of shutting down the economy shouldn't be worse than the problem. It was assumed that the labor market would improve as people were vaccinated, businesses reopened, and injections of aid encouraged spending.

Three dangers loomed. First, the increasing prevalence of virus variants, which could be more contagious than and resistant to vaccines than COVID-19. Second, the possibility, even likelihood, of states allowing people to engage in or countenancing risky behavior, such as prematurely abandoning mask mandates, restrictions on indoor gatherings, requirements for social distancing, and other protective measures, as people rushed to return to normal living, work and school.

Third, nationwide testing to determine who has or had the virus seemed to be a baseline requirement for reopening a locked-down economy. Especially given the outbreak of virus variants, an accurate diagnostic test produced on a mass scale and deployed to labs across the country to identify and isolate the infected is necessary. Routine screening of students and educators should be a precursor to opening schools and the economy. Testing will identify people exposed to the virus, with or without knowing, or those who have overcome it; will indicate who may have developed immunity and can return to work; will trace and, if necessary, treat or isolate infected people's contacts. The Biden administration's provision of $10 billion for testing was only a start.

At first, all went well for the new president. Vaccines became widely available and proved effective against COVID-19 infections, reduced hospitalizations, and protected against death. Returning to normalcy, people began to venture out mask-free.

But the situation changed drastically. Causing the change was the advent of the extremely contagious and evolving Delta variant of the virus. Caseloads climbed from a daily average of nearly 12,000 new infections in early July 2021 to 80,000 in August 2021. Overwhelmingly, the victims were the unvaccinated. Vaccination campaigns sputtered, especially in the South, where hesitation about vaccination, resistance to being vaccinated, and skepticism about vaccines were prevalent.

Abetting these doubts was misinformation spread by some Republican politicians and pundits appearing on local media, publications, radio, and cable television.

Consequently, around25 percent of eligible Americans remained unvaccinated, although the figure began to decline as more people began to be convinced of vaccination's urgency.

By early September 2021 there were more than 160,000 new cases daily, some 100,000 patients hospitalized nationwide, and more than 1,500 Americans dying each day.

Conflicts involving federalism persist between and within different levels of government; some governors defy the federal government; state authorities are defied by educators at the local level. Issues include whether to require children to return to school and under what conditions and circumstances: mask wearing, vaccinations required, classrooms ventilated, social distancing, infected children quarantined.

Policy contradictions and reversals from the White House and the CDC sowed confusion about mask wearing and social distancing, and booster shots—for whom and when should they be administered? Should people go back to work? Gather in large crowds? By early September 2021, the U.S. had experienced 40 million cases and 640,000 deaths.

On September 9, 2021, President Biden announced the following measures: new vaccination requirements, easing access to booster shots, keeping schools free of the virus, increasing testing and masking, improving virus response and treatment, and aiding the economic recovery.

## Key Takeaways

A global pandemic has challenged the blurred authority of the branches and levels of the U.S. government. They have been shown to be more or less equipped to combat it, as the fight has entailed conflict, competition, and cooperation between and among them. Issues have involved leadership, directives and guidance to people, and the availability and distribution of medical equipment and supplies. Difficult decisions have to be made in attempting to balance public health and perpetuate the economy. Politics has inevitably obtruded. The news media have bestowed coverage and dispensed praise and, more often, blame. The number of sick and dying soared during 2020 without much help from President Trump. The Trump administration's Operation Warp Speed program provided effective vaccines in record time. The effort was hampered, however, by inadequate distribution of the vaccinations, thus leaving a public-health and economic disaster up to the incoming Biden administration to try to resolve. Initially President Biden's campaign against the COVID-19 virus was successful. But it was upended by the advent of the Delta variant and people's failure to be vaccinated. He proposed new measures in response.

## Exercises

1. Characterize President Trump's leadership in the battle against the coronavirus.
2. Assess the media coverage of the coronavirus.
3. What will it take to achieve an economic recovery?
4. What has been the impact of the coronavirus on federalism?

# 16.7 Recommended Reading

Baumgartner, Frank R., and Bryan D. Jones. *Agendas and Instability in American Politics*, 2nd ed. Chicago: University of Chicago Press, 2009. Theory and evidence showing that, in part because of the media, sudden policy changes occur.

Day, Phyllis J. *A New History of Social Welfare*, 7th ed. New York: Pearson, 2012. Social welfare policies from a historical perspective.

Howard, Christopher. *The Hidden Welfare State: Tax Expenditures and Social Policy in the United States*. Princeton, NJ: Princeton University Press, 1997. A compelling argument that government welfare (defined broadly) policies overwhelmingly favor business and the affluent.

Jones, Bryan D., and Frank R. Baumgartner. *The Politics of Attention: How Government Prioritizes Problems*. Chicago: University of Chicago Press, 2005. An information-processing approach to policymaking.

Mayer, Martin. *The Fed: The Inside Story of How the World's Most Powerful Financial Institution Drives the Markets*. New York: Free Press, 2001. A detailed discussion of the Fed's history, workings, and influence.

Speth, James Gustave. *Red Sky at Morning: America and the Crisis of the Global Environment*, 2nd ed. New Haven, CT: Yale University Press, 2005. A scholarly and frightening overview of threats to the environment.

Wilson, William Julius. *When Work Disappears: The World of the New Urban Poor*. New York: Knopf, 1996. An analysis of poverty and jobs in the inner city.

# 16.8 Recommended Viewing

*The China Syndrome* (1978). Television news reporters (Jane Fonda and Michael Douglas) uncover a nuclear power scandal.

*The Day after Tomorrow* (2004). Hollywood's hyperbolic depiction of the horrors of global warming (e.g., New York City is devastated by a huge tidal wave and an ice storm) in the face of an indifferent U.S. president and a reactionary vice president.

*Grass* (1999). A documentary about the government's marijuana policy in the twentieth century.

*Green* (2000). A disturbing documentary about the effects of the 150 petrochemical plants between Baton Rouge and New Orleans.

*Inside Job* (2010). Charles Ferguson's riveting, powerful, and polemical documentary argues that the financial crisis of 2008 was avoidable and casts the blame on Wall Street.

*The Insider* (1999). True story of a tobacco industry whistle-blower who works with a *60 Minutes* producer on a story that CBS executives only broadcast belatedly.

*Patch Adams* (1998). Robin Williams treats patients with humor in this sentimental examination of U.S. health policy.

*Public Housing* (1997). Fred Wiseman's patient and probing documentary on life in public housing.

*Silkwood* (1983). Story of Karen Silkwood, who died mysteriously after exposing radiation leaks at the nuclear plant where she worked.

*Stand and Deliver* (1988). New teacher at a drugs and guns–dominated Los Angeles barrio school elevates his students into an educational elite.

*Traffic* (2000). A conservative judge, appointed by the president to lead the war against drugs, discovers his daughter is a user.

*Wall Street* (1987). Megavillain financier draws naive broker into his immensely profitable illegal practices (insider trading) but gets his comeuppance when the conscience-stricken broker informs the Securities and Exchange Commission.

# Endnotes


1. David L. Altheide, *Creating Fear: News and the Construction of Crisis* (New York: Walter de Gruyter, 2002).
2. Timothy O. Lenz, *Changing Images of Law in Film & Television Crime Stories* (New York: Peter Lang, 2003).
3. Elayne Rapping, *Law and Justice as Seen on TV* (New York: New York University Press, 2003).
4. Sara Sun Beale, "The News Media's Influence on Criminal Justice Policy: How Market-Driven News Promotes Punitiveness," *William and Mary Law Review* 48, no. 2 (2006): 397–480.
5. James Surowicki, "The Financial Page: The Pay Is Too Damn Low," *New Yorker*, August 12 & 19, 2013, 35; the number directly employed may be 66,000.
6. Binyamin Appelbaum and David M. Herszenhorn, "Congress Passes Major Overhaul of Finance Rules," *The New York Times*, July 16, 2010, A1.
7. Joe Nocera, "Dubious Way to Prevent Fiscal Crisis," *The New York Times*, June 5, 2010, B1, 7.
8. Ron Suskind, *Confidence Men: Wall Street, Washington, and the Education of a President* (New York: Harper-Collins, 2011).
9. Timothy F. Geithner, *Stress Test: Reflections on Financial Crises* (New York: Crown, 2014).
10. For a comprehensive analysis of federal budgeting, see Dennis S. Ippolito, *Why Budgets Matter: Budget Policy and American Politics* (University Park, PA: Penn State University Press, 2003).
11. Jeffrey D. Sacks, "Our Dangerous Budget and What to Do About It," *New York Review*, February 6, 2014,
12. Michael D. Shear, "An Obscure Law Unravels Obama's Legacy, One Rule at a Time," *The New York Times*, May 2, 2017, A1(20).
13. Christopher Jencks, "The Immigration Charade," *New York Review*, September 27, 2009, 49–52.
14. *United States v. Texas,* 579 US (2016).
15. David Pace, "House Takeover Led to Spending Plan," Associated Press Online, August 6, 2002.
16. EME *Homer City Generation v. EPA* (2014).
17. Trudy Lieberman, *Slanting the Story* (New York: New Press, 2000).
18. Eric Lipton, "Fight Over Wage Illustrates Web of Industry Ties," *The New York Times*, February 10, 2014.
19. Pew Research Center survey in association with the *National Journal*. Not surprisingly, members of Congress were more positive toward the public, with 31 percent agreeing and an additional 17 percent volunteering that "it depends," compared to 13 percent and 7 percent, respectively, of presidential appointees and 14 percent and 3 percent, respectively, of civil servants. Pew Research Center 1998: 1.
20. Brian F. Schaffner and Mary Layton Atkinson, "Taxing Death or Estates? When Frames Influence Citizens' Issue Beliefs," in *Winning with Words: The Origins and Impact of Political Framing*, ed. Brian F. Schaffner and Patrick J. Sellers (New York: Routledge, 2010), 121–35.
21. Program for Public Consultation, "Major Report Shows Nearly 150 Issues on Which Majorities of Republicans & Democrats Agree." *PPC*, August 7, 2020. Retrieved from: https://publicconsultation.org/defense-budget/major-report-shows-nearly-150-issues-on-which-majorities-of-republicans-democrats-agree/.
22. Stephen J. Farnsworth, *Spinner in Chief: How Presidents Sell Their Policies and Themselves* (Boulder, CO: Paradigm Publishers, 2009), 22.
23. For their development of the idea of "punctuated equilibrium" applied to public policies, see Bryan D. Jones and Frank R. Baumgartner, *The Politics of Attention: How Government Prioritizes Problems* (Chicago: University of Chicago Press, 2005).
24. Thomas A. Birkland, *Lessons of Disaster: Policy Change after Catastrophic Events* (Washington, DC: Georgetown University, 2006).
25. Eric M. Patashnik, *Reforms at Risk: What Happens after Major Policy Changes Are Enacted* (Princeton, NJ: Princeton University Press, 2008), especially 2–6, 11–15, and 155–75.
26. Christopher G. Faricy, *Welfare for the Wealthy: Parties, Social Spending, and Inequality in the United States* (New York: Cambridge University Press, 2015).
27. Theodore R. Marmor, Jerry L. Mashaw, and John Pakutka, *Social Insurance; America's Neglected Heritage and Contested Future* (Washington, DC: CQ Press, 2013).
28. Jason DeParle and Robert Gebeloff, "The Safety Net: Across U.S., Food Stamp Use Soars and Stigma Fades," *The New York Times*, November 8, 2009, accessed June 6, 2011, http://www.nytimes.com/2009/11/29/us/29foodstamps; and Jason DeParle and Robert Gebeloff, "Once Stigmatized, Food Stamps Find New Users and Acceptance," *The New York Times*, February 11, 2010, A1.
29. "Welfare Reform: With TANF Flexibility, States Vary in How They Implement Work" (Washington, DC: General Accounting Office, 2002), accessed June 6, 2011, http://www.gao.gov/new.items/d02770.pdf.
30. For an overview of the origin of the Social Security System, see Edward D. Berkowitz, *Robert Ball and the Politics of Social Security* (Madison: University of Wisconsin Press, 2003).
31. For a contrary view, see Joseph White, *False Alarm: Why the Greatest Threat to Social Security and Medicare Is the Campaign to "Save" Them* (Baltimore: Johns Hopkins University Press, 2001).
32. For details of President Bush's campaign, see George C. Edwards III, *Governing by Campaigning: The Politics of the Bush Presidency* (New York: Longman, 2007), 216–80.
33. The Cato Institute, a conservative think tank, has been a major proponent of privatization. Its recommendations can be found at Cato Institute, "Social Security," http://www.socialsecurity.org.
34. Edmund L. Andrews, "As White House Begins Campaign for Overhauling Social Security, Critics Claim Exaggeration," *The New York Times*, January 10, 2005, A15.
35. Jim VandeHei and Peter Baker, "Social Security: On with the Show: President's 'Conversations' on Issue Are Carefully Orchestrated, Rehearsed," *Washington Post*, March 12, 2005, A3.
36. Gallup/CNN/USA Today poll, January and May 2005.
37. An account of education policy and politics is Patrick J. McGuinn, *No Child Left Behind and the Transformation of Federal Education Policy* (Lawrence: University Press of Kansas, 2006); a critique of the law and suggestions of ways to improve it is Scott Franklin Abernathy, *No Child Left Behind and the Public Schools* (Ann Arbor: University of Michigan Press, 2007); and a slashing attack on education policy, including NCLB, as more spectacle than rational is Mary Lee Smith with Linda Miller-Kahn, Walter Heinecke, Patricia F Jarvis, and Audrey Noble, *Political Spectacle and the Fate of American Schools* (New York: Routledge/Falmer, 2004).
38. For example, see the radio addresses of January 4, 2003, September 6, 2003, and January 3, 2004; the Rose Garden speech of June 10, 2003; and the speech on May 12, 2004.
39. Sam Dillon, "Students Ace State Tests, but Earn D's From U.S.," *The New York Times*, November 26, 2005, A1, 10.
40. Ford Fessenden, "How to Measure Student Proficiency? States Disagree on Tests," *The New York Times*, December 31, 2003, A16; and for a typical piece by education writer Michael Winerip, see "On Education; A Pervasive Dismay on a Bush School Law," *The New York Times*, March 19, 2003, A24.
41. Sam Dillon, "Most States Fail Demands Set Out in Education Law," *The New York Times* July 25, 2006, A14.
42. Andrew J. Rotherham, "No Pundit Left Behind," *The New York Times*, January 12, 2005, A23
43. Julie Hirschfield Davis, "Revamping of No Child School Act Is Signed," *The New York Times*, December 11, 2015, A24 (32).
44. Erica L. Green, "Trump Orders Review of Education Policies to Bolster Local Control," *The New York Times*, April 27, 2017, A14.
45. Eric L. Green, "Rules on For-Profit Schools Are Repealed," *The New York Times*, June 29, 2019, A15.
46. Robert Pear, "Medicare Costs Expected to Soar in Coming Years," *The New York Times*, March 24, 2004, A1, 15.
47. Jacob S. Hacker, *The Road to Nowhere: The Genesis of President Clinton's Plan for Health Security* (Princeton, NJ: Princeton University Press, 1997).
48. Jacob S. Hacker, "The Road to Somewhere: Why Health Reform Happened," *Perspectives on Politics* 8, no. 3 (September 2010): 865.
49. David D. Kirkpatrick, "Groups Back Health Overhaul, but Seek Cover," *The New York Times*, September 12, 2009, A1.
50. *National Federation of Independent Business et al. v. Sebelius, Secretary of Health and Human Service et al.*, 567 US (2012).
51. *King v. Burwell*, 576 U.S.________(2015).
52. Sue Halpern details the incompetence, the many problems with developing and trying to fix HealthCare.gov in "The Flop," *New York Review*, December19, 2013, 22.
53. Ron Suskind, quoting John DiIulio, in "Why Are These Men Laughing?" *Esquire*, January 2003 99.
54. See Stephen Coleman, "The Internet as a Space for Policy Deliberation," in Frank Fischer and Herbert Gottweis, eds., *The Argumentative Turn Revisited: Public Policy As Communicative Practice* (Durham, NC: Duke University Press, 2012) 149–79.
55. Regina G. Lawrence, "Defining Events: Problem Definition in the Media Arena," in *Politics, Discourse, and American Society*, ed. Roderick P. Hart and Bartholomew H. Sparrow (Lanham, MD: Rowman & Littlefield, 2001), 92.
56. W. Lance Bennett and Regina G. Lawrence, "News Icons and the Mainstreaming of Social Change," *Journal of Communication* 45, no. 3 (Summer 1995): 20.
57. Frank R. Baumgartner and Bryan D. Jones, *Agenda and Instability in American Politics* (Chicago: University of Chicago Press, 1993), 124.
58. Rodney Barker, *Political Legitimacy and the State* (Oxford: Clarendon Press, 1990).
59. For an overview of policy evaluation, see B. Guy Peters, *American Public Policy: Promise and Performance*, 9th ed. (Washington, DC: CQ Press, 2012).
60. Patricia Aufderheide, *Communications Policy and the Public Interest* (New York: Guilford Press, 1999).

61. Jonathan D. Glater, "Texas U. Fires Aid Officer over His Ties to Lender," *The New York Times*, May 15, 2007, A13; and Karen W. Arenson, "Columbia Will Pay $1.1 Million to State Fund in Student Lending Scandal," *The New York Times*, June 1, 2007, A23.
62. Jonathan D. Glater, "G.A.O. Study Cites Loose Oversight of College Loans," *The New York Times*, August 2, 2007, A1.
63. Diana Jean Schemo, "Congress Passes Overhaul of Student Aid Programs," *The New York Times*, September 8, 2007, A12.
64. Peter Baker and David M. Herszenhorn, "Obama Signs Overhaul of Student Loan Program," *The New York Times*, March 31, 2010, A14.
65. Joel Best and Eric Best, *The Student Loan Mess: How Good Intentions Created a Trillion-Dollar Problem* (Berkeley: CA: University of California Press, 2014).
66. Ashley Parker, Yasmeen Abutaleb and Josh Dawsey, "Trump administration has many task forces-but still no plan for beating Covid-19," *Washington Post*, April 111, 2020, 1ff.
67. Sharon LaFranier and Chris Hamby, "Preying on the Panicked, Scammers and Con Artists See a Bonanza in Covid-19, *The New York Times*, April 6, 2020, A6.
68. John Meyers, "California loans 500 ventilators to New York, other areas in immediate need amid coronavirus," *Los Angeles Times*, April 6, 2020, https://www.latimes.com/california/story/2020-04-06/california-loans-500-ventilators-to-new-york-other-areas-in-immediate-need-amid-coronavirus.
69. For a description of the negotiations involving Treasury Secretary Mnuchin, Senate Republican Majority Leader Mitch McConnell (R. KY), Senate Minority Leader Chuck Schumer (D. N.Y.), House of Representatives Speaker Nancy Pelosi (D. Cal.), and others, over the contents of the legislation, see Carl Hulse and Emily Cochran, "Passing the Stimulus: Non-starter at 9 A.M.. To 96-0 at Midnight," *The New York Times*, March 27, 2020, A6-7.
70. See Tara Siegel Bernard and Ron Lieber, "In the Rescue Plan: Checks, Unemployment Benefits and More," *The New York Times*, March 27, 2020, A6-7.
71. Beth Cameron, "I ran the White House pandemic office. Trump closed it," op. ed., *Washington Post*, March 13, 2020.
72. Donald J. Trump (@realDonaldTrump) March 18, 2020.
73. Politifact, The Pointer Institute, https://www.politifact.com/factchecks/2020/feb/27/rush-limbaugh/fact-checking-rush-limbaughs-misleading-claim-new-/.
74. Thomas Kaplan, "Cuomo Laments Mismatched Distribution of Cash Aid Between States," *The New York Times*, April 15, 2020, A15.
75. J. David Goodman, "How Outbreak Kept New York a Step Behind," *The New York Times*, April 8, 2020, A1, 12.
76. No author, "Around The Region," *The New York Times*, March 31, 2020, A13.
77. Trip Gabriel and Lisa Lerer, "Trump's Boost in Approval Is Not Surprising. The Boosters Are," *The New York Times*, April 1, 2020, A1 (22).
78. Jennifer Steinhauer and Zolan Kanno-Youngs, March 27, 2020, A1 (11).
79. Ron Lieber and Alan Rappeport, April 3, 2020, B6.
80. April 3, 2020, B1(7).
81. April 3, 2020, B1 (8).

CHAPTER 17

# Foreign and National Security Policies

## 17.1 Preamble

On January 31, 2001, the U.S. Commission on National Security/21st Century released its report warning that foreign terrorists would soon attack and kill many people in the United States.[1] The commission was the brainchild of President Bill Clinton and Speaker of the House Newt Gingrich, mandated by Congress, and chaired by two former senators, Warren Rudman (R-NH) and Gary Hart (D-CO). It spent $10 million and worked for three and a half years. To ensure widespread coverage of the report, its chairmen hired a public relations firm, visited newspapers' news bureaus in New York and Washington, DC, briefed key members of Congress, and unveiled it at a news conference on Capitol Hill.

The report was not entirely ignored, but it never received the media attention it warranted. The wire services reported it, as did the *Washington Post*, the *Los Angeles Times*, and CNN. *USA Today* published a short piece. But there were few stories in the rest of the news media when the commission reported or later. Nothing about it was reported in the *New York Times*. Most Americans were unaware of the report and of the deadly danger it warned of.

Interviewed a year later, journalists regretted the limited coverage. They attributed it to various factors. One was timing: the press covers only a few major stories at any time, and the cut in interest rates and the electricity crisis in California were deemed more newsworthy because of their immediate effects on people. The apparent lack of interest from public officials was another explanation. The news media would have covered the report far more if President Clinton, who had just left office, had promoted it or if his recently inaugurated successor George W. Bush had held a news conference about it or invited the two senators to the White House or had highlighted terrorism in a speech. President Bush did none of these things. Nor did Congress hold a hearing on the report or make terrorism a priority. The report also lacked immediacy: it was a prediction about an event that *might* happen.

The media failed to connect the report to past events: terrorists had previously staged several attacks against the United States, including destroying two U.S. embassies and damaging the World Trade Center. "In the three months leading up to 9/11, the phrase al-Qaeda was never mentioned on any of the three evening news broadcasts—not once."[2]

This case shows that not reporting or insufficiently reporting stories can be significant. The news media put no pressure on President George W. Bush to take action to try to forestall terrorist attacks. They denied people information and understanding about the terrorist threat and limited their ability to hold the administration accountable for a policy failure when the attacks occurred. After the attacks, they arguably gave excessive and positive coverage to the Bush administration's responses to terrorists and terrorism.

## Enduring Image

### The Twin Towers

On 9/11 al-Qaeda terrorists armed with primitive box cutters took over four passenger planes, transforming them into lethal weapons. They flew two of the jets into the Twin Towers of the World Trade Center in New York City, killing 2,823 people from around the world and injuring many more. They flew the third jet into the Pentagon, causing more casualties and serious damage to the building. Passengers prevented the terrorists from flying the fourth plane to Washington, DC, and it crashed in the Pennsylvania countryside. Shown throughout the world, the horrifying shots of the planes flying into the Twin Towers and of the towers' destroyed remnants are enduring images of a spectacular attack on the symbols of U.S. economic might. They graphically demonstrated the ability of terrorists from abroad to attack on U.S. soil. They shocked Americans into realizing their country's vulnerability, with its six thousand miles of land borders and three hundred ports of entry.

This video shows the south tower impact during the September 11, 2011, terror attacks.

View in the online reader

To a nation accustomed to Hollywood disaster blockbusters, the 9/11 attack was harsh reality.[3] Yet the phrases used by television commentators had an eerie familiarity: they recalled Hollywood's fictional movie *The Siege*, a 1998 thriller about terrorists attacking targets in New York City.

President Bush and other U.S. government and military leaders responded to the attacks depicted in the devastating images and words of the media. Their themes were American national identity, strength, and power. Their purpose was to unite the American public and mobilize support for a "war on terrorism" to be waged abroad and at home.[4] In their stories, journalists repeated and thereby reinforced these themes and supported the purposes.[5]

The United States is the global superpower and world leader. The world in which it exists is a wondrous place. It is also beset by famine, poverty, disease, and catastrophes both natural (tsunamis, earthquakes) and man-made (global warming, pollution of the seas and skies, and release of radioactive materials from nuclear plants). It is a world of genocide, regional and ethnic strife, terrorism, and refugees; of conflicts and violence in Syria, Iraq, Afghanistan, Yemen, and elsewhere. The nuclear weapons program of North Korea, the proliferation of weapons of mass destruction ("loose nukes"), the Arab–Israeli conflict, and instability in and challenges to regimes throughout the world are some of the foreign-policy issues that affect the United States. Others are economic upheavals, the rise of China to world economic and political power, relations with Russia (e.g., over Ukraine), AIDS in Africa, the availability and price of oil, the importation and availability of dangerous illegal drugs, and the annual U.S. trade deficit of around $800 billion. And now there is the virulent coronavirus and its variants.

At the same time, the United States is extraordinarily active, often militarily, in international affairs. Since 1989, it has intervened in Panama, Kuwait, Somalia, Bosnia, Haiti, Kosovo, Afghanistan, and Iraq.[6] On the other hand, it stood aside as hundreds of thousands of people were killed in the Rwandan genocide. President Clinton later apologized for doing nothing in that state.

America's military expenditures are enormous. The annual defense budget is around $711 billion plus more billions for the Homeland Security and intelligence agencies. That's about ten times greater than any other nation. The United States has around eighty major weapons programs under development with a collective price tag of $1.3 trillion. It has formal or informal agreements to defend thirty-seven countries. It has nearly 800 bases, ports, and airfields abroad, and its military personnelare deployed in approximately 130 countries, including South Korea, Germany, and autocracies such as Uzbekistan. Excluding Iraq and Afghanistan, some 200,000 American military personnel plus a roughly equal number of dependents and civilians are stationed abroad. At roughly forty billion sold, the United States is the world's leading supplier of weapons to the world, selling around half of the annual total.[7]

### Link

**U.S. Department of Defense Budget**

View the defense budget here.

According to an investigation by the *Washington Post*, the government responding to the terrorist attacks of 9/11 has created a top-secret America:

- "1,271 government organizations and 1,931 private companies work on programs related to counterterrorism, homeland security and intelligence in about 10,000 locations across the United States."
- "An estimated 854,000 people . . . hold top-secret security clearances."
- "Many security and intelligence agencies do the same work. . . . For example, 51 federal organizations and military commands . . . track the flow of money to and from terrorist networks."[8]

This chapter explains why the United States has become so involved in the world, how the government is organized to make foreign and national security policies, and the most important policies that result.

# 17.2 The Executive Branch Makes Foreign and Military Policies

## Learning Objectives

After reading this section, you should be able to answer the following questions:

1. Who is involved in making foreign policy?
2. How do the president and the bureaucracy interact in constructing foreign policy?
3. What are some of the causes of competition or disagreement among the makers of foreign policy?

Foreign policy is made by the president, presidential advisors, and the foreign policy bureaucracies. Individuals and agencies compete for power and supremacy in the making and the contents of foreign policy decisions. Their effectiveness depends on their closeness to and confidence from the president, their reputation and prestige, their skill at bureaucratic in-fighting, and their personality and style.

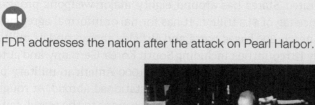

FDR addresses the nation after the attack on Pearl Harbor.

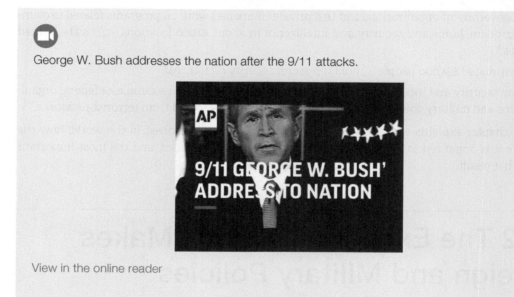

View in the online reader

George W. Bush addresses the nation after the 9/11 attacks.

View in the online reader

## The President

Formal powers specified in the Constitution put the president at the center of foreign policy. They include being commander in chief of the armed forces, negotiating treaties, and appointing ambassadors. The president is also the spokesperson for and to the nation: notable presidential addresses have been made by Franklin D. Roosevelt after the Japanese attack on Pearl Harbor in 1941 and by George W. Bush following the 9/11 attacks.

How presidents manage the bureaucracy influences the information they receive and their range of policy options.[9] Franklin Roosevelt opted for overlapping jurisdictions, with departments competing for influence and his attention. Other presidents established rules and procedures for processing information and vetting opinions. President Clinton sought out independent-minded advisors and gave them some leeway to decide policy. President George W. Bush relied on a few advisors, particularly the dominating, self-confident Vice President Dick Cheney and Secretary of Defense Donald Rumsfeld.[10] President Donald Trump seemed to have supreme confidence in his own judgment and to have little compunction about changing or removing cabinet members and advisors.

# National Security Advisor

Foremost among the president's foreign policy advisors is the **national security advisor**. Issues the advisor faces include how to serve and protect the president's interests and how to deal with other makers of foreign and defense policy in the government.

**national security advisor**

Leading advisor to the president on national security and foreign policy.

Some national security advisors have built a large staff to help them formulate options and oversee policy implementation. They have been vocal in espousing and expressing their views. One of the most powerful and forceful national security advisors was Henry Kissinger, who served Presidents Richard Nixon and Gerald Ford. He understood the job as requiring him to interact frequently with the news media to communicate his and the president's policy views. He was famously successful in dealing with reporters, especially the three television networks' correspondents and the influential Washington columnists specializing in foreign affairs. He was able to "disarm them with his wit, intimidate them with his brilliance, flatter them with his confidences and charm them with his attention."[11] His critics were likely to be telephoned, cajoled, stroked, invited to dine, and visited at their homes.

The national security advisor is often in competition with the secretary of state. In the starkest example, President Jimmy Carter's national security advisor, Zbigniew Brzezinski, clashed frequently with Secretary of State Cyrus Vance. He tried to manage policy in the White House and did not always communicate decisions to other policymakers. Vance resigned in protest over not being informed in advance about the attempt to rescue the American embassy personnel held hostage in Iran in 1980.

Some national security advisors try to be neutral facilitators in policy debates between the heads of the major foreign policy bureaucracies. They are not always successful. President Ronald Reagan's national security advisors were unable to mediate between the constantly warring Secretary of State George Shultz and Secretary of Defense Caspar Weinberger or control Director of Central Intelligence William Casey.

The trend in recent administrations has been to select knowledgeable and low-key individuals who can provide the president with expert advice but not invite or engage in running conflicts with the other foreign policy bureaucracies. Sometimes this turns into catering to the president's wishes, as Condoleezza Rice did with President George W. Bush's wish to go to war with Iraq. After his reelection in 2004, he appointed her secretary of state.

Led by the national security advisor, the National Security Council's Principals Committee consists of the president's senior security advisors, relevant cabinet members, and military and intelligence advisors. The president's principal forum for considering national security and foreign policies, it is supposed to ensure consensus on and coordinate the policies among the various government agencies. But it is not easy to avoid internecine warfare among its participants, and discourage (let alone prevent) the secretaries of defense and state and the vice president, as well as special envoys to trouble spots, from communicating to the president unilaterally to influence and make policy.

# The State Department

The State Department is the oldest cabinet-level department. It has primary responsibility for managing the foreign affairs budget and resources, leading and coordinating other U.S. agencies in developing and implementing foreign policy, leading and coordinating U.S. representation abroad, and negotiating with foreign countries.

In none of these areas is its leadership unchallenged. Within the United States, the national security advisor has often eclipsed the secretary of state and the State Department as the principal source of policy ideas. The Defense Department has long been a competitor in national security policy, and the U.S. special trade representative has provided an alternative source of economic advice for the president. Abroad, the ambassador's authority in the U.S. embassy is often resisted by personnel assigned to it by other agencies, such as those responsible for spying.

The State Department's lead position in foreign affairs has also been compromised by congressional reluctance to pass foreign affairs appropriations, restrictions it imposes on how the funds can be spent, and micromanaging of the foreign affairs budget.

Congress also requires the State Department annually to certify countries as meeting targets on human rights, arms control, reducing drug trafficking, and other areas in order to remain eligible for foreign aid. An escape hatch does allow presidents to certify a country for aid if it is in the "national interest" to do so.

# Defense Department

For most of its history, the military was organized under the separate commands of the War Department and the Navy Department. No political or military authority other than the president existed above these departments to coordinate and direct them. This changed after World War II, when the 1947 National Security Act established the cabinet-rank position of the secretary of defense. In 1949, an amendment to the 1947 National Security Act established the Defense Department and the post of chair of the Joint Chiefs of Staff.

Exercising command authority over the military on behalf of the president, the secretary of defense participates in making and executing foreign policy, especially when it requires the use of force. Thus, Secretary of Defense Donald Rumsfeld was intimately involved in the decision to attack Iraq and was responsible for the 2003 execution of the policy.

The chair of the Joint Chiefs of Staff plans and coordinates the deployment of American forces, the unified command's conduct of these operations, and how the military services train and equip the necessary forces. Since the 1980s, a dominant issue within the Defense Department has been improving the operational efficiency of the armed forces.[12] The concern for operational efficiency is joined by a concern for cost. Almost half of the Defense Department's annual budget goes to salaries and a quarter to operating and maintaining military forces.

The twin concerns for efficiency and cost have been combined in three debates over the ability of the United States to fight wars today. One debate is between defense hawks, who want increased defense spending to ensure U.S. security, and deficit hawks, who wish to reduce all areas of government spending. A second debate is over military readiness. Does the military consist of "hollow forces" that look robust on paper but lack training, modern weapons, and effectiveness? The third debate is over the impact of modern technology on how the United States organizes, prepares for, and fights wars.

All three debates took place over the Iraq War. Deficit hawks reacted with great concern to the Bush administration's continuously rising price tag for the war and the occupation and attempted reconstruction of Iraq. The second debate was seen in the concerns expressed by National Guard units over the length of time they were serving in Iraq and the refusal of the military to allow many career soldiers to leave, resign, or retire. The debate over the role of technology in warfare was central to the dispute between Secretary of Defense Donald Rumsfeld and many senior military officers over how to conduct the war and how large a military force was necessary.

# The Central Intelligence Agency

The Central Intelligence Agency (CIA) was created by the National Security Act of 1947. Its main task was to correlate, evaluate, and disseminate intelligence.[13] It was not explicitly authorized to engage in covert action or to collect its own information. Both of these tasks, however, quickly became part of its mission.[14]

The CIA's directorate for operations engages in covert operations. By the 1970s, the cumulative effect of two decades of covert action and of news stories about them produced a media and thus public image of the CIA as a "rogue elephant" that was out of control. Congress then created two special committees, one in each chamber, to oversee intelligence. It also insisted that covert actions be accompanied by an explicit "Presidential Finding" that the covert actions are in the national interest. The CIA was involved in secret prisons established abroad by the United States during the Iraq war and in "enhanced interrogation" like waterboarding that arguably reached the level of torture. (See the discussion in our Chapter 14.)

## Other Intelligence Agencies

The CIA is one of several intelligence agencies. Others are

- the State Department's Bureau of Intelligence and Research;
- the agencies of the military services;
- the Defense Department's National Security Agency (NSA), which is charged with maintaining the security of U.S. message traffic and intercepting, analyzing, and cryptanalyzing the messages of other states;
- the Defense Intelligence Agency (DIA);
- the Federal Bureau of Investigation (FBI); and
- the Department of Homeland Security.

They operate independent of the CIA.

After the 9/11 terrorist attacks, the CIA's intelligence estimating abilities and procedures came into question. Of concern was the absence of clandestine collection capabilities (spies) in many parts of the world that harbor anti-American terrorist movements or possess weapons of mass destruction. Also questioned was the CIA's lack of cooperation with the FBI and other intelligence agencies. Perhaps most devastating was the finding of the 9/11 Commission that investigated the terrorist attacks: "a failure of imagination" kept the intelligence agencies from anticipating and thwarting the attacks.

### Link

**The 9/11 Commission**

Read the findings of the 9/11 Commission here.

The Iraq War brought forward new charges of intelligence failures. At issue was the quality of the intelligence that contributed to the decision to go to war and the failure to find evidence of weapons of mass destruction in Iraq. Their supposed existence and the imminent threat posed by them to the United States had figured heavily in President Bush's justification to Congress and the American people for the war.

### Director of National Intelligence

In response to intelligence failures, Congress passed and President Bush signed legislation creating a Director of National Intelligence (DNI) in December 2004; the DNI was to be the president's chief intelligence advisor, with substantial control over the government's annual intelligence budget of at least $40 billion. The DNI would be the overall leader of fifteen independent and rival agencies. The CIA director now reports to the DNI. In practice, the power of the intelligence job depends on the director's relationship with the president.

## Department of Homeland Security

This newest part of the foreign policy bureaucracy was conceived in response to the 9/11 attacks and became effective in November 2002.[15]

The Department of Homeland Security combines activities from twenty-two different federal agencies with a total workforce of 170,000 employees. Agencies incorporated in the department include the Immigration and Naturalization Service (INS), the Secret Service, the Customs Service, the Federal Emergency Management Agency (FEMA), the Transportation Security Administration (TSA), the Coast Guard, and the Border Patrol. Some observers are concerned that the combination of foreign policy and domestic missions in the same department limits its effectiveness. That is, the capacities to meet the challenges posed by earthquakes, floods, blackouts, and storms (tasks that are central to FEMA's mission) have been underdeveloped as more resources and attention are given to fighting terrorism, or that the need to respond to these catastrophes will divert attention away from fighting terrorism.

## The U.S. Trade Representative (USTR)

This is the title given to both an agency located within the Executive Office of the President and to the individual who heads the agency.[16]

Congress created the office in 1962 largely out of frustration with the State Department's handling of international trade. It felt that the State Department was too concerned with the policy positions of foreign states and was not responsive enough to American business interests. The USTR is responsible for developing and coordinating U.S. international trade policy. This includes all matters that fall within the jurisdiction of the World Trade Organization, which establishes the rules of trade between states.

### Key Takeaways

Foreign and military policies are made and carried out by the executive branch, particularly the president, with the national security advisor, the State Department, the Defense Department, the Department of Homeland Security, and the intelligence agencies. The National Security Act of

1947 and recent bureaucratic reorganization after 9/11 reshaped the structure of foreign policy-making. The individuals, departments and agencies involved often disagree over policies, military spending, military goals, and much more.

## Exercises

1. What formal powers put the president at the center of foreign policy? How might being the head of the executive branch give the president an informal advantage in making foreign policy?
2. How did the National Security Act reorganize the national security establishment? What do you think the idea behind the National Security Act was?
3. What are the responsibilities of the Department of Homeland Security? Do you think it makes sense to have one department handle all those jobs? Why or why not?

# 17.3 Influence from Congress and Outside Government

## Learning Objectives

After reading this section, you should be able to answer the following questions:

1. How does Congress influence foreign policy?
2. How have presidents attempted to deal with congressional involvement in international affairs?
3. What nongovernmental groups influence foreign policy, and how?

The constitutional division of power between the president and Congress is an "invitation to struggle over the privilege of directing U.S. foreign policy."[17] This struggle is most likely to take place when different political parties control the presidency and Congress, when powerful members of Congress disagree with the administration's policies, and when these policies are controversial or unpopular.

The ability on occasion to make decisions and take action quickly gives the president more power over foreign policy than Congress, which takes more time. Nonetheless, Congress can be influential by asserting its amending, oversight, and budgetary powers.

By attaching amendments to pieces of legislation, Congress has directed foreign aid funding for specific countries or purposes such as aid for Israel, buying products made in America, and prohibiting money from being spent on family planning programs.[18] But amendments are normally limited to relatively minor policies.

Congress can also exercise influence through oversight of the executive branch's implementation of foreign or military policy.[19] During the Vietnam War, the Senate Foreign Relations Committee, chaired by Senator J.W. Fulbright (D-AR), held hearings critical of the administration's conduct of the war. During the George W. Bush administration, committees in the House and Senate held hearings on the abusive treatment of prisoners by U.S. soldiers at the Abu Ghraib prison in Iraq and what higher-ups in the command knew about them. But hearings usually take place after policies have been implemented or too late to change them significantly.

Congress can also influence foreign policy through its budgetary powers. It can reduce or even refuse to fund programs. But congressional budgetary powers are blunt and not fine-tuned to the particulars of a policy. Cutting off funding is particularly difficult when it makes members vulnerable to accusations (especially in campaign advertisements directed against them by their opponent) of failing to fund the troops, as happened during the Iraq War. Budgetary controls also do little to offset the president's authority to commit the United States to a course of action by announcing such policy decisions as a war on terrorism.

The struggle between Congress and the president to control American foreign and military policy can also take place over three constitutional powers that the president and Congress share: appointments, treaties, and war.

## Appointments

The president appoints but the Senate has the constitutional authority to approve the appointment of ambassadors and those charged with running government departments. (Many ambassadors are wealthy campaign contributors.) This gives the Senate a voice in how these organizations are run. The Senate does readily and routinely confirm most appointees who deal with foreign policy, but this is often because the president, anticipating objections, usually makes unobjectionable appointments.

In addition, presidents often evade the appointment problem by using people whose appointment is not subject to Senate approval as negotiators. These people may be trusted allies of the president or have expertise in the issue being negotiated. In the Reagan administration, National Security Council staffer Lt. Col. Oliver North was the driving force in the ill-fated Iran–Contra deal that would have freed American hostages held (in Lebanon) by an organization with ties to Iran and funded the Contras in Nicaragua through secret weapons sales to Iran.

### Link

**Oliver North**

Read a related interview with Oliver North here.

## Treaties

The Constitution states that it is the president who by and with the advice and consent of the Senate negotiates treaties. The approval of two-thirds of the senators voting is required. The Senate does not always consent. The Republican-controlled Senate, for example, rejected the Treaty of Versailles negotiated by the Democratic president Woodrow Wilson following the end of World War I. This treaty created the League of Nations, the forerunner to the United Nations, but with the treaty's rejection the United States did not join. Today, presidents routinely include key members of the Senate on negotiating teams as a means of obtaining advice before and easing consent after a treaty is signed.

The Senate has rejected few treaties outright, but presidents have learned that approval is not assured even when senators are involved or at least consulted in advance.[20] For example, in 1999 the Senate rejected, by a vote of fifty-one to forty-eight, the Comprehensive Nuclear Test Ban Treaty, which would have banned all tests of nuclear weapons.[21] Even without rejecting a treaty, the Senate may modify it by making amendments and thereby undermine a complex international agreement and bring about a diplomatic or security crisis.

The Senate's power of **advice and consent** is somewhat negated by the president's increased reliance on executive agreements over treaties as a means of entering into agreements with other states.[22] Unlike treaties, **executive agreements** do not require the consent of the Senate before becoming law. Presidents are free to enter into them at their own discretion and to end them when they see fit. Congress has tried to curb this power but with little effect. In the 1970s, it passed the Case–Zablocki Act that requires presidents to inform Congress of any and all executive agreements they enter into.

**advice and consent**

Constitutional authority of the Senate to approve treaties—approval from two-thirds of the senators voting is required.

**executive agreements**

Agreements that the president enters into with other states; unlike treaties, they do not require the consent of the Senate before becoming law.

# War Powers

The Constitution grants Congress the power to declare war and to raise and maintain armed forces. But when does a state of war come into existence? The United States has sent troops into battle over 125 times in its history, yet Congress has declared war only five times: the War of 1812, the Spanish-American War, the Mexican War, World War I, and World War II. No declaration of war preceded the entry of American forces into the Korean War. President Harry Truman all but ignored Congress, basing his use of force on a UN Security Council resolution, an argument that would be used again later in the Persian Gulf War and the Iraq War. Vietnam, too, was fought without a declaration of war. When the legality of this war was challenged, defenders pointed to the Gulf of Tonkin Resolution, in which Congress authorized the president to take whatever steps he felt necessary to protect and defend American forces in South Vietnam; the war's defenders also pointed to congressional votes authorizing funds for fighting the war. The argument was that if Congress did not support the war, all it had to do was stop authorizing funds to fight it. Such an action is far easier said than done.

The congressional-presidential struggle over war-making powers came to a head during the Vietnam era and led to Congress passing the War Powers Resolution over President Richard Nixon's veto. This resolution effectively allows the president ninety days to wage war without congressional approval. No president has recognized the constitutionality of the War Powers Resolution, though none has openly challenged it either.[23] (See Chapter 13.)

# Influence from Outside Government

Influence can be exerted on foreign and national security policy by think tanks, interest groups, and the public through opinion polls and elections.

## Think Tanks

Think tanks are private research organizations that seek to influence public policy. They have been referred to as "idea brokers" because they help define the issues on the policy agenda and options for addressing them.[24]

Foreign policy is an area in which think tanks have become especially active for several reasons. First, it has become much more complex: no longer restricted to national security, foreign policy encompasses trade, finance, human rights, the environment, and cultural issues. Second, the information abilities of the government have been overwhelmed by this expanded foreign policy agenda. Long-range planning and strategic speculation are now commonly produced by think tanks, as is current information on breaking issues. Third, think tanks provide multiple and competing policy recommendations backed up with supporting information. Of course, as we discussed in the previous chapter, think tanks can be ideological, providing partisan policy analyses and proposals.

## Interest Groups

A wide variety of groups try to influence U.S. foreign policy. There are economic groups such as the Chamber of Commerce and the American Farm Bureau Federation. There are ethnic groups representing Arab, Greek, Turkish, Chinese, Cuban, and Eastern European Americans.[25] Public interest groups seek to influence U.S. foreign policy in such areas as human rights (Amnesty International) and the environment (the Sierra Club).

As documented in Chapter 9, foreign governments can also behave as interest groups. After 9/11 and during the Iraq War, Saudi Arabia came under harsh criticism in the United States for its failure to crack down on terrorist groups. Part of the Saudi response was to engage in a large-scale media and lobbying campaign to improve its image and relations with government and the public in the United States.

Interest groups often conflict on an issue. In the debate over creating free trade areas such as the North American Free Trade Agreement (NAFTA), business groups were pitted against labor and environmental groups. In other cases, one interest group seems to dominate a policy area. This has long been the case with the Arab-Israeli conflict, where Jewish American groups, notably the American Israel Public Affairs Committee (AIPAC), have been particularly influential. (See Chapter 9.)

## Public Opinion

Americans have "limited attention and low levels of knowledge about the details of foreign affairs."[26] Nonetheless, they have views about foreign policy. These are influenced by the opinions of trusted elites as communicated, not always accurately, by the media.[27]

More generally, Americans would like their country to pursue national security and international justice through participation in treaties and agreements and collective decision making within international organizations. They would also like the country to combat terrorism, prevent the spread of nuclear weapons, reduce levels of immigration, and protect the country's borders.

Many of these opinions are neither detailed nor intensely held. The public therefore usually goes along with America's foreign policies or at least gives policymakers the benefit of the doubt unless the media tell them that things have gone wrong. Nonetheless, the public can sometimes initiate and constrain foreign policy.[28]

The timing of elections is one way public opinion influences the president's willingness to undertake foreign policy initiatives and exercise military force. Presidents become increasingly hesitant to take foreign policy risks as elections approach for fear of having their leadership called into question. Even successes can be criticized as being too costly. So deep-seated is this reluctance to act that a common complaint from foreign leaders is that U.S. foreign policymaking grinds to a halt every four years.

For a different view, there is the film *Wag the Dog* (1997), in which a president's aides invent a war with Albania to distract media and public attention from his involvement in a sex scandal that is about to derail his reelection.

**Vietnam syndrome**

Post-Vietnam assumption by U.S. policymakers that Americans would not support military action if it resulted in significant casualties to U.S. troops.

One question that has received considerable attention is the American public's opinions about the use of military force. The conventional wisdom after Vietnam was that Americans would not support military action if it resulted in significant casualties to U.S. troops. This was called the **Vietnam syndrome**.

As a result, any military involvement in the future would have to be short and involve the overwhelming application of force.[29] The George W. Bush administration's decision to minimize the number of U.S. forces on the ground in the Iraq War and the heavy use of air power as a prelude to the ground war reflected this syndrome.

The American public's willingness to tolerate casualties does depend on the reasons for military action.[30] People are most supportive of the use of military force when they believe it is to protect the United States against attack. Nonetheless, protracted conflicts lower presidential popularity: witness Korea and President Truman, Vietnam and President Johnson, and Iraq and President George W. Bush.

## Key Takeaways

Congress is involved in foreign and military policies through its amending, oversight, and budgetary powers and through the constitutional power related to appointments, treaties, and war it shares with the president. While Congress has sometimes worked to limit the president's autonomy in foreign policy, the use of executive orders and the ability to enter military engagements without formal declarations of war have ensured the president's continued primacy in international affairs. Forces that sometimes influence foreign and military policies from outside government are think tanks, interest groups, and public opinion.

## Exercises

1. What formal constitutional powers does Congress have that allow it to influence foreign policy?
2. Why might it be difficult for Congress to limit the president's power to send troops into combat, even though it is Congress that has the formal power to declare war?
3. Why do you think the American public is relatively uninterested in foreign affairs? What foreign policy issues do you think Americans care about and should be concerned about the most?

# 17.4 The Major Foreign and National Security Policies

## Learning Objectives

After reading this section, you should be able to answer the following questions:

1. What are isolationism and internationalism? How have they been incorporated into U.S. foreign policy?
2. How did World War II change the direction of U.S. international involvement?
3. What policies guided U.S. action during the Cold War and the Vietnam War?

In this section, we move from the makers of U.S. foreign and national security policies to the policies they have made.

# From Isolationism to Internationalism

**isolationism**

Belief that U.S. national interests are best served by avoiding involvement with foreign countries.

Two visions have competed for how the United States should orient itself to world politics. They are isolationism and internationalism. **Isolationism**, the policy of trying to stay aloof from foreign entanglements, has long roots in American foreign policy.[31] Many date it back to George Washington's Farewell Address, which warned Americans to "steer clear of permanent alliances with any portion of the foreign world."

During the period between World War I and World War II, the United States pursued a largely isolationist foreign policy. It refused to join the League of Nations, and Congress passed a series of bills in the 1930s that imposed a policy of neutrality on the United States in foreign conflicts.

Isolationism ended with U.S. involvement in World War II. It may regain some favor now as Americans react negatively to the financial and human cost of involvement in Iraq and Afghanistan. Media stories about outsourcing, in which American companies give the jobs of their American employees to low-paid workers overseas, may add to the isolationist impulse.

**internationalism**

Belief that U.S. national interests are best served by involvement with foreign countries.

Meanwhile, internationalism reigns. **Internationalism** means involvement in events beyond one's borders to accomplish and protect the national interest.[32] It has dominated American foreign policy since 1955, a decade after World War II ended. Internationalists favor democratization, free trade, and a policy of global military activism designed to maintain America's dominant position in world affairs. But specific policies have varied depending on the administration in power.

We discuss the most important of these policies: containment, deterrence, détente and arms control, and the use of military force by the United States, particularly in Vietnam and Iraq.

# Containment

**Cold War**

The rivalry and consequent arms race between the United States and its allies and the Soviet Union and its allies, which lasted from the end of World War II until the late 1980s.

**containment**

The U.S. policy of vigilance and alliances to prevent the spread of Communism.

The World War II alliance between the United States and the Soviet Union soon gave way to a series of international crises that divided the victors into two opposing blocs. The result was a **Cold War** of the United States and its allies against the Soviet Union and other Communist countries.

The concept guiding American foreign policy in this global struggle with the Soviet Union and its allies was **containment**.[33] It held that the United States did not need to engage in a war to defeat the Soviet Union. Instead, it could adopt a policy of constant vigilance and the creation of alliances in which American power would be used to contain and counter Soviet aggressive moves.

During the Cold War, the news media focused on the conflict between the United States and Communist countries. The main stories were the Communist takeover of China, the Korean War, U.S. relations with Cuba, and the Vietnam War. Thus, until the collapse of the Soviet Union in 1991, the U.S. media depicted the world in general and the preceding stories in particular from the American side of the Cold War frame.

# Deterrence

Another concept guiding U.S. foreign and military policy during the Cold War was **deterrence.**[34] According to deterrence theory, nuclear weapons were too powerful and destructive to be used as instruments of warfare. They were best suited to holding an opponent (here, the Soviet Union) in check by threatening it with destruction should it engage in an act of nuclear aggression.

Deterrence strategies are designed to prevent an opponent from undertaking an objectionable course of action. It was an article of faith during the Cold War that nuclear deterrence could not be assumed to exist through the possession of a large nuclear arsenal. The United States adopted a second strike strategy: to deter an attack by possessing the capability to absorb an enemy's nuclear attack and retaliate with so much force that it could inflict an unacceptable level of damage on its society. Stability was assumed to be assured when both sides adopted such a strategy.

**deterrence**

The assumption that U.S. possession of nuclear weapons would hold the Soviet Union in check by threatening it with destruction should it engage in nuclear aggression.

### Link

**Deterrence Strategy**

Click here to read about deterrence strategy.

This created a situation of **mutual assured destruction (MAD).** Thus a major concern of policymakers in the United States was that the Soviet Union not be allowed to gain a significant advantage over the United States in the size of its nuclear inventory. Because Soviet leaders shared the same goal, the result was an arms race.

**mutual assured destruction (MAD)**

Deterrence by being able to absorb a nuclear attack and have enough nuclear weapons left over to inflict an unacceptable level of damage on the enemy.

# Vietnam

As the Cold War expanded in the late 1950s and early 1960s, containment entered the Third World. Already the United States had been involved in helping bring down anti-American governments in Guatemala and Indonesia. Now newly independent states in Africa and Asia became political and military battlegrounds in which the United States and Soviet Union supported competing local leaders.

The most enduring and significant extension of containment to the Third World came in Vietnam.[35] The Geneva Peace Accords envisioned a country temporarily divided at the seventeenth parallel, with Communist forces in control of North Vietnam and pro-Western forces in control of South Vietnam. But North Vietnam and its Communist allies in South Vietnam began a military campaign to unify all of Vietnam.

## U.S. Involvement in Vietnam

When President Dwight Eisenhower left office, the United States had one thousand military advisors in South Vietnam. President John F. Kennedy authorized an additional fifteen thousand advisors. Under President Lyndon Johnson, the war became increasingly Americanized as U.S. forces carried out sustained and massive bombing campaigns against the North and U.S. ground troops began fighting in the South.

## The Tet Offensive

A turning point in the war came in late January 1968. Seeking a final, decisive victory, the Communists launched a massive simultaneous attack, known as the Tet Offensive, on major cities throughout the country. In the attack on Saigon, the South Vietnamese capital, soldiers temporarily invaded the American embassy grounds, in full view of American reporters and television news crews.

From a purely military standpoint, Tet was a disaster. Nearly two-thirds of the Communist troops were killed or captured. The expected popular uprising against the Americans and South Vietnamese government did not take place.

## Media Response to Tet

Yet by the end of the Tet Offensive, significant segments of the media and thus the American public had turned against the administration's conduct of the war, if not the war itself. In February 1968, the *Wall Street Journal* warned readers in an editorial that the effort in Vietnam may be "doomed." Following a visit to Vietnam, CBS Evening News anchor Walter Cronkite famously declared that "it is increasingly clear to this reporter that the only rational way out will be to negotiate, not as victors, but as an honorable people who lived up to their pledge to defend democracy and did the best they could."[36] And a special report on NBC television declared the war a failure.[37]

**FIGURE 17.1 Footage that Galvanized U.S. Opposition to the Vietnam War**
The photograph and television footage of the execution by the director of South Vietnam's national police force of a Viet Cong prisoner on the streets of Saigon during the Tet Offensive helped galvanize U.S. opposition to the Vietnam War.

Source: Eddie Adams/Associated Press.

Even before Tet, media coverage of the war was becoming more critical. The media's response was driven by a cumulative reaction to the "credibility gap" that had existed for many months between the optimistic statements of the administration and the military command and the experiences of reporters and soldiers in the field. This critical reporting was indexed to growing dissent within the Johnson administration and the Democratic party, evidenced by Minnesota Senator Eugene McCarthy seeking the presidential nomination on an antiwar platform. It was also represented and reinforced by images capturing the brutality and horror of the war.

**FIGURE 17.2 Vietnamese Children Fleeing Napalm**

This legendary photo, showing a naked Vietnamese girl and other children fleeing napalm, challenged the justification for the U.S. involvement in Vietnam by graphically exposing the cruelty of the war on innocent children.

Source: Associated Press.

By late March, approval of President Johnson's "handling of the situation in Vietnam" had dropped to 26 percent and disapproval swelled to 63 percent.[38] On March 31, 1968, the president announced he would not run for reelection and that U.S. bombing of North Vietnam would be restricted.

After he took office in 1969, President Richard Nixon pursued a policy of Vietnamization. It was designed to create conditions so that by 1972 the South Vietnamese army would be able to hold its own when supported by U.S. air and sea power. Congress held hearings and cut off some funds. There were demonstrations against the war (see here), especially on college campuses. Nixon's strategy failed, and in spring 1972 North Vietnam attacked South Vietnam, forcing Nixon to re-Americanize the war. By the time the war finally ended, 55,000 U.S. troops had lost their lives in Vietnam; as many as 541,000 Americans were fighting there at the war's height, and $150 billion was spent on the war effort.

# Détente and Arms Control

**détente**

U.S. policy of cooperating with the Soviet Union within the context of continuing competition and conflict.

President Nixon redirected American foreign and national security policy. He sought to minimize future Soviet challenges by treating the Soviet Union less as a rival and more as a partner in the international system. Known as **détente**, the goal was to create a framework of limited cooperation between the two superpowers within the context of ongoing competition and conflict.[39]

Détente's greatest success was in the area of arms control, most notably with the signing of the SALT I and SALT II agreements (see here), which placed outer limits on the size of the American and Soviet nuclear forces.[40] These agreements slowed the arms race while maintaining the fundamental symmetry in U.S. and Soviet nuclear forces around which deterrence had been built decades before.

# The Carter Administration

President Jimmy Carter's foreign policy emphasis on human rights pushed U.S.–Soviet competition into the background.[41] He criticized the human rights abuses of leaders who had loyally stood by the United States in its containment of the Soviet Union. One of those criticized was the shah of Iran. Put into power through a coup engineered by the Central Intelligence Agency (CIA) in 1953, the shah had been one of America's staunchest Cold War allies. But by the 1970s, he had become increasingly isolated within his own country.[42]

In January 1979, a revolution ousted the shah, who was replaced as leader in Iran by the exiled Ayatollah Ruhollah Khomeini. When news broke in October that the shah was coming to the United States for medical treatment, Iranian militants seized the U.S. embassy and held fifty-two Americans hostage. The Carter administration placed economic sanctions on Iran and undertook a hostage rescue mission in 1980 that failed. The hostages were not released until January 20, 1981, thirty minutes after Ronald Reagan became president.

Night after night, the media reminded American policymakers and the public of the continuing hostage situation in Iran and of the inability of the U.S. government to end it.

View in the online reader

The media reported the crisis night after night under such titles as "America Held Hostage."

Only a few diplomats were being held hostage, not the entire nation. Nonetheless, the media depiction conveying the impression of American impotence probably precipitated the rescue mission and contributed to making Jimmy Carter a one-term president.

# The Reagan Administration

President Reagan rejected the notion that the United States could cooperate or work with the Soviet Union. Under Reagan, détente and arms control ceased guiding American foreign policy.

The deathblow to détente had come during the Carter administration, when the Soviet Union invaded Afghanistan in 1979 in order to prop up pro-Russian Communist political forces. Within a year, the Soviet Union occupation army grew to 110,000, and it had to bear the primary responsibility for fighting the guerrillas, or Mujahedin, who were supported by U.S. funds. American military aid to the Mujahedin rose from $120 million in 1984 to $630 million in 1987.

Support for the Mujahedin was consistent with the Reagan Doctrine that the purpose of American foreign policy was not only to contain the spread of Communism but also to assist in bringing down Communist rulers.[43]

Most controversial was the administration's support for anticommunist forces in Nicaragua, where the Sandinistas had overthrown forty years of arbitrary, oppressive, and corrupt family rule in July 1979. The Sandinistas were sympathetic to Cuba's Castro and hostile to the United States. In

November 1981, Reagan authorized spending $19 million to transform a small and largely ineffective fighting force into one (the Contras) that would be more capable of ousting the Sandinista regime. In response, Congress passed the Boland Amendment, which barred the use of CIA or Defense Department funds for the purpose of overthrowing the Nicaraguan government or provoking a military exchange between it and Honduras. Chafing under this restriction, the Reagan administration devised a covert plan for increasing the amount of funds available to the Contras. At the heart of the administration's plan was a scheme to divert money to the Contras from the covert sale of weapons to Iran. When it became public, the Iran–Contra affair produced widespread and mainly critical negative media coverage and a storm of controversy.

# An Uncertain New World Order

On December 26, 1991, the Soviet Union collapsed. The end of the Cold War brought forward expressions of hope that America's military involvement in the world might be lessened. For some this meant that a return to isolationism was possible; for others it meant that the United States would be able to engage in building democracy and promoting peaceful change.

These alternative visions of America's role in the world were soon challenged by the reemergence of traditional national security concerns. The event that sparked this challenge was Iraq's August 2, 1990, invasion of Kuwait. It led to the Persian Gulf War, the first major international conflict of the post–Cold War era.[44]

The UN Security Council set January 15, 1991, as the deadline for Iraq's peaceful exit from Kuwait and authorized member states to "use all means necessary" to bring about Iraq's complete and unconditional withdrawal. When Iraq did not withdraw, the United States launched Operation Desert Storm. On February 28, after less than one month of fighting, Iraq announced a ceasefire; on April 6, Iraq accepted the UN's terms to formally end the war. The war was a diplomatic and military success for the United States, which had put together a global coalition against Iraq and conducted a military campaign that produced relatively few American casualties.

Before the war, media coverage generally reflected the views of U.S. policymakers and the military; it generated little debate over policy alternatives. The war itself was overwhelmingly reported from the perspectives of U.S. policymakers and the military.[45]

## Key Takeaways

Two visions of foreign policy are isolationism and, dominant since World War II, internationalism. The main policies during the Cold War were containment, deterrence, détente and arms control, and the use of military force, as in Vietnam.

## Exercises

1. Why do you think the United States has historically been isolationist? Why might this have changed after World War II?
2. What was the idea behind the Cold War policy of containment? How did the United States try to contain Soviet influence?
3. What was the Reagan Doctrine? How did Reagan put it into practice?

# 17.5 The George W. Bush Administration

## Learning Objectives

After reading this section, you should be able to answer the following questions:

1. What was the Bush Doctrine?
2. How did military operations in Afghanistan and Iraq under George W. Bush begin?
3. How have the media portrayed the U.S. military engagements in Afghanistan and Iraq?

After the 9/11 terrorist attacks, President George W. Bush focused on a policy of global leadership in a war on terror.[46] Media coverage and depictions would exaggerate terrorism and add to the importance of the war.[47]

## The Afghanistan War

The first confrontation in this war came in Afghanistan, where Osama bin Laden, the acknowledged mastermind of the 9/11, attacks, had taken refuge and where his terrorist organization, al-Qaeda, enjoyed support and protection from the ruling Taliban government.[48]

**FIGURE 17.3**
**Osama bin Laden**
The Saudi Arabian leader of al-Qaeda and mastermind of the 9/11 attacks symbolized terrorism for U.S. policymakers and the media.

Source: World History Archive / Alamy Stock Photo

President Bush demanded that the Taliban expel Osama bin Laden and al-Qaeda and sever its ties with international terrorism. When this did not happen, the United States and its allies began aerial strikes against terrorist facilities and Taliban military targets inside Afghanistan on October 7, 2001. Ground forces were supplied largely by the Northern Alliance, a coalition group that had opposed Taliban rule. Its efforts were aided and guided by the Central Intelligence Agency (CIA) and U.S. military forces. The Taliban soon surrendered, but its leader and Osama bin Laden remained at large.

In covering the war in Afghanistan, the U.S. media reported a consensus among policymakers and the public on the need to defeat the Taliban; the media also focused on military strategy and its execution and paid little attention to the loss of life and the destruction caused by the war. As the CNN chairman wrote in a memo instructing its correspondents not to focus excessively on Afghan suffering, "We must redouble our efforts to make sure we do not seem to be simply reporting from their vantage or perspective."[49]

Nation-building turned out to be far more difficult than simply overthrowing the Taliban. Some roads and buildings were rebuilt, and some girls, excluded from education by the Taliban, returned to school. Presidential elections were won by more or less pro-U.S. candidates. But there was little "security, stability, prosperity, or the rule of law."[50] Outside the capital of Kabul, Afghanistan was a collection of fiefdoms run by warlords and an opium-growing economy that fueled lawlessness and funded terrorists. The country's Supreme Court was controlled by Islamic fundamentalists. Except for its elections, Afghanistan would be overshadowed by Iraq, to which the U.S. news media's attention largely turned.

# The Bush Doctrine

President George W. Bush outlined a new direction for American foreign and military policy. Known as the Bush Doctrine, it contained three interrelated themes.[51]

First, predominance was the necessary foundation of American military strategy. The United States must possess a significant military power advantage over all other states so that it could act unilaterally (alone) to defend its national interests when and where it saw fit.

Second, the strategy for employing military power was **preemption**. Rather than containment and deterrence, the United States would act first to remove threats before they were capable of wreaking harm.

**preemption**

President George W. Bush's policy, exemplified in the war against Iraq, of removing threats before they harm the United States.

Third, in addition to reducing the military threat posed by other states, preemption had the goal of fostering regime change. Regime change was necessary because hostile states and terrorist organizations, the two principal threats to the United States through their possession of or attempts to possess weapons of mass destruction, were unlikely to change their ways. Only by removing them from power could the threat be eliminated.

Critics pointed out the limitations of preemption as a policy. In theory it should be applied to Iran and North Korea, which are hostile to the United States. But Iran could attack Israel and strike back against U.S. forces in the region, and North Korea could unleash its nuclear weapons and invade South Korea. So under what circumstances and when should the policy be applied?

Given its heavy involvement of military and money in Iraq, moreover, did the United States have the resources to apply a preemption policy to any other countries? The National Guard and Reserve made up approximately 40 percent of U.S. forces in Iraq and Afghanistan. The system was not designed to keep reservists on duty in a campaign against terrorism and fighting abroad for an extended period. Reservists trained one weekend a month and two weeks a year, accelerated before deployment; thus many of them were ill prepared and lacked combat skills.[52]

# The Iraq War

The Bush Doctrine provided the strategic rationale for the Iraq War.[53] The diplomatic maneuvering leading up to war entered into the final phase on March 17, 2003, when President Bush addressed the nation and gave Saddam Hussein forty-eight hours to leave Iraq. Hussein rejected Bush's ultimatum.

The first blow in the war was struck in the early morning hours of March 20, when President Bush ordered an air strike against the Iraqi leadership. The ground war began early in the evening of the same day, as American and British forces crossed into Iraq from Kuwait. Baghdad fell on April 9. On May 1, aboard the USS *Abraham Lincoln*, President Bush declared an end to major hostilities. In Iraq, celebrations of peace were short-lived, as looting and anarchy soon became the order of the day, followed by insurgency and sectarian conflict. The United States soon went from liberator to occupier.

To build support for the war, the administration had claimed that Iraqi dictator Saddam Hussein was a major threat to the United States because he possessed biological, chemical, and perhaps nuclear weapons of mass destruction and was likely to supply them to terrorists. To make its case, the administration treated unclear or ambiguous information as certain facts (e.g., that Iraq had attempted to obtain uranium from Africa). It ignored intelligence questioning whether Iraq possessed weapons of mass destruction and implied links between Saddam Hussein, 9/11, and terrorists that were never proven. The administration also used inflammatory language (e.g., "We don't want the smoking gun to be a mushroom cloud" said National Security Advisor Condoleezza Rice).

## The Media in Support

Before the war, there were some critical newspaper articles. Nonetheless, the media transmitted, parroted, promulgated, generally confirmed, and rarely challenged the administration's scare campaign.[54] The television news networks' coverage of domestic dissent was minimal, although they did report opposition from countries such as France, which argued for a diplomatic solution.[55]

The *New York Times* in particular supported the administration's rationale for going to war with Iraq by accepting U.S. government sources and Iraqi exiles' claims at face value, displaying them on the front page under heavy-breathing headlines. The *Times* gave glowing coverage to Secretary of State Colin Powell's speech and presentation of February 5, 2003, to the United Nations supposedly documenting Iraq's weapons of mass destruction.

The *Times* undermined the credibility of Iraqi government denials by following them with challenges from U.S. officials, and it discredited U.S. and foreign sources critical of the administration's argument. Stories challenging the administration's case for war were downplayed: James Risen's "C.I.A. Aides Feel Pressure in Preparing Iraqi Reports," completed several days prior to the invasion, was not printed until three days after the start of the war and was then relegated to page B10.[56] Dissenters received little coverage.

Because the *Times* has a reputation for occasional skepticism about people in authority, its coverage gave credibility to the administration's arguments. Moreover, many news organizations, such as CNN and National Public Radio, follow the *Times*'s lead.

The lack of vigorous challenges by leaders of the Democratic Party to the Bush administration in the run-up to the war left little criticism of the Bush policy for the news media to transmit. But the *Times* coverage contributed to the Democrats' docility. If the *Times* had published more critical stories, some Democrats might have been emboldened to attack the war policy.

### Comparing Content

#### The Iraq War

Media coverage of the war itself was dramatically different depending on whether one was exposed to U.S. or Arab media.[57]

In general, the U.S. media supported the war, presenting it as "America against the enemy," or as "us versus them." Complexities were ignored: there were no in-depth stories on the history of Iraq, its factions (Kurds, Shiite and Sunni Muslims), no understanding that, despite their hatred of Saddam Hussein, many Iraqis would not welcome the United States.

Television was most enthusiastic. Morning shows depicted the attack on Iraq as right and proper. Cable stations were unabashedly patriotic: Fox News titled its coverage "Op. Iraqi Freedom: War on Terror." American flags were part of on-screen logos and backdrops. Many of the expert commentators were former high-ranking officers in the U.S. military who were enthusiastically, or at least guardedly, pro-war.

American reporters embedded with the invasion forces gave the troops' perspective to their American audience. Reporters framed the conflict the same way as U.S. officials and military commanders.

The war shown on American television networks and on cable was almost entirely bloodless. It featured the "video game" aspects of the technical wizardry of American military power.[58] There was a dearth of gruesome or grisly footage. Reports repeated the Pentagon's sanitized language: "degraded" for slaughtered Iraqi units, "softening up" for the exploding of Iraqi soldiers in their bunkers.

In dramatic contrast was the depiction of the war by Al Jazeera, the Qatar-based satellite television channel dominated by Arab nationalists and Islamists, transmitting to a daily audience of thirty-five million across the Arab world. (The channel is barely seen in the United States.) It showed a different version of the war with different subjects and frames.

Al Jazeera had access to the Iraqi leadership. It placed correspondents and cameras in the Iraqi cities under attack and reported from the inhabitants' perspectives. Its staff gave an Arab point of view to an Arab audience.

Al Jazeera did not ignore the American side. It reported the allied advances, had a reporter embedded with U.S. forces, and broadcast sound bites from President Bush. But it debated rather than interviewed American spokespersons. It featured critics of the United States, took Iraqi government statements at face value, and highlighted any setbacks of the coalition forces.

Al Jazeera barely mentioned that the United States was opposing a brutal dictatorship. It depicted the U.S. military as an invading, occupying force of ruthless killers. It broadcast a report from Iraqi television of pictures of dead U.S. soldiers and interviews with captured ones. It showed raw and graphic footage of the destruction inflicted on Iraq and the pain and suffering of its civilians: charred bodies, mourning families, hospitals choked with bleeding and burned civilians.

## It's Not Over Until It's Over

President Bush announced victory, but Iraq remained a country with ethnic and tribal divisions and religious fanatics following the dictates of clerics. Conflict continued, with insurgents attacking and killing U.S. troops, Iraqi police, and public officials. Weapons of mass destruction were not found. The condition of the country's infrastructure was dire. Many more billions of dollars were needed to pay for the war and reconstruction and to keep U.S. troops in Iraq.

Elite consensus over the war evaporated. The revitalized Democratic opposition was reflected in Vermont Governor Howard Dean's campaign for the party's 2004 presidential nomination. He called the war precipitous and poorly prepared. The 9/11 Commission found that Iraq had no collaborative relationship with al-Qaeda and no involvement in the attacks on the World Trade Center. The former head of counterterrorism at the National Security Council contended that before the attacks, the Bush White House did not treat the danger of Osama bin Laden and al-Qaeda as urgent. He confirmed that the possibility of attacking Iraq was on the administration's policy agenda before 9/11.[59]

Media coverage of Iraq turned critical. There were frequent reports of bombings, suicide attacks, and stories of people kidnapped and beheaded. There was a media feeding frenzy of revelations about and photographs of torture by U.S. military personnel and private contractors in the Abu Ghraib prison in Iraq and in Afghanistan.[60]

**FIGURE 17.4**
**Abu Ghraib Prisoner "Gilligan" Hooded, Caped, and Wired on His Box**

Photographs such as this, shown around the world, undermined the U.S. claim to be a liberator not an occupier of Iraq.

Source: U.S. Army. Via Wikimedia: https://commons.wikimedia.org/wiki/File:Abu_Ghraib_34.JPG.

## Key Takeaways

The Bush Doctrine was three-pronged: it featured predominance, preemption, and regime change as the pillars of U.S. foreign policy. The United States therefore conducted military operations in Afghanistan in response to the 9/11 attacks. President George W. Bush's doctrine of preemption then involved the United States in a war to overthrow the ruling regime in Iraq. While the media initially gave favorable coverage to the decision to go to war and to the military operations in Iraq, subsequent revelations about false assumptions and errors made both before and during the war brought about media criticism.

## Exercises

1. What is meant by preemption? What are some potential problems with a policy of preemption?

2. What was the justification for invading Afghanistan? How did the American media cover the war in Afghanistan?
3. What was the justification for invading Iraq? Why do you think the American media were reluctant to challenge the Bush administration's arguments for going to war in Iraq?

# 17.6 President Obama, President Trump, and President Biden

## Learning Objectives

After reading this section, you should be able to answer the following questions:

1. What were the most challenging foreign policy issues the Obama administration faced?
2. What were important differences between the foreign policies of Presidents George W. Bush and Barack Obama?
3. What were the Obama policies toward Libya, Syria, and Ukraine?
4. What were President Trump's foreign policies?
5. What were President Biden's initial foreign policy changes?

## President Obama

President Barack Obama once described his guiding principle of foreign policy as "Don't do stupid shit." Easier said than done. He inherited challenging foreign policy problems from his predecessor, particularly repercussions of the war in Iraq, where al-Qaeda–connected jihadists operated and the governing regime was increasingly allied with Iran; the war in Afghanistan, where the Taliban were resurgent; and a global war on terrorism. Other bequeaths relevant to foreign policy from President Bush were a secret document authorizing the capture, detention, and lethal action against al-Qaeda terrorists, and a Special Operations Command to launch attacks anywhere in the world. He would also have to try to deal with the revelations by Edward Snowden of U.S. electronic surveillance of millions of people in this country and abroad.

President Obama also faced persistent issues that had beset his predecessors, including the Arab-Israeli conflict, the rise of China, and the proliferation of nuclear weapons, their possession by North Korea, and their development by Iran.

Further complicating foreign relations for the Obama administration would be unexpected challenges, as in what to do, if anything, about the explosion of popular outrage against some of the autocratic rulers of the Middle Eastern states—states replete with corruption, unemployment, and inequality—of Bahrain, Egypt, Libya, Syria, Tunisia, and Yemen. Turmoil and conflicts in some of these states were exacerbated by divisions between Sunnis and Shias, Muslims and Christians, and other ethnicities and religions. (For a parody of how U.S. policies differ toward each state, depending on U.S. interests, see "John Oliver, America's Freedom Package," *The Daily Show with Jon Stewart*, March 21, 2011.)

As with all his predecessors, the national interest was the essential criterion President Obama applied in deciding U.S. foreign and national security policies. A state's national interest does not necessarily change when a new president takes office. But what might that national interest be? How much flexibility would the president and his administration have (or display) to redefine it? To what extent would the Obama administration, especially the president and his secretary of state—first Hillary Rodham Clinton, then John Kerry—continue, change, or even repudiate some of the Bush policies?

Influencing the Obama responses were two obvious factors. First, the president was on record, from speeches during his presidential campaign and other statements, proposing policies to deal with some of these foreign policy challenges; for example, withdrawing all U.S. combat forces from Iraq by a specific date and a phased withdrawal from Afghanistan. Second, many Americans were disenchanted with the military losses, huge costs, irresolution, and lack of success in America's wars, and therefore were reluctant about new military involvements abroad.

In May 2010, the White House released a white paper detailing the Obama administration's national security strategy. It endorsed engagement, cooperation, and coordination with other states. It rejected the unilateralism, the (supposed) go-it-alone policy of the Bush administration. It committed to exhausting other options before war whenever possible. It identified the proliferation of weapons of mass destruction as the gravest danger facing the country.

So the Obama administration's foreign and national security policies would not be identical with its predecessor's. They would be less bellicose and unilateral, more diplomatic and multilateral. Examples were an arms control agreement with Russia that resulted in a substantial reduction in the countries' nuclear weapons, negotiating with Iran to reduce that country's nuclear program, a bilateral agreement with China on climate change, and re-engagement with the United Nations. The president did not speak about "spreading democracy around the world" and expressed a willingness to talk directly with countries with which the United States has disagreements. In December 2014, he would normalize relations with Cuba.

President Obama removed U.S. combat brigades from Iraq by August 2010, and all U.S. troops were out by the end of 2011; but personnel remained in the country to try to help ensure its stability and favorable relations with the United States. He increased the number of U.S. troops in Afghanistan by thirty thousand, doubling the overall American deployment (President Bush had begun a more modest buildup), but announced in May 2014 that all U.S. troops would be withdrawn by the end of 2016. This did not take place.

The Obama administration intensified the war on terrorism against al-Qaeda and its allies (although without torture). It vastly expanded the use of drones against them in Pakistan's tribal areas, Somalia, Yemen, and elsewhere but then reduced them during the president's second term. Arguably, these attacks were targeted assassinations. Moreover, drones will not necessarily remain a weapon for the United States: they are becoming available to most of the developed world.[61]

On May 1, 2011 (May 2 in Pakistan), U.S. special forces killed Osama bin Laden in his compound located roughly one mile from the Pakistan Military Academy.

The administration continued to give billions of dollars to Pakistan to combat terrorism despite questions about their effectiveness and effects.[62]

The Obama administration's policies did not produce success in all or even most areas. For example, stalemates continued in the peace negotiations it brokered between Israel and the Palestinians, and the talks were suspended in 2014. Relations with North Korea did not improve.

In February 2015, the administration issued a new security strategy, the first in five years and its last. The United States would continue its strong leadership in the world but recognize the limits of its power; confront short-term threats but not lose sight of long-term issues. Such issues included "climate change, trade, poverty, cybersecurity and global health."[63]

**FIGURE 17.5** Death of Osama bin Laden

Osama bin Laden was killed on May 1, 2011, by U.S. Navy Seals in his hideaway in Pakistan. In this photograph, released by the White House and shown around the world, we see the president, Vice President Joe Biden, Secretary of State Hillary Clinton, Secretary of Defense Robert Gates, and other members of the president's national security team in the Situation Room as cameras mounted on the helmets of the attackers send video footage of the assault narrated from CIA headquarters by Director Leon Panetta.

Source: Obama White House Archives. P050111PS-0210. President Barack Obama and Vice President Joe Biden, along with members of the national security team, receive an update on the mission against Osama bin Laden in the Situation Room of the White House, May 1, 2011. (Official White House Photo by Pete Souza). Via Flickr: https://www.flickr.com/photos/obamawhitehouse/5680724572/.

## Libya, Syria, Ukraine, and the Islamic State

In March 2011, President Obama ventured into uncharted territory by intervening militarily in Libya (see here). Arguably inspired by news media coverage of the events in Libya, his announced purpose was humanitarian: to prevent the dictator Muammar Gaddafi from massacring the Libyans rebelling against his regime. The intervention, taken over by the North Atlantic Treaty Organization (NATO), of which the United States is the most important power, involved missile strikes against Gaddafi's forces, then the imposition of a no-fly zone. It did not entail U.S. troops on the ground.

The intervention's ultimate intention, indicated by the bombing of Gaddafi's compound and by the president's later statements, was regime change—that is, to force Gaddafi to give up his rule. Given his superior firepower and the rebels' disorganization and lack of weapons, it was not clear that Gaddafi would depart voluntarily without further pressure from the United States and its allies or what any successor regime might be. In the end, Gaddafi was overthrown mainly by the NATO air strikes.

Anarchy resulted. State authority was not restored. A 2012 attack on the U.S. diplomatic mission in Benghazi killed U.S. Ambassador J. Christopher Stevens and Sean Smith, U.S. Foreign Service information management officer. Following the next day was an assault on a nearby CIA annex in a different compound about one mile away, killing two CIA contractors. These deaths and how they were explained by administration officials would be a continuing source of dispute with Republicans in Congress, resulting eventually in contentious congressional hearings in 2014.

After initially drawing a (metaphorical) red line and threatening to attack if the Syrian government used chemical weapons, President Obama responded with caution to the civil war in Syria. He sought approval from Congress for a strike and then allowed the United Nations the opportunity to identify Syria's chemical weapons and dismantle the program. In following this process, the president resisted calls by Republicans for more aggressive action and, not incidentally, adhered to the Constitution.

President Obama was similarly restrained in responding to a challenging situation in Ukraine when that country's president was ousted in February 2014 and fled to Russia, and Russia's President Vladimir Putin annexed Ukraine's Crimea. It was unclear whether Eastern Ukraine, with its large Russian-speaking population, would become part of Russia or stay with Ukraine. The United States organized an international coalition to apply sanctions against Russia for threatening Ukraine.

Meanwhile, in a jihadist insurgency, a group known by its initials, ISIS or ISIL (Islamic State of Iraq and the Levant), took over vast swaths of territory in northern and western Iraq and eastern Syria and also obtained pledges of allegiance in Nigeria, Libya, and Yemen. It proclaimed an Islamic state, or a caliphate.[64] Its media department disseminated slick videos on social media to raise funds, send messages, and recruit members from Europe and other parts of the world. It targeted and brutally killed members of ethnic groups, religious minorities, and forces opposed to it, as well as westerners, including freelance journalists from the United States. It attracted horrific worldwide attention by posting gruesome videos on social media showing executions, severed heads impaled on railings, and decapitated bodies. It could not be ignored.

On September 10, 2014, in a televised address, President Obama announced that the United States and its allies would undertake air strikes against key positions aimed to "degrade and ultimately destroy" ISIS. Although U.S. advisors would work with Syrian rebels and Iraq troops, there would be no U.S. troops on the ground.

In sum, President Obama eschewed direct U.S. military involvement—yes to drones to target terrorism suspects; no to sending troops to battle on the ground—although he did unobtrusively assign Special Operations Forces selectively to Afghanistan, Syria, and Cameroon.[65] Nonetheless, Republicans portrayed him as weak and indecisive. From the president's perspective, he was pursuing a foreign policy that avoided errors.

# President Trump

President Trump inherited a government involved in conflicts in Afghanistan, Iraq, Libya, Somalia, Syria, and Yemen. The modes of involvement were public (by land, from sea, by air) and secret (drone strikes, special forces). He could conduct these actions and others he may have decided to undertake relatively unbound by Congress and with a security establishment that had close to doubled in size since 2001 and that included nuclear, conventional, and cyber weapons.[66]

Aside from his commitment to increase substantially the defense budget, however, and his penchant for oral bellicosity, the president's inclination seemed to be to disengage militarily from the countries in which the United States was engaged. He rejected globalism and was indifferent to nation-building, democratizing, or promoting freedom in other states. He was a unilateralist who promised a foreign policy of "America First" but with few specifics, such as what to do about an increasingly geo-politically assertive China.[67]

We can, however, specify several policy areas that the president articulated. First was a much belabored promise to construct a wall along the southwestern border with Mexico, to keep out undocumented immigrants from Central America and for which the Mexican government would pay, one way or another. Relatedly, he proposed to change immigration policy to prevent terrorists or potential terrorists, who might include Muslim refugees from Syria and elsewhere, from entering or living in the country. In this respect, in June 2018, the Supreme Court voted 5–4 to uphold his ban on travel from several predominantly Muslim countries, on the grounds that it is part of his powers to conduct the nation's international affairs (Trump v. Hawaii, 585 U.S.).

Second was his promise to destroy ISIS. Since President Trump took office, ISIS had been driven out of its territory by a combination of U.S. air power, Kurdish Peshmerga forces, and Iraqi troops. But it still attracted adherents and remained a terrorist threat.

**FIGURE 17.6 Death of Islamic State Leader Abu Bakr al-Baghdadi**

October 26, 2019. A posed photo showing President Trump and his team monitoring developments in the hunt for the ISIS leader. It seeks to emulate the famous, spontaneous photo of President Obama and his national security officials monitoring the search for Osama bin Laden (see Figure 17.5).

Source: Trump White House Archived. President Trump Watches as U.S. Special Operations Forces Close in on ISIS Leade, October 26, 2019. (Official White House Photo by Shealah Craighead). Via Wikimedia: https://commons.wikimedia.org/wiki/File:President_Trump_Watches_as_U.S._Special_Operations_Forces_Close_in_on_ISIS_Leader_(48967991042).jpg.

Third was to end North Korea as a nuclear threat to the United States and its allies. President Trump travelled to North Korea twice to meet with the North Korean dictator in pursuit of this goal, but was unsuccessful. (Revealing the vicissitudes of foreign relations, the second meeting was held in Hanoi in Vietnam, the country against whom the United States had once waged a bloody war.)

Fourth was to withdraw or renegotiate the United States from treaties that, he claimed, did not serve American interests. Some were trade agreements that, according to the president, penalized America economically. He could leave these treaties because undoing them did not require congressional approval.[68] He withdrew the United States from the Trans-Pacific Partnership (TPP) of twelve nations, covering 40 percent of the world's economy, and renegotiated NAFTA, the agreement that abolishes tariffs between the United States, Canada, and Mexico.

President Trump also withdrew the United States from the Paris Accord, by which most countries agreed on a series of measures to battle climate change. He identified himself as a climate change skeptic, calling it a "Chinese hoax," although his stated arguments for withdrawal were essentially economic.

President Trump questioned another treaty, the North Atlantic Treaty Organization (NATO), describing it as obsolete. By this he could have meant that its emphasis on territorial defense in Europe was no longer necessary (as America pivoted to Asia). This overlooked the alliance's military operations in Afghanistan. More specifically, he complained about burden sharing, charging that most of NATO's other members failed to live up to their financial commitments to the organization's military spending.

He imposed economic sanctions on Iran and also withdrew from the agreement reached by the Obama administration and other countries with Iran limiting the latter's development of nuclear weapons. As the Trump administration moved through its third year, tensions exacerbated, the administration increasingly viewed Iran as its antagonist in the Middle East, as the threat to its interests, and as the enemy of its allies and friends, such as Israel and Saudi Arabia.

Fifth, President Trump promised to try to bring about peace between the Israelis and Palestinians. Giving lip service to this objective is expected by American presidents of all stripes, and the effort almost always ends in frustration, if not in failure. The president did not help himself by bestowing favors on the Israeli prime minister and punishing the Palestinians. But he achieved a modicum of success in 2020 by brokering treaties between Israel and several Arab states.

Sixth was U.S. relations with Russia. The president's rhetoric about President Vladimir Putin was sympathetic, even admiring. But there was the investigation into the Trump campaign's possible involvement with the Russian hacking of his opponent's presidential campaign and publicizing of the stolen contents through WikiLeaks. Russia had annexed Crimea, invaded Eastern Ukraine, provided air support to the Syrian dictatorship, and gotten friendly with Iran. Venezuela was another source of conflict, with the U.S. favoring the overthrow and Russia the retention of the incumbent repressive ruler.

Seventh, attempting to cut the country's sizable trade deficit with China, President Trump imposed huge tariffs on Chinese exports to the United States, against which China retaliated, provoking a trade war and stock market gyrations, as well as economic losses for American farmers widely reported in the media. The president also lay blame on China for the creation and circulation of the coronavirus.

## President Biden

As discussed in our Presidency chapter (13), President Biden began his presidency by rejoining the Paris Climate Accord and the World Health Organization, and extending the nuclear arms control treaty with Russia. He reaffirmed America's commitments to its international alliances and disavowed the isolationism of his predecessor. He opted for diplomacy over tariffs with China. Otherwise, he moved cautiously to deal with the foreign policy issues he had inherited from President Trump, who had inherited many of them from President Obama.

### Key Takeaways

President Obama inherited foreign and national security policy issues such as the wars in Afghanistan and Iraq. He also faced persistent problems and unexpected challenges. His policies were less bellicose and more multilateral than that of his predecessor. Particularly in response to the situations in Libya, Syria, and Ukraine, he rejected U.S. military involvement in favor of diplomacy, negotiations, and sanctions. President Trump imposed several foreign policies that fall under his rubric of "America First."

## Exercises

1. What were the most important foreign policy issues faced by President Obama?
2. How would you define the U.S. national interest?
3. How did President Obama's foreign policies differ from President George W. Bush's?
4. What policies would you have pursued in Libya, Syria, Ukraine, and against ISIS?
5. What do you think of President Trump's "America First" policies?

# 17.7 Foreign and National Security Policies in the Information Age

## Learning Objectives

After reading this section, you should be able to answer the following questions:

1. How and what do the media report from abroad?
2. How do the media interact with the military?
3. What are the consequences of the media's depictions of U.S. foreign and national security policies?

The United States government tries to promote a favorable image of its policies and actions to more than 200 million people abroad through such news media, run by the Broadcasting Board of Governors, as the Voice of America, Radio Free Europe/Radio Liberty, the Middle East Broadcasting Network, and Radio Free Asia. The effectiveness of these outlets against their Russian (Russia Today and Sputnik News), Chinese, and other rivals is debatable.

That said, Libya, Afghanistan, Iraq, 9/11, and the other cases we have discussed show the ability of the executive branch to impose its preferred frames, at least in the United States, if not abroad, and at least for a time, on an international crisis. Four factors are involved.[69]

First, the executive branch has an enormous advantage in the early collection and analysis of information, especially when the crisis erupts on short notice. Second, when they are united and their campaign is coordinated, the president and his senior advisors can dominate the rhetoric and speeches about the crisis. The alternatives are leaks and breakdowns in message cohesion. Third, the administration can manipulate intelligence reports favoring its views and discount ones that contradict or weaken them. Fourth, if the crisis is brief, opponents lack the time and opportunity to mobilize public opinion. But if the crisis lingers, they can obtain their own information and undermine the administration's initial framing.

As explained in Chapter 3, the news media usually index story frames to the range of viewpoints—the agreement and disagreement—among high-ranking U.S. officials.[70] As time goes on, however, they may collect and disseminate information critical of the administration's frame and expose any disconnect between official claims and the reality on the ground. This assumes they have access to the events, resources to cover them, and the expertise to understand them.

# Media Interactions

U.S. foreign and national security policies are made and largely articulated in the United States. Policymakers and members of the media interact in Washington and in related places such as the United Nations in New York City. But the policies are often executed, have their effects, and thus must be reported from abroad.

## Reporting from Abroad

Aside from the *New York Times*, most U.S. newspapers, magazines, and television networks and cable stations have few foreign bureaus with correspondents. Some television news operations (e.g., ABC, CBS, NBC, and CNN) send reporters (known as "one-man bands") equipped with computers and cameras to report from foreign locations, thereby gathering the news while avoiding the costs of bureaus. For foreign news, the bulk of the U.S. news media rely primarily on the wire services, such as the Associated Press and, for visuals, on Associated Press Television News (APTN) and Reuters Television.

For U.S. news organizations with reporters abroad, London is the central location: it is the source of around 25 percent of all bureau-based reporting. Bureaus, or half-bureaus with no permanently stationed correspondent, are established at other locations for several reasons: in Moscow, Beijing, and Tokyo because of their important relations with the United States; in jumping-off points such as Johannesburg, South Africa, for covering the rest of the region; and in Jerusalem to cover the continuing story of the Arab–Israeli conflict. Roughly a quarter of foreign correspondents are stringers or freelancers—more or less knowledgeable locals. Most of them receive low pay, no benefits, and have a precarious relationship with their employers.[71]

Around 50 percent of television's foreign coverage portrays violence.[72] This often occurs where news bureaus are not located. For example, the main news in late December 2004 and into 2005 concerned the horrifying death of at least 150,000 people and the destruction at the shorelines of several Asian countries caused by the tsunami waves that resulted from underwater earthquakes in the Indian Ocean.

To cover stories from such "hot spots," reporters often have to parachute (not literally) in from their bases. They spend time on logistics, getting from place to place, booking hotel rooms, and hiring drivers and translators.[73] Because they lack knowledge of local conditions and don't stay long, they tend to rely on a few sources, mainly U.S. embassy officials, aid workers, and spokespersons from the government of the country.

Wars and conflicts involving (e.g., Iraq) or potentially involving (e.g., Libya) the United States are the exception; they are covered extensively by journalists assigned there or reporting from as near as possible. But media coverage of such conflicts is limited in two ways. First, it focuses on no more than one or two countries at a time. In recent years this has meant Afghanistan, then Iraq, then Libya, then Syria, then Ukraine, and now? Second, it emphasizes violence over politics and religious and ethnic divisions.

But even in Iraq, most reporters for the U.S. news media had little knowledge of the region's history, Islamic fundamentalism, the resurgence of Arab nationalism, or, indeed, of Iraq. Nor did they speak or read Arabic, which limited their ability to obtain information from native sources.

**FIGURE 17.7 Covering News Outside of the United States**

Because the U.S. news media do not have bureaus in most countries, they must dispatch reporters to cover disasters such as the tsunami waves that wreaked death and destruction on the countries bordering the Indian Ocean.

Source: Photo by Michael L. Bak, http://commons.wikimedia.org/wiki/File:Bodies_in_Banda_Aceh_after_2004_tsunami_DD-SD-06-07373.JPEG.

Accurate and comprehensive or not, news from overseas can be transmitted instantly to twenty-four-hour cable channels and thus to American policymakers and the public. This is facilitated by the combination of new communications technologies and global media systems. Satellite telephones, digital cameras, videophones, laptops with uplink capacities, computers, videos, and blogs from people on the scenes provide vivid images and descriptions of events as instant news for the media to transmit and for people to access on the internet. The first video and photos of the tsunami and its dire destruction of late 2004 came from the camcorders of tourists caught in the deluge. The destruction and horror of terrorists' attacks on the London subway on July 7, 2005 (known commonly as 7/7), was reported first by people trapped underground.[74]

A wealth of information about international affairs is thus available on the internet from domestic and foreign media: television clips, radio interviews, and reports and stories in newspapers and magazines. People interested can learn about policymakers from around the world and the contents and effects of their foreign and national security policies.

However, satellite television, YouTube, bloggers, and social media are also used to spread propaganda, lies, and hate. And the flow of information is repressed by the state, in the person of security and military forces, and their control of information through such weapons as censorship, imprisonment, torture, and execution.

# Media Interactions with the Military

The Defense Department interacts with the media to produce highly positive depictions in several ways. One is through the Hollywood films that "depict and glorify the heroic exploits of U.S. military power."[75]

A second way the Pentagon generates positive coverage of an administration's national security policies is through the special briefings it provides to the retired officers who appear thousands of times on television and radio as "military analysts." Many of them have ideological agreement with and allegiance to the Pentagon. They also have financial ties, as lobbyists for, senior executive or board members of, or consultants to military contractors that benefit from the policies the "analysts" assess.[76] It is in their interests to maintain their access to and stay on the Pentagon's right side. Consequently, many of them repeat administration talking points on the air. The largest group was affiliated with Fox News, then NBC and CNN. The Pentagon paid a private contractor to search databases and track all the analysts' comments.[77]

Positive portrayals of the military by the media may be unusual. The view of Civil War Union General William Tecumseh Sherman may be more typical: upon hearing that the Confederate army had shot two reporters, he remarked, "Great. Now we'll have the news from Hell by noon." This suggests the perennial conflict between the military and the media. From the military perspective, reporters should be "part of the team." For most correspondents, their coverage can only be restrained if it would jeopardize an operation or the lives of troops. Traditionally, however, the military denies them access, limits their reporting to official sources, engages in obfuscation and delay, and censors their stories.

**embedded**

The Defense Department's innovation of placing reporters with military units during the Iraq War.

So it may seem surprising that the military allowed some six hundred reporters to be **embedded** with the U.S. troops during the war in Iraq. Secretary of Defense Donald Rumsfeld and Assistant Defense Secretary for Public Affairs Victoria Clarke pushed the decision through. It turned out to be a shrewd move. Reporters were co-opted by the troops with whom they were embedded. They reported from the perspective of the U.S. forces winning the war. And they were kept away from places the Pentagon did not want them to go.

Reporters who were not embedded had a tough time getting into and around Iraq and obtaining cooperation from the U.S. military. Many of them were located at U.S. Central Command forward headquarters in Doha, Qatar, where at press conferences generals summarized the success of military operations on a high-tech set designed by a show-business professional at an estimated cost of $250,000.

Still, reporting from war zones and repressive regimes is dangerous. Aside from censorship, journalists live and work under constant threat of violence, kidnapping, and murder. Many have been killed or wounded.[78] As one horrifying example, in April 2011, photojournalists Tim Hetherington (see *Diary* and *Restrepo* in Section 9) and Chris Hondros were killed by a grenade in Libya. Marie Colvin, who had covered conflicts in Chechnya, East Timor, Kosovo, Libya, Sierra Leone, and Zimbabwe, was killed in Homs, Syria.[79]

**FIGURE 17.8 Dangers of Reporting in Conflict Zones**

The dangers of reporting in conflict zones is exemplified in the death of photojournalist Chris Hondros, who was killed by a grenade in Libya not long after taking this photo of a rebel fighter in Misurata.

Source: Chris Hondros/Getty Images.

# Revelations

New technology can be used to disclose information, particularly that involving national security, that the government wants kept secret. It is appropriate for us to return briefly to them. As we discussed in Chapter 3, WikiLeaks (http://wikileaks.org) was founded by Julian Assange to achieve transparency in government activities by exposing official secrets. In 2010, it released to selected news organizations about 90,000 documents prepared by the U.S. military about the wars in Iraq and Afghanistan. Then later in the year, WikiLeaks released a trove of around 260,000 U.S. diplomatic cables. The cables show that candor exists behind closed doors; they reveal confidential conversations, accounts of meetings, and appraisals of foreign leaders.

The *New York Times*, which received the reports directly from WikiLeaks and the cables from the United Kingdom's *Guardian* newspaper, published articles detailing and interpreting the leaked documents.[80] It also put selected items online, as did WikiLeaks, with redactions to remove the names of the diplomats' confidential sources.

Some of the material consisted of low-level gossip. Other parts were more intriguing, such as the following:

- The Saudi royalty encouraged the United States to attack Iran, as did the leaders of Egypt, Jordan, and Israel.
- The Yemeni government covered up the U.S. missile strikes against the country's local branch of al-Qaeda by claiming that its own forces had carried out the attacks.
- The U.S. ambassador made scathing comments about the lavish lifestyle of the rulers of Tunisia.
- Corruption exists in the Afghan government.
- China was involved in global computer hacking.
- How to placate China if North Korea collapsed and was unified with South Korea.

There were repercussions. The U.S. ambassador to Mexico resigned as a result of information released. Ecuador expelled the U.S. ambassador, who in a cable had referred to high-level police corruption that the country's president possibly knew about. The U.S. government identified security gaps and further limited the availability of classified information.

As also discussed in Chapter 3, in 2013, Edward Snowden, a former contractor with the National Security Agency, started to release to selected newspapers (notably, the *Washington Post* and the *Guardian* in London) a vast trove documenting the agency's monitoring of communications, data mining of online activity, and secret tracking of billions of phone calls and emails. The programs took place in the United States and worldwide.

It can be time consuming, but there are legitimate ways of extricating information from the U.S. military that it is obdurate about revealing. After years of legal back-and-forth with the Special Inspector General for Afghanistan Reconstruction, the *Washington Post*, through a Freedom of Information Act request, finally obtained and released thousands of pages of documents revealing how the public had been deceived about the war in Afghanistan. Instead of the progress claimed by senior American officials, the reality was a pessimistic assessment of mistakes and failures, of a few troops executing an unclear mission.[81]

# Terrorists' Use of New Technology

Osama bin Laden's associates in their compound watched Hollywood movies, including *The Siege* (see Section 9) as they devised and refined the plot that would result in 9/11.[82] But their use of new technology was far more advanced than that. They used it to collect information about targets such as ports, airports, and nuclear power plants and to communicate about, plan, and coordinate attacks. They circulated a manual prepared by al-Qaeda, nicknamed "The Encyclopedia of Jihad," that detailed how to establish an underground organization and engage in attacks.

There are more than four thousand terrorist websites in different languages. They change their addresses to avoid being hacked by intelligence agencies and freelance vigilantes but still retain much of their content. These sites free the terrorists from dependence on the media for coverage and framing of their deeds. They are aimed at current and potential supporters, governments they oppose, and worldwide public opinion. They are used to raise funds, recruit terrorists, and mobilize support, also to express the terrorists' views and objectives, threaten their enemies, and show videos of their actions.

Through their video units, the terrorists send messages to receptive broadcasters like Al Jazeera, messages that are reported and rebroadcast by media outlets throughout the world. These videos are carefully staged: the backdrop is designed, weapons pointed, and the shot framed. When kidnapped victims are shown, their statements are scripted as they plead for their lives before sometimes being decapitated on camera. Western media do not show the horror, but the videos are sold in Iraq and throughout the world.[83]

No extremist organization was more effective at communicating its message than ISIS. It has so outraged the American public and people throughout the world with its violence and horrific videos, that Presidents Obama and Trump inevitably condemned and vowed to destroy it. Which brings us to media consequences.

# Media Consequences

As with the outbreak of Ebola in West Africa, coverage from abroad can be excessive and fear-mongering, and induce panic, even if only briefly. It demands attention from public officials in the United States no matter how few the cases in the country.

More important, coverage from abroad can undermine U.S. foreign and national security policies. By depicting the Tet Offensive as successful, the media made it difficult for President Johnson to send more troops to Vietnam and encouraged the eventual withdrawal of U.S. forces. The nightly stories about U.S. embassy personnel held captive in Iran, often under the heading "America Held Hostage," probably provoked President Jimmy Carter into allowing a risky rescue effort that turned into a debacle.

Media depictions of events abroad can encourage or compel U.S. policymakers to take action by sending aid personnel, or even troops. This occurs under two conditions.

Media coverage, however, often comes after—not before—the government's decision to take action. Thus, news coverage of the humanitarian crises in Somalia was a response to the first President Bush's decision to deploy ground troops. Then news stories supported the decision by framing the famine there as a desperate crisis in which the United States had an obligation to intervene. Later news coverage, however, did affect policy. Reports of the killing of eighteen U.S. Army Rangers and the showing of the body of one of them being dragged through the country's capital of Mogadishu, resulted in the Clinton administration's decision to withdraw U.S. troops.

Media coverage or lack of coverage of an event can allow and even encourage government inaction. In Rwanda in 1994, Hutu extremists slaughtered eight hundred thousand Tutsis and Hutu moderates, their countrymen, women, and children. The news media depicted this genocide, when they covered it at all, as part of an endless tribal struggle the United States could not much affect. Besides, it was only a few months since the media had reported the killing of American soldiers in Somalia. The United States never intervened in Rwanda. As National Security Advisor Anthony Lake said later, "We didn't make any decision." He did not ask his staff to consider options and make a policy recommendation to President Clinton.[84]

On occasion, as currently in Belarus and Venezuela, an autocratic regime will use force to try to stay in power—or, as with the military in Myanmar, take over the government and violently repress dissent. Even when the media report these events, their coverage allows the American government the discretion essentially to stay uninvolved.

Generally, by what they cover and how they frame it, the U.S. media support the president's foreign and national security policies and priorities.[85] Their coverage of the terrorist attacks of 9/11 helped justify the war on terrorism against Osama bin Laden and al-Qaeda and the attack on the Taliban in Afghanistan. By depicting war against Iraq as desirable, the media facilitated the Bush administration's policies of preemption and regime change. When military operations began on March 19, 2003, nearly two-thirds of Americans polled favored the president's policies toward Iraq, and 71 percent supported the use of force.[86]

The media's impact continues in the form of fiction. In 2017, the drama 24 returned to television on the Fox channel in a new version, under the title *24 Legacy*. Featuring a super-competent Islamic terrorist organization, it perpetuated Islamophobia and the identification of Islam with terror. It thereby reinforced President Trump's attempt to institute a ban on travel to the United States from citizens from several predominantly Muslim countries.[87]

Meanwhile, websites like Breitbart News and Infowars have featured alarmist stories about a rape crisis, a flesh-eating crisis, and the risk of female genital mutilation—all involving refugees and none of them true.

## Afghanistan

In February 2020, President Trump kept a campaign commitment by negotiating America's departure from Afghanistan with the Taliban. It would be May 1, 2021. In return, the Taliban committed not to harbor terrorists and to negotiate with the Afghan government, but not to stop its military campaign.

Determined to end his country's twenty years' war expeditiously, President Biden set August 31 as his deadline for American troops and officials to withdraw.

However, the Taliban forces swept across the country as the Afghanistan military melted away and the country's president fled. The U.S. evacuation was fraught. The Taliban gained control of Afghanistan's capital, Kabul, and access to its airport, where thousands gathered at its gates waiting or hoping to leave the country. Many Afghans were stymied by U.S. red tape from obtaining visas for departure.

In justifying and defending his policy, in two televised addresses (transcripts available from the *New York Times* for August 17 and September 1, 2021), the president argued that almost twenty years of war had been more than enough; that the Taliban's fast takeover of the country and of Kabul had been unexpected; and that he had not been warned by his intelligence services that it was possible. Nor had the chaos at the city's airport been predictable. He claimed that, given the circumstances, the evacuation to safety by air of around 20,000 Americans and 100,000 Afghan allies and interpreters in seventeen days had demonstrated the evacuation's success. The people left behind could be saved later. The only alternative to the departure was further escalation. The resources saved could be spent on competition with China, Russia, and defeating terrorists elsewhere.

The president's policy, conduct of the evacuation, and arguments and defense were contested. There were conflicts within his administration, some of which were played out in the press. For example, from different sources, the *New York Times* issued conflicting headlines and stories such as "Contradicting Biden, Reports Warned of Rapid Collapse,"[88] and "Intelligence Agencies Did Not Predict Swift Collapse, Officials Say."[89]

Another source of criticism emanated from the president's political opponents and their allies in conservative media. Although they had supported the departure policy when it was promoted by President Trump, they now criticized both the policy and its execution, claiming, for example, that they would have demanded more concessions from the Taliban.

Finally, there were the conventional news media. Their coverage was sometimes positive, but often negative, reminiscent of America's hasty retreat from its Saigon embassy in Vietnam in 1973. Typical was the *Times*'s David E. Sanger's conclusion: "Biden Owns Final Failure in Afghanistan."[90]

The most devastating negative depictions undermining the president were visual. CNN's on-the-ground correspondents at the Kabul airport showed thousands of people massed together, a horrific shot of two people clinging to then falling from the outside of planes in flight, and the death and devastation caused by suicide bombers at an airport gate.

Afghanistan may not be over with. At the least, we can expect hearings by congressional committees on the withdrawal policy and its execution.

## Key Takeaways

The president's policymaking ability is buttressed by advantages in information gathering, public appeal, manipulation of intelligence, and the media's practice of indexing. While the media usually support the administration's policies, at least at first, they can also provide important criticism: for example, by publishing revelations from WikiLeaks and Edward Snowden, undermining policymakers and casting doubt on some of their policies. The media have influenced policy decisions and their execution.

## Exercises

1. What are the strengths and weaknesses of the U.S. media's reporting from abroad? How could it be improved?
2. How does the Defense Department influence the way the media report military actions? What is the advantage of allowing reporters to "embed" in military units?
3. What are the advantages and disadvantages of new technology in reporting events from abroad?
4. Who benefits and who suffers from the revelations of WikiLeaks and Edward Snowden?

# 17.8 Recommended Reading

Art, Robert J. *A Grand Strategy for America*. Ithaca, NY: Cornell University Press, 2003. A forceful presentation of America's national interests and how to defend them.

Baum, Matthew A., and Tim J. Groeling. *War Stories: The Causes and Consequences of Public Views of War*. Princeton, NJ: Princeton University Press, 2010. Argues that journalists' assessments of stories' newsworthiness and people's assessments of the stories' persuasiveness influence public support for U.S. foreign policy.

Bennett, W. Lance, and David L. Paletz, eds. *Taken by Storm: The Media, Public Opinion, and U.S. Foreign Policy in the Gulf War*. Chicago: University of Chicago Press, 1994. Essays by leading scholars on the war's political communication elements.

Draper, Robert. *To Start a War: How the Bush Administration Took America Into Iraq*. New York: Penguin Press, 2020. The explanation based on interviews with all the crucial witnesses.

Entman, Robert M. *Projections of Power: Framing News, Public Opinion, and U.S. Foreign Policy*. Chicago: University of Chicago Press, 2004. A thoughtful effort to explain why the media accept or reject the White House version of foreign policy.

Hallin, Daniel C. *The "Uncensored War": The Media and Vietnam*. New York: Oxford University Press, 1986. The definitive study of media coverage of the Vietnam War.

Hannerz, Ulf. *Foreign News: Exploring the World of Foreign Correspondents*. Chicago: University of Chicago Press, 2004. Based on interviews, describes the backgrounds and working lives of foreign correspondents.

Hess, Gary R. *Presidential Decisions for War: Korea, Vietnam, and the Persian Gulf*. Baltimore: Johns Hopkins University Press, 2001. How Presidents Truman, Johnson, and the first President Bush brought the United States into and conducted these wars.

Hess, Stephen, and Marvin Kalb, eds. *The Media and the War on Terrorism*. Washington, DC: Brookings Institution Press, 2003. Journalists discuss and comment on media coverage of the war on terrorism.

Jenkins, Tricia. *The CIA in Hollywood: How the Agency Shapes Film and Television*. Austin, TX: University of Texas Press, 2012. From negative to positive to mixed.

Mermin, Jonathan. *Debating War and Peace: Media Coverage of U.S. Intervention in the Post-Vietnam Era*. Princeton, NJ: Princeton University Press, 1999. Finds that the government sets the terms and boundaries for media coverage of the policy debate about military intervention.

Thrall, A. Trevor. *War in the Media Age*. Cresskill, NJ: Hampton Press, 2000. A critical study of the evolution and implementation of government press strategy from Vietnam through the Gulf War.

Western, Jon. *Selling Intervention and War: The President, the Media, and the American Public*. Baltimore: Johns Hopkins University Press, 2005. Discusses and explains how presidents often succeed in selling their intervention and war policies to the media and the public.

# 17.9 Recommended Viewing

*Apocalypse Now* (1979). In Francis Ford Coppola's visually dazzling take on the Vietnam War, an American captain is sent to assassinate a renegade colonel waging an unsanctioned war.

*Atomic Café* (1982). A compilation of film clips mocks the propaganda films made in the 1940s and 1950s to reassure Americans about nuclear weapons.

*Bearing Witness* (2005). A moving documentary on the lives and experiences of five war correspondents, all of them women.

*Casablanca* (1942). Classic Hollywood film with memorable dialogue and acting, in which a cynical American expatriate in Morocco embraces idealism and engagement. A metaphor for the United States moving from isolationism to internationalism in World War II.

*Control Room* (2003). A documentary on the war in Iraq from the Al Jazeera and Arab perspective.

*Diary* (2011). Photojournalist Tim Hetherington (codirector of *Restrepo*) contrasts scenes from the war zones he covered to his life in London and New York. Soon after making the film he, was killed in Libya.

*Dr. Strangelove, or: How I Learned to Stop Worrying and Love the Bomb* (1964). Stanley Kubrick's (and Terry Southern's) ultimate Cold War black comedy features a demented general, a befuddled U.S. president, bellicose advisors, military paranoia, and bravado.

*Duck Soup* (1933). The Marx Brothers spoof diplomacy, nationalism, patriotism, law, and—above all—America's wars. President of Freedonia Rufus T. Firefly (played by Groucho Marx) justifies war: "It's too late. I've already paid a month's rent on the battlefield."

*The Fog of War* (2003). In Errol Morris's documentary, former Secretary of Defense Robert McNamara reflects on his involvement in decisions that resulted in death and destruction (the fire bombing of Japan during the Second World War, the Cuban Missile Crisis, the Vietnam War).

*The Great Dictator* (1940). Charlie Chaplin's powerful parody of Hitler, Mussolini, the Nazi regime, and fascism.

*Hearts and Minds* (1974). A remorseful anti–Vietnam War documentary with devastating images and interviews with policymakers, militarists, and ordinary people involved.

*Home of the Brave—Land of the Free* (2003). Mordant documentary look at a U.S. Special Forces unit in Afghanistan.

*The Missiles of October* (1974). Documentary that profiles President John F. Kennedy and his associates and describes their actions during the Cuban missile crisis.

*Reporting America at War* (2003). A basic history of the reporting of American wars from the Spanish-American War through the invasion of Iraq that focuses on legendary correspondents and thus minimizes reporters' self-censorship and the acceptance of official perspectives and naive notions of wartime glory.

*Restrepo* (2010). This harrowing documentary follows a combat team of American soldiers deployed in a lethally dangerous remote valley in Afghanistan.

*Return with Honor* (1998). First-person survival accounts of U.S. pilots held captive in North Vietnam and testimonies of their wives are joined to Vietnamese archival footage in a moving documentary of mental, physical, and emotional resilience.

*Seven Days in May* (1964). Military leaders plot to overthrow the president after he concludes what they think is a disastrous nuclear disarmament treaty with the Soviet Union.

*The Siege* (1998). Terrorists blow up a federal building in Manhattan, resulting in a crackdown on civil liberties and terror suspects.

*The Unknown Known* (2013). In this Errol Morris documentary, the sophistical longtime public official and shrewd politician Donald Rumsfeld, whose career culminated as George W. Bush's secretary of defense, tries to justify and defend his actions, particularly his conduct of the war against Iraq.

*Wag the Dog* (1997). Shortly before an election a spin doctor and Hollywood producer fabricate a war to cover up a president's sex scandal.

*War Feels Like War* (2003). Firsthand immediacy and detail fill this documentary showing "unilateral" correspondents (those not embedded) as they report the Iraq War.

*Which Way Is the Front Line from Here? The Life and Time of Tim Hetherington* (2013). Moving documentary about the photojournalist.

*Why We Fight* (1942–1945). Seven documentary films made by Frank Capra for the U.S. Department of War for American troops during the World War II.

*Zero Days* (2016). Alex Gibney's documentary about the U.S.–Israeli development and use of the offensive cyber-weapon "Stuxnet" to slow down the Iranian nuclear project.

# Endnotes

1. This account and the interviews appear in Stephen Hess and Marvin Kalb, eds., *The Media and the War on Terrorism* (Washington, DC: Brookings Institution Press, 2003), 113–20.
2. Tom Fenton, *Bad News* (New York: Regan Books, 2005), 4.
3. See Anthony Lane, "This Is Not a Movie," *New Yorker*, September 24, 2001, 79.
4. For a useful collection of studies, see Alex P. Schmid, ed., *The Routledge Handbook of Terrorism Research* (New York: Routledge, 2011).
5. John Hutcheson, David Domke, Andre Billeaudeaux, and Philip Garland, "U.S. National Identity, Political Elites, and a Patriotic Press Following 9/11," *Political Communication* 21, no. 1 (January–March 2004): 27–50.
6. On the justifications for war since 1990, see Nicholas Kerton-Johnson, *Justifying America's Wars: The Conduct and Practice of US Military Intervention* (New York: Routledge, 2010).
7. Thom Shanker, "U.S. Leads Arms Market With Sales Of $40 Billion," *The New York Times*, December 27, 2016, A6.
8. Dana Priest and William M. Arkin, "Top Secret America," *Washington Post*, July 19, 2010, 1ff.
9. Gary R. Hess, *Presidential Decisions for War: Korea, Vietnam, and the Persian Gulf*. (Baltimore: Johns Hopkins University Press, 2001).
10. Thomas Preston and Margaret G. Hermann, "Presidential Leadership Style and the Foreign Policy Advisory Process," in *The Domestic Sources of American Foreign Policy*, 4th ed., ed. Eugene R. Wittkopf and James M. McCormick (Lanham, MD: Rowman & Littlefield, 2004), 363–80.
11. Walter Isaacson, "The Senior Official," *Washington Journalism Review* 14, no. 9 (November 1992): 30; see also Walter Isaacson, *Kissinger* (New York: Simon & Schuster, 1992).
12. Eliot A. Cohen, "A Revolution in Warfare," *Foreign Affairs* 75 (1996): 37–54; and Thomas G. Mahnken and James R. FitzSimonds, "Revolutionary Ambivalence," *International Security* 28 (2003): 112–48.
13. John Ranelagh, *The Agency: The Rise and Decline of the CIA* (New York: Simon & Schuster, 1986); and Arthur S. Hulnick, *Fixing the Spy Machine: Preparing American Intelligence for the Twenty-First Century* (Westport, CT: Praeger,1999).
14. See Gedeon Naudet and Jules Naudet, *The Spymaster: CIA in the Crosshairs*, 2015. A documentary about the agency with appearances by all twelve of its living directors.
15. Glenn P. Hastedt, "Homeland Security," in *Contemporary Cases in U.S. Foreign Policy: From Terrorism to Trade*, 2nd ed., ed. Ralph G. Carter (Washington, DC: CQ Press, 2005); Harold Relyea, "Organizing for Homeland Security," *Presidential Studies Quarterly* 33 (2003): 602–24.
16. Steven Dryden, *Trade Warriors* (New York: Oxford University Press, 1995).
17. Louis Henkin, *Foreign Affairs and the Constitution* (Mineola, NY: Foundation Press, 1972), 131; and Lee Hamilton, *A Creative Tension: The Foreign Policy Roles of the President and Congress* (Washington DC: Woodrow Wilson Center Press, 2002).
18. Ruth Berins Collier, "Foreign Policy by Reporting Requirements," *Washington Quarterly* 11 (1988): 74–84.
19. Loch K. Johnson, "The U.S. Congress and the CIA: Monitoring the Dark Side of Government," *Legislative Studies Quarterly* 4 (1980): 477–99.
20. Loch K. Johnson, *The Making of International Agreements: Congress Confronts the Executive* (New York: New York University Press, 1984).
21. Stephen I. Schwartz, "Outmaneuvered, Out Gunned, and Out of View," *The Bulletin of the Atomic Scientists* 56 (January 2000): 24–31.
22. Lawrence W. Margolis, *Executive Agreements and Presidential Power in Foreign Policy* (New York: Praeger, 1986).

23. See William G. Howell and Jon C. Pevehouse, *While Dangers Gather: Congressional Checks on Presidential War Powers* (Princeton, NJ: Princeton University Press, 2007).
24. Donald E. Abelson, *Think Tanks and Their Role in U.S. Foreign Policy* (New York: St. Martins, 1996).
25. Tony Smith, *Foreign Attachments: The Power of Ethnic Groups in the Making of American Foreign Policy* (Cambridge, MA: Harvard University Press, 2000); and Alexander DeConde, *Ethnicity, Race, and American Foreign Policy* (Boston: Little Brown. 1992).
26. Benjamin I. Page with Marshall M. Bouton, *The Foreign Policy Disconnect: What Americans Want from Our Leaders but Don't Get* (Chicago: University of Chicago Press, 2006), 226; see also Benjamin I. Page and Tao Xie, "Purposive Mass Belief Systems concerning Foreign Policy" in Paul M. Sniderman and Benjamin Highton, eds., *Facing The Challenge of Democracy: Explorations in the Analysis of Public Opinion and Political Participation* (Princeton: Princeton University Press, 2011), 47–65.
27. Matthew A. Baum and Tim J. Groeling, *War Stories: The Causes and Consequences of Public Views of War* (Princeton, NJ: Princeton University Press, 2010).
28. Andrew Johnstone and Helen Laville, eds., *The US Public and American Foreign Policy* (New York: Routledge, 2010).
29. Bruce W. Jentleson, "The Pretty Prudent Public: Post Vietnam Public Opinion on the Use of Military Force," *International Studies Quarterly* 36 (1990): 49–74.
30. Peter D. Feaver and Christopher Gelpi, *Choosing Your Battles: American Civil-Military Relations and the Use of Force* (Princeton, NJ: Princeton University Press, 2004).
31. Selig Adler, *The Isolationist Impulse* (New York: Praeger, 1957).
32. David A. Baldwin, ed., *Neorealism and Neoidealism: The Contemporary Debate* (New York: Columbia University Press, 1993); and Joseph S. Nye Jr., *The Paradox of American Power* (New York: Oxford University Press, 2002).
33. John Lewis Gaddis, *Strategies of Containment* (New York: Oxford University Press, 1993).
34. Patrick M. Morgan, *Deterrence: A Conceptual Analysis* (Beverly Hills: Sage, 1977).
35. Robert L. Gallucci, *Neither Peace nor Honor* (Baltimore: Johns Hopkins University Press, 1975); and Leslie H. Gelb with Richard K. Betts, *The Irony of Vietnam: The System Worked* (Washington, DC: Brookings Institution Press, 1979).
36. CBS News Almanac: Walter Cronkite. Accessed July 5, 2019 at https://www.cbsnews.com/news/almanac-walter-cronkite/.
37. Editorial, *Wall Street Journal*, February 23, 1968, 14; CBS News Special: *Report From Vietnam*, February 27, 1968; and NBC News *Special Report*, March 10, 1968.
38. Gallup Organization, *Vietnam War: A Compilation, 1964–1990. Public Opinion and the Vietnam War: National and International Opinion*, vol. II (Princeton, NJ: Gallup, 1992).
39. Coral Bell, *The Diplomacy of Détente: The Kissinger Era* (New York: St. Martin's, 1977).
40. Thomas C. Schelling and Morton H. Halperin, *Strategy and Arms Control* (New York: Pergamon-Brassey's Classic, 1985).
41. Robert C. Johansen, *The National Interest and the Human Interest: An Analysis of U.S. Foreign Policy* (Princeton, NJ: Princeton University Press, 1980); Debra Liang-Fenton, ed., *Implementing U.S. Human Rights Policy* (Washington, DC: United States Institute of Peace Press, 2004).
42. Stephen Kinzer, *All the Shah's Men: An American Coup and the Roots of Middle East Terror* (New York: John Wiley & Sons, 2002).
43. James M. Scott, *Deciding to Intervene: The Reagan Doctrine and American Foreign Policy* (Durham, NC: Duke University Press, 1996).
44. Michael J. Mazarr, Don M. Snider, and James A. Blackwell Jr., *Desert Storm: The Gulf War and What We Learned* (Boulder, CO: Westview, 1993).
45. W. Lance Bennett and David L. Paletz, eds., *Taken By Storm: The Media, Public Opinion, and U.S. Foreign Policy in the Gulf War* (Chicago: University of Chicago Press, 1994).
46. For criticism of the Bush policy, see John E. Mueller, *Overblown: How Politicians and the Terrorism Industry Inflate National Security Threats, and Why We Believe Them* (New York: Free Press, 2006); and Louise Richardson, *What Terrorists Want: Understanding the Enemy, Containing the Threat* (New York: Random House, 2005).
47. Brigitte L. Nacos, *Mass-Mediated Terrorism: The Central Role of the Media in Terrorism and Counterterror* (Lanham, MD: Rowman & Littlefield, 2007).
48. Bob Woodward, *Bush at War* (New York: Simon & Schuster, 2002).
49. Alessandra Stanley, "Battling the Skepticism of a Global TV Audience," *The New York Times*, November 1, 2001, B4.
50. The quote and information in this paragraph come from J. Alexander Thier, "A Chance of Success Slips Away," *The New York Times*, September 23, 2004, A27.
51. John Lewis Gaddis, "A Grand Strategy of Transformation," *Foreign Policy* 130 (2002): 50–57.
52. Ivo H. Daalder, James M. Lindsay, and James B. Steinberg, "The Bush National Security Strategy: An Evaluation," Policy Brief #109 (Washington, DC: Brookings Institution Press, 2002).
53. Glenn P. Hastedt, *Understanding the War in Iraq* (Upper Saddle River, NJ: Prentice Hall, 2004); Bob Woodward, *Plan of Attack* (New York: Simon & Schuster, 2004).
54. Stanley Feldman, Leonie Huddy, and George E. Marcus, *Going To War in Iraq When Citizens and the Press Matter* (Chicago: University of Chicago Press, 2015); Michael Massing, "Now They Tell Us," *New York Review*, February 26, 2004, 43–49; also his exchanges with journalists from *The New York Times*, March 25, 2004, 45–46, and the *Washington Post*, April 8, 2004, 74–77; and Massing's "Unfit to Print?," *New York Review*, May 27, 2004, 6–10. For a strong dissent, arguing that media coverage of his speeches was biased against President Bush, see Jim A. Kuypers, *Bush's War: Media Bias and Justifications for War in a Terrorism Age* (Lanham, MD: Rowman & Littlefield, 2006).
55. Danny Hayes and Matt Guardino, "Whose Views Made the News? Coverage and the March to War in Iraq," *Political Communication* 27 (2010): 59–87.
56. Daniel Okrent, "Weapons of Mass Destruction? Or Mass Distraction?" *The New York Times*, May 30, 2004, sec. 4, p. 2.
57. This is based on Rami G. Khouri, "For the Full Story, Watch US & Arab TV," *Pacific News Service*, March 26, 2003; James Poniewozik, "What You See vs. What They See," *Time*, April 7, 2003, 68–69; and Jacqueline E. Sharkey, "The Television War," *American Journalism Review* 25 (May 2003): 18.
58. Sean Aday, "The Real World Will Never Get on Television: An Analysis of Casualty Imagery in American Television Coverage of the Iraq War," in *Media and Conflict in the 21st Century*, ed Philip Seib (New York: Palgrave Macmillan, 2005), 141–56.
59. Richard A. Clarke, *Against All Enemies: Inside America's War on Terror* (New York: Free Press, 2004); for a more sympathetic view of President Bush, see Bob Woodward, *Bush at War* (New York: Simon & Schuster, 2002).
60. Seymour M. Hersh, *Chain of Command: The Road from 9/11 to Abu Ghraib* (New York: HarperCollins, 2004).
61. On the issues raised by the use of drones, see John Kang and Sarah Kreps, *Drone Warfare* (Malden, MA: Polity Press, 2014); Hugh Gusterson, *Drone: Remote Control Warfare* (Cambridge, MA: MIT Press, 2016).
62. Lawrence Wright, "The Double Game," *New Yorker*, May 16, 2011, 91–94.
63. See Peter Baker, "Top Aide Leaps to Defense of Obama Security Stance," *The New York Times*, February 7, 2015, A7.
64. Fawaz A. Gerges, *ISIS: A History* (Princeton, N.J.: Princeton University Press, 2016).
65. Mark Mazzetti and Eric Schmitt, "Obama's 'Boots on the Ground': Special Forces," *The New York Times*, December 28, 2015, A1(9).
66. See Sue Halpern, "US Cyber Weapons: Our 'Demon Pinball,'" *New York Review of Books*, September 29, 2016, 26–30.
67. See his address of September 25, 2018 to the United Nations General Assembly.
68. Justin Wolfers, "Presidents Have Surprising Power to End Trade Deals," *The New York Times*, September 20, 2016, A3.
69. This discussion is based on Jon Western, *Selling Intervention and War: The President, the Media, and the American Public* (Baltimore: Johns Hopkins University Press, 2005), 224.
70. W. Lance Bennett, Regina G. Lawrence, and Steven Livingston, "None Dare Call It Torture: Indexing and the Limits of Press Independence in the Abu Ghraib Scandal," *Journal of Communication* 56 (2006): 467–85; for a different approach, see Robert M. Entman, *Projections of Power: Framing News, Public Opinion, and U.S. Foreign Policy* (Chicago: University of Chicago Press, 2004).
71. Stephen Hess, *International News & Foreign Correspondents* (Washington, DC: Brookings Institution Press, 1996).
72. William A. Hachten and James F. Scotton, *The World News Prism: Global Information in a Satellite Age*, 7th ed. (Malden, MA: Blackwell, 2007), 9. "Man-made and natural disasters—with their villains, victims, and heroes—are also news." Robert I. Rotbeg and Thomas G. Weiss, eds., *From Massacres to Genocide* (Washington, DC: Brookings Institution Press, 1996).
73. Ulf Hannerz, *Foreign News: Exploring the World of Foreign Correspondents* (Chicago: University of Chicago Press, 2004), 44.
74. William A. Hachten and James F. Scotton, *The World News Prism: Global Information in a Satellite Age*, 7th ed. (Malden, MA: Blackwell, 2007), 47.2007), 47.
75. Carl Boggs and Tom Pollard, *The Hollywood War Machine: U.S. Militarism and Popular Culture* (Boulder, CO: Paradigm Publishers, 2007), ix.
76. This paragraph is based on David Barstow, "Message Machine: Behind TV Analysts, Pentagon' Hidden Hand," *The New York Times*, April 28, 2008, A1ff.
77. This paragraph is based on David Barstow, "Message Machine: Behind TV Analysts, Pentagon's Hidden Hand," *The New York Times*, April 28, 2008, A1ff.
78. See the annual reports of the Committee to Protect Journalists.
79. Marie Colvin, *On The Front Line: The Collected Journalism of Marie Colvin* (New York: Harper Press, 2012).
80. Scott Shane and Andrew W. Lehren, "Leaked Cables Offer a Raw Look Inside U.S. Diplomacy: Dispatches Chronicle Threats and Tensions," *The New York Times*, November 29, 2010, A1ff.
81. Thomas Gibbons-Neff, " Public Was Duped On Afghan War," *The New York Times*, December 10, 2019, A1 (9).

82. Lawrence Wright, *The Looming Tower: Al-Qaeda and the Road to 9/11* (New York: Knopf, 2006).
83. Gabriel Weimann, "www.terror.net: How Modern Terrorism Uses the Internet," Special Report 116, United States Institute of Peace, March 2004; and Danny Schechter, *Media Wars: News at a Time of Terror* (Lanham, MD: Rowman & Littlefield, 2003).
84. John Darnton, "Revisiting Rwanda's Horrors with a Former National Security Advisor," *The New York Times*, December 20, 2004, E1.
85. Jonathan Mermin, *Debating War and Peace: Media Coverage of U.S. Intervention in the Post-Vietnam Era* (Princeton, NJ: Princeton University Press, 1999).
86. Richard Morin and Claudia Deane, "71% of Americans Support War, Poll Shows," *Washington Post*, March 9, 2003, A14.
87. James Poniewozik, "'24' Reboot Has a Dire Ring to It," *The New York Times*, February 6, 2017, C1(6).
88. Mark Mazzetti et al., August 18, 2021, A1 (6).
89. Julian E. Barnes, August 19, 2021, A9.
90. August 16, 2021, A1 (9).

APPENDIX A

# The Constitution of the United States

We the People of the United States, in Order to form a more perfect Union, establish Justice, insure domestic Tranquility, provide for the common defence, promote the general Welfare, and secure the Blessings of Liberty to ourselves and our Posterity, do ordain and establish this Constitution for the United States of America.

## A.1 The Constitution of the United States

Section. 1. All legislative Powers herein granted shall be vested in a Congress of the United States, which shall consist of a Senate and House of Representatives.

Section. 2. The House of Representatives shall be composed of Members chosen every second Year by the People of the several States, and the Electors in each State shall have the Qualifications requisite for Electors of the most numerous Branch of the State Legislature.

No Person shall be a Representative who shall not have attained to the Age of twenty five Years, and been seven Years a Citizen of the United States, and who shall not, when elected, be an Inhabitant of that State in which he shall be chosen.

Representatives and direct Taxes shall be apportioned among the several States which may be included within this Union, according to their respective Numbers, which shall be determined by adding to the whole Number of free Persons, including those bound to Service for a Term of Years, and excluding Indians not taxed, three fifths of all other Persons. The actual Enumeration shall be made within three Years after the first Meeting of the Congress of the United States, and within every subsequent Term of ten Years, in such Manner as they shall by Law direct. The Number of Representatives shall not exceed one for every thirty Thousand, but each State shall have at Least one Representative; and until such enumeration shall be made, the State of New Hampshire shall be entitled to chuse three, Massachusetts eight, Rhode Island and Providence Plantations one, Connecticut five, New York six, New Jersey four, Pennsylvania eight, Delaware one, Maryland six, Virginia ten, North Carolina five, South Carolina five, and Georgia three.

When vacancies happen in the Representation from any State, the Executive Authority thereof shall issue Writs of Election to fill such Vacancies.

The House of Representatives shall chuse their Speaker and other Officers; and shall have the sole Power of Impeachment.

Section. 3. The Senate of the United States shall be composed of two Senators from each State, chosen by the Legislature thereof, for six Years; and each Senator shall have one Vote.

Immediately after they shall be assembled in Consequence of the first Election, they shall be divided as equally as may be into three Classes. The Seats of the Senators of the first Class shall be vacated at the Expiration of the second Year, of the second Class at the Expiration of the fourth Year, and of the third Class at the Expiration of the sixth Year, so that one third may be chosen every second Year; and if Vacancies happen by Resignation, or otherwise, during the Recess of the Legislature of any State, the Executive thereof may make temporary Appointments until the next Meeting of the Legislature, which shall then fill such Vacancies.

No Person shall be a Senator who shall not have attained to the Age of thirty Years, and been nine Years a Citizen of the United States, and who shall not, when elected, be an Inhabitant of that State for which he shall be chosen.

The Vice President of the United States shall be President of the Senate, but shall have no Vote, unless they be equally divided.

The Senate shall chuse their other Officers, and also a President pro tempore, in the Absence of the Vice President, or when he shall exercise the Office of President of the United States.

The Senate shall have the sole Power to try all Impeachments. When sitting for that Purpose, they shall be on Oath or Affirmation. When the President of the United States is tried, the Chief Justice shall preside: And no Person shall be convicted without the Concurrence of two thirds of the Members present.

Judgment in Cases of Impeachment shall not extend further than to removal from Office, and disqualification to hold and enjoy any Office of honor, Trust or Profit under the United States: but the Party convicted shall nevertheless be liable and subject to Indictment, Trial, Judgment and Punishment, according to Law.

Section. 4. The Times, Places and Manner of holding Elections for Senators and Representatives, shall be prescribed in each State by the Legislature thereof; but the Congress may at any time by Law make or alter such Regulations, except as to the Places of chusing Senators.

The Congress shall assemble at least once in every Year, and such Meeting shall be on the first Monday in December [Modified by Amendment XX], unless they shall by Law appoint a different Day.

Section. 5. Each House shall be the Judge of the Elections, Returns and Qualifications of its own Members, and a Majority of each shall constitute a Quorum to do Business; but a smaller Number may adjourn from day to day, and may be authorized to compel the Attendance of absent Members, in such Manner, and under such Penalties as each House may provide.

Each House may determine the Rules of its Proceedings, punish its Members for disorderly Behaviour, and, with the Concurrence of two thirds, expel a Member.

Each House shall keep a Journal of its Proceedings, and from time to time publish the same, excepting such Parts as may in their Judgment require Secrecy; and the Yeas and Nays of the Members of either House on any question shall, at the Desire of one fifth of those Present, be entered on the Journal.

Neither House, during the Session of Congress, shall, without the Consent of the other, adjourn for more than three days, nor to any other Place than that in which the two Houses shall be sitting.

Section. 6. The Senators and Representatives shall receive a Compensation for their Services, to be ascertained by Law, and paid out of the Treasury of the United States. They shall in all Cases, except Treason, Felony and Breach of the Peace, be privileged from Arrest during their Attendance at the Session of their respective Houses, and in going to and returning from the same; and for any Speech or Debate in either House, they shall not be questioned in any other Place.

No Senator or Representative shall, during the Time for which he was elected, be appointed to any civil Office under the Authority of the United States, which shall have been created, or the Emoluments whereof shall have been encreased during such time; and no Person holding any Office under the United States, shall be a Member of either House during his Continuance in Office.

Section. 7. All Bills for raising Revenue shall originate in the House of Representatives; but the Senate may propose or concur with Amendments as on other Bills.

Every Bill which shall have passed the House of Representatives and the Senate, shall, before it become a Law, be presented to the President of the United States; If he approve he shall sign it, but if not he shall return it, with his Objections to that House in which it shall have originated, who shall enter the Objections at large on their Journal, and proceed to reconsider it. If after such Reconsideration two thirds of that House shall agree to pass the Bill, it shall be sent, together with the Objections, to the other House, by which it shall likewise be reconsidered, and if approved by two thirds of that House, it shall become a Law. But in all such Cases the Votes of both Houses shall be determined by yeas and Nays, and the Names of the Persons voting for and against the Bill shall be entered on the Journal of each House respectively. If any Bill shall not be returned by the President within ten Days (Sundays excepted) after it shall have been presented to him, the Same shall be a Law, in like Manner as if he had signed it, unless the Congress by their Adjournment prevent its Return, in which Case it shall not be a Law.

Every Order, Resolution, or Vote to which the Concurrence of the Senate and House of Representatives may be necessary (except on a question of Adjournment) shall be presented to the President of the United States; and before the Same shall take Effect, shall be approved by him, or being disapproved by him, shall be repassed by two thirds of the Senate and House of Representatives, according to the Rules and Limitations prescribed in the Case of a Bill.

Section. 8. The Congress shall have Power To lay and collect Taxes, Duties, Imposts and Excises, to pay the Debts and provide for the common Defence and general Welfare of the United States; but all Duties, Imposts and Excises shall be uniform throughout the United States;

To borrow Money on the credit of the United States;

To regulate Commerce with foreign Nations, and among the several States, and with the Indian Tribes;

To establish an uniform Rule of Naturalization, and uniform Laws on the subject of Bankruptcies throughout the United States;

To coin Money, regulate the Value thereof, and of foreign Coin, and fix the Standard of Weights and Measures;

To provide for the Punishment of counterfeiting the Securities and current Coin of the United States;

To establish Post Offices and post Roads;

To promote the Progress of Science and useful Arts, by securing for limited Times to Authors and Inventors the exclusive Right to their respective Writings and Discoveries;

To constitute Tribunals inferior to the supreme Court;

To define and punish Piracies and Felonies committed on the high Seas, and Offences against the Law of Nations;

To declare War, grant Letters of Marque and Reprisal, and make Rules concerning Captures on Land and Water;

To raise and support Armies, but no Appropriation of Money to that Use shall be for a longer Term than two Years;

To provide and maintain a Navy;

To make Rules for the Government and Regulation of the land and naval Forces;

To provide for calling forth the Militia to execute the Laws of the Union, suppress Insurrections and repel Invasions;

To provide for organizing, arming, and disciplining, the Militia, and for governing such Part of them as may be employed in the Service of the United States, reserving to the States respectively, the Appointment of the Officers, and the Authority of training the Militia according to the discipline prescribed by Congress;

To exercise exclusive Legislation in all Cases whatsoever, over such District (not exceeding ten Miles square) as may, by Cession of particular States, and the Acceptance of Congress, become the Seat of the Government of the United States, and to exercise like Authority over all Places purchased by the Consent of the Legislature of the State in which the Same shall be, for the Erection of Forts, Magazines, Arsenals, dock Yards, and other needful Buildings;—And

To make all Laws which shall be necessary and proper for carrying into Execution the foregoing Powers, and all other Powers vested by this Constitution in the Government of the United States, or in any Department or Officer thereof.

Section. 9. The Migration or Importation of such Persons as any of the States now existing shall think proper to admit, shall not be prohibited by the Congress prior to the Year one thousand eight hundred and eight, but a Tax or duty may be imposed on such Importation, not exceeding ten dollars for each Person.

The Privilege of the Writ of Habeas Corpus shall not be suspended, unless when in Cases of Rebellion or Invasion the public Safety may require it.

No Bill of Attainder or ex post facto Law shall be passed.

No Capitation, or other direct, Tax shall be laid, unless in Proportion to the Census or Enumeration herein before directed to be taken.

No Tax or Duty shall be laid on Articles exported from any State.

No Preference shall be given by any Regulation of Commerce or Revenue to the Ports of one State over those of another; nor shall Vessels bound to, or from, one State, be obliged to enter, clear, or pay Duties in another.

No Money shall be drawn from the Treasury, but in Consequence of Appropriations made by Law; and a regular Statement and Account of the Receipts and Expenditures of all public Money shall be published from time to time.

No Title of Nobility shall be granted by the United States: And no Person holding any Office of Profit or Trust under them, shall, without the Consent of the Congress, accept of any present, Emolument, Office, or Title, of any kind whatever, from any King, Prince, or foreign State.

Section. 10. No State shall enter into any Treaty, Alliance, or Confederation; grant Letters of Marque and Reprisal; coin Money; emit Bills of Credit; make any Thing but gold and silver Coin a Tender in Payment of Debts; pass any Bill of Attainder, ex post facto Law, or Law impairing the Obligation of Contracts, or grant any Title of Nobility.

No State shall, without the Consent of the Congress, lay any Imposts or Duties on Imports or Exports, except what may be absolutely necessary for executing it's inspection Laws; and the net Produce of all Duties and Imposts, laid by any State on Imports or Exports, shall be for the Use of the Treasury of the United States; and all such Laws shall be subject to the Revision and Controul of the Congress.

No State shall, without the Consent of Congress, lay any Duty of Tonnage, keep Troops, or Ships of War in time of Peace, enter into any Agreement or Compact with another State, or with a foreign Power, or engage in War, unless actually invaded, or in such imminent Danger as will not admit of delay.

## A.2 Article II

Section. 1. The executive Power shall be vested in a President of the United States of America. He shall hold his Office during the Term of four Years, and, together with the Vice President, chosen for the same Term, be elected, as follows:

Each State shall appoint, in such Manner as the Legislature thereof may direct, a Number of Electors, equal to the whole Number of Senators and Representatives to which the State may be entitled in the Congress: but no Senator or Representative, or Person holding an Office of Trust or Profit under the United States, shall be appointed an Elector.

The Electors shall meet in their respective States, and vote by Ballot for two Persons, of whom one at least shall not be an Inhabitant of the same State with themselves. And they shall make a List of all the Persons voted for, and of the Number of Votes for each; which List they shall sign and certify, and transmit sealed to the Seat of the Government of the United States, directed to the President of the Senate. The President of the Senate shall, in the Presence of the Senate and House of Representatives, open all the Certificates, and the Votes shall then be counted. The Person having the greatest Number of Votes shall be the President, if such Number be a Majority of the whole Number of Electors appointed; and if there be more than one who have such Majority, and have an equal Number of Votes, then the House of Representatives shall immediately chuse by Ballot one of them for President; and if no Person have a Majority, then from the five highest on the List the said House shall in like Manner chuse the President. But in chusing the President, the Votes shall be taken by States, the Representation from each State having one Vote; a quorum for this Purpose shall consist of a Member or Members from two thirds of the States, and a Majority of all the States shall be necessary to a Choice. In every Case, after the Choice of the President, the Person having the greatest Number of Votes of the Electors shall be the Vice President. But if there should remain two or more who have equal Votes, the Senate shall chuse from them by Ballot the Vice President.

The Congress may determine the Time of chusing the Electors, and the Day on which they shall give their Votes; which Day shall be the same throughout the United States.

No Person except a natural born Citizen, or a Citizen of the United States, at the time of the Adoption of this Constitution, shall be eligible to the Office of President; neither shall any Person be eligible to that Office who shall not have attained to the Age of thirty five Years, and been fourteen Years a Resident within the United States.

In Case of the Removal of the President from Office, or of his Death, Resignation, or Inability to discharge the Powers and Duties of the said Office, the Same shall devolve on the Vice President, and the Congress may by Law provide for the Case of Removal, Death, Resignation or Inability, both of the President and Vice President, declaring what Officer shall then act as President, and such Officer shall act accordingly, until the Disability be removed, or a President shall be elected.

The President shall, at stated Times, receive for his Services, a Compensation, which shall neither be increased nor diminished during the Period for which he shall have been elected, and he shall not receive within that Period any other Emolument from the United States, or any of them.

Before he enter on the Execution of his Office, he shall take the following Oath or Affirmation:—"I do solemnly swear (or affirm) that I will faithfully execute the Office of President of the United States, and will to the best of my Ability, preserve, protect and defend the Constitution of the United States."

Section. 2. The President shall be Commander in Chief of the Army and Navy of the United States, and of the Militia of the several States, when called into the actual Service of the United States; he may require the Opinion, in writing, of the principal Officer in each of the executive Departments, upon any Subject relating to the Duties of their respective Offices, and he shall have Power to grant Reprieves and Pardons for Offences against the United States, except in Cases of Impeachment.

He shall have Power, by and with the Advice and Consent of the Senate, to make Treaties, provided two thirds of the Senators present concur; and he shall nominate, and by and with the Advice and Consent of the Senate, shall appoint Ambassadors, other public Ministers and Consuls, Judges of the supreme Court, and all other Officers of the United States, whose Appointments are not herein otherwise provided for, and which shall be established by Law: but the Congress may by Law vest the Appointment of such inferior Officers, as they think proper, in the President alone, in the Courts of Law, or in the Heads of Departments.

The President shall have Power to fill up all Vacancies that may happen during the Recess of the Senate, by granting Commissions which shall expire at the End of their next Session.

Section. 3. He shall from time to time give to the Congress Information of the State of the Union, and recommend to their Consideration such Measures as he shall judge necessary and expedient; he may, on extraordinary Occasions, convene both Houses, or either of them, and in Case of Disagreement between them, with Respect to the Time of Adjournment, he may adjourn them to such Time as he shall think proper; he shall receive Ambassadors and other public Ministers; he shall take Care that the Laws be faithfully executed, and shall Commission all the Officers of the United States.

Section. 4. The President, Vice President and all civil Officers of the United States, shall be removed from Office on Impeachment for, and Conviction of, Treason, Bribery, or other high Crimes and Misdemeanors.

# A.3 Article III

Section. 1. The judicial Power of the United States shall be vested in one supreme Court, and in such inferior Courts as the Congress may from time to time ordain and establish. The Judges, both of the supreme and inferior Courts, shall hold their Offices during good Behaviour, and shall, at stated Times, receive for their Services a Compensation, which shall not be diminished during their Continuance in Office.

Section. 2. The judicial Power shall extend to all Cases, in Law and Equity, arising under this Constitution, the Laws of the United States, and Treaties made, or which shall be made, under their Authority;—to all Cases affecting Ambassadors, other public Ministers and Consuls;—to all Cases of admiralty and maritime Jurisdiction;—to Controversies to which the United States shall be a Party;—to Controversies between two or more States;—between a State and Citizens of another State;—between Citizens of different States;—between Citizens of the same State claiming Lands under Grants of different States, and between a State, or the Citizens thereof, and foreign States, Citizens or Subjects.

In all Cases affecting Ambassadors, other public Ministers and Consuls, and those in which a State shall be Party, the supreme Court shall have original Jurisdiction. In all the other Cases before mentioned, the supreme Court shall have appellate Jurisdiction, both as to Law and Fact, with such Exceptions, and under such Regulations as the Congress shall make.

The Trial of all Crimes, except in Cases of Impeachment, shall be by Jury; and such Trial shall be held in the State where the said Crimes shall have been committed; but when not committed within any State, the Trial shall be at such Place or Places as the Congress may by Law have directed.

Section. 3. Treason against the United States shall consist only in levying War against them, or in adhering to their Enemies, giving them Aid and Comfort. No Person shall be convicted of Treason unless on the Testimony of two Witnesses to the same overt Act, or on Confession in open Court.

The Congress shall have Power to declare the Punishment of Treason, but no Attainder of Treason shall work Corruption of Blood, or Forfeiture except during the Life of the Person attainted.

# A.4 Article IV

Section. 1. Full Faith and Credit shall be given in each State to the public Acts, Records, and judicial Proceedings of every other State. And the Congress may by general Laws prescribe the Manner in which such Acts, Records and Proceedings shall be proved, and the Effect thereof.

Section. 2. The Citizens of each State shall be entitled to all Privileges and Immunities of Citizens in the several States.

A Person charged in any State with Treason, Felony, or other Crime, who shall flee from Justice, and be found in another State, shall on Demand of the executive Authority of the State from which he fled, be delivered up, to be removed to the State having Jurisdiction of the Crime.

No Person held to Service or Labour in one State, under the Laws thereof, escaping into another, shall, in Consequence of any Law or Regulation therein, be discharged from such Service or Labour, but shall be delivered up on Claim of the Party to whom such Service or Labour may be due.

Section. 3. New States may be admitted by the Congress into this Union; but no new State shall be formed or erected within the Jurisdiction of any other State; nor any State be formed by the Junction of two or more States, or Parts of States, without the Consent of the Legislatures of the States concerned as well as of the Congress.

The Congress shall have Power to dispose of and make all needful Rules and Regulations respecting the Territory or other Property belonging to the United States; and nothing in this Constitution shall be so construed as to Prejudice any Claims of the United States, or of any particular State.

Section. 4. The United States shall guarantee to every State in this Union a Republican Form of Government, and shall protect each of them against Invasion; and on Application of the Legislature, or of the Executive (when the Legislature cannot be convened), against domestic Violence.

# A.5 Article V

The Congress, whenever two thirds of both Houses shall deem it necessary, shall propose Amendments to this Constitution, or, on the Application of the Legislatures of two thirds of the several States, shall call a Convention for proposing Amendments, which, in either Case, shall be valid to all Intents and Purposes, as Part of this Constitution, when ratified by the Legislatures of three fourths of the several States, or by Conventions in three fourths thereof, as the one or the other Mode of Ratification may be proposed by the Congress; Provided that no Amendment which may be made prior to the Year One thousand eight hundred and eight shall in any Manner affect the first and fourth Clauses in the Ninth Section of the first Article; and that no State, without its Consent, shall be deprived of its equal Suffrage in the Senate.

# A.6 Article VI

All Debts contracted and Engagements entered into, before the Adoption of this Constitution, shall be as valid against the United States under this Constitution, as under the Confederation.

This Constitution, and the Laws of the United States which shall be made in Pursuance thereof; and all Treaties made, or which shall be made, under the Authority of the United States, shall be the supreme Law of the Land; and the Judges in every State shall be bound thereby, any Thing in the Constitution or Laws of any State to the Contrary notwithstanding.

The Senators and Representatives before mentioned, and the Members of the several State Legislatures, and all executive and judicial Officers, both of the United States and of the several States, shall be bound by Oath or Affirmation, to support this Constitution; but no religious Test shall ever be required as a Qualification to any Office or public Trust under the United States.

# A.7 Article VII

The Ratification of the Conventions of nine States, shall be sufficient for the Establishment of this Constitution between the States so ratifying the Same.

# A.8 Bill of Rights

**Article the third [Amendment I]**

Congress shall make no law respecting an establishment of religion, or prohibiting the free exercise thereof; or abridging the freedom of speech, or of the press; or the right of the people peaceably to assemble, and to petition the Government for a redress of grievances.

**Article the fourth [Amendment II]**

A well regulated Militia, being necessary to the security of a free State, the right of the people to keep and bear Arms, shall not be infringed.

**Article the fifth [Amendment III]**

No Soldier shall, in time of peace be quartered in any house, without the consent of the Owner, nor in time of war, but in a manner to be prescribed by law.

**Article the sixth [Amendment IV]**

The right of the people to be secure in their persons, houses, papers, and effects, against unreasonable searches and seizures, shall not be violated, and no Warrants shall issue, but upon probable cause, supported by Oath or affirmation, and particularly describing the place to be searched, and the persons or things to be seized.

**Article the seventh [Amendment V]**

No person shall be held to answer for a capital, or otherwise infamous crime, unless on a presentment or indictment of a Grand Jury, except in cases arising in the land or naval forces, or in the Militia, when in actual service in time of War or public danger; nor shall any person be subject for the same offence to be twice put in jeopardy of life or limb; nor shall be compelled in any criminal case to be a witness against himself, nor be deprived of life, liberty, or property, without due process of law; nor shall private property be taken for public use, without just compensation.

**Article the eighth [Amendment VI]**

In all criminal prosecutions, the accused shall enjoy the right to a speedy and public trial, by an impartial jury of the State and district wherein the crime shall have been committed, which district shall have been previously ascertained by law, and to be informed of the nature and cause of the accusation; to be confronted with the witnesses against him; to have compulsory process for obtaining witnesses in his favor, and to have the Assistance of Counsel for his defence.

**Article the ninth [Amendment VII]**

In Suits at common law, where the value in controversy shall exceed twenty dollars, the right of trial by jury shall be preserved, and no fact tried by a jury, shall be otherwise re examined in any Court of the United States, than according to the rules of the common law.

**Article the tenth [Amendment VIII]**

Excessive bail shall not be required, nor excessive fines imposed, nor cruel and unusual punishments inflicted.

**Article the eleventh [Amendment IX]**

The enumeration in the Constitution, of certain rights, shall not be construed to deny or disparage others retained by the people.

**Article the twelfth [Amendment X]**

The powers not delegated to the United States by the Constitution, nor prohibited by it to the States, are reserved to the States respectively, or to the people.

# A.9 Additional Amendments to the Constitution

**Amendment XI [Proposed 1794; Ratified 1798]**

The Judicial power of the United States shall not be construed to extend to any suit in law or equity, commenced or prosecuted against one of the United States by Citizens of another State, or by Citizens or Subjects of any Foreign State.

**Amendment XII [Proposed 1803; Ratified 1804]**

The Electors shall meet in their respective states, and vote by ballot for President and Vice President, one of whom, at least, shall not be an inhabitant of the same state with themselves; they shall name in their ballots the person voted for as President, and in distinct ballots the person voted for as Vice President, and they shall make distinct lists of all persons voted for as President, and of all persons voted for as Vice President, and of the number of votes for each, which lists they shall sign and certify, and transmit sealed to the seat of the government of the United States, directed to the President of the Senate;—The President of the Senate shall, in the presence of the Senate and House of Representatives, open all the certificates and the votes shall then be counted;—The person having the greatest number of votes for President, shall be the President, if such number be a majority of the whole number of Electors appointed; and if no person have such majority, then from the persons having the highest numbers not exceeding three on the list of those voted for as President, the House of Representatives shall choose immediately, by ballot, the President. But in choosing the President, the votes shall be taken by states, the representation from each state having one vote; a quorum for this purpose shall consist of a member or members from two thirds of the states, and a majority of all the states shall be necessary to a choice. And if the House of Representatives shall not choose a President whenever the right of choice shall devolve upon them, before the fourth day of March next following, then the Vice President shall act as President, as in the case of the death or other constitutional disability of the President.—The person having the greatest number of votes as Vice President, shall be the Vice President, if such number be a majority of the whole number of Electors appointed, and if no person have a majority, then from the two highest numbers on the list, the Senate shall choose the Vice President; a quorum for the purpose shall consist of two thirds of the whole number of Senators, and a majority of the whole number shall be necessary to a choice. But no person constitutionally ineligible to the office of President shall be eligible to that of Vice President of the United States.

**Amendment XIII [Proposed 1865; Ratified 1865]**

Section. 1. Neither slavery nor involuntary servitude, except as a punishment for crime whereof the party shall have been duly convicted, shall exist within the United States, or any place subject to their jurisdiction.

Section. 2. Congress shall have power to enforce this article by appropriate legislation.

**Amendment XIV [Proposed 1866; Ratified 1868]**

Section. 1. All persons born or naturalized in the United States, and subject to the jurisdiction thereof, are citizens of the United States and of the State wherein they reside. No State shall make or enforce any law which shall abridge the privileges or immunities of citizens of the United States; nor shall any State deprive any person of life, liberty, or property, without due process of law; nor deny to any person within its jurisdiction the equal protection of the laws.

Section. 2. Representatives shall be apportioned among the several States according to their respective numbers, counting the whole number of persons in each State, excluding Indians not taxed. But when the right to vote at any election for the choice of electors for President and Vice President of the United States, Representatives in Congress, the Executive and Judicial officers of a State, or the members of the Legislature thereof, is denied to any of the male inhabitants of such State, being twenty one years of age, and citizens of the United States, or in any way abridged, except for participation in rebellion, or other crime, the basis of representation therein shall be reduced in the proportion which the number of such male citizens shall bear to the whole number of male citizens twenty one years of age in such State.

Section. 3. No person shall be a Senator or Representative in Congress, or elector of President and Vice President, or hold any office, civil or military, under the United States, or under any State, who, having previously taken an oath, as a member of Congress, or as an officer of the United States, or as a member of any State legislature, or as an executive or judicial officer of any State, to support the Constitution of the United States, shall have engaged in insurrection or rebellion against the same, or given aid or comfort to the enemies thereof. But Congress may by a vote of two thirds of each House, remove such disability.

Section. 4. The validity of the public debt of the United States, authorized by law, including debts incurred for payment of pensions and bounties for services in suppressing insurrection or rebellion, shall not be questioned. But neither the United States nor any State shall assume or pay any debt or obligation incurred in aid of insurrection or rebellion against the United States, or any claim for the loss or emancipation of any slave; but all such debts, obligations and claims shall be held illegal and void.

Section. 5. The Congress shall have power to enforce, by appropriate legislation, the provisions of this article.

**Amendment XV [Proposed 1869; Ratified 1870]**

Section. 1. The right of citizens of the United States to vote shall not be denied or abridged by the United States or by any State on account of race, color, or previous condition of servitude.

Section. 2. The Congress shall have power to enforce this article by appropriate legislation.

**Amendment XVI [Proposed 1909; Questionably Ratified 1913]**

The Congress shall have power to lay and collect taxes on incomes, from whatever source derived, without apportionment among the several States, and without regard to any census or enumeration.

**Amendment XVII [Proposed 1912; Ratified 1913]**

The Senate of the United States shall be composed of two Senators from each State, elected by the people thereof, for six years; and each Senator shall have one vote. The electors in each State shall have the qualifications requisite for electors of the most numerous branch of the State legislatures.

When vacancies happen in the representation of any State in the Senate, the executive authority of such State shall issue writs of election to fill such vacancies: Provided, That the legislature of any State may empower the executive thereof to make temporary appointments until the people fill the vacancies by election as the legislature may direct.

This amendment shall not be so construed as to affect the election or term of any Senator chosen before it becomes valid as part of the Constitution.

**Amendment XVIII [Proposed 1917; Ratified 1919; Repealed 1933 (See Amendment XXI, Section 1)]**

Section. 1. After one year from the ratification of this article the manufacture, sale, or transportation of intoxicating liquors within, the importation thereof into, or the exportation thereof from the United States and all territory subject to the jurisdiction thereof for beverage purposes is hereby prohibited.

Section. 2. The Congress and the several States shall have concurrent power to enforce this article by appropriate legislation.

Section. 3. This article shall be inoperative unless it shall have been ratified as an amendment to the Constitution by the legislatures of the several States, as provided in the Constitution, within seven years from the date of the submission hereof to the States by the Congress.

**Amendment XIX [Proposed 1919; Ratified 1920]**

The right of citizens of the United States to vote shall not be denied or abridged by the United States or by any State on account of sex.

Congress shall have power to enforce this article by appropriate legislation.

**Amendment XX [Proposed 1932; Ratified 1933]**

Section. 1. The terms of the President and Vice President shall end at noon on the 20th day of January, and the terms of Senators and Representatives at noon on the 3d day of January, of the years in which such terms would have ended if this article had not been ratified; and the terms of their successors shall then begin.

Section. 2. The Congress shall assemble at least once in every year, and such meeting shall begin at noon on the 3d day of January, unless they shall by law appoint a different day.

Section. 3. If, at the time fixed for the beginning of the term of the President, the President elect shall have died, the Vice President elect shall become President. If a President shall not have been chosen before the time fixed for the beginning of his term, or if the President elect shall have failed to qualify, then the Vice President elect shall act as President until a President shall have qualified; and the Congress may by law provide for the case wherein neither a President elect nor a Vice President elect shall have qualified, declaring who shall then act as President, or the manner in which one who is to act shall be selected, and such person shall act accordingly until a President or Vice President shall have qualified.

Section. 4. The Congress may by law provide for the case of the death of any of the persons from whom the House of Representatives may choose a President whenever the right of choice shall have devolved upon them, and for the case of the death of any of the persons from whom the Senate may choose a Vice President whenever the right of choice shall have devolved upon them.

Section. 5. Sections 1 and 2 shall take effect on the 15th day of October following the ratification of this article.

Section. 6. This article shall be inoperative unless it shall have been ratified as an amendment to the Constitution by the legislatures of three fourths of the several States within seven years from the date of its submission.

**Amendment XXI [Proposed 1933; Ratified 1933]**

Section. 1. The eighteenth article of amendment to the Constitution of the United States is hereby repealed.

Section. 2. The transportation or importation into any State, Territory, or possession of the United States for delivery or use therein of intoxicating liquors, in violation of the laws thereof, is hereby prohibited.

Section. 3. This article shall be inoperative unless it shall have been ratified as an amendment to the Constitution by conventions in the several States, as provided in the Constitution, within seven years from the date of the submission hereof to the States by the Congress.

**Amendment XXII [Proposed 1947; Ratified 1951]**

Section. 1. No person shall be elected to the office of the President more than twice, and no person who has held the office of President, or acted as President, for more than two years of a term to which some other person was elected President shall be elected to the office of the President more than once. But this Article shall not apply to any person holding the office of President when this Article was proposed by the Congress, and shall not prevent any person who may be holding the office of President, or acting as President, during the term within which this Article becomes operative from holding the office of President or acting as President during the remainder of such term.

Section. 2. This article shall be inoperative unless it shall have been ratified as an amendment to the Constitution by the legislatures of three fourths of the several States within seven years from the date of its submission to the States by the Congress.

**Amendment XXIII [Proposed 1960; Ratified 1961]**

Section. 1. The District constituting the seat of Government of the United States shall appoint in such manner as the Congress may direct:

A number of electors of President and Vice President equal to the whole number of Senators and Representatives in Congress to which the District would be entitled if it were a State, but in no event more than the least populous State; they shall be in addition to those appointed by the States, but they shall be considered, for the purposes of the election of President and Vice President, to be electors appointed by a State; and they shall meet in the District and perform such duties as provided by the twelfth article of amendment.

Section. 2. The Congress shall have power to enforce this article by appropriate legislation.

**Amendment XXIV [Proposed 1962; Ratified 1964]**

Section. 1. The right of citizens of the United States to vote in any primary or other election for President or Vice President, for electors for President or Vice President, or for Senator or Representative in Congress, shall not be denied or abridged by the United States or any State by reason of failure to pay any poll tax or other tax.

Section. 2. The Congress shall have power to enforce this article by appropriate legislation.

**Amendment XXV [Proposed 1965; Ratified 1967]**

Section. 1. In case of the removal of the President from office or of his death or resignation, the Vice President shall become President.

Section. 2. Whenever there is a vacancy in the office of the Vice President, the President shall nominate a Vice President who shall take office upon confirmation by a majority vote of both Houses of Congress.

Section. 3. Whenever the President transmits to the President pro tempore of the Senate and the Speaker of the House of Representatives his written declaration that he is unable to discharge the powers and duties of his office, and until he transmits to them a written declaration to the contrary, such powers and duties shall be discharged by the Vice President as Acting President.

Section. 4. Whenever the Vice President and a majority of either the principal officers of the executive departments or of such other body as Congress may by law provide, transmit to the President pro tempore of the Senate and the Speaker of the House of Representatives their written declaration that the President is unable to discharge the powers and duties of his office, the Vice President shall immediately assume the powers and duties of the office as Acting President.

Thereafter, when the President transmits to the President pro tempore of the Senate and the Speaker of the House of Representatives his written declaration that no inability exists, he shall resume the powers and duties of his office unless the Vice President and a majority of either the principal officers of the executive department or of such other body as Congress may by law provide, transmit within four days to the President pro tempore of the Senate and the Speaker of the House of Representatives their written declaration that the President is unable to discharge the powers and duties of his office. Thereupon Congress shall decide the issue, assembling within forty eight hours for that purpose if not in session. If the Congress, within twenty one days after receipt of the latter written declaration, or, if Congress is not in session, within twenty one days after Congress is required to assemble, determines by two thirds vote of both Houses that the President is unable to discharge the powers and duties of his office, the Vice President shall continue to discharge the same as Acting President; otherwise, the President shall resume the powers and duties of his office.

**Amendment XXVI [Proposed 1971; Ratified 1971]**

Section. 1. The right of citizens of the United States, who are eighteen years of age or older, to vote shall not be denied or abridged by the United States or by any State on account of age.

Section. 2. The Congress shall have power to enforce this article by appropriate legislation.

**Amendment XXVII [Proposed 1789; Ratified 1992; Second of twelve Articles comprising the Bill of Rights]**

No law, varying the compensation for the services of the Senators and Representatives, shall take effect, until an election of Representatives shall have intervened.

APPENDIX B

# Articles of Impeachment Against President Donald John Trump

## B.1 H. Res. 755—116th Congress (2019–2020)

**RESOLUTION**[1]

Impeaching Donald John Trump, President of the United States, for high crimes and misdemeanors.

*Resolved*, That Donald J. Trump, President of the United States, is impeached for high crimes and misdemeanors and that the following articles of impeachment be exhibited to the United States Senate:

Articles of impeachment exhibited by the House of Representatives of the United States of America in the name of itself and of the people of the United States of America, against Donald J. Trump, President of the United States of America, in maintenance and support of its impeachment against him for high crimes and misdemeanors.

**ARTICLE I: ABUSE OF POWER**

The Constitution provides that the House of Representatives "shall have the sole Power of Impeachment" and that the President "shall be removed from Office on Impeachment for, and Conviction of, Treason, Bribery, or other high Crimes and Misdemeanors". In his conduct of the office of President of the United States—and in violation of his constitutional oath faithfully to execute the office of President of the United States and, to the best of his ability, preserve, protect, and defend the Constitution of the United States, and in violation of his constitutional duty to take care that the laws be faithfully executed—Donald J. Trump has abused the powers of the Presidency, in that:

Using the powers of his high office, President Trump solicited the interference of a foreign government, Ukraine, in the 2020 United States Presidential election. He did so through a scheme or course of conduct that included soliciting the Government of Ukraine to publicly announce investigations that would benefit his reelection, harm the election prospects of a political opponent, and influence the 2020 United States Presidential election to his advantage. President Trump also sought to pressure the Government of Ukraine to take these steps by conditioning official United States Government acts of significant value to Ukraine on its public announcement of the investigations. President Trump engaged in this scheme or course of conduct for corrupt purposes in pursuit of personal political benefit. In so doing, President Trump used the powers of the Presidency in a manner that compromised the national security of the United States and undermined the integrity of the United States democratic process. He thus ignored and injured the interests of the Nation.

President Trump engaged in this scheme or course of conduct through the following means:

(1) President Trump—acting both directly and through his agents Within and Outside the United States Government corruptly solicited the Government of Ukraine to publicly announce investigations into—

(A) a political opponent, former Vice President Joseph R. Biden, Jr.; and

(B) a discredited theory promoted by Russia alleging that Ukraine—rather than Russia—interfered in the 2016 United States Presidential election.

(2) With the same corrupt motives, President Trump—acting both directly and through his agents within and outside the United States Government—conditioned two official acts on the public announcements that he had requested—

(A) the release of $391 million of United States taxpayer funds that Congress had appropriated on a bipartisan basis for the purpose of providing vital military and security assistance to Ukraine to oppose Russian aggression and which President Trump had ordered suspended; and

(B) a head of state meeting at the White House, which the President of Ukraine sought to demonstrate continued United States support for the Government of Ukraine in the face of Russian aggression.

(3) Faced with the public revelation of his actions, President Trump ultimately released the military and security assistance to the Government of Ukraine, but has persisted in openly and corruptly urging and soliciting Ukraine to undertake investigations for his personal political benefit.

These actions were consistent with President Trump's previous invitations of foreign interference in United States elections.

In all of this, President Trump abused the powers of the Presidency by ignoring and injuring national security and other vital national interests to obtain an improper personal political benefit. He has also betrayed the Nation by abusing his high office to enlist a foreign power in corrupting democratic elections.

Wherefore President Trump, by such conduct, has demonstrated that he will remain a threat to national security and the Constitution if allowed to remain in office, and has acted in a manner grossly incompatible with self-governance and the rule of law. President Trump thus warrants impeachment and trial, removal from office, and disqualification to hold and enjoy any Office of honor, trust, or profit under the United States.

**ARTICLE II: OBSTRUCTION OF CONGRESS**

The Constitution provides that the House of Representatives "shall have the sole Power of Impeachment" and that the President "shall be removed from Office on Impeachment for, and Conviction of, Treason, Bribery, or other high Crimes and Misdemeanors". In his conduct of the office of President of the United States and in violation of his constitutional oath faithfully to execute the office of President of the United States and, to the best of his ability, preserve, protect, and defend the Constitution of the United States, and in violation of his constitutional duty to take care that the laws be faithfully executed—Donald J. Trump has directed the unprecedented, categorical, and indiscriminate defiance of subpoenas issued by the House of Representatives pursuant to its "sole Power of Impeachment". President Trump has abused the powers of the Presidency in a manner offensive to, and subversive of, the Constitution, in that:

The House of Representatives has engaged in an impeachment inquiry focused on President Trump's corrupt solicitation of the Government of Ukraine to interfere in the 2020 United States Presidential election. As part of this impeachment inquiry, the Committees undertaking the investigation served subpoenas seeking documents and testimony deemed vital to the inquiry from various Executive Branch agencies and offices, and current and former officials.

In response, without lawful cause or excuse, President Trump directed Executive Branch agencies, offices, and officials not to comply with those subpoenas. President Trump thus interposed the powers of the Presidency against the lawful subpoenas of the House of Representatives, and assumed to himself functions and judgments necessary to the exercise of the "sole Power of Impeachment" vested by the Constitution in the House of Representatives. President Trump abused the powers of his high office through the following means:

(1) Directing the White House to defy a lawful subpoena by withholding the production of documents sought therein by the Committees.

(2) Directing other Executive Branch agencies and offices to defy lawful subpoenas and withhold the production of documents and records from the Committees—in response to which the Department of State, Office of Management and Budget, Department of Energy, and Department of Defense refused to produce a single document or record.

(3) Directing current and former Executive Branch officials not to cooperate with the Committees—in response to which nine Administration officials defied subpoenas for testimony, namely John Michael "Mick" Mulvaney, Robert B. Blair, John A. Eisenberg, Michael Ellis, Preston Wells Griffith, Russell T. Vought, Michael Duffey, Brian McCormack, and T. Ulrich Brechbuhl.

These actions were consistent with President Trump's previous efforts to undermine United States Government investigations into foreign interference in United States elections.

Through these actions, President Trump sought to arrogate to himself the right to determine the propriety, scope, and nature of an impeachment inquiry into his own conduct, as well as the unilateral prerogative to deny any and all information to the House of Representatives in the exercise of its "sole Power of Impeachment." In the history of the Republic, no President has ever ordered the complete defiance of an impeachment inquiry or sought to obstruct and impede so comprehensively the ability of the House of Representatives to investigate "high Crimes and Misdemeanors". This abuse of office served to cover up the President's own repeated misconduct and to seize and control the power of impeachment—and thus to nullify a vital constitutional safeguard vested solely in the House of Representatives.

In all of this, President Trump has acted in a manner contrary to his trust as President and subversive of constitutional government, to the great prejudice of the cause of law and justice, and to the manifest injury of the people of the United States.

Wherefore, President Trump, by such conduct, has demonstrated that he will remain a threat to the Constitution if allowed to remain in office, and has acted in a manner grossly incompatible with self-governance and the rule of law. President Trump thus warrants impeachment and trial, removal from office, and disqualification to hold and enjoy any office of honor, trust, or profit under the United States.

# B.2 Articles of Impeachment Against President Donald John Trump

**In the House of Representatives, U. S., January 13, 2021.**[2]

*Resolved*, That Donald John Trump, President of the United States, is impeached for high crimes and misdemeanors and that the following article of impeachment be exhibited to the United States Senate:

Article of impeachment exhibited by the House of Representatives of the United States of America in the name of itself and of the people of the United States of America, against Donald John Trump, President of the United States of America, in maintenance and support of its impeachment against him for high crimes and misdemeanors.

**ARTICLE I: INCITEMENT OF INSURRECTION**

The Constitution provides that the House of Representatives "shall have the sole Power of Impeachment" and that the President "shall be removed from Office on Impeachment for, and Conviction of, Treason, Bribery, or other high Crimes and Misdemeanors". Further, section 3 of the 14th Amendment to the Constitution prohibits any person who has "engaged in insurrection or rebellion against" the United States from "hold[ing] any office . . . under the United States". In his conduct while President of the United States—and in violation of his constitutional oath faithfully to execute the office of President of the United States and, to the best of his ability, preserve, protect, and defend the Constitution of the United States, and in violation of his constitutional duty to take care that the laws be faithfully executed—Donald John Trump engaged in high Crimes and Misdemeanors by inciting violence against the Government of the United States, in that:

On January 6, 2021, pursuant to the 12th Amendment to the Constitution of the United States, the Vice President of the United States, the House of Representatives, and the Senate met at the United States Capitol for a Joint Session of Congress to count the votes of the Electoral College. In the months preceding the Joint Session, President Trump repeatedly issued false statements asserting that the Presidential election results were the product of widespread fraud and should not be accepted by the American people or certified by State or Federal officials. Shortly before the Joint Session commenced, President Trump, addressed a crowd at the Ellipse in Washington, DC. There, he reiterated false claims that "we won this election, and we won it by a landslide". He also willfully made statements that, in context, encouraged—and foreseeably resulted in—lawless action at the Capitol, such as: "if you don't fight like hell you're not going to have a country anymore". Thus incited by President Trump, members of the crowd he had addressed, in an attempt to, among other objectives, interfere with the Joint Session's solemn constitutional duty to certify the results of the 2020 Presidential election, unlawfully breached and vandalized the Capitol, injured and killed law enforcement personnel, menaced Members of Congress, the Vice President, and Congressional personnel, and engaged in other violent, deadly, destructive, and seditious acts.

President Trump's conduct on January 6, 2021, followed his prior efforts to subvert and obstruct the certification of the results of the 2020 Presidential election. Those prior efforts included a phone call on January 2, 2021, during which President Trump urged the secretary of state of Georgia, Brad Raffensperger, to "find" enough votes to overturn the Georgia Presidential election results and threatened Secretary Raffensperger if he failed to do so.

In all this, President Trump gravely endangered the security of the United States and its institutions of Government. He threatened the integrity of the democratic system, interfered with the peaceful transition of power, and imperiled a coequal branch of Government. He thereby betrayed his trust as President, to the manifest injury of the people of the United States.

Wherefore, Donald John Trump, by such conduct, has demonstrated that he will remain a threat to national security, democracy, and the Constitution if allowed to remain in office, and has acted in a manner grossly incompatible with self-governance and the rule of law. Donald John Trump thus warrants impeachment and trial, removal from office, and disqualification to hold and enjoy any office of honor, trust, or profit under the United States.

# Endnotes


1. H.Res. 755 – 116th Congress (2019-2020). Articles of Impeachment Against Donald John Trump, President of the United States, for high crimes and misdemeanors. https://www.congress.gov/bill/116th-congress/house-resolution/755/text.
2. H.Res. 24 – 117th Congress (2021-2022). Article of Impeachment Against Donald John Trump, President of the United States, in maintenance and support of its impeachment against him for high crimes and misdemeanors. https://www.congress.gov/bill/117th-congress/house-resolution/24/text.

# Index